THE HUNDRED YEARS WAR
VOLUME III
Divided Houses

THE
HUNDRED YEARS
WAR

JONATHAN SUMPTION

VOLUME III
Divided Houses

faber and faber

First published in 2009
by Faber and Faber Ltd
Bloomsbury House
74–77 Great Russell Street
London WC1B 3DA

Typeset by Donald Sommerville
Printed in England by CPI William Clowes, Beccles, NR34 7TL

A CIP record for this book
is available from the British Library

ISBN 978-0-571-13897-5

2 4 6 8 10 9 7 5 3 1

To Jude

Contents

List of Maps, Plans and Tables ix
Preface xi
Synopsis to 1369 xv

  I Neighbours and Enemies 1
  II Return to Arms, 1369 18
  III Pontvallain and Limoges, 1370–1371 61
  IV Poitou, 1372 115
  V John of Gaunt in France, 1373–1374 171
  VI The Congress of Bruges, 1374–1377 212
  VII England's Barbicans, 1377–1378 281
  VIII Brittany, 1379–1381 351
  IX The Revolt of the Towns, 1380–1382 413
  X The Path of Flanders, 1382–1383 456
  XI The Shadow of Invasion, 1383–1385 511
  XII The Path of Portugal, 1385–1388 558
  XIII War and Peace, 1387–1389 624
  XIV The Gascon March, 1381–1393 679
  XV Men-at-Arms 723
  XVI The Truce of Leulinghem, 1389–1396 774
  XVII Epilogue, 1396–1399 834

Note on Money 876

Abbreviations 878
References 879
Bibliography 949
Index 978

Maps, Plans and Tables

In the text

1 Quercy and Rouergue, 1369–1370   23
2 Poitou: the northern march, 1369–1371   30
3 The Pontvallain campaign, December 1370   89
4 The reconquest of Poitou, April–September 1372   147
5 Principal *routier* garrisons of the Gascon march, 1370–1373   167
6 John of Gaunt's *chevauchée*, August–December 1373   190
7 The crossing of the Allier, October 1373   193
8 Principal *routier* garrisons in Auvergne, Quercy and Limousin, 1374–1377   209
9 The siege of Saint-Sauveur-le-Vicomte, August 1374–July 1375   220
10 Calais and the Pale, September 1377   293
11 The Duke of Anjou in Gascony, July–October 1377   298
12 The conquest of the Navarrese castles of Normandy, April–June 1378   319
13 The assault on Saint-Malo, August–September 1378   326
14 Campaigns in Navarre, June 1378–March 1379   335
15 The Earl of Buckingham's campaign in France, August 1380–May 1381   389
16 The siege of Nantes, November 1380–January 1381   398
17 The Roosebeke campaign, November 1382   481
18 The Norwich crusade, May–September 1383   499
19 Sluys, Damme and the Vier Ambachten, 1385   542
20 The Castilian invasion of Portugal, July–August 1385   561
21 The battle of Aljubarrota, 14 August 1385   565
22 The Anglo-Portuguese invasion of Castile, March–June 1387   608

23 The Radcot Bridge campaign, December 1387   640
24 The French invasion of Guelders,
    September–November 1388   663
25 Principal territories of the Counts of Armagnac and Foix,
    1375–1382   681
26 Principal *routier* garrisons, 1379–1392   685
27 Cities under siege, 1379–1389   697
28 *Routier* operations, autumn 1383   700
29 French territorial proposals, 1377–1393   808

    General maps
  I France   xviii
 II Aquitaine   870
III Paris   871
 IV Brittany and the Cotentin   872
  V Flanders and the Low Countries   873
 VI The Scottish border   874
VII Castile, Navarre and Portugal   875

    Family trees
  A Royal House of England   866
  B Royal Houses of Castile and Portugal   868

Preface

There are few darker periods of England's history than the last three decades of the fourteenth century. The famous victories of Edward III and the Black Prince had set standards of achievement which their successors could never hope to match. The one-sided treaty of Brétigny which followed them had embodied England's territorial claims at their grandest and most ambitious, drawing lines across the map of France from which another generation of English diplomats was unable to retreat with honour. Prisoners of their own triumphs, the English were condemned to see the conquests of the past thirty years overrun by the armies of the King of France in less than ten. Edward himself, a senile, pathetic symbol, outlived all the companions of his great years, and finally his son the Black Prince as well. Rarely has *nemesis* followed so quickly and directly upon *hubris*. When Edward died in 1377, he was succeeded by a vulnerable child, who was destined to grow into a neurotic and unstable adult presiding over a divided nation, until he was finally deposed and murdered by his cousin.

Although these were years of defeat for England, they were not sterile years. The conduct of the war passed into the hands of the growing class of career soldiers and adventurers. Their leaders were men of courage, determination and strategic imagination, who ensured that England remained an effective belligerent even against the background of financial penury and persistent retreat. Great maritime bases were established on the Atlantic coast of France from Calais to Bayonne. English war fleets operated from Dordrecht to Lisbon. English armies operated not only in France but in Flanders, Portugal, Navarre and Castile, and as free companies in Italy and Germany. English diplomats were active in every European country. Yet all this effort was destined to end in failure. For in the fourteenth century, as in almost all periods, the chief material of war was money. England was among the most intensively governed states of contemporary Europe, but it lacked the resources to fight an aggressive war of conquest against a country with three times its wealth and population. For much of this period England also had to take on Castile, the principal naval power of the Atlantic seaboard; Flanders, still the greatest industrial and commercial power of Europe outside Italy; and Scotland, a constant menace in her rear.

However, France too paid a heavy price for her success. On the surface, these were glittering years for France: years of extravagant ceremony at the grandest court of Europe, of great palaces, of famous paladins making their reputations as far afield as Naples, Hungary, Poland and Constantinople, of astonishing artistic creativity among painters, sculptors, jewellers, poets and novelists. Yet beneath the surface the French government lived constantly at the edge of bankruptcy and the population subsisted in fear and insecurity. Large parts of the country, especially in the south, were ruined and depopulated by the burden of war taxation. In the wealthier northern provinces around the capital there were co-ordinated movements of rebellion and social revolution. These pressures would have been difficult for any government to contain. But the inexperience of Charles VI and his gradual relapse into insanity after 1392 divided the French political world, as the King's relatives competed for the plunder of the state, sowing the seeds of disintegration and civil war in the following century. Like England in the dotage of Edward III, France was destined to destroy herself by the completeness of her victory.

The late fourteenth century was above all a self-conscious age. Its achievements and failings were remorselessly analysed by the chroniclers, lawyers, social commentators and poets of the time. From Chaucer and Gower in England to Eustache Deschamps and Christine de Pisan in France, contemporary writers were convinced that they were living through fascinating times: times of great wickedness and great achievement, of intense personal heroism and collective mediocrity, of extremes of wealth and poverty, fortune and failure. More than six centuries later, it is possible to agree with all of these judgments. It is also possible to reconstruct the mood of the time with the aid of a range of narrative, literary and record sources far wider than those available for any earlier period of medieval history, and drawn from the whole of western and southern Europe. I have made use of all of this material. But the narrative is shaped mainly by the extensive record sources of England, France and Spain. In this and other respects, the principles on which this history is written were explained in the preface to the first volume, and have not changed.

I should like to thank Sir William Harding for making many helpful suggestions about the text, and saving me from countless solecisms.

J.P.C.S.
Greenwich
February 2008

Synopsis to 1369

After three decades in which the ambiguous status of the duchy of Aquitaine had poisoned relations between England and France, Philip VI of France decreed the confiscation of the duchy in 1337 and Edward III declared war. Edward's initial strategy was to stir up the internal political tensions of France, encouraging rebellions against the authority of the French Crown with promises of military support. Between 1338 and 1340, the English King concentrated his efforts on Flanders where the revolt of the towns against their count, Louis of Nevers, provided him with a rich and powerful ally on France's northernmost province. To provide the Flemings with a justification for making war on Philip VI and to encourage other provincial rebellions, Edward revived the claim which he had made at the beginning of his reign to be the rightful king of France through his mother (the eldest daughter of Philip IV of France). In 1340 he proclaimed himself King of France at Ghent. But apart from the famous sea-battle at Sluys in 1340, which resulted in the destruction of the French fleet, Edward III's northern strategy was a failure which ended in military stalemate and bankruptcy.

The English King turned next to Brittany, where a war of succession broke out in 1341 between the house of Montfort, backed by England, and the French King's candidate, Charles of Blois. Strategically, this was more productive. The English occupied much of Brittany, including the important coastal fortress of Brest. Finally, in 1346, Edward III landed in Normandy with a large English army to take advantage of an incipient rebellion among sections of the Norman nobility. The rebellion never materialised, but Edward marched through northern France and, confronted by the numerically superior army of Philip VI north of the Somme, defeated and largely destroyed it at the battle of Crécy. He went on to capture Calais in 1347 after a siege of eleven months. These events coincided with important developments in other theatres. In England, an attempt by France's long-standing Scottish ally to mount a diversion in Edward's rear ended with their defeat at Neville's Cross in 1346 and the capture of the King of Scotland, David II. Henry of Lancaster took an army to Bordeaux in 1345, and over a period of some eighteen months recovered much of the territory in the lower valleys of the Garonne and the Dordogne which had been lost to the French in the early years of the war.

The following decade was dominated by the attempts of Edward III and the Prince of Wales to exploit the prolonged and destructive rebellion of Charles of Evreux ('the Bad'), King of Navarre, which began with the assassination of the Constable of France, Charles of Spain, in 1354. In 1356, John II of France arrested Charles in Rouen castle, and put a number of his principal supporters to death. These events provoked the greatest civil war in France's medieval history. As France subsided into anarchy, the English planned co-ordinated invasions of northern France by three English armies operating from Calais, Brittany and Aquitaine. The only part of this ambitious plan to be carried through to a conclusion was the southern invasion, which was conducted by the Prince of Wales with a combined English and Gascon army from Bordeaux. John II marched against the Prince, and caught up with him east of Poitiers in September 1356. The battle of Poitiers ended with the loss of John's army and his own capture. It also led to four years of civil war in the course of which Paris was taken over by a revolutionary regime led by Charles of Navarre and the demagogue Étienne Marcel. Much of northern France was occupied by English garrisons, Navarrese armies, and German, English and Gascon free companies. This disastrous period in French history was brought to an end by the treaties of Brétigny (1360) and Calais (1361). By these treaties, John II obtained his own release and Edward III's promise to abandon his pretension to be King of France. But in return he had to promise a crushing ransom and to cede about a quarter of the territory of his kingdom to create an enlarged duchy of Aquitaine, free of all feudal dependence on France. In 1363, the duchy became an independent principality, which was settled on the Prince of Wales.

The treaties failed to bring peace to France, mainly because it proved impossible to control the ravages of the English, Navarrese and Gascon companies still operating there. John II never formally renounced his sovereignty over Aquitaine, because Edward III continually put off his own renunciation of the title of King of France in the hope that the continuing threat that he might resume it would keep the French government compliant. But, with John II's premature death in 1364, power passed to his son Charles V who set about unpicking the settlement of 1360–1. In 1367, the Prince of Wales invaded Castile in the name of King Pedro, who had been deposed and expelled by his illegitimate half-brother Henry of Trastámara with French backing. The Prince defeated Henry and his French allies at the battle of Nájera but the expedition bankrupted him. In an attempt to recover his finances the Prince imposed, with the support of the Estates of Aquitaine, a *fouage* or hearth tax on his subjects. Two principal noblemen of the south-west, the Count of Armagnac and the lord of Albret, took the opportunity to test the effectiveness of the settlement of 1360–1. They appealed to the King of France against the tax. Charles V's acceptance of these appeals effectively repudiated the treaties of Brétigny and Calais. When the Prince declined to answer to the appeals Charles declared the duchy forfeited in May 1369. Edward III resumed the title of King of France three weeks later.

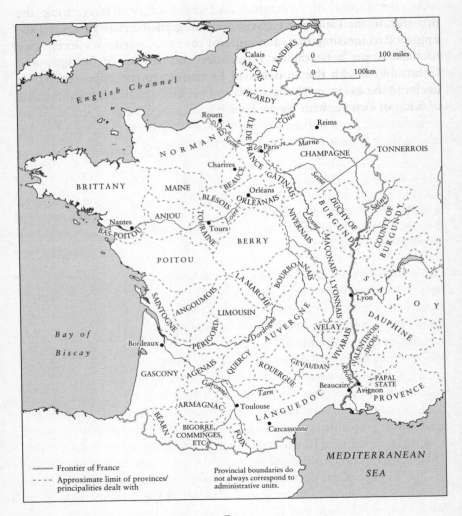

1 France

CHAPTER I

Neighbours and Enemies

In 1389, in the Celestine Convent in Paris, an old man imagined the English Parliament gathered in London before Queen Truth. The young Richard II sat beneath her throne wearing the crown and a tunic embroidered with the leopards of England. Opposite him stood his uncles John of Gaunt, Thomas of Woodstock and Edmund Langley, sons of the warrior-king who 'by God's will had broken the close of the gilded *fleurs de lys*'. Around them the chivalry of the land stood, stained to the tips of their fingers with the blood of their enemies.

Who can count how many churches you have left in ruins . . . how many widows, beggars, cripples and orphans you have made in Scotland and France, the Queen asked them . . . but although you succeeded in capturing the King of Scotland and triumphed by God's leave on the awful battlefields of Crécy and Poitiers, yet now as we speak you hold scarcely a hundredth part of these two kingdoms.[1]

Philip de Mézières, the sombre spirit who composed this allegory, had been a minor witness of the great reversal of fortunes which the Queen described: a soldier in Normandy at the lowest point of the civil war of the 1350s, a councillor of Charles V in the time of victories and a recluse watching events from his cell during the troubled reign of Charles's son. He was a moralist, an advocate of ancient ideals of chivalry which had perhaps never existed, and he was readier than most of his contemporaries to discover the hand of God in recent events. But he could see as well as the English noblemen in his arresting parable the scale of the transformation which had come about in just twenty years.

At fifty-six Edward III was past the age when he was physically capable of fighting in France although it would be some time before he realised it. The English King passed much of his time at the royal manors of Havering and Sheen. On his rare visits to the great public palaces at Westminster, Windsor and Eltham he tended to remain secluded in his chamber away from the noise, gossip and publicity of the court. The daily

I

business of government was left to his Council. Edward's Council was ill-suited to the conduct of a major war. In 1369 the dominant figure there was William of Wykeham, Bishop of Winchester. Wykeham was a man of modest origins who had had been Edward's Chancellor since 1367. He was 'head of the King's privy council and controlled his great council' according to the complaints made at his impeachment in 1376. William of Wykeham loved power. But he was not good at using it. Although only moderately venal himself, he proved to be a poor administrator and a bad judge of subordinates and he presided over a notable decline in the administration's traditionally high standards of competence and honesty. He was also completely inexperienced in foreign affairs.

With the reopening of the war with France political influence progressively passed to another of the King's ministers, William Lord Latimer. He was a very different kind of man. Latimer was a professional soldier who had fought with English armies in Scotland, France and Gascony during the 1350s before making his reputation as the leading English captain in Brittany during the 1360s. He returned to England at about the end of 1367 aged thirty-eight with a large personal fortune and high ambitions. Shortly after his return he was appointed Steward of the royal household, a powerful position which gave him the ear of the King and a large measure of control over other people's access to him. When the break with France came in 1369 Latimer threw himself into the daily grind of military administration with all the energy and efficiency that was not forthcoming from William of Wykeham. He was continually conducting musters, inspecting ships, directing requisitions, paying troops and transacting the miscellaneous diplomatic affairs which the Exchequer clerks darkly referred to as the 'King's secret business'. So far as anyone maintained a continuous surveillance over the English war effort in these years it was Latimer.[2]

But if the English King had servants what he lacked was friends and colleagues. Edward had survived most of the men who had helped him to defeat the French in the 1340s and 1350s. William Bohun, Earl of Northampton, who had commanded his armies in Scotland and Brittany, had died campaigning with the King in France in 1360. Henry, Duke of Lancaster, Edward's ablest strategist and diplomat and perhaps the real architect of the treaty of Brétigny, had died of plague in 1361 within a year of its conclusion. Not one of the six earls whom Edward had created in 1337 to serve as partners in his great enterprise was still living in 1369. In his prime Edward's partnership with the English nobility had depended on a certain personal chemistry, a generous purse, a splendid court and a high degree of accessibility. His relations with a younger generation were inevitably more distant. The vacuum left in his counsels was never filled. The Prince of Wales, who as Edward's heir could have been expected to succeed to Henry of Lancaster's influence, was an outstanding military commander but a man of poor political judgment who had been away in Aquitaine since 1363 and eventually returned, broken in health and spirit, in 1371. In his absence the dominant figure at court and occasionally in government was the King's second surviving son, John of Gaunt.

John of Gaunt was a controversial figure in his own day and has remained one ever since. His historical reputation has suffered from the fact that he was a mediocre soldier in an age of great ones and from his obstinate pursuit of what seems in retrospect to be the doomed project to make himself King of Castile. It has suffered also from the persistent vituperation to which he was subjected in his lifetime by the most eloquent chronicler of the period, Thomas Walsingham of St. Albans. The fact that Shakespeare gave him some of his greatest lines has only partly redeemed him. Gaunt deserved better. He had been born in Ghent in 1340, shortly after his father had assumed the title of King of France, and had passed his whole youth amid the clash of arms: at the sea fight off Winchelsea in 1350, in the abortive expedition to Normandy of 1355 and in the army of Reims in 1359–60. But he retained throughout his life a rare scepticism about what armed force could achieve and a clearer view than most of his contemporaries of the long-term interest of England. He owed his position in English public life to a number of factors: his unshakeable loyalty to the dynasty even in the darkest period of Edward III's dotage and Richard II's infancy; his intelligence, articulateness and relative freedom from received opinions; and a hot temper combined with an imposing physical presence which silenced dissent and made him both respected and hated. To these advantages he added the indispensable condition for all political power in the middle ages, a great personal fortune.

John of Gaunt had married in 1359 Blanche of Lancaster, one of the two surviving daughters of the great Henry of Lancaster and co-heiress to the immense properties of the palatinate of Lancaster and the earldoms of Leicester, Derby and Richmond. When Blanche's sister died of plague in April 1362 the entire inheritance fell into Gaunt's hands. He owned land in almost every county of England, producing a net income of between £8,000 and £10,000 a year.[3] With wealth on this scale he could hold his own regardless of the transient phases of royal

3

favour. He could put a military retinue into the field on a scale unequalled by any others apart from the King and the Prince of Wales. He could deploy influence and patronage not just at court but across much of provincial England. His wealth and power were highly visible: the great palace of Savoy on the Strand which symbolised the evils of the realm in the eyes of the rioters who destroyed it in 1381; the castle which he built at Kenilworth in Warwickshire whose splendid ruins can still be seen; the immense fortresses at Lancaster, Pontefract, Knaresborough, Tutbury, Leicester and some two dozen lesser strongholds; the resounding titles and clattering escorts of liveried retainers; the publicly flaunted mistress and bastards. John of Gaunt's role as the main executant of England's foreign policy in the last years of Edward III and for much of the reign of Richard II inevitably invited resentment and hostility when things went wrong.

When Charles V repudiated the treaty of Brétigny in 1369 the English held about a quarter of the territory of the French kingdom. South of the Loire the treaties of Brétigny and Calais had created a vastly enlarged territory of Aquitaine which had been erected into an autonomous principality in 1363 and granted to the Prince of Wales. In normal times the Prince's territory was financially and administratively self-sufficient and in the course of the 1360s it had acquired many of the trappings of a sovereign state. The Prince had his own Chancellor and Treasurer, his Constable and Marshal, his provincial seneschals and from 1370 his 'Court of Sovereignty' to hear appeals without recourse to Edward III in England. Many of these institutions were miniatures of the corresponding organs of the government of France. His officers controlled with greater or lesser degrees of tenacity the whole of the Atlantic coast of France from the Vendée to the Pyrenees, including the three major Atlantic ports of La Rochelle, Bordeaux and Bayonne. From the coast his territory extended inland through the basin of the Garonne and its tributaries beyond Montauban, Millau and Rodez, penetrating in long fingers across the map towards the Cevennes and the high plateau of Aubrac, and up the Dordogne valley to the foothills of the mountains of Auvergne. North of the Dordogne the Prince's dominions embraced the whole of the marshy lowlands of Saintonge and the rich, undulating plains of Angoumois and Poitou. Further east, comparatively inaccessible from Bordeaux, lay the high, inhospitable Limousin plateau.[4]

North of the Loire England's strength was concentrated in four areas: the fortress town of Calais, the county of Ponthieu at the mouth of the

Somme, the castle of Saint-Sauveur-le-Vicomte in Normandy and the duchy of Brittany. These territories were less extensive than the holdings of the English royal house in the south-west but they represented a more formidable threat to the French monarchy.

Calais was the greatest strategic asset of the English in France. The town, only twenty miles by sea from the Kent coast, was protected by a powerful circuit of walls and ditches, by marshes which surrounded it on all sides and by a ring of outlying forts which pushed the border of the English pale out for ten miles into the hinterland. Its garrison had a normal wartime strength of about 1,200 professional soldiers and 300 armed citizens, which made it the largest permanent concentration of troops in Europe. The main problem about Calais was its dependence on England for supplies. In 1369 and for most of the following decade the garrison benefited from the benevolent neutrality of Louis de Mâle, Count of Flanders, who allowed his subjects to bring supplies to the town and to buy English goods there. But the Count was a fickle friend, whose support might be withdrawn at any moment. During the 1370s successive aggressive captains were able to replenish their stores by mounting powerful cattle-rustling raids far into northern France and driving the herds back to the town. But, as the neighbouring parts of Artois and Picardy were progressively impoverished and depopulated, the returns from these operations diminished and the burden of victualling the town mounted.

Economically Calais contributed little to its own survival. Its civilian population consisted of English colonists, who lived on the garrison, on passing travellers and on England's export trades. A staple was established, or rather re-established, at Calais by royal ordinance in 1370. It was in theory the compulsory transit point of all English exports. But in practice the staple ordinances could never be rigorously enforced because Calais was a war zone. In the early 1370s less than half the trade which should have gone through Calais actually did so. The production of the Calais mint, usually a faithful barometer of economic activity there, fell to a historically low level. But, in spite of the high cost of maintaining Calais and the occasional misgivings expressed by English politicians, its possession was invaluable to the English. It provided them with a secure base on the coast of France. And the expense which it forced on France was at least as great as the cost to the English Exchequer. To contain the continual threat from the town the French kings were obliged to maintain what amounted to a standing army in Picardy and Artois, based on Boulogne and Saint-Omer and at least a dozen smaller places in between.

There would never be peace, sang the French courtier-poet Eustache Deschamps, while the English held Calais.[5]

The county of Ponthieu had been inherited in 1279 by Edward I's wife, Eleanor of Castile. Apart from more or less lengthy periods of confiscation, it had belonged to the kings of England ever since. The territory, standing at the mouth of the Somme less than ninety miles from Paris, might have been as significant as Calais if it had been better fortified and if Edward III's officers had got on better with its inhabitants. The ford of Blanchetaque and the bridge at Abbeville were the only crossings of the Somme west of Amiens. Le Crotoy on the northern shore of the estuary was a walled harbour town with a powerful castle, which had been an important French naval base. During the 1360s Edward III had spent a great deal of money on the defences of these places and had considerably reinforced their garrisons as the diplomatic situation deteriorated.[6]

Saint-Sauveur by comparison was an anomaly. The great Norman fortress occupied a strong position in the centre of the Cotentin peninsula, dominating the road to Cherbourg at the point where it crossed the River Douve. It had belonged to that perennial rebel Godfrey of Harcourt who had bequeathed it to Edward III at his death in 1356. With the peace of 1360 the rest of the region moved into the obedience of the King of France. But Edward was allowed to retain Saint-Sauveur on condition that he granted it to a man of his choice. He chose Sir John Chandos, hero of the battles of Poitiers and Auray and the Prince's Constable of Aquitaine. Chandos, although heavily engaged in the affairs of the Aquitaine, spent much of his time at Saint-Sauveur. He commissioned substantial works including the reconstruction of the keep and the strengthening of the curtain wall with new towers. As a result the fortress had become a serious menace. Its garrison had recently been strengthened and had begun to operate in concert with the last remnant of the English wing of the Great Company of 1367–8, which was based not far away at Château-Gontier in Maine. The Great Company, which was led by the experienced professional *routier* Sir John Cresswell, was at this stage probably about a thousand strong. Together, the garrisons of Saint-Sauveur and Château-Gontier represented a disciplined force of nearly 1,500 English soldiers standing across the main road communications of western France close to the great arteries of the Seine and the Loire.[7]

Brittany had for many years been regarded as a vital strategic interest of the English. It lay across their land and sea communications with Gascony. It provided a broad, accessible invasion route overland into

Anjou, Maine and Lower Normandy. Brittany was one of the great fiefs of France, administratively autonomous and ruled by its own dukes. The current duke, John IV de Montfort, was a highly intelligent, ambitious young man who was determined to revive the ancient strength of his duchy and preserve its historic independence. In the long run that required an accommodation with the French Crown as John was well aware. But his hands were tied by his past. John owed his position to the armed intervention of England in the long civil war which had divided the province between 1341 and 1364. After the death of his father in 1345, when he was about five years old, John had been taken to England and brought up at Edward III's court while the English fought their battles in Brittany in his name. He had married Edward's daughter Mary and then, after her premature death, the Prince of Wales's step-daughter Joan Holand. As Edward himself would declare in 1372, the Duke of Brittany was 'doubly made our kinsman and not only strove continually to accommodate himself to our wishes but, even when he was far away and surrounded by enemies, never ceased to labour in our interest'. There was a fair measure of hyperbole in this statement. But the bond of sentiment undoubtedly existed and was acknowledged by John himself. As he once told the King of France, 'if he surrounded himself with Englishmen it was because they had nourished him as a child and they are his servants and officers and those of his wife the duchess, who is herself English.'[8]

In his dealings with John de Montfort Edward III had some important bargaining counters in addition to kinship and affection. The honour of Richmond in Yorkshire, which the dukes of Brittany had held for most of the past three centuries, was sadly decayed, but had once yielded more than the entire revenues of Brittany. It was currently in Edward's hands and occupied by John of Gaunt. Edward also had in his custody the two sons of John's defeated rival Charles of Blois, who had been killed at the battle of Auray in 1364. They had been held in England since 1357 as security for their father's unpaid ransom. They would have been natural figureheads for John's many enemies in France and Brittany. The implicit threat to release them could be relied on to bring John to heel. In addition the English maintained an important military presence in the duchy. Edward III still controlled the great castle of Bécherel in eastern Brittany. Its large and unruly English garrison was answerable in practice to William Latimer who had been granted the captaincy of the place in June 1368. Sir Robert Knolles, the famous English *routier*, kept another powerful military establishment in his castle at Derval on the eastern march of the duchy. Other Englishmen controlled castles in the Duke's name and farmed much of his revenue. They filled his household. A small group of them still sat in his council. The Duke's English friends were too visible to be liked. They occupied honourable positions which might have gone to Bretons. They held land in the duchy whose former owners had not forgotten that it had once been theirs. English garrisons had pillaged and impoverished the duchy during the civil war and after it had ended they continued to do so. At Latimer's impeachment in 1376 the Bretons alleged that his officers at Bécherel had taken £83,000 in four years from *patis*, as the protection money exacted from local communities was called. The figure is impossibly high, but even a modest fraction of it would have made Latimer an exceptionally rich man. John de Montfort's dependence on the English was controversial among his subjects and he tried to reduce it. He pursued a deliberate policy of Bretonisation, edging Englishmen out of most government offices and the principal ducal fortresses. He protested with real anger at the incursions of the largely English bands occupying Château-Gontier and armed his subjects against the garrisons of Derval and Bécherel. But it would take him many years to shake off the tutelage of England entirely.[9]

France had no strategic positions within the British Isles comparable to the great fortresses and provinces which the English controlled in France. The most serious threat to the English homeland came from Scotland. The long vendetta between the two kingdoms of the British Isles, which had begun with Edward I's attempt to conquer the Scottish kingdom two generations before, was destined to continue until the sixteenth century and arguably until 1746. For most of this period the Scots were allies of France. The 'auld alliance' was of critical importance to the Scots, who regarded it as the main guarantee of their continuing independence. For years they had maintained a constant pressure on England's northern border. They had mounted major invasions to coincide with English offensives on the continent. These offensives had never seriously threatened the political heart of England, which lay beyond the reach of Scottish armies. But they were nevertheless a serious problem for the English government. The security of the Scottish border had a big impact on English political sentiment. Scotland was an ancient enemy, far more intensely feared and hated than France. England's continuing acceptance of Edward III's heavy military expenditure on the continent always depended on his being able to persuade his subjects that the northern march of the kingdom was secure. This meant that when tensions between the two British realms were high it was necessary to divert a large part of the country's military resources to the defence of the border. In the 1340s and 1350s and again in the 1380s virtually all the manpower and tax revenues of the counties north of the Trent had to be reserved for this purpose.

Recently relations between France and Scotland had been under strain. The defeat of John II at the battle of Poitiers in 1356 had seriously dented the Scots' loyalty to the 'auld alliance'. The treaty of Berwick of 1357, which was the direct result of the French defeat, was ostensibly no more than a ransom agreement for David II, held in England since the battle of Neville's Cross. It did not resolve any of the secular issues between England and Scotland. But, by spreading the ransom of David II over ten years, during which by the law of arms David would not be at liberty to make war on his captor, the treaty ensured a long period of truce. In the event it proved to be even longer than ten years because of the difficulty that the Scots experienced in paying the ransom instalments from the meagre resources of their country. In 1365, when only a fifth of it had been paid, the Scots were obliged to agree to a substantial increase in order to be allowed to spread out the payments over twenty-five years. They also accepted a continuation of the truce until at least February 1370. These instruments made a legal obligation out of a policy which suited David II for other reasons: his troubled relations with leading Scottish nobles and the highlanders, the economic travails of his people in the face of the burden of taxation, and his own relations with the English court, a famous centre of European chivalry where the Scottish King felt at home. Charles V sent an embassy to Scotland in the spring of 1369. It landed at Aberdeen at about the end of April only to find that the Scottish King was in London with his principal advisers negotiating a reduction of the instalments of his ransom and a further fourteen-year truce with England, which was ultimately agreed in June.[10]

War and peace had always been relative concepts on the Scottish march. The heavily wooded hills of southern Scotland and the English border counties had been devastated by decades of warfare. A large proportion of the population on both sides lived at the margins of banditry and had come to depend on the traditional life of raids and counter-raids, cattle rustling, kidnapping and gang warfare across the border. These incidents constantly threatened to erupt into open war between the two countries. The difficulty of controlling the situation was increased by the fact that the fortunes of both kings were in the hands of local men with interests of their own in the wars of the border. The

English government was obliged to delegate the day-to-day defence of the region to the leading families of the north, Percy and Neville in Northumberland, Clifford, Dacre and Lucy in Cumberland and Westmoreland. These were families which owed their wealth and influence to the border war. By 1369 they had built up great power-bases in the north which would eventually undermine the stability of the English government itself. The Percys, a Yorkshire family which had only established itself in Northumberland at the beginning of the fourteenth century, were by 1369 by far the most powerful lords of the north and virtually hereditary wardens of the east march. Their personal military following was among the largest in England. On the Scottish side very similar personal fiefdoms were being built up by the ambitious and aggressive lords of the house of Douglas and the Dunbar Earls of March. Their interests by now extended along the whole length of the border. Their relations with the English border lords were poisoned for much of this period by a growing and intensely personal animosity.

The instability of the border region was aggravated by its openness. The border was rarely marked or guarded. It was inhabited on both sides by people who shared a common language, culture and social attitude. There were English allies living among the Scots in parts of the Lowlands. There were Scottish sympathisers in Carlisle, Hexham and Newcastle. In 1369 there were still four important enclaves of English-held territory north of the border, which were to prove a constant irritant. Berwick, on the north shore of the Tweed estuary, was an important commercial town which contained the largest English garrison in Scotland. Roxburgh, at the junction of the Tweed and Teviot valleys, was a powerful garrisoned fortress, partially rebuilt by the English in the past decade. At Jedburgh in Teviotdale, a Percy lordship, an English garrison held out deep in Douglas territory. Finally there was the lordship of Annandale in Galloway, north of the Solway Firth. Almost inaccessible from England and serving no strategic purpose apart from its own defence, most of Annandale had been occupied by the English families of Bohun and Dacre in the early fourteenth century. Their territory had been much reduced by the encroachments of the Douglases. But the Bohuns still held and garrisoned the fortress of Lochmaben on the south-east side of the loch at the headwaters of the River Annan.[11]

Edward III was never willing to make the compromises that might have brought a permanent peace with Scotland. But he attached extreme importance to holding the truce on the march. He deprecated the tendency to retaliate unthinkingly for every Scottish border raid and did his best to impose a framework of law and diplomacy on the borderers' violent instincts. A system of peacekeeping, originating in much older traditions of march law, had been developed since 1357 into one of the most elaborate of its kind on any of the march zones of western Europe. The wardens of the march, almost always now selected from the ranks of the great border families, were armed with power to suppress disorders and bring the perpetrators to justice. Regular 'march days' were held at points along the border, at which disputes were submitted to special tribunals and settled by joint juries of English and Scots. They were supplemented by 'great days of the march' at which the ambassadors of the two kings dealt with matters of national significance. These measures were remarkably successful. For nearly a decade after 1369 the perennial lawlessness of the border was prevented from erupting into open war. The disarming of Scotland, a relatively new element in the European strategic balance, was one of the main advantages that Edward III enjoyed when the war with France resumed in 1369.[12]

At the same time new threats were beginning to emerge from other parts of the British Isles. Nearly a century after Edward I had completed the conquest of Wales the country was entering upon a period of economic and political tension which would eventually explode in 1400 with the rebellion of Owen Glendower. The enforcement of seigneurial rights upon a resentful peasantry was a fertile source of violence and unrest in many parts of Europe. But the situation was aggravated in Wales by the fact that the English landowners who exercised them were almost all beneficiaries of the wholesale disinheritance of the native Welsh princes in the 1280s and the slow, persistent tide of forfeitures, purchases and exchanges which had followed ever since. The resentment which their officials, who were usually Englishmen, aroused was fortified by nostalgia and myth and by a powerful sense of collective identity among the native Welsh. To these were added the tensions arising from the plantation of fortified boroughs in the midst of a wholly rural society, governed and largely populated by English immigrants and enjoying monopolies extending well beyond their walls; and from the appointment of Englishmen to all the highest positions in the Welsh Church, which created a frustrated underclass of educated and half-educated Welsh clergymen with no prospects of advancement and every reason to share their frustrations with their flocks.

The English were well aware of the problems of Wales. Their officials in the principality had for many years been nervous about the threat of localised risings, and from time to time violent incidents occurred to remind them of it. The danger of a wider revolt had been contained mainly by the fragmented character of Welsh society and by its difficult geography, which made national movements of rebellion hard to organise and sustain. But it had been contained also by a measure of sensitivity on the part of the agents of the English government and the leading territorial magnates. There had been judicious patronage of influential Welshmen and opportunities for well-paid service and looting in the continental armies of Edward III. In the last years of Edward III, however, conditions became harsher. The decline of agricultural and pastoral incomes, a general phenomenon in late medieval Britain, was felt badly in Wales, much of which was infertile and far poorer than England. The progressive pressures on aristocratic incomes in the last three decades of the fourteenth century led everywhere to the more systematic enforcement of seigneurial rights. The disappearance of infantry from England's continental armies deprived humbler men of many of the opportunities which their fathers and grandfathers had enjoyed.

The lordship of Ireland was an older and in some ways a more intractable problem, but an increasingly significant one. Ireland had its own administration, its own Chancery and Exchequer and its own courts. It had its own Parliament presided over by a Lieutenant sent out from England. The golden age of the English lordship had been the reign of Edward I at the end of the thirteenth century when the island had been relatively peaceful and had yielded substantial profits to the Anglo-Irish colonists and revenue surpluses to the Crown. The fourteenth century by comparison was a tale of continual decline. Devastating raids from Scotland in the early years of the century, plague and recession and the rise of the Gaelic chiefs, as well as persistent rebellions among sections of the Anglo-Irish themselves, had reduced much of the English lordship to an anarchic wasteland. Edward III's preoccupation with Scotland and France had starved the Irish Lieutenants of attention and funds, and his reign witnessed a sharp deterioration in an already difficult situation. The revenues of the Irish lordship collapsed. Some of the Anglo-Irish sold up and withdrew to England. Others merged with the native Irish population. Ireland became a significant liability for the English Crown. In 1360 a Great Council at Kilkenny had presented Edward III with a catalogue of the ills of the country and a warning that, unless serious steps were taken to arrest the decline, the King's lordship in Ireland would not survive.

Ireland was always a politically marginal factor in England's relations with other European powers. The Gaelic Irish were never a threat to

England itself. Nor was the island ever likely to be a back-door route for invasion, as Wales and Scotland were. Its significance was that it was an increasingly expensive distraction at a time when England's resources were already tightly stretched. The petition of the Kilkenny Council marked a turning point in the relations of England and Ireland as the English kings started to invest substantial sums trying to re-establish their authority in Ireland. In June 1369, at the moment when the declarations in Paris and London completed the breach with France, the latest Lieutenant to be charged with the government of Ireland sailed for Dublin with more than 600 men.[13] These men could not easily be spared.

The final piece of the western European jigsaw was Flanders, which like Brittany occupied an ambiguous political position between the two main belligerents. Nominally a fief of France, Flanders had achieved practical independence under the rule of Louis de Mâle, the last and ablest of the Dampierre counts. Ill-tempered, autocratic, and unscrupulous, Louis de Mâle had governed the county ever since the death of his father on the battlefield of Crécy more than twenty years earlier. In that time he had transformed Flanders into the principal political and economic power of the Low Countries. In 1356 Louis had greatly increased his power by invading the Imperial duchy of Brabant, lying east of Flanders, traditionally the strongest principality of the German Low Countries. The result of this calculated act of violence was the treaty of Ath in the following year by which two of the principal cities of Brabant, Antwerp and Mechelen, were transferred to Flanders and Louis was recognised as heir to the rest. This consolidated block of territories would in due course fall to Louis's sole heiress, Margaret. Twelve years after the treaty of Ath Louis achieved his greatest diplomatic coup when he recovered the three French-speaking castleries of Lille, Douai and Orchies, which had been annexed by France at the beginning of the fourteenth century. Their restitution was part of the terms which Louis exacted in return for agreeing to marry Margaret to Charles V's brother Philip instead of to an English prince. The cession of the three castleries had caused great grief to Charles V. So much so that he had exacted a secret promise from his brother that he would sell them back to France after Louis de Mâle's death. But Philip made an equally secret promise to his father-in-law on the eve of his wedding that he would never do it. Nor would he ever appoint any man to govern them but 'Flamens flamengans nés de Flandre' ('Flemings, speaking Flemish and born of Flemish stock'). Louis was determined that Flanders would survive as a political force independent of France even after his domains had passed to a prince of the *fleurs de lys*.

The prosperity of Flanders after decades of destructive civil wars and foreign invasions was due in large part to the fact that Louis de Mâle had succeeded in staying out of the Anglo-French wars. Flanders was an infertile, densely populated land dominated by politically self-conscious industrial towns whose main trade was the manufacture of high-quality woollen cloth. They depended on France for a large part of the grain supplies which fed their populations and on England for their industry's main raw material, wool. Flanders, said Froissart, 'stands on the frontier of England and because of the great trade that its inhabitants do with England their hearts are more English than French.' This was true, at least among the commercial oligarchies of the towns. In the 1330s and 1340s the determination of Louis's father to cut off his subjects' economic relations with England had led directly to his defeat and exile at the hands of the three 'great towns' of Ghent, Bruges and Ypres. Louis de Mâle never forgot this. When the war between England and France broke out afresh in 1369 he adopted a policy of neutrality, unacknowledged and often deviously pursued, but consistently observed in spite of his status as a vassal of France and his daughter's marriage to the French King's brother. Louis refused to distribute Charles V's manifesto against England on the outbreak of war, observing disingenuously that his subjects were 'simple fellows' who would not understand such things. He declined to lend any military or naval assistance to France or even to let French diplomatic agents pass through his domains. He turned a blind eye to the activities of English agents who openly recruited troops, chartered ships and bought victuals and war materials in Flanders under the noses of his officials. This behaviour generated much ill-feeling between France and Flanders. For the time being, however, there was nothing that the French King's ministers could do about it.[14]

France in 1369 remained the varied patchwork of regions which it had always been, a country of many languages, disparate laws and cultures and intense local patriotisms. In some ways the French nation remained an official abstraction, familiar to the kings, their servants and propagandists and a few churchmen. To most other people the very word 'France' meant no more than the Île de France, a region around Paris. With the accession of Charles V five years before, the monarchy had become once more an essentially Parisian power as it had been in the days of Louis IX and Philip the Fair. The vast royal palace on the Île de la Cité, overshadowed by memories of the revolution of 1358, was abandoned to lawyers and officials. The French war effort would be directed from the Hôtel Saint-Pol, a rambling mansion surrounded by gardens in eastern Paris, which Charles had rebuilt and extended during the 1360s; and from the principal royal mansions of the Île de France: Saint-Germain-en-Laye, Melun, Creil and Montargis. Charles's methods marked in some ways a return to the secretive policy-making of his grandfather Philip VI, involving a small number of close relatives and trusted officers. His delicate health meant that he travelled little, never led his own armies and had a relatively short attention span when it came to public business. Meetings of his Council began at about 9.00 a.m. and were generally over by 10.00. These habits would have counted as defects in another ruler. But they were compensated in Charles's case by an acute intelligence, an outstanding discernment in choice of subordinates and a facility with public opinion which deserted him only in the final months of his reign.

The French King was an enigma to the English as he was to many of his subjects. John of Gaunt had once dismissed Charles as 'a lawyer', a remark which was not intended to be flattering and caused much amusement when it was repeated to him. Ostensibly the French King's war aim was to enforce the confiscation of the English domains in France which had been pronounced by his judges in June 1369. What he really hoped to achieve is less clear. For, if the ultimate fate of England's French possessions has made their disappearance seem inevitable, Charles was a man of his time who did not necessarily see it that way. He certainly wished to reduce the extent of English holdings in western France, especially in Poitou with its great open frontier to the Loire provinces and its long-standing connections with the royal house, and in Artois where Calais was a constant threat to the security of his realm. He never shifted from the demand that whatever territory the English king held in France should be held as a vassal of the French Crown and not, as the treaty of Brétigny laid down, as part of an autonomous state. But he did not wish to condemn France to generations of attrition with her closest and most powerful neighbour, and throughout his reign proved willing to make large concessions of territory for the sake of peace.

Although virtually without military experience of his own, Charles took a personal interest in the prosecution of the war. Christine de Pisan called him 'principal captain' of his armies, observing that wars were 'better fought by the power of the mind than by brute force of arms'. The

King made some serious mistakes, especially in the first year of the war when he was too ambitious and hasty. But he learned quickly. Cunning, ruthless, highly intelligent, with the flexibility to respond to the changing military situation, he would not be rushed into decisions. He was very conscious of the military strength of England and had a good deal of respect for Edward III, whose portrait stared at him from a four-leaf panel hanging in his study in the Hôtel Saint-Pol. Charles appears to have been personally responsible for what remained the military orthodoxy of the next forty years, that the English were not to be confronted in battle unless it was on overwhelmingly favourable terms. The policy was more or less forced on him by his country's failure to develop a strong indigenous tradition of military archery to match that of the English longbowmen. It remained an article of faith among his circle that Philip VI had gambled his crown by giving battle at Crécy and it was obvious that John II had done so at Poitiers. The King's defensive response to successive English invasions was to prove politically controversial both among the nobility, whose aggressive instincts had to be contained, and among the mass of ordinary Frenchmen, who were obliged to flee to nearby refuges as the open country (*plat pays*) was systematically devastated by the enemy. But it ensured that the French were able to fight the kind of war at which they excelled: a war of sieges, surprises, and harassment, of persistent pressure on the marches which gradually wore the enemy down.[15]

A medieval ruler was expected to take counsel. It was what distinguished monarchy from despotism. Charles V's principal advisers were his immediate family: his brothers the Dukes of Anjou, Berry and Burgundy, and his brother-in-law Louis, Duke of Bourbon. These were the same men who served as his lieutenants in the main theatres of the war and as executants of his decisions. With the possible exception of the Duke of Berry, they were all competent soldiers, skilful politicians and diplomats and, at least while Charles V was alive, loyal pillars of the revived monarchy. The most significant influence on the course of the war was undoubtedly Louis, Duke of Anjou. This able and ambitious but impulsive thirty-year-old, the second son of John II, had been royal Lieutenant in Languedoc since 1364. He had been the most vigorous advocate of war with England before 1369 and he probably entertained more radical ambitions than the King for expelling the English from France. He was also well placed to realise them since his lieutenancy gave him viceregal powers in all the provinces bordering on Aquitaine from the Dordogne to the Pyrenees, together with the complete disposition of the Crown's revenues there. However, as well as being the most formidable adversary of the English in France, Louis of Anjou was also a perennial source of instability at the heart of royal policy-making. His personal appanage was limited to the small, war-damaged duchy of Anjou on the lower Loire, which brought him much less revenue than either of his younger brothers drew from their great domains. Anjou was always looking for a stage on which to cut a bigger figure. He was also jealous, quarrelsome and vindictive, allowing his actions to be influenced by personal vendettas, with Charles of Navarre and John de Montfort for example, which cut across royal policy towards these difficult but important vassals. Occasionally he conducted what amounted to a foreign policy of his own with the English, the Castilians and the Aragonese, and later the Italians.

Beneath the royal princes there was a large corps of ministers and administrators on whom the King depended for the ordinary functioning of his government and increasingly for advice on major issues of policy. Over the years its membership was remarkably stable. Almost all of them were men who had served Charles V's father in the last years of his reign. The Archbishop of Sens, Guillaume de Melun, was a soldier-prelate who had led his retinue at the battle of Poitiers and shared John II's captivity in England. He had sat on the French royal Council since 1351. John, Count of Sarrebruch, the Butler of France, was another prisoner of Poitiers who had acquired great influence with the old King during their exile in England and went on to serve on Charles V's Council and in a succession of delicate diplomatic missions. Jean de Dormans, who became Bishop of Beauvais and ultimately a cardinal, had lived through the crisis of 1356–8 with Charles when he was Dauphin and then served both John II and his son as Chancellor. Bureau de la Rivière had begun his career as the Dauphin's squire and trencherman in 1358 when he must have been in his late teens and held the King in his arms as he died, twenty-two years later. This shadowy but influential individual, who became Charles V's principal chamberlain in about 1372, was virtually first minister at the end of the reign. Between them these men brought a remarkable continuity to the conduct of affairs in France at a time when England was riven by political crises and undermined by constant changes of personnel. Their personal opinions on policy are rarely recorded. But their experience of the long political crisis of the 1350s had made them share both the King's ambition to undo the effects of defeat and his willingness to compromise with the enemy when the occasion arose.[16]

CHAPTER II

Return to Arms
1369

Charles V originally envisaged a short war. When he and his advisers laid their plans they conceived a series of bold strokes involving the deployment of overwhelming force on several fronts at once. The command of the armies was assigned to the King's three brothers. Louis of Anjou was given sole charge of the war on the south-east march of Aquitaine which bordered on his lieutenancy in Languedoc. The Duke of Berry was appointed lieutenant-general with authority to conduct the war across the whole basin of the Loire from Auvergne to Anjou. Between them Anjou and Berry proposed to mount simultaneous invasions of Aquitaine from all sides. But the main enterprise, which was entrusted to the Duke of Burgundy, was nothing less than a seaborne invasion of England. In March 1369 a Great Council attended by the leading noblemen of the realm met in the King's presence to approve this venture. At beginning of April orders were given to concentrate all available shipping in the mouth of the Seine. The transports were to be requisitioned in the seaports of France while the escorting warships would be hired from the Castilians and the Genoese. Agents were sent into the Low Countries and Burgundy to buy arms and equipment in bulk. A huge depot for victuals and stores was organised in the Seine port of Harfleur. Philip of Burgundy's orders were that the armada should be ready to sail by the beginning of September.[1]

By the time that the formal breach with England occurred in May 1369 the Duke of Anjou's officers had already been waging open war in Quercy and Rouergue for four months. Anjou was not a man to let an opportunity pass him by. He was well aware that these would be the most difficult provinces for the English to defend. In neither of them was there a historic tradition of loyalty for the English to draw on. Quercy was the one province whose cession to the English in 1362 had met with significant local resistance. Rouergue had never previously belonged to the English duchy even in its heyday at the end of the thirteenth century. The lords of Armagnac and Albret, who were the leading figures behind the rebellion, had a large network of kinsmen and clients in both provinces.

So far, the Duke of Anjou's officers had been able to take over much of the region without invading either province in force. They operated by a combination of blandishments and threats, supported by small packets of men sent from the Toulousain to occupy crucial towns and castles as they submitted. In Rouergue the defence was in the hands of the Prince of Wales's seneschal, the Cheshire knight Sir Thomas Wettenhall. By March 1369 Wettenhall had lost control of most of his province and was attempting to hold out with a small English garrison in the citadel of Villefranche. The inhabitants of the town below were already in touch with the Duke of Anjou. They had no interest in a government that was incapable of defending them. They told Wettenhall that they would surrender unless help came quickly. The place was in French hands by May. Another Cheshire man, James Mascy, commanded the English garrison at Millau. His relations with the town seem to have been rather better than Wettenhall's and they remained loyal for longer. But it was a fragile loyalty which owed very little to sentiment. Mascy had a strong garrison and controlled the twin forts of Compeyre and Paulhe which stood on opposite sides of the Tarn four miles upstream. If the townsmen had defected to the French these places would have been a serious threat to their livelihoods. So for the time being Millau fended off the approaches of Anjou's officers, offering evasive reassurances and sending agents to take legal advice in distant places. There was a handful of other places in Rouergue where the English still clung on: the tower of Sauveterre on the south-east march of the province; the remote castle of Castelmary in the valley of the Viaur; and two small manors belonging to the Anglophile Bishop of Vabres who was now their only significant ally in the province. The situation was almost as bad in Quercy. In the north the English had more or less retained control of the Dordogne valley but had lost most of the rest. The only significant English garrison in the south was the important town of Montauban, where the English Seneschal, Sir Thomas Walkefare, was still holding out surrounded by territory which had submitted to the agents of the Duke of Anjou.[2]

In the face of the crisis the Prince's government was paralysed. Its financial position was catastrophic. In round figures, in the financial year ending 29 September 1369 the domestic revenues of the principality stood at 276,000 *livres* of Bordeaux (about £55,000 sterling). This represented a fall of 40 per cent from their highest point three years earlier. Almost three-quarters of these revenues came from just two regions, Poitou and Saintonge, out of the ten into which the principality was divided for accounting purposes. The collapse everywhere else was due to a combination of factors but mainly to the unstable political situation. The five easternmost regions, Limousin, Périgord, Agenais, Rouergue and Quercy, had ceased to account at all owing to administrative chaos and war. Much of the Bazadais, south-east of Bordeaux, was Albret country and had contributed nothing to the Prince's treasury since the lord of Albret's appeal. Collection of the notorious *fouage*, which had provoked the appeals, had ceased almost everywhere. The result, as the Prince told his father, was that his principality was no longer capable of defending itself. Complete collapse was averted only by large subsidies from England. In addition to about £22,500 contributed by the English Exchequer to the cost of sending out troops from England in March 1369, another £20,000 was shipped out in coin in June.[3]

Two years after the end of his ill-judged Castilian adventure the Prince of Wales was a shadow of his former self. His health had continued to deteriorate. He was now bedridden at Angoulême and only intermittently capable of directing affairs. Day-to-day business was carried on by his principal councillors, who were able men but lacked his presence and his natural authority. The chief figure on his Council was the Seneschal of Aquitaine, Sir Thomas Felton. Felton, who was destined to be the dominant figure in the government of the principality for the next decade, was the kind of man on whom the English war effort in France had always depended. A Norfolk knight of modest fortune, he came from a family with a long tradition of royal service who had made his whole career in the Prince's following. He was one of the few men in a court of stooges and flatterers to give his master unvarnished advice. Felton was a competent soldier who had fought with distinction at Poitiers and Nájera but he was primarily an administrator rather than a general. The principal military leaders on the English side were Sir Hugh Calveley and Sir John Chandos. Both of them had come relatively late on the scene. Calveley had been in Aragon, where he had been engaged in consolidating a fortune made in the wars of Spain. He had recrossed the Pyrenees and placed himself at the Prince's disposal at the end of the previous year. Chandos was probably the ablest captain in English service anywhere as well as an astute politician who had warned against the Prince's insensitive treatment of the Gascon nobility. He was urgently recalled to the Prince's court from his estates in Normandy in December shortly after Calveley's arrival.[4]

When Sir John Chandos arrived at Angoulême he found the government demoralised by the speed of the collapse in Quercy and Rouergue. The administration of the outlying provinces was in disorder. There was no clear plan of campaign and very few troops. Sir Hugh Calveley was engaged in wasting the lands of leading appellants in the Landes and southern Gascony, a useless enterprise which neither won over the rebels nor deterred others. The defection of the lord of Albret with much of his great network of kinsmen and allies had deprived the Prince's officers of one of their richest sources of military manpower. Except in Poitou and the Bordelais, which remained conspicuously loyal to the Prince's cause, noblemen across the principality were holding their breath and waiting to see which way events would turn before committing themselves. Reinforcements had been promised from England. But most of them were still waiting for their passage at Southampton.[5]

The main priority of the Prince's councillors was to hold the valleys of the Dordogne and Garonne which were the main east–west arteries leading to Bordeaux; and the plains of Saintonge, Angoumois and Poitou in the west of the principality which were its richest and most populous regions and the source of most of its grain. In January 1369, as Anjou's offensive gathered pace, Chandos resolved on a counter-attack in the south-east. It was a courageous decision. In spite of intensive recruitment no more than about 500 men-at-arms could be found for his army. Chandos was obliged to make good the shortage by forging an alliance with less conventional warriors, the survivors of the *routier* bands of the Great Company. They had come to life again with the collapse of the Anglo-French treaty and many were returning to their old hunting grounds. Chandos's chief recruiting agent was Bertucat d'Albret, the illegitimate half-brother of the lord of Albret. One of the most successful professional *routiers* of the previous generation, Bertucat had recently re-formed his company and begun to infiltrate the mountains of Auvergne, revisiting scenes of his profitable spoliations after the battle of Poitiers. In January 1369 he was persuaded to bring his companies down from the hills to reinforce the English in Quercy and Rouergue. Chandos arrived in Quercy at about the beginning of March 1369 and established his headquarters at Montauban. A few days later Bertucat d'Albret crossed the Dordogne at Bergerac and invaded the province by the north.[6]

The situation which Chandos found at Montauban was very unsatisfactory. The city was the most important English stronghold in Quercy and the key to their position on the south-east march of the duchy. Yet the walls of the town were weak. The Prince had begun to construct a citadel (now incorporated in the Musée Ingres) at the east end of the bridge over the Tarn but it was probably still incomplete in 1369. Within the town the war was provoking bitter divisions among the citizens as local politicians jockeyed for position with an eye on the next regime. Chandos secured the English hold on the lower valley of the Tarn by occupying the monastic town of Moissac, a walled town dominated by its famous Benedictine abbey which was strategically placed at the confluence of the Tarn and the Garonne. At same time he took possession of the massive fortress of Richard I at Saint-Nicolas-la-Grave, which guarded the confluence from the south side. These moves made Montauban difficult to reach by river from Toulouse and for the time being made its position reasonably secure.[7]

No French field army had yet set foot in the province, but by April 1369 the French were preparing an invasion in force from two directions. The Duke of Berry and Marshal Sancerre were assembling an army of some 2,000 men-at-arms in Auvergne ready to descend on Rouergue by the valley of the Dordogne. A second army was being organised by Louis of Anjou around the cathedral city of Albi in northern Languedoc. Like Sir John Chandos the Duke of Anjou had to resort to the companies to make up his numbers. The army incorporated several famous brigands from the worst years of the past decade. They were supported by a corps of sappers and a siege train from the Duke's arsenal at Toulouse. The total strength of this force is uncertain but with the men already in the field it may well have matched the 4,000 or so men whom the English reckoned to be operating under Anjou's orders.[8]

Chandos's first instinct was to avoid challenging Anjou's army directly but to counter-attack towards the centre of Anjou's lieutenancy in the Toulousain in the hope of drawing it off. On about 20 March 1369 he marched out of Montauban up the valley of the Tarn towards Toulouse wasting the land as he went. There is no reliable record of this campaign but it undoubtedly caused great destruction in the northern Toulousain and according to Froissart came within a few miles of Toulouse itself. What it completely failed to do was disturb Anjou's plans. The forces at Albi pressed on with their purpose, marching on Montauban a day or two after Chandos had left it. In Chandos's

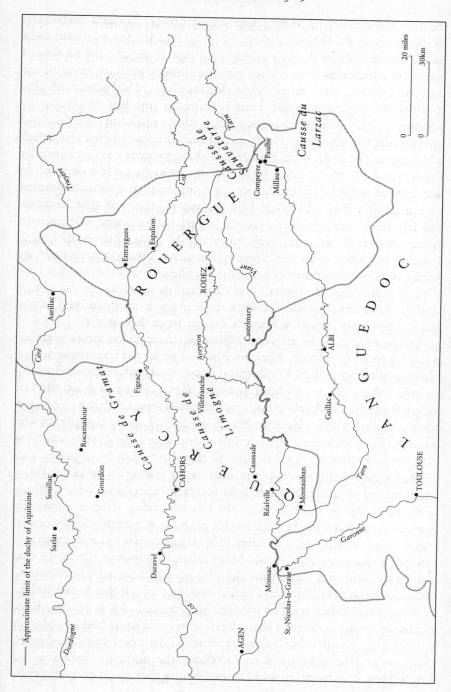

1 Quercy and Rouergue, 1369–1370

absence the defence of Montauban was left to Sir Thomas Walkefare. Walkefare was an experienced soldier who had fought a famous fight at the battle of Poitiers. He put part of his garrison into the *bastide* of Réalville which was then a river port standing at a sharp bend of the Aveyron, some nine miles from Montauban. The object of this manoeuvre was to stop the French bringing supplies downriver to support a siege. It meant that the French were obliged to take time and effort to capture the place. Réalville resisted with ferocity for more than a fortnight. The walls were battered by stone throwers, undermined by sappers and eventually taken by assault in about the middle of April. In accordance with the pitiless laws of war the defenders were massacred to a man. But they had saved Montauban. By the time that Réalville fell Chandos had returned, placed a garrison of some 200 men in Montauban and then withdrawn into the hills to harass the French siege lines. The French were unwilling to besiege a solidly garrisoned city with Chandos still in the field nearby. For the moment they gave up the idea of attacking Montauban and marched north towards the Lot to deal with the few towns and castles, most of them comparatively minor places, which still flew the Prince's banner from their walls.[9]

At Angoulême the Prince's councillors had managed to scrape together a few hundred more men. They were placed under the command of that old war-horse Sir Robert Knolles who had recently arrived from Brittany to offer his assistance. In April 1369 Knolles made his way up the Lot valley from the Bordelais. About twenty miles west of Cahors he found his path blocked by a detachment of the French army comprising the bands of Petit Meschin, Perrin de Savoie and three other *routier* captains who had been sent forward to close the River Lot to supplies and reinforcements coming from the west. They had occupied Duravel, a small walled village dominated by a fortified Benedictine priory, which then stood on the right bank of the Lot beneath a steep escarpment. Knolles was forced to lay siege to this place. In about the third week of April 1369, having failed to carry it by assault, he set about starving it out. Chandos came north from Montauban to join him. The siege was a disaster. Within a short time the English had run out of everything except wine. It rained day and night, soaking their clothes beneath their armour. Finally they tried to suborn the defenders. Most of them were old companions in arms of Bertucat d'Albret and some had served with Chandos in Castile. The facts are obscure. It seems that the French captains at Duravel agreed to surrender the place to Chandos and Knolles but were betrayed and arrested before they could carry out their bargain. At about the beginning of May the English abandoned the siege and marched off to the north. As for the *routier* captains they were sent to Toulouse. There on 11 May 1369 Louis of Anjou had Perrin de Savoie and Petit Meschin drowned in the Garonne and three other captains hanged and quartered.[10]

Lacking a supply train or heavy siege equipment and faced with growing difficulty in foraging for food, Sir John Chandos's forces were compelled to split up into small groups remaining constantly on the move. Within a few days they were scattered across the *causses* from the Dordogne to the Lot. They tried to surprise some of the more substantial places which had surrendered to the French. But they were consistently unsuccessful. The first target was Domme, an important walled town standing on a cliff-top over the Dordogne at the eastern march of Périgord, which had recently accepted a French garrison. Chandos failed to take the place by assault and was obliged to abandon the siege after a few days. Other places were successfully occupied, often without resistance, but proved impossible to hold. The inhabitants simply bent before the wind. Rocamadour was a typical case. The famous pilgrimage town at the northern extremity of the Causse de Gramat was defended by a local garrison which had been retained at the Duke of Anjou's wages when the place submitted to his officers in March. When Chandos's men arrived they resisted for long enough to say they had done their duty but no more. Next morning they agreed to admit the English and swear loyalty to the Prince, just as they had two months before to the King of France, and to supply fifty donkey-loads of victuals to Chandos's army for ready cash. 'And thus', says Froissart, 'Rocamadour remained in peace.' The pattern was the same everywhere else. Men fled to the village tower on the appearance of men-at-arms shouting 'Guyenne! Saint-Georges!' one day and 'Montjoie! Saint-Denis!' the next, swearing whatever oaths of loyalty were asked of them.[11]

On 8 May 1369 Chandos briefly reunited his dispersed forces for an attack on the cathedral city of Cahors. A powerful mounted raiding force was created, led by Chandos himself and the Gascon paladin Jean de Grailly, Captal de Buch. They arrived suddenly beneath the walls of the cathedral city a week later, achieving complete surprise, and launched an immediate assault, hoping to carry the walls before the defence was ready. They failed. The attack occasioned a brief panic among the Duke of Anjou's councillors. He sent all available men to the city and even called on his brother John of Berry to bring reinforcements from Auvergne. Barges were sent urgently up the Aveyron with supplies. He need not have bothered. Chandos lacked the means to undertake a siege. Once the assault had failed he withdrew. Joining forces with Knolles he returned north to the Causse de Gramat. On 19 May 1369 there was an attempt on Figeac which also failed. The two commanders are next reported moving east towards the march of Rouergue. Thus did the grand strategic idea conceived in January peter out in June in a series of improvised pinpricks. The campaign established what was to be pattern of the next phase of the war: on the English side the rapid movements of a *guerre de course* and some brilliant strategic thinking, but without the time or resources to follow anything through; on the French side the slow, overwhelming concentration of forces and progressive rolling back of frontiers. Sir John Chandos had already decided that he was wasting his time on the south-eastern march of the principality. Towards the end of May he sent his herald to Angoulême to ask for instructions.[12]

The long-awaited expeditionary force from England finally sailed from Southampton at the beginning of March 1369. There must have been between 800 and 1,000 men in all, most of them recruited in the English and Welsh lands of the Prince of Wales.[13] The commanders were Edmund Langley, Earl of Cambridge, and John Hastings, Earl of Pembroke. Cambridge was the third of the English King's four surviving sons, then twenty-eight years of age, an easy-going mediocrity with no military experience except for his participation as a teenager in his father's campaign of 1359–60. Pembroke was an abler man. Intelligent, self-confident and ambitious, he was a great favourite of Edward III and with a longer apprenticeship might have been an effective commander. But, still only twenty-two years old, Pembroke had even less experience than Cambridge. The choice of these two men is eloquent evidence of the lack of experienced talent among the English court aristocracy after the passing of the great generation which had fought in Edward's wars before 1360.

The army disembarked from its ships in the roads of Saint-Malo on the north coast of Brittany. The Earls' first task was to make contact with the main English garrisons of the region. Latimer's garrison at Bécherel appears to have been resupplied and possibly reinforced. Cambridge briefly joined forces with Sir John Cresswell's company at Château-Gontier to help them consolidate their positions in Anjou and Maine. The army then turned south. John de Montfort later denied that he had connived in these operations and declared that he had had no choice but to let Cambridge cross his territory once he had landed. But no one believed him. The English had discharged their ships under the noses of John's garrison at Solidor in the bay of Saint-Malo and were allowed to cross the Loire by the great fortified bridge at Nantes.[14]

The two Earls must have reached the Prince's court in late April 1369. Their arrival coincided with a series of fresh setbacks for the English cause. The first came in Périgord. So far the Duke of Anjou's agents had made very few inroads in this province and none at all north of the Dordogne. The English remained securely in possession of the river as far as Domme, with their allies holding all the principal fortresses along its course and a significant garrison guarding the main bridge at Bergerac. Even the Count of Périgord, Archambaud V, a declared enemy of the Prince who had promised the year before to adhere to the appeals against the hearth tax, sat on his hands until it became clearer which side was winning. Towards the end of March 1369 Archambaud made up his mind. He and his brother Talleyrand led their retinues into Quercy to join the Duke of Anjou's army. On 13 April the Count formally adhered to appeals in the French encampment outside Caussade and appointed his proctors to represent him before the Parlement. Charles V promised him a war subsidy of 40,000 francs and urged him to open hostilities against the Prince in Périgord at once. As a result the first task assigned to the Earls of Cambridge and Pembroke after they reached Angoulême was to mount a punitive raid against the possessions of both brothers, much as Calveley had been doing against Albret and Armagnac in the foothills of the Pyrenees. They brought fire and sword to the family's properties in the province and passed the best part of May in besieging the impressive thirteenth-century castle of Bourdeilles above the River Dronne west of Brantôme before an incautious sortie by the garrison enabled them to take the place. Pembroke won his spurs in this engagement, receiving his knighthood at the hands of his fellow commander.[15]

These agreeable acts of war were suddenly interrupted towards the end of May 1369 by a much more serious threat to English interests in Poitou. Poitou was strategically and politically crucial to the English government of Aquitaine. It was a convenient gateway for French armies coming from the north. It was by far the richest province of the Prince's domains. It was also, of all the provinces ceded by the treaty of Brétigny, the most consistently loyal to the Prince. None of its towns had yet abandoned their allegiance. The nobility had taken to the life of the

Prince's court, receiving grants and offices at his hand. They had rallied round the Prince in his troubles. An important Poitevin contingent was even then serving with Sir John Chandos in Quercy. The only significant noble families of Poitou who supported the cause of Charles V in 1369 were those, generally living on the north and east marches of the province, whose main domains lay outside the principality in areas controlled by the French Crown.[16]

Early in May 1369 the French embarked on a series of needling raids on English positions on the northern march of the province. Within a few days of the start of this campaign a small force collected by the captain of Tours surprised La Roche-Posay and captured it by escalade in a daring night attack. La Roche-Posay was a powerful fortress sited on a spur of rock above the left bank of the Creuse guarding the Roman road from Tours to Poitiers. Technically just beyond the limit of Aquitaine, its occupation by partisans of the Prince had been a bone of contention between England and France for many years. Its loss seriously seriously weakened the northern defences of the principality. Charles V put a garrison into it and used it as a base from which to mount further incursions towards Poitiers and Châtellerault. The easy terrain, which made the region so prosperous, also made it difficult to defend. There were no mountains or major rivers presenting any serious obstacle to an invader.

Shortly, an even more menacing series of raids was organised from Anjou in the lower Loire by two local captains in French service, Jean de Bueil and Jean de Kerlouet. Jean de Bueil was a nobleman of Touraine serving as captain of Angers. Jean de Kerlouet was a relative unknown. He was a squire from northern Brittany of no great wealth or lineage who had served Charles of Blois for the last eight years of his life and then, after Charles's death in 1364, had followed Bertrand du Guesclin to Castile. He seems to have based himself at Saumur. Between them De Bueil and Kerlouet built up a raiding force which was estimated by Froissart at 1,000 men-at-arms and may well have been close to that. Many of these men were footloose Bretons who had recently fought with the companies, like Kerlouet himself. They began to penetrate deep into the western march of Poitou. The English were caught off balance. Cambridge and Pembroke were still tied down outside Bourdeilles; Calveley was still in the foothills of the Pyrenees; Chandos was in Quercy with much of the baronage of Poitou. The only significant forces at the Prince's disposal in the province were the garrisons of the principal towns and a company of some two or three hundred men under command of his friend Sir Simon Burley and his long-standing Welsh retainer Sir Digory Say. Both men were based at Montreuil-Bonnin, a garrisoned fortress ten miles west of Poitiers. Towards the end of May 1369 this force was annihilated by a large raiding party led by Jean de Bueil and Jean de Kerlouet which had managed to penetrate some fifty miles into the principality without being noticed. The English, who were conducting a sweep west of Poitiers, rode into a well-laid ambush. They were heavily outnumbered and swiftly overwhelmed with the loss of 140 men killed or captured. Say escaped with a handful of companions to the nearby fortress of Lusignan. Burley was among the prisoners.[17]

This event caused panic in Angoulême and an abrupt change of direction as the Prince's officers stripped resources from every other front to defend the northern march of Poitou. Sir James Audley, another close friend of the Prince, was appointed as his lieutenant in the province. The Poitevin barons were brought back from Quercy and placed under his command. By the beginning of June a second army was being formed from the troops of the Earls of Cambridge and Pembroke with some additional companies raised in Poitou itself. Sir John Chandos was withdrawn from the southern front to join them.[18]

Audley's army was the first to see action. He established his headquarters at Poitiers and then struck east in about the middle of June into the valley of the River Creuse, which marked the limit of the province. Audley's first target was the town of Le Blanc, an enclave of Poitou on the right bank of the Creuse which was under siege by the French. The place was temporarily relieved (it fell a few months later). Then, turning north, Audley attacked Le Soudun, now an insignificant hamlet, which was then the site of an important castle guarding the left bank of the river eight miles upstream of La Roche-Posay. This place appears to have been carried by assault and garrisoned against the French. Turning back on his tracks Audley launched a punitive raid against the territory of Guy de Chauvigny, one of the few prominent noblemen of Poitou to have defected to Charles V. Guy's castle at La Brosse was taken by storm on the day after Audley's arrival. Audley hanged sixteen of the Breton company which Guy had left to guard the place and put in a garrison of his own. Many years later the Cheshire knights serving in Audley's army would recall this incident as one of great feats of arms of their careers.[19]

The Earl of Cambridge's army entered the Vendée at about the end of June 1369. The region, lying between the Sèvre Niortaise and the

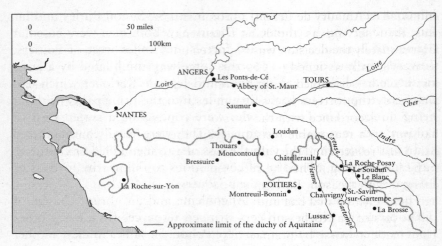

2 Poitou: the northern march, 1369–1371

Bay of Bourgneuf, had never been fully absorbed by the Prince's administration. The French had hung on to some important lordships there which they contended were not included in the territorial settlement at Brétigny. The most significant of these enclaves was the great fortress of La Roche-sur-Yon which was the centre of the road system of the region and the key to the defence of Poitou against any invasion force approaching from Nantes. The place belonged to no less a person than the Duke of Anjou and was defended by one of his retainers, Jean Belon. He commanded the largest French garrison of the region. When, in about the second week of July, Cambridge brought up his siege engines against the walls, Belon faced a dilemma common to many garrison commanders of the late middle ages. Reluctant to face an assault which would put his life at the mercy of the enemy, yet seeing no relief in prospect, he entered into negotiations with the English Earls. In the middle of July he agreed to surrender La Roche-sur-Yon in one month unless he was relieved beforehand. If no relief came he was to be paid 6,000 francs for the stores in the castle and allowed to leave freely with his men. Belon was permitted to send a message to the French King informing him of these terms. Cambridge for his part summoned reinforcements to help him fight off any attempt to relieve the place. Audley brought his own army across from Poitiers to join him. Their combined strength must have amounted to more than 2,000 men.

In spite of the French King's aversion to pitched battles a serious attempt was made to relieve Belon before the deadline. The task was entrusted to Amaury de Craon, a prominent magnate from Maine who was then serving as the King's lieutenant in Lower Normandy. Unfortunately the decision was not taken until a very late stage and the force originally assigned to Craon was too small. Precious days were lost while he scrambled about for reinforcements. By the time that he was ready the fortress had surrendered. The whole transaction was strictly in accordance with the laws of war provided that the garrison had put up a reasonable resistance. But the short time during which Belon had resisted and the value of the stores he had left behind proved to be his undoing. When he returned to Angers he was arrested and charged with treason. Early in the following year the Duke of Anjou had him sewn up in a bag and drowned in the Loire.[20]

The loss of La Roche-sur-Yon was a serious reverse for the French. They made it worse by prematurely withdrawing Amaury de Craon's force from the Loire valley and redirecting it northward into Maine to deal with the English garrisons of Château-Gontier and Saint-Sauveur. This decision appears to have been made by Charles V himself, almost certainly because of the threat which these places posed to the assembly area of the army of England. However, the operation was badly mishandled. The English companies at Château-Gontier abandoned the place without waiting to be attacked and escaped. Most of them made their way north to reinforce the garrison of Saint-Sauveur. Amaury de Craon was ordered to pursue them and force them to battle but was unable to catch up with them in time. He reached Saint-Sauveur towards the end of August and began to make dispositions for a siege. Shortly, he was joined there by much of the baronage of Lower Normandy as well as by a large contingent from Brittany and both Marshals of France. It was an impressive force. But there had not been time to prepare a proper siege train. The leaders of the besieging army fell out. Then the Bretons withdrew. Without them the Marshals considered that their forces were not strong enough. So in about the middle of September they abandoned the siege. Charles V was furious. He ordered them to return. But they do not seem to have done so.[21]

The cost of Craon's unsuccessful attempt on Saint-Sauveur was high, for while the French commanders in the west had their backs turned the Earl of Pembroke followed up the capture of La Roche-sur-Yon with a highly successful campaign along the lower Loire. He first tried to capture the bridge-town of Saumur but was beaten off by its garrison. However, both of the crossings of the river between Saumur and Nantes fell into his hands: the ford by the fortified abbey at Saint-Maur; and the great fortified bridges at Ponts-de-Cé. These places were strengthened and garrisoned. Their capture made it much more difficult for the French to continue their raids into the western march of Poitou and gave the English a clear line of communication to the substantial army which was now crammed into the fortress of Saint-Sauveur.[22]

With the Loire front secure, companies of English and Gascon troops now began to penetrate east into the neighbouring French provinces of Berry and Bourbonnais. Most of these raids were pinpricks whose impact was small and brief. But one company achieved something more spectacular. The Gascon captain Bernard de la Salle had fought under the Prince in Castile before becoming one of leaders of the Great Company. He joined forces with his brother Hortingo and an adventurer called Bernard de West, who may have been an Englishman. Together they recruited a company of about 120 men-at-arms and 200 archers out of the large Anglo-Gascon garrison based at Niort and invaded the Bourbonnais. There had been no recent operations in the area, so the custodians of its castles were not on their guard. The principal territorial magnate of the region, the Duke of Bourbon, was away with the King at Rouen accompanied by most of his retainers. They were waiting to embark for England. The raiders arrived outside the Duke's castle of Belleperche, on the bank of the Allier north of Moulins, in about the middle of August. Dressed as peasants they tricked the gatekeeper into admitting them, swiftly overpowered the small garrison and took over the castle. Inside they found Isabelle de Valois, dowager Duchess of Bourbon, Charles V's mother-in-law, whom they took prisoner. A large supply of victuals had been laid in for her court, which enabled the invaders to establish a permanent base. From Belleperche they occupied a string of castles regularly spaced across the western Bourbonnais and the neighbouring regions of Berry and the Limousin. At the western extremity of this line of strongholds they joined forces with the Herefordshire knight Sir John Devereux, a colourful protégé of the Prince of Wales, who commanded a large *routier* company based in the great fortress of La Souterraine on the northern march of the Limousin. For more than a year to come the French were obliged to divert considerable effort and manpower to contain the operations of these captains.[23]

The concentration of virtually all the resources of Aquitaine in its northern march meant that the defence of Quercy and Rouergue was practically abandoned. What little remained of English-held territory in these provinces was swiftly gobbled up by the officers of the Duke of Anjou. The process was highly sensitive to expectations. It was clear that the English were not in a position to defend the more distant outposts of their territory. For small communities concerned above all about their own security and anxious to avoid a return to the catastrophes of the 1350s, this was decisive. Patriotic sentiment rarely entered into it. At Montauban the townsmen had remained loyal to the Prince while Sir John Chandos was in the province, in spite of being threatened by Anjou's agents with confiscations and enormous fines. But as soon as Chandos left they opened negotiations and made the best bargain they could. A local nobleman, Ratier de Belfort, who had once served as the lieutenant of the English seneschal of Quercy, was now performing the same office for the French. He distributed money liberally among the townsmen and made lavish promises of privileges and favours. In June 1369, as the French closed in on Montauban, Sir Hugh Calveley arrived in the region from the Landes. He tried to shore up Montauban's defences by establishing forts on the River Tarn upstream of the town. It appears to have been while he was engaged in these operations that Montauban opened its gates to the French. The place was certainly in their hands by the end of the month. Inside the town the change of allegiance was followed, as it often was in the divided communities of the south-west, by the wholesale replacement of the consuls and an orgy of private vendettas. The only surviving English presence in Quercy was now the garrison of Moissac, which held out for another year before surrendering in its turn. But the region was given up for lost well before that. Calveley withdrew into the Agenais. Sir Thomas Walkefare, whose office as seneschal of Quercy had by now become an empty symbol, fled to Rouergue to join Sir Thomas Wettenhall, but he was a marked man. The French blamed him (probably wrongly) for the imprisonment and death of the two royal officers who had served the appeal papers on the Prince the year before. When some months later he was captured in a skirmish in Rouergue he was sent to Toulouse, kept in prison for a year and then hanged from a high scaffold specially built for him in a public square.[24]

The collapse of the English cause in Rouergue followed shortly after their final expulsion from Quercy. The catalyst was a struggle for the possession of Compeyre, a small walled town with a thirteenth-century keep built on steeply rising ground on the right bank of the Tarn, which was the key to the river defences of Millau. The inhabitants of Compeyre had no reason to feel grateful to the Prince's government.

Their town had once been an important place, one of the few possessions of the French Crown in the heart of the Count of Armagnac's great fief. But, with the arrival of Gascon and English officials after 1362, it had been forced to accept the 'many insults' heaped upon it by the larger and richer town of Millau. Its local court was suppressed. It was obliged to accept Millau's protection, to pay its taxes, to resort to its tribunals and to accept a garrison under the orders of its English captain, James Mascy. On 22 June 1369 a small troop of French soldiers under the command of a local nobleman appeared outside the gates of Compeyre and was promptly admitted by the citizens. The incident was a miniature of the tensions in the region which had undermined the English administration for years. Mascy, who was at Compeyre when the town defected, found himself blockaded in the castle from the streets below. Judging his position untenable he agreed to surrender the place unless he was relieved by 1 July and handed over his son, who was with him in the keep, as a hostage. The deadline was only a week away. There was a desperate scramble among the scattered groups of English soldiers and officials in the province to organise a relief force. Sir Thomas Wettenhall marched as fast as he could to Millau, where he arrived on 26 June. Some small companies of *routiers* arrived from Auvergne with an English captain, Hugh Russell. The French for their part collected their own reinforcements. In Rodez the Count of Armagnac's lieutenant raised what local forces he could. The Count himself, who was with the Duke of Anjou at Toulouse, prevailed upon him to send 400 Breton *routiers*. The Count's son John, who was at Clermont-Ferrand with the Duke of Berry, was urgently recalled. On 16 July 1369 the combined French force arrived without warning at Compeyre. The English were heavily outnumbered and caught between the attacking force and the French troops in the town. There was a bloody battle in which they were badly mauled. As darkness fell they tried to slip away. But they were noticed and pursued. They lost their baggage train and many of their men. Russell escaped with part of his company across the Tarn and took refuge in the castle of Paulhe on the opposite bank. Mascy and Wettenhall found their way by a circuitous route back to Millau where they decided, perhaps unwisely, to struggle on. A few weeks later, as Wettenhall led a raiding party across the *causses*, he was confronted near Montlaur by a detachment of men under one of Louis of Anjou's captains and routed. Wettenhall himself was mortally wounded. He was carried to a nearby house where he died. It was some evidence of the regard in which Wettenhall had been held at Millau that they paid for a sung mass in his memory in the town church at which the whole clergy and leading citizens of the town were present.[25]

At Westminster Edward III's councillors had tried to follow events as reports reached them from France, generally late, inaccurate and confused. They conceived and jettisoned fresh plans with bewildering rapidity in response to each new setback. In March and April 1369 they were still transfixed by the deteriorating situation in Aquitaine. No sooner had the Earls of Cambridge and Pembroke sailed from Southampton but plans were drawn up for another army to leave for Gascony in June under the command of John of Gaunt. These plans were suddenly overtaken by the news of the French occupation of Ponthieu, which occurred at the end of April. This had been planned in Paris for at least two years and anticipated by Edward's officers in the county for months. But its timing and speed still came as a shock to the English. Hugh de Châtillon, the Master of the Royal Archers, arrived outside Abbeville at dawn on 29 April. The town at once opened its gates. Most of the garrison fled. The governor and his staff were arrested. The first reports of these events reached Westminster at the beginning of May followed swiftly by further tidings of disaster. Le Crotoy was stormed on 5 May. The garrison in the castle was the largest in the county and one of the largest in France but they abandoned it within hours of the French occupation of the town and sloped away. Airaines was abandoned on the next day. The remaining garrisons of Ponthieu held out hopelessly for another month. The last English refugees from the county arrived at the gates of Calais on 1 June.[26]

There was a sudden panic at Westminster. If Ponthieu could fall so easily could Calais be next? There were disturbing reports of French military activity at the edge of the pale. The walled town of Ardres, which marked the south-eastern extremity of the English territory, was attacked over five days in May and remained under a loose siege for several weeks thereafter. The English castle of Audruicq five miles east of it was captured at about this time. Plans to prop up the Prince in Aquitaine were dropped. John of Gaunt's expedition to Aquitaine was cancelled and the companies originally assigned to it were redirected to Calais. The Earl of Hereford was appointed captain of Calais. On 2 May he was ordered to raise an extra 900 men and to proceed urgently to hold the town against the French. A number of old soldiers were brought out of retirement to man the breaches of the town's defences, including Sir Frank Hale, one of the great figures in Aquitaine of the 1340s, and the aged paladin Sir Walter Mauny who had begun his military career in Scotland in the 1330s. They were to be followed by a large expeditionary army, at least 6,000 strong, which would cross the Channel later in the summer and invade northern France. The King intended to take command of this force in person. The calculation seems to have been that it would both secure Calais against attack and present a sufficiently serious threat to draw off French attacks on Aquitaine.[27]

It was in this highly charged atmosphere that Parliament met at Westminster on 3 June 1369. The assembled members received a sombre report from the Chancellor, William of Wykeham, about the breakdown of diplomatic relations with France and recent events in Aquitaine and Ponthieu. The Prince of Wales, said Wykeham, had taken advice from the wisest men about him and concluded that the time had come for Edward III to resume the title of King of France. The Chancellor did not spell it out but everyone must have realised that this formal step would mark the final repudiation of the treaties of Brétigny and Calais and a return to the old war aims of the 1350s. It was probably the only realistic response to events on the ground in France. Three days later, on 6 June 1369, the King was advised to take this momentous step by both Houses.[28]

It is obvious from the terms in which Wykeham addressed his audience that the English government was still unaware of the French King's invasion plans. Their eyes were shortly opened. The French invasion fleet began to assemble in the Seine in June. Within a few days the English government was informed that a 'large fleet of sailing ships and galleys' was being created to invade their island. Whether the news would have altered their plans if it had come earlier is an interesting question, but coming at this late stage it was received with surprising equanimity. Attack was thought, rightly as it turned out, to be the best form of defence. So John of Gaunt continued with his plans, crossing discreetly to Calais with a small entourage at the beginning of July. The Earl of Hereford left at about same time to take up his command in the town. A fleet of nearly 300 ships, ranging from small crayers to monsters of 300 tons, gathered in the Bay of Sandwich to carry their men in relays across the Channel. A raiding squadron was detached from the fleet at Sandwich and sent to reconnoitre the French coast. They succeeded in causing a fair amount of disruption to the French King's invasion plans. About a dozen French ships were caught in the mouth of the Somme. A landing was briefly effected at Saint-Denis in the Chef de Caux (modern Sainte-Adresse) within sight of the French fleet's anchorage.[29]

There was something curiously unreal about the French invasion plan of 1369. It must have engrossed the efforts of many officials and soldiers during the summer, but has left little trace in the surviving records. The enterprise had been controversial from the outset. As the Breton magnate Olivier de Clisson had pointed out in the Great Council which approved the project in March, the French had limited experience of major seaborne expeditions. It is clear that they greatly under-estimated the scale of the undertaking. At an early stage things began to go wrong, mainly on the maritime side. Like their English rivals, the French had traditionally relied on requisitioned merchantmen to supply both transports and warships for their fleets. However, no great naval campaign had been attempted since the 1340s and since then the maritime geography of France had changed beyond recognition. Calais had been an English port since 1347 and La Rochelle since 1362. These had previously been the leading mercantile ports of the French Atlantic coast. Brittany and Flanders were neutral. That left the French government with only the ports of Normandy and Picardy, principally Boulogne, Saint-Valéry and Dieppe. Even in these places the abrupt ending of trade with England in 1369 and the dangers of running the gauntlet between Calais and the Kent ports had dealt a severe blow to France's merchant marine. French naval resources in 1369 consisted of a modest fleet of requisitioned ships most of which were too small for efficient war service. Of those whose size is recorded, none exceeded fifty tons burden and most carried less than half of that. The famous royal arsenal at Rouen had not been used for construction or repair work for a decade. The royal galley fleet comprised just ten vessels, half of them based in the Mediterranean and the rest in a poor state of repair. None of these problems appear to have been considered when Charles V formulated his invasion plans.[30]

The King was counting on his allies to make good the deficiencies in France's indigenous naval resources. In this he was sorely disappointed. Flanders, which had been expected to provide much of the transport fleet, appears to have contributed little or nothing. The Grimaldi of Monaco and Menton had furnished war fleets of up to thirty-two galleys to Philip VI, but their maritime strength was only a shadow of what it had been. They controlled just ten galleys in 1369 and were unable to commit more than half of them to the invasion fleet. In the event they supplied none at all. Castile, the other traditional source of war galleys, did no better. Henry of Trastámara, the French-backed pretender to the Castilian throne, had undertaken the previous autumn to provide at his own expense two galleys for every one that Charles V could find from other sources. He was unable to live up to his promises. Seville, the largest city of Castile and the site of its principal naval arsenal, was securely held by his partisans and about twenty galleys were still there more or less intact. But the supporters of the murdered Don Pedro had disabled most of them by removing their oars and their Portuguese allies were blockading the mouth of the River Guadalquivir. The invasion fleet waiting in the Seine was apparently an impressive sight. The French King took parties of distinguished visitors out to watch the spectacle from the shore. Not many of them can have realised how many ships were required to carry even a modest army encumbered with its stores, horses and equipment.[31]

On 16 July 1369 the leaders of the French army of invasion received the Oriflamme at the abbey of Saint-Denis and prepared to set out for Harfleur. The King and the Duke of Burgundy established their headquarters in the citadel of Rouen at the end of July. The army was already encamped in the meadows of the Seine. Its final strength was the result of decisions made in Paris a month before, when it was known how much shipping was available. It must have fallen well short of the numbers originally envisaged in March. There were about 2,000 men-at-arms, most of them retainers of the Dukes of Burgundy and Bourbon. They were supported by several hundred crossbowmen, including some Genoese companies recruited by Rainier Grimaldi, and by the crews of the ships, who would be expected to fight with the army once it had landed. The whole force, including seamen, probably numbered between 4,000 and 5,000 men.

At Calais the English army had crossed the Channel by the end of the month. Its total strength according to French estimates was about 4,000, which is consistent with the English records. Their first task was to consolidate the English hold on the territory around Calais before Edward III arrived to take command. He was expected to follow in the autumn with fresh contingents which could be expected to bring the army's payroll strength to between 8,000 and 10,000 men, plus between 4,000 and 5,000 servants ('varlets') who were not counted on the paid strength but were in fact combatants. On about 1 August 1369 John of Gaunt rode out of Calais with the Earl of Hereford on the road to Ardres. The French commanders on this front were Gui de

Luxembourg, Count of Saint-Pol, and John, lord of Sempy, captain of Boulogne, both of them prominent magnates of the region who were destined to spend much of their lives guarding the barren marshes of the Pas-de-Calais. They were supported by Moreau de Fiennes, the rather ineffectual Constable of France. Froissart's estimate of the troops at their disposal was about 1,000 men, thinly spread in a great arc between Boulogne and Saint-Omer. As the chronicler pointed out, it was enough to contain raiding parties but not to confront a major field army. Gaunt's forces swept aside the French troops besieging Ardres. They retook the keep of Audruicq. About ninety smaller fortified places were captured and either manned or destroyed. Then the army burned a path eastward towards the ancient and dilapidated episcopal city of Thérouanne and the walled town of Aire, and south into the county of Saint-Pol.[32]

The French government's intelligence had proved to be even worse than that of the English. They had known nothing of the arrival of an English army at Calais until John of Gaunt rode out of the gates of the town. The news was brought to the King at Rouen. At the time Charles was presiding over a great assembly of notables in the Norman capital and was in the midst of some delicate negotiations about the financing of the invasion force. The timing could not have been worse. Most of the King's Council was for postponing the expedition to England at once and sending the Duke of Burgundy north to confront John of Gaunt instead. A commission was appointed from the ranks of the assembly to deliberate on the matter. After a certain amount of hesitation they agreed with the advice tendered by the Council. Charles reluctantly put off the invasion until the autumn. The army was ordered north to the Somme. Philip of Burgundy left Rouen on 7 August and reached Abbeville two days later. The French garrisons of the Calais march were ordered to withdraw south to meet him at Hesdin. A general summons was issued to the nobility of northern France and the inhabitants of the major cities. With these additions to his strength the best estimate that can be made is that the Duke of Burgundy had between 8,000 and 10,000 men under his command. On 19 August 1369 Philip marched north out of Hesdin.[33]

Four days later, on 23 August 1369, the English army was resting from its labours in the fields between Ardres and Guines when the French army was reported a short distance away. John of Gaunt and his captains were at dinner. They rushed to grab their arms and their horses. Within a few hours each army had fortified itself against the other. The

English concentrated their strength around the hamlet of Balinghem. They drew themselves up in battle formation on flat ground protected by an impassable marsh. The French took up position on a steep hillside above a stream behind the village of Tournehem, where they dug deep ditches around their positions. About six miles of gently undulating ground lay between them. Neither side moved, except for skirmishes between scouting parties and exhibitionists and the occasional mounted raid. Philip of Burgundy sent his interpreter, an English squire, to mingle among his countrymen and report back. There were desultory negotiations for an arranged battle which came to nothing as such exchanges almost always did. Both commanders were later criticised for their immobility. Part of the problem was the inexperience of the English commanders. John of Gaunt had fought in several campaigns but was exercising his first command. The Earl of Hereford was Constable of England but had inherited his office and at twenty-seven had never been to war. But there was not much that even a more enterprising general could have done. The English were outnumbered. Their men were experiencing difficulty in getting supplies through the waterways from Calais. Many of them had fallen ill in the still, stinking swamp. As for the French, Philip of Burgundy, although a good deal more experienced than the opposing commanders, was never an inspired general. According to Froissart he had been ordered by his brother not to start a pitched battle without his express permission. His father-in-law, Louis de Mâle, plied him with advice to the same effect. The advice, if it was given, was sound. Philip's advantage of numbers was not enough to force the narrow passages through the marsh. But the absence of movement quickly undermined the morale of his men. Discipline began to break down. There was much murmuring in the ranks about the delay in paying their wages. Quarrels broke out within the French army.[34]

In England chaotic attempts were being made to accelerate the assembly of the second army which would give them the decisive advantage of numbers. They were hindered by the usual logistical difficulties. A renewed epidemic of bubonic plague began without warning and infected a number of people close to the court including the Queen. Meanwhile, a steady stream of intelligence was coming in from spies planted in the entourage of Charles V and his captains. By 7 August 1369, the day that the Duke of Burgundy left Rouen, it was already known at Westminster that the French army of invasion was being diverted to the march of Calais. Across the English counties men-at-arms who had been holding themselves ready for orders were directed urgently to join the King at Sandwich. A week later on 14 August these orders were countermanded and embarkation delayed. Then, later on the same day, the timetable was accelerated once more. The King had received a report, which was probably false, that the French fleet had sailed from Harfleur and was about to attack the Solent ports or, worse, the crowded mass of transports gathered in the Downs off Sandwich. Men-at-arms were ordered to the coast as soon as possible. On 18 August Edward's ministers learned that the Duke of Burgundy had left Abbeville and was expected to reach John of Gaunt's army within three or four days. Edward was by now at Eltham. From here he issued a fresh round of commands, telling his commanders that they must be at sea by the 20th in order to reach Gaunt in time. In the event the second army was still not ready by the second week of September when it was decided to send those who had mustered across the Channel straight away without waiting for the rest.[35]

Edward had by now abandoned his plans to command them in person and resolved to stay in England. So the second wave of English troops to reach Calais was commanded by the Earl of Warwick. Warwick was very different from the two young *ingénues* currently commanding in France. He was a popular and flamboyant figure, an experienced soldier and an aggressive commander, who had fought at Crécy and Poitiers. He was accompanied across the Channel by the Earls of Salisbury, March and Oxford and by a large number of household troops and experienced veterans, about 2,000 men in all. They reached Calais on about 12 September 1369. While the army was laboriously disembarked from the ships Warwick rode out of the town with a small escort to confer with John of Gaunt at Balinghem. He was not impressed by what he saw. He enquired sarcastically of Gaunt and Hereford how long they planned to stay put in their tents. He swore a 'great oath' to have the enemy dead or alive if they remained where they were for another two days. This was bravado. But it was never tested, for the enemy did not remain where they were for two days. Reports of the scale of the reinforcements, which may have been exaggerated, persuaded the Duke of Burgundy that his situation had become untenable. On the following day before dawn the French army set fire to their stores, abandoned their positions and marched south to Hesdin. They left in such haste that the English were able to salve sixty barrels of wine, another sixty of beer and huge supplies of bread, meat and fish, on which they gorged themselves till nightfall.[36]

When the French army reached Hesdin most of it was disbanded, leaving the whole of northern France at the mercy of the large English army standing on the march of Calais. The Duke of Burgundy returned to Paris. Charles V, who had been waiting upon events at Rouen, cancelled the invasion of England and began to devise other plans for the fleet that was still lying at anchor in the Seine. Then, on about 18 September 1369, he too left for Paris.[37] On the face of it, these were extraordinary decisions. The most plausible explanation is a sudden cash-flow crisis which prevented the Duke of Burgundy from paying his men. But if the French King and his brother thought that John of Gaunt was about to return to England they were gravely mistaken. Some English companies did return home. But the Earl of Warwick had landed all his men by 15 September and fresh contingents were now reaching Calais every day. They were joined in the town by a large body of German troops, the results of an energetic campaign of propaganda and recruitment in the Low Countries during the summer. The leaders of the English army resolved to strike against the Seine base of the French fleet. The whole army must by now have had a payroll strength of about 6,000 strong or about 8,000 with additional combatants. On about 15 September they formed themselves into three divisions and advanced south on a broad front more than twenty miles wide, burning everything before them. Towards the end of September Edward III's Council decided to support their operations with a fleet. Forty-three ships were selected from the transports recently returned from Calais and placed under the command of the two admirals. They sailed from Rye on 1 October and began to loot their way down the coast of Picardy and Normandy towards the mouth of the Seine.[38]

The French defence in the Pays de Caux was in the hands of the Count of Saint-Pol, the commander on the march of Calais. Although largely deprived of men by the dispersal of the army, Saint-Pol performed his task with great skill. He was forbidden, just as Philip of Burgundy had been, to engage the English in battle. But he retreated before John of Gaunt's army, keeping a few hours' march ahead of them, slowing up their advance, making long-distance foraging impossible by picking off isolated groups. The French either knew or guessed that Harfleur was Gaunt's destination. The delay which Saint-Pol inflicted on the invader won them precious time in which to strengthen its defences. The King sent Pierre de Villiers, master of his household and a close confidant in the crises of the late 1350s, to prepare the place for a siege. He built a flour mill and temporary defences around the gates and brought in vast quantities of artillery and ammunition from the arsenal at Rouen. The French fleet, which was still anchored in the estuary, was sent out to sea for safety.[39]

At about the beginning of October 1369 the English army arrived outside the walls of Harfleur. The English fleet must have arrived off the harbour at almost the same moment. The Count of Saint-Pol had by now shut himself in the town with 200 men-at-arms. He left another 100 men under the command of Baudrain de la Heuse in a fortified village north of the town to harass the English lines from the rear. The English commanders ordered an immediate assault on the walls. When this failed several more were attempted, equally unsuccessfully. The ferocity of these attacks can be judged by fact that the defenders expended 12,000 crossbow bolts in repelling the first one alone and 44,000 more in the later ones. John of Gaunt could have undertaken the siege of Harfleur, as the French plainly assumed that he would. He had carpenters and sappers with him. He had plenty of time. But his men were suffering from disease, not only the dysentery which was endemic among armies on campaign, but in some cases bubonic plague which was active in London and Calais. With the French fleet dispersed and the army of invasion disbanded, the strategic objective of his campaign had largely disappeared. So, in the third week of October, after just four days outside the town, John of Gaunt turned back towards Calais.[40]

The retreat proved to be more difficult than the advance. It involved marching back across land which had been devastated by both armies. The French made a serious attempt to block Gaunt's path and break up his army. Hugh de Châtillon, the Master of the Royal Archers, who was still holding Ponthieu, barred the western crossings of the Somme. All the bridges of the Oise were blocked in order to stop the invaders moving east. Gaunt's men were ambushed by the garrison of Abbeville a few miles east of the town as they headed for the ford of Blanchetaque. There was a bloody battle in which the English eventually beat off their assailants and captured a number of prisoners, including Hugh himself. By an irony which was no doubt delicious to him, Hugh's captor was none other than Nicholas of Louvain, the former governor of Ponthieu whom Hugh had surprised and captured at Abbeville in April. Hugh was taken back to Calais and sold to Edward III, who ordered him to be locked up in Nottingham castle. By the middle of November Gaunt and his sickly army had returned to Calais. Warwick died there of plague before he could get back to England. By the end of the month most of the survivors had returned to their homes.

It may be wondered what John of Gaunt had achieved for his pains. He had demonstrated his father's military power. He had forced the abandonment of Charles V's invasion plans. In a pungent return to the strategy of the 1350s he had dented the prestige of the French monarchy, which had stood by and allowed northern France to be burned and pillaged under the noses of its commanders. But Charles V was strong enough to live with that. It was the English who needed to force a decision. In this sense they had failed. The decisive battle had eluded them.[41]

Charles V felt keenly the loss of face involved in the cancellation of the invasion. But his alternative plan for the fleet proved to be an even more humiliating failure. It was devised during the autumn of 1369 in conjunction with two Welsh adventurers called Owen Lawgoch (or Owen of Wales) and Jack Wyn. Owen was the great-nephew of the last native prince of Wales, who had been killed in 1282 in the final stages of Edward I's conquest of the country. Since then his family had lived in impoverished obscurity, owning small parcels of land in Wales and the marches and in Surrey. According to Froissart, Owen himself had been brought up at the French court and as a young man had fought at the battle of Poitiers on the French side before following the Anglo-Gascon companies into Italy in the early 1360s. At some stage he fell in with Jack Wyn, a colourful professional mercenary calling himself 'Le Poursuivant d'Amours' who was probably the best-known Welsh captain in France. Wyn had served with the English companies in eastern France in 1359 and 1360 and had settled permanently in Burgundy after the peace. There he served as the custodian of John of Gaunt's possessions in Champagne, including the important castle of Beaufort east of Troyes. When the war resumed in 1369 Wyn declared for the King of France. Together with Owen of Wales he began to recruit a following among Welshmen in France, including a number of prisoners of war in French hands and others who had deserted from the Prince's companies in Aquitaine. They persuaded Charles V that Wales was ready to rise against the English if only help could be brought to them from outside.

Their pretensions were much exaggerated but they were not complete bluff. There were in fact prominent men in north Wales who were ready to rise against the English. And, although Owen had not been in Wales for many years, except perhaps briefly in 1365–6, his name still counted for something there. Without knowing or understanding more than a smattering of this, Charles V was persuaded in the autumn of 1369 to use the fleet which he had assembled for the invasion of England to carry Owen and Jack Wyn to Wales. They were to embark at Harfleur on 6 December 1369. The preparations were even more hurried and unsatisfactory than those which had preceded the attempt to invade England in the summer. It would be interesting to know if anyone other than the silver-tongued Owen counselled the cautious King to finance an expedition across more than 500 miles of sea in the middle of winter in order to land a tiny army in one of the remotest parts of Britain.[42]

The whole venture was a disaster. Owen's Welsh companies began to arrive at the port in the second half of November 1369. They were reinforced over the following fortnight by some companies of Genoese crossbowmen and French men-at-arms as well as infantry contingents recruited in the towns of northern France. Victuals and equipment were procured and loaded. More than 100,000 francs was said to have been disbursed. December is squally on the Atlantic coast. Some of the urban contingents, appalled by the weather conditions in which were expected to sail, deserted. But Owen of Wales and Jack Wyn pressed on. They put to sea with a somewhat reduced army more or less on time on about 7 December 1369. But they were driven back by difficult weather conditions after about twelve days at sea during which they failed to make a landfall. In England the government learned about Owen's treason by the beginning of November 1369 and of his planned invasion of Wales about six weeks after that. They confiscated his meagre lands. They reinforced the coastal garrisons of Wales and arrested the Anglesey man who was supposed to organise the rising in the west. It was not until much later that they learned to take Owen of Wales seriously. It says something for his persuasiveness that the fiasco did nothing to dent his reputation with the King of France. But Charles V never embarked on such a reckless operation of war again.[43]

The travails of the English King and his captains in the north were not enough to halt the progressive collapse of the English position on the south-east march of Aquitaine. Quercy was already lost and the only significant town which remained to them in Rouergue was Millau. The opinions of the doctors of law at Bologna, which the consuls of Millau had commissioned in the spring, had now been received. They were found to be unconditionally favourable to Charles V. The opinions, which had been commissioned mainly in order to put off importunate representatives of the Duke of Anjou, now eased the path of surrender.

The consuls negotiated a short truce with Anjou's officers at the end of September 1369. The captain of the town, James Mascy, left for Angoulême to impress upon the Prince the seriousness of his situation. When the truce expired no answer had come from Angoulême. So the consuls resolved to surrender the town. The opinions of the doctors of Bologna were read out at a general assembly of the citizens and the populace with one voice ratified the decision. The small English garrison in the citadel continued to hold out, but the end when it came was surprisingly amicable.

Mascy returned to Millau from Angoulême at the end of December to find that the townsmen had manned the walls and gates against him. As he stood outside the consuls invaded the citadel. In a tense exchange in the hall of the castle Mascy's wife, who had been left in command during his absence, refused to hand over the keys. But she ostentatiously left them on the table to be taken. Mascy had a substantial company of men-at-arms with him but he made no attempt to force the issue. The townsmen allowed him to enter the town with his son and a page and they agreed over a meal that the best thing would be for him to negotiate the peaceful departure of all the remaining English troops in the province. The garrisons in Castelmary and Sauveterre had already agreed to sell out. The two garrisons maintained in the English interest by the Bishop of Vabres were disbanded. Over the next few days Mascy negotiated the surrender of Paulhe. He was eventually escorted under safe-conduct from Millau to Castelmary where the remaining English troops in the province had assembled for their final departure. After they had gone the arms of Edward III and the Prince were ceremonially taken down from the gates of Millau and smashed. It was almost exactly eight years since Sir John Chandos had put them there.[44]

In Poitou the glow of success left by the English operations of the summer had already faded. The French troops of the march did not disband at the onset of winter. They concentrated on long-distance raiding from Touraine and Berry, the only regions where the march remained easily penetrable after Pembroke's campaigns along the Loire. The main centres of operation were Saumur, the westernmost bridge over the Loire still in French hands, which was the base of Jean de Bueil and the Marshal, Louis de Sancerre; and La Roche-Posay on the Creuse, where Jean de Kerlouet and his troops established themselves in September. Shortly afterwards Kerlouet created an important subsidiary base at Saint-Savin-sur-Gartempe, a walled town on the west bank of the Gartempe about fifteen miles south of La Roche-Posay.[45]

On the English side the defence of the whole march was nominally the responsibility of the Prince's lieutenant, Sir John Chandos. In reality Chandos commanded only his own retainers and garrisons and, when they were summoned, the Poitevin retainers of the Prince. The Earl of Pembroke, who commanded the English expeditionary force, took the view that it was beneath him to serve under a mere banneret, however famous. In practice the task was informally divided between them, Pembroke maintaining a screen against Jean de Bueil and the garrisons of the Loire valley while Chandos defended the eastern march against Kerlouet's garrisons on the Creuse and the Gartempe.

Pembroke may have had the grander name but his inexperience showed. In December 1369, shortly before Christmas, he conducted a fire-raising raid across the Loudunois and encamped with a force of about 500 men around the village of Purnon. He stayed there for long enough to enable Jean de Bueil to gather 600 men-at-arms from the garrisons of the Loire to surprise him. Pembroke's men were still struggling to form lines across the village street when the French horsemen charged into them, killing or capturing about a hundred. Pembroke abandoned his supplies and several hundred war-horses to the enemy and fled to a fortified house at the edge of the village where he had to be rescued by Chandos and the garrison of Poitiers. The French withdrew to their bases. 'We have acquitted ourselves honourably,' they told each other; 'now let us make off with our loot and prisoners while we still have them.' Pembroke's enemies, a growing band by now, could scarcely conceal their satisfaction.[46]

Chandos's own days, however, were numbered. On the last day of December 1369 he tried to trap the company of Jean de Kerlouet as it entered Poitou by the bridge over the River Vienne at Lussac. The bridge, which carried the old Roman road from Limoges to Poitiers, consisted of a timber carriageway supported on four great stone piles rising out of the water. As the French captain approached with his men he found the carriageway blocked at the western end by about 140 men commanded by Sir Hugh Stafford and Sir Digory Say. There was a fierce fight for possession, but before the French could break out they were attacked from behind by Chandos, who had brought the rest of his troops round by the other bank of the river. The French were crushed between the two English forces. Casualties were exceptionally heavy on both sides. They included both of the principal commanders. Jean de Kerlouet was one of the large number of prominent French prisoners. Chandos, who like many professional soldiers never wore a vizor, was run through the head with a sword. He died a few hours later without recovering consciousness. In English eyes his loss far outweighed any gain made in the fight. They would later say that had he lived he would have turned the tide and saved Aquitaine. That perhaps was self-deception. But Chandos's death, following upon that of Audley five months earlier, deprived the Prince of his wisest political counsellors and his only outstanding generals.[47]

The English probably had the better of the war of raid and counter-raid in Poitou. But whatever advantages they derived from it were dissipated in the first three months of 1370 by a disastrous adventure of the Earl of Cambridge in the Bourbonnais. The capture of Belleperche in the previous summer had been a humiliation keenly felt by Louis, Duke of Bourbon. As soon as the army of the north was disbanded in September Louis set about recovering the place. At the end of December 1369, after long preparations, he and Marshal Sancerre laid siege to Belleperche with an army of about 1,000 men. The siege was methodically pursued. Bourbon had trenches dug around the castle. He built elaborate field fortifications ('*bastides*') opposite the gates. He brought in siege engines to batter the walls day and night until the captive Duchess, terrified by the constant crashing of masonry about her, sent a message begging her son to stop. The Duke, who had committed his reputation to the recapture of the place, ignored her.[48]

The Earl of Cambridge was with the Prince at Angoulême when the news of Bourbon's operations reached them. A better strategist might have been satisfied that a substantial French force was being tied down by a garrison of just 120 *routiers* in a place which was marginal to the wider course of the war. But it was decided that it should be relieved. Froissart, who was well informed about this campaign, says that it was the Prince who made the decision, it is not clear on whose advice. The main reason was probably a desire to force a pitched battle, a form of warfare in which the English had excelled for two generations and in which victory would count for a great deal in the contest for local loyalties. It was a bold strategy. It involved redeploying most of the English expeditionary force and raising the largest locally recruited army that the Prince's states had produced since the ill-fated invasion of Castile. They would have to march 200 miles through inhospitable territory in mid-winter in order to reach Belleperche. Unfortunately the Prince was in no state to execute the plan himself. He depended on the

48

generalship of his brother, who had neither the experience nor the skill for the task and was poorly served by his advisers.[49]

At the beginning of February 1370 the Earl of Cambridge, accompanied by most of the English expeditionary force, the Prince's household troops and the baronage of Poitou, arrived at Limoges. The rest of the nobility of Aquitaine had been ordered to join him there. Reports reaching the French commanders put his strength at about 4,000 men, which accords broadly with Froissart's information but may have been rather more than the true figure. In the course of February and early March the Duke of Bourbon's army was heavily reinforced from Burgundy and the northern provinces in order to meet the new threat. As a result, when Cambridge reached Belleperche, probably towards the end of February 1370, he found himself facing a French army of about 1,500 men-at-arms and 300 archers, well dug-in on one side of the castle and defended at the front and rear by rings of trenches and field-works. The French artillery train included a huge fixed arbalest made in Genoa which had been brought from the Duke's castle of Chantelle and was still talked of two centuries later in the time of Rabelais.

The English had expected to be able to bring the besieging army to battle or force them to withdraw. However, to the surprise of his troops and the indignation of some of them, the Earl of Cambridge declined to order a full-scale assault on Bourbon's positions. Instead he began a laborious counter-siege, punctuated by sharp skirmishes and exchanges of artillery fire. After two weeks of this Cambridge finally changed his tactics and tried to provoke a battle on open ground. He sent Sir John Chandos's herald into the French lines to challenge them to come out. The Duke of Bourbon was having none of that. 'Chandos,' he replied, as the herald later told Froissart, 'you may tell your masters that I shall not fight to suit them.' After digesting this answer Cambridge tried to provoke the French to break cover by using Bourbon's mother as a bait. He drew up his men in battle order in front of the French positions. On the other side of the castle, which the French army had been forced to leave uncovered in order to face the English, the garrison brought the Duchess of Bourbon out of a postern gate and led her under heavy escort through the deserted French siege lines. The French told the Chandos herald that they thought this a discreditable trick 'unheard of in a war of gentlemen'. The Prince of Wales agreed with them when he was told about it later. At any rate it did not work. The Duke of Bourbon's men held their ranks and the

Duchess was carried off into the Limousin. Shortly afterwards, in about the middle of March 1370, the English companies at Belleperche set fire to the castle and escaped. As they left the French stormed the walls under the noses of the Earl of Cambridge's army and planted Bourbon's standards on top of the towers.

After a few days of confused counsels and bitter internal wrangling among the English leaders Cambridge's army abandoned the campaign. The retreat was very difficult. The English withdrew under cover of a heavy snowstorm. Entering the Limousin they were forced by appalling weather and shortage of victuals to divide their army into small groups which were harassed by a skilful French pursuit directed by Marshal Sancerre. Deserters told the French that Cambridge was suffering heavy casualties and had lost a great number of horses. As for the men who had occupied Belleperche, they were cornered in the small town of Lesterps in the county of La Marche and all but annihilated. Their leaders were taken to Paris to be beheaded for treason. Only Bernard de la Salle escaped. All that the English gained from the Belleperche campaign was the Duchess of Bourbon. She was placed at the disposal of the Prince, who gave her to his friend Simon Burley to enable him to pay his own ransom. The Duchess was eventually released in 1372 after three years in captivity in exchange for Burley plus a large sum in cash. Militarily the campaign had been a disaster. It had cost the Prince many men and emptied what remained of his treasury as well as inflicting a public humiliation on a son of the King of England.[50]

While the Earl of Cambridge was marching across the Limousin plateau to Belleperche the French extended their power into the Agenais. This region, which bordered on Quercy to the west, stood across the routes to Bordeaux by the valleys of the Lot and the Garonne. It was a region of countless small, subdivided lordships many of whose possessors were old allies of the Albret or Armagnac families and had adhered to the appeals from the outset. The leaders of the towns had waited upon events like so many others. Anjou's agents had been pressing for their submission for some months. In February 1370 the pace of events sharply accelerated. Anjou bought the submission of the provincial capital at Agen by lavish gifts to influential figures in the town and extraordinarily generous grants to the inhabitants, including a perpetual exemption from all royal taxation. He thought well enough of his prize to come to the town to receive its submission personally in the middle of February. The Prince's officers appear to have made a deliberate decision to concentrate their whole remaining strength in the region in the walled towns of Aiguillon and Port-Sainte-Marie by the confluence of the two rivers. This was no doubt realistic. But it involved allowing the French to walk in to the rest of the province. The Count of Armagnac took charge of this process. Once the men of Agen had submitted he found that other places were very ready to follow their example. All the significant towns of the region submitted in the course of the month.[51]

In Périgord a similar story was unfolding. Arnaud d'Espagne, Seneschal of Carcassonne and marshal of Anjou's army, was the Duke's captain-general in the province. A number of castles were occupied and garrisoned by his officers. In the uplands north of the Dordogne the Prince's subjects and allies now deserted him in droves. Périgueux, the provincial capital, had already decided that the safest course was to submit. The consuls were only holding out for suitable terms. Like everyone else their main concern was to ensure that they received proper military support to secure them against the Prince's revenge. On 28 February 1370, the place formally submitted. The citizens were summoned by trumpets to the cloister of the monastery of Saint-Front to hear the summons of the King and the Duke of Anjou read out and to ratify the consuls' decision. The bishop's palace in the Cité, which the English had used as a fortress and an occasional residence for the Prince and the Earl of Cambridge, was demolished and its materials carried away lest either side should use it again to overawe the citizens.[52]

The English had now lost control of most of the hill country of Périgord and the whole of the valleys of the Lot and the Garonne east of the confluence, with the isolated exception of Moissac where the garrison left by Chandos was still courageously but pointlessly holding out. The process accelerated as each submission brought more in its wake and the inhabitants of the English principality lost whatever confidence they had ever had in the Prince's ability to defend them. It was not at all clear that the French advance could be stopped even at Aiguillon or Bergerac which were now the outer barbicans of the Prince's domains. The lord of Albret had returned to Gascony after his long and highly profitable stay at the court of Charles V with a promise of 60,000 francs a year towards the cost of making war on the Prince in the Landes and the Bazadais where his family's lands were concentrated. But in the event no war was required. In about February 1370 Albret occupied the important walled city of Bazas. The language of the records suggests that some force was necessary but not much.

Albret had already distributed 2,000 francs among the leading citizens for their co-operation and it is likely that the only resistance came from the garrison in the citadel. By the beginning of March he had his own garrison of 100 men there. Bazas was just forty miles from Bordeaux.[53]

The lack of any serious resistance from the Prince's officers in these places is remarkable. There is no trace of any fighting, even on the modest scale which Wettenhall and Mascy had managed in Rouergue. Shortage of money and manpower is the most likely explanation. The domestic revenues of Aquitaine, which had fallen to a historic low in the year ending 29 September 1369, fell by another third in the following year. The main reasons were the progressive disintegration of the Prince's administration and the collapse of the wine trade as a result of the war. The tonnage of wine passing through Bordeaux fell by 70 per cent by comparison with the year before and the proceeds of the wine customs by four-fifths. Unpaid men might still serve out of loyalty but there was little enough of that. None of the cities occupied by the French in February and March 1370 had had garrisons to defend them, with the possible exception of Bazas, and no field army was within reach. Major towns, long-standing allies, powerful castles, were simply abandoned to the Duke of Anjou.[54]

As the formal structure of the Prince's government collapsed in the outlying regions of Aquitaine his officers were gradually replaced by irregulars: self-employed captains of free companies operating in a loose alliance with the English, and local lords pursuing their own interests under English colours. In Quercy Bertucat d'Albret joined forces with Bernard de la Salle after the latter's escape from Belleperche. The two of them commanded a combined company of 200 men-at-arms with perhaps 500 hangers-on which established itself in the Figeac area. From here they raided over the whole region. In Périgord the towns which submitted to the French in the Vézère valley were mercilessly harried by the Montaut lords of Mussidan, who remained the standard-bearers for the Prince in the valleys of western Périgord. The royal garrison in Périgueux kept the raiders away from the immediate vicinity of the city, but within three months of its submission the citizens were complaining that raiding parties were penetrating to within ten miles of its walls. The Prince's dependence on men like Bertucat and the Montauts was the only alternative to deploying proper garrisons and field armies, but their use inevitably meant treating the populations of these provinces as enemies.[55]

In both England and France the campaigns of 1369 were followed by a period of reflection and reassessment. Both governments had entertained hopes of a swift knock-out blow. Both had been disappointed. In France, which had spent more and run out of money first, serious thought was already being given to the implications of a political stalemate and a long war of attrition. The lack of an effective system for imposing and collecting taxes had been the single most important factor in the military failure of France in the 1340s and 1350s. In just the same way the development of an efficient tax system in France in the next two decades, coinciding with systemic failures of the English system, is central to an understanding of the French military revival.

The financial demands of the war were conditioned by significant changes in the way it was fought. In the 1340s and 1350s the main military operations had been conducted by very large armies operating for short periods, generally in summer. The French army at Crécy had been at least 20,000 strong and was in being for just one month. But the great battles fought by these slow-moving hordes were a thing of the past by 1369. The French, having rejected the pitched battle as the main end of warfare, concentrated instead on the effective control of territory. The army commanded by the Duke of Burgundy in September 1369 was the largest that Charles V deployed in the whole of his reign. After that he never deployed more than about 4,000 men-at-arms in a single army and rarely had more than 6,000 on his payroll at any one time, divided between all theatres. On the other hand these armies remained in the field for much longer periods. Although the rhythm of expansion in spring and contraction in the autumn continued, there were always substantial forces serving at the French King's wages even in winter. The consequence of these developments was that the trend towards the professionalisation of war, which had been evident in most European countries for many years, was sharply accelerated in the last three decades of the fourteenth century. The maintenance of standing forces of professional fighters called for a steady, predictable stream of funds, month in, month out, every year. The laconic Bertrand du Guesclin is said to have reminded Charles V of this at the time of his appointment as Constable. 'Qui bien ne les paie, ils ne veulent servir,' he said.[56]

Before 1360 the French tax system had consisted of a bewildering variety of taxes granted either by the Estates-General of one or other of the two great administrative divisions of France, Languedoc and Languedoil, or more commonly by smaller assemblies representing a single province or region. The great majority of these taxes were local, temporary, and hedged about with conditions which took a long time to negotiate and greatly reduced their value. The inadequacy and unpredictability of these sources of revenue had been an abiding problem for French governments, which had been unable to engage in the most basic financial planning and had been forced to resort to coinage manipulation to fill the funding gap in times of crisis. By 1369, however, the French state was collecting three permanent taxes, all of which had come into existence during the past nine years. The main decisions were due to the much-maligned John II, or perhaps to his more far-seeing advisers. In December 1360, immediately after his release from captivity in England, John issued the ordinance of Compiègne which introduced special taxes in order to raise the money owed to Edward III for his ransom. These took the form of indirect taxes on goods exposed for sale (known as '*aides*') and a surcharge on the salt tax (or *gabelle*). The *aides* were levied at the standard rate of 12d in the pound (5 per cent) on all commodities except wine which paid one penny in the shilling (8.3 per cent). After a number of experiments with higher rates the *gabelle* had been fixed by 1369 at 10 per cent.[57]

The payment of a king's ransom was one of the few unconditional financial obligations of a subject to his lord. The *aides* and the *gabelle* had therefore simply been imposed by royal decree without the consent of any representative assembly and without the prolonged and expensive negotiations which had preceded the collection of earlier taxes. In theory this was an extraordinary and strictly temporary state of affairs. The ransom was supposed to be paid by 1366 and payments in fact ceased early in 1368. By this time, however, the ransom *aides* had been tacitly recognised as an additional war tax of indefinite duration. Money raised from the ransom taxes was repeatedly diverted by the King or his lieutenants to military expenditure during the successive crises of the 1360s. Latterly, a significant proportion (generally a sixth) of the revenues raised from *aides* had been spent with the government's permission on the defences of the towns where they were collected. Other grants were being made from the receipts of the *aides* for war damage repairs and the military expenses of favoured noblemen and princes of the blood. This state of affairs appears to have been more or less accepted by the regional assemblies which had met at Compiègne, Chartres and Sens in 1367. They complained about several aspects of the new tax regime. But they did not complain about the continued collection of the *aides* nor about its diversion to war expenditure.[58]

From the beginning of 1364 the ransom taxes were supplemented by an even more important source of revenue, the *fouage* or hearth tax. The *fouage* was a traditional form of taxation in Languedoc which had been accustomed for many years to frequent, heavy war taxes. Hearth taxes had considerable advantages. They broadened the tax base, enabling the burden to be spread on a more or less uniform basis across a whole region. The lion's share of every hearth tax came from taxpayers in the *plat pays* where most people lived. For these reasons they were complementary to the *aides* which were collected mainly in market towns. In November 1363 the Estates-General of Languedoil meeting at Amiens ordained a hearth tax to be levied on each household at a graduated rate more or less related to ability to pay, which was designed to yield an average of three francs per hearth across the whole of Languedoil. It was explicitly a war tax, intended to finance a standing army of 6,000 men to deal with the free companies then at the height of their power. The introduction of the *fouage* depended on consent at the outset, but no term was set on it. It was an indefinite tax and shortly became a permanent one, unlike previous grants of taxation by the Estates-General of Languedoil which had always been made for a limited period, and unlike those of Languedoc which still were.

All three of the new taxes of the 1360s were designed for particular purposes. But their collection was under the control of the Crown which in practice applied them as it saw fit. Salaried royal commissioners (*élus*) in each diocese let the taxes in their districts to tax farmers, financiers who promised to pay fixed sums at fixed times to the district receiver, taking their profit or loss from any difference. The *élus* and the treasurers-general in Paris supervised the process of assessment, enforced the obligations of the farmers and resolved the innumerable disputes which arose in the course of collection. It is clear that in the first few years these functionaries encountered serious problems which were only gradually surmounted. But they were not responsible for the main weakness of the system, which was the large number of exemptions. The clergy were exempt from hearth taxes on the footing that they paid clerical tenths. Noblemen were also exempt both from direct taxation and from sales taxes on the produce of their domains. However, the most significant exclusions were geographical. The counties of Artois, Boulonnais and Saint-Pol, which bordered on the English pale of Calais and were constantly fought over, had to be allowed to commute their liability for comparatively modest sums. The newly conquered regions of the south-west were generally given extensive tax exemptions for an initial period in order to induce them to support the new order. Flanders and Brittany were practically independent states contributing neither service nor revenue. The Dauphiné and Burgundy east of the Saône were technically beyond the frontiers of France. More significantly the administrative service which collected the taxes in Languedoil did not extend to the appanages of the royal princes, the duchies of Burgundy and Anjou, the county of Blois and the extensive territories in central and western France belonging to the Duke of Berry. The *aides* were collected in the appanages. But they were collected by the officers of the princes who ruled them. They were generally entitled to take all or a large part of the proceeds as the price of their acquiescence. As for the *fouage*, that did not extend to the appanages at all. However, for all their drawbacks these were highly productive taxes and the administrative apparatus which was devised to enforce them was an immeasurable improvement on anything that had existed before. By 1369 they had already enabled Charles V not just to finance the elaborate bureaucratic structure of his government and to spend large sums on war and building, but to accumulate a reserve of about 400,000 francs in cash stored in sacks in the castle of Melun and in the towers of the Hôtel Saint-Pol and the Louvre in Paris.[59]

The breakdown of relations with England in 1368 and the reopening of the war in the following year were inevitably accompanied by a rapid acceleration in the rate of government expenditure, which quickly outstripped current receipts from the collectors. Without a major campaign of borrowing or an increase in tax rates this state of affairs could only last as long as the reserve. In round figures, out of the reserve of some 400,000 francs accumulated by 1368, 249,000 francs had been spent on military operations by July 1369 and 121,000 francs on diplomacy, in addition to small sums on building and personal expenditure of the King. The reserve was exhausted at the precise moment when Charles V's army of invasion was mustering by the Seine and John of Gaunt was marching out of Calais at the head of his army.[60]

It was against this background that the King's great assembly of notables met in the hall of Rouen castle at the beginning of August 1369. The precise status and powers of this assembly are uncertain because the summonses which called it into being have not survived. It was probably not technically a meeting of the Estates-General but a more limited gathering of selected interests, the sort of gathering which Charles V, with his acid experience of the representative assemblies of the 1350s, found it easier to manipulate. The King's spokesman was Jean de la Grange, the Benedictine Abbot of Fécamp, who had emerged as one of the King's most astute financial advisers. He told the assembly that the *fouage* of 1363, although intended to finance an army of 6,000 men, had in fact yielded barely enough to pay a quarter of that number. This may have been an exaggeration. But there is little doubt that the yield of the *fouage* had been disappointing and it had certainly not been designed to sustain a war against England. So the Abbot proposed that the *fouage* and the *gabelle* should continue to be collected but that they should be supplemented by fresh indirect taxes at much increased rates. This proposal caused great ill-feeling in the assembly and all three Estates objected to it. As ever, a large part of the problem was the difficult balance between urban and rural taxpayers. In the event the representatives were prepared to agree to an increase in the *aides*, including the doubling of the rate on wine sold wholesale, but only on the basis that these impositions were levied in place of the *fouage*, not in addition to it. To make the *plat pays* bear its share of the burden once the *fouage* had gone a new tax (the *molage*) was introduced on grain brought to the mills, which bore mainly on grain-growers and rural consumers for whom bread formed a larger part of the diet.[61]

This compromise proved to be highly unsatisfactory for taxpayers and ministers alike. It may even have diminished the government's net tax revenues. The truth was that the war could not be financed without imposing direct taxes on the great majority of French households located outside the towns and their immediate suburbs. The *molage*, which was designed to be the main tax imposed on the *plat pays*, was a disaster. It was so unpopular that in at least one diocese of northern France (Noyon) the *élus* could find no one willing to farm it. In November 1369 the government was forced to abandon the *molage* after only three months and to reinstate the *fouage*.

The whole question was revisited at a meeting of the Estates-General of Languedoil in Paris early in December 1369. The Chancellor of France opened the proceedings on 10 December in the palace on the Île de la Cité with an explanation of the government's predicament. The object was still the maintenance of a standing army of 6,000 men, but this time the King's ministers made it quite clear that a mere return to the pre-August situation would not do. There would have to be a large overall increase in the tax burden. The Estates deliberated for more than a week before agreeing on 19 December to a new package of fiscal measures. The *molage* was abolished. The *aides* were reinstated at the rates in force before August. And the *fouage* was reimposed at rates which reflected the contrasting fortunes of urban and rural households but were very high in both cases. The towns were to pay an average of six francs per hearth and the *plat pays* an average of two. Individual assessments were, as always, dependent on the taxpayer's resources, 'le fort portant le faible'. Even so the new scheme almost immediately ran into stiff resistance from taxpayers, so much so that for the first few months it was necessary to order a large abatement in the rates. But they remained in force without any further authority from the Estates-General, which never met again in Languedoil until after the King's death.[62]

The Duke of Anjou never freed himself from the need to engage in regular bargaining with representative assemblies as his brother had done in the north, but he proved adept at manipulating and bullying them when he needed to. Languedoc paid the *aides* like the rest of France and, like the rest of France, tacitly accepted their transformation into a permanent war tax. Their yield in the region was estimated at about 200,000 francs a year, most of which was reserved for paying the great pensions and subsidies promised to the counts of Armagnac and Périgord and the lord of Albret for bringing their appeals against the Prince of Wales. Languedoc also paid the *gabelle*, which needed to be regranted from time to time but invariably was. The *fouage* had a more chequered history. Collection was for some time held up by the lack of any up-to-date census of taxable households. Migration, plague and financial misfortune had made the existing assessments unusable. The practice had therefore been for the Estates of Languedoc to grant fixed sums which most communities then collected internally by imposing a hearth tax at whatever rate was required to satisfy their share. Between 1364 and 1374, however, a new census was carried out and thereafter periodically updated. It embraced all households with at least 10 *livres* worth of moveable property. This established a somewhat arbitrary but serviceable basis for collecting hearth taxes and enabled the Estates of Languedoc to start granting them again. The Duke of Anjou obtained a *fouage* of one franc per hearth in March 1368, the equivalent of another of two francs in October, and an extra half franc in January 1369, two francs and one gros more in May, making a total of just over five and a half francs per hearth payable over a period of eighteen months.[63]

The real turn of the fiscal screw, however, in Languedoc as in the north, came in the autumn of 1369 after the early campaigns. The Estates of Languedoc sat in successive sessions over a period of six weeks between September and November, first at Carcassonne, then at Toulouse. The outcome was a grant of 430,000 francs payable over one year, the largest grant ever made by the Estates of Languedoc, which was to be raised by indirect taxes on wine and a *molage* on grain. This grant was originally intended to replace the *aides* (worth about 200,000 francs in Languedoc) and to make about 230,000 francs of new money available for war purposes. The scheme was somewhat similar to the one ordained for Languedoil at the assembly at Rouen in August and it ran into much the same difficulties when they tried to enforce it. The collectors advised that the new taxes would not even raise half the amount promised. The Estates had to be recalled to Toulouse in February 1370 to revise the terms of the grant. They suppressed the *molage*, increased the rate on wine, and authorised a fresh hearth tax at the high rate of three francs per hearth. For one major city, Montpellier, these taxes represented a liability six times what the city had paid from a much larger population in 1328 before the war began, and three times what it had paid in 1348 when the war was still in its early stages. Yet Montpellier is exceptional only in the wealth of its surviving records.[64]

For their scale and persistence these changes represented a historically unprecedented burden of taxation in north and south alike. Moreover, it proved to be no more than a minimum in many parts of France, for the practice grew up of imposing local and temporary additional taxes, usually with the sanction of local assemblies, in order to fund particular operations of war which were important to the region, such as the siege of a nearby fortress or the pursuit of a local company of *routiers*. The major theatres of the war, in particular Lower Normandy and, later, Auvergne, therefore paid much higher taxes overall than others, in addition to bearing the brunt of war damage. The disappearance of most of the financial records of the time means that the yield of war taxes can be only very roughly estimated. In 1372 the combined receipts of the *aides*, *gabelle* and *fouage* in Languedoil were estimated by the King's Council at about 1,640,000 *livres*. In Languedoc, where the rates varied from year to year, the yield of all direct and indirect taxes other than the *gabelle* was estimated at 430,000 francs in 1370. This assumed a hearth tax of three francs over a year which was less than the Duke of Anjou was usually able to extract. Even allowing for the perennial optimism of such estimates these figures suggest total revenues from general taxation of at least 2,000,000 *livres,* or £400,000 sterling. This takes no account of taxes on the clergy, which were negotiated with the Pope and separately administered, nor of extraordinary taxes voted by local assemblies for special purposes.[65]

Of course not all of these large sums were available for war expenditure. The Estates-General of Languedoil in December 1369 had expressly authorised the use of at least part of the yield of the *gabelle* and of the tax on wine sales to support the cost of the royal household. In practice tax revenues were also spent on the salaries and expenses of the civil service, on pensions and gratifications for the princes of the blood and on satisfying the King's taste for jewellery, books and palaces. It is a striking fact, and some evidence of the natural buoyancy of French tax revenues, that the most intensive and continuous period of military activity in French history coincided with the construction of the King's great Parisian palaces and fortresses at Saint-Pol, the Louvre, the Bastille Saint-Antoine and Vincennes, as well as the creation of a new wall around the right-bank quarters of Paris; not to speak of the fine royal residences at Saint-Germain-en-Laye, Creil, Montargis and Melun and the princely constructions of the Duke of Berry at Mehun and Bourges. Louis of Anjou was less interested in building than his brothers but he appropriated a substantial part of the *aides* and the *gabelle* of Languedoc to the cost of his magnificent personal household. For all this, however, the evidence indicates that a high proportion, about two-thirds, of the tax revenues of the French state was in fact devoted to the prosecution of the war. This would in most years have amounted to somewhere between 1,200,000 and 1,500,000 *livres*, say £240,000 to £300,000 sterling. There was no prospect of Edward III matching war expenditure on this scale. England had only ever held its own against the superior economic resources of France in the late 1350s when France was divided by civil war and wrecked by brigandage. Excluding the cost of guarding the coasts and defending the Scottish march, the English government spent an average of about £90,000 a year on the prosecution of the war on land and sea between 1369 and 1375, which was about a third of the amounts available for war purposes to Charles V. The whole history of these years is written in these figures.[66]

CHAPTER III

Pontvallain and Limoges
1370–1371

According to Froissart, when the French King had been considering whether to receive the appeals of the Gascon lords one of the people whom he consulted was the Count of Saint-Pol, who had been a hostage in England for several years and was then in Paris on parole.

He said that England was only a little country by comparison with France, for he had ridden the length and breadth of it several times and had given much thought to its resources. Of the four or five regions into which one could divide the kingdom of France the poorest would offer more revenue, more towns and cities, more knights and squires than the whole of England. He was amazed at how they had ever mustered the strength to achieve the conquests that they had.[1]

It was an exaggerated picture but recognisable. England did not have anything like the wealth or taxable capacity of France.

In an age of limited credit, when governments lived like most of their subjects from hand to mouth, the conduct of England's long war with France was always dependent on the state of its public finances. In England as in France the costs of the king's household and the administration consumed far more than the 'ordinary' revenues of the crown, essentially the income generated by the royal demesne and the king's prerogative rights. For nearly a century these revenues had had to be supplemented by a number of permanent taxes. Unusually among European states these included duties levied on the country's export trade. The so-called 'great and ancient custom' had been levied on the export of wool, pelts and hides since the reign of Edward I. Miscellaneous duties on wine, cloth and other goods had been added over the years. The most recent of these was the wool tax, in effect a supplementary customs duty on wool exports. Initially granted as an extraordinary measure to fund war expenditure, the wool tax had in effect become part of the Crown's permanent revenues since 1362, when Parliament recognised that the King could not do without it even in peacetime. The war Parliament of June 1369 regranted it at increased rates.[2]

The customs revenues were always the largest single source of revenue available to the English kings. But they were sensitive to economic conditions and the yield was correspondingly variable. Between 1353 and 1362, in retrospect the golden age of English public revenues, they had yielded an average of about £88,000 a year, an unprecedented figure which was never attained again. The 1360s and 1370s were more difficult times for English trade. The average annual yield of the customs between 1368 and 1375 was about £67,000 and the tendency was downward. When the revenues of his demesne and prerogative rights and exactions are added, the total revenues on which the King could count came to between £80,000 and £100,000 a year. Of this sum the ordinary overheads of the King's household and government consumed at least £55,000 a year, sometimes more.[3]

This meant that the English King was wholly dependent in the long run on Parliamentary taxes to finance the conduct of the war. Parliamentary taxes were traditionally levied as a proportion of the value of moveable property. They were collected at standard rates, a tenth in the towns and a fifteenth in the country, according to an assessment originally made in 1334 which was now becoming out of date. They were granted for short periods, usually a year, occasionally two or even three years. A single tenth and fifteenth (which was as much as Parliament had ever granted for a year) had a nominal value of about £38,000 and in practice brought in almost that much. In addition the Church granted clerical tenths which were voted by the convocations of the ecclesiastical provinces of Canterbury and York, generally in conjunction with Parliamentary subsidies. The clerical tenth had a nominal yield of £18,000. But it was collected by the Church itself, not very efficiently, according to an even more antique assessment dating from 1291. In practice it brought in rather less than the nominal yield.[4]

In the aftermath of the break with France Edward was unwilling to ask his subjects for war taxes. Like his adversary he expected the war to be short and decisive. He probably believed that a demand for a lay subsidy would be resisted. If so he was almost certainly right. The outbreak of the war coincided in England with a series of natural misfortunes. A fresh epidemic of bubonic plague, the third to hit England in a generation, had begun early in 1369. Torrential summer rains had broken the grain crop and food prices were rising to levels not seen for half a century. Cattle disease and stagnating wool prices added to the woes of English producers.[5] Edward III's war propaganda seems to have had little impact on public opinion. There had been very little war damage in England. The Scots were quiescent. The mass of the population appear to have been no more impressed by the threat of invasion from France than Edward III himself was. There was nothing to bring home to them the menace of war. Unlike Charles V's subjects Englishmen had become unused to heavy taxation. In the 1350s the war had been financed mainly from customs revenues, the pain of which was too indirect to be noticed by the population at large. Apart from a conspicuously unsuccessful emergency levy in 1360 there had been no Parliamentary subsidy since 1357 and there would not be another until 1371. For the time being the English were content to watch with anxiety the progress of a war that they could still regard as the King's personal affair.

At this stage of his long reign Edward III was extremely cautious with his finances. He made no attempt to repeat the rash financial experiments by which he had funded his early campaigns in France. Like his adversary, Edward paid for the opening campaigns of the war at a rate greatly in excess of his revenues by drawing on a reserve accumulated in the 1360s. Edward's reserve had been funded not from a surplus of tax revenues, as Charles V's had, but from the windfall receipts such as ransoms and dowries which could be regarded as belonging to the King personally. In the year 1369 Edward III's war expenditure was financed almost entirely from this accumulated hoard and from other one-off gains of the same kind which were continuing to come in. He spent £42,000 on supporting the defence of Aquitaine, at least £75,000 on John of Gaunt's campaign in Picardy and Normandy, about £20,000 on the garrison of Calais and £10,000 on Ireland. Including money spent on coastal defence, for which no adequate record survives, the King's total war expenditure for the year must have been in the region of £160,000. Of this, nearly nine-tenths (£135,650) was covered by payments made between November 1368 and August 1369 from the King's personal resources. Although Edward continued to make modest personal contributions to the cost of the war during the following years he exhausted most of his personal liquid assets in the first year. He had nothing like the regular inflow of funds to fall back on that his rival could command. This inevitably operated as a powerful constraint on his conduct of the war. 'I counsel that ye begin no war in trust of your riches,' said Dame Prudence in Chaucer's *Melibee*; 'for they . . . suffice not wars to maintain.'[6]

*

Edward III faced the same strategic dilemma after 1369 as he always had done. His main object was to defend the possessions of his house in south-western France. This was exceptionally difficult and expensive to do directly. Defensive warfare required a large number of permanent garrisons and an army ready to appear at short notice to meet threats which would materialise at a time and place of the enemy's choosing. A generation of English and Gascon soldiers had grown used to wars of rapid movement by heavily armed cavalrymen supported by mounted archers, the traditional techniques of aggressive warfare. Defensive warfare, with its static forces and its scraps and sieges, was not the kind of fighting at which they excelled. Moreover it could never be decisive. The war would be won, if at all, by bringing political pressure to bear on the French King, which necessarily involved invading France by the north. The northern provinces were the richest parts of France and politically the most sensitive. The march of Aquitaine by comparison was politically marginal and difficult to reach from England. The sea route was long and hazardous. The passage of an army of any size required great numbers of the largest kind of ships, of which England never had enough. The overland route was blocked by the Loire, rising in the hills of Auvergne and descending in a great arc north then west to the Atlantic. The river was a formidable barrier: broad, fast-flowing and treacherous, exceptionally difficult to ford and guarded at every crossing by fortified bridges and walled towns. Invading northern France by Calais or with local support through Brittany or Normandy was a more inviting strategy.

The English King was well aware that internal divisions within France had in large measure accounted for his successes in the 1350s and sought out the fault lines which might enable him to repeat them. His plans for 1370 revolved around that French Alcibiades, Charles of Evreux, King of Navarre. Charles had been living in his Spanish kingdom for the past eight years nursing his grievances against the Valois kings of France. The loss of his valuable domains in the Seine valley in 1364 had left him with nothing more in France than the Cotentin peninsula, the city of Evreux and a claim to the lordship of Montpellier in Languedoc, which Charles V had promised him in 1365 but never delivered. Charles of Navarre was another man who looked back nostalgically to the 1350s, when, by playing off England and France against each other and recruiting supporters among the natural enemies of the Crown, he had briefly been the arbiter of France's destinies. In mid-June 1369, five weeks after Charles V had declared war on England, the King of Navarre crossed the Pyrenees with his ministers and counsellors and returned to France. There is some evidence that his return was suggested or at least encouraged by the Prince of Wales. In July 1369 he arrived in Brittany and at once made contact with potential allies.[7]

Charles of Navarre's first stop was the castle of Clisson in Bas-Poitou. Its owner, Olivier de Clisson, offered to serve as a go-between with the Duke of Brittany. The two men travelled together to Nantes, where the Duke was staying, and finalised their negotiations in great secrecy in the citadel. The outcome was an agreement, supported by the oaths of both parties, that each would come to the aid of the other. The detailed terms have not survived and Charles's chancellor never dared to reduce them to writing. Charles then went to Cherbourg, which was the principal fortified town of his shrunken domain. From there he sent his ambassadors to Edward III and Charles V in order to lay out his stall.[8]

In the last week of August 1369 two of Charles of Navarre's councillors appeared before the French King at Jumièges, the beautiful Benedictine abbey on the banks of the Seine to which the King had retreated after the sessions of the assembly at Rouen. Their demands when they came were predictable: the restoration of all Charles's lost possessions in Normandy, the recognition of his rather remote claim to the duchy of Burgundy, and the delivering up of the promised lordship of Montpellier. Charles V did not overreact as his father would have done. He was a cleverer diplomat and quickly took the measure of the King of Navarre. His representatives rejected outright Charles's demands for the recovery of his lands in Normandy, pointing to the treaty by which Charles of Navarre had ceded them in 1365. As for his other claims, the French King played for time while he set about outmanoeuvring the ambitious prince. He suborned the King of Navarre's principal negotiator. And he quickly squashed Charles's alliance with John de Montfort and Olivier de Clisson. The agreement had come to the ears of the Marshals during the siege of Saint-Sauveur in September 1369. They reported it to Charles V. John de Montfort took fright and was forced into a public declaration of loyalty to the Crown. He sent Olivier de Clisson, that practised trimmer, to deliver a complaisant message to the King in Paris.[9]

Charles of Navarre's emissaries to Edward III arrived in England towards the end of August 1369 in the midst of the clang of arms surrounding the final preparations for the despatch of the army to Calais. They were accompanied by a Gascon knight in the service of the Prince of Wales. Their instructions were to pave the way for a grander Navarrese embassy which arrived in the autumn, in which the leading light was Charles's subtle confidential secretary Pierre du Tertre.

The King of Navarre's dealings with the English court were devious even by his standards. In the first place, although his emissaries were there to interest the English King in a military and political alliance, he did not really want one. His real object was to strengthen his bargaining position with the King of France in order to obtain a better settlement of his claims. Edward, who had been double-crossed more than once by Charles in the 1350s, can hardly have been unaware of this. He simply had to hope that intransigence on one side or the other would bring about a breakdown of relations between the King of Navarre and his cousin of France and open an opportunity for him. Secondly there was a major bone of contention between Charles and Edward in the shape of the garrison of Saint-Sauveur-le-Vicomte, which was situated in the heart of the Navarrese domains in Normandy. Since the departure of Sir John Chandos for Aquitaine the fortress had been governed in their own interest by the two principal captains in command there, Chandos's sometime lieutenant John Cocking and a man called Roger Hilton, who had emerged as the leader of the free companies from Château-Gontier. They were a law unto themselves. Their men ranged over the whole of the Cotentin, raiding up to the walls of Cherbourg. Charles's officers could not move about his domains without a safe-conduct from Cocking and Hilton. There was 'not a foot of land belonging to him which was not subject to ransom', his ambassadors complained. During the winter the garrison of Saint-Sauveur had carried out extensive works around the fortress to improve its defences and accommodate the enlarged garrison. The monks of the abbey outside the gates had been expelled and their buildings fortified. A subsidiary fort had been constructed at the manor of Garnetot on the opposite bank of the River Douve. To prevent further destruction of his territory Charles of Navarre was obliged to pay protection money, levying the cost in taxes from the inhabitants. Between December 1369 and September 1370 the captains of Saint-Sauveur were able to extract promises of 17,000 francs (about £2,800) in this way, of which more than ninety per cent was actually paid. The effect was to divert substantially the whole taxable capacity of Charles of Navarre's domains into the pockets of the English.

There is no record of the work of Pierre du Tertre's embassy of September 1369. However, it is clear from the sequel that Charles's agents offered his domains in Normandy as a base for English operations against the King of France, provided that suitable terms could be agreed. They also made it clear that an end to the depredations of the garrison of Saint-Sauveur would be one of those terms. During the winter English emissaries continually passed between Southampton and Cherbourg with plans for military action. They received discreet encouragement from the sinuous King of Navarre but they got no further towards a firm agreement than Edward had.[10]

The English government's military plans for 1370 were put before the assembled baronage at a Great Council held in London at the beginning of February. An English agent by the name of John Paulesholt had recently returned from Cherbourg, where he had passed several weeks in discussion with Charles's councillors and the captains of Saint-Sauveur. He reported on the situation in Normandy for the benefit of the assembled magnates. Provided that suitable terms could be worked out with the King of Navarre it was agreed that the main enterprise of the summer should be the landing of an army of 2,000 men-at-arms and 2,000 archers in the Cotentin. The plan was to disembark the army in the great open bay of La Hogue on the east side of the Cotentin peninsula, where Edward III himself had landed in 1346. They would then join forces with the King of Navarre and the garrison of Saint-Sauveur and invade France through the Seine valley. Arrangements were immediately made to requisition the necessary shipping and to send out weapons and other equipment to fill the stores of Saint-Sauveur. Sir Robert Knolles, who had left Aquitaine in the previous autumn to return to Brittany, was now recalled to England. With the approval of the Great Council he was offered the command of the proposed army of invasion. The details were not worked out until later, but in their final form what was proposed was that Knolles should serve as the King's lieutenant in France with a general commission to carry on the war in Edward's name for a period of two years. Knolles's commission did not extend to Aquitaine. But everywhere else he was to have authority over all other English captains fighting in France.[11]

Sir Robert Knolles was a skilful and experienced professional soldier, but in an age when great commands went with social rank he was a surprising choice for a commission like this. He was a man of modest origins, now about fifty years old, who had made a fortune as an independent captain in the Breton civil wars. He was best known for his capture and sack of Auxerre in January 1359 and for his audacious *chevauchée* in Auvergne and Velay at the head of a great coalition of freebooters later in the same year. His selection as commander of the army severely limited the range of potential recruits, since none of the great magnates whose retinues traditionally supplied the backbone of the King's armies could be expected to serve under a man of his rank. The reason for the choice was the penury of the King and the remarkable way in which it was proposed to finance the campaign. It was conceived as a business venture. Knolles was to be paid a fee of £1,000 a year. He was authorised to recruit his own army in any part of England except for Northumberland, Westmoreland and Durham, whose manpower was reserved for the defence of the Scottish march. The King agreed to supply shipping to carry his army to the continent and to pay wages and recruitment bonuses ('regards') at double the traditional rates but only for the first three months. Thereafter the army would have to pay its own way from plunder and other profits of war.

Knolles's particular military experience made him the obvious choice for a long plundering campaign of this sort and his wealth enabled him to bear the financial risk of a project representing a total financial commitment of at least £10,000 a month. His personal contingent was 600 strong. He spread the risk by entering into subcontracts with three prominent knights, Sir Alan Buxhill, Sir Thomas Grandison and Sir John Bourchier. Buxhill was an influential courtier who had been Constable of the Tower since 1366 and was currently serving as under-chamberlain of the royal household. Bourchier had served for many years with the Prince of Wales in Gascony and fought at Nájera. Grandison was a nephew of the aristocratic Bishop of Exeter. He had fought at Poitiers, Reims and Nájera and had recently been admitted to the Order of the Garter. Knolles's agreements with these men provided for the four of them to share the profits of the venture in proportion to the size of their retinues. They were appointed deputy royal lieutenants by the King and made to swear oaths that in spite of the division of authority they would make their decisions collectively and keep the army together throughout the campaign. This was a prescient precaution as it turned out, but useless. The four commanders in turn entered into agreements with a number of other captains. The full agreements have not survived but the likelihood is that all of those involved were providing their companies at their own cost and risk after the first three months just as Knolles was.

The captains were an interesting group. Some, like the two bannerets Walter Lord Fitzwalter and William Zouche of Harringworth, were noblemen of the sort who would have accompanied an expedition of the more traditional kind. Some were professional freebooters after the model of Knolles himself, like Thomas Caun, one of the more notorious captains who had terrorised the Île de France and Normandy in the 1350s. Most were ambitious young men for whom the campaign was a speculative venture offering fame and fortune far ahead of their rank and experience. Sir John Clanvowe was nineteen years old. Sir Walter atte Lee was just seventeen. His participation in John of Gaunt's campaign of the previous year must have been his first experience of war. Mathew Redmayne, who agreed to answer for 150 men-at-arms and 150 archers, belonged to a prominent military family in the north-west but he was still only a squire and cannot have been any older than Clanvowe. Some of these men must have staked a large part of their wealth on the enterprise. Sir John Minsterworth, an ambitious hothead from the Welsh march, was a man of very modest means but contracted for 200 men-at-arms and 300 archers, the largest company in the army after Knolles's own. His subsequent career suggests that he may have been unbalanced. How these men recruited their companies is unclear. Most were probably recruited in the ordinary way by contracts of indenture. But it is clear that a fair number were outcasts, apostate clergymen and criminals on the run or emptied out of the jails, who served for loot and pardons.[12]

Aquitaine was a distraction in this scheme, but as spring approached it became a more significant distraction. At the time when the Great Council was considering the plans for the coming year, the defence of Aquitaine was believed to be in a reasonably satisfactory state. The news of Chandos's death had not yet reached England and the disasters of February and March had not yet occurred. It was therefore decided to send only modest assistance to the principality. About 300 men recruited in England by the agents of the Prince and the Earl of Pembroke were due to sail in the next few weeks. Another 500 were due to follow in the spring under the command of Sir Walter Hewitt. The choice of Hewitt was probably influenced by much the same sort of considerations which had pointed to Knolles as the captain of the larger expedition. He was another successful professional who had made a fortune in Brittany in the 1360s. He was in a position to lend the government almost half the cost of taking his company to Gascony. These plans had to be radically revised in April 1370 when the collapse of the Prince's position in the Garonne valley became known in England. It was now obvious that neither the Prince nor the Earl of Cambridge was capable of controlling the situation there. So it was resolved in about the middle of April to send John of Gaunt to

Aquitaine with a further 800 men in addition to the 800 or so already planned. Gaunt was chosen at least in part because he was thought to be a better diplomat than either of his brothers. He was armed with extensive powers to grant pardons and concessions to those whom the Prince of Wales had offended and driven into the arms of the French.[13]

By the standards of the past three decades these were not particularly ambitious operations. Even so, financing them was never going to be easy in the conditions of 1370. The initial funding of Knolles's army cost about £35,000 plus associated shipping expenses of about £3,500. Reinforcing Gascony on the scale originally envisaged represented a commitment of about £10,000. But John of Gaunt's expedition, given the exalted status of its commander, would have to be funded on a grander scale. The immediate cash cost in advances of wages and shipping expenses amounted to nearly £17,000 and the ultimate cost was nearly twice that figure. In addition there were other expensive distractions. From February 1370 onwards Edward III's government was spending large sums in keeping two fleets amounting to more than thirty vessels at sea with full complements of soldiers and seamen in order to defend the coasts against French seaborne raids. Unfortunately Edward's resources were at a low ebb. He had spent his reserves. It was a poor year for customs revenues. The only taxes being collected were a clerical tenth granted by the Convocation of Canterbury with exceedingly bad grace and after more than a week of argument in St. Paul's cathedral in London. The province of York followed suit. The figures suggest, when account is taken of the ordinary overheads of government, not just a cash-flow problem but a revenue deficiency of at least £50,000.[14]

It was made good by a systematic campaign of borrowing from Edward's subjects. This began in a small way in the new year. By March 1370 Exchequer officials were touring the country with demands for loans against the future receipts of the clerical tenth and the customs in order to finance the down-payments on Sir Robert Knolles's contract. The receipts proved quite inadequate. In June the Exchequer reported a 'tresgrande et hastife effusion de despenses' and began to panic. The King declared that he had to have the enormous figure of 100,000 marks (£66,666) by 5 July or be forever dishonoured. The response was impressive. The largest contribution came from a single individual, the famously rich Richard Fitzalan, Earl of Arundel, known as 'Copped Hat'. Arundel, who had inherited the vast estates of the Mortimers of Chirk and the Warenne Earls of Surrey and made a profitable career as a soldier in his younger years, was an astute financier who stored up cash in chests and sacks in the high tower of Arundel castle, in his castles on the Welsh march and with churches and merchants in London. He had already lent the government 10,000 marks (£6,666) in September 1369. Between May and September 1370 he lent another 30,000 marks (£20,000), all secured on the London customs. Even on this munificent scale the King's borrowings were very much a hand-to-mouth affair. Much of Arundel's money had to be laboriously carried to Westminster in wagons from the Earl's stores at Shrewsbury, escorted by an Exchequer clerk and a company of archers, before being distributed to soldiers and seamen at the ports.

The rest of Edward's requirements were supplied by another, more insistent round of borrowing. The King's ministers opened up their own chests. The city of London organised syndicated loans. Collectors of the customs and the clerical tenth were pressed for advances on their receipts. But the most productive form of pressure and the most widely resented was the appointment of commissioners for each county to assess the richest men of the community according to their reputed wealth. Refusals were not to be tolerated. The target of 100,000 marks may have represented an opening bid, but in fact Edward III raised about two-thirds of that amount by the end of September from more than 200 bishops, abbots, landowners, urban corporations and merchants. This was more than the value of a Parliamentary subsidy. Indeed part of it might as well have been a subsidy. For, although favoured or secured lenders received repayment of their loans quite quickly, many of the smaller lenders were still unpaid a decade later. Most of them never saw their money again.[15]

Charles of Navarre was told about the English King's military plans in February 1370, shortly after the Great Council had approved them. About a month after this he received what amounted to Charles V's final offer. It was not generous. After a long-drawn mediation in Paris the French King's councillors promised no more than that the King would observe his existing obligations under the treaty of 1365. What he would not do was restore the valuable domains which Charles of Navarre had possessed in Normandy before the civil war of 1364–5. A delegation of Charles V's Council was sent from Paris to Cherbourg to discover Charles's reaction and make arrangements for him to do homage. They found him, as always, dissatisfied, inscrutable and devious. He put off doing homage on various pretexts, dragging out the preliminaries while he set about making himself a bigger threat to Charles's security, in the hope of provoking a better offer.[16]

In England the first companies of Knolles's army began to muster in the course of May 1370. The Admirals' officers were working to assemble the large fleet of ships required to carry it to La Hogue but there was still no agreement with the King of Navarre. After a series of inconclusive messages had passed back and forth across the Channel it was decided to invite Charles of Navarre to come to England in person, since 'they would seal their alliance more quickly and with less contention in person than by intermediaries.' On the assumption that something would come of this the Council announced that Southampton would be the army's port of embarkation and ordered the transports to proceed there by 1 July. The delay was only partly due to the gyrations of the King of Navarre. There had also been serious problems in the requisitioning process. It had been assumed in February that a fleet large enough for an army of 4,000 men with horses and equipment could be assembled just from the larger ships of the ports of East Anglia. This proved to be a serious mistake, and the Admirals' officers were to spend most of the next three months turning merchant ships out of ports in the west country and up the east coast as far north as Berwick, some of them as small as twelve tons. In the end it was necessary to make up the strength of the transport fleet by chartering ships in Holland and Zeeland.[17]

As time went on it became increasingly doubtful whether the King of Navarre would commit himself even by July. When Edward's messengers arrived at Cherbourg they found him preoccupied with the problem of Saint-Sauveur. His officers had recently spent two weeks in the company of the French Marshal Moutier de Blainville, recapturing the castle of Eroudeville outside Montebourg, where the captains of Saint-Sauveur had tried to set up a satellite garrison. Charles was also facing demands from Cocking and Hilton for a large increase in the *patis* payable to them once the existing ransom treaty expired in late May. His response to Edward III's invitation was to send his private secretary, Pierre du Tertre, back to England, accompanied by his equally conspiratorial chamberlain, Jacques de Rue, and a number of other councillors. Their instructions were to arrange a personal meeting with Edward III. First, however, they were to impress on the English King the importance of doing something about Saint-Sauveur. Otherwise there would be no point in going on. 'You would not believe the damage and dishonour that they are inflicting on us and plan to inflict in future,' they were to say, '. . . it is martyrdom to have to endure such shame. No man could be expected to put up with it.'[18]

Charles's ambassadors landed at Newport, Isle of Wight, early in June 1370. Passing through Southampton they were able to see for themselves the gathering of Knolles's army and the assembly of the fleet. Edward III received them at Westminster. The first and most urgent item of business as far as the English were concerned was to make the arrangements for the King of Navarre's visit to England. These were extremely elaborate. Charles never put himself in anyone's power without taking hostages for his safety and Edward III had to agree that a large number of imposing personages, including the Earls of Warwick and Suffolk and the Bishop of Durham, would be held in Cherbourg castle until his return. To serve Charles's dignity and protect him from French naval operations in the Channel, a fleet of eighteen of the King's own ships, streaming with coloured pennons and stuffed with armed men and artillery, was made ready at Southampton to bring him to England. The projected cost of this state visit was so great that the King was obliged to call for an extra 25,000 marks (£16,666) of loans to cover it. Once all this had been agreed the ambassadors turned to the question of Knolles's expedition to France. This was a delicate matter. Charles of Navarre was anxious that Knolles should enter the field as soon as possible, but he did not want him in the Cotentin. He was afraid to burn his boats with the King of France by publicly receiving an English army in his territory. Edward III reluctantly accepted reality. Knolles's destination was changed to the Pays de Caux, north of the Seine estuary. This was very much second best. It would be practically impossible for the army to reach southern Normandy as long as the French held the bridge-towns of the Seine. It also necessitated a change of embarkation point. On 26 June 1370 the revised orders reached the fleet and the ships began to head east out of the Solent ports towards Winchelsea and Rye, which the Council had appointed for the purpose. The army followed along the shore. A whole month was lost.[19]

By the time that Charles of Navarre arrived in England the original point of his meeting with Edward III had disappeared. Knolles's army sailed from Winchelsea and Rye in stages between mid-July and 2 August 1370. There were about 2,000 men-at-arms and 2,000 archers on the payroll, making a total of about 6,000 mounted men with pages and varlets. The weather was atrocious. At least one ship laden with horses foundered in high winds off Rye. In the end it became necessary to abandon the plan to land in Normandy and to ship the army to

Calais instead. Walter Hewitt's companies had already sailed for Gascony from Dartmouth at the end of June and Gaunt's larger force followed him about a month later. The course of events for the next year was fixed as far as it could be. Charles of Navarre arrived in England on 21 July 1370 while the embarkation of Knolles's army was in progress. On 1 August he came before Edward III with a crowd of gentlemen, servants and minstrels at the royal manor of Clarendon, the famous hunting lodge of Henry II and Henry III in Wiltshire, where they could be assured of some privacy. But the outcome hardly warranted the secrecy. The two men agreed on a truce in the Cotentin for a limited period, which was roughly drafted out by them and handed to Latimer to be formalised. They spoke vaguely of 'alliance and friendship' but Edward III found it impossible to pin Charles down on any point of real importance. Everything was to be settled between the councillors of the two kings in due course. It was, as Edward euphemistically observed, 'a start'. Nothing was recorded in writing. No witnesses were present except, apparently, Latimer. On about 12 August Charles of Navarre left Clarendon for the ships.[20]

In the middle of April 1370 Charles V, his three brothers, the Dukes of Anjou, Burgundy and Berry, and his brother-in-law, the Duke of Bourbon, gathered in Paris to celebrate Easter and to take stock of the strategic situation. The main lines of the French government's strategy in the coming six months were laid down at a series of meetings after Easter, attended by most of the leaders of the military aristocracy. They resolved to concentrate their efforts on completing the conquest of Aquitaine. Two armies were to be formed. The Duke of Anjou would invade the principality from the south-east by the Garonne and make for La Réole and Bergerac, while the Duke of Berry entered the Limousin to penetrate into the heart of the principality from the east. The two wings were to meet at Angoulême where it was hoped to lay siege to the Prince in his capital. At some stage the plan was expanded to embrace a third attack on the principality by the north from the fortresses of the Loire and the Creuse under direction of the Marshal Mouton de Blainville. The Duke of Anjou, who was the hero of the hour after his bloodless conquests of the past three months, ventured to predict that the English would be driven out of Aquitaine within two years.[21]

Another momentous decision was made at the same time. It was resolved to dismiss the Constable, Moreau de Fiennes. The Constable's office was traditionally held for life but Moreau was not thought to have distinguished himself on the march of Calais over the past year. He was 'half-asleep', they said. Instead it was proposed to recall Bertrand du Guesclin from Castile and to appoint him in Fiennes's place. It was an unconventional choice. By tradition the Constable was a great noblemen, not a man like Du Guesclin whose only claim was that he was an outstanding professional soldier. But there was serious concern in Paris about the plans of Knolles, whose very name had sown terror in France since 1359. No obvious alternative candidate existed among the higher nobility. According to Froissart, Du Guesclin's promotion was the work of Louis of Anjou. There is some support for this from Du Guesclin himself, who would always look on Anjou as his patron and protector at court.

Now in his mid-forties, Bertrand du Guesclin was already a famous figure. He had been largely responsible for placing Henry of Trastámara on the throne of Castile, overthrowing the English-sponsored candidate in a campaign which, although supported and subsidised by the French government, was very much a personal venture. He had made himself in the process the richest of all the soldiers of fortune who had flourished on the margins of the Anglo-French war in the 1350s and 1360s. In one sense he was the French counterpart of Robert Knolles, a man of humble origins (though not as humble as Knolles's) who had made his reputation and his fortune as an independent captain. The line between public war and brigandage had been extremely uncertain in the careers of both men. And they had traits of personality in common. Both were grasping, self-reliant men whose taciturn manner probably reflected their discomfort in the presence of the great magnates who traditionally dominated the counsels of kings. Bertrand, as Christine de Pisan described him in her portrait of the ideal constable, was 'dignified and spare with words, never talking of trifles'. But if Du Guesclin had these things in common with Knolles he was a much greater soldier. He was not, it is true, a good battlefield tactician like Chandos or the Prince of Wales, both of whom had had the better of him in the field. But these experiences had led him to share the misgivings of Charles V about the risk of fighting battles against the English. His war was not to be a war of battles. He understood the value of a war of attrition which in the long term the English could not win. His strengths were his tight control over the forces under his command, his meticulous planning of his campaigns, his mastery of a war of rapid movement and a grasp of the wider strategic object which was equalled only by the late Henry of Lancaster or by Edward III in his prime.[22]

The first of the three attacks on Aquitaine to materialise was the attack on Poitou from the north. Jean de Kerlouet, who had been ransomed almost immediately after being captured at the bridge of Lussac, was the prime mover. With the advantage of speed and surprise he achieved a notable victory at the outset of the campaign. In the first week of July a raiding force drawn from his garrisons at La Roche-Posay and Saint-Savin appeared without warning outside Châtellerault at dawn. They seized the walls with ladder parties and quickly took possession of the town. Châtellerault was an important walled town at the confluence of the Vienne and Clain in north-eastern Poitou, which commanded the main road from Tours to Poitiers and a fortified bridge over the Vienne. It belonged to Louis of Harcourt, one of closest of the Prince's Poitevin councillors, who was in the town at the time. He had to flee in his nightshirt through the gardens of his neighbours' houses. Harcourt's garrison held out for some weeks in the towers of the bridge until they too were obliged to abandon the place and flee. The French strengthened the fortifications of Châtellerault and put in a large garrison. It became the base of Marshal Sancerre. These events made a serious dent in the defences of Poitou and caused much concern for the security of Poitiers, which was only fifteen miles away. Shortly afterwards the Prince's officers in Poitiers unearthed a plot to surrender the city, organised by three senior clerics. For the time being the establishment of the town remained loyal to the Prince. But it was a fragile loyalty. 'A fine outline of a bishop' was what one of the plotters called the Bishop of Poitiers.[23]

In spite of the ambitious target announced by Louis of Anjou at the Paris assembly, his own campaign in the Garonne valley achieved little more than the consolidation of previous gains. It was mainly important as a spectacular demonstration of Du Guesclin's capacity to be everywhere at once. The Breton captain came over the Pyrenees from Castile in June 1370. He brought with him his entire company of about 1,000 French and Breton retainers, a sprinkling of Castilian fortune-hunters and the huge sum of 120,000 *doblas* (just under £30,000) in cash paid to him by the grateful King of Castile. He arrived at Toulouse in about the middle of July. On about 15 July Anjou and Du Guesclin moved north from Toulouse down the valley of the Garonne. Their total strength must have about the same as the 4,000 or so men who had been deployed in 1369. On the 23rd they captured Moissac at the confluence of the Garonne and the Tarn. The garrison, the only one still holding for the Prince of Wales in Quercy, surrendered without a blow when it became clear that the townsmen would not support them. The capture of this place enabled supplies to be carried downriver after the army. At the beginning of August Anjou's army moved into the Agenais and then thrust north into the valley of the Dordogne. Anjou's council had already agreed deals with some major defectors from the English cause, which were dependent on his showing his face there. The lord of Beynac had recognised Charles V since the previous autumn. Sarlat had declared for the King of France by July. Nicholas de Beaufort, who was probably serving in the French army, brought into the French allegiance the huge inheritance of his wife, Marguerite de Galard, dame de Limeuil, in return for a lump sum, a handsome pension and a contribution to the cost of defending his lands. This great lordship comprised more than thirteen castles on the north side of the Dordogne valley in addition to the town and castle of Limeuil guarding the confluence of the Dordogne and the Vézère. The French were now in control of the whole course of the Dordogne upstream of Lalinde.[24]

Louis of Anjou and Bertrand du Guesclin entered Sarlat in the second week of August 1370. From here they penetrated rapidly west into the heart of Périgord. At Périgueux Du Guesclin separated himself from Anjou. Using the city as his base he divided his troops into a number of separate raiding forces and launched rapid attacks on English-held towns in the lowlands to the west. Brantôme on the Dronne and Montpon on the Isle were both occupied in the space of a few days, together with a large number of smaller places around them. According to the versifier who wrote Bertrand's life he 'seemed to multiply himself everywhere and from all directions men came out to offer him the keys of their towns'. The main object of these moves seems to have been to obstruct the routes from Bordeaux towards Angoulême and Limoges in order to hamper the communications of the Prince's armies on the eve of the Duke of Berry's operations in the Limousin. A brief and unsuccessful attempt was even made to take Bergerac, the principal English garrison town on the Dordogne. This was beaten off by the Seneschal of Aquitaine, Sir Thomas Felton, without much difficulty. But the English very nearly lost the nearby town of Lalinde, an important *bastide* town on the north bank of the Dordogne, whose inhabitants resolved to admit the French. Felton arrived in the place only just in time to avert this disaster.[25]

The Limousin was the province which the English had taken over last and absorbed least. It was high, infertile and heavily wooded. It generated very little revenue for the Prince's coffers. The surviving accounts of the principality suggest that it had been virtually ungarrisoned before the outbreak of the war. Given the financial state of the principality things were probably no better afterwards. At an early stage Charles V had begun to prepare the ground for its reconquest. As in Poitou, the first wave of defections consisted for the most part of men whose main landed interests lay elsewhere, in territory controlled by the King of France. They began to adhere to the appeals against the Prince's *fouage* in large numbers from May 1369, encouraged by generous promises of pensions and grants. Some did much more than just adhere to the appeals. Louis, Viscount of Rochechouart, whose most valuable domains lay in Berry and southern Touraine, had fled to Paris and taken service with the King of France. He returned with 120 French troops to occupy his great thirteenth-century castle at Rochechouart which guarded the western approach to Limoges by the valley of the Vienne. The fortress of Chalusset, eight miles south of Limoges, with its vast thirteenth-century curtain walls, is still one of the most impressive military ruins in France. Charles V acquired possession of this place in October 1369 from Rochechouart's cousin, Louis de Sully, together with the important castle of Châlus, standing over the road from Limoges to Périgueux.[26]

When it became known in the spring of 1370 that the Duke of Berry was to invade the Limousin and no steps appeared to be planned by the Prince of Wales to defend it, the trickle of deserters became a flood, even among those who had no significant interests outside the province. Most of these men were moved by the conviction that the Prince's rule was doomed. This applied particularly to those whose domains lay in the east and south of the province, regions whose natural lines of communication with the rest of Aquitaine lay through the valleys of Périgord and Quercy, now for the most part occupied by the French. Raymond de Mareuil, whose family originated in the Angoumois but had large possessions in the Limousin, had begun the war as a stout adherent of the Prince of Wales. He had served with Chandos in Quercy, participating in the defence of Montauban and the siege of Domme. He submitted to the King of France in June 1369 as soon as Chandos abandoned Quercy. In July 1370 he brought his retinue to Auvergne to join the army of the Duke of Berry. He was typical of his kinsmen and neighbours. When the Duke of Berry marched south out of Bourges at about the end of the first week of August his army included a large number of barons of the Limousin, several of whom had been with Chandos the year before. They were determined to be on the winning side. The English had 'lost too much to recover now', they reasoned, according to Froissart. Berry's agents toured round the towns and leading magnates of the Limousin encouraging others to follow suit. By the time the Duke himself arrived in the province most of it was ready to drop like ripe fruit into his lap.[27]

The Duke of Berry was joined on his march by the Duke of Bourbon, who brought more men from Bourbonnais, and by the Count of La Marche with the men of his county. At same time the Marshal Sancerre entered the Limousin from the north-west with troops drawn from French garrisons in northern Poitou. The total strength of the forces converging on the Limousin was probably about 2,000 men-at-arms. Their objective was Limoges, the provincial capital. Like many cities of southern France, Limoges was a double town comprising two distinct built-up areas, each with its own circuit of walls. The larger and more ancient of the two, which was known as the Château, had grown up around the old Roman city and the Benedictine abbey of St. Martial on high ground about half a mile from the River Vienne. Below the Château, on the right bank of the river, the smaller Cité had grown up rather later around the cathedral of St. Etienne and the bridgehead. Between the two enclosures lay a dense undefended suburb where the butchers and tanners carried on their noxious trades. The Château was a commune governed by its consuls, where most of the population and the commercial wealth of Limoges was concentrated. It was defended by a powerful circuit of walls built in the thirteenth century, about a mile and a half long and forty feet high, with more than two dozen towers and eight fortified gateways. The Cité by comparison was essentially an ecclesiastical enclave, overshadowed by the unfinished bulk of the cathedral and a cluster of urban monasteries, and dominated politically by its bishop. It was weaker. It stood on lower ground. Its walls, although more recent than those of the Château, had not been maintained and were 'notoriously insufficient' according to its inhabitants. Neither the Château nor the Cité appears to have had any significant garrison.[28]

On the evening of 21 August 1370 the Duke of Berry arrived at the head of his army after a march of two weeks in which he had encountered no serious opposition. He set up his headquarters in the Dominican convent, among the vineyards and suburban gardens, and opened negotiations with the defenders. The Bishop, Jean de Cros, had traditionally enjoyed cordial relations with the Prince of Wales and had recently stood godfather to his youngest child. Nevertheless he agreed to surrender the Cité to the French. His motives were never clearly established. There is some evidence that he was won over by his kinsman Roger de Beaufort, a member of the powerful family of the lords of Turenne, who was with the Duke of Berry's army. He probably decided, like so many other territorial magnates in south-western France, that English rule in the Limousin was doomed. On the morning of 24 August 1370 the population of the Cité gathered in the square in front of the Porte de l'Escudière on the west side of the Cité to formalise their submission in the presence of the Duke of Berry and the leaders of the French army and to receive them into the streets to cries of 'Montjoie!' and 'Saint-Denis!' The ceremony must have been visible and audible from the towers of the Château, just 200 yards away. But the Château did not follow Jean de Cros into the French King's allegiance. Its inhabitants defied the Duke of Berry and held out for the Prince.[29]

At the end of August 1370 the great French campaign devised in Paris in April came to a sudden end. The plan for the forces of Berry and Anjou to join up in Périgord was abandoned along with the idea of confronting the Prince of Wales at Angoulême. Precisely how and when this change of plan was decided is difficult to say. The reasons were almost certainly financial. The Duke of Berry depended for the financing of his campaign on grants from Charles V's treasury in Paris. Charles V had paid the advances of part of his army and contributed 2,000 francs per month to the cost of paying his personal retinue up to the end of November. But Berry had great difficulty in paying the balance and was short of cash throughout the campaign. The Duke of Anjou's financial position was even worse, for although his resources were greater he had seriously overstretched them. The nobility of Languedoc had been paid their advances on mustering in July but many of them were still waiting for the rest. This was a serious embarrassment since some of their captains were great figures among the nobility of Languedoil. The Duke extracted himself from it only by heavy borrowing. A loan was raised from a syndicate of Florentine bankers organised by the Pazzi agent at Avignon. Bertrand du Guesclin made another substantial loan from the hoard which he had accumulated in Castile, rather as English captains like Hewitt and Knolles lent their war profits to Edward III. Even so the French campaigns in the Midi could not continue without large subsidies from the Treasury in Paris, which Charles V was unwilling to provide with Knolles's army in his front garden. In that sense Knolles may have achieved more for his master than he realised. Louis of Anjou withdrew from Périgord at the end of August 1370 and returned to

Toulouse. Du Guesclin marched at high speed up the valley of the Isle towards the march of the Limousin and briefly joined the Duke of Berry at about the time that the Cité of Limoges surrendered. But the two of them then went their separate ways. Berry turned north on the day he received the surrender, without making any attempt on the Château of Limoges and leaving only a modest garrison in the Cité. He paid off his army at Bourges at the beginning of September. Du Guesclin turned south and was back in Toulouse by the end of the month to collect his pay. His company received their wages from the Duke of Anjou's treasurers on 14 September and then left for the north.[30]

The first ships of John of Gaunt's fleet must have reached Bordeaux in mid-August 1370 just as the French campaign was beginning to wind down. Early in September he appeared with his army at Cognac, where the Prince of Wales was waiting with the Earls of Pembroke and Cambridge. Gaunt must have been shocked by the sight of his elder brother, whom he had last seen in England at the height of his powers seven years before. Reduced to being carried in a litter, the Prince lay surrounded by attendants and councillors who were obliged to take most of his decisions for him. They had mustered as large an army as would serve, given the rather distant prospect of payment. Its strength is a matter of conjecture but, allowing for the troops serving in garrisons and on the northern march of Poitou, there must have been about 3,000 men, including those who had recently arrived from England. The original objective had been to confront the troops of the Duke of Anjou in the valleys of the Dordogne and the Garonne before they could join up with those of the Duke of Berry. But it was too late for that now that both enemies had melted away. So the decision was taken to mount a powerful punitive raid into the Limousin. The intention was to make an example of the Cité of Limoges which would echo through every other town in the south-west that contemplated joining the steady tide of defections to Charles V. The leaders of the army of retribution included some of greatest names of European chivalry: three sons of Edward III, Walter Hewitt, the Captal de Buch, Guichard d'Angle and most of leading barons of Poitou. At some time in the second week of September 1370 the Anglo-Gascon army arrived outside Limoges. It was less than three weeks since the Duke of Berry had left. The Prince sent his messengers into the Cité to summon the townsmen to surrender. He told them that otherwise he would destroy their homes with fire and sword.[31]

The Duke of Berry had left the Cité in the hands of three captains, Roger de Beaufort, his brother-in-law Hugh de la Roche, and Jean de

Villemur, a confidant of his from Berry. They commanded a garrison of just 140 men. It was enough to overawe the citizens, who were beginning to regret their support for the surrender of August, but it was not enough to hold out against a determined assault by the Prince's army. The siege lasted just five days. John of Gaunt directed operations. A careful survey of the defences was carried out, which revealed that one section of the high city wall was built on foundations of soft tufa, not rock. Gaunt sent in miners to tunnel underneath it. The defenders detected the mine and tried to countermine, digging tunnels beneath those of the besiegers. According to one report Gaunt himself was in the tunnel when the counterminers succeeded in breaking through the gallery walls. They had to be beaten off in hand-to-hand fighting in the cramped underground space. On 19 September 1370 the besiegers fired the timber supports holding up the mine and brought down about a hundred feet of wall. The English and Gascons, who were gathered in battle order outside, launched an immediate assault which was repulsed. But a second assault overwhelmed the defenders and brought the attackers into the streets of the city. It happened so quickly that the defenders did not have time to set up an inner line of defence. The soldiers poured into the conquered place, killing and looting wherever they went. The population, swollen by the influx of refugees from the surrounding *plat pays*, was defenceless.[32]

The capture of cities by assault was routinely followed by appalling scenes of looting, rapine and murder. Contemporaries shrugged their shoulders. By the laws of war it was the proper fate of a city which had been summoned to surrender and then been taken by assault. The inhabitants had defied the Prince's justice and could hope for nothing. Froissart was a historian all of whose instincts lay with the men-at-arms of the besieging army. Yet he was one of the few to spend tears on the fate of these nameless victims of the customs of medieval warfare. His account, although exaggerated and embroidered with much imaginary detail, is one of the most famous pages of his chronicle:

The Prince, the Duke of Lancaster, the Earl of Cambridge, the Earl of Pembroke, Sir Guichard d'Angle and the rest entered the city on foot with their companies and their hordes of hangers-on. All of them were equipped for evil and ready to spread out across the city, killing men, women and children as they had been ordered to do. It was heart-rending to see the inhabitants throwing themselves on the ground before the Prince as he passed, crying out 'Mercy, noble lord, Mercy'. He was so enraged that he heard them not. No one listened to their appeals as the invaders ran through with their swords everyone they found in their way. These people had had nothing to do with the city's treason but paid a dearer price than the great figures who had really been responsible. There is no man who, if he had been at Limoges and remembered the name of God, would not have wept over the tragedy that happened there, for more than three thousand people, men, women and children, died on that day. Let the Lord receive their souls for they were all martyrs . . . And the looting did not stop until the whole city was stripped and left in flames.

In fact the most reliable figure for casualties, which is given by a monk of St. Martial's abbey writing shortly after the event, suggests that some 300 people, perhaps a sixth of the normal population, lost their lives. About sixty members of the garrison, almost half its strength, also perished in the assault.[33]

Most of the leading figures in the city were taken prisoner. The Bishop was found in his palace by a company of soldiers who grabbed him and brought him before the Prince of Wales. The Prince abused him to his face and swore by God and St. George that he would have him beheaded. But he too was to be spared, saved by the intervention of John of Gaunt who claimed him as his prisoner. Roger de Beaufort, Hugh de la Roche and Jean de Villemur had had their headquarters in one of the monasteries of the city. They emerged from the building, unfurled their banners and drew up the eighty or so surviving members of the garrison in formation in an open square, where they fought off the English and Gascons until they could carry on no longer. Then they appealed to be received as prisoners. 'My Lord,' they said to the Duke of Lancaster according to Froissart, 'you have defeated us and we are at your mercy. Deal with us now according to the laws of arms.' The Prince, who had watched the fight from his litter, felt his anger sated and allowed them to be spared and taken. Jean de Cros bought his release early in the following year. Hugh de la Roche was put to a 'great and excessive' ransom but was free by 1372. The other captains of the garrison were taken to England where they were held while interminable negotiations continued about their ransoms. Jean de Villemur appears to have died in captivity. Roger de Beaufort and the son of Hugh de la Roche had still not succeeded in agreeing a ransom in 1375, when they were finally released on parole. The damage to the city, although probably exaggerated by first reports, was certainly very severe. The timber houses of the inhabitants were burned out. All the churches except for the cathedral were sacked. Many of them were left burned out and derelict. Parts of the city still bore the marks of the sack seventy-five years later. The bishop's palace remained uninhabitable until the sixteenth century. From what was left to them inhabitants were required to pay an indemnity of 40,000 *écus* to the Prince's treasury.[34]

Sir Robert Knolles landed at Calais during the first week of August 1370. After resting his men for five days he marched out of the gates on about the 9th. The campaign was conducted as it had been conceived, as a large-scale plundering raid. The route taken almost exactly followed that of Edward III's great raid of 1359. The army, all mounted, struck out east across Picardy past Saint-Omer, Arras and Noyon. They passed north of Paris making for Reims, describing the same great arc around the capital. Knolles's methods were those of the free companies of the 1350s. It was just before the harvest and the ripe grain was standing in the fields. The army demanded protection money wherever it went. Major garrisoned places, towns, castles and fortified abbeys, which rarely paid ransom money, saw their suburbs and outbuildings attacked and burned. Weaker places generally paid if they could. 'How much will you pay us to leave you alone?' was the question which Knolles's harbingers put to successive village communities. He was reported to have taken 100,000 francs personally. The French adopted what had now become their traditional strategy. They brought the population of the *plat pays* into the walled towns and castles. They used sortie parties and small mounted forces to harass stragglers and foragers. But they made no attempt to put an army into the field to challenge the advance of the invaders. On 22 September, after six weeks on the march, the English army arrived on the left bank of the Seine close to Corbeil, south-east of Paris, where Edward III's army had encamped almost exactly eleven years before.[35]

Much had changed in the silhouette of the capital since the last occasion when an English army had stood before it. The walls and towers showed off the recovery of the Crown, the fruit of Charles V's obsession with building and his concern for the security of his capital. On the north side a new circuit of walls, hardly begun in 1360, was now approaching completion. The left-bank quarters were still defended by the thirteenth-century walls of Philip Augustus but they had been improved and strengthened and a substantial *bastide* built at the Porte de la Bordelle, opposite where the English army now stood. The great circular keep of Philip Augustus's Louvre, which had once dominated the skyline at the western extremity of the city, was now almost hidden by Charles V's high curtain wall, the 'beaulx murs et maçonnages' which Charles V would proudly display to the Holy Roman Emperor in 1378 and which the Limbourg brothers would illustrate in Jean de Berry's *Très Riches Heures*. At the opposite end of the city the sky was marked by the towers of Charles V's new buildings at Saint-Pol, extending down to the waterfront and dominated by its great square bell-tower. The slate roof of the new Celestine church just east of them had been built under the King's patronage and dedicated by the Archbishop of Sens only the week before Knolles's arrival. Close to the Porte Saint-Antoine, marking the eastern limit of the city and the scene of the disorderly events of 1358, it was possible to see the footings of the new Bastide Saint-Antoine (the Bastille of later notoriety) whose foundation stone had been laid just six months earlier. Beyond, rising above the forest east of the new walls, was the great keep of Vincennes, just completed at prodigious cost to serve as the core of a new official city and a refuge for the revived monarchy in time of disorder, one of many symptoms in dressed stone of the historic distrust between the King and the citizens of his capital.[36]

Paris was defended by its citizens, supported by about 1,200 professional men-at-arms. Most of them had been withdrawn from the army of the Count of Saint-Pol on the march of Calais. In fact Knolles had no thought of besieging the city. He did not have the equipment, the manpower or the time. His object was to provoke an engagement. On 24 September he drew up his army on the south-east side of the city between the Seine and the Orléans road. But the French King ordered his men to remain within the walls. 'Let them go,' Olivier de Clisson is reported to have said, 'they cannot take the land away with them.' At the gates there was much discontent among the men-at-arms and some overt disobedience. A few men came out of the Porte de la Bordelle and engaged in bloody skirmishes with detachments of the English force outside, but in general the King's order was obeyed. When it became clear that French were not willing to fight on Knolles's terms, the English began to destroy suburban villages and houses under the noses of the defenders in hope of forcing them out. Villejuif, Gentilly, Arcueil, Bicêtre and other places that had survived the debacle of the 1350s went up in flames. The King watched the ring of fire from the upper windows of the Hôtel Saint-Pol. In the evening Knolles's army withdrew to the heights of Anthony overlooking the city from the south-west. Early on the following day, 25 September, they had gone. They split up into at least two columns. One of them marched rapidly west into lower Normandy and began to plunder around the cathedral city of Sées. The rest hung around the Beauce and the southern Île de France, returning briefly to try the defences of Paris again at the end of the month. By the middle of October 1370 the English had regrouped and were heading south towards Vendôme.[37]

Bertrand du Guesclin arrived in the capital from Languedoc just as Knolles was retreating. In the Hôtel Saint-Pol, on 2 October 1370, the King formally invested him with the sword of office of the Constable. The great captain's arrival had an immediate impact on the conduct of the war. His first task was to deal with the English army before it did irreparable damage to the King's authority in the northern provinces or linked up with his internal enemies. This meant raising substantial fresh forces and paying them at least their advances. The decisions were made in the first few days of October and approved by another of the carefully stage-managed assemblies in which Charles V specialised: a session of the royal Council, swelled out with noblemen at court and leading citizens of the capital. The King's treasury was exhausted. He needed to associate his subjects with the conduct of the war as the prelude for the renewed financial exertions which would be required to finance it. The method chosen was the same as the one to which Edward III had resorted in England: a forced loan from his subjects. Commissioners were sent into each diocese of Languedoil to raise cash loans from rich townsmen, ecclesiastics and functionaries. They were assessed according to their wealth and required to advance a sum equal to the wages of a certain number of men-at-arms for a standard period of six weeks. The French commissioners, like their English counterparts, were told not to take No for an answer. They were especially tough on those perennial butts of popular ire, lawyers and bureaucrats, 'fur hats' as Du Guesclin contemptuously called them.[38]

The main concern of the French ministers was that Knolles might join forces with Charles of Navarre and re-establish the grip which the English had held on Lower Normandy at the end of the 1350s. The King of Navarre had so far declined to declare himself for either side, while holding out prospects to both. He had promised many months ago to come before the French King to resolve their differences personally if satisfactory arrangements for his safety could be worked out, but discussion of the arrangements had been deliberately drawn out. Jean du Tertre and two other confidential advisers were closeted with Edward III's councillors, while in France other councillors of the King of Navarre haggled with Charles V's ministers over the terms of a safe-conduct that would enable him to come to court. A safe-conduct was eventually issued by the King at the end of October and oaths exacted from prominent French commanders that it would be honoured. But Charles of Navarre showed no signs of acting on it.[39]

In the meantime Knolles's army marked time. They passed the whole of October in the Vendômois and Touraine, where they would be well-placed to co-ordinate operations with the English forces in Poitou and Saint-Sauveur or to march into lower Normandy once a deal was done with Charles of Navarre. Knolles tried to established a secure base between the Loir and the Loire. He captured and garrisoned a number of castles and monasteries there in the course of October and divided the territory up into ransom districts. But his long-term intentions were entirely unclear even to those around him. There were tensions between the English commander and his subordinate captains, which came to the surface as the autumn wore on. Most of the captains were much younger men than Knolles and some, at least in their own estimation, were better-born and better formed in chivalry. They were dissatisfied by the results to date, which they attributed to Knolles's misjudgments and his lack of experience of commanding properly constituted armies. Sir John Minsterworth had conceived a virulent hatred of his commander, constantly criticising his generalship and referring to him as the 'Old Freebooter'. He made himself the leader of the malcontents.[40]

The French did not stand still while the English commanders exposed their differences. Their main force in the field was the army of the Count of Alençon, the King's lieutenant in Lower Normandy, who was based at Caen. Alençon was actively recruiting troops in Lower Normandy from late September. As autumn turned to winter substantial reinforcements were brought in from elsewhere. Bertrand du Guesclin and the Marshal Mouton de Blainville arrived at Caen with their retinues in early November. The aged Marshal Arnoul d'Audrehem came out of retirement to join them. Olivier de Clisson brought his men from Brittany. Troops were stripped from the French garrisons of the Breton march. The King had authorised Bertrand du Guesclin to raise 2,000 men, but his total strength by the end of November was probably about twice that number. While this force gathered at Caen a second army was formed at Châtellerault in Knolles's rear under the command of Marshal Sancerre. Sancerre stripped every available man from the garrisons in the marches of Berry and Poitou to increase his numbers. With these men at his back he moved down the Loire valley and established his headquarters at Vendôme. With fresh troops arriving daily from Paris his total strength rose to nearly 1,200 men.[41]

These troop movements began to cause serious concern to the English commanders, who were in danger of being caught between the Marshal's forces at Vendôme and the Constable's at Caen. Knolles called for help from other English forces in western France. The main English force within reach was the garrison of the fortified abbey of Saint-Maur, west of Saumur, one of the northern barbicans of Poitou which guarded the only usable ford over the lower Loire. Sir Hugh Calveley, who was in command at Saint-Maur, joined Knolles with some of his men in November. Co-ordinating operations with the companies at Saint-Sauveur proved to be more difficult. They were further away and most of them were not in the King's pay. So, using his powers as royal lieutenant, Knolles sent one of his deputies, Sir Alan Buxhill, with a troop of 100 men to take command of the fortress. Buxhill left Knolles at the end of November and reached Saint-Sauveur on 1 December 1370.[42]

Sir Alan Buxhill was a considerable figure among the petty captains around Knolles, and it may well have been his departure which precipitated the break-up of the army. The occasion was a violent dispute between Knolles and his colleagues about where the army was to winter. Knolles belonged to a tradition of guerilla warfare whose tools were surprise and concealment. He was as suspicious of pitched battles as the French commanders were for their own, very different reasons. He was unwilling to hang around while the French concentrated their forces around him. He proposed to withdraw into Brittany where he could lodge his profits in safety. The army could then re-form to resume the campaign in the following spring. His officers took a different view. They were in a rich, strategically central region close to the northern march of Aquitaine. They preferred to find themselves defensible winter quarters from which they could continue to ransom the country. They were willing to accept the challenge of a pitched battle. There was something to be said for both views. Knolles persisted in his own and when his colleagues refused to accept it he told them that he would go to Brittany without them. Knolles left four garrisons to hold his conquests on the march of Anjou, in the abbey at Vaas on the Loir, at Louroux (north of La Chartre-sur-le-Loir) and at the castles of Rillé and Beaufort-la-Vallée further south. He then marched off to the west at the beginning of December, taking with him his own retinue, the largest in the army, and several other companies.[43]

The rest of the English army divided itself into three independent corps. One was jointly commanded by Grandison and Calveley and the

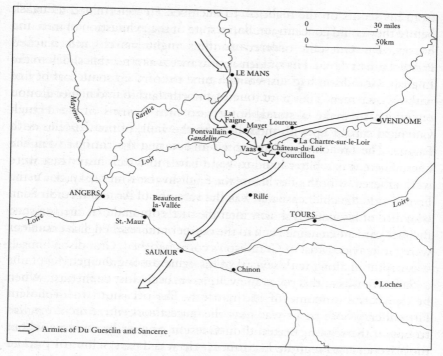

3 The Pontvallain campaign, December 1370

other two by Fitzwalter and Minsterworth. They resolved to separate in order to make their own wintering and foraging arrangements, but before they could act on this plan Bertrand du Guesclin was upon them. On 1 December 1370 he left Caen with his army and marched south at great speed night and day. On the evening of 3 December, after covering more than thirty miles a day, he arrived in the area of Le Mans. On the 2nd or early on the 3rd Sancerre left Vendôme with his own smaller army and approached the English positions from the other side. The English captains had no warning of the threat from either direction. Knolles was by now well west of Le Mans. Grandison's corps, variously estimated at 600 or 1,200 men, was spread out in disorderly encampments along the banks of the River Gandelin between the villages of Pontvallain and Mayet, flat featureless land now densely planted with pine forests but which in the fourteenth century was largely given over to marsh and scrub. Fitzwalter's corps was encamped a few miles further south. The exact whereabouts of Minsterworth's corps is not clear. Du Guesclin received reports of the English positions from his scouts on the night of 3 December. He determined to attack before they could concentrate. So, in spite of the exhaustion of men and horses, Du Guesclin ordered another night march and reached Pontvallain at dawn. His sudden appearance was a terrible shock to the English. Grandison had just enough time to form up some sort of line with his own men. They tried to retreat northward to find higher ground on which to make a stand. Some 300 men-at-arms of the French vanguard caught up with them beneath the walls of the Château de la Faigne. The Frenchmen dismounted and rushed the confused English lines. There was a bitter hand-to-hand battle in which heavy casualties were suffered by both sides before the English were overwhelmed. On the French side the chief casualty was the valiant old Arnoul d'Audrehem, who died of his wounds shortly after the battle, the end of a distinguished military career extending back to the outset of the war. English casualties were far heavier. Most of Grandison's corps perished. Grandison himself was captured along with several of his principal lieutenants.[44]

Sancerre was at this point a few hours' march away to the east. When he heard the outcome of the battle he turned south to deal with Fitzwalter, whose corps was now the largest concentration of English troops in the region. Bertrand du Guesclin paused briefly to sort out the prisoners and regroup his men. He detached part of his army under Olivier de Clisson and sent them off to the west after Knolles. Then he took the rest of his exhausted troops to join in the pursuit of Fitzwalter. Fitzwalter had no intention of being caught on open ground like Grandison. He fled south with his men towards the abbey of Vaas on the Loir, a large, partly fortified abbey which was held by one of Knolles's garrisons. He just had time to get within the abbey walls before Sancerre's men caught up with him. But he did not have time to organise its defence. Sancerre ordered an immediate assault. There was fierce fighting on the walls before the French finally forced their way into the enclosure as darkness fell and began to massacre the defenders. Du Guesclin arrived on the scene with his men at the end of the fighting to complete the rout. Reliable estimates put Fitzwalter's casualties at over 300 men killed and an unknown number of prisoners, including the commander. Du Guesclin claimed Fitzwalter for himself, a privilege of his office which led to some ill-feeling among the men who had borne the brunt of the fighting. Perhaps he thought, like the old soldier who tells us this, that Fitzwalter was the Marshal of England.[45]

The survivors of the English army scattered in confusion after the battles of Pontvallain and Vaas. Sir John Minsterworth's corps, which had not fought in either battle, fled into Brittany as soon as the issue was known. The rest spread across the country in all directions. A few made their way to Saint-Sauveur. Hugh Calveley found his way back to Poitou. About 300 men managed to form themselves into a company and occupied the castle of Courcillon, just south of Château-du-Loir. Here they rested briefly before making their way towards the Loire with Sancerre's cavalry snapping at their heels. Knolles's garrisons at Rillé and Beaufort-la-Vallée abandoned their walls and joined them. The combined group, several hundred strong, headed south pursued by Du Guesclin. They lost much of their strength in ambushes and cavalry attacks as they fled. In the end about 400 men succeeded in reaching the ford of Saint-Maur, where they were able to cross the Loire under the protection of the English garrison in the abbey. From here some of the survivors made their way east towards Auvergne. The rest headed for Bordeaux. But they were not safe even now. Du Guesclin and Sancerre had reached the bridge-town of Saumur, where they rested their men for a couple of days while scouts collected intelligence about the fugitives' movements. Then, on about 8 December, they crossed the Loire at midnight to continue the pursuit. They caught up with the largest group of English refugees deep inside Poitou by the fortress of Bressuire. The castle was garrisoned for the Prince of Wales but its defenders would not open the gates to admit the fugitives for fear of letting in the French as well. As a result the English were caught beneath the walls and wiped out almost to a man.[46]

As for Knolles he safely reached his castle at Derval on the Breton march, where he passed the winter in comfort. Most of his troops, together with those of Sir John Minsterworth, resolved to return to England. Several hundred formed themselves into companies and marched across Brittany making for Saint-Mathieu, the harbour at the tip of Finistère which was the traditional stopping place for ships passing between England and the Biscay ports. They were continually harassed on their way by the cavalry squadrons of Olivier de Clisson. Many were killed before reaching their destination. At Saint-Mathieu they found just two ships in the harbour on which some of them, including Minsterworth, were able to buy a passage to England. The rest were left behind on the beaches where they were shortly afterwards cornered by Clisson and massacred. For the dead there was nothing to be done. The prisoners were taken to Paris in carts and thrown in prison where most of them remained for several years. Grandison's health was destroyed by prison conditions. He died shortly after his release, not yet forty years old. Fitzwalter had to mortgage most of his land to moneylenders to pay the crippling ransom demanded of him. Sir Geoffrey Workesley may have been one of the lesser captains of Knolles's army but he had to encumber his estates to buy his liberty and in the end lost almost everything to his creditors. Years after the disaster several of their companions were said in Parliament to have returned to England ruined men.[47]

The French withdrew from Bressuire in about the middle of December 1370. Du Guesclin then turned north to deal with the garrison of Saint-Maur, a major source of instability in western Touraine and a valuable strategic asset to the English who could use the ford to co-ordinate their operations north and south of the Loire. In the event Saint-Maur hardly resisted. The garrison had been weakened by Calveley's departure in November and demoralised by the defeat of their companions. Sir John Cresswell, who took command in Calveley's absence, fought off one assault and then sold the place to the Constable. The whole campaign from beginning to end had been an extraordinary demonstration of Du Guesclin's unconventional skills as a commander. He had covered several hundred miles of ground in about two weeks, marching at night in driving rain in the middle of winter. By sheer force of personality he had driven his men to do the same. By the speed of his movements, the quality of his reconnaissance, the boldness of his decisions and his ruthless persistence in carrying them out, he had frustrated the main English military enterprise of 1370 and had not just defeated but destroyed an army of 4,000 men. 'I tell you,' said the Breton knight who showed Froissart the scene of these events many years later, 'this Constable Bertrand was a gallant man who did great things in his time for the honour of France.'[48]

The return of the remnants of the army with their conflicting tales of discord, incompetence and betrayal began a long period of recrimination in England. The King's Council ordered an inquiry. In the absence of the principal actors, who were either serving in France or languishing in French prisons, their main source of information was Sir John Minsterworth who was as much responsible for the disaster as any man. His main object was to exculpate himself. In July 1372, more than eighteen months after the disaster, the Council concluded that the fault lay with Knolles and to some extent with Buxhill, who had failed to maintain discipline in the army and abandoned the enterprise without the King's leave. Edward censured both men. He also confiscated the land which Knolles had been granted as his fee for organising the campaign. This act aroused much indignation among Knolles's many friends in England. The Prince of Wales and John of Gaunt protested. Knolles and Buxhill sent men from France to plead their cause. Edward III eventually relented, although Knolles never recovered his fee and had to disgorge the 10,000 marks in profit which he was thought to have made out of the campaign. As for Minsterworth, he was arrested and charged before the Council with traducing Knolles. His ultimate fate is perhaps the oddest postscript to the campaign of 1370. Humiliated by the King and frustrated in his ambitions, Minsterworth fled to France and began a new career in the service of Charles V.[49]

The immediate consequences of the destruction of Knolles's army were more serious than the saving of reputations at Westminster. It ended the myth of English invincibility on the battlefield, which had for years been among their most valuable military and diplomatic assets. Particularly striking was the ineffectiveness of the English archers, who had constituted about half the army. They had admittedly been badly positioned, but what struck at least one contemporary was that their arrows failed to penetrate the armour of Du Guesclin's troops or to break up their lines. The disaster brought an end to Edward III's hopes of an alliance with Charles of Navarre. On 2 December 1370 Edward III's councillors had put their seals to a draft treaty. Under its terms Charles of Navarre undertook to do homage to the English King as King of France and to support him against Charles V in ways that his wily ambassadors had contrived to leave largely undefined. In return Edward III offered a cash subsidy, possession of Saint-Sauveur, large territorial concessions in the principality of Aquitaine subject to the consent of the Prince of Wales, and more in northern France should Edward III ever conquer it. In the meantime Edward promised to take firm measures against the garrison of Saint-Sauveur. The King sent abrasive instructions to Sir Alan Buxhill requiring him to reduce the garrison to the minimum required for its defence and to withdraw the satellite garrisons from the abbey buildings outside the walls and the manor of Garnetot across the river. The battles of Pontvallain and Vaas were fought just two days later while Charles's ambassadors were waiting at Southampton for a fair wind to take them back to Normandy. The whole transaction was ultimately vetoed by the Prince of Wales, who objected to the territorial concessions which had been made at his expense. But the alliance was already dead by then. With the destruction of Knolles's army there was no point in it for either side.[50]

Charles of Navarre lost no time in responding to the new strategic reality. He dismissed the many English mercenaries serving in his garrisons in the Cotentin. They left to swell the garrison of Saint-Sauveur. For his part Edward III made no further attempts to restrain the operations of the garrison of Saint-Sauveur, which became more aggressive than ever. In the spring of 1371, the only period for which accounts survive, the garrison was exacting ransoms of more than 6,000 francs in cash and kind from a total of 273 villages of the Cotentin. A few months later the King of France was obliged to remit most of the tax liabilities of the inhabitants of the region on account of the 'misery and poverty of men pillaged and ransomed day and night and living continually under the threat of violent death'. On 25 March 1371 the long deferred meeting of Charles V and Charles of Navarre took place in the castle of Vernon, overlooking the Seine west of Paris. It was a frigid occasion. The two men did not even exchange the kiss of peace and Charles of Navarre declined to take supper with his host. They had a series of private meetings over the following days. Charles V conceded virtually nothing to his cousin apart from a promise to put him in possession of Montpellier, to which he was already entitled under earlier agreements. On 29 March Charles of Navarre did homage to the King and left.[51]

The Prince of Wales was carried back from Limoges in his litter followed by his entire army. In the first week of October 1370 he arrived at the small town of Cognac where he disbanded his Gascon troops. The campaign had sapped what remained of his physical strength. It was apparent that he was no longer capable of performing even the outward gestures of government. His doctors advised him that he must return to England, and after the ordeal of Limoges he was disposed to agree with them. The Prince's inclination to give up the government of his principality may well have been reinforced by pressure from his father and his father's ministers in England. They were beginning to understand something of the political misjudgments which had brought the affairs of Aquitaine to their present pass. At about this time the notorious *fouage*, which was hardly being collected any more, was formally annulled, apparently at Edward III's insistence, and an amnesty declared for the many people in Aquitaine whom the Prince had alienated since his return from Castile. Without further warning or discussion with his courtiers and captains the Prince announced at Cognac that John of Gaunt would take over the government of the principality as his lieutenant. Gaunt was reluctant to accept the appointment for more than an interim period. It would call for heavy expenditure and keep him away from England. So he insisted on a document which would entitle him to be released from his responsibilities and to leave if the wages of his retinue fell more than a month in arrears and in any event by 24 June 1371. These decisions were formally ratified at about the end of November 1370 at an assembly in Bordeaux attended by the baronage of the surviving provinces of Aquitaine. The Prince embarked in the Gironde at about Christmas-time, accompanied by his wife and by the Earl of Pembroke, who had resolved to return to England with him. They arrived at Plymouth soon after the new year. The long sea journey was a fresh blow to the Prince's weakened frame. It was some three months before he could be moved from his bed in the priory of Plympton overlooking the sound. On 19 April 1371 he entered London in obvious discomfort, to be met at Southwark bridge by the Mayor and a crowd of citizens and dignitaries and escorted to the Savoy Palace. It was a stark contrast to the last occasion when the Prince of Wales had entered the city in state, in 1357 after the battle of Poitiers. After the ceremonies the Prince retired to his manor at Berkhamsted. He remained nominally Prince of Aquitaine for the next eighteen months. Even after that he presided occasionally at meetings of the Council and made rare appearances on state occasions, but it was for practical purposes the end of his public career. He was forty-two years old.[52]

John of Gaunt's immediate priority when he took over the government of the Prince's domains was to recover some of the ground lost to the French in the eastern highlands of the principality. The recapture of Limoges, followed by the abrupt withdrawal of the Prince and his army, had left the English in possession of the provincial capital while most of the rest of the province was controlled by local noblemen committed to the King of France. Sir Richard Abberbury, a retainer of the Prince who had come out to Aquitaine with the Earl of Cambridge, was appointed Seneschal of Limousin and put in charge of a rudimentary administration. He was probably based at Limoges. The reconquest of the rest of the province was left to Eustache d'Aubricourt. He was appointed as lieutenant in Limousin and in the adjacent parts of Périgord, with Walter Hewitt as his assistant and several hundred English men-at-arms under his command. Unfortunately it was not enough to persuade the inhabitants of the Limousin that the English government was serious about defending the province, and without that their task proved hopeless.

Shortly after the departure of the Prince, Aubricourt and Hewitt laid siege to the castle of Rochechouart, which was the seat of the largest French garrison in the province. The captain of Rochechouart was a Breton companion of Bertrand du Guesclin called Thibault du Pont, who was away in the north with the Constable. His deputy, an illegitimate half-brother of the Viscount of Rochechouart, agreed to surrender the place if it was not relieved within a limited period. Charles V sent Thibault urgently back to the Limousin with a relief force, which succeeded in entering the castle and raising the siege. The bastard of Rochechouart, who was thought to have made terms a bit too readily with the besiegers, was charged with treason.

Not long after this reverse Aubricourt's career in the Limousin came to an abrupt close. He was tricked into entering the French castle of Pierre-Buffière, south of Limoges, and ambushed by its garrison. He was ransomed for an enormous sum and made to withdraw from Aquitaine. Hewitt left the Limousin soon after this. By the spring of 1371 the formal structure of English government in the Limousin had collapsed. The citizens of Limoges sent one of their number to England to protest to Edward III about the way his representatives had abandoned them. They could not be expected to remain in his obedience, they said, unless they received some protection. Edward wrote to Abberbury about it but very shortly Abberbury himself left.[53]

As in Quercy and Rouergue, once it became clear that the Limousin could not be held, the English abandoned it to guerillas. Aubricourt was replaced as lieutenant by Sir John Devereux, the English captain of the *routier* garrisons at La Souterraine and Sainte-Sévère on the northern march of the province. Devereux terrorised the northern parts of the Limousin. He forged alliances with the Gascon companies, who did the same in the south. Early in 1371, Bertucat d'Albret and Bernard de la Salle began to penetrate into the Limousin from Quercy and the Cantal. Ussel, a small walled town on the old Roman road from Clermont to Bordeaux, was seized and garrisoned at the beginning of the year by Perrot de Galard, a Gascon confederate of Bertucat's. Many of the small towns of the southern march which had submitted to Charles V's officers were occupied and garrisoned by small groups of soldiers drawn from the military underworld of displaced Gascon and French ruffians that men must have remembered from a decade before. By the summer of 1371 the Anglo-Gascon companies were holding a ring of forts around Limoges itself even though the place was still nominally a possession of the Prince of Wales.[54]

Périgord was an easier province than the Limousin for the English to operate in. It was more accessible from the Atlantic regions where their strength was concentrated. They also had more significant alliances there. At beginning of December 1370 John of Gaunt and the Earl of Cambridge laid siege to the town of Montpon with a large army of Englishmen, supported by many of the principal lords of Aquitaine. Montpon was a small walled town dominated by a strong castle, guarding the bridge over the River Isle only twenty miles from Libourne. It had been captured by Bertrand du Guesclin earlier in the year. He had left it to be defended by Sylvester Budes, a cousin of his who commanded one of the Breton companies in the service of the Duke of Anjou. Budes's relatively small garrison tied down Gaunt's forces for more than two months. Gaunt, intensely irritated, methodically filled in the ditches of the castle with tree trunks covered with earth. There followed a series of assaults launched from specially constructed mobile shelters and ramps while the English archers tried to force the defenders away from the battlements with showers of arrows. The assailants came up over the walls. They broke their way through at ground level with pickaxes. The defenders fought them all off.[55]

In January 1371 the siege of Montpon seemed likely to turn into a major operation. Bertrand du Guesclin regarded its relief as a debt of honour. He began to raise troops in December. In about the middle of December Anjou decided to raise the stakes. He not only resolved to direct the relief of the town in person but persuaded his brothers the Dukes of Berry and Burgundy to join him with their own troops. The raising at short notice of a large army in several parts of France to fight a winter campaign in the south-west put a great strain on Anjou's finances, for he had to undertake to pay not only his own contingents but those of his brothers. The enormous hearth tax voted by the Estates of Languedoc in 1370 had already been committed to the repayment of loans and arrears of wages outstanding from Anjou's campaign in the summer. Armed with the news that three royal princes and the Constable of France were to descend on Montpon, Anjou's councillors were able to extract an extra two francs per hearth from the representatives of Languedoc, bringing to more than five francs the total of hearth taxes imposed over the past year.[56]

Considering the scale of the operation, the distances involved and the financial embarrassment of the Duke of Anjou, the relief army was collected with impressive speed. But it proved not to be fast enough. The Constable marched south from Paris, joining forces with the Duke of Berry at Bourges and with Philip of Burgundy at Clermont in Auvergne. The whole army gathered on open ground outside the city gates on 17 February 1371. The Duke of Anjou's army began to muster at Montauban on 19 February. The French garrison of Montpon knew that relief was on the way but after eleven weeks of siege they could hold out no longer. On about 19 or 20 February 1371 John of Gaunt launched the fiercest assault on the walls so far. Seeing that they were in no position to resist, the defenders sent a herald to parley with the besiegers. The attack was briefly called off while the captains of the garrison bargained for their lives. Froissart gives a detailed account of the negotiations which is probably fanciful but reveals much about the growing formality which governed the conduct of war, at least among those who fought for princes rather than for themselves. The defenders were initially told by Gaunt's marshal, Guichard d'Angle, that the Duke would not even concede their lives after all the trouble that they had caused him. One of the Breton captains, who was acting as spokesman, replied:

Sir Guichard, we are soldiers in the pay of the King of France and we have sought to do our duty to our lord as you would do for yours. We call on you to deal with us justly according to the law of arms, as knights and squires ought to deal with each other and as you would expect us to deal with you if you were in the pass to which we have come.

It was eventually agreed that the town and castle would be surrendered at once and the garrison taken as prisoners of war. They were promised their lives, with the exception of the lord of the place who had originally opened the gates to Du Guesclin's troops the year before. He, however, had already escaped by a postern gate during the final assault and was nowhere to be found.[57]

   The Duke of Anjou abandoned the campaign as soon as the news reached him. This left his brothers in the lurch. They were approaching from Auvergne by two separate routes. The Duke of Berry and the Constable had taken the northerly route by the Roman road to Bordeaux while Philip of Burgundy passed further south through the valley of the Lot. Rather than turn back with nothing to show for their pains Berry and Du Guesclin resolved to continue their advance and attack the town of Ussel, the main *routier* garrison in southern Limousin, which lay a few miles ahead of them. Ussel was vigorously defended. The French launched an assault against the walls as soon as they arrived but when it failed they had to sit down for a siege for which they were ill-prepared. They had no heavy siege equipment and very limited supplies of food. It was bitterly cold. During the first night a blizzard began to blow. 'God the Father, King of the firmament, was an Englishman that night,' the French said, according to Du Guesclin's biographer. A few days later Philip of Burgundy came up to join them. His appearance on the scene may have saved the face of the French. The garrison were there for money not honour. They agreed to sell the place while they could still expect reasonable terms. They exacted a high price and a safe-conduct through the length of the Limousin to join Sir John Devereux at Sainte-Sévère. On 4 March the French army departed. Within a few months, Ussel had been reoccupied by another Gascon company.[58]

On 24 February 1371 the English Parliament met in the Painted Chamber at Westminster beneath the famous paintings of battle scenes from the wars of Ptolemy and Judas Maccabaeus. William of Wykeham gave the opening address as he had done in 1369. He had a sombre message to deliver. Since their last meeting, he said, when they had approved the King's resumption of the arms and title of France, Edward had sent his captains overseas to recover his rights at enormous cost. But the King of France had become so strong that he was now in a position to reconquer the entirety of Edward's continental dominions and to gather a fleet large enough to destroy the whole navy of England and carry an invading army over the Channel to pillage and conquer the realm. This was a gross exaggeration, as Edward III's ministers must have known, but the true situation was serious enough. For two years Edward III had been trying to fight a war on several fronts, financed mainly by savings and borrowing. By now it was clear he was dealing with a far more formidable and powerful enemy than John II. The war was going badly and a substantial increase in taxation was unavoidable. The King's Council told the Commons that the government urgently required a subsidy of £100,000, half of which was expected to come from the laity and half from the clergy, who were due to meet after Parliament had been dissolved. This was an exceptionally steep demand. It represented nearly twice the conventional value of a Parliamentary subsidy.

Nothing is known about the deliberations which followed except that they were acrimonious and lasted more than a month. It was not that there was any serious opposition to the war itself, which had so far been fought with only limited demands on the purses of the King's subjects.

If the chroniclers are any guide there was widespread resentment of the way that the French had undone the settlement of 1360. Ill-feeling against France was aggravated by the disruption of the wool trade with Flanders and the threat and occasional reality of naval raids on the coast of England. This was reflected in fierce hostility to French nationals in England, whose presence as businessmen, monks, spouses, domestic servants or prisoners of war had been an ordinary feature of life for many years. If the Commons had had their way they would all have been interned or expelled in 1371. Edward III's remarkable record as a war leader was still remembered and still inspired confidence. But it also meant that the run of minor defeats and the progressive loss of territory was received with widespread incomprehension and far too readily attributed to corruption or incompetence. This was one reason why there was so much resistance to the proposed tax. The Commons called it an 'oppressive ransom'. The Council responded with menaces. The Commons assumed that the King's revenues must have been diverted to improper purposes. They prepared a petition, which they were not allowed to present, demanding that the proceeds of all future taxes should be paid over to commissioners to be disbursed only for war expenditure.

When it became clear that the government would brook no refusal of its demands, the ecclesiastical peers fell to quarrelling with the Commons about the increased share which the clergy were being asked to bear, half instead of a third. They declined to commit the clergy in advance of the meeting of Convocation. This in turn provoked ugly outbursts of anti-clerical feeling, and calls from some quarters for the dispossession of the Church. To the general feeling that the clergy were not bearing a fair share of the national burden was added an unreasoned instinct that the fighting men had been let down by greedy churchmen and incompetent clerical administrators. This view was common enough in wartime in both England and France, and would become more so. Du Guesclin's views about 'fur hats' were widely shared on both sides of the Channel. The knight in the famous French allegorical tract Le songe du vergier spoke for many when he said that the clergy 'reposed peacefully beneath shady canopies elegantly scoffing fat delicacies' while he and his kind spilled their blood and fortunes in their defence. At Westminster in 1371 it was characteristically the young, hot-headed Earl of Pembroke, just returned from the frustrating and underfunded campaigns in south-western France, who apparently suggested the scheme to increase the clergy's share. The King's ministers, who included prominent clergymen, found themselves attacked from all sides. It is reasonably clear that the Commons refused to grant a subsidy until they were removed. The ministers preferred not to provoke a crisis on an issue which was known to be extremely sensitive with the King. So, on 24 March 1371, William of Wykeham resigned as Chancellor. He was followed three days later by the Treasurer, the competent and honest Bishop Brantingham of Exeter. Both men were replaced by laymen.

On 28 March, the day after Brantingham's resignation, the Commons agreed to grant its half of the subsidy. The two convocations followed suit but with extreme reluctance. The southern convocation listened stony-faced in St. Paul's cathedral to the appeals of the King's councillors. They had to be adjourned to the Savoy Palace where the sick Prince of Wales, surrounded by ministers and noblemen, browbeat them in person, 'first earnestly requesting then demanding' a subsidy, before they would consent. In the northern province it took two assemblies and two months to persuade the clergy to comply. The Parliament and convocations of 1371 proved to be the first of a succession of assemblies in which defeat and insecurity provoked discord and mutual recrimination among the English.[59]

The government had hoped to get the first instalment of the new taxes into its coffers by Whitsun and the rest by midsummer. It quickly became apparent that this would not be achieved. The first problem was that both the lay and clerical subsidies were being levied on a different basis to their predecessors which required fresh assessments. The clerical subsidy extended to unbeneficed clergy and clergy who had previously been exempt. The lay subsidy was granted as a lump sum of £50,000 to be raised by a levy on parishes at an average rate of 22s 3d per parish. This scheme was designed to deal with the effect which plague, migration and exemptions had had on the traditional tax assessments, now nearly forty years old. But it assumed that there were 45,000 parishes in England, a figure which the Commons appear to have got from the widely read chronicle of Ranulph Higden of Chester. Unfortunately it had no empirical basis at all. Within a month of the grant the government realised that it was uncollectable. They ordered an urgent survey of parishes and summoned the sheriffs to send one of the two burgesses from each town and one of the two county representatives who had made the original grant to attend a new assembly. On 8 June this semi-Parliament met at Winchester. They were presented with evidence that the true number of parishes in England was about 8,600, less than a fifth of the number previously assumed. The assessment was therefore increased from 22s 3d to 116s, which was probably more than the Commons would have granted on the first occasion if they had known what they were doing. New assessments were then commissioned to enable it to be properly distributed. Ultimately, in spite of the resistance of taxpayers, nearly £92,000 of the £100,000 was actually collected. But it took a long time. The bulk of the proceeds did not become available until the summer of 1372 and collection was not completed until 1374. This ruled out any ambitious military ventures in 1371.[60]

Fortunately for the English the French government was also in financial difficulty in 1371. The effort involved in mounting two major campaigns in mid-winter had drained the French treasury. In February 1371 Charles V's Council suspended payment of civil service salaries. During the summer unexpected difficulties were encountered in collecting the *aides*. The nature of these difficulties is not disclosed by the rather fragmentary sources, but what is clear is that a major enquiry into the falling off of yields was under way in most of the provinces of Languedoil. Charles V was obliged to anticipate the flow of tax revenue by borrowing 100,000 francs from a syndicate of Italian bankers at Avignon. Even this did not enable him to pay the wages of his troops regularly. The wages of the army on the march of Calais were in arrears. Some of his captains were still waiting to be paid for their service in the campaigns of 1369. As a result the French King was not in a position to carry out any of the menacing operations with which William of Wykeham had tried to frighten his audience in the Painted Chamber in February. After the rapid movements of the past two years a stagnant calm, born of exhaustion and financial paralysis, fell on all the main theatres of war.[61]

The summer campaigning season was largely taken up with the painstaking and unproductive sieges of the handful of fortresses in western France, where English garrisons and the remnants of the Great Company of 1367–8 had continued to hold out in the midst of French territory. The castle of Thury-Harcourt on the River Orne south-west of Caen had been occupied since the summer of 1370 by two retainers of Charles of Navarre, the cousins Jean ('Le Moine') and Eustache ('Rifflart') de Pollehay. Jean de Pollehay called himself an officer of the King of England, which he was certainly not, at least in any formal sense. The garrison, which was probably an offshoot of the garrison of Saint-Sauveur, was a mixed rabble of Englishmen, Normans and

Navarrese *routiers* and, although not large, it had devastated much of Lower Normandy since the summer of the previous year. One of Charles of Navarre's first public acts as a vassal of the King of France was to negotiate its surrender on 12 April 1371. The terms made it clear that although the place had been under loose siege for several months it was by no means at the end of its resistance. The English in the garrison would not contemplate surrender without a safe-conduct to Saint-Sauveur or Bécherel and payment of the arrears of their *patis* and ransoms. This liability, amounting to 14,000 francs, ultimately had to be met by the long-suffering taxpayers of the five dioceses of Lower Normandy.[62]

In about April 1371 Du Guesclin turned his attention to the twin castles of Conches and Breteuil on the edge of the Pays d'Ouche. These places nominally belonged to Charles of Navarre, but had been granted by him to Edward III's famous Gascon captain Jean de Grailly, Captal de Buch, during the civil wars of the 1360s. They were still commanded by his captains. When summoned to surrender at the beginning of April 1371 they replied that they would take no orders but his. They were allowed a six-week truce in which to obtain the Captal's instructions. The French entertained some hopes that the Captal would surrender the castles. He had been captured commanding Charles of Navarre's army at the battle of Cocherel in 1364 and released without ransom by Charles V. There was a school of thought at the French court which considered that this prevented him fighting directly against the King. The Captal did not agree. He declined to surrender either fortress. There was some inconclusive skirmishing around the walls of both places in the second half of May. At the beginning of June the Constable set about organising a formal siege of Conches, digging trenches around its walls, strengthened at critical points by stone *bastides*, and fortifying churches and other buildings around the perimeter. A looser siege was maintained around the castle of Breteuil. The sieges were interrupted by frequent diversions on other fronts and the two fortresses held out until early in the following year. The garrison of Conches eventually surrendered at the beginning of February 1372 after the French had brought up heavy reinforcements and gunpowder artillery. They were granted honourable terms and were allowed to leave in peace. The garrison of Breteuil made an even better deal. They were allowed to remain in occupation on behalf of the Captal de Buch provided that they undertook not to make war on the King of France and his subjects. It was a small reward for nearly a year of effort.[63]

*

Charles V had adroitly countered the schemes of the King of Navarre. The tragedy of his reign was that he was never able to do the same with John de Montfort. The French King lived in perennial fear that John would align himself with his old champions and let English armies into France across the open march of the duchy. The King's fears were very wide of the mark. In fact the Duke's great object was to keep out of the war and avoid antagonising either side. He had no desire to become an English client again unless he had to. Charles V never really understood this or realised how difficult John's position was. He was shocked by the Duke's decision to allow the army of the Earls of Cambridge and Pembroke to land at Saint-Malo and cross Brittany on their way to Aquitaine in the spring of 1369.[64] He was infuriated by John's brief dalliance with the King of Navarre. These were acts which branded John de Montfort at the court of France as an enemy for the rest of Charles's reign. The result was to bring about the very thing that Charles most feared. It was a serious misjudgment.

A large part of the explanation for it lay in the presence of influential Bretons at Charles V's court and in his army, men who had never really accepted John de Montfort's legitimacy as Duke. The cause of Blois was dead, but it would be many years more before its partisans were ready to forget. Jeanne de Penthièvre lived in Paris but retained the enormous possessions of her family in northern Brittany. She was still a power in the duchy and a focus of loyalty among the former supporters of her husband. Her daughter was married to Louis of Anjou, whose appanage bordered on Brittany to the south-east and who stirred up difficulties for John de Montfort whenever he could. It was Louis and his mother-in-law, and the Franciscans of Guingamp in whose church the dead hero was buried, who were the main drivers behind the attempt to promote the canonisation of Charles of Blois in the decade after his death. The sanctity of politicians and war leaders was a delicate matter in an age which believed that God was the arbiter of men's political fortunes, as the myths surrounding Joan of Arc were to demonstrate in the following century. John de Montfort regarded the cult of his old enemy, with its attendant eulogies and miracle stories, as a direct challenge to his authority.

Others were willing to challenge it more directly. Bertrand du Guesclin had been a supporter of Charles of Blois. He always refused to do homage to John de Montfort for his lands in Brittany. His retinue and the many Breton companies who fought for Charles V on the marches of Aquitaine were full of men who had fought for the House of Blois and had chosen to make a career outside Brittany since Charles's death. John de Montfort might try to steer a difficult path between England and France but the leading noble houses of Brittany, Laval, Beaumanoir, Rohan and Retz, who had recognised Charles of Blois in his lifetime, were never favoured by John de Montfort as his own supporters were. They all rejected neutrality for themselves and fought in the armies of the King. Charles V exploited these natural tensions within the Breton aristocracy. He plied Montfort's enemies with favours. He flattered the oligarchies of the towns. He played on the traditionally royalist sentiments of the bishops. Many of them became the King's familiars and friends. They were probably the real authors of his Breton policy.[65] John de Montort for his part reacted very defensively. He could not afford to abandon his residual links with the English while his enemies were so powerful at the court of France.

Ironically by far the most persistent and dangerous of the Duke's Breton enemies was a man whose father had been executed for treason by Philip VI and whose family had been as closely associated with the English as John de Montfort himself. Olivier de Clisson, then thirty-five years old, was a tempestuous spirit who was destined to become one of the pivotal figures in French politics of the late fourteenth century. He was the leading territorial magnate of Bas-Poitou, an appendage of the duchy of Brittany extending south from the estuary of the Loire to the Bay of Bourgneuf. His hereditary domains included the great castle of Clisson, which still stands above the road from Nantes to Poitiers, and the fortress of Champtoceaux, guarding the eastern frontier of the duchy on the Loire. He had been brought up in England after his father's execution and had gained his first experience of war in English armies. He had lost an eye while fighting with Sir John Chandos at Auray, and served under the Prince of Wales at Nájera. For the first year of the war Clisson had tried to stay in with both sides, a prudent course perhaps for a man whose territory lay on the marches of the enlarged duchy of Aquitaine. All this ambiguity stopped around the end of 1369 when it became clear that the English were in difficulty. Olivier de Clisson decided that his ambitions would be better served by allying himself with the French royal house. Charles V drew him to his service by well-judged grants and favours and flattered his vanity with a series of important commands and diplomatic missions. As Clisson became more closely identified with the King's cause his relations with John de Montfort deteriorated. It is hard to say which was the cause and which the effect. There may also have been other, more personal factors at work: obscure jealousies at the Breton court, aggravated by Clisson's short temper and notoriously prickly personality. There was persistent gossip that Clisson had made advances to John's wife. What is clear is that the two men became not just political adversaries but bitter personal enemies. Their prolonged vendetta, which lasted in one form or another for three decades, would be a source of serious instability in the politics of Brittany and later in those of France.[66]

In 1370 Clisson set about creating a coalition against John de Montfort among his enemies within the duchy. His first step was to procure his own appointment as the lieutenant of Jeanne de Penthièvre in Brittany. Shortly after this he became Charles V's lieutenant in Bas-Poitou. In the summer of 1370, he acquired control of the great fortress of Josselin in the central highlands of the Breton peninsula. Josselin had recently passed by marriage to the Count of Alençon. Charles V, observing that it was 'essential' to have control over the place, pressed Alençon to exchange it for two royal castellanies in Normandy and a cash income, and then granted the place to Olivier de Clisson. Then in October 1370 Clisson went further by concluding a remarkable personal alliance with Bertrand du Guesclin. The two men agreed to defend each other's interests against all others except for the King of France, to come to each other's assistance whenever they were in danger, and to share equally all their profits of war. The agreement did not name John de Montfort but it was clearly directed against him and appears to have provoked the final breakdown between the two men. John summoned Clisson before his court to answer for his 'gross disloyalty', and when he failed to appear decreed the confiscation of all his possessions in the duchy. The Duke's officers were never able to take control of Clisson itself but they occupied Champtoceaux and put a garrison into it. Clisson appealed to the Parlement of Paris, thus challenging the tacitly accepted immunity which Brittany had long enjoyed from the jurisdiction of the courts of the King of France. When his lawyer tried to serve John de Montfort with the papers, the Duke had him drowned in the Loire with the documents around his neck. The breach was complete.[67]

The presence of English-controlled garrisons in Brittany gave Du Guesclin and Clisson plenty of occasions for making war in John de Montfort's duchy. This process ultimately destroyed the delicate balance by which John de Montfort had sought to distance himself from both sides in the wider war. In December 1370 Clisson led a French army across the whole length of the Breton peninsula in pursuit of the fleeing remnants of Robert Knolles's army. The garrison of Pontorson, which was directly controlled by Bertrand du Guesclin, nibbled away at the marches of the duchy. John de Montfort completely lost control of Bas-Poitou, which became for practical purposes part of the French march opposite Aquitaine. The coastal fortress of Collet in the Bay of Bourgneuf, the only important place in the region not already in the hands of Charles V's allies, was taken from its English garrison by French troops and held in the King's name in spite of Montfort's protests. The retreat of English arms encouraged many Bretons hitherto loyal to Montfort to identify themselves with the renascent power of the French Crown and to join in the attack on English interests in Brittany.[68]

Early in 1371 Olivier de Clisson decided to lay siege to the English fortress at Bécherel. It was an astute move. The garrison of Bécherel was deeply unpopular in Brittany. Clisson's venture not only had the support of the traditional allies of the King of France in the duchy but of many who had been firm partisans of John de Montfort. But Montfort, although he resented the ransoming of the land by Latimer's garrison as much as any man, could see that he himself was Clisson's real target. He had spent three years avoiding a choice but, when forced to choose between the occupation of Bécherel by a French garrison controlled by Olivier de Clisson and its possession by an English minister, he decided that the second was the lesser evil. He forbade the operation. His objections were brushed aside. The siege of Bécherel was a running sore between John de Montfort and Charles V for more than a year. Olivier de Clisson's army arrived outside the fortress in about April 1371. The place was defended by a garrison of some 300 freebooters under the command of Latimer's deputy, Sir John Pert. He was later to be accused of greed and corruption in the House of Commons and it may well have been his fault that the castle's stores were low when Clisson's siege began. But whatever his faults he redeemed them by the skill of his defence. Pert led repeated sorties into the siege lines and generally had the better of the fighting. He certainly received no help from Latimer or anyone else in England. In late July 1371 an attempt was made to create an army of relief out of other English garrisons in western France. About 700 men are said to have been found for this venture. The relief plan was thwarted by Du Guesclin, who drew off large numbers of troops from the sieges of Conches and Breteuil, recruited more in Lower Normandy, and then invaded the duchy. For a short time in the first half of August 1371 the Constable took command of the siege of Bécherel in person. For want of money to intervene, the English were impotent spectators of these events. An emissary from the beleaguered garrison penetrated through Clisson's lines and reached England in June 1371 during the sessions of the Winchester Parliament. He brought personal letters addressed to the King and every one of his councillors pleading for help. But the Treasury was empty. They refused 'utterly' and sent him away.[69]

John of Gaunt passed most of the year 1371 in the Atlantic provinces of his brother's principality, endeavouring to put some sort of order into its government, but he undertook no major military operations. His relative immobility was due to the dire financial problems of the principality, the full measure of which was still not appreciated by his father's ministers at Westminster. The English expeditionary force which had come to Aquitaine with Gaunt and Hewitt in 1370 had been paid for the first six months of its service from June 1370. It had received nothing since. John of Gaunt's appeals presumably had a more courteous hearing in England than those of the captain of Bécherel, but he got the same answer. By the spring of 1371 he was becoming concerned that the men would start to support themselves by pillaging the Prince's domains, thereby accelerating the rate of defections among the local nobility. He borrowed heavily on his own account in order to pay them at least part of their due. He had cash shipped out by his treasurer in England. He raised what revenues he could in the duchy. An assembly of the Estates of Poitou voted him a sales tax of five per cent for a year but not much of it appears to have been collected and there is no evidence of any similar grants in other parts of the principality. Under the terms of his appointment by the Prince of Wales, John of Gaunt had agreed to serve as his brother's lieutenant for a limited period and then only if his wages and those of his men were paid. So, on 21 July 1371, he called the Prince's councillors before him in Bordeaux and announced his resignation. He then formally surrendered his powers into the hands of the Prince's officers. The melodrama at Bordeaux was designed mainly to make an impression in England. John of Gaunt made it clear that he would continue to do what he could to defend the principality while he remained there. But his main preoccupations as the summer wore on were his designs on the Crown of Castile, of which more will be said in the following chapter, and his preparations to return to England.[70]

The only notable military operation conducted by the English in Aquitaine in 1371 was due to the Seneschal of Poitou, Sir Thomas Percy.

He was probably the nearest that England came to finding a successor to the military tradition of Audley and Chandos. A cadet of the famous Northumberland clan, he was the only member of his family to make a career fighting in France. In August 1371 Percy laid siege to Moncontour, one of a number of places on the northern march of Poitou which the French captains of the march had strengthened and garrisoned to serve as forward bases for penetration into Poitou. Moncontour was a small town dominated by the massive fortress built by that great castle-builder Fulk Nerra, Count of Anjou, in the eleventh century. Percy arrived there in early August with a scratch army drawn from nearby garrisons and from the retinues of the leading Poitevin barons, together with a battery of stone-throwing artillery. Charles V and his commanders made a serious effort to relieve the place. Their problem, like Gaunt's, was a severe shortage of cash. It was estimated that 2,000 men would be required for the operation. There was no money to pay them. The Constable, who was then at Bécherel, left a screen of troops around the castle and marched south with Olivier de Clisson and the rest of the army. The Marshals stripped men from the garrisons of the Loire and northern Poitou to reinforce him. But they were too late. In about the middle of September 1371 Moncontour was stormed by Percy's troops. The entire French garrison was killed apart from the captain and five or six of his companions. When the Constable reached the town, four days after it had fallen, he found it defended by a large English garrison. He ordered an assault, but his officers thought better of this idea. They had no crossbowmen with them. The task was hopeless. So the French turned round and marched away.[71]

On 23 September 1371 John of Gaunt entered La Rochelle to embark for home, accompanied by most of the army that he had brought with him from England. His departure must have resulted in the withdrawal of at least a third of the English troops then serving in southern France. Gaunt made what arrangements he could for the defence of Aquitaine in his absence. Lieutenants were appointed for each province of the principality, all of them prominent local noblemen, a notable break with the Prince's practice of appointing Englishmen to such posts. Most of the available resources were concentrated on the defence of Poitou. On the northern march a number of semi-autonomous captaincies were created under the command of contractors who agreed to guard the march in return for what profits they could make from the land around them. A partnership of military contractors comprising Thomas Percy, the Seneschal of Saintonge John Harpeden, and the Poitevin nobleman

Renaud de Vivonne took over responsibility for the fortress of La Roche-sur-Yon together with much of the north-western march. They were to meet all their own costs and pay a rent of 500 marks a year from the forfeitures of traitors in their area and the profits of raiding into Anjou and Bas-Poitou. Moncontour was exploited for their own account by another syndicate organised by Walter Hewitt. Other castles of the march were assigned to other captains on much the same basis. Garrisons were left in the main surviving fortresses of the Garonne and the Dordogne. The rest of the principality was left to fend for itself.[72]

The citizens of Limoges had had enough. While John of Gaunt waited at La Rochelle for shipping and a fair wind, a delegation came before Charles V in Paris to press him to take possession of their city and restore order in the region. Marshal Sancerre gathered 200 men-at-arms and left for Limoges so quickly that there was not even time to take the muster of his company. On 14 November 1371 Limoges formally submitted to the King of France. Experience had made the citizens wary of submitting too completely. They would not let Sancerre and his men within their gates at once. He had first to procure the confirmation of their ancient privileges and the grant of new ones, then to pass the winter months removing the Anglo-Gascon *routiers* from the castles which blockaded the road and river routes around the city. As a result the Marshal did not formally take possession until 26 April 1372. Even then the citizens of Limoges would not remove the arms of the Prince of Wales from their gates. They simply placed those of the King of France above them. For many years this symbol remained the last vestige of an official English presence in the Limousin.[73]

Three decades earlier, when Edward III had only just embarked on his great adventure in France, Benedict XII, the shrewdest of the Avignon Popes, had warned him in prophetic tones of its ultimate outcome. The King of France, he said, was fighting in his own country surrounded by his own people. He could lose many battles without losing the war, suffer huge casualties and yet recover. But Edward, fighting with expeditionary armies in a foreign land, could win fight after fight and yet ultimately lose everything he had in France.[74] Like all the Avignon Popes Benedict had been bound to France by strong ties of sentiment, political calculation and financial interest. But there was also a more disinterested reason for the attention which they paid to the Anglo-French war. In spite of the manifest sympathy of the Avignon Popes for France the papacy remained the only organisation with the international prestige to organise a major peace initiative. The 1370s was the last period of European history in which it was to play this role.

When the war reopened in 1369 the reigning Pope was Urban V. Urban had been elected in Avignon but he had returned to Italy in June 1367, accompanied by some of the cardinals and a skeleton administration. The experiment had failed for a number of reasons: persistent war between the major cities of the papal state, the growing threat from Bernabò Visconti, the ambitious despot of Milan, and the poverty and anarchy of Rome and Viterbo where Urban resided. These factors might have driven him from Italy even if the Anglo-French war had not suddenly reignited in his absence. But when he did finally announce his intention of returning to France, well-informed contemporaries believed that the main reason for his decision was a genuine desire to reconcile Edward III and Charles V and a naive belief that he could do it. The French government, which had been unspeakably dismayed by Urban's departure and had done its best to dissuade him, was overjoyed. They sent a fleet of galleys to escort him back across the Mediterranean to Marseille. At the end of September 1370, while Robert Knolles was burning villages along the roads south of Paris and the Prince of Wales was returning from the destruction of Limoges, Urban V entered Avignon.[75] As soon as he had arrived he began to plan a fresh round of peacemaking. He wrote to the two kings. He selected his mediators. But he got no further with his task. The voyage had broken his already delicate health. He fell ill in November and died on 19 December 1370.

Urban's successor, elected on 30 December 1370, was Pierre Roger II de Beaufort who took the name Gregory XI. Gregory was the nephew of an earlier Pierre Roger who had been Chancellor of France before reigning for ten years as Pope Clement VI (1342–52). The new Pope had much in common with Clement: intelligent, cultivated, charming, he impressed even his enemies by his princely manner. The Chancellor of Florence, Salutati, no friend of the papacy, called him 'cautious and wise, modest, devout, charitable, charming and, which is fitting in such a magnificent ruler, completely trustworthy and reliable'. These genial qualities were attested by others and Gregory undoubtedly possessed them. But they did not prevent him from being a determined politician and a shrewd diplomat. Gregory's political life was dominated by two great obsessions. The first was an unwavering ambition to take the papacy back to Rome, as his predecessor had tried and failed to do. To this end he needed to consolidate the papal state in central Italy and to defend it against the expansive dictatorship of the Visconti lords of Milan and, later, against the self-governing cities of his own dominions. This meant that in his time the budget of the papacy was largely committed to the prosecution of a succession of expensive wars in Italy.

Gregory's second obsession was his family. The Rogers had once been a minor noble family from the region of Bas-Limousin, more or less corresponding to the modern *département* of the Corrèze. Their rapid ascent in the middle years of the fourteenth century was entirely due to the patronage of Pierre Roger I when he was Chancellor of France and at Avignon once he became Pope. In 1350, in one of the more spectacular property transactions of the period, Clement arranged for his nephew (Gregory XI's older brother) to purchase the viscounty of Turenne from the bankrupt house of Comminges. Turenne was the richest and most powerful lordship of Bas-Limousin. It included the great fortress of Turenne itself, numerous subsidiary forts, castles and manors, and vast domains extending from Brive on the River Corrèze to Beaulieu on the Dordogne. At the time of Gregory's election Guillaume Roger, Viscount of Turenne, was a loyal but inactive vassal of the Prince of Wales. He eventually made his submission to the French crown in January 1373. Two of the Pope's younger brothers were determined partisans of the Duke of Anjou. Nicholas de Beaufort, who had been married to the heiress of the great lordship of Limeuil on the Dordogne, had recently put French garrisons into all his castles. Roger de Beaufort was one of the captains of the Cité of Limoges who was captured fighting against the Prince of Wales in September 1370.

These events gave Gregory a more direct emotional interest in the course of the war than any of his predecessors. Partly because it suited his political ambitions, partly from personal sentiment and family interest, partly also because of the francophile mood of the papal court where he had passed his adult life, Gregory was wedded to the interests of France. At his coronation procession in January 1371 the Pope gave the place of honour to the Duke of Anjou, who held the bridle of his horse. He passed part of the hot Rhône summers in the Duke's mansion at Villeneuve-lès-Avignon. He addressed unsolicited advice to Charles V about the importance of watch duty at his castles. He wrote fulsome letters of congratulation to French commanders on their victories and tipped 200 florins to the messenger who brought him news of an English defeat.[76]

Gregory believed, as Urban had done, that he could not leave Avignon while the Anglo-French war continued. He also needed the political support of France and the financial resources of the French Church in order to restore his authority in Italy, both of which were bound to be limited while France was torn apart by war. One of the first steps which Gregory took after his coronation was to write to both kings to inform them of Urban V's plans for a peace conference and to tell them that he had appointed the mediators whom his predecessor had selected before falling ill. He also sent an emissary to sound out Louis of Anjou and John of Gaunt in Gascony. The selection of suitable mediators had always proved difficult. But the choice made by Urban and confirmed by Gregory was remarkable. Simon Langham, the only English member of the college of cardinals, was an austere and independent-minded Benedictine who had formerly been Archbishop of Canterbury and Chancellor of England. Langham's relations with Edward III were poor. He seems to have had reservations about Edward's foreign policy. Edward for his part distrusted the papacy and had disapproved of Langham's promotion to the cardinalate. In spite of his English nationality and official background Langham's appointment is unlikely to have been welcomed at Westminster. By comparison the other mediator, Jean de Dormans, 'Cardinal of Beauvais', was extremely close to Charles V. He had been one of his most intimate counsellors when he was Dauphin. He had been present at the negotiation of the treaty of Brétigny. He had been Chancellor of France since 1361. He had been involved in all Charles V's dealings with England and had delivered the opening address at the assembly of May 1369 in Paris at which war had been declared. Dormans had been promoted cardinal in the same year as Langham but, unlike Langham, he retained his position within Charles V's government after his appointment and stayed in France instead of moving to the papal court. These appointments can only be explained on the footing that the Pope's advisers thought that Edward III was shaken by the experience of the last two years of war and was ready to compromise on something like Charles V's terms.[77]

If so it was a serious mistake. Among the English King's ministers there were undoubtedly some who thought that England would have to surrender some of the gains made at Brétigny for a durable peace. There is some evidence that they included the leading figures in the government of Gascony, John of Gaunt and the Seneschal, Sir Thomas Felton, both of whom had struggled to defend Aquitaine without money and welcomed the appointment of mediators.[78] They could see, as the King himself could not, that there was only one direction in which events in the south-west could move. In England, however, the political community was still transfixed by the victories of 1346 and 1356. The reality of Edward III's position in France was little understood. The subsequent course of events suggests that at this stage Charles V was no more willing to compromise than his opponent. Gregory XI's first attempt at peacemaking was doomed to failure before it began.

The 'Cardinal of Canterbury' left Avignon on his mission of peace at the end of March 1371, accompanied by his learned secretary Adam Easton. They met Jean de Dormans at Melun about a month later. Charles V received them graciously in Paris. He assured them that his Council was in principle content to negotiate with his adversary. But he made no other commitments. The English government would not at first go even this far. Leaving his colleague in Paris, Langham travelled to Calais where he passed several months trying in vain to obtain a safe-conduct to visit the English court. It was not until October that he was allowed to cross the Channel, and when he arrived it was to receive a humiliating rebuff. The cardinal made a series of proposals for submitting the dispute with France to arbitration. According to a French chronicler the Pope himself was suggested as arbitrator, or a tribunal of Christian monarchs or perhaps a commission of dignitaries recruited equally in both countries. All of this was entirely unrealistic. Edward III would never have put his fortunes in the hands of Gregory XI, whose French sympathies were well known. The idea of arbitration by the Pope was not even acceptable to Charles V. The Pope responded by suggesting another approach, a diplomatic conference, the first of many that was to grapple with the problems of sovereignty and territory during the 1370s and 1380s. This was eventually and rather grudgingly agreed. But the prospects were poor. Langham's problem was that at the time he was in England the strategic situation was particularly fluid. Both governments were planning major campaigns for the year 1372. At the same time the geographical range of the fighting seemed likely to expand with both Brittany and Castile being drawn into the war as active belligerents for the first time since 1369. Both sides had strong hopes that the coming year would see dramatic changes in their fortunes and were inclined to defer serious negotiation until events had improved their bargaining position.[79]

CHAPTER IV

Poitou
1372

When John of Gaunt took over the government of the principality of Aquitaine at the end of 1370, he took over with it the traditional responsibility of the officers of the principality for the conduct of England's relations with the kingdoms of the Spanish peninsula. From England's point of view the situation which he found could hardly have been worse. Edward III and the Prince had backed the losing side in the Castilian civil war, as a result of which the richest and most powerful of the Iberian kingdoms had become a French protectorate. The Prince had continued to foment domestic opposition to Henry of Trastámara's rule in the hope of recovering some of his financial losses but that policy simply made the position worse. Two years after murdering his rival Pedro I at Montiel in 1369, Henry of Trastámara had established a large measure of control over his kingdom. His many enemies, within and beyond its borders, had proved unable to act together and he had prevailed over all of them separately. The King of Portugal had suffered a series of humiliating defeats on land and sea before finally making peace in March 1371. The King of Aragon had withdrawn from the fray. Within Castile Henry's enemies had hung on to a number of fortresses from which they were gradually extruded in the course of the year 1371. Zamora fell in February. Carmona fell in May and with it most of the surviving leaders of the resistance.

The English had only one bargaining counter in the affairs of Castile. They were in possession of King Pedro's two surviving daughters, Constanza and Isabel, who had been delivered up to the Prince five years before as security for their father's debts and were currently living at Bayonne. The two girls were the children of Pedro's mistress Maria de Padilla, and their legitimacy had once been a debatable issue. But in 1362 the Cortes of Castile had formally accepted Pedro's statement that he had been through a ceremony of marriage with their mother and had accepted her children as his legal heirs. In his will Pedro had declared that the eldest surviving daughter and her husband should she have one were to inherit his kingdom. There could be little doubt, so far as the law mattered, that if Pedro had been rightful King of Castile then the elder of the two girls, Constanza, was entitled to be Queen. She was then seventeen years old and wholly without political experience. But her birth alone ensured that she would become the standard-bearer of the *emperogilados*, as the supporters of the dead King Pedro were called. At some time in 1371 John of Gaunt decided to marry her.[1]

When and how this plan took shape in his mind is impossible to say. The Duke of Lancaster had been a widower since 1368, when his first wife Blanche had died at the age of twenty-two. Gaunt was an ambitious, flamboyant man who was never likely to be satisfied by the secondary role reserved for the younger sons of kings. Like Louis of Anjou, that other ambitious dreamer whom he in many ways resembled, he wanted to carve out a principality for himself and to play a great part in the politics of Europe. He might have become King of Scotland if the idea had not been rejected by the Scottish Parliament in 1364. He had already toyed (like Anjou) with the idea of asserting an ancient and rather technical claim to the county of Provence. To such a man the prospect of becoming King of Castile in his wife's right was infinitely enticing. Gaunt must have consulted his father about it, but it is not at all clear that England's strategic interests were uppermost in the mind of either of them.

As for Constanza, her marriage can never have been a source of much personal happiness. It was a union of political convenience. Her relations with her new husband would always be distant and formal. But the marriage would give her what she wanted most, a champion who would avenge her father's death. Constanza was intensely loyal to his memory and surrounded by dispossessed Castilian noblemen and clerics who encouraged her resentments. Her marriage may well have been suggested by one of them, Juan Gutiérrez, Dean of Segovia, the conspiratorial Castilian cleric who had been a confidant of King Pedro's and briefly his ambassador to the English court in 1369. He was almost certainly a member of Constanza's tiny court at Bayonne in 1371. Gutiérrez would in due course emerge as John of Gaunt's Castilian secretary and chief adviser on the affairs of the peninsula. Doña Constanza and John of Gaunt were married, probably at Roquefort in the southern Landes, on about 8 September 1371.[2]

John of Gaunt's ambition to make himself King of Castile was to absorb most of his energies for the next eighteen years. It was not as unrealistic a project as it now seems. Henry of Trastámara had imposed his will on almost all of Castile, but he was by no means secure on his throne. He had usurped it without the shadow of a claim with the aid of an army composed mainly of French *routiers*. Doubtless long tenure would in due course bring the house of Trastámara legitimacy and security, but for the time being Henry's hold on the Castilian throne depended on the continuing presence of French captains in his service. Even after Bertrand du Guesclin's departure with his retinue in June 1370 there were believed to be at least 1,000 French men-at-arms serving in Castile. The true number may have been larger. Yet Henry's dependence on them was a source of weakness as well as strength. Most of them were independent captains with few natural loyalties who had been recruited by Du Guesclin from the ranks of the Great Companies. Henry did his best to bind their interests to his cause. He poured wealth and titles over them. Pierre de Villaines was now a rich man and Count of Ribadeo. Bernard of Béarn, a professional brigand and an illegitimate son of the Count of Foix, was Count of Medinaceli. Arnaud du Solier, who had once led a notorious band of *routiers* in Languedoc under the nickname 'Le Limousin', was lord of Villalpando. These men were unlikely to stay if ever the flow of largesse dried up. Constanza no doubt lacked allies in Castile capable of fighting the French on equal terms but she was a potent symbol. Her claims enjoyed a good deal of latent support among Henry's subjects which a change in his fortunes or the departure of his French protectors could be expected to bring to the surface. The Cortes of Toro claimed in 1371 that there were still many towns of the kingdom where venomous disputes were provoked by friends of the 'tyrant who called himself King'. There were disturbances in Murcia and probably in other towns, whose authors were found with letters from John of Gaunt in their possession. The province of Galicia in the north-west had supported King Pedro at the lowest periods in his fortunes and had never learned to accept his successor. At the end of the year 1371 a fresh rebellion, fomented by *emperogilados* based in Portugal, was to throw over the authority of Henry's officers and put the province once again in the hands of the late King Pedro's partisans.[3]

Henry of Trastámara was surrounded by external enemies whose hostility was constrained only by fear and by treaties of convenience. The kingdom of Aragon-Catalonia, with its great maritime wealth and powerful navy, had been the leading light in most of the anti-Castilian coalitions of the 1350s and 1360s. Her cautious ruler had privately concluded by 1371 that Henry of Trastámara was there to stay. But he was too canny to admit the change of policy to the outside world and no one doubted that he would be there for the pickings if Henry's government collapsed. Navarre remained a critical piece in the Spanish chequerboard, for it controlled all the passes of the western Pyrenees and was still occupying a substantial slice of Castilian territory which it had seized during the blackest period of the civil war. However, the most dangerous enemy of Trastámaran Castile was Portugal, which was gradually emerging as a force in the affairs of the peninsula.

Since the opening up of the straits of Gibraltar in the middle of the thirteenth century Portugal had become a significant staging post for trade between the Mediterranean and the Atlantic and a base for the first European explorations of the Atlantic coast of Africa, developments which would briefly make Portugal a world power in the fifteenth and sixteenth centuries. The maritime communities of the Portuguese coastal strip, where most of population was concentrated, were already waxing rich. In the 1360s up to 450 merchant ships at a time could be seen lying off Lisbon and significant communities of Italian, Catalan and southern French merchants resided there. Lisbon and Oporto were both important shipbuilding centres. As a naval power Portugal was second only to Castile, with a fleet of about twelve fighting galleys, commanded and probably built by Genoese specialists. King Pedro of Portugal, who died in 1367, was said to have enjoyed an annual income of about 240,000 *dobras* (about £45,000) at the time of his death and to have left a hoard of 800,000 pieces of gold and 400,000 marks of silver in the keep at Lisbon.[4]

The fifteenth-century chronicler Fernão Lopes, who tells us all this, was making a point. Portugal had traditionally avoided the international entanglements of the other Iberian kingdoms and Pedro had grown rich mainly by keeping his country out of the Castilian civil wars. His son Fernando, who succeeded him at the age of twenty-two, reversed his father's policy and dissipated his fortune in the process. Handsome, self-confident and ambitious, Don Fernando was also impetuous, easily led and wholly lacking in judgment. His sixteen-year reign was a catastrophe for Portugal and an opportunity for the English which they would grasp with both hands. As the nearest surviving male relative of Pedro of Castile, Fernando had a colourable claim of his own to the Castilian succession. His first intervention in Castile in 1369 was a disaster. To begin with there had been some easy successes on land. But within a short time the tables were turned. In the autumn of 1370 the Castilians scattered the Portuguese fleet at Sanlucar de Barrameda at the mouth of the River Guadalquivir. Fernando's country was invaded and partly occupied by Henry and his French auxiliaries. At the treaty of Alcoutim in March 1371 he publicly renounced his claims to Castile, abandoned his Aragonese allies and made peace with Henry of Trastámara, promising to marry the Castilian pretender's daughter. For the moment peace reigned between Castile and its chief Iberian rival. But Fernando had not reconciled himself to defeat or abandoned his hopes of glory. There was plenty of scope for Henry's enemies to make trouble for him at the court of the impulsive and ill-advised young King of Portugal.

When John of Gaunt left La Rochelle for England in October 1371, his first objective was to persuade his father's government to give a higher priority to the defence of Aquitaine. Gaunt no doubt genuinely believed in this, but he was also well aware of the value of Aquitaine as a base from which to invade Castile. He was dismayed to discover when he reached England that the main preoccupation of Edward III and his ministers was not Aquitaine, still less Castile, but Brittany. Forced by the operations of Clisson and Du Guesclin to make the choice which he had been avoiding since 1369, John de Montfort had finally resolved to appeal to the English. During the autumn of 1371 he retreated to the security of the great castle overlooking the harbour of Vannes, the old headquarters of the English lieutenants of the civil war period. From there he sent two emissaries to England to plead his cause with Edward III: his treasurer, Thomas Melbourne, and the Admiral of Brittany, John FitzNicol. His selection of two members of the small surviving caucus of Englishmen on his council speaks volumes about his plight. They arrived in England in October 1371, about a month before John of Gaunt.[5]

The English King's councillors were keen to intervene in Brittany. But they were also determined to exploit John de Montfort's political weakness. Edward III's terms were put to Melbourne and FitzNicol by his Council at the beginning of November 1371. The English King was willing, they said, to send English troops to the Duke's assistance in the following year. When the garrison of Bécherel had been rescued from Olivier de Clisson the place would be delivered up to John de Montfort, thus removing a major bone of contention between the Duke and his subjects. But in return he would be required to do liege homage for his duchy to Edward III as King of France and to support his war with Charles V. In addition he was to surrender twelve major fortresses in the duchy to Edward III's officers for the duration of the war, including the three main harbours of western Brittany at Brest, Morlaix and Hennebont. They were to be occupied immediately by the garrison evacuated from Bécherel. Edward appointed two ambassadors to carry these terms to Brittany and obtain the Duke's agreement. One of them, Robert Neville, was the younger brother of the prominent northern baron John Neville, lord of Raby, a close friend of Latimer's and a rising figure at court. He knew the Duke well, having briefly served as Marshal of Brittany some years before. His colleague, Ralph Barry, was a chamber squire and veteran of many clandestine missions to Charles of Navarre, one of those reliable servants of the King who so often acted as the executants of his secret diplomacy.[6]

On 6 November 1371 John of Gaunt disembarked at the Cornish harbour of Fowey. With him came the two princesses of Castile; some prominent Gascon and Poitevin noblemen; and several of the leading English captains who had served with him in Gascony, including Sir Hugh Calveley and the English Lieutenant in the Limousin, Sir John Devereux. Gaunt was also accompanied by a small group of Castilian exiles. They included two men who were to be prominent among the makers and executants of Gaunt's great project: the indispensable Dean of Segovia, Juan Gutiérrez, and a charming and colourful adventurer from Galicia called Juan Fernández Andeiro. Andeiro was exceptionally good at ingratiating himself with men of power in every country where he lived. He had served King Pedro until his death and then fled to Portugal, where he had rapidly become a personage of some influence. He soon became equally intimate with John of Gaunt. His presence in the Duke's inner circle signalled a new interest in what Portugal could contribute to the Duke's ambitions.[7]

The Duke of Lancaster reached London about a week after Neville and Barry had left for Brittany. He had a difficult meeting with the King on 25 November 1371. The Marshal of Aquitaine, Guichard d'Angle, and Guiraud of Tartas, lord of Poyanne, one of the few significant lords of the Landes still loyal to the Prince, were also present. The main purpose of this meeting was to impress upon Edward the urgent need to fund the defence of Aquitaine before it was lost. There was no possibility of the necessary funds being found in the principality. They would have to come from England. The Gascons present also wanted a prominent leader in the King's confidence to be charged with their defence, if not one of his sons then the Earl of Pembroke who was known to be close to Edward III and had made a favourable impression during the two years which he had passed in the principality. Gaunt believed that if the duchy was properly defended in the coming year there was a chance of bringing back into the English allegiance some of those who had deserted it since 1368. Even the lord of Albret, who had recently become discontented by the Duke of Anjou's growing rapprochement with his ancient enemy the Count of Foix, might be drawn back to the fold. There is a rather cryptic report of the discussion in a letter which Edward III wrote to Albret a few days later which suggests that Gaunt had already made overtures to him. But it was obvious that everything depended on a dramatic improvement in England's military fortunes. It is probable that Gaunt raised with his father on the same occasion his other great project of invading Castile and deposing Henry of Trastámara. All that is known is that Edward III would not be rushed into a decision. These were, he said, 'difficult matters'. An enlarged meeting of the Council, attended by the leading bishops and nobles, would be summoned to Westminster to consider them.[8]

The Great Council was the traditional forum in which the major decisions on the conduct of the war were made. It met at Westminster on 13 January 1372 and remained in session for about two weeks, one of the longest meetings of its kind that had ever been held. The proceedings are not recorded. The main outlines have to be inferred from the orders which were issued after it closed. The main military operations of the coming year were to be in Brittany. A great fleet was to be requisitioned in every port of England and directed to four assembly points in the Solent to embark troops at the beginning of May. An army of about 6,000 men was planned, which the King intended to command in person. Initially two of his sons, the Prince of Wales and the Earl of Cambridge, were expected to accompany him. The Earl of Pembroke was appointed as the Lieutenant of the King and the Prince and ordered to return to Aquitaine as soon as possible. Pembroke proposed to sail to La Rochelle with no more than a small personal retinue but with enough coin and bullion to recruit an army of 3,000 men locally. Once he had secured the defence of Aquitaine he was to head north and cross the Loire to join forces with the King. The strategy was very similar to that of 1356, in which the Prince and Henry of Lancaster had tried to mount simultaneous campaigns in Brittany and Gascony and to join their armies near the Loire. The King went to great lengths to keep these decisions secret. Guichard d'Angle and Giraud de Tartas, who had been present at the Council, were sworn to secrecy and authorised to disclose the King's plans to no one but the Prince's principal officers in the duchy.[9]

*

The Great Council made one other decision of great moment. It was by the 'common counsel of England' that on 29 January 1372 John of Gaunt publicly declared himself to be King of Castile and León in right of his wife and quartered his arms with those of the Spanish kingdom. It is not clear what if any decisions were made about how that claim was to be made good, but it was widely believed, both in France and in Spain, that Gaunt intended to invade Castile later in the year. There is a good deal of evidence that he did. His plan seems to have been to recruit his own army of about 1,200 men to embark at Plymouth in the summer and land in Gascony. He proposed to take with him that experienced warrior William Montague, Earl of Salisbury, and Sir Hugh Calveley, a veteran of Hispanic affairs who had fought on both sides of the Castilian civil wars of the 1360s. They expected to be able to recruit additional forces in Gascony and to invade Castile across the Navarrese passes. The King of Navarre, whose co-operation in the scheme was essential, was then on his way back to his kingdom from Normandy and was expected to pass through Barcelona. Agents were despatched to Catalonia to meet him there. John of Gaunt had ambitious plans for fomenting simultaneous invasions of Castile from east and west as he entered the kingdom from the north. His representatives in Aragon were instructed to try to interest the Aragonese King, Peter IV, in this scheme. But the western wing of this strategy, which depended on the goodwill of Portugal, had much more promise. Portugal, unlike Aragon, was accessible by sea from England or Gascony. John of Gaunt had already received an indirect indication of support from Don Fernando, who had secretly written to his old friend Juan Fernández Andeiro in England suggesting some form of joint military action against Castile. The Great Council was persuaded to approve the despatch of a small force of men-at-arms to Portugal to encourage Don Fernando's aggressive instincts. Gaunt appointed ambassadors to leave for Portugal as soon as possible. The leader of the embassy was none other than Andeiro himself.[10]

On 9 February 1372, a few days after the Great Council closed, Constanza made her ceremonial entry into London as Queen of Castile, accompanied by the Prince of Wales, an exotic mixture of English and Castilian retainers and a great escort of city dignitaries. Crowds lined the streets to see her as she processed along Cheapside and the Strand to be received by her husband at the Savoy Palace. In the next few weeks John of Gaunt set about giving himself the ways of a king. He was henceforth referred to in English official documents as 'King of Castile and León' and was orally addressed as 'Monseigneur d'Espagne'. He gathered around himself a small court of Castilian knights and ladies, some of whom had accompanied him from Gascony. Others joined him over the following years as successive disasters forced them to flee from Castile and from neighbouring kingdoms where they had taken refuge. Within Gaunt's household a small Castilian chancery was set up under the supervision of Juan Gutiérrez, which prepared documents in his name according to the traditional style of King Pedro's chancery, dated after the Castilian era, sealed with a silver seal of the royal arms of Castile and England and signed in John's hand with the traditional formula 'Yo El Rey', possibly the only words of Spanish that he ever knew.[11]

John of Gaunt's marriage and his designs on the throne of Castile proved to be a serious political mistake from every point of view but his own. It cemented the alliance of the Trastámaran dynasty with its French protectors and made Castile an enemy of England for a generation. Castile was a formidable adversary. The country was relatively infertile and it had suffered as much as anywhere in western Europe from the economic misfortunes of the fourteenth century: plague and depopulation, declining production, persistent inflation, all of them accompanied by severe social tensions. But its population was about twice that of England and its resources, although laid waste in the civil wars, were potentially very large. Henry of Trastámara had begun his reign with a heavy burden of debt which he had funded, as weak rulers tended to do, by lavish disposals of assets and devaluing the coinage. But by the time that John of Gaunt chose to pick his quarrel with the new dynasty the Castilian crown was already well on the way to recovery and disposed of revenues substantially exceeding those of England. The Cortes which met in the northern town of Toro in September 1371 resumed the periodic grants of direct taxes on non-nobles (*servicios*) and reintroduced a permanent sales tax (the *alcabala*) at the historically high rate of ten per cent. Over the following years Castile, although lacking the pervasive bureaucracy of England and France, would gradually join the ranks of the western European countries to whom war brought intensive government and crushing levels of taxation. The tax revenues of the Castilian Crown had stood at 500,000–600,000 *doblas* (about £100,000–£120,000) before the civil war, which was roughly comparable to the annual revenues of the kings of England in wartime. They rose to well over twice that level at their peak in the 1380s.[12]

Castile was the principal naval power of the Atlantic seaboard. She was a major exporter of primary commodities, particularly wool and iron, with a large and growing merchant fleet. The Biscay ports of Santander, Bermeo, Bilbao and Castro Urdiales were a significant force on the Atlantic trade routes. Their ships, built for carrying bulk cargoes, were among the largest vessels afloat, immense sailing vessels carrying 200 tons and upwards which were much prized as fighting vessels. In addition Castile maintained the largest permanent war fleet of any Atlantic power. At its peak, before the civil wars of the 1360s, it had comprised at least thirty fighting galleys based at Seville, where a large naval arsenal existed to service them. They were designed, managed and commanded by Genoese experts, the acknowledged masters of galley fighting in the late middle ages. Gil Boccanegra, Admiral of Castile and younger brother of the Doge of Genoa, who died in 1367 after a quarter of a century of service to the kings of Castile, had been among the most famous galley commanders of his day. His son and successor Ambrogio was an enterprising and ingenious naval commander in the same tradition.[13]

Henry of Trastámara had been under contract to supply his galley fleet to the King of France since the naval treaty of 1368. It is possible that he would have done so even if John of Gaunt had not publicly claimed his throne but it is by no means certain. Henry had been in a position to send naval assistance to France ever since the conclusion of the treaty of Alcoutim with Portugal in March 1371 but had done very little about it. During the summer of that year there was a good deal of diplomatic traffic between Paris and the Castilian court. The instructions of these emissaries have not survived but the naval question was certainly part of them. Yet Charles V was so uncertain of Castilian support that he applied to the Republic of Genoa to furnish the required twenty galleys instead. There is every reason to believe that Henry of Trastámara's rather cool attitude to his obligations was transformed, late in the day, by the news of John of Gaunt's marriage to his niece. The event evidently caused real consternation among his councillors. They had not forgotten the Prince of Wales's devastating invasion of 1367 and, like much of Europe, they entertained exaggerated notions of England's military capacity. In September 1371, Henry told the Cortes at Toro that he had resolved to send a fleet to support the King of France in the following year. Part of the exceptionally heavy taxation authorised by the Cortes was required in order to equip and man it. Towards the end of the year a 'solemn' embassy arrived at the French court from Castile to confirm the naval treaty and enlist the support of France against what was obviously thought to be a grave and imminent peril.[14]

This happened at a critical moment for France, whose maritime fortunes were then at a low ebb. After the humiliating abandonment of the King's project for invading England in 1369, an attempt had been made to address the problem by a programme of new construction at the royal arsenal at Rouen. Initially the workforce concentrated on making Norman barges, long clinker-built ships somewhat like Scandinavian longships, with raised stern and forecastle, powered by up to 200 oarsmen and an auxiliary sailing rig. Three of them were built during the winter of 1369–70 and two more in the following winter. These were the traditional workhorses of French royal fleets but they were slow and notoriously short-lived. At the beginning of 1370 a Genoese shipwright was hired to supervise the construction of proper Mediterranean galleys, smooth-sided, faster and more robust. Six of these vessels were built in 1370 and three more in 1371. In addition there were five Mediterranean galleys hired from the Grimaldi of Monaco and about five older Rouen galleys, probably dating from the 1340s and 1350s, of the type knows as *galées huissières* with broader hulls and stern gates for loading horses.[15]

This was a significant force but it had not been well used. The first two years of the war was an undistinguished period for French naval operations. The only notable feat of arms was the destruction of part of Portsmouth by a cruising squadron detached from the invasion fleet of 1369. This had done nothing to divert the English from their purpose and subsequent events showed it to be a flash in the pan. The reasons for this are unclear. The lack of experienced galley captains and crews was certainly part of the problem. Aimery of Narbonne, who was appointed Admiral of France at the end of 1369, was a valiant knight but completely without specialised skills. Although he went to sea with his fleet his functions as a commander in practice appear to have been exercised by his deputy, Jean de Coulombier, a shipmaster from Montpellier, who was relieved of his duties after a year.

There were many problems, which the French government had never really mastered, associated with the deployment of galleys and other oared ships. They were ideal for coastal raiding because of their shallow draft, manoeuvrability and large armed crews. However, they required regular maintenance and frequent refits. They had limited storage space, which meant that they could not remain at sea for very long without returning to port to take on victuals and drinking water. They were vulnerable to attack by sailing ships which, although less manoeuvrable, had the advantage of height and could be built up with raised timber superstructures fore and aft. This was an important consideration at a time when bows and arrows were still the main weapons of naval warfare. The greatest medieval sea captains fought with oared vessels and sailing ships in combined fleets. But French efforts in this direction continued to be addled by the shortage of large French sailing vessels.

In 1370 the French did nothing with their fleet until mid-July when a squadron of twenty-four ships eventually sailed from the Seine. The squadron comprised ten of the sixteen galleys in French service, together with thirteen large sailing ships and a seagoing barge chartered in Castile. The returns from all this effort were meagre. In the first few days of their cruise the fleet burned the village of Gosport outside Portsmouth and captured a large merchantman of Bayonne. But although they were at sea on and off until early November the rest of their cruise was uneventful apart from pinprick raids on undefended settlements. They failed to intercept the King of Navarre on his return from Southampton to Cherbourg. The record was worse in 1371. French strength in galleys and oared barges now stood at between twenty and twenty-five vessels, and along the south and west coasts the English were bracing themselves for a savage campaign of coastal raids. In fact the French ships passed the whole year in lay-up, probably because they had not been properly maintained.[16]

The Castilian naval alliance, coupled with the gradual revival of France's indigenous maritime strength over the next decade, shifted the strategic balance in France's favour. The Castilians not only threatened England's ability to move armies more or less freely to any point on Europe's long Atlantic coast-line as she had done since the battle of Sluys in 1340. The constant threat to England's maritime counties profoundly altered English attitudes to the war, forcing English governments to concentrate more of their financial and military resources on home defence and severely limiting their capacity to defend Aquitaine or send great expeditionary armies to France.

The Christmas festivities at the French court in 1371 were especially splendid and more than usually significant politically. They were attended by all of the King's closest advisers, his brother the Duke of Berry, the Duke of Bourbon, the Constable Bertrand du Guesclin, and most of the captains who had borne the burden of the war. The plans formulated among small groups of councillors over the past month were now submitted to those who were to carry them out, part of the formalities of consultation on which medieval government depended even in an age of autocracy. The main military operation proposed for 1372 was to be the reconquest of Poitou, a project which had been close to the King's heart since the early months of the war. Poitou had ancient connections with the royal house. It had been formally added to the appanage of the Duke of Berry as early as November 1369, together with the neighbouring provinces of Angoumois and Saintonge, in expectation of their swift recovery from the English. These regions constituted the heart of English Aquitaine, where the Prince's government maintained significant garrisons and had the support of almost all the nobility. It was not going to be possible to detach them by covert negotiations with local potentates followed by limited military operations, in the way that had proved so effective in Quercy, Rouergue or the Limousin. After the halting start of the past three years tax revenues were now flowing strongly into the King's coffers. It was intended to invade Poitou with a field army of some 4,000 men. The command would be given to the Duke of Berry in deference to his rank and his position as nominal overlord of the region to be conquered. But its real leaders would be the Constable, the Duke of Bourbon and Marshal Sancerre.[17]

The Duke of Anjou was not present at the festivities and was not party to these decisions. But Charles V intended to maximise the pressure on the English administration by getting Anjou to mount a simultaneous invasion of Aquitaine from Languedoc, the first significant operation there since 1370. The King had been negotiating directly with a delegation of the towns of the seneschalsy of Toulouse in Paris over his brother's head and had persuaded them to grant a special war tax of 350,000 *livres* of Tours. In January 1372 this arrangement was ratified in Anjou's presence by the Estates of Languedoc. They granted the Duke a hearth tax of three francs per hearth (later increased to four) for a period of a year and the *gabelle du sel* for the same period on the strict condition that the proceeds were to be spent exclusively on the prosecution of the war. This represented almost as heavy a burden of taxation as they had experienced in the first two years of the war.[18]

Four thousand men was not a large force for the reconquest of Poitou even with a major diversionary campaign in the Garonne valley. Success depended on preventing the English from sending large-scale reinforcements to Aquitaine or mounting a major invasion of France by the north. Over the past few months Charles V had returned to the project for invading England. He no longer imagined, if he ever had, that the country could be conquered, but he believed that a landing in force on the English coast would tie down English forces in the defence of their homeland and prevent his adversary from sending expeditionary armies to the continent.

Initially the French King had pinned his hopes on the Scots. David II had unexpectedly died at the age of forty-seven in February 1371 and had been succeeded by his amiable but unwarlike nephew, Robert Stewart. The French King had made a serious bid for Scottish support in the first few months of the new reign. In June 1371 he had received a Scottish embassy at Vincennes which had come to notify him of Robert's accession and to renew the long-standing treaty of friendship between the two countries. The embassy was led by the experienced and loyal Bishop Wardlaw of Glasgow. Its members included Archibald Douglas, a good friend of France who had fought in the French army at the battle of Poitiers. It was probably Douglas who was responsible for the secret agreement made with Charles V's councillors at Vincennes on 30 June 1371. By this document Charles V agreed to arrange for the Anglo-Scottish truce to be annulled by the Pope. As soon as this had been achieved the French King would pay 100,000 nobles (£33,000) to enable Robert to salve his honour by paying off his predecessor's ransom before making war on England. Charles was prepared to send 1,000 French men-at-arms to Scotland for two years and to pay the wages of 1,000 Scots to support them. Whether Robert authorised Douglas to make any such agreement is not at all clear, but he certainly did not ratify it when the ambassadors returned to Scotland in the autumn. In the event the project came to nothing. The Scottish King was content to confirm the French alliance but only in the most anodyne terms. He would not promise to fight the English unless they were foolish enough to repudiate the truce.[19]

Spurned by the Scots, Charles V turned to the possibility of fomenting a rebellion in Wales, a plan which had already failed in 1369. Once more the instruments of Charles's plans would be the persuasive Owen of Wales and his companion in arms, Jack Wyn. Since the fiasco of 1369 Owen had succeeded in expanding his influence in Wales. Periodic indictments disclose the existence of small cells of Owen's supporters in north Wales, some of whom sent him money and recruits. Many more must have escaped the attention of the Prince's officers. Owen had kept his largely Welsh company of some 200 men in being by taking employment as a jobbing mercenary wherever he could find it. In the autumn of 1371 he was one of a number of mercenary captains of diverse nationalities in the service of the German city of Metz. Towards the end of 1371, however, he was recalled to France. He was probably among the councillors with the King at Christmas. His role in the coming campaign would be to take command of a small army which was to sail for Wales as soon as shipping could be found for it. When the Castilian ambassadors arrived in Paris, probably during December, with their fears of invasion and their offers of naval assistance, Charles seized the opportunity. Henry of Trastámara's emissaries received prompt and generous assurances that Charles would if necessary send a French army to Castile to frustrate any Lancastrian invasion. In return he exacted a promise that twelve Castilian galleys and eight sailing carracks would be sent urgently to join the French fleet at Harfleur. Their first task would be to escort Owen's army to Wales, perhaps as early as February or March 1372.[20]

Charles V was well informed about what was happening in England. The 'notable persons well disposed to us in whom we have every confidence', whom the King identified as the source of his intelligence, may have included people close to the English court or they may simply have been Anglophone spies sent to pick up the gossip of Westminster. Whatever the source, within days of the dispersal of Edward III's Great Council the French King had received more or less accurate reports of its proceedings in spite of all the English King's precautions. By the end of January 1372 he knew about his enemy's plans for landing an army in Brittany. Either then or soon afterwards he learned about the mission of the Earl of Pembroke to Aquitaine.[21] As a result his scheme for a diversionary landing in Wales became more ambitious. In about March 1372 the size of the landing force was trebled and the scheme radically altered. The new plan was that Owen should sail first with his company to northern Castile, where he would be joined by the promised Castilian ships and by 1,000 men-at-arms recruited from among the French mercenaries in the service of Henry of Trastámara. The diversion would also have the advantage of enabling the fleet to approach the Scillies on its way to Wales from the south with the aid of the prevailing westerly winds instead of laboriously tacking into them from the east and running the gauntlet of England's western fleet.

The task of persuading Henry of Trastámara to co-operate in these plans was confided to an emissary sent from Paris, the Burgundian knight Jean de Rye. He was a veteran of Castilian affairs whose knowledge of the country went back to the siege of Algeciras in 1344. He knew Henry of Trastámara well, having been present at the negotiation of the naval treaty of 1368. This was just as well for he had an exceptionally difficult mission to perform. Henry had to be persuaded to part with most of the foreign mercenaries who were keeping him on his throne. The mercenaries themselves had to be induced to leave a country where they were living off the fat of the land in order to embark on a perilous voyage to one of the poorest regions of Europe. If this proved too much to ask, Jean de Rye was instructed to press for Owen to be reinforced with Castilian troops instead. In either case it would be necessary to spend large sums of money in Castile on shipping, crews and soldiers. Charles hoped that Henry of Trastámara might meet the cost himself, if necessary by setting it off against the debts which he owed to Charles V and Louis of Anjou for their past support. But if Henry would not pay, Jean was empowered to raise the money from moneylenders on the French King's credit or in the last resort by taking up to 60,000 francs from the proceeds of Bertrand du Guesclin's Castilian estates, which the Constable was in the process of selling. In about March 1372 Jean de Rye left Paris for Castile.[22]

Against this unpromising background, the cardinals of Canterbury and Beauvais opened the long-planned diplomatic conference beneath the walls of Guines on 1 March 1372. Neither side was represented by men who were particularly close to the counsels of the kings. Charles V's instructions to his own representatives were calculated to ensure that nothing of much importance would occur. They were told to manoeuvre the English into making the running and to confine themselves to bland professions of goodwill without making any proposals of their own. Any suggestion of arbitration was to be resisted. If the English complained about the repudiation of the treaty of Brétigny the French were to respond with the same legal arguments and counter-accusations as Charles V had deployed during the acrimonious diplomatic exchanges which had preceded the outbreak of war in 1369. As for the English ambassadors, they are said by a French source to have spoken 'more graciously than usual', but it is unlikely that their instructions were any more accommodating. The two sides exchanged their incompatible views about the legal basis of Edward III's claim to the French Crown. There is some evidence that they agreed on a proposal to be presented to the kings for suspending the war for the lifetime of Edward III, an interesting idea which at least one and probably both kings rejected. The conference broke up after five weeks at the beginning of April.[23]

*

John de Montfort's position in Brittany deteriorated rapidly during the winter of 1371–2. The siege of Bécherel was still continuing. A succession of inconclusive embassies passed between Paris and Vannes, in which each side aired the grievances built up over the past three years and John sought to fend off French intervention in his duchy. But, however desperate he was for military assistance, John de Montfort was not prepared to accept it on the demeaning terms offered by Edward III's ministers. The surrender of twelve fortresses to the English would have discredited him in the eyes of his subjects. John also thought, rightly as it turned out, that the English were at least as keen to get a foothold in Brittany as he was to have their support, and that better inducements would be offered if he held out for them. Neville and Barry, who must have reached Vannes at about the beginning of December 1371 with the Council's proposals, were obliged to call for more convenient instructions. The broad lines of an agreement only emerged in the course of February 1372, after the Great Council had resolved upon an invasion of Brittany and Edward's ministers had become anxious about the timetable. Edward's ambassadors were authorised to drop all of their more objectionable demands. The Duke was promised an advance guard of 600 men to defend the duchy against the French. He was given the ultimate control over their operations. The demand for the surrender of ports and castles was abandoned. Instead the English agreed to surrender on demand any places which they occupied in the course of the campaign. The price paid for John's alliance was increased. He was now to have the honour of Richmond restored to him and a complete release of his debts to Edward III. In return for all this the Duke would be expected to allow the English King's host to land in the duchy and use it as a base from which to invade France. John himself was expected to contribute 1,000 men-at-arms of his own to the venture. After four months in Brittany Neville and Barry returned to England. They reported to the Council on about 28 March.[24]

They found Edward III's ministers preoccupied with the problems of shipping and coastal defence. England's island position made her uniquely dependent on being able to deploy very large fleets of transports and escort ships, which had to be requisitioned from commercial shipowners. The limiting factors in the planning of any overseas expedition were the availability of ships and seamen and the length of the sea passage. Shipping an army to Brittany across more than 200 miles of sea was a much more difficult undertaking than crossing the Channel to Calais, as Edward III might have recalled from his first campaign there, thirty years before. In 1342 at least 440 ships had been requisitioned to carry an army of about 7,000 men to the peninsula. Most of the ships had had to perform the passage twice and even so about 1,400 men had been left behind. The whole process had taken three months from the time the ships were assembled. The army of 1346, which was probably about 14,000 strong, had crossed to the Cotentin in one passage but had needed about 750 ships to do it. The transport of armies to Gascony was even more difficult. The English had never succeeded in shipping much more than 3,000 mounted men across the Bay of Biscay in one go even when they controlled its entire coast-line.[25]

According to the complaints of the Commons at the end of 1372, the growing difficulty which the English encountered in transporting their armies to the continent was due to a serious decline of their merchant marine. The evidence, although incomplete, bears this out. In 1347 Edward III had deployed 737 ships for the epic siege of Calais, the largest English fleet for which there is reliable evidence in the whole medieval period. Of these ships 682 were requisitioned merchantmen and the rest were either the King's or chartered in from abroad. By comparison in the early 1370s the Admirals, with much effort and barrel-scraping, were able to requisition about a third of this number, between 200 and 250 ocean-going hulls. Moreover their average carrying capacity, although larger than it had been in the early years of Edward III, was still too small for effective use as transports. The shipowners of Venice, Genoa and the Biscay ports of Castile routinely traded vessels of 300 tons burden and upwards. But the merchant fleet which carried John of Gaunt to Calais in 1369, at 255 hulls the largest that the English assembled in this period, included only eight vessels of more than 200 tons burden. Seventy per cent of the requisitioned merchantmen were under 100 tons.[26] The comparatively small size of English ships posed special problems in an age of all-mounted armies. Large numbers of horses had to be shipped: generally one for an archer and three for each man-at-arms.[27] They had to be stowed below deck in dismantlable wooden pens. English ships were designed for carrying bulk cargoes in deep holds and had only very limited deck space, which made them particularly unsuitable for carrying passengers with animals. In the early years of Edward's reign the average carrying capacity of English ships had been no more than about eighteen to twenty men with their horses per hull. In the later years of the century it was between twenty and thirty men with horses, depending on the length of the sea passage. This meant that it took between four and six tons of cargo capacity to carry one man and his horses.[28] Most of this was for the horses. Up to six times as many men could be carried if horses were not required or were to be found at the destination.[29]

The supply of seamen proved to be as critical as the supply of ships. Medieval merchant ships were labour-intensive. The English had been forced by shortage of manpower to abandon the earlier practice of sending ships to sea with double crews working in shifts. But, as a broad generalisation, even with single crews they needed at least one crewman for every four tons of carrying capacity. Crewing ratios were higher on the smaller vessels. Unlike soldiers, who were recruited almost entirely from volunteers, the seamen serving on requisitioned ships were conscripted men. They were obtained by press gangs working their way along the coast from port to port clearing the menfolk from coastal villages and towns. The administrative records of the 1370s are full of imprecations hurled at harassed officials, complaining about the slow and inadequate results produced by the press gangs. For all their efforts, the returns diminished with the fortunes of English merchant shipping generally. More than 13,300 English seamen had manned the fleet of 1347. Yet the largest number of seamen raised at one time in this period was just over 5,000 men in 1369.[30]

The shipowners of England repeatedly petitioned Parliament for a solution to their woes and the Commons took up their cause at almost every session. They pointed to requisitioning and impressment as the main cause of the destruction of their fortunes. It had led, they said, to the decline of the English merchant marine and the abandonment of the seafaring life by growing numbers of young men. These claims oversimplified a complex problem, for other factors were also at work including the general contraction of England's foreign trade and the devastating impact of the Black Death on English coastal communities. But the Commons' diagnosis is plausible. On average a large ocean-going merchant ship represented an investment of about £500, which had to be recovered over the relatively short life of a wooden, clinker-built ship. Requisitioned ships were taken without hire or any other form of compensation, often for long periods. They served for at least four months in 1369 and 1370 and would serve for six in 1372. This represented a heavy annual tax on England's shipowners which in the longer term reduced their profits and inhibited investment in new hulls. Seamen, unlike shipowners, were paid but the rate was low. Moreover, until the system was changed in 1373, paid time ran only from the date when operations began. Weeks and sometimes months which seamen passed in port waiting for orders were in principle entirely unpaid. In 1372 one group of 620 west country seamen complained that they had been kept idle without pay from April to July awaiting orders. We know this because the King made them an *ex gratia* payment which is recorded in the accounts. But their experience was fairly common and others in their position did not even get a tip. There is a good deal of anecdotal evidence of resistance to war service among seamen, who escaped from the ports in growing numbers as the King's sergeants approached and occasionally tried to fight them off by main force. In 1372 the Admirals' officers encountered serious resistance in the ports. Although the evidence is sparse there seems to have been something approaching a strike in the west of England. By the end of March, after two months of effort, the ports from the Thames to Bristol appear to have produced fewer than fifty ships between them. The masters and crews were reported to be breaking their bonds and escaping to sea to fish or trade.[31]

Determined efforts had been made since the previous year to obtain fully manned galleys from the republic of Genoa, the only source of such ships which was not already beholden to France. Early in 1371 Edward III had taken into his service an Italian by the name of Jacopo Provana who offered to negotiate an arrangement with the Genoese. He left England in the spring carrying the enormous sum of £9,500 to cover advances to the shipmasters. Provana was the kind of shadowy adventurer to whom the English government often turned in order to make up for its ignorance of Italian affairs but he was not an ideal choice. He was a Piedmontese nobleman and a stranger to the turbulent and clannish politics of Genoa. He also had the misfortune to begin his task just after a revolution had brought a new plebeian government to power in the city. Provana's contacts were with the ousted patrician opposition. In December 1371 he concluded a treaty in Florence with two prominent patrician politicians from Genoa, Antonio Fieschi and Marco Grimaldi, both of whom were at war with the current government of the republic. They promised to furnish eight to ten war galleys for four months in the summer of 1372. Provana promised them generous advances and mobilisation fees in addition to a substantial monthly hire once they reached England. Some of this may even have been paid. But the agreement was never implemented, probably because of the failure of the Fieschis' plans to seize power in Genoa. It must have been clear by March 1372 that the Genoese would not be coming. The English turned for help to Bayonne. At the end of the month an agent was sent there to hire carracks and ocean-going barges urgently for the King's service.[32]

At about the end of April 1372 the English government became aware that the French and their Castilian allies were preparing a major naval campaign. The precise nature of their plans was still unclear but it was assumed that there would be large-scale coastal raids against southern England. On 26 April orders went out to array men for coast-guard duty and to make beacons on hilltops along the Kent coast. The ships of the Cinque Ports were sent out to patrol off the Kent coast. All of this seriously aggravated the Admirals' difficulties in finding shipping for three continental campaigns. On 10 and 11 May the current demands on available shipping were reviewed at a two-day session of the Council at Westminster attended by all the King's principal advisers. The special arrangements for the defence of the coasts, hitherto limited to Kent, were extended to Surrey and Sussex. It was decided to try to concentrate on despatching the smaller forces planned for the continent. The Earl of Pembroke left at once for Plymouth. His shipping needs were very modest, about fifteen vessels, but they would not be met until well into June. Another eight or ten ships would be needed to carry the small corps destined for Portugal. The advance guard of 600 men-at-arms which had been promised to John de Montfort was being put together under the command of the Steward of Edward III's household, Sir John Neville, the ambassador's elder brother. Thirty to forty ships would be needed to carry them. Unfortunately there were not enough ships even for these modest task forces, let alone the 6,000 men whom the King proposed to lead into Brittany. A fresh round of requisitioning was ordered. Agents were sent to hire ships on the continent in Holland and Zeeland. The King still clung to the hope that the main expedition might embark in mid-June.[33]

On 10 May 1372 Owen of Wales issued his manifesto in Paris announcing his ambitions to his own people and incidentally to his English enemies:

Whereas the Kings of England have in the past, moved by intemperance and greed, wrongly and without cause treacherously killed or put to death my forbears the Kings of Wales and expelled them by force from their kingdom and subjected a kingdom that is rightly mine as their lineal descendant and closest blood relation, I have petitioned various Christian princes, declaring my right and humbly beseeching their help. Lately I came before my most powerful and well-regarded lord Charles by the grace of God King of France and Dauphin of Vienne and showed him my right, and he taking pity on my estate and considering the great wrong that the kings of England have done to my forbears and that the present king still does to me . . . has supported me with his men-at-arms and ships to recover my kingdom.

The French King, according to Owen, had already committed himself to expenditure of 300,000 francs on men-at-arms, archers, shipping and equipment to support his venture, which was to be repaid from the revenues of Wales after the conquest. But the contrast between this grandiose declaration and the meagre forces at Owen's disposal was striking. In addition to his own company, now 200 strong, Owen had been given a French company of 165 men under one of Charles V's chamberlains, Morelet de Montmor, and a fleet of eight galleys and four barges under the command of the Monegasque admiral, Rainier Grimaldi.[34]

In the last week of May 1372 Owen of Wales's tiny force sailed for Castile from Harfleur. They rounded the Cotentin peninsula, turned south and fell on Guernsey at the end of the month, landing their whole force near St. Peter Port. Guernsey was ill-prepared for an invasion. Castle Cornet, the most substantial place on the island, was in an appalling state of disrepair, its towers falling in and the gates, portcullises and drawbridge broken. Beauregard was a modern keep at the south-east end of the town which had recently been constructed as a refuge. Both had nominal garrisons in 1372. It was necessary to get help from Jersey. Sir Edmund Rose had just taken over as captain of Gorey castle on Jersey, the strongest fortification in the Channel Islands. He crossed urgently to Guernsey with his garrison. He also brought eighty men borrowed from the companies at Saint-Sauveur, who were increasingly used as a reserve of manpower to support England's military ventures in western France. Rose led his troops against the invaders, supported by about 800 islanders. About five miles from St. Peter Port they suffered a bloody defeat. Much of the island army was killed. Rose fled from the field with the survivors and took refuge in the ruins of Castle Cornet. Here he defied Owen's army, in spite of the dilapidated state of the defences, until they withdrew to their ships to continue on their voyage.[35]

In the meantime a highly effective softening-up operation was in progress on the march of Poitou. Bertrand du Guesclin and the Duke of Bourbon had established their headquarters since the end of March in the fortress of Chinon on the northern march of Poitou. They commanded a raiding force of about 1,000 men-at-arms and a company of Genoese crossbowmen. They also had the large French garrisons on the northern march at Châtellerault and La Roche-Posay to draw on. Du Guesclin launched the rapid raids over great distances which had become characteristic of his military method. The first of them, up the river valleys of the east march of Poitou, was conducted at such speed that the troops were unable either to forage or feed themselves properly and lost many of their horses. This campaign left the French in control of all the major river crossings into Poitou from the east except for Chauvigny. Bertrand du Guesclin's purpose was as much diplomatic as military. His agents and those of the Duke of Berry had been active in Poitou for several months, making emollient offers in return for promises of submission. The Poitevin nobility rejected his approaches to a man. But the towns, which had never been as committed to the Prince, were not so sure. Poitiers was left increasingly exposed by the French conquests on the eastern march. The city was divided between two parties whose relative strength fluctuated with the military situation. The Mayor, Jean Renaud, the officers of the city and the richest citizens were loyal to the Prince. But most churchmen and some leading merchants openly declared their preference for the King of France. By now they were probably supported by most of the population.[36]

Pending the arrival of the Earl of Pembroke from England the defence of Aquitaine was in the hands of Jean de Grailly, Captal de Buch, and the Seneschal of Bordeaux, Sir Thomas Felton. The Captal, who took command of the military operation, had many advantages for the task. His family had never wavered in its support of the English dynasty even in the darkest days of the 1330s. He was a soldier of courage and experience with a European reputation. But he had been formed in the school of the Gascon companies of the 1350s, like many of his contemporaries, and he was not a particularly skilful strategist or field commander. He also had very few troops at his disposal, a few hundred at the most, and those probably unpaid. His main problem was the uncertain loyalty of the towns, which made it necessary to detach large numbers of men to serve in the four main garrisons at Poitiers, Thouars, Niort and La Rochelle. The Captal's response to the French raids of the spring was, perhaps understandably, to sit tight in the walled towns and castles until the promised subsidies arrived from England and to conserve his strength for the main French assault which was known to be in preparation.

In June 1372 the Constable sent Olivier de Clisson to lay siege to Moncontour, now the only significant English garrison north of Poitiers, while he and the Duke of Berry conducted a powerful military demonstration beneath the city walls. Moncontour was held by Sir John Cresswell with a garrison of sixty mainly English troops. The prospect of losing it was sufficiently serious to provoke the English into attempting its relief. With Bertrand du Guesclin and Louis of Bourbon prowling outside Poitiers, the relief had to be attempted from Niort, the only other large garrison which was close enough. Walter Spridlington, the captain of Niort, managed to collect a field force of several hundred men and briefly established a counter-siege at Moncontour. Shortly after this the French launched a ferocious assault on the castle. Once they had carried the outer bailey Cresswell sued for terms. His men were allowed to withdraw with their arms (but not their booty) to Poitiers. The capture became known for a famous incident which illustrated the notorious prickliness of the low-born Constable about his chivalric reputation. One of the garrison had taunted him during the siege for fighting against the Prince when (it was wrongly alleged) his ransom from the battle of Nájera remained unpaid. This man disgraced Bertrand's arms by hanging them upside down from the battlements. When he fell into the Constable's hands after the fall of the outer bailey he was hanged from the walls with his helmet around his neck.[37]

In about the second week of June 1372 the Earl of Pembroke sailed out of Plymouth for La Rochelle. He was accompanied by Sir John Devereux and a number of Gascon notables. They brought with them a treasury of £12,000 in cash, enough to pay the projected army of 3,000 men for more than four months. Considering the importance of Pembroke's mission and the information that the English government now had about the strength of enemy forces at sea, Pembroke's forces were extraordinarily vulnerable. Froissart says that there were about fourteen ships, which is consistent with other evidence. Most of them were quite small. The requisitioning orders had insisted that the vessels assigned to Pembroke should not exceed fifty tons burden. An escort was provided of just three large fighting ships with built-up towers. To defend these vessels Pembroke had eighty English men-at-arms and eighty archers, plus the Gascon notables and their companions and a small company charged with guarding the cash, fewer than 200 men in all. He plainly did not expect to encounter more than pirates on his route.[38]

The harbour of La Rochelle is sited at the head of a deep inlet giving onto the great open bay between the islands of Ré and Oléron. The approaches to the port were narrowed by sandbanks close to the shore which became treacherous at low tide, creating difficulties for the heavily laden English cogs with their deep draft and inability to sail close to the wind. Pembroke's squadron entered the bay on the afternoon of 22 June 1372. As the ships passed south of the Île de Ré they saw the whole Castilian fleet lying at anchor off the mouth of the harbour, twelve galleys and at least eight carracks. Ambrogio Boccanegra had brought them across the Bay of Biscay to blockade the Gascon ports against Pembroke's fleet as soon as his plans became known. They had been lying in wait for him for several weeks. When Pembroke arrived the tide was high but ebbing and the Castilian ships lay across the channel.

In spite of the inferiority of his forces Pembroke seems to have decided to try to force his way past the Castilian squadron into the safety of the harbour. The soldiers armed themselves. Several squires of Pembroke's retinue were knighted on the deck of his flagship. The men-at-arms were concentrated on the larger ships, the archers positioned in the forecastles. As they sailed towards the entrance the Castilians moved into formation, hoisted their banners, pennons and streamers from their masts and came forward to meet them. The probable site of the battle lies about two miles west of the harbour, off the promontory on which the modern port of La Pallice now stands. The English were caught between the enemy and the sandbanks and found themselves attacked at close quarters by the Castilian carracks. These towered over the much smaller English vessels. Their upper decks were filled with crossbowmen and a rain of arrows came down on the exposed English soldiers and seamen. The Castilian galleys were equipped with heavy mounted arbalests and stone-throwers which cast huge stones and lead projectiles to crush the timbers of the English decks. For their part the English archers made little impression on the Castilian archers and crews, who were high up and well protected by timber breastworks and large 'pavois' or shields. After several hours of fierce fighting the English had lost two of their ships. Night fell and the Castilians withdrew. The English squadron anchored in its awkward position for the night, cut off from the open sea by the Castilian fleet around them. In La Rochelle the senior English officer was the English Seneschal of Saintonge, Sir John Harpeden. He was making desperate efforts to find reinforcements for Pembroke's tiny army before the fight resumed in the morning. He pleaded with the townsmen to supply him with men and ships. But the English government had few friends in La Rochelle. Its shipmasters had no desire to risk their ships and their lives against an experienced Castilian war fleet. Harpeden eventually managed to collect together a force of Gascon men-at-arms from nearby garrisons. They commandeered four barges and succeeded in reaching Pembroke's ships shortly after dawn. Meanwhile messengers were sent urgently to the Captal de Buch and to Sir Thomas Felton to bring in reinforcements from further afield.

As the sun rose on 23 June the English found themselves held against the sandbanks by the wind and the incoming tide, unable to move. The Castilians were lying upwind of them. During the morning the Castilians closed again. Once more it seems to have been the carracks, not the galleys, which took the lead. Pembroke put his largest ships and the barges newly arrived from the town in front of his line and posted all his archers in them. The Castilians concentrated the entire force of their attack on these vessels. At least four Castilian vessels attached themselves to Pembroke's flagship with grappling irons and poured arrows into the ranks of the defenders. Eventually they succeeded in casting oil over the decks of the leading English ships and setting fire to it with burning arrow-heads. Pembroke fought them off for several hours with a handful of men-at-arms and some archers but, as the flames spread, their resistance began to fail. The horses in the holds began to shriek in agony, forcing their way out of the pens in which they were confined and breaking the timbers at the side of the holds. Men threw themselves into the sea to escape the heat. Pembroke surrendered and was taken onto a Castilian vessel. All the Gascon notables were captured. The other large ships suffered the same fate. Sir John Harpeden, who was in one of the barges of La Rochelle, was captured along with several of the knights who had come out with him from the town. Once the larger and better-manned English ships had been overcome the Castilians made short work of the smaller ones behind. By mid-afternoon it was all over. The Castilians took possession of the surviving English ships, crewed the ones that they could use and burned the rest. Pembroke's treasury was captured intact. About 160 prisoners were taken, including seventy knights. A handful of men escaped after the battle, among them the resourceful John Devereux. But apart from these there were hardly any survivors. Boccanegra's ships remained at anchor for the following night, the sounds of revelry floating across the bay. Then on the following day they left with the tide and sailed for Castile to join forces with Owen of Wales.[39]

The sea battle off La Rochelle is sometimes regarded as a vindication of the fighting galley against the sailing ship as an instrument of war. There is some evidence that the English themselves took this view. But it is hard to justify. The leading role in the battle on both sides was taken by sailing ships and it was their height and manpower which won the day. The English were defeated mainly because they had chosen to send a small, lightly protected squadron to Gascony, counting on the good fortune which had enabled their ships to cross the Bay of Biscay without mishap so many times before. The folly of this decision should have been obvious. The real lessons of the battle were the importance of good intelligence and the superiority of experienced professional admirals. Boccanegra's strategic judgment had been faultless. His ships were in the right place at the right time as those of the French and English admirals hardly ever were.

On the evening of 24 June 1372, midsummer night, Sir Thomas Felton and the Captal de Buch arrived in La Rochelle with a large body of troops which they had recruited with admirable speed in Saintonge and the Bordelais. They found the town a scene of confusion. The Castilian fleet had vanished. No one seemed to know what had happened. Eventually one of John Harpeden's Gascon companions appeared. He had managed to persuade his captor to accept his parole and had found his way back to the town. From him they heard the story of the gravest strategic set-back that the English had yet suffered in the war.[40]

The French fleet of Owen of Wales and Rainier Grimaldi arrived in the Basque port of Santander at the end of June 1372, shortly before Ambrogio Boccanegra's triumphant return from La Rochelle. The courteous conventions which usually prevailed between English and French gentlemen had no appeal for the Castilians. The visitors were appalled to see famous knights such as the Earl of Pembroke and his companions bound together by chains round their necks 'like dogs on their leads'. 'They know no finer courtesy,' Froissart remarked, 'just like the Germans.' The prisoners were taken to Burgos to be exhibited to Henry of Trastámara. He was quite as rough a man as his admiral and had no intention of releasing them even for ransom while there was political advantage to be gained from holding them. The Gascon knight Florimond de Lesparre was released fairly quickly by the good offices of Matthew Gournay, one of the English knights who had fought for Henry in the 1360s. Most of the others had to wait many years.

The Earl of Pembroke's fate was particularly wretched. He was sent to the grim fortress of Curiel above the River Duero, east of Valladolid.

There he was kept in appalling conditions which broke his health within six months. He was ultimately given to Bertrand du Guesclin in 1374, together with twenty-six other prisoners, in partial discharge of the debt owed to him by the Castilian King. Pembroke agreed to pay the Constable a ransom of 130,000 francs (about £22,000). His English friends arranged for a large sum in cash and promissory notes to be deposited with an Italian banker at Bruges and released to the Constable's agents provided that the Earl was delivered into English custody at Calais by Easter 1375. But the Earl was obviously dying. He was carried north in a litter 'in short stages as kindly and gently as could be', but died six days before Easter as the cortege reached Amiens. Du Guesclin never got his money.

The Poitevin nobleman Guichard d'Angle got out of Castile under another complicated commercial deal in return for the surrender to Henry of Trastámara of the Castilian estates of the French *condottiere*, Olivier de Mauny, notorious as the 'evil nest' (*Mau Nid*) whom Chaucer accused of having lured King Pedro to his death. Olivier exchanged the prisoner for Mathieu, lord of Roye, one of the surviving hostages for the treaty of Brétigny, who was still in captivity in England. Mathieu in turn paid for his release by marrying his daughter with a large endowment to Olivier's brother. As for Sir John Harpeden he remained in captivity until 1378. According to a story circulating in England, which must have been apocryphal, he earned his freedom by volunteering to champion the divinity of Christ in single combat against two 'Ethiopian' heathens. Humbler men died in captivity or were released many years later when it became obvious that they were no longer worth their keep. Eight years after the battle there were still west country seamen captured at La Rochelle who were believed by their friends and families to be rotting in Castilian jails.[41]

In Aquitaine the battle of La Rochelle had a shattering effect on the Prince's officers and their allies. Without Pembroke's treasury or a commander of his political stature it was far from clear that an army could be found to resist the coming invasion. Sir John Devereux, the only notable survivor of the battle, was appointed as captain of La Rochelle with as large a garrison as could be spared. Sir John Cresswell and Sir Thomas Percy took command in Poitiers. The Captal de Buch remained in the field, keeping the advantages of mobility. It is not clear what kind of force he had under his command. But the signs of desertion among hitherto loyal subjects of the Prince were now multiplying ominously. On 9 July 1372 Bertrand du Guesclin and

Olivier de Clisson met prominent churchmen and noblemen of the province at Loudun to discuss what terms would be available to them if they defected. The two French commanders saw the prospect of a bloodless conquest of the province if they stayed their hand. They granted a truce to all Poitevins. The terms have not survived but the sequel suggests that they were granted protection from forfeiture if they promised not to take up arms in the Prince's interest. On the south-eastern march of Aquitaine the impact of the destruction of Pembroke's fleet was just as dramatic. Louis of Anjou brought forward his preparations in order to take advantage of the disarray of the defenders. Mustering relatively modest forces at Moissac and Agen he entered the valley of the Garonne at the beginning of July encountering no resistance at all. Aiguillon, at the confluence of the Garonne and the Lot, and Port-Sainte-Marie, the river port on the Garonne downstream of Agen, had resisted him in 1369 and 1370 but surrendered in 1372, apparently without a blow. At least six other places followed their example.[42]

At Westminster English policy underwent a bewildering series of changes as Edward III and his ministers, without accurate or up-to-date information about their enemies' plans, groped about for a response to these events. They learned very quickly that the French fleet had sailed from the Seine. But they do not seem to have realised how small it was nor that it was bound for Castile rather than England. Until the first reports arrived of the invasion of Guernsey they do not even seem to have known of Owen's involvement. The scraps of information that they had, more menacing for being incomplete, provoked a panic in England out of all proportion to the immediate threat. From 9 June onwards a stream of commands issued to royal officials in Hampshire, the Isle of Wight and the west country. They were warned that the French and their allies would shortly descend on them in a 'great fleet of ships and galleys packed with fighting men' to invade the realm and eradicate the English tongue. Coast-guard levies were called out in all the maritime counties of southern England. The order to array men for coast-guard service and prepare beacons on hilltops, hitherto limited to the south-east of England, was extended to the whole of the south and west coast as far as the Bristol Channel. Wales was recognised as a target as soon as Owen's participation was known and all fortified places there were ordered to be manned and equipped against a landing.[43]

On 22 June, as Owen of Wales sailed south across the Bay of Biscay and the Castilian fleet opened its two-day engagement against the Earl of Pembroke, Edward III decided to assemble all the shipping which was being made ready for his passage to Brittany in the Downs off Sandwich. He resolved to postpone his continental campaign and instead use the ships to carry out a sweep of the Channel with a view to finding out and destroying the enemy's fleet. The main companies who were holding themselves ready to invade France, including those of the Prince and the Earl of Cambridge, were summoned to Sandwich bringing four months' provisions but leaving their horses behind. Many others, who were preparing to embark at Southampton with the advance guard destined for Brittany, were diverted to join the King. John of Gaunt, the Earl of Salisbury and Sir Hugh Calveley were recalled from their Iberian fantasies and given the same instructions. No less than twenty-nine iron 'gonnes' firing lead shot were brought out of the arsenal at the Tower to be mounted on the decks of the ships. The increased scale of the operation, the need to reposition ships and the grinding deliberation of the English administrative machine forced on Edward the usual frustrating delays. The best that could be done was to have the men ready at Sandwich for the new enterprise in the second week of August.[44]

Juan Fernández Andeiro, oblivious of the disaster at La Rochelle and the mounting hysteria at Westminster, arrived at the Portuguese court in the cathedral city of Braga at the beginning of July 1372, accompanied by one of John of Gaunt's squires. The situation which they found would have been extremely promising if England's military fortunes had been better. The Portuguese treaty of peace with Castile, although barely a year old, was already looking threadbare. Within six months of sealing it Don Fernando had repudiated his promise to marry Henry of Trastámara's daughter in favour of his mistress, Leonora Teles de Meneses, a promiscuous and dominating married woman whose uncle was the King's principal councillor. This misalliance was not well received in Portugal. It provoked sullen hostility among the nobility and riots in the streets of Lisbon. But Leonora's marriage to her previous husband was duly annulled by royal order towards the end of 1371 and shortly afterwards Don Fernando married her. The new Queen of Portugal and her aged and inept uncle now became the most powerful figures in Portuguese politics. They filled the court and council and the major castles of the Crown with her relations and friends. They pursued an actively anti-Castilian policy. They showed special favour to the exiled partisans of King Pedro of Castile, who now gathered in growing numbers at the fringes of the Portuguese court. On 10 July 1372 the two envoys from England entered into a formal military alliance with Portugal which envisaged a joint invasion of Castile.[45]

In about the middle of July reports reached Westminster that the garrison of Bécherel had entered into a conditional surrender agreement. Sir John Pert had done more than his duty. His men had been reduced to eating their horses and hunting for rodents in the cellars of the castle. They finally agreed to surrender the place unless the King or one of his sons appeared with a relief force by an agreed date. The news provoked yet another panic at Westminster and a reversion to the plans which had been jettisoned in the last panic only three weeks before. The army would land in Brittany after all. The King urged his ministers on to fresh efforts in the hope of getting there in time to relieve the beleaguered garrison. The treaty between Edward III and the Duke of Brittany, which had been so long in the making, was sealed in St. Stephen's chapel at Westminster on 19 July. On 25 July there was a hastily convened meeting of the Council at Westminster at which the latest plans were approved. Sir John Neville, who was to command the advance guard, was dispatched at once to Southampton. There a desperate scramble was in progress to find ships for him. A fleet of barges, which was being made ready in Plymouth and Dartmouth, was directed to the Solent. A squadron of chartered merchantmen which had recently reached Sandwich from Holland and Zeeland was sent to join them. When these proved to be insufficient the Admirals' clerks were sent round the west country ports yet again to search for ships which had evaded previous sweeps. The King himself proposed to follow as soon as the fleet and army gathering at Sandwich were ready.[46]

The Duke of Bourbon took the field with Bertrand du Guesclin and Marshal Sancerre in the first half of July 1372, probably at Bourges. They were joined towards the end of the month by the Duke of Berry. Their combined force was estimated at about 3,000 men-at-arms and 800 crossbowmen. The army's first task before invading Poitou was to deal with the fortress town of Sainte-Sévère on the River Indre in southern Berry, a thorn in the flesh of the Dukes of Berry and Bourbon and their subjects for several years and a serious threat in the army's rear. They arrived there in about the middle of July. A subsidiary force was sent to invest La Souterraine, thirty-five miles away across the plateau of Bas-Berry. The captain of both fortresses, Sir John Devereux, was at La Rochelle. In his absence the command of Saint-Sévère was assumed by John Fotheringhay, a notorious figure from the past who had achieved brief fame and a considerable fortune as the captain of the *routier* garrison of Creil at the end of the 1350s. He commanded a garrison of 140 *routiers* of diverse nationalities including many local men. On about 30 July 1372, after the siege had been in progress for about two weeks, Sainte-Sévère was taken by storm in an operation which was long remembered as a model of its kind. The French undermined the outer curtain wall at several points. They then divided the circuit into three sectors and, as the mines were fired, launched simultaneous assaults with scaling ladders on all three. The defenders of the curtain wall were overwhelmed too quickly to be able to withdraw to the citadel. Nearly half of them were killed in the fighting and many more were cut down as they tried to escape into the fields. The rest were left to the mercy of the conquerors in accordance with the pitiless laws of war. The French attitude to *routiers* had hardened since the 1350s. They hanged every one of them, apart from those who were judged to be soldiers in the service of Edward III rather than brigands fighting for themselves. Fotheringhay's position was perhaps ambiguous. But he had crossed Marshal Sancerre at an earlier encounter and was put to death with the rest. Another English brigand was only spared by order of the Duke of Bourbon, who recognised him as a man who had served him in England during his years as a hostage in the 1360s. Recalling these events many years later as an old man, Bourbon's standard-bearer thought that only four of the defenders had left the place alive.[47]

The Captal de Buch was at Saint-Jean d'Angély in northern Saintonge. As soon as he knew that the French army had left Bourges he called a council of war. The moment of crisis had clearly arrived. The assembled captains resolved to summon every available man-at-arms from Poitou and Saintonge to confront the invaders. It is impressive that even at this stage and against such long odds the Captal was able to gather most of the more famous names of the Poitevin nobility under his banner. But many of their followers stayed away. By the end of July the Captal is reported to have had about 900 men-at-arms and 500 archers under his command and many of those had been taken from garrisons. Froissart says that the Captal's army had planned to attack the French siege lines at Sainte-Sévère. Sir John Devereux, whose garrison had been holding the place, and Sir Thomas Percy, one of whose cousins was there, were the main supporters of this plan. It

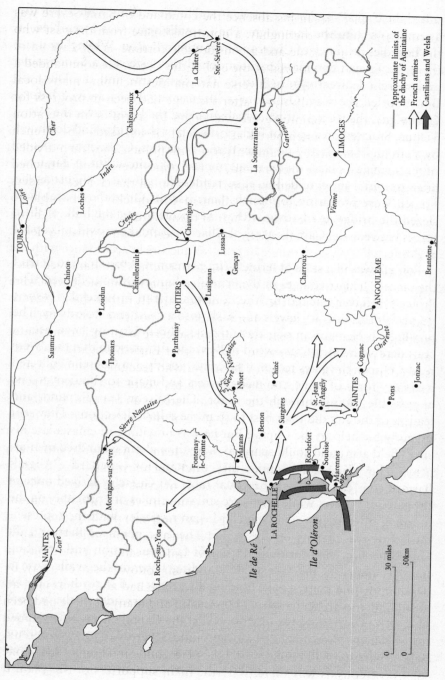

4 The reconquest of Poitou, April–September 1372

Legend:

- Approximate limits of the duchy of Aquitaine
- French armies
- Castilians and Welsh

POITOU 1372

147

suited the Captal's aggressive instincts and he went along with it. But the attempt cost him the campaign. The Captal's army was assembled at the Benedictine abbey of Charroux in southern Poitou. While they were there the French commanders abandoned the siege of La Souterraine and marched directly into Poitou. The Constable and the Duke of Bourbon led the way. On about 1 August 1372 they arrived before Chauvigny, the fortress-town which guarded the bridge over the River Vienne. Situated on a spur of high ground over the bridge and defended by a circuit of walls and no fewer than five castles, Chauvigny was one of the strongest places on the eastern march of Poitou. But its garrison, after an initial show of defiance, surrendered on about 5 August as the French were preparing to launch their assault. Once the French had siezed the bridge at Chauvigny they were able to put the bulk of their forces between the Captal's army at Charroux and the provincial capital at Poitiers.[48]

Poitiers was in a state of ferment. Its garrison was too small to defend the place. The last vestiges of the Prince's administration collapsed. The Prince's receiver packed up the contents of the provincial treasury, 30,000 florins in gold, jewels and cash, into a chest and stole away. The pro-French element among the citizens, who must now have been a considerable majority, sent word to Bertrand du Guesclin that they were ready to open the gates to him if he came quickly. Du Guesclin collected a cavalry force of some 300 men-at-arms and made for Poitiers as fast as possible, riding through the night. The Mayor, Jean Renaud, and leaders of the city did their best to stem the tide of defections. They sent urgently for help to the Captal. But he was unwilling to emasculate his small field army and could spare no more than about a hundred men-at-arms. They rode north under the command of Guichard d'Angle's bastard son Jean. It was an unequal race. Du Guesclin arrived outside the gates of Poitiers while they were still some miles off, probably on the morning of 6 August. Du Guesclin began to parley with the representatives of the citizens on the walls. The epic poem of Bertrand du Guesclin's life, that curious mixture of fact and fiction and arresting images, describes the Constable standing beneath the walls with a handful of attendants, a page holding his helmet as if in readiness for an assault, and offering the city a choice between surrender or the horrors of a sack. They asked for time to deliberate. By now even Renaud and his colleagues recognised defeat. Cautious to the end, they resolved not to surrender to such a small force for fear that the city would be retaken by the Captal before the main French army could arrive. They told the

Constable that they would open their gates when they saw the banners of the Duke of Berry on the horizon. They also made it a condition that the French were not to depart without dealing with the English garrison. As soon as this decision had been made the handful of English soldiers in the city fled for the citadel. Those who failed to make it were seized and bundled out of the gates. On 7 August 1372 the Duke of Berry, having ridden at more than his usual dignified speed from Chauvigny, arrived outside the city. He solemnly received the keys from the Mayor before riding through the streets to cries of 'Montjoie!' from the assembled crowds. The citadel was assaulted from the streets shortly afterwards and after resisting for a day and a half surrendered on terms. Inside the French found just eighteen men, a magnificent ceremonial sword, and the seals of the principality of Aquitaine. In Paris Charles V ordered masses to be celebrated at Notre-Dame.[49]

The news of the fall of Poitiers caused consternation among the Captal's army. The leaders held another council of war. They decided to split the army into two groups, small as it was, and to cling on to a small number of fortified places until help could reach them from England. The Poitevin companies withdrew to the northern march to shut themselves in the fortress-town of Thouars. The rest of the Captal's army, comprising the English and Gascons, withdrew west towards Saintonge and the coast. These dispositions seem to have been made with a view to holding territory through which a relief force might reach Poitou overland from Brittany or by sea from England. But the English encountered considerable resistance in the west. The inhabitants of the walled towns had no desire to see their homes turned into a battlefield. They wanted to surrender to the dominant army, which was manifestly Du Guesclin's. The men of La Rochelle would have declared for Charles V at once if they had not been overawed by the Anglo-Gascon garrison in the citadel. Walter Hewitt, who arrived at Niort with an advance guard of 200 men, found the great citadel on the bank of the Sèvre held by Walter Spridlington's garrison. But the gates of the town were closed in his face. The citizens intended, they said, to receive the French as Poitiers had done. The Captal, who arrived at Niort shortly after Hewitt, was in no mood for this. He was able to enter the citadel from outside the town through a wicket gate and invaded the town from the other side, killing large numbers of the inhabitants in the streets and ordering the summary execution of the ringleaders. A large garrison was left to hold Niort and the road from Poitiers while the rest of the army occupied the surrounding strongholds. Sir Thomas Percy made for La Rochelle. The Captal occupied Saint-Jean d'Angély. Hewitt took a company of men to the south end of the bay of La Rochelle and occupied the fortress of Soubise at the mouth of the Charente.[50]

Owen of Wales and the Welsh and French troops who had sailed with him from Harfleur were still kicking their heels in Santander, while attempts were made to find money to pay them and reinforcements for the invasion of Wales. The French government's commissioner, Jean de Rye, had raised substantial sums by collecting various debts owed to Louis of Anjou by the King of Castile and by realising the remaining value of Bertrand du Guesclin's Castilian estates. But the main obstacle to the enterprise proved to be Henry of Trastámara. He was alarmed by Andeiro's noisy intrigues in Portugal. He had sent an ambassador of his own to Portugal, ostensibly to reconfirm the peace treaty, but in fact to find out what was going on. The ambassador, Diego Lopez de Pacheco, was a venerable figure, by birth Portuguese, who had served as a minister of Don Fernando's grandfather before making his career in Castile. He must have been there while Andeiro and Hore were concluding their business at Braga. On top of the rumours from Portugal came the first reports of Edward III's naval build-up in southern England, which had reached Paris by the last week of July and Burgos by early August. In both places it was believed that Edward III's objective was La Rochelle. With all these pressures crowding in on him Henry was unwilling to allow his galley fleet and his French auxiliaries to leave for Wales on an expedition of doubtful strategic value. As for his subjects, none of them was willing to go. They would rather fight in Granada 'or Persia', they said, than in Wales. Early in August 1372 Henry of Trastámara went in person to Santander to confer with Owen of Wales and the French naval commander Morelet de Montmor. He told them that he would honour his obligations to Charles V and put a fleet of forty Castilian sailing vessels at their disposal. But their destination would be La Rochelle, not Wales. Shortly after this Henry moved his headquarters close to the Portuguese border at Zamora to wait upon events.[51]

Forced to abandon their Welsh project, Morelet de Montmor and Owen of Wales sailed from Santander for La Rochelle in about the middle of August 1372. Their original fleet was reinforced with Castilian merchant ships stuffed with soldiers. Shortly, the ships anchored in the sheltered waters between the Île d'Oléron and the mainland. They landed their men near the small harbour of Marennes.

The Constable and the Duke of Bourbon were still nearly a hundred miles away around Poitiers, suppressing pockets of resistance which might threaten the newly won capital. Learning of Owen's landing on the coast of Saintonge, Du Guesclin detached about 300 men. He put them under the command of the Breton captain Thibault du Pont and Renaud, lord of Pons, and sent them to the coast to support Owen's operations there. In the third week of August the combined French, Welsh and Castilian force laid siege to Hewitt's garrison in the castle of Soubise.[52]

The Captal de Buch was anxious not to find his small army caught between two French ones. He determined to snuff out this second front before it could be built up any further. So he collected as many troops as could be spared from the garrisons of Saintonge and western Poitou. With these men at his back the Captal set off on the evening of 22 August on a bold night-time attack on the French lines around Soubise. It was a dark night in the waning phase of the moon. As they approached the enemy siege lines they tightened the straps of their armour to stop them clinking in the silence. They achieved complete surprise. Shortly after midnight the Anglo-Gascon force, commanded by the Captal in person, fell without warning on the French encampments while Hewitt led a sortie out of the castle with about thirty men-at-arms. The first encampment which the English and Gascons came upon was that of Thibault du Pont and the lord of Pons, who were lodged in the buildings of a monastery church just outside the town. The Captal assaulted the building, scattered the French troops sleeping in the courtyard and captured both commanders. The survivors fled to the encampment of Morelet de Montmor and Owen of Wales, which was a short distance away in a group of suburban buildings.

Owen and Morelet had been warned by the noise and had had time to organise their men. When the Anglo-Gascon attack came it was met with volleys of crossbow fire in front while Owen and Morelet took their men-at-arms around the rear of the attackers and counter-attacked. They fought the assailants hand-to-hand in the dark. The cries of 'Notre-Dame' and 'St. George' were the only means of identification. The Anglo-Gascons were driven back, lost their way, and then found themselves trapped in a dead end in the village of Soubise. Sir Thomas Percy was captured by a Welshman. The Gascon lord of Mareuil surrendered with him. The English Seneschals of Saintonge and Angoumois were both taken. The Captal sold himself dearly. He laid about the French to right and left with his axe, felling any who approached him until he too was overpowered. Like King John at the battle of Poitiers, the Captal is said to have demanded to know whether his captor was a gentleman, 'for I refuse to surrender save to a gentleman though I die by it.' His captor was in fact an extremely impoverished man-at-arms but he could truthfully say that he was 'nobly born, of a knight and a lady'. Once the Captal had been taken the rest of his army disintegrated. The men submitted or fled. Hewitt, who knew the ground better, found his way back across the ditch into the castle. Sir John Cresswell, Sir John Devereux and a few others managed to follow him. As the French prepared to assault the walls of the castle Hewitt and his companions bargained with the enemy for a safe-conduct out. They were the only captains of the Anglo-Gascon army to escape. As day broke the gates of the castle were opened and the French took possession.[53]

Although the battle of Soubise involved very few men, perhaps 600 or 800 on each side, it marked the end of the last hope that the English might have entertained of saving Poitou and Saintonge. With the towns in no position to resist a siege, the Captal had had no realistic alternative but to stake everything on a surprise attack on the enemy in the field. The gamble had almost succeeded. But in the event defeat deprived the English at a stroke of almost all their leaders and probably about half of their reliable troops in the south-west. In Bordeaux the government was in the hands of the Seneschal, Sir Thomas Felton. He was now little more than a caretaker. There was a handful of garrisons left north of the Gironde but they had been stripped to skeleton strength to reinforce the Captal's army. Loyalty was the only currency left to pay them with. The money salvaged from the treasury at Poitiers, which would have paid a thousand men for a quarter, was lost when the receiver of Poitou was murdered by robbers as he tried to reach La Rochelle. In the west the islands and coastal areas of Saintonge surrendered to Morelet de Montmor and Jean de Rye immediately after the battle. The combined French and Castilian fleet then sailed north to blockade La Rochelle. On 30 August 1372 the main body of the French army, with the Dukes of Berry, Burgundy and Bourbon and the Constable at its head, marched west from Poitiers to confront the surviving pockets of English and Gascon troops. On the same day the Duke of Anjou mustered the army of Languedoc at Agen and prepared to march down the Garonne valley. 'Alas, Guienne, now you are truly lost', the Captal is said to have exclaimed to Morelet de Montmor after his capture. 'What are you saying?' replied Morelet, 'Guienne is won.'[54]

In England Edward III's efforts were lost in a chaos of conflicting objectives and administrative disorder. The stream of terrible news from Aquitaine reached Westminster always at least two weeks out of date and often inaccurate. The King's ministers realised by now that the invasion scare of June and July had been a delusion and that the whole of Aquitaine might be lost unless drastic measures were taken to reinforce it. It was probably in the second week of August that they devised yet another strategic plan, the fourth since the beginning of the year. A very large army, about 6,000 men-at-arms and archers, perhaps 8,000 combatants altogether, was waiting on the coast of Kent by the Downs. The new plan appears to have been to land them on the north coast of Brittany and, after relieving Bécherel, to march overland into Poitou, presumably crossing the Loire by the bridge of Nantes. On 11 August 1372 the King left Windsor for the coast. He informed the two archbishops that he had resolved to take the war to the enemy 'manu forti'. Unfortunately Edward's frequent changes of plan had left him badly placed to do this. Many of the men waiting by the Downs had no horses because they had expected to be fighting at sea. There was a large fleet waiting to embark them, 376 ships according to reports reaching the generally well-informed Italian community at Avignon. But they were in the wrong place for a descent on Brittany. Edward arrived at Sandwich on 27 August and boarded his flagship, the *Grace Dieu*. But his ships were pinned to their anchorage in the Downs by stiff contrary winds which continued to blow for a month. John Neville on the other hand, who was waiting at Southampton with his men, was in the right place to reach Brittany but had no ships. None of the west country barges assigned to him had arrived. Some of them had absconded. The chartered ships of Holland and Zeeland were just enough to carry Neville's horses. They were sent ahead. Neville and his companions were compelled to kick their heels in the fields about Southampton 'pur defaute de navye', as he explained when years later he was charged with misconduct by a vengeful Parliament.[55]

On 5 September 1372 the French army arrived before La Rochelle. The citizens had already made up their mind to surrender. They had taken over the town and overpowered its English garrison, who were being held in the cells of the town jail. Froissart tells a pretty story that the captain of La Rochelle, the Englishman Philip Mansel ('not a very intelligent man'), was invited to dinner by the Mayor and tricked into organising a review of the garrison. The review occurred in the plain outside the castle gates on the following morning while the townsmen broke into the castle behind his back. The truth was probably more prosaic, a matter of sleepy sentries and scuffles at night. What is certain is that when the French arrived the citizens were furiously engaged in demolishing the citadel so that they would never again be overawed by the garrison troops of either side. Only on 8 September, when they had completed this task, did they open their gates to admit the French army. The English captain was delivered up to the Duke of Berry and the Duke's troops processed in triumph through the town.

In the rest of Poitou resistance swiftly collapsed. As at Poitiers, the French set about capturing all the small satellite garrisons around La Rochelle which might otherwise have made life intolerable for the newly surrendered town. The isolated castle of Benon, east of La Rochelle, was taken by storm and the entire garrison put to the sword. Marans, north of the town, was held by a garrison of Brabant mercenaries who surrendered it and threw in their lot with the French rather than suffer the same fate. The lesson was not lost on the nobility of Poitou who were still holding out in Thouars. The Duke of Berry had written to their leaders suggesting that they should come to an accommodation. The Poitevins kept their distance but were careful not to lose contact. In the middle of September the majority of them decided to sue for terms. A few dissentients withdrew from the fortress and joined the English garrison at Niort. The rest, the Bishops of Luçon and Maillezais and twenty-three of the leading lay barons of Poitou, appointed plenipotentiaries to negotiate for them. They came before the Dukes of Berry and Burgundy in their camp outside Surgères, a small walled town east of La Rochelle, where the French army was engaged in the siege of the Anglo-Gascon garrison. On 18 September 1372 a truce was agreed for the whole province of Poitou until 30 November. Unless Edward III or the Prince in person relieved Thouars by that date the signatories agreed to submit to Charles V. Charles's lieutenants undertook that they would all recover their possessions and hold them in peace as vassals of the King. At the same time their leader Louis d'Harcourt, having secured his right to be restored to his domains in Poitou, entered into a private convention of his own by which the French King's lieutenants promised him the return of all his confiscated domains in Touraine and the revenues of his family's barony of Saint-Sauveur in the Cotentin as soon as it should be recaptured from the English.[56]

On the following day, 19 September 1372, Surgères surrendered and the French invaded Saintonge and Angoumois. The conquest of these provinces was even swifter than that of Poitou. Saint-Jean d'Angély, which was defended by the remnants of the Captal's garrison, surrendered as soon as the French army came before the walls. At Saintes the acting seneschal, William Farringdon, determined to resist. His men put up a fierce fight from the fortified bridge over the Charente. But the citizens seized the captain at night and forced him to surrender. The conquest of Angoumois was left to subordinate commanders with quite small companies of men but this was enough. Angoulême, the Prince's old capital, which more than any southern town had witnessed the magnificence of the Prince's court in his prime, surrendered at about the same time as La Rochelle. Pons was reoccupied by its lord, Renaud de Pons, after more than a year in which it had been held against him by his estranged wife. The only notable town which still held out for the Prince was Cognac. Its citizens would gladly have surrendered like those of so many other southern towns, and at one point agreed to do so. But the English recovered control in time to stop them and the garrison maintained an isolated defiance there until 1375. Further south, in the valley of the Garonne, another body of French troops under the Duke of Anjou edged closer to Bordeaux, capturing the great border fortress of Le Mas d'Agenais on the western edge of the Agenais. The whole of the remaining holdings of the English in the Agenais had been overrun by the end of September 1372 with the solitary exception of the fortress of Penne on the left bank of the Lot, where an isolated Anglo-Gascon garrison continued to hold out. Penne ultimately surrendered by agreement on New Year's Day.[57]

By this time any prospect of help from England had disappeared. On the day that the magnates of Poitou made their conditional surrender to the Duke of Berry, Edward III's flagship the *Grace Dieu* reached Winchelsea, a progress of barely fifty miles after two weeks of beating into the wind. Nine months after they had been presented to the Great Council at Westminster, the King's ambitious plans for the year had come to nothing. More than £60,000 had been spent on the fleet and the armies of invasion but not a single company of men had left England apart from the companions of the Earl of Pembroke and some minor reinforcements for the garrison of Calais. It was getting late in the season. The requisitioned merchantmen which provided the bulk of Edward III's transports were urgently required for the annual wine fleet to Bordeaux. The King would probably have had a mutiny on his hands if he had not released them. Most of the ships and the men serving in them were paid off on 6 October. Edward himself refused to give up. He insisted that the campaign was not over and declared that he expected to be at sea for another three weeks. It was not until 14 October that he agreed to disembark from the *Grace Dieu* after seven weeks on board.

The Prince recognised defeat earlier than his father. On 5 October he came before a packed meeting of the Council at Westminster bearing the charters investing him with the principality of Aquitaine. He declared to the assembled prelates, peers and royal officials that he was resigning all of his continental titles and possessions into Edward's hands. One of the Council, Guy Brian, a respected veteran of Edward's wars whose service dated back to the Scottish campaigns of the 1330s, asked the Prince whether that was really his wish. The Prince replied that it was. Less than a fifth of the great territory which he had ruled in 1364 now remained under English control.[58]

England's only continental allies, Brittany and Portugal, were swiftly engulfed in the disaster. On 16 October 1372, six months late, Neville finally sailed from Southampton with the wine fleet, escorted by ships of war of England and Bayonne. He landed at Saint-Mathieu at the western tip of Finistère with just under 1,000 men. From here he swiftly took possession of Brest and a number of other walled places of the far west. A well-trained force even of this modest size might have made a great difference to John de Montfort's fortunes in the summer, but in October it was too late. Bécherel had surrendered. In vain John de Montfort pleaded with the besiegers to take possession of it in his name. They claimed it for the King of France. The news of Neville's arrival completed the destruction of the Duke's cause. There was uproar among the prelates and leading noblemen of Brittany when they heard about it. The French King moved swiftly to exploit their anger. He had a large army at his disposal in north-western Poitou which was waiting for 1 December, the date appointed for the surrender of Thouars. On 22 October 1372 these forces were diverted north. On the 28th the Constable, the Dukes of Berry, Burgundy and Bourbon, and the Marshal Louis de Sancerre invaded Brittany. On the 30th they were before Rennes. Their suspicions about John de Montfort were soon confirmed. The march had been so swift that John's English Duchess, who was in Rennes when their approach was reported, only just had time to flee. She was caught a few miles south of the city on the road to Vannes by soldiers of the Duke of Bourbon. Many years later, when he was an old man, the Duke of Bourbon's standard-bearer recalled that when her baggage was searched they found a copy of her husband's treaty with Edward III which Neville had brought with him from

England. 'Am I a prisoner?' the Duchess asked the Duke of Bourbon when she was brought before him. 'No, Madam,' he replied. 'We do not make war against women.' But her husband, he added before releasing her, was 'playing a foolish game from which he will not easily extricate himself'.[59]

John de Montfort tried to extricate himself, but as the Duke of Bourbon had foreseen it was not easy. He wrote to the King of France admitting that he had invited the English in, but saying that he had done it only in order to maintain his authority against Olivier de Clisson and other rebellious barons. He entered into direct negotiations with the leaders of the French army outside Rennes, protesting his good faith. A compromise was eventually patched up under which John agreed that he would expel the foreigners from his duchy and the French agreed to withdraw their army from Rennes. But he never intended to honour it. Instead he made his way to the fortress of Brest, where he met Neville and his officers and secretly ratified the treaty with Edward III. Charles V's emissary, Guillaume Mauvinet, who came before the Duke to deliver the King's protest against this treachery, was treated to a charade in which John called the English captains before him and ordered them to depart. The only reason, he explained, why they were slow in complying was that ships could not be found to carry them back to England. In fact John did nothing to expel Neville's men and according to reports reaching Paris had even appealed to Edward III to send more.

The French made the most of their discovery of John's secret diplomacy. The text of the Anglo-Breton treaty was widely distributed in Brittany and provoked mass desertions among the Breton nobility. Several of them swore never to serve him again. By the end of the year John de Montfort's administration was still effective in Finistère, around Vannes and in the Guérande peninsula west of Nantes, but almost nowhere else. Neville succeeded in occupying a handful of ducal castles in the extreme west but his garrisons were confined there by a wall of local hostility.[60]

Fernando of Portugal suffered his own nemesis shortly afterwards. He may not have known about the battle of La Rochelle when he sealed the treaty of Braga with John of Gaunt's emissaries in July. But he does not seem to have been shaken by the news of the battle, which must have reached him shortly afterwards, nor by the succession of reverses which the English suffered in south-western France in August and September, nor even by the growing signs of unrest in his own kingdom.

His marriage and the large-scale changes of personnel at court which had followed it remained profoundly unpopular with the Portuguese nobility. His aggressive foreign policy was equally unwelcome to the mercantile oligarchies of the towns. Diego Pacheco reported to Henry of Trastámara on his mission to Portugal at Zamora at about the end of August 1372. He advised an immediate invasion of Portugal. Don Fernando was too weak at home to put up any serious resistance. He thought that disaffection was so strong in Lisbon that a fifth column in the Portuguese capital might rise up on Henry's approach and deliver it to him. Pacheco's advice provoked vigorous debate in the Castilian King's council. Ultimately Henry resolved to advance into Portugal. He had the same exaggerated view of England's capacity to launch an army across a thousand miles of ocean as Fernando did and was determined to snuff out the Anglo-Portuguese alliance before the English arrived. At the end of November 1372 Fernando began to realise the seriousness of his position. Juan Fernández Andeiro, who was still at the Portuguese court, was sent back urgently to England to get help.

In about the middle of December 1372 Henry of Trastámara crossed the frontier west of Ciudad Rodrigo with a mixed army of his Castilian vassals and French mercenaries. Pacheco's assessment of the country's defences proved to be correct. The French and Castilians swept aside resistance around the frontier fortress of Almeida, captured the city of Viseu and then turned south. A second Castilian army, largely recruited in Andalusia and commanded by the masters of the military orders of Santiago and Calatrava, entered Portugal at the same time by the Tagus valley at Alcántara. The two wings joined forces at Coimbra at the end of the year and prepared to advance on Lisbon. In Seville, where the Castilian fleet was being refitted and resupplied after the exertions of the summer, twelve galleys were being made ready to attack the Portuguese capital from the sea. Fernando stood by helplessly.[61]

In Poitou the end had come. In the last days of November 1372 the French army began to gather outside the walls of Thouars. Inside the fortress the leaders of the local nobility were waiting for 1 December, the day appointed for them to submit to the Crown of France unless Edward III or the Prince got through to them with a relief force. The abandonment of Edward III's seaborne expedition was known in the principality by now. In Bordeaux Sir Thomas Felton was desperately trying to assemble a relief force from the shrunken remnant of the principality still under his control. He succeeded in raising a small scratch army from the loyal nobility of the Bordelais and southern

Périgord. With only a short time to go before the deadline Felton marched north to Niort. There he found the remaining English captains waiting for him: Sir Digory Say, Sir John Devereux and Sir John Cresswell. They had a handful of Poitevin loyalists with them. The total strength of the English and their allies was about 1,200 men-at-arms. Felton and his colleagues sent a herald forward to the Poitevins in Thouars. He knew, he said, that they had bound themselves to surrender the town if they were not relieved by the King or the Prince in person. But only the 'fortunes of the sea' had stopped them from coming to the Poitevins' aid. He urged them to make a sortie from the walls and join forces with him to confront the French in battle. These proposals provoked agonised debate inside the citadel of Thouars where the sentiments of the Poitevins were still very much with Edward III. The lord of Parthenay spoke strongly for accepting Felton's proposal and offered various reasons why it was consistent with the oaths that they had sworn to the French. But no one else took this view. The herald returned to Niort bearing their excuses and a copy of their treaty with the French leaders. Felton contemplated challenging the French army. But his scouts reported that there were more than 3,000 French troops drawn up in battle order in the plain south of Thouars with their banners unfurled. His men refused to continue against such odds and he was forced to withdraw. On 1 December 1372 the Poitevins came out of the gates of Thouars unarmed and rode into the French camp. Later that day, in the Franciscan church at Loudun, they did homage to the Duke of Berry as Count of Poitiers. On 11 December the three royal dukes and the Constable entered Paris, accompanied by the leading barons of Poitou and bringing the prisoners of Soubise in their train. On the following day there was a magnificent ceremony in the great hall of the Louvre. The Duke of Berry did homage for Poitou to his brother the King. The Poitevins for their part swore oaths of loyalty to the Crown, promising to uphold its rights against all persons, 'especially the King of England and his children'.[62]

The surrender of Thouars left the English with just five places of any military value in Poitou: La Roche-sur-Yon and Mortagne-sur-Sèvre in the Vendée; Lusignan and Gençay, south of Poitiers; and the walled town of Niort in the west. Felton left Sir John Devereux in command of these places when he returned to Bordeaux in December. The combined strength of their garrisons seems to have been between 1,000 and 1,200 men. Devereux did what he could to hang on to these enclaves. He established his headquarters at Niort and maintained a spirited guerilla war for another four months, but he was in an impossible position. The hostility of the inhabitants of Niort made the place difficult to defend. The scattered distribution of his forces made it equally difficult to fight in the field. In February 1373 Bertrand du Guesclin returned to the province with an army largely composed of Breton companies and converts among the local nobility to mop up Devereux's garrisons. Olivier de Clisson laid siege to Mortagne-sur-Sèvre and La Roche-sur-Yon. The French Seneschal of Poitou laid siege to Lusignan. The Constable himself prowled about Niort with a field force of some 500 men.[63]

By denuding his garrisons Devereux succeeded in collecting together a field force of about 800, just enough to achieve local superiority against the dispersed French forces. With these he embarked on a campaign of rapid spoiling raids against the French siege operations in a style reminiscent of Du Guesclin's own. He attacked Clisson's detachment in early March and forced him to abandon the siege of Mortagne. Clisson had to flee in the middle of his dinner. At about the end of the month Devereux almost achieved the same thing against the Constable, but this time the outcome was disaster. It happened at Chizé, a small walled town about fifteen miles south of Niort on the banks of the River Boutonne, where an isolated company of English troops was defying the much larger forces of the Constable from the walls. Devereux's army outnumbered the Constable's and initially had the better of the encounter but the French rallied and drove them back, eventually putting them to flight. Devereux lost almost all of his men in this battle and he himself was taken prisoner along with most of his captains. The men of Niort opened their gates as soon as the news of Devereux's fate reached them. La Roche-sur-Yon surrendered to Olivier de Clisson in the summer after a siege of some five months. Mortagne was recovered by the French at about the same time, after Devereux had accepted a 10,000 gold francs reduction of his ransom in return for ordering the garrison to surrender.

Lusignan held out for longer by dint of its powerful situation, but the garrison had suffered grievous losses at Chizé and was confined to the walls by the *bastides* which the French constructed across the approaches. Lusignan had once been among the most profitable centres of brigandage in southern France. Its powerful position and prodigious walls and ditches became the stuff of legend within a generation of these events. But, by the spring of 1374, the garrison was unable to raid or forage and the place remained in English hands after 1372 only by virtue of a subsidy from Bordeaux. Even that was not enough. The fortress opened its gates to the Duke of Berry in September 1374. In his later years the Duke encouraged the story that that tough old freebooter, Sir John Cresswell, had decided to surrender it when, lying in bed with his mistress, he saw a vision of its mythical creator the enchantress Mélusine. The truth is more prosaic. Cresswell had been captured by Marshal Sancerre while trying to ambush the cortege of the Duchess of Berry. He was persuaded to surrender Lusignan in lieu of his own ransom and that of Sir Thomas Percy, one of the leading prisoners of Soubise.

Only one notable Anglo-Gascon garrison now survived in Poitou, at Gençay, the great triangular fortress whose ruins still stand on a rocky outcrop above the River Cloyère south of Poitiers. Gençay belonged to the Welsh knight Sir Digory Say and his Poitevin wife and step-daughter. The three of them defended it for nearly two years after the battle of Chizé with the aid of a garrison of Englishmen and Gascons. It finally surrendered in February 1375.[64]

The English had put down deeper roots in Poitou than in any other part of France and for them the loss of the province was unexpectedly painful. Prominent Englishmen had acquired land in Poitou. They had become closely integrated with the indigenous nobility in a way that they had never done even after two centuries of possession in the Gascon heartland of the principality, with its pride of place, self-contained clans, awkward dialect and reputation for difficult friendships. Sir Digory Say had held three substantial lordships in Poitou either through his wife or by grant of the Prince. Sir Simon Burley, the future tutor of Richard II, was another Englishman who had married a rich Poitevin widow and settled agreeably in the province. Walter Spridlington, who had been captain of Poitiers since 1361, was a modest squire but he married a local widow of fortune and became in a decade one of the richer English settlers, with lands scattered across the province. Robert Granton, one of the Prince's clerks who served as his receiver for Poitou, had grown fat on grants made by the Prince from the confiscated lands of those who had gone over to the French. These men lost everything in 1372.[65]

Their losses were perhaps the ordinary fortunes of war, which such men had to accept as risks of their profession. The position of the indigenous nobility of Poitou was more complicated. After the surrender of Thouars they kept their lands and almost all of them served Charles V and the Duke of Berry as loyally as they had previously served the Prince. Louis d'Harcourt and the lord of Parthenay were prominent among the Poitevin contingents fighting with Bertrand du Guesclin at Chizé. One Poitevin member of John of Gaunt's household in England, hearing of the fall of Poitiers, resolved to join his next campaign in France with the express purpose of deserting as soon as he could. Only a handful of men followed the English into exile and most of these were humble men with little to lose and strong attachments to English patrons. But a few were considerable figures who might have made a different choice. Guichard d'Angle, perhaps the closest of the Prince's Poitevin confidants, never returned to Poitou after his release from captivity in Castile. He ended his days in England as Earl of Huntingdon, a curious evolution for a man who had spent his whole adult life before 1360 fighting against the English. Even that great Anglophobe, the poet Eustache Deschamps, found time to write a lament for him after his death in 1380, calling him Poitou's finest soldier for whom there was nothing to reproach. Guichard's bastard son Jean remained, like his father, loyal to the English for the rest of his days and his nephew William probably also accompanied him to England. But his legitimate daughters and their husbands promptly switched their allegiance to Charles V and received a grant of his confiscated lands.

Even more difficult were the dilemmas of the families of English settlers, who found themselves inhabiting an unfamiliar twilight world, neither English nor wholly French. Sir John Harpeden, the Prince's Seneschal of Saintonge in 1372, had married a sister of Olivier de Clisson in the 1360s at a time when Clisson was an intimate of the Prince of Wales. His son was brought up in Clisson's household, became a Frenchman and founded a distinguished Poitevin dynasty. When John the elder returned to Aquitaine as Richard II's Seneschal in 1385 John the younger was a prominent figure at the court of Charles VI, enjoying his father's forfeited estates in Poitou, serving as French seneschal in the march province of Périgord and fighting in French armies, as his descendants continued to do until the twentieth century. So far as we know father and son never met again after 1372.

Poitevin women who married English soldiers and administrators felt these dilemmas acutely, especially when they had property and kin in the province. Guichard d'Angle's wife hung on to her husband's castle at Château-Larcher during his captivity in Castile and was able to negotiate a personal truce with the Duke of Berry, for Guichard, says Froissart, 'although a loyal English partisan was not excessively hateful in French eyes'. She seems to have stayed in France once her husband was released from captivity. Simon Burley's wife also seems to have stayed behind when he returned to England. The elder Harpeden's second wife, Catherine Senechal, was still in her early twenties when her husband was captured at the sea battle of La Rochelle. She commanded the brief defence of the citadel of Fontenay-le-Comte against the Duke of Burgundy in October 1372 after the town below had been surrendered by its citizens. Her mother married Sir Digory Say. Mother and daughter played a prominent part in the defence of Gençay against the French. And when the end came both of them followed their husbands to England. Catherine later claimed always to have been a Frenchwoman at heart, which may well have been true, for she returned to France as soon as her husband died and married a retainer of the Duke of Berry. But her mother stayed on in England after the death of Sir Digory, where she kept a comfortable household and survived into the following century. Humbler women fared less well. Agnes Forget, a widow of Fontenay-le-Comte, had married an English soldier of the garrison and had a son by him. When the place fell her husband vanished. Her fellow citizens gleefully seized her property and drove her out of the town to beg for alms in the streets of Paris. We cannot know what hidden rancours had built up over the decade in which the English had occupied Fontenay-le-Comte and similar places, but Agnes's story was probably not unusual.[66]

With the reconquest of Poitou and Saintonge Charles V and his captains had succeeded in recovering substantially all of the territory ceded to England at the treaties of Brétigny and Calais. Unable for logistical and financial reasons to counter-attack in force, the English resorted increasingly to irregular warfare fought in their name by free companies of Gascons. Their operations followed a consistent geographical pattern which reflected the declining fortunes of the English principality. They were concentrated in the *massif* of Auvergne, which had never been ruled by the English, and in the provinces of Aquitaine from which the English King's officers had been progressively expelled since 1369. Auvergne was still the natural fortress that it had been when the Arverni tribes had held out against the Romans. Although relatively poor, its remote valleys and difficult terrain made it an ideal defensive redoubt. Its position at the head of all the great river valleys of western France enabled the companies to launch raids into the surrounding lowlands over considerable distances from their bases.

In the reconquered provinces the main factors were political. The French reoccupation of Quercy, Rouergue, Limousin and Périgord had been achieved mainly by forging alliances with prominent local noblemen and leading figures in the towns. These men expected to emerge as dominant figures in the politics of their regions, which by and large they did. But what they gained in the process their local enemies and rivals lost. The massive disturbance of local patterns of power which usually followed the restoration of French administration tended to create a class of losers who provided the essential support for the local operations of the Gascon companies. Only in Poitou did a different pattern emerge, and that was because it was the only province of Aquitaine which the French recovered by force of arms alone. Its nobility and its towns remained completely loyal to the Prince until the end; and when the end came the whole political community accepted the incoming regime. The old solidarities survived. The impact of the change was therefore smaller in Poitou than it was anywhere else and the companies never made any significant inroads there.

In the early 1370s the major figure among the captains operating in south-western France was Bertucat d'Albret. He was one of the few independent captains with a clear strategic vision. His force of personality enabled him to impose it on other captains in a way that no one else had done since the days of Arnaud de Cervole and Séguin de Badefol. Like many of the leading Gascon *routiers* Bertucat was the acknowledged bastard of a noble father. But although nobly born and brought up in the profession of arms, he was excluded by convention from a share of the landed wealth of his family. Bertucat was truly rootless, a professional captain living on the spoils of his company. His position was very similar to that of the many other captains in the irregular war who were either illegitimate or else younger sons in regions where primogeniture was the rule of succession. Philippe de Mézières, an astute observer of the habits of his class, put his finger on their dilemma. They were men who

by the custom of the land have little or no portion of the inheritance of their fathers and who are often forced by poverty to follow unjust and tyrannical wars in order to sustain their nobility, for they know no other trade than the profession of arms. In this way they do so much harm that I dare not relate all the looting and violence by which they oppress the poor.[67]

After the collapse of English rule in Quercy the province remained the main centre of Bertucat's operations for the next four years. The combined strength of his company and Bernard de la Salle's was reported in 1371 to be about 160 men-at-arms and about 500 mounted infantry, a very substantial force by the standard of fourteenth-century companies. At least eleven garrisons in Quercy are known to have operated under their control in this period, in addition to the important bridge town of Espalion on the Lot in western Rouergue. The list is certainly incomplete. As the English progressively retreated from the eastern provinces of Aquitaine the *routiers* expanded the range and scale of their operations to fill the void. A loose federation of Gascon companies occupied fortresses distributed in a broad arc extending from the Tarn in the south to the Vienne in the north. Their methods were the classic methods of irregular soldiers throughout the Hundred Years War. They spied out the defences of castles and small towns, suborned the defenders or introduced their companions on market days disguised as merchants or peasants. They clambered over dark sections of the walls from ladders at dead of night or forced their way through gateways opened for them from within. They put small groups of men into well-sited castles within easy marching distance of each other. Their garrisons had their own captains and operated more or less autonomously. But they worked together, dividing the region into ransom districts which they shared out among themselves and joining forces to mount long-distance raids or to fight off attacks from the armies of the King's lieutenants. They strangled the commerce of the greater commercial towns, preying on merchants, ransoming travellers and carrying off townsmen working in the vineyards and vegetable plots by the walls. Then, when conditions became difficult, they sold out, took their profit, and re-established themselves elsewhere.[68]

On 14 October 1371, shortly before dawn, Bertucat d'Albret and Bernard de la Salle captured Figeac. Figeac was an important market town on the western march of Quercy with substantial walls, a rich Benedictine abbey and a fortified bridge over the River Célé. Its prosperity was measured by the loot. The immediate haul of jewellery, plate and other valuables was reckoned at 50,000 francs plus 4,000 florins worth of foodstuffs. Bernard de la Salle commemorated the event by receiving his knighthood from his companion in arms in the public square of the town (the modern Place Carnot). They had good reason to be satisfied with their work. They moved their headquarters into the town, recruited fresh gangs of adventurers across Gascony and used the place as a base for long-range raiding. For the inhabitants of the surrounding region it was a disaster. Most of the population of the town abandoned it to the conquerors and settled temporarily in a hill-town five miles away. The rest of northern Quercy was parcelled out into ransom districts and shared among Bertucat's captains. The records of the small town of Martel in northern Quercy tell us something of what it meant to live in the region during the occupation: sentries standing guard day and night on the walls and towers; continual reports of cavalcades leaving Figeac two, three or five hundred strong; speculation about the direction in which they were going; frightened letters between the towns of the region asking for news; delegations sent with bags of cash to redeem their friends from the cells of Bertucat's castles; and the perennial fear of spies and traitors within their own walls ready to let in Bertucat's bands in return for a share of the spoil. Further afield the threat was more sporadic. But over the following months mounted raiding forces from Figeac penetrated deep into southern Quercy. The revenues of the cathedral chapter of Cahors fell to less than a sixth of their pre-war levels.

The French response perfectly illustrated the impotence of the King's officers in the face of well-organised guerilla operations away from the main theatres of the war. The fall of Figeac had not come as a bolt from the blue. The place was known to be vulnerable, a low-lying valley town with no professional garrison whose population had been much reduced by plague and war losses. Bertucat d'Albret and Bernard de la Salle had prowled around the walls for more than a year before they finally took it. Yet the French King's officers in the region did nothing to save it or to recover the place after it was taken. This was probably a rational decision. It would have required a large army to lay siege to a town the size of Figeac. Neither the King nor his Lieutenant in Languedoc was willing to divert resources from other tasks of greater strategic value. They treated the elimination of *routier* garrisons in the former English provinces as a problem for the local communities, to be financed out of local revenues on top of the ordinary burdens of war taxation. For their part the local communities usually preferred to buy the *routiers* out, which was cheaper and surer than a major siege even if the result was to swell the raiders' profits and encourage them to resettle elsewhere.[69]

In the case of Figeac even a buy-out took more than eighteen months to organise. It involved the representatives of at least five provinces within riding range of Figeac: Quercy, Rouergue, Auvergne, Limousin and Gevaudan, none of whom could agree about the amount to be paid or its distribution among the various contributors. They appealed for help to the King, who referred them to the Duke of Anjou, who referred them on to the Count of Armagnac and his son. There was a succession of ill-tempered meetings and at least two abortive treaties with the

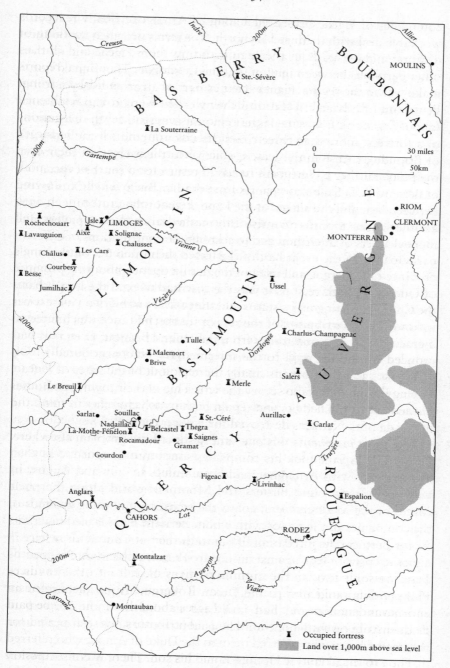

5 Principal *routier* garrisons of the Gascon march, 1370–1373

companies of Figeac before the Count of Armagnac finally reached a workable deal with them in May 1373. The terms provided for Bertucat d'Albret and Bernard de la Salle to withdraw from Figeac and all their other garrisons between the Lot and the Dordogne. They agreed not to make war in the region again except as part of an army led by a son or lieutenant of Edward III. For this they were to be paid 120,000 francs (about £20,000). It was the largest amount ever paid for the evacuation of a fortress, more than three times the amount paid for the *videment* of Brioude or Anse in the 1360s, which had themselves set records in their day. Further payments must have been exacted for the evacuation of Bernard de la Salle's companies from the Limousin, which was agreed between him and the agents of the Pope at about the same time. It took another three months to raise the money from the taxpayers and moneylenders of the region and to sort out the contributions of different participants. In the event half of the immense burden fell on the single province of Rouergue and most of the rest on the neighbouring province of Quercy. In both regions it was the towns who paid the lion's share, the Church insisting on its status and the military nobility on its services in kind. The contribution of the rest of southern France was limited to a gracious aid of 4,000 francs from the Duke of Anjou. Even that was reduced by the fee paid to the intermediary who negotiated it. On 3 August 1373 the Gascons finally marched out of the gates of Figeac, leaving the inhabitants to survey the wreckage of their town: 500 houses burned out or trashed beyond repair, both parish churches in ruins and the trade of the citizens destroyed for a generation.[70]

Like most *videments* this one simply shifted the problem elsewhere. Bernard de la Salle took his companies south into Languedoc as soon as the treaty with Armagnac had been sealed. In July and August he was operating around Béziers and Montpellier and along the trade routes of the Mediterranean coast, the traditional hunting grounds of the companies of the 1360s with whom Bernard had learned his trade. As for Bertucat, he hired himself out to the city of Cahors for service in a vicious private war against an unruly French nobleman, Philippe de Jean. At some time in the autumn of 1373 he fell into the hands of Philippe who sold him to the Duke of Anjou. Anjou demanded an enormous ransom and had him held in chains in the fortress of Roquemaure on the Rhône until he paid it. He was not seen again until the beginning of 1377.[71]

The Provençal lawyer Honoré Bonet was not the only contemporary to ask himself why lowly peasants and townsmen should have to suffer

for the quarrels of their sovereigns. Nor was he the only one to answer
that by the fruits of their labour they gave their rulers the means to fight
their wars. It followed that 'if on both sides war is decided upon and
begun by the councils of the two kings the soldiery may take spoil from
the kingdom at will and make war freely.' In contemporary eyes the
men responsible for these acts were 'English' although, as Froissart's
good knight Bonne-Lance observed, they were 'not English by
nationality, but Gascons fighting the Englishman's wars'. In fact many
of them were not even Gascons but Béarnais or even Bretons. Yet the
label was in a larger sense justified. Bertucat d'Albret and Bernard de la
Salle, like almost all the *routier* captains operating in the south-west,
declared themselves to be Edward III's captains, proclaiming their
allegiance on their banners and in their treaties and safe-conducts. They
needed the legitimacy which these symbols conferred on their violence.
A lawful war in the eyes of medieval men meant a war, however
indiscriminate its violence or innocent its victims, which was fought by
the authority of a sovereign prince. If a *routier* captain was ever
captured his allegiance might make the difference between being
ransomed as a prisoner of war or being hanged or drowned as a bandit.
Not for nothing did Charles of Artois, a French nobleman who fought
a long guerilla war against the Valois monarchy in the lower Loire with
a mixed band of English and French soldiers, come before Robert
Knolles during the campaign of 1370 to ask for a banner and a tunic
with the King of England's arms. Many years later when the Limousin
routier Mérigot Marchès was on trial for his life in Paris, his defence
consisted of a string of incidents designed to demonstrate that his wars
were authorised by John of Gaunt and Richard II of England.[72]

Such claims were often justified, as indeed they had sometimes been
in Mérigot's case. The belligerent status of the leading Gascon *routiers*
was tacitly and sometimes overtly recognised at Westminster and
Bordeaux, a symptom of the increasingly close relations between the
English government and the companies. A small number of *routier*
garrisons which were conceived to be important to the defence of the
Bordelais were subsidised from the revenues of the duchy. Well-known
routiers were appointed as royal captains in distant provinces, as Sir
John Devereux had been in the Limousin and Bernard de la Salle would
be after him. They appeared as the English King's representatives on
the joint commissions which enforced truces. They dealt regularly with
the English King's Council in Bordeaux. Indeed Bertucat ended his
career in the 1380s as one of them. Some even visited England and

maintained direct relations with the court at Westminster. In return the English King's ministers, although they could never control the operations of the companies, enjoyed a degree of influence over many of them. Active co-operation between the English King's officers and the free companies, which had once been rare, became normal and even indispensable in the 1370s and 1380s. English and Gascon captains co-ordinated their military enterprises with those of English armies in the field. Bertucat d'Albret had fought with Sir John Chandos in Quercy. Bernard de la Salle supported John of Gaunt's operations in the Massif Central at the end of 1373. The companies at Saint-Sauveur received nothing from the English Exchequer and not all of them were English. But they accepted captains appointed by Edward III and in 1370 they even complied with instructions to moderate their looting when it briefly became a diplomatic embarrassment. This was perhaps the ultimate test for garrisons whose main purpose was looting. Yet it was by no means uncommon. In 1372 Bernard de la Salle was ordered by the Prince's representatives in Gascony to withdraw from one of the towers of Merle in Bas-Limousin, which he had taken from a kinsman of the Pope. Eventually and with ill grace, he did so.[73]

CHAPTER V

John of Gaunt in France
1373–1374

When Parliament opened at Westminster at the beginning of November 1372 it was Guy Brian, an experienced and well-liked soldier with no personal responsibility for the disasters of the summer, who was charged with the task of explaining what had gone wrong. There were in fact a large number of reasons for the English defeat, including misfortunes and misjudgments of a sort inseparable from the conduct of war. But the main themes of Brian's address, which extended over the best part of two sessions, were the lack of means to defend Aquitaine and the poverty of England's naval resources. Parliament sat for three weeks. Most of this time must have been devoted to a lengthy post-mortem on the events of the summer and plans for recovery in the following year.[1]

Guy Brian's diagnosis of the problems of Aquitaine is confirmed by the copious records generated by the English war effort. The loss of Poitou and Saintonge had deprived the principality of its most productive provinces and what remained was incapable of financing its defence. The clerks who reported on the revenues of Aquitaine after the Prince's resignation found that they amounted to less than £1,500 sterling a year which was barely a twentieth of the Prince's internal revenues in 1368–9. Only the districts around Bordeaux still accounted to the Treasurer of the duchy. The wine customs, which accounted for most of the duchy's receipts, had fallen catastrophically. The pound of Bordeaux, traditionally worth 4s sterling, had by now been devalued to 2s 8d, a fall of a third. This was perhaps the lowest point of the duchy's financial fortunes, but they never improved by much. For the next two decades its revenues would never exceed about £2,500 sterling a year which was hardly enough to pay for internal administration let alone defence. Between October 1372 and April 1374 the Seneschal, Sir Thomas Felton, personally funded the government of Aquitaine to the tune of more than £8,000, presumably by borrowing on his own credit and paying his retinue from his own pocket, an extraordinary contribution for a Norfolk knight with broad acres and rich patrons but no great fortune. The duchy was now more heavily dependent on England than it had ever previously been in the three centuries of its history. Felton's enormous deficit was ultimately repaid from the English customs. In the long run Exchequer subsidies would be required to pay most of the ongoing costs of the duchy's government.

Nor was Gascony's dependence on England only financial. Almost all the famous Gascon captains were dead or in prison or had transferred their allegiance to the French. In the following years the English kings found themselves employing Englishmen not just as provincial seneschals and receivers, as the Prince had done, but as captains of most of the significant garrisons. The defence of the region against any major French offensive would depend on the despatch of troops from England. Even the duchy's food supplies depended in difficult years on exports of grain from England now that the grain-growing regions had been lost and the traffic of the river valleys was disrupted by war.[2]

The other element of Guy Brian's lament, the decline of English seapower, probably struck a stronger chord than the fate of Aquitaine. The main conclusion which the English ministers drew from their defeats in 1372 was that their naval forces were completely inadequate for confronting the French and Castilian galley fleets now ranged against them. This was a more intractable problem. Or rather it was two problems: one relating to the protection of English seaborne trade, the other to the defence of the long, exposed English coast-line. Chaucer's merchant was not the only Englishman who 'wolde the see were kept for any thing bitwixte Middelburgh and Orewelle'. By 1372, and probably earlier, armed convoys were operating both in the North Sea and across the Bay of Biscay. The expense of the escorting ships and their complements of soldiers was met by a special levy (tunnage and poundage) on cargoes, which was passed straight on to shippers in higher freight charges together with the cost of the double crews required by merchant ships in wartime. The result was a rise in costs which fell ultimately on producers, depressing their margins in already difficult trading conditions. Coastal raids added to their woes. There had been one damaging attack on the Solent by French galleys and barges in 1369 and another, less damaging, in 1370. In the following year there had been a brief and violent naval war with Flanders, provoked by some piratical incidents between English and Flemish seamen. Squadrons of Flemish merchantmen had landed raiding parties several hundred strong in Yorkshire and in Dorset and escaped with impunity after inflicting a good deal of damage on nearby settlements.

The political impact of even occasional coastal raids or losses at sea was out of all proportion to the damage actually done.[3]

The most effective defence was to attack the enemy's ships in their ports. The English had often tried to do this but had only once succeeded, in January 1340, when they had destroyed almost all of the French galley fleet as it lay beached in Boulogne harbour. The French were not caught out like that again. In the late fourteenth century their war fleet was well protected in the arsenal at Rouen or within the sea-walls of Harfleur. Generally, the English admirals were obliged to conduct erratic scouting expeditions with fast barges, and sweeps of the Channel with small fleets of requisitioned merchant ships, all in the hope of a chance encounter with the enemy at sea. These campaigns were exceptionally expensive and almost always fruitless. They required a carelessly exposed enemy, outstanding intelligence and a fleet armed and ready to act on it quickly, ideal conditions which were rarely encountered. So in times of danger coast-guards waited day after day beside unlit beacons on cliff-tops waiting for the appearance of French raiders. Coastguard duty was boring, unpopular and often evaded. The Commons complained about this too. Yet the results of so much effort were notoriously patchy. The Solent was heavily defended after 1370. Elsewhere it took up to twenty-four hours to collect the local levies and even longer to bring in reinforcements from inland. By the time they arrived the invaders had usually taken their spoil and vanished.[4]

After the disasters of 1372 the English government devoted a growing share of its slender resources to naval operations. The solution according to Edward's ministers was to build up a specialised fleet of oared vessels on the model of other Atlantic powers. They might have been less impressed by the potential of these vessels if they had known about the difficulties which France and Castile had encountered in operating them in northern waters. But one advantage which they undoubtedly possessed was that they were less affected by the caprice of the winds. Guy Brian blamed the 'contrariouseté de vent' for the naval disasters of 1372, and this became an article of faith with Edward III's Council. England already had about twenty relatively small oared barges, most of which belonged to the Cinque Ports or various private entrepreneurs. In the first days of the new Parliament the King was authorised to order the construction of fifteen large new barges in designated ports of eastern and southern England at the expense of the ports themselves. Several ministers and courtiers, including Latimer, Buxhill and William Neville, also built and fitted out barges at their own expense. Some of these were very substantial ships. The *Paul of London*, of which we have a particularly complete description, was to be eighty feet long with eighty oars, equipment for sixty archers and a great mast with three fortified topcastles. At the same time the King embarked on the construction of the 'new galley' of 180 oars in a great pit by the River Stour outside Canterbury. This vessel, later called the *Katherine*, was comparable in size to the standard Mediterranean galleys of Genoa and Castile. She was for some years the pride of the royal fleet.[5]

The government hoped for greater things by forging an alliance with Genoa, the major galley power of the Mediterranean, which Edward III's ministers hoped might play the same role for England as Castile did for France. In spite of the botched intrigues with disaffected Genoese exiles earlier in the year, relations with the republic were reasonably cordial. Genoese merchants had important commercial interests in Bruges and the Low Countries which depended on the free passage of their merchant fleets through the Channel. The republic was sensitive to this fact now that the English controlled both sides of the Narrows. The new Doge, Domenico de Campo Fregoso, had already undertaken not to support the French or Castilian war effort and there is some evidence of active support for the English cause. Martin Cataneo, a member of a prominent Genoese mercantile family, recruited more than 450 crossbowmen and oarsmen for the English government during the winter of 1372–3. Most of them appear to have been found in France and the Low Countries among the Genoese mercenary companies in French service. Antonio Doria, who brought a company of ninety men to England, had been the captain of the Duke of Anjou's crossbowmen on the march of Gascony two years before. In the autumn of 1372 the Doge's brother Pietro, Admiral of Genoa, let it be known that he was willing to bring a whole squadron of fighting galleys to England on suitable terms. It was decided to take him up on his offer. Jacopo Provana was sent back to Italy, this time accompanied by a prominent Genoese merchant who was in with the regime and the poet Geoffrey Chaucer, then a squire in the royal household. The high priority now being assigned to the war at sea was signalled early in 1373 by the appointment of William Montague, Earl of Salisbury, to command an enlarged Channel fleet during 1373, with both Admirals serving under him. Salisbury was one of England's most experienced commanders with a distinguished military career going back to the Crécy campaign of 1346. He also had a certain amount of experience of fighting at sea, having commanded squadrons in the Channel in 1370 and 1372. He was a much more considerable figure than the men who were customarily entrusted with purely naval operations.[6]

The English government's ambitious plans for fighting at sea in 1373 were combined with fresh projects of conquest on the continent. In the final days of the autumn Parliament it was decided to approve the despatch of a large expeditionary force, initially expected to be about 4,000 men, under the command of John of Gaunt. The plan appears to have been to land this army in Brittany and re-establish John de Montfort's position in his duchy. Gaunt would then cross the Loire at Nantes, invading Aquitaine through Bas-Poitou. It was essentially a fresh attempt at the strategy of 1369 and 1372.[7] In Gaunt's own mind this venture was probably intended to be the prelude to a yet vaster enterprise, namely the invasion of Castile over the Pyrenean passes from Gascony.

The weakness of these grandiose designs, as always, lay in the arrangements for financing them. The Commons remained intensely suspicious of the government's financial management and inclined to look for cheap victories. They renewed the wool tax for another two years and grudgingly added a lay subsidy of one tenth and fifteenth when told that that would not be enough. Even so, tax revenues and customs combined could be expected to bring in barely £100,000 in the course of the year 1373, of which about two-thirds would be available for war expenditure on past experience. A comparison with the French government spending plans is revealing. Although 1373 was to be a lean year for the French government's finances after the prodigious efforts of 1372, Charles V's Council, meeting at the same time as the English Parliament, resolved upon a budget for the coming year in which 600,000 francs (about £100,000) was allowed from the royal treasury for field and naval operations alone, on top of the cost of maintaining some fifty garrisons. A rough estimate of French war expenditure in this period, which is all that can be attempted, suggests that it was running at at least twice the level of England's.[8]

How much Edward III himself contributed to the plans for a military recovery in 1373 is difficult to say. It may not have been much. The King was now sixty. The abandonment of the great seaborne expedition of 1372 marked the beginning of his decline into weary senility, a development which was to have baleful consequences for the conduct of the war and the stability of English politics over the following years. Nominally the principal officers of the Council were now the Chancellor, Sir John Knyvet, and the Treasurer, Richard Lord Scrope of Bolton. Knyvet was a former royal justice, an ineffectual mediocrity who owed his appointment to the need to find a layman to placate the anti-clerical Parliament of 1371. Scrope, who had been promoted on the same occasion, was a much abler man but was either unable or unwilling to take a grip on the government's financial administration. Access to the King was tightly controlled by a small group of dominant councillors who took responsibility for the conduct of the war, pre-eminently the Chamberlain William Latimer, the Steward Sir John Neville and the King's long-standing diplomatic adviser Sir Richard Stury, Edward's 'familiarissimus' as a malicious chronicler called him.[9] These men all came from the ranks of the lesser nobility where the King's administrative household had traditionally been recruited. They were joined in the inner recesses of government by two less conventional figures, Richard Lyons and Alice Perrers.

Lyons was a London vintner of obscure origins who had made a fortune from commodity-dealing and money-lending. There is some evidence that he may have been a Fleming. Lyons owed his influence to his ability to raise large loans in the city at short notice, to his inventive way with money, and to the favour of Latimer. He was involved in most aspects of royal finance. He farmed part of the customs revenues. He was the largest of the Crown's commercial creditors, earning attractive rates for well-secured loans. He acted as the Crown's agent for mulcting the Italian merchant community in London. He supervised the system of selling licences to export goods without going through Calais. He also operated a debt-broking business in the course of which he made large sums by buying up ancient unpaid debts of the Crown. These debts were acquired at discounts as large as 95 per cent or 99 per cent and then repaid to Lyons in full, presumably by Latimer's direction. Much of the proceeds of these operations went straight into the Chamber where it escaped the audit controls of the Exchequer and passed under the direct control of Latimer. But part of them almost certainly went into Lyons's pocket.[10]

In the nature of things most of Lyons's activities were carried on in dark corners. Alice Perrers on the other hand exercised her power with a brazenness that shocked her contemporaries. She had originally come to the King's attention as a lady-in-waiting to Queen Philippa and at some time in the early 1360s became his mistress, bearing him three children over the following years. Edward's infatuation with Alice, hitherto comparatively discreet, became notorious in the last five years of his life. This was partly because she began to take a prominent part in the public ceremonies of the court, which was tactless but not in itself exceptional. What was exceptional by the standard of past royal mistresses was the determination with which this intelligent and greedy woman used her access to the King to obtain favours for her clients, amass wealth for herself, and advance her own political objectives. In 1376 it was alleged in Parliament that Alice relieved the King's Treasury of £2,000 to £3,000 a year. Alice Perrers's presence about the King did more than anything else to discredit him in the eyes of his subjects. It was also directly related to the declining fortunes of England in the war as the King progressively withdrew from day-to-day decision-making and, in the words of the poet John Gower, 'abandoned his buckler to seek battle in bed'. This was unfair. But there was a larger sense in which Edward III's partial retreat from public life was profoundly damaging to England's fortunes. At the height of his powers the King's skill in managing his own patronage had been the key to his close relations with the nobility and to his ability to muster support for an onerous war. His inaccessibility in the 1370s and the diversion of royal favour to a small group of self-interested ministers and cronies undermined the political order in much the same way as Gaveston's power had done in the previous reign and Simon Burley's would in the next. Moreover it meant that there was usually no decisive voice to resolve the doubts and squabbles of those who had the day-to-day conduct of affairs.[11]

At about the end of the year 1372 Juan Fernández Andeiro returned to England accompanied by a Portuguese royal clerk, Vasco Dominguez, precentor of Braga cathedral. They brought with them the text of the treaty with the Portuguese King and the news that Gaunt's ally was in danger of being conquered by Henry of Trastámara before he could perform it. These reports presented the English government with fresh dilemmas. Some way would have to be found of shoring up the Portuguese kingdom while John of Gaunt fought his way across France. At Westminster Edward III's ministers were prevailed upon to promise that an army would be sent to Don Fernando's assistance as soon as possible. This decision was made rapidly, probably under pressure from John of Gaunt, and without any real thought for the logistical problems involved. Originally fixed at 1,600 men, the army was placed under the command of one of Gaunt's retainers, Sir Nicholas Tamworth. He was a dependable captain who had begun his career as a freebooter in Burgundy in the 1350s and had been captain of Calais since 1370. His army would probably have enabled Fernando to match the French mercenaries of Henry of Trastámara if it had arrived in time. But there was little chance of that. Winter gales and recruiting problems in England were likely to delay any attempt to ship troops across the Bay of Biscay until May at the earliest. In mid-January 1373 Gaunt sent two emissaries back to Portugal to urge patience and endurance on his ally.[12]

Unfortunately neither Don Fernando nor John of Gaunt anticipated the scale or the speed of Castile's pre-emptive strike. When the Castilians crossed the Portuguese border in December 1372 the Portuguese King had made no serious preparations to defend his country. He then conducted the campaign with the greatest possible ineptitude. Having initially resolved to confront the invaders at Coimbra, he changed his mind, abandoned his wife in the citadel and retreated hurriedly south. There he shut himself in the royal castle of the old Moorish capital of Santarém overlooking the vast plain of the Ribatejo north of Lisbon, while his enemies swept past him to attack his capital. By the time that Tamworth received his orders Henry of Trastámara was already at Lisbon. The city, by far the most considerable in Portugal, dominated the economy of the country by virtue of its new-found maritime wealth and its expanding population. But its defences had not kept pace with its prosperity. The city had been built up on terraces on the north shore of the Tagus around the fortified cathedral and the Moorish castle of St. George, but the crumbling walls protected only the upper town. The rest was completely open. On 23 February 1373 the Castilian King occupied the lower town without difficulty. Two weeks later his Admiral, Ambrogio Boccanegra, appeared in the Tagus with the Castilian galley fleet to complete the investment of the city from the sea. The population of Lisbon withdrew into the upper town and put up an unexpectedly stout resistance. Don Fernando sent a handful of knights from Santarém to support them and a modest fleet of four galleys and fifteen sailing ships under the command of the Admiral of Portugal. But it was an unequal fight. The Castilians threw assault parties against the fragile gates. They brought up stone-throwers which cast great boulders into the wooden houses and narrow streets. The Portuguese Admiral panicked. He refused to obey an order to attack Boccanegra's ships before they concentrated beneath the city, lost half his galleys in a fight and then left his sailing fleet beached and poorly guarded so that much of it was captured by the enemy. By the beginning of March 1373 Lisbon was all but lost.[13]

Henry of Trastámara had no desire to get bogged down indefinitely in Portugal. From the first days of the campaign he had been looking for a way of neutralising Portugal so that he could withdraw his troops and turn his strength against England. In Avignon his ambassadors prevailed on the Pope to intervene. Like his predecessor, Gregory XI had always supported the Trastámaran dynasty against its internal enemies and had encouraged Henry's alliance with France. He was quite as concerned as Charles V was that the continuing hostilities between the Iberian kingdoms might end up by letting the English into the peninsula. Gregory had a legate at the Castilian court, the aristocratic French cardinal Guy of Boulogne, a crafty diplomat who was related to the King of France and well in with his ministers. On 1 March 1373 Guy arrived unannounced at the castle of Santarém where Don Fernando was still cowering with his councillors. He delivered a flowery oration before the court about the horrors of war and the distress of the Holy Father and offered his services as a mediator. But it was more mundane considerations than these which decided the Portuguese King and his advisers to agree. Don Fernando must by now have been told that help would not reach him from England until the spring. His kingdom was incapable of continuing the war alone and his capital was likely to fall very shortly. There followed some two weeks of intense negotiation between the Cardinal and the agents of both kings in the Franciscan monastery outside Lisbon where Henry of Trastámara had set up his headquarters. Don Fernando's capitulation when it came could not have been more complete. By the treaty sealed at Santarém on 19 March 1373 he agreed to make peace with Castile and to join the Castilian King in an alliance against Edward III and John of Gaunt. He was to expel from his kingdom twenty-eight named partisans of the late King Pedro of Castile and John of Gaunt including Andeiro. He was also required to hand over as security for his good behaviour a large number of hostages and seven of Portugal's principal frontier fortresses. Any English troops arriving in Portugal were to be treated as enemies and expelled, if necessary with Castilian military assistance.[14]

This blow to John of Gaunt's Spanish ambitions was quickly followed by another. Without disbanding his army Henry of Trastámara returned to his kingdom and made for the march of Navarre. Charles of Navarre was still holding a number of border towns and castles taken from the Castilians under cover of the Prince of Wales's campaign of 1367. They included the fortress-town of Logroño on the River Ebro, and the walled towns of Vitoria and Salvatierra, which controlled the approaches to the Navarrese kingdom from the west. The time had come to deal with this continuing sore. Henry encamped his men in the great oak forest of Bañares near the monastic town of Santo Domingo de la Calzada on the pilgrimage road, where six years before he had had his headquarters before the disastrous battle of Nájera. From here he issued an ultimatum to the King of Navarre to surrender his gains and make a permanent peace with his larger neighbour or suffer the consequences. Charles was in no position to resist. He submitted almost as completely as Don Fernando had done. Once again it was Guy of Boulogne who negotiated the final deal. After several months of patient diplomacy Charles of Navarre had to surrender the disputed border fortresses and to agree to a marriage alliance. Both John of Gaunt's points of entry into Castile were now closed.[15]

The result of the new treaty of Santarém was to release the Castilian galley fleet for service against England. By May 1373 it had been agreed that Castile would send at least six war galleys to fight with the French fleet in northern waters for the next three summer seasons. In the event Henry decided to send fifteen. The King of Portugal marked his change of allegiance by promising to add two more galleys of his own each year at Henry of Trastámara's expense. Unfortunately for the English, at much the same time Jacopo Provana's attempts to hire a galley fleet in Genoa ended in failure. When the English King's agents reached Italy they found that war had broken out between the Genoese republic and the kingdom of Cyprus. It was an absurd dispute, arising from an argument about the order of precedence between the Genoese and Venetian delegations at the coronation of the King of Cyprus. But it ended in a riot, the death of several Genoese and the collapse of Edward III's plans to employ a galley fleet in the Channel in 1373. The Admiral of Genoa was ordered to the eastern Mediterranean with every available fighting ship.[16]

Within weeks of the treaty of Santarém Brittany too was closed against the English. John of Gaunt's plans to land there had become known in Paris, at least in outline, by Christmas 1372. Charles V's councillors were under no illusions about John de Montfort's dealings with the English. Two months after the arrival of Neville's troops in the duchy the Duke had been unable to produce either an acceptable explanation of their presence or a convincing promise to get rid of them. Over the new year, the traditional season for planning military operations, it was decided to have done with him. The Duke of Brittany wrote to the King of France in February 1373 with a gift of fresh fish and hypocritical professions of goodwill. The English, he said, would be gone as soon as the weather enabled them to embark. In March 1373 the King resolved upon the immediate occupation of Brittany.[17]

In the event the first English troops and the van of the French army of invasion arrived in Brittany almost simultaneously. The English had decided to land their army at Saint-Malo, where the Earl of Cambridge had arrived in 1369. The island port had obvious advantages for Gaunt's purposes. It was more accessible from England than Brest. It also possessed the only first-rate harbour on the rocky north coast of the peninsula. But it had never been firmly under the control of the Duke. The townsmen, aided by their geographical situation, had for years refused to recognise John's overlordship or admit his officers. John had responded by waging open war on them from the garrisoned keep which he had built at Solidor at the mouth of the River Rance. In 1373 his lieutenants there were constructing a line of temporary forts along the shore. These measures are likely to have been co-ordinated with the English. For, in about the middle of April 1373, an English fleet appeared in the bay under the command of the Earl of Salisbury accompanied by both Admirals. They had forty-five ships and barges under their command with more than 1,700 English soldiers on board in addition to some 2,000 seamen and several companies of the King's newly hired Genoese crossbowmen. In the harbour the English found seven Castilian merchantmen which they boarded, killing their crews and seizing their cargoes. They then landed on the island. From here they landed raiding parties on the mainland to forage for supplies and reconnoitre the area. Their task was to secure the landing area for John of Gaunt who was due to follow with the main body of the army in May.[18]

The French army of Brittany was already gathering at Angers when Salisbury landed at Saint-Malo. The bulk of its strength had been recruited from Charles V's allies among the Breton nobility and from the retainers of the Duke of Bourbon, who had been appointed to command it. When the news of the landings arrived Bertrand du Guesclin was hurriedly recalled from Poitou to join them. The whole army must have numbered about 3,000 men. They entered the duchy in the last week of April. The Constable made directly for Rennes, which was the principal city of francophone Brittany and the hub of the road system of the region. The Duke of Bourbon headed for the north coast to contain Salisbury's force. The Viscount of Rohan marched on Vannes where John de Montfort was staying. They encountered no resistance at all. For most Bretons the news of the arrival of a second English army and the prospect of a third was decisive. Almost all the fortresses of the nobility and even the garrisoned castles of the Duke opened their gates as the French approached. John de Montfort's authority was repudiated everywhere. He packed up the contents of his treasury and chancery and fled, leaving his personal possessions to be looted by his enemies. He only just managed to reach Brest before they caught up with him. In the citadel the Duke was received by Sir John Neville. He appointed the Englishman as his lieutenant in Brittany and charged him to hold Brest in his name until he could get help. He left his treasury, more than 20,000 francs in cash (about £3,300), in Neville's hands as an earnest of his return. Then, on 28 April 1373, he took ship for England.[19]

Once John de Montfort had left, the last of his partisans melted away. Those castellans who did not surrender at once usually did so once they had been shown copies of the Duke's treaty with Edward III. Nantes appears to have admitted the French before the end of the May, thus putting an end to Gaunt's hopes of an uncontested crossing of the Loire. In the north of the peninsula Salisbury's men at Saint-Malo found the whole shoreline opposite them occupied by the enemy. Only the small and dispersed English forces in the peninsula continued to fight for the disgraced Duke. At Hennebont a largely English garrison was forced to surrender by the townsmen after the walls and keep had been undermined. Concarneau was carried by assault and its English captain captured. The Duke's favourite residence at the castle of Suscinio was defended to the last man by one of John de Montfort's Breton squires and a group of English retainers. Only three places still flew the Duke's banner at the end of June. A large and well-supplied *routier* garrison defended Sir Robert Knolles's fortress at Derval on the eastern march of Brittany. John de Montfort's English Duchess commanded a small, loyal garrison at Auray in the Gulf of Morbihan. And Neville concentrated what remained of his army behind the walls of Brest in the far west. Knolles, although not the most senior English soldier in the province, practically assumed the command of all English forces there. After seeing to the defence of Derval and Auray he made his way to Brest with the Duke's English treasurer, Thomas Melbourne, and joined Neville in the keep. On 1 June 1373 Bertrand du Guesclin laid siege to Brest. At about the same time the lord of Laval besieged Derval with the retinues of the Breton nobility.[20]

All of these terrible tidings reached Westminster at about the same time in the middle of May 1373. John de Montfort must have arrived in England in early May. He was followed within days by Provana and

Chaucer, returning empty-handed from Italy, and by the first reports of Portugal's repudiation of the English alliance. Suddenly the world seemed a very different place. On about 20 May John of Gaunt's plans to land in Brittany were abandoned. Not long afterwards the Earl of Salisbury's force was recalled from Saint-Malo. Sir Nicholas Tamworth's army of Portugal, which was already beginning to gather at Southampton, was cancelled. Only the Portuguese ambassadors, Juan Fernández Andeiro and his colleague, declined to recognise reality. They pressed on with the conclusion of the Anglo-Portuguese alliance even after they knew that Fernando had allied himself with the King of Castile and that Andeiro had been forbidden to return to Portugal, simply deleting the clause of the draft treaty which provided for an English expeditionary force to operate in Portugal. The treaty was solemnly executed in that form in St. Paul's cathedral in June. But it was a dead letter from the moment that the seal was attached. It was never ratified.[21]

With the limited number and low tonnage of the ships available there could be no question of sending John of Gaunt's army to Gascony across the Bay of Biscay. He would now have to enter France through Calais. This meant that it would be necessary to reach Aquitaine by marching round the north and east of Paris and passing across the Massif Central, the only region where it was feasible for an English army to cross the Loire. It also necessitated a change of embarkation port from Plymouth to Sandwich and Dover. These changes of plan caused chaos. At least 200 transports had been requisitioned for Gaunt's passage, more than eighty of which were already lying at Plymouth. More were on their way there. The ships were left idle in the Sound while the rest of the requisitioned fleet was ordered to the Downs. Nearly 4,500 men were making their way to Plymouth from all over England. The men were stopped on the roads and redirected to Kent. The date of Gaunt's embarkation, already some three weeks late, had to be put back to the middle of June. The army was eventually carried to Calais in relays by a smaller fleet requisitioned in the east coast ports and about a hundred vessels chartered by the English government's agents in Holland, Zeeland and Flanders. Shiploads of equipment and supplies followed: trains of carts, great quantities of tenting, mobile grain mills and ovens, and bridging equipment.[22]

The most difficult question for Edward's ministers was what to do about John de Montfort once the Breton campaign had been abandoned. He was burning to get back to his duchy to support the hard-pressed garrisons still holding out for him. He had also promised

Neville to relieve him in Brest. John determined to raise an army of his own. His plan was to embark the men at Plymouth and Dartmouth on the ships which had been requisitioned for John of Gaunt. His recovery of the honour of Richmond in the previous year meant that he had dilapidated but potentially valuable assets in England against which he could borrow to finance this project. At first Edward's government was willing to support him. They agreed to let him recruit 600 men-at-arms and 400 archers in England. They made a large grant towards his expenses and lent him £9,000. Neville lent £2,000 more out of his own pocket. Then suddenly, on about 10 June 1373, the whole project was cancelled. The reason is not recorded but the likelihood is that the English government was unable to agree terms with the Duke for the reoccupation of his duchy. For the truth was that their interests were directly opposed. John wanted to be reconciled to his subjects, whereas Edward III's ministers wanted to obtain military control of the peninsula. So John was forced to drop his plans to return to Brest and his strength was added to John of Gaunt's army, probably against his wishes. He was destined to pass the next few months marching through France in Gaunt's shadow. The job of relieving Brest was assigned to the Earl of Salisbury.[23]

Inside the castle of Brest Neville and Knolles knew little or nothing of what was going on in England. They did not know that the Duke of Brittany had been diverted to Calais or that the Earl of Salisbury's fleet was being prepared in Southampton to relieve them. Their men had exhausted their stores and their hopes. By July 1373 they were reduced to eating their horses. On 6 July the garrison entered into a conditional surrender agreement with Bertrand du Guesclin in a form which had by now become conventional. A truce was agreed for the area around Brest, which would allow the garrison to resupply itself. The fortress was to be abandoned a month later on 6 August unless by then the Duke of Brittany had appeared in person with enough men to hold his own against the French army on open ground outside the gates of the town. The Bretons in the garrison were to be pardoned and allowed to keep their lands while the English were to be given a safe-conduct to go wherever they wished with everything they had. To secure their performance of these promises the English commanders delivered six hostages and furnished undertakings from six more to surrender if they were called for.[24]

While he waited for the month to pass Bertrand du Guesclin occupied his men by raiding the Channel Islands. He captured and briefly occupied the lower wards of the coastal fortress at Gorey on Jersey while the garrison held out from the keep. He then attacked Guernsey, which was virtually undefended, and seized the dilapidated fortifications of Castle Cornet. The inhabitants were obliged to enter into a *patis* agreement to pay protection money to the Constable. Crops, villages and farm buildings were so completely devastated that the King's revenues there yielded almost nothing for years afterwards.[25]

The Earl of Salisbury sailed out of Southampton with the relief force for Brest towards the end of July 1373. After joining the ships of the western admiralty at sea his fleet comprised more than fifty vessels with nearly 3,000 soldiers on board and several shiploads of stores. When the fleet entered the great roadstead at Brest it was received with ecstatic joy by the garrison. Salisbury's own joy must have soured when he saw the terms of the conditional surrender agreement. The place had not been relieved in the manner required because John de Montfort was not there in person. Faced with this unexpected difficulty the English decided to repudiate their agreement with the Constable. Their pretext was a series of minor disputes about the truce around the town, which they said that the French had failed to observe. On 4 August 1373 Neville wrote to the French commanders in the name of the three captains who had sealed the agreement, declaring that since they had received no satisfactory answer on these points they considered that were no longer bound to surrender. They demanded the return of the hostages in French hands. Meanwhile preparations were made to defend Brest. The stores were unloaded from the ships. Artillery was distributed about the walls and bows, arrows and cords among the archers. The French were outraged. On 6 August, the day appointed for the surrender, Bertrand du Guesclin, fresh from his conquests in the Channel Islands, appeared before the town with the whole of the French army in Brittany, about 3,000 men. They found Neville's garrison and Salisbury's relief army drawn up in their lines in front of the gates. The numbers on each side were roughly matched. But neither was willing to be drawn into a battle. Most of the English were equipped for service at sea and had no horses. As for the French, they did not care to lose the advantage of the defensive by attacking an enemy in prepared positions beneath their own walls. After a few days the French army withdrew. The Earl of Salisbury's men boarded their ships in the second week of August and returned to England, leaving Neville to defend the place with a normal wartime garrison, probably no more than about 200 men, which was periodically resupplied from England. The six English hostages in French hands were left to their fate. They became prisoners of war and were held in harsh conditions for four years until Neville was eventually persuaded to pay £4,500 for their release from his own pocket. For John de Montfort and Edward III the whole affair had probably been worth the effort. John never settled his debt to Neville and Brest was destined to remain in English occupation for almost a quarter of a century.[26]

The year 1373 was one of the best years for English naval operations in Edward III's reign. The English fleet had, as the Chancellor told Parliament in November 1373, 'confronted the enemy with skill and enterprise'. Much of this was due to the Earl of Salisbury. What was perhaps most remarkable was that his operations had been carried out with much the same forces as had so completely failed the year before. None of the new barges ordered the previous November was ready in time to take part in the capture of Saint-Malo and only three were ready for the relief of Brest. The rest were delivered late and in some cases incomplete and without their tackle. Crewing difficulties were a serious constraint on the use of these vessels even when they had been delivered. The Admirals did not have nearly enough Genoese oarsmen to man them. Most of the crews were pressed men, drawn from the small pool of English seamen who were not already serving on requisitioned merchantmen.[27]

The main reason for England's success at sea in 1373 was the strange passivity of their French and Castilian enemies. Early in the year the mere threat of their appearance had emptied the sea lanes along the south coast of England. Yet the galleys did nothing to justify their fearsome reputation. The French barges spent most of the summer at their bases in the Seine as a result of a backlog of maintenance work in the Rouen arsenal. There is some evidence that they also experienced the same sort of difficulty in recruiting local oarsmen as the English did. The ships eventually succeeded in putting to sea in mid-July, by which time it was too late to interfere with the English expedition to Saint-Malo. There was no attempt to disrupt the long-drawn-out process of transporting John of Gaunt's army to Calais. There were no recorded raids on the English coast. When the 'army of the sea' returned to Harfleur to revictual, in early August, many of the troops assigned to it were recalled to reinforce the defences of the north against John of Gaunt. The Monegasque Admiral Rainer Grimaldi undertook another short cruise in the middle of the month with the six Italian galleys of his own squadron. But after three weeks they were back in port preparing for winter lay-up. As for the Castilians, their galley fleet had arrived in the Seine in June accompanied by a number of sailing ships. The Castilians probably participated in Grimaldi's two cruises. There was at least one direct encounter with Salisbury's fleet which resulted in the capture of three of the Castilian sailing ships. Otherwise they seem to have done very little. The absence of Ambrogio Boccanegra with his aggressive tactics and skill in handling large fleets at sea may have had something to do with this. He had retired from Castilian service after the siege of Lisbon. The fleet sent to the Channel was commanded by his successor, Fernán Sánchez de Tovar. Sánchez was a soldier, not a seaman, and a native Castilian in an office traditionally monopolised by Genoese. He would later prove himself to be a competent practitioner of naval guerilla warfare and a master of the coastal tip-and-run raid, but neither skill was much in evidence in this first campaign.[28]

Yet, for all their ineffectiveness at sea, the French and Castilian fleets achieved their purposes by their mere existence. In the long run their impact would not be measured in burning villages, captured hulks or bloated corpses washed up on the beaches of southern England but in money. Leaving aside shipping costs associated with John of Gaunt's expedition, English naval operations in 1373 cost Edward III's government more than £40,000.[29] This was more than the entire yield of the Parliamentary subsidy for the year. It was nearly half of the government's average annual expenditure on warfare. The weight of naval expenditure in the government's accounts had grown substantially since 1369, a tendency which persisted for many years and was not matched by any increase in the government's resources. This seriously inhibited the conduct of military operations in France.

John of Gaunt crossed the Channel in about the middle of July 1373 followed shortly by the Duke of Brittany. Three English earls joined the army as well as Henry, Lord Percy, the greatest figure on the Scottish march, who had the standing of an earl. Several of the great captains of past campaigns were there, including Calveley and Hewitt. The whole army numbered about 6,000 men-at-arms and archers on the payroll, half as many again as the number originally planned back in November. With the mass of pages, varlets, clerks and artificers, there must have been about 9,000 mounted men altogether. The process of shipping the whole force across the Channel, with all its horses, equipment and stores, was not completed until 9 August. On the following day the army formed itself into two columns. One, under the command of the Duke of Brittany, marched directly south towards Hesdin and then turned

south-east, skirting around Amiens and reaching the Somme just east of
the city. The other, under John of Gaunt himself, followed a roughly
parallel route about forty miles east of them via Saint-Omer and Arras.
The army covered about ten miles a day, leaving villages and farms in
flames across a broad front. Gaunt was keen to get to the south-west
and made no attempt to attack any of the walled towns or castles on the
route. On about 19 August the two columns met on the Somme.[30]

The appearance of an English army in Calais wrong-footed the
French King's ministers. They were still expecting a landing in Brittany.
As a result almost all the available troops were in the peninsula, tied
down by the sieges of Brest and Derval. There were barely 600 men on
the Calais march. It was not until the first week of July that the French
King, alerted by the scale of English troop movements in the Channel,
realised what was happening. A second army was summoned to
assemble at Amiens in August. The Duke of Burgundy, who was on his
way to Brittany, was abruptly recalled and put in command of it. Duke
Philip entered Amiens with about 700 men-at-arms on 14 July 1373. He
was obliged to pass more than a month idle in the city as the laborious
process of recruitment was put in hand and troops made their way
across northern France to join him. He still had only about 4,000 men
under his command when John of Gaunt marched out of Calais.[31]

The English forded the Somme not far from the walled town of Bray.
A few miles further south they burned the town of Roye as the terrified
population crowded for safety into the tower of the fortified church.
Then they paused for a week by the banks of the River Avre in the open
plain of Vermandois, daring the Duke of Burgundy to attack them.
While they waited the Duke of Brittany composed a letter of defiance
to Charles V, the formal renunciation of his homage which the law
required of any man who intended to fight against his lord. But John's
letter was more than a point of form. It was an angry and self-righteous
denunciation of the French King for invading his duchy, capturing his
walled towns and castles, imprisoning and killing his supporters and
committing every other 'irreparable villainy'. 'I hold you to be my
enemy,' John wrote; 'do not be surprised if I come now to injure you
and your supporters and avenge the wrongs you have done to me.'[32]

The French army left Amiens on 17 August 1373 and headed south-
east, reaching Soissons on the 22nd. Philip of Burgundy followed what
had become the traditional French strategy of avoiding battle. He kept
his distance from the English, moving from one walled town to another,
always keeping the bulk of his army between the enemy and Paris. The

population of the *plat pays* was ordered into the towns and castles. Garrisons were put into all the more significant walled places. Unprotected bridges were broken. In the French capital the King and his advisers struggled to reinforce him. The northern cities were commanded to find infantry and crossbowmen. The troops of the 'army of the sea' were urgently recalled from Harfleur. A new corps was raised from late arrivals and placed under the command of Charles V's youthful and mediocre uncle, Philip, Duke of Orléans.[33]

All the indications are that the French commanders thought that John of Gaunt and John de Montfort were heading for Brittany. They therefore had a difficult dilemma. The Constable's army in Brittany was badly needed to help keep the English away from Paris. But withdrawing it would expose the major cities of the duchy to attack. With some misgivings, Charles V decided towards the end of August to recall it. Olivier de Clisson paused before leaving to patch up a truce with Knolles's garrison at Derval. Knolles himself was far away at Brest. His lieutenants had given up hope of relief. They cannot have known how tightly stretched French resources were. So they agreed to surrender the castle on 29 September if no relief force had appeared by then. Clisson took hostages for the performance of these undertakings but he must have wondered, after the affair at Brest, whether they were worth much. In early September he too was on the road to Paris. The Viscount of Rohan was left to defend the Crown's interests in Brittany with a retinue of just 300 men. To fill the gap Charles took the remarkable step of summoning the Duke of Anjou from Languedoc. Anjou was ordered to leave at once for Brittany bringing every available man with him. He received this summons towards the end of August in the Dordogne valley. He was on his way by the beginning of September with 2,500 men at his back.[34]

On about 23 August 1373 John of Gaunt's great column began to head east from the Vermandois. They crossed the Oise south of Saint-Quentin, passing well north of Philip of Burgundy's headquarters at Soissons. They then made for Laon and Reims, leaving behind them a broad swathe of looted barns and burning farmsteads and villages. On about 3 September they passed Laon. A few days later they crossed the Aisne by the bridge at Vailly and marched south towards Épernay. The terrain was easy. The only serious obstacles were the many river crossings. A corps of carpenters proved adept at throwing bridges across the ruptured ends of masonry which the French had left behind them. Supply was a more difficult problem. To feed an army of this size off the

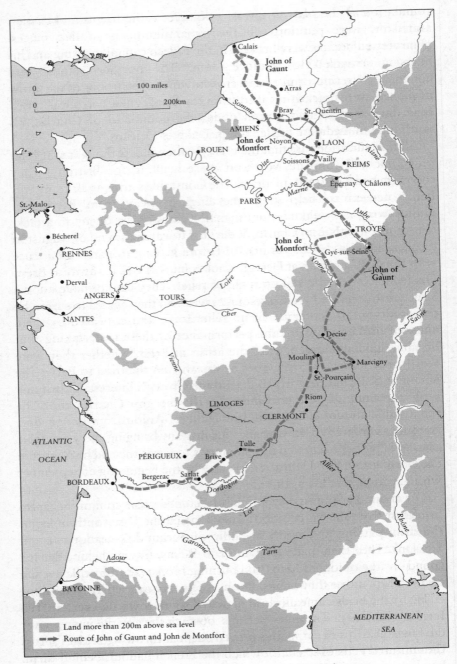

6 John of Gaunt's *chevauchée*, August–December 1373

country it was necessary to spread it out over a broad front and to send armed foraging expeditions some way from the main body. They proved to be very vulnerable. As the English moved into Champagne they began to encounter increasing resistance and suffered heavy losses of men and horses. The French formed harassing forces of a few hundred mounted men to pick off stragglers and foraging parties one by one. At the beginning of September Jean de Bueil surprised a company of English north of Laon and took a large number of prisoners. On the 9th another English detachment commanded by Walter Hewitt was ambushed near Oulchy-le-Château, south of Soissons. Hewitt was killed in this encounter and more than thirty of his men-at-arms were captured. Bands of peasants hidden in the forests fell on anyone wearing the cross of St. George or speaking English ('or any other strange and horrible language'), battering them to death, drowning them or slitting their throats. It was to be the pattern of the campaign.[35]

In the middle of September 1373 the French forces in the north were ordered to concentrate at Troyes, the cathedral city on the left bank of the Seine in southern Champagne. The strategy appears to have been to prevent the English army from swinging round to the west and approaching Paris through the Gâtinais as Edward III had done in 1359, or from making a dash for Brittany as Knolles had done in 1370. The King's orders were that they were to delay, harass and exhaust the enemy but on no account to give battle. Once again the policy was controversial, especially among its victims in the undefended countryside of northern France whose murmurings were becoming too loud to be ignored. At a council of war in Paris the Constable had to remind his fellow councillors about Crécy and Poitiers and the many pitched battles which the French had fought and lost against the English. Olivier de Clisson, who was 'brought up with the English and knows their ways better than any of you', would back him up, he said. According to Froissart's much embellished account of this meeting the King declared that he 'would not risk the lives of his knights and the fate of his realm for a corner of land'. The Duke of Burgundy left Soissons on 10 September, shortly after the council of war had concluded, and joined forces with the other French corps during the next few days. On the 15th they entered Troyes.[36]

The two armies came as close at Troyes as they would ever do. The English began to cross the River Aube, north of the city, a few days after the French had arrived. On about 22 September the vanguard of John of Gaunt's army penetrated into the undefended suburbs of Troyes, breaking into the rich suburban monasteries and mansions and throwing themselves against the outworks which the French had built in front of the bridgehead on the right bank of the river. They paid heavily for their indiscipline. A sudden sortie from the city caught them unawares, killing 120 of them and capturing eighty more. Three Bretons, presumably retainers of John de Montfort, were found among the prisoners and summarily executed as traitors. John of Gaunt tried to provoke a battle outside Troyes. He halted the main body of his army in the plain north of the city. From the city walls they could be seen through the haze of smoke rising from the wreckage of the suburbs, standing in formation for three days in succession and daring the French to attack them. The French refused to move. On about 25 September the English marched away up the valley of the Seine. The army crossed the river beneath the walls of the fortress of Gyé-sur-Seine, thirty miles upstream, at about the end of the month. But Gaunt did not attempt to turn west as the French must have expected him to do. Instead he made a dash southward into the Nivernais and along the upper valley of the Loire towards Auvergne, pursued at a distance by the Duke of Burgundy. By the first few days of October it was clear that John of Gaunt was looking for a crossing of the Loire and that he was heading not for Brittany but for Gascony.[37]

The Duke of Anjou had by now reached Brittany. He arrived at Derval shortly before the date fixed for its surrender. He was joined there by Olivier de Clisson. Anjou's long march from Languedoc had been a mistake as events had turned out. The region which he had come to defend was no longer threatened. The garrison of Derval added to his frustrations by refusing to surrender according to their agreement. Knolles had re-entered the fortress and repudiated the treaty which his lieutenants had made. They had acted without his authority, he said. The Duke of Anjou had the hostages brought out and beheaded beneath the walls in full view of the defenders. In law he was within his rights, although there were plenty of men in his army who protested at his act. According to report it was Clisson who insisted on their execution. 'If they do not die I shall not so much as put a helmet on my head for your war,' he is said to have told the Duke. Knolles responded by having an improvised scaffold built out from a high window of the keep, where four French prisoners of war were promptly beheaded and thrown into the castle ditch. It was the second time in as many months that Knolles had dishonoured the conventions on which war between noblemen was founded.[38]

On about 10 October 1373 John of Gaunt's army, having left a trail of devastation in the Charolais, crossed the Loire by the bridge at

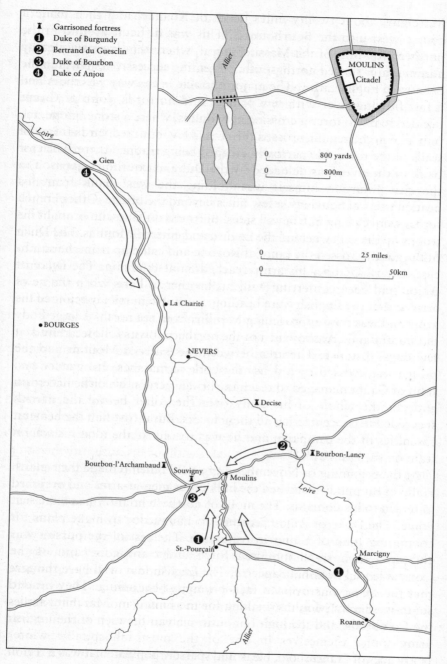

Garrisoned fortress
❶ Duke of Burgundy
❷ Bertrand du Guesclin
❸ Duke of Bourbon
❹ Duke of Anjou

7 The crossing of the Allier, October 1373

Marcigny, about twenty miles north of Roanne, and then made a course west into the Bourbonnais. This was difficult ground in the northern foothills of the Massif Central, where the rivers swollen by autumn rains flowed north–south, presenting successive barriers to the exhausted English army. The major obstacle in the way was the Allier, a fast-flowing river with few bridges and no fords. John of Gaunt decided to try to force a crossing at Moulins, where a stone bridge, the only one in the region, crossed the river a few hundred yards from the walls of the town. He narrowly escaped being trapped there. The east bank of the river was defended by the Duke of Bourbon's garrison in the city. Bourbon himself was holding the west bank from his headquarters at Souvigny, a few miles beyond the bridge. Other French forces were closing in from all sides. Bertrand du Guesclin brought his troops up the valley behind the English and entered Moulins. The Duke of Burgundy crossed the Loire at Roanne and came up from the south-east. On 18 October his army reached Saint-Pourçain. The Duke of Anjou had been conferring with his brother in Paris when the news arrived that the English were heading south. He hurriedly rejoined his army and was now approaching Moulins from the north. A large body of infantry and crossbowmen of the northern towns followed him at a few days' distance. The area between the walls of Moulins and the bridge was crossed by a dense network of marshes and waterways. John of Gaunt managed to reach the bridge across this difficult terrain and got the whole of his army over the Allier before the French succeeded in concentrating all these forces. But it cost him the heaviest casualties of the campaign and he was forced to abandon his wagon train on the east bank.[39]

At the beginning of November 1373 the French remade their plans. Philip of Burgundy dismissed the bulk of his men-at-arms and prepared to return to his domains. The mobs of northern infantrymen were sent home. The Duke of Anjou returned to Languedoc to make plans for containing John of Gaunt in Aquitaine. The rest of the pursuit was entrusted to a small mounted force under the command of the Constable and Marshal Sancerre. The English may well have thought that the worst was over. In fact it was just beginning. They headed south-west from Moulins, making for the Limousin. Marching across the Combraille and the high Limousin plateau the men of the English army found themselves in one of the most inhospitable winter landscapes of France: cold, bleak and sparsely populated, it was a region of dense forest with no food for men or beasts. The rain fell in torrents, turning the roads into marshes and filling the streams with undrinkable mud. Foraging was impossible. The troops were strictly forbidden to stray from the main force. Anyway they no longer had any carts. The Constable's mounted raiders clung to their flanks, picking off those who ignored these orders. Everywhere that the English had passed the French found the route marked by the corpses of their starved horses.[40]

John of Gaunt was welcomed nowhere until the beginning of December 1373 when, reaching the valley of the Corrèze in Bas-Limousin, the army entered the last part of the province to accept French rule. In these remote regions there was still a fund of residual loyalty to be tapped. Gaunt was able to pause for about three weeks while his men rested and raiding parties spread out across the neighbouring parts of the Cantal and northern Quercy. The city of Tulle put up no more than a perfunctory resistance. Brive willingly opened its gates and accepted an English garrison. Several noblemen received him in their castles. But these were the solitary (and as it turned out short-lived) gains of Gaunt's campaign. 'Honourable to their arms but disastrous to their interests' was the balanced verdict of the official chronicler of the French royal house.

The army which entered Bordeaux at the end of December 1373 was a shadow of the one which had left Calais five months before. Although they had not succeeded in engaging the enemy on any substantial scale they looked like beaten men. More than half of the thirty thousand horses with which they had set out from Calais had been lost. Much of the army, including 300 belted knights, entered the city on foot. Others were without their armour, which they had thrown away en route to lighten their loads. Their clothes were filthy and torn and their faces drawn with hunger. It is impossible to be precise about the scale of the human casualties. Hundreds had succumbed to injury or disease on the march or had been killed in skirmishes with the French. A large number of veterans were prisoners in French hands. Most of them were still prisoners three years later.

Bordeaux was in no position to take on the burden of feeding a mass of men roughly equal to its ordinary population. The city was in the grip of a renewed epidemic of bubonic plague from which many of the troops would die in the following weeks. The harvest had been poor throughout southern France. Food prices rose to astronomic levels which Gaunt's followers were quite unable to pay. They had long since spent their advances and were forbidden to raid and steal in friendly territory. In the next few weeks famous knights, rich men with broad acres in England, were to be seen begging for food in the streets of the duchy's capital.[41]

The sorry condition of John of Gaunt's army, although obvious to its commanders, did not become generally known for some time. Contemporary opinion, both in England and on the continent, assumed that, with an army of nearly 10,000 Englishmen and the support of an aggressive Gascon nobility, John of Gaunt had the whole of the south-west at his mercy. On 22 November 1373, as Gaunt's army marched across the Limousin plateau nursing the injuries of the crossing of the Allier and battered by rain and high winds, Edward III's Chancellor was telling Parliament at Westminster that the Duke of Lancaster's outstanding qualities of command and fine feats of arms had inflicted serious damage on the French. The King, he said, intended to make Gaunt's army the focus of military operations on the continent for 1374. He asked for a Parliamentary subsidy to keep it in being until the following November, some six months beyond the service specified in the men's indentures.[42]

The Chancellor did not tell Parliament that the main objective for 1374 was the invasion of Castile. But this was by now becoming obvious. At the papal court it was taken for granted. In Castile the partisans of the dead King Pedro were stirring in the towns. Five people were executed in Murcia early in 1374 for organising demonstrations in favour of John of Gaunt. There is some evidence of similar disturbances in other places. On the march of Navarre Henry of Trastámara's military governor at Logroño had already written off his master's chances of survival and agreed with Charles of Navarre to bring his own troops over to the enemy when the invasion came. At about the end of the year Henry had his young heir, the future John I, crowned as his successor, the traditional resort of rulers who felt unsteady on their thrones. At about the same time the Castilian King summoned the largest army that he could gather to defend his kingdom and sent his agents to the Duke of Anjou in Toulouse with appeals for help. In February 1374 some 6,200 Castilian cavalry and 5,000 infantry had gathered around Burgos. They were advancing towards the River Ebro, where Henry of Trastámara could cover the approaches to his kingdom from the north and east.[43]

The carrion crows were gathering in both of these directions. Peter IV of Aragon had followed the progress of John of Gaunt's army with intense interest. Unlike the rulers of Portugal and Navarre he had resisted the attempts of the papal court to bring about an accommodation with Henry of Trastámara. He was determined to hang on to the frontier regions of Castile which he had occupied during the Castilian civil wars of the late 1360s. For the moment Peter dithered, uncertain whether to risk the security of his kingdom by publicly throwing in his lot with an invader who might never appear or to stand on the sidelines and lose the chance of consolidating his gains at Castile's expense. But even this master of procrastination seems to have decided that Henry of Trastámara's days might now really be numbered. In November 1373 all three of the principal officers of the duchy of Aquitaine, the Seneschal Sir Thomas Felton, the Constable and the Mayor of Bordeaux, were locked in negotiations with Peter's representatives in the Pyrenean town of Jaca, planning the conquest and partition of Castile. Peter's agents tentatively promised a corps of 1,500 cavalry to support an English invasion, provided that he should not have to declare himself until John of Gaunt had actually reached the Ebro. Peter was plainly assuming that the Duke of Lancaster was planning to enter Castile through Navarre. He was almost certainly right about this. One of the first acts of John of Gaunt after arriving in Bordeaux was to send five of his councillors to conclude matters with the King of Aragon. Some members of this mission appear to have been charged with negotiating with the King of Navarre as well.[44]

All of these plans, however, depended for their execution on the English army in Bordeaux, which was sick, demoralised and mutinous. There was a rash of desertions. Those who could afford it found passages on ships bound for England. Refugees from Gaunt's army began to appear on the streets of London. The Duke of Brittany sailed for Brittany at the beginning of February 1374 taking at least part of his retinue of 1,000 men with him. Many of the rest were incapable of fighting, even if they had been fit and willing, for want of horses and equipment. But the Duke's gravest problem was the want of money to pay their wages. According to their indentures the men were required to serve for a year to the end of June 1374. They had been paid a quarter's wages in cash before leaving England and another quarter's worth in assignments on government revenues. They were now due their wages for the third quarter. A substantial proportion of them were not willing to serve unless they were paid. The King had promised John of Gaunt to 'refresh' the army by sending out £12,000 in cash as a payment on account for the rest of their service. But his ministers did nothing about it. They said that this was because they had not known where to send the money. In fact it seems clear that they did not have it. This turn of events was deeply embarrassing to John of Gaunt. He was not inclined to drive a hard bargain with his captains even if he had been able to. His own claims against the government amounted to nearly £25,000, much of which was still outstanding from his previous expedition to Aquitaine.[45]

At Westminster the Council had no idea of the condition of John of Gaunt's army until a messenger arrived in England in mid-January 1374 with the Duke's letters containing his report on the state of affairs in Gascony. These were forwarded post-haste to the King at Langley, north of London, and read out before him on 17 January 1374. Their contents caused consternation. The Duke told his father that he could not even ensure that the troops would serve what remained of their indentures let alone an extra six months. The Council chewed over the options during the last ten days of January and eventually resolved to send a commission of three knights out to Bordeaux to reason with the Duke and his captains. The leader of this group, Sir Nicholas Dagworth, was a soldier of renown with a talent for delicate diplomacy. But his most persuasive argument was the missing £12,000, which he was to take with him to Gascony in coin and pay out to John of Gaunt's captains on the strict condition that they undertook to serve at least until June. In addition he was to take an extra 2,000 marks to be distributed among the men at John of Gaunt's discretion. Dagworth and his colleagues received their instructions on 1 February 1374. But it proved impossible to find the £12,000. By 24 February their mission had been cancelled.[46]

The ultimate cost of John of Gaunt's expedition was at least £100,000, of which it seems likely that about half had been paid in cash or assignments in the course of 1373. The whole of the duties and subsidies which had been voted for war purposes had been spent, leaving the cost of paying Gaunt's army in 1374 unfunded. As the Chancellor had hinted in his opening address to the Parliament of November 1373, tax revenues were simply not enough to cover the cost of the war and were quite unequal to the combined resources of France and Castile. Confronted with these gloomy facts Parliament had responded by authorising a subsidy for 1374 and another for 1375 if the war was still continuing. The clergy matched this by granting their own tenth in the following month. With these grants the government could expect to enjoy receipts of about £120,000 in the course of 1374, of which on past reckoning about £80,000 might be available for war expenditure. Since it cost between £8,000 and £9,000 a month to keep John of Gaunt's army in being this would just about enable it to operate until November, assuming no other military expenditure at all. But that of course was an impossible assumption and no one at Westminster was making it. There were past debts and arrears to be settled. There was the steady drain of money on the defence of Calais (currently about £20,000 a year). There were fresh commitments in Ireland (more than £11,000).

In addition to all this Parliament had required the King to take proper measures for the 'keeping of the sea'. Reports had reached England shortly before the Parliament of November 1373 that the King of Castile had recently agreed with Charles V to send another galley fleet to the Channel in 1374. This news, which was substantially correct, had provoked the usual panic among the Commons when it was reported to them. At the beginning of February 1374 the Admirals were preparing what the Council believed to be the largest fleet of barges and 'great ships' ever assembled for the defence of the coasts save when the King or the Prince had commanded in person. As a result the money coming into the Exchequer was at once claimed for seamen and men-at-arms recruited for the fleet, who would otherwise have deserted. More than £10,000 was paid to them in advances in February. By the time that the Admirals put to sea in the second half of March, the cashiers of the fleet had drawn nearly £29,000 from the Treasury. The difficulty encountered in paying the army of Aquitaine reflected a permanent deficiency in the government's war accounts, of which the most important single cause was the cost of financing naval operations for the defence of England.[47]

In Bordeaux John of Gaunt was oblivious to the travails of the Exchequer at Westminster. He assumed that the money was on its way and played his cards with some skill while he waited for it to arrive. He persuaded his captains to be patient and managed to form some effective units from companies which were still able and willing to fight. With these he made a show of force in about the middle of February against the castles of French partisans within reach of Bordeaux. This brief campaign was brought to an end towards the close of February by a controversial agreement with the Constable and the Duke of Anjou. The terms were that there was to be a truce covering the whole of the south-western theatre, including Castile, until Whitsun, 21 May 1374. The two royal dukes promised to appear with their entire armies at their backs for an arranged battle near Moissac on Easter Monday,

3 April, on open ground in the flat meadows at the confluence of the Tarn and the Garonne.

The truce was for different reasons in the interest of both sides. John of Gaunt, whose position was weaker than Louis of Anjou or Bertrand du Guesclin realised, obtained a respite of more than a month to rest and supply his army and resolve his financial problems, and nearly three months to complete his preparations for the invasion of Castile. The arranged battle, a traditional tool of English military diplomacy, is unlikely to have represented Anjou's preference. But he had virtually no troops under arms. The battle probably represented John of Gaunt's price for the truce. There is no doubt that Anjou took it seriously and believed that it could be won. His financial officials passed much of March negotiating loans and advances against the tax revenues of Languedoc. His marshals recruited troops throughout Languedoc. Louis's domains in Anjou and Maine were scoured for recruits. A thousand men were hired from the Breton companies operating in the south and centre. The Duke of Burgundy promised to join him with several hundred more. The Count of Savoy came from beyond the Rhône. About 3,500 men had been retained for Anjou's army by the end of March. But the main force with which Anjou proposed to confront the English at Moissac was the large Castilian army of Henry of Trastámara, which was already assembled near the southern frontier of Navarre waiting for the threatened English invasion. Anjou persuaded Henry to bring these men over the Pyrenees through the passes of Navarre. Charles of Navarre, faced with the threat of a Castilian invasion, reluctantly agreed to allow them through in small groups of 300 at a time against strict promises of good behaviour and the delivery of suitable hostages.[48]

John of Gaunt's agreement with the Duke of Anjou ultimately foundered on the objections of the King of France, who had not been consulted and strongly disapproved when he was told. The arranged battle was inconsistent with his firm policy of avoiding all major engagements with English armies. As for the truce, Charles V consulted his councillors and the jurists of the Parlement of Paris and pronounced it to be neither binding nor expedient, mainly on the ground that it was inconsistent with his treaty obligations to Castile. The Duke of Anjou must have learned of his brother's reaction in about the middle of March.[49]

In the third week of March John of Gaunt, accompanied by Sir Thomas Felton and some of the principal captains of his army, travelled across the windswept wastes of the Landes to the southern march of the English duchy. In the cathedral city of Dax on the Adour he met Gaston Phoebus, Count of Foix, and Charles, King of Navarre, the two great territorial princes of the western Pyrenees whose support would be indispensable for any successful invasion of Castile. The meeting was also attended by uninvited guests, three councillors of the Duke of Anjou led by the Marquis of Cardaillac, who appeared on behalf of their master. Their instructions were to ask Gaston Phoebus to use his good offices with John of Gaunt to have the arranged battle, now only a fortnight away, cancelled or at least postponed. They were also charged to discuss certain 'secret business' with the Count of Foix and the King of Navarre which can only have concerned the projected invasion of Castile. They appear to have had some success in the matter of the battle, which was becoming an embarrassment to all parties. John of Gaunt must have begun to fear that he would be outnumbered at Moissac. Anjou for his part had certainly under-estimated the time required to bring troops from Anjou and Bourbonnais and evidently had no conception of the logistical difficulties of bringing a Castilian army across the Pyrenean passes in early spring. So the battle was cancelled and Louis of Anjou withdrew his request for Castilian reinforcements. The terms of the new agreement are obscure, but it is clear that in spite of the French King's repudiation of the truce it was agreed to observe it.[50]

On the projected invasion of Castile, however, Louis of Anjou's envoys achieved nothing. The terms of John of Gaunt's agreement with the King of Navarre have not survived and it would be characteristic of Charles's ways if they were never recorded. But the outline was disclosed four years later by his Chamberlain, Jacques de Rue, to the interrogators of the Châtelet prison in Paris. John of Gaunt was to be allowed to cross the Pyrenean passes and to use Navarre as a base from which to enter Castile in return for his assistance in recovering Logroño and certain other border towns which Charles had been forced to restore to Henry of Trastámara in the previous year. John of Gaunt's treaty with the rich, powerful and notoriously independent-minded Count of Foix was in some ways an even more striking demonstration of the respect in which the English army was held among experienced observers in the region, in spite of its internal dissensions and battered condition. Gaston Phoebus opened his chests to lend the Duke money. He agreed to a marriage between his eldest son and John of Gaunt's daughter Philippa, with a comparatively modest dowry. And he proposed to put his powerful army at John of Gaunt's disposal for the campaign against

Henry of Trastámara in return for a fee of 12,000 *doblas* (about £2,300) plus the wages of his men. The agreement records that the invasion of Castile was expected to begin within two months of Easter, in other words in late May when the truce with the Duke of Anjou expired. As for the King of Aragon, he was still formally uncommitted to John of Gaunt's cause. But by the time Gaunt's emissaries left Barcelona on 10 March 1374 Peter IV had made it reasonably clear that he was likely to support the English invasion. The issues in Barcelona had been not whether but how: the strength of Peter's military contribution, the extent of his territorial rewards in eastern Castile, the delicate question of timing. All of Gaunt's diplomatic arrangements for invading Castile seemed to be falling into place.[51]

Yet they fell apart within a week. John of Gaunt was back in Bordeaux by 26 March. There he abruptly abandoned all his plans for campaigning in southern France and Spain and resolved to return at once with his army to England. The only possible explanation for this remarkable volte-face is that he had now learned that funds to pay his army's war wages were not after all on their way from England. Peter IV's ambassador was on the point of leaving for Bordeaux with his master's agreement to join in the invasion, on Gaunt's terms if necessary, when the first reports of Gaunt's decision reached Barcelona. The Aragonese King declined to believe it and sent the ambassador on his pointless mission anyway. But within days it became obvious that he was wasting his time. At Burgos Henry of Trastámara stood down part of the army which he had recruited to meet the Lancastrian onslaught. Some time after 8 April 1374 John of Gaunt boarded his ship in the Gironde. Sir Thomas Felton went with him, apparently in order to recruit troops in England to strengthen the duchy's defences. On 25 April they landed at Dartmouth.[52]

It would be a long time before England's reputation recovered from the humiliation. The Count of Foix abandoned his treaty with the Duke. The King of Navarre complained of betrayal and resigned himself to observing the hated treaty with Castile. His eldest son, the future Charles III, married Henry of Trastámara's daughter Leonora in the Castilian town of Soria in May of the following year. The King of Aragon cancelled his embassy. Eventually, when threatened with imminent invasion from Castile, he too made terms with Henry of Trastámara, surrendering all the Castilian border fortresses which he had occupied since 1369. A month after Leonora's marriage to the heir of Navarre, Soria witnessed another royal wedding between the

Castilian King's own heir and the daughter of the King of Aragon. These treaties reflected the growing military strength of Trastámaran Castile within the Iberian peninsula, just as the large dowry which Henry of Trastámara paid for his daughter's marriage signified its progressive financial recovery from the disasters of the civil war. But the skin-deep reconciliations with Navarre and Aragon were agreeable to no one but Henry of Trastámara. Charles of Navarre dreamed of revenge. Peter IV made no bones about his own position. Writing to his official biographer the Aragonese King said that he had never trusted Henry of Trastámara and had married his daughter to Henry's son only because the impoverishment of his kingdom left him with no choice. As for John of Gaunt, his Castilian projects were virtually abandoned. In the following year the English government made a discreet approach to Henry of Trastámara through the King of Navarre, suggesting that the Duke might be prevailed upon to drop his claims in return for Castilian withdrawal from the French alliance and payment of the debts owed by King Pedro to the Prince of Wales. No doubt these demands would have been negotiable if Henry had shown any interest. But he did not. He replied, according to the Castilian source which tells us this, that while England and France remained at war he 'would not abandon the French alliance for all the world'.[53]

As soon as the news of John of Gaunt's departure was confirmed the Duke of Anjou sent his agents into Castile to press upon Henry of Trastámara a new project for a joint invasion of Gascony. Anjou was keen to take advantage of the disarray in the English duchy and the presence of a large Castilian army in the southern foothills of the Pyrenees. The idea was for the Castilians to enter the duchy across the mountains from the south while Louis of Anjou attacked with his own army through the valley of the Adour and joined forces with them outside Bayonne.[54] Bayonne would have been a great prize for both men. It was the principal maritime city of Gascony and the chief commercial rival of the Basque ports. Its galleys and merchantmen represented the main threat to Castilian command of the sea lanes across the Bay of Biscay. Its capture would probably have led to the loss of the whole of the Adour valley, loosening English control in the south of the duchy and making it exceptionally difficult to attempt another invasion of Castile.

But if the plan was well conceived its execution was not. The first Castilian forces to appear were a fleet of eight galleys from the arsenal at Seville, which were on their way to join the French fleet in the Channel. They arrived off Bayonne in about the middle of June 1374 under the command of the Admiral of Castile, Fernán Sánchez de Tovar. Henry of Trastámara followed shortly afterwards with his army. He took the coast road from San Sebastian, difficult terrain where the foothills of the Basque mountains descend steeply to the sea. Conditions were particularly bad in 1374. It had been a late spring. The melting snows had turned the rivers into torrents, spreading out when they reached the coast into impassable tidal swamps. The Castilian King had made no preparations to supply his army by land or sea. As a result the troops were already in a wretched state when they crossed the Bidasoa. Bayonne had never been directly attacked before and it was usually ungarrisoned. Some prominent inhabitants of the town, including the Bishop, assumed that all was lost and fled when the Castilians arrived beneath their walls. But they under-estimated the resilience of the English government in a region which had always belonged to it even in the darkest hours of the Gascon duchy. In Bordeaux the government was in the hands of two caretaker lieutenants, the Mayor of Bordeaux Sir Robert Roos, and the Gascon veteran Florimond de Lesparre. They had enough warning of what was afoot to organise the defence. The suburbs of Bayonne were flattened. The citizens were organised in districts under their own captains and artillery distributed among them. Reinforcements were sent from Bordeaux under the command of Sir William Elmham, a confidant of John of Gaunt who was one of a small band of soldiers that the Duke had left behind to stiffen the defence of the duchy. Another of them, Sir Matthew Gournay, was sent to Dax to hold the valley of the Adour against the approach of the Duke of Anjou. Florimond de Lesparre occupied the territory of Marensin around Soustons, whose lord, the Viscount of Castelbon, had chosen this moment to throw in his lot with the Duke of Anjou. When Henry of Trastámara arrived outside the walls of Bayonne on 21 June, he found the whole region well defended and completely cleared of supplies.[55]

The Duke of Anjou, who should have been on his way with help and stores, was nowhere to be seen. He had been sidetracked in May by a quixotic project for the invasion of Aragon by a confederation of Aragonese exiles and *routier* bands which predictably dissolved in chaos and recrimination, leaving large parts of the Rhône valley at the mercy of companies of frustrated brigands. Anjou was obliged to pass several weeks in large-scale police operations in eastern Languedoc. As a result he was away from Toulouse until 22 June 1374. No sooner had he returned than he was diverted from his purpose by fresh reports of *routier* activity, this time around Montauban. The envoys of the King of Castile demanded to know what had happened to his plan to meet Henry outside Bayonne. The truth was that Anjou had lost interest in Bayonne. He sent his apologies to Henry of Trastámara and turned north to face the new threat in Quercy. The Castilian King refused to wait. He folded his tents and marched home in disgust.[56]

These distractions prevented the French from mounting any serious military operations against the English in the south-west until late July 1374. By this time the possibility of military assistance from Castile had passed. On about 22 July the Duke of Bourbon arrived outside Brive, the only notable conquest which John of Gaunt had made on his great march through France. The place was defended only by its citizens and a small English garrison of fifty men. Bourbon's troops assaulted the walls from two sides at once and fought their way over the top and into the streets. The garrison fled to the church where they tried to bargain for their lives from the top of the tower but the building was stormed and every one of them was killed. A relief force was despatched by the English lieutenants from Bordeaux but it was still some thirty miles away when the town fell. The consuls who had let in the enemy were beheaded beside the gate through which the English had entered eight months before. Their remains were exhibited on the walls as a warning to others who might mistake the fleeting appearance of English armies for a permanent revival of their fortunes. About a week later Bourbon joined forces with Anjou at Toulouse. The two royal dukes marched out of the city on 1 August, accompanied by the Constable and the leading magnates of the south-west with about 4,000 troops. The army moved west down the valley of the Garonne and in about the middle of the month appeared outside La Réole.[57]

La Réole was the strongest English fortress of the Garonne valley and the main barbican of the east march of the duchy. The town, itself defended by three circuits of walls, was dominated at its western extremity by the great square citadel with its four towers planted on the rock, originally built by Richard Coeur-de-Lion and continually strengthened by his successors to defend the approaches to Bordeaux. Since any French army operating in the region would need to be supplied by river, the capture of La Réole was the essential preliminary to any French invasion of the Bordelais. As at Bayonne the English had had plenty of time to prepare the defence. The citadel had been revictualled and armed with artillery. A large garrison was put into it under the command of the redoubtable Sir Hugh Calveley. But the outcome was very different. Shortly after the siege had begun the English attempted a sortie against the encampment of the Duke of Bourbon. They were beaten back and when they tried to return through the gate by which they had left they were unable to stop the French from coming in after them. The outer circuit of the walls was lost together with some of the richest quarters of the town and a large quantity of stores. Calveley did not have the support from the town that Elmham had enjoyed at Bayonne. The leading citizens went out to parley with the French commanders. They agreed to open their gates. On 21 August 1374 the Duke of Anjou entered the town. It was only a matter of time before the citadel followed. As the French had discovered when they lost the place to Henry of Lancaster in 1345, the citadel was weaker on the town side than towards the river and was overlooked by the tower of the church of St. Pierre. On 28 August Calveley decided that it could not be defended. A conditional surrender was agreed by which the garrison undertook to surrender on 8 September if Edward III or one of his sons had not come to its relief by then. It was pure face-saving. Calveley knew perfectly well that no relief force could be organised within ten days, even without Edward III or one of his sons. On 8 September 1374 the Duke of Anjou was master of La Réole.[58]

This left as the only real obstacles to a French advance on Bordeaux the twin fortresses of Saint-Macaire and Langon on either side of the Garonne, some thirty miles from the city. The English took urgent measures to reinforce both places, while Florimond de Lesparre set about organising the defence of the capital. A few days after Calveley's surrender at La Réole the French host arrived before the walls of Saint-Macaire. A better planned and more persistent campaign might have brought the war to the suburbs of Bordeaux. But quite suddenly, towards the end of September, the French withdrew. The reason for this sudden change of plan is far from clear. Saint-Macaire was not strong and English forces in the region were thinly spread. Nor was Anjou short of money. The Estates of Languedoc had been milked for subsidies. Anjou's treasurers had been busy sending money to the front since the beginning of the campaign. The explanation probably lies in the Duke's unwillingness to spend it. He was an instinctive hoarder of treasure and had his own ambitions as well as his brother's to fulfil. By early October he was back in Toulouse where he paid off the troops, pressing lavish gifts on their commanders. The English lieutenants must have been extremely relieved. But only the immediate threat had gone.

To well-informed observers the future of the English in Gascony must have seemed bleak.[59]

According to reports reaching the French court John of Gaunt returned to a glacial reception in England. The King and the Prince of Wales thought that he had squandered the fine army placed at his disposal. They were angered by his refusal to fight on in the south-west during the summer. Scurrilous rumours circulated about the arranged battle at Moissac, which Gaunt was widely believed to have shirked, leaving the Duke of Anjou with the honours of the field. Yet, for most of those in England who knew the facts, the failure of the campaign raised more important issues than John of Gaunt's qualities as a military commander. The easy assumption of 1369 that the English could repeat their triumphs of the 1350s had gone. Ultimately Gaunt's experience was to have a profound effect on his own strategic thinking and that of his contemporaries. The main consequence was the virtual abandonment of any attempt to conduct major military operations in south-western France. Gaunt himself was wholly committed to retaining the French possessions of his house. But he had been shocked by the disorder in which he found the affairs of the duchy and despaired of being able to find the resources to defend it against the constant and wearing pressure of France on its borders. Edward III promised that he would send Sir Thomas Felton back to the duchy with reinforcements, and tried to do so, but the usual administrative and financial problems intervened and other projects took priority. Felton did not in fact get back to Bordeaux until the summer of 1375, more than a year after he had left, and then with very few troops. For years to come Gascony would be starved of funds and reinforcements to finance campaigns in northern France, in Brittany and at sea. Gascon lords who visited England were received, according to an acute observer, with embarrassed silence and confessions of impotence and sent on their way with nothing more helpful than a smile and reassuring verbiage. Drafts of men, a few hundred strong, would be sent out from time to time to reinforce the defences of the English duchy at critical moments. But after John of Gaunt's departure in the spring of 1374 no major English expeditionary army would set foot there again until the arrival of Thomas, Duke of Clarence, in 1412.[60]

The main result of this neglect of Gascony was a fresh chapter in the operations of the Gascon free companies. When John of Gaunt had arrived in Aquitaine in December 1373 the region had recently been pacified by the agreements which the Count of Armagnac and the Pope had made with the two principal captains, Bertucat d'Albret and Bernard de la Salle. They had reserved the right to fight with any army led by the King of England or one of his sons. So the arrival of John of Gaunt effectively released them from their engagements. Bernard de la Salle left the Mediterranean and returned to the Gascon march. By the beginning of December 1373 his companies and the remnants of Bertucat's had joined forces with the English army in the Limousin. He himself was with John of Gaunt at Brive. Gaunt followed a deliberate policy of trying to hold the regions lying east of the shrunken borders of the duchy with the aid of Gascon companies like his. He appointed Bernard as captain for the King of England in the Limousin and appears to have given him a general commission to operate on Edward III's behalf in the neighbouring provinces of central France. In mid-December 1373 Bernard took his companies and some detachments of the English army and marched south into the Cantal, a region of steep valleys and dense forest, pock-marked with ancient forts, where the western foothills of the mountains of Auvergne gradually flattened out into the bleak *causses* of Quercy. Here he occupied a number of strongholds which became the main centre of *routier* activity in southern France for nearly twenty years.[61]

The most important of these places was Carlat, a remarkable natural fortress built on top of a sheer basalt rock rising 130 feet above the valley, some ten miles east of Aurillac. The castle was systematically demolished in 1604 by the engineers of Henry IV and almost nothing remains of it. But in the late fourteenth century it must have been an impressive sight, defended by stone ramparts extending for 300 yards along the cliff-tops on either side. Carlat had been occupied before by Gascon companies, in 1369, and had been bought out at much expense in 1371 by the Estates of Auvergne. Its reoccupation in December 1373, together with about a dozen other places around Aurillac, gave the Gascons a formidable base at the cross-roads of the road and river routes between Auvergne, Limousin and Quercy. The man put in command of these places in 1373 was Garcie-Arnaud, bastard of Caupenne, an associate of Bernard de la Salle who came from the Pyrenean march of Gascony. His family had been associated with the English government in Bordeaux for generations.

Surviving accounts of Garcie-Arnaud's occupation of Carlat suggest that there was more to it than the indiscriminate pursuit of plunder which had characterised earlier operations of the Gascon companies.

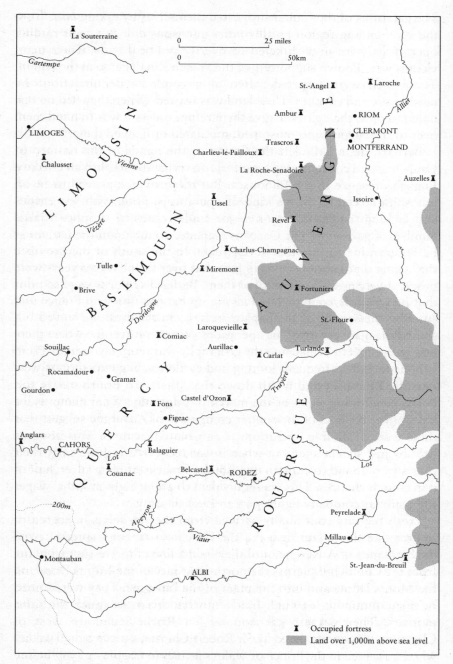

8 Principal *routier* garrisons in Auvergne, Quercy and Limousin, 1374–1377

The garrisons of the Cantal supported themselves by taking *patis* from the surrounding region as all *routier* garrisons did. But their raiding operations were now directed to overtly political ends. Their main victims were known supporters of the French King's cause in the region. These men were targeted, often as a result of denunciations by neighbours and enemies. Their land was wasted. When they fled no one dared to open their gates to give them refuge unless it was to hand them over to the enemy who ransomed, mutilated or hanged them.[62]

Bernard de la Salle left the Cantal in the hands of the bastard of Caupenne and concentrated his efforts on trying to establish an effective English presence in the Limousin. But the province proved to be an inhospitable centre for his kind of operations, poor, with few castles and lacking the resources or major trade routes to support a large number of garrisons. The Gascons managed to maintain themselves at La Souterraine for another seven years. In the south of the province they clung on to about six small forts but over the next two years were progressively pushed out of all of them. Bernard's returns were so poor that he seriously contemplated giving up his profession in France and entering the service of the papacy in Italy. In the event he stayed but shifted the main centre of his operations east into Auvergne where there was more spoil to be had and the geography was more favourable. From here he launched frequent looting and cattle-rustling expeditions west into the Limousin and north down the Allier into Bourbonnais and Berry, penetrating as far as the march of Burgundy. What glimpses we have of the receipts of the *routier* companies of Auvergne suggest that these were profitable operations. The isolated castle of Trascros was held by just sixteen men but when it was recovered in June 1375 their chests were found to contain two hundred marks of plate silver, half of it in church chalices. This was equivalent to about eight months' wages for a similar company fighting in an English army.[63]

Fresh recruits continually arrived from the Bordelais in search of returns like these. During 1374 the Gascon companies spread across the highlands of Auvergne until they held a line of fortresses extending from the Cantal hills across the north-west face of the Monts Dore and the Monts Dôme and into the plain of the Limagne. They were joined by a small number of English adventurers driven by much the same motives. Their largest garrison, at La Roche-Senadoire west of Clermont, was commanded by Sir Robert Cheyne, a professional soldier who had served in the Prince of Wales's armies in Castile in 1367 before leading a division of the Great Company of 1368 and then returning to the Prince's service in Quercy and Rouergue when the war broke out in 1369. Cheyne was typical of an expanding class of English professional soldiers, following in the tracks of more famous opportunists like Knolles, Calveley, Hewitt, Devereux and Cresswell, men who moved freely between the paid service of the Crown and the freebooting of the companies. One of Cheyne's lieutenants at La Roche-Senadoire was Richard Craddock, a younger man whose career followed the same pattern in the next generation. His father had been the Prince's lieutenant seneschal in Rouergue in the last months of English rule there and ultimately became Mayor of Bordeaux. Richard himself found profit and excitement in Auvergne but would pass most of his time in royal service in England and at Bordeaux. In an increasingly fluid war the distinction between the way of life of the free companies and that of the King's paid soldiers was less certain than it had seemed to an earlier generation.

By the end of 1374 there must have been several thousand *routiers*, predominantly Gascons, based in Auvergne and operating in the English interest. The situation had so far deteriorated that in the following spring it was necessary to send the Duke of Bourbon with another army against the intruders. During May and June 1375 Bourbon passed through the mountains of Auvergne, capturing six of the principal *routier* fortresses on the north face of the *massif* in less than two months. Cheyne appears to have ended his career in the Duke of Berry's prison in the Tour de la Monnaie at Clermont. But most places surrendered on terms, usually after a nominal resistance. At the last fortress to be reached before Bourbon paid off his army the captain opened his gates on the Duke's approach and led his company away without a word.[64] These men were there for profit, not for glory. There were better ways of carrying on their trade than fighting hopeless actions against superior forces. The Duke of Bourbon brought some relief to the battered provinces of the region but he never penetrated to the Gascons' principal redoubts in the Carladais and within months of his departure the companies were flowing back into the mountains of Auvergne as if he had never been there.

CHAPTER VI

The Congress of Bruges
1374–1377

'War at his beginning hath so great an entry and so large that every wight may enter when him liketh and lightly find war,' wrote Chaucer, 'but certes what end shall thereof befall it is not light to know.' Since 1369 there had been few attempts to find a negotiated end to the war and none that had proved productive. Two short conferences, at Guines in March 1372 and Bruges in January 1373, were all that diplomacy had achieved, and these had consisted largely of reiterated exchanges of the two governments' public positions. A year later growing pessimism about England's ability to defend its possessions in Aquitaine naturally encouraged thoughts of a negotiated settlement.

John of Gaunt had his own interest in promoting peace with France. It was becoming increasingly clear that while the war continued the French government would have the strongest reasons for supporting Henry of Trastámara with money and manpower. Over the following years the Duke of Lancaster became the foremost English advocate of peace with France, to the irritation of many of his more bellicose compatriots. At about the beginning of December 1373, when he was at Brive on his march through France, he made contact with the local representatives of Guillaume Roger, Viscount of Turenne, the Pope's brother and principal political adviser. Gaunt wanted it to be known in Avignon that he was interested in the idea of a fresh diplomatic conference under papal auspices. This roundabout method of dealing with the papal court was probably dictated by the limitations of the Duke's authority, but it was good enough for the purpose. The message reached Gregory at about Christmas-time. His reaction was extremely guarded. He discussed it with the Duke of Anjou and eventually sent an agent to Bordeaux with a cautious response. There was not the slightest prospect, he said, of the French King compromising on his claim to ultimate sovereignty over Aquitaine, which was the point on which previous Anglo-French conferences had foundered. Louis of Anjou had made this perfectly clear. So if another attempt was to be made with any chance of success John of Gaunt would have to press Edward III and his ministers to make concessions. Was the Duke prepared to do that, the Pope wondered?[1]

After his return to England in April 1374 John of Gaunt took a more decisive and persistent role in the direction of English foreign policy than he had ever done before. After resting in the west country he went straight to London at the beginning of May and passed most of the next three months there. Although there is no direct record of his role in Edward's counsels events to some extent speak for themselves. The Archbishop of Ravenna, Pileo de Prata, a shrewd Italian prelate from the Veneto who was serving as one of the Pope's legates in France, arrived in London in May. He brought with him proposals for a long truce and a diplomatic conference at which Edward III and Charles V would each be represented by one of his sons. The plan probably reflected Gaunt's discussions with the Pope's representatives in Bordeaux earlier in the year and it was presumably Gaunt whom the Pope had in mind as the royal prince who would lead the English delegation. Pileo proved to be a skilful diplomat. At the conclusion of his visit Edward told him that he was prepared to agree to a general truce until Easter 1375 in order to enable a diplomatic conference to be convened at Bruges in Flanders. He proposed to nominate a distinguished embassy with full powers to commit him. He promised to nominate the Duke of Lancaster as its leader. His only condition was that the King of France would give a similar commitment.[2]

The immediate obstacle to a diplomatic solution was Brittany. John de Montfort had arrived in Brittany by sea from Bordeaux in about mid-February 1374 to try to revive his friendships in the duchy from which he had fled nearly a year before. The visit served only to confirm the destruction of his authority. He landed at Auray, the fortress town in the Gulf of Morbihan which his wife was defending with the aid of an English garrison. There he summoned the Estates of Brittany. However, none of them would come without the leave of the King of France. Charles had no interest in giving it. The Breton duchy had not formally been confiscated but the King had refused to recognise John de Montfort as Duke since his letter of defiance of the previous year and was in practice treating the duchy as vacant. Far from permitting the Bretons to go before John at Auray he sent Bertrand du Guesclin and Olivier de Clisson into Brittany in April with heavy French reinforcements to remind them of their duty. At about the same time John withdrew to England, determined to return at the head of an English army. In May, while Pileo de Prata was working on the English King's ministers, John was bargaining for the support of Edward's Council. John of Gaunt is unlikely to have favoured this project, which cut across all his plans for a diplomatic conference. But the English government seems to have been divided on the issue. John de Montfort was a great favourite of the King's. He also had allies on the Council including its two most assiduous members, Neville and Latimer, both of whom were steeped in the affairs of Brittany and reluctant to abandon the Duke to his fate.[3]

The inner history of policy-making in this period is even more obscure in France than it is in England. The papal legates had consulted Charles V in advance about their proposed conference and he had given it his blessing, at least outwardly. Charles V was reappraising his war aims. Having recovered almost all the territory ceded by the treaty of Brétigny he was willing in principle to compromise with the English for the sake of peace. France had lived through five years of almost continuous fighting. The war was expensive and locally destructive. The taxes which supported it were unpopular. Renewed bouts of bubonic plague depopulated villages and towns and made hearth taxes harder to collect. The *aides*, which were levied on transactions and tended to fall in times of depression, experienced a sharp reduction in 1373 and 1374 from which they would not recover for some years. In spite of the failure of English arms since 1369 the English were still feared for the damage that they could do to the land of France and to the delicate balance of its internal politics. Charles V, although only thirty-six years old, was a sick man. Gouty and unhealthy for many years, he was afflicted in the summer of 1374 by an obscure but apparently serious malady. He was thinking about the political situation which he would bequeath to his six-year-old son if he died prematurely, and was already preparing the great series of ordinances which would attempt to control the rivalries of his three brothers during what might be a long regency.[4]

These changes of mood at the Hôtel Saint-Pol coincided with the emergence of tensions within the French royal family. Louis of Anjou remained as uncompromising as ever in his hostility to England but he was marginalised by his distance from Paris, by doubts among Charles's councillors about his political judgment and by his facility for making influential enemies. More significant as a factor in French thinking about war and peace was the personality and ambition of his youngest brother, Philip, Duke of Burgundy. Philip was emerging as the most influential of the royal princes. He was with the King for much of June and July 1374, when the French response to the papal legates' plans was being considered. His main interest in the peace process arose out of his marriage to Margaret of Flanders, daughter and sole heiress of Louis de Mâle. He was on good terms with his father-in-law and listened to him. As the heir to Louis's territories he was the heir to many of Louis's political preoccupations. He was also a subtle diplomat with an instinct for compromise and an intelligent grasp of the political dilemmas of the English. He had known most of the leading figures at Edward III's court during his long captivity in England after the battle of Poitiers. Alone among Charles V's councillors he retained the forgotten commonplace of an earlier age that the royal princes of England and France belonged to one cousinhood. Philip of Burgundy became the most persistent advocate at the French court of a negotiated settlement with England, very much as John of Gaunt did for quite different reasons on the other side of the Channel.[5]

For the French King the main problem about the conference lay in its timing and in the English demand for a general truce while it was being organised. The French government wanted to negotiate from a position of strength. In particular, if there were to be negotiations for a permanent peace, it was important to eliminate the surviving English positions outside the heartlands of the Gascon duchy and the pale of Calais. In the north this meant the fortress of Saint-Sauveur-le-Vicomte in the Cotentin and the surviving English garrisons at Brest and Auray in Brittany. In the south-west the military situation was even more delicately balanced. The Duke of Anjou was on the point of invading the Garonne valley. The garrison of Lusignan, the most dangerous of the surviving English enclaves north of the Gascon march, was negotiating for its surrender. Sir Digory Say was still holding out in the castle of Gençay in the heart of Poitou. So was the important walled town of Cognac on the Charente east of Saintes. All of this unfinished business made the timing of any truce a critical issue. When the King received the legates again at about the end of June 1374, he played for time. He told them that he needed to reflect. In the meantime he began to make preparation for a fresh military campaign.[6]

On about 12 July 1374 Pileo de Prata's letters arrived at Westminster, reporting that there would be a delay while the French King made up his mind. The English King's Council knew nothing about the French government's plans but they assumed, quite correctly, that Charles V was not interested in freezing the current military balance and naturally turned to their own projects. The tepid French response tipped the balance on the King's Council in favour of John de Montfort's project.

John received the go-ahead for his invasion of Brittany less than a week after Pileo's messenger had left England. On 17 July the first orders were given to requisition shipping for his men. The expedition was conceived on an ambitious scale. The army was to comprise 4,000 men under the joint command of John de Montfort himself and the King's son Edmund Langley, Earl of Cambridge. Their personal retinues accounted for about two-thirds of its strength. The rest was provided by the 22-year-old Edmund Mortimer, Earl of March, and by Edward, Lord Despenser, an accomplished courtier and patron of Froissart, who called him 'the finest knight and the most gallant and courteous man in England'. This was gross flattery, but Despenser was certainly an experienced captain, having fought in all the major English campaigns on the continent since 1356. The four captains contracted to serve for a full year, the first six months at the King's expense. After that they would be expected to maintain themselves from the plunder and ransoms of Brittany and France, an echo of Knolles's disastrous campaign of 1370 which was likely to destroy whatever goodwill John de Montfort still had among his subjects. But the English government was less interested in re-establishing Montfort's authority in his duchy than in improving their bargaining power at Bruges by a decisive stroke against France. The campaign was always seen as the complement to a long diplomatic game. The captains' indentures made express provision for the recall of the army if a truce or peace was made. So when, in the middle of August 1374, the legates finally reported to the English Council that Charles V was ready to discuss the general truce and the conference it was Edward's turn to temporise. The legates were told that the King would need the advice of the leading men of the realm. They had unfortunately dispersed to the country for their holidays. There would be no response until early October. With the optimism that had become habitual among English military planners, it was hoped that by early October John de Montfort's expedition would already have sailed.[7]

These decisions came at an exceptionally difficult time for the English government, which was experiencing a cash-flow crisis of a kind which was becoming familiar to the harassed officials of the Exchequer. Naval operations in the Channel had been wound down three months early in July 1374 and the fleets of both admiralties paid off, leaving only the King's ships and barges and the service of the Cinque Ports to defend the coasts. Since the threat from the French and Castilian fleets was then at its height, financial stringency is likely to have dictated this decision. The Breton campaign presented the Exchequer with a serious financial headache. Most of the cost had to be paid in advance. Up-front pay-ments of more than £32,000 to the troops would be required in the next few weeks in addition to the wages of the crews of the 200 or so ships which would be needed to carry them across the Channel. In August, as the captains were recruiting their retinues in the shires, there was a scramble for ready money at Westminster. A syndicate of London merchants with interests in the Calais staple offered to come to the King's aid with an interest-free loan of £10,000 if the government would agree to enforce Calais' theoretical monopoly of the English export trade. This was thought to be too expensive a concession, and in the event an even larger loan was made, ostensibly by another London merchant, John Pyel, in partnership with the financier Richard Lyons. They combined to lend the government £20,000 to pay the advance due to John de Montfort. It was a characteristically murky transaction. Lyons's participation was real enough but Pyel was simply a front for Latimer. Moreover only two-thirds of the loan was actually received in cash from the two lenders. The rest was set off against the face value of some ancient royal debt which the lenders had bought up, presumably at a heavy discount, from the Bardi bank and other creditors of the Crown. This represented an implicit rate of interest of something like 50 per cent per annum. Although extortionate on the face of it this probably represented the going rate for a government whose credit was weak and whose military fortunes were low. More controversial was the source of the money. Some of it certainly came from the private fortunes of Latimer and Lyons, both of whom were rich men. But much of it appears to have been taken by Latimer from cash balances of the King's Chamber so that the King was effectively lending money to himself for the profit of his ministers. In round figures a total of about £46,500 inclusive of interest was borrowed for the Breton campaign from various ministers, courtiers and professional financiers between August and December 1374, of which about £8,800 represented very short-term finance (a matter of days) and about £9,300 was never actually received but settled on account in discharge of ancient debt. The balance, about £28,400, was new money which was effectively being advanced against the receipts of the following year.[8]

The first military objective of the French government was Saint-Sauveur, a running sore in the French flank for many years. There had been three previous attempts to capture the fortress: one in August 1369, which had dissolved in disputatious chaos after less than a month; another in

1372 when a much smaller French force tried to surprise the place but was detected as it approached and wiped out; and a third early in 1373 when elaborate preparations were made for a siege, only to be abandoned as a result of the political crisis in Brittany. These failures at least made it clear what scale of operations would be required. Saint-Sauveur occupied a strong position. It had vast store-rooms, plentiful supplies of water and a garrison large enough to mount formidable sorties against a besieging army. At the end of 1372, Charles V had been advised that its reduction would require a force of 3,000 men-at-arms and 600 crossbowmen in addition to the horde of labourers and artificers required to build field-works and artillery. The cost was estimated at 40,000 francs (about £6,700) and even that was a serious under-estimate. This advice probably explains why for a long time afterwards the French government balked at the idea of a siege in spite of the loud and persistent complaints of the Normans.[9]

In July 1374 Charles V ordered his officers to undertake the siege of Saint-Sauveur. They were to invest it as soon as possible and to keep to the task 'day by day' until it was captured. The man put in charge of this operation was Jean de Vienne, a Burgundian knight who had made his military reputation as a young man in the civil wars of the 1360s and had been employed virtually full-time since 1369 as a professional captain in French armies. In about December 1373 he had been appointed Admiral of France. Jean de Vienne was given as his lieutenants a number of prominent Norman magnates and a rising figure in the royal bureaucracy, Jean le Mercier, who was coming to be regarded as the King's chief financial technician. Charles V had no intention of paying for the operation from his own resources if he could avoid it. He proposed to lay the whole burden of the siege on the corner of western France which had suffered most from the depredations of the English garrison, as if its capture would benefit no one else. The siege operations were expected to cost about 15,000 francs (about £2,500) a month. On 24 August the representatives of the six dioceses of Lower Normandy gathered before the King's commissioners in the royal castle at Caen and after a week of deliberation agreed to authorise the collection of this sum in September and October on top of the usual taxes. They cannot have imagined that the operation would last almost a year.[10]

The main reason why it took so long was that Charles V ignored the advice which he had received and tried to retake the fortress with insufficient resources. Jean de Vienne arrived in the Cotentin in about the middle of August 1374 with no more than a few hundred men. He set up his headquarters in the village of Pont-l'Abbé by the River Douve, about five miles east of Saint-Sauveur. Workmen began to construct a large *bastide* there under the protection of his troops. Another was built at Beuzeville a little further east, whose ruins can still be seen in the fields; and a third at Saint-Sauveur-de-Pierrepont, some five miles south of the fortress. Garrisons were put into the principal seigneurial castles of the region. The Castilian galleys, which arrived in the Channel in July, were detailed to lie off the Cotentin to intercept any attempt by the English to reinforce Saint-Sauveur by sea. This kind of loose siege was a technique often employed to limit the depredations of an enemy garrison and obstruct their foraging and pillaging expeditions. But it was not likely to recover the fortress in the face of determined opposition from its garrison. In the event it did not even significantly restrict their operations.[11]

The defence of Saint-Sauveur in 1374 was nominally the responsibility of its captain, Sir Alan Buxhill, a courtier who had taken a lease of it from Edward III at a rent of 1,000 marks a year in return for the profits of war. But Buxhill had returned to England some years before, leaving the defence of the place to be directed by his deputy, Thomas Catterton. Catterton was an obscure English squire who had originally been sent to Saint-Sauveur by Latimer in 1370 to take control of the garrison's lucrative revenues and had stayed there ever since. According to a jaundiced English chronicler his job was to do the minister's bidding 'in peace and war, in justice and injustice, in true and false alike'. He was assisted by a Somerset knight, Sir Thomas Trivet, and by a Breton called Hennequin Vallebreton. Nothing is known of Vallebreton, but Trivet was a considerable figure. He had been a professional soldier since he was about sixteen. He had fought with the Prince at Nájera and with Knolles at Pontvallain. He also had some experience of siege warfare, having taken part in the long defence of Bécherel and received his knighthood there. These three men commanded an ill-assorted group of adventurers: well-born fortune-hunters from the margins of Edward III's court, refugees from the former garrison of Bécherel and survivors from the military underworld of the Great Companies of the 1360s. The total strength of the garrison was about 300 men. They were to be much reviled for their role in the events of the next few months, but the truth is that they conducted the defence of the Saint-Sauveur with remarkable courage and endurance.

In any medieval siege the strongest weapons of the besiegers were psychological: the constant threat of an assault, which spelled capture,

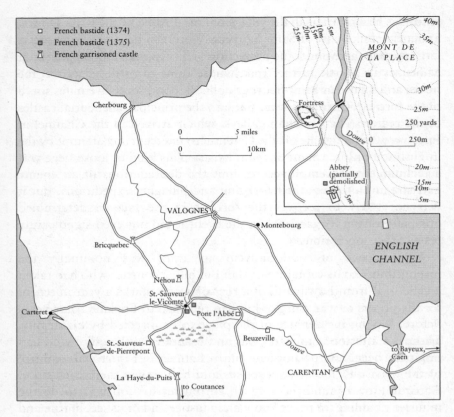

9 The siege of Saint-Sauveur-le-Vicomte, August 1374–July 1375

ruin or death to the defenders if it succeeded. Most garrisons in this period surrendered after a largely symbolic resistance when confronted by overwhelming force, bargaining for their lives before opening their gates. But by the time that the defenders of Saint-Sauveur were summoned to surrender by Jean de Vienne they were prepared for a long fight. They had already demolished the buildings within bowshot of the walls. They had dismantled the nearby Benedictine abbey to prevent the French from occupying it, taking the dressed stones into the castle to serve as projectiles for their mangonels. They launched powerful raids against French positions and supply lines and took a number of important prisoners from under Jean de Vienne's nose. They even continued their booty runs, taking cattle from the surrounding countryside for their stores and burning the suburbs of Saint-Lô and Bayeux during the siege. There were 'many fine feats of war and chivalry' around the beleaguered town, according to reports reaching England.[12]

Edward III's ministers were counting on the expedition of John de Montfort and Edmund of Cambridge to draw off most of the French forces around the fortress. But the English had, as usual, under-estimated the logistical difficulties. The Admirals seem to have been intending to commandeer the annual wine convoy to Gascony, which normally left England with empty holds in early October and called at Saint-Mathieu in Finistère on the way. But the requisitioning officers appear to have encountered unexpected resistance from the shipmasters. Many of them had already had their ships requisitioned once that year for coastal defence. Many seem to have sailed away while they could. Others accepted their advances and absconded. About 200 large ships were needed, but by the end of September, after two months of intensive requisitioning in every maritime county, the Admirals' officers had managed to find just sixty.[13]

The long-awaited Great Council met at Westminster on 6 October 1374 to consider the papal legates' proposals for a peace conference. Pileo de Prata was present in the English capital in October and probably attended it. Its decisions were no doubt carefully prepared by the King's ministers. The upshot was that the English magnates agreed to negotiate with France at Bruges. They also agreed to the reappointment of John of Gaunt as Edward's chief negotiator. However, they were not now willing to agree to a general truce. Instead there would be only a local one on the march of Picardy to enable the representatives of both sides to reach Bruges without interference. The reservation must have dismayed the legates. It meant that the conference would take place against the background of a fluctuating strategic situation. But both sides now had large-scale military enterprises on foot which they were unwilling to abandon. At the end of November 1374 the French King gave his formal consent to proceed with the conference on these terms. Both sides were playing for time. The dense preliminaries, the negotiation of the truce and the issue of safe-conducts and procurations were not completed until well into the new year. Right up to the last moment the French had doubts about how serious the English really were. The opening of the conference was eventually fixed for 11 March 1375.[14]

As autumn turned to winter and the date of the conference approached there was a palpable sense of frustration in both capitals. At Saint-Sauveur the French commanders were making no progress. By October Jean de Vienne had succeeded in persuading the King that he did not have enough troops for the job and that the *bastides* around the fortress were too small and perhaps too far away to contain the English garrison. Fresh troops began to arrive during the second half of October but the numbers still fell far short of what was required. The representatives of Lower Normandy had appeared before Jean de Vienne at Saint-Lô, the principal town of the Cotentin, on 16 October in order to be bullied into authorising the continued collection of 15,000 francs a month from their province until the end of December. Yet the end of December came and the garrison of Saint-Sauveur, now in the fifth month of the siege, showed no signs of exhaustion. In January 1375 the French King sent a testy message to Jean de Vienne ordering him to increase the pressure on the fortress and speed up the campaign. The King's Council decided to increase the size of the army to 2,000 men in addition to the crowd of workmen employed on the siege works. A close siege (*siège fermée*) was to be undertaken instead of the strategy of loose encirclement followed since the previous summer. A major deployment of gunpowder cannon was planned, in addition to the more familiar mechanical stone-throwers which were already in use. The King's 'great cannons', which were stored in the Louvre, were loaded onto barges, carried down the Seine and dragged across the rough roads of southern Normandy. An expert from Languedoc was hired to set up an iron foundry at Saint-Lô to build more of these crude ancestors of modern field artillery. One of them was designed to fire balls weighing a hundred pounds (45 kg). Two more foundries, one for iron and one for brass, were created at Caen to cast artillery pieces under the supervision of another specialised 'cannon-master', who appears to have been an Italian. All of this cost the equivalent of a major campaign. The long-suffering Estates of Lower Normandy met for a third time at Bayeux at the end of January 1375 to authorise another two months' worth of emergency *fouages*. Similar taxes were now exacted for the first time from the rest of Normandy north of the Seine. The King even loosened his own purse-strings and allowed contributions to be made from central funds.[15]

In England John de Montfort and his companions had still not embarked for Brittany. The winter weather may have contributed to the delay but shortage of shipping was the main reason. By the end of the year there were 115 ships in the harbour, barely half of what was required, and many of these had only skeleton crews on board. John de Montfort and the Earl of Cambridge, who had hung about London with their retinues while their transports were being found, finally left for Plymouth after Christmas with orders to embark as many men as they could in whatever ships were available. Two senior knights, Guy Brian and Ralph Ferrers, were instructed to hurry them on and take their musters as they embarked. The shipping situation improved in January with the return of the wine fleet from the Gironde and muscular recruitment by the press gangs in ports across southern England. There were nearly 170 ships at Plymouth by the end of January, most of which now had full crews. But now it was the turn of the troops to cause delay. A month after the arrival of the leaders at Plymouth stragglers from their retinues were still being turned out of London hostelries and packed off to join their companions. Despenser's company did not start arriving until several weeks later. Bored and idle men waiting by the coast took readily to cattle-rustling and house-breaking. The delays greatly aggravated the government's already serious financial problems because the men had to be paid for sitting around uselessly in London and the west country. Some of the loans which the King's ministers had arranged in the autumn were already falling due. The government had no choice but to pay those who were secured and leave the rest of their creditors to go without. The garrison of Ireland was peremptorily informed that because of the 'great outpouring' of money occasioned by the Breton campaign their pay-bills could not be met. At the beginning of March there was an explosion of anger at Westminster. In a letter addressed to Guy Brian and Ralph Ferrers, which has the authentic ring of Edward's drafting, the King expressed his astonishment at their 'slackness' and threatened retribution if things did not improve. Similar letters went to the commanders themselves.[16]

Outside Saint-Sauveur the measures taken by the French royal Council in January were beginning to bite. By the end of February the besieging army had reached its full strength and had moved into positions close to the walls of the fortress, among the ruins of the town. A mass of workmen recruited in the towns of Normandy were digging trenches and building shelters. A new *bastide* was built in the ruins of the abbey, some 500 yards from the walls on the south side. Several of the 'great cannons' brought from Paris were in place. They shortly began to do serious damage to the roofs of the fortress and the topworks of its walls. The main keep had to be abandoned owing to its vulnerability to artillery fire. Most of the garrison was sheltering in the wall-turrets which were thought to be stronger.[17]

We cannot know whether the men who witnessed these engines in action understood the significance of what they were seeing. Ever since its first significant appearance on a European battlefield, at Crécy in 1346, gunpowder artillery had been used mainly as infantry weapons, against men rather than masonry. In sieges they were weapons of defence, used to fire iron quarrels from the walls into the ranks of the besieging army and, slightly later, round cannonballs into its flimsy timber field-works. The single artillery piece which the French deployed in front of the southern castle of Puyguilhem in 1338, a precocious case, and the two pieces used against Melun in 1359 were designed for firing metal shot at wooden doors and sortie parties, not for battering stone walls. Gunpowder artillery had a dark reputation. An English writer of the time referred to it as 'that devilish instrument of war'. Yet the recorded instances of its use are more interesting for the later developments that they foreshadow than for any effect that they had at the time. The use of cannon against masonry was a more recent and potentially more fertile development, requiring much larger and more powerful machines made of iron rather than brass. They called for foundry skills of a high order as well as prodigious expenditure on saltpetre, a rare and costly commodity. Their deployment presented many difficulties. Siege cannon were heavy machines, difficult to transport, relatively inaccurate, with a slow rate of fire and a horizontal trajectory which tended to reduce the range. Their barrels were rarely completely regular and projectiles, generally cut stone balls, were a poor fit. Powder and ball had to be muzzle-loaded with gas-tight tampons of earth rammed into place between them. But it was at Saint-Sauveur that the new weapon first played a decisive role in siege operations. The transformation of siege tactics and fortress design, which was to be the main contribution of the next century to the technology of warfare, had begun.[18]

The great Carolingian church of St. Donatien in Bruges has long since been demolished. The largest and grandest of the city's sixty churches, it stood close to the town hall on the site of the open square known as the Burg. The diplomatic conference which had been in the making for the past year opened in its cavernous interior some two weeks late on 27 March 1375. Both governments had sent impressive embassies. The French delegation was led by the Duke of Burgundy and Jean de la Grange, a highly political Benedictine, now Bishop of Amiens. The English were represented by the Duke of Lancaster and the Bishop of London, Simon Sudbury. Sudbury was an able lawyer with a broader outlook on the European scene than most of his colleagues. He was one of the last English bishops of the middle ages to take his degree at the

University of Paris and one of the few Englishmen to have made a career in the largely French bureaucracy of the Avignon papacy. The third important member of the English team was Latimer who, although not formally named as an ambassador, was present among the English representatives and served as the main link between the negotiators and the Council at home. Both embassies were supported by a small army of councillors, military commanders, lawyers, clerks and attendants, swelling the numbers in the church and filling the lodging houses of Bruges. The French ambassadors, whose safe-conduct allowed for up to 500 followers, appeared in magnificent style. The Duke of Burgundy received an allowance of 5,000 francs a month for his expenses. A special livery was designed for his retainers, who included his entire adminis-trative household, complete with heralds, trumpeters, minstrels and harpists. Three carts drawn by fifteen horses were required for his robes and tapestries. John of Gaunt's allowance was less than half his opposite number's; but even in his case there were mutterings in England about his 'vast' retinue and its 'horrible, incredible cost'. The papal legates went to some lengths to stage-manage the proceedings so as to accommodate the pride of these magnificent personages. They met the rival delegations on successive days at precisely the same distance from the gates of Bruges and arranged for them to enter the church at precisely the same moment from different sides. They refused to adjudicate on the question which team should sit on the right-hand side of the church at the plenary sessions, ordering both teams to stand, alternately on the right and the left, until they had sorted this out for themselves. The Archbishop of Ravenna delivered the opening sermon. The Bishops of Amiens and London followed with stately homilies. The two royal dukes delivered 'most eloquent' speeches declaring their devotion to the cause of peace.[19]

There was an established procedure at such conferences which was modelled mainly on the methods of courts of law. That was the problem. Both sides conceived the process as a sustained appeal for justice rather than a search for the fertile compromise which might fall short of both sides' expectations. Much energy was applied to nice questions of precedence and procedure. This considerably lengthened the formal sessions while ensuring that the more productive exchanges occurred elsewhere. The real business began on the second day, 29 March, when the spokesmen of the two embassies stated their opening positions before the whole assembly. The English demanded that either Edward III should be recognised as King of France or else the treaty of Brétigny should be observed and all their territorial losses since 1369 restored to them. The Bishop of Amiens responded that Charles V was the sole lawful King of France and that there could be no question of returning to the treaty of Brétigny, which the English had repudiated by their continued fighting in France during the 1360s. Everyone knew that these declarations were being made for form. Simon Sudbury's reply 'passed lightly over' the claim to the Crown of France before broaching other, more tractable issues. The legates proposed that the broad lines of a peace should be discussed before the embassies got down to detail and on the following day they put the outlines of two proposals before the assembly. The first was that the English should simply sell their remaining territories in south-western France to Charles V for cash. The second was that the provinces which had been ceded to Edward III in 1361 should be partitioned between England and France. The latter option, which was the only one likely to interest the English, left open the critical question whether those parts of Aquitaine which the English retained should be held as fiefs of the French Crown in return for homage and service, or in full sovereignty. The legates addressed this problem two days later at the next plenary session. They were well aware that the dual status of the English dynasty as kings in England and vassals in France had been the origin of the war. A clean juridical separation between the crowns was plainly required. There were two possibilities, they suggested. One was that the English should have only the reduced territories in the south-west which they still occupied, essentially the coastal strip from Bordeaux to Bayonne and the lower reaches of the Dordogne valley, but in full sovereignty. The alternative was a more controversial proposal, now suggested for the first time, that the duchy of Aquitaine should be enlarged by the restoration of some at least of the territories lost to the French but that it should be settled on the Duke of Lancaster. He would then do homage for it to the King of France and would renounce all his domains in England, a solution which could be expected over the generations to transform the house of Lancaster into truly French princes.

The legates held a series of sessions with each side separately to receive the ambassadors' initial reactions. These proved to be entirely incompatible. The Duke of Burgundy insisted that all territory within the traditional borders of France had to be held as a fief of the French King. For their part, the English refused to contemplate any kind of dependent status for the duchy of Aquitaine. As far as they were concerned the real issue was what should be the territorial limits of an English sovereign state in south-western France. Over the following days both sides moderated their positions. The French declared that they would consider dividing the enlarged duchy of Aquitaine created by the treaty of Brétigny into three parts, one to be ceded to the French Crown, one to be held by the English in full sovereignty, and a third to be settled on an English prince (a son or nephew of Edward III) as a fief of France. The English countered with a proposal to divide it into two parts: the territory which they still held would be retained in full sovereignty, while the rest of the vast domains once ruled by the Prince of Wales would be held by an English prince as a fief of France. The legates proposed a number of variants for consideration. Alternatively, if the issue of sovereignty could not be resolved, the parties might consider a forty-year truce during which each side would hold the territory presently under its control and the French would make an annual payment to the English King in compensation for his territorial losses.

It is worth dwelling on these exchanges since they encapsulated the war aims of both sides as well as the difficulty of finding a solution short of total victory for one of them. The proposals put forward by the papal legates at Bruges may not have found favour at once but they supplied the themes for every Anglo-French negotiation until the end of the fourteenth century. The immediate problem, however, was that all of them went beyond the current instructions of the ambassadors. The conference therefore adjourned on 8 April 1375 to enable them to consult their governments. The principals were to remain at Bruges while their subordinates returned to Paris and Westminster. The men who left swore mighty oaths to put the proposals fairly to their masters and the principals to consider them with open minds at the next session. At Avignon rumours that peace was imminent began to circulate among the mercantile and diplomatic communities. The date fixed for the next session of the conference was 6 May 1375.[20]

By the time that the delegations reassembled, however, the political situation had changed and the auguries were much less favourable. Latimer returned to Westminster from Bruges as soon as the conference had adjourned, accompanied by one of lawyers of the English delegation. They reported to Edward III and his Council in the middle of April. The Council's response was consistent with the line which the English had taken for many years. They were not prepared to separate the duchy of Aquitaine from the English Crown. Nor would they agree that the English King should hold it as a vassal of France. But they were prepared to accept a substantial reduction in its geographical extent by comparison with the vast territories held by the Prince of Wales in his heyday. They were interested in the three-part division of the duchy suggested by the French delegation, under which the part held in full sovereignty by the King of England would have been limited to the area of the south-west which the English currently controlled.

Unfortunately a more absolute line was taken in Paris. The French King's Council, its numbers swollen by prominent figures from beyond the royal court, received a report of the conference from the Bishop of Amiens. Philip's tentative compromises received a sour reception, which probably owed something to the presence of his brother, Louis of Anjou. But whatever the dynamics of the assembly there could be no doubt about the outcome. 'With one accord' they rejected any solution which left part of French territory in the hands of the English Crown free of homage to the King of France. This effectively marked the repudiation of the three-part division which the French delegation had itself put forward. It was not the first time that Philip of Burgundy's desire to bring an end to the war had put him ahead of sentiment in Paris and it would not be the last. Perhaps the English would have given more serious consideration to the idea of settling Aquitaine on a son or nephew of Edward III if they had not been encouraged to hope for better. As it was the conference was doomed to failure when it reconvened in May. By then, however, events on the ground had added fresh bones of contention.[21]

The army of Brittany finally embarked at Plymouth at the beginning of April 1375. They landed a few days later at Saint-Mathieu at the tip of Finistère. If John de Montfort expected to find loyalists waiting to rally to his flag he was quickly disabused. His arrival in his duchy with a foreign army was sullenly received even among his natural supporters. But there was no organised opposition. The defence of Brittany had been left to Olivier de Clisson with a scratch army of about three or four hundred men-at-arms formed from the retinues of the leading royalist houses of Brittany: Rohan, Beaumanoir, Rochefort and Laval. The only the major concentrations of French royal troops in the field were around Saint-Sauveur, where Jean de Vienne had about 2,000 men under his command, and on the march of Gascony, where another army, probably rather smaller, was operating under Bertrand du Guesclin. At the time of the English landings Du Guesclin had his hands full. He had just taken the surrender of Sir Digory Say's castle at Gençay, the last surviving English enclave in Poitou, and stormed Montreuil-Bonnin, a walled town west of Poitiers which an English company had surprised a few weeks earlier. In the middle of March Bertrand du Guesclin had arrived before Cognac, by then the only remaining English stronghold north of the Gironde.[22]

John de Montfort's invasion had come some six months later than planned. But with 4,000 men at his back and several hundred English garrison troops in Brest and Auray he might have achieved great things even now. The problem was that he had a more limited strategic view than the English government. His object was to reassert his authority within his duchy. He had no conception of using the largest army currently operating in France for any wider ends. More might perhaps have been expected of his fellow commanders. But the Earl of Cambridge was not a man to press his own view even if he had one. The army began by invading the northern part of the peninsula where opposition to John's rule had traditionally been concentrated. The Earl took the small harbour town of Saint-Pol de Léon by assault, massacring much of the population. He then marched along the rocky north coast, wasting the land as he went. In about the second week of May, after six weeks in his duchy, John de Montfort arrived outside Saint-Brieuc, a small episcopal town on the north coast whose inhabitants closed their gates against him. Saint-Brieuc was a place of no importance. But the Duke could not lose face by letting the challenge pass. So he laid siege to it. In spite of the enormous size of his army he failed to make any impression on the place. Two weeks after the beginning of the siege John de Montfort was still patiently pushing mines through difficult terrain towards the walls while his army sat idle around him. [23]

In the church of St. Donatien at Bruges the papal legates sensed the change of mood as soon as the diplomatic conference reopened in the second week of May. The delegations seemed 'much harsher and more obdurate than before', they wrote in their report to Gregory XI. They rapidly reached an impasse on the question of sovereignty. All the compromises considered before the adjournment were rejected by one side or the other and neither had any fresh proposals to offer. The only course which remained open was a long truce of at least forty years, in effect a provisional peace treaty with the French government paying an annual quit-rent for the parts of the duchy of Aquitaine that they had reconquered. This was really a device for bringing peace while leaving the insoluble issues unsolved. The English response was not encouraging. They had come to discuss a peace treaty, they said. They were fed up with the turn the proceedings were taking and were thinking of going home. On 15 May 1375 the conference was

suspended for three days of festivities and jousting in the market of
Bruges organised by Philip of Burgundy, an occasion for the champions
to show off their skills and for the Duke to impress onlookers and
enemies with the splendour of a prince of the *fleur de lys*. On the 16th,
while these celebrations were in progress, a Great Council met in
England to receive what must have been a rather gloomy report on what
was happening in the Flemish city. Its proceedings are not recorded but
the outcome is likely to have reflected the government's instincts,
fortified by John of Gaunt's reports from Bruges. No one seems to have
thought that the time had come to buy peace at the price that the French
were now demanding, but neither did they want to see the conference
collapse in disarray after its promising opening. It was decided to
authorise John of Gaunt to negotiate a truce for one year, which would
at least enable the conference to limp on into another session at which
the French government might prove more accommodating. This could
also be expected to save Saint-Sauveur and possibly Cognac as well.[24]

Even this modest proposal generated fresh contention when it was
discussed at Bruges a few days later. The problem was that the
negotiations were being conducted against an unstable military
background, with each courier from Paris, Westminster or Brittany
changing the bargaining position of the parties. The siege of Saint-
Sauveur was approaching its critical moment. A large English army was
operating in Brittany under the command of a man driven by his own
political objectives who was not represented at Bruges. In the south-west
the courage of the garrison of Cognac had lasted just two months. After
fighting off a number of assaults and watching the Constable's engineers
assembling the stone-throwers on the plain beneath their walls they
agreed in about the middle of May to surrender the place to Bertrand du
Guesclin on 1 June if it was not relieved by then. This passed
responsibility for its fate to the English government in Bordeaux. In the
second half of May, as discussions resumed at Bruges, the Constable and
Marshal Sancerre were recruiting substantial forces in the Loire valley
and across central France in order to head off any attempt at relief.[25]

A week of acrimonious argument at Bruges finally concluded with an
exceptionally obscure document. What appears to have happened is
that the two national delegations, unable to settle the terms of the truce
among themselves, agreed to leave them to be determined provisionally
by the legates themselves. The legates published their decision on 26
May 1375 in the form of an arbitrators' award. This document was a
brave but hopeless attempt to freeze the military situation as it was,

before fresh developments once more undermined their efforts. The legates declared a truce of one year to take effect immediately. But it would be subject to confirmation by the two kings when they had had a chance to consider it. The ambassadors on each side promised to send some of their number home to deal with this. They were to return with their governments' instructions by 17 June. In the meantime the document made elaborate provision for the sieges of Cognac and Saint-Sauveur. Cognac was to be surrendered into the hands of the Pope and his legates for the duration of the truce. At Saint-Sauveur the French siege was to be lifted. The siege works around the walls of the fortress would be abandoned but left intact and the French allowed to reoccupy them when the truce expired. The *bastides* east and south of the town would remain in the hands of their French garrisons but they would be forbidden to engage in any acts of war.[26]

Unknown to the negotiators at Bruges these provisions were already redundant. It was too late to stop the surrender of Cognac and there is no evidence that the French government even tried. The Duke of Berry, to whose appanage the town belonged, was already on his way there. The citadel was given up by its garrison on the appointed day, 1 June, in accordance with their agreement. As for Saint-Sauveur, Catterton and his companions had entered into a conditional surrender agreement five days before the legates' award. After nine months of siege operations they had reached the limits of their endurance. Physical exhaustion, empty store-rooms and relentless bombardment had all taken their toll. The first of the great iron cannon ordered earlier in the year had been dragged into position in the ruins of the abbey buildings on 4 May and embedded in its prepared timber and earth position. It began firing immediately. Another of these monsters was sited on the Mont de la Place, east of the fortress, a few days later. They brought to about eight the number of large artillery pieces and mechanical stone-throwers around the fortress. The high walls of Saint-Sauveur had not been designed to withstand this battering. They began to suffer serious damage. According to reports subsequently made to the King of France the walls, roofs, bridges and gatehouses were all 'grandement demolie' by artillery. Thomas Catterton was nearly killed when a large cannonball came in through the window of the tower in which he was sleeping.

Almost as serious as the artillery damage was the progress being made by French sappers now that they could start their mines just an arrow's shot from the walls. At about this time they succeeded in undermining part of the curtain wall, bringing one of the towers crashing over and opening a breach. Shortly after this incident the garrison sent a herald into the French camp to tell the French King's officers that they wanted to treat. Terms were finally agreed on 21 May 1375. Unless the fortress had been relieved by an English army by 2 July the fortress would be surrendered on the following morning, 3 July. Eight prominent members of the garrison, including Sir Thomas Trivet, were to be delivered up as hostages to secure the punctual performance of this engagement. In the meantime there was to be a cease-fire around the fortress.

More controversially, the agreement provided for large payments to be made to the defenders once they had surrendered. The garrison was to receive 40,000 francs (about £6,700), which Jean de Vienne and the leading men of Normandy swore to pay them 'by the faith we owe to God, to Our Lady, to the profession of arms and to the bonds of honour and chivalry'. In addition, 12,000 francs (about £2,000) was to be paid to Catterton personally, 2,000 francs (about £330) to Trivet, and 1,000 francs (about £170) to Vallebreton. The garrison was also to be paid the ransoms of some its more prominent prisoners, which were said to be worth another 4,500 francs. Finally, they were to have a safe-conduct home with transport laid on.

Payments to garrisons for surrendering their fortresses were not uncommon in the late middle ages. The payments to Catterton and his colleagues, however, were unusually large and naturally provoked accusations of collusion when they became known. Yet Catterton's accusers ignored the circumstances in which the agreement was made. The garrison knew nothing of the negotiations at Bruges. For them what mattered was that they had obtained a six-week respite from the pressure of artillery bombardment and mining and from the constant threat of assault. They knew that John de Montfort and the Earl of Cambridge were in Brittany with an army twice the strength of Jean de Vienne's; and they fully expected to be relieved before the date fixed for the surrender. One of Catterton's first acts after the agreement was made was to send a messenger to the two commanders informing them of the terms and calling on them to come to his aid. Of course John de Montfort might ignore their appeal or march on Saint-Sauveur and fail beneath the walls. But in that case the fortress was doomed anyway.[27]

As for the French, the agreement had obvious advantages in spite of its high cost and the progress that they had made on the ground. 'That which may be bought ought not to be bought with men's blood,' Charles V used to say to those who thought it shameful to trade places with the enemy. The composition with Catterton and his men preempted the negotiations at Bruges. And it could be expected to draw the English out of Brittany and force them to confront a French army on ground of its own choosing. Charles V's commanders were just as convinced as Catterton was that John de Montfort and the Earl of Cambridge would attack their siege lines at Saint-Sauveur. They were preparing for the fight. The first step was to bring the Constable's army north from the march of Gascony. The King ordered him to join Jean de Vienne in Normandy as soon as Cognac was in his hands. This would bring the strength of the French army at Saint-Sauveur to at least 4,000 men-at-arms. Three more large artillery pieces were ordered from the foundries of Caen and no fewer than twenty-nine smaller artillery pieces armed with lead shot. These last were infantry weapons, destined to reinforce the fixed positions of the army against a relief force. What was probably envisaged was a double line of defences around the fortress: one facing inwards to contain a sortie by the garrison, the other facing outward towards the troops of the relieving army.[28]

The news of Catterton's agreement with Jean de Vienne reached Westminster and Bruges at about the same time in the last few days of May. It caused consternation in both cities. The great question for the French government was whether to ratify the deal set out in the legates' award. If they did they would lose the fruits of nine months of expensive effort at the moment when Saint-Sauveur was about to fall into their hands. If not, then there would probably be an attempt to relieve the place, which could only lead to a large-scale pitched battle between the English and French armies in Normandy and the end of any prospect of peace. But if the French had a dilemma the English had a worse one. At Westminster the Council's immediate reaction was to organise a relief force. The exact plans are not known, but they must have involved the use of the English army in Brittany. There was no other way in which a large enough force could be got to Saint-Sauveur in time. The Council also proposed to send additional troops from England. On 31 May orders were given to organise a small expeditionary force to sail from Southampton by the middle of June. The requisitioning officers moved fast. At least fifteen ships were requisitioned within a week and more were being found.[29] It was the best opportunity that the English had had since 1369 to force a decisive battle on their enemies. Unfortunately for them, however, their leaders failed to rise to the opportunity. And as they hesitated, the French were able to outmanoeuvre them.

John of Gaunt's messengers appear to have arrived in England in the first days of June bearing the text of the legates' truce. It was apparent that to continue with the relief operation now would be tantamount to repudiating it. It would also be quite unnecessary if the truce was respected by the French, as John of Gaunt plainly assumed it would be. So the Council reconsidered its decision. On 5 June 1375 its orders were revoked. The officers charged with finding men and ships were ordered to return immediately to Westminster 'because of the truce with France'. But what if the French repudiated it? That question had already occurred to the papal legates. They left Bruges at the beginning of June and made for Paris, where they arrived unannounced on 6 June and sought an immediate audience with the King. There they learned that their worst fears were about to be realised. Charles had no intention of ratifying the legates' terms. The siege of Saint-Sauveur would not be lifted. The *bastides* would not be evacuated. The iron founders of Caen and Saint-Lô continued to work shifts day and night. On about 15 June 1375 the French King issued a general summons to all men-at-arms in the provinces of Languedoil to muster beneath the walls of Saint-Sauveur by 2 July.[30]

News of the legates' truce was brought to John de Montfort and his companions in Brittany in the first few days of June by a herald sent by John of Gaunt from Bruges. He found them still engaged in the siege of Saint-Brieuc. John de Montfort had no interest in relieving Saint-Sauveur. The Earl of Cambridge lacked the will or force of personality to insist. After a certain amount of debate the leaders of the army decided to put off a decision until they had completed the siege of Saint-Brieuc, which they believed (wrongly as it turned out) to be on the point of falling. In the event they did not even do that.

Early in June Olivier de Clisson decided to attempt a spectacular diversion. At this stage the captain of the English garrison of Brest was that resourceful survivor, Sir John Devereux. He had built a *bastide* known as the 'New Fort' about five miles north of the town of Quimperlé by the south coast. Here he had installed a subsidiary garrison to prey on the citizens of the town and to maintain communications between Brest and the other major English garrison in Brittany at Auray. Clisson detached about 200 men-at-arms from the tiny French army in Brittany. It included the leading Breton lords who were with him. They marched some seventy miles to the south coast to surprise and capture Devereux in his lair. John de Montfort saw a chance to capture all of his principal aristocratic opponents at a stroke. So, leaving a detachment of troops to carry on the siege of Saint-Brieuc, he abruptly left with the main body of his army and pursued Clisson south. As the Duke approached the New Fort, Clisson and his companions fled and took refuge behind the walls of Quimperlé. They only just had time to close the gates and draw up the bridges before the English rushed the walls. John de Montfort methodically surrounded the town, which was not much more important than Saint-Brieuc, and set about starving his enemies out. The Breton barons inside did not give much for their chances of defending it with their small troop of men-at-arms and the uncertain aid of the inhabitants. But John de Montfort left them no alternative. When they sent a herald into his camp to ask for ransom terms the Duke sent him away with the response that he would take no prisoners unless they submitted unconditionally to his mercy. It seemed cruel, the herald is said to have answered, to deal thus with men who had only been loyally serving their lord. 'Their lord?' said John. 'They have no lord but me and when I lay hands on them they will know it.'[31]

Shortly after 17 June 1375 the messengers from Westminster and Paris returned to Bruges with the instructions of the governments. The delegations at once fell to bitter argument, barely concealed by the cryptic documentation which records the ultimate outcome. On 27 June 1375 a truce of a year was sealed by John of Gaunt and Philip of Burgundy. A separate document contained the terms relating to current operations in Normandy and Brittany. These terms represented a complete defeat for the English. Edward III was required to recall his army to England immediately, thus sealing the fate of Saint-Sauveur and depriving John de Montfort at a stroke of all his strength. John was to be allowed to keep just 200 men-at-arms, Breton or English, to garrison the handful of places under his control, and a small personal retinue to support his dignity, but that was all. The diplomats devised a face-saving charade for Saint-Sauveur. It was agreed that the gathering of the French army at Saint-Sauveur on 2 July would be cancelled. The payments due to the garrison and its commanders were to be made on the appointed day in accordance with the agreement made with Catterton in May. But the fortress was to be delivered up to the two papal legates to be held temporarily in the name of the Pope. He was to hold the place as stakeholder. If there was a permanent peace its terms would ordain the fate of Saint-Sauveur. But if no peace had been made by 1 June 1376 the place would be delivered by the Pope's custodian to the King of France on payment of a further 40,000 francs to Edward III. The real effect of this agreement was that the English sold Saint-Sauveur to Charles V for 40,000 francs with a year to pay. To underline the point it was agreed that the Pope's custodian would be none other than Bureau de La Rivière, the French King's principal chamberlain.[32]

The painful process of extracting from taxpayers the funds to pay the garrison of Saint-Sauveur was already almost complete. On 4 June 1375 the Estates of Lower Normandy gathered before the King's commissioners in the cathedral city of Bayeux, their fifth meeting since the start of the siege. They confessed themselves incapable of raising the 60,000 francs required. Instead they offered a third of it, which they proposed to borrow from the royal treasury and repay over a period of time by raising a forced loan from the richer inhabitants. The rest of the sum due to Catterton and his men, together with the enormous cost of recruiting troops for the *journée de Saint-Sauveur*, was contributed by the King. The total cost of the siege operation, the surrender payments and the *journée* can only be guessed. But the amount which fell upon the six dioceses of Lower Normandy alone amounted to 150,000 francs (about £25,000) in supplementary taxes and forced loans, in addition to the ordinary burden of war taxation. This represented about four times the normal burden of the province's hearth taxes on top of the *aides* levied on sales.[33]

The truce came into force in Normandy on 2 July 1375, the day by which Saint-Sauveur had to be relieved if it was not to be surrendered. Ignoring its terms, the French had assembled a huge army, between 6,000 and 10,000 strong in the fields about the fortress. The garrison were confused. The messenger sent from England with the King's instructions had not arrived. The men inside the fortress appear to have had little information about the truce and none about the supplementary declarations which regulated the fate of the fortress. According to Froissart they fell to arguing about whether the truce had superseded the surrender agreement or whether the earlier agreement prevailed over the later. But Bertrand du Guesclin cut short the argument, telling the garrison that unless they surrendered he would kill all their hostages and launch an immediate assault on the walls in which no quarter would be given. On the following morning Saint-Sauveur was surrendered at the appointed time. The cash was counted out in coin and paid to the garrison. In a curious gesture of complicity, Thomas Catterton presented a tip of 2,000 francs to Jean le Mercier, one of the French commissioners who had negotiated the surrender agreement in May, as if to show what a good bargain Le Mercier had made for the defenders. He received it with condign embarrassment and paid it into the funds of the province of Lower Normandy. The baggage and spoil accumulated in years of successful plundering operations was loaded onto several dozen open carts flying pennons painted with the arms of France and escorted to the nearby harbour of Carteret to be loaded into ships for England.[34]

In Brittany a similar scene was played out a few days later before the gates of Quimperlé but with a very different outcome. On about 30 June Olivier de Clisson and his companions had made their own conditional surrender agreement with the Duke of Brittany. They accepted the bleak terms which he had offered at the outset of the siege and agreed to surrender to his mercy. But they asked for a delay of two weeks to uphold their honour and allow the King of France to send a relief force. John de Montfort offered them eight days and so it was agreed. Neither side knew anything yet about the truce, which was due to come into force in Brittany on 7 July. Unfortunately for John de Montfort this was just before the agreed date for the surrender of Quimperlé. Shortly after the agreement with Olivier de Clisson had been made, two English knights arrived exhausted from Bruges with an escort of French sergeants. They had covered some 450 miles in five days to bring a copy of the truce. They also brought the Duke of Lancaster's orders that the army should leave immediately for England. They were followed soon afterwards by Sir Mathew Redmayne, who arrived from England with a similar message from Edward III.

John de Montfort was speechless with frustration and rage. If he had not made a composition with the defenders of Quimperlé the town and his leading enemies in the duchy would have been in his hands. After a long silence he said to Gaunt's emissaries: 'Cursed be the hour when I granted this respite to my enemies.' The thought may have occurred to him to ignore the truce, which was not directly binding on him, and carry on the fight with the aid of those of his men who were willing to join him in his defiance. Edward III had to send direct orders under his privy seal on 20 July commanding the English captains in peremptory terms to cease fighting. In about the middle of August Sir Philip Courtenay arrived off Brittany with the ships of the western admiralty to bring the army back home. Deprived of his army, John de Montfort acceded to the truce with ill grace. But he would not back it with a public oath and he kept with him rather more than the 200 garrison troops allowed by the terms. He even tried to form a fresh army in conjunction with the former English captain of Lusignan, Sir John Cresswell.

These attempts at continued resistance were snuffed out by Bertrand du Guesclin and Olivier de Clisson, who arrived in the duchy with a substantial force at the end of August 1375. John de Montfort's duchy was now for all practical purposes bounded by the walls of Auray and Brest. Knolles's castle at Derval is no longer heard of and had probably been abandoned. The only conquest which John de Montfort had to show for three months in the field was the small coastal fort at Saint-Mathieu. Early in the following year the Duke left Brittany and withdrew to the court of Flanders. It was to be two years before he returned to his duchy.[35]

The truce was received in England with intense dissatisfaction. The general opinion was that the conference had been a collusive sham in which the English ambassadors had got too close to their French counterparts. Their days were reported to have been filled with 'japes and jollities' and their nights with 'revelry and dancing'. The elaborate formulae obscuring the surrender of Saint-Sauveur deceived no one, and the abandonment of John de Montfort was seen as a shameful waste of a golden opportunity. Some said that the Duke of Lancaster had been duped, others that Latimer had been bribed. No one had a word to say for the garrison of Saint-Sauveur, whose courageous defence of the fortress over ten months was forgotten. Catterton himself suffered particular abuse because he was a protégé of Latimer's and had made more money than anyone else from the surrender. He was destined to pass the rest of his life in and out of prison before being killed in a duel by one of his traducers.[36]

During July and August 1375 the heralds passed through the war zones of western France proclaiming the truce of Bruges to the sound of trumpets in the market squares of provincial towns and before the closed gates of countless garrisoned fortresses. As a result of successive extensions formal hostilities between England and France were to be suspended for a period of almost exactly two years. Conceived in an untidy compromise, the truce of Bruges was seen in England as a triumph of French diplomatic guile. Yet it ended by disappointing even French expectations.

The first problem about it became apparent almost immediately. Although the truce extended in theory to Castile, Henry of Trastámara had not been represented at Bruges and never regarded it as binding upon him. The ink was scarcely dry on the document before a fleet of some eighty galleys and carracks sailed from the Biscay ports of Castile under the command of the Admiral of Castile to prey on English shipping. On 10 August 1375 they sighted a large English convoy which had put into the Bay of Bourgneuf to take on cargoes of salt on its way back from Gascony. The heavily laden English ships, cornered in the confined space of the bay, were sitting targets for the galleys. Thirty-nine of them were captured, including twenty-two of more than 100 tons burden whose loss would be felt by requisitioning officers for years to come. In another incident, a few weeks later, two ships bound for England were captured in the Bay of Biscay by armed Castilian merchantmen. On board one of them was Florimond de Lesparre, Edward III's former acting seneschal in Bordeaux, who was on his way to England for discussions with the Council. He appealed in vain to the truce. They took him back to Castile as a prisoner. The King of Castile was unrepentant. As long as John of Gaunt continued to claim his crown he would have his own quarrel with England whatever Charles V chose to do. At the end of the year he informed the ambassadors of the King of France and the Duke of Anjou that he regarded himself as still being at war with the English.[37]

A more persistent threat to the truce came from the continuing operations of the Gascon companies in central and southern France. The terms did not require them to surrender their captured fortresses in French territory but they did restrict their operations. Apart from enforcing arrears of *patis* under existing agreements the companies were forbidden to ransom the country around them or to engage in acts of violence against the French King's subjects. This was a severe test of their rather ambiguous relationship with the King's councillors at Westminster and Bordeaux. The trouble, as Froissart judiciously observed, was that these professional brigands 'did not know how to stop fighting'. At the beginning of 1376, when the truce had been in force for six months, the French complained that the war was still being fought across the provinces of the south-west in Saintonge, Périgord, Quercy, Limousin and Auvergne.[38]

Politically the most sensitive of these regions was Périgord, which was close to Bordeaux and to the main road and river routes between Gascony and the central highlands. The truce was hardly noticed there. The English still securely held the Dordogne valley below Lalinde. Further north their cause was sustained by a large Anglo-Gascon garrison at Brantôme on the River Dronne and by Raymond de Montaut, lord of Mussidan. Raymond was a formidable guerilla leader who had been one of the Prince of Wales's closest companions and remained loyal to his successors long after most men in his position had recalculated their advantages. His partisans were active in the valleys of the Isle and the Vézère throughout the truce. Their main target was the provincial capital, Périgueux, rich by the standards of a poor province, insecure behind its dilapidated walls and reduced by the misfortunes of past wars to little more than 500 households. As the autumn evenings drew in the citizens were obliged to mount watches as if in time of war and make bonfires in the ditches beyond the walls to light up the approach of ladder parties on moonless nights. Within a few weeks of the proclamation of the truce in Périgord Marshal Sancerre had to be sent into the region to enforce it. Unfortunately the forces at his disposal were not nearly adequate to the task and he was never able to make much impression, except in the immediate vicinity in which he was operating. The French protested bitterly to Sir Thomas Felton in Bordeaux and endeavoured to put into service the creaking machinery for enforcing the truce. The joint commission of conservators of the truce met in late November 1375 in the small village of Caudrot, half-way between La Réole and Langon, which marked the boundary between English and French territory so far as it was possible to speak of one. The lawyers made promises of amendment and damages. The raids continued. Fresh complaints followed within three weeks.[39]

The French government was unbending in its insistence that the cost of defence against the companies would have to be met on top of the *aides* and *fouages* by special contributions from the regions directly affected. The policy applied as much in Périgord as anywhere else. In December 1375 Charles V recalled Sancerre and announced that the Constable would be sent to the south-west with a much larger army in the new year. But when Du Guesclin arrived in February 1376 his first act was to haggle about money. He told the consuls of Périgueux that he was in principle willing to concentrate his efforts in their area but it would depend on what they could offer him. The neighbouring province of Saintonge had also asked him to intervene and had offered him attractive grants. What was it worth? In the event it took a promise of free supplies for his army and the yield of a one-franc hearth tax for their wages.

Whether the taxpayers of Périgueux got value for money is a difficult question. The Constable laid siege to Brantôme at the beginning of March 1376 and the Anglo-Gascon garrison was eventually bought out six weeks later. But the long-suffering inhabitants of the region had to pay the cost of this composition on top of the expenses of his army. Moreover the Constable's operations lit as many new fires as it extinguished old ones. While his men were encamped around Brantôme he formed raiding parties to descend on the valley of the Dordogne, in much the same way as Raymond de Montaut had done in the valley of the Isle. Du Guesclin denied that he was breaking the truce and he may well have been right. The distinction between offence and reprisal was almost impossible to draw. The result, however, was to spread the fighting into the Bergeracois and southern Périgord, where persistent dogfights would break out between English and French for several months to come. Without troops or money Edward III's representatives in Bordeaux were powerless to intervene. 'I think that the Constable will do much evil before he withdraws,' the Mayor of Bordeaux resignedly wrote to Archbishop Sudbury, as if he was speaking of another country.[40]

Périgord got off lightly by comparison with the provinces of the central highlands, where the truce was broken with a savagery and persistence that matched the worst years of King John II. The valleys of the upper Dordogne and the Céré and their tributaries were dominated by the enormous presence of Garcie-Arnaud de Caupenne's garrisons at Carlat and its satellites. The truce had been publicly proclaimed throughout this region on 6 July 1375. But an inquiry commissioned by the French seneschal of Rouergue reported that over the next three months eight major raids had been carried out against targets in his province alone. Behind this dry document, full of wordy legal formulae and arid calculations, lay thousands of ruined lives. Mounted men would appear in small villages with little or no warning in formations up to 500 strong to round up the horses and cattle, breaking into the larger houses to find money or jewellery, commandeering carts and dragging them away filled with all the stores they could lay hands on. Straw, grain, loaves, cheeses, barrels of vinegar, logs, boots, blankets and tablecloths, candlesticks, swords, clothing are all mentioned in the catalogues of lost possessions. A few miles away the raiders would pause to make their camp, sort out the spoil and decide how much of it they wanted for themselves. Then, from all around, the villagers would come to claim the rest, paying ransoms for their goods according to a rough appraisal of their value. The hidden savings of the richer peasants and village squires were dug out by their owners to redeem farm animals: forty gold florins in one case to recover eleven cattle and six horses, five florins in another for a prized plough ox. Two neighbouring hamlets which had fallen behind in their payment of *patis* lost more than a hundred stolen cattle, five burned-out houses and most of their stores of rye and straw in a single raid. They had their losses assessed at 1,193 gold florins, a considerable fortune. One broken farmer told the investigators that, although the eight cows and two plough oxen which he had lost were worth fifty florins, he could not begin to estimate his real loss. Without a full plough team he could not till his land and so lost his crop as well. Yet he was by no means the worst off. Some men who tried to resist the raiders were hacked to death. Any who looked prosperous enough were seized and taken away with their legs tied together under the belly of a horse and then left in leg-irons in a cellar until their ransoms were found. Some of these men were worth no more than twenty-five francs, scarcely more than the cost of feeding them. But even in small farming villages there were rich peasants who could be sold back to their families for as much as 1,000 francs.

The same scenes must have been repeated across most of Gevaudan and Auvergne. In about August or September 1375 the bastard of Caupenne fought a pitched battle near Saint-Flour against an army raised by the Estates of Auvergne. In the course of this engagement he captured the commander of the Auvergnats and several prominent local noblemen. Some of these men remained in captivity for eighteen months while the garrison raided their lands to force them to ransom themselves on the ruinous terms demanded. Others were put to work to procure supplies, mounts and medical services for the garrison's needs. It is some indication of the prosperity of the garrison of Carlat and its satellites in this period that part of the *patis* exacted from the town of Saint-Flour was demanded in bales of silk which had to be bought from a wholesaler near Montpellier and in decorative silver objects specially commissioned from jewellers at Le Puy.[41]

In the spring of 1376 raiding parties from Carlat began to penetrate into Quercy, a province which had been more or less left alone by the Gascon companies since Bertucat d'Albret's treaty of 1373. Bernard Douat, a young protégé of Bertucat's then at the outset of his career as a professional *routier*, captured the castle of the Marquis of Cardaillac at Balaguier on the left bank of the Lot near Figeac. Douat is known to have been operating in Auvergne and there is some evidence that his men came from Carlat. Within three months there were reported to be more than 500 men at Balaguier and the place had become a base for fresh conquests. Belcastel, an austere thirteenth-century castle whose ruins still stand above the Aveyron between Rodez and Villefranche, was captured during the summer, thus bringing all of Rouergue within riding range of Carlat's satellites. Over the following weeks Bernard Douat's men established at least six satellite garrisons in Rouergue.

The provincial Estates strained every muscle to raise a permanent force of just 100 men-at-arms to patrol the province. A tentative project for laying siege to Belcastel was abandoned, apparently for want of money. The royal authorities in the region did almost nothing. In

November 1376 the Duke of Anjou assured the Estates of Quercy, who had come before him at Toulouse, that he was ready to chastise the truce-breakers 'so that they would never have seen the like'. But, like Du Guesclin's clients in Périgord, they would have to pay for it. He was not willing, he said, to subsidise the defence of Quercy from the tax revenues of the rest of Languedoc. His officials added that they would need to raise the equivalent of a two-franc hearth tax and a five per cent sales tax on commodities from the population of the province. It would be cheaper, they observed, than paying *patis* to the enemy. But when the delegates withdrew to the Carmelite convent nearby to discuss the idea they at once fell to violent quarrels about the distribution of the burden. Cahors, the richest community in Quercy but far away from the raiders and well protected by its walls, refused to make more than a modest financial gesture. Although abused on all sides as '*fous et buzes*', they stuck to their position. In the end Louis of Anjou got no more than the sales tax. The promised campaign against the companies of Quercy never happened. Most of the places in Quercy occupied by the Gascons in 1376 and 1377 were still in their hands a decade later.[42]

For the French King's ministers the Gascon companies were just part of a broader problem to which their own troops contributed as much as anyone. The growing dependence of both governments on full-time professionals to fight their wars meant that any prolonged period of truce was bound to release large numbers of armed men into idleness and crime. On the French side the most problematic group were the Bretons. Brittany was a poor and densely populated region with a large nobility, serious war damage and deep political divisions. These conditions had created a great military diaspora as Breton soldiers formed themselves into self-governing companies to job for work in the service of the King of France. They were employed on all fronts: on the march of Brittany itself, in garrison duties in the Loire provinces, in the personal retinues of Du Guesclin and Clisson. After the reconquest of Poitou most of them found employment in the armies of Louis of Anjou in Languedoc. The ravages of the Breton companies had fewer diplomatic ramifications than those of the English and Gascons because their victims were usually other subjects of the King of France. But sound judges, such as the poet Eustache Deschamps, thought that they were the worst of all.[43]

Louis of Anjou had released almost all the professional companies in his service in the course of 1374. Most of them were Bretons. Some of them crossed the Pyrenees to support a hopeless rebellion against Peter IV in Aragon and then drifted back to Languedoc in the following spring. Some made their way into Berry, Limousin and Auvergne, the traditional hunting grounds of the Gascon companies. Most eventually found their way across the Rhône to loot the papal state under the leadership of Olivier du Guesclin and Sylvester Budes, the Constable's brother and cousin. By the time of the truce of Bruges the Breton bands in the south had already been unemployed for several months and were becoming a serious problem. They went, says Froissart, 'to serve the lords from whom they expected the biggest profits'. But the truth was that there were no lords in France with work to give to them or indeed to the hundreds of others who were paid off after the truce of Bruges was proclaimed.[44]

The French government responded as it had done in the 1350s and 1360s. It tried to push the companies out of France to do their worst elsewhere. Louis of Anjou paid the leading Breton companies operating beyond the Rhône not to come back into France and took steps to obstruct the crossings of the river if they should try. The Queen of Sicily's seneschal in Provence successfully blocked the crossings of the Durance to prevent them from moving south. The Pope paid them ransom money to go away but then found that it was impossible for them to leave. In the following spring most of them were cantoned in the papal state around Carpentras and on the east bank of the Rhône at Pont-Saint-Esprit. Meanwhile news arrived of fresh bands of soldiers making their way down the Rhône towards Avignon apparently in the hope of finding work in Spain. Most of these men had probably been laid off from garrisons in northern France.[45]

In about May 1375 Charles V promoted a scheme to enrol several thousand unemployed soldiers into a private army and send them into Germany under the command of Enguerrand de Coucy. Enguerrand was one of the more remarkable of the rootless adventurers of the period. By birth one of the leading barons of Champagne, he owed his fame and fortune to the favour of Edward III. He had arrived in England at the age of twenty-one in 1360 as one of the hostages for the performance of the treaty of Brétigny and had made a great impression at Edward's court, then at its most glamourous. Froissart, who met him there, described him as a graceful courtier who sang and danced beautifully and filled the needy historian's hand with silver. In 1365, still ostensibly a prisoner, he married Edward III's eldest daughter Isabel. He was admitted to the Order of the Garter and in the following year became Earl of Bedford. Not content with making Enguerrand by rank one of the leading barons of England, Edward III bought his son-in-law the rich county of Soissons in northern France. The outbreak of war between the country of his birth and that of his adoption was a cruel blow for Enguerrand de Coucy. He responded to it by declaring that he would fight for neither King. Instead he led an errant life in Bohemia and Italy before returning to France in about the middle of 1374.

Coucy had inherited from his mother a rather tenuous claim to a group of territories beyond the eastern march of France, in the Breisgau, Alsace and the German-speaking regions of Switzerland, which were currently occupied by the Habsburg dukes of Austria. It was two of Charles V's councillors, Bureau de la Rivière and Jean le Mercier, who apparently suggested that the King might be prepared to contribute to the cost of employing the Breton and Gascon companies in a campaign to recover these places by force. The plan was for Coucy to take into his service as many as possible of the companies operating in central France and the Rhône valley. To these would be added a second army of about 1,500 men-at-arms, most of whom were drawn from the troops concentrated in Normandy for the surrender of Saint-Sauveur. They included about 500 Burgundian men-at-arms led by Charles V's lieutenant in Normandy, Jean de Vienne, and the 400-strong Welsh companies of Owen of Wales. The French King, we are told, 'did not care what the terms were provided that his kingdom was rid of them'.[46]

Early in June 1375 the Breton companies cantoned by the Rhône began to move north. The Pope paid them 5,000 francs to speed them on their way and then hired the Gascon companies of Bernard de la Salle to guard the northern limits of his dominions and prevent them coming back. Originally about 2,000 strong, as they advanced the Breton companies were joined by other bands of unemployed soldiery. By the time they passed Lyon, at the beginning of July, their estimated strength was about 4,000 men-at-arms in addition to 800 Genoese and the huge mob of pages, 'pillagers' and hangers-on who always followed in the wake of *routier* armies. They swarmed across the Dombes and the county of Burgundy during July and August. The grapes were ripening on their stalks and the harvest was about to begin as the Bretons burst into the Barrois at the beginning of September. Everywhere they passed they left a trail of burning buildings and uprooted vines. On 31 August 1375 Coucy issued a wordy manifesto from Paris proclaiming his grievances against the dukes of Austria and declaring his intention with God's help of recovering his own. Then, in the first few days of

September, he marched through Champagne into the great plain of the Sundgau west of Basel and waited for the companies to join him.[47]

The outcome was an almost exact repetition of the disasters which overcame Arnaud de Cervole's attempt to lead the French companies into Germany in 1365. Instead of joining Enguerrand de Coucy in the Sundgau, the companies split up into some twenty-five separate groups and rampaged over Alsace and Lorraine, burning and looting the open country, blackmailing the cities and extracting *patis* from those they left alone. The population fled to the walled towns and castles with all that they could carry. They referred to their tormentors as 'English'. The very word had become synonymous with violence and looting, although few of the attackers had ever been in English service and most were known to be 'Bretons from Brittany'.

It took nearly two months to gather these unruly tribes together under Coucy's banner. By then Duke Leopold of Austria had arrived to direct the defence of his domains. Large garrisons had been raised by all the major cities of the Rhine. Every crossing of the river had been blocked. Balked in his original plans, Coucy was compelled to take his ramshackle army further south through the passes of the Jura mountains and across the valley of the Aare into the Swiss canton of Berne. The defenders cleared the countryside of men and supplies and destroyed what they could not take, as men had learned to do in France. As a result the army was left to wander about the region without an enemy to confront, spoil to take, or food to eat. They broke up into small groups, forcing the defences of the smaller towns, burning villages, breaking into abandoned houses and monasteries, and making empty demonstrations of force outside the closed gates of walled towns. At the end of December 1375 the men of Berne launched a series of ferocious surprise attacks against detachments of Coucy's army and slaughtered a large number of them. Owen of Wales was caught with his own company and a large part of the Breton contingent encamped around the Cistercian convent of Fraubrunnen north of Berne. Several hundred of them died in the burning wreckage of the convent or were hacked to death by the furious Swiss as they tried to escape. On 13 January 1376 Coucy made his peace with Leopold in the small town of Wattwiller and turned back, empty-handed, for home.[48]

His army, some 4,000 men-at-arms with great mobs of angry, leaderless and hungry followers, were left to fend for themselves. They flowed back westward into Alsace inflicting appalling destruction on the region as they passed. Charles V was forced to raise another army under Marshal Sancerre to head off those who seemed intent on re-entering France and keep them beyond its frontiers. Sancerre raised his banner at Reims on 1 March 1376. The Breton companies turned away, heading south. For two months Sancerre kept them on the Empire side of the Saône and the Rhône, shadowing them from the west bank as far as Vienne. Part of his force continued the pursuit to Pont-Saint-Esprit. In the course of March and April 1376 most of the Breton companies arrived back where they had started on the northern march of the papal state. There they were joined by fresh *routier* bands from Languedoc, mostly Bretons like themselves. These men had been paid the equivalent of a quarter-franc hearth tax by the Estates of Languedoc to leave France. In April they marched across the bridge over the Rhône at Pont-Saint-Esprit. At the end of the month there were some 5,000 mounted *routiers* and perhaps the same number of hangers-on crammed into the Comtat Venaissin north of the papal city of Avignon.[49]

Some of these exiled veterans of the wars of France melted into the countryside, making new lives in the Imperial territories beyond the Rhône. Many more must have slipped away and found their way back to their homes in Brittany and other parts of France. But, as in the 1360s, the ultimate destination of most of them was Italy, where the endemic wars of the papacy against the cities and despots of the north offered evergreen opportunities for professional warriors in one of the richest parts of Europe. Sir John Hawkwood's 'Company of the English Men-at-Arms in Italy', which had come to Italy with the first wave of English and Gascon mercenaries in 1362, was by now indisputably the largest and most effective mercenary company in the peninsula with some 2,500 men-at-arms and 500 archers. Injury and disease had taken its toll of Hawkwood's men and many of them must by now have been Italian, French or German. But the officers and council of the Company were certainly Englishmen and it is clear that a steady trickle of English recruits must have been reaching them from England and Gascony. The famous English *condottiere* was well informed about the progress of negotiations at Bruges and understood perfectly the implications for Italy. 'You will have plenty of trouble on your hands if peace is made between England and France,' one of his lieutenants told the ambassadors of Florence.[50]

In the winter of 1375–6 the fortunes of the papacy in Italy were at their lowest point for many years. Gregory XI's representatives in the peninsula were locked into a fresh war, this time with the Florentine republic. Most of the principal cities of the papal state had rebelled and joined forces with Florence. Urbino rose in November, Perugia, the seat of the papal vicar, in December. Viterbo and Orvieto followed. In March 1376 the papal vicar lost control of Bologna, the principal papal city of the Romagna and the northern barbican of the Pope's dominions. In desperation, the Pope turned to the free companies. Sir John Hawkwood, the principal *condottiere* in Gregory's service, was pressed into service against the recalcitrant cities of the papal state. Bernard de la Salle, still the leading light among the Gascon companies operating in southern France, was called into the Pope's presence at his summer residence at Pont-de-Sorgues, north of Avignon, and persuaded to undertake the task of taming the Florentines. He crossed the Alps with a company of about 1,000 Gascons in about November 1375. In the spring of 1376, with most of Coucy's companies from Switzerland encamped in the Rhône valley at Gregory's back door, the Pope resolved to add their numbers to the horde of brigands operating in his name in Italy. Gregory appointed a new legate to represent his interests in the peninsula, Robert, Cardinal of Geneva. The son of the Count of Geneva, Robert was a ruthless and worldly ecclesiastical politician then aged thirty-four. He struck a deal with the two leading Breton captains in the Rhône valley, Jean de Malestroit and Sylvester Budes. They agreed to take command of all the *routier* companies then occupying the Pope's dominions in France and lead them across the Alps. The total strength of their force, according to Italian estimates, was between 10,000 and 12,000 men, which was comparable to the largest armies that the English and French kings had deployed in France since 1369. Somehow money was found to pay their advances. At the end of May 1376 Malestroit and Budes made their way out of the Comtat and through the Susa pass into the great plain of Lombardy.[51]

These events rid France and the French-speaking regions to the east of most of the free companies who were not established in garrisons. But they achieved very little for Gregory XI. The cities of Italy had learned much since the first great military migration from France in 1362. Native Italian companies were better armed and organised than their predecessors and the inhabitants of the cities were better at defending their walls. In principle the Cardinal of Geneva had between 15,000 and 20,000 mercenaries at his disposal but ambition and jealousy got in the way of his attempts to co-ordinate their movements and none of them would undertake any major operation while their pay was in arrears, as it generally was. Hawkwood made a private truce with the

Bolognese and withdrew. The Bretons and Gascons prowled about the walls of Bologna, destroying farms and vineyards, until the beginning of 1377 when lack of pay and supplies forced them to withdraw eastward towards the Adriatic coast. There they joined forces with some of Hawkwood's followers and supported themselves by looting. The result was to provoke fresh rebellions against the Pope's authority in one of the few regions which had remained loyal. The sack of Cesena in February 1377, in which a combined force of English and Breton mercenaries massacred an estimated 4,000 citizens as the Cardinal of Geneva urged them on from the citadel, was shocking even by the standards of a region hardened to the atrocities of professional soldiers. The rhyming verses in which a French poet celebrated the deed reveal all the contempt of an aristocratic cardinal and a band of professional men-at-arms for the menial townsmen who refused to feed and pay them for their pains. 'Strike and kill, strike and kill,' Sylvester Budes is said to have shouted at his men at Cesena as they passed through 'streets paved underfoot with the dead and mutilated of the town'.[52]

At Christmas 1375 the English ambassadors returned to Bruges for the next session of the peace conference. John of Gaunt was once again the leading member of the delegation, accompanied this time by his brother Edmund, Earl of Cambridge. They were supported by Simon Sudbury, the ubiquitous Latimer and other prominent councillors of Edward III. A Florentine merchant who witnessed their entry into the city was not impressed. They arrived from Calais with a suite of 300 horsemen looking like a company of soldiers, armed and dressed in campaign leathers, the Duke of Lancaster carrying a hawk on his arm.

By comparison Charles V's representatives, who arrived a few days later on 29 December, lost no opportunity to exhibit the revived wealth and power of France. Two hundred horsemen in the Duke of Anjou's livery rode through the city gates on chargers with surcoats embroidered with the arms of France, followed by 250 liveried pages riding four or six abreast. Then came 30 carriages of luggage, drawn by teams of four; 40 liveried falconers, each carrying two large birds on his arm, one with a leopard draped over the cropper of his horse, all surrounded by packs of greyhounds and hunting dogs; 150 squires dressed in black and blue coats of silk and satin and 80 knights in scarlet and black, riding four abreast; 8 mace-bearers in the livery of the King of France; 30 bandsmen in gold robes and jewelled collars; 6 noblemen on great war-horses, some in robes trimmed with fur, others with jewelled collars and headbands; and 2 men holding drawn swords upright before them. Behind this great cavalcade rode the Dukes of Anjou and Burgundy and the cardinal Bishop of Amiens, Chancellor of France, all three of them dressed in cloth of gold and blue damask, and wearing hoods studded with precious stones. The French ambassadors' cavalcade was immediately followed by the two papal legates with their own great suite of bishops and clerks and an escort of 1,600 horsemen. The English delegation had hired a house on the route to watch the spectacle discreetly from behind the curtains of an upper room. But their hiding place was pointed out to the French royal dukes as they passed. The watchers had to save their dignity by pulling the curtains aside, bowing deeply and engaging in unrehearsed banter through the window.[53]

The conference reopened against an unpromising political background in both countries. Originally fixed for 15 September, the opening had been repeatedly adjourned, generally at the insistence of the French. They had refused to agree to reconvene at Bruges on the ground that they felt unsafe there, whereas the English refused to meet them anywhere else. For some two months Anjou had kicked his heels in Saint-Omer and John of Gaunt in Calais while this dispute was resolved. The row had all the hallmarks of Anjou's negotiating style, as the Duke of Lancaster recognised when he was told about it. Anjou had recently been cultivating his influence in Paris after years of relative neglect. His emergence as the 'chef et principal' of the French delegation was a bad omen. 'Let us at least have goodwill in time of peace and fighting in time of war,' the Duke of Lancaster is reported to have said, his head sunk in his hands. [54]

On 30 December 1375 the two embassies entered the church of St. Donatien simultaneously by separate staircases. The ambassadors of each side raised their hats, bowed low and kissed each other on the lips. But their negotiations made no progress at all. The legates made no attempt to resolve the issue of sovereignty. They moved straight to the proposal which they had floated back in March for avoiding the issue. This envisaged a forty-year truce, in effect a peace, but one which preserved the territorial status quo, broadly favourable to the French. Discussion, however, was overshadowed by venomous disputes about the failures of the current, temporary truce. The English delegation produced two rolls of complaints about French breaches of the truce in the south-west, to which the French responded with their own roll of counterclaims about the operations of the Gascon companies. After what the legates delicately called 'many disputes and debates' they finally produced a wordy draft of the proposed truce. The practical effect of this document was to confirm the French in their occupation of all the reconquered provinces and to remove the Anglo-Gascon garrisons from the reconquered territories. In return the legates proposed that the French should pay the English King a lump-sum 'rent', spread over the forty years of the truce. All *patis* and personal ransoms already due at the date of the truce would remain due but new exactions would cease. Broadly similar arrangements were proposed for Brittany. John de Montfort was to be allowed to retain the three places of Auray, Brest and Saint-Mathieu which were occupied by English garrisons on his behalf, and to receive a pension from the revenues of the duchy. Otherwise he was expected to leave the province and reconcile himself to the loss of his lands, in theory for the duration of the truce, in effect for ever. In about the middle of February the two delegations were charged to send some of their number home for instructions on these proposals.[55]

The English King and his advisers studied the legates' proposals during the last week of February 1376. They were realistic about them. An air of weariness can be detected in their answers, which quibbled on detail but accepted the main principles. They were not, after all, being required to concede anything that they had not lost already. They had given up what hope that they had once entertained of reversing their fortunes in the field. They were even willing to abandon John de Montfort if they could hold on to Brest for themselves. Their main interest was to secure the largest possible 'rent' for their lost provinces. However, when the sessions resumed, on 4 March 1376, it became apparent that the misgivings of the French were more fundamental. They were concerned about the English King's status in the provinces which he would continue to occupy for the next forty years. They were not prepared to agree to his calling himself King of France there. They would make no promises about whether appeals would be received from the English duchy during the truce. So the problem of sovereignty had not, after all, been avoided. The second session of the conference ended as the first had done with a stalemate and a temporary truce. On 12 March 1376 it was agreed to extend the existing truce by nine months to 1 April 1377. The ambassadors were to meet again on 1 July to give their governments' final answers to the legates' proposals. In the meantime the French royal dukes promised to do their best to restrain Bertrand du Guesclin, news of whose operations in Périgord was beginning to reach the delegations at Bruges; and to prevail on Henry of Trastámara to cancel the naval campaign that he was planning for the summer. But they gave no guarantees on either count. When the English delegation returned to Westminster in early April 1376 they must have felt that they had achieved very little for their pains.[56]

Three weeks after the return of the English delegation the storm of frustration and anger provoked by seven years of ineffective government and military defeat broke over the heads of Edward III's ministers. On 28 April 1376 Parliament opened at Westminster. On the next day, the first day of business, the Chancellor, Sir John Knyvet, made the traditional speech explaining the reasons for the summons. The King's main concerns, he declared, were the defence of England and the prosecution of the war on the continent. The government, as always, needed fresh grants of war taxation to meet these burdens. Knyvet asked for a tenth from the clergy, a tenth and fifteenth from the laity and an extension of the customs for at least a year. These demands were comparatively modest. But they were the prelude to a major political crisis, the first of a succession of internal tumults which was destined to cripple the English war effort over the next two decades and to transform the English government's attitude to the peacemaking process.

After the Chancellor's speech the Commons withdrew to their habitual meeting place in the great polygonal chapter house of Westminster Abbey. There the government's demands immediately encountered an avalanche of objections. The first break with tradition came almost immediately when someone proposed that the Commons should all swear an oath to speak their minds candidly and to give each other mutual support against the King's anger. Members delivered their speeches behind closed doors, addressing the crowded chamber from the large carved lectern by the central pillar. The first to speak, an unnamed knight, opened by declaring that the people were so enfeebled and impoverished by past grants of taxation that they could no longer pay. 'What is more,' said this man, 'for many years all that we have paid for the prosecution of the war has been squandered by incompetence and treachery.' The King should be able to live from the revenues of the royal demesne without 'ransoming' his subjects. There was plenty of gold and silver belonging to him which he had only to retrieve from the secret hoards of the ministers who had embezzled it. Another knight came to the lectern after him to take up the theme. £8,000 a year, he alleged, was being spent by the King on the defence of Calais when the whole cost could be borne by the merchants of the town if only the government would enforce the staple ordinances which were designed to give them a monopoly of England's foreign trade. He was followed by a succession of speakers making the same points in increasingly accusatorial tones. It was eventually agreed that these were difficult matters on which it would be necessary to canvass support among the Lords. On 3 May 1376, after three days of discussion among themselves, the Commons began to draw up a list of the frauds and other misdeeds which they would lay at the charge of the King's ministers and officers. This exercise was still in progress on 9 May when one of the King's household knights, Sir Alan Buxhill, arrived at the doors of the chapter house with a testy message from the King. He wanted to know why they were taking so long to agree to his demands and summoned them to appear before the King and the peers. The Commons elected the first known Speaker of the House to act as their spokesman. He was Sir Peter de la Mare, the steward and friend of the Earl of March.[57]

The 'Good Parliament', as it came to be known, met at a time of widespread discontent in England, the consequence of a long agricultural depression, aggravated by plague, cattle disease and harvest failures. But the anger of the Commons was due to grievances most of which were directly related to the war. They included weariness at the high level of taxation since 1371, disgust at the small military return for so much effort and resentment against ministers who had presided over the succession of expensive defeats. There was as yet no inclination to question the wisdom of the war itself. The complaints were about means not ends. The disappointing outcome of the peace conference at Bruges added force to their anger and discredited its leading architect, the King's son John of Gaunt. The English seemed to have cravenly given up a promising military position for nothing. The French had outmanoeuvred them completely. Much of this was misconceived. The Commons did not know about the diplomatic revolution in Paris which had replaced the Duke of Burgundy by Louis of Anjou as the main architect of French diplomacy just as John of Gaunt's peace policy seemed to be on the point of success. They knew even less about the government's financial difficulties. Edward III's annual expenditure on Calais was not £8,000 as the Commons believed but nearly three times that amount, and the cost had always fallen on the King's Treasury and not on the merchants of the Calais staple. The King's government had never been able to pay for the war without Parliamentary subsidies, except briefly in the 1350s during a period of exceptionally buoyant customs revenues. There was not the slightest prospect of its being financed now from the modest revenues of the royal demesne, however carefully husbanded. The King's ministers had indeed lined their own pockets, as ministers had often done in the past, but not on anything like the scale imagined by the Commons and certainly not on a scale which could explain the King's current penury. Nor was there any great store of gold and silver to be found in their chests if they were to fall. The real problem, as the chronicler Froissart perceived, was that the victories of Edward III's prime had come back to haunt him. They had set a standard of achievement which was hard to meet but equally hard to abandon.

In the time of good King Edward III and of his son the Prince of Wales the English had so many fine victories over the French and made so many great conquests, taking so much money from ransoms and *patis* that they became marvellous rich. Many who were no gentlemen by birth had won so much gold and silver by their boldness and courage that they became noble and rose to great honour. And so those who came after them naturally wanted to do the same, howbeit that ... by the wisdom and cunning of Sir Bertrand du Guesclin and by the aid of other good knights of France the English were sorely worsted.[58]

To the Commons, who did not understand the exceptional conditions in which England had triumphed in the 1350s, there seemed to be no explanation short of treachery and folly for the turn which the war had taken two decades later.

These prejudices were not new. If they proved more dangerous in 1376 than before it was because they were skilfully exploited by men with strong vested interests and more focussed complaints about the policies of the King's government. There were three main groups at work. The first and most active were the merchants of the Calais staple, who were closely connected with the mercantile community of the city of London. By 1375 the staple merchants were disappointed and resentful men. They believed that their business had been ruined by the government's sale of licences to export English goods to other ports. One side-effect of these licences had been to bypass the indigenous English wool wholesalers, since most of the licences were bought by foreign merchants, generally representatives of the great Italian trading houses. This aggravated the discontent and spread it beyond the tight circle of staple merchants to the wholesalers of the provincial market towns. In Parliament Latimer and Lyons, who had been closely associated with the sale of licences, found themselves the main targets of the staplers' anger. It is tolerably clear that the staplers were behind most of the allegations of financial peculation levelled at both men.[59]

The second notable group of opponents was the clergy, who had their own reasons to be suspicious of the diplomatic manoeuvrings at Bruges. They associated them with an obscure deal which Edward III had negotiated with the papal legates in parallel with the better known dealings with the French. For more than a century successive English kings had sought to conserve the taxable resources of the Church for themselves by limiting the power of the Popes to levy their own taxes on the clergy. These arrangements had come under pressure with the Pope's growing need of money to fight his wars in Italy during the 1370s. As a result relations between England and the papacy had become increasingly strained at a time when Edward III's ministers were trying to negotiate a peace with France under papal auspices. In June 1375, at about the same time as the conclusion of the truce at Bruges, Edward III's representatives had executed an unexpected volte-face. They reached a deal with the legates by which the Pope would be allowed to collect a subsidy of 60,000 florins (about £8,500), in return agreeing to a series of promotions of royal servants to English bishoprics, including the pliable Simon Sudbury, who had been prominent among the English negotiators at Bruges and now became Archbishop of Canterbury. The result was to expose the Church to simultaneous demands from both Pope and King after five years in which the Church had been heavily taxed to pay for the war with France. Many of the clergy were thrown into alliance with other opponents of royal taxation. The clergy were not of course represented in the Commons. Their own assemblies were being held at St. Paul's cathedral and in York Minster. But many of the prelates sitting in the Lords overtly sympathised with the government's critics and others were active in influencing opinion at Westminster. On 18 May 1376 the learned Benedictine Thomas Brinton, Bishop of Rochester, delivered a sermon in London which, although wrapped in the allusive conventions of formal preaching, offered an unmistakably hostile message. Brinton lambasted the King for allowing the spoliation of the Church for the benefit of a few ambitious officials in search of bishoprics. He took up many of the Commons' grievances against corrupt and self-serving ministers. It was the duty of Parliament, he said, to remedy these scandals.[60]

The third and perhaps the most formidable group to join this miscellaneous coalition of the government's enemies comprised a large section of the English military nobility. They were well represented not only in the Lords but among the knights of the shires sitting in the Commons. Of the seventy-two representatives of the shires who sat in

255

the Good Parliament at least forty-four were real knights. Their collective experience embraced the whole course of England's war over the past forty years from the highest points to the lowest. Some of them looked back on military careers extending back to the beginning of the King's reign. William Haselrigg, a squire who sat for Northumberland, had fought at Halidon Hill in 1333 when he was seventeen years old. Sir John Eynesford, one of the members for Herefordshire, had begun his career at the age of thirteen at the siege of Perth (1335) and had been with the King in Flanders in 1339. Four members of the Commons had fought at Crécy, seven at Poitiers and five at Nájera. Sir Richard Waldegrave, one of the members for Suffolk, was one of several possible originals for Chaucer's 'veray parfit gentil knight', for after serving in the English army which attacked Paris in 1359, he had fought under the Earl of Hereford with the Teutonic Order in Lithuania and been present at the storming and sack of Alexandria in 1365. But some of these men, including Sir Richard, had also stood with younger men in the bleak marshes of the pale of Calais in 1369 waiting for the decisive engagement which never came. Others had fought in the army which Du Guesclin had defeated at Pontvallain in 1370; embarked on ships in 1372 which never left the English coast; joined the fruitless march of John of Gaunt across France in 1373–4 or the abortive expedition of John de Montfort to Brittany in 1375. The knights were not a monolithic political block. Many were retainers of the King or the Duke of Lancaster, who are likely to have supported the court. But all of them belonged to a demoralised and disappointed caste. As the Commons would put it early in the following reign, they 'longed to participate in great adventures and achieve famous feats of arms each in the sight of the others.'[61]

John of Gaunt was initially inclined to dismiss these men as country bumpkins ('knights of the hedgerows'). This was a mistake, as one of his squires told him to his face. They were 'no common men but experienced and powerful men of war' with friends and kinsmen among the most powerful men in the land. It soon became clear that these friends and kinsmen included much of the lay peerage and all the King's sons other than Gaunt himself. The Prince of Wales, a dying man but a powerful symbol, ostentatiously refused to support the King's ministers in their troubles. The Earl of March would not have allowed his steward to serve as the Commons' spokesman unless he was of the same mind. Indeed in some ways his career exemplified the disappointments which the lay peerage shared with the knights. A man of large ambitions, he had a name to live up to. He was too young to have shared in the achievements of Edward III's prime, yet his military achievements at the age of twenty-three consisted of his participation in the abortive naval expedition of 1372 and the unsuccessful campaign in Brittany in 1375. He had raised his own company of 800 men to fight in Brittany and would have fought on in the service of John de Montfort if he had not been peremptorily recalled to England. It was a loss of face which he obviously felt personally.[62]

On 9 May 1376 Sir Peter de la Mare came before the Lords in answer to the King's summons. The Lords sat in the White Hall, a bare stone hall next to the Painted Chamber in the heart of the palace. When he entered the intimidating surroundings of the chamber, the doors were closed after him and most of his colleagues shut out. John of Gaunt, presiding, commanded him to state his business. De la Mare refused to be browbeaten. He would not speak until the whole Commons was present 'for what one of us says we all say'. When the rest of the Commons were eventually brought into the hall the Speaker presented the Commons' request for the appointment of a committee of peers to deliberate with them. The Commons, he said, wished to discuss with them 'many faults and grave problems' which they had identified in the King's administration and which would have to be remedied before they could deal with the King's demands for a subsidy. The Lords, after discussing this briefly among themselves, agreed; and after obtaining the King's consent the Commons nominated four bishops, four earls and four barons whom they wished to see on the 'intercommuning committee'. The bishops selected included none of the men most closely connected with the royal administration and one (Courtenay of London) who had already shown himself to be one of its most articulate opponents. The earls and barons were all men who had made a name for themselves as soldiers in past campaigns.[63]

The King and the Prince had both been present for the opening sessions of Parliament. But they were sick men who could no longer attend to business for more than short periods. Edward withdrew shortly afterwards to his private apartments in the palace of Westminster and the Prince to the manor of Kennington. They featured in the unfolding crisis as distant figures, informed and consulted at critical moments, but for ever off-stage. In their absence the defence of the government's interests fell to John of Gaunt. He played a weak hand badly. Gaunt did not have the same status and authority as his father and elder brother and his dominant role at the peace conference had identified him too closely with the perceived limpness of English policy towards France. Moreover he was not by nature a conciliator. His exalted conception of royal authority was outraged by the presumption of the knights and his first instinct was to try to overawe the Commons by a show of force. 'I do not think they realise how powerful I am,' a hostile source records him as saying. He was dissuaded from this course by the advice of his own men. They pointed out to him that the Parliamentary knights had too much support to be intimidated in this way. Apart from the Prince and much of the nobility they had important allies in the city of London. If they were threatened the Londoners would be likely to come to their defence. Gaunt himself and his friends and allies would be in serious danger.

The twelve members of the Lords' committee conferred with the Commons on the morning of 12 May. They fell in with the proposals of the knights after what appears to have been a very perfunctory discussion. Later that day the Commons, accompanied by the twelve, appeared before John of Gaunt and the peers to present the Commons' response to the government's opening statement. Sir Peter de la Mare spoke for them. The Lords, he said, could have no idea how heavily the burden of past war taxation year upon year had weighed on the Commons. Even this they would have borne with patience if the war had gone well. Indeed they could have borne defeat as well if their money had been well spent. But they wanted a full account of where the money had gone. With the great sums which had been received from the ransoms of the kings of France and Scotland and from past grants of taxation there ought to be immense sums still unspent in the Treasury without any need for further taxation. If there were not, then the King was being defrauded by his servants. The Duke of Lancaster asked for names. Sir Peter named Latimer, Lyons and Alice Perrers. Then he expanded on the charges against them, persisting in the face of constant heckling by John of Gaunt, Latimer and other peers who claimed to know the facts. Latimer and Lyons, Sir Peter alleged, had undermined the Calais staple, thereby impoverishing the merchants of the kingdom and increasing the burden of defending the town on the royal Treasury. They had rejected an offer of an interest-free loan which the staple merchants of Calais had offered on condition that the government abandoned the sale of licences to avoid the staple ordinances. Instead they lent the money themselves at an extortionate rate of interest. The Commons wanted to conduct a full investigation of this transaction and called for the last two Treasurers, both of whom were sitting among the Lords, to give evidence about it. Next Sir Peter turned to the systematic buying up of dishonoured royal debts at a discount which Latimer and Lyons had procured to be paid by the Treasury at par for the benefit of themselves and their friends. This was likely to be a popular theme, for many of those present had lost money by the King's repudiation of his debts. Sir Peter's final charge was levelled against an equally unpopular target, the King's mistress Alice Perrers. Sir Peter demanded an end to the flow of gifts to Alice and declared that it would be 'a great advantage to the realm if she were removed from the King's company'.[64]

For most of the next two weeks the Commons worked with the designated committee of the Lords on the preparation of their case against the King's ministers. They looked for material to discredit them wherever they could find it, without much care for accuracy or objectivity. The Commons already knew a fair amount about the loan of August 1374 because both aldermen who sat for the city of London had been involved. Some further information came to light on 19 May when they took evidence in the White Hall from both men and from Richard Scrope, who had been Treasurer at the time. The Commons 'cried out with one voice' when this evidence established that Latimer and Lyons had been behind the loan and that the money might have come from the King's Chamber. Fresh material came into their hands when Sir John Annesley, a Nottinghamshire knight whose wife had inherited a share of the barony of Saint-Sauveur, publicly accused its captain, Thomas Catterton, of having treasonably sold the place to the French. Catterton had been and possibly still was a retainer of Latimer. The Commons saw the chance to broaden the inquiry to cover Latimer's responsibility for the collapse of English positions in France. They resolved to accuse him of being privy to the sale of Saint-Sauveur. At the same time they began to look into the custody of Bécherel, which had been lost three years earlier at a time when Latimer was nominally its captain. A roll was obtained, apparently from the records of the Exchequer, recording ransoms collected at Bécherel in Latimer's time, which provided the basis for charges of extortion and embezzlement going back to the early 1360s. To this was added accusations that he had procured the release of French spies caught in England, that he had failed to supply the fortress properly or to pay its garrison and even that he had deliberately frustrated the naval expedition of 1372, which had been intended to relieve the place. These weighty, though unsubstantiated, allegations were filled out with a variety of petty charges of embezzlement or misuse of office against Latimer and Lyons themselves and various minor officials who could be shown to have some connection with them. By comparison the most that they could find to throw at John Neville, the other man associated with the direction of the war on the King's Council, was that his retinue had pillaged the villages of Hampshire while waiting to embark for Brittany in 1372 and that he had obtained repayment in full of two ancient royal debts which he had bought at a discount.[65]

On 24 May 1376, at a joint session of both houses of Parliament, Sir Peter de la Mare formally presented the Commons' charges before the Lords. He called for the impeachment of Latimer, Lyons, Neville, Catterton and Alice Perrers. To these were added a number of lesser victims of the in-fighting in the city of London: the skinner Adam Bury, who held the office of King's mayor at Calais and like Lyons had fallen foul of the staple merchants; a wealthy London fishmonger, a crony of Lyons who had offended some of the staplers' allies on the court of aldermen; and several petty officials who had suddenly found their minor peculations caught up in larger events. Sir Peter called for the dismissal all the King's principal councillors on the grounds of venality or incompetence and the removal of Alice Perrers from court. In their place the King was invited to appoint a permanent council of three bishops, three earls and three barons who would reform the royal administration, stop improvident grants to favourites and 'not fear to tell the King the truth'. Until this was done they would not consider any further grant of tax revenues. The Lords approved both courses.

Over the following days Edward III's government capitulated. Steps were taken to secure the accused and their property. Latimer was placed in the charge of the Earl of March as Marshal of England until the conclusion of the proceedings and released on bail. Lyons was arrested and held in honourable custody in the Tower, to the disgust of the Commons who wanted him closely confined. Catterton was found in the city and taken by boat to the King's great fortress of Queensborough on the Isle of Sheppey. Adam Bury fled to Flanders. On 26 May the King agreed to dismiss Latimer and Neville. He also swore to remove Alice Perrers from his household and never to allow her in his company again. The new permanent council demanded by the Commons was appointed at once. John of Gaunt, too angry to accept any part in this revolution, refused to be appointed. The new council was therefore largely filled with the government's critics. Most of them were members of the Lords' committee which had worked with the Commons on their charges.[66]

The trial of the disgraced ministers and officials occupied substantially the whole of the month of June and the first few days of

July. It occurred in an atmosphere of intense hostility to the accused. William of Wykeham, who had never forgiven his own dismissal from office five years before, hectored Latimer when he was called on to answer Sir Peter's charges. If he had had his way the charges would have been determined summarily without allowing Latimer either counsel or time for preparation. The accused were interrupted as they presented their case. From time to time the Lords broke off to investigate absurd rumours discreditable to one or other of the accused: that Latimer had imprisoned a messenger coming from La Rochelle with unspecified tidings from the King; that he had betrayed the King's secret dealings with Charles of Navarre to the King of France and made away with a witness who could have proved it; or that Alice Perrers employed a Dominican friar to cast spells on the King to entice him into her arms. Many of these reports seem to have originated in London, where lampoons and jingles against the court were everywhere and ugly mobs gathered in the streets. In the event something approaching justice seems to have been done. Catterton came before the Lords in the middle of June but refused to give any account of his conduct at Saint-Sauveur. Since there was no evidence against him, no verdict on him was ever reached. He was returned to his prison cell and released shortly afterwards. Latimer stoutly defended himself before the Lords and was acquitted of the charges of betraying Saint-Sauveur and Bécherel, which would have carried the penalties of treason. He was convicted on only two charges, one relating to the sale of licences to avoid the Calais staple, the other to the loan of August 1374. For these he was fined a sum to be determined by the King and declared ineligible to hold public office again. Lyons admitted most of the acts charged against him but claimed the King's authority to do them. Since he had no official position and could produce no warrant this was difficult to sustain. He was found guilty on all the charges against him and sentenced to be imprisoned at the King's pleasure and to lose all his property. Several of his associates suffered imprisonment and fines. Neville was ordered to make restitution of his gains on one of the debt discounting transactions but otherwise seems to have got away scot-free. Alice Perrers never appeared before her judges, perhaps because of the embarrassment which the proceedings would have caused to the King, but a statute was passed excluding her by name from the confines of the court.[67]

The last weeks of the Good Parliament were overshadowed by the slow decline of heroes. At the end of May 1376 the Prince of Wales's health suddenly deteriorated. It became clear that he was dying. There was a pathetic scene as the King, himself increasingly infirm, came to Kennington to take leave of his favourite son, surrounded by weeping attendants. On 8 June 1376, Trinity Sunday, he died. 'On his death,' wrote the chronicler Thomas Walsingham, 'the hopes of England utterly perished.' Contemporaries vied with each other to heap conventional praise on a man who 'never attacked a nation which he did not defeat nor besieged a city which he did not take', knowing that their words would be heard as an oblique commentary on modern times. Bishop Brinton, who had preached against the court during the early sessions of the Good Parliament, composed a eulogy of the dead man with an overtly political message addressed to his successors. Brinton drew on a timeless theme which had been used to explain military decline ever since the age of Tacitus. There had been a time, not so long ago, he told his hearers, when God had favoured the just cause and French armies had been 'wonderfully scattered' by English arms. Was it surprising that noblemen and knights of a later generation had failed in war when they had become soft, abandoning the hardy ways of their forbears in favour of luxury and vice, or when the bishops themselves no longer dared to rebuke the powerful for their misdeeds? 'Power without wisdom', said Brinton, 'was a like a sword in the hands of a madman.' Like others who wrote obituaries of the Prince, Brinton drew a veil over the political follies and misgovernment which had cost him most of Aquitaine and the enduring hostility of Castile. In Paris, which the Prince had once threatened to take with his helmet on his head and an army at his back, a magnificent requiem mass was said in the Sainte Chapelle in the presence of the King of France and his court.[68]

Edward III was not strong enough to attend the final session of the Good Parliament at Westminster. He withdrew to the palace of Eltham where, in obvious discomfort, he received the Lords and Commons in the great hall to respond to their petitions. The Parliament had been a disaster for Edward's government; and in its final days it completed the rout of the ministry by refusing to grant taxation. Although the King had yielded before the storm at every point the Commons would agree only to extend the collection of the customs for a further three years, which was no more than tradition entitled the King to have in any event. They refused to grant a lay subsidy, pleading plague, poverty, cattle disease and harvest failure. Then they withdrew. This was a serious break with constitutional tradition, the only occasion in the past generation when the Commons had failed in its duty to aid the King in his necessity. It was also a grave political misjudgment. If the Good

Parliament had ended with the grant of a subsidy the government might have felt bound to leave the rest of its work intact. As it was, the withholding of taxation alienated the lay peerage, who had been broadly supportive of the Commons' position. Those close to the King came to the same view as John of Gaunt, that the whole episode was an act of insubordinate and unconstitutional meddling. Parliament closed on 10 July 1376. It was the last episode of Edward's public life. Some time after this the King moved to his favourite residence at Havering where, at the end of September, his health suddenly deteriorated. For some months he lay, apparently on the verge of death and barely able to exercise even the desultory and intermittent influence over affairs which had been characteristic of the past few years. His physicians melted away for fear of being blamed for his death. Effective power passed to John of Gaunt.[69]

On 5 October 1376 the Prince of Wales was splendidly interred at Canterbury in the presence of the great men of the land and a dense crowd of onlookers. His body was carried through the city on a hearse, preceded by two great war-horses dressed in his arms and two men in armour and helmets, one bearing the Prince's heraldic arms of war with all its quarterings, the other with the arms of peace with ostrich plumes. It was laid to rest between the high altar and the choir of the cathedral, surmounted by the armour which he had worn in life, while his tomb was prepared in the Trinity Chapel beside the shrine of Thomas Becket.

John of Gaunt launched his counter-revolution as soon as the obsequies were over. The members of the permanent council were curtly notified that the King had no further need of their advice and steps were taken to refuse them access to him at Havering. Gaunt himself came to Havering on about 7 October and appeared before the King, accompanied by the Chancellor and the principal officers of the royal household, proffering a petition that Latimer should be pardoned for all the offences that the Good Parliament had found proved against him. The King gave a sign that he granted it. Latimer formally submitted to a fine of 20,000 marks which Edward at once graciously remitted. The royal Council was then reconstituted and the disgraced minister restored to his old place on it. A few days later Alice Perrers was restored to favour. She received a pardon for all the money, gold, silver, cloth and jewellery that she had taken over the years from the Chamber or the Exchequer and an ample grant towards a new wardrobe.[70]

Shortly, John of Gaunt turned his attention to the men whom he regarded as the chief authors of the parliamentary revolution. His first target was William of Wykeham, Bishop of Winchester. Wykeham had been the most overtly hostile of Latimer's opponents in the Lords and had emerged as the senior member of the permanent council which the Commons had foisted on the King. There is some evidence that he had also been spreading gossip casting doubt on the legitimacy of John of Gaunt's birth, a perennial rumour which regularly reappeared among the Duke's enemies and always provoked him to paroxysms of anger.

On 13 October 1376 a Great Council met in the White Hall at Westminster. It had been summoned in order to take stock of the peace negotiations with France and to make plans for the resumption of the war if it should come to that. In fact its first business was to be Wykeham's impeachment. The charges, which were promoted by John of Gaunt and Latimer, all related to Wykeham's misconduct of the King's business during the period when he had been a minister between 1361 and 1371. The staleness of these charges and the fact that they were the mirror image of those advanced against Latimer in the Good Parliament made it perfectly clear that revenge was the main motive of the prosecutors. When Wykeham asked for time to prepare his defence William Skipwith, a compliant lawyer recently appointed to the bench who was present to advise the magnates on the law, reminded him that he had spoken against a similar application by Latimer in May and declared that the Bishop was no more entitled to the indulgence than Latimer had been. In fact Wykeham got a brief adjournment at the insistence of John of Gaunt and was defended by six sergeants-at-law when the council resumed. It did him no good. On 23 October he was sentenced to be deprived of the temporal possessions of his see. Wykeham was obliged to dismiss his personal household, to disperse the scholars of New College, his foundation at Oxford, and to wander for several months from house to house in search of a roof over his head. Peter de la Mare, whose forthrightness had so outraged Gaunt, did not even receive the favour of a trial. He was arrested by royal warrant at the end of November 1376 and sent to the grim castle of Nottingham. His patron, the Earl of March, was deprived of the office of Marshal of England.[71]

William of Wykeham had never been a popular figure and his own reputation for honest administration was no better than Latimer's. But it is clear that the main reason for his fall was a change of political sentiment in the short period since the dissolution of the Good Parliament. The only contemporary chronicler who ventured to comment suggested that opinion had been turned by an outbreak of violent disorder in the west country instigated by tenants of the Earl of

Warwick, one of the permanent councillors appointed in the Parliament.[72] This incident may well have seemed symptomatic of a wider breakdown of law and order in the provinces, of which there is some evidence. But a more significant factor in the change of mood was the deterioration of the international situation. The truce was breaking down across south-western France and hopes of a compromise on sovereignty at Bruges were receding. The grievances of those who had objected to the mishandling of the war and the terms of the truce faded away with the prospect of renewed fighting.

The reversal of the Good Parliament's work was not accepted by everyone. Resentment of John of Gaunt's ruthless exercise of power earned him the life-long distrust of many of his contemporaries. Among Gaunt's increasingly vocal enemies it was widely believed that he was making a bid to succeed his father as King. The St. Albans chronicler Thomas Walsingham believed that John of Gaunt planned to elbow his young nephew Richard of Bordeaux aside and perhaps even to poison him. The Commons' concern about this was probably what lay behind their request, which was duly granted, that Richard should be brought before them in the last days of the Good Parliament to be honoured as the King's heir. The Duke of Lancaster understood the point that they were making and deeply resented it. As he would later say in Parliament after Edward's death, he was the son of a King and one of the greatest men of the realm after the King. He had more to lose by an act of treason than any man living. Yet the gossip of Westminster and the London streets quickly became the orthodoxy of European courts.[73]

By the autumn of 1376 Gregory XI had lost whatever hope he had ever entertained of brokering a permanent peace. Having more than once postponed his return to Italy to follow the tortuous course of the Bruges conference, the Pope left Avignon for the last time on 13 September 1376, brushing aside the lamentations of the cardinals, the court of France and the tradesmen of the city. A few days later he embarked with his court at Marseille. The facts fully justified his pessimism. There had been some brief and unsatisfactory negotiations at Bruges in August. Since neither side brought any fresh proposals and none of the royal princes on either side attended, these discussions were never likely to be fruitful. Most of the time was taken up with mutual recriminations about breaches of the truce. 'I really do not know what news to give you,' one of the French ambassadors wrote to a friend; 'our days are filled with speeches but none that offers any prospect of peace.' The conference adjourned at the beginning of September 1376 for the two governments to consider another ingenious proposal of the legates. The idea was that the territory currently occupied by Edward III should continue to be held in full sovereignty but only for the lifetime of Edward himself. After that sovereignty would either vest in the King of France or be awarded to one or other King by arbitrators or possibly by the Pope. The English ambassadors laid this scheme before the Great Council in October after the trial of William of Wykeham. It was completely rejected. The reaction of the King of France was equally uncompromising.[74]

In the middle of November 1376 the delegations made their way back to Bruges. Once again the princes on either side stayed away. The business was handled by royal councillors with strictly limited instructions. As soon as the question of sovereignty arose it became obvious that the gap between them was unbridgeable. If they compromised on this, the English said, they would be lynched on their return to England. The legates proposed to write to both kings asking for the appointment of new and grander emissaries with wider discretion. The English replied that no one else was likely to be given wider discretion. They added that since they were obviously wasting their time they would prefer to go home. The French ambassadors were more tactful but no more pliable.

Recounting all this in a private letter to the King of France, the legates pressed him to make concessions. 'Think', they wrote, 'of the supreme blessings of peace and tranquillity for a Christian people who have suffered so much by this war.' Charles V laid the letter before his Council. His answer was brought to Bruges on 7 December 1376 by Jean le Fèvre, Abbot of Saint-Vaast, a civil lawyer recently admitted to the French King's Council. Le Fèvre delivered the King's message to the legates and the French ambassadors in a private session on the following day. It was a remarkable statement. Charles V set out his views with brutal candour and without any of the crafted legal arguments and diplomatic obfuscation which had characterised his earlier pronouncements. There were no circumstances, he said, in which he would concede sovereignty over any part of France. The chronicles of France showed that even the Viking invaders who settled in Normandy in the ninth and tenth centuries had acknowledged the ultimate sovereignty of the kings. None of his predecessors had ever been willing to deal with the holders of the great fiefs on any other basis and he himself had sworn at his coronation that he would never alienate the rights of his crown. If he were to refrain from exercising his sovereignty in Aquitaine he would dishonour himself, encourage other rebellious princes in France and prejudice the rights of third parties, namely the inhabitants of Aquitaine to whom he owed justice. What was more, there was no obvious advantage in compromise, for if the English were allowed unfettered dominion of any of the French provinces they would sooner or later use them as a base from which to make war on him or his successors. As for the terms agreed at Brétigny and Calais they were past history now. If Charles himself had sworn to honour them that was only in order to get his father out of captivity in England. Fortunately the English had spared him the moral dilemma by delaying John II's renunciations of sovereignty over the provinces ceded to England. They had never been made. There was once a Roman emperor, the Abbot said, who asked a captured prince how long, if he made peace with his people, he could expect it to last. The prisoner answered: 'for as long as it remains founded in reason and justice and no longer'. The same would be true, he said, of any treaty made with the English.

The French King knew the strength of his own position. His understanding of his adversaries was less impressive. He seemed oblivious to the real difficulties which the feudal relationship between France and Aquitaine had caused in the half-century before 1337 or of the importance which the English had always attached to the question of sovereignty. His ministers made no attempt to follow the complex internal politics of England and had no idea of the extent to which John of Gaunt had gone out on a limb to support a compromise peace at the English court. Charles V's view about the cause of the present impasse was simple and wrong. He held the Duke of Lancaster personally responsible for it. His view was that Gaunt was a great captain whose influence in England depended on being able to find employment for his vast military retinue. He therefore had a vested interest in the continuance of the war. Charles had heard the reports of the Duke's ambition to succeed his father and believed them. Comparing the Duke to Julius Caesar, returning from Gaul to suppress the Roman Republic, Charles told the papal legates that Gaunt's ultimate object was to keep an army in being with which he could seize the throne when the moment came. The peace conference might as well have closed at this point. In fact it limped on at Bruges until the new year, mainly because neither government was willing to incur the odium of publicly breaking off negotiations. It was then adjourned until 1 March 1377. This was just one month before the expiry of the truce.[75]

*

Charles V's intransigent line was explained by his strong strategic position and his well-filled war chest. While the English House of Commons had maintained its traditional hostility to the collection of subsidies in time of truce, the system of permanent taxation which now operated in France was not dependent, at least in the north, on regular consent from representative assemblies. This meant that between 1375 and 1377, when war expenditure had been running at a comparatively low level, French tax revenues had continued to flow in at wartime rates. There is much evidence that, even after meeting his swelling personal commitments, Charles V had accumulated a large surplus since the proclamation of the truce. In Languedoc and in the Duke of Berry's appanage in central France consent to taxation continued to be required, but even in these regions the persistence of *routier* operations had made it possible to go on obtaining grants at the high levels which had been traditional before the truce. The Duke of Berry received larger and more frequent grants of taxation during the truce than ever before. Much of it was earmarked for financing *videments* which never actually occurred. Louis of Anjou secured four grants from the Estates of Languedoc during the truce, amounting to eight and a half francs per hearth altogether, at a time when his only significant war expenditure was the financing of small-scale cat-fights in Périgord and the bribing of the companies in the Rhône valley. There were plausible reports of a great hoard of cash accumulated in his castle at Roquemaure on the Rhône.[76]

When the French King's ministers began to prepare for the resumption of the war after the Christmas festivities of 1376, the main focus of their plans was the preparation of a large fleet and an 'army of the sea'. For the past three years Charles V had been making strenuous attempts to reform the French war fleet. Jean de Vienne, who had been Admiral of France since 1373, was no seaman. But he was a bold military commander and a competent administrator. He had addressed the endemic corruption of the arsenal at Rouen. He had put in hand a proper programme of maintenance to keep the King's galleys and barges seaworthy. In about February 1376 the arsenal had begun an important campaign of new building. Great quantities of timber had been cut down in the forests of the Seine valley and floated down the river to be seasoned for new hulls. The skilled workforce had been increased to about 160 men. Ten new clinker-built oared barges had been laid down. More had been ordered in 1376 and yet more in 1377. Plans were being made with the Castilians for a large reinforcement of Mediterranean galleys from Seville. The Castilians were in turn applying pressure to the Portuguese to contribute their own contingent.[77]

The exact nature of their plans for using this formidable navy is as uncertain as anything else which has to be deduced from the evidence of intercepted correspondence and interrogated agents. The south coast of England was an open, accessible and inviting target. The evidence is that Charles V initially proposed that the ships should burn their way west along the south coast and then land an army at Milford Haven in Pembrokeshire under the joint command of Owen of Wales and the renegade English knight Sir John Minsterworth. For Owen this marked a return to the abortive plans of 1369 and 1372 and to the dream of restoring an indigenous principality of Wales. What Minsterworth could contribute, or indeed expected to get out of this adventure, is more difficult to say. He must have been a plausible talker in spite of his shady past. Early in 1377 Minsterworth was sent by Charles V to Castile with instructions to organise the hire of transports and troops and the purchase of arms and equipment to be distributed among the Welsh after they had landed.[78]

At the same time the French were hoping, not for the first time, to reawaken the Scottish lion, which had been such a valuable ally before 1357. The Scots had a far greater potential than the Welsh for drawing English efforts away from France, as even Owen admitted. The main obstacle to France's ambitions in this direction was the unwarlike King, Robert Stewart. Robert's family interests lay north of the Forth. He had never had much time for the complex politics of the border or been willing to risk his security by repudiating the truce with England. When the Scottish borderers launched occasional forays into the north of England, his reaction was to abuse them as 'wicked drunkards' and disavow them. Yet there were signs, to which Charles V's advisers may have been more sensitive than Edward's, that the mood in Scotland was changing. Edward III in his dotage was not the terrible figure that he had been in his prime. The Scots had noticed the divisions of the English political community once his firm hand was removed. The lords of the Scottish border were impatient with the stalemate and less amenable than they had been to control by the King. These men relied for their power on extensive networks of dependants: kinsmen, tenants, friends and followers who looked to them for leadership and patronage and for opportunities which in a poor country only war could provide. Yet they were more than gang leaders and freebooters. Sir Archibald and his cousin William, Earl of Douglas, had both been brought up in France and fought with John II at Poitiers. They and their kind lived in the harsh world of the border. But they shared a European outlook and were treated by Froissart with the respect due to those who belonged to the world of European chivalry. At some time early in 1377 Charles V sent an agent to Edinburgh to persuade Robert II to repudiate the truce. He promised to send another embassy with more detailed proposals. According to Froissart, Robert summoned a council of the Scottish baronage and agreed, on their advice, to reopen the war. If this is true then he shortly thought better of it. But his subjects were increasingly inclined to take matters into their own hands irrespective of his views. They had the support of prominent officers of his court. John Mercer, the richest merchant in Scotland and a long-standing friend of France, travelled to France in the spring, visited the French court and personally inspected the preparations of the French 'army of the sea'.[79]

With high hopes that the English would have their hands full with major raids on southern England, a rebellion in Wales and possibly a Scottish invasion in the north, the French ministers set about planning their own operations for the summer of 1377. The main lines of their strategy seem to have been laid down at the beginning of February, when the Dukes of Burgundy, Berry and Bourbon and the Constable Du Guesclin were all with the King in Paris. What was envisaged was no fewer than four royal armies, in addition to Jean de Vienne's 'army of the sea'. Two major offensives were planned, one under Louis of Anjou against the remaining English strongholds of the south-west, the other under the Duke of Burgundy against Calais. At the same time it was intended that Olivier de Clisson would attack the two surviving fortresses held for John de Montfort in Brittany, at Brest and Auray; and that the Dukes of Berry and Bourbon would march on Carlat and its satellite fortresses in the foothills of Auvergne. 'Never in the memory of man had such a great enterprise been undertaken,' declared the official chronicler of the reign.[80]

1377 was the year of the English King's jubilee. By now Edward had become a remote figure in his own kingdom, moving at irregular intervals between the royal manors around London and keeping to the shadows, out of sight of his subjects. There is some evidence of an improvement of his health early in 1377 but he seems to have remained incapable of giving more than passing attention to public affairs and access to him was strictly controlled by his household. There are vivid but pathetic glimpses of his life: Alice Perrers, a manipulative presence standing at the head of the King's bed as officials came before him; the Chamberlain quarrelling with petitioners outside his room until the King came to the door to find out what was going on and silenced them by taking the petition out of their hands; the old man propped upright on his chair at formal audiences, looking 'like a statue' and unable to speak, as his sons and selected bishops, officials and courtiers stood around him; a hooded barge bearing the prostrate King up the Thames from Havering to Sheen during the sittings of Parliament, making its way through the mass of boats lying off the palace of Westminster, all filled with people trying to catch a last glimpse of him.[81]

Parliament opened at Westminster in the absence of the King on 27 January 1377. The Council had been forced to summon it by shortage of funds to fight a war that now seemed inevitable. According to Thomas Walsingham, John of Gaunt brought pressure to bear on the electors of the shires to return more amenable knights than those of 1376. But even without interference the imminence of the threat from France would probably have been enough to produce a more compliant mood. The opening address was delivered by the newly appointed Chancellor, Adam Houghton, Bishop of Saint David's. His words were calculated to darken the menace and loosen men's purses. He dwelt on the enemies that now encircled England: France, Scotland, Castile. The Council, he said, had received 'several letters and private reports' about the progress of French and Castilian naval preparations. The English King's barges were already being mobilised. A comprehensive programme of requisitions began in early February while Parliament was sitting. Yet the main difference between the new Parliament and its predecessor lay not in the personnel or attitudes of the Commons but in the position of the Lords. Their support for the Parliamentary revolution of 1376 had been indispensable but they were no longer inclined to favour a radical programme of reform in the face of the government's obvious financial need. This time the 'intercommuning committee' which the Lords appointed to assist the Commons in their deliberations was stuffed with government supporters. Even the Earl of March seems to have rallied to the government's cause. In most respects both houses showed themselves willing enough to do the government's bidding. Gaunt's counter-revolution was completed with the reversal of all proceedings in the last Parliament against Alice Perrers and Richard Lyons and his associates and the restoration of most of their sequestered assets. A few members of the Commons, including some veterans of the previous Parliament, raised their voices to protest about the treatment of Peter de la Mare, but they were cowed into silence. The leadership of the opposition passed from the Commons to an unlikely coalition of the Church and the citizens of London.[82]

The leading figure among the government's clerical opponents was William Courtenay, the impulsive and ambitious but extremely able younger son of the Earl of Devon. Courtenay had recently been appointed at the age of thirty-four to the bishopric of London, a promotion which he probably owed to the patronage of the Black Prince. He was already known as an outspoken opponent of royal taxation and a vocal enemy of John of Gaunt. He had sat on the intercommuning committee of the Good Parliament and on the short-lived permanent council which emerged from it. He had also acted as William of Wykeham's counsel at his trial. None of these things can have endeared him to the ministry. Courtenay's continued acceptance of the programme of the Good Parliament became apparent quite early in the Parliament of 1377, when he raised objections to the grant of any subsidy at all even with the war about to restart. At least three bishops supported him. Their opposition intensified when the southern convocation assembled in its traditional meeting place at St. Paul's in London on 3 February, a week after the opening of Parliament at Westminster. The presiding bishop, Archbishop Sudbury, was a dependable supporter of the government and made no secret of the fact. Walsingham calls him a 'hireling drunk with the poison of greed'. But Sudbury proved quite unable to manage one of the most unruly clerical assemblies for many years. The first bone of contention was the position of William of Wykeham, whom the government had refused to allow to come within twenty miles of Westminster. At Courtenay's urging convocation refused to transact any business until the government relented and allowed him to join their deliberations. At Courtenay's urging again they opened proceedings for heresy against a royal clerk and protégé of John of Gaunt's, John Wycliffe. Wycliffe would later become a much more celebrated figure than he was in January 1377, but he was already the author of some government-inspired tracts and a remarkable academic treatise, *De Civili Dominio* ('Of Temporal Power'), which advocated the political subordination of the Church to the civil power and the use of its property for public purposes. For a few days Wycliffe's prosecution, like Wykeham's, acquired a symbolic importance in the eyes of all the main protagonists, for reasons which had little connection with either the man or his views. Courtenay and his supporters saw in Wycliffe's writings signs of what they perceived to be the wider political threat to the autonomy of the Church. For his part Gaunt saw the heresy charge as an indirect attack on himself.[83]

The other force involved in the confrontation was the London mob. London had been a significant factor in the revolutions of the thirteenth century and in the deposition of Edward II. Yet its re-emergence as a force in English politics during the last three decades of the fourteenth century took John of Gaunt's generation by surprise. Perhaps it should not have done. With an estimated population of about 45,000 souls, London was only about a quarter of the size of Paris but it was still among the largest European cities at a time when urban unrest was becoming an endemic problem for most western monarchies. The city's oligarchic organisation and social divisions made it as vulnerable as any of them to crime and disorder. Political power was concentrated in the hands of the mayor and aldermen, themselves drawn from a small group of rich merchants belonging to the major guilds. The mass of the population consisted of unenfranchised apprentices, journeymen, labourers, servants and beggars, most of whom lived close to subsistence levels at the best of times. The physical fabric of the city aggravated the natural tensions of this world. People lived packed together in a dense network of narrow lanes and alleys interrupted by the gardens of monasteries, churchyards and aristocratic mansions. The city's ancient and extensive liberties deprived the King's ministers of any real measure of control over this crowded and intensely political place. There was no equivalent in London of the Paris Châtelet, installed in the heart of the city, with its royal judges, jailers and sergeants. The only visible signs of royal power were at the edges of the city: the Tower of London on the east, a royal fortress, arsenal and zoo; and the Marshalsea and King's Bench prisons south of London Bridge in Southwark.

London had done well by the war. It was an important entrepôt for the sale of armour, equipment and looted objects. The building trade had prospered by the magnificent spending of successful captains returning from France and merchant capitalists grown fat on the profits of the government's financial operations. Calais was virtually a London colony. Yet Londoners had felt the decline of English arms since 1369 as much as any group of Englishmen. The disruption of English trade and shipping had badly affected the city's interests. The return of heavy annual taxes bore hard on mercantile cities which paid both Parliamentary tenths and customs duties. The city government had promoted most of the charges against Lyons and his associates in the Good Parliament and when they were convicted it had gleefully degraded them from their offices in the city. The Duke of Lancaster was not popular in London. He suffered the obloquy reserved for all politicians with high pretensions and more power than status. As the effective ruler of England, the principal commander of its armies and the author of its recent policies towards France, it was perhaps inevitable that he should become the focus of popular resentment. Bishop Courtenay's challenge to the government in convocation provided an unexpected catalyst for these emotions. Lampoons against the Duke appeared in public places. Banners were carried about insulting his name. Posters repeating the old fable that he was the son of a Ghent butcher were nailed to the doors of St. Paul's and Westminster Abbey.

John of Gaunt responded to the challenge with all the injured majesty and impulsive anger which his staff had managed to restrain during the sessions of the Good Parliament. On 19 February 1376 he proposed a bill in Parliament which would have effected a revolution in the city's relations with the Crown, transferring the powers of the mayor and aldermen in matters of public order to a royal captain and conferring on the Marshal of England the same power to make arrests within their jurisdiction as he already enjoyed in most of the realm. On the same day Gaunt personally escorted Wycliffe to St. Paul's cathedral to meet his judges. He came mob-handed with the Marshal, Henry Lord Percy, his baton held before him, four doctors hired for Wycliffe's defence, and a mass of noblemen and liveried retainers. Inside the cathedral he and Percy heckled the proceedings and exchanged undignified abuse with the Bishop.

On the following day London erupted into violence. A meeting of prominent citizens was called to organise the city's defence against what appeared to be a systematic assault on its privileges. They were addressed by two disaffected lay peers, Guy Brian and Walter Fitzwalter. Both were experienced military men who had been prominent supporters of the Parliamentary attack on the court in the previous year. Brian was a well regarded veteran of Edward III's early campaigns and a former knight of the royal household. Fitzwalter was an ambitious and disappointed cavalier who had been captured in the battle at Vaas in 1370 and had had to mortgage his Cumberland estates on ruinous terms to Alice Perrers to raise money for his ransom. He took the lead with an inflammatory speech against John of Gaunt. At the end of the meeting the Londoners present grabbed what weapons lay to hand and went in search of their enemies. They broke down the doors of Henry Percy's house in Aldersgate and forcibly released a prisoner whom he was detaining there. Then they went in search of Percy himself, rampaging through the bedrooms and piercing the beds with their lances. Thwarted of their prey, they made their way through Cheapside towards John of Gaunt's palace of Savoy, gathering the crowds about them as they went. They swarmed down Ludgate Hill, declaring their intention to seize the Duke. They reversed Gaunt's arms whenever they found them. They beat up anyone seen wearing his badge. They battered to death a clerk who gave it as his opinion that De la Mare was a traitor who deserved all that he had got. The Duke was dining with Henry Percy at the house of a friend. They had not yet finished their oysters when the mob was heard approaching. The two men got up so fast that the Duke cracked his shins against the table. Running to the nearby quays of the Thames, they commandeered a boat and rowed themselves across the river to Kennington where the dowager Princess of Wales gave them sanctuary in the Prince's manor. Only the personal intervention of Bishop Courtenay saved the Savoy from being torched.

How far the city government was behind these events is hard to judge. 'So large a crowd cannot be calmed even by the pleas of the mayor,' the aldermen protested after the event; 'a riot, once it has begun, rages like a whirlwind to one side then the other, provoked by mindless cries of different ringleaders, until eventually they inflict some terrible injury.' Edward's ministers did not proceed with the plan to appoint a royal captain, perhaps because they were chastened by the rioters or perhaps, as Thomas Walsingham says, because the King in an interval of lucidity forbade it. But the city government was forced to dismiss the Mayor and to earn the Duke's pardon by carrying a large wax candle impressed with his arms through the streets to St. Paul's, where it was to be kept ever lit. The common people of the city never accepted the submission of their leaders. Although summoned by the town crier to join the procession behind Gaunt's armorial candle, all but the city's office-holders stayed away. The mob remained as dangerous a threat as it ever had been. For some time Gaunt and Percy were obliged to pass between their mansions and the palace of Westminster through the back streets, accompanied by an escort carrying shields and drawn swords.[84]

Ultimately the success of the Duke's policy of repressing dissent was measured by his ability to obtain grants of taxation. By that test the results were very mixed. Speaking in Prince Richard's name Gaunt had called at the outset of the Parliament for larger subsidies than the Commons had ever voted in a single session. The government, he said, needed to raise two tenths and fifteenths in a single year. But if the

Commons were reluctant to grant a subsidy in the traditional form he invited them to consider alternative ways of raising the same money: a general purchase tax of 5 per cent, a hearth tax of one groat (four pence) per household or a tax of one pound per knight's fee on holdings of land. It would be better, he said, 'to give voluntarily than to lose everything to the enemy'. The Commons declined to grant a double subsidy. They had endured some 'difficult years', they said. They singled out in particular the heavy loss of ships to the enemy, almost certainly a reference to the fleet lost in the Bay of Bourgneuf. In the event, after discussing the possibilities for a long time, the Commons chose a form of taxation which the government had not suggested. On about 22 February they granted a poll tax of four pence per head on every man and woman in the country, which they appear to have believed was the equivalent of one tenth and fifteenth. There were to be no exemptions apart from children under fourteen years old and honest beggars. Convocation, in spite of the ill-feeling generated by recent events, or perhaps because of it, made its own grant four days later: a poll tax of twelve pence from each beneficed clergyman, inclusive of the four pence granted by the Commons.[85]

The poll tax was condemned by the chronicler Thomas Walsingham, that arch-conservative and acerbic anti-government man, as 'an unheard-of tax', which it was. Nevertheless it had a number of attractions for those who devised it. It offered, like the parish tax of 1371, an escape from the outdated standard assessments of 1334 on which the tenths and fifteenths had been based for the last forty years. It substituted a broader tax base defined on the simplest possible principle. It had the advantage of being a regressive tax, unrelated to income or assets, which bore lightly on the landowners and substantial townsmen represented in the Commons. It also bore very lightly on the Church, even at three times the rate payable by laymen. No doubt many men agreed with John Robynet, a young domestic servant in Nottingham, who protested, as he was arrested for non-payment, that it was 'unjust and irrational for him to have to pay as much as a richer citizen ought to pay'. Yet four pence was not an enormous sum, about a day's wages for a carpenter or two-thirds of a day's wages for an archer. The Commons was well aware of the upward pressure on wages since the great epidemics, which had contributed to the declining profitability of land since the middle years of the century. They must have believed, like their predecessors in 1371, that there was a large number of people who had fallen outside the tax net under the old system but who could afford to pay. In prosperous years this calculation would probably have been justified. But it proved to be a serious misjudgment in 1377. There would have had to be about 2,300,000 adult lay taxpayers to justify the Commons' expectations. In fact some 1,355,000 laymen were assessed for a total of £22,586 which was less than two-thirds of the value of a traditional subsidy. The discrepancy was due partly to the fact that the Commons had over-estimated the adult population of England and partly no doubt to indulgent local assessors and a measure of evasion and fraud. The clerical poll tax brought in just £800 as compared with the £15,000 which a clerical tenth traditionally yielded. These exceptionally poor receipts coincided with one of the worst periods for the customs receipts in recent memory. As a result the English government faced a reopening of the war in 1377 with total revenues from taxation of less than £60,000, about half the average level for the period.[86]

Early in March 1377, a few days after the dissolution of Parliament, the Council received its first inkling of the scale of French military plans for the summer when it discovered about the projected invasion of Wales. A report was received from Sir Thomas Felton, the Seneschal of Gascony, that Sir John Minsterworth had been captured by a Gascon squire in Navarre on his way to the Castilian court. He was brought back to Bordeaux and put on a ship bound for England. Minsterworth's papers told most of the story and the rest was extracted from him under torture in the Tower of London. He was drawn and hanged and his quarters distributed to the four corners of the realm to warn others of the perils of treason. Shortly after this the French government's negotiations with the Scots became known when Charles V decided to send one of his private secretaries, Pierre Bournaseau, on a secret mission to concert plans with the Scots. Unfortunately for Bournaseau his flamboyant manner and princely dinner plate betrayed him. He was stopped at the port of Damme by the officers of the Count of Flanders as he was about to board a ship for Edinburgh and accused of conducting the French King's business in Flanders without its ruler's consent.[87]

These reports intensified the English sense of vulnerability. The King's Council was in almost continual session during the spring. The great men of the realm assembled roughly once a month to consider the state of negotiations with France and the conduct of the war which would follow their collapse. The garrisons of Berwick and Lochmaben on the

Scottish march were reinforced. Although the French ministers abandoned their designs on Wales once the secret was out, the Welsh paladin Sir Digory Say was sent to take charge of its defence. Three hundred English troops were sent to the principality. All the major Welsh castles were repaired and revictualled, their garrisons brought up to strength and equipped with artillery. At least in Wales the English had the advantage of intelligence telling them where to expect an attack. The problem everywhere else was the immense length of coast to be defended against an attack whose exact direction was impossible to predict. Coast-guards were arrayed along the south and east coasts. Garrisons were put into the Isle of Wight and the ports of Devon and Cornwall, all of which had been the targets of earlier French raiding campaigns. London, which had not been a target for thirty years, was put in a state of defence with watches kept on the walls and the citizens formed into units to resist an attack. The whole fleet of the northern admiralty and most of the ships of the western one were concentrated in the Thames.[88]

What the Duke of Lancaster needed above all was more time. For five months, from February to June 1377, the English tried to put off the coming conflict by breathing life into the moribund negotiations with France. The papal legates had passed much of January and February in Paris trying to persuade Charles V to extend the truce. The difficulty, as they discovered, was the long lead time required for any major naval campaign, which meant that Charles V was for practical purposes committed already. The Castilians were in the same position. Henry of Trastámara's fleet was being made ready for action at Seville. His ambassadors in Paris objected to any discussion with the English at all. From Westminster the Council sent a herald to Paris to listen out for news. They authorised the Earl of Salisbury, who had been permanently residing at Bruges since the previous autumn, to agree a truce of two years. But when the conference at Bruges reopened in early March the French ambassadors had nothing to offer except for an invitation to meet again on the march of Calais and an extension of the truce for just one month until 1 May. This was shortly afterwards extended to midsummer, 24 June. Early in April the ambassadors of both nations left Bruges for the last time.

There was a brief epilogue in Picardy. The papal legates installed themselves in May in the town of Montreuil in Ponthieu and tried to reopen the conference there. Both governments sent 'solemn' embassies to signify the importance that they attached to the occasion. The English sent the Chancellor and the Chamberlain as well as the Earl of Salisbury, the Poitevin nobleman Guichard d'Angle and a host of clerks and officials including the poet Chaucer. Charles V was represented by his own Chancellor, Pierre d'Orgemont, his principal Chamberlain, Bureau de la Rivière, together with two bishops and two counts. Edward III's son-in-law Enguerrand de Coucy, although formally part of the French delegation, acted as a neutral intermediary as far as he could. The French Chancellor's account of the proceedings more or less admits that the whole thing was a grandiose charade.[89]

As Orgemont wrote, and probably said, there was no reason for the French King to be particularly accommodating. In mid-May, while the diplomats were arguing at Montreuil, Charles V travelled to Normandy to review the royal fleet of galleys and barges in the arsenal at Rouen. They moved downstream to their sea base at Harfleur at the beginning of June. They were joined there in the next few days by the combined galley fleets of Castile and Portugal. The whole international force comprised between fifty and sixty ships, including thirty-six galleys. Six of the cannon made for the siege of Saint-Sauveur, two armed with stones and four with lead shot, were hauled over from the Cotentin to be mounted in the bows of the leading French vessels. A huge 'army of the sea' was mustered at the beginning of June to fight from these ships: no fewer than 3,500 crossbowmen, the largest concentration of bowmen which the French had ever assembled; several hundred men-at-arms; and at least 3,000 armed seamen.[90] On the other side of the Channel more than 150 requisitioned merchant ships had been collected in the Thames off the Tower and at Rotherhithe. Nearly 4,000 men-at-arms and archers had been retained to fight on board these ships. The Admirals were working towards an embarkation date in the middle of July.[91]

Whether by accident or design Charles V's ministers timed their diplomatic manoeuvres perfectly. On 21 June 1377, just three days before the expiry of the truce, the papal legates at Montreuil communicated Charles V's final offer to the English ambassadors. The King of France, they said, would not restore any of the conquered provinces north of the Dordogne apart from the strip of southern Saintonge along the right bank of the Gironde. The most that he would do was buy out the English claims for 1,200,000 francs (£200,000) in cash. He was also willing to consider a marriage between the young Prince Richard and his daughter Catherine, with the Angoumois as the bride's dowry. South of the Dordogne he was prepared to cede all the provinces which had been held by the Black Prince before 1369 provided that the English abandoned Calais. According to the French ambassadors' evaluation the territories which they were offering comprised sixteen or seventeen walled cities and at least 4,000 fortresses. The proposal fell well short of the Englishmen's minimum demands. Edward's representatives had been instructed to draw out the negotiations for as long as possible and they were careful not to reject it whatever their private thoughts. They said that they would give their answer by 15 August at Bruges. They presumably asked for an extension of the truce at least until then. But if so it was refused.[92]

In the event the slow progress of England's naval preparations made no difference to the outcome because the whole English plan of campaign was thrown into disarray by the death of Edward III. The King's health had appeared to be mending recently. He had been rowed upriver for the annual festivities of the Order of the Garter at Windsor on St. George's Day. In what proved to be the last great pageant of his reign Edward knighted his grandson Richard of Bordeaux, together with his youngest son, Thomas of Woodstock, John Sotherey his bastard by Alice Perrers, and the heirs of the houses of Lancaster, Oxford, Stafford, Salisbury, Percy, Mowbray and Beaumont: a whole generation of young men destined to participate in the defeats and divisions of the next two reigns. Two months later, on 21 June 1377, the day that the last French offer was put forward, Edward III suffered a stroke at the royal manor of Sheen near Richmond. Paralysed and speechless, he declined rapidly and died before the night was out. His death was as pathetic as the final years of his life. The malicious Thomas Walsingham reported that the knights and squires of his household slipped away to safeguard their fortunes in the new reign. Alice Perrers was said to have fled from the house, taking the rings from his fingers as she went. The King died attended by a single priest. His death could not have come at a worse moment. It was out of the question for the leading members of the English political community to be away from the seat of government at such a time. The English naval expedition therefore had to be cancelled. The troops mustered for it were stood down before they reached the port. Most of the ships were held in the Thames to await further orders. The powers of the English ambassadors at Calais automatically lapsed on the death of the king who had appointed them. The Earl of Salisbury and his colleagues, unable even to procrastinate, crossed the Channel to England on 23 June to find the country filled with lamentation and foreboding. The truce expired at dawn on the following day.[93]

CHAPTER VII

England's Barbicans
1377–1378

Richard II came to the throne of England in the middle of one of the gravest military crises of the war. On 29 June 1377 the French and Castilian admirals landed at dawn beneath the ruins of Winchelsea. The invaders beached their ships and made their way in the early light along the marshy estuary of the Rother to fall on Rye. Rye was vulnerable, as those who remembered the French raid of 1339 knew. It was a small river port which then stood about a mile inland on a low cliff above the river estuary, gnawed by the tides on its eastern side. The municipality had levied money to build a circuit of walls but the defences were still incomplete when the French returned. The inhabitants at first resisted with ferocity. But after the first assault, in which many of them were killed, the rest fled into the country around or surrendered to the invaders. The French Admiral, Jean de Vienne, occupied the town. He sent most of his army back to the ships to continue their cruise west towards Hastings. He himself planned to dig his force in at Rye and use it as a base for wasting the surrounding region. He expected to be able to hold his own for a good ten days before the English succeeded in concentrating their forces against him. He would then withdraw and repeat the operation elsewhere. In fact he lasted less than two days.

The English system depended on having men armed and ready in their homes to be called out for a swift counter-attack before the invader had securely established himself ashore. In this at least it was moderately successful. The local commissioner of array was Hamo of Offington, the Abbot of Battle, a prominent figure in the county 'beneath whose monkish habit', says a contemporary, 'was a soldier of mark and a stout defender of home, neighbours and coast.' On the day after the landing, Hamo occupied Winchelsea. The town, which had been abandoned since the French raid of 1360, stood directly above the beached galleys and barges of the French fleet. Faced with a threat to his ships and his line of retreat, Jean de Vienne immediately moved against Winchelsea.

His first step was to parley with the Abbot. When this got him nowhere he launched a full-scale assault on the defenders' positions. The departure of most of his force and the need to use others to guard the ships appears to have left him insufficient manpower for this operation. After several hours of fighting his men were forced to retreat. That evening Jean de Vienne ordered his men to withdraw to their ships. The decision was not popular with some of his companions but French coastal raiders tended to be nervous of being stranded in enemy territory. In the early evening of 30 June the French systematically set fire to Rye, reducing the town to ashes. They then took forty-two casks of wine and their richest captives and sailed away.[1]

The price that the English had to pay for Hamo's success at Winchelsea was the destruction of Hastings. While the battle was being fought at Winchelsea, the other detachment of Jean de Vienne's army landed outside the town. Hastings was a much decayed community. Its great days as one of the leading members of the Cinque Ports were long since past. Its harbour was almost entirely silted up and its trade had been lost to its rivals. Like Winchelsea and Rye, it was unwalled. The inhabitants fled inland as the raiders approached. The French and Castilians were able to burn the town without resistance. During the next few days the two squadrons of the enemy fleet were reunited and the 'army of the sea' carried out a third landing at Rottingdean, just east of what was then the insignificant village of Brighton. The defence here was supposed to be the responsibility of Richard Fitzalan, the young Earl of Arundel, who was the leading magnate of Sussex, a commissioner of array and the owner of the principal castle of the district at Lewes. But Lewes was undefended and its castle in disrepair. The Earl was away, engrossed in the preparations for the forthcoming coronation at Westminster. In his absence the defence of the district was taken in hand by another martial cleric, John of Charlieu, Prior of Lewes. That this role should fall to him was ironic, for John was probably by birth a Frenchman and some of his personal retinue certainly were. He was assisted by two experienced English knights, Sir John Fawsley, a retainer of the Earl of Arundel, and Sir Thomas Cheyne, famous as one of the men who had captured Bertrand du Guesclin at Nájera. They tried to stop the French on the beaches. But they arrived too late with only 500 men and walked straight into an ambush. A hundred of the English force lost their lives in the ensuing battle and all three captains were taken prisoner. The Prior remained in captivity in France for a year before being released against a ransom of 7,000 nobles

(£4,666), thereby saddling Lewes priory with a liability which would cripple it for a generation. The French marched inland as far as Lewes, which they entered without difficulty and burned before retreating to the coast to leave by the next tide.[2]

Edward III's body lay in state in St. Paul's cathedral and Westminster Hall as the news came in of successive French landings on the south coast. On 5 July 1377 the old King's body was escorted across the palace yard to be interred in Westminster Abbey in the presence of most of the lay magnates and prelates of the kingdom and the whole of the royal household. Eleven days later his ten-year-old grandson was anointed and crowned King in the same place in a ceremony at once traditional and embellished with symbolic statements of the God-given authority which the child was incapable of exercising. Immediately after the coronation the new King created four earls, among them his uncle, Thomas of Woodstock, who became Earl of Buckingham and Marshal of England, and Henry Percy, who became Earl of Northumberland. The ceremonies were overshadowed by the threat of the French fleet which was now believed to be heading for the Thames. Forty miles away at Sheerness and Shoebury Ness, watchmen with drums and trumpets stood by the huge beacons which had been built to warn of an enemy attempt to force the estuary. In the riverside villages at Greenwich, Woolwich, Thurrock and Gravesend, men were preparing to resist a landing near the capital.[3]

Edward III had made no provision for a regency. To devise one after his death would have provoked a serious political crisis. John of Gaunt would have been an unpopular choice and does not seem to have pressed for it. No one else had the necessary status and authority. Instead the prelates and lay peers who had attended the coronation gathered on the following day and conferred the day-to-day conduct of government on the two principal officers of state, the Chancellor and the Treasurer, assisted by a 'continual council'. These arrangements, which amounted to a regency in all but name, remained in place until the beginning of 1380. The Council was a coalition on which both sides of the political divisions of the past eighteen months were represented. But the most influential and cohesive group in the new government were the former friends and retainers of the Black Prince. The Queen Mother, Joan of Kent, had taken charge of her son's affairs after her husband's death and had done much to keep the Prince's household together. She remained a discreet but powerful presence behind the scenes. Former clerks and officials of the Black Prince and his widow moved into

positions of influence across the whole of the government service. Simon
Burley, the new King's tutor, who carried the boy back to the palace in
his arms after the coronation ceremony, had been the Black Prince's
childhood friend and one of his few confidants during the years in
Aquitaine. He remained the most powerful man at court for a decade.
The opinions of these men, most of whom had never previously tasted
power, are impossible to discover. But many of them had personally
experienced the bitterness of defeat in France and it is hardly
conceivable that it had not left its mark on them. Burley had been a
prisoner of the French for three years and had then lost everything in the
debacle of 1372. Sir John Devereux, another councillor, had served as
one of the Prince's last lieutenants in Limousin and fought at La
Rochelle. Bishop Harewell of Bath and Wells, who had been the Prince's
chancellor in Aquitaine at the time of the rebellion of Albret and
Armagnac in 1368, joined the Council in October 1377.[4]

The most notable absentee was John of Gaunt, whose rule thus came
to an abrupt end after barely eight months. There is nothing to suggest
that the Duke tried to cling to power. He was weary of the grind of
active government and distressed at the unpopularity which his
vindictive and high-handed ways had brought him. He obtained leave
to withdraw to his estates and gave himself up to hunting with hawk
and hound. Gaunt would never lack influence. His position as a prince
of the blood guaranteed that. But he never again dominated the
government as he had done since October 1376. The new Council
moved swiftly to undo his work. They ordered the seizure of Alice
Perrers's assets within days of the old King's death. They made peace
with the Londoners. William of Wykeham was pardoned and restored
to his confiscated temporalities. Peter de la Mare was released from
Nottingham castle and given a hero's welcome in the streets of London.
The Council later characterised his imprisonment as 'irrational' and
paid him compensation.[5]

The Council had no alternative but to prosecute the war as vigorously
as it could afford, a course which in any event corresponded to the
instinct of most of its members. They reinforced the county levies and
commissioners of array with experienced captains and paid troops in
the places thought to be most vulnerable to attack. More troops were
sent to Pembrokeshire, where the government was still troubled about
the possibility of a landing by Owen of Wales. The Earl of Cambridge
was put in command of 1,000 men and sent to hold Dover castle and
the Kent coast. The Earl of Salisbury was put in charge of the coast of

Hampshire and Dorset. John of Arundel, the brother of the Earl of Arundel, was made keeper of Southampton which was regarded as the prime target. He entered the town at the beginning of July, accompanied by a large body of soldiers including a company of Genoese crossbowmen and an artillery train.[6]

The exact movements of the enemy fleet cannot be traced behind the generalised lament of the chronicles about the wasting of the south coast. The rather sparse evidence that exists suggests that their ships penetrated into the west country as far as Plymouth but achieved nothing more of note after the sack of Lewes. In the second half of July 1377 they returned to Harfleur to rest their crews, land prisoners and spoil and take on stores for a second cruise which was expected to last for six weeks. Jean de Vienne attended a conference with Charles V and his advisers early in August. It was decided that the main purpose of the second cruise would be to support the Duke of Burgundy's operations against Calais. But the Duke's army had not yet mustered for the campaign. In the meantime, therefore, it was proposed to concentrate the fleets against Southampton.[7]

As the French and Castilians completed their preparations for the second cruise the Scots, sensing a new vulnerability in English affairs, began to mount raids into the surviving English enclaves of the Scottish lowlands and the counties of Cumberland and Northumberland. There was an escalating series of incidents on the border in July 1377, inflaming tensions on both sides. The man behind these raids was George Dunbar, Earl of March, the most powerful magnate of East Lothian, who was then one of the Scottish wardens of the east march. Ostensibly, his grievance was the failure of the English to give redress for a brawl at the Roxburgh fair some weeks earlier, in which his chamberlain had been killed. But the timing of the raids and the fact that a French herald had recently been captured on the march suggest that the initiative may have come from France. Dunbar surrounded Roxburgh before dawn on 10 August 1377. When the sun rose he broke into the town, massacred the inhabitants and burned the place to the ground. It was almost certainly his men who ambushed and killed much of the English garrison of Berwick as they rode through the country north of the fortress a few days after this. Sir Thomas Musgrave, the English captain of Berwick, was among the prisoners. Writing to the English government to justify his operations, March threatened to take Berwick, which 'stands in Scotland, the which town ye call yours'. These incidents led to a ferocious and inconclusive sequence of reprisals.

Within two weeks Henry Percy, Earl of Northumberland, was harrying Dunbar's lands with several thousand borderers at his back. The escalation of the crisis provoked alarm at Westminster and prayers across the whole of England before a tense truce was eventually restored on the border in the course of September.[8]

Percy's first report from the north, which was received at Westminster on 19 August, coincided with the news that the French and Castilian 'army of the sea' had landed on the Isle of Wight. In fact Jean de Vienne had not planned this. His ships had been driven onto the island by high winds and his men forced to disembark there. The island was strongly defended and its garrison had enough warning of the attack to assemble close to the shore. But they lost this advantage by a serious tactical misjudgment. They decided to allow part of the French and Castilian force to land before attacking them on the beach, in the belief that they could defeat them in detail before the rest had landed. The enemy thwarted this plan by storming the beach with their whole force at once. The defenders found themselves heavily outnumbered. They turned and fled inland. Jean de Vienne's men pursued them, killing and burning as they went. A subsequent royal inquiry found that every substantial settlement in the east and south of the island was 'utterly burned and destroyed'. The only serious resistance was at Carisbrooke castle, the principal fortress of the island, where the captain, Sir Hugh Tyrell, led his garrison in a bold sortie as the enemy approached and inflicted heavy losses on them. He then withdrew behind his walls as they burned the town beneath his nose. After passing several days on the island the French negotiated the payment of *patis* of 1,000 marks (£666) and re-embarked on their ships.[9]

The sack of the Isle of Wight was a victory of sorts, but it lost Jean de Vienne whatever chance he ever had of surprising Southampton. By the time that his ships penetrated into Southampton Water John of Arundel and Robert Knolles were waiting for them. Their troops could be seen from the ships following them along the shore. A landing was attempted near Southampton but it was repulsed at the water's edge. Another attempt, at Poole, was frustrated by the troops of the Earl of Salisbury. In the last days of August 1377 the fleet turned east along the coast of Sussex and Kent where they did no better. The French finally succeeded in landing a raiding force at Folkestone on 31 August. They burned much of the town before they were driven off by local levies under the command of the Abbot of St. Augustine's, Canterbury. The Abbot followed along the coast as the ships cruised east towards Dover. The

French ships waited for three days here, looking for a chance to land. But the great royal fortress at Dover was one of the few castles in England which had been kept in proper repair, and there was a large garrison on its walls in addition to the Abbot's host. We cannot know how long the stand-off would have continued. On about 3 September 1377 the Duke of Burgundy invaded the Pas-de-Calais and the French and Castilian fleets sailed across the Narrows to support his operations from the sea.[10]

The Franco-Castilian campaign of 1377 was the most powerful naval assault on England since the reopening of the war. The physical damage, although worse than anything since the burning of Southampton in 1339, was comparatively modest. But the effect of the raids on the course of the war was far greater than its immediate military impact. The French became more confident of their ability to cross the 'moat defensive' which had for decades protected their enemy from effective retaliation. Over the following years their projects would become bolder. In England the defence of the coasts had been a source of concern for many years but the sudden realisation of these fears still came as a shock. Public anger broke out in venomous bursts of indignation against anyone who could be blamed and many who could not. Several citizens of Rye were hanged for failing to defend the place energetically enough. The men of Kent blamed the leading landowners of the county, who had left their castles unrepaired and ungarrisoned. This was obviously a widely held view. The Earl of Arundel was abused for failing to garrison Lewes. Scurrilous and almost certainly untrue stories circulated about the insouciance of John of Gaunt, who was in the north when the French landed, 'enjoying his parties and hunts', according to Thomas Walsingham. He was supposed to have declared that for all he cared the French could wreck his castle at Pevensey. He was rich enough to rebuild it. Gaunt was sufficiently stung by these grumbles to put a garrison into this ancient and indefensible pile for the first time in many years. In the longer term French coastal raids were probably the largest single factor behind a fresh shift in English attitudes to the war towards a predominantly defensive outlook and ultimately to a weary resentment of the war. There was a further increase in the proportion of English war expenditure which went on the defence of the south and east coasts. More and larger fleets patrolled the Channel for longer periods in spite of all the experience which showed that forward defence was virtually impossible against coastal raiders. For the first three years of the new reign no major continental campaign was undertaken or even planned.[11]

Across southern England a rash of castle-building marked a substantial investment in fixed defences by both the King and his subjects. The concern was that next time the raiders would not content themselves with mounting smash-and-grab raids on small coastal towns but would attempt a permanent occupation, ransoming the home counties as the English and Gascons had done in so many provinces of France. Kent and the neighbouring areas of East Sussex saw some of the heaviest expenditure. As the Commons pointed out in 1378 this area was thick with unmanned and dilapidated castles, most of which could easily be surprised by night with the aid of a few men and a local guide. There is a good deal of evidence to support this complaint. It was so long since there had been any persistent warfare in the south of England that most of the castles and town walls of Kent dated from the twelfth and early thirteenth centuries. A few, such as Gaunt's castle at Pevensey, dated from Roman times. Probably only Dover and Queensborough had permanent garrisons. In the next decade the town walls of Winchelsea, Rye and Sandwich would all be strengthened. Canterbury was surrounded by an almost entirely new circuit of walls, constructed between about 1378 and 1390, in which gun-ports made one of their first appearances in England. The castle of the archbishops at Saltwood received a massive towered gateway. Sir Edward Dalyngrigg, successful man of war, confidant of John de Montfort and household knight of Edward III and Richard II, was licensed to build the fortress of Bodiam 'in defence of the surrounding country against the King's enemies'. Sir Roger Ashburnham's moated castle at Scotney was built at the same time, probably for the same reason. John Lord Cobham, veteran of the Bruges conference, made no secret of his reason for building Cooling Castle in the north Kent marshes. 'I am made in help of the country,' proclaims the inscription in enamelled copper which can still be seen on the front of the gatehouse. Kent was the extreme example but not the only one. In the following year the Council began a systematic survey of coastal castles in all counties south of the Trent and of walled towns as far inland as Oxford. Important works were undertaken at the royal castles near the Solent and in Cornwall. Southampton, which was already well-walled by English standards, was continuously strengthened during the 1380s and equipped with gun-ports. A new citadel was ordered to be 'quickly made' on Castle Hill by the greatest English architect of the day, Henry Yevele. This great cylindrical keep has long since vanished but in its time it was regarded as one of the wonders of English castle-building, 'large, fair and very stronge, both by worke and the site of it', as the Elizabethan antiquary Leland described it.[12]

The frame of mind in which these defences were constructed was reflected in a growing fear of foreign spies and fifth-columnists, an abiding characteristic of insecure societies at war. 'Whenever there is war and whenever there is fear of war,' wrote Philippe de Mézières, one of Charles V's councillors, 'the first and chief rule is to arm yourself with information from loyal spies.' Dedicated agents could be sent into enemy territory. Merchants from neutral countries, especially Italians, could be used to gather information or to spread misinformation. Men could be sent to mingle with the crowds who pressed about the open courts of medieval kings or hang about their armies. A generation later Christine de Pisan recorded in her eulogy of Charles V that spies were thought to be specially important in advance of naval raids to report where the defenders were thinnest on the ground. There undoubtedly were real French spies in England as well as a much larger number of imagined ones. The English ministers, who used all of Philippe de Mézières's techniques themselves when they could, were well aware of the threat and went to some lengths to meet it. Bailiffs in the ports kept watch on unusual comings and goings. Innkeepers were required to be native Englishmen and expected to report foreigners and other suspicious persons. It may have been an innkeeper who denounced the Frenchman found near Salisbury in July 1377 and his two compatriots arrested in Southampton in December 1378. They were interrogated by the Council as spies, which they probably were. So, without doubt, was the Englishman Robert Rillington, who was convicted before the King's justices in 1382 of serving in the crew of a French raider and 'leading them secretly by night to inspect the town and castle of Scarborough'; and Hughlin Gerard, a merchant of Bologna settled in London who confessed to reporting the 'secrets of the realm' to his Paris correspondent.[13]

The pressure to find out enemies within the realm came mainly from below and resulted in a large number of baseless accusations. The Commons had always believed that the heads of alien priories, however long naturalised, were 'French in their bones' (*fraunceys en lour corps*). They were convinced that these men reported on English coastal defences to their superiors in France. In 1373 they had petitioned for the removal of all those living within twenty leagues of the sea. In 1377 they called for their complete expulsion. A single foreign monk with a knowledge of the coast-line and the tides, they later declared, could organise the landing of a thousand enemy troops on a tide or two thousand at night. There had in fact been one notorious case, which the Commons did not allow the government to forget, involving John Boquet, the French prior of the Benedictine monastery on Hayling Island in the Solent, who was removed to an inland house after he had been found with incriminating correspondence in his possession in 1369. But there was no evidence of widespread treachery among foreign churchmen and the government had hitherto been content to exact an oath from them that they would not 'reveal the state, affairs or secrets of the realm to any foreigner'. Even Boquet, who was probably a fool rather than a traitor, was eventually allowed to return to Hayling on giving security for his good behaviour. The Benedictine Prior of Pembroke, John Rougecok, who came from Normandy, was arrested and sent to London for interrogation in April 1377 at a time when the French were thought to be about to land in South Wales, but nothing seems to have been found against him. He too was allowed to return.

There was, however, a notable change of mood in the autumn of that year after Jean de Vienne's raids on the south coast. In December the government reluctantly agreed to expel foreign clergymen with the exception of heads of houses, employed chaplains and beneficed clergymen who were 'known good and loyal men not suspected of spying'. The exceptions ironically covered most of the more prominent targets of the Commons' ire including Boquet and Rougecok, both of whom stayed behind. But some hundreds of others sailed from Dover early in the following year, 'violently expelled' as a Norman abbot complained to the Pope.

Thus ended another of the many cultural and economic links which had joined English and French society since the eleventh century. It was characteristic of the popular animosities behind this policy that most spy scares of the following years were the result of denunciation rather than official action. Walter Wareyn, an archer from Warwickshire who had fought at the battle of La Rochelle, found himself arrested as a spy when he returned with a French accent after six years of captivity. His relatives vouched for him but others were less fortunate. They were arrested on suspicion and held in prison indefinitely because they were friendless strangers or too poor to find sureties. In 1380 it was reported that Newgate prison in London was packed with a 'great number' of these wretches. The sheriffs eventually called on anyone who had any evidence against them to produce it. This resulted in just eight of them being prosecuted, all of whom were acquitted. According to the sheriffs' report nothing was found against any of them except that they were strangers in the city at a time when enemy galleys were known to be cruising off the coast and that they were 'running hither and thither about the place like spies'.[14]

The first major offensive since 1350 against the English positions at Calais opened at the beginning of September 1377. The Duke of Burgundy appeared with his army at Thérouanne on the edge of the English pale on 2 September 1377. Plausible English estimates put its strength at 2,600 men-at-arms, 700 Genoese crossbowmen and a horde of infantry and hangers-on from the villages and towns of a region that had suffered for a generation at the hands of the English of Calais. The French and Castilian fleets were recalled from the Kent coast and on the following day anchored off the town with another 3,000 to 4,000 troops on board, most of them bowmen. The Duke's combined strength must have been between 7,000 and 10,000 men. He had also brought an impressive siege train comprising at least six and probably nine cannon, one of them designed to fire projectiles of 130 pounds; and what the English described as a 'trebuchet of unimaginable size such as we have never seen in these parts'. The campaign was to be a classic illustration of the truism of fourteenth-century military commanders that great fortresses were usually taken by psychological pressure, not by force.[15]

The garrison of Calais had expected to be attacked since April. Yet the simultaneous appearance of these great forces by land and sea plainly shocked them. The defence was in the hands of Sir Hugh Calveley, still a formidable military figure, who had been captain of the town for the past two years. He commanded one of the strongest fortresses in Europe. The town itself was surrounded by a circuit of walls and towers on which Edward III had lavished money year after year ever since he had captured it thirty years before. Beyond the walls of the town lay a water-filled moat and an expanse of soft, marshy ground which made it difficult for an attacker to approach and almost impossible to set up siege equipment. The harbour, which was outside the walls, was defended on the seaward side by a long spit of sand known as the Rysbank, built on artificial foundations and culminating at its eastern end in a stone tower. On the landward side a ring of garrisoned castles, linked by a network of rivers and canals, guarded all the approaches. These places would have to be captured if a way was to be opened to the town and a besieging army supplied there. By the time that the Duke of Burgundy arrived Calais had been heavily reinforced. It was defended by about 1,800 men of whom rather more than half served in the town and castle of Calais itself and the rest in the outlying forts.[16]

On 4 September 1377 the Duke of Burgundy laid siege to Ardres, the largest of the outlying forts of the Calais pale. Ardres stood on flat ground south-east of Calais separated from the town by ten miles of bleak scrub and marsh. Its situation was not strong. But substantial sums had recently been spent on strengthening the walls and barbicans and the place was apparently well victualled. The garrison had been progressively increased over the years and now stood at the considerable figure of 360 in addition to the inhabitants of the town. In the opinion of sound judges the place was twice as strong as it had been in 1369 when Sir Ralph Ferrers had successfully defended it against the French for more than three months. The captain of the place in 1377, however, was a very different kind of man. Jean de Jauche, lord of Gommegnies, was a soldier of fortune from Hainault who had been in English service since 1369 and had served as captain of Ardres for most of that time. He regarded the place mainly as a base for kidnapping and cattle-rustling and had no desire to risk his life and fortune in a heroic defence. He was badly rattled by the sight of the French setting up their artillery and preparing their assault. A messenger from the Duke of Burgundy added to his unease, appearing at the barriers in front of the gate to tell the garrison that no prisoners would be taken if Ardres fell. Gommegnies assembled the garrison and the leaders of the town and told them that the place was too weak to withstand an assault. Some of the defenders were surprised and tried to argue with him. Undeterred, on 7 September he surrendered the town to the Duke of Burgundy without striking a blow.

The French occupation of Ardres made much of the eastern sector of the march indefensible. Two small forts nearby surrendered on the same day and a third was abandoned by its garrison. The only other significant place in the sector was Audruicq, a castle built on rising ground about five miles east of Ardres, which was now cut off from Calais by French troops. Audruicq was commanded by a squire called William Weston with a garrison of fifty men, half what he considered to be necessary. He had asked Calveley for more but had been told that none could be spared. After three days of continuous assaults the French artillery had wrecked part of the walls. Their sappers had drained the moat and filled it in at three points. More than a quarter of the garrison

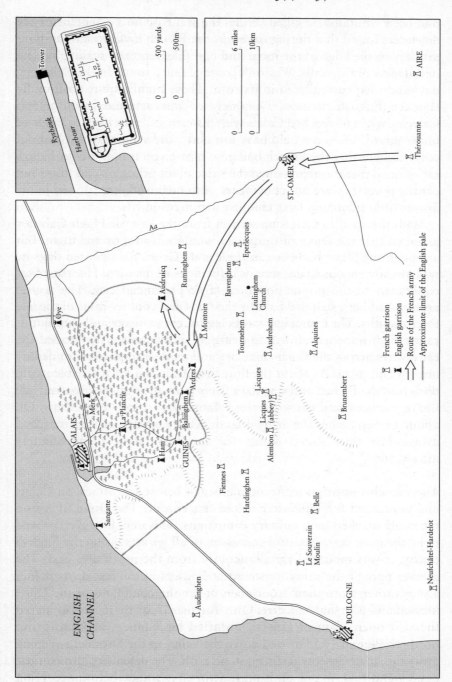

10 Calais and the Pale, September 1377

Tower

Rysbank

Harbour

0   500 yards
0   500m

0   6 miles
0   10km

ENGLISH CHANNEL

Aa

Oye

Merk

CALAIS

Ham

La-Planche

GUINES

Sangatte

Audinghen

Le Souverain Moulin

Neufchâtel-Hardelot

BOULOGNE

Belle

Hardinghen

Fiennes

Balinghem

Ardres

Alembon

Licques

Licques (abbey)

Brunembert

Alquines

Audrehem

Tournehem

Leulinghem Church

Bavenghem

Montoire

Audruicq

Ruminghem

Eperlecques

ST.-OMER

Thérouanne

AIRE

French garrison
English garrison
Route of the French army
Approximate limit of the English pale

293

had been wounded or killed. When the sun rose on 11 September the defenders found that during the night the French had brought up their artillery to the edge of the moat and had piled up their scaling ladders in full view of the walls. Weston's courage failed him. On the following day Audruicq surrendered in its turn. These humiliations profoundly shocked English opinion. Gommegnies was arrested by Sir Hugh Calveley when he reached Calais with his men and sent back to England under guard. Weston would have aroused more sympathy if it had not come to light that the French had paid him 2,500 francs (about £400). He claimed that this represented the value of his prisoners and stores but contemporaries were not convinced. Both men were imprisoned in the Tower of London and later charged with treason.[17]

With the road to Calais now open from the east Sir Hugh Calveley assumed that the Duke of Burgundy would advance on the town. But although the Duke had been in the Pas-de-Calais for only ten days he was already encountering serious difficulties of his own. His army was equivalent to the population of a large provincial city. The region around had been stripped bare by the raids and counter-raids of the last three months. The campaign was being fought in heavy and continuous rain which impeded efforts to bring in supplies. It also flooded the causeways across the Calais marshes and made it impossible to deploy heavy equipment. At about the time that Audruicq fell a terrible storm dispersed the French and Castilian fleets from their anchorages outside Calais harbour and caused serious damage to some of the ships. On about 13 September the army abandoned the campaign and marched away. The fleet sailed south for its bases almost immediately afterwards.[18]

The French campaign in Aquitaine began before the attack on Calais and continued for long after it had fizzled out. The Duke of Anjou famously disliked long military campaigns. This one, however, proved to be the most sustained and successful of all his attacks on the English duchy. It was mounted simultaneously from the north and east. The greater part of the army mustered at Poitiers in the last days of July 1377: rather more than 2,000 men under the command of the Duke himself and Marshal Sancerre. On 1 August Anjou marched out across the rich open plain of Poitou, unfurled his banners at Nontron in northern Périgord and moved down the valley of the Dronne, sweeping away the small Gascon garrisons in his path. The defenders burned their castles and fled or put up a perfunctory resistance before accepting terms. This was a region which had been controlled for years by the garrisons and guerilla bands of Raymond de Montaut, lord of Mussidan. But even Raymond's great fortress at Bourdeilles resisted for only seven days before the garrison sued for terms and opened their gates. In the next few days Louis of Anjou was joined by a smaller army coming up from Languedoc under the command of the Seneschal of Beaucaire. The combined force, now nearly 3,000 strong, marched across the heavily wooded valleys of western Périgord towards Bergerac, the main English garrisoned town on the Dordogne.[19]

Like the defenders of Calais, the English in Bordeaux had had several months' warning of what was afoot, but like them they received the news of the enemy's arrival with something like panic. In Bordeaux, however, there was better reason for it. A year of stalemate and two years of truce had done nothing to improve the duchy's defences or the parlous state of its finances. The English Exchequer was responsible for paying about 250 English troops in Gascony, distributed between the garrisons of Bordeaux and Bayonne. In addition John of Gaunt, who was the lord of Bergerac, paid for the garrison of its castle from the revenues of his English estates. Otherwise, all military expenses had to be met from local revenues. In 1377 the Constable of Bordeaux, the duchy's chief financial officer, could afford to pay only two garrisons, at Saint-Macaire on the Garonne and Dax on the Adour. The remaining castles of the duchy were defended by their lords and the towns by their inhabitants with locally recruited troops. Some of them received a subsidy from the duchy's revenues, which is likely to have been substantially less than the cost of defence and was generally paid late or not at all. It was of course in their interest to defend themselves anyway. But unlike the English they had the alternative of submitting to the King of France.

Even the cash-strapped ministers of Edward III realised that urgent steps would have to be taken to send money out to Bordeaux. Since the Italian banking network no longer extended to wartime Bordeaux this had to be done laboriously and expensively by sending coin and bullion across the Bay of Biscay in heavily armed ships. A total of £5,755 in coin was scraped together at Westminster, which was probably all that could be spared. The Great Council which met in April 1377 had their own ideas on how this money should be spent. They thought that to pit a field army against the Duke of Anjou was unrealistic. They told Felton that the money was to be used for static defence and proposed that he should raise an extra 700 troops to boost the garrisons in the duchy.

They even specified the places where these troops were to be posted. Whether this was the wisest way to run a campaign 500 miles away may be doubted but Felton was an experienced enough soldier to ignore the Council's prescriptions when he wanted to.[20]

When the money arrived at the end of May he was getting confused messages from his spies about the Duke of Anjou's plans. But early in June he learned that the main French objective was the valley of the Dordogne and by early July he knew that they intended to lay siege to Bergerac before advancing down the valley towards Bordeaux. To meet this threat Felton disposed of just 860 men-at-arms and an uncertain number of archers, perhaps about a thousand men in all, of whom about half were Gascons. Some of those present must have reflected on the decline of England's affairs since the Black Prince had fought with 4,000 Gascons at Poitiers and nearly twice as many at Nájera. Felton reinforced the garrison of Bergerac. But he was obliged to withdraw troops from most of the remaining garrisons to create a small field army. Even this rapidly exhausted his funds. The money from England was swallowed up in arrears almost as soon as it arrived. By mid-August Felton was desperately urging the Constable of Bordeaux to find more money by whatever means he could before even this small army deserted him.[21]

In these difficult conditions the continuing loyalty of the Gascons was very much an unknown factor. Felton was in the same position as Sir Oliver Ingham had been forty years before. Bordeaux and Bayonne were thought to be reliable, although there had been obscure plots and treasons even in Bordeaux. Left to themselves, most of the smaller towns of the duchy would have been happy to make terms with the stronger power. The nobility had closer links with the English administration, but they were staking all that they had on a successful English defence against a much stronger enemy. For some the risk seemed too great. In March 1377 Guillaume Sans de Pommiers, whose family had a long tradition of loyalty to the English duchy, secretly agreed to admit 300 French soldiers into his castles including the strategically vital fortress of Fronsac on the north bank of the Dordogne opposite Libourne. He had been worked upon over several months by the lord of Albret. The King of France, said Albret, intended to take Bordeaux and all the territory around it in which Guillaume Sans's lands were located. If he changed sides in time he would keep what he had and receive a grant of 20,000 francs as well as a pension large enough to garrison all his castles against the English. In one form or another these arguments must have occurred to every prominent Gascon nobleman in the English allegiance. After much hesitation Guillaume Sans succumbed. But he was the only one. And before he could do anything Felton appeared without warning at Fronsac and arrested him. He was tried in Bordeaux in April and beheaded.

Felton could not have carried out this swift and brutal act of repression unless he was confident of the support of the rest of the nobility, many of whom were jurors at Guillaume Sans's trial. Their position is a reminder that beyond a point political allegiance cannot be analysed simply in terms of self-interest. Men like the new Captal de Buch, Archambaud de Grailly, came from families which had never deserted the cause of the English kings even in the darkest hours of the duchy's history. Archambaud's father had died in a French prison rather than reach an accommodation with Charles V. He himself had attended the coronation of Richard II at Westminster. Raymond de Montaut, lord of Mussidan and Blaye, was the standard-bearer for the English cause in Périgord. He had visited England, mixed with the English nobility, lived well on grants and borrowed money and trafficked in prisoners of war. He returned to fight for Richard II against the Duke of Anjou in 1377. Yet he might have served his own interest better by abandoning the English long before.[22]

The Duke of Anjou arrived before Bergerac on 22 August 1377. Bergerac was a compact walled town of some 1,500 souls on the north bank of the Dordogne, which was situated in the most fertile part of the valley and controlled the only bridge over the Dordogne in Périgord. Its brick houses and public fountains proclaimed its prosperity to the world. But in spite of its wealth and its strategic importance very little had been done to improve its defences since the Earl of Derby had overwhelmed them in a few hours in 1345. They consisted of the joined up facades of buildings with gaps filled by a low, thin brick wall protected by an earthwork and a water-filled ditch. At critical points there were fortified gateways and curious free-standing towers which had been built as refuges from raiders but were useless against a properly equipped army. The citadel, which stood at the water's edge upstream of the bridge, was an ancient structure dating from the eleventh century. But it was well-manned and equipped with stone-throwers and cannon. The captain of Bergerac, a Gascon retainer of John of Gaunt, was away in England. He had left the castle to be defended in his absence by a kinsman. But the leading figure in the defence was the *routier* captain Bertucat d'Albret. Bertucat had purchased his release from the Duke of Anjou's prisons at about the

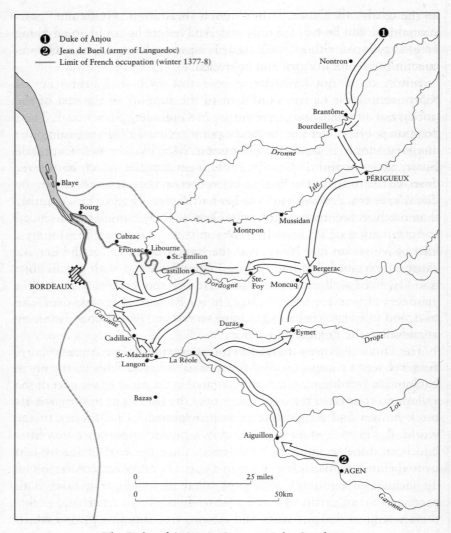

① Duke of Anjou
② Jean de Bueil (army of Languedoc)
——— Limit of French occupation (winter 1377-8)

Nontron

Brantôme
Bourdeilles

Dronne

PÉRIGUEUX

Isle

Blaye

Bourg

Mussidan

Cubzac
Montpon
Fronsac Libourne
   • St.-Emilion
Castillon   Bergerac
BORDEAUX   *Dordogne* Ste.-
        Foy Moncuq

Garonne

Cadillac   Duras
               Eymet
St.-Macaire   *Dropt*
Langon   La Réole

Bazas

Lot

Aiguillon

② •AGEN

0   25 miles

0   50km

Garonne

11 The Duke of Anjou in Gascony, July–October 1377

end of 1376 and put himself at Felton's service as soon as the truce had failed. Felton put him in command of the town with about 270 men-at-arms, most of them belonging to his own company. In addition several companies of Gascons who had abandoned their garrisons in northern Périgord took refuge in the town and joined in the defence.[23]

Disaster struck the English and their Gascon allies almost immediately. The first assault, against the Porte de Clairac, by the river in the south-east corner of the town, was repulsed with heavy French casualties. The Duke of Anjou ordered Jean de Bueil to bring heavy siege equipment from La Réole. This involved dragging cumbersome machines, trebuchets and the massive covered battering rams knows as 'truies', across some thirty-five miles of poor roads between the Garonne and the Dordogne. The main obstacle in their path was the rocky, fast-flowing stream of the River Dropt. It had to be crossed by a long stone bridge beyond the bastide of Eymet, about fifteen miles from Bergerac. Jean de Bueil had been provided with 400 men-at-arms to escort the siege train. Sir Thomas Felton collected together about 700 men, virtually all that he had available, and set up an ambush near the bastide. Felton's movements had been noticed. The French escort force was doubled before it reached the river. It now included some of the most famous knights in Louis's army: apart from Jean de Bueil himself there were his brother Pierre, the elderly paladin Le Bègue de Villaines, Bertrand du Guesclin's long-standing Breton adjutant Thibaut du Pont, and Owen of Wales. When the two armies came in sight of each other they both dismounted. There was a fierce soldiers' battle between well-matched enemies with roughly equal numbers. The decisive moment came when the French pages, who had been sent to the rear with the horses, appeared on the field and the English thought that a fresh corps had arrived to reinforce their enemies. They fell back, trying to disengage. But they were overwhelmed. A large number of Felton's troops were killed. Many of those who escaped from the battlefield were drowned in the river as they tried to get away. Only about 200 survived. Felton himself was taken prisoner, along with Raymond de Montaut, lord of Mussidan; Bérard d'Albret, lord of Langoiran, the only member of his clan apart from Bertucat who had maintained his English allegiance; and the lords of Duras and Rauzan, who were the leading Anglo-Gascon barons of the Agenais.

When the news reached the defenders of Bergerac, Bertucat d'Albret tried to persuade them that all was not lost. They were not convinced. Two days later, on 3 September, the citizens awoke to find that the artillery from La Réole had been erected in front of their walls and that trumpets were sounding in the French camp to signal the assault. Bertrand du Guesclin sent a parlementaire into the town to persuade them that further resistance would only lead to their town being sacked. The citizens briefly deliberated among themselves and agreed. Bertucat was not consulted but he could see which way events were moving. He gathered his men and rode out of the town across the stone bridge onto the unguarded south bank. From there they fled to the nearby fortress of Moncuq. As they left the French entered Bergerac.[24]

The Duke of Anjou called a council of war in his tents. He decided to press on westward down the Dordogne towards Bordeaux. The situation was unusually favourable. In contrast to the north, where Philip of Burgundy had been driven from the field by bad weather and supply problems, southern France was enjoying fine weather and one of the most bountiful harvests in recent memory. Fresh troops were on their way from the north and more had been summoned from Languedoc. Towards the end of the first week of September Edward III's son-in-law Enguerrand de Coucy arrived from the Île de France with 700 men-at-arms. Enguerrand had admired Edward III and refused to break with him while he lived. These ties would never be inherited by the child-king of England. Charles V had persuaded Enguerrand to enter his service within a fortnight of the death of the old King. As he prepared to fight against his former friends he sent his English page north to deliver a letter to Richard II renouncing his English lands and his membership of the Order of the Garter. It was his duty, he declared, to fight for the King of France as his 'natural and sovereign lord'. His wife, Edward III's daughter, who had been in England when the truce expired, joined him in France after Edward III's funeral, but ultimately returned to England early in 1379 shortly before her death. Of their two daughters, the elder was brought up in France and married into the French nobility while the younger stayed in England, becoming Countess of Oxford and a prominent figure at the court of her cousin. It was a symbolic division.[25]

The Château de l'Ombrière in Bordeaux was a scene of confusion and panic when Bergerac fell. The Seneschal's Council met on 3 September. They issued an appeal for help to the nobility and towns and sent urgently to England for instructions. The strongest personality among them was Sir William Elmham, the governor of Bayonne, who seems to have appointed himself as acting Seneschal. His main priority was the defence of Bordeaux. He gathered together the remnants of Felton's army and the few remaining garrison troops. From these he formed two companies to defend the western and northern approaches to the city. One, under his own command, was to hold the walled towns of Libourne and Saint-Emilion at the western end of the Dordogne valley where the main thrust of the Duke of Anjou's offensive was expected. The second, under two of his lieutenants, Edmund Cresswell and William Chandler, was ordered to hold the north shore of the

Gironde at Bourg and Blaye. This strategy was forced on Elmham by lack of manpower. But it tacitly abandoned the whole of the Dordogne valley above Saint-Emilion to the French. It also left Bordeaux itself 'without captain or garrison', as the Council acknowledged. The city would have to be defended by its citizens. They hired men-at-arms wherever they could find them but had no money with which to pay them. Unless they received 4,700 *livres bordelais* (about £630) immediately, the jurats of the city declared, the defence of the city would collapse. The Council told the Constable that somehow or other this sum would have to be found. Somehow or other it was.[26]

Money, however, was no longer the Council's main problem. As the implications of the loss of Bergerac and Felton's army sank in, the loyalty of the Gascon nobility and towns began to drain away. The Gascon prisoners of Eymet were taken before the Duke of Anjou in his camp after the battle. Several of them later claimed that they had been threatened with death unless they abandoned their English allegiance. This was probably untrue. But Anjou is known to have bought them from their captors in order, he said, to 'turn them to the King's and our allegiance'. He may well have applied to them the policy which Charles V had applied to the Captal de Buch, refusing to let them ransom themselves unless they submitted. For whatever reason they did submit within a few days. The two barons of the Agenais, the lords of Duras and Madaillan, took their new homage lightly in the fickle tradition of the region from which they came. They returned to the English fold almost immediately in return for a bribe of 600 *livres bordelais* (£80). 'Better to perjure ourselves to the Duke of Anjou than to the King of England, our natural lord who has been so good to us,' they reasoned according to Froissart. Bérard d'Albret and Raymond de Montaut of Mussidan were more considerable figures, long-standing allies of the English whose defection was a serious and public blow. Bérard delivered up the powerful castle of Cubzac on the north shore of the Dordogne, a serious impediment to Elmham's efforts to hold the lower reaches of the river. He also made himself responsible for recruiting fresh converts to the French cause in the Entre-Deux-Mers east of Bordeaux, where his main influence lay. Raymond de Montaut delivered up much of western Périgord to the French. When Cresswell and Chandler arrived with their troops at Blaye, Montaut territory for many years, the citizens shut the gates in their faces. They later submitted to the Duke of Anjou. Defection is contagious. Soon after withdrawing to Moncuq Bertucat d'Albret, whose career in English service dated back to the 1350s, made his own submission to the French Crown, undertaking to hold as many as twenty-seven castles on the Gascon march for the Duke of Anjou. This, the most remarkable submission of all, was certainly voluntary. It was Bertucat's judgment of the way things were going.[27]

The French army swept effortlessly down the Dordogne. Sainte-Foy surrendered the morning after the French arrived. Castillon, although virtually abandoned by Elmham, was defended by its inhabitants for twelve days. It surrendered only after the lower town had been lost and the great double keep had been severely battered by the French trebuchets. Anjou sent raiding forces downstream to try out the defences of Libourne and Saint-Emilion. But instead of trying to force his way past Elmham's companies he unexpectedly turned south and marched cross-country towards the Garonne. This move wrong-footed Elmham, whose forces were distributed along the north shore of the Dordogne and the Gironde, well away from the Duke's new line of attack. The Garonne was hardly defended at all. The last notable fortifications on the Garonne east of Bordeaux were the twin towns of Saint-Macaire and Langon, with their great thirteenth-century keeps standing on either side of the river some thirty miles away from the capital. The Council in the Château de l'Ombrière hurriedly recalled Cresswell and Chandler from Bourg and commandeered ships to carry their men upriver to Saint-Macaire. Elmham marched after the Duke and shut himself in the *bastide* of Cadillac, a short distance downstream. The south bank of the river was abandoned. Langon remained entirely undefended except by its inhabitants. In the third week of September the French army appeared before Saint-Macaire for the second time in two years. This time, the inhabitants of the lower town entered into negotiations as soon as the Duke arrived. The town surrendered after four days. The garrison plundered the town and retreated with their spoil into the citadel, an enormous square keep with walls ten feet thick built on a projecting rock at the western extremity of the town. Anjou erected eight large trebuchets around the keep which battered the walls day after day. The garrison finally surrendered on about 7 or 8 October after two weeks of this. Langon, on the opposite bank, opened its gates without waiting to be attacked.[28]

The French army was now reaching the limits of its endurance. Winter was closing in. Supply problems intensified. At the siege of Castillon forage parties had had to range more than thirty miles from the army to find food. By October horses were dying for want of fodder.

The Duke of Anjou decided to call an end to the campaign. The last episode was an act of personal revenge. On 9 October 1377 he appeared before Duras, the castle of the lord of Durfort. The great square castle of the Durforts, with its four corner towers, was impressively strong but of little strategic value. Yet Anjou spent three weeks battering it into submission with his artillery and launching bloody assaults against the walls. The survivors of the garrison retreated to a tower after the rest of the castle had been overrun and finally surrendered at the end of October 1377. Louis of Anjou then turned for home.[29]

In the midst of his Italian preoccupations Pope Gregory XI found time to write to the Duke of Anjou from his summer palace at Anagni, south of Rome. He was fulsome in his congratulations. The capture of so many places in so short a time and of almost all the leaders of the enemy army had caused him 'inexpressible joy and satisfaction, for which we give thanks to the Lord, hoping only that He has destined you for some yet greater triumph.' It had been an exceptionally well-managed campaign which had skilfully exploited the weaknesses of an admittedly outnumbered enemy. The whole of the valley of the Garonne was opened up to future French armies. Bordeaux, the main political pillar of the English duchy, became a frontier town. Detachments of Anjou's army raided across Entre-Deux-Mers and the western Bazadais and into the Médoc, forcing the surrender of many smaller places. According to the official count no fewer than 134 castles and walled towns were taken. The result was to consolidate the Duke's grip on a great swathe of territory all round the city. When he turned for home in mid-October, instead of paying off the whole of his army as he had done in 1374, he put part of it into winter quarters, distributing men among garrisons close to Bordeaux. The *bastide* of Cadillac, abandoned by Sir William Elmham, was turned into a depot for stores and equipment waiting for the great siege which Anjou intended to undertake the following year.

In due course, Anjou's garrisons were succeeded by the lords of countless small towns and castles who received them as confiscated lands. They carried on the unending war of raid and reprisal which had been an ordinary feature of the life of Périgord, Quercy, Rouergue and Auvergne for two decades. The estate accounts of the archbishops of Bordeaux, who were among the largest landowners of the region, tell the story in the laconic marginal notes which their clerks addressed to the auditors. This tenant has not paid his dues because 'everything has been destroyed by the French'; that estate produces 'no revenues on account of the war'; another has been 'wasted by the French' and lies empty and uncultivated, the grapes rotting on their stalks; many are marked with the increasingly familiar refrain, *'deserta est'* ('abandoned'). The accounts of the papal collectors in the region tell the same tale: 'a wasteland', 'utterly abandoned', 'devastated by war'. A large part of the diocese of Bazas, lying south-east of Bordeaux, was described in 1379 as 'charred and ruined'. Some of these places did not recover for more than a generation. In 1384 the Soudan de Trau, one of the biggest lay landowners of the Bordelais, explained to Richard II's officials why he could not repopulate the deserted parishes of his demesne. This man looked back on the fall of Saint-Macaire and the defection of Bérard d'Albret as the turning point in the fortunes of the district. The inhabitants had fled. Raiders of both sides were apt to appear without warning. The soldiers of the duchy had demolished the only castle in which the peasants could take refuge. So land once yielding 300 marks a year had become worthless. There were many other tales like his. Surveys carried out at the end of the fourteenth century were still reporting farms invaded by brambles which had gone out of cultivation twenty years before. It is true that the picture was not uniform. The Médoc north of Bordeaux largely escaped the problems elsewhere. And between the wrecked farms there were islands of prosperity where men still made a living from the land. But part of the problem was the very caprice of war, which left buildings intact in sight of burned-out shells and neatly tended rows of vines next to hillsides from which everything had been grubbed up by soldiers.[30]

During the first few months of the reign of Richard II the English government, frustrated by the problems of reinforcing Gascony and frightened by the coastal raids of Jean de Vienne, adopted the strategy which was to dominate their conduct of the war with France for the next decade. They set about acquiring a chain of garrisoned fortresses, clones of Calais, along the Atlantic coast of France: Brest, Cherbourg, Le Crotoy and Saint-Malo. Brest and Cherbourg were successfully occupied and held against the French for many years. Two major attempts against Saint-Malo failed. Designs against Le Crotoy were abandoned. The Channel Islands, after a long period of neglect by the English Crown, were built up as a victualling centre and a staging post for operations in Normandy and Brittany, developments which had already provoked powerful raids against the islands by French commanders. By 1377 the two major castles of the Channel Islands, Castle Cornet on Guernsey and Gorey on Jersey, both had substantial garrisons. A future English Chancellor would refer to all these places as England's 'frontiers and barbicans beyond the sea'. As the phrase suggests, the authors of English policy thought of the 'barbicans' as the first line of defence against French attacks on England. They served as bases from which to control the English Channel. They maximised the threat from English expeditionary armies, which now had a choice of places by which to enter France, thereby tying down large French forces in their own country.[31]

Whether this scheme was coherently thought out from the beginning or came about by trial and error as opportunities arose, is a question which the sources, always fuller on actions than designs, do not directly answer. It was certainly a policy deliberately promoted and to some extent financed by powerful mercantile interests, mainly in London, which had lost heavily by French piracy and naval raids and were keen to reassert English control of the narrow seas. But it also reflected long-standing frustrations among those who were concerned with the fortunes of the land war. The easiest point of entry into France was through Calais and Picardy. The short sea crossing required only local command of the sea and could be achieved with relatively modest fleets of transports operating in relays. But England's strategic interests were now concentrated in the Atlantic provinces of Normandy, Brittany and Gascony, which were difficult to reach from Calais. The lower reaches of the Seine and the Loire, with their broad, fast-flowing streams, represented an impassable barrier for an army. Brittany could be reached from Calais only by taking the long way round, north and east of Paris as Edward III had done in 1359 and Knolles in 1370 and as the Earl of Buckingham would do in 1380. To reach Gascony, as John of Gaunt learned in 1373, an even more circuitous route was required through the upper valley of the Loire and the western slopes of the Massif Central.

The first objective was Brest and its outlying harbours in western Brittany. The fortress had been held by English garrisons for many years. But its captains were answerable to John de Montfort, who was in principle responsible for paying their wages, maintaining the defences and directing operations. In 1377 he was in no position to do any of these things. Shortly before the expiry of the truce, the English government sent an armed escort to collect him from Bruges, where he had been living in exile for the past year, and bring him back to England through Calais. He arrived a ruined man. His only English asset, the honour of Richmond in Yorkshire, was mortgaged to Sir John Neville as security for the great sums which were owed to him for his service in the duchy before 1374. Brest and Auray were the only places in Brittany where his flag still flew. Neither of them seemed likely to survive for long. Auray was besieged by Olivier de Clisson at the beginning of July 1377. Its English garrison opened their gates to the French within a month and took ship back to England. At Brest, the *bastides* in front of the gates had already been reoccupied by Olivier de Clisson's Breton companies. A squadron of Castilian merchant ships arrived to blockade the harbour from the sea. If the English Council had not taken swift action the place would almost certainly have gone the way of Auray. They paid off part of his debt to Neville, redeemed Richmond and assumed responsibility for the cost of defending the fortress. In return John de Montfort was obliged to cede the town and castle and the famous harbour to the English for the duration of the war. A squire, John Clark, was sent out to the town at the beginning of September with supplies, reinforcements and orders for the garrison. He was to be followed by a large seaborne expedition in October. The object was to break the blockade, lift the siege on the landward side and occupy as much as possible of the territory in western Finistère which had traditionally been controlled from Brest. For shipping, the Council proposed to use the fleet which had been assembled in the Thames in June. It was still being held there under requisition, abandoned by its crews and depleted by desertions. A fresh round of requisitions was put in hand to reinforce them. The Admirals concentrated on the larger vessels that could be built up for fighting at sea. Press gangs were sent through the maritime communities to find seamen. Nearly 4,000 troops were recruited.[32]

The chief figures behind this enterprise were Edward III's youngest son Thomas of Woodstock, Earl of Buckingham, and Richard Fitzalan, Earl of Arundel, two men who were to be closely associated with the new naval strategy. They had much in common. Arundel had recently succeeded to his father's earldom at the age of thirty. Intelligent and ruthless, Arundel was one of the richest men in England, with ambitions to match his fortune. Buckingham, who was to command the expedition to Brest, was a more enigmatic figure. Only twenty-two years old at Richard's accession, he had hitherto lived in the shadows of the royal court. There is some evidence that the old King thought ill of his abilities. He had been dubbed a knight comparatively late and became an earl only at his nephew's coronation. Although he had been Constable of England since 1376 he had acquired no military or political experience at all in his father's time and never had an endowment to match his status. Yet throughout his life he had a stately manner and a strong attachment to the conventions of chivalry and the forms of courtly behaviour. He spoke 'like a king's son', said Froissart. Thomas of Woodstock was perhaps the extreme example of the young noblemen of his generation who struggled against the frustrating limitations of English power that deprived them of the chances of glory that their fathers and grandfathers had enjoyed. The frustration was intensified in his case, as it was for so many of his contemporaries, by expensive tastes, a profound sense of lineage and a perennial shortage of money. 'The best of men' was the chronicler Walsingham's judgment of him. But his career shows him to have been an assertive and quarrelsome man with a high opinion of his own talents which was never entirely justified by his acts.[33]

The first Parliament of the new reign opened at Westminster on 13 October 1377. It was, perhaps inevitably, affected by the unresolved tensions of the past. A large number of the knights of the shire who had sat in the Good Parliament were re-elected to the Commons, including Sir Peter de la Mare, who was once again elected Speaker. Their instincts were in some respects a reversion to those of 1376. Alice Perrers was once again brought before Parliament to hear herself banished and her property forfeited. The Commons grumbled about Lyons's pardon, which they blamed on Alice. They procured the removal of their old enemy William Latimer and a number of his friends from the continual council. Their hostility to John of Gaunt was unspoken, but palpable. The Commons' radicalism, like that of their predecessors, was founded on strong support for the war and on a conviction that the ministers of Edward III had been half-hearted about prosecuting it. With memories of the French raids on the south coast still fresh, this proved to be one of the most warlike assemblies of the late fourteenth century. They complained about the decline of ancient chivalry, about the losses of the warrior class in France, about the end of what they supposed to have been England's former mastery of the seas. They were merciless in their judgment of recent failures, which they were inclined to blame this time on captains in the field rather than the comparatively new ministers at Westminster. The defenders of Ardres and Audruicq were tried in Parliament for treason and sentenced to death. They were only saved by the intervention of John of Gaunt.[34]

The real test of Parliament's support for the war, however, was its willingness to pay for it. Richard II had inherited an empty treasury from his grandfather. Richard's ministers told Parliament that they needed no less than 400,000 marks (£266,666) to refill his coffers and prosecute the war. The Commons responded, as they had so often done, with suggestions that more money could be derived from the royal demesne and the Church. They prepared a rather unrealistic table to show what riches these sources could be expected to produce but they were finally persuaded to make a grant of two tenths and fifteenths. These were declared to represent two years' worth of direct taxation. But they were to be collected in one payment by 2 February 1378. It was less than the government had wanted but still the largest single tax payment which the Commons had ever authorised.

True to their instincts, the Commons did not trust the government to spend it well. They made it a condition of the grant that the entire proceeds of the tenths and fifteenths as well as the wool subsidy and the clerical tenth should be paid to two special treasurers acceptable to themselves, who were to make disbursements only against warrants for military expenditure. William Walworth and John Philpot, who were appointed to perform this office, were both prominent London financiers who were among the members sitting for the city in the Commons. Walworth was a former mayor who had made his fortune as a victualler and wool merchant. Philpot was a rich and well-connected grocer. Both men belonged to the well-organised group of Calais staple merchants which had dominated the city's government for years and had a direct interest in the policy of concentrating resources on the war at sea. In the first three years of Richard's reign about three-quarters of the total receipts of the English state passed through their hands and were applied to war purposes. This was a substantial increase on the proportion, generally about 60 per cent, which had hitherto been normal. It was achieved mainly at the expense of the royal household and the ordinary internal administration of the country, both of which were severely squeezed. The absolute sums involved were high by historic standards. Between 14 December 1377, when they took up their functions, and 4 February 1379, when they delivered their first accounts, the special treasurers spent £145,651 on the war, the largest figure for any comparable period since 1370. For a brief period England was able to spend money on the war at a rate not far short of that of France.[35]

The Earl of Buckingham had originally planned to sail to Brest with the annual wine convoy bound for Gascony, which usually left in early October. He missed the convoy, which sailed without him, taking some of his troops and most of his ships with them. As a result, the Earl was

forced to postpone his expedition until the end of the year. He decided
to make use of the ships and troops still waiting in London by taking
them on a plundering raid against the Flemish port of Sluys, where a
large number of Castilian merchant ships were reported to be waiting,
laden with cargo, for a favourable wind. Since the English government
was endeavouring to maintain good relations with the Count of Flanders
and his subjects, this was not a wise decision and it is quite possible that
Buckingham consulted no one but his fellow captains. In the event they
never reached Sluys. In the last week of October Buckingham and his
companions mustered their men outside the half-finished buildings of
Edward III's Cistercian foundation of St. Mary Graces, east of the Tower
of London, and further down the Thames at Ratcliffe, a bleak area of
wharves and boat-yards in Stepney Marsh. The men were crammed onto
thirty large warships and a number of smaller barges and supply vessels.
They put to sea on 7 November 1377. After three days they encountered
a terrible storm. Driving rain and gale-force winds scattered the fleet.
Several of the supply ships took in water and were abandoned by their
crews, who took refuge on the crowded decks of the warships. The
survivors limped home with broken masts and torn sails. The fiasco was
rather unfairly blamed on the two Admirals, both of whom were
removed at the beginning of December after only a few months in office.
They were replaced by the Earls of Arundel and Warwick, who were
expected to bring more energy to their task.[36]

Buckingham's fleet was repaired and reunited at Sandwich in the
course of the following month and sailed again in the middle of
December 1377. Shortly afterwards it successfully joined forces with
the western fleet in the Channel. The combined armada then headed
south for Brest, between sixty and eighty strong. The ships must have
reached the town at about Christmas-time. They found the approach to
the harbour blocked by the Castilian squadron lying off the town.
Seeing the great carracks ahead of them, a large part of the English fleet
mutinied and refused to fight. One of Buckingham's subordinate
commanders was threatened with death by his crew unless he agreed to
turn back. Undeterred, Buckingham sailed ahead with the rest of his
ships and broke through the enemy line. Eight armed Castilian
merchantmen were captured in this fight and a number of others put to
flight. When Buckingham and his companions entered the harbour they
encountered opposition of a more unexpected kind. The garrison in the
castle consisted mainly of Englishmen, commanded by a former
associate of Robert Knolles called John Lakenheath. They were in an

ugly humour. They claimed to be owed more than 22,000 francs (about £3,700) in back wages and refused to open their gates unless it was paid. The leaders of the army had to guarantee this sum personally before they were allowed to take possession. Once inside, Buckingham appointed Robert Knolles as temporary captain. He filled the stores of the castle from the supplies which he had brought with him. He increased the garrison's strength. He began to push out the limits of the garrison's effective control in Finistère. The new base was swiftly turned into a centre for English commerce raiding. Cargoes were commandeered from passing ships to add to the garrison's stores. Making north into the Channel with a galley and two barges, Sir Thomas Percy was able to disperse a convoy of fifty unarmed Flemish and Castilian merchantmen, sinking several of them and capturing at least two entire cargoes. This short campaign was one of the most successful naval enterprises of the English since 1369. On 25 January 1378 the fleet returned in triumph to England.[37]

Brest was destined to remain in English hands for just over twenty years. It never did serve as a point of entry into France. The sea journey always proved to be too long for the carriage of a large army. The fortress played a modest part in supporting English naval operations in the Channel and maintaining communications with Gascony. Like Calais, it became a largely military town, economically dependent on its garrison. Knolles held the town and castle with 240 men and the garrison was probably maintained at something like that level until the end of the 1380s. The local civilian population was progressively driven out by the hardships of frequent French raids and sieges and persistent requisitioning and billeting by its English captains. Victualling and supply proved to be a major operation, managed by the King's receiver, a full-time official, and by a network of suppliers in Dartmouth and Fowey, Bayonne and Bordeaux. Regular works had to be carried out on the walls and towers. Gunpowder artillery was manufactured in England and laboriously hauled to the coast to be shipped out to the town. At least two ships were kept permanently in the harbour to maintain communications with the mainland and capture prizes at sea. Whether all this justified the expense may be doubted. In the first few years the net cost of the English occupation of Brest was between £6,000 and £8,000 a year, which was substantially more than the English government spent on Gascony over the same period.[38]

The main beneficiaries of the occupation of Brest were its captains. Much of the seaborne commerce of western Europe was carried past the fortress and it offered rich spoils. Inland the garrison gradually established a ransom district extending north to the coast and south as far as the Bay of Bénodet. Knolles's successors as captains of Brest, who relieved him in June 1378, were two Oxfordshire knights close to the King, Sir Richard Abberbury and Sir John Golafre. These men, neighbours at home, had probably entered into a partnership to exploit the profits of war together. They entered into a fixed-price contract with the King under which they agreed to man and defend the fortress at their own expense in return for an annual fee of 10,000 marks (£6,667), plus a proportion of the spoil which was calculated according to a complicated formula leaving them with about half. During the eleven-month tenure of the fortress by Abberbury and Golafre the spoil declared to the King's receiver came to £1,727, of which rather more than half was derived from *patis* and the rest came from ships and cargoes captured at sea. Of this sum £875 went into the captains' pockets, a considerable fortune by the standards of the time. Abberbury and Golafre were followed by another business partnership of Sir Hugh Calveley and Sir Thomas Percy, who took the contract at a slightly reduced fee with a larger share of the spoil. These were all essentially financial transactions. The captains of Brest rarely visited the fortress and generally performed their duties through deputies who accounted to them for the profits. Calveley and Percy declared less than half the spoil that their predecessors had done but must have made far more. In 1384, when Percy held the contract alone, the Bretons claimed that the garrison was taking *patis* from 160 parishes and reckoned the proceeds at 35,000 francs (about £5,800) a year in cash and 1,200 barrels of fish, meat and grain. There is no record of the costs incurred by the early captains of Brest, but the fact that the government was able to drive a much harder bargain with their successors suggests that they did very well for themselves. Richard Abberbury was already a rich man when he went to Brest, but it is not fanciful to see the grand gatehouse of Castle Donnington in Berkshire, which was ostentatiously rebuilt for him in the 1380s, as a monument to the profits of a successful war contractor even at a time when English fortunes were waning.[39]

With Brest and its hinterland under English control Richard II's Council turned their attention to the Cotentin peninsula and its absent lord, Charles of Navarre. Charles was now fifty-five years old, an embittered figure who had passed most of his adult life in exile in Navarre. He had not given up hope of recovering the great appanage in southern

Normandy which he had enjoyed until the civil wars of the 1360s. According to his secretary and chamberlain, whose confessions in the following year are the main source for his acts in this period, Charles of Navarre still thought of himself as the rightful King of France. He still hoped for some catastrophic event, perhaps a great defeat or the death of the King, which would plunge France back into the civil disorders of the 1350s and create an opening for his ambitions. From his castles at Pamplona, Estella and Olite he maintained a regular correspondence with the citadel of the town of Évreux, where a small group of soldiers and administrators ran what remained of his French domains and handled his difficult relations with the court of France. But Charles had long ago lost what friends and influence he had ever had in Paris and was increasingly out of touch with events there. Distance and frustration magnified his illusions. As a well-placed observer remarked during a candid exchange with the King of Navarre's representatives in Paris, the truth was that Charles of Navarre was profoundly hated at the Hôtel Saint-Pol and too far away to need appeasing. The hatred was fully reciprocated. The King of Navarre had made at least two attempts to have Charles V poisoned since his return to Navarre in 1372 and had encouraged a variety of obscure and unsuccessful plots. His only real bargaining counter was his capacity to make trouble by intriguing with the English and even that was a weapon to be used with caution. Charles of Navarre's French domains were poorly defended and vulnerable to reprisals if he should press his chances too far. Even in his Navarrese kingdom he was exposed to attack from Castile, an ancient and powerful enemy and a compliant ally of France, whose hostile presence on his southern border always inhibited his more aggressive plans.[40]

As far as the English were concerned Charles of Navarre was an untrustworthy politician who had double-crossed them several times. But he possessed important harbours in Lower Normandy, in particular Cherbourg and Barfleur, which made him worth courting in spite of the risks and frustrations involved. In the spring of 1377, with the end of the truce of Bruges in sight, the King's councillors at Westminster began to take a more active interest in him. Sir Edward Berkeley, a former retainer of the Black Prince who was to become something of an expert on southern Europe over the following years, spent the best part of a year in Gascony and Navarre trying to pin down the slippery King of Navarre. Charles played his usual game of hinting at an alliance with England without actually making one in the hope of persuading the French King to buy him off with fresh concessions. He received Berkeley with every outward show of warmth while in Paris his agents covertly renewed their demands on the French King, offering a military alliance against the English. In August 1377 Charles's tactics changed. A profoundly gloomy report arrived from his agents in Paris, followed in due course by the French King's official rejection of all of his demands. Suddenly he declared his willingness to join forces with England. He began to press forward with his plans with an impatience and enthusiasm that must have taken Berkeley by surprise. He would return to Normandy, he said, with a corps of Navarrese troops, 300 or 500 men, in ships that the English government in Gascony would be expected to find for him in Bayonne. He would put the harbours of the Cotentin and the Navarrese castles of southern Normandy at the disposal of an English army for a joint invasion of France. As an earnest of his intentions Charles proposed a marriage between his daughter and Richard II.[41]

In about early October 1377 these proposals were carried to Westminster by one of Charles of Navarre's Norman squires. His arrival coincided with the opening of Parliament. The Parliamentary peerage was enthusiastic. They were even prepared to waive a dowry for Charles's daughter, an extraordinary concession bearing in mind that Richard was one of the most eligible princes of Europe. Progress, however, was slow. Communications across the Bay of Biscay in winter were difficult. The emissary sent with the English answer, a Gascon squire called Garcie-Arnaud de Salies, left as soon as he could for Bordeaux, accompanied by an English knight, Sir John Roches. But it took them nearly two months to find a passage to Bordeaux. In Pamplona Charles of Navarre became nervous. The long silence from England troubled him. The French government, although lacking precise information, had already become suspicious of the diplomatic bustle around Navarre and began to stir up trouble on Charles's southern front. The French Admiral Jean de Vienne was in Castile at the end of the year. There were rumours of Castilian troop movements south of the Ebro. Regular messengers passed between the Duke of Anjou and Henry of Trastámara, many of whom had to go through Navarre. Some of them certainly had their letters opened by Charles of Navarre's officials. On 6 January 1378 Henry of Trastámara declared himself. From Toledo he issued orders for the invasion of Navarre in the spring. The army was ordered to muster at Logroño on 1 April. This time, Henry said, he would not just harass Charles of Navarre's kingdom but annex it to his own.[42]

These machinations in Charles's rear forced him to drop his plans to go to Normandy in person. In the new year he decided to send to France in his place his eldest son, also called Charles, an inexperienced youth of eighteen whose arrival, he thought, would seem less threatening than his own. The young prince was given a retinue so grand that Charles's Navarrese subjects had to submit to a special tax to pay for it. But the purpose of his visit was characteristically obscure. The young prince appears to have known nothing of his father's dealings with the English. The real business of the mission was left to his entourage who did. One of them was carrying a satchel of documents for Pierre du Tertre, the King of Navarre's secretary, who had been involved in Charles's covert dealings with the English for nearly a decade and was currently based in western France. His task was to fill the store-rooms of the Navarrese castles in Normandy and make sure that their garrisons held fast behind their walls until the English arrived. The King of Navarre proposed to send his chamberlain, Jacques de Rue, to join him with his final instructions as soon as he had done the deal with the English. He would also be joined by one of Charles's French wardrobe servants, who was going to insinuate himself into the royal kitchens in Paris and poison the King of France.[43]

On 6 January 1378, the day that the Castilian mobilisation orders were sent out, Charles the Younger set out from Navarre with his companions. A few days later Garcie-Arnaud de Salies finally arrived in Pamplona with the English Council's proposals, only to find that they had been overtaken by events. The King of Navarre's most urgent need now was for help in defending his southern frontier against Castile. He wanted reinforcements from England or Gascony to be sent to him across the Pyrenees. He clearly entertained quite unrealistic notions about how long they would take to get there. So Garcie-Arnaud was sent straight back to England with pressing demands for military assistance. With him went yet another Navarrese emissary, Charles's councillor the lord of Garro. He brought with him powers to reach agreement on all outstanding matters.[44]

At Westminster the English King's ministers were devising their plans for the coming season. Their ideas were on a scale to match the lavish financial resources recently made available by Parliament. At the end of January 1378 it was resolved to raise an army of 6,000 men. Part of this host was to be put on board some large vessels of Bayonne and employed in patrolling the south coast of England in the hope of intercepting French raiders. The rest was to be mobilised in two stages. The first contingent would be employed in a purely naval operation in the Channel. Some 2,700 troops, about half of the English army, were assigned to this operation and placed under the temporary command of the Admiral of the West, Richard Earl of Arundel. The plan appears to have been to launch a pre-emptive strike against the French fleet while it was still at its home ports in Normandy. The second stage of the campaign was expected to open a month later in the middle of April. Arundel's squadrons were to return to England and join forces with the rest of the army and fleet at Southampton. The whole fleet would then sail out from the Solent on what their indentures called a 'great expedition' under the command of the Duke of Lancaster. The English administrative sources are extremely discreet about the objective of Gaunt's 'great expedition'. The contemporary chroniclers clearly did not know, which suggests that only a handful of the participants did. But it is clear that the plan was to land his army at the newly acquired base at Brest and invade Brittany. Between March and June 1378 seven ships were continuously engaged in ferrying Gaunt's victuals and war stores to the port.[45]

In March 1378 this already overloaded programme was burdened with a fresh project when the King's ministers were forced to turn their attention to Gascony. The duchy had been leaderless and almost denuded of troops for some six months. The French were expected to resume their offensive in the south-west in the summer. The issue could not be put off any longer. A new Lieutenant was appointed, Sir John Neville. He had already shown himself in Brittany to be a skilful organiser of rearguard actions. It was proposed to assign to him an army of 1,000 men, bringing to 7,000 the total for which shipping would have to be found. It was a modest force with which to face the hordes likely to be available to the Duke of Anjou. But the Council planned to strengthen Neville's hand by co-ordinating his operations with those of the companies operating beyond the Gascon march. Several prominent Gascon *routier* captains were in England over the winter of 1377–8 to discuss the possibility of mounting diversionary raids on the Duke of Anjou's northern flank, the first time that these irregulars had been so formally acknowledged as part of the English King's forces in France. Bertucat d'Albret had ostensibly made his peace with the Duke of Anjou and stayed away. But two of his principal lieutenants, Bernard Douat and Perrot de Galard, were at Westminster. They commanded two important fortresses in Quercy: Montvalent, high above the Dordogne east of Souillac; and Balaguier, on the left bank of the Lot near Figeac. Between them these places controlled about a dozen satellite garrisons and could raise a raiding force of up to 500 mounted men. With Galard and Douat in England were at least two other significant figures from the shadowy world of the Gascon free companies: the notorious Limousin brigand Mérigot Marchès, one of a handful of English partisans who were still resisting the officers of the French King in his native province; and Raymond de Custon, one of the captains of Charlus-Champagnac, an ancient castle of the Viscounts of Turenne dominating the gorges of the Dordogne in Bas-Limousin.[46]

Given the unhappy history of large-scale requisitioning programmes in England the arrangements for the Earl of Arundel's Channel fleet proceeded with unusual efficiency. Most of the troops assigned to him were ready at the ports by the end of March 1378. By early April nearly sixty requisitioned ships and barges were available. Nicholas Hakenet, a Norman spy in English service, had passed much of the winter watching for signs of activity in the French Channel ports. He returned to England in late April to report. Yet nothing happened. It is possible that Arundel was waiting for the French galley fleet to leave the arsenal at Rouen before sailing for the French Channel ports. But this is speculation. Public opinion, which had been led to expect great things and knew nothing of all this, began to grumble against the leaders of the army 'as common people are wont to do as their moods change', wrote the snobbish Thomas Walsingham, who actually agreed with them. There was unconcealed anger when the Scottish adventurer Andrew Mercer, son of the famous merchant of Perth, began to raid along the coast of north-east England with a squadron of ships put together from the ports of Scotland and from French and Castilian merchant ships in Flanders.

In late April, while the Earl of Arundel was still waiting with his ships in the Thames, groups of adventurers began to put to sea to pursue their own private enterprises. The London merchant John Philpot took some ships and about a thousand seamen and soldiers north and captured Mercer at sea together with several Castilian merchant ships of his squadron. The Bayonne squadron, which was probably by now being employed to escort Gaunt's victualling ships to Brest, broke off to prey on Castilian merchant convoys entering the Channel. The seamen of the Cinque Ports carried out a series of hit-and-run raids around Fécamp on the coast of Normandy. One of them even succeeded in recovering the bells of Rye church, carried off by the French the year before.[47]

*

While the English plans hung fire a major political crisis developed in France. At the end of March 1378 the French government uncovered the whole of Charles of Navarre's plans for joint operations with the English in Normandy. This appears to have happened because of some ham-fisted diplomacy by English agents in southern France. In February Sir John Roches was in Béarn trying to involve Gaston, Count of Foix, in the Anglo-Navarrese scheme. He seems to have upset his host by threatening reprisals if he failed to co-operate. As a result Gaston sent a confidential message to the French King appealing for protection and disclosing the King of Navarre's 'horrible and detestable' plot against the Crown. He also told him that he thought that Jacques de Rue, then travelling through France, was part of it. Charles V knew by now about the armies gathering in southern England. When he received Gaston's message in the first week of March he assumed that they were intended for Normandy. This sealed Charles of Navarre's fate. Charles V immediately ordered the French garrisons in winter quarters east of Bordeaux to be prepared to go to the Count of Foix's assistance if he was attacked. The fleet of galleys and oared barges based at the arsenal of Rouen was told to put to sea as soon as it could be made ready. Commissioners were sent to ensure that all royal fortresses in Normandy were provisioned and garrisoned against an invasion. Meanwhile the royal *baillis* were instructed to scour the roads for Jacques de Rue and his party. Within a few days they were found at an inn at Nemours, south of Paris, and arrested. In their baggage the King's officers found a roll containing copies of draft treaties and correspondence which disclosed much of Charles of Navarre's recent dealings with the English government. Jacques himself was taken first to the castle of Corbeil on the Seine and then to the Châtelet prison in Paris. Here in a succession of confessions he admitted the plot to poison Charles V. He revealed the plan to put English garrisons into the Navarrese castles of Normandy and described with a wealth of circumstantial detail the story of his master's negotiations with the English going back to 1369, much of which the French King and his councillors were now learning for the first time.[48]

At the end of March 1378 Charles V summoned Charles the Younger before him. The scene was the old twelfth-century palace of Louis VI at Senlis north of Paris, whose ruins can still be seen rising above the ramparts of the town. The young prince of Navarre appeared under the protection of a safe-conduct. He was accompanied by the Bishop of Dax, a learned Norman cleric who had travelled with him from

Navarre, by the Navarrese military governor of Normandy, Ferrando d'Ayens, and by several of his father's officials and captains in France. The Navarrese prince came ready to complain about the arrest of Jacques de Rue. But he was abruptly reduced to silence by the King's councillors. One of them produced the document recording Jacques's confession. He took the prince through the history of his father's plots, all of which appears to have been news to him. The King of France, he said, had decided to take over the seven principal Navarrese fortresses in Normandy including Cherbourg and Avranches and to install his own garrisons in order to prevent them falling into the hands of the English. The Duke of Burgundy had already been appointed to receive their surrender. All those present in his entourage would have to swear to open their gates when they were summoned to do so. The captains of the remaining Navarrese garrisons would be left in possession, but only if they swore not to admit the King of Navarre or the enemies of the realm or to make war against France.

Charles the Younger and his companions, evidently taken aback, swore the oath demanded of them on a copy of the Gospels and fragment of the True Cross, the holiest relic that could be found. Most of the young prince's attendants were then released to tell the garrison commanders what to do. But the prince himself and Ferrando d'Ayens were held at Senlis to accompany the Duke of Burgundy into Normandy. Charles was a willing guest. He was obviously shocked by the contents of Jacques de Rue's confession and over the following weeks he threw his lot in with his uncle. He was handsomely rewarded for his loyalty with an income, a retinue and a mansion in Paris. Ferrando d'Ayens was a different quantity. He had been the principal Navarrese captain in France during the civil wars of the 1350s and was known to be close to the English. Indeed he had once briefly been a mercenary in their service. He was arrested as soon as he had sworn his oath and accompanied the French army as a prisoner.[49]

The pre-emptive strike against the Navarrese castles in Normandy had been improvised at very short notice and took some time to gather pace. Philip of Burgundy had to send to Dijon for his body armour and to borrow horses from the King's stables. Initially he had no more than a few hundred men and a modest artillery train. He opened his campaign on 12 April 1378 at Breteuil, some twenty miles south of Evreux. Breteuil was the strongest of the group of Navarrese fortresses in eastern Normandy. The King of Navarre's second son, Pierre, had taken refuge there with most of the officers of the King of Navarre's

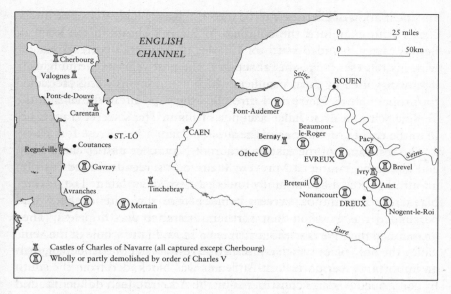

12 The conquest of the Navarrese castles of Normandy, April–June 1378

French domains. Two other detachments of Philip's army laid siege on the same day to the Navarrese headquarters at Evreux and the fortress of Beaumont-le-Roger. On 14 April it was the turn of Bernay. In spite of the oaths which had been sworn at Senlis, none of these places would comply with the prince of Navarre's orders to surrender. But none of them resisted for very long. Some of the Navarrese troops were prepared to fight but by and large the King of Navarre's Norman subjects were not. Evreux, which had never been a strong place, had already been abandoned by most of its defenders. Its Navarrese captain persuaded his companions to open their gates. At Bernay the *basse cour* of the castle surrendered as soon as the French arrived. The keep was defended by the King of Navarre's secretary, Pierre du Tertre. He knew what fate would be in store for him if he fell into the French King's hands. But he could not persuade the garrison to hold out. On 19 April, after the walls had been battered by trebuchets for two days, Bertrand du Guesclin arrived with reinforcements to mount an assault. The defenders sent Pierre out to parley with the French and then pulled up the drawbridge behind him so that he could not return. The garrison surrendered later that day. Pierre was arrested and sent to Paris to be delivered to the jailers of the Temple prison. The Constable and the Duke of Burgundy had promised to put in a good word for him and no doubt did so. But any inclination of Charles V to be merciful was quickly dispelled by the clerks who examined the contents of Pierre's chests in the keep of Bernay. They included much of Charles of Navarre's correspondence with his representatives in France over the past year, its meaning only lightly disguised by a crude code in which pseudonyms were substituted for proper names. Pierre du Tertre filled the gaps out in the cells of the Temple with an even fuller account of his master's secret diplomacy than the earlier revelations of Jacques de Rue.

The resistance of the eastern group of Navarrese castles came to an end at the beginning of May 1378. Breteuil surrendered for cash on about the 3rd. Beaumont followed a few days later. The former Navarrese captain of Evreux came before the gate of Pacy and persuaded the garrison that further resistance was hopeless. They abandoned their posts without striking a blow. In the whole of the Seine valley the only place which continued to resist was Pont-Audemer, then an important river port. Pont-Audemer was blockaded from the south by garrisoned *bastides* constructed by the Admiral, Jean de Vienne, and from the river by four galleys of Monaco. Its Navarrese captain declared that as long as Charles of Navarre was alive he would surrender only on his personal instructions. But even he was not willing to chance his life for long. At the beginning of June the French brought up cannon against the walls and increased their strength around the town. The defenders surrendered on the 15th in return for pardons, three months' wages in their pockets and safe-conducts to Cherbourg.[50]

In the Cotentin the French invasion began in the last week of April 1378. It was conducted by about 1,000 local troops recruited in Lower Normandy. The principal towns, Carentan, Valognes and Avranches, surrendered rapidly. They were all substantial places whose populations probably refused to defend them against a royal army. In most cases the King of Navarre's captains in the citadels were bought off. The only resistance came at the smaller places whose garrisons were less dependent on popular support for their defence. The castle of Gavray, which housed Charles of Navarre's Norman treasury, was defended by a garrison of just thirty-four men for nearly a month. The defenders sold the place at the end of May but only after its powder magazine had blown up and its food stores had been exhausted. By June only Mortain and Cherbourg still held out for the King of Navarre. Mortain was already under siege and preparations were in hand for an attack on Cherbourg.[51]

After four civil wars in a quarter of a century Charles V had resolved to be finished with Charles of Navarre. On 16 June 1378, as the campaign in the Seine valley was drawing to its close, the King presided at a public session of the Parlement of Paris, attended by the whole royal Council, many of the leading noblemen of the French court and representatives of the municipality of Paris, the usual chorus summoned to witness the great occasions of the French state. The notarised confessions of Jacques de Rue and Pierre du Tertre were read out to the assembled gathering. Copies were distributed among the crowd outside. The two men were brought in to acknowledge the truth of their contents. They were then condemned to be beheaded in the market of Les Halles and their dismembered bodies exhibited at the four principal gates of Paris.

As the King of Navarre's ministers were taken to the scaffold the last Navarrese garrison to hold out against the French onslaught was coming to the end of its resistance. The defenders of Mortain sued for terms after artillery had been brought up and sappers had undermined the walls and towers. Of the twenty-one fortresses seized by royal forces, fourteen were wholly or partly demolished over the next two months and royal garrisons were put into the others. Ferrando d'Ayens, who had proved either unable or unwilling to procure the surrender of a single castle, was locked up in the citadel of Caen and then in Rouen castle where he appears to have passed the rest of his days.[52]

With his French domains facing extinction at the hands of Charles V and his Navarrese kingdom threatened with invasion from Castile, the King of Navarre was now in a desperate position. The military forces at his disposal were divided between Normandy and the Ebro frontier of Navarre, and were too weak to defend either. Charles's nephew Charlot de Beaumont was sent into Gascony in April to recruit men among the *routier* companies. The companies of Bertucat d'Albret and several other Gascon captains, together with a handful of English and Aragonese, were hired for service on the Ebro front during the summer. Artillery was mounted on the walls of the principal towns and castles, the first time that it had been seen in Navarre. Emissaries were sent in all directions with appeals for help: to Aragon, to the Count of Foix, to the English council in Bordeaux. These were all powers with a natural interest in containing the overweening strength of Castile in the Iberian peninsula. But none of them was strong enough to save Navarre on its own. At the beginning of May 1378 Henry of Trastámara was reported to be marching north with substantial forces and a powerful siege train to join the Castilian troops already gathered on the Navarrese march.

The King of Navarre and his councillors fled over the Pyrenees to the small town of Saint-Jean Pied-de-Port, where his dominions met those of the King of England and the Count of Foix. Here at least he was safe from capture and better able to follow the complex diplomatic traffic which he had set in motion.[53]

Charles of Navarre's latest emissary to the English court, the lord of Garro, had arrived at Westminster in March 1378. Since he had left Navarre before the arrest of Jacques de Rue his instructions were already out of date. But even without instructions it must have been clear to him that unless the English intervened quickly his master's domains in Normandy would be lost. The English Council knew that too. They drove a hard bargain. They offered to send supplies and reinforcements urgently to Cherbourg and to lend the impecunious King of Navarre 25,000 francs (about £4,200) to help him confront his enemies in Spain. They were also willing, although this would take longer, to send an army of 1,000 men to Gascony to be placed at Charles's disposal for up to four months if the Castilians invaded Navarre. But they were not prepared to depend on the King of Navarre's goodwill. The price of their help was the immediate transfer of Cherbourg to English control for a period of three years, together with any other Navarrese fortresses in Normandy that survived the French onslaught.

Cherbourg was a great prize. The walls of the town had been largely rebuilt in the 1360s. The immense wedge-shaped castle dominated the harbour from the eastern end of the town with its great keep, the twelve towers of the curtain wall, the lines of ditches and the cavernous stores, all just seventy miles by sea from England. It was one of the strongest places in western France. The lord of Garro appears to have agreed with the English proposals. But he could not commit Charles of Navarre without his authority. In about the middle of April, as the Duke of Burgundy's officers negotiated the surrender of Evreux, Breteuil and Bernay, the lord of Garro left England for Navarre on a fast armed merchantman of Bayonne.[54]

It shortly became clear that there would not be time to wait for the King of Navarre's answer. So the English Council resolved to take control of Cherbourg in any case. In this they were abetted by the Navarrese captain of the town, Ramón de Esparza. His garrison was too small to defend the place against a large French army even with the aid of the refugees flooding in from other Navarrese castles in Normandy. His stores were also perilously low. At the end of April 1378, shortly after the lord of Garro's departure, Ramón sent one of his lieutenants to England to plead for help. The Council were only too pleased to take the opportunity of putting their own troops into Cherbourg. Sir William Farringdon, a knight of the royal household, and Garcie-Arnaud de Salies, the former English ambassador to Navarre, were sent to the town on a fact-finding mission and returned, accompanied by Ramón himself, towards the end of May. While Ramón toured the apothecaries of London buying sulphur and saltpetre to replenish his stores of gunpowder, Farringdon and Garcie-Arnaud set about recruiting troops.[55]

On 1 June 1378 a Great Council gathered at Westminster. The situation before them was very different from the one which they had contemplated when their plans were first laid earlier in the year. The Earl of Arundel's fleet was still idle in its ports. The Duke of Lancaster's 'great expedition' had been delayed by shortage of shipping. The Admirals had been able to requisition a total of 211 transports, which were scattered between half a dozen ports from Norfolk to Devon. But it was not enough to carry John of Gaunt's army to Brest with its horses. Some of the ships were still without crews as press gangs struggled to fill their quotas from the reluctant youth of the east coast ports. There is no record of the deliberations of the Council, but the outcome is known from the stream of instructions which issued from the King's ministers as soon as it dispersed. The Earl of Arundel was ordered to proceed with his operations against the French fleet immediately and then to take possession of Cherbourg. Troops to reinforce the town and castle would follow as soon as stores could be collected to support them. The landings at Brest were cancelled. Gaunt's 'great expedition' was redirected against Saint-Malo in northern Brittany, an operation which would require fewer horses and therefore less shipping space. At the same time the Council proposed to try to occupy another 'barbican' further north, namely the small but strategically valuable fortified harbour of Le Crotoy, at the mouth of the Somme in Picardy. Le Crotoy was to be attacked by Sir Hugh Calveley with a raiding force from Calais, probably in conjunction with part of the English fleet. Sir John Neville was instructed to proceed urgently to Bordeaux to take up his lieutenancy and charged to support the defence of Navarre against Henry of Trastámara. Since only thirty-four ships could be spared to carry Neville's men with their horses and stores, his retinue had to be reduced to about half the strength originally planned. Somehow or other he would have to find 1,000 men to send to the defence of Navarre when he got there.[56]

The Earl of Arundel and that veteran of past marine expeditions, William Montague, Earl of Salisbury, sailed from Southampton in the first few days of June 1378 with all the ships and men which were ready at Southampton. There were about 2,000 soldiers, carried on some eighty vessels. On about 7 June the English fleet entered the estuary of the Seine and appeared off the French naval base at Harfleur. Arundel landed at least part of his army near the town and began to try its landward defences. The French had no coast-guard system comparable to the one which operated in southern England. The old marshal, Mouton de Blainville, who was in command in Pays de Caux, was taken completely unawares with only 100 men-at-arms under his command. But he valiantly fought off Arundel's force from the walls of Harfleur. With no siege equipment the English were unable to make any impression on the modern defences of the town. On about 21 June they retreated to their ships, pursued by sortie parties from the town which inflicted heavy casualties on the encumbered soldiers as they struggled through the water to clamber over the ships' sides. From Harfleur, Arundel sailed westward across the great bay of the Seine towards Cherbourg. There Ramón de Esparza let them pass into the harbour and admitted them to the castle. A few days later a small squadron from Bayonne arrived, bringing the lord of Garro back from Navarre with Charles's authority to agree to what had by now become a done deed. With him came Charles's nephew Charlot de Beaumont and some Navarrese troops. On 27 June the Navarrese agents formally handed possession to the English King's commissioners in the name of their master. The first English garrison troops arrived in the town shortly afterwards.[57]

Arundel had been lucky. It was only in the last few days of his cruise that he encountered any serious opposition at sea. The mobilisation of the French galleys and barges had been severely delayed. The oarsmen were in the process of mustering. The ships themselves were probably still in the covered halls of the arsenal at Rouen. The Castilians arrived in the Channel in about the middle of June and beached their ships at Saint-Malo, but they did not receive their orders until the end of the month. It was only at the very end of June that they caught up with part of Arundel's fleet as it withdrew from Cherbourg. Early in August, as John of Gaunt completed the final preparations at Southampton for the departure of his armada and Neville mustered his men at Plymouth to sail for Bordeaux, the Castilian galleys descended on the west country. The English had expected them to attack the ports of embarkation and had called out the levies of the coastal counties to defend them. But the Castilians preferred booty and easy targets. They carefully avoided both ports. A number of landings occurred along the Dorset coast. But the brunt of the enemy's attack fell on Cornwall. With almost all their ships and seamen pressed into the King's service elsewhere, the Cornish harbours were wide open to the invader. Several of them were burned, including the important river port of Fowey. Others had to pay heavy ransoms to be spared the same fate.[58]

John of Gaunt's army finally sailed from the Solent on about 10 August 1378 with some 5,000 troops on board and probably about the same number of seamen, in addition to pages and varlets, artillery and stores. Judging by the size of the fleet only a small part of this great host can have been mounted. When the English entered the great bay of Saint-Malo they achieved complete surprise. They boarded the merchant ships in the roads, pillaged their cargoes and burned the hulls. Then they landed on the eastern shore of the bay, took possession of the spit of land which linked the island town to the mainland and began to deploy their artillery against the walls. Saint-Malo was protected by modern ramparts and, at the eastern end facing the spit, by a powerful castle held by a large French garrison. At first the inhabitants panicked at the sight of such a large host and sued for terms. Then they recovered their nerve and broke off negotiations. On about 14 August the English delivered their first assault. They were thrown back with heavy losses. Several more assaults followed but all were unsuccessful. The English then set to work at the slow business of undermining the walls. Their mine was almost finished when a night-time sortie from the town destroyed it. Dissensions began to arise in the English camp. John of Gaunt fell out with the Earl of Arundel, whom he blamed for the disaster of the mine.[59]

For the first two weeks after their arrival the French did very little to interfere with John of Gaunt's operations. The Castilian fleet was away burning the villages of Cornwall. The French galley fleet had by now been mobilised but has left no record of its deeds and was certainly not present at Saint-Malo. The Constable of France was with his army in the Cotentin, where the main thrust of the English attack had been expected to come. He was forced to bring his men hurriedly south to meet the new threat. On about 24 August Du Guesclin arrived at Dinan, at the head of the estuary south of Saint-Malo. He was joined there by Olivier de Clisson with more troops raised in Brittany itself.

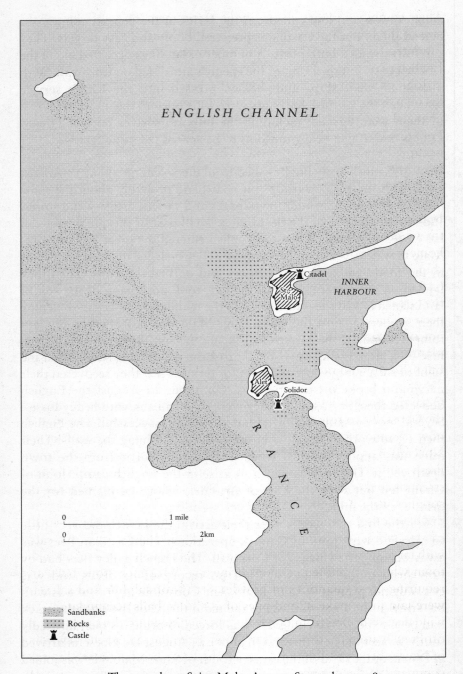

13 The assault on Saint-Malo, August–September 1378

Their combined strength was about 1,500 men, about a third of the size of the English army. They occupied the south of the bay and sent mounted raiders across the sands at low tide to carry out raids in the English rear.

John of Gaunt now found himself severely hampered by the size of his own army, which was far too large for the operation in which it was engaged and required an enormous flow of supplies to maintain it. Foraging inland became exceptionally difficult once the Constable had occupied the shoreline opposite. The victuallers ferrying in supplies from the south of England and the Channel Islands were unable to keep up with the demand. Gaunt was running out of time. He had set out late in the season. The shipmasters would have to be back by the beginning of October to join the wine fleet for Bordeaux. In September the whole campaign was abandoned. Some retinues had already gone home, probably because of supply problems. The rest reboarded their ships in the middle of the month and sailed away. The planned attack on Le Crotoy was quietly abandoned. It was an anti-climactic end to the 'great expedition'. The general view in England was that they had been defeated by 'incompetence and inertia'. John of Gaunt, who had not only commanded the expedition, but played the leading role in planning it, received most of the blame. He never commanded an English army in France again.[60]

Once the English had withdrawn from Saint-Malo Charles V ordered the Constable to resume his operations against Cherbourg. This had by now become a much more formidable task. Between September and November 1378 the English poured men and supplies into the town. Fresh reinforcements from England during the autumn brought the peak strength of the garrison to 760 men. Twelve shiploads of victuals and supplies were brought in from Southampton. Vast amounts of wine, dried vegetables and salted meat and fish were accumulated in the castle's stores. An armoury of crossbows and longbows was created with large stocks of spare bolts and arrows. A foundry was set up in the town which forged ten cannon, firing 15- or 24-inch stone balls and requiring great quantities of powder. Stocks of sulphur and saltpetre were laid in to make it, and piles of cut stone balls accumulated. The wine fleet returning from Bordeaux was diverted into the roads to hold off French attempts to seal off the town from the sea. At the beginning of November 1378 John of Arundel, the Earl's brother, arrived to take command of the defence.[61]

Bertrand du Guesclin's preparations were conceived on an equally impressive scale. The harbour of Saint-Vaast-la-Hougue and the town of Carentan became advanced depots, to which great quantities of war materials were shipped by sea or carted overland. At least twenty large cannon were ordered from foundries across Normandy. Great swathes of the forest of Montfort were felled to heat the furnaces. An army of craftsmen and labourers dragged them through the Cotentin and into position about the town. Massive mobile shelters made of timber were built to protect the assault parties. Between 17 and 20 November 1378 the French army mustered at Valognes. There is no reliable record of its strength but it must have been considerable, for the cost of their wages came to well over twice what the English had spent on occupying, supplying and defending the town since the summer. As at the siege of Saint-Sauveur the burden of financing the host fell on the communities of Lower Normandy, who had most to lose by the existence of an English garrison in their neighbourhood. They were relentlessly squeezed for cash grants, requisitioned materials and pressed labour.[62]

The French siege went badly from the start. The advance guard of the Constable's army was ambushed as it approached the town and more than sixty men-at-arms captured, including his brother and his cousin. Du Guesclin eventually set up his headquarters in the ruins of the twelfth-century abbey of Notre-Dame du Voeu on the west side of the town, protected by lines of trenches and palisades. But repeated sorties from the town caused heavy losses and much damage to tents, shelters and equipment in the unprotected French encampments. The supply train failed within days. Food began to run out. The Constable was not used to failure. He lost his temper with Jean le Mercier, the official responsible for the supply organisation, who was abused as a 'shit, a thief and a traitor'. In the first week of December the English garrison was reinforced by another 200 men. Hunger, bitter cold and high winds finally broke the morale of the besiegers. Less than three weeks after the start of the siege Du Guesclin suspended operations.

In the hope of at least containing the English garrison Du Guesclin fortified the abbey buildings of Notre-Dame du Voeu and left a garrison there under one of his lieutenants, Guillaume des Bordes. But the abbey's improvised fortifications were weak and its garrison too small to hold its own against the powerful English force in the castle. Not long after the end of the siege Guillaume des Bordes abandoned it to the enemy and retreated to a line about fifteen miles south running across the Cotentin peninsula through Valognes and the abbey town of

Montebourg. Immense works were undertaken in the new year to transform Montebourg into a garrisoned fortress to serve as his new headquarters. More than 1,000 French troops were assigned to him to hold it. But the new line proved to be little more defensible than the old. The garrison of Cherbourg was able to launch foraging raids deep into French-held territory with impunity. In July 1379 a French force of 500 men-at-arms and 600 crossbowmen tried to cut off John of Arundel's successor Sir John Harleston as he returned from one of these raids with a thousand head of plundered cattle in his train. Although the French heavily outnumbered their enemy they suffered a costly defeat near Saint-Vaast-la-Hougue, with more than a hundred men killed and many more captured, including Guillaume des Bordes himself. Pitched battles were rare in this period and this one must have served as an unpleasant reminder of the devastating effect of massed longbowmen on men and horses. The French were forced to abandon Montebourg and withdraw their forces further south while the English garrison acquired practical control over most of the territory between Cherbourg and Carentan. As for Guillaume des Bordes, he was sold to the English government who gave him to Sir Thomas Felton as a contribution to the cost of his own ransom.[63]

Cherbourg became another frontier town like Calais, Brest or Berwick, whose main business was the service of a large military establishment and the trade in looted goods. At the time of the siege there was still a large number of Navarrese in the garrison as well as some of Charles of Navarre's Norman retainers. But the Norman soldiers were ambivalent about the English occupation and almost all the Navarrese returned to Navarre with Charlot de Beaumont early in 1379. They were replaced by Englishmen, rubbing shoulders with a population that remained entirely French. Charles V commanded all his subjects in Cherbourg to withdraw after the arrival of the English or be treated as traitors. A few of them complied, adding to the number of empty shops and abandoned houses in what had once been a thriving commercial port, but most of the inhabitants had nowhere else to go. They stayed as long as they could still make a living. They reached an unheroic but workable compromise with the English captains. They received guarantees for their possessions and limited commercial privileges in England. They negotiated terms for the billeting of soldiers in their houses, always a delicate problem in garrison towns. They submitted to a modest duty on wine, which was certainly less onerous than the taxes they would have paid to the King of France. They did watch duties for the English captains just as they had done for Charles of Navarre.[64]

How much Cherbourg contributed to England's war effort was a controversial question even at the time. The English government thought well enough of the place to hang on to it until 1394. It became a staging post for English naval operations in the Channel and a base for mounted raids into France. It also tied down French forces who would otherwise have been available for service on other fronts. But Cherbourg never fulfilled its promise as a point of entry into France any more than Brest did, in spite of being larger and closer to England. Its defence was extremely expensive. For the first eighteen months of the occupation the garrison was maintained at 560 men, more than twice the garrison of Brest. In addition to their wages there was the regular drain of money to pay for building works and repairs, victuals and equipment, most of which had to come from England, and for ships and crews which were constantly employed in ferrying goods and men to and fro across the Channel. In the first year after the end of the siege Cherbourg cost the English government about £10,000. Thereafter the garrison was reduced and the cost fell to about £8,000 a year until the end of 1382 when dramatic reductions were achieved by putting the captains onto fixed price contracts. The profits of Cherbourg went into the captains' pockets. They must have made even larger profits than those of Brest, for the loot of the Atlantic sea lanes was just as plentiful and the Cotentin was a richer region than Finistère. Although there are no figures for profits at Brest their value can be judged from the fact that Sir Hugh Calveley, one of the shrewdest military entrepreneurs of his day, at one point agreed to take the Cherbourg contract at 5,700 marks (£3,800) a year, less than half what the government had been paying to defend the town. In 1386, after complaints in Parliament about the cost of England's continental barbicans, it was successfully let at just £2,000 a year. As at Brest these contracts were essentially financial transactions. The prominent public figures who obtained them rarely if ever commanded the defence in person. They took the profits, sometimes paid their men and performed their duties through deputies.[65]

Sir John Neville's fleet, carrying the new Lieutenant, 560 English troops and £6,000 in cash, arrived off Bordeaux on 7 September 1378 as the bells of the city's churches were ringing for vespers. Neville found the duchy in a state of exhausted stalemate. Since the capture of Sir Thomas Felton a year before, the King's affairs in Bordeaux had been in the hands of a caretaker administration in which the leading figure was the acting Seneschal, Sir Matthew Gournay. Gournay was a professional soldier with more than thirty years' experience of fighting in France who had been at every great battle of the previous reign from Sluys to Nájera. Since his main centre of operations was the southern city of Dax his direction of business must have been remote. But there was in any event very little for the administration to do. Much of its staff had been laid off for want of funds. Military expenditure was reduced to keeping skeleton garrisons in a handful of walled towns and paying modest subsidies to help the territorial lords of the Bordelais to defend their own. The few military operations undertaken by the Anglo-Gascons had been essentially private enterprises, funded by loot. The citizens of Bordeaux, who had been told that the government could do nothing for them, were obliged to organise their own defence. They did it with verve and some success. At the end of June 1378 they had launched a remarkable campaign of their own against the French garrisons along the Garonne which resulted in the recovery of the fortress-town of Langon. Further east a group of lords of the Agenais led by Gaillard de Durfort, lord of Duras, even reoccupied the cathedral city of Bazas.[66]

Gascony owed its survival mainly to the distractions of the Duke of Anjou. He had professed since the end of the previous year to be planning the great campaign that would achieve the 'final conquest of the duchy of Guienne' and had obtained unusually generous grants of taxation with which to fund it. But it is clear that Anjou had lost interest in Gascony. Much of the summer of 1378 had been taken up with the Duke's latest plan for acquiring a kingdom for himself, a quixotic design to seize the Aragonese territory of Mallorca and make himself its King. There is no evidence of any serious preparation for a campaign in Gascony until July. It is unlikely in the circumstances that his army was particularly strong and his progress was certainly exceptionally slow. His intention, according to reports reaching Bordeaux, was to lay siege to the city. This operation would have called for a fleet to blockade the Gironde and a very elaborate supply operation, no easy task in the difficult conditions of Languedoc that summer. At the beginning of August Anjou opened his campaign at La Réole. Then instead of marching towards Bordeaux he turned aside to recapture Bazas, a place of secondary importance whose defenders resisted for about three weeks and then sold out. By the time Bazas fell Neville was in Bordeaux. Neville's army may have been too small to challenge the Duke in the field. But it represented a substantial garrison for a city with a modern circuit of walls and direct access to the sea. In about the middle of September Anjou abandoned his campaign and withdrew to Toulouse.[67]

Like the Earl of Derby in 1345 and the Black Prince in 1355 Neville resolved to make an impression on the French before they had time to concentrate their strength against him. North of Bordeaux, on the opposite shore of the Gironde, the French Marshal Louis of Sancerre was engaged in the siege of the coastal fortress of Mortagne. This place had been a thorn in the side of the French administration in Saintonge and a major source of disruption on its roads ever since the French had reoccupied the province in 1372. Apart from the cliff-top castle of Talmont, a little further north, it was the last foothold of the English on the north shore of the estuary. The place was defended by just forty men-at-arms commanded by its owner, the Soudan de Trau, 'one of the world's most valiant knights' according to a sound judge, and now the only notable English ally left in Saintonge. Neville resolved to mark his arrival in the duchy by breaking the siege. Within two weeks of disembarking he had doubled the size of his army by drawing on the handful of English troops serving in garrisons in the Bordelais, on the retinues of the Gascon nobility and the corps of crossbowmen hired by the city of Bordeaux. A fleet of more than fifty vessels was collected from ships waiting for the vintage in the Garonne ports. In the last week of September 1378 Neville sailed north down the Gironde. In spite of the scale of his preparations his arrival seems to have taken the besiegers of Mortagne by surprise. They abandoned their *bastides* around the town and melted into the countryside. Some of them fled to a nearby priory and took refuge in a fortified tower. The English destroyed the *bastides* and stormed the priory. Neville then led his men back across the estuary and conducted a sweep of the French garrisons in the Médoc north of Bordeaux, capturing them all one after the other.[68]

The relief of Mortagne made a considerable impression on the Gascon nobility, especially in Saintonge where ambitious men had written off the English since the disasters of 1377. Shortly after the relief of Mortagne Raymond de Montaut, lord of Mussidan and Blaye, who had defected to the French after the battle of Eymet, returned to his old allegiance bringing both of his principal lordships with him. Raymond had always said that his original defection was forced on him by threats to his life. But there is little doubt that his real reasons for doing a deal with Neville were the revival of English arms on the right bank of the Gironde, where his interests were concentrated, and the enormous bribe (more than £1,000 sterling) which the Seneschal paid to bring him and his many kinsmen and clients back to the English side.[69]

The struggle for Mortagne was famous for another reason. It was the occasion for the death of one of the best-known soldiers of fortune in French service, Owen of Wales, who was assassinated by an agent of the Council in Bordeaux in early September. The assassin was an impecunious Scottish squire by the name of John Lamb, who had been planted by the English in Owen's company in the early stages of the siege. He stabbed Owen in the back as he sat on a tree trunk combing his locks in the early morning sun. This unchivalrous proceeding was much criticised by the flamboyant Welshman's many admirers in France, including the chronicler Froissart and the Soudan de Trau. But Neville had no time for this kind of sentiment. Owen was a traitor whose activities in France and Castile and in Wales itself had been followed with fear and anger in England. He rewarded Lamb handsomely and sent him back to England to tell his tale in person to the young King. Owen was laid to rest by his companions in a nearby chapel which has long since vanished. The Welsh companies, however, did not vanish as they had perhaps been expected to. They were taken over by Owen's companion-in-arms Jack Wyn, who had probably always been the main organising force. Wyn died in about 1385. But the Welsh companies continued to fight as an organised corps in French service until the 1390s. Owen's memory lived on and when, at the beginning of the next century, a far more terrible Welsh leader arose to challenge the English with French support, he claimed to have been inspired by his example.[70]

The main purpose of Sir John Neville's presence in Gascony was to organise an expedition to prop up the kingdom of Navarre. But by the time he reached the duchy the Castilian invasion was already in its third month and Charles of Navarre's affairs had come to a critical pass. Henry of Trastámara, who was in declining health, had left the conduct of the campaign to his eldest son John, a delicate young man of twenty now exercising his first military command. In June 1378 John had reached the western march of Navarre with about 4,000 cavalry and a large number of infantry and archers. The King of Navarre was bereft of allies. He was on bad terms with his neighbour and brother-in-law the Count of Foix. The English had not yet appeared. The King of Aragon would do nothing without an English lead and a reasonable assurance of success. At about the beginning of July 1378, the Castilians crossed the frontier of Navarre.[71] Charles of Navarre was able to muster about 1,450 men in his kingdom. In addition he had about 500 Gascon, Béarnais and Catalan mercenaries in his pay, about half the number who had contracted to serve him earlier in the year. The rest had taken their advances and sent their excuses when the time came. In the first week of July Charles still hoped to make a stand at the royal castle of Olite south of Pamplona, where most of his army was concentrated. But at the last moment the King changed his mind and decided to spread the available manpower thinly among a large number of garrisons with a few larger contingents in the main towns. He himself retreated north to Pamplona. In the last week of July 1378, as the Castilians closed in around his capital, Charles abandoned the defence to Roger-Bernard of Foix, Viscount of Castelbon, the mercenary captain who served the unmilitary King as his 'lieutenant in time of war'. Taking with him his principal advisers and a small escort, he fled north across the Pyrenees. For the next four months he lived at Saint-Jean-Pied-de-Port while the Castilians occupied most of the southern and western part of his kingdom. The only determined resistance which is recorded occurred at Estella and Pamplona, where predominantly Gascon garrisons, supported by some English archers and Gascon crossbowmen hired in Bordeaux, fought off the Castilians from the walls.[72]

The Castilians spread out across the plain of Navarre, seizing walled towns and castles, destroying villages, barns and crops. It was the first time for half a century that the country had suffered systematic looting and destruction on the scale of which a great army was capable. In the province of Estella, one of the most fertile regions of Navarre which accounted for nearly a quarter of its taxable wealth, the peasants' stories are told in the reports of the tax collectors who passed from village to village after the invaders had gone. Out of nearly 200 parishes all but ten were unable to pay and had to have their assessments reduced by amounts which varied from twenty to a hundred per cent. The accounts explain why in the usual laconic phrases: 'destroyed by war', 'nothing to eat', 'all their goods carried off', 'everything lost'. The country around Pamplona fared even worse. More than thirty suburban villages were razed by the invaders. Some of those who took their animals and goods into nearby castles for safety lost everything when the castles were stormed. Only the mountains of the north offered any refuge.[73]

The new English Lieutenant in Gascony was preoccupied by the problems of the duchy for some time after his arrival. As a result Navarre received very little attention until late October, when Charles

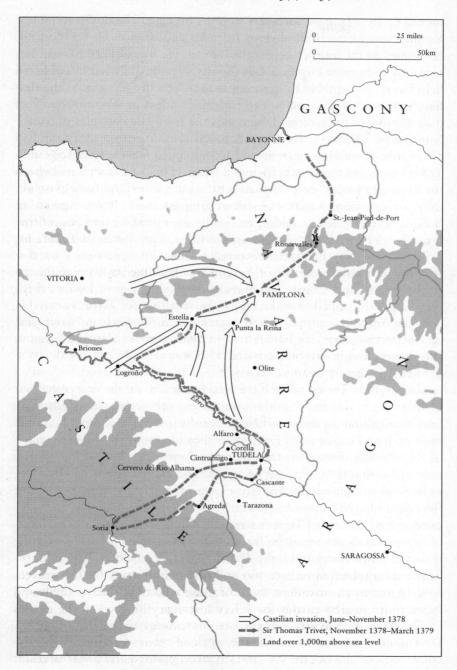

14 Campaigns in Navarre, June 1378–March 1379

turned up in person in Bordeaux to press his case. The dire state of his fortunes must have been obvious from his appearance. He had lost all his horses on the journey across the Landes. He was obliged to send his secretary to borrow money about the city. Neville did what he could to help but he was unable to spare more than 400 of the 1,000 men who had been promised to the Navarrese ambassadors at Westminster. The man appointed to command them was the erstwhile defender of Saint-Sauveur Sir Thomas Trivet, a resourceful captain with a sharp eye for the chance of enrichment, who had accompanied Neville from England. Trivet's task was to escort the King of Navarre back to Pamplona before the Pyrenean passes were blocked with winter snow and to help break the Castilian siege which was still in progress there. It was agreed in Bordeaux that when he had done this he would take command of the great border fortress of Tudela on the Ebro. The choice of Tudela as Trivet's base was probably dictated by its close proximity to the Aragonese frontier. Peter IV of Aragon was building up his own forces in the region and Charles of Navarre is likely to have known this. Neville plainly hoped to make up for the small size of Trivet's army by enlisting Aragonese support for an attack on Castile. Early in November an embassy departed for Barcelona, led by Geraud de Menta, a Gascon lawyer on the Lieutenant's council who was regarded as the duchy's principal expert on Spanish affairs.[74]

Sir Thomas Trivet must have left Bordeaux in the last week of October 1378. He led a motley company south across the windswept Landes. In about the middle of November he joined the King of Navarre at Saint-Jean-Pied-de-Port. From there they filed south through the pass of Roncevalles. But when they descended into the plain of Pamplona they found that the Castilians had gone. The Trastámarans had learned to be wary of fighting pitched battles against English armies, even with the advantage of numbers. It is probable that they had also received exaggerated reports of Trivet's strength. There were some among John of Trastámara's advisers who feared that they would look like cowards if they did not stand and fight. But they were in the minority. John of Trastámara retreated to Logroño and paid off his army for the winter, leaving garrisons behind in the more important conquered towns of Navarre. He expected to be back in the spring.[75]

The King of Navarre returned to his capital at the beginning of December 1378 and set about the work of reconstruction. A hastily convened assembly of the Navarrese Cortes granted him a war subsidy of 60,000 florins (about £8,500), the largest single grant that Charles's small kingdom had ever made and well beyond the population's capacity to pay in the current state of the country. His mercenary companies ate up his available funds without having very much to do now that the enemy had withdrawn. After resting at Pamplona, most of the Gascon companies were assigned to garrison duties. On about 11 December 1378 the rest marched out of Pamplona with the King, the Viscount of Castelbon and Sir Thomas Trivet. The whole force must have numbered between 800 and 1,000 men including about 400 Englishmen. In about the middle of December they crossed the great thirteenth-century bridge over the Ebro and entered the fortress city of Tudela.[76]

Tudela was the second city of Navarre. A population of about eight or nine thousand people, Christian, Jewish and Muslim, was crammed into a maze of brick streets on the south bank of the Ebro, surrounded by high walls and heavily fortified gateways and overlooked by the great royal castle crowning the hill on which the town was built. The city was the capital of the southernmost of Navarre's *merindades* (or provinces), a salient which extended south of the river across the flat plain towards the sierras of northern Castile. Bounded on one side by the kingdom of Aragon and on the other by Castile, it was at once the wealthiest and the most vulnerable part of Charles of Navarre's kingdom. Trivet was assigned the castle of Tudela itself while the Viscount of Castelbon took his own company and part of Trivet's and garrisoned the important fortress of Cascante about five miles away on the Aragonese border. The Catalan soldier of fortune Raymond de Pailhas installed himself in the castles of Corella and Cintruénigo on the River Alhama which marked the border with Castile.[77]

Trivet was restless for action and, no doubt, for loot. On Christmas Eve he rode out of Tudela with both his fellow captains and about 300 mounted men. Their objective was the Castilian town of Soria, some sixty miles away by the headwaters of the Duero, which was (and is) the nodal point of the road system of the region. The raiders had reckoned without the treacherous climate of northern Spain. They left the plain of Tudela in weather so warm that it was possible to eat outside in the winter sun. But as they rode up into the sierras the temperature dropped. Trivet decided to ride through the night to surprise Soria in the morning but he was caught in a snowstorm. His guides lost their way. His men were scattered over a considerable distance. By the time they reached the town, late on Christmas morning, the defenders were ready for them. There was a violent skirmish at the gates in which both sides suffered casualties. The invaders, seeing that they had lost the advantage of surprise, withdrew and arrived exhausted at Cascante on the following day. Charles of Navarre was there to welcome and congratulate them but apart from the burning of some Castilian border towns Trivet had achieved nothing. His next venture, a few days later, was hardly more successful. The objective this time was closer at hand, the small town of Alfaro on the Ebro, just beyond the border. Trivet drew the garrison out of their gates into an ambush and killed and captured a large number of them. But the women of the town succeeded in closing the gates before he could force his way in. Once again he returned empty-handed to Tudela.[78]

In Barcelona the English embassy had arrived in about the middle of December. The King of Aragon, who had been expecting Neville himself, was unimpressed by Geraud de Menta's appeal for armed support. The small scale of England's military intervention so far cannot have helped. In any event the immediate threat to Navarre had passed with the withdrawal of the Castilians for the winter. Peter said that he would consider the English request again in May. At the beginning of January 1379 Charles of Navarre sent the Viscount of Castelbon and several members of his Council to Barcelona to intercede with Peter. They brought with them proposals which would have been attractive at any other time. But they fared no better than Geraud de Menta.[79]

On 12 February 1379 Henry of Trastámara announced his intention of sending his son back into Navarre in the spring. His army was ordered to appear at Logroño in April. At this the King of Navarre resolved to abandon the fight. He sent a messenger to the Castilian King to ask for terms. He was accorded a truce of six weeks for talks. The negotiations were conducted at Burgos in the course of March. Charles of Navarre's principal representative was Juan Ramírez de Arellano. He was a prominent figure at Charles of Navarre's court, who had spread his loyalty widely in the course of his long career. He had commanded Navarrese armies in France and served the English as a contract captain in Brittany. He was also in high favour with Henry of Trastámara, having fought for him in the Castilian war of succession. But however warm Ramírez's welcome at Burgos he could do nothing to disguise his master's nakedness. Henry's terms were a terrible humiliation for the defeated King of Navarre. The Castilian King was determined that Navarre should be disabled as a political power. Charles was required to enter into a military alliance with Castile and France against every other power, 'especially the King of England'. As security for his good behaviour he was to surrender twenty of the principal fortresses of southern Navarre, including Tudela, for ten years. Estella was to be surrendered to Ramírez himself and held on behalf of both kings. All of these places were to receive Castilian garrisons. These measures effectively put Charles of Navarre at the mercy of Castile and France if ever he should threaten the security of either country again. The terms required Charles to expel the English and Gascon companies from Navarre as soon as possible. Henry of Trastámara lent Charles 20,000 *doblas* in order to pay their arrears and speed them on their way. On 31 March 1379 the plenipotentiaries of the two kings sealed the treaty containing these terms in the village of Briones on the Ebro, close to the Navarrese border. On 18 April the King of Navarre came to Tudela to complete the formalities and to engage in the skin-deep expressions of goodwill which were expected of defeated princes on such occasions as these. John of Trastámara escorted him from the frontier to the Castilian pilgrimage town of Santo Domingo de la Calzada where his father was staying. There the two men ratified the treaty and feasted together for a week.[80]

For the English the treaty of Briones was a serious strategic setback. It meant that for as long as the Anglo-Castilian war continued the only practicable route by which they could attack Castile overland was closed to them, while the Castilians were in a position to enter Gascony across the Pyrenean passes at will. Charles's English and Gascon captains were furious. Trivet had begun to raid in Navarrese territory around Tudela as soon as the preliminary truce was announced. He challenged the Castilian governor of Logroño to an arranged battle with 100 men on each side. He even made contact with Peter IV of Aragon in the hope of continuing the war under his auspices. But Peter had no intention of provoking the rampant lion in its moment of triumph and refused. So Trivet withdrew from Tudela in May and hung about the treasury offices in Pamplona while his accounts were settled. By July 1379 he was back in Bordeaux.[81]

The treaty, one of Henry of Trastámara finest moments, was also his last great public act. Although only forty-six years old, Henry was worn out by a lifetime of fighting and hardship. Shortly after the feasting at Santo Domingo he fell ill and on 28 May 1379 he died. With his dying breath he ordered the release of all his English and other Christian prisoners of war and urged his son to 'be for ever loyal to the house of France'. Charles of Navarre still had eight years to live but the treaty of Briones marked the end of his political career. He had retained his crown. But he had lost almost everything else: Cherbourg to the English and the rest of his Norman domains to the King of France. Navarre was economically ruined for a generation and his control over it had to be shared with the officers of the King of Castile. His heir was a pensioner of France, living in Paris and fighting in French armies. Charles felt the loss of status keenly. He became increasingly bitter about it, dreaming impossible dreams of murder and revenge and even, in brief moments of anger, returning to his old conspiratorial ways. In January 1387 he died prematurely, aged fifty-five, when a servant accidentally set fire to his bed with a candle. 'I have few friends in France and many enemies,' he had said a few years earlier to a passing English musician who played for him at dinner in the hall of the castle at Olite. 'Some of my enemies are your enemies too,' he added; 'for I have had a great deal to do with the English in my time and lost much of what I had on their account.'[82]

On 27 March 1378 Pope Gregory XI died in the Vatican palace in Rome just fourteen months after arriving in the city from Avignon. He was buried on the following day in the church of S. Maria Nuova (now S. Francesca Romana) in the Forum where, two centuries later, a grandiose marble tomb would be erected to honour the Pope who brought the papacy back to Rome. Gregory's death precipitated a major crisis in the affairs of the Latin Church which was destined to have a profound effect on all the participants in the European war. The return of the papacy had been a very personal ambition of the Pope's. But in the course of the fourteenth century the power of the college of cardinals had immeasurably increased and they had appropriated a growing proportion of the papacy's resources. Overwhelmingly French, richly endowed and comfortably installed in palaces at Avignon and Villeneuve, the cardinals had never shown the same interest in returning to Italy. After more than seventy years in France the rest of the papal court was as French as the college of cardinals. The ruinous condition of Rome, the disorders of central Italy and the dying spasms of the war with Florence all combined to accentuate their insecurity. The Romans knew as well as anyone that when the cardinals met to elect Gregory's successor there would be a strong movement to find a candidate who would lead them back to France.

On 7 April 1378 the cardinals entered the conclave in the Vatican. There were sixteen cardinals present, of whom eleven were French. The preponderance of Frenchmen would have been even greater if seven cardinals, all of them French, had not been away, either in Avignon or on diplomatic business. The French cardinals in Rome could have carried the day without their absent colleagues if they had been united behind a single candidate. But they were not. The seven 'Limousin' cardinals, who were either related to the last two popes or came from the same region of France, formed a faction within the French group which was bent on the election of one of their own number and succeeded in alienating the rest. A two-thirds majority was required. No one faction had a sufficient majority. These differences had to be resolved in exceptionally difficult conditions. Ever since the announcement of Gregory's death the streets of the *borgo* around St. Peter's had been filled with roving mobs of armed men, their numbers swollen by peasants from the surrounding Campagna, baying for a Roman or at least an Italian pope. The city authorities, who were responsible for the security of the conclave, said that they could not guarantee to maintain public order unless they got their way. As the doors to the conclave were being sealed the Roman mob broke into the Vatican palace and occupied the chambers beside and beneath the conclave, shouting and beating on the walls and floors throughout the night and the following day. On 8 April the cardinals lighted upon a compromise candidate, Bartolomeo Prignano, Archbishop of Bari. As the conclave ended the crowd finally broke down the doors of the conclave and the proceedings lost their last shreds of dignity. A group of cardinals took it into their heads to placate them by seizing an aged Roman cardinal and presenting him to the Romans with the tiara on his head and the papal robes thrown over his shoulders while their colleagues fled in the confusion.[83]

Over the following years several careful investigations by national governments and other bodies failed to produce a conclusive answer to the question whether Prignano was lawfully elected. But most of the evidence suggests that he was. He had been identified as a suitable candidate with some support among all factions several days before the conclave in the course of preliminary discussions among the cardinals. The atmosphere of the conclave, although certainly intimidating, does not seem to have had a decisive effect on the electors. The worst scenes of violence occurred after Prignano had been chosen. The cardinals participated in his enthronement, ten days after the conclave, and later put their seals to the letters which announced his election to the world. The main reason for the crisis which followed was not the manner of the new Pope's election but his rebarbative personality.

Bartolomeo Prignano, who took the name Urban VI, was a Neapolitan canon lawyer of humble origins, then aged about sixty, who had been a senior official of the papal chancery for many years. He was an able administrator and a learned man of irreproachable morals who was known to all the cardinals but not well enough to have made enemies among them. They may well have thought that he would be easily dominated. If so they were quickly disabused. Prignano had not been a cardinal and within a very short time of his election it became apparent that he strongly disapproved of the cardinals' magnificent way of life, their grand palaces, their trains of attendants and courtiers and their princely incomes. There were plenty of people who could have been found to support his views in Rome and elsewhere. But Urban was not one to choose his time or his language. He was a squat, rude man with a loud voice and a foul temper. He addressed those who stood in his way with 'a face red as a lamp and a voice hoarse with rage', according to a curial official who had often witnessed such scenes.[84] From the moment he was crowned Urban made his views about the cardinals known in a succession of venomous outbursts in private, in consistory and in his public sermons. These were accompanied by overt threats to curb their privileges. The natural resentment of the aristocratic French cardinals was aggravated by their ill-concealed contempt for the undignified bearing and crude manner of the jumped-up Italian official whom they had elected. But there was much more to the cardinals' resentment than snobbery and defensiveness. Urban VI was in fact wholly unfit to govern the Church. He lost no time in making enemies not only among the French cardinals but among their Italian colleagues, the princes of Europe, their ambassadors in Rome, numerous bishops, and influential figures of all nationalities in the papal administration. His impulsiveness and lack of self-control, his ignorance of affairs and his impatience of advice, all of which were revealed within days of his enthronement, would lead him and his supporters to the brink of disaster more than once in the course of his twelve-year reign.

The cardinals shortly concluded that they had made a serious mistake. The prime mover in the events which followed appears to have been Jean de la Grange, Cardinal of Amiens, a pensioner and former councillor of Charles V of France, whose princely manner was imposing even by the standards of his colleagues. He had been in Tuscany at the time of Gregory's death and reached Rome about a fortnight after the election. According to the evidence later collected for the King of Castile, La Grange was irritated that his colleagues had not been able to procure the election of a Frenchman.[85] He also found himself almost immediately embroiled in a series of bruising arguments with the new Pope, in whose eyes he represented everything that was worst in the college of cardinals. La Grange's palace in Trastevere became the meeting place of ambitious clerics and soldiers with whom he floated the idea of declaring the decision of the previous conclave void and proceeding to a fresh election. One by one the cardinals left Rome over the following weeks and repaired to the small town of Anagni east of the city, where they installed themselves in the old palace built at the end of the thirteenth century by the last Pope to reign in Italy. On 2 August 1378 the twelve French cardinals in Italy and the Cardinal of Aragon issued a declaration from Anagni calling on Urban to abdicate. This was followed by an inflammatory manifesto and a circular addressed to the princes of Europe, denouncing Urban as 'antichrist, demon, apostate and tyrant' and declaring his election void on the only ground known to canon law, namely that it had been imposed on them by force. In the next six weeks they were joined by three of the four Italian cardinals.

The decisive consideration now was the attitude of the King of France. Charles V did not receive a full account of the cardinals' position until August, when an emissary arrived in Paris from Italy. He gave the King their version, suitably embellished, of the circumstances in which Urban had been elected in April. He was followed within a few days by two more emissaries from Anagni. Their instructions were to tell the King that the cardinals proposed to repudiate Urban and proceed to another election. They needed to know whether he would support them. Charles V, who had previously been inclined to temporise, was now forced to a decision. His relations with the French cardinals were close. As he himself acknowledged, 'he had many friends among them, several of whom had been his ministers and others his pensioners.' His brother Louis of Anjou was a determined and avowed partisan of the cardinals. Before August was out Charles V had resolved to support them in their defiance of the Pope. The decision was not made public. But it was communicated to them in a private letter written in the King's own hand. At the same time the French King arranged for 20,000 francs to be sent to Italy for the cardinals' physical protection and ordered the Breton companies quartered in the papal state to be ready to go to their assistance if they were needed. Charles cannot have known, any more than the cardinals did, that they were starting a schism that would last for forty years. These men were concerned only with the immediate issue. They thought that Urban VI would quickly be ousted from Rome and his election expunged as the mistake which it undoubtedly was.[86]

In late August 1378 Urban VI fell out with Jeanne of Anjou, Queen of Naples, his only important protector in Italy apart from the people of Rome. She transferred her support to the cardinals, who left Anagni for the small cathedral town of Fondi at the southern extremity of Latium close to the boundaries of her kingdom. Events then moved rapidly. On 18 September 1378 Urban VI appointed twenty-nine new cardinals, twenty of whom were Italian. It was a decisive shift in the balance of the papal court. On the same day the King of France's letter reached Fondi. Two days later, on the 20th, the dissident cardinals, French, Italian and Aragonese, held a new conclave in the palace of the Counts of Fondi. Their choice fell on Robert, Cardinal of Geneva, a man as different from Bartolomeo Prignano as it was possible to be. A bishop at nineteen and a cardinal at twenty-nine he had made a charmed progress through the ranks of the Church. He was still only thirty-six years old at the time of his election. To the world at large he was notorious as the papal legate in the Romagna who had been one of the chief authors of the massacre of the population of Cesena. But it is not difficult to see why the cardinals should have chosen this supremely political priest at this crisis of their affairs. Robert was an intelligent diplomat with a commanding presence and an excellent grasp of languages. He could be expected to sympathise with the aspirations of the French cardinals and to outmanoeuvre Urban VI in the royal courts of Europe, especially that of France. Indeed there is some evidence that the choice had been made much earlier and discussed with Charles V in August.[87] On 31 October 1378 Robert was enthroned in Fondi cathedral. He took the name Clement VII.

Once the cardinals had taken the irrevocable step of electing a second pope the issue necessarily moved to the international stage, where decisions were guided by the political interests of the main actors. There was never any real doubt about the outcome in England, where scarcely a single voice was raised in favour of Clement VII. The visible and powerful position which the French government and its representatives had enjoyed for decades at the papal court in Avignon was notorious in England. It was widely assumed that the cardinals had turned against Urban because he was not French. There were even reports that they had fallen out with him because of his sympathy for England. He was said to have criticised the diplomatic activities of the Cardinal of Amiens at the conference of Bruges, where he had been one of Charles V's ambassadors. These were fanciful notions and Richard II's ministers no doubt knew better. But the end of the French domination of the papacy after three-quarters of a century can only have been welcome to them. Their discussions are not recorded but their actions speak for themselves. In October a prominent Gascon clergyman who had once served in the administration of the Black Prince, arrived in England as the official emissary of the cardinals of Fondi. This man was well-placed to get a hearing if anyone was but he was arrested by the sheriffs of London and sent under guard to appear before the Council, who had him locked up in Gloucester castle. His attendants were thrown into Newgate prison. The English bishops declared without hesitation for Urban. Parliament, which was then in session, endorsed their decision and the government proceeded to enforce it not only in England but in those parts of France which it controlled.[88]

Charles V had a more difficult task. Opinion about the merits of the issue was much more sharply divided in France than it was in England. A group of bishops and scholars whom the King had consulted in September, before the second election, declared the question of Urban's legitimacy to be 'moult haulte, perilleuse et doubteuse' and declined to express a view until the facts were better known. Very few of them knew how far their King had already committed himself to Clement VII. As time went on the Urbanist version of the events of April 1378 began to circulate in France and the cardinals' case began to look somewhat threadbare. The University of Paris reported that its members and faculties were unable to agree. Its internal debates probably mirrored those of the rest of the clergy. Most Frenchmen who had an opinion on the subject appear to have assumed that Urban VI was the true pope, nine out of ten according to reports reaching his rival from Avignon. 'Misguided they may be,' wrote Clement's informant, 'but this Bartholomew has a lot of supporters.' On 16 November 1378 an enlarged session of the royal Council met in the King's presence at the castle of Vincennes, to which the King invited selected churchmen. Charles no doubt made his wishes clear. The outcome was the formal recognition of Clement as Pope and an order to publish his election in all French churches. The decision was said to have been unanimous, but not everyone was convinced. In the following year it was necessary to convene a much larger assembly at the Louvre at which no fewer than three Clementist cardinals related their experiences during the conclave of April 1378. It was one of those tremendous public occasions at which Charles V and his ministers were so adept: superbly stage-managed before a carefully selected audience. Among the noblemen, prelates and lawyers present, there was an impressive show of unity. The churchmen 'shared the King's opinion', a contemporary recorded, 'for fear of losing their benefices'. The assembly was followed by grandiose ceremonies in front of Notre-Dame cathedral in which Clement was declared to be the true Pope and all who declined to acknowledge him condemned as schismatics.[89]

Charles V denied that political calculation had anything to do with these decisions. He would have supported any properly elected candidate, he said, 'even an Englishman'. It is probably true that he was persuaded by his friends in the college of cardinals that their hand had been forced when they elected Urban VI. He may even have believed that this would be as obvious to everyone else as it was to him. But he cannot have overlooked the great diplomatic advantages which he and his predecessors had derived from their close relationship with the six French popes who had reigned at Avignon. Certainly his brothers and ministers did not. The timing of the conference at Vincennes was largely dictated by the need to bolster Clement's position internationally. England's support for Urban was a foregone conclusion. So was that of Rome and much of Italy. The German Emperor, Charles IV, had declared for Urban a month earlier. He was followed by the great majority of the lay and ecclesiastical princes of Germany. No one had yet declared for the French Pope apart from France and the Angevin kingdom of Naples. Unless action was taken quickly it would be too late. As soon as the Council had dispersed ambassadors were despatched to every country in which France might be thought to have any influence in order to press Clement's case.[90]

Clement VII's problem was that to establish himself as the undisputed head of the Church he had to snuff out his rival's cause in Italy. In particular he had to extinguish it in Rome. This proved to be Clement's earliest and most damaging failure. He depended entirely on force. The Castel Sant' Angelo had been held since the death of the last Pope by a French nobleman with a largely Breton garrison. Their frequent sorties and artillery fire from the walls had made the Vatican *borgo* uninhabitable. A steady flow of funds from the King of France and the Duke of Anjou enabled Clement to recruit heavily among the Gascon and Breton companies in central Italy at the beginning of 1379. In April Clement increased his dependence on French arms still further by entering into a secret deal with the agents of the Duke of Anjou of which even the cardinals were unaware. Under the terms of this agreement

Louis agreed to enter Italy with a large French army to expel Urban from Rome and install Clement in his place. In return Louis's long-standing dream of a kingdom of his own was to be gratified by the creation of the 'Kingdom of Adria', a new central Italian state which was to be carved out of the northern and eastern provinces of the papal state.[91]

In the event there would be no time for these plans to mature. On 30 April 1379 the French captain of the Castel Sant' Angelo surrendered to the Romans after withstanding a siege of more than six months. On the same day a relief force commanded by Clement's French nephew Louis de Montjoie and comprising between 500 and 1,000 Breton and Gascon *routiers* was wiped out by the Italian mercenaries of Urban VI, the first major engagement of the fourteenth century in which Italians had triumphed over foreign mercenaries. The battle occurred at Marino, south of Rome on the shores of Lake Albano. Montjoie, Sylvester Budes and Bernard de la Salle were all captured, together with some 300 of their followers. Many of the rest were killed. Urban VI's legates across Europe had good reason to crow about this 'fortunate massacre' (*felix extermin[at]io*). Within a few days of the battle Clement fled by sea to Naples. There he was greeted by Queen Jeanne on the quays of the Castel dell'Ovo, the great royal fortress projecting into the Bay of Naples. But the Neapolitans had not forgotten that Urban VI was one of them. They erupted in violence. French property in the city was looted. The Clementist archbishop was driven from the city and replaced by Urban's nominee. On the foreshore the mob yelled 'Death to the Antichrist' at the windows of the Castel dell'Ovo and made preparations to storm the walls. After three days Clement was forced to re-embark on his ships. At the end of May he left Italy for good on a fleet of galleys hired in Provence and Catalonia and escorted by what remained of the Breton company of Sylvester Budes. With him went the French cardinals who had elected him and much of the French personnel of the papal court. On 20 June 1379 Clement re-entered the city of Avignon which Gregory XI had left nearly three years before.[92]

Amid these great events the gradual dissolution of the Breton and Gascon companies which had fought in Italy since 1376 passed almost unnoticed. The captains were swiftly ransomed after the disaster at Marino but most of their followers were dispersed or dead. Sylvester Budes returned to a life of brigandage in France and was beheaded by order of the *bailli* of Mâcon early in 1380. Some of his followers who had stayed in Italy reformed themselves into new companies. They were still active in Tuscany in 1381, but eventually faded into the military underworld of the peninsula. Jean de Malestroit and Bernard de la Salle entered the service of the Queen of Naples with what remained of their companies. Malestroit died in Italy in 1382. La Salle passed the rest of his life in Italy and in the Provençal territories of the crown of Naples. He eventually married an illegitimate daughter of the despot of Milan, Bernabò Visconti, thus becoming a brother-in-law of that other successful adventurer, Sir John Hawkwood.[93]

Seated in the great palace of the popes on the east bank of the Rhône, Clement VII was visibly the creature of France which, in English and German eyes, he had always been. Beyond Provence and the valley of the Rhône Europe divided along lines which more or less corresponded with its existing political divisions. Clement VII was acknowledged in countries that were aligned with France but almost nowhere else. The French Queen of Naples supported him from the outset. Scotland was among the first to place itself in the French camp. The French rulers of Savoy and Cyprus followed suit. In Germany Clement had very little support but what he had came from clients of France. The rest of Germany and the Latin churches of central Europe were overwhelmingly for Urban VI. At the imperial Diet at Frankfurt in February 1379 the ambassadors whom Charles V had sent to press Clement VII's cause among the German princes found themselves lectured on their errors at the public sessions and cold-shouldered at banquets, where they were made to sit at a table on their own like lepers or heretics.[94]

In two regions, Flanders and Spain, the dilemmas arising from the schism were directly related to political problems generated by the Anglo-French war. Flanders was legally part of France. Its territory was divided between four French dioceses, all of which had Clementist bishops. The Count, Louis de Mâle, may have been inclined initially to adhere to Clement VII like his French kinsmen. But he knew that he could not deliver the support of his subjects and hardly tried. In June 1379 Louis accepted the decision of an ecclesiastical council meeting at Ghent to acknowledge Urban VI.[95] His decision reflected the same political imperatives which had kept him out of the Anglo-French war for thirty years. The stability of his government depended on the populations of the industrial cities, pre-eminently Ghent, where suspicion of France was a long-standing tradition and economic and political ties to England were strong. Clement VII never had much support in Flanders.

The situation was more complicated in the Iberian peninsula where opinion was divided at every level. All four Iberian kingdoms initially adopted a policy of neutrality, in most cases for genuinely conscientious reasons. Yet all four were ultimately shifted from it by pressures arising from the war between England and France. Don Fernando of Portugal was the most inconstant of the Iberian rulers and the most overtly opportunistic. He declared for Clement VII at the beginning of 1380, contrary to the sentiments of most of his subjects and to the advice of most of his councillors, at a time when he hoped to forge a closer relationship with Castile and France. The main proponent of this policy in Don Fernando's council gave a flowery account of the decision to the French court later in the year, in which he acknowledged that relations with France had been a major factor. Yet within months Fernando was already trying to revive the English alliance and negotiating secretly with Rome. Portugal was destined to change its allegiance three times in five years in response to the exigencies of diplomacy and defeat. In Castile John of Trastámara commissioned much the most thorough investigation of the circumstances of Urban's election but then ignored its results. When he finally recognised Clement VII in May 1381 it was because of relentless pressure from France on which the Castilian King depended for his defence against the increasingly aggressive plans of John of Gaunt and Don Fernando. John of Trastámara's decision, like Don Fernando's, was controversial in his own country and made against the advice of many of his councillors. The chronicler Ayala, a noted francophile who served several times as John's ambassador to France, took little trouble to conceal his disgust at a decision which was designed for an audience outside Castile. Only the kings of Aragon and Navarre managed to avoid a final commitment. Both rulers, however, had heirs who were closely aligned with France and who brought their countries into the Avignon camp as soon as they came to the throne.[96]

The papal schism destroyed the international influence of the papacy for more than a century by turning both contestants into clients of the states which chose to recognise them. This was a serious setback to the cause of peace. The Avignon popes, for all their partiality, had been responsible for the only serious attempts at a diplomatic settlement between England and France over the past forty years. The final chapter in the peace conference at Bruges had occurred in the last weeks of Gregory XI's pontificate. The exiled Poitevin baron Guichard d'Angle, now Earl of Huntingdon, represented Richard II. He was accompanied by the usual group of lawyers. Opposite them sat the Bishop of Bayeux with his own lawyers. But they were only there for form. Both sides had major military enterprises in hand. The proceedings broke up in May 1378 after the news arrived of Gregory's death. Nothing was agreed other than the arrangements for the next meeting. These were quickly overtaken by the schism. Of the two legates, Pileo da Prata was later made a cardinal by Urban VI and became one of his most active agents. His colleague, Guillaume de l'Estrange, threw his lot in with Clement VII. He made a heroic attempt to carry on the process on his own and a series of inconclusive conferences occurred under his auspices on the march of Picardy and Calais. It was a hopeless task.[97]

The schism not only marginalised the one institution with the prestige to force talks on the warring parties. It contributed to a significant diplomatic realignment among the leading European powers. It created new bonds between England and Germany, thirty years after the last alliance between a king of England and a German emperor. And it revived the old political alliance between England and the cities of the Low Countries, which were strongly Urbanist, widening the ancient breaches between France and Flanders. These developments were sedulously encouraged by both of the rival claimants to the papal tiara, each of whom hoped to prevail through the armed force and diplomatic influence of his secular champions. At a popular level there is little doubt that the travails of the Church added another source of venom to the relations of England and France, as the official propaganda of each side branded the other as patrons of schism and heresy and as each Pope blessed the wars of his own sponsors, offering crusading indulgences to their soldiers and excommunicating their opponents.

CHAPTER VIII

Brittany
1379–1381

In retrospect the closing years of the reign of Charles V can be seen as the last occasion when the war might have been decisively concluded on France's terms. That it was not was due to two serious misjudgments on the part of the King of France. The decision to reignite the civil war in Brittany by annexing the duchy to the Crown's domain gave England a fresh opportunity to prolong the war in France's Atlantic provinces. It provoked what proved to be the last great English campaign in France in the fourteenth century. This final push, on which the English expended much treasure, ended in a humiliating failure. But it cost France two critical years and its government a serious loss of face. The virtual abandonment of the attempt to eject the English from Gascony was a less dramatic and perhaps less obvious mistake but in the long term proved to be even more significant. Louis of Anjou's failure to press the invasion of Gascony to a conclusion encouraged England's latent supporters in the south-west and brought back to the English camp most of the trimmers who had made their peace with the Duke of Anjou after the victories of 1377. It was a missed opportunity which France would not make good until the middle of the fifteenth century. The struggle between the two countries subsided by 1380 into a tired stalemate, followed by two decades in which public opinion became increasingly hostile to the war in both countries. Governments presided over by incapable monarchs were weakened by internal dissension, deficits and the distracting personal ambitions of the princes who stood behind the thrones: Louis of Anjou and Philip of Burgundy in France, John of Gaunt and Thomas of Woodstock in England.

In the closing days of the campaign against Charles of Navarre's garrisons in Normandy, in June 1378, a royal official passed through Brittany, reading out in the public places of the towns a summons requiring John de Montfort to appear in Paris to answer charges of treason. The proclamation passed almost unnoticed at the time. John was in England and did not hear of it for several months. But it proved to be among the most controversial decisions of the King's reign, dividing his Council, his family, his supporters in Brittany and political sentiment in France. The trial opened on 4 December 1378 in the great chamber of the Parlement of Paris before the King and the handful of the peers of France who had not sent their excuses. The King's proctor read out a formidable list of treasonable acts extending back to 1370, while the ushers went through the motions of calling out the Duke's name in the courtyards outside. The outcome would have been a foregone conclusion even if John had been there to answer. On 18 December 1378 he was condemned in default and the duchy was pronounced forfeited into the King's hands.[1]

In one sense all this was an empty formality. The French royal chancery had referred to John as the 'former' duke ever since he had renounced his homage in 1373. French armies had already overrun the whole of the duchy except for the western extremity of the peninsula which was controlled by the English garrison of Brest. But for all that the King of France did not control Brittany. It remained an autonomous duchy even in the absence of a duke. The ducal demesne, which included John's castles and the principal towns of the peninsula, was administered by the Viscount of Rohan in effect as regent for the next duke, whoever that should be. The duke's courts continued to operate. There was a shadow administration in the castle at Nantes, staffed by former clerks of his government. Most of the Breton leaders seem to have assumed that John de Montfort would eventually make his peace with the King and return to his duchy. But there was a significant minority who favoured the transfer of the duchy to the house of Blois, which still commanded a good deal of emotional support in parts of the duchy. By the terms of the treaty of Guérande the heirs of Charles of Blois were entitled to succeed John de Montfort if he should die without male heirs. Since John was now nearly forty years old and had no children by either of his marriages this seemed much the most likely outcome.[2]

Charles V had accepted this state of affairs for five years after his break with John de Montfort. But in 1378 he resolved to bring matters to a conclusion. The genesis of this decision is obscure but there are good reasons for associating it with two of Charles's closest councillors in his final years, his First Chamberlain Bureau de la Rivière and that restless spirit, Olivier de Clisson. With the death of many of Charles V's older councillors Bureau had emerged as the guiding figure on the royal Council, overtly exercising the influence which he had always had in private. Olivier de Clisson, whose charm and military ability had made him an influential member of the royal circle, was probably at this stage the King's main source of information and advice about Brittany. Several of the allegations made against John de Montfort at his trial reflected Clisson's particular grudges.[3]

Why did Charles choose to bring an end to the awkward interregnum of Brittany and annexe it to his demesne? There seem to have been two main factors at work. In the first place there was no plausible claimant to the ducal title. The King was determined not to let John de Montfort return. The only alternative contender was the house of Blois which suffered from a major disability. Its candidate, John of Blois, was a prisoner in England. In 1378 John of Blois must have been in his late thirties. For a quarter of a century he had known little else but the walls of the grim state prisons of Devizes and Nottingham. He knew little or nothing of Brittany and few Bretons had set eyes on him. The danger was that John de Montort might die while his heir was still under English control. But to obtain his release it would be necessary to do a deal with Richard II's ministers, a bargaining counter which they could be expected to exploit for all that it was worth. At one point a proposal was canvassed for disinheriting John of Blois and promoting the candidature of his younger brother Henry. But legitimacy mattered too much in fourteenth-century minds for this idea to take root. Henry did not even have the support of his mother. She was determined to try to ransom her eldest son and had no compunction about negotiating with the English if she had to.[4]

There was a second reason for Charles's action in 1378. He was under severe financial pressure. With no end to war in sight he was having to spend large sums on military and naval operations while at the same time trying to build up his reserves. He had reached the limits of his subjects' taxable capacity. Even present levels of taxation were not likely to be maintainable for long. Charles's failing health added to his concerns. The oppressive fiscal regime which he had created troubled his soul and threatened to leave his young son with an inheritance of bitter public hostility when eventually he mounted the throne. Other sources of revenue had to be found. In his last years Charles increasingly turned to the royal demesne, badly damaged by war, reduced by grants to friends and councillors and inefficiently managed by his servants. The confiscation of Charles of Navarre's possessions in Normandy had shown the way. The annexation of Brittany would be the largest accretion of territory to the Crown since the annexation of Languedoc a century before. It would enable him to appropriate the ducal revenues, whose management was even poorer than his own but which were potentially very lucrative. And it would enable him to levy war taxes in the duchy on the same basis as other provinces which were directly governed by the Crown.[5]

Charles V does not seem to have anticipated the fierce resistance which his project was bound to arouse among the Breton nobility. The first to declare her opposition was Jeanne de Penthièvre. She was outraged, for the confiscation decree would extinguish not just John de Montfort's rights but also those of her son as his heir presumptive. When the Parlement was considering the charges against John she instructed her lawyers to oppose the proceedings. But their objections were brushed aside. Jeanne had many allies. The principal noblemen of Brittany had been conspicuously loyal to the Crown ever since John had thrown in his lot with the English but they were also strong supporters of the duchy's political autonomy, on which their local influence largely depended. They declared that they had no desire to see Brittany absorbed into the intrusive administrative and fiscal regime of France, 'like Normandy'. The leaders of the opposition in Brittany were John, Viscount of Rohan, and Guy, lord of Laval, both of them long-standing supporters of the house of Blois and experienced politicians with great domains in eastern and central Brittany. They had as much to lose as anyone if the duchy was extinguished as a political entity.[6]

In the spring of 1379 the English government was grappling with a financial crisis of its own. The double subsidy of 1377 had been intended to finance a decisive offensive against France during the following year. But by the time that the ineffectual Chancellor, Adam Houghton, Bishop of Saint David's, rose to address the Parliament of October 1378, it had all been spent. Parliament was meeting at Gloucester, an unpopular venue which had been chosen mainly to avoid the anger of the London mob. The proceedings were overshadowed by John of Gaunt's defeat at Saint-Malo. It was a difficult time at which to ask for another subsidy. Much of Houghton's address was devoted to undignified recriminations against the tide of 'bacbyters' who were spreading calumnies against the King's officers.

The defence of the government's position fell to the Steward of the royal household, Richard Lord Scrope of Bolton, a conspicuously able politician who was widely respected. Faced with a hostile Commons Scrope adopted a mixture of firmness and tact. His main theme was the number and geographical spread of England's enemies. Scrope under-

354

stood the anxiety and insecurity provoked in England by the raids of the French and the Scots. He suggested that the war was essentially defensive and emphasised the heavy cost of garrisons: £24,000 a year at Calais, £12,000 at Brest and 'great sums' at Cherbourg, Bordeaux and Bayonne in addition to the growing expenditure on the defence of Ireland, the Scottish march and the south coast of England. Every penny of the lay subsidies and wool duties, Scrope said, had been spent on legitimate operations of war. The Commons were incredulous. They called for the accounts and appointed a committee to examine them. These more or less bore out what Scrope had said but only served to open up fresh lines of complaint about strategy. The Commons acknowledged that the high cost of John of Gaunt's expedition to Saint-Malo was money properly expended in an honourable venture in spite of the disappointing outcome. But like so many critics of war expenditure, before and since, they could not accept that a large proportion of any war budget is inevitably consumed by overheads rather than offensive operations. They identified no less than £46,000 of improper expenditure, about thirty per cent of the whole. Most of it had gone on garrisons and embassies. Such operations, they declared, were not the kind of 'grant voiage et forte guerre' that they had had in mind in granting the double subsidy. Scrope protested that the coastal garrisons in France were essential forward bases and that their presence was the main thing that stopped the French from taking the war into England. The Commons were sceptical, perhaps rightly so. They pointed out that the government had had two years' worth of lay subsidies and they declined to grant another after only a year.

The King's ministers took it badly. According to one report, they threatened to issue commissions of trailbaston, a profitable but highly unpopular procedure which had not been used for many years, by which the King's judges were empowered to tour the counties imposing rough justice for real or alleged incidents of violence. If this threat was really uttered their bluff was called. The government received only a modest and temporary increase in the rate of the wool duty, which was reckoned to be worth no more than £4,000 in a full year. The main outcome of the Gloucester Parliament was the resignation of Chancellor Houghton a week into the sittings, followed by the removal of the entire continual council and its replacement by a new one, the third to hold office since Richard's accession. The assembly was hurriedly dissolved in mid-November before worse befell.[7]

The result was that no military operations were planned for the summer of 1379. When the Great Council, which traditionally applied itself to strategic planning in the new year, met rather later than usual in February 1379, they were told that the Treasury was empty and that nothing could be done. Yet even without aggressive plans England could not stand still. There had been a brief but embarrassing incident at the end of November, when a handful of Scottish borderers tunnelled their way by night into the cellars of Berwick castle, the principal English fortress of the Scottish march, and overcame the garrison as they slept. The raiders were disavowed by the Scottish wardens of the march. The Earl of Northumberland retook the place by storm within ten days and executed the culprits. But the affair was a dramatic warning of the danger of allowing garrison strengths to decline. The cost of maintaining Calais was rising. Cherbourg and Brest were in urgent need of resupply. Sir John Neville in Gascony, with fewer than 1,000 troops at his disposal, most of them tied up in garrison service, was pleading for reinforcements and money.[8] At Westminster the Great Council regarded the war at sea as having first call on its limited funds. Two new English Admirals had recently been appointed, both chosen from among the most experienced commanders in English service, Sir Thomas Percy and Sir Hugh Calveley. Calveley was already the keeper of the Channel Islands. The two Admirals were now made joint captains of Brest and given authority over the garrison of Cherbourg, in what was obviously an attempt to create a unified Channel command operating from both sides of the straits.

The problem of finance was for the moment deferred. The Great Council advised that Parliament would have to be summoned in the spring. In the meantime, they suggested, the government would have to borrow. A great campaign of forced loans was launched at the end of February 1379. The peers present at the Council were the first to put their hands in their pockets. The representatives of the Corporation of London were summoned to declare how much they would find for the King's needs. Commissioners toured the country with blank summonses executed under the privy seal in which they filled in the names of men reported to be rich enough to pay. Cash-rich war contractors, like Sir Robert Knolles, invested their profits in government loans against good security and promises of interest rates exceeding fifty per cent. More than £13,000 was raised. Most of it was spent on raising a fleet for Percy and Calveley.[9]

How far the English followed events in Brittany and Paris over the winter is not at all clear. But they began to take notice during the six weeks which followed the dispersal of the Great Council. In March 1379 the master of Jeanne de Penthièvre's household arrived in England to hold preliminary discussions with Richard II's Council about the situation in the duchy. The main purpose was to obtain the release of John of Blois. The course of the discussions is impenetrably obscure but it is known that Jeanne's agents had John transferred to the royal castle of Marlborough and obtained permission to interview him there. The discussions came to nothing. The English had no reason to sell their help cheaply. They were certainly not willing to release the sons of Charles of Blois while there was any chance of restoring their own candidate to the duchy. By the end of March the Council at Westminster had resolved to support a fresh invasion of Brittany in the hope of exploiting what seemed to be highly promising developments there. Preliminary plans were made for an expeditionary army of 4,000 men provided that some means could be found to pay for it.[10]

Charles V probably got wind of these discussions, for before anything could come of them he resolved to bring the burgeoning crisis in Brittany to a head. Early in April 1379 the French King appointed four commissioners to take possession of the duchy in his name. Their leader was Louis, Duke of Bourbon, one of the peers who had sat in judgment on John de Montfort. The others were the indispensable Bureau de la Rivière, the Admiral of France Jean de Vienne and the Marshal Louis de Sancerre. A small force of men-at-arms was placed at their disposal and plans were made to invade the duchy from the south-east by way of the ducal capital at Nantes. Charles V did not expect to encounter any serious resistance.[11]

Bertrand du Guesclin and the leading Breton magnates, Rohan, Laval and Clisson, were summoned before the King in Paris. There was a chilly interview in one of the council chambers of the palace on the Île de la Cité. The King informed them of the steps which he was taking to enforce the judgment of December and asked them whether they intended to co-operate. Through gritted teeth they said that they would. When the King required them to swear an oath they did that too. But in the event only Olivier de Clisson, who had supported the confiscation from the outset, honoured his word. Rohan and Laval fled back to Brittany, claiming that they had sworn in fear of their lives. Bertrand du Guesclin, who commanded a number of important royal fortresses on the north-east march of Brittany, was in a difficult position. He was the principal military officer of the Crown. But his heart was with Rohan and Laval. He stayed sullenly in Paris.

Towards the end of April 1379 a large part of the Breton baronage gathered in the presence of Rohan and Jeanne de Penthièvre, probably at Rennes. They put their name to a document in which they swore to oppose the French invasion and created a league to organise the defence of Brittany. Four of their number were elected as marshals to recruit an army. The handful of royal garrisons in the peninsula were expelled and their castles occupied by the rebels. A hearth tax of one franc was ordered to be levied throughout the duchy to finance its defence against the Crown. Finally, after some further deliberation, the Bretons resolved to send an embassy to John de Montfort in England to invite him to return as soon as possible to his duchy. Neither Laval nor Rohan formally acceded to the league although many of their kinsmen and friends did. Their consciences were probably troubled by their oaths. Whatever they may have thought about the man whose alliance with England had caused such outrage five years before, all of these men were realistic enough to see that he was now the only champion of Breton autonomy available. Some of them were even prepared to contemplate the return of an English army. When, at about this time, Sir Hugh Calveley landed a raiding party from the sea to pillage villages on the Breton coast, he was astonished to find himself welcomed as a liberator. Jeanne de Penthièvre's attitude was particularly remarkable. She did not formally join the Breton league, perhaps because of her close relations with the court. But she gave it her blessing and seems at one point to have agreed to her third son, Henry, assuming the nominal command of the Breton army. Charles V had succeeded in uniting the whole political community of Brittany for the first time in nearly forty years.[12]

While the Breton leaders were deliberating Olivier de Clisson arrived in Nantes with a small troop of soldiers and royal officials to secure the city in the path of the French army. Clisson was the captain of Nantes and its citadel was held by his men. But the town and the vital bridge over the Loire were firmly under the control of its inhabitants. They were courteous but inflexible. They told Clisson that they had no intention of admitting the English but neither would they acknowledge Charles V's commissioners. Over the following days they expelled all royal officers from the town and forced Clisson to withdraw. The Duke of Bourbon had mustered his small army at Le Mans on 30 April and was already on his way. Clisson met him in the fortress of Champtoceaux on the Loire at the border of the duchy. He recounted the scale of the Breton rebellion and his own failure at Nantes. Shortly afterwards, a delegation arrived from the Breton league. They left Louis of Bourbon in no doubt that any attempt to enter the duchy would be resisted. With the modest forces under his command there was no question of forcing the issue. Bourbon withdrew to Angers and then north into Maine to wait for further instructions.[13]

The English Parliament met at Westminster on 25 April 1379. They were once again addressed by Richard Scrope, this time as Chancellor. Scrope spoke on the now-familiar text of heavy expenditure, public danger, and poor tax yields. But he had not forgotten the suspicions of the Commons at Gloucester. He invited them to nominate a commission of peers to examine the government's finances for themselves. All the accounts would be laid before them, he said. They would have power to enter government offices without warning to pursue their investigations. They would find no hidden caches of money, no undisclosed sources of revenue and no corrupt transfers to the King's household. The commission was duly nominated and passed the best part of a month buried in the government's accounts. They seem to have been satisfied.

The turning point came with the arrival at Westminster in the middle of May of the ambassadors of the Breton league. The Bretons found John de Montfort sitting as Earl of Richmond among the Lords. They seem to have had no difficulty in persuading him to fall in with their plans. The more delicate question was what role the English would play in his return. John could not appear in Brittany at the head of an English army without alienating most of the Breton nobility and probably all of the towns. On the other hand he did not wish, once he was back on Breton soil, to be left at the mercy of his new friends, some of whom had been his worst enemies only a few months before. His first instinct was that it was too dangerous to go back to Brittany without a large armed force of his own. This was also the view of the Duke of Lancaster and Richard's other councillors. They were naturally more concerned with England's interests than John's. Within a few days of the Bretons' arrival they were talking in terms of sending John de Montfort back to Brittany with the projected expeditionary army of 4,000. In return for this assistance and shipping to get it to Brittany, they proposed to appoint him as Richard II's lieutenant in the duchy and to require him to carry the fight into France as soon as he was secure in his possession of it.[14]

Assuming that the army was paid for six months' service, a campaign on the scale envisaged was expected to cost £50,000 on top of the government's other commitments. This was a substantial sum, the equivalent of a standard Parliamentary subsidy and a corresponding grant from the Church. A difficult and long-drawn negotiation began with the representatives of the Commons. Finally they were persuaded that the opportunity was worth the cost. On 27 May 1379 they granted not a standard subsidy but a poll tax, the second experiment of its kind. Like its predecessor of 1377, the new tax was to be levied at the rate of four pence a head. But, remembering the unpopularity of the earlier poll tax, the Commons made some changes. They raised the qualifying age from fourteen to sixteen years and exempted married women. They also added a crudely graduated income tax on the better-off. Twenty-two categories of taxpayer were identified who were thought to be able to afford more than four pence. These were assessed at rates which were designed to mulct the commercial and professional classes in the towns, who did not do military service and were believed to have got away lightly under the old regime of standard taxes on moveables. The rates varied from five pounds for a judge (more than twice the rate of the richest advocate, be it noted) to a shilling for the keeper of a small inn. An earl paid four pounds and a knight one. John of Gaunt and John de Montfort occupied a special category of their own. They paid ten marks (£6 13s 4d) each. The Church, which had done well from the previous poll tax, was pressed into granting an equivalent income tax of its own at steeply graduated rates which bore heavily on the bishops and greater monastic houses. The government's financial officers were very confident. They were brought before Parliament to swear an oath that at these rates the tax would yield enough to finance the Breton campaign as well as the repayment of the forced loans. They were just as optimistic about the timing. The assessments were expected to be completed and the first half of the subsidy collected within a month.[15]

In the course of June 1379 John de Montfort's negotiations with his subjects came to the attention of the French government. Charles V revoked the powers of his commissioners. In their place he appointed his brother Louis of Anjou, who had been in the north since the spring. Anjou was assigned an army of nearly 2,500 men-at-arms. Part of this force was placed under the command of the Duke of Bourbon and immediately ordered to Avranches, where he could cover both the Cotentin and the north coast of Brittany if the English tried to land troops. Eight Castilian galleys, which reached the Gulf of Saint-Malo in July, were set to guard the approaches to the peninsula by sea. In the arsenal at Rouen shipwrights were working hard to complete the construction of new oared barges and to repair and equip the rest. But in spite of these warlike preparations the Duke of Anjou's instructions were more pacific. Better, it was said, to try to soften the resentment of the Bretons with tact and recover the castles of the duchy with money.

This almost certainly represented Louis of Anjou's own preference. His misgivings about the confiscation of Brittany were well known. He also had many friends and kinsmen who were now prominent in the ranks of the rebels, including his mother-in-law Jeanne de Penthièvre. At the beginning of July he established his headquarters in the border fortress of Pontorson on the north-east march of Brittany and opened negotiations with the leaders of the Breton league. Louis's diplomatic approach provoked divisions among the Breton nobility, as no doubt it was intended to. The league's most powerful supporters were the first to secede. Rohan and Laval, who had never formally adhered to it but had publicly supported its objects, were persuaded to return to their previous alliance with the Crown. The doubts about whether John would return in time and the prospect that he would come with a large English army are likely to have been the main factors in their decision. Jeanne de Penthièvre might have followed their example if she had been able to. She was passing through Dinan with her son Henry on her way to Pontorson when the local leaders of the league invaded the town with their retainers and refused to let her leave.[16]

In England the plans for John de Montfort's return to Brittany were encountering the usual administrative and financial obstacles. The poll tax, the first instalment of which was due in late June, did not begin to come in until August and early reports from the collectors suggested that the amounts would fall a long way short of the confident predictions of the Exchequer. The Council attributed this to the laxness and incompetence of the assessors. But all the evidence suggests that it was in fact due to gross misconceptions on the part of the Commons and the Exchequer officials who advised them. They had under-estimated the effect of raising the qualifying age and exempting married women and had greatly over-estimated the number of higher-rate taxpayers. The full extent of the disaster took some time to become apparent, but the total assessment ultimately proved to be only £19,304, not much more than the cost of repaying the forced loans raised to finance the fleet. The result was that by July there was no money left to pay for the Breton expedition and neither ships nor troops had been recruited for it. The embarkation date had to be deferred until the autumn.[17]

Seeing the prospect of a triumphant return slipping away, John de Montfort took the greatest gamble of his career. In about the middle of July 1379 he announced his intention of leaving for Brittany immediately, almost unescorted. He proposed to take hostages from the Bretons for his own safety and to bring just seventy English soldiers, a handful of Breton retainers and no horses. Richard II's Council appears to have accepted this change of plan with some misgivings. They assigned two representatives of their own to accompany him: Sir Richard Abberbury, until recently captain of Brest and something of an authority on Breton affairs, and the civil lawyer Walter Skirlaw, a rising star on the diplomatic side of the English royal Chancery. John had to agree to be 'guided' by these men. Their real function was to keep an eye on him and to negotiate a deal with the Breton league which would serve the wider strategic interests of England. According to reports later circulating in Brittany, which were almost certainly true, the Council also exacted a promise that John would return to England in September to assume the command of the larger expedition. On 22 July 1379 John and his small company sailed from Southampton with the two Admirals and thirty-nine ships of the Channel fleet on what had originally been planned as a routine coastal raid in the estuary of the Seine. On 3 August, in the late afternoon, they arrived in the great open roads off Saint-Malo.[18]

The English fleet sailed in line past the town with a following wind, making for the channel which led into the estuary of the River Rance. The Castilian and French galleys appear to have been beached, either in the inner harbour or south of the town in the inlet of Bas Sablons. They made no attempt to intercept the leading ships, which were large fortified hulls under the command of Sir Hugh Calveley. But once these had gone past they made for the transports, most of them simple cargo barges which were following on behind with the Duke's furniture, armoury and treasury. The galleys assailed the transports with cannon, terrifying the crews and doing serious damage. Disaster was only avoided when Calveley turned his ships back and, tacking into the wind, succeeded in rejoining the rest of the fleet. There, their greater height gave them the advantage over the galleys. The French and Castilian crews suffered heavy casualties from arrows shot from the towers and masts of the English ships and were eventually forced to withdraw to the shelter of the harbour. Cannon had been mounted on ships for some years, but this was one of the earliest recorded naval engagements in which they played a significant part. It also illustrated the weakness of an all-galley fleet, even in the age of gunpowder, when pitted against large sailing ships with searoom and wind. By nightfall the whole of the English fleet was anchored in the Rance by the keep of Solidor, which was firmly under the control of the Breton league. John had dropped a messenger ashore in Normandy to tip off the league's local leaders. Within a short time the beach had been secured by Breton troops and invaded by a crowd of well-wishers from the region around.[19]

The sudden appearance of John de Montfort in Brittany took the French by surprise. The first contingents of Louis of Anjou's army were just beginning to muster on the border some twenty-five miles away. Anjou himself had left for consultations with the King and his councillors at the royal castle of Montargis, south of Paris, where the government had temporarily taken refuge from the plague which was raging in the capital. The only prominent representative of the Crown in the region was the Constable, who was in the citadel of Saint-Malo with a retinue of just 200 men-at-arms, enough to defend the town but not enough to interfere with John de Montfort's progress on the mainland. From Montargis Anjou wrote hurriedly to the Viscount of Rohan, ordering him to make at once for Saint-Malo and drive the 'former duke' back into the sea. Rohan did not receive this missive until 6 August and it took him three days to raise his retainers. Few other Breton noblemen could have achieved even that much. On 9 August Rohan set out from his castle at La Chèze at the head of 400 men-at-arms.[20]

John de Montfort played his cards with consummate skill. As soon as he had landed he despatched a circular to the baronage of Brittany, announcing his return and calling on them to come before him at Dinan, a walled town at the head of the estuary of the Rance some fifteen miles south of Saint-Malo. On 6 August John entered Dinan and installed himself in the house of the Franciscans. Most of the nobility of the region was already in the town. About ninety more arrived over the next few days, bringing their military retinues with them. On the 9th John was able to preside over a council which could have passed for a general assembly of the Breton nobility. The only famous names who were absent were Olivier de Clisson, who was sulking in the citadel of Nantes, and the Viscount of Rohan, who was a day's march from the town with his men and whose intentions were still uncertain. Rohan did not take long to realise that it was too late to drive John de Montfort back into the sea. With the strength of the rebellion growing daily even the greatest noblemen were obliged to bend with the wind if they were to conserve their influence and their followers. Guy de Laval had already resiled from his deal with the Duke of Anjou and submitted to John de Montfort. When Rohan reached Dinan on the 10th he sized up the situation and did the same, putting his whole force at John's disposal. Both of these men were clearly terrified by their own boldness and desperate to avoid an irrevocable breach with the King of France, at least until the direction of events became clearer. Even after they had submitted to John de Montfort they were writing to assure the Duke of Anjou that it was all dissimulation. Disentangling the truth from the lies is not easy.

Some of the men who were with John de Montfort at Dinan would no doubt have abandoned him at the first signs of failure. But, as the bandwagon gathered speed and Louis of Anjou failed to intervene, it became increasingly difficult for them to withdraw. John gave them few excuses and did much to disarm old criticisms. He promised to govern by the advice and counsel of the nobility and to abandon his English advisers. 'I'll believe that when I see it,' Bertrand du Guesclin remarked when this was reported to him. Yet on 10 August, the day of Rohan's submission, John felt strong enough to dispense with Calveley and Percy and send the fleet back to England. On 16 August the assembled Bretons listened in the packed church of the Franciscans to a rousing speech in which the Duke recounted the injustices which he had suffered at the hands of Charles V and robustly defended the historic independence of the duchy. Jeanne de Penthièvre appeared before the crowd to support him. Plans were announced for an army to hold Brittany against the French. Nearly 1,000 men were promised from the retinues of those present. Rohan alone committed 300.

On 20 August John de Montfort entered Rennes, the principal city of eastern Brittany. Its captain, Thomas de Fontenay, a former officer of Charles V's household, was not a signatory of the league but had been among the first to offer his submission. He opened the gates upon John's arrival. Here John de Montfort began to behave like a ruler. The rudiments of an administration were put together. Instructions were despatched to ducal officials in every part of the duchy. An attempt was made to address the rebels' chronic shortage of funds by doubling the rate of the hearth tax. All available troops were summoned to assemble before John's marshals at Vannes. From Rennes John set out on a month-long tour of his duchy, passing through the great Penthièvre fief in the north, the vast Rohan domains of the centre and along the south coast. On 26 September he entered Vannes in triumph. He had been in Brittany for less than two months.[21]

Charles V's councillors at Montargis watched these events from a distance with growing incredulity. Accusations of treachery and connivance were already being made against Bertrand du Guesclin at the beginning of August. Bureau de la Rivière was foremost among the Constable's detractors. He would probably have said the same about Anjou if he had dared. And it is true that neither of the two principal executants of royal policy in Brittany had his heart in the job. The Constable had no wish to see another civil war in Brittany. Nor did his followers, who deserted his standard at an alarming rate during the autumn. Du Guesclin maintained his contacts in the rebel camp and looked for openings that might lead to a compromise. He even came down to the beach as the English fleet was leaving to talk to Sir Hugh Calveley from the water's edge. The two men were old enemies and friends. Du Guesclin had been Calveley's prisoner in the Breton wars of the 1350s and his companion in arms in Castile in the following decade. They were men of the same bent of mind who had always got on well. The English, Du Guesclin reported, seemed willing to consider a negotiated solution. The first approaches from John de Montfort's camp reached the Duke of Anjou in mid-August when two prominent members of the Breton league came before him with proposals. Louis's response is not known but he certainly did not reject them out of hand. He was obviously in no hurry to resort to force. He did not leave Montargis until the third week of August and then dallied for several days in Anjou while the Duke of Bourbon and his men kicked their heels uselessly on the Breton march. When he finally arrived back at Pontorson at the end of the month he embarked on a long series of discussions with the Bretons.

On 17 October 1379, without a blow being struck, a truce was agreed, initially for a period of a month, to allow for a conference between the principals. Under the terms of this agreement both sides agreed to submit to the mediation of the Duke of Anjou and John de Montfort's long-standing protector Louis de Mâle, Count of Flanders. In point of form nothing had been resolved. But everyone knew that the decree of confiscation was a dead letter. On 18 November 1379 the French army at Pontorson was disbanded and no further attempt was made against the Bretons. The French government retained one significant town, Saint-Malo, and a handful of small garrisons scattered across eastern Brittany. Apart from Brest, which was still securely held by the English, and Nantes, which declined to deal with either side until the outcome was clear, the whole of the rest of the peninsula was in the hands of John de Montfort. If the recollections of an old man, recorded many years later, are to be trusted, Bertrand du Guesclin believed that the debacle had cost him the confidence of the King. He even endeavoured to return his sword of office.[22]

If John's bloodless triumph was a reverse for the French it was ironically just as problematic for the English. He had recovered almost

DIVIDED HOUSES

all of Brittany with very little assistance from them, and no agreement
had been reached with the Breton league for future operations against
the French Crown. John's English advisers, Abberbury and Skirlaw,
followed him about his duchy until mid-September when they returned
empty-handed to England. In his current situation it was very much
against John's interest to lift a finger against the King of France. Once
he had sealed his truce with Anjou he was not in a position to do so.
This left the status of England's great expeditionary army rather
uncertain. The requisitioning of shipping had been in progress since
June but no troops had been recruited for lack of funds to pay their
advances. On 9 September another Great Council met at Westminster
to review the government's military plans in the light of the continuing
problems with the poll tax. The strength of the army of Brittany was
reduced by two-thirds from 4,000 to 1,300 men and its cost was cut to
less than half the original estimate. As reports of events in Brittany
reached England there were further changes. The command was
switched from John de Montfort to the Marshal of England, John of
Arundel, and the destination was changed from Saint-Malo to Brest.
No one seems to have applied their minds to the strategic purpose which
this army was now supposed to achieve.[23]

In any case another, more unusual, project was now competing with
Brittany for the attention of the Council and the limited resources of the
Treasury. This arose from some characteristically devious dealings
between the King's ministers and a prominent French prisoner of war. It
is a romantic story. Waleran de Luxembourg, Count of Saint-Pol, was a
rash young man who had been captured in a skirmish in the Pas-de-
Calais in 1374. He had had great difficulty in ransoming himself, partly
because he was one of the richest territorial magnates of Picardy and his
captors were expecting a steep ransom; and partly because of the
unwillingness of the French government to exchange this raw soldier for
more distinguished prisoners. Increasingly resentful of his fate, Saint-Pol
was bought and sold and finally acquired by the King, who allowed him
to live at court at Windsor castle. There he fell in love with a young
widow, Matilda Courtenay, 'la plus belle dame de toute Engleterre'
according to Froissart. Matilda was Richard II's half-sister, the child of
his mother's earlier marriage to Sir Thomas Holand. Public opinion
disapproved of the match and the Queen Mother shared their opinion.
But the Council had their own ends in view. They agreed to ransom the
Count for 100,000 francs (£16,666) and to allow him to marry his

366

betrothed on highly unusual terms. Saint-Pol agreed to renounce his homage to the King of France, to do liege homage to Richard II for all his domains and to hold his many fortresses in Picardy and the march of Flanders at the disposal of the English government. Within fifty days of his release he was required to seize the town and castle of Guise, one of the major fortresses of the Vermandois, which belonged to his relatives of the house of Châtillon and to make war on the French Crown from its walls and those of his own castles in the vicinity. For this purpose he was to be supplied with a small army of 300 English men-at-arms, supported by 300 mercenaries from the Low Countries under the command of a turncoat of an earlier generation, Thierry ('Canon') Robesart.[24]

The plan came to grief as almost all such adventures did. The Count of Saint-Pol was taken to Calais and released in September 1379. But rumours about the terms of his liberation had already reached the ears of the French ministers. At the beginning of October royal officials seized the Count's castles in Picardy and Enguerrand de Coucy put royal garrisons into the fortresses of the Vermandois. The Count and Robesart got as far as Hainault, where they planned to begin recruiting their mercenaries. But Robesart was arrested by the regent of Hainault at the request of the French government and locked up in the castle at Mons. The Count fled back to Calais and returned to captivity in England. He eventually married Matilda Courtenay in the following year and succeeded in paying the rest of his ransom. But he was banished from France until after death of Charles V. 'Age and maturity', it was said when he was finally pardoned, 'would soften his impulsive spirit.'[25]

With the return of the Count of Saint-Pol to England events moved from farce to tragedy. The English army of Brittany gathered in the Solent in October only to find that there were not enough ships to carry even the reduced numbers with their horses and equipment. Bored and frustrated, the men mutinied and took to looting the villages and churches of Hampshire while the Admirals' officers combed the ports of England for more ships. By the beginning of December about ninety ships had been found, most of them quite small, plus thirty-five larger hulls hired in Bayonne and the Low Countries to carry the horses. It was a difficult time of year, with long nights and unpredictable weather. John of Arundel's sea captains thought that a storm was coming and advised him to wait. But he was under strong pressure to make up for lost time. He felt he had waited long enough. On 6 December 1379 the English fleet sailed out of the Solent. On the following night the storm struck. The ships were scattered before the wind and driven out into the Atlantic, then back onto the coasts of Ireland, Wales and Cornwall. At least seventeen troop-carrying ships were wrecked off Ireland. Nineteen more, laden with horses, foundered on the coast of Cornwall. Sir Hugh Calveley, a man now well into his fifties, survived clinging by a cable to a broken mast. John of Arundel was drowned trying to reach the shore. Hundreds of soldiers and seamen lost their lives. It was several years before England's self-confidence as a naval power recovered from this blow.[26]

The French ministers were preoccupied with their own problems. The Duke of Anjou was still at Pontorson when a messenger arrived with news of a serious rebellion against his authority in Languedoc. The background to this event was a tragedy which was only beginning to be understood in Paris. Languedoc had for years been taxed more heavily in proportion to its resources than any other part of France with the possible exception of Normandy. It had borne substantially the whole burden of prosecuting the war against the English in Gascony and of fighting off the companies operating on the fringes of the region. It had also had to fund the cost of maintaining Louis of Anjou, a royal prince with a magnificent household and international ambitions. The tax base from which all this had to be financed was shrinking rapidly as successive censuses showed a steep and persistent decline in the number of taxable households. In the three seneschalsies of Languedoc the number fell from about 84,000 in 1370 to about 31,000 nine years later. Medieval tax censuses were notoriously fallible but on any view these were remarkable figures. Part of the fall was due to the three great agents of depopulation: plague, famine and war. There is also anecdotal evidence of large-scale migration into neighbouring regions which were more lightly taxed. But the main factor at work is likely to have been the progressive impoverishment of both town and country, resulting in a high proportion of households falling below the threshold of ten *livres*' worth of moveable property at which liability to pay tax began.

In the face of this catastrophe the Duke of Anjou was determined to maintain the absolute level of his tax receipts. He responded with a sharp increase in the rate of taxation. In the early part of the decade the Estates-General of Languedoc had generally met twice a year, granting hearth taxes at a rate which amounted to about five francs per hearth per year. In December 1377 the Estates-General, meeting at Toulouse, was induced to grant a new *fouage* at one franc per hearth per month, more than double the traditional level. Since this coincided, as it turned out, with the virtual suspension of large-scale military operations on the march of Gascony it proved extremely difficult to get the grant renewed at the same rate in the spring. No fewer than three meetings of the Estates-General were required before Louis of Anjou got his way. Even then the city of Nîmes refused to agree until the Duke threw their representatives in prison and suspended their consulate. When, in October that year, Louis of Anjou demanded the extension of the tax at the same rate for a full year, the cowed representatives at Toulouse did not dare to challenge him. But the tensions generated by these debates were felt well beyond the churches and palaces in which the Estates-General met. Urban mobs were less easily intimidated. Overt signs of resistance multiplied. Le Puy erupted into riots in April 1378 as the *bailli* and chief judge of the Velay discussed the collection of the tax with the consuls of the town. In November 1378, after a poor harvest had left men with no means of paying, the inhabitants of Alès assaulted the town hall. A 'nest of thieves', they called it.[27]

Instead of moderating his demands Louis of Anjou responded by trying to dispense with the Estates-General altogether. In the autumn of 1379 he demanded an extension of the tax for yet another year. Commissioners were appointed to browbeat each community individually. These proceedings brought ill-feeling in Languedoc to a new pitch of intensity. A number of towns sent delegates to the north to protest to the King. Louis of Anjou, who was engrossed with the negotiations with the Bretons, brushed their complaints aside. He told his brother that the complaints were exaggerated and that he would deal with them when he had time. Time was not to be given to him. On 21 October 1379 six of Anjou's commissioners, led by his chancellor and his treasurer, arrived at Montpellier with a large escort of clerks, officials and servants. Montpellier was the largest city of the province after Toulouse and had once been the richest. But it had probably suffered more than any other place by the misfortunes of Languedoc. The town had had more than 10,000 taxable households in 1345 compared with fewer than 1,000 now. The consuls had protested against the current tax, declaring that the inhabitants had not enough to live on. On the day after their arrival the Duke of Anjou's commissioners met the consuls in the chapter house of the Franciscan convent and presented their demands. The consuls declined to answer at once. They said that they would think about it and return with their answer. When they returned it was with a large armed mob at their backs. There was an ill-tempered argument. As voices rose the crowd forced its way into the building. They fell on the Duke's officers and commissioners and their staff and lynched them. Many were hacked to death as they lay on the ground. Their bodies were dragged through the streets and thrown into wells. The carnage continued all night. Then in the sober morning they set about putting the city in a state of defence and called upon the other cities of the province to rise with them in defiance of Anjou's government.[28]

For a few days it looked as if the rising might spread to other cities. The consuls of Nîmes reported 'murmurings' throughout the province. The King's proctor there had his house sacked. The consuls temporarily suspended all taxation for fear of imminent revolution. At the edge of the plain, twenty miles from Montpellier, the inhabitants of Clermont de l'Hérault rang the tocsin, set fire to houses and assaulted the castle of the Count of Clermont, shouting: 'Kill all the rich like the men of Montpellier did.' The slogan, although hardly an accurate statement of the motives of Montpellier, was a reminder that underlying many tax rebellions there were profound social divisions. The root cause was that the tax census was used as a measure of the taxable capacity of the whole community, not as a basis for collecting from individual households. The money was in practice paid to the government by the municipal authorities and recouped from the inhabitants on principles which were decided locally by urban elites who knew how to look after their own interests. Montpellier was comparatively unusual in recouping the cost with a mildly progressive income tax. Local sales taxes on commodities, which bore particularly hard on the poor, were far more common. Latterly, the Duke of Anjou had exploited these internal divisions, encouraging the use of indirect taxes by municipal authorities. It was easier to obtain their consent if the full weight of the tax fell on others. As a result when violence broke out in the towns it was often directed as much against fellow citizens as against the local representatives of the government. The riots at Le Puy and Clermont-de-l'Hérault in 1378 had both been aimed at the consuls and the rich. How are we to feed our children, the rioters prayed to the famous black statue of the Virgin in the cathedral of Le Puy, in the face of taxes 'inflicted on us by the rich to lighten their own burden'?[29]

The repression, when it came, was savage. In January 1380 Louis of Anjou, accompanied by 1,000 men-at-arms and a large force of crossbowmen, was received into the city of Montpellier by a crowd of women and children prostrating themselves on the ground and crying for mercy. A few days later the Duke decreed the penalties of *lèse-majesté* from a vast scaffold in a carefully contrived ceremony every detail of which had been agreed in advance. Six hundred citizens who had been involved in the rebellion were to be executed: 200 would be beheaded, 200 hanged and 200 burned alive. Montpellier would lose its consulate and part of its ramparts. The assembled consuls removed their robes of office and surrendered the clapper of the town bell and the key of the gates to give symbolic effect to these decrees. As for the rest of the citizenry, they would be required to pay an indemnity of 600,000 francs to the King in addition to payments to the kinsmen of the dead men and the cost of endowing chapels to pray for the repose of their souls. On the following day most of these penalties were remitted. The executions were limited to a small number of ringleaders and the indemnity, which the town had never had the least prospect of paying, was reduced to 130,000 francs. Even the reduced penalties were remitted in the following reign.[30]

The government received a shock. Charles V did not overlook the real lesson as Anjou had. In January 1380 a delegation of the principal cities of Languedoc travelled to Paris to put their grievances before him. Their intervention seems to have been decisive. In April 1380 the King removed the Duke of Anjou from the lieutenancy of Languedoc after sixteen years in the job. Shortly after his recall the delegates reached agreement with the King on a new tax regime. The rate of the *gabelle du sel* in Languedoc was doubled, but the *aides* were halved and the hearth tax was reduced to three francs per year, a quarter of the rate which Anjou had demanded. The King also undertook that the revenues derived from these taxes would be applied exclusively to the prosecution of the war. It may be that even Anjou came to acknowledge the adverse impact of his rule, for among the many acts of reparation for public and private misdeeds which later appeared in his will was a bequest of 50,000 francs (£8,333) to the poor of Languedoc on account of their sufferings under his government. Anjou remembered in particular the victims of his onerous taxes and the men and women who had abandoned their homes rather than pay them, 'for which things we may have been responsible'. In his agreement with the towns of Languedoc Charles V undertook not to burden the province again with a prince of the royal family as his lieutenant but to appoint a competent captain of lesser rank to conduct the war on the marches in his name. Shortly afterwards Bertrand du Guesclin was nominated as Captain-General in Languedoc with most of Anjou's functions.[31]

It was a significant retreat which must have been profoundly wounding to the King's brother. Yet Languedoc was far from unique. In the neighbouring provinces of Auvergne and Bas-Berry the records reveal the same shrinking tax base, aggravated by far more serious physical damage from *routier* operations. The number of taxable households in Auvergne fell during the 1370s by about a third and in parts of the province by more than half. Depopulation caused by disease, war and emigration to the more peaceful and lightly taxed domains of the Duke of Bourbon were all significant factors. As in Languedoc, however, the major cause seems likely to have been the impoverishment of those who stayed behind but disappeared below the tax threshold. The Duke of Berry, whose appanage included these provinces, had responded in the same ruthless fashion as his brother in Languedoc by tightening the fiscal screw yet further. In the course of the 1370s, as the wealth and population of Auvergne diminished, the frequency and rate of hearth taxes rose inexorably. By 1378 the towns of Auvergne were paying hearth taxes at approximately the same rate as those of Languedoc in addition to the *aides* on essential commodities and the *gabelle* on salt. The Duke reacted to the protests of the Estates of Auvergne by ordering the arrest of the protesters, who were held in prison until they consented to further grants. It was one thing to extract consent from terrified representatives in the provincial capital but another to collect it from their constituents. Large numbers of peasants and townsmen fled from their homes into the hills and forests of Auvergne, where they formed themselves into bandit armies known as *tuchins*, often commanded by indigent noblemen with their own grievances against the government. According to the fullest contemporary account to survive they were united by 'awful oaths never to bow their heads to the yoke of taxes'. By the end of the 1370s the *tuchins* had become almost as great a menace in Auvergne and northern Languedoc as the Anglo-Gascon companies.[32]

Most popular resistance to taxes occurred not in provincial assemblies or even in the streets of the towns but in the face of the collectors and the officers whose job it was to enforce payment against defaulters. According to the petition of the Estates of Auvergne to the King in 1379 a poor man who had been unable to pay could be confronted at his door by ten or twelve 'sergeants, commissioners and bailiffs' whose ruinous charges would be added to the sum due. The system invited violence on both sides. In Languedoil, the recorded opposition to taxation took the form of attacks on collectors and the occasional articulate personal protests which are recorded in the registers of the French Chancery because over-zealous officials charged the offender with *lèse-majesté*. Such incidents became more common as fiscal pressure on the population intensified and the brutality required to extract payment increased. Charles V's financial officers in Paris were well aware of the problem and their master was more sensitive to it than his brothers. For the past three years the King and the Chambre des Comptes had been trying to lighten the burden without conceding the principle, by granting temporary or localised exemptions and reducing the number of hearths for which the worst-affected communities were assessed. On 21 November 1379 Charles V published a great ordinance on the reform of the French tax system, which declared in its opening paragraph the King's desire to relieve the 'grief and oppression' of his subjects. Yet these reforms were too capricious in their incidence. The administrative measures consisted only of moderating or sometimes punishing the abuses of officials and trying to address the imbalance between rich and poor taxpayers. They barely scratched the surface of the underlying grievances. The day would come when the protests would coalesce into large-scale rebellions, even in the traditionally loyal cities of the north.[33]

The English Parliament which opened at Westminster on 16 January 1380 was overshadowed, like so much political discussion in France, by financial crisis. Addressing the assembled Lords and Commons in the presence of the young Richard II, Chancellor Scrope declared that the government was bankrupt. He recounted the history of the poll tax of 1379, which had raised less than half its expected yield. The wool duties had been reduced to a trickle by unrest in Flanders. The forced loans raised to anticipate the receipt of the poll tax were still outstanding. There was no money to pay garrisons on the Atlantic seaboard of France or the march of Scotland and nothing to defend the coast of England, let alone to finance a campaign on the continent. There were no hidden reserves. The Commons were angry and frustrated. They pointed to the scale and frequency of Parliamentary taxation, going back to the early years of the previous reign. The burden, they said, could not be sustained indefinitely. Unless the war came to an end shortly the realm would be ruined. They demanded another special commission to examine the accounts and to review the whole financial history of the war. They called for the dismissal of the 'continual council'. The government bowed before the storm. The 'continual council' resigned *en masse* and was replaced by the five principal officers of state with a smaller council of administrators and members of the King's household. Chancellor Scrope was dismissed in favour of the amiable and honest but ineffectual Archbishop of Canterbury, Simon Sudbury. The financial commission was duly appointed and given extensive powers of inquiry. But there was no escaping the facts, which were substantially as Scrope had described them.[34]

In spite of their lack of funds, the English King's Council had vast strategic ambitions, focussed on Gascony and Brittany. Sir John Neville had been pressing for money and reinforcements for Gascony ever since his arrival in the duchy in September 1378. The march had been comparatively stable for two years and Neville himself had made remarkably effective use of the tiny forces at his disposal. He had harassed the forward positions of the French, recapturing some of the smaller places close to the city and taking a great quantity of pre-positioned stores and artillery which Anjou had left in readiness for a future offensive. An extra 400 troops had been sent out from England in the previous autumn, bringing the total strength of English forces in the duchy to just over 1,000 men, still a pitifully small number. But the enemy was uncomfortably close to Bordeaux and no one believed that the present torpor on the front would last. In the longer term the security of the city depended on recovering control of the lower valleys of the Dordogne and the Garonne, and that called for a major campaign in the south-west.

Richard II's ministers were devising an ambitious plan for co-ordinated campaigns against the French, with an English army operating from the Gironde and an Aragonese army operating simultaneously from Roussillon. This was an old dream which successive English ambassadors had canvassed in Barcelona for years. In the autumn of 1379 Geraud de Menta, the Gascon diplomat responsible for these negotiations, had been in England for consultations. It had been decided that the time had come to press the project to a conclusion. It would be the main military enterprise of 1380. Gerald returned to Barcelona with a promise that the plan would be put before Parliament.

But how were the English to get an army to southern France? The sea route was ruled out by want of shipping. The long overland route via the Massif Central was regarded as impossible after John of Gaunt's experience in 1373. The English would need an accessible port in Brittany and access to the city of Nantes with its great bridge over the Loire. When Geraud de Menta left England for Barcelona in October

1379 John of Arundel's fleet was about to sail for Brittany. But by the time he reached Aragon it had been destroyed at sea. Before any major expedition to Gascony could be contemplated it would be necessary to complete the business of the previous year and re-establish control over the Breton peninsula.[35]

Once again Charles V eased the English government's difficulties by throwing the Bretons into their arms. The long-delayed mediation between John de Montfort and Charles V had just come to the end of its opening session in the northern town of Arras, having probably got no further than the opening statements. Frustrated by the obduracy and dilatoriness of French diplomacy, John de Montfort appointed ambassadors to conclude a military alliance with England. There is little doubt that he had the support of the Breton nobility for this move. The leading figure in his embassy at Arras was Jean de Beaumanoir, an old partisan of Blois who had been a leading light in the leagues of the previous year. Beaumanoir arrived at Westminster towards the end of January and was in the English capital for more than a month. On 1 March 1380 a perpetual alliance between England and Brittany was sealed. Both sides had learned some lessons. This time, John de Montfort's ambassadors did not commit him to participating in an English invasion. But it was agreed that an English army would be received in the peninsula and that English troops would be given transit rights through John de Montfort's dominions on their way to France or Gascony. In return John received a guarantee of English military assistance in the event of a French invasion of his duchy. The command of the new expedition was conferred on the Earl of Buckingham. Twenty-five years old and with little military experience, Buckingham was not an ideal choice. But his deficiencies were to some extent made good by the formidable group of veteran captains which was assigned to accompany him. They comprised almost all the notable English commanders then living, including Sir Hugh Calveley, Sir Robert Knolles, Sir John Harleston, Sir Thomas Percy and William Lord Latimer. The size of the army was eventually fixed at 5,000 English troops, in addition to a force of mercenaries which it was proposed to recruit in the German Low Countries. It was expected to serve on the continent for a full year.[36]

Buckingham's retainer and friend Sir John Gildesburgh, a veteran of Crécy and Poitiers, was Speaker of the House of Commons. He laboured mightily to procure the necessary finance. The Commons eventually succumbed, as their predecessors had so often done, to the instinct that one more spasm of financial exertion, one more tremendous military offensive might enable the war to be brought to a close on acceptable terms. They granted a standard subsidy and, unusually, a further half-subsidy which was to be collected with the rest but treated as an advance on any tax which might be granted in the next Parliament. The proceeds of these impositions, together with the arrears of the poll tax of the previous year, were strictly reserved for the proposed expedition. And, the Commons warned, they would have to be enough for that purpose. There was to be no new Parliament before the autumn of 1381. As for the cost of garrisons, that would have to be met from the modest proceeds of the additional wool duty voted in the previous year. The Commons were interested only in large-scale offensive operations. It is clear that great hopes were invested in Buckingham's enterprise. He was charged, said his letters patent of appointment, to 'bend all his efforts to the bring the war to its ultimate conclusion'.[37]

The planning of the Earl of Buckingham's expedition to France brought the English government up against the abiding problem of the new maritime strategy. Although the English had successfully acquired the bases in France they never acquired the shipping resources which were necessary to make effective use of them. The decline of the King's own fleet was symptomatic. In 1369 Edward III had owned twenty-seven ships and barges, including five with a carrying capacity of more than 200 tons apiece. By the time of his death this had been reduced by losses and decay to four sailing ships, four barges and a galley. In 1378 only the great 300-ton sailing carrack *Dieulagarde* was fit for service. Two years later, in 1380, the *Dieulagarde* had been given to Sir William Elmham and the remnants of the fleet had been sold to pay the debts of the office of the King's ships. This marked the end of the 'royal' navy until the next century.

Much the same fate had befallen the fleets of oared barges which Edward III had ordered from the principal maritime towns in 1372. Some of them had served in the fleets of the following year but very few of them reappeared later. The experiment was repeated in the autumn of 1377 by the authority of the October Parliament but the results were no better. Forty-two cities and towns were commanded between them to build twenty-seven small barges ('balingers') of forty to fifty oars each and to meet the cost by levying contributions from their richer inhabitants. This was a substantial burden for most of them.

Cambridge, for example, commissioned its barge from a London shipbuilder at a cost of £142. This was three times the town's contribution to a standard Parliamentary subsidy and had to be paid on top of the double subsidy granted by the same Parliament. The balingers were destined to serve in the fleet of 1378 and some of them reappeared in 1379. But thereafter they vanished as completely as their predecessors. The ministers of Richard II ordered an inquiry into what had become of them. The truth was that most of them had rotted away. The English government had no specialised repair facilities, such as the French maintained at Rouen or the Castilians at Seville. They had a storage depot and a yard at Ratcliffe in Stepney, the London suburb where most of the commercial shipbuilding and repairing trades of the capital were concentrated. But it was probably no more than a group of open docks cut out of the mud and was never properly funded or manned. However, the decisive factor in the decline of the royal fleet is likely to have been a shortage of crewmen. England had no native tradition of operating oared vessels. Conscripting seamen merely diverted the available manpower from requisitioned merchantmen without achieving any net increase in the number of operational ships. Without adequate crews it was hardly worth spending money on maintenance.[38]

More fundamental than the problems of the royal and municipal fleets was the continuing decline of the English merchant marine, measured in both ships and seamen. In the course of the 1370s the number of English ocean-going hulls available for requisition declined from about 250 at the beginning of the decade to about 190 at the accession of Richard II and about 120 three years later. The reality was even worse than these figures suggest, for the average carrying capacity of the surviving ships declined from 70 to 55 tons over the same period. It is clear that losses and depreciation were not being made good, particularly among the largest ships.[39]

Many shipowners responded to the heavy loss rates among traditional deep-hold ships by abandoning the trade and investing in oared vessels instead. Barges accounted for about a quarter of requisitioned ships in the early years of Richard II. These were small, short-lived vessels whose growing importance in the English merchant fleet was due mainly to the fact that they were cheap to build and offered some prospect of a return even if half the year was spent in the service of the King. The more robust of them could be used for commercial service, like the *Maudelayne*, which Chaucer's shipman traded 'from Grootland to the cape of Finistère' and in 'every creek in Brittany and Spain'. But their main value was that they could also be used for privateering expeditions against foreign cargo ships, an increasingly profitable alternative to trading. At the end of 1379 a commercial syndicate led by the rich Dartmouth shipowner John Hawley put together a small private war fleet of two sailing ships and five oared barges, which was commissioned to cruise off the south coast of England and western France. The system was extended and formalised in 1382 when the west country ports from Southampton to Bristol clubbed together to defend their coasts. These groups of naval entrepreneurs paid all their own costs in return for the spoil and the local proceeds of the tonnage and poundage duties. In the following year a similar deal, covering the Channel and the North Sea, was agreed with another commercial syndicate organised by the London ironmonger Robert Parys. For the government, privateers were cheap. But they had serious disadvantages. They were not amenable to strategic direction and were apt to embroil the King with neutral powers.[40]

In the longer term the solution was for the government to pay hire to English shipowners as it already did to foreign ones. After years of holding out against this reform, a hesitant step was taken in March 1380. Responding to the latest Parliamentary petition from the beleaguered shipowning community, Richard II agreed to pay them for the use of their ships at 3s 4d per ton per quarter from the day the vessel arrived at the designated assembly point. Even at that low rate the burden proved to be beyond the cash-strapped English government. Hire was discontinued in subsequent years and only reintroduced in 1385 at the even lower rate of 2s per ton. It would take many more years to remedy half a century of indifference to the plight of shipowners. In the meantime, as a naval power England spent its capital at home and looked for shipping abroad. Bayonne was an occasional source of fighting ships and seamen. Ships were regularly chartered by English agents in the Low Countries, generally for carrying horses. But even with these additions to England's naval strength the 'lift' of English fleets in the early 1380s was only about 4,000 fully equipped troops, about 1,000 less than it had been in the last years of Edward III and less than a third of the corresponding figure in the 1340s. The Admirals' officers succeeded in requisitioning only 123 English ships for Buckingham's army in 1380, the lowest point to which the merchant fleet sank in the late middle ages. Even this required a good deal of barrel-scraping. Some of the ships taken were as small as ten tons. The numbers were made up by chartering at great expense no fewer than 156 merchant ships in the Low Countries in the course of March and April, much the largest foreign contingent which had ever served in an English fleet.[41]

The original plan was to embark Buckingham's army at Plymouth and Dartmouth in May 1380 and sail directly for Brittany. This would probably have required more ships than the government could produce, even with the addition of chartered foreign tonnage. But in the event it proved to be impractical for other reasons. On 4 February 1380 the Castilian ambassador in France, Pedro Lopez de Ayala (also one of the principal chroniclers of his time), had sealed a new naval treaty with Charles V. This provided for the Castilians to furnish France with a fleet of twenty galleys with a total complement of 4,600 seamen and soldiers, more than twice the squadron which had served in previous years. The treaty also envisaged the possibility that the Castilian vessels might over-winter in French ports, instead of returning to their home bases, thus considerably extending the campaigning season. When the news of these arrangements reached England in the second half of April, the Council lost its nerve. Their confidence had been undermined by the fate of John of Arundel's fleet. They were afraid that Buckingham's transports might be dispersed by bad weather on the passage and its scattered fractions picked off by the more agile galleys of Castile. So they resolved to carry the army in relays to Calais instead. This meant that Buckingham would have to reach Brittany by the long land route round the north and east of Paris. It also meant switching the port of embarkation to Sandwich and postponing it while the ships were repositioned. These difficulties, which would delay the army's arrival in Brittany by more than three months, must have provoked a fresh round of reflection about England's strategic vulnerability at sea. They were among the main reasons for a sudden revival of English interest in Portugal.[42]

Of all Castile's unequal relationships with its neighbours, none was more problematical than the relationship with Portugal. Henry of Trastámara had twice humiliated Portugal by force of arms. The country had for practical purposes been a client of Castile ever since the treaty of Santarém in 1373. Don Fernando had accepted his diminished status with apparent good grace but inward fury, a difficult pretence for this impulsive and unstable ruler to maintain. The Portuguese King was discreetly rearming throughout this period. The walls of Lisbon and the citadel of San Jorge, whose dilapidated state had proved to be his greatest weakness in 1373, had been entirely rebuilt. An ambitious programme of fortification was undertaken in the main provincial towns and castles. Much attention was devoted to the organisation of Portugal's military nobility and urban levies. Ordinances were issued for their re-equipment along the lines of the French troops, whose service in Henry of Trastámara's armies had made such an impression on the Portuguese. From 1377 the maritime towns were encouraged with commercial and fiscal privileges to build ocean-going ships which would be available to the King for naval service in wartime, concentrating on the largest ships of 100 tons burden or more. Twelve of these ships were built for the King's own account in addition to his fleet of specialised war galleys. Don Fernando was waiting for the chance to use them.

The death of Henry of Trastámara in May 1379 changed many things. His son and successor was a very different kind of man. Twenty-two years old at his accession, John of Trastámara was morbidly religious and introspective, somewhat unsure of himself and subject to frequent and debilitating bouts of illness. He was surrounded by his father's ministers and advisers and remained loyal to his father's policies, but he had none of his father's iron determination and few of his skills as a military commander. Within days of his accession Fernando cast off the mask. He withdrew the five Portuguese galleys which were being fitted out for service with the Castilians in the Channel. Then, without consulting his council, he began to devise plans for reviving the ill-fated Anglo-Portuguese alliance of 1372 and making war on his neighbour with English assistance.[43]

There was more to Portuguese policy in these years than opportunism and a frustrated desire for revenge. Don Fernando, then aged thirty-five, had been afflicted for a number of years with a severe wasting disease which seems to have been a form of tuberculosis. His illness intermittently deprived him of control over the affairs of his kingdom and concentrated the minds of those about him on the succession. The King's only legitimate child was a daughter, Beatrice, born in 1373. His will designated her as his successor and appointed the Queen, Leonora de Teles, as regent until she was of age. But the prospects of both mother and daughter once Don Fernando was dead were extremely uncertain. Leonora was an ambitious, manipulative and grasping parvenue who was no more popular now than she had been when her marriage to the King had provoked riots in the streets of Lisbon. As for Beatrice, she was a child of seven of whom little was known. She had been betrothed to a bastard of Henry of Trastámara, Don Fadrique, since she was three. She faced formidable rivals in Don Fernando's half-brothers, the Infante João and his younger brother Dinis. These two princes were the sons of King Pedro I's tragic second marriage to Inez de Castro.* Dinis had lived in exile in Castile under the protection of the Trastámaran court for years and the Infante João would shortly be forced to join him there. João was a kingly figure, then in his late twenties, with a strong following among the Portuguese nobility and the Lisbon mob. The one constant theme of Don Fernando's inconstant final years was the determination of the Queen to find a protector with the strength to assure Beatrice's succession and to support her own position as regent. On the face of it the obvious answer was a dynastic alliance with Trastámaran Castile. There would have been some support for this among the Portuguese aristocracy and the higher clergy. But it would have been personally repellent to Don Fernando and risked provoking a civil war upon his death. S. Fernando and Leonora persuaded themselves that an alliance with an English prince might provide another way of securing Beatrice's inheritance while conserving the independence of Portugal from its larger neighbour.[44]

In the autumn of 1379 the Portuguese King had made contact with his old favourite Juan Fernández Andeiro, the Galician adventurer who had negotiated the Anglo-Portuguese treaties of 1372 and 1373. Andeiro was now living in exile in the Duke of Lancaster's household in England. Fernando suggested to him that he should use his influence with the Duke to persuade him to bring an English army to Portugal. It was probably at the same time that Fernando first mooted the possibility of a marriage between Beatrice and the seven year-old son of Edmund Langley, Earl of Cambridge. Andeiro took up the Portuguese King's proposal with enthusiasm. It seems likely that his first approach was met with either rejection or evasion. The Duke of Lancaster had been losing interest in the Iberian peninsula for some time. His claim to the Castilian throne must by now have been recognised in England for the grave political blunder that it was, and John of Gaunt himself had done little to further it since 1374. Geraud de Menta in Barcelona was

---

* Inez de Castro's life is one of the great medieval romances. She was the illegitimate daughter of a Galician nobleman, who came to Portugal as a lady-in-waiting of Don Fernando's mother, Constance of Castile. She became the mistress of Don Fernando's father, the future Pedro I, and secretly married him after Constance's death. In 1355 she was murdered on the orders of Pedro's father, Alfonso IV, after Pedro had refused to abandon her. Something of Inez's beauty can be seen in the exquisite limestone tomb which stands close to Pedro's own in the Cistercian church of Alcobaça, north of Lisbon.

actively trying to settle the dispute between England and the Trastámaran dynasty. Peter IV of Aragon, who was John of Trastámara's father-in-law, had offered to act as mediator. In March 1380 Peter approached the King of Castile with a veiled proposal, apparently endorsed by John of Gaunt and Richard II's Council, that the Lancastrian claim should be dropped in return for peace between England and Castile and the abandonment of Castile's military alliance with France.[45]

Early in 1380 Andeiro was instructed to carry the English response back to the Portuguese King. The text has not survived, but whatever its terms it caused Don Fernando to conclude that there was no alternative to a dynastic match with Castile. Fernando, whose health was now visibly declining, could not afford to wait for the slow evolution of Lancastrian foreign policy. In about April 1380 he let it be known that he would be willing to cancel Beatrice's betrothal to Don Fadrique and to promise her instead to John of Trastámara's six-month-old son and heir Henry. On 21 May 1380 the two kings concluded a treaty in which it was agreed that Beatrice would be married to Henry as soon as they were both of age. What was envisaged was nothing less than the union of Portugal and Castile within a generation. The point was driven home by another provision. If Beatrice should die before the marriage was solemnised, leaving Don Fernando with no other heir of his body, John of Trastámara himself would succeed him as King of Portugal. The unspoken bargain was that the King of Castile would connive in the exclusion of the children of Inez de Castro from the Portuguese throne.[46]

Meanwhile English attitudes were undergoing a fundamental change. John of Trastámara rejected the King of Aragon's attempt at mediation and ratified the naval treaty with France. Frenetic preparations for a naval campaign against England were in progress in the arsenal of Seville and the port of Santander in the spring of 1380. A Portuguese alliance began to look more attractive in English eyes. Portugal was a significant naval power with a galley fleet which was as large as Castile's even if it was not as professionally managed. A war between Castile and Portugal could be expected to detain the Castilian fleet far from the Channel. And even if it did not, the galleys would have to make their way from headland to headland up the hostile Portuguese coast for more than 500 miles in order to get from their base in Seville to the Bay of Biscay. In a short time John of Gaunt moved from a position of resigned indifference to the affairs of the Iberian peninsula to one of energetic enthusiasm. According to the chronicler Thomas Walsingham, a prejudiced but well-informed source, it was Gaunt who pressed on Richard II's councillors the value of a Portuguese alliance as a means of parrying the naval threat from Castile. Like most later historians contemporaries probably assumed that he had his own interests in mind as much as England's. There was something in this. With the Navarrese passes now firmly closed to English armies, a Portuguese alliance would open up another route into Castile which could transform John of Gaunt's claim from a legal abstraction to a serious strategic venture. His obsession with what came to be known as the 'path of Portugal' became one of the dominant themes in English political discussion about the war. In late May 1380, at about the time that Don Fernando's representatives were sealing their agreements with John of Trastámara, Juan Fernández Andeiro was told to return to Portugal, this time with a more accommodating message, an armed escort and extensive diplomatic powers on behalf of both Richard II and John of Gaunt.[47]

Andeiro conducted his mission in the cloak and dagger fashion which became him. No one wanted to see a repetition of the debacle of 1372, when the Anglo-Portuguese alliance had been prematurely disclosed and Castile had launched a pre-emptive invasion before help could arrive from England. So Andeiro discreetly disembarked at Oporto in the north of the kingdom and made his way unannounced to the thirteenth-century fortress of Estremoz in eastern Alemtejo, where the King and Queen were staying. Here he was received in the utmost secrecy and accommodated in their private apartments while the business was discussed. Andeiro's mission was as successful as John of Gaunt could have wished. No doubt much of this was due to the ambassador's natural persuasiveness. But it seems likely that the main reason for his success was the influence which he acquired over Queen Leonora. Those who knew of their relations 'kept their thoughts to themselves', wrote the well-informed fifteenth-century chronicler Fernão Lopes. There is little doubt that during his short stay at Estremoz Andeiro made the Queen his mistress. On 15 July 1380 the Portuguese King renewed the Anglo-Portuguese treaty of June 1373. At the same time he entered into a number of additional agreements. These were crudely drafted documents leaving many matters undefined. They bear all the marks of a private negotiation conducted without any of the usual legal and bureaucratic assistance. Beatrice, who had been betrothed successively to three Castilian princes in her short life, was now promised to the seven-year-old son of the Earl of Cambridge. The

Earl was to come in person to Portugal bringing with him his son and an army of 2,000 men, which the Portuguese King undertook to pay at the usual English rates for three months. Andeiro had obviously been told not to promise more than England's resources of shipping could perform. It was therefore agreed that they would come without horses or bulky equipment, which Fernando would provide for them at reasonable prices when they arrived. The Portuguese King and the Earl of Cambridge would then mount a joint invasion of Castile in the name of John of Gaunt.[48]

Andeiro and Fernando set about covering his return to England with a theatrical gesture. The ambassador travelled secretly to the river port of Leiria, north of Lisbon, and announced himself to local officials as if he had just arrived by sea. The King then ordered his arrest, had him pulled from his bed in a local hostelry and pretended to expel him from his dominions on pain of death. To reassure the Castilians Fernando sent his ambassadors before the Castilian Cortes, which was about to meet at Soria. There they solemnly confirmed the betrothal of Beatrice and the Infante Henry which the Portuguese King had already committed himself to repudiate. Don Fernando's council were not let into the secret until after Andeiro had left Portugal. It was probably in September 1380 that the King summoned them to the castle of Santarém, the scene of his humiliation at the hands of Henry of Trastámara in 1373. He told them that it was time to get even with Castile and disclosed the substance of the arrangements which he had made with the English. The councillors were aghast. They demanded time for reflection. When they reconvened after three days of discussion they were unanimous in their opposition. All of them had sworn to honour the treaties with Castile, as indeed Don Fernando himself had done. Castile, they said, was a much stronger kingdom than Portugal. It had prevailed over stronger kings than Don Fernando. His last alliance with the English had been followed by a Castilian invasion from which Portugal had only recently recovered. All of this was sound advice. But Don Fernando brushed it aside. He had not asked them, he said, whether to make war on Castile but only how to do it.[49]

Amid the alarms of the summer of 1380 the death of one of the greatest soldiers that France had produced caused barely a ripple in the strategic calculations of each side. In the spring Bertrand du Guesclin left to take up his appointment as Captain-General in Languedoc. On his way south he paused to lay siege to a company of *routiers* occupying the castle of

Châteauneuf-de-Randon in the Gevaudan. While he was there he contracted dysentery and died on 13 July. It was an inglorious end. His body, unskilfully embalmed by local apothecaries, was borne through the mountains of Auvergne, drawing crowds of the curious and the star-struck on the way. His bones were eventually brought across the Beauce and the Île de France only days before the same regions were wasted by the army of the Earl of Buckingham. They were laid to rest by the King's order next to the place in the abbey church of Saint-Denis which Charles had appointed for his own tomb.[50]

The Earl of Buckingham's army, with its horses, equipment, wagons and stores was laboriously ferried in relays across the Channel from Sandwich to Calais in the course of June and July 1380. The Castilian galley fleet arrived too late to interfere. They did not reach La Rochelle until 8 July and were obliged to pause there for several days for orders and supplies. Then, as they made their way round the Breton peninsula with their small escort of French ships, they were blown off course by a storm and driven onto the Irish coast near Kinsale. As a result it was not until the end of July that they arrived at the principal French naval base at Harfleur. Whether the outcome would necessarily have been different if they had arrived earlier is not at all clear. The French tended to regard seapower mainly as an instrument of economic attrition and strategic retaliation. The Castilian captains' orders from the outset had been to devastate the Channel Islands and the Isle of Wight and to burn English coastal towns, not to engage the English fleet or to co-ordinate their operations with the army on land. On 24 July 1380 all twenty galleys, accompanied by five smaller oared ships fitted out by the French, sailed out of Harfleur on the first of a series of hit-and-run raids in the English Channel. A prisoner who had been captured at sea and then escaped brought the news to England just as the last of Buckingham's troops and horses were being unloaded at Calais.[51]

In the last few days of July 1380 the Castilians and their French auxiliaries landed in Sussex, in Rye Bay, burned Winchelsea and moved up the Rother valley, destroying a large number villages on the way. Although the English had had several months' warning the defences failed completely. The Earl of Arundel, who was the local commander in Sussex, commandeered some ships and tried in vain to attack the raiders from the sea. The Abbot of Battle, who had successfully defended Winchelsea in 1377, arrived with his troops too late and was put to flight.[52] After returning to resupply their ships in the Seine the

Castilians launched a second raid in the last week of August. This time they entered the Thames estuary and penetrated upriver as far as Gravesend, within twenty miles of London. They boarded two ships lying in the river, pillaged some cargoes of cloth and did a great deal of damage on both the Kent and Essex shores. In London there was an outburst of indignant patriotism. The aldermen arrayed their men in the streets. A pair of stone towers was ordered to be built downstream of the Tower, one on either side of the river, from which chains could be stretched across the water to stop enemy ships. John Philpot, the wealthy London grocer and one of the dominant figures of the city's politics, indulged his own brand of demagogic capitalism, lending £1,000 to the government's rapidly draining war chest and paying for one of the two defensive towers out of his own pocket.[53]

When the French government came to review the naval operations of this year they concluded that they had got poor value for money from the Castilians. In terms of spoil this was true. The declared yield was only about 2,000 francs (£333). The galleys were said to have been small and old. Their endurance had proved to be only about two weeks before it was necessary to return to their bases to take on supplies. There was therefore time for only two raids before they had to leave for Castile to avoid the winter gales. The French ministers complained about the long transit times between France and Castile and the short period of service in the Channel. It compared unfavourably, they said, with the record of the Genoese fleets employed by Philip VI and John II a generation earlier. The idea of over-wintering the fleet in the north, which had been canvassed with Ayala in Paris in February, came to nothing. The strategic benefit, however, was greater than the French realised. The mere threat of a Castilian fleet had forced Buckingham to take a long and circuitous route to Brittany instead of the direct crossing by sea, and would shortly lead England into an expensive and ultimately fruitless adventure in Portugal. The raids on the south and east coasts provoked angry protests in Parliament and in the longer term accelerated the trend in England towards a more defensive strategy. These were substantial advantages.[54]

Moreover they were achieved at minimal cost. The French King had agreed to pay half the operating costs of the Castilian fleet, which came to just 62,000 francs (about £10,000). By comparison the great sums invested over the years in building up an indigenous war fleet in the arsenal at Rouen brought him hardly any return at all. The Admiral, Jean de Vienne, has acquired a historic reputation as the architect of

French naval power which is hardly borne out by the facts. In spite of their excellent repair facilities the French were no better at maintaining their fleet in good condition than the English. In the previous year they had built seven new oared barges in the arsenal at Rouen but allowed eight more to rot away in lay-up at Harfleur. There were only five serviceable French galleys in 1380, most of which were fitted out at their own cost by the seamen of Harfleur. The arsenal had only one seaworthy vessel to offer. Among the naval powers of the fourteenth century it was only the southern Europeans, Venice and Genoa and the Italian-trained navies of the Iberian peninsula, who really understood the importance of continuous maintenance and knew how to organise galley fleets efficiently.[55]

The Earl of Buckingham was already marching through France when the Castilian raids struck England. He had finally set foot in Calais on 19 July 1380 and raised his standard at the edge of the pale three days later on the 22nd. A forward company commanded by Sir Thomas Percy had already secured the first major river crossing on the army's route, sixty miles away at Cléry on the Somme west of Péronne. The main body of the army set out across the plain of Artois and Picardy, where abandoned fields, burned out buildings and fortified church-towers testified to thirty years of continual raid and counter-raid. Buckingham, says Froissart, had never previously been in France unless his two brief visits to Brittany counted. He was curious to see the powerful walled towns of the war zone, with their thickets of bell-towers, their walls built up with timber outworks bristling with archers and men-at-arms and great fortified gateways of a kind which was only just beginning to be seen in England. In the first few days of August the English army crossed the Somme and headed south-east towards Champagne, following much the same route as Robert Knolles had done in 1370 and John of Gaunt in 1373.[56]

The French King's ministers were initially taken by surprise. The English had closed their ports since early May to prevent reports of Thomas of Woodstock's preparations from reaching the continent. As a result the French were still expecting the main landings to occur in Brittany. Even after the first companies landed at Calais, it was thought to be no more than a diversionary raid. Enguerrand de Coucy was sent to the Somme to contain it. The true scale of the English operation did not become apparent until the arrival of Buckingham himself. Overall direction of the defence was then passed to the Duke of Burgundy. He was appointed Captain-General of all French forces in France. In early August, as soon as his army was strong enough, Burgundy set out in pursuit. Both sides employed the strategy which had become familiar from past English *chevauchées* in France. The French garrisoned the towns and defensible castles in the invaders' path. The open country was emptied of valuables, animals and consumable stores and the population herded into the walled places. The English burned crops and villages for miles around and conducted demonstrations in front of the walls in the hope of provoking a battle. But the French refused to be drawn. At first the Duke of Burgundy's army, at about 3,000 men, was much smaller than Buckingham's. It followed the English cavalcade at a cautious distance on parallel courses in two divisions, one on each flank, preventing the enemy from foraging for supplies, picking off stragglers and isolated companies, but avoiding all engagements with the main body of the enemy. The English were passing through some of the richest landscapes of France but they had great difficulty in replenishing their stores. They marched in disciplined ranks and battle order. Froissart thought this admirable, but the truth was that they had no choice.[57]

The familiar story of destruction and ruin is traced in the records of the towns and churches of Picardy. After the whirlwind had passed by, the Benedictine monks of Mont-Saint-Quentin left their refuge behind the walls of Péronne to survey the damage. The English army had advanced across a front at least twenty-five miles wide, leaving in their wake barns, farmhouses, mills and bakehouses reduced to burned-out stumps. Hundreds of acres of prime farmland were wasted so completely that it was years before tenants could be found for them. Villages had been abandoned by their inhabitants which would not be reoccupied for a generation. When the English army reached the open plain of Champagne they took to demanding food from walled towns as the price of leaving the villages around untouched. There was no response, and the destruction continued unabated. The smoke rising from sixty villages whose inhabitants had taken refuge in Reims failed to persuade the city to send out supplies. As the English marched on, the scale of the destruction mounted. In mid-August the town of Vertus was reduced to a charred waste as the inhabitants looked on from the walls of the citadel, the second time in a generation that this had happened to them. The fine suburban properties which they destroyed included the home and vineyards of the courtier and poet Eustache Deschamps. All that he had there was 'burned and charred, captured or destroyed'.[58]

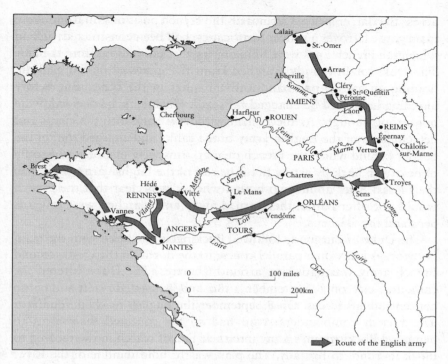

15 The Earl of Buckingham's campaign in France, August 1380–May 1381

On the evening of 24 August 1380, after four weeks on the march, the Earl of Buckingham's army forded the Seine and arrived before the walls of Troyes, the cathedral city at the southern edge of the great chalk plain of Champagne. The Duke of Burgundy had crammed all his troops into the city. With him were Enguerrand de Coucy, the Dukes of Bar and Lorraine, a Marshal and the Admiral of France and a host of famous knights. The Dukes of Berry and Bourbon joined them there with reinforcements from the central provinces. The total strength of the French army had by now risen to about 4,000 with more reported to be on the way. The French leaders were under strong pressure from their men to fight the invaders. They had sent a messenger to the King to seek his permission to offer battle. In the English camp expectations were high. That night an order of battle was agreed between the captains. New knights were made from ambitious squires and bannerets from knights. The sun rose on the following morning, 25 August, to reveal the English army drawn up in three broad lines of men-at-arms with the archers stationed behind them, all advancing slowly on foot

389

across the flat, empty plain towards the French positions. In front of the main gate of Troyes a timber fortification had been constructed, behind which the French lines were filling up as men poured out from the city. The Duke of Burgundy watched from the gateway in full armour, holding an axe in one hand and a banner in the other. But before anything happened he changed his mind. His forces, he decided, were not strong enough. As the French withdrew back into the city, some detachments of the English army broke ranks and charged the timber barrier behind which the French men-at-arms were manoeuvring, only to be driven back by arrow fire. The rest of the English army waited in their lines. After about two hours, when it was clear that the French would not offer battle, they turned away and marched west towards Sens and the Gâtinais.[59]

The Duke of Burgundy followed Buckingham's march with the main body of his army on a parallel course to the north. In the west a second French army was gathering around Chartres. The Duke entered the cathedral city on 6 September 1380 and paused for a few days to concentrate his forces. On 8 September the English reached Vendôme. The French commanders, who had so far confined themselves to hemming Buckingham's army into their line of march, now resolved to block its route to Brittany. The plan was to hold the line of the River Sarthe, then a broad and fast-flowing river with few fords or bridges. During the following days the bulk of the French army crossed the Sarthe at Le Mans to take up their positions on the west bank. These manoeuvres were still in progress when, on 14 September, the news arrived that the King had suffered what appears to have been a severe heart attack on the previous night. Two days later he was dead at the age of forty-four. The final act of Buckingham's campaign was destined to be played out against a background of mounting political crisis in Paris.[60]

'When great men die everything changes,' wrote Christine de Pisan. Like many of her contemporaries she would one day look back on the death of Charles V as 'the gateway to all our later misfortunes'. The King had died at the royal manor of Beauté overlooking the Marne east of Paris. The body was brought back to Paris for burial and remained for a week in the abbey church of St. Antoine by the eastern gate of the capital while the royal dukes, Anjou, Berry, Burgundy and Bourbon gathered. The new King, Charles VI, was a little less than twelve years old when his father died, slightly younger than his distant English cousin Richard II. He had passed the whole of his short life amid the public rituals of the French court, seen by thousands but observed by none. Physical strength, a sunny temperament and a precocious interest in hunting, armour and weaponry are the only personal characteristics of the young Charles VI which are known. Everything else is obscured by the conventions of princely life and the overbearing presence of his father, uncles, tutors and household officers. As yet he was little more than a symbol of authority.[61]

The dead King had given much thought to the government of France during a minority. Yet, when the time came, he bequeathed a poisonous legacy to his son. In August 1374, shortly after his health had begun to fail, Charles had issued an ordinance fixing the age of majority of the kings of France at thirteen, as compared with the traditional age of fourteen for kings and twenty for noblemen. The King cited thirteen as the 'age of discretion' and recalled the example of Louis IX, who was said to have taken the government of the realm into his hands at that age. But his real motive was his fear of a regency and the uncertainty and instability that went with it. A series of ordinances followed in the autumn of 1374 whose main object was to achieve a carefully contrived balance of power within his family. Louis of Anjou, the oldest of his brothers, was to be Regent, while the Dukes of Burgundy and Bourbon were to act jointly as the young King's guardians and tutors. In principle the Regent was to have all the powers of the Crown. But the revenues of the royal demesne in Paris, Normandy and the Île de France were to be assigned to the King's two guardians to pay the expenses of his household, while the other public revenues of the realm were reserved for meeting the cost of administration and defence. The late King's favourite, Bureau de la Rivière, was given a pivotal role in the new regime. He was the principal executor of the late King's will. He was to serve as First Chamberlain to the new King until he came of age. Nothing of importance affecting the young Charles VI or his brother Louis was to be decided without his approval. He was also given custody of the King's personal treasury. These complex arrangements called for a degree of co-operation between the late King's brothers and ministers of which they were no longer capable. They were also completely unsuitable for a nation at war.[62]

The obsequies of the dead King took place over three days between 24 and 26 September 1380. The four royal dukes followed the coffin through the streets of Paris from Notre-Dame to Saint-Denis and stood at the grave in the abbey church, next to the one which had recently been made for Bertrand du Guesclin. In a world where symbols sometimes counted more than facts the burial of a king conventionally marked the true end of his reign. As soon as the ceremony was over the survivors fell to quarrelling over the spoils of power with a fury intensified by the suppressed jealousies and antagonisms of the previous reign. The Duke of Anjou, still smarting from his disgrace earlier in the year, relished the chance of power too much to accept the limitations placed on him by his dead brother. The Duke of Burgundy claimed precedence at public ceremonies as the first peer of France, the Duke of Anjou as the senior member of the royal family. Their retinues almost came to blows on a famous occasion when the two men tried to sit in the same seat next to the King. The Dukes of Burgundy and Bourbon, supported by the Duke of Berry, claimed to be entitled as the King's guardians to appoint his principal officers while the Duke of Anjou claimed the same right as Regent. This issue quickly came to a head since it was necessary to choose a Constable to succeed Bertrand du Guesclin, an urgent item of business with an English army marching through France. Before his illness Charles V had decided on Bertrand's fellow Breton and long-standing brother-in-arms, Olivier de Clisson. But his appointment was only confirmed after a bruising row between the King's uncles. Finally there was the delicate status of the Duke of Berry, who had been regarded by the late King as a political incompetent and ostentatiously excluded from any part in the minority. He was bent on obtaining a place in the councils of the realm in keeping with his rank. As for Bureau de la Rivière, he was brushed aside. Years of whispering in the late King's ear had won him too many enemies. The royal dukes regarded him as a manipulative upstart. The Duke of Berry cordially loathed him.[63]

These apparently trivial disputes were based on more than personal animosity and wounded pride. Behind them lay the opportunities which the death of the single-minded Charles V had opened up for his three brothers. All of them had personal ambitions which depended to a greater or lesser degree on their being able to lay hands on the resources of the French Crown. The Duke of Berry wanted to be lieutenant in Languedoc, an appointment which, when added to his appanage in Berry and Poitou and his existing lieutenancy in Auvergne, would give him the resources of about a third of France. The Duke of Burgundy was constantly looking over his shoulder at Flanders, destined to be his wife's inheritance and the main pillar of his own fortune. However, the most ambitious and destructive of the royal dukes' personal ventures was, characteristically, the Duke of Anjou's. For some months Anjou had been secretly negotiating to acquire the succession to the Kingdom of Sicily, the latest of his many attempts to find a realm of his own. The Kingdom of Sicily was the name given to the great southern Italian territory ruled by the descendants of Louis IX's brother Charles of Anjou, although Sicily itself had not formed part of their domains for a hundred years and the kingdom was ruled from Naples. The Queen, Jeanne of Anjou, still childless at fifty-three in spite of her four marriages, had been gravely weakened by the divisions in Italy which followed the papal schism. Her steadfast support for the Avignon Pope had exhausted her treasury and cost her a good deal of support among her subjects. It had also naturally earned her the venomous hostility of Urban VI, who set about destroying her.

In the autumn of 1379 Urban found a formidable champion in the royal house of Hungary. In the longer term the engagement of the Hungarian dynasty in the affairs of southern Italy was to be a fateful step for the papacy. But at the time its advantages seemed more obvious than its disadvantages. Hungary was the most powerful and expansive state of eastern Europe. The King, Louis the Great, was himself descended from a cadet branch of the Angevins of Naples and had for some time had designs in Italy. His armies had recently penetrated into northern Italy, where they had conquered the region of Friuli from the Venetian Republic. Louis of Hungary was no friend of Jeanne of Anjou. His brother had been her first husband and the effective ruler of her kingdom until he was murdered with her connivance in 1345. He resolved to overthrow her. Louis's chosen instrument was his cousin Charles of Durazzo, a young man of twenty-five who had been brought up at Jeanne's court and was married to her niece but had made his career in Louis's service. Charles was then in north-eastern Italy, where he was serving as the King of Hungary's captain and viceroy. He was a skilful diplomat, a cunning and ruthless politician and an effective military commander as well as a natural focus of loyalty for Jeanne's many domestic enemies. Urban VI offered to transfer the crown of Naples to him if Louis of Hungary would provide him with the troops to conquer it. By early 1380 the deal seems to have been done.

In Avignon Clement VII responded by turning to the Duke of Anjou. Clement had everything to gain by tempting the house of France into Italy. French intervention in the peninsula offered the only prospect of dislodging his adversary on his home territory. Negotiations began in January 1380 and by June had resulted in an agreement in which Jeanne adopted Louis as her son and declared him heir to all her dominions in southern Italy and Provence. In return Louis undertook to arm a small squadron of war galleys at his own expense for the defence of Naples and, if her dominions were invaded, to help her with troops and money. Even with the generous subsidies promised by Clement VII these undertakings were far beyond Louis's personal resources. They proved to be the beginning of a long and costly entanglement of the French state in Italy which would last in one form or another until the middle of the sixteenth century.[64]

Immediately after the funeral of Charles V the late King's brothers met in the palace on the Île de la Cité in the presence of a great gathering of courtiers, prelates, officials and lawyers. Their spokesmen traded demands. Cabals were formed. Gossip began to spread through the city. No decision was reached. On about 28 September it was finally agreed to submit their disputes to a body of arbitrators. The arbitrators devised a solution which was untidy but probably the best available. It was decided to declare the young King to be of age and to have him crowned at Reims at once. It was not of course anticipated that he would actually govern. The declaration of majority was simply a legal device for bringing all of Charles V's arrangements for the regency to an end and terminating Bureau de la Rivière's authority over the royal household and treasury. Instead the four royal dukes agreed to partition the government among themselves. The Duke of Anjou would continue to call himself Regent while the Dukes of Burgundy and Bourbon would continue to act as the King's guardians. Anjou was to have the day-to-day conduct of the government and control of all the financial resources of the Crown which were not required for the upkeep of the King's household. But all important decisions would be made by the four royal dukes jointly with the assistance of a council of up to twelve others chosen by them. It was probably part of this deal that the Duke of Berry should have the lieutenancy of Languedoc, for the appointment was announced shortly afterwards. These awkward compromises did little to calm the ill will between the strong personalities involved. Within days of the agreement the Duke of Anjou seized the personal treasure of the late King, consisting of plate and jewels in the Hôtel Saint-Pol and 200,000 francs in cash which had been lodged in the tower of Vincennes. Learning that there was more concealed in the castle of Melun, he forced the official responsible for its safe-keeping to disclose its whereabouts and took that too. Froissart says that he wanted the money to fund the defence of Naples, which may well be true. What is known is that for the next six weeks, until Anjou partially backed down, government business was paralysed as every council meeting was dominated by the furious demands of the Duke of Burgundy for its return. Part of it was never accounted for.[65]

The task of Charles V's successors would have been difficult in any circumstances, but he had left them another problem which was entirely unexpected even by his closest advisers. About two hours before his death Charles had decreed the abolition of the hearth tax and remitted all outstanding arrears. He had long been troubled by the growing signs of revolt against the weight of royal taxation and the legacy of disorder which he was storing up for his successor. But this was not an act of considered policy. It was the gesture of a frightened man who knew that he had little time left in which to efface the sins of power. The ambiguous record of his words suggests that if he had had his way he would have abolished the *aides* as well. But, even in the attenuated form represented by his ministers' drafting, the King's final act of personal expiation was a disaster from which the French state took three years to recover. The instrument was at first kept secret, but it was a valid act and in October the new government decided that it would have to be published. The news spread rapidly across France. Official copies were sent to all the main provincial centres. Unofficial rumour exaggerated the news elsewhere.[66]

The abolition of the hearth tax not only removed the most important single source of war finance. It gravely unbalanced the French tax system. The hearth tax, however imperfect, was the only direct tax. It represented the most effective means of reaching the pockets of the better-off and of the mass of the population residing in the countryside. Without it the government was almost entirely dependent on the two indirect taxes, the *aides* and the *gabelle du sel*. Both of them fell mainly on the populations of the towns, where most salt was consumed and where the wholesale markets for food and wine were located. They also bore heavily on the poorest members of the urban community, who spent a relatively high proportion of their income on food and drink. In many places it was believed that all taxes, direct and indirect alike, had been abolished. The public crier of Montpellier went through the streets announcing the end of the *gabelle*. In Nîmes there were processions to mark the end of all royal taxation. The Estates of Auvergne took the news of the dead King's ordinance as their excuse to reject all war taxes. In some of these places the wish was probably father of the thought. But when the truth became known there was a spontaneous and violent protest. The first signs of trouble occurred in the north. In the towns of

Picardy and the Île de France men rose up and threw out the collectors of the *aides*. At Compiègne and Saint-Quentin rioters took over the streets. At Saint-Denis the dead King had hardly been buried before mobs invaded the market-place and attacked the collectors of the *aides*. Tensions rose in Paris. Collection in most parts of France ground to a halt. In one of their first acts the Council resolved to summon the Estates-General of Languedoil to meet in the following month. They counted on the atmosphere of goodwill that would be generated by the coronation of his successor. With good management the assembly might be persuaded to re-grant at least part of the taxes abolished by Charles V.[67]

Meanwhile the King's treasury was bare. The French army abandoned its stations on the River Sarthe. Some companies melted away. The rest made their way, leaderless and confused, to Paris and encamped in the suburbs, demanding their pay, looting the villages and barns and the traffic on the roads and shouting support for one or other faction of the royal family. On 13 October 1380 Louis of Anjou disbanded the army and dismissed the men unpaid to their homes. The only organised forces now remaining under French command were a company of a few hundred men under the command of Olivier de Clisson and the scattered garrisons of Anjou and the Breton march.[68]

The English army was able to ford the Sarthe without opposition and crossed the swamps of the Mayenne, advancing west towards Brittany. In early October 1380 they entered the duchy south of the fortress-town of Vitré and moved slowly towards Rennes. Here they were surprised and vexed to find that no arrangements had been made to receive them. There was no Breton army with which to join forces. The towns closed their gates in Buckingham's face. John de Montfort, the ally whom Buckingham had come to support, was at Hennebont in the south-west of the peninsula. He seemed to be in no hurry to welcome Buckingham. The truth was that the death of Charles V had changed everything. The new government was unlikely to be as stiff-necked in its opposition to John de Montfort as Charles V and Bureau de la Rivière had been. John enjoyed reasonably good relations with the French royal dukes. The Duke of Anjou had been personally committed to finding a negotiated solution to the Breton problem since the previous October. Philip of Burgundy's wife was John's cousin and his father-in-law was John's principal protector. Now, charged with the government of France but without troops or money to defend it, the royal dukes had little choice but to do a deal with him. John's private preferences are not known. But he was under strong pressure from his baronial supporters to dispense with English military assistance and heal the breach with France. So he did as Charles of Navarre had so often done in his heyday. He used Buckingham's presence as a bargaining counter to help him strike a deal with the French and as an insurance against the possibility of failure.[69]

For the moment nothing could be done in Paris. The princes were too preoccupied with the struggle for power and the approaching coronation of the King. So John played for time. He sent Buckingham his excuses. He promised to meet him to discuss plans, but not yet. He travelled slowly. The English army passed most of October kicking their heels around Rennes, moving on every three or four days as they exhausted the supplies around them. It was not until the end of October 1380 that the two men finally met. The scene was the thirteenth-century fortress of Hédé, north of Rennes. John was suave and full of reassurance. After several days of forced conviviality Buckingham managed to pin him down to operational detail. It was agreed that in the next few days the English army would lay siege to Nantes. The city was of vital interest to both men, to John because it was one of the few places that was still refusing to admit his officers, to Buckingham because of its important bridge over the Loire. The English proposed to march on it at once. John would join them with his own army within two weeks of the opening of the siege. He also undertook to organise a fleet of armed barges in the Loire to prevent the city from being resupplied by river. But even as he discussed these things with the English commander John was preparing to double-cross him. In his private chamber in the citadel of Rennes he put his seal to a curious notarial act of a kind which he had more than once employed to ease his conscience before some gross breach of faith. In it the Duke recited all that he owed to the advice and support of the kings of England over the years, declaring to the notary and perhaps to posterity that if he were now to break his word to the English and strike a deal with the French it would only be because his hand had been forced.[70]

Three hundred miles away, on the morning of 4 November 1380, Charles VI of France was being anointed and crowned in the great Gothic cathedral of Reims, a spectacular ceremony sanctified by tradition, which he can only dimly have understood. The banquet which followed was interrupted by the arrival of three successive messengers from Brittany with the news that the English were marching on Nantes. The dukes and the military officers of the Crown discussed what to do

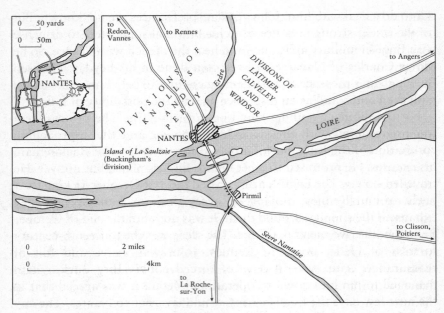

16 The siege of Nantes, November 1380–January 1381

amid the revelry and noise. There was a small garrison in the citadel of Nantes which was answerable to Olivier de Clisson but was certainly not large enough to fight off an assault alone. There were thought to be about 400 men available in garrisons of the Breton march. Two officers of the Duke of Bourbon who were present at the banquet were ordered to leave at once for the west to bring these men into the city before the English invested it. They did their work well. The first English troops reached Nantes on the morning of Sunday 4 November 1380. By the time that the rest of Buckingham's force arrived the French had put some 600 professional troops into the city.[71]

Nantes was a rich city, living well on the trade in wine and salt, which had suffered comparatively little from war damage. It was a difficult place to besiege. It had a powerful and complete circuit of walls. It was relatively compact, not much more than a thousand yards in circuit, which meant that it could be defended by a modest garrison with the support of the citizens. The town and the plain north of the walls were divided by the River Erdre. The Loire, then unembanked and more than a mile wide, was divided into fast-flowing branches running between a number of large islands. The Earl of Buckingham was obliged to divide his army around Nantes into three more or less independent forces.

Latimer, Calveley and Sir William Windsor encamped on the eastern side of the town. Knolles and Percy covered the west beyond the Erdre. The Earl himself occupied La Saulzaie, an inhabited island in the Loire directly opposite the river gate of the town. None of these divisions were in a position to reinforce each other quickly in the event of an attack and even with 5,000 men they were unable to seal off the whole city. At the outset of the siege the Earl sent a hurried appeal to England for reinforcements. He said that he needed at least 2,000 more men urgently. While the Council struggled to provide them, his operations depended on the promises of the Duke of Brittany. But John de Montfort was nowhere to be seen. The Earl sent him a stream of messages, none of which was answered. In Paris the newly crowned King made his *joyeuse entrée* into the capital on 11 November, welcomed by ecstatic crowds and by innumerable petitioners waiting for the ordinary business of government to resume. Among the petitioners were the ambassadors of the Duke of Brittany. As soon as the festivities were over they agreed an indefinite truce with the French royal Council. On 19 November 1380 John de Montfort appointed four prominent noblemen, all of them associated with the Breton league of the previous year, to negotiate in the utmost secrecy a permanent settlement with the Regent.[72]

John's hand was strengthened by the developing financial crisis of the French government. On 14 November 1380 the Estates-General of Languedoil met for the first time since 1369 in the palace on the Île de la Cité. The four royal dukes presided impassively as the Chancellor, Mile de Dormans, outlined the government's dire financial situation. The proceedings of the assembly are poorly documented and its decisions are difficult to reconstruct from the terse formulae of the closing ordinances and the misleading gossip of the chroniclers. But some common themes emerge from all the national and provincial assemblies which would meet during the first year of the new reign to grapple with the problems of war finance. It was generally accepted that financial assistance to the Crown in time of war was an obligation of every subject. The complaints were not so much about the principle of war taxation as about the way in which Charles V had transformed the grants of the 1360s into permanent taxes. The assemblies were determined to re-establish the principle that taxation was not a prerogative of the Crown. It was a grant from its subjects, made for a limited period and subject to review and to the redress of their grievances. The real division was between the majority which accepted that the current crisis justified a grant of taxation and a small but powerful minority which considered that in its present state France could bear no extraordinary taxation at all. They thought, like the Parliamentary opposition in England, that the King should be compelled to live off the ordinary revenues of his demesne. The leaders of this group were the city of Paris, which traditionally dominated the deliberations of the third estate. They were supported by a powerful caucus of the nobility. However, before the Estates-General could reach a conclusion, the issue was taken out of their hands by the Paris mob.[73]

In spite of war and plague Paris was as populous at the end of the fourteenth century as it had been before the first outbreak of the Black Death. The new rampart of Charles V had roughly doubled the area of the city on the right bank of the Seine, enclosing ancient suburbs, allotments and vineyards and provoking a prolonged building boom. Apart from the cemeteries, the gardens of the monasteries and aristocratic mansions and the drained marshland still known as Marais, almost every available space within the walls was built over by 1380. Houses rose two, three and sometimes as many as six stories above tiny plots of ground, separated by dark and filthy lanes. Some 200,000 people lived in this place, one of the densest concentrations of humanity in Europe. Even in more ordered times Paris had always been an intensely political city. Its main business was government, as it always has been. Its economy was sustained, directly or indirectly, by the service of the King; the great noblemen and ecclesiastical princes who attended on him; and the judges, lawyers, administrators and courtiers who waxed rich on the business of the Crown. The King, the Dukes of Anjou, Berry, Burgundy, Bourbon and Brittany, the Counts of Alençon, Artois, Armagnac, Flanders, Hainault and Auvergne, a dozen other noblemen and nearly thirty bishops and abbots maintained their own palaces in the capital, some of them built and staffed on the grandest scale. These men were actors on a national stage. They were visible symbols of power, targets for social grievances and political complaint. More than a hundred bell-towers tolled the great occasions of the political and ecclesiastical calendar. Rumours and grievances magnified among the tightly packed residents of the alley tenements. Crowds quickly gathered in the few open spaces within the walls. The fortunes of war heightened public emotions, threatening the security of the city and interrupting the distant network of suppliers which fed its immense population. Sharp contrasts of wealth and poverty were all too obvious where slums grew up beside palaces, noblemen pushed through the crowds on horseback escorted by liveried outriders, and the fortunate of whatever origin exhibited their prosperity with coloured silks and jewellery and extravagant hats and shoes. In the 1380s a rising tide of migration into the city combined with economic contraction to produce high levels of unemployment among the mass of insecure journeymen and labourers and mounting class hostility among the poor and the young. Hard times made yesterday's workmen into today's mobsters, the carrion of tomorrow's gallows.

Charles V had passed more of his time in his capital than any of his predecessors, and the tumults of the 1350s had taught him the power of the mob. He had devoted much attention to the security of the city. The main agent of royal control in Paris was the Provost. The office was held from 1367 to 1381 by the formidable and authoritarian Hughes Aubriot, a self-made man of modest origins whose father had been a Dijon money-changer. He made a bigger difference to the appearance of the capital than any one man before Baron Haussmann and, like Haussmann, most of his acts were directed in one way or another to holding down the city of revolutions. He was responsible for a raft of ordinances and decrees regulating disorderly conduct, idleness, prostitution, taverns and gaming houses, and the bearing of arms in the streets. A reformed police force, consisting of 220 sergeants serving in shifts, was based at the Châtelet. Their efforts were supplemented by the sergeants employed by the various abbeys exercising criminal jurisdiction in the city, and at night by the watch, a militia drawn from the richer householders and organised by the city guilds in units of ten and fifty. But even in Aubriot's time the government had no way of confronting a serious outbreak of urban violence without raising an army to overawe the city from the outside. By the time of Charles V's death the city's defences, which Aubriot largely rebuilt, were directed as much against the inhabitants as any external enemy. The Louvre lay well within the new rampart but survived, rebuilt and enlarged as a garrisoned refuge, prison, treasury and arsenal. The towers of the Châtelet looked down on the butchers' quarter, famous to generations of Parisians as the home of its most violent mobs. Opposite, on the left bank, Aubriot had constructed a smaller urban fortress, the Petit Châtelet, to allow the authorities to seal off the riotous students of the university quarter of the left bank from the rest of the city. At the eastern edge of the city the intimidating mass of the Bastille Saint-Antoine, whose foundation stone had been laid in 1370 by Aubriot himself, was rising from its foundations.[74]

On the morning of 15 November 1380 a large crowd gathered in the Place de Grève to protest against the burden of war taxation. Many of them were wearing parti-coloured hoods and tunics of green and white, the city's colours. On the eastern side of this large open space stood the Maison aux Piliers, the seat of the Provost of the Merchants and the four *échevins*, a body drawn from the higher ranks of the Parisian guilds who over a period of more than a century had gradually come to assume the powers of a municipality. These men represented the aristocracy of the city's trades. Most of them had done well by the Crown's policies in the past two decades and their interests had been well satisfied by the abolition of the hearth tax. But their main concern in November 1380 was to preserve their own authority, caught as they were between the demands of the government and the anger of the masses. The Provost of the Merchants came to the front of the building to address the crowd. He tried to persuade them to disperse and leave the issue to their betters. He was greeted by a ferocious harangue from a leather-dresser in the crowd. This man inveighed not just against taxes but against the rich of the city and the conspicuous consumption of the royal court. 'Will we never see an end to the mounting greed of these lords?' this man asked according to the appalled chronicler of Saint-Denis. They 'feed off our goods, these people whose only thought is to decorate themselves with gold and jewellery, surround themselves with trains of flunkeys, put up superb palaces and devise fresh taxes with which to crush this city.' He finished with a call to arms. About 300 men surged forward with weapons in their hands. They seized the Provost of the Merchants and marched him across the bridge to the palace on the island, where the Estates-General was meeting. They invaded the courtyard and then the great hall, shouting their demands so that they could be heard by the young King and his four uncles, gathered in an upper room with their advisers and officials.

Whatever else might be said of the Duke of Anjou he did not lack courage. Accompanied by the Dukes of Berry and Burgundy, the Constable and the Chancellor, he entered the hall and confronted the mob. The Provost of the Merchants made a long speech. He described the misery and poverty of the population in graphic language. He called for an immediate end to war taxation. The Provost was a reluctant protester but he played his part well. A great roar of approval went up when he had finished. The Duke played for time. He told them that their case would be considered by the Council. The truth was that the Council was divided. Many of its members were concerned about the precedent which would be set by yielding to threats of violence. What would the mob demand next? Their doubts were silenced as the crowd outside grew larger and more menacing. The Chancellor emerged once more, this time to pronounce the abolition of the *fouage*, the *aides* and the *gabelle*. An ordinance confirming the decision was hastily prepared.

The Council's judgment of the mood of the mob was borne out by what followed. After the shouts of 'Noel!' and 'Montjoie! Saint-Denis!' came the cry 'Aux Juifs!' The main Jewish quarter of Paris lay on the right bank between the Place de Grève and the Châtelet, a district of narrow lanes and crowded tenements. The crowd streamed across the Pont aux Changeurs and invaded the Juiverie, killing Jews, forcibly baptising their children, wrecking their houses, tearing up loan books and carrying off jewellery and plate left as pledges. They were urged on from the streets outside by the young noblemen who were the Jews' main clients. The rest of the Île de France took their cue from Paris. As the news of these events spread across northern France, in one town after another the celebrations turned into pogroms against the Jews.[75]

The Council had no intention of accepting the situation. The abandonment of taxation was plainly not an option for a nation at war. They viewed their concessions as no more than a tactical retreat and greatly resented the threats by which they had been obtained. They resolved to try again, this time in stages. The Estates-General was reassembled and persuaded to agree to the principle of war taxation. But they were invited to consult their constituents about its exact form. On 17 November 1380, as the representatives returned to their homes, orders went out to all the *baillis* of northern France requiring them to convene local assemblies to consider the financial needs of the government away from the pressures of the Parisians. The idea was to set the provinces against the capital. Unfortunately the government had under-estimated the intensity of public hostility, which was by no means confined to the poor of Paris. In many towns of northern France the assessments were believed to have been distorted in favour of the wealthy mercantile elite and social resentments were as strong as anywhere. 'By God's Blood, the fur-hats never pay their due,' one man shouted through the streets of Sens. The government's cause was not helped by exaggerated reports about the size of the dead King's hoarded treasure and the widespread knowledge of the Duke of Anjou's thefts from it. The threat from England did not always seem to be a good answer to men who had never understood the logic of avoiding battle. In Normandy the assembly met in the archbishops' palace at Rouen on

10 December 1380. They were pressed by the King's commissioners with the urgent need to raise an army of 8,000 men against the English. The clerical contingent was stuffed with royal officials and the nobility with men had been prominent in the wars of the Cotentin and the Breton march. They urged their colleagues to accept a sales tax, if not at the traditional rate then at least at a reduced one. But the towns and a substantial part of the nobility would have none of it. 'Rien, rien!' they cried. If Normandy, with its close association with the Crown, could not be persuaded, there was not much chance of a better answer elsewhere. None of the local assemblies whose proceedings are recorded was prepared to make a grant. They all referred the decision back to the next meeting of the Estates-General.[76]

The representatives reassembled in Paris shortly before Christmas 1380. Their deliberations, which extended over about two weeks, are not recorded. But the outcome can be deduced from successive ordinances issued in the first three months of 1381. It was a firm reassertion of the principle of control over taxation by representative assemblies. The government had to submit to the abolition not just of the *fouages* covered by the dying declaration of Charles V but of the *aides*, the *gabelle* and all other taxes levied on the Crown's authority going back to the beginning of the century. In return the King was granted a war tax for a limited period of one year, starting from 1 March 1381, to cover the cost of a standing army of 4,000 men-at-arms and 2,000 crossbowmen. The precise basis of assessment was left to the Estates of each province to decide and might differ from one province to the next. The assessment and collection of the new tax, moreover, was to be left in the hands of local officers answerable to their own provincial assemblies and not to the King. These people were charged with ensuring that every penny collected was spent on the prosecution of the war and the cost of the King's household. Nothing was to be diverted into the pockets of the King's relations and ministers. The ordinances, if they had lasted, would have marked the dismantling of the system of national taxation devised by the ministers of John II and Charles V in the 1360s, which had been the foundation of France's military recovery. There would have been a reversion to the old system which had applied before 1360, when for practical purposes grants of the Estates-General had operated as decisions in principle only, to be followed by a wearing and time-consuming round of local negotiations. Few men outside the Chambre des Comptes can have recalled how far that process had paralysed successive French kings in every crisis. On

404

this occasion, even with a large English army besieging Nantes, it was to take more than two months to negotiate a variety of different regional taxes in several provincial cities with different groups of interested parties, each with their own grievances to be redressed, before any funds came into the Treasury. Some local assemblies insisted that the proceeds of local collections should be reserved not just for war expenditure but for particular kinds of war expenditure of specifically local concern. Thus the taxes of Champagne were earmarked for the defence of the northern frontier, opposite Calais and Flanders; and those of Normandy for the garrisons on the Cherbourg front. These concessions no doubt had to be made to get the tax grant through. Even so receipts must have fallen far short of the minimum required to defend the frontiers of France. The Estates-General of December 1380 marked the shift of power by insisting on the King's formal confirmation of the charters and liberties of every province of Languedoil. It was a symbolic act but an important one nonetheless. Most of these instruments dated back to the rebellions of 1314–15 which had followed the death of Philip the Fair. They were still remembered as the high-water mark of regional autonomy in France.[77]

By the end of 1380 England's financial and military resources were more tightly stretched than they had been at any time in the past forty years. In addition to the 5,000 English troops serving under the Earl of Buckingham in France, there were about 2,000 men distributed between the garrisons of Calais, Cherbourg and Brest, and another 1,000 in Gascony, making a total of about 8,000 men serving in France. The Council was also having to meet growing demands for troops at home. A deteriorating situation in Ireland had made it necessary to send Edmund Mortimer, Earl of March, there with 1,000 men, the largest English garrison force to serve in the island for many years. A far graver threat, because it was closer to home, had erupted on the Scottish march. In reprisal for the loss of two of their merchant ships at sea, the Scots captured Ralph Lord Greystoke and his entire retinue of 120 men in the Glen valley south of the border as he was on his way to take up his duties as captain of Roxburgh castle. The haul also included a great quantity of tapestries and plate with which Greystoke intended to decorate his austere quarters. This incident was followed by a large-scale Scottish raid into Cumberland, led by the Earl of Douglas, which resulted in the almost total destruction of Penrith and a retaliatory raid by the English wardens into the western lowlands. Faced with the prospect of a breakdown of the truce in the Scottish march Richard II's Council decided to take the conduct of affairs out of the hands of the border lords. In September they appointed John of Gaunt as royal lieutenant on the march and sent him hurriedly to the north with as many troops as could be found. By the end of October there were some 3,000 men serving on the Scottish march in addition to the locally recruited hordes of the Percys and Cliffords. This brought the total number of troops maintained in arms by the English government to about 12,000, divided between four fronts, an exceptionally high proportion of the tiny section of the population with skills and aptitudes to fight as men-at-arms or archers. It was the most difficult possible moment to have to meet further demands from lieutenants and allies. Yet the government was now committed to sending another 2,000 men to reinforce Buckingham in Brittany and at least 2,000 more to Portugal in the following spring.[78]

Encouraged perhaps by early reports of the troubles of France, the English government had assumed some exceptionally heavy financial commitments. The cost of the Earl of Buckingham's campaign had been grossly under-estimated. About £76,000 had already been spent on the expedition up to the end of September 1380 including shipping costs. If it lasted the full year envisaged by the men's indentures, the final bill would be twice as much even without the promised reinforcements. In addition about £40,000 had to be paid out on claims for soldiers' and seamen's wages accumulated from past campaigns dating back to the beginning of the reign and in some cases even earlier. The rest of the government's military commitments brought the total to about £280,000. This figure was roughly comparable to the annual war budget of France. It was more than England had spent in any comparable period since the campaigns in the Low Countries which had bankrupted Edward III in the early years of the war. To meet it, the government had revenues available for war expenditure amounting to about £100,000. A combination of high overheads, over-ambition and lack of candour in its dealings with the Commons had put Richard's Council in an impossible position. The Parliamentary subsidy of March 1380 had represented a substantial commitment by the Commons, which they had given on the express understanding that they would be asked for no further funds until the autumn of 1381. In August 1380, less than a month after the Earl of Buckingham had marched out of Calais, the Council was obliged to summon a new Parliament for early November, a full year before the appointed time.[79]

The assembly opened on 8 November 1380 in the unfamiliar surroundings of the Cluniac priory of St. Andrew's in Northampton, which had been chosen, like Gloucester two years earlier, in order to escape the London mob. It was not a happy choice. Winter storms and flooding had made it hard to get to. Accommodation, food, forage and fuel were all in short supply. When Chancellor Sudbury rose to explain why the assembly had been summoned his opening address mentioned no figures. But he left no doubt about the gravity of the crisis. The Council had already spent more than the entire proceeds of the last subsidy on the Earl of Buckingham's army. Their wages for the second six months of the campaign would fall due in December. The pay of the King's garrisons in France, Scotland and Ireland had fallen far into arrears and some of the men were threatening to desert. The coasts were defenceless. The King's creditors were demanding repayment. Some of them had liens over the King's few remaining jewels and were threatening to sell them. A further large grant, said Sudbury, was unavoidable. The loyal Sir John Gildesburgh, who was once again elected Speaker, came before the Lords and asked the King's councillors for a precise statement of the government's financial needs. The Commons, he said, wanted a figure in which they could have confidence, not something that would simply serve as the prelude to further demands later. He was given a copy of a schedule prepared by the King's financial officers. It showed that there was a deficiency in the government's war accounts of £160,000. This figure broadly accords with the surviving financial records.[80]

The Commons were stunned. The government's demands were 'outrageous and insupportable', they said. They represented between two and three years' worth of war subsidies at the customary rates. The Commons insisted that the figure should be reduced and invited the Lords to consider how this could be done. They seem to have expected the Lords to consider what military expenditure could be dispensed with. In fact the peers responded with alternative proposals for raising the whole sum. One was the traditional tenth and fifteenth on moveable property. At least three tenths and fifteenths would have been required. This was, as always, profoundly unpopular with the interests represented in the Commons because of the anomalies associated with the antique assessment of 1334. The second possibility was a general sales tax after the model of the French *aides*, which would have fallen disproportionately on the towns and required the creation of a new and expensive fiscal administration. The third was a graduated poll tax assessed on each community at a flat rate of four or five groats (1s 4d or 1s 8d) per head but distributed among individuals according to ability to pay. After much deliberation the Commons decided on the poll tax. At the beginning of December 1380 they resolved upon a grant of 100,000 marks, or £66,666. They proposed that the clergy should contribute half as much again, making a total of £100,000. The poll tax of 1377 had been levied at an average rate of four pence a head and had produced a total assessment of £22,586. So the Commons simply trebled the rate and imposed an average payment of twelve pence a head. At the same time they withdrew the expensive concessions which had reduced the yield of the tax of 1379: the age of eligibility was reduced from sixteen to fifteen and the exemption for married women was abolished. The result was a highly regressive tax, born of the Commons' conviction that traditional taxes let wage earners off too lightly at a time of strong wage inflation. 'All the money of the realm has passed into the hands of labourers and craftsmen,' as they had complained two years earlier. The Commons at Northampton declared that, within every community, the strong should aid the weak. But there was no graded table of contributions as there had been in 1379, and no other mechanism for requiring the rich to pay more. In the poorest communities there simply were not enough rich taxpayers to carry their neighbours' burden.[81]

The size of the grant made by the Northampton Parliament, coming so soon after the generous grant made earlier in the year, was a measure of the commitment which the English political community still felt to the war. If the grant fell well short of what the government had asked for it still represented the maximum that the Commons thought that taxpayers could bear. The proceeds were to be strictly reserved for the Earl of Buckingham's army in France, for the defence of England and for operations at sea. The Commons at Northampton were no more interested in England's continental 'barbicans' than their predecessors had been and presumably did not regard the expedition to Portugal as being in anyone's interest but John of Gaunt's. The clergy were pressured into making their own grant more promptly and generously than had been their habit. The convocation of Canterbury met in the parish church of All Saints, Northampton, immediately after the dissolution of Parliament. To raise the £33,334 expected of them they had to authorise a poll tax at even higher rates than those payable by the laity: 6s 8d for every monk, nun or priest in the land with a reduced rate of a shilling for those in deacon's or other lesser orders. Thus was born one of the most hated and destructive taxes in England's history, whose very name could be invoked to discredit other capitation taxes more than six centuries later.[82]

Measures to reinforce Buckingham's army in Brittany were put in hand as soon as the King's ministers and officials had returned to Westminster. Sir Thomas Felton, the former Seneschal of Gascony, was appointed to command a force of 2,000 men to sail to the Loire. He was to take with him a fleet of armed barges to close off Nantes from the river and £10,000 in gold coin to be distributed among the men already there. Felton's expedition was not, however, the only military enterprise planned for the following months. In spite of the Commons' misgivings and the fact that funds had not been voted for it, the Council decided to go ahead with the expedition to Portugal. Indeed they increased its size from the 2,000 men promised by Juan Fernández Andeiro to 3,000. Both of these forces were expected to leave in the spring from the ports of Plymouth and Dartmouth. The attempt to pursue both enterprises at once proved to be too ambitious.[83]

It soon became clear that Felton's army would be too late. The Earl of Buckingham was already having great difficulty in maintaining the siege of Nantes. The French garrison in the city fought off one assault after another and began to launch sorties into the besiegers' encampments, some of which inflicted heavy losses. The English tried to undermine the walls of the city, only to find their mines destroyed by French countermines. The new Constable, Olivier de Clisson, and the Marshal, Louis de Sancerre, arrived in December 1380 with fresh troops to harass the English lines from the outside and attack foraging parties which strayed too far from their bases. Supplies continued to flow into the city by river while the besiegers starved. English morale sank to new lows every day. It was a bitterly cold winter. Frequent night attacks deprived the men of sleep. During December dysentery began to spread through the army. By the beginning of January 1381 Buckingham was faced with disaster. He had lost a fifth of his men and almost all of his horses to disease, exposure, desertion and battle casualties. On about 6 January 1381 he abandoned the siege.[84]

There was worse to come. On 15 January 1381 John de Montfort reached agreement with the council of regency in Paris. The terms were the fruit of more than two months of negotiation between his representatives and a group of royal councillors led by that other sometime ally of England, Enguerrand de Coucy. John de Montfort agreed to come before Charles VI to do homage for the duchy of Brittany and obtain the King's pardon for his many acts of treachery. For this he was to pay an indemnity of 200,000 francs (about £33,000). The French government for its part agreed to recognise the liberties and immunities of the duchy of Brittany as they had stood before the decree of confiscation. The towns and castles which the French still occupied in the duchy would be surrendered. The great border fortress of Champtoceaux on the Loire would be restored to the Duke, together with all the domains which had been confiscated from him in other parts of France. The treaty marked the surrender of the Crown on every point of substance. But for all that it was a diplomatic masterstroke. John was required to renounce all his agreements with England, to dismiss all Englishmen in his employment apart from his household officers and personal servants, and to turn his arms against his erstwhile ally and 'damage them in every possible way'. The only qualification, recorded in a secret clause, was that John would not in practice be required to fight personally against the English. At a stroke the foundation of England's strategy in France was shattered. A shrewder man than the Earl of Buckingham might have guessed that some such thing was afoot when John de Montfort declined to lift a finger to help him during the siege of Nantes. But there is no reason to doubt the reports of the chroniclers that he was thunderstruck when the news was brought to him.[85]

The immediate question was what to do with the English army. It was nominally the strongest armed force in France and likely to remain so while the French government's current financial crisis persisted. But it was broken, as completely as John of Gaunt's army had been after its long march through France in 1373. For a few weeks Richard II's Council at Westminster refused to recognise facts. They appear to have thought that, with pay in the men's pockets and fresh troops and horses from England, Buckingham could simply resume the siege of Nantes in the spring. They pressed on with their plans as if nothing had changed. Felton's men were signed up to their indentures and received their advances. Ships began to assemble at Plymouth. Horses were procured across England and arrangements were made to ship them to the Loire. In late March and early April 1381 Felton and his fellow captains were ordered to proceed to their ports of embarkation. But there were not nearly enough ships for them, let alone for the army of Portugal as well. They were obliged to wait idly by the seashore for several weeks while the Admirals' officers tried to find more.[86]

The Council had misjudged the mood of Buckingham's men, possibly because Buckingham himself had misjudged it. At least one company, Hugh Calveley's, withdrew at the beginning of February and made their way back to England. The rest waited despondently for orders. Without money they could not buy food. Without horses they could not even steal it. Finally Buckingham decided to march on the seat of John de Montfort's administration at Vannes and confront the Duke in person. John met him on the road. It must have been a difficult encounter. The Duke of Brittany explained that he had had no choice but to strike a deal with the French. The towns and the Church had been adamantly opposed to the English alliance. The nobility were occupied in defending the frontier of the duchy. Without a deal with the French there was no prospect of his being able to maintain himself in power. Buckingham was unimpressed. There were '*grandes paroles*' between the two men. But there was nothing that the Earl could do other than negotiate the best possible terms for his orderly departure for England. In early March Sir Thomas Percy and William Lord Latimer agreed a deal. They promised to withdraw peacefully in return for 50,000 francs (£8,333), 30,000 of it in prompt cash. Part of this money was spent in hiring ships in the ports of southern Brittany for the army's return to England. The rest was promised by Whitsun. Two days were passed in jousting with selected champions from the ranks of the French army according to the elaborate procedures of the heralds, the kind of event which Buckingham loved all his life. The results of these heroic exhibitions of strength and skill were as dismal for the English as the real war had been. In about the second week of March the English army marched off west towards Brest.[87]

Buckingham's agreement with the Duke of Brittany provoked much irritation at Westminster. On about 15 March 1381 the Council decided to send the money collected for Buckingham's army to Brittany in advance of Felton's army. Sir John Kentwood, the Steward of the duchy of Cornwall, sailed from Dartmouth with two Exchequer officials, an escort of archers and a chest of gold at the end of March and landed at Brest. His instructions were to find out how many troops Buckingham still had and to persuade them to stay in France until their indentured service was complete in June. No money, they insisted, was to be paid to any captain who refused. At Brest Kentwood found the Earl of Buckingham installed in the fortress and delivered the Council's unpalatable message. The Earl was immoveable. He had given his word to the Duke of Brittany. His army was fed up. Part of it had already sailed for England in Breton ships. Shipping was being found for the rest. On 30 April Kentwood gave up. He paid over the money to the Earl and watched the last of the English army boarding the ships in the harbour beneath the castle walls. On 2 May 1381 Buckingham landed with his men at Falmouth in Cornwall. The campaign had been Buckingham's opportunity to do great deeds in the image of his dead father and brother. Its failure was to weigh on him for the rest of his life. Thirteen years later, when he founded the college of secular priests which was destined to be his principal monument, its statutes called for daily masses for the souls of those who had died in the army of 1380–1.[88]

English policy was now a picture of disarray. The 2,000 troops of Felton's army of Brittany were kept at Dartmouth for several weeks while the Council considered what to do with them. The possibility of shipping them to Gascony appears to have been considered. Felton's men were joined on the Devon coast in the course of May by the Earl of Cambridge and some 3,000 troops of the army of Portugal who milled about the town competing with them for food, shelter and shipping space. No firm plans had been made when Gaunt, the moving spirit behind both the Portuguese and the Breton projects, left for talks with the Scots on the northern march. In June Felton's army was disbanded. As for John de Montfort he became a loyal but unenthusiastic vassal of the King of France, protected by Charles VI's uncles and treated as a pariah by his old enemy Olivier de Clisson and the party at the French court who clustered round him. The English never forgave John for deserting them. His close personal connection with the English royal family, his English peerage and his friendship with prominent figures at the English court only aggravated the sense of betrayal. Until the Anglo-Breton alliance was revived in the next generation relations between England and the court of Brittany remained extremely cool. The government confiscated John's honour of Richmond and forfeited the property of the handful of Englishmen who remained in his service. The English clung on to their expensive outpost at Brest, although events had now greatly reduced its value to them. They intrigued with Olivier de Clisson and from time to time toyed with the idea of promoting the claims of John of Blois. Even the Duchess, Joan Holand, the English King's half-sister, became a focus of the new antagonism. She stayed in England in spite of John's attempts to have her returned. Joan would not rejoin her husband in Brittany until late 1383, when she was dying. Medieval marriages are hard for a historian to penetrate. Convention, duty and discretion make an opaque barrier, especially among those whose marriages were essentially political acts. Like Enguerrand de Coucy, another French nobleman who had once been prominent at the English court and married an English princess, John found that their relationship would not bear a change of allegiance.[89]

CHAPTER IX

The Revolt of the Towns
1380–1382

The disturbances in Languedoc in 1379, like the urban tax strikes of 1380, were warnings of a more profound crisis as perhaps only Charles V himself had understood at the time. They occurred against a difficult economic background: disease, depopulation and a deepening recession characterised by falling agricultural prices, industrial stagnation and a severe shortage of gold and silver coin. All contributed to the growing crisis of Europe's cities. The physical destruction wrought by war in England, France and Italy and later in Flanders, Spain and Portugal, aggravated the effects. In England, rich in statistical evidence, almost every indicator of economic activity in this period shows a marked decline. Anecdotal evidence and sporadic outbreaks of violence confirm the pattern elsewhere. The popular revolt of the *ciompi* in Florence in 1378 had been a major crisis in the affairs of one of Europe's principal industrial centres which passed virtually unnoticed outside Italy. Yet over the next four years similar urban revolts, generated by unemployment and crushing burdens of war taxation, would shake the instincts of the governing classes in both France and England. Beyond the walls of the towns, the Peasants' Revolt of 1381 in England and the rebellion of the peasant *tuchins* of central France proved to be even more disturbing to societies whose wealth was still founded on agricultural production. These rebellions marked the beginning of a period in which popular violence became once again a major factor in the fortunes of European states. The world is old, the times infirm, sang the poet Eustache Deschamps, voicing the joyless pessimism which, however conventional, clearly struck a chord among his aristocratic audience and is matched in the works of his English contemporaries.[1]

In September 1379 the three 'great towns' of Flanders, Ghent, Bruges and Ypres, rebelled against the authority of the Count, Louis de Mâle. The great towns were the leading industrial and commercial cities of

Flanders and among the largest in Europe. Their wealth and concentrated populations made them a formidable political force, especially when they were united. They had played the leading role in all the civil wars of Flanders in the past eighty years. They had established themselves as an intermediate level of government, carving the county up into 'quarters' over which they asserted and intermittently exercised intrusive powers of control. Yet their fortunes had been in precipitate decline for some years. To some extent this was due to the general contraction of the western European economy in the late fourteenth century. But there were other, peculiarly local factors at work. The three great towns and Courtrai, a protégé of Ghent that almost ranked as a fourth, specialised in the manufacture of luxury woollen cloths. Their costs were high, mainly because of their resistance to technological change and dependence on high-quality raw wool imported from England. By the 1370s they were being undercut in their main export markets by luxury woollen cloth made in Italy and by the silks and velvets which were increasingly favoured by fashion-conscious buyers. Lower-quality stuff was also encountering intense competition from the rural villages and smaller towns of Flanders and, increasingly, from the fledgling cloth industries of Brabant and England. These changes undermined the delicate social balance on which the internal peace of the Flemish towns depended. Masters responded to the shrinkage of their trade with tighter restrictions on entry into the craft guilds, as a result of which a growing proportion of those engaged in the textile industry were casually employed artisans and unskilled labourers. Meanwhile inflation ate into the real value of textile workers' wages. The effect was aggravated by Louis de Mâle's frequent devaluations of the coinage and by a sharp rise in the level of taxes.

The municipal authorities, especially in Ghent and Ypres, responded to the threat to their position by exercising tighter control over their 'quarters' in order to limit competition from smaller cloth-making centres. This tutelage, supported by armed force when necessary, was a source of much of ill feeling and brought the great towns into collision with the officers of the Count. Louis de Mâle had not forgotten the role of Ghent, Bruges and Ypres, and of their weavers in particular, in the revolutions of his father's reign. He deliberately set out to undermine them, supporting the pretensions of the smaller centres with privileges and protecting them in his courts. The rapid development of the county's administrative and judicial institutions gave Louis far more effective means of intervention than his predecessors had enjoyed. In the long term these trends would reduce the ancient autonomy of the cities to nothing. Their immediate effect was to provoke a final spasm of revolt against the Count's authority, led by the town which was most directly affected, Ghent.

In Ghent, the largest of the three great towns, the contraction of the textile industry had been more rapid than anywhere else. In the 1370s the population of the town was probably no more than about 30,000, about half what it had been thirty years before. Unemployment and poverty were serious and growing problems. Like other Flemish towns, Ghent was governed by councils dominated by the landowning patriciate and by shifting coalitions of craft and trade guilds. In a contracting economy political power became the means by which rival groups sought to line their pockets and protect their commercial interests at the expense of others. These rivalries quickly spilled out into the streets and workshops. Conspiracies, strikes and street violence between rival interests were aggravated by personal rivalries within the major guilds and by blood-feuds between prominent patrician and mercantile families. These conditions provided ready opportunities for demagogues and mobsters.

The catalyst for the rebellion of 1379 was the construction by the men of Bruges of a navigable canal from the Zwyn to the Lys. The canal, which had been authorised by Louis de Mâle, was regarded by Ghent as a direct assault on their interests, as indeed it was. It would have established a direct link by water between Bruges and the granaries of the northern French plains, bypassing Ghent and diverting business away from the town's powerful grain wholesalers. In Ghent opposition to the canal was led by Jan Yoens, a grain shipper in straitened circumstances with a gift for oratory, who had recently assumed the leadership of his guild. He was supported by the weavers, some of whom had a broader political agenda, and by the 'White Hoods', a semi-autonomous urban militia which had traditionally been used to impose the city's will on the countryside around. In July 1379 Yoens broke up the canal works with the aid of the White Hoods, killing and mutilating many of the men who were working on it. Faced with the prospect of retaliation by the Count, the city councillors of Ghent rapidly lost control of the situation. Hotheads in the streets broadened the rebels' support, appealing to a wider range of interests and grievances, some of which were potent echoes of earlier civil wars: taxation, infringements of the city's juridical privileges and the perennial fear that its charters would be revoked and its inhabitants laid at the mercy of the Count's officials, judges and tax-gatherers. At the beginning of September 1379 the councillors were swept aside in favour of Yoens and his allies. The Count's bailiff, who tried to restore order, was lynched and his master's banner torn in pieces and trampled underfoot. Shortly after this incident Yoens joined to his cause two men who were to be among the guiding spirits of the revolution in the following years: the weaver Francis Ackerman and a violent gang leader called Peter Van den Bossche, probably a baker, who had taken over the leadership of the White Hoods. They put the town in a state of defence. They razed the houses of the Count's officers and expelled them from the town. Then they led the White Hoods and a large mob of townsmen against the fortified places of the district around, demolishing manor houses, farms and castles in a campaign which had more to do with class hatreds than defence. The Count's favourite residence, at Wondelgem, just beyond the northern suburbs, was sacked and left gutted by fire.[2]

Louis de Mâle had already begun to prepare a punitive expedition against the recalcitrant town. But before he was able to gather his forces Yoens had succeeded in spreading the rebellion to the rest of Flanders. The other towns were governed, like Ghent, by conservative oligarchies with close links to the nobility and the Count. But they had important minorities, often associated with the weavers' guilds, who were desperate enough to believe that they could improve their fortunes by taking control of Flanders out of the Count's hands in alliance with the men of Ghent. In September 1379 Courtrai, a long-standing ally of Ghent whose government overtly sympathised with the revolution, opened its gates to the White Hoods. Ypres was taken over by its weavers as the men of Ghent stormed the gates. Attacked from front and rear at once, the Count's garrison fled. Most of the smaller towns along the coastal plain submitted in the wake of Ypres. Only Bruges and its dependent towns in the north now remained.[3]

Bruges had nothing to gain by falling in with the plans of Ghent. Politically the town was an ally of the Count and it had many bones to pick with Ghent. With its large shipping, brokerage and banking businesses, it was also less dependent on textiles than any other major Flemish town. When the horde of Ghent approached, Louis de Mâle's captain resolved to fight. He had the support of most of the town and the surrounding *franc* (as Bruges's quarter was known). But as he drew up his men in front of the walls the weavers mounted a *coup d'état* behind his back. They took over the administration, pushed the Count's officers aside and threw open the gates to the captain of Ghent. Bruges's outports at Damme and Sluys were occupied without difficulty shortly afterwards. Jan Yoens died, apparently from natural causes, in his moment of triumph on about 1 October 1379. In Ghent they buried him 'as if he had been Count of Flanders'. But his work was done. In the space of three weeks Louis de Mâle's authority had been eliminated in most of Flanders. The Duke of Burgundy, who had been summoned to his father-in-law's assistance, arrived with an advance guard of his army in November in time to broker a humiliating peace in which Louis was compelled to concede almost all of Ghent's demands. The peace was widely regarded as a sham. Few people believed that Louis de Mâle intended to be bound by it for any longer than it took him to recover his strength. And so it proved.[4]

At the court of France the significance of these events was little understood. Louis de Mâle came to Paris in March 1380, his first visit for many years, to find support for his cause. He was frigidly received. His practical neutrality in the Anglo-French war and his support for John de Montfort had provoked bitterness and rage in the French capital. His recent recognition of the Roman Pope seemed to Charles's ministers to fall little short of treason. In consequence his difficulties were viewed with indifference by the King's Council and with discreet satisfaction by many others. In spite of the advocacy of his mother, Margaret of Artois, and his son-in-law, Philip of Burgundy, he appears to gave gained nothing for his trouble apart from vague assurances of future help which were themselves dependent on the state of the war with England.[5]

At the beginning of April 1380 Louis left Paris empty-handed but bent on revenge for the humiliations of the previous autumn. His appeals for help were received more sympathetically in the other principalities of the Low Countries, where the threat of urban revolution was better understood than it was in France. He called to his standard all the embittered tribe of exiles who had lost their homes, wealth and influence at the hands of the revolutionaries. The treaty with Ghent and its allies was torn up. The Count's supporters were given free rein to launch a savage war against the undefended villages of southern Flanders, in which great numbers of largely innocent peasants were murdered. They laid waste the country around Ghent, cutting off the town's river trade and destroying the windmills on which it depended for its grain. The men of Ghent responded with attacks on the castles and manors of the nobility throughout Flanders.[6]

Louis resolved to pick off Ghent's allies first. Bruges, the latest and most reluctant of them, was the first to secede. The town was controlled by a minority regime dominated by weavers and dependent on the armed support of Ghent. In May 1380 it was overthrown by the other guilds. An army sent from Ghent to restore the ousted faction was scattered outside the gates of the town. At the beginning of June Louis de Mâle returned to Bruges in triumph. The Count moved against Ypres two months later in the middle of August. The men of Ghent tried once more to intervene. But they unwisely divided their forces. As a result part of their army was wiped out by the Count's cavalry while the rest were forced to withdraw. The Count arrived at Ypres to find the leading citizens on their knees in front of the gates, clutching the keys of the town and begging for mercy. Louis, however, was not inclined to be merciful. Over the following days between 300 and 400 supporters of Ghent were identified and rounded up in the streets of Ypres. They were beheaded one after the other on a huge scaffold erected in the market-place. Within days of this demonstration Louis de Mâle's officers had recovered possession of most of Flanders with the exception of Ghent itself.

On 2 September 1380 the Count of Flanders laid siege to Ghent with a huge army drawn from every part of the region. However, Ghent proved to be a tough antagonist. The townsmen were more united and more committed to their cause than the populations of Bruges and Ypres. And in spite of the size of his army the Count was unable to seal off their supplies. Early in October 1380 he was obliged to concede another dishonest armistice. Penury and the logistical problems of feeding an army through the long winter months were the main factors at work but political calculation was another. There were 'other means of imposing my will on the land', as the Count wrote to his cousin shortly after these events. At the time that this letter was written Charles V was dead and the new King's uncles had taken control of the government of France. Ultimately it was Louis's son-in-law Philip, Duke of Burgundy, who would furnish Louis with his 'other means'.[7]

The English political community did not imagine that the revolt of Flanders held any lessons for them, any more than the court of France had done. When popular rebellion erupted in their own island, the event took them by surprise. But it did not come out of a clear sky. Most of the economic problems of the countryside ultimately sprang from the drastic depopulation which followed the Black Death: falling rents and agricultural prices, accompanied by strong upward pressure on wages. The lords of rural manors responded by systematically enforcing their surviving manorial rights and zealously invoking the Statute of Labourers which had been enacted in the aftermath of the first epidemic in order to limit the wage demands of labourers and restrict their mobility. These measures were only partly effective but they provoked sharp conflicts, sometimes breaking out into physical violence. The shadow of the Jacquerie of 1358 darkened men's thoughts and fear of revolution became a recurring theme of political discourse. That lugubrious conservative poet John Gower warned that the common people would one day break their bonds, 'which hath befalle in sondri londes'. France was undoubtedly the chief of the sundry lands that Gower had in mind. He was not alone. After a rash of incidents in the south and west in 1377 the Commons in Richard II's first Parliament reported that peasants were forming sworn associations to oppose the demands of their lords and were openly resisting the bailiffs of the manors. They voiced their fear of rural revolution 'as happened some time ago in France', even as they called for stronger measures of repression.[8]

There had been outbreaks of popular unrest in England before. But they had generally been localised riots, directed against targets which were close at hand. The Peasants' Revolt was unique in its geographical spread and in its adoption of a broader political and ideological programme. The immediate occasion for it was the poll tax voted by the Northampton Parliament. The tax was profoundly hated. It was hated for its exceptionally high rate and the regressive basis of its assessment. It was hated for the intrusive way in which it was assessed and collected, by officious outside commissioners instead of the local men who had traditionally been employed on this delicate and uncongenial task. But the revolt was more than a protest against taxation or even against the reassertion of manorial control over unfree and partly free men. The impact of the Good Parliament had extended well beyond the classes represented in Parliament and it inaugurated a tradition of popular radicalism surviving long after it was dissolved. The rebels were concentrated in the capital and in the regions around where national politics had their most powerful resonance. They railed against the diversion of the King's tax revenues into the pockets of his ministers and the treachery and corruption which they believed had undermined the war effort, just as the Commons of 1376 had done. From these specific grievances they moved to a generalised resentment of the whole class from which the King's servants and soldiers were drawn. When, after the young King's coronation, Bishop Brinton of Rochester preached against taxes 'taken from the poor and spent on supporting the pride of the rich', he filled his sermon with overt references to the disputes of the previous year, and his words achieved a fame extending well beyond Palace Yard where it was probably delivered. The same themes achieved even wider distribution at the hands of popular preachers like John Ball or satirists like the widely read author of *Piers Plowman*.[9]

It became apparent as early as February 1381 that the poll tax was being evaded on a large scale. When the collectors came to the Exchequer to present their accounts for the first instalment it was found that local communities had been declaring on average about two-thirds and in some places less than half of the number of taxpayers who had been counted at the time of the first poll tax in 1377. On 16 March the Council appointed special commissions in fifteen counties to tour the towns and villages, armed with formidable powers of compulsion, taking sworn evidence from local officers and producing lists of undeclared taxpayers to be passed to the collectors. Their operations were never likely to be popular. But the problem was aggravated by their high-handed behaviour. As Chancellor Pole would later observe in a rare moment of reflection, if the lesser officials of the Crown misbehaved the King and his ministers found themselves forced to back them up, thus drawing the fury of the populace upon themselves.

This is what happened at Brentwood in Essex on 30 May 1381. One of the commissioners for Essex had arrived in the town to review the tax rolls in the hundred of Barstaple. The response of the surrounding villages was carefully planned. Their men appeared en masse, armed with old bows and sticks, determined to resist. The men of Fobbing, a large village on the north shore of the Thames Estuary, were the first to be cited. Their spokesman was one Thomas Baker, who appears to have been one of the chief organisers of the revolt in Essex. He declared that Fobbing had paid under the existing assessment; that they had their receipt; and that they would have nothing to do with the inquiry. The commissioner had come with just two royal sergeants and a handful of clerks for an escort. He ordered the sergeants to arrest Baker. At this the furious peasants fell on him and his staff, beat them up and chased them out of town. Several of his jurors were captured and beheaded. Three of his clerks were lynched and their heads carried around the neighbouring villages on poles. An overtly political direction was given to the rebellion three days later at a large meeting which was held more than twenty miles away in the village of Bocking. Here, according to a hostile source, the rebels of Brentwood and malcontents drawn from across the county swore to act together 'to destroy certain lieges of the King and his common laws and all lordship and to have no law in England except only those which they had themselves ordained.'[10]

The rebellion in Kent began two days later on 2 June 1381. It was Whit Sunday, the time of crowds and summer games. The first incidents were deliberately co-ordinated with the actions of the men of Essex. The rioting began in the north of the county along the Thames, as the men of Essex were gathering at Bocking. On 4 June the Kentishmen, reinforced by about a hundred Essex men, invaded Dartford. They forced their way into Rochester and laid siege to the ancient Norman keep, which was shortly surrendered to them by its terrified constable. During the next few days men flocked to the rebels' standard from across Kent. On about 7 June they held a great public meeting at Maidstone at which they elected as their leader an obscure adventurer called Wat Tyler. Tyler, who was in fact a tiler, appears to have hailed from Essex. According to reports reaching Froissart he had fought in France, presumably as an archer. He was chosen because he had a ready tongue and a forceful personality, which shortly transformed the formless mob about him into a more or less organised army. Tyler's 'programme', so far as it can be called that, was more ambitious than anything put forward by the rioters of Brentwood or even the conspirators of Bocking. He wanted to remove the 'traitors' about the King and to abolish serfdom together with all the other incidents of the manorial system.

Tyler first led his horde south through Kent towards the coast. The most serious incidents occurred at Canterbury, where some 4,000 rebels entered the town, looking for Archbishop Sudbury. As Chancellor of England he was a convenient scapegoat for the failures of the ministry. Sudbury was away in London. But the crowd sacked his palace and invaded the cathedral, threatening him with a traitor's death when they found him. 'Ah, this Chancellor . . . shall give us an account of the revenues of England and of the great profits that he has gathered since the King's coronation,' they cried according to Froissart's informants when they saw the luxurious decorations of the Archbishop's palace. Then they went to occupy the castle and break open the town jail. In the streets of the town the sudden collapse of order brought opportunities to settle old grudges. 'Have you no traitors here?' the crowd yelled as they passed through the streets. Houses were pointed out and their occupants dragged into the streets and their heads hacked off on the ground.[11]

Over the following days mobs moved through Essex and Kent, gathering strength as they went. They were armed with sticks, battle axes, rusty swords, half-plumed arrows and bows 'reddened with age and smoke'. In general their targets were carefully selected. The rebels were interested mainly in the destruction of documents: the county records kept in Canterbury castle, the muniments which the sheriffs of Essex and Kent kept in their homes, judicial and financial records of every description. Documents sealed in green wax, the colour used by the Exchequer, were specially singled out for destruction as they were assumed to relate to tax. They attacked the manors and urban mansions of the sheriffs and other royal officials, the King's judges and the justices of the peace, lawyers and poll tax commissioners. Anyone connected with the Crown or John of Gaunt was vulnerable. The perpetrators of these acts were not drawn only from the poorest or most desperate sections of the community. Some of them, including many of the ringleaders, were people of substance on a village scale, who had held office in the manor as reeves, bailiffs or constables. Some were free tenants with large holdings of land and beasts. Such men must have found it relatively easy to pay the poll tax. But they came from the very groups of successful rural entrepreneurs who had found the constraints of the manorial courts and the intrusions of the royal officials most irksome. They also represented the most politically informed sections of village society.[12]

On about 10 June 1381 Tyler resolved upon a co-ordinated march on the capital by rebel forces from Essex and Kent. Tyler himself took command of the men of Kent, who approached the city from the south. On his march he was joined by a man of whom rather more is known, John Ball, 'the mad priest of Kent'. Ball belonged to the pervasive clerical underworld which flourished throughout England in the late middle ages and gave a large number of local leaders to the revolt of 1381. He was an ordained priest and itinerant preacher who had been spreading his heterodox message for some twenty years and was currently languishing in Maidstone jail. The rebels found him there and forcibly released him. Ball was not an organiser. He was an ideologue, a prophet and a seer. His traditional target had been the wealth and corruption of the higher clergy. But under the impulsion of the events of June 1381 he broadened his theme to embrace an intense, messianic utopianism which ultimately rejected all political authority, lay and ecclesiastical. In a series of broadsheets, which were widely distributed across England, he denounced in obscure and allusive rhyming couplets the sinfulness of power. The most famous statement of his views was the sermon that he preached to the rebels of Kent on Blackheath on the text:

> Whan Adam delved and Eve span
> Who was then a gentilman?

God had made all men free, said Ball, but men had fashioned the bonds which now held them. Once oppressive lords, corrupt judges and dishonest ministers had been removed, all would be free and all would have 'the same nobility, rank and power'. What Ball seems to have meant by this was that there should be no intermediaries between the King and the mass of peasants, labourers and craftsmen. His programme was summed up in the slogan: 'With King Richard and the true commons of England.' It became the watchword of the revolution.[13]

When the rebels began their double march on London the King was at Windsor. On 11 June 1381 he was brought to London and taken to the Tower, which was thought to be the safest refuge in southern England. He was joined there over the next day or two by his mother Joan of Kent, the Chancellor Archbishop Sudbury, the Treasurer Sir Robert Hales, the Earls of Arundel, Salisbury, and Warwick, the young Earl of Oxford, and a small group of attendants and professional soldiers including Sir Robert Knolles, Robert of Namur and the Gascon *routier* Bertucat d'Albret, who was then staying at the English court. The only organised bodies of troops in the capital were the small garrison of the Tower, the knights with the King and about 150 men-at-arms with an uncertain number of archers. There was also a band of retainers of Robert Knolles whom he had stationed in his London mansion.[14]

Much depended on the attitude of the mass of Londoners. This was extremely uncertain. The regressive character of the poll tax had been particularly jarring in the capital, with its stark contrasts of wealth and poverty. The richer merchants, who had previously been assessed on the value of their stock in trade, got away with a few shillings for themselves and their immediate families. These men, who included the dominant figures in the guilds and city government, were the main beneficiaries of the poll tax. They had driven forward the enrolment of taxpayers with energy, organising house-to-house visits which ensured that the scale of evasion was lower there than in most parts of the country. The anger of the undeclared taxpayers who were found out was so strong that the sheriffs of London and Middlesex had refused to collect their names for fear of riots. It is, however, clear that a significant number of Londoners supported the rebel cause for reasons far more diverse than the poll tax. Some, mainly drawn from the poorest classes, sympathised with the grievances of the peasants and may have shared their utopian visions. Serfdom was not a problem in London but relations between the mass of labourers and journeymen were no easier for that. However, most of the peasants' supporters in the capital appear to have been motivated not by social grievances at all but by the same political animosities which had provoked the disorders in London in 1376 and 1377. This was, for Londoners, unfinished business. The notion of a corrupt court, betraying the country to the French and out for its own enrichment, had never died.[15]

The group of ministers gathered round the King in the Tower played for time in the hope that the rebels would run out of supplies and enthusiasm. They sent a messenger to meet the Kentishmen on the road in order to find out their demands. The messenger found the rebels encamped on Blackheath. Their spokesman's answer was chilling. They had come, they said, to 'save the King and destroy the traitors to him and his realm'. They asked for a meeting with the King. In spite of the misgivings of Sudbury and Hales the King's councillors made a serious attempt to satisfy this request. On 13 June the King took a barge from the Tower and sailed downriver to Greenwich. The rebel host came down the slope from Blackheath towards the water's edge. Richard tried to parley with them from the security of the barge. But the rebels refused to talk unless Richard landed. So the King's companions ordered the barge about and returned to the Tower.[16]

They arrived only just ahead of the first detachments of the Kent army. In the early afternoon of 13 June 1381 the rebels entered Southwark, which was unwalled, and broke open the prison of the King's Marshalsea. At about the same time an even larger host of men from Essex was making its way along the Mile End Road towards the fields outside Aldgate, north of the Tower. On Mayor Walworth's orders all the city gates had been secured. London Bridge was defended by a gate-tower in midstream. The drawbridge was up. But as the mob approached it was lowered. The rebels poured across the bridge into the city. The hands of the bridge keepers appear to have been forced by an organised rising within the city. Once inside the walls the mob moved west past St. Paul's and down Ludgate Hill. They broke open the Flete prison. Their numbers swollen by released criminals, they made for John of Gaunt's Palace of Savoy. The palace stood on the Strand by the Thames, between London and Westminster, the most magnificent private residence in England, built on the ransoms of war in more fortunate times and only recently refurnished and decorated by the Duke. The rioters prohibited looting. Their object was to make a political point by methodically, almost ritually destroying everything in the palace. The Duke's plate was cast into the Thames. The costly hangings were torn apart. The furniture was thrown from upper windows to be hacked to pieces below. The artefacts were smashed with hammers and the jewels ground up in mortars. The Duke's armoured jacket was found and set on a lance to be used for target practice. The whole building was then set on fire and the remnants blown up with gunpowder seized from the Duke's armoury.

The rest of the army of Kent poured through the city and joined forces with the men of Essex who had by now been let in through Aldgate. They broke open Newgate prison, the third London prison to have its contents discharged into the streets. They wandered through the streets, hunting down unpopular officials and 'traitors' and those singled out for death by their enemies within the city. The priory of St. John's Clerkenwell, the headquarters of the Hospitallers, was sacked because Treasurer Hales was the head of the order in England. Seven Flemings who had taken refuge there were butchered to satisfy the perennial resentment of Londoners for foreign competitors. That evening the leaders of the rebels met at the house of a prominent London citizen. There they drew up lists of people to be beheaded as soon as they could be found: John of Gaunt, Sudbury and Hales, Sir Robert Bellknap, Chief Justice of Common Pleas, Bishop Courtenay and others. These were symbolic victims. Few of them were chosen for what they had done. Indeed Hales had only been Treasurer since February and had no responsibility for either the poll tax or the conduct of the war. They were proscribed because they were leading current ministers of a government which had failed. In the Tower the author of the *Anonimalle Chronicle*, who was present, watched the young King climb to the top of a turret to gaze over the burning buildings and the glowing embers of the Savoy Palace.[17]

The occupation of London by the rebels was the signal for fresh outbreaks of violence across much of eastern and central England. There was a series of risings in Hertfordshire, most of them directed at the great monastic landowners. In Suffolk the leader of the rebellion was a renegade priest called John Wraw. He invaded the town of Sudbury and sacked the manor of Richard Lyons, the corrupt financier at the centre of the protests of the Good Parliament of 1376. Both the Prior of Bury St. Edmunds and Sir John Cavendish, Chief Justice of King's Bench (who lived in the neighbourhood) were hunted down and butchered. Cambridgeshire was raised a day or two later by two emissaries from the rebels of London. Throughout East Anglia mobs gathered under a variety of local demagogues to hunt down justices of the peace, poll tax commissioners and local officers of John of Gaunt. Further north the arrival of news from London was followed by serious urban risings in Scarborough, Beverley and York.[18]

Gaunt himself was at Berwick on the march of Scotland when the first reports of the rebellion reached him. His first instinct was to head south towards the capital. But it quickly became clear that he was a marked man. Wild rumours were heard about armed posses hunting for him. The Earl of Northumberland heard that the King had made common cause with the rebels against his uncle. Fearing to be too closely associated with a man whose days seemed numbered, Northumberland turned the Duke away from the gates of Alnwick castle, urging him to head for the royal castle at Bamburgh and stay there until the crisis was over. Gaunt eventually fled with a handful of retainers and servants into Scotland and threw himself on the charity of the Scottish King Robert Stewart. The Duchess was obliged to flee from Hertford castle, only to find herself refused admission to her husband's own fortress at Pontefract. She was eventually offered shelter in the decrepit castle of Knaresborough in Yorkshire. Catherine Swynford, the Duke's mistress, went into hiding.[19]

In the Tower counsels were divided. Sir Robert Knolles suggested a night-time attack on the rebels led by the garrison of the Tower and the troops at his mansion. Mayor Walworth thought that he could raise six or seven thousand reliable men from the wealthier households of the city once the fuse had been lit. But the rest of the company, whose voice ultimately prevailed, was appalled at the idea of staking everything on this one throw of the dice. If it failed the Tower would become their prison. They counselled concessions. A first attempt was made to persuade the rebels to disperse voluntarily by inviting them to formulate their demands in writing and offering them a general pardon. But the two knights who were sent out of the Tower to announce this offer were unable to make themselves heard above the barracking of the crowd. A second, more risky strategy was therefore tried. A meeting was proposed between the rebels and the King at Mile End, east of the walls. The idea was to draw the rebels out of the streets and enable the ministers cowering in the Tower to escape. Early on the morning of 14 June the King left the Tower with a tiny armed retinue and rode down the Mile End Road to meet the rebels. Several hundred of them were gathered at Mile End to meet him. Their main demands were the immediate abolition of serfdom; the repeal of all laws 'except the statute of Winchester' (which dealt with defence against foreign invasion); the end of the Statute of Labourers; and a universal rent for agricultural land fixed by law at four pence an acre. A number of lesser demands followed. The King conceded all of them one after another. He handed to the rebels the banners that his attendants were holding as token of his good faith and promised charters of freedom to all who asked for them. The only thing that he would not concede was the demand that the rebels should be allowed to deal with 'traitors' as they deserved. Richard replied to this that they would have the heads of such men as had been adjudged traitors by due process of law.

Whether Richard was sincere or his concessions were simply a device to buy time is impossible to say. He certainly succeeded in thinning out the ranks of the rebels, many of whom began to drift back to their homes. But he did not satisfy the more extreme of the peasants' leaders or the more radical Londoners. Nor did he sate the demand for blood. While Richard was at Mile End a mob of some 400 men rushed the gate which guarded the bridge serving as the main point of access to the Tower of London. The drawbridge had been lowered and its portcullis raised in expectation of the King's return. No attempt was made to stop them, which suggests that the common soldiers in the fortress may themselves have sympathised with the rebels' cause, just as the defenders of Rochester, Maidstone and other castles had done. Sudbury and Hales were found in the chapel of the White Tower, where they had passed their final hours saying one mass after another. 'Here I am, your archbishop,' Sudbury is said to have declared as they broke their way in. They dragged him out of the building, across the courtyards of the Tower and onto Tower Hill and beheaded him on a log of wood. Treasurer Hales suffered the same fate immediately after him. So did the Franciscan William Appleton, who was killed for no other reason than that he was John of Gaunt's physician; and John Legge, a royal sergeant who was believed, probably wrongly, to have been responsible for the special commissions to find out evaders of the poll tax. Their heads were mounted on poles and set over the gate of London Bridge. Across the capital the streets exploded with violence. Wat Tyler, accompanied by several hundred men, went in search of further traitors. Richard Lyons was pulled out of his home and taken to Cheapside to be beheaded. Richard Imworth, the Marshal of the Marshalsea, was dragged from sanctuary at Westminster Abbey and followed him to the block on the next day. Numbers of lawyers, city jurymen and supposed retainers of the Duke of Lancaster were found out and murdered. The rebels fell on any foreigners that they could find.

The policy of concessions having been discredited, the King's advisers appear to have gone back to the more aggressive plans previously pressed upon them by Walworth and Knolles. On the night of 14–15 June a plan was laid to trap and kill Wat Tyler. The rebel leader was invited to attend another meeting with the King to discover what further demands his followers might have. The meeting was to take place at Smithfield, a large open space surrounded by buildings outside the city walls where a weekly cattle market was held. Inside the city a large force of Londoners was recruited from the richer households and told to come out when the signal was given. In the early afternoon Richard rode to Smithfield in the intense summer heat, accompanied by about 200 mounted men. They wore armour and weapons concealed beneath their robes. They took up a position beneath the buildings of St. Bartholomew's Priory. On the other side of the open space the rebels were drawn up in military order. Tyler came forward, riding upon a little hackney and accompanied by a single attendant bearing his banner. Richard asked him why his followers had not dispersed, since he had conceded all their demands at Mile End. Tyler replied that there were other matters that remained to be settled. These included the redistribution of land among the population; the confiscation of the estates of the Church; the abolition of all bishops save one; and that 'all men should be equally free with no distinctions of status between man and man save in the case of the King.' There was a pause, followed by an altercation. A scuffle broke out. In the mêlée Walworth struck Tyler with a cutlass and one of the King's squires ran him through twice with his sword. Tyler, badly wounded, managed to turn his horse around and escape into the open ground between the two groups of armed men, crying 'Treason!' He fell from his saddle to the ground. Panic gripped the massed ranks of Tyler's supporters. Many of them began to bend their bows. But they were stopped by Richard himself, who rode out to them and cried: 'I will be your chief and only captain and from me you shall have all that you seek.' He urged them to reassemble in a few minutes in the fields to the north, by the walled enclosure of St. John's Clerkenwell. But by the time that they regathered there, about half an hour later, Walworth and Knolles had arrived with several thousand loyal citizens at their backs. Overawed by this mass of armed men, the rebels agreed to disperse. The Essex men made their way east across the fields and the Kentishmen were escorted through the city and over London Bridge. Mayor Walworth was knighted by the King on the spot.[20]

The government quickly re-established control. Wat Tyler was pulled, half-dead, out of St. Bartholomew's hospital, where his friends had taken him, and beheaded at Smithfield. The ringleaders still in London were arrested. Some of them were summarily put to death. Elsewhere the repression was taken in hand by the Council under the impulsion of William Courtenay, who had succeeded Sudbury as Archbishop and Chancellor. They sent to every corner of England the news of Tyler's death and the dispersal of the rebels in London. This rapidly chilled enthusiasm in the outlying areas where the revolt was just taking wing. Sir Thomas Trivet was sent into Kent to put out the dying embers of revolt there. The companies of Felton's army of Brittany, some of whom were still at Dartmouth, were sent to restore order in Hampshire and Wiltshire. Only in Essex was there any serious attempt at organised resistance and that was put down with much brutality under the nominal command of Richard himself. Real control may have been with his captains but there is little doubt that Richard himself had his heart in the business. 'Wretches!' he is said to have told a peasant delegation who came before him to ask for the confirmation of the concessions made at Mile End, '. . . peasants you are and peasants you will remain.' The rebels made a brief last stand with an improvised army on a hilltop by the village of Billericay. The Earl of Buckingham dispersed them with a cavalry charge, killing a large number. Over the following weeks several hundred of the leading figures were found and brought before the King's justices. John Wraw tried in vain to save his skin by turning King's evidence. John Ball was discovered in Coventry and brought to St. Albans for trial. He openly avowed his actions and invoked the pardon promised by the King. But he was executed nonetheless.[21]

The revolt had lasted barely a month. Yet it was to have profound consequences for England's ability to prosecute the war. Sir Richard Waldegrave, the Speaker, delivered the Commons' diagnosis of the country's ills when Parliament met the following November. The main factors in the recent revolt had been civil disorders within the country, caused he thought by the higher nobility's maintenance of the quarrels of its inferiors; by intensive and heavy-handed government; and by excessive taxation for a particularly poor return. Waldegrave's analysis was neither complete nor in all respects fair but the perception that it was right became one of the orthodoxies of contemporary politics. Perhaps even more significant was the growing recognition of the Parliamentary Commons that England simply lacked the resources to support a long-term war against the richest and most populous European nation. The country, they declared, had become progressively impoverished since the 1360s. The continual export of gold and silver coin (much of it in the pockets of English soldiers) had provoked a serious deflation. The terms of trade had changed against England as exports of wool, tin and lead had declined both in volume and in unit value. These problems were aggravated by war damage by land and sea, by enemy attacks on the coasts and sea-lanes and by the inexorable decay of the English merchant fleet. The Commons' solution was that the scale of the King's wars should be 'carefully but substantially reduced'. They adjourned on 6 December until the new year to consult their constituents about the government's financial needs. Current tensions within the realm, they said, ruled out another Parliamentary subsidy for the moment.[22]

For the first time since the ill-fated Congress of Bruges, the Council seriously contemplated making peace with France. Diplomatic contacts between the English and French courts had never entirely ceased. There had been desultory meetings between English and French diplomats year upon year at the edge of the pale of Calais. But the fragmentary records of these conferences suggest that, although the French were genuinely anxious to achieve a negotiated settlement, the English were not. Their ambassadors had edged their way towards accepting some kind of compromise on the question of sovereignty in south-western France but they had very limited authority and were in no position to pursue these openings. After the Peasants' Revolt there was a marked change of tone. With the Commons refusing to finance another large continental expedition, the councillors of the young Richard II were hamstrung as completely as those of the King of France. In March 1382 an English embassy was on the march of Picardy trying to agree arrangements with their French opposite numbers for a major diplomatic conference in the summer. A cease-fire was agreed. The two principal belligerents promised to recruit no new armed forces on land or sea until at least 1 June 1382. Terms of peace were put forward on each side together with a fall-back proposal involving a twelve-year truce, the terms of which had evidently been worked out in some detail. For the first time since the mid-1370s the English agreed to send ambassadors of sufficient status and authority to conclude a deal. Shortly afterwards the government announced that it would be represented by the Duke of Lancaster, the Earl of Buckingham and Thomas Holand, Earl of Kent, as grand an embassy as could have been contrived. According to reports picked up by Aragonese agents at Avignon both sides were confident of an imminent end to hostilities.[23]

The expedition to Portugal was the only continental venture to survive from the grandiose plans of the previous winter. The Earl of Cambridge's army, 3,000 strong, remained by the shore at Plymouth and Dartmouth throughout the month of June 1381, held up by adverse winds blowing in from the south-west. The whole army finally sailed south at about the end of June crammed into just forty-one exceptionally large ships. It is some sign of the diminished fortunes of the English merchant marine and the growing weight of Portugal in the trade routes of the Atlantic that sixteen of these vessels were Portuguese. The Earl himself was a political figurehead who had shown himself to be a soldier of very mediocre talents on the only previous occasion when he had exercised independent command, in Gascony in 1369 and 1370. He had been appointed because he was the only man who could convincingly represent his brother. But he came with a distinguished company. Sir William Beauchamp, a veteran of Nájera and long-standing military retainer of John of Gaunt, was the constable of the army and commanded the largest retinue after Cambridge's own. The marshal of the army, Sir Matthew Gournay, then more than seventy years old, had fought at Sluys, Crécy, Poitiers and Nájera according to the brass which once covered his grave in the church of Stoke-sub-Hamdon, Somerset. This old hand at Iberian politics had fought on both sides in the Castilian civil wars and had lived briefly at the Portuguese court in the time of King Fernando's father. Sir Thomas Symonds was charged by Gaunt with bearing his Castilian standard, which was to be unfurled as the army entered Castile. The Duke's Castilian secretary, Juan Gutiérrez, was there with the exiled Castilian knights from his court, including Juan Fernández Andeiro himself. To these were added a handful of well-known soldiers of fortune including the Gascon captain the Soudan de Trau and the Hainaulter Thierry Robesart. The Earl travelled with his wife, Isabella of Castile, and their

431

young son Edward, a diplomatic bargaining counter then only eight years old.[24]

In spite of the elaborate measures of deception by which Fernando had attempted to conceal his alliance with the English, rumours about it had been circulating for several months. The Castilians received reports in February 1381, probably from England, that an expedition was being prepared against them but they had no details of its route. By the following month they had obtained details of the Anglo-Portuguese treaty with its arrangements for a joint invasion of Castile through Portugal. The full strength of Cambridge's army must have become known at the Castilian court during the summer. John of Trastámara was alarmed. The English enjoyed a formidable military reputation, for all their recent reverses. Cambridge's army was half as big again as that specified in the treaty. It was substantially larger than the French mercenary corps which his father had deployed in the final stages of the civil war and most of those had by now returned to France. It was more than enough to turn the military balance in the Iberian peninsula even without the phantom English army which the Castilian King persuaded himself was assembling in Gascony in order to open a second front in Galicia or Navarre. John made an urgent appeal for troops to the French government, probably through Ayala, who was in Paris to negotiate the renewal of the Franco-Castilian alliance. Ayala formally sealed the new treaty in the Duke of Berry's grandiose mansion at Bicêtre, north of Paris, on 22 April. Less than a month later John publicly declared for the French candidate to the papal throne. Unfortunately for John none of this produced the immediate reinforcements that he needed. In Paris the Council was disabled by the continuing tax strike in the French provinces and absorbed by the Duke of Anjou's efforts to promote his ambitions in Italy. It was as much as they could do to allow a handful of volunteers to recruit their own companies to go to John's aid.[25]

Thrown back on his own resources, the Castilian King resolved to repeat the strategy which his father had used in 1373 by knocking Portugal out of the war before the English could arrive. He summoned his army to muster on 20 April 1381 on the banks of the Duero, the traditional invasion route into northern Portugal. The King proposed to take command here in person. Meanwhile another Castilian army was formed further south at Badajoz under the command of the Master of the Castilian Order of Santiago and Fernando's exiled half-brother the Infante João. These two men began to penetrate into the Alemtejo in

May. At sea the Castilian King planned to create one of the largest war fleets that Castile had ever deployed. John told the Cortes, which was summoned to the northern city of Medina del Campo to authorise emergency taxes, that as many as forty galleys were being made ready by an army of shipwrights at Seville and the Biscay ports of the north. This was approximately double the King's existing strength in galleys. A fleet of 130 sailing ships and barges was being collected to support them. For John's subjects these plans entailed yet another turn of the fiscal screw. The Cortes granted John a subsidy of no less than four *monedas* (the conventional unit in which *servicios* were expressed). It also authorised a heavy forced loan secured on the future yield of the *alcabala* (or sales tax).[26]

If the Castilian strategy failed in 1381 it was partly because there was insufficient time to prepare and partly because the Portuguese King had learned something from the disasters of 1373. The southern arm of the Castilian pincer movement was stopped by a series of vigorous Portuguese counter-attacks along the valley of the Guadiana. The northern arm was delayed for two months when the Portuguese successfully fomented a rebellion in León and the Asturias behind John's back. Castile was, however, able to strike one effective blow against Portugal before the Earl of Cambridge arrived. On 12 June 1381 the Portuguese war fleet, comprising twenty-two galleys and four sailing ships, sailed south from the Tagus under the command of the Queen's brother, João Afonso Telo. Their object was to stop the Castilian fleet leaving Seville by blockading the mouth of the River Guadalquivir. The fleet rounded Cape St. Vincent at the south-west tip of Portugal and penetrated into the Gulf of Cadiz on 17 June 1382. Their arrival caught the Castilians at a disadvantage. The vast armada planned by John of Trastámara was still being fitted out. There were only seventeen serviceable galleys at Seville with full complements of soldiers and seamen. These had been brought down to the open sea and anchored off the island of Saltes at the mouth of the Río Tinto. The tips of their masts could be seen by the Portuguese as they approached along the coast of the Algarve from the west. Outnumbered by the enemy, the Castilian Admiral Sánchez de Tovar resorted to guile. He feigned a withdrawal in the hope of drawing the Portuguese on. The Portuguese commander, seeing his prey escaping, fell into the trap. He ordered his ships forward without pausing to draw them up in formation. There was not even time for the crews to drink some water or the troops to finish arming themselves. The result was a disaster for the Portuguese. A large part of

433

their rowing crews was made up of conscripted peasants and beggars pressed into service in the streets of the towns. This hindered the complex business of manoeuvring these large oared ships. Half of the Portuguese galleys, passing too close to the shore, got their oars caught in the nets of some fishermen and had to stop to extricate themselves. The rest closed on Sánchez de Tovar's tightly arrayed fleet in complete disorder and were boarded and captured one by one. By the time the other galleys had freed themselves from the nets they were heavily outnumbered and suffered the same fate. The entire Portuguese navy had been lost in an afternoon. Twenty galleys were captured and one destroyed. Some 6,000 Portuguese soldiers and seamen were killed or taken. The Portuguese commander was among the prisoners. The damage to the morale of the King, who had devoted much treasure and time to building up his fleet over the past few years, weighed on him for the remainder of the war.

John of Trastámara was exultant. He believed that the victory would prevent the English from landing in Portugal. And so it might have done if it had been followed up straight away. A Castilian blockade of the entrance to the Tagus or the Duero at this stage would have been difficult for the English to force. But Sánchez de Tovar was determined to return to Seville to land his prisoners and spoil and secure the captured galleys. The Portuguese Prince Don João, who was fighting with the Castilian armies, could see that an opportunity was being missed. He rushed to Seville, armed with royal letters of authority, gathered together six of the captured Portuguese galleys and persuaded some of the Portuguese prisoners to join him in an attack on Lisbon. The small squadron entered the Tagus in the middle of July and made for Lisbon. Don João believed that the men of the capital would rise in support when he appeared. But they probably never even discovered who was in command. As soon as Don João's ships were recognised as enemies they were driven off in a hail of artillery fire and crossbow bolts and forced to withdraw to Seville. Unknown to the Castilians, the Earl of Cambridge's fleet was already approaching Lisbon. The ships arrived safely in the roads and anchored beneath the city walls on 19 July 1381.[27]

Things began to go wrong as soon as the English army landed. Several weeks were taken up with processions and feasting and with diplomatic business. Don Fernando had declared his allegiance to the Avignon Pope early in 1380 at a time when he was trying to improve relations with France. The English Council, however, were determined to present the invasion of Castile as an Urbanist crusade. They may well have thought that this would add to their support in Castile. The Portuguese King therefore had to be detached from his allegiance to Avignon. On 29 August he duly abjured Clement VII and declared once more for Urban. Fernando's declaration cleared the way for the formal betrothal of the Earl's eight-year-old son Edward to Princess Beatrice, which was to seal the Anglo-Portuguese alliance. Edward was acknowledged as the heir presumptive to the Crown of Portugal and received the homage of the leading noblemen and walled towns of the realm. The two small children were then ceremonially installed in a vast bed in a chamber of the royal palace, covered by a magnificent black heraldic tapestry with figures worked in pearls. A crowd of courtiers stood around as prayers were said over them by the Bishop of Lisbon, an ardent partisan of Avignon, and by Juan Gutiérrez, who was even then plotting to supplant him. On 8 September 1381, at a great gathering of Fernando's councillors and the captains of the English army, a letter from Urban VI was read out in which the Roman Pope authorised his adherents everywhere to seize the property of Clementists for themselves and to make war on them everywhere with the same privileges and indulgences as crusaders in the Holy Land.[28]

This was mere rhetoric. The Earl of Cambridge's army was in no position to take the field for they had no horses. They had come expecting that mounts would be ready for them in accordance with the treaty. But Fernando had done nothing about this. The Portuguese Cortes met, probably early in September, to authorise a mass requisition of horses and mules. Finding at least 3,000 animals in a country as small as Portugal without dismounting Don Fernando's own troops was a major undertaking which took some time. Many of them proved to be of low quality or unbroken. The English won many admirers among the Portuguese for the skill with which they managed these wild and unsuitable beasts. But the whole process cost them another two months of campaigning time. The leaders of the army passed most of this time comfortably installed in the suburban monasteries of Lisbon while their men camped in the fields by the Tagus, north of the city. But as the autumn wore on they grew bored and ran out of money. Discipline broke down. The English and their Gascon and Hainault auxiliaries began to break into suburban houses and rural farms, to sack the outlying villages and pillage along the roads around the capital. The Earl of Cambridge proved quite incapable of restoring order. Stories of appalling atrocities began to circulate, which no doubt grew in the telling. Within a few weeks the English were profoundly hated around Lisbon.[29]

Meanwhile the Castilian offensive had made a halting start. John of Trastámara entered Portugal with the main body of his army towards the end of July 1381, attacking west of the Castilian city of Ciudad Rodrigo and laying siege to Almeida. In the southern sector the Master of the Castilian Order of Santiago launched a simultaneous offensive from Badajoz and besieged Elvas. These two border fortresses, repeatedly expanded and rebuilt, had been the principal eastern defences of Portugal since the twelfth century and would remain so until the nineteenth. Almeida was poorly defended. The town surrendered to the Castilians on 9 August and the castle some three weeks later. But further progress then came to a halt. King John, whose constitution was never up to the rigours of a campaign, fell ill. Then, when the news of the English landings reached him, he lost his nerve. The southern arm of the Castilian pincer movement was abandoned and the troops around Elvas were brought north to reinforce the army at Almeida. A messenger was sent to the Earl of Cambridge at Lisbon with a challenge to fight an arranged battle somewhere between Lisbon and the frontier. It was an empty gesture. The Earl ignored the challenge and Fernando had the unfortunate Castilian messenger who delivered it flung into prison. Towards the end of September 1381 the Castilian King withdrew to the castle of Coca, north of Segovia. The financial strain was more than the Castilian treasury could bear. The troops at Almeida, the seamen and shipwrights in Seville and the Basque ports and the permanent garrisons on the frontiers of Navarre and Granada, were all clamouring for their pay. The Castilian Cortes sat intermittently for some two months at Avila between October and December before authorising another large increase in taxation.[30]

John of Trastámara could not believe that his enemies would remain immobile throughout the winter. He made plans to deploy a great army 5,000 strong along the border to contain them. In fact, a winter campaign never seems to have been contemplated. Since English armies were famous for their indifference to the seasons this was presumably Fernando's decision. A more vigorous proconsul might have shifted the Portuguese King from this position but the Earl of Cambridge simply accepted the situation as he found it. His army remained in its encampments around Lisbon until the end of the year. They were needed there to defend the capital and the English fleet against Sánchez de Tovar's Castilian galleys cruising offshore. In December 1381 the galleys finally returned to Seville to be laid up for the winter and the English ships were able to leave for home. As soon as they had gone

Fernando left to celebrate Christmas at Santarém while the Earl of Cambridge departed with his unruly troops for winter quarters in the valley of the Guadiana, close to Portugal's eastern frontier. The Earl established his headquarters in an Augustinian monastery outside the walled town of Vila Viçosa, about ten miles behind the frontier, and waited for the spring.[31]

Early in December 1381 a squire arrived in England from Lisbon with a report to the Council and the Duke of Lancaster. It must have made sombre reading. The Earl of Cambridge took the blackest possible view of his situation. He seems to have concluded that nothing could be expected from the Portuguese army and that his own force was at risk of destruction unless it received rapid and powerful reinforcements from England. For an army which had not even taken the field this was an extraordinary statement. John of Gaunt felt that his great adventure ought to be on the verge of triumph. He was determined that the chance should not escape him now. So he resolved to take command in Portugal himself. He would bring another 4,000 men with him. These plans were completely unrealistic. The main problem, as always, was finance. The Earl of Cambridge's army had been paid a quarter's wages in advance before leaving England. The next quarter's wages were supposed to come from the Portuguese King's treasury. Thereafter the position was somewhat uncertain, no one having anticipated that the army would have to spend so long in Portugal. The men were now pressing for their third quarter's pay. The cost of meeting the arrears and sending a second army out under Gaunt himself was reckoned at another £60,000 for six months.[32]

Parliament returned from its Christmas adjournment on 24 January 1382. The business of the new session was dominated by John of Gaunt's great project. The Duke's unpopularity was always at its strongest when he was seen to be controlling the business of government. The mood in London was highly charged. Six hundred members of the London guilds appeared before the young King at Kennington manor to ask that they might have 'only one King'. The message was too obvious to be missed. In the palace of Westminster John of Gaunt gave the peers the substance of the Earl of Cambridge's bleak message. He told them that it was essential to 'rescue' the army in Portugal. He argued that this was in England's interests not just his own. A successful war against the Trastámaran dynasty in Castile was the best way of assuring the defence of the seas and coasts around England. Gaunt was realistic enough not to suggest that the Commons should finance his Portuguese venture outright. What he proposed was that the money should be lent to him by the Crown for three years with repayment secured on the income of his English estates. The details of the scheme have not survived, but Gaunt appears to have envisaged that the Crown would raise the £60,000 from taxation and that his repayments would then be used to reduce the need for further Parliamentary taxes in future. But, however ingeniously wrapped up, what John of Gaunt was really asking for was a new Parliamentary subsidy following hard on the disastrous poll tax of the previous year. His demands generated acrimonious discussion at Westminster which continued for more than a fortnight. It divided the Lords, where Gaunt's natural supporters were to be found. Most of them accepted his arguments. But an important minority was afraid of another popular uprising and unwilling to denude the country of troops. The Commons rejected the proposal on more fundamental grounds. War taxation had continued year on year for too long, they said. They would not authorise a new subsidy, whether by way of loan or grant. All that they would do was extend the modest supplementary export duties originally granted at Gloucester in 1377 for another four and a half years in order to finance the defence of England. If the government wanted to mount offensive operations it would have to find some other way of paying for them. As for Gaunt's pursuit of the Castilian throne, that they declared to be his own affair and nothing to do with them. On this note the proceedings were brought to a close.[33]

At almost the same moment the attention of the French government was fixed upon the personal venture of another royal uncle, which had even less to do with French interests than the succession of Castile had to do with English ones. The adoption of the Duke of Anjou as the heir to the kingdom of Naples had been intended to secure Queen Jeanne on her throne. In the event it destroyed her. Urban VI had learned about the Queen's negotiations with the Duke in March 1380 from a disaffected ally. On 11 May 1380 he had purported to depose her and declare her throne vacant. A year later he patched up a squalid deal with Charles of Durazzo. In return for the grant of the Neapolitan crown Charles promised to conquer it and then to cede large parts of its territory to the Pope's worthless nephew. Urban for his part raided the treasuries of the Roman churches to raise the money needed to pay Charles's troops and offered them the indulgences of crusaders. On 2 June 1381 Charles of Durazzo was crowned in the old basilica of St. Peter's in Rome before an audience consisting largely of Magyar soldiers.

Jeanne despatched a messenger to France with a desperate appeal to Louis of Anjou to rescue her. She invoked the military clauses of their agreement of the previous year. As an additional inducement she offered to share the government of her domains with Louis in her lifetime. But events moved too fast for either Jeanne or Louis. On 8 June 1381 Charles marched out of Rome with about 7,000 Magyars and some 1,000 soldiers of fortune to take possession of his new kingdom. The Queen's armies, such as they were, tried to halt his advance at the border but they were swept aside. On the evening of 16 July Charles of Durazzo entered Naples. The inhabitants refused to defend the capital. Jeanne fled with her closest supporters to the protection of the Castel Nuovo. The castle was powerfully fortified. But it had not been victualled for a siege. After five weeks it became clear that it could hold out no longer. Jeanne was forced to enter into a conditional surrender. She was given just five days to organise a relief force. Her husband, Otto of Brunswick, made a valiant attempt to relieve her in time. But on 24 August he was routed beneath the walls of the Castel S. Elmo and captured. At the beginning of September 1381 Charles took possession of the Castel Nuovo and the Queen became his prisoner.[34]

These events were the prelude to a sustained campaign of lobbying by Jeanne's partisans in France. Her Provençal subjects undertook to support a French expedition to Italy with money and men. From Avignon Clement VII ceaselessly pressed the French court to intervene. He also greatly enlarged his own financial commitment, offering to place substantially the whole revenues of the Apostolic Chamber and the taxes levied on the French Church at Louis's disposal. Meanwhile Jeanne's agent in Avignon supplied a steady stream of reassuring (but false) reports that the inhabitants of the Neapolitan kingdom and most of the states of Italy would support an Angevin invasion. These reports, amplified by Clement's agents in Paris, had a considerable impact on the decision-makers at the French court. On 4 and 5 January 1382 there was a long and difficult session of the French royal Council in the castle of Vincennes. All the royal princes were there apart from the Duke of Berry. So were King's councillors, the Constable Olivier de Clisson, the lord of Coucy and some of the government's most experienced soldiers and diplomats. A delegation of five prominent members of the papal court hovered between the council room and the ante-chambers of the palace. By a majority, and with express misgivings about the difficulty of the undertaking, the Council gave it as their opinion that Louis of Anjou was bound to go to the aid of the Queen of Naples. He had already committed himself too far to withdraw with honour now. They advised that an expeditionary force should be prepared as rapidly as possible. Some of Louis's advisers urged caution. But their reservations were brushed aside. On 7 January 1382 the Duke of Anjou resolved to conquer Naples and rescue its Queen from her prison. The decision was announced to the King and his Council on the following day. In the middle of February 1382 Louis left Paris for Avignon. Three weeks later, in the consistory hall of the papal palace, he swore before the assembled court of Clement VII that he would not leave the papal city until the time came for him to take the road to Italy.[35]

Louis of Anjou marched to the Alps from the papal city of Carpentras in the middle of June 1382. Initially his army comprised some 12,000 mounted men. The Council, although they had urged the expedition upon the Duke, forbade the King's subjects to join it for fear of denuding the country in the face of the English. As a result, most of Louis's army had been recruited in the francophone territories of the Empire east of the Rhône. More were hired by his Italian allies. He was also joined by most of the surviving Gascon and Breton companies in Italy, including the band of Bernard de la Salle and the Italian and German companies operating in the papal state in Jeanne's name. With these accessions of strength Louis commanded one of the largest armies gathered together in the fourteenth century, about 60,000 mounted men by the time he reached the marches of the papal state according to his own estimation. His numbers, he wrote to the city of Marseille, increased daily as men came into his camp 'like vultures gathering around a corpse'.[36]

It was a curious phrase to use and as it turned out a prophetic one. The Angevin invasion was a disaster for all the main protagonists. It was a death sentence for Queen Jeanne. She had been held in the remote castle of Muro in the Apennines ever since the Duke of Anjou's preparations had become known in Italy. There, at the end of July 1382, she was smothered by her jailers on the orders of Charles of Durazzo. The body was brought back to Naples to be exposed in the ghastly candle-lit gloom of the convent church of Santa Chiara as Louis pressed on towards his southern kingdom. There was little armed resistance. But the Duke encountered growing difficulty in feeding his immense host. He was obliged to divide his forces in order to ease his supply problems. Less than a third of his men followed him into Neapolitan territory at the end of September 1382. Charles of Durazzo fought a skilful rearguard action. He was supported by the English *routier* captain Sir John Hawkwood with a company of more than 2,000 mercenaries. Heavily outnumbered, they adopted much the same tactics as the French had in the face of the English invasions of 1373 and 1380. They wasted the earth in front of the enemy, harassed his flanks at every turn and persistently refused battle. At the end of the year most of Louis's troops had deserted him. The rest were sick, starving and unpaid. Louis decided that his great venture had failed. Writing from Benevento, where he had established his winter quarters, he called on the French Council to send funds urgently. Failing that, let them at least find some excuse to recall him for service in France so that he could withdraw without disgrace. The Council never received his plea. The messenger was intercepted and the letter delivered instead to Urban VI. In the new year Louis approached Charles of Durazzo to ask for terms. According to reports reaching Rome he was ready to abandon his claim to the Neapolitan kingdom in return for Provence and a safe-conduct out of Italy.[37]

The immediate consequence of Anjou's Italian adventure was to remove the dominant figure on the French Council from the political scene. Power passed into the hands of Anjou's brothers, the Dukes of Berry and Burgundy. Berry was the older brother. But he was an idle man without Philip's political acumen and ambition. He was generally content to defer to him provided that he was given a free hand in the provinces of the south. No one doubted that the real seat of government was now the Hôtel d'Artois, the luxurious mansion north of Les Halles, surrounded by gardens and outbuildings, where Philip established his Parisian residence. It would, however, be a mistake to suppose that Philip could do as he liked. The administration and the Parlement were still full of Charles V's old servants who were loyal to his memory. There were military leaders and territorial magnates of considerable stature who were not beholden to him and whose views could not be ignored: the young King's maternal uncle and guardian, the Duke of Bourbon; the Constable, Olivier de Clisson, a natural contrariant whose office, wealth, and close personal relationship with the young King made him largely independent of other men's patronage; the Marshal, Louis de Sancerre, and the Admiral, Jean de Vienne, who were closely associated with the victories of the 1370s; courtier-captains like Enguerrand de Coucy and that grizzled veteran of three decades of French and Castilian civil wars, Pierre de Villaines, both of them highly regarded by the military nobility and the population of Paris. The Duke of Burgundy's decisions were always constrained by a weight of consensus which represented a strong brake on personal government. Over the years, however, the transfer of power from Anjou to Burgundy would have a significant impact on the direction of French policy. Philip of Burgundy did not share Anjou's personal loyalty to the Avignon papacy. He was much less interested in the Gascon march and the affairs of the Iberian peninsula. His interests were concentrated in the north, where he was intent on restoring Louis de Mâle's authority in Flanders. Philip had never felt his brother's animosity against England. In the long term he realised that an accommodation with England would be necessary if he was to take effective control of his wife's inheritance in the Low Countries.

The Duke's of Burgundy's first challenge was the financial condition of the French state, which Louis of Anjou had left unresolved. The partial re-establishment of the tax system by the Estates-General of Languedoil at the beginning of the year had failed. After a halting start the flow of receipts appears to have settled at about a tenth of the sums anticipated.[38] The standing army of 6,000 men which the delegates in Paris had envisaged never came into being. Apart from the defence of Nantes in January 1380, which had involved only limited forces, no significant military enterprise had been attempted since the King's accession. A large part of the problem was the reduced geographical area from which the King's taxes were now drawn. With the attempt to introduce royal taxation into Brittany abandoned, the revenues of southern and central France reserved to the Duke of Berry, Burgundy supporting the increasingly magnificent train of life of its Duke and the revenues of the Loire provinces assigned to the Italian campaign of the Duke of Anjou, substantially the whole burden of fighting the English had to be borne by the taxpayers of a very limited region: Paris and the Île de France, Normandy, Picardy and Champagne. These provinces comprised perhaps a third of France's population, its most fertile agricultural areas and most of its richest cities. But they were also the most politically organised regions of France, where opposition to royal taxation after the death of Charles V had been strongest.

On 14 January 1382 the Provost of the Merchants and the representatives of Paris were summoned to Vincennes, where the court was residing. When they arrived they were brought before the King. He was attended by his uncles and the rest of the royal Council. The Parisians were told that the King required them to re-grant all the taxes in force before the death of Charles V. They asked for time to consider this and were given one day. When they returned on 16 January they were admitted to the council chamber one by one and required to give their answer without knowing what the others had said. The cowed Parisians submitted. On the following day the Council published the new taxes. It was a hole and corner affair, for the government needed time to manage public opinion. A crier appeared in the enclosed courtyard of the Châtelet. Another mounted the marble platform in the great hall of the palace on the island during the lunch hour and made the proclamation to the empty chamber. With effect from 1 March 1382 the sales taxes on wine and other goods exposed for sale were to be reinstated at the rates in force under Charles V. The *gabelle* would be reimposed at an increased rate. Equally high-handed but less well recorded negotiations were conducted with the provinces of Languedoil with the same outcome. The news of what had happened only gradually spread through the capital and then from town to town across northern France. During the next six weeks, as the government looked for tax farmers willing to collect the new revenues, tensions rose in the northern towns, each waiting to see what others would do.[39]

During the terrible week when London had been under the control of Wat Tyler and his allies, Michel Pintoin, the future chantor of the abbey of Saint-Denis and official historian of Charles VI, was in England on the financial affairs of his house. The murder of Archbishop Sudbury was reported to his little group of Frenchmen on the day it happened. Someone said: 'I tell you that before long worse things than these will come to pass in France.' 'God forbid that France's ancient loyalty should be defiled by such horrors,' replied the deeply conventional Pintoin. Yet his interlocutor proved to be the better prophet.

The violence began in Rouen. The largest city of the kingdom after Paris, Rouen lived mainly on shipbuilding and the manufacture of coarse woollen cloth, both labour-intensive industries in decline. The city suffered from many of the same problems as the cloth towns of Flanders: high unemployment, large-scale migration from the country-side, widening social divisions. Tensions were aggravated by the tight control exercised by the rich ecclesiastical corporations which owned most of the city and the small merchant patriciate which dominated the commune, two groups which were much resented by the lowlier inhabitants and notoriously at loggerheads with each other. On 24 February 1381, a week before the new taxes were to come into force, a group of men led by a draper called Jean le Gras sounded one of the great bells of the commune, calling the population to arms. Their confederates closed the gates of the city to stop people leaving and opened up the prisons. A great mob took over the streets. They were drawn from the poorest sections of the city's population, '*la merdaille*' as a local chronicler called them. Their main targets were the rich: leading wholesale merchants, Jews, town councillors past and present, the wealthier churches, the farmers of the *aides* and the collectors of the *gabelle*. There were few casualties but a great deal of destruction. The cloister of the Franciscan convent was filled with refugees as houses were sacked, furniture smashed and stock carried off. The looting continued all day and throughout the following night until the watch, composed of householders and guild members, finally recovered their nerve and managed to restore order. They then set about turning the chaos to their own advantage, paying off scores of their own and pursuing old rivalries. The cathedral and the abbey of St. Ouen were invaded, their archives and muniments burned, and the canons forced to put their names to acts signing away rents, lawsuits, rights and privileges. On the hill of Bihorel, by the Abbeville road north of the city walls, men hacked down the immense triangular gallows by which the abbot of St. Ouen flaunted his jurisdiction to the townsmen below. The famous charter extracted from King Louis X in the rebellion of 1315, which had achieved a symbolic importance far exceeding its legal effect, was paraded through the cemetery of St. Ouen, one of the largest open spaces of the city, while reluctant officials and ecclesiastics swore to respect it. The Harelle, as the revolt of Rouen came to be called, had lasted for just three days.[40]

The Duke of Burgundy's first reaction to the news from Rouen was to face down the opposition by force. On 1 March the young King, accompanied by his uncle and the lords of Coucy and Albret, set out from Vincennes with an armed escort to intimidate the Rouennais before their example spread to the capital. They had only got as far as Saint-Denis when it became clear that they were too late. Early that morning, when the collectors of the *aides* had arrived in the market of Les Halles to begin their work, some 500 furious young men looking for trouble had already gathered there. The first trader to be asked to account for the tax was an old woman selling cress. As they approached her stall the collectors were attacked, covered in blows and left for dead. The mob, now blooded, poured out of the market-place into the Rue Saint-Denis and spread through the narrow streets, yelling abuse, gathering recruits as they went and carrying bystanders along in their path. Within a short period there were several thousand rioters on the streets. They converged on the Place de Grève looking for weapons. Some years before, when Paris was threatened with attack by the English, Hughes Aubriot had stocked in the Maison aux Piliers a large number of *maillets*, street-fighting weapons consisting of cylindrical lead cudgels fitted with wooden handles. The mob broke down the doors of the building, forced their way into the tower where the *maillets* were stored and distributed them among the crowd outside: hence the name *maillotins*, which was subsequently conferred on the rebels. As at Rouen, the violence was begun by the poor. They were drawn mainly from the mass of young journeymen and unemployed, recent migrants from the country, beggars and criminals. Here were the *popolo minuto*, according to the Florentine merchant Buonaccorso Pitti, who was in Paris at the time and remembered the revolt of the *ciompi* of Florence, four years earlier.

Armed with their lead cudgels the mob spread through the right-bank quarters of the capital, wrecking houses and breaking into church treasuries. The first victims were the officials charged with collecting the *aides*. Tax collectors and farmers seen in the streets were cut down where they stood. Others were hunted down in their houses or found clinging to the altars of the city's churches. They were dragged out to meet the same fate. Their registers were torn in pieces or burned. Then the mob turned its wrath against the rich bourgeois: moneylenders, royal judges and officials. All fled as their houses were broken open and pillaged. The mansion of the Duke of Anjou was taken over and transformed into a meeting place for leaders of the mob. Some of the rioters made for the Jewish quarters, sacking their houses, destroying their records and pledges and killing those who would not declare their conversion to Christianity. The forces of order vanished. The royal Provost, the Bishop of Paris, the Provost of the Merchants and the remaining royal councillors all fled with what possessions they could carry. Only the old Breton *routier* Maurice de Tréséguidy, now the royal captain of Paris, tried to stem the violence. His men were quickly overwhelmed.

The King's cavalcade had by now turned back towards Vincennes. The Duke of Burgundy left the main party, accompanied by the Chancellor, the lord of Coucy and a small group of officials. They rode to the Porte Saint-Antoine at the eastern end of the city to find out what was happening. A group of Parisians appeared at the gate to speak to them. These men were prominent members of the Paris guilds. They had nothing to say for the rioters and certainly could not speak for them. But they were just as hostile to the new taxes. They hoped by mediating between the mob and the government to extract concessions. They made three demands of the Duke: the immediate abolition of all taxes introduced since the beginning of the century; the release of four citizens who had been arrested for organising resistance to the taxes in February; and an amnesty for the events of the day. Later that morning the Council met in the castle of Vincennes to consider these demands. They decided that there would be no compromise. The answer was sent back that the King would concede nothing apart from the release of the four citizens. When this was reported to the leaders of the mob there was a fresh explosion of violence. The *maillotins* headed for the Châtelet, the seat of the Royal Provost and the symbol of royal power in the city. They broke down the gates and opened up the cells as the sergeants fled for their lives. After this it was the turn of the city's other prisons, most of which belonged to the Bishop and the great abbeys. They were broken open and their prisoners released onto the streets. [41]

Within the walls the householders and guildsmen had already begun to reassert control. The watch was called out, armed, and placed under the control of the guild captains. During the night and the following day they gradually recovered possession of the streets as the violence of the mob burned itself out. But once the municipality had put a stop to the violence, as that shrewd observer Buonaccorso Pitti noted, they simply took over the rebels' cause as their own. They kept the city gates firmly closed and set about bargaining with the government about the taxes. For its part, the Council at Vincennes maintained its defiance. Royal troops were sent to occupy the bridge of Charenton, upstream of the city, and began to stop river traffic carrying in food. The Duke of Burgundy summoned his Burgundian retainers. Rumours got about that John de Montfort and even Louis of Anjou were on their way with troops to suppress the resistance of the capital. A show of force suited the authoritarian instincts of Philip of Burgundy and he may well have contemplated one. But it was no longer realistic. As the news of the rising in Paris spread through the northern provinces the new taxes were rejected everywhere. At Amiens, where the violent party conflicts of 1358 still lay just below the surface of civic life, men went through the streets shouting out their support for the rioters of Paris. At Dieppe the town gates were closed in the collectors' faces. At Falaise in Normandy rioters broke up the auction of the tax farm for the district. At Caen the collectors were abused and manhandled. Angry crowds took to the streets at Orléans and Reims. Similar scenes were enacted in countless other towns of the north. The government was forced to compromise. On 4 March 1382 the Council announced the temporary suspension of the taxes and a partial amnesty for the rioters. The Parisians for their part agreed to submit to mediation by the University and to deliver up forty of the ringleaders of 1 March, who had been arrested by the watch and shut in the Châtelet. They were beheaded or hanged at the gates of the city in small groups over the following days until the threat of fresh riots made it necessary to suspend the executions.[42]

The uneasy stand-off in Paris enabled the government to make an example of less formidable antagonists. On 17 March 1382 the King and the Duke of Burgundy left Vincennes for Rouen for the second time. A fortnight later, on 29 March, the gates of Rouen were thrown down and symbolically trampled underfoot by the royal party as they rode in with helmets on their heads and drawn swords in their hands. Only twelve ringleaders were executed at Rouen. But the bourgeois who had tried to make use of the popular violence were humbled. The municipality was abolished and its powers transferred to the royal *bailli*. The town bells and coat of arms were confiscated. A vindictive fine of 100,000 francs was imposed, nearly half of which was actually enforced.[43]

The authority of the Crown had been upheld. But the issue of taxation remained unresolved. No attempt was made to recall the Estates-General, which had shown itself to be largely ineffective in 1380. Instead a series of provincial assemblies was summoned in April 1382, starting with the five *baillages* of Champagne and Picardy. Their representatives gathered before the King and his ministers at Compiègne. The president of the Parlement, Arnaud de Corbie, like most fourteenth-century lawyers profoundly conservative and authoritarian, harangued the delegates about the desperate state of the government's finances. But the most that they would agree to do was consult their constituents. In the event four of the five *baillages* refused a grant outright. The fifth, Sens, conceded a sales tax that proved impossible to collect. The reception of the King's demands in Amiens, the only city whose deliberations are recorded, suggests that the problem was not necessarily the principle of taxation but its distribution among the population. The King's need was acknowledged at Amiens. There might have been popular support for a direct tax which would not fall chiefly on the poor but that was unacceptable to the merchant oligarchies who dominated the civic life of the town. So nothing at all was agreed.[44]

The Parisians had not been represented at Compiègne but they were asked to grant their own tax at the rate promised by the province of Sens. The captains of the watch summoned a large assembly to consider this demand. It was rejected by an overwhelming majority. A few voices were raised in support of the government. More would have been if they had not been silenced by the ugly mood of the gathering. At Vincennes the Council refused to take No for an answer. They sent Enguerrand de Coucy to reason with the Parisians. Enguerrand was a popular figure in the capital, one of the few men associated with the court who had been able to circulate freely during the March riots. But even he could only obtain a derisory offer of 12,000 francs. At the end of April 1382 the Council resorted in frustration to more abrasive measures. Once again the river traffic serving the city was cut off at the bridge of Charenton and this time at the downstream bridge of Saint-Cloud as well. The court moved to Melun, south of the city. From there the troops of Philip of Burgundy began a campaign of harassment against the Parisians, stopping road traffic around the city and wasting the suburban farms and orchards of prominent bourgeois. There was even talk of an assault on the walls. There was a long conference in the refectory of the monastery of Saint-Denis at which the spokesmen of the King and the city addressed a panel of mediators as if they were ambassadors of rival nations. The Parisian guild leaders, caught between their fear of the government and their fear of the mob, finally agreed in the middle of May 1382 upon a subsidy of 80,000 francs. But they had no public support for this deal and probably knew it.[45]

When, on 1 June 1382, Charles VI made his formal entry into Paris to mark his reconciliation with the capital, the councillors who were most closely associated with the Crown's attempt to repair its tax system stayed away for fear that their presence would provoke violence. Normandy, aristocratic, conservative, closely associated by tradition with the monarchy's fortunes, followed the example of Paris with better grace. The Estates of Normandy granted 30,000 francs at an assembly held at Pontoise at the beginning of June. The murmurings of revolt when this decision was first reported at Rouen suggest that it was no more popular among urban taxpayers than the Parisian grant. Some weeks later, when the tax began to be collected, a mob of journeymen and servants led by a butcher invaded Rouen's cloth market, overturned the stalls and broke up the market. It is probable, although the evidence is sparse, that similar grants were being made at provincial assemblies across northern France and meeting with similar resentments. By midsummer tax revenues had begin to flow again, but tensions were high and the proceeds disappointing.[46]

Much of the resistance to emergency taxation in France was inspired by the continued defiance of the Count of Flanders by the city of Ghent. Ghent, the original author of the urban revolutions of 1379, had suffered much since Louis de Mâle had brutally suppressed the rebellion in every other part of Flanders. It had seen its trade ruined by confiscations and boycotts. It had been defeated in battle. In a war of raid and counter-raid characterised by savagery on both sides, the town had suffered heavy casualties. In June 1381 it lost its last ally when Grammont was captured and burned and its inhabitants butchered by Louis de Mâle's captains. Yet Ghent itself, protected by walls and marshland and by its situation at the confluence of two great rivers, beat off every attempt by the Count's armies to capture it.

The cities of Flanders, the German Low Countries and northern France belonged in many respects to the same economic community, and the progress of the civil war in Flanders was followed with intense interest among its neighbours. Contemporaries, who rarely understood the dynamics of urban revolt, were profoundly conscious of the contagion of popular revolution. Buonaccorso Pitti was no doubt mistaken when he reported that the risings in Rouen and Paris had been provoked by agents of Ghent. But his opinion probably reflected the conventional wisdom of the political class in Paris and certainly their worst fears. Events seemed to bear their view out. At Amiens the rabble-rousers passed through the streets calling out their supporters with cries of 'Up with Paris! Up with Ghent!'[47]

In July 1381 the Count of Flanders had begun a systematic blockade of Ghent. With garrisons in Courtrai, Oudenaarde and Dendermonde, Louis was able to cut the river routes to Ghent by the Lys and close the Scheldt on both sides of the city. This left Ghent's dense population dependent for its food supplies on provisioning raids by mounted parties from the city; and on supplies carted overland from Hainault and Brabant or shipped to the harbours of Holland and Zeeland and smuggled across the low-lying region north of the city known as the Vier Ambachten. Raw materials for the city's workshops had to get in by the same routes. Gradually, over the next six months, all of these lifelines failed. Louis de Mâle's garrisons patrolled the territory around Ghent, attacking supply trains and killing or imprisoning the men in charge of them. He pressed the rulers of the neighbouring states to forbid their subjects to trade with Ghent. All of them did so with more or less effect. The grain traffic from Hainault was the first to dry up. Supplies from Brabant and from Holland and Zeeland continued in spite of the decrees of their rulers, but at irregular intervals and on a much reduced scale. As the city's distress mounted the Count's attitude became progressively harsher. There were a number of attempts to find a negotiated solution. All of them failed in the face of Louis's intransigence. He would accept nothing short of unconditional surrender.

By the end of 1381 the tragedy of Ghent had polarised opinion across northern Europe. Louis de Mâle recruited knights and squires to his standard from well beyond his own domains. Many of them were not simply earning their pay but intent on supporting the social order. 'Noblemen stick together,' as Froissart observed. On the other side of the divide a wave of solidarity united urban radicals in the self-governing cities. In Brabant the citizens of Louvain and Brussels supported the provisioning efforts of Ghent in defiance of their Duchess. Liège, a city controlled by its guilds with a long tradition of political radicalism and social discord, wrote letters of support and promised 600 cartloads of wheat and flour at the lowest point of the city's fortunes. Even in places which enforced the blockade and supported the Count with money and troops, the city magistrates grew frightened by the strength of feeling in the streets and tenements.[48]

Louis de Mâle's refusal to grant terms to the men of Ghent merely drove them to ever more desperate measures. The last serious attempt to find a compromise solution occurred in October 1381. The Flemish towns and the princes of the Low Countries, desperate for a solution to a conflict which was beginning to infect their own domains, convened a fresh peace conference. It was held at Harelbeke, a small village on the banks of the River Lys outside Courtrai. Ghent was represented there by twelve prominent members of the city government led by the two senior aldermen, Simon Bette and Gilbert de Grutere. A conditional agreement was made, subject to confirmation by the general assembly of the town. It provided for the complete submission of the city and for the surrender to the Count of 200 ringleaders to be nominated by him in due course and dealt with as he saw fit. Most of the city government was behind the agreement. They were supported by the grain shippers' and victuallers' guilds, whose members had been ruined by the blockade. The mass of inhabitants, says Froissart, were for peace 'except for the rabble who liked nothing better than a riot'. But it was not only the rabble who were opposed to the terms. The main opponents of the peace were the weavers, who saw nothing in the terms to ameliorate their desperate economic plight and every sign that the Count meant to suppress the autonomy of the city government. They were egged on by prominent politicians who had been heavily implicated in the events of the past two years and suspected that their names would be included in the Count's list of 200 victims. The municipality did their best to suppress opposition to the treaty. Peter Van den Bossche, the most prominent opponent, was imprisoned. On 2 January 1382 a mob consisting mainly of members of the grain shippers' guild invaded the town hall to attack the opponents of the peace. They murdered the town clerk, who was believed to be one of them, and threw his body into the street. Two wretches were seized and tortured until they confessed to a conspiracy against the peace, before being killed in their turn. Outside in the streets a pitched battle was fought between the partisans of the weavers and the grain shippers.

On 13 January 1382 a messenger arrived from Louis de Mâle with an ultimatum requiring the city to ratify the terms of the peace and deliver up hostages to secure its observance. On the 24th, the day before the aldermen were due to consider this demand, a general assembly was called in the Friday Market, the largest open space in the city. The opponents of the peace came well prepared. As the citizens stood in formation under the banners of their guilds they read out a declaration to the assembled multitude urging them that if they wanted their city to survive they should place all the powers of government in the hands of one man. They had their candidate ready: Philip Van Artevelde. Philip was a gang leader associated with Peter Van den Bossche and the weavers' faction, who had recently begun to take part in the councils of the city. His main claim to fame was that he was the son of Jacob, the famous dictator of Ghent who had led the city's rebellion against the Count's father forty years before. About half of those present in the Friday Market were opposed to his nomination. But the proposal had the appeal of novelty in a desperate situation and it began to gather momentum among the crowd. Perceiving this, his opponents sought to diminish the authority of the assembly by walking out of it. This was a mistake, as such decisions usually are. The effect was to leave the field clear for Van Artevelde's partisans.

Philip himself had been waiting for his moment in a public bathhouse nearby. He was fetched and taken in triumph to the town hall. There he was sworn in as captain of Ghent. An emergency government was set up, consisting of the new captain and four councillors of his

451

choice. But real power lay with Van Artevelde himself and with Peter Van den Bossche, who became his constant adviser and colleague. They made short work of the treaty. The terms were formally put to the aldermen on the day after Van Artevelde assumed power and rejected. A reign of terror was inaugurated against its authors. Simon Bette was lynched. His colleague Gilbert de Grutere was accused of being in league with the Count and killed by Artevelde's own hand. Three men, including the dean of the grain shippers' guild, were thrown into the city prison and then beheaded. Over the following weeks Van Artevelde claimed a large number of other victims who were either killed or forced to flee: rival politicians whom he wanted out of the way, personal enemies who had crossed him in the past and a large number of others whose main offence was that they or their forbears had participated in the movement which had deposed and murdered his father back in 1345.[49]

Philip Van Artevelde's methods were in some respects strikingly similar to his father's, on which they were probably based. He set about creating a new solidarity among the inhabitants. Men wore their allegiance on their sleeves, which were inscribed with the motto 'God sustain us.' The councils of the city were thrown open to the poor. There were tough measures to suppress the endemic private feuds and gang wars of fourteenth-century Ghent. A succession of populist measures reinforced his power. For the first time a true siege economy was imposed. The private grain stores of the monasteries and richer citizens, who had farms beyond the walls, were requisitioned and sold off at fixed prices. Steeply progressive taxes were levied, which shifted the burden of financing the war onto the possessors of the great commercial and landed fortunes. Ghent's procurement methods became even more aggressive than they had been before. A fleet of shallow-draft boats was organised to bring in supplies under heavy guard across the Vier Ambachten. Francis Ackerman led a large armed force across the territories of Brabant and the prince-bishopric of Liège in order to find grain and escort it back to Ghent. Louis de Mâle responded by tightening the blockade. His officers broke the bridges over the River Dender, by which the convoys were getting through from Brabant. They hired their own fleet of boats to stop the traffic from the north. The flow of goods was reduced once more to a trickle.[50]

Froissart thought that 'in his heart Philip Van Artevelde was an Englishman' ('*avoit le corage trop plus englois que franchois*'). There is no doubt that he was right about this. Philip had been named by his father after Edward III's Queen, Philippa, who had been his godmother. He had passed his early years in England, where his mother had taken refuge after Jacob's death. But there was more to Philip's loyalty to England than sentiment. He had been in the pay of the English government from 1369, if not earlier, at the substantial rate of 100 marks a year. In the longer term he knew that his measures would not save the town unless he could draw England into the Flemish civil war. So, in February 1382, a month after assuming power, he sent three of his associates to Westminster to open negotiations with the English Council. He offered to recognise Richard II as Count of Flanders and King of France if the English would supply weapons to the men of Ghent and bring a fleet and an army to the Low Country in the summer.[51]

Hitherto the English government had made no attempt to exploit the travails of Flanders. The region was economically important to England, but it was a distraction from the main object of dealing with France. It suited the English ministers better to maintain cordial relations with Louis de Mâle. When Philip Van Artevelde's emissaries reached England they found Richard II's ministers occupied with plans for the forthcoming peace conference. The problem with all peace initiatives, as John of Gaunt had learned at Bruges, was that without a credible military threat the ambassadors would have little to bring into the conference chamber. So the Great Council which approved the arrangements for the conference also resolved to raise an army of 6,000 men to invade France under the young King himself in the event that diplomacy failed. Unfortunately the noblemen gathered at Windsor had no power to make a grant of taxation and no other proposals for financing this army. The King's ministers had no money and no continental allies other than Portugal. In March 1382 they were ruefully contemplating the possibility that they would be unable to make war and unable to make peace either. For those at Westminster who were looking for an escape from this predicament the appearance of Philip Van Artevelde's emissaries some days after the Great Council had closed was a godsend. It offered the prospect of invading France by the north with Flemish support, in much greater strength than England could have mustered from its own resources. A campaign in the north was also more likely to find support in Parliament and among the financiers of the city of London, where the impact of the Flemish civil war on the wool trade and the Calais staple was already causing concern.[52]

Richard II's Council took up Van Artevelde's initiative. But the Council was a coalition of disparate interests and prejudices. Those who wanted to make a success of the peace conference supported the Flemish proposals for tactical reasons. But over the following weeks they were displaced by others with larger ends in view. Some of them thought that the revolt of Ghent might really supply the means of redressing the strategic balance with France. Some were more interested in spoiling the southern strategy favoured by John of Gaunt. As a result, interest in peacemaking began to recede. An assembly of shipmasters was summoned to advise about the logistical problems of sending a seaborne force to eastern Flanders. Preliminary plans were made to embark the proposed army of 6,000 on eighty large ships and to land them at Antwerp in the mouth of the Scheldt. The expedition was expected, rather optimistically, to cost about £60,000. Another assembly, of merchants and financiers, was convened to consider ways of raising this sum without Parliamentary taxation. They included representatives of all the mercantile cities of England and the Italian banking houses in London. The financiers thought that the money could be borrowed but only if Parliament was willing to underwrite the loan with promises of fresh taxes, later if not sooner. So, on 24 March 1382, Parliament was summoned to meet once more in the hope that they would reconsider their previous decision. The opening was fixed for 7 May. Van Artevelde's emissaries were told that they would have a firm answer a week after that. The English ambassadors were still in Picardy, putting the final touches on the arrangements for the peace conference, but by the time they returned to Westminster at the end of March the Council had already privately abandoned the policy of settling with France. It was replaced by a policy which was characteristic of the aimlessness and opportunism of English thinking: a programme of diplomatic evasion and temporising extending into the summer, which was designed to gain time while Richard II's ministers argued about whether to intervene in Flanders or Castile and looked across the Channel to see what could be extracted from the increasingly confused situation in France.[53]

Philip Van Artevelde's agents left England on 7 April 1382. About a fortnight later the last hope for peace in Flanders vanished. A conference, at least the third of its kind, had been convened in the cathedral city of Tournai under the auspices of the rulers of Holland, Hainault, Brabant and Liège, all of whom were concerned about the destabilising effect of the civil war. All the major towns of Flanders sent representatives. At Ghent there were high hopes. The streets and gateways of the town were crowded with people praying for its success as Philip Van Artevelde left for Tournai with the town's delegation. But when it came to the point Louis de Mâle declined to negotiate. He had never wanted the conference. He knew by now about the negotiations of Philip Van Artevelde with the English government, which had been reported to him by spies in London. He was actively recruiting troops for a final trial of strength. He was confident of victory. From the distance of the Château de Mâle Louis announced that his council would declare his wishes in due course. His wishes, when they were eventually made known, were bleak. He would accept the surrender of Ghent, he said, provided that all adult males in the city appeared before him to repent their acts, dressed in their shirtsleeves with bare heads and nooses around their necks. He would decide their fate on the day. The *bailli* of Hainault tried to persuade the men of Ghent to submit even on these terms. Philip Van Artevelde replied that he and his colleagues had no authority to dispose of the lives of their fellow citizens and then left.[54]

CHAPTER X

The Path of Flanders
1382–1383

On 3 May 1382, a few days after the collapse of the talks at Tournai, Philip Van Artevelde gambled the fate of Ghent on a single desperate stroke. About 4,000 men from Ghent appeared without warning outside the walls of Bruges. They were led by Philip himself and his two principal lieutenants, Peter Van den Bossche and Francis Ackerman. They had left Ghent on the previous day and had marched unseen through the night. Most of them were citizen soldiers. But there was also a small corps of German and English mercenaries and an artillery train. It was the day on which the Brugeois traditionally stopped work early to take part in the procession of the Holy Blood and to drink themselves senseless. Towards the end of the afternoon the army of Ghent halted in a large meadow south-west of the town known as Beverhoutsveld. The Count of Flanders was in the castle on the eastern side of the town when the news was brought to him. There was a hurried conference with the guild leaders and the captain of the town. The captain wanted to close the gates and take his time to organise the defence. But the Count favoured a more aggressive response. So the trumpeters passed through the crowded streets to call men to arms.

Towards the end of the afternoon Louis de Mâle led his army, a mixed crowd of experienced soldiers and armed townsmen out of the gates. They moved forward without order or discipline, 'full of meat and wine'. It was an unseasonally warm day and the sun was already low in the sky, shining into their faces as they marched. The army of Ghent was waiting in battle order. Their archers were drawn up at the front together with the artillery. As the horde of Bruges approached, the archers and cannon simultaneously opened fire. The Count's army reeled before the shock. Its front lines thinned out as men and horses fell to the ground beneath the volley of missiles. Then the men of Ghent advanced in a body and began to slaughter the Brugeois. The Count's own company was surrounded and Louis himself briefly unhorsed. At this point some of the Brugeois deserted to the other side. They were almost certainly the members of the weavers' and fullers' guilds, men who had supported the cause of Ghent in 1379. In the confusion the whole mass turned and fled towards the town, pursued by the victorious men of Ghent. When they reached the gate the enemy pressed in after them. The cloth-workers appeared on the streets to welcome them. 'Tout un!', they shouted. Louis de Mâle managed to escape from the press of men and find his way back to the castle. There he tried to organise a counter-attack. In the market-place, under the shadow of the great belfry of the cloth-hall, the loyal guilds, the butchers, fishmongers, cutlers and furriers gathered in their lines to defend their town. The Count led his men-at-arms through the streets to reinforce them. But before he could reach the market-place the men of Ghent and cloth-workers of Bruges invaded the square. The Count's allies were massacred. His troops were forced to turn back. Louis himself took refuge in a hovel built into the city walls. That night he escaped through a window, swam the moat and made off on foot into the open country.[1]

In spite of the support he had received from the cloth-workers Philip Van Artevelde treated Bruges as a conquered city. A garrison was installed. Two captains, Peter Van den Bossche and a dyer called Peter de Winter, were appointed as governors. On the day after the battle the inhabitants were assembled in the great open space in front of the monastery of St. Catherine, outside the walls, and made to swear an oath of loyalty towards the new regime. A heavy indemnity was laid upon the town and many prominent inhabitants were rounded up and sent off to Ghent as hostages for its payment. Three of the gates were demolished together with thirty feet of wall on either side and the spoil used to fill up the ditches. The men of Ghent sacked the Count's residence in the castle. For three days they went through the streets looting the houses of the rich and those associated with Louis's government. But their main objective was the food stores. Grain, flour, wine and salted meat was seized and loaded into hundreds of carts to relieve the hunger of Ghent.

The political consequences of the battle were dramatic. The blockade of Ghent was broken. In Ypres the cloth-workers took over the town and sent their submission to Philip Van Artevelde. He was received there as a hero. The whole of the maritime region to the west followed the lead of Ypres. Courtrai threw out the Count's officers. By the end of May 1382 Louis de Mâle's government had collapsed in most of Flemish-speaking Flanders. After a number of adventures Louis de Mâle eventually reached the French-speaking city of Lille. From here he withdrew at about the beginning of June to his castle at Hesdin in Picardy.[2]

Louis de Mâle's officers retained control of the three Walloon-speaking castleries of southern Flanders. But the only places in the Flemish-speaking regions which were still held by his partisans were the two towns of Oudenaarde and Dendermonde. They were minor places, but of incomparable strategic value for they enabled Louis to close the River Scheldt to navigation on both sides of Ghent. The focal point of the struggle which followed was Oudenaarde. The town had suffered more than any place in Flanders in the three years since the civil war began. Repeatedly fought over, it had been battered by artillery, its walls partially demolished and its trade ruined. Much of its population had abandoned it and migrated elsewhere. Louis sent a corps of 450 elite soldiers under a Flemish nobleman called Daniel de Halewyn to hold the husk of walls, buildings and frightened inhabitants. Halewyn and his companions prepared to fight to the end. They demolished every building outside the walls within arrow-shot. They sent away most of their horses. Women and those too old or young to fight were expelled. Stores were laid in. Ghent threw all its strength against the town. Early in June 1382 a vast army appeared outside the walls, raised from the citizens of Ghent and its subject towns. It was stiffened with a corps of professional mercenaries including some 300 English archers, most of them deserters from the garrison of Calais drawn by the high rates of pay on offer. They invested Oudenaarde from both sides of the Scheldt. Bridges of boats were thrown across the river upstream and down to seal off access by water. Siege engines were sited around the walls and hurled great stones into the town. Gunpowder artillery was placed in front of the main gates, including a huge 'bombard' whose roar could be heard more than twenty miles away. Across Flanders the struggle took on all the savagery of a class war. The Count's supporters were proscribed. Many of them fled to the Walloon regions or France. The rural mansions of the nobility and the rich were attacked and burned by raiding parties from the towns. At the Count's castle at Mâle the mob of Bruges were shown the cradle in which Louis had been nursed as a baby and the font in the chapel in which he had been baptised. They smashed them into small pieces and sent them off as trophies to Ghent.[3]

The collapse of Louis de Mâle's government in Flanders occurred just as the English Parliament was about to assemble at Westminster. It opened up a strategic opportunity barely dreamed of when Philip Van Artevelde's emissaries had been in England. Yet it also provoked a bitter debate, which was to continue in one form or another for the next three years, between those who wanted to grasp the opportunity of intervening in Flanders and those, associated with John of Gaunt, who were determined that any English army available for service overseas should be used to shore up the position of the Earl of Cambridge in Portugal. The Portuguese Chancellor, Lourenço Fogaça, an engaging diplomat and a firm anglophile, had recently arrived in England to add his own voice to the clamour for a southern strategy. He was once described by his master as a man with 'the cross of St. George graven on his heart'.[4]

When Richard Scrope stood up on 8 May 1382 to deliver the traditional address he told the assembly of the plan to send the young King abroad with an army of 6,000 men but he was no more precise about the army's destination than 'France'. This must have added to the suspicions of an assembly which had learned to distrust the government's military enterprises and had already washed its hands of the Duke of Lancaster's Castilian ambitions. In the event it did not matter. The Commons were unwilling to contemplate any grant of war taxation at all except for purely defensive purposes. The discussion turned mainly on a plan to borrow £60,000 on the security of a Parliamentary guarantee, a variant of the scheme which Parliament had already rejected when John of Gaunt proposed it in February. It was a difficult time at which to borrow money, let alone such a great sum. The knights invited the Lords to appoint a commission of merchants to advise them. Fourteen merchants were nominated, half of them Londoners. They included John Philpot, the former mayor who had been involved in a number of previous royal loans, and the rich grocer Nicholas Brembre. They were more pessimistic than the financiers who had considered the question in March. They declared that the money could not be raised even with a Parliamentary guarantee. They reminded the Commons of the fate of the bankers who had bailed out the government in previous financial crises: Pole, Wesenham, Walwain, Chiriton. All of these princely merchants of the last generation had been rewarded with persecution and bankruptcy. The most that their successors would do was guarantee the repayment of such loans as the Parliamentary peers and knights might care to make out of their own pockets. The peers and knights did not take the hint and the projected loan was abandoned.

The government tried to find money by other methods. They raised a modest loan from the London branch of a Genoese banking house.

They offered discounts to exporters for paying the wool tax in advance. They sold off yet more of Richard II's jewels. Even with these expedients the English government's total receipts in the six-month period from April to September came to less than £22,000, one of the lowest figures for any corresponding period since the 1330s. By the time Parliament was dissolved on 22 May 1382, it was clear that no offensive operations would be possible for several months. The Council appointed three representatives to report the disappointing outcome to the leaders of the rebellion in Flanders. They left at the end of the month. As for Fogaça, he remained in England, buying horses and weaponry in London and confecting plans with John of Gaunt to send a second army to Castile in the following year if not in this one.[5]

Balked in the direction of England, Philip Van Artevelde proferred an olive branch to the government of France. He wrote a 'mild and friendly' letter to Charles VI inviting him to order the Count of Flanders to return to his domains and govern them 'in justice'. Failing that, Van Artevelde proposed that the French King should take the county into his own hands and appoint a royal governor. The French King's councillors laughed at his impertinence when the letter was read to them, and the messenger who delivered it was thrown into prison. Yet Van Artevelde's assumption that the French government might help him was by no means absurd. Louis de Mâle had a firm ally in his son-in-law, Philip of Burgundy, who had promised him his support soon after his withdrawal to France. But in spite of his dominant position in the King's Council there was a heavy weight of consensus against him. Louis de Mâle had never been a popular figure at the French court. There were still plenty of influential noblemen who found a certain satisfaction in his misfortunes. They were strongly opposed to allowing France to become involved in a ferocious and apparently endless civil war against rich and populous towns which had shown themselves to be resourceful antagonists. Some of these men also took the view, for which there was much to be said, that Louis's intransigence towards Ghent had contributed largely to his problems and that France could play a more productive role by broking a settlement.[6]

The French ministers were of course aware of the English government's intrigues with Philip Van Artevelde in March, for the Count must surely have told them, but at this stage they took the threat of English intervention lightly. They no doubt learned about the debates in Parliament in May. The forthcoming peace conference was the main focus of attention. After successive postponements it was now due to open on 20 June. John of Gaunt was still expected to attend and the Duke of Burgundy had been nominated as the head of the French delegation. No one seems to have been very sanguine about the prospect of a permanent peace. But great hopes were invested in the fall-back proposal for a twelve-year truce, which had been one of the ideas discussed during the preliminaries in March.[7] This had obvious attractions for the French. It would indefinitely defer the thorny issues which had frustrated previous conferences. It would make it unnecessary for them to surrender territory as the price of peace. And it would leave the English King with no more than the insignificant ribbon of land that he still held in the south-west. Some thought was given to what would happen if the conference failed but current French military planning did not contemplate a campaign in Flanders. The government had resolved as long ago as April 1381 that the King would lead an army into the south as soon as money could be found to pay for it. Their main priorities were to suppress opposition to the Duke of Berry's authority among the cities of Languedoc and to apply pressure to the English in the march of Gascony. This remained their position after the expulsion of Louis de Mâle from the Flemish regions of Flanders and indeed throughout the summer of 1382.

In spite of the great expectations which had built up around it the peace conference came to nothing. At the last moment the English downgraded the negotiations by announcing that John of Gaunt would not, after all, be coming. Instead it was the familiar and competent but less august figure of John Gilbert, Bishop of Hereford, who appeared at Calais. He, according to the malicious Thomas Walsingham, was a man who 'liked blather better than truth'. The Duke of Burgundy accordingly remained at court and sent less impressive personages to represent France in his place. Gilbert's instructions have not survived but it is plain that he had very little authority. The discussions appear to have broken down over the issue of Castile. John of Trastámara had made it clear to the latest French ambassador to visit his court that he would not agree to any truce unless it extended to Castile. But that was unacceptable to John of Gaunt. It would have halted the operations of the Earl of Cambridge in Portugal at the very moment when the long-delayed invasion of Castile was expected to start and would have obstructed preparations for the second army which Gaunt was bent on sending out in the following spring.

Faced with this impasse Richard II's Council was forced to decide whether it would back John of Gaunt's plans or not. At about the beginning of July 1382 they met at Westminster to try to give some clear direction to English diplomatic and military planning. John Gilbert returned from Picardy, leaving his fellow ambassadors to carry on the argument with the French. Fogaça was still at Westminster pressing for intervention in Castile at the earliest possible moment. There is no surviving record of the outcome but there are good reasons to believe that John of Gaunt's allies prevailed. The Council appears to have decided that their first priority would be to send Gaunt with an army to Gascony in the spring of 1383, provided that Parliament could be persuaded to vote funds for it. Gaunt planned to cross the Pyrenean passes into Castile while his brother and King Fernando launched a simultaneous invasion from Portugal. The Council proposed to keep open the alternative strategy in the north, partly no doubt because the Commons' hostility to Gaunt's Castilian ambitions was well known; and partly because the more optimistic among them thought that it might be possible to run with both projects at once. After the meeting had closed a herald was sent into the siege lines at Oudenaarde to propose that Philip Van Artevelde should come to England in person to concert plans. Fogaça sailed for Portugal to report to Fernando. These decisions went some way to resolve the division among Richard II's advisers between the partisans of a northern and a southern strategy by conceding something to each. But they condemned the conference in Picardy to failure. John Gilbert returned to the march of Picardy with nothing to offer. The cease-fire was extended to October 1382, effectively writing off the campaigning season for that year, but nothing more could be agreed.[8]

Unknown to the English Council the future of the Anglo-Portuguese alliance on which the southern strategy depended had already become extremely uncertain. In Portugal the war with Castile was proving to be destructive and unpopular. With the coming of spring some eighty Castilian sailing ships and oared barges had appeared in the Tagus and begun to blockade Lisbon. Every day Castilian men-at-arms and Basque mountain troops landed from the ships to plunder and burn. They sacked the suburbs of Lisbon. They destroyed the fine mansions of the King and the nobility which stood along the banks of the river from Lisbon to Santarém. They launched large-scale mounted raids across the Ribatejo opposite the city. Much of this was cattle country which was rapidly denuded of its herds. There was no Portuguese fleet to resist them. It was more than a month before there was any organised defence even on land.[9]

Away in the east the English army passed six months, from January to June, by the Castilian frontier. Fernando had given strict instructions that the English were not to raid into Castile for fear of provoking a counter-attack for which his army was not prepared. His orders were not consistently obeyed. Early in the year 'Canon' Robesart led some 800 men across the Guadiana and into the foothills of the Sierra Morena. Another raiding force in the spring briefly penetrated into Castile north of Badajoz, supported by Portuguese frontier troops. But for most of the time the English sat unpaid and bored in their winter quarters waiting for orders and staring at the great featureless plain of the Alemtejo. Since they could not support themselves at the expense of their enemies they had little choice but to live off their hosts. Their encampments were situated in the richest agricultural region of Portugal. The English ranged through it, breaking into houses, stealing cattle, raping women. They tortured those who hid their goods and killed those who resisted them. An English chronicler, who presumably got his information from men serving with the army, reported that his countrymen treated the Portuguese 'like worthless serfs'. The Portuguese King repeatedly complained to the Earl of Cambridge. But although the Earl issued orders that the offences were to stop he was not a man to make his wishes respected. After the outrages which had occurred around Lisbon the previous autumn relations between English and Portuguese sank to new lows. Englishmen travelling on their own were attacked and murdered. They were given poisoned bread to eat. Town gates were closed in their faces. Some of these were stormed by undisciplined mobs of English soldiers as if they were enemy strongholds.[10]

In the spring of 1382, at a critical stage of the preparations for invading Castile, a court scandal gravely weakened the Portuguese government. John of Gaunt's Galician retainer Juan Fernández Andeiro had taken advantage of his return to Portugal with the English army to resume his affair with the Queen, Leonora Teles. With the King visibly ailing and only intermittently capable of directing affairs, Leonora had become the dominant voice in the Portuguese government. Most of Don Fernando's councillors and professional advisers and much of the court nobility were by now her clients and protégés. Andeiro moved into residence at court and began to receive lavish grants on his mistress's nomination. When, in the spring of 1382, it became obvious that the Queen was pregnant the gossip surrounding her relationship with Andeiro could no longer be contained. In about March 1382 the

Portuguese court moved to Evora, a substantial city dating from Roman times standing at the edge of the Alemtejo. As a result of some indiscreet words of Andeiro the truth about his affair with Leonora became known to one of her ladies-in-waiting, who was married to the King's private secretary, Gonçalo Vasques de Azevedo. She repeated the story to her husband and he let a hint of what he had learned drop in the Queen's presence. Vasques was a venal man who owed much to Leonora's favour. But he was also close to the King, having served as confidential adviser to both Fernando and his father before him. Leonora panicked. She seems to have thought that she was about to be denounced and disgraced. So she attempted what amounted to a *coup d'état*. She prevailed on Fernando to order Vasques's arrest. The King's half-brother, John of Avis, who was the only other member of the royal Council with the stature and independence to stand up to her, was arrested at the same time. The sick King was then packed off to the castle of Vimieiro, a day's ride away, leaving Leonora and Andeiro in control of Evora. The two prisoners were taken to the citadel under armed guard and loaded with chains while the Queen plotted their execution on trumped-up charges of treason.

Leonora might have got away with the destruction of Gonçalo Vasques but she had overreached herself in attacking John of Avis, who was a considerable figure in Portugal. John was the bastard son of the previous King of Portugal, Don Pedro. His father had appointed him at the age of six as Master of the military order of Avis, an office which gave him control of the order's great wealth and assured him of a substantial position independent of the factions at court. Now twenty-five years old, John was a popular figure in the cities and among the nobility. The noblemen about the court protested. The captain of Evora refused to carry out the executions without the King's personal warrant. Even the Earl of Cambridge, who had originally refused to become involved, was induced to intervene on the prisoners' behalf. After three weeks both men were released. It is unclear how much Fernando ever knew about his wife's conduct. Leonora eventually bought the complicity of Gonçalo Vasques. As for John of Avis, he withdrew from court, a confirmed enemy of the Queen, and joined the Earl of Cambridge on the eastern march. An uneasy calm descended on Evora.[11]

Shortly afterwards discipline finally collapsed in the English army. The long months of inactivity had been bad for the men's morale. Many of them died during the winter from malnutrition and disease, and heavy casualties were suffered in a succession of violent incidents with the Portuguese. The army's numbers had fallen to about a thousand men, a third of its original strength. The survivors were angry about their pay. They had received nothing since the autumn of the previous year. It was far from clear whether their wages were a Portuguese responsibility or an English one. Fernando appears to have accepted responsibility in principle but declined to pay, ostensibly because they had ignored his prohibition against raiding into Castile, in fact because he was struggling to raise his own army and did not have the money. At about the end of May 1382 malicious reports began to circulate among the men that the Earl of Cambridge had received the money to pay them but failed to distribute it. This provoked a serious mutiny in a large section of the army encamped around the town of Estremoz. A mass meeting was called. A surprising leader emerged in the shape of Sir John Sotherey, the seventeen-year-old bastard son of Edward III and Alice Perrers. He persuaded his fellows to confront the Earl in his quarters and if they received no satisfaction to turn their arms against the King of Portugal. The men formed up around Sotherey. They unfurled the banner of St. George and marched in warlike array on Vila Viçosa, crying out 'A Sotherey! A Sotherey, the brave bastard!' As they approached the town they were met on the road by the marshal of the army, Sir Matthew Gournay, and two of his captains. The ringleaders were brought before the Earl in his quarters. He had nothing to offer them. But they were eventually persuaded to send a delegation of three men to petition the King of Portugal. Fernando was alarmed by the prospect of an uncontrolled English army marauding across his realm. He received the representatives of the men and promised that they would receive some money within a fortnight. To make good his promise the King's officers had to plunder the silver from church treasuries. 'You see what a little trouble-making will do,' Sotherey is said have remarked when the delegates returned with the news.[12]

In fact the mutineers had destroyed the last shreds of goodwill which the English enjoyed in Portugal. Fernando himself remained loyal to the alliance in spite of the difficulties that it had brought him. He too had 'the cross of St. George graven on his heart', as he later told Lourenço Fogaça but he was no longer in control of events. His councillors had unanimously objected to the English alliance when it was first made for reasons that had been largely borne out by events. A few noblemen, like John of Avis and the future Constable of Portugal Nun' Alvarez Pereira, enjoyed war with a relish that they had learned from their English mentors. But most of the Portuguese nobility regarded the conflict with Castile as pointless and damaging. The prime mover behind the English alliance had been the Queen, who had persuaded herself that the English offered a better guarantee than the Castilians of her daughter's succession to the throne. This calculation had never been very realistic and it seemed particularly threadbare now. The Earl of Cambridge's army was a shadow of what it had been and arguably represented a greater threat to Portugal than to Castile. John of Gaunt's promised army of reinforcement had been postponed to the following year with no assurance that it would come even then. Andeiro could see all this. He was the author of the Anglo-Portuguese treaty in 1380 but he had shed whatever loyalty he had once felt for John of Gaunt when he tied his fortunes to the Queen's. In June Leonora was already looking for an alternative match for her much betrothed daughter. The campaign against Castile would probably have been abandoned before it started but for the Portuguese government's fear of the English army on their soil and the uncertainties arising from the Queen's pregnancy. What if the child was a boy? Unless Fernando repudiated him, he would displace Beatrice as the heiress of Portugal and all the carefully laid plans of the past two years would fall away.[13]

The fortress-town of Elvas stood on a hillside crowned by a powerful thirteenth-century fortress overlooking the plain of the Alemtejo. Ten miles of wheat fields and olive groves separated it from the River Guadiana and the Castilian city of Badajoz. It was here that the English and Portuguese armies finally joined forces on 6 July 1382. The King was now very ill. His distended belly made it painful for him to move and difficult to receive visitors. He installed himself with his household in the citadel while the Earl of Cambridge occupied the Dominican convent in the lower town. Their followers were kept well apart. The Portuguese troops encamped around the base of the town while the English spread themselves along the road to Badajoz. Estimates of their strength varied but the English appear to have had about 1,000 men at their disposal plus the usual pages and camp-followers, and the Portuguese about 6,000 men equally divided between cavalry and infantry. John of Trastámara's army was substantially larger: about 5,000 men-at-arms including some French companies, in addition to about 1,500 light horse and a horde of archers and infantry. But they were still more than a hundred miles away at Ciudad Rodrigo in the north.[14]

Although there were no Castilian troops opposite them apart from the garrison of Badajoz, the Anglo-Portuguese army made no attempt to enter Castile. Instead their leaders took up a Castilian proposal to fight an arranged battle on the frontier as soon as John of Trastámara arrived with his army. He did not reach Badajoz until 31 July. In the early hours of the morning the whole of the Anglo-Portuguese army advanced towards the frontier to meet him. The appointed place was a flat expanse of open ground by the small hamlet of Caia, three miles west of Badajoz. They drew themselves up in their battle lines, the English in the van and the Portuguese behind. Don Fernando stirred himself to appear on the battlefield and began to confer knighthoods on ambitious young men, English and Portuguese, until it was pointed out to him that he was not entitled to do so, never having taken knighthood himself. The Earl of Cambridge dubbed him on the field so that he could repeat the process properly. It was a day rich in symbols. In the front line Sir Thomas Symonds unfurled John of Gaunt's Castilian banner as the English stood behind him roaring out: 'Castile and León for King John, son of Edward of England.' Then they brought forward the banner presented by Pope Urban VI to mark the crusade against the Castilian adherents of the Avignon Pope. On the opposite side of the field no one stirred. The King of Castile was represented by a solitary pavilion which had been erected that morning by his officers. Shortly they were seen to dismantle it and withdraw towards Badajoz. The Anglo-Portuguese waited in line for several hours. Then, in the early afternoon, they withdrew to Elvas. Although they did not yet know it the campaign was over.[15]

On 19 July 1382 the Queen had given birth to a baby boy who died four days later. The child was generally assumed to be Andeiro's, but the King marked the birth and death with extravagant displays of joy and sorrow. Beatrice was once again an heiress. For the more calculating men about the Queen the event paved the way for the reconciliation with Castile which must have been planned within her circle for weeks. The probability is that the first approach was made while the Castilian army was on its way south to Badajoz at the end of July, and that the abortive arranged battle at Caia was no more than a charade for the benefit of the English. What is clear is that, shortly after the retreat from Caia, the Constable of the Portuguese army, accompanied by Gonçalo Vasques de Azevedo, brought a formal proposal into John of Trastámara's headquarters. Ten days of intensive negotiation followed. The Portuguese emissaries received their instructions by word of mouth. To avoid attracting the attention of the English they travelled by night with a single squire for an escort. The precise source of their instructions is something of a mystery. Fernando later told the English that he had

had nothing to do with the negotiations. This statement was received as mere subterfuge, designed to hide his embarrassment, but it may well have been true. There is a weary, resigned quality about many of Don Fernando's pronouncements at this time. He was certainly not incoherent or incapable of following what was going on about him, but he was racked with pain and quite unable to stand up to the Queen and his household officers. For his part, John of Trastámara had good reasons to make peace with Portugal in spite of the numerical superiority of his army and the enthusiasm of his leading captains. He did not wish to risk a battle against an English army even in its present sorry state. Moreover, after maintaining an army and a fleet in almost continuous service for more than a year, he was in serious financial difficulty. He could probably not have kept his army in being for much longer anyway.[16]

The treaty between Castile and Portugal was finally concluded in the early hours of 10 August 1382. The terms were extremely favourable to Portugal. It was agreed that Beatrice's engagement to the Earl of Cambridge's son would be repudiated and that instead she would be betrothed to the Castilian King's second son, the Infante Fernando. Since he was barely a year old Leonora was assured of a long regency after her husband's death, with some prospect of Castilian support against her internal enemies. The Castilians agreed to restore all that they had gained during the war, including the fortress of Almeida, the whole of the Portuguese fleet captured at Saltes and all prisoners of war in their hands. The English army was to be bundled out of Portugal as soon as possible. John agreed to make available ships of his own fleet to carry them back to England. The English knew nothing about any of this until, on the morning of 10 August, the trumpeters passed through their lines proclaiming the peace. They were astonished. They cried out that they had been betrayed. Men were seen flinging their helmets to the ground and striking them with their axes. The Earl of Cambridge angrily declared that the treaty was not binding on him. If he had not lost so much of his army, he said, he would have carried on against the Castilians on his own. As it was there was nothing he could do. During the following weeks Portugal completed its diplomatic realignment by repudiating the obedience of the Roman Pope and declaring itself for Avignon. The Earl took a frigid leave of the King. Some of his Gascon men-at-arms and English archers decided to stay behind and take service with the Portuguese. Most of the Castilian exiles who had come with him to Portugal also stayed and some of them later made their own peace with the Trastámaran dynasty. Sir John Sotherey, the leader of the mutineers at Vila Viçosa, fled rather than face disgrace in England. Two years later he was tracked down in Aragon and kidnapped by the English government's resident agent there, but he appears to have died before he could be sent home. The rest of the English army followed the Earl of Cambridge west to the small port of Almada at the mouth of the Tagus opposite Lisbon to await their passage to England.[17]

The diplomatic conference in Picardy came to a close at the beginning of August 1382 while the furtive negotiations for the treaty of Badajoz were still in progress. The French, who had expected more from it than the English, reacted angrily to what they regarded as a grave breach of faith. In about the middle of August 1382 Charles VI's Council met, probably in the royal castle at Compiègne on the Oise north of Paris. They resolved to go ahead with the long-standing plan, which had been suspended during the conference, to send an army to Languedoc and invade the English duchy of Aquitaine. There is no evidence of dissent or even serious debate. If the Duke of Burgundy would have preferred a punitive expedition against Ghent he certainly did not press the point. Charles VI, who was to assume the nominal command of the army, received the Oriflamme at Saint-Denis on 18 August. A week later the decision was announced in Paris at one of those theatrical gatherings which lent weight to so many of the great moments of the Valois monarchs. The young King sat in the great hall of the palace on the Île de la Cité. His uncles the Dukes of Burgundy and Bourbon, the Constable Olivier de Clisson, the leading citizens of Paris and a crowd of councillors, lawyers and prelates, gathered round the steps of the throne as Philip of Burgundy declared that the English had rejected both peace and truce in spite of the generous territorial concessions which had been made to them. The King, Philip said, intended to defend his realm and carry the war to the English in Aquitaine. The army was summoned to muster on the Loire at Orléans on 20 September.[18]

Freed from the constraints of the peace conference and still ignorant of the disaster unfolding in Portugal, the English ministers pressed ahead with their preparations for the expedition of John of Gaunt to Gascony and Castile. Charles of Navarre's old mercenary captain Bertucat d'Albret was sent to Pamplona to persuade him to open the Pyrenean passes to Gaunt's army. Geraud de Menta, the veteran of so many fruitless diplomatic missions to Barcelona, was instructed to make yet another attempt to interest the cautious King of Aragon. On 9 August

1382 writs were issued for the election of a new Parliament, the third in a year, which was expected to approve these plans and to make a grant of taxation to pay for them. Both countries seemed to be moving towards a decisive trial of arms in south-western France, the first major campaign there since 1377.[19]

John of Gaunt passed the month of September 1382 on his estates in Yorkshire while at Westminster the assiduous lobbying for a southern strategy in which he and his supporters had been engaged for most of the year was undone by events. In the middle of the month Lourenço Fogaça returned to England, accompanied by a squire from the English army in Portugal. They brought with them the embarrassing news of the treaty of Badajoz. The Duke's reaction when the news was brought to him in the north was an obstinate refusal to face facts. He would not accept that the fiasco cast any doubt on the feasibility of his ambitions in Castile. He would not even accept that the Portuguese alliance was at an end or that the Earl of Cambridge's days in Portugal were numbered. Instead he set about recruiting reinforcements and endeavoured to stiffen his brother's resolve. Fogaça, who never accepted his country's diplomatic volte-face and knew Don Fernando's private views, may well have encouraged him in this. But to most observers it must have been obvious that the case for sending an army across the Pyrenees had been much weakened by the fate of the other arm of the pincer in which Gaunt had hoped to crush the Castilian King. As the fortunes of the southern strategy waned those of northern one flourished. The Council had maintained contact with Philip Van Artevelde. Although the captain of Ghent was unable to come to England there had been busy diplomatic traffic across the Channel throughout the summer. Three councillors of Ghent were at Westminster in late September. A draft treaty between England and the rebel towns was ready by the end of the month. The Council, which had hitherto been dealing only with the agents of Ghent, invited him to send a delegation representing all three of the great towns of Flanders to conclude the matter.[20]

At this point a new element was injected into the situation by one of the most unusual and controversial personalities of the late fourteenth century. Henry Despenser, Bishop of Norwich, was a worldly and flamboyant prelate then in his early forties. He belonged to one of the great military families of England and, as his contemporary, the chronicler Thomas Walsingham, observed, he was cut out to be a soldier rather than a priest. In the 1360s he had in fact briefly fought by the side of his brother Edward, then a professional captain in Italy. Two decades later Walsingham described him leading the gentry of Norfolk into battle during the Peasants' Revolt, wearing a steel helmet and body armour and laying about him right and left with a double-edged sword, 'gnashing his teeth like a great boar'. Despenser was by all accounts a man of rather wooden intelligence. There is good reason to believe that his intervention in the war with France was really the doing of his chaplain, Henry Bowet, a cunning and ambitious clerical politician who ultimately rose to be Archbishop of York. In March 1381, when Bowet was in Rome on a routine diplomatic mission for the government, he persuaded Urban VI to issue two papal bulls in favour of the Bishop, empowering him to proclaim a crusade at a moment of his own choosing against supporters of the Avignon Pope anywhere in Europe. He was authorised to grant the indulgences of a crusader in the Holy Land to volunteers who were willing to enlist for a full year or make a suitable financial contribution. He was allowed to dispense clerks who volunteered from their obligations of residence and to release them from the authority of any of their superiors who might object. A third bull, issued more recently, conferred on him extensive disciplinary powers over the English Church for the purpose of forwarding the enterprise.

Despenser had hitherto made no use of these instruments and it is quite possible that the English government knew nothing about them. But on 17 September 1382, sensing that his moment had come, he declared himself to be Pope Urban's nuncio in England. He published his bulls to every diocesan bishop and had them nailed up on church doors and public places across the country. Despenser (or more probably Bowet) perceived that the best way to obtain support for his crusade was to adopt the northern strategy. Some of Richard II's Council had been advocating it for months. The Commons, with their traditional concern for the wool trade and the Flemish markets, were more likely to contribute to the cost. So he proposed to the government to recruit an army of crusaders and lead them into Flanders via Calais. The irony of leading an Urbanist crusade against the Count of Flanders, one of the leading Urbanist princes of northern Europe, was not lost on contemporaries. Once Despenser had occupied Flanders he proposed with the support of the rebellious Flemish towns to invade schismatic France. He promised to keep his army in the field for a full year. But the most attractive part of his offer was that the taxpayer would have to meet only part of the cost of the enterprise. Many of the participants would be serving without pay for the salvation of their souls. By selling crusading indulgences the Bishop expected to be able to make a substantial financial contribution to the cost of the others.[21]

Bishop Despenser's proposal was most unwelcome to John of Gaunt. It reignited all the old strategic divisions which had apparently been laid to rest in the summer and threatened the prospect of getting Parliamentary approval for his plans in Castile. Behind his difficulties lay the beginnings of a significant shift of power which made it increasingly difficult for Gaunt to impose his will on the English government. In the absence of any formal arrangements for a minority or a regency Gaunt's influence depended on the continued passivity of the boy King. By 1382 this passivity could no longer be taken for granted. Richard II was fifteen years old, a year past the age which tradition was beginning to recognise as the age of majority for rulers. His own personality, wilful, self-conscious, impulsive, keen to impress, was already beginning to make itself felt beyond the confines of his household. The Peasants' Revolt, in which he had played a prominent role largely of his own making, had matured him. It had also dramatically brought home to him the significance of his own status as King. In January 1382 Richard took another step towards emancipation when he married Anne of Bohemia, the sister of the German Emperor Wenceslas. The match, which was a considerable personal success in spite of its unpopularity in the country, had been arranged mainly by Richard's household officers with the strong personal support of the King himself. It brought him a degree of emotional independence and a larger and more organised household, both developments which encouraged him to take control of affairs into his own hands. It also distanced him from his uncles and the great magnates who had dominated his early years. In July 1382 the King astonished the political community by dismissing the Chancellor, Sir Richard Scrope, a friend and former steward of John of Gaunt, who had refused to give effect to what he regarded as feckless royal grants in favour of Richard's friends.[22]

This was one of a number of incidents which made the role of Richard's friends more noticeable. Foremost among them were two men of conspicuous ability who were destined to play a major part in the political controversies of the following years: Sir Simon Burley and Sir Michael Pole. Burley was a former retainer of the Black Prince who had made and lost a fortune in the wars of Poitou before becoming the boy King's tutor and mentor and ultimately his vice-chamberlain. Pole was the son of the famous wool merchant of Hull who had been the old King's principal banker in the early years of the war. He was another man who had made his career as a professional soldier in France. Now in his early fifties, he had served with the Black Prince and John of Gaunt in Gascony. Pole had been assigned to the royal household by Parliament in 1381 to 'advise and govern' the King and he quickly acquired a strong personal influence over him. Burley and Pole had a vested interest in the effective exercise of power by the King and became notorious for their willingness to use it in their own financial interests. But they were also intensely loyal to Richard. They brought to his counsels an intelligence and a detachment from past controversies that enabled them to see the issues more clearly, perhaps, than the King's uncles or the great magnates who had dominated the government at the beginning of the reign. Neither Richard nor his advisers had yet developed the pronounced views about the war which they would hold later, but they were far less inclined than before to defer to the opinions of the Duke of Lancaster.[23]

Although Burley and Pole were for the time being Richard's pre-eminent political advisers there were other men about the King, less involved in the day-to-day conduct of government, whose role was becoming important. Some of them were knights of his household, the kind of men who had been the executants of royal policy for generations and whose comparatively modest origins made them dependent on royal favour. Some of them were young noblemen of Richard's own age: men like Ralph Stafford, the fifteen-year-old son of the Earl of Stafford, who was probably closer to the King than anyone until his premature death in 1385; or the sixteen-year-old Thomas Mowbray, later Earl of Nottingham. More significant because he was more ambitious than these two, and at twenty rather older, was Robert de Vere, Earl of Oxford, who had ridden with Richard to Mile End in 1381 and shortly became his inseparable companion. These and other immature young men fed the King's self-confidence and lapped up honours and grants at his hand.

The relations between the Crown and the nobility were critical to the political stability of late medieval England and depended in large measure on the even-handed distribution of the patronage of the Crown. The use of that patronage to build up power and wealth for a handful of privileged individuals and their dependents was bound to make enemies among older men excluded from favour. In the 1380s these resentments burned with special bitterness in the breast of

Richard's uncle, the ambitious and assertive Earl of Buckingham. One of the most prominent men in the kingdom by right of birth, Buckingham was condemned to watch impotently as his views were ignored and lesser men's claims on Richard's largesse were satisfied in offensive abundance. For different reasons the cliquishness of the King's circle also had the effect of progressively isolating John of Gaunt. He had become a lonely figure by 1382. His great wealth made it unnecessary for him to forge alliances among his fellow magnates. His very qualities repelled friendship. As an astute contemporary remarked, the English nobility were frightened and jealous at the spectacle of Gaunt's 'great power, sure judgment and outstanding intellect'.[24] Nowhere was this fear and jealousy more strongly felt than among Richard II's inner circle. While the King lived in Gaunt's shadow he could not truly reign. Richard's own isolation from his contemporaries and his emotional instability make it hard to identify any consistent theme in his behaviour but his occasional outbursts against his uncles were to become more frequent and more violent.

Towards the end of September 1382 the French court left Paris and travelled south towards Orléans, the assembly point of the army of Aquitaine. At about the same time they began to receive reports of intense diplomatic activity in England and Flanders. Louis de Mâle had his agents among the Flemish community in London. Some at least of the Flemings' discussions with English agents had occurred in Bruges, a porous, international town, where few things remained secret for long. At Montargis, the pleasure palace of Charles V east of Orléans, the King's Council met to consider the implications of these reports. In some ways the debate mirrored the one which had occurred at Westminster three months before. The Duke of Burgundy, who had hitherto been obliged to go along with the Council's southern strategy, was now seriously alarmed for his wife's inheritance in Flanders. He pleaded for French intervention in the county in support of Louis de Mâle. He urged on those present the principle that a lord should support his vassal. To those who recalled Louis's past disloyalties he replied that the Count was ready to make amends and serve the King as he ought. His audience remained sceptical and reluctant to change their plans so late in the day. For the moment the Duke was overborne by the consensus around him. The Council believed that the best course was to send a commission of councillors into Flanders to try to offer terms to the men of Ghent and broker a settlement with Louis de Mâle. The muster at Orléans was postponed until the situation became clearer. But the King's advisers resolved, 'firmly' according to the most authoritative report, to go ahead with their original plan to attack the English in the south-west.[25]

When Parliament assembled at Westminster, on 8 October 1382, the opening address was delivered by the new Chancellor, Bishop Braybrooke of London. Braybrooke was a convenient placeman with none of his predecessor's parliamentary skills. His lacklustre performance was evidently regarded as falling well short of the occasion, for it was followed by a fiery oration in the White Hall by John Gilbert, Bishop of Hereford. England, said Gilbert, had never been in so much danger from its enemies. Without vigorous measures the kingdom was 'on the point of being conquered and left at the mercy of its foes and the nation and language of England utterly destroyed'. Two 'noble paths' offered an escape from the perils around them, each blessed by the Pope with the indulgences of a crusade. The 'path of Flanders', proposed by the Bishop of Norwich, was a 'fine and broad' avenue into France offering the chance to inflict grave damage on the enemy in alliance with the Flemish towns provided that the effort could be sustained for long enough. The 'path of Portugal', on the other hand, offered the prospect of ending the war altogether by forcing England's enemies to battle and putting John of Gaunt on the Castilian throne. There was no better way of bringing the issue with France to a decision. The Duke, according to Gilbert, was ready to take an army of 2,000 men-at-arms and 2,000 archers to Spain. The cost would come to £43,000 assuming that double rates were paid to the men and that the campaign lasted six months. This sum, Gilbert proposed, would initially be raised from taxation. But provided that Gaunt survived it would all be repaid in due course from his assets in England.

The very fact that such a debate was occurring was symptomatic of the paralysis of the King's Council. There was no precedent for a major strategic decision of this kind being laid before both houses of Parliament. The outcome was deadlock. In the Lords the views of John of Gaunt prevailed. The peers advised that an army of 4,000 men was not large enough but they accepted the argument that the 'path of Portugal' could decide the war with France. They also thought that it was essential to go to the aid of the Earl of Cambridge. They obviously had an altogether unrealistic idea of Cambridge's situation. The Commons took a different view. With some trepidation, remembering the rebellion of 1381, they voted a subsidy of one tenth and fifteenth, suggesting ways of reducing the share of the burden borne by the peasantry. Although they did not restrict the use of the funds they made it clear that they preferred the 'path of Flanders'. The autonomy of Flanders, they said, was an essential interest of England. It was also easier to support by force of arms. An expeditionary army would have a shorter sea passage. The draw of the crusading indulgence would be a powerful aid to recruitment among Englishmen and foreigners alike. It would be a great deal cheaper. Finally there would be indirect benefits for other fronts. An English invasion of Flanders would force the French government to cancel its plans to invade Gascony and deter them from providing military assistance to Castile.[26]

The Commons were shrewder in their assessment of the strategic position than the Lords but neither assembly had reckoned with the speed of the French reaction. In the first few days of October 1382 the commissioners whom the French royal Council had appointed to reason with the Flemings arrived in Tournai on the march of Flanders. It was an impressive group, led by Mile de Dormans, Chancellor of France, and Arnaud de Corbie, First President of the Parlement. From Tournai they addressed letters to the three great towns asking for safe-conducts. They had come, they said, on behalf of the King to make peace between the Flemings and their Count and to discover whether there was any substance in the rumours that they were negotiating an alliance with England. They forwarded a conciliatory letter from Charles VI. Philip Van Artevelde received this missive in Ghent. He travelled to Oudenaarde, where the siege was now entering its fifth month, to consult the captains of the Flemish army. Together they committed themselves to the course which was to lead them to disaster. They did not recognise the olive branch for what it was. They seem to have realised that an outright rejection risked provoking a French invasion but they were confident in the ability of the great horde of men gathered outside Oudenaarde to resist. They persuaded themselves that the English, who were in fact deeply divided on the merits of a Flemish alliance, were so desperate for access to the Flemish market that they would send an expeditionary army to Flanders on any terms. They also believed that they had more time than they really did. Philip Van Artevelde wrote to the French commissioners from Ghent that he would not negotiate with them unless they first procured the surrender of the Count's garrisons at Oudenaarde and Dendermonde and reopened the River Scheldt to navigation. The commissioners replied with incredulity that they were only seeking a safe-conduct to discuss such matters. But Philip repeated his refusal. 'Believe us when we say that we mean it,'

Van Artevelde wrote to them on 14 October, 'for although we are poor and humble men we know how to speak like princes.'

On the same day the Flemish delegation which was to seal the articles of agreement in England received its instructions. Philip showed no sign of realising that he depended for survival on English support. The delegates were instructed to offer the English a military alliance on land and sea but only on exacting terms. Among other things they were to require the extradition of all exiles who had fled to England from the revolutionary governments of the towns. They were to insist on the removal of the English wool staple from Calais to Bruges for three years and thereafter to a place appointed by Ghent. Finally they were to demand the repayment of no less than £140,000 which the Flemish towns were believed to have lent to Edward III in 1340 in the time of Philip's father. Power had evidently gone to Philip's head. Three days after receiving this document, on 17 October, the Flemish delegates left for England.[27]

Opinion on the French royal Council was now turning rapidly against the Flemings. Between 5 and 10 October 1382 the King left Montargis and began to head north. At some stage reports must have reached him of the proceedings at Westminster, where the English government had been quite open about the state of their negotiations with Philip Van Artevelde. In about the middle of October the court reached Compiègne, north of Paris. There they received Philip Van Artevelde's intemperate letters. This time there appears to have been little if any argument in the Council. The attack on Aquitaine was cancelled. The assembly of the army was moved from Orléans to Péronne and Corbie in northern Picardy and fixed for the end of October. In order to block the passage of troops from England a subsidiary force was sent to Thérouanne, in the wedge of territory between the pale of Calais and the ditch of the Aa which marked the western extremity of Flanders. From the siege lines at Oudenaarde Philip Van Artevelde breathed defiance. Writing to the councillors who had been at Tournai, he declared that there would never be peace in Flanders while the Count tried to strangle the commerce of Ghent by maintaining his garrisons on the Scheldt. If the French army invaded, the Flemings would defeat them as they had done before. Van Artevelde was thinking, as perhaps others were, of 1302, the *annus mirabilis* of Flemish endeavour, when the great towns had destroyed the chivalry of France at the battle of Courtrai.[28]

The ambassadors of the three great towns of Flanders arrived at Westminster on about 25 October 1382. They received a warm welcome in the streets of London, where support for Ghent was running high. The politicians were more equivocal. The Commons' support for the 'path of Flanders' had shifted opinion within the Council and fortified the opponents of the 'path of Portugal'. But John of Gaunt was fighting a rearguard action with the support of his brothers and a number of other magnates. The Flemings, who seem to have been largely unconscious of these divisions, were received by the Council shortly after their arrival. Two of the King's uncles, Lancaster and Buckingham, were present, together with the Earls of Salisbury and Kent, Simon Burley and the Steward of the royal household, John Montague, as well as a number of other councillors. It must have been a difficult meeting for John of Gaunt but his position was eased by the extravagant demands which Philip Van Artevelde had instructed the ambassadors to make. The councillors were taken aback by the suggestion that the English should pay £140,000 for the privilege of sending military assistance to Flanders. They began to smile as the ambassadors' message was being read out. When the Flemings left the room they burst out laughing. Early in November the Flemings were escorted to Dover. They took with them another draft treaty for submission to the captain of Ghent, without the offending provisions. They got no further than Calais. When they reached the English enclave they found that their route home was already blocked by the French army assembling on the march of Flanders.[29]

Charles VI arrived with his entourage at Arras on 1 November 1382 and installed himself in the monastery of St. Nicholas, beyond the northern suburbs of the town. There he received Louis de Mâle, who performed the act of homage which this proud man had not proffered to a King of France for thirty years. The King was only fourteen years old but, like Richard II in England, he was already more than a richly dressed doll who presided at Council meetings mouthing assent to his tutors' summary of decisions. In the course of a brief childhood dominated by the rituals and symbols of military life, Charles had learned to love the trappings of war. He was fascinated by armour and weaponry and obsessed with jousts and tournaments. A miniature suit of chain mail was made for him every year as he grew, with a steel helmet enamelled with gold *fleurs de lys*. It was characteristic of him that he had insisted, in spite of the objections of some of his Council, on taking part personally in the campaign against the Flemings. 'If I am to reign in power and glory,' he said, 'I must learn the profession of arms.' Charles had been too young at his father's death to have experienced the frustrations of a subordinate position at the royal court. Like most infant kings he had been brought up to an exalted idea of the royal majesty, which could be uncomfortable for the experienced commanders and administrators who governed in his name. It could also generate intense, uncompromising anger against rebellious subjects of whose lives and motives he knew almost nothing.[30]

In the plain south of Arras the Marshals' officers were beginning to take the musters of the largest army to be assembled by France since 1356. It was a remarkable feat of military logistics. Companies of men-at-arms continued to arrive during the first three weeks of November, bringing its effective strength to nearly 10,000 men. They came from every part of France. The Duke of Burgundy, the strongest proponent and main beneficiary of the campaign, contributed more than a fifth of the army from the territory of his duchy and from his retainers among the French nobility. He had taxed his subjects, borrowed heavily from moneylenders and melted down his gold and silver plate to pay their wages. Of the whole force 6,500 were men-at-arms, with more than 2,000 pikemen and about 1,200 archers and crossbowmen. To the north, at Lille, a second, smaller army was being assembled by the officers of Louis de Mâle from the French-speaking castleries of southern Flanders and the ranks of the exiled nobility of the county as well as from his allies among the neighbouring principalities of the Low Countries.[31]

These were above all cavalry armies, recruited from the nobility. The anger and fear provoked among these men by the defiance of Ghent had proved to be a powerful recruiting agent. Although the King's Council had drawn on selected towns for infantry and bowmen their numbers were kept to a minimum. They were uncomfortably aware of the hostility to the whole enterprise in the cities of northern France, where there was strong fellow-feeling for the men of Ghent. The stories of some of the men arriving at the musters bore out their concerns. In the village of Attichy, near Compiègne, the local lord's demand for the traditional cart and team to take his equipment to the army was obstructed by local men who protested that the men of Ghent were 'no enemies of the King but allies of Paris and Rouen'. The company of the Marshal of Burgundy was attacked by a mob as it passed through Reims on the way to join the army and prevented from going any further. The arrival during the autumn of commissioners charged with exacting supplementary *aides* aggravated the grievance of men like these. In Paris, now denuded of troops, tensions were running high. Leagues were being formed in every quarter to organise resistance to the collectors. Plans were laid to take over the streets and kill the King's officers. Spies and delators reported plots to storm the Louvre and the castle of Vincennes. 'Wait and see how the King fares in Flanders,' said Nicholas Flamenc, an old conspirator who had been a ringleader of the lynch mobs of 1358; 'if Ghent prevails, as we all hope, then will be the time to rise.'[32]

Outside Oudenaarde Philip Van Artevelde was planning his own campaign. The best estimates of his strength suggest that he had between 30,000 and 40,000 men under arms, a vast host but consisting almost entirely of raw, urban levies. The two captains of Bruges, Peter Van den Bossche and Peter de Winter, were detailed to hold the line of the River Lys. The eastern end of this sector was defended by the walled town of Courtrai and the western one petered out into the marsh and dense forest beyond Merville. All the bridges over the river were broken except for those at Comines and Warneton, which carried the two roads leading north from Lille. Peter Van den Bossche set up his headquarters at Comines and concentrated the bulk of his forces there. De Winter's men guarded the crossing at Warneton. A curtain of troops was left to contain the garrison of Oudenaarde. Meanwhile Van Artevelde formed the rest of his forces into a great field army in the valley of the Scheldt west of Lille. His main problem was the loyalty of the other towns. Probably only Courtrai could be counted on. Bruges and Ypres were divided communities, ruled by commissioners from Ghent with the support of the cloth-workers' guilds. In the last days before the French invaded Van Artevelde visited both towns to rally his supporters and raise morale among the frightened inhabitants. As the crisis approached he became increasingly hysterical. He spent five days haranguing the populace of Ypres in the market-place. He told them that the French would never succeed in crossing the River Lys. He promised that help was on its way from England. Like the French King's ministers he had no idea of the time required to recruit an army in England and ship it across the Channel.[33]

The French army's strategy was devised by the Constable, Olivier de Clisson. His objective was to engage the Flemings as early as possible. Daniel Halewyn's garrison at Oudenaarde was at the end of its endurance. The season was late. Heavy rainfall made the going difficult for the French army's horses and supply trains. The army could probably not have withstood a prolonged campaign. So, spurning suggestions that he should take the long way round by Saint-Omer,

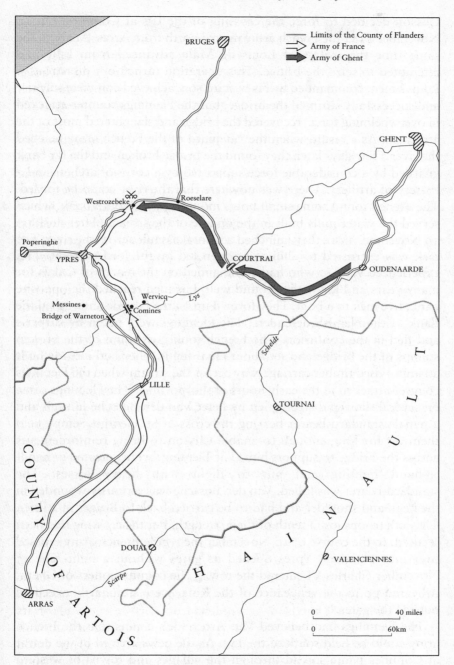

BRUGES

Limits of the County of Flanders
Army of France
Army of Ghent

GHENT

Westrozebeke
Roeselare

Poperinghe
YPRES

COURTRAI

OUDENAARDE

Messines
Wervicq
Comines
Bridge of Warneton

Lys

Scheldt

LILLE

TOURNAI

H A I N A U L T

C O U N T Y   O F   A R T O I S

DOUAI

VALENCIENNES

Scarpe

ARRAS

0   40 miles
0   60km

17 The Roosebeke campaign, November 1382

481

Clisson decided to force the crossing of the Lys at Comines. On 12 November 1382 the French army moved north from Arras. At about the same time the troops of Louis de Mâle advanced from Lille and attempted to seize the bridge. This operation turned out disastrously. Louis's men, commanded by his bastard son, achieved complete surprise and successfully stormed the bridge, but the Flemings counter-attacked in overwhelming force, recovered the bridge and slaughtered most of the attackers. As a result, when the vanguard of the French army reached the river a few days later, they found the bridge broken and the far bank guarded by a considerable force supported by a corps of archers and a battery of artillery. There was nowhere that the river could be forded. The French found some small boats moored by the south bank, which served the water-mills built in the middle of the stream. After dusk on 19 November 1382 they launched a frontal assault across the river. The task was entrusted to about 600 men led by the lord of Sempy, an experienced veteran who had commanded on the march of Calais for many years and knew the ground well. His men reached the opposite bank, five men to a boat. They formed up on the far side and rushed the flank of the Flemish defenders. The Flemings were taken by surprise and fled in the confusion. The French took possession of the broken stumps of the bridge and set about repairing it. They had already built an improvised timber carriage-way across the stream when the Flemings counter-attacked in the early hours of the morning. The Flemings came on several thousand strong, led by Peter Van den Bossche himself and a female standard-bearer bearing the cross of St. George. Sempy held them off for long enough to enable Clisson to bring reinforcements across the bridge to support him. The Flemings were defeated in hand-to-hand fighting and put to flight with heavy losses. The standard-bearer was killed. Van den Bossche was seriously wounded in the head and shoulder and had to be carried back to Bruges in a litter. Clisson's troops lost a tenth of their strength, but the crossing had been secured. In the course of 20 November the whole French army crossed over into Flanders. Ypres opened its gates without a fight. On 23 November Charles VI entered the town. The commissioners of Ghent, delivered up to the vengeance of the King, were summarily executed outside the gates.[34]

The Flemings had believed Van Artevelde's claims that the French army could be held south of the Lys. As the news arrived of the defeat at Comines panic spread through the villages and towns of western Flanders. The first reports were quickly followed by advance detachments of the French army, which fanned out across the country, fired by anger against people whom they had learned to hate as anglophiles, Urbanists and revolutionaries. The towns sent delegations before the King bearing the keys of their gates. Everywhere the inhabitants declared their French allegiance with white crosses sown onto their clothes. It was useless. The soldiers looted and burned everywhere they went. Three substantial clothmaking towns, Poperinghe, Wervicq and Messines, were sacked in the first forty-eight hours.

The destruction of Poperinghe, a town of some 4,000 souls, set new standards of brutality. The Duke of Bourbon's division arrived outside the walls shortly after midnight on 24 November and fell on the night watch, which was guarding the barricades at the main gate. They killed as many as they could catch while the rest fled through the streets waking their fellow citizens. The inhabitants grabbed as much of their plate and cloth as they could carry and made for the other gates while the soldiers spread through the town breaking open and looting houses. Then they lit fires systematically across the town before withdrawing to Ypres with their booty. As they left a fresh horde of soldiers arrived, mostly Flemish noblemen in the service of Louis de Mâle. The flames were already taking hold as the newcomers passed through the town breaking into every house that could still be entered in search of loot. A graphic account was given a few weeks later at a popular shrine in Touraine by a Welsh pilgrim who had fought with the French army. He had arrived at Poperinghe with Bourbon's men and got trapped by the fires. He described the streets and open spaces, filled with soldiers shouting and panic-stricken townsmen running about looking for a way out of the inferno. The narrator took refuge in the cellar of a burning house. When he emerged the next morning the whole area was a desert of charred wood and cinders with a few of the larger buildings still standing, engulfed by flames. He followed behind a stream of people making their way through the intense heat towards a gate and, passing into the open country outside, threw himself into the river. Emerging from the water on the opposite bank he found himself surrounded by the frightened and angry inhabitants of the town who had passed the night in the meadows watching the destruction of their homes. He fled for his life, pursued by a furious crowd of refugees with pikes and axes.[35]

Philip Van Artevelde was in Ghent when the news came that the French had crossed the Lys. He left at once to rejoin the army at Oudenaarde. An English herald (the former Chandos Herald, biographer of the Black Prince) succeeded in making his way there from

Calais under cover of his immunity, bearing news of the current state of discussions with Richard II's Council. For the first time Van Artevelde realised that there was no chance of help arriving from England in time. If he had been wise he would now have fought a defensive campaign in the boggy terrain around Oudenaarde, grinding down his enemy over the winter months. But the battle of Beverhoutsveld had swelled Van Artevelde's confidence and sapped what wisdom he had ever had. He put his host in marching order and advanced west to seek out the French army in the plain north of Ypres. On 20 and 21 November 1382 the Flemings left Courtrai. On the 25th they passed through Roeselare. Towards dusk they halted on a high ridge overlooking the road from Ypres, just south of the village of Westrozebeke, which the French called Roosebeke. The place lay about six miles north of the French encampment. Here they began to dig themselves in. On the following day, 26 November, the French, many of whom had been hurriedly recalled from plundering raids across western Flanders, formed up in battle order and advanced north towards the enemy. A steady drizzle fell as they came to a halt in the sodden plain in front of the Flemish positions. A group of Louis de Mâle's Flemish-speaking knights passed through the whole length of the Flemish camp in disguise to reconnoitre the enemy's positions. They reported that there were about 40,000 men in the Flemish host. Apart from about sixty English archers they were untrained townsmen in disorderly formations with rough weapons. They were occupying a strong position on rising ground, their flanks protected by woodland and thick hedges and their front by a line of trenches. But there was no natural protection for the Flemish army from behind. In spite of their superiority of position and their vastly greater numbers Clisson resolved upon a frontal attack on the following morning.

In the early hours of 27 November the French moved slowly forward in three divisions. The vanguard was commanded by the Constable and the Marshals. The largest division was in the centre. It included the King, riding with his three uncles and the lord of Coucy. They were surrounded by a personal bodyguard of 400 men including the Welsh companies of Jack Wyn. The rearguard was taken up by the companies from the western provinces, Artois, Picardy and Normandy. A contemporary described the eerie sound of metal on metal as the links of ten thousand tunics of chain mail shifted against each other and steel helmets clinked against shoulder armour. At the foot of the ridge on which the Flemings were standing the French halted, dismounted and sent their horses to the rear. About a thousand feet now separated the two armies but each was concealed by a thick mist. Arrows and other missiles were hurled aimlessly into the opposing lines. Then, as the King's standard-bearer unfurled the Oriflamme, the mist suddenly lifted and the bright winter sun lit up the two armies. The first French division pounded up the slope of the ridge to assail the Flemings. Van Artevelde had drawn up his men in a single mass with his strength concentrated in the centre around a banner of St. George. Their ordered formation and strict line discipline were far more impressive than the French had been led to expect. Several batteries of artillery covered the ground by which the French were approaching. A hail of arrows and metal shot struck the first groups to reach the crest. Several prominent knights fell dead. The centre of Clisson's line was forced back and began to retreat down the slope, but the French men-at-arms were still advancing at the wings. Then the second French division, commanded by the Duke of Bourbon and the lord of Coucy, outflanked the Flemings and fell on their unprotected rear. Many years later the Duke of Bourbon's standard-bearer recalled seeing the two divisional commanders swing their axes left and right through the dense ranks of the enemy. The King and the Duke of Burgundy had withdrawn from their division to a nearby hillock. They watched as the wings of the French first line enveloped the Flemings and the men of Coucy and Bourbon crushed them from behind.

The French now began a methodical massacre of their enemy. The Flemings panicked. Their line broke and they disintegrated into a terrified, formless mass, fleeing wherever they could find an opening. Enguerrand de Coucy organised companies of men-at-arms in pursuit squads to chase those who had managed to get away from the mêlée. They hacked them to the ground as they fled across the fields. A group of several hundred Flemings tried to rally in a copse of woodland, only to be surrounded and cut down like their fellows. The slaughter continued until nightfall. The battle had lasted less than two hours. As always in medieval battles, most of the casualties were suffered in the final stages and almost all on the defeated side. The macabre count of bodies organised by the heralds after it was over found only about a hundred French casualties but no fewer than 27,500 Flemish dead according to the Florentine Buonaccorso Pitti, who was present at the battle. Nine-tenths of the Flemings' corpses bore no wounds. They had been crushed to death in the press of the defeated army, drowned as they tried to cross a large pond in their rear or smothered face down in the mud as their companions trampled over them in the bid to get away. About 3,000 Flemings were found wounded but alive on the battlefield. They were finished off with knives or axes as they lay on the ground. A handful of prominent Flemish survivors were taken prisoner and later beheaded on the orders of the Count of Flanders. The body of Philip Van Artevelde was found in a ditch, smothered beneath the corpses of his bodyguards. The body was identified by a wounded Flemish prisoner and brought to the fourteen-year-old King. He had it hanged by the neck from a nearby tree. Later it was delivered up to Louis de Mâle, who sent it to Ypres to be broken on the wheel in the market-place together with the bodies of two of his lieutenants. Some, even among Louis's supporters, believed that greater honour was due to men however lowly born who had died in battle.[36]

The battle of Roosebeke was followed by the collapse of the rebellion throughout Flanders. At Oudenaarde most of the soldiers manning the Flemish siege lines abandoned their posts as soon as the news arrived. A sortie by the garrison dispersed the rest. Courtrai was sacked by the troops of Louis de Mâle on the day of the battle. Bruges, the richest city of Flanders, would have suffered the same fate but for the intervention of the Count. He persuaded the King to receive the town's submission, but on exacting terms: an indemnity of 120,000 francs, an undertaking to make good the damage done to the Count's property in the town and a promise to sever all relations with the English. It was Louis's only act of mercy. There was no amnesty for the friends of Van Artevelde's regime. In the public places of the towns the train of executions continued for several months as Van Artevelde's friends and supporters were rounded up and hanged, beheaded, buried alive or broken on the wheel by the officers of Louis de Mâle: 92 victims at Bruges, 55 at Ypres, 28 at Oudenaarde, 16 at Aalst, 32 at Dendermonde, 17 at Bergues and so on.[37]

On 1 December 1382 the King and his principal advisers entered Courtrai while the French army encamped in the fields beyond the walls. They remained there for more than two weeks while desultory negotiations began with the men of Ghent and plans were laid for a siege of the town. Ghent had lost much of its male population in the battle. It had lost all its allies in Flanders. It was vulnerable to the re-imposition of the blockade. For several days after the battle the inhabitants did not know what to do. Their first instinct was to submit even on the bleak terms offered by the French. The French leaders and the aristocratic exiles around the Count hated Ghent with a passion which even now can shock those who read the venomous verses penned by Eustache Deschamps against that 'root of treason . . . of Cain and Judas born'. Yet, as December wore on, the French threat to Ghent began to seem less credible. It was very cold. The heavy rain flooded the plain around the town and turned the valleys of the Lys and the Scheldt into basins of mud. The horses suffered badly. The captains of the army, many of whom were serving on credit, wanted to go home. Inside the beleaguered town the citizens recovered their self-confidence after the first impact of the disaster. Reports of the executions and confiscations in the rest of Flanders served as a reminder of the fate which awaited the town's most prominent citizens and stiffened their resolve. Peter Van den Bossche, still suffering from the wounds received at the bridge of Comines, arrived from Bruges in a litter a few days after the battle. He took over the role of Van Artevelde and began to organise the defence.

In about the middle of December 1382 the French King's Council resolved to abandon the campaign and pay off most of the army. As soon as this news reached Ghent the town's leaders broke off negotiations. On 18 December the French withdrew from Courtrai to pass Christmas in the more congenial atmosphere of Tournai. Their last act before leaving was to take down the spurs and armour pieces stripped from the bodies of French knights killed at the battle of Courtrai, eighty years before, which were still hanging in the church of Notre-Dame. This famous battle, one of the most humiliating defeats suffered by French arms in the middle ages, had achieved a symbolic importance in the minds of both sides. Now it was avenged. As the King and his entourage departed, the troops entered through the newly demolished gateways and completed the devastation begun by the Count of Flanders's men three weeks before. The town was systematically pillaged. Those of the inhabitants who had not managed to hide or flee were murdered in the streets and houses. Most of the built-up area was left in flames.[38]

Ghent fought on for nearly three years after the battle of Roosebeke but it fought alone. Politically the French victory was complete. French sovereignty over Flanders became a reality for the first time in more than a century. The Count, although nominally restored to his former authority, withdrew to the francophone castleries of the south. In *Flandre flamengeante* power was shared between his officers and the ministers of the King of France. The terms of Bruges's submission, which served as the model for those granted to other towns, provided that the Brugeois would 'acknowledge the King of France as their sovereign and obey him and his lieutenants, bailiffs, officers and sergeants . . . in the same way as the subjects of other peers of France are bound to do.' The appellate jurisdiction of the Parlement of Paris in Flanders, which had been a dead letter for most of the fourteenth century, was restored. The French took control of most of the major garrisons. They appointed their own captains at Bruges and its two outports of Sluys and Damme. Aardenburg, then a seaport on the broad estuary of the River Zwyn, received a garrison of 200 Bretons. Courtrai was placed under the command of a protégé of the Duke of Burgundy. Ypres and Gravelines became part of the military command of the lord of Sempy and were incorporated in the ring of French fortresses around Calais.[39]

One of the first acts of the French government after its victory was to extend the trade embargo against England into Flanders where it had never previously been applied. All dealings with the English were forbidden. The decision, followed shortly by the withdrawal of the merchants of the Hanseatic ports, was profoundly damaging to the Flemish cloth industry. It was a commercial disaster for Bruges, which had become the cross-roads of north European trade. The flourishing English commercial community in Flanders was destroyed overnight. John Salomon, the doyen of the English merchants at Bruges, who had lived there for a quarter of a century and served as the English government's shipbroker and paymaster in Flanders, loaded all his goods and money into ships at Sluys and fled to London as the French entered the town. Others, who moved less fast, lost all their stock and property as English assets were confiscated by the Crown and bestowed on the Constable of France. At least four Englishmen in Bruges were executed as supporters of the regime of Ghent. With the Calais staple cut off from Flanders and all the ports of the county in French hands, the wool trade between England and the Low Countries virtually ceased until, in the spring, the English managed to establish an informal staple port for their exports at Middelburg in Zeeland. This enabled the trade to be carried on via Antwerp. But volumes were well down on previous years and prices were low.[40]

The French occupation of Flanders, following on the submission of the Duke of Brittany the year before, was a major strategic reverse for England. It brought all the maritime provinces of France north of the Gironde under effective French control for the first time in nearly half a century. It put an end to an alliance which had been one of the sheet-anchors of English policy since the outset of the war. It also touched the English population more closely than any of the successive misfortunes of recent years. The Flemish towns had been not only allies but major markets for English exports and shipping and banking centres of European importance. Perhaps no other event so potently symbolised the new international alignment of Flanders than its nominal conversion to the cause of the Avignon Pope. Clement VII had every reason to shower largesse on the messenger who brought him the first report of the battle. Charles VI gave the inhabitants of Bruges 'five or six days to think about it' before submitting to his command that they recognise Clement VII. The men of Ypres were told by the King's spokesman that it was 'proper for them to think as the King thought' on such a matter. The rest of Flanders was given until Easter to declare themselves for a cause which had become one of the main tools of France's foreign policy and the badge of its system of alliances.[41]

The battle of Roosebeke proved to be an equally fateful moment for France. The defeat of Ghent was a severe set-back to radical politicians in the French towns, who had emerged as the chief internal enemies of the monarchy. They had been counting on a French defeat in Flanders in order to pursue their campaign against war taxation. The outcome of the battle dashed their hopes and enabled the King's ministers to avenge all the humiliations of the past two years. About a third of the army was retained about the King after the rest had been disbanded. They accompanied him south across the plain of Picardy, making for Paris.

On 11 January 1383 Charles VI and his uncles appeared outside the capital at the Porte Saint-Denis with about 2,000 soldiers wearing full body armour, arrayed in divisions as if for battle. The leading citizens had gathered outside the gate to receive them as tradition demanded. They were curtly ordered to return to their homes. The troops threw aside the chains and barriers across the gateway and marched in with drawn swords, led by the Constable, the Admiral and the two Marshals. Detachments occupied the principal buildings, public places and road crossings. This was not an operation of war. It was a political demonstration, calculated to overawe the inhabitants of France's most intensely political city. Troops of soldiers passed through the streets, arresting all those who were thought to have organised or encouraged resistance to the new taxes of the previous year. The principal opposition politicians were taken to the cells of the Châtelet, where they found themselves rubbing shoulders with a mass of small-time agitators and others who had had the misfortune to provoke the grudges of the King's uncles. The proscriptions extended to malcontents and demagogues, some of whom had last challenged the Crown as long ago as 1358. The Parlement, which had tried to play a moderating role in the arguments, fell under special suspicion. One of its presidents was arrested together with two prominent advocates. One of these was Jean des Marets, advocate to three successive kings of France and councillor of the Duke of Anjou, who had aroused the ire of the Duke of Burgundy by speaking too well for the citizens of Paris during their negotiations with the government.

The executions began on the following day. The first victims were two drapers and a jeweller. They were followed to the scaffold at intervals of a few days by groups of six or eight victims at a time. Jean des Marets was beheaded, in spite of the widespread sympathy which was felt for him at court. According to Froissart he refused to express contrition for his acts, declaring from the scaffold that he had done nothing to deserve his fate. Several prisoners committed suicide in their cells before their time came. Meanwhile the customary rituals of civic humiliation were put in hand. The principal gates of Paris were taken off their hinges and thrown to the ground. A section of wall was demolished by the Porte Saint-Antoine. Nearby, the Bastille was redesigned to resist attack from the city side and provide royal forces with a means of entering the city 'even against its inhabitants' will'. The chains which were traditionally piled up at street corners to be stretched across the streets in times of trouble had become a symbol of the Parisians' possession of their own city. They were confiscated and carried off to Vincennes. Soldiers were billeted on the inhabitants. Every citizen was ordered to surrender his armour and weapons. On 17 January 1383 the King entered the great hall of the palace on the island to announce the suppression of most of the civic institutions of the capital: the offices of the Provost of the Merchants and the *échevins* were abolished and their functions transferred to the King's Provost. The masters of the city guilds and the *quarteniers*, *cinquanteniers* and *dixeniers* who commanded the citizen militia were dismissed. The activities of the religious confraternities, pillars of the capital's communal life, were indefinitely suspended. Heavy fines were levied on prominent citizens, assessed at a level designed to pay the outstanding accounts of the captains who had fought in Flanders.[42]

The object of the repression was not just revenge, welcome as that was to the Duke of Burgundy who had personally endured the pretensions of the Parisians in the spring of 1382. The government was determined to make taxation a royal prerogative, unfettered by any requirement of consent. A majority of the royal Council had apparently objected to this policy but the Duke of Burgundy and his aristocratic allies overruled them. It was the principal theme of the tremendous oration listing the sins of the Parisians which was delivered by the Chancellor, Pierre d'Orgemont, on 1 March from the marble steps of the palace before a great crowd of citizens, one from every household of the city. The prime count in the charge against them was that they had refused to consent to the taxes required for the defence of the realm. Their refusal was now labelled treason. It would have been difficult to devise a more radical or explicit repudiation of the traditional consensual basis for royal taxation. The Chancellor's recitation was followed by a characteristic piece of political theatre, in which the royal princes fell to their knees to beg the child King to pardon his erring subjects. Charles pardoned them. But the Chancellor had made the point which mattered and the King's officers were already acting on it. On 20 January 1383 the *aides* and the *gabelle* had been reimposed in Paris by royal proclamation at rates even higher than those previously in force.[43]

Proceedings very similar to those in Paris were conducted by special commissioners and local *baillis* in most of the major cities of the north. At Rouen the King's officers arrived in March with a military escort commanded by the Admiral of France. Three hundred citizens were pulled out of their houses and thrown into prison. Those who were thought to have organised resistance to the taxes were summarily executed. At Amiens an oligarchy of the richest citizens was given control of the municipal institutions. Proscriptions and executions were ordered at Reims, Châlons, Troyes and Sens, all places where riots had attended the government's attempts to collect war taxes in 1381 and 1382. The King himself presided over the punishment of Orléans for offences against the Crown which went back to the civil wars of the 1350s. All of these visitations were followed by ritual pardons, heavy fines, forced loans and the reinstatement of the *aides* by royal proclamation. Languedoc did not have to wait long before meeting the same fate. There was no invasion of the south and no campaign of executions there, but the Estates of Languedoc were summoned to Lyon in July 1383 to hear the King's commissioners announce the reimposition of the *aides* and the suppression of all the self-governing consulates of the towns. Early in the following year they recovered their consulates but were made to submit to a fine of 800,000 francs for acts of rebellion going back to the tax strikes of 1378. This enormous sum, equivalent to a hearth tax of six francs a year on every taxable household for the next four years, represented a crushing burden, made worse by the fact that its collection was concentrated in a handful of cities such as Toulouse and Carcassonne which were thought to bear most of the blame for recent opposition to royal policies. The principle of taxation by royal command, which had never quite been acknowledged under Charles V, was now overtly established throughout the realm. Meetings of the Estates-General of Languedoc became less frequent and more compliant. Those of Languedoil would not meet at all until 1413 and only infrequently thereafter.[44]

The Earl of Cambridge arrived in England with the remnants of his army a few days before the battle of Roosebeke. The men returned in Castilian ships, in poor health, without mounts or equipment, bringing with them their tales of mutiny and betrayal. They were also sadly reduced in numbers. Forty-one large ships had carried them to Portugal but only twelve were required to bring them back. John of Gaunt had been counting on Cambridge to cling to his foothold in Portugal while he planned his next move against Castile. He was furious. He washed his hands of the returning army and refused to meet their outstanding wage bills.

Even now the Duke of Lancaster's cup of bitterness was not yet full. The treaty of Badajoz proved to be only the first stage of a closer alliance between Portugal and Castile. During the winter of 1382–3 Fernando's health continued to deteriorate. He ceased to take even an intermittent part in the direction of his government, which was conducted in his name by Leonora Teles with the aid of a small coterie of close advisers: her lover, Juan Fernández Andeiro; her brother, João Afonso Telo, Admiral of Portugal; Gonçalo Vasques de Azevedo, the King's confidant and now the Queen's; the Constable, Alvaro Perez de Castro, who had helped him to negotiate the treaty of Badajoz; and Martin, Bishop of Lisbon, the de facto leader of the Clementist party in Portugal. Several of these men were in fact Castilians: ecclesiastics like the Bishop of Lisbon or old *emperogilados* like Andeiro and Castro who had supported King Pedro's cause in Castile until his death and then made new careers as exiles at the court of Portugal. All of them owed their positions to the Queen's patronage. All were desperate to find a way of holding on to power after Don Fernando's death.

In October 1382 they hit upon a radical solution. The Queen of Castile had recently died. Their plan was that John of Trastámara should himself marry Princess Beatrice in place of his infant son. John, they reasoned, was far more likely to apply the resources of his realm in defending Beatrice's interests if he were her husband than if he were only her prospective father-in-law. In particular he could be expected to restrain the ambitions of Inez de Castro's sons, both of whom were living in his realm. Moreover, since John had two sons by his first marriage, his descendants by his two marriages would found distinct dynasties ruling in Castile and Portugal. In November 1382 Juan Fernández Andeiro led a magnificent embassy to Castile to present the Queen's proposals to John of Trastámara. Wind of these events probably reached England early in 1383, when yet another emissary of Fernando's arrived at Westminster to wring his hands before the King's ministers. He was shortly followed by Florimond, lord of Lesparre, a Gascon prisoner of war in Castile, bearing proposals from John of Trastámara himself for a peace conference at which the Lancastrian claims to his kingdom might be bought out.[45]

On 21 December 1382 Bishop Despenser formally took the cross at St. Paul's Cross in London. Shortly afterwards his commissioners began to tour the provinces, preaching and granting absolution to all who signed up to fight in his army or contributed to the cost. A national sales campaign was launched, supported by meretricious marketing and mendacious claims for the indulgences which went well beyond anything authorised by the Pope's bulls. The number of crusade preachers was swollen by imposters and confidence tricksters who forged their commissions and pocketed their receipts. The results were spectacular. A horde of men came forward, gentlemen, monks and priests, ruffians, peasants, apprentices and tradesmen, rich and poor, all buying paradise. According to Froissart, however, professional men-at-arms held back. 'Soldiers never go to war without money up front,' he observed; 'they cannot live on pardons.' But the Bishop's chests were filled with coin, gold and silver, and jewellery contributed by the faithful. He could afford to pay them.[46]

The King's ministers, as ever responding to events as they happened, were in a quandary. They were vitally affected by the fortunes of the Flemish rebels and by English mercantile interests in the Low Countries. Moreover, with the demise of the 'path of Portugal' the 'path of Flanders' was the only aggressive strategy open to them. But in the Council's view the Bishop of Norwich was the wrong man for the job. They had serious misgivings about the sort of amateur soldiers which he was likely to recruit and about his own suitability as a commander. They were also concerned about allowing him to roam over the continent free of any direct political control by the King's officers. So, on about 12 December 1382, a week after authorising the Bishop's recruitment campaign, the Council tried to upstage him. They announced that the King would raise his own army and lead it to Flanders in person. The object would be to relieve the blockade of Ghent and expel the French from Flanders. The government's plan must have been to absorb the crusaders into the ranks of the royal army. They probably hoped to appropriate the Bishop's funds as well. This scheme was endorsed by the lay and ecclesiastical magnates and a great body of military men at a Great Council which met in January 1383. A knight was sent to Ghent with a message that help would soon be on its way. A committee of representatives of Ghent and exiles from Bruges and Ypres established itself in London to support the enterprise. Francis Ackerman, one of Ghent's three captains, had appointed himself 'Admiral of Flanders'. He arrived in England at the beginning of January with a squadron of nine ships raised in the harbours of the Vier Ambachten, and put them at the disposal of the English government. Meanwhile, Peter Van den Bossche in Ghent was planning to seize a port in western Flanders by which contact could be maintained with England and troops and supplies brought to the city. On 26 January 1383 a large force of citizens and mercenaries of Ghent fell on Aardenburg, then an important harbour town in the estuary of the Zwyn opposite Sluys. They took it by assault three days later, massacring its French garrison.[47]

The Council's plan to make the invasion of Flanders a royal enterprise had much to be said for it, but it foundered on two obstacles. The first was the opposition of the King. Richard did not share Charles VI's enthusiasm for war and was reluctant to go. Without him there was no one who could take the command out of Despenser's hands as of right. The second problem was money. The single tenth and fifteenth voted by the Commons in the autumn was not enough to support the army of 6,000 men which the Council had in mind. The Great Council advised that without a fresh Parliamentary grant it could not be done. Yet the chances of another grant seemed remote given the ill grace with which the last one had been approved. And so it proved.

When Parliament met at Westminster on 23 February 1383 competing proposals were put before them by the Council and the Bishop of Norwich. The Council tried to drum up support for a royal expedition funded by fresh taxation. The Bishop offered to lead his own army into Flanders, financing the campaign from the funds raised by the sale of indulgences together with the proceeds of the taxes voted in the previous Parliament. In its final form Despenser's proposal was to raise an army of 5,000 men and to keep them in the field for a full year. As soon as the subsidy was paid over to him an advance guard of 2,000 men would leave to relieve the blockade of Ghent. The rest would follow in the spring to occupy the rest of Flanders. The Bishop's pretensions caused intense irritation among the Lords, most of whom supported the Council's proposals. Despenser was testily cross-examined by his fellow peers. They declared that if France were to be conquered by English arms it should be conquered for the King, not the Church. They thought that it was asking for trouble for a bishop with limited military experience to exercise a major command. If the crusade went ahead Despenser should at least be made to delegate his military functions to a suitable lay commander. The Lords were the King's traditional advisers on such matters but their views were rejected root and branch in the Commons. They felt as strongly as anyone about the French occupation of Flanders but they thought that if the Bishop of Norwich was willing to recover Flanders without asking for further funds he should be allowed to do so. Finance, however, was not the only factor in their minds. A vocal faction in the Commons, led by the Archbishop of Canterbury's brothers Philip and Peter Courtenay and supported from the streets by the mobs of the city, was openly contemptuous of the military skills of the King's uncles and doubted the Council's good faith. They suspected (probably rightly) that the royal army which the Council was proposing was really intended to serve the ambitions of John of Gaunt in Castile. They were determined to have nothing to do with it. Not content with commending Bishop Despenser's enterprise, the Commons demanded that the King and all three of his uncles should remain in England to watch the border with Scotland. For good measure they added that in their view the Castilian King's offer of negotiations should be accepted. John of Gaunt became increasingly ill-tempered as the session continued and eventually walked out in disgust.[48]

Without the funds to finance its own plans the Council was obliged to submit to the Commons' will. A week after Parliament closed the Exchequer paid over nearly £30,000 to the Bishop's commissioners from the proceeds of the last Parliamentary subsidy. The rest was paid in stages over the following weeks. Despenser even managed to escape any real supervision over his military command. With obvious reluctance he had told the Lords that he would accept a royal lieutenant with ultimate authority over all military matters. He would put forward four names, he said, from which the King might choose one, but in the document ultimately agreed there was a proviso that if he could not reach agreement with the nominated lieutenant then 'the King will be content in such a case for the said Bishop to have the governance and disposition of the army . . . in all respects.' Despenser had no intention of making any agreement which would enable someone else to supplant him and in the event no royal lieutenant was ever appointed. Instead Despenser nominated four men as his lay captains: Sir Hugh Calveley, Sir William Farringdon, Sir William Elmham and Sir Thomas Trivet. They were later joined by Sir Robert Knolles, who had lost none of his appetite for fighting although he must by now have been in his sixties. These were all experienced professional soldiers whose presence in the army must have done something to inspire confidence among critics of the enterprise. But none of them had the rank to dominate Despenser.[49]

On 2 April 1383 the final act of Portugal's reconciliation with Castile was played out at the royal manor at Salvaterra de Magos on the left bank of the Tagus. The marriage treaty between the two countries was sealed in the hall as Fernando languished, ill and unseen in another part of the building. It was a remarkable document. The Princess Beatrice was to be married to John of Trastámara as soon as the ceremonies could be organised. When Fernando died they would reign jointly as King and Queen of Portugal. The real beneficiaries of the treaty were to be the Queen and her lover. Under the terms of the agreement neither John nor his child-bride was to have any control over the government, which was to be carried on by Leonora until they had an heir who survived to the age of fourteen. The most elaborate provisions were included to secure the autonomy of Portugal and the independence of its institutions. Leonora's chief Portuguese rival, the Infante João, openly declared that the marriage could not have been approved by Fernando. He also thought that it would be profoundly unpopular in the cities of Portugal. He was probably right on both counts. But Don João was completely dependent on John of Trastámara and could do nothing. He was rewarded for his candour by being lured to the royal castle of Ciudad Rodrigo, where he was arrested and his movements restricted on the orders of the King. On 17 May 1383 Beatrice was married to the Castilian King in the cathedral of Badajoz amid extravagant celebrations which cost so much that John was obliged to anticipate half a year's taxation to pay for them. As for Fernando, he declined to attend. He mustered just enough energy to send a personal emissary to carry yet more apologies to John of Gaunt in England.[50]

On 17 March 1383 messengers were despatched to all the county towns of England summoning the crusaders to make for the coast at Sandwich. Exactly two months later about 8,000 men had reached Calais and another 3,000 or so were gathering by the Kent and Essex coasts. It was a sign of the enthusiasm which had driven recruitment in England that most of these men were volunteers serving without pay and that archers greatly outnumbered men-at-arms, perhaps by as much as three to one. On 16 May 1383 the Bishop of Norwich hurriedly crossed the Channel to open the campaign, fearing, it was said, that if he hung around for too long the Council would relieve him of his command.[51]

Despenser's strategy was largely determined by the agents of the Flemish rebels. A large Flemish mission had arrived in England at the beginning of March, thirteen merchants of Ghent and various exiles from Bruges. Seven of them stayed in London to advise the Council while the other six accompanied the Bishop on his adventure. Despenser's first priority was to break the French blockade around Ghent. So, on 19 May 1383, without waiting for the rest of the army to arrive, he led his troops out of Calais and along the coast road to Gravelines. It was perhaps unfortunate for Despenser that his enterprise began with a series of spectacular successes, for hubris was a large part of the explanation for the disasters which followed. On 20 May Bourbourg, a major fortress guarding the road to Bruges beyond the River Aa, surrendered without striking a blow. Gravelines was defended by its inhabitants, supported by a large Breton garrison, but it fell to the first assault. In the harbour the crusaders captured seven large cargo ships as well as a large number of fishing smacks. So many horses were taken that they were going for a shilling apiece. Dunkirk, the next town along the coast, was invested by land and sea but surrendered rather than suffer the same fate. The army entered the town, probably early on the morning of 25 May.

The French King's ministers had had at least six months' warning of what was afoot but they do not seem to have taken Despenser's crusade seriously until the last moment and had taken no steps to recruit an army. The defence was left to local forces. They were organised by one of Louis de Mâle's bastard sons, Louis de Hase, and by the lord of Dixmude, who was the principal territorial magnate of south-western

Flanders. These two men assembled an army which was by all accounts substantially larger than Despenser's. But it was of very uneven quality. The core of their force consisted of aristocratic retainers of the Count of Flanders and about 1,900 French garrison troops stationed in Flanders. The rest were raw local levies from the *franc* of Bruges and the nearby towns of Ypres, Furnes and Bergues. At least one of its captains was secretly in touch with Despenser. Even those who were loyal had doubts about their men. Many of them were Urbanists and others had more sympathy for the English than for their new French masters.

On 25 May 1383 the Bastard of Flanders advanced across the flat scrubland south of Dunkirk a few hours after the English had occupied the town. Despenser and Calveley marched their men out of the gates and drew them up in battle order beneath the walls. A banner with the papal crossed keys was carried aloft in front of them and another with Despenser's family arms. A herald was sent across to parley with the approaching horde and perhaps persuade them to come over to their side. But he was seized and killed by a group of Flemish knights before he reached the enemy line, a rare breach of the convention which protected heralds from violence in wartime. Watching this incident from their lines the English at once attacked. The Flemings came forward in a disorderly mass to meet them. Few of them reached the English lines. They were cut down in thousands by dense volleys of arrows from the English archers. The urban troops in the Flemish ranks fled. The professional soldiers behind them tried to hold their ground but they were by now heavily outnumbered. Their line broke and they were overwhelmed. A violent thunderstorm broke out as the English finished off the survivors. The English claimed to have taken ten thousand lives. Priests, monks and friars, the chronicler Thomas Walsingham recorded with satisfaction, inflicted more casualties than any other group. Within a few days most of the walled places of the region had submitted, including the fortress of Cassell and the towns of Nieuport, Poperinghe, and Bergues. Meanwhile Sir Thomas Trivet arrived from England with the rest of Despenser's professional troops. In Paris Charles VI's ministers were appalled. The whole work of Roosebeke was being undone before their eyes. On 27 May, two days after the battle of Dunkirk, they ordered the recruitment of a fresh army in northern France, the second to invade Flanders in a year.[52]

Early on the morning of 9 June 1383 the English army appeared outside the western gates of Ypres. The decision to attack this large and populous city had been pressed on Despenser by the representatives of

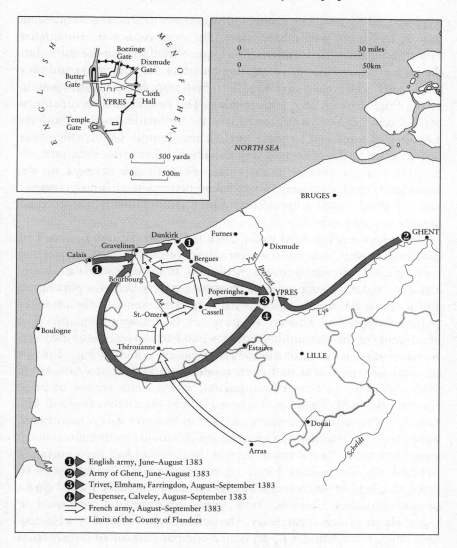

18 The Norwich crusade, May–September 1383

Ghent and Peter Van den Bossche. Peter arrived almost simultaneously
from the east with a large force of his own to support the Bishop's
operations. Failure would one day make the decision controversial but
at the time it was supported by all Despenser's English advisers for good
political and strategic reasons. Ypres was the major cross-roads of
eastern Flanders. Its occupation by an English army would not only

have opened up road communications between Ghent and the English base at Calais but would have barred the most convenient route for a French army entering Flanders. The English tried to rush the gates. But the men of Ypres had been expecting an attack for some days and they were ready. The great bell of the Cloth Hall rang out the alarm as soon as the English were seen approaching. The first English company to reach the Butter Gate was greeted with a cannonade. Further south an assault was launched in force against the Temple Gate, which was beaten off. On the following day the English launched simultaneous assaults against several gates, this time with the support of the contingents of Ghent. They succeeded no better. On 11 June Despenser and Van den Bossche disposed their forces around the town and settled down for a long siege.[53]

Ypres was a substantial town defended by a continuous circuit of walls and towers and two concentric lines of ditches. The Bishop had been told that the garrison was weak and its stores low. He probably also expected some support from the town's largely Urbanist population and its powerful guilds of cloth-workers. The events of the previous year, however, had shaken support for Ghent and England. The inhabitants of the surrounding country had been brought into the town with all the food and animals that they could bring. Known sympathisers of Ghent had been rounded up and driven out. Huge stocks of grain had been accumulated and a strict regime of price control instituted. The English arrived to find the ditches flooded. The town's extensive suburbs, where much of its industry was concentrated, were partially demolished, a sacrifice which would finally ruin its once-great cloth trade. In the town, gaps in the defences had been hurriedly patched up. Carpenters laboured to reinforce the ramparts with projecting timber structures from which rocks could be hurled down on assault parties. Cannon, firing pebbles or grapeshot, were sited on top of all the principal gateways. The defence was directed by a Flemish nobleman, Peter Van der Zype, with a company recruited largely from Flemish retainers of the Duke of Burgundy. But the backbone of the resistance was the local patriciate, the nobility of the surrounding region and the population of the town, who had been armed and drilled for days before the English arrived. They manned their stations with fierce determination.[54]

Although the bulk of the besieging army had crossed the Channel with Despenser it was the men of Ghent who took the leading role in the siege. They were far better equipped than their allies and had more experience

of conducting siege operations in the difficult, marshy terrain of eastern
Flanders. The few buildings which were still standing outside Ypres were
fortified and armed with artillery. Trenches were dug around the town
and reinforced by improvised timber forts at regular intervals. Mines
were dug towards the walls. Immense stone-throwers were constructed
in front of the main gateways, which progressively reduced them to
rubble. Teams of water engineers laboured to divert the local streams
away from the town and drain the ditches protecting the walls. Labour
and materials were requisitioned across western Flanders. Great timber
pontoons were constructed to enable assault parties to reach the base of
the walls. The defenders did their best to obstruct these efforts. Sortie
parties set fire to the enemy's siege works. The mines were captured and
destroyed. Repair crews worked through the night to make good the
damage before dawn brought a renewed barrage of rocks crashing into
the walls and gates. But the advance of the besiegers seemed inexorable.
Within two weeks the flow of supplies into the town had been cut off.
Both rings of ditches had been drained and partially filled with timber
and rubble. The main fighting occurred in the northern sector around the
Dixmude and the Boezinge gates. At dawn on 24 June, midsummer day,
seven pontoons were dragged into place between the two gates. The
English swarmed across them and tried to fight their way over the walls
with scaling ladders. They were met with a barrage of flanking fire from
cannon mounted on both gateways and suffered terrible casualties before
the retreat was eventually sounded. It was the first recorded occasion
that these weapons had played a decisive part in the defence of a walled
stronghold. A few days after this reverse the English tried again. The
assault parties approached the walls from north and south. This time
they were protected from the rain of missiles and grapeshot by four huge
timber shelters on wheels. But they had not reached the base of the walls
before sorties from the town attacked their shelters and forced them to
retreat. Five hundred men were lost in this attack.[55]

The failure of these assaults proved to be the turning point of the
campaign. The besiegers had suffered heavy casualties on the walls. Over
the following weeks many more succumbed to disease as dysentery took
hold in their lines, where at least 20,000 men were concentrated in the
usual insanitary conditions. Supplies were rapidly exhausted. To make
matters worse reports of the easy victories and golden spoils in the first
week of the campaign had tempted large numbers of fresh men from
England to take the cross and join the army. They had heard reports that
Ypres was about to fall and wanted to be in on the sack. The great

majority of these men were useless mouths: London servants and apprentices, roughs and criminals, absconding clergymen, men with no experience of war. Many of them arrived without weapons. They brought no more food than they needed for their passage. Despenser was quite unable to manage the situation. Morale collapsed. Sharp words were exchanged between the Bishop and his men and sharper ones were muttered in corners. Quarrels broke out about the distribution of booty. The Bishop was reported to have appropriated three barrels of gold for his own use. Sir Thomas Trivet, one of the few captains who succeeded in making money during the siege, had almost certainly got it by long-range raiding into northern France but was widely believed to have been trafficking with the defenders. The new arrivals from England, intensely disappointed by what they found in Despenser's camp, deserted in their thousands. Many of the original troops made off with them. Damaging stories began to circulate in England about Despenser's incompetence and the divisions among his men.[56]

Meanwhile the English army's position was becoming increasingly insecure as the French pressed forward with their own plans to re-invade Flanders. At the end of June, after a month of intensive recruitment, the French government proclaimed the *arrière-ban*. The troops were ordered to assemble at local mustering centres across France in the last week of July. At Westminster these developments were followed with dismay, mingled with a certain satisfaction among those who had always regarded the Bishop of Norwich as an interfering amateur. At about the end of June the Council made another attempt to wrest control of the army from him. They offered to send out the Earl of Arundel as a royal lieutenant and invited Despenser to transfer the command to him. But Despenser, ever jealous of his authority and distrustful of his captains, sent an evasive answer which was interpreted as a refusal. Arundel remained in England.[57]

In the last week of July 1383 the Bishop of Norwich, conscious of the progress of French preparations, turned to negotiation. He declared a local truce and sent a messenger into the town to offer terms to the defenders. Their lives and property would be safe if they surrendered, he said. Otherwise the whole town would be reduced to ashes and its inhabitants killed. 'Kill your captains! Think of the future!' Despenser's Flemish allies yelled across the empty ditches. The delegates of the town came out to the Bishop's tents to be plied with wine and cherries and treated by turns to flattering speeches and hectoring threats. Inside the walls, conditions were deteriorating. The defenders were exhausted. Their stores were running out. The few streams which still entered the town had become stagnant and foul. The streets stank with sewage. At length a provisional agreement appears to have been reached by which the town agreed to surrender on 20 August unless it was relieved by the King of France before that date. But either the townsmen refused to ratify it or their captains repudiated it. What is clear is that on 30 July 1383 discussions were abruptly broken off. The Bishop raised his arm as the townsmen left him and excommunicated them in the name of the Roman Pope. The provost of the abbey of St. Martin, who was as good an Urbanist as Despenser, responded by appealing to the same Pope against the legate's acts. As the delegation re-entered the town the Bishop's banners were being unfurled to show that the truce had ended.[58]

On 2 August 1383 Charles VI received the Oriflamme from the abbot of Saint-Denis and on the following morning set out for the north, accompanied by the Duke of Burgundy and the troops of his household. An advance guard was sent ahead under the command of the Admiral of France, Jean de Vienne, with 600 men-at-arms and some companies of Genoese crossbowmen to secure the crossings of the Lys. The rest of the army received orders to be at Arras by 22 August. From Avignon Clement VII promised them indulgences to match the pardons distributed by his rival. On the day the King left Paris the English hurled themselves against the walls of Ypres in a final attempt to capture the place before the French arrived. The assault, which had been in preparation for much of the previous month, engaged the whole of the Anglo-Flemish army. Five gateways were attacked at once. The men-at-arms approached with scaling ladders, covered from the rear by dense cohorts of archers and protected from above by wheeled timber shelters. Fire wagons, stuffed with wool and powdered sulphur, were pushed forward against the gates. The defenders, unable to break the shelters with stones, sallied from the gates to attack the fire wagons with lances, axes and swords. The crews of the wagons were driven back in hand-to-hand fighting and their loads tipped into the ditches. Terrible casualties were once more inflicted by the cannon mounted on the gates, which fired co-ordinated barrages of shot into the attackers' lines. Repeatedly forced back from the gates, the English and their Flemish allies renewed their attacks on six successive days. Towards the end they succeeded in getting a great wheeled siege tower, fitted with a trebuchet and heavy iron bombard known as the Canterbury Gun, up against one of the gate towers. But they were unable to fight their way over the walls. On 8 August, after several hours of desperate fighting, the final assault was called off.[59]

A council of war was held in the Bishop's tents on the following morning. It was an acrimonious occasion. The English had borne the brunt of the assaults and their losses had been heavy. Jean de Vienne was reported to have reached the Lys, just fifteen miles south, with the advance guard of the French army. The King of France had left Senlis two days before. The captains of Ghent wanted to press the attack on Ypres. They believed that the defenders had reached the limit of their endurance. But the English had had enough. They were determined to abandon the siege. Unfortunately they were unable to agree on an alternative strategy. Bishop Despenser wanted to confront the French King on the Lys. Sir Hugh Calveley had worked out a bold scheme for attacking the van of the French army by night. Peter Van den Bossche refused to participate in this scheme and the three other English captains on the Bishop's council, Trivet, Elmham and Farringdon, all advised against it. Their main concern was that their line of retreat to the coast might be cut off by the advancing French army. They regarded Calveley's plan as suicidal. In the end everyone stuck to his own view. On the following morning, 10 August, the army broke up in disorder. The stores were burned and the siege works abandoned, together with the artillery and much of the booty. Peter Van den Bossche left in disgust for Ghent, taking most of the Flemish contingent with him. The volunteers who had enlisted for the sake of the crusading indulgences were dismissed to make their way back to England as best they could. Trivet, Elmham and Farringdon withdrew west with the bulk of the professional companies and established their headquarters in the fortress of Bourbourg, south of Gravelines. As for Bishop Despenser, he marched south to the Lys, accompanied by Calveley, the rest of the Flemings and the handful of English companies whom he could persuade to go with him. They hovered about Jean de Vienne's force, daring them to attack. Then they put away their standards and retreated to the coast.[60]

In England the King's uncles, Lancaster and Buckingham, were alarmed for the fate of the army and the defence of Calais. They were determined to take over the enterprise from the hapless Bishop of Norwich before the latest reverses turned into a rout. Nothing, however, could be done quickly in England in August. The King and his councillors were at their pleasures, scattered across the country. John of Gaunt, who had passed most of the summer on the Scottish border, received the news of Charles VI's advance at his castle at Pontefract in the Midlands. He summoned his military retinue on his own initiative on 22 August. At Westminster steps were taken to charter merchant-men, the fastest way to get troops across the Channel. On 24 August Gaunt and Buckingham wrote to Richard, who was in Yorkshire, urging him to come south and assume the command of a fresh expeditionary army in person.[61]

In the plain north of Arras the French army was already gathering for the invasion of Flanders. It was the largest armed force that the French Crown had raised for a generation and more than twice the size of the army which had fought at Roosebeke the year before. A new enthusiasm for royal service had been generated by the victories and loot of 1382. The rates of pay offered for men-at-arms were considerably increased, making military service a paying proposition for the first time in many years for men who were neither great noblemen nor full-time soldiers. According to the Marshals' reckoning 16,000 men-at-arms appeared at the musters in addition to some 6,000 infantry and archers, enough, as a contemporary remarked, to subdue 'many barbaric nations'. Allowing for pages and varlets the army's total strength must have been well over 30,000. They came from every part of France and the francophone territories of the Empire. The fog of smoke from so many camp fires and the clutter of carts and animals filling the plain made it impossible for the young King to review his men as he had planned. The banners of seven dukes and twenty-seven counts could be seen floating above the mass of men. In a great show of unity the King was joined by all three of his uncles who were in France. Even John de Montfort was there, making his first appearance in a French army after a lifetime in the service of England.[62]

On 25 August 1383 the whole host of France moved slowly out of its encampments and marched north. A week later, on 1 September, the van of the army reached the River Aa in a confused mass of men, horses and baggage carts, shrouded by a thick autumnal mist. They began to cross into Flanders. The English had patched up their quarrels well enough to attempt some sort of defence. They created a line of improvised forts in churches, castles and monasteries on the north side of the Aa to hold up the French advance. They drew up the rest of their forces in battle order a short distance away on the southern slopes of Mont Cassell, the steep hill rising nearly 600 feet above the coastal plain of Flanders, which served as the anchor of the region's defence from classical times to the First World War. But their courage failed them when they saw the strength of the enemy army. They set fire to the town of Cassell and, fighting off the townsmen who tried to stop them, they withdrew under cover of night towards the coast. The French rapidly mopped up the isolated English garrisons of the Aa valley and advanced north in pursuit, heading for Dunkirk. Sir Robert Knolles with 500 English and about 1,000 Flemish troops fought a vigorous rearguard action while his companions hurriedly prepared to defend the two principal strongholds of the district, Bourbourg and Gravelines. On 7 September the French King arrived outside Bergues, then a substantial river port handling much of the wool trade of western Flanders. Knolles toyed with the idea of defending this place but, finding himself surrounded on three sides, he set fire to the timber houses of the town and ordered his men to make off. As they struggled, laden with booty, out of the gates the French came over the walls. Most of Knolles's Flemish auxiliaries and much of the population of the town were either burned to death or cut down in the streets. The fall of Bergues opened up the road to Dunkirk. The French occupied the port without resistance on the following day, thus enabling supplies for their army to be brought in by sea.[63]

In England the fifteen-year-old King reacted to the stream of dismal tidings from Flanders in the erratic way that would soon become familiar to his subjects. Having done nothing in response to his uncles' messages for more than two weeks he panicked as the unfolding disasters were reported to him. When the news of the French occupation of Dunkirk was brought to him at his dinner table in the town of Daventry, near Northampton, he kicked away the table, called for his horse and rode post-haste to London to meet his Council. At St. Albans the Abbot was woken in the middle of the night to find him a change of mount, 'as if he planned to slay the King of France that very night' said the waspish Thomas Walsingham, who witnessed the scene. On the following day, 12 September 1383, the King of France encamped with his host in the meadows outside Bourbourg, where most of the English companies had taken refuge. Richard II, having recovered from his ride, was presiding over an emergency session of the Council at Westminster. It was a difficult meeting. Richard's ardour had cooled overnight. The plans of his uncles to send him to Flanders encountered resistance among his other advisers. There was no time to recruit an army big enough to confront the host of Charles VI with credit. It would be wrong, they said, to expose the King to ridicule by sending him overseas with anything less. Instead it was decided to reinforce the garrison of Calais and its outlying forts and to send Lancaster and Buckingham to rescue the Bishop of Norwich with whatever troops could be found in time. A messenger was sent over the Channel with letters urging Despenser to hold out until they could arrive. Meanwhile the two royal dukes established their headquarters on the Isle of Thanet in north Kent, while their marshals mustered their men and the London merchant John Philpot struggled to find ships to carry them. But they had not anticipated the speed with which the Bishop of Norwich's enterprise would collapse.[64]

Bourbourg was a small town with powerful walls and a water-filled moat. Its compactness made it comparatively easy for even a small garrison to defend, let alone the force of some 3,000 men which was crammed into it in September 1383. The captain of the town was an officer of the Calais garrison called William Hoo but real command was exercised by the triumvirate of knights, Trivet, Elmham and Farringdon, who had served on Despenser's council before abandoning him at Ypres. They returned a curt answer to the summons to surrender which was addressed to them on the first day by the herald of the King of France. The assault came that evening. It began with a heavy artillery bombardment. Volleys of arrows tipped with burning pitch set fire to the thatched roofs of the houses in the town. The French advanced to the edge of the ditch dragging timber and stones to construct a makeshift causeway to the foot of the walls. These men suffered terrible casualties from the archers on the walls above. As darkness began to fall the Bretons of John de Montfort's retinue came forward with their scaling ladders. They reached the summit of the walls, only to be thrown back in bloody hand-to-hand fighting. The Duke of Brittany's banner was wrested from his standard-bearer at the edge of the battlements and taken into the town. As the Bretons fell back others took their place only to be forced back in their turn. By the time the attack was called off some 500 French soldiers lay dead in the ditch.

On the following morning John de Montfort advised the leaders of the French army to strike a deal with the garrison. The French captains had no desire to become bogged down in a long siege in the marshes of coastal Flanders at the onset of winter. John for his part did not believe that Bourbourg could be taken by storm. He was also concerned by the threat in the French army's rear from the troops of Despenser and Calveley in Gravelines, only five miles away. On 14 September 1383 Montfort negotiated a treaty with the garrison. Its terms were extremely favourable to them. It was agreed to proclaim a truce for three days. At the end of that time, on the 17th, the captains of Bourbourg would surrender the place to the French and do their best to bring about the surrender of Gravelines as well. They were to be allowed to take away their booty and even their prisoners, who included many of the more wealthy inhabitants of the town. On top of that, by a secret side agreement the Duke of Brittany paid them a lump sum of 28,000 gold francs (£4,700) for their complaisance.[65]

After the surrender of Bourbourg most of its garrison made for Calais. They found themselves refused admittance to the town and forced to wait, hungry and exposed, on the beaches for events to determine their fate. Meanwhile their captains repaired to Gravelines in accordance with their agreement with John de Montfort, to urge upon Bishop Despenser the wisdom of surrendering the town. By his own account Despenser was prepared to fight. When the French army appeared before the walls, on 19 September 1383, he defied the French herald's summons to surrender, declaring that he had acquired the place at much cost in blood and cash and had bound himself to hold it for Pope Urban and King Richard. But his men would not support him. They had lost all interest in continuing the campaign, which they regarded as doomed. They were not prepared to wait for John of Gaunt to cross the Channel. There was also concern about the fate of the men huddled on Calais beach, who would be defenceless if the French turned on them. Shortly the leaders from Bourbourg took the issue out of the Bishop's hands. A brief truce was negotiated so that Despenser could call on the English government to relieve him, but without waiting for it to expire the captains struck another deal with the Duke of Brittany. They agreed to surrender Gravelines for 10,000 gold francs (£1,700), which was said to be the value of the provisions left in the town. On about 23 September the English demolished the fortifications of Gravelines and marched out of the gates with their gains. The inhabitants, whom the French regarded as traitors, were abandoned to their fate. They were massacred by the Bretons of John de Montfort, who began to sack the town as soon as the English left. Within a few hours much of it had been reduced to ashes. Shortly afterwards Charles VI disbanded his army and turned south.[66]

The campaign was followed by bitter recriminations on both sides. The leading figures in the French army were profoundly dissatisfied by the lack of any decisive engagement. They believed that the deal struck with the English garrisons of Bourbourg and Gravelines had cheated them of a valuable haul of ransoms. The Florentine merchant

Buonaccorso Pitti, who had volunteered to serve with the French army for adventure and loot, spoke for many of these men when he complained that they had left with 'heavy losses and little honour'. More than one voice accused John de Montfort of colluding with his English friends to let them escape. The accusation, magnified by rumour and malice, was destined to haunt him for years. But the terms were approved by the Duke of Burgundy for sound reasons of policy. Philip was a politician and a diplomat with little interest in military glory. The campaign had been one of the most expensive ever fought by the French Crown, costing well over 2,000,000 *livres* (£400,000). The treasury was out of cash in spite of the reimposition of the *aides* and heavy borrowing. The fear of provoking another taxpayers' revolt was still a powerful restraint on the French government's acts. It was cheaper to buy out Despenser's captains than to keep the French army in the field and essential to do so before the Duke of Lancaster's army could arrive to reopen the campaign on more equal terms.[67]

Philip also had an eye to his own interests. The men of Ghent were still holding out against the French occupation of Flanders. While Charles VI and his uncles had been preoccupied with operations at Bourbourg they had taken advantage of the situation to recapture the strategic town of Oudenaarde and re-establish their control over the upper valley of the Scheldt. The manner of their entry into Oudenaarde spoke volumes about the continuing resilience of the Flemish opposition. A small force of men under the command of Francis Ackerman had been let into the town at night by the citizens. The garrison was massacred. Every Frenchman who could be found within the walls was hunted down and killed, together with their supporters among the Flemish population. The English were widely believed to have inspired this coup. English merchants were the first on the scene to exploit the buyer's market for looted objects. And, once in possession, the first act of the leaders of Ghent was to make another appeal to England for military assistance. In spite of the humiliating outcome of the Bishop of Norwich's crusade England still seemed to be the key to the pacification of Flanders. Within days of the fall of Gravelines messengers were on their way to Westminster bearing the Duke of Burgundy's proposals for an immediate truce and an invitation to a fresh diplomatic conference on the march of Calais.[68]

In October Despenser's army returned in small groups to England. They encountered a glacial reception. John of Gaunt, still smarting from the rejection of his southern strategy by Parliament, had nursed hopes to the very end that they might be diverted to Gascony and used to mount another attempt upon Castile. He and his friends were infuriated by the thought that an opportunity had been lost for the sake of an enterprise which had proved to be a waste of money and effort, all for reasons that they had predicted. Gaunt's own plans had been no more realistic than Despenser's but his anger was widely shared. The public, which had applauded Despenser's adventure and generously contributed to its cost, found it hard to understand its inglorious end. Anger turned to outrage when the terms of surrender and the scale of the bribery became known, as they soon did. When Parliament opened at Westminster, on 26 October 1383, the debacle in Flanders dominated all discussion. The Commons made it a condition of their grant of a fresh subsidy that those responsible for the disaster should be brought to book. As a result the main business of the session proved to be the long and acrimonious trial of Despenser himself, together with his chaplain Henry Bowet, his campaign treasurer, the three principal captains on his council, Trivet, Elmham and Farringdon, and several lesser figures who were thought to have disgraced themselves in one way or another. It was an unedifying spectacle. The defendants had been incompetent and dishonest but they were being tried as scapegoats for the failure of a misconceived plan which had been supported by most of the political community. Bowet, who was charged with being involved in the receipt of the French bribes, managed to establish an alibi and was acquitted, although as the real author of the scheme he was in a sense more guilty than anyone. The campaign treasurer and the military men were all sentenced to be imprisoned at the King's pleasure. Despenser defended himself with verve in the face of constant heckling, bandying points with the prosecutors. He blamed his captains, the men of Ghent and the government at home, everyone in fact but himself. As a bishop he was immune from punishment but the temporal assets of his see were confiscated and he himself returned to the humdrum business of diocesan administration for the remaining twenty-three years of his life. Of all the participants in the affair only Calveley and Knolles, those aged heroes of the 1350s, emerged with their reputations intact.[69]

CHAPTER XI

The Shadow of Invasion
1383–1385

Richard II, now fifteen years of age, was already showing himself to be an erratic ruler, by turns diffident and impulsive. But his most consistent trait was his intense loyalty to individuals whom he trusted. The King's principal minister at this stage was Michael Pole, who had been appointed as Chancellor of England in March 1383. Pole's administration was the first since the King's accession which he could properly regard as his own. Pole was an intelligent and diligent man with a clear conception of where England's interests lay. He understood the limits of England's power better than most of his contemporaries. Addressing the assembled Lords and Commons at the opening of the Parliament of October 1383, he laid bare the problems posed by the war with compelling candour. England, he pointed out, was at war with 'three of the greatest nations of Christendom, France, Castile and now Flanders as well'. The English had traditionally treated attack as the best form of defence and there was much to be said for fighting on the enemy's territory. It was the best guarantee against invasion. It was more profitable and more honourable for those who fought in English armies. It was also the only way of achieving England's aggressive war aims. Yet it was impossibly expensive. The essential problem, as he would point out in the following year, was an economic one. It lay in the multitude of England's enemies and their 'great strength and wealth compared with the weakness and poverty of this realm'.[1]

The facts which lay behind these statements were not spelled out but they hardly needed to be. Each of England's two principal enemies, France and Castile, had public revenues considerably exceeding those of England. With the re-establishment of the French tax system Charles VI's ministers were now deploying armies with a payroll strength of fifteen or twenty thousand men year after year, three or four times the largest field armies of the previous reign. The French annexation of Flanders had more than doubled their shipping resources and made it possible for them to contemplate major seaborne expeditions for the first time since the 1340s. While France's military and naval resources were increasing exponentially, England's capacity for offensive operations was in steep decline. Buckingham's campaign had been one of England's most costly military undertakings since 1369 but the payroll strength of his army had been only about 5,000. Another expedition on that scale would not have been nearly enough to confront the enlarged armies of France. In current conditions the exercise could not have been repeated anyway. Well over half of Buckingham's transports had been hired in the ports of the Low Countries, mostly in Flanders, which was now closed to English agents, or in Holland and Zeeland whose rulers were no longer willing to antagonise the mighty Duke of Burgundy. Nor was the money there to pay for it. The English government's revenues were just about enough to support the permanent garrisons on the coast of France and in the Scottish march. There was nothing left over for offensive operations. At least two Parliamentary subsidies would have been required to fund another continental campaign on the scale of Buckingham's. But in the three years since the disastrous poll tax of 1380 the Parliamentary Commons had granted only one, in October 1382. In November 1383 they would grant another but only after the King had declared that none of them would be allowed to leave Winchester until they had agreed. The option of fighting a purely defensive war did not exist. Once the English abandoned large-scale offensive operations on the continent there would be nothing to stop the enemy from turning their vast resources to the invasion of England itself.

These problems had been developing for some years but became critical in the autumn of 1383 as a result of the deterioration of relations with Scotland, which threatened to open a new front in England's rear, the worst nightmare that could be imagined as Pole told Parliament. The current truce with the Scots, which had been in force since 1370, was due to expire on 2 February 1384. Medieval truces were notoriously fragile but this one had held remarkably well. Since the death of Edward III, however, things had become more difficult. The Scottish cross-border raids of 1380 had marked a change of mood which was noticed and taken seriously in England. Expenditure on border castles was increased. John of Gaunt was appointed as the King's lieutenant on the border, a notable mark of the priority now accorded to England's northern frontier. Gaunt established cordial personal relations with many of the leading Scottish lords of the march, something which the great English families of the border had never succeeded in doing. He spent long periods each year in the north trying to maintaining order by a mixture of diplomacy and intimidation. As time went on this delicate balance became increasingly difficult to sustain.[2]

In about 1381 Robert II's eldest son John, Earl of Carrick, who had been the chief Scottish representative at many of the march days with England, became his father's lieutenant on the marches. Carrick could hardly have been more different from his cautious and vacillating father. He was an ambitious politician with all the impatience for power of the middle-aged heir, and he was determined to build up a power-base for himself on the Scottish march. He forged a close political alliance with the Douglases, now the dominant figures on the march and much the most aggressive proponents of war with England. By 1383 the political pressure on the Scottish King from the marcher lords had become irresistible. In June 1383 there was a heavy Scottish raid into Northumberland which ended with the capture and partial destruction of the castle of Wark on the Tweed. This incident was patched up by the Duke of Lancaster at a march day in the following month, but it was the last time that this well-tried technique worked. At the time William Wardlaw, Bishop of Glasgow, the Scottish King's long-standing diplomatic adviser, was in France. At Orléans in April he had renewed the ancient alliance between the two kingdoms and secretly agreed with the French government to reopen the war with England as soon as the truce expired in the following year. In return France was to support the Scots with experienced commanders, a thousand men-at-arms, equipment for another thousand and a cash subsidy of 40,000 gold francs (£6,700). Once they had resolved not to renew the truce the Scots rapidly lost interest in enforcing the law of the march. In November 1383 there was another heavy raid into Northumberland which captured no castles but did serious damage to towns and villages across the county. The English captains on the border warned the government at Westminster that the Scottish raiding activity was intensifying. Unless firm steps were taken to reinforce the border they could not answer for the security of the north.[3]

Pole believed that peace with France had become indispensable. For the next three years his view became the corner-stone of English policy. In this he was supported by the King and by an increasingly influential group of courtiers and ministers who were convinced that the war could not be won. They resented the entanglements in Flanders and Castile that seemed to be artificially prolonging it. They found allies in some surprising quarters. According to Froissart, who was well informed about affairs at Richard's court, they included a number of prominent professional soldiers who had borne much of the burden of the last decade of fighting, among them the vice-chamberlain Simon Burley and two of the disgraced leaders of Despenser's crusade, Thomas Trivet and William Elmham, both of whom were shortly released from the Tower and restored to favour. The government was also able to forge an alliance with the great London wool merchants. They had been vocal in their support of Despenser's enterprise, but they were also among the first to recognise that the defeat in Flanders was likely to be permanent. The London grocer Nicholas Brembre, who became Mayor of London in 1383 with the support of the court, was a stalwart supporter of the government. Even with these allies, however, neither the King nor his principal minister were entirely free agents. The nobility resented their progressive exclusion from power and their diminished role in the King's counsels as Richard came to rely increasingly on his own intimates. Many of these disaffected men still hankered after the brilliance of Edward III's golden years. The King's growing estrangement from his uncles, Lancaster and Buckingham, now largely bereft of influence, was symbolic of a larger shift of power. In the autumn Parliament of 1383 there was an angry protest in the Lords against the narrowness of the King's circle. The anger tended to merge with a more general frustration provoked by the government's conduct of foreign policy and the visible signs of England's military and diplomatic decline. Richard brushed their objections aside. But as England's misfortunes accumulated they became more difficult to ignore.[4]

During the winter of 1383–4 the Council embarked on a policy of progressively withdrawing from continental commitments, negotiating with France and concentrating their military resources against Scotland. At the beginning of October they accepted the Duke of Burgundy's invitation to participate in a fresh diplomatic conference. The French messengers brought preliminary proposals with them which were regarded in England as surprisingly favourable in the circumstances. Pole even called them 'handsome'. Both sides appointed impressive delegations to represent them. Ghent's appeals for help, which reached Westminster shortly afterwards, were ignored and their representatives in London were sent packing. Meanwhile the Council cancelled the next march day on the Scottish border and declined to receive the ambassadors whom the King of Scotland had sent to London with his explanations and proposals. Instead the Earl of Buckingham was sent northward to stand on the border with an army of 3,000 men.[5]

The 'handsome' proposals apparently made by the Duke of Burgundy have not survived, and although the diplomatic conference which followed was the most important since the proceedings at Bruges in the 1370s almost nothing is known about it. It opened shortly before Christmas at Leulinghem, an unprepossessing mining village south of Calais. The village church, which was to serve as a conference centre for successive Anglo-French exchanges over the following years, was a modest building with a thatched roof standing in the middle of country devastated by the raids of the Calais garrison and long ago abandoned by its inhabitants. Its sole advantage was that its location avoided disputes about diplomatic precedence. It stood at the edge of the English-occupied county of Guines and had an entrance on each side by which the opposing delegations could enter simultaneously, each negotiating on its own territory. The Duke of Berry led for France. John of Gaunt, who for all his declining influence was still the only man in England with the stature to negotiate on equal terms with the French royal princes, was the leader of the English embassy. The Count of Flanders attended as part of the French delegation. So did John de Montfort, whose ambiguous past enabled him to present himself as a friend of both sides, who proved to be a skilful moderator.

In January 1384 the delegates reached a provisional agreement about terms for a final peace. They were recorded in a draft treaty together with a number of matters which it had not been possible to agree and had to be reserved for further discussion. Oblique references to the contents of this document suggest that the French had offered the return of at least some of the provinces of Aquitaine reconquered since 1369 on the basis that the enlarged duchy would be ceded to John of Gaunt. He would hold it as a fief of the French Crown. This was somewhat similar to the proposal which the French government had aired at the Bruges conference a decade before. The English reaction is not recorded, but they certainly did not reject it out of hand, as they had in 1375, and there is some evidence that they accepted it in principle. It was a major advance on a point which had frustrated every previous attempt to negotiate an end to the war. The matters reserved for further discussion are more difficult to identify but the main one appears to have been John of Gaunt's continuing claim to the throne of Castile. This, the French declared, would have to be discussed with John of Trastámara. The Castilian King had four representatives at the conference but they were without instructions. So the delegates agreed to disperse to consult their governments and allies and to reassemble

on 1 June 1384. To cover the position until then they put their seals to
a truce covering the whole of France, including Flanders, and the seas
around both countries. More controversially Ghent was protected by
the truce after a prolonged and ill-tempered debate which nearly
wrecked the conference. The truce was to last for eight months until
1 October 1384.[6]

Within days of the delegates putting their seals to the truce the ground
moved beneath them. Louis de Mâle, Count of Flanders, died suddenly
at Saint-Omer on 30 January 1384. Louis's death led to a major change
in the political geography of Europe. He was succeeded as ruler of
Flanders and Artois by his daughter, Margaret, and her husband, Philip
Duke of Burgundy. The couple also inherited Louis's right to the
succession of the neighbouring duchy of Brabant, which was effectively
a protectorate of Flanders. These territories now passed irrevocably into
the orbit of a French state already dominated by the Duke of Burgundy.
On 7 February Philip procured an order for the payment to himself of
100,000 francs (about £16,600) out of the French royal treasury to
meet the cost of taking possession of his new dominions.[7] For the next
five years the Low Countries would remain the chief focus of French
foreign policy as the Duke ruthlessly deployed France's wealth and
military strength in support of his efforts to build a brilliant new
principality for himself in north-west Europe. The shift in French
priorities was bound to create fresh occasions for conflict with England,
whose interests were directly engaged by the fortunes of the Low
Countries. The control by a hostile power of the coastal regions of the
North Sea posed much the same threat to England's security in the
1380s as it would do later in the reigns of Queen Elizabeth and
George III. Philip of Burgundy understood perfectly that the economies
of Flanders and England were inextricably linked and had always
shared his father-in-law's instinct that in the longer term peace with
England was indispensable. The immediate problem was that England's
championship of the urban revolutions in Flanders and her alliance with
Ghent were a direct challenge to his power in Flanders. The English
garrisons in Calais and its surrounding forts, technically part of Philip's
new county of Artois, were a permanent threat to the prosperity of the
surrounding region and a base for future military intervention in the
Low Countries. Until he had secured his grip on his new dominions
Philip could not take the accommodating line on peace with England
which had characterised his diplomatic activity before the revolt of the
Flemish towns.

At the end of April 1384 the Duke and Duchess of Burgundy rode through the Flemish-speaking regions of Flanders to make their ceremonial entries into Ypres and Bruges and receive the submissions of the smaller towns on their route. Only Ghent continued to hold out against Louis de Mâle's successor. Ghent was protected by the truce of Leulinghem, but Philip had no intention of allowing that to prevent him from subduing the recalcitrant town. His first acts showed where his instincts lay. Preliminary survey work was ordered for the Groot Kasteel of Sluys, which would start to rise from the ground on either side of the Zwyn later that year and ultimately cost Philip nearly 200,000 francs (about £33,000). These immense fortifications (the Groot Kasteel had a flooded moat, sixteen towers and walls twelve feet thick and fifty feet high) were designed to secure Philip's possession of the principal harbour of Flanders and to stop supplies coming in by sea for Ghent. On 10 May Philip issued a general pardon to all those who had participated in the rebellion against Louis de Mâle in return for a special tax at the enormous rate of 14,000 francs each month to pay for the subjugation of Ghent. On 17 May 1384 Oudenaarde, Ghent's vital outpost on the upper Scheldt, was surprised by a joint force of French and Flemish soldiers commanded by a Flemish nobleman. They employed the old trick of blocking a gateway with laden carts and then rushing the entrance before the defenders realised that they were under attack. Within a short time the attackers had taken over the town and planted the banners of Flanders and Burgundy in the market-place. The Ghent garrison was massacred. Philip probably sanctioned this blatant breach of the truce in spite of his denials.[8]

For the Scots the truce which their allies had agreed at Leulinghem could not have come at a worse time. The English were in the process of assembling more than 4,500 men in the north in addition to several hundred garrison troops and the horde of borderers raised by the wardens of the march. To meet this threat the Scots had been counting on receiving substantial financial and military assistance from France under the terms agreed at Orléans the previous April. Instead they lost the support of their ally a week before their own truce with England was due to expire. In the closing moments of the Leulinghem conference the Duke of Berry had promised to send an embassy to persuade the Scottish King to accede to the truce. But although the ambassadors were nominated almost immediately they had to wait several weeks in Paris for their instructions while other more pressing matters occupied the attention of the French royal Council. In the meantime open war broke out on the Scottish border.

In the circumstances the Scots did better than might have been expected. The men mainly responsible for the Scottish operations on the march were Sir Archibald Douglas and George Dunbar, Earl of March. Seeing that the English field army was concentrated in the eastern march they gathered the border lords from the whole length of the march and struck in the west. On 27 January 1384, a few days before the truce expired, they fell on Lochmaben. The old Bohun castle on its wooded promontory jutting into the south end of the loch was the last vestige of the fifty-year-old English presence in Annandale. It was a powerful fortress with a keep and fortified entrance bridge, which had been largely rebuilt in the last years of Edward III's reign, but it was poorly supplied and garrisoned and surrounded by territory controlled by Archibald Douglas. The demoralised garrison surrendered on 4 February after a siege of barely a week. The castle was partly demolished and made indefensible. The lowlanders then invaded Cumberland, burning part of Penrith and briefly attacking Carlisle.

The ambassadors sent by the King of France to extend the truce to Scotland finally left Paris in the middle of March. By this time it suited the English to delay their mission. They were detained at Westminster for several weeks while their hosts prepared their response to the loss of Lochmaben. This proved to be slow in coming and lumbering in execution. On 24 March 1384 John of Gaunt arrived at Newcastle with his brothers the Earls of Cambridge and Buckingham. A week later the three princes crossed the Tweed with some 4,000 men and marched on Edinburgh. The inhabitants of the Scottish capital abandoned it to the enemy, taking with them everything that they could carry. On 10 April the English army occupied the city without opposition and advanced north towards the retreating Scots as darkness fell. John of Gaunt stood his men in battle order throughout the night in temperatures so cold that several of the men and many of their horses died of exposure. But in the morning it was found that the Scots had stolen away across the Firth of Forth. In about mid-April the campaign was abandoned and the Duke retreated into England. It had been an embarrassing failure. Gaunt had not forced the Scots to terms. Nor had he deterred them from vigorously prosecuting the northern war in future. As soon as he left Scotland William, Earl of Douglas, overran Teviotdale, one of the few regions of lowland Scotland where the English still had partisans. The only remaining English enclaves in the Scottish lowlands were now the areas within sight of their three surviving garrisons at Jedburgh, Roxburgh and Berwick.[9]

On 22 October 1383 King Fernando of Portugal had finally died in Lisbon at the age of thirty-eight. His last recorded words were an appeal for God's forgiveness for the condition in which he left his kingdom. In accordance with the treaty sealed at Salvaterra de Magos in April, Princess Beatrice was now proclaimed Queen of Portugal and Leonora Teles became regent. Leonora was little loved in Portugal but for a brief moment she seemed invulnerable. Her government had the merit of legitimacy and it was supported by the whole political establishment, including almost all of the nobility, the higher clergy and the councillors of the dead King. It could also count on political and military assistance from Castile. Yet it was destined to last for less than three months. Ironically the agent of its destruction was John of Trastámara. He had probably never intended to be bound by the restrictions in the treaty even at the time it was made. Its terms reduced him to a titular sovereign while real power was enjoyed by Leonora and her manipulative lover. A vocal minority on his council regarded these provisions as dishonourable and urged him to take possession of his wife's kingdom at once. It soon became clear that John himself was of their mind. He sent a representative to attend the dead King's funeral with instructions to call for declarations of allegiance from the leading magnates of the kingdom. He quartered the arms of Portugal with his own. He issued orders directly to Leonora's garrison commanders and began to recruit troops in both kingdoms. During November 1383 it dawned on many people that the Castilian King intended to annex Portugal to his Crown.[10]

John of Trastámara's menacing attitude gravely undermined Leonora's government. It also provoked an immediate rebellion in the main cities of Portugal, where the prospect of a Castilian dynasty aroused strong passions and Inez de Castro's son Don João had many friends and allies. The main centre of opposition from the outset was Lisbon. Like most great European cities Lisbon was an oligarchy ruled by a small body of rich, conservative merchants whose natural inclination was to support Leonora. But the mass of the population had loathed the Queen ever since her marriage to Fernando a decade before. In the last few years the population of the capital had been swelled by migration and radicalised by economic depression. The densely crowded streets could produce violent, highly politicised mobs as readily as those of Paris, London or Florence. Its newly built walls gave them the confidence to defy any external power whether Portuguese or Castilian. There were demonstrations in the capital against the regent and her Castilian advisers as soon as the King's death was announced. The leading merchants of the city were forced to follow. They proclaimed their support for Don João and began to organise opposition to Leonora's government.[11]

Shortly they acquired a more formidable leader. John, the Master of Avis, the young illegitimate half-brother of the late King, had initially pledged his support like the rest of his class to Beatrice and John of Trastámara. But he was no friend of Leonora and had been a marked man since Leonora's failed *coup d'état* of 1382. He believed, probably rightly, that Andeiro was out to kill him. John of Avis made contact with the leaders of the opposition in Lisbon. He recruited supporters among the gang leaders who controlled the mob. On 6 December 1383 he forced his way into Leonora's apartment in the royal palace with a band of armed men and murdered Andeiro before her eyes, while a great crowd gathered outside the building baying support. John of Avis had not foreseen that his pre-emptive attack on Leonora and her lover would lead to a political revolution. He thought that any organised resistance to the Castilians was hopeless and had planned to flee to England to take service as a mercenary with Richard II. But events quickly moved out of his control. When the news of Andeiro's death spread through the capital the streets exploded into violence. The bishop, a Castilian and a Clementist as well as one of Leonora's closest confidants, was lynched in his own cathedral and his body thrown from the top of a tower. The Jewish quarter was pillaged. Known friends of Castile and supporters of the regent fled for their lives. Leonora herself withdrew to Santarém, the strongest fortress in the Tagus valley. From there she addressed a panicked appeal for support to her son-in-law in Castile.

In fact John of Trastámara had already entered Portugal. On about 13 December 1383 he established himself in the northern fortress town of Guarda with a small military retinue while an army was urgently recruited for his service in Castile and among his aristocratic supporters in Portugal. In Lisbon the city council met three days later on 16 December 1383 in the chapter house of the Dominican convent. They were profoundly suspicious of popular movements. All their instincts were for Beatrice and Leonora, and they were terrified of the prospect of armed intervention by the King of Castile, but their hand was forced by an intimidating crowd of citizens gathered in the open space outside the monastery. The Master of Avis was proclaimed 'regent and protector' of Portugal. Leonora's garrison in the citadel of Lisbon surrendered within a few days.[12]

To begin with John of Avis declared himself to be holding office on behalf of Don João. One of his first acts was to write to the exiled prince in Castile acknowledging him as King. Don João was in no position to respond. He received the Master's missive in the heavily guarded citadel of Toledo, to which he had been confined on John of Trastámara's orders as soon as it was known that King Fernando was on his deathbed. John himself described it as a necessary betrayal but regretted it to the end of his days. It was not the last. At the beginning of January 1384 the Castilian King advanced from Guarda to Santarém with about 1,000 men-at-arms at his back. Leonora Teles had begged him to come and she greeted him as a saviour. But John had no interest in propping up the unpopular regent. After a brief and brutal negotiation in his pavilion the hapless Leonora was forced to resign her office. The King took possession of her treasury, put his own troops into the citadel and assumed the functions of government himself. Shortly afterwards Leonora was bundled off to the Franciscan convent of Tordesillas in Castile, the traditional place of banishment for powerful women who had crossed the Castilian kings.[13]

Each side in this new conflagration at once appealed to its natural patron beyond its borders. In the third week of January a French embassy led by an experienced diplomat, Jean le Fèvre, Bishop of Chartres, caught up with the King of Castile at Santarém after spending the best part of six weeks on their travels. Le Fèvre's main task was to interest John of Trastámara in the diplomatic conference at Leulinghem, but the probability is that he was also instructed to discuss naval co-operation between France and Castile in the event that peace negotiations failed. His staff included a French knight, Jacques de Montmor, who had made a speciality of fighting at sea. The ambassadors found John preoccupied with plans to lay siege to Lisbon, for which he would need all his ships. He was in no mood to discuss proposals for a permanent peace. John appointed his councillor, the chronicler Pedro Lopez de Ayala, to represent him at the peace conference. However, by the time Ayala set out in February the conference at Leulinghem was over. He crossed with a messenger sent post-haste from Paris with a copy of the truce. There is no evidence that John ever ratified it.[14]

For his part the Master of Avis appealed for English support as soon as he had taken control of Lisbon. He despatched one of his squires to

England, accompanied by a Bristol cloth merchant with business interests in Portugal. The lowly status of these ambassadors is eloquent evidence of the Master's lack of aristocratic support in the first days of his revolution. They made contact with the English court by February 1384 but their appeals for assistance seem to have fallen on deaf ears. In March, however, John of Avis was able to replace them with more substantial figures. Lourenço Fogaça, Don Fernando's Chancellor, had initially served under the regency of Leonora like the rest of his caste, but he defected to the Master of Avis after witnessing the Castilian King's brutal seizure of power at Santarém and agreed to return once more to England to represent the pretender. He was accompanied by another recent convert, Fernando Afonso de Albuquerque, Master of the Portuguese military order of Santiago, a former protégé of Leonora Teles, who, like Fogaça, had been outraged by the proceedings at Santarém. Their instructions were to press for a fresh English expeditionary force to be sent to Portugal. In the meantime they were to raise whatever mercenaries they could hire in England on their own credit. In return they were authorised to offer Portuguese support for the Duke of Lancaster's claims in Castile and the service of a Portuguese galley fleet in northern waters.[15]

Fogaça and Albuquerque left Lisbon at the end of March 1384 at a time when their exact status was uncertain and the outlook for the man who had appointed them was bleak. John of Avis directly controlled only Lisbon and the territory on the opposite bank of the Tagus. In addition there were independent risings in his favour in Oporto, Portugal's second port, and in a number of towns of the Alemtejo including Evora. There were thirteen war galleys in the harbour at Lisbon but few experienced crews to man them. The royal treasury was empty and the rebels were obliged to resort to moneylenders and coinage operations to make ends meet. A handful of prominent figures had rallied to John's cause after the events at Santarém in January 1384 but apart from Fogaça and Albuquerque the only man of real consequence among them was the 23-year-old Nun' Alvarez Pereira. He became the Master's principal military adviser. Few could have foreseen at the time that he would become the only military genius that Portugal has produced. The nationalist movement drew its support from the mercantile classes, the maritime cities and the urban mobs, while ranged against them were all the interest groups which had traditionally exercised power in Portugal: the Church, the civil service and the nobility. The Portuguese nobility may have been dismayed by

John of Trastámara's willingness to ride roughshod over the country's institutions and to tear up a treaty which he had sealed less than a year before, but they liked the alternatives still less. They feared and suspected urban revolutions. They were disturbed by signs of rebellion among the peasantry of the open country. Above all they wanted to safeguard their property by supporting what seemed likely to be the winning side. No fewer than fifty-four garrisoned towns and castles had declared for the Castilian King by the spring of 1384. Almost all of the nobility acknowledged him. Many of them brought their retainers to serve in his army. John of Trastámara appeared to have overwhelming strength on his side.

In March 1384 the Castilian King marched on Lisbon from Santarém with the modest forces he had with him. By now they must have numbered about 2,000 men-at-arms including the French companies still in his service. In Castile another army was being recruited to swell his numbers. In spite of the patchy response of his over-taxed subjects, by the end of May the Castilian King had some 5,000 men-at-arms and 1,000 light horse encamped around Lisbon in addition to 'numberless' crossbowmen and infantry. A vast victualling operation was under way to supply this host by sea from Seville. As many as forty Castilian galleys lay off the city, blocking the mouth of the Tagus.[16]

On 5 May 1384 the English Parliament met in the unfamiliar surroundings of the great hall of the bishop's palace at Salisbury. The main business of the session was the draft treaty which had been provisionally agreed at Leulinghem in January. The government was not required to submit its treaties to the scrutiny of Parliament, as Chancellor Pole pointed out in his opening address, but Pole made it perfectly clear why he was doing it. Whatever the outcome of the current negotiations with France Pole wanted Parliament to accept responsibility for the financial consequences. Over the past year the Treasury had been able to get by only by deferring payments to captains of companies and borrowing against future revenues from Italian bankers in London and war contractors like Knolles and Philpot. If peace was made the debts accumulated from past campaigns would still have to be met. On the other hand if the talks failed considerable sums of money would be required to defend England against the fleets of Castile and now Flanders, and against invasion from Scotland and France. The most interesting feature of Pole's account of the situation was that it went without saying that there would be no money to finance offensive operations on the continent even if the desired subsidy was granted. The government was now budgeting for a purely defensive war.[17]

There was another, unspoken reason why Pole was determined to consult Parliament. The draft treaty was controversial. Richard's ministers were not secure enough to force the terms through on their own responsibility. Their judgment was borne out in the event, for when the document was laid before Parliament it provoked acrimonious debate in both houses which continued for more than a fortnight. In the Lords the debates degenerated into undignified squabbling in which arguments about the merits of the treaty were overlaid by strong personal antagonisms. The Earl of Arundel had been prominent in the Councils and campaigns of Richard's first three years. He felt more than anyone the loss of influence which, like other prominent noblemen, he had suffered since 1380. He was also one of the largest wool exporters in England with a strong personal interest in the fate of Flanders. Always an outspoken advocate of an aggressive war policy, Arundel made an intemperate speech blaming the decay of England's strength on bad government and warning of crippling losses and imminent national collapse. The sixteen-year-old King, who was present, took this as a personal attack. White with anger he turned on Arundel. 'Liar! Go to Hell!' he shouted. There was a hushed silence, which was eventually broken by John of Gaunt. He rose to his feet and made an emollient speech which for the time being placated both men, but the tensions persisted.

Shortly afterwards there was an extraordinary incident in the Earl of Oxford's rooms as another day's proceedings were about to begin. An Irish Carmelite friar called John Latimer, who had been saying mass before the King, approached him after the service and said that he had information proving that the Duke of Lancaster was plotting to depose him and seize the throne. The King responded by ordering Gaunt to be summarily executed. He was made to back down by the shocked protests of the other noblemen who were present and eventually acknowledged that the accusations against Gaunt were unfounded. The evidence, such as it is, suggests that Latimer was mad. But the Duke's friends believed that he had been put up to it by Richard's courtiers. Latimer was later seized by some of Lancaster's retainers, who tried to make him implicate those who were behind him. They took him off to Salisbury castle, where he was so badly tortured that he later died of his injuries.[18]

At the conclusion of the debates, the most that the Lords could be persuaded to say about the negotiations with France was that 'considering all the issues and difficulties, if they were in the King's position they would be more inclined to peace than war'. They refused to comment on the particular terms which were before them. At first the Commons would not express even this guarded opinion. An honourable peace, they said, would be the 'most noble and gracious aid and comfort that could be devised' but they would not presume to assess the merits of this one. In any event, they added, the territorial settlement in France was nothing to do with England or them. To some extent this answer reflected a reluctance to take responsibility for a decision of such consequence. But it is also clear that the Commons were as divided as the Lords. They enquired about the possibility of deferring the issue between the two nations by settling upon a long truce. The King's spokesman (presumably Pole) testily informed them that the French would not agree to that because it would not be acceptable to their allies. A choice had to be made, he said, between peace and war. Which was it to be? The Commons protested that they could not understand the obscure legal language in which some of the terms were drafted. They then offered some tentative criticisms. They had misgivings about the proposal that Richard should do homage for territory in Aquitaine and thought that he should certainly refuse to hold Calais as a fief of France. This was not what the King's ministers wanted to hear. The only terms on offer, they said, were those of the draft treaty. Remember, they added, the 'multitude of wars waged on every side against this small kingdom . . . the great strength and wealth of their enemies and the weakness and poverty of their own kingdom.' But the Commons would do no more than associate themselves with the mealy-mouthed answer already given by the Lords.

The proceedings in Parliament had revealed how desperate Richard II's ministers were to make peace with France even on terms which conceded the issue of sovereignty. But it was equally clear that the compromise negotiated at Leulinghem commanded at best lukewarm support among the English political community and that there was strong opposition to the idea of making concessions on Calais. Neither the Commons nor the convocation of the clergy of Canterbury (which was meeting across the close in the cathedral) were willing to face up to the financial implications of their position. The Commons initially hoped to limit their support to allowing the collection of the half-subsidy conditionally granted in the previous November. Only when the King threatened to send judicial commissions into the provinces to boost his revenue from fines and forfeitures did they agree to vote another half-subsidy. Even this was deferred to the following year and conditional on the country being still at war. The clergy after 'much deliberation and speech-making' followed suit. These two grants between them added a mere £25,000 to the government's revenues for the year.[19]

In Edinburgh another acrimonious debate was taking place between the partisans of peace and war. A small troop of French men-at-arms, about twenty strong, landed in May 1384 in the small east coast port of Montrose in Angus, hoping to take advantage of the fact that the truce had not yet been proclaimed in Scotland. They had come to fight as volunteers in Scottish service without official sanction from the French government, but there was little doubt that they had its tacit consent. Their leaders, Geoffrey de Charny and Jean de Blaisy, were both prominent royal officials and they had embarked at Sluys, a port which was tightly controlled by Philip of Burgundy's officers. Their arrival coincided with the long-delayed appearance of Charles VI's ambassadors bearing the text of the truce and the French King's invitation to accede to it.

Robert II wanted to comply. The French were obviously not going to honour their promise of 1,000 men-at-arms. Without the protection of the truce his realm would be exposed to the full weight of England's revenge. But the Scottish lords of the march were furious. Sir Archibald Douglas had always favoured a more aggressive strategy against England. His cousin James, who had succeeded to the Douglas earldom in April, was described as an 'energetic knight, ever an enemy of England'. He became the leading advocate of a war policy in the councils of the Scottish King. According to Froissart, not always a reliable source for Scottish affairs but well-informed about this period, the Douglases and their allies argued that the truce of Leulinghem had been made without their consent. They pointed out that it had not protected them when they needed it in April. Now that they had tasted blood and pushed the English back they wanted to carry on what they had begun. When the King rejected their advice they withdrew from his council to confer with the French knights in the church of St. Giles in Edinburgh. There they agreed to fight on regardless of Robert's views. At the beginning of June they mounted a powerful raid across the eastern march into Northumberland. The French company rode with them. Robert II wrung his hands and sent a herald to Westminster to disavow the acts of his subjects. In point of form the Scottish King got his way. Scotland finally acceded to the truce on 7 July 1384. Sir Archibald Douglas was one of the commissioners appointed to execute the instrument, which he did with gritted teeth in the parish church at Ayton, north of Berwick. But neither he nor his fellow borderers had the slightest intention of observing it. One of his fellow commissioners at Ayton was his cousin, Douglas of Dalkeith. Within days he was leading a major raid against Berwick which resulted in the burning of part of the town. He wrote to Richard II claiming to be retaliating against similar outrages committed by the English, adding that Berwick was part of Scotland anyway. The pattern of heavy raids across the border at intervals of six to eight weeks was extended into the autumn as if nothing had happened.[20]

For a quarter of a century the English had made their plans against France on the assumption that they could count on the relative quiescence of the Scottish border. Now much of the military manpower of England beyond the Trent had once again to be assigned to the defence of the north as it had been in the early part of Edward III's reign. The Scottish march, which had cost less than £1,000 to defend in the last year of Edward III's reign, was consuming more than £20,000 a year by the end of 1384, roughly the same as Calais. On top of this came heavy expenditure on repairing and modernising the defences of Berwick, Carlisle and the royal castles on the march, most of which had been badly neglected in the long years of half-peace. For Richard II's ministers the events of 1384 marked a grave military and financial set-back.[21] For the French the short campaign in June was a reminder of strategic possibilities that they had almost forgotten and which they would exploit far more energetically in the following year. 'You have seen the manner and condition of our country but you have not seen the full extent of our power,' the Scots told Geoffrey de Charny and Jean de Blaisy as they departed, according to Froissart. Scotland, they added,

is of all countries the one which the English fear most, for as you have seen we can ride deep into their country without having to face the perils of a sea crossing . . . If we had but a thousand lances of French knights and squires, with the people that we already have here we should do such a deed in England that it should be spoken of forty years after.[22]

The diplomatic conference reopened on the march of Calais more than two months late in the first week of August 1384. The Duke of Lancaster once again led the English delegation, accompanied this time by his brother the Earl of Buckingham. Their instructions appear to have been to obtain an agreement on something like the terms agreed in January. The Duke of Berry was still the senior representative of the King of France. Reports from his entourage suggest that he was full of optimism about the outcome. But Berry was no longer in control. The dominant figure in the French delegation was his brother Philip of Burgundy, who had not been present in January. He had his own objectives. The proceedings opened with a series of ill-tempered exchanges which set the tone for what followed. The French insisted that the conference should begin with low-level meetings between councillors at Leulinghem while the principals on either side remained in their headquarters at Boulogne and Calais. The English delegation, who were furious at having been made to kick their heels for several weeks in Calais waiting for the French to turn up, regarded this proposal as another delaying tactic. The status of the various allies gave rise to venomous bickering. The English wanted to negotiate directly with their French opposite numbers and then sort out the allies later. They delayed issuing safe-conducts for the ambassadors of Scotland and Castile. They particularly objected to the presence of the Scots. The French would probably have been willing to push the Scots to one side and virtually told them so. But they were not willing to negotiate without the Castilians, whose quarrel with John of Gaunt they regarded as their own. For their part the French objected to the presence of the representatives of Ghent, who were there as allies of England but were regarded by the Duke of Burgundy as rebellious subjects.[23]

While these preliminaries were being argued out a great throng of courtiers, clerks, servants and followers milled around Boulogne waiting for something to happen. The poet Eustache Deschamps, who was on the staff of the French delegation, took the opportunity to visit Calais accompanied by an English knight of his acquaintance. He was dismayed by what he saw. Here was a French town populated by Englishmen, where it was impossible to sleep at night for the biting of fleas and the sound of crashing waves, braying horses and mewling babies. He was abused as a French 'wine bibber'. Soldiers watching out for spies stopped him in the street and demanded to see his papers. By the end of his visit the few words of English he had picked up included 'Franche dogue', 'goday' and 'commidre' [come 'ere]. The English, he reminded himself, had tails. Four centuries before Hogarth and Sterne Calais was already the meeting point of alien cultures.[24]

The journal of the Bishop of Bayeux, which is the main source for the diplomatic gatherings of these years, has a gap corresponding to the last three weeks of the conference. As a result all that is known for certain about the rest of the discussions is that they ended in failure. However, the account which Michael Pole later gave to the English Parliament is consistent with all the other evidence. According to him the conference never moved beyond the preparatory discussions. The French councillors would not negotiate on the basis of the draft provisionally agreed in January. Nor would they agree to a direct meeting between the principals. As a result the sessions were taken up with procedural wrangling and filibustering and the royal princes never met. The main bone of contention was Calais. The draft treaty of January had conceded the town and its dependent forts to England but left open the question whether it would be held as a fief of France or as (so to speak) an annexe of the city of London. In August and September, however, the French appear to have insisted on its complete surrender. The Duke of Burgundy had good reason to regard Calais in English hands as a serious threat to his interests, but it was an issue on which the English political community felt just as strongly, as they had shown during the Salisbury Parliament. Philip must have known that there was no prospect of their agreeing to surrender Calais, nor did he ever insist on it again. Why should he have wanted to wreck the conference in 1384 by making such an obviously unacceptable demand? The most plausible hypothesis (but it is no more than that) is that he was concerned about the position of Ghent. Philip's authority in Flanders and Brabant depended on putting an end to the five-year rebellion of the town. He evidently believed that he had to do it before accounts were settled between England and France. To some extent he misread the situation. Philip failed to see the weakness of his enemies, as adversaries commonly do in wartime, and did not realise how desperate the English were for peace. The upshot was that John of Gaunt and his colleagues had to content themselves with an extension of the truce for another seven months until 1 May 1385.

As in January, it proved difficult to find a formula that covered the position of Ghent during the truce while respecting Philip's refusal to treat the rebels like a sovereign power. Ultimately the town was excluded from the truce. Instead, a separate declaration was executed by the Duke of Berry, who promised that his brother would take no measures against the men of Ghent during the truce provided that they showed a similar restraint on their side. The exact legal status of this document was never clear. The ambassadors of Scotland and Castile sealed the truce along with those of France. The position of the nationalists in Portugal was passed over in silence. The French said that they were not ruling out the possibility of further peace talks during the truce. In reality the arrangements were regarded on all sides as no more than a pause to prepare for the resumption of the war in earnest.[25]

For once the public pronouncements of Richard II's ministers departed from the stock phrases which had become usual in English propaganda. They were intensely disappointed by the outcome, very much as the French had been in 1382. John of Gaunt reported to the Council at the end of September that the French had obviously been intent on war. But the councillors were at a loss to know what to do about it. A Great Council had already been arranged for 11 October. Parliament was summoned to meet at Westminster a month later in November. Both assemblies met in an atmosphere of crisis. In his opening address to Parliament Chancellor Pole deployed all the arguments which had traditionally been used to justify emergency grants of taxation. He told the assembled peers and Commons that the King had resolved to take the field against his enemies in person and needed to do so in proper state, though he was not specific about the destination of the King's expedition. He reminded his audience that they were surrounded by 'deadly enemies, all in league with one another': 'the French with their great resources of manpower, the Castilians with their galley fleet, the Flemings with their many large ships and the Scots who can invade the kingdom across a land border at will.' The peers continued their deliberations until shortly before Christmas. We know nothing of their debates except that they were acrimonious and inconclusive. As for the Commons, they were shocked into making the largest grant since the notorious poll tax of 1380. The half-subsidy outstanding from the Salisbury Parliament was revoked. In its place two tenths and fifteenths were voted, the first to be collected in March 1385 and the second in June. Together with the clerical subsidy which was voted a few days later this amounted to rather more than £100,000. The second subsidy was subject to the usual conditions and one unusual one. The King, said the Commons, must take the field in person as his Chancellor had promised. Otherwise the grant would be void.[26]

During the sittings of the English Parliament there was an unpleasant reminder of the truths uttered by Pole in his opening address. The Scottish Parliament was in session at the same time. They too had to consider what to do when the truce expired in May. But they were more single-minded about it than the English, with their more complex dilemmas, could ever be. Robert II, who had never been cut out to be a war leader, was made to surrender much of his power to his heir, the Earl of Carrick. The surrender, ostensibly limited to the administration of justice, in practice made Carrick the ruler of Scotland. The conduct of the war on the border passed to the lords of the march, in particular to Carrick himself and the Douglases. At the beginning of December 1384, in spite of the truce, the Scots captured Berwick castle for the second time since the accession of Richard II. There were reports that the deputy who held the castle for the Earl of Northumberland had taken a bribe to let the invaders in. Rumours of this sort commonly circulated after any humiliating reverse. But John of Gaunt took the chance to press a personal vendetta against the Earl of Northumberland, who was sitting among the peers at Westminster. Gaunt had him arraigned before the Lords for dereliction of duty and sent north to recover the place on pain of forfeiture of his assets. Berwick castle had been considerably strengthened since the last time it had fallen to Scottish raiders in 1379. Rather than take the risk of an unsuccessful assault Northumberland paid 2,000 marks out of his own pocket to buy the invaders out.[27]

Unfortunately for Richard's ministers the double subsidy voted by the Commons created expectations which were hard to live up to. Even a double subsidy would no longer pay for a continental campaign if substantial forces had to be maintained on the Scottish border as well. In fact receipts from the new grant were partly offset by a steep decline in customs revenues, which was probably due to the rigorous enforcement of the boycott on English goods in the new domains of the Duke of Burgundy. Pole's opening address to Parliament had revealed a man terrified by the threat of encirclement by Flanders, Castile and Scotland. His view was widely shared. The Council was not willing to denude England of troops at such a moment. So the promised continental army was quietly dropped.[28]

Lisbon had held out on dwindling rations through the summer as John of Trastámara reinforced his army on land. The Castilian fleet beat off attempts to relieve the city by sea from Oporto and progressively tightened the blockade in the Tagus. But the besiegers were unable to make any impression on the walls of the city; and in spite of the straits to which the defenders were reduced time was on their side. The financial strain on the Castilian treasury of keeping these great forces in the field month after month was becoming intolerable. As the summer wore on the besiegers began to suffer even worse privations than their enemies. Food became increasingly difficult to find as the men exhausted the supplies within foraging range, the common problem of large-scale siege operations in the fourteenth century. Disease, another perennial hazard of medieval sieges, took a heavy toll on weakened men working in hot weather. 'Plague' (probably dysentery or typhus) spread rapidly through the confined and insanitary Castilian encampments and the ships of the fleet. By the beginning of September 1384 the Castilians were losing more than 200 men a day to disease. Some of John of Trastámara's best captains succumbed, including the famous Castilian admiral, Fernán Sánchez de Tovar. John, who believed that the city was on the point of defeat, refused to raise the siege until finally his wife Beatrice showed signs of having contracted the disease. On 3 September he bowed to the advice of his council and abandoned the campaign. The Castilians burned their tents and withdrew. A permanent force was left in Portugal to contain the supporters of John of Avis. They were put into winter quarters in garrison towns to the north and west of Lisbon. The galleys withdrew to their dockyards in Seville. John himself returned to Castile, promising to be back with even larger forces in the spring.[29]

For the time being the most that the English government could do to support the Master of Avis was encourage men to sign up as volunteers. The two Portuguese ambassadors were allowed to recruit men-at-arms and archers at their own expense in England. To pay their advances they borrowed money from a syndicate of London merchants organised by the Mayor, Sir Nicholas Brembre, and from a group of moneyed courtiers. They appear to have had authority to offer the goods of Portuguese merchants in England as security as well as guarantees from the cities of Lisbon and Oporto. These transactions and the rather shadowy character of the security were destined to generate unpleasant disputes when the loans went unpaid and the creditors began to seize Portuguese ships and cargoes. But they enabled Fogaça and Albuquerque to recruit a substantial force of mercenaries among the mass of unemployed professional soldiers loitering around London. Most of them were men who no longer had much prospect of profitable employment in France: English and Gascon soldiers of fortune with a motley gathering of Dutch, German, Italian, Portuguese and even Castilian adventurers. At least six shi-loads of troops sailed for Portugal in the course of the winter. In the spring Portuguese merchantmen calling at English ports were being requisitioned by the Admirals' officers to carry more. In addition to the recruitment campaign in

England, to which Richard's government had agreed, a fair number of English soldiers doing tedious garrison duty in Calais, Cherbourg and Brest deserted their posts and made their way overland to Bordeaux to take ship to Portugal. We cannot know how many Englishmen fought in Portugal in 1385 but the English records and the accounts of their doings in Portugal suggest that there must have been at least 1,000 including a significant number of archers.[30]

John of Trastámara received prompt and on the whole accurate reports about the activities of Fogaça and Albuquerque from Castilian merchants in England. Over the winter he appealed once more to the French King for support. He wrote directly to several prominent captains in France to ask them to come to his aid. The French King's ministers were in no position to organise an expeditionary force but, like Richard II's Council, they did what they could to encourage volunteers. Jean de Rye, one of Charles VI's chamberlains and a veteran of Castilian affairs, was at the court of John of Trastámara in the new year on another fruitless quest for the loan of galleys. He stayed behind to serve with his company in the coming campaign, although he was over sixty years old. He also took an active part in arranging for mercenaries to be recruited for the Castilian King's service in France. A number of Breton companies, said to be 800 strong, were recruited by the joint efforts of Jean de Rye and a Poitevin captain called Geoffrey de Parthenay. More Bretons were raised by the son of the King of Navarre. John of Trastámara's recruiting agents crossed the Rhône, hiring men-at-arms from among the companies of brigands operating in Provence. Even in Béarn, where Gaston de Foix was overtly hostile to the whole enterprise, 300 men-at-arms were found to go to the aid of the King of Castile including Froissart's informant the Bascot de Mauléon. 'Either you will return impoverished in rags and covered in fleas,' Gaston told them after a farewell banquet in the castle of Orthez, 'or you will all be killed or captured.'[31]

In Ghent Peter Van den Bossche and Francis Ackerman were struggling to hold the town together after the disaster at Roosebeke. They refused to contemplate surrender, which would almost certainly have entailed their own execution. They were also by instinct committed to the English alliance and to the survival of the wool trade with England. Ackerman, like Van Artevelde before him, drew a pension from the English Treasury. The growing difficulty in provisioning the town had undermined his authority during the summer. More moderate spirits were beginning to suggest an accommodation with the Duke of Burgundy. But Ackerman had lost none of his power to move the crowd. On 12 July 1384 he summoned a large armed mob led by the weavers and their allies to the Grain Market, near the town hall. He spoke darkly of the traitors within who had taken the Duke of Burgundy's money to deliver up the town. When he had whipped up their temper, he and Peter Van den Bossche led them to the house of Rees Van Herzele, an urban nobleman who had become the leader of the peace party. The mob beat him to death and raised up Richard II's standard in the market-place.[32]

Desperate to provoke another English military intervention Ackerman resolved to place Ghent under the direct authority of the King of England. At the end of the summer messengers were sent urgently to England to put this proposal before the English ministers. In October Richard II's ministers, still furious about the outcome of the peace conference, agreed. They undertook direct responsibility for the defence of Ghent and promised to appoint an English Ruwaert (or Governor). Ackerman had asked for a prince of the King's blood, but that would have entailed a firmer political commitment and a larger army than the English government was willing to contemplate. Instead Richard appointed Sir John Bourchier, a competent but unremarkable soldier in late middle age who had been one of Knolles's captains in the campaign of 1370. Froissart thought him 'adequate', which is a fair summary of his talents. Bourchier embarked with a wool convoy from Harwich in early November, accompanied by 100 English men-at-arms and 300 archers. He reached Ghent shortly afterwards via Middelburg under the noses of Philip of Burgundy's spies.[33]

Louis of Anjou died on 20 September 1384 in a chamber overlooking the Adriatic from the keep of Bari. He had been in southern Italy for two years, penned to the eastern seaboard of the kingdom he had come to conquer, outmanoeuvred by a cunning adversary, perennially starved of funds and forgotten by most of France. Many of those who remembered him would have agreed with the verdict of the poor wretch arrested after an evening in a drinking house in Orléans, who had called Louis 'dead and damned'. 'What did he think he was doing down there, looting and pillaging, draining us of cash and trying to grab someone else's country?' At the time of his death Louis still had a substantial army in the field, including important companies of French and Gascons. Another army, commanded by Enguerrand de Coucy, had left

France in July and was currently in Tuscany on its way south. Over the next few weeks desperate efforts were made by Louis of Anjou's widow and Bernabò Visconti, despot of Milan, to salvage Louis's quixotic enterprise for the benefit of his younger son.[34]

Philip of Burgundy was no more interested in diverting France's resources into Italy than he had been in organising an expeditionary army to rescue John of Trastámara in Castile. His eyes were fixed on the north. He and his brother Berry stood by as Louis's army disintegrated over the winter. They actively obstructed the valiant efforts of Louis's widow to keep his project alive. 'Forget all these little ventures and do something that will live in history for ever,' Philip is supposed to have declared. In Paris plans were being laid for a double invasion of England in the following year. An advance guard would sail for Scotland in the spring and invade the north of England in conjunction with the Scots. Jean de Vienne, the Admiral of France, was designated as the commander of this force. He was to be followed by a much larger army under the nominal command of Charles VI himself, whose precise landing point was not disclosed and may not yet have been decided. Although the political initiative had come from the Duke of Burgundy there are good reasons for regarding the Constable, Olivier de Clisson, as the main author of the invasion plan. According to Froissart he told Jean de Vienne that he would rather meet the whole strength of the enemy in their own land than half of it in his homeland, 'as my master, Henry of Lancaster, used to say, who brought me up in my youth'. What made this a feasible strategy in 1385, apart from England's declining capacity to make war in France, was the acquisition of direct control over Flanders, with its long coast-line on the North Sea, its convenient harbours and its vast shipping resources. Clisson's project was by far the most ambitious conceived by the French government since the beginning of the war half a century before. It had all the features which the English chronicler Thomas Walsingham regarded as hallmarks of the French military method: 'expense, shrewdness, forethought and planning'.[35]

Of these four it was expense which counted most. The restored *aides* and *gabelle*, now re-established as permanent taxes, brought in about 2,000,000 *livres* a year to the French Treasury net of collection costs. On top of these, on 19 October 1384, Charles VI announced a special, supplementary levy 'for the passage of the sea'. The *taille* (as it came to be called) was an *ad hoc* tax not a permanent one. But it was collected like the *aides* and the *gabelle* by the King's order without the authority of any assembly of the general or provincial estates. It was an impressive demonstration of the new-found power and self-confidence of the French Crown after the crushing of the urban insurrections. Over the next five years, until the suspension of the war in 1389, successive *tailles* would bring the French government's total revenues from taxation up to an average of about 3,000,000 *livres tournois* (or £600,000 sterling) a year. The corresponding figure for England, taking customs revenues and Parliamentary and clerical subsidies together, was less than a sixth of that sum. The disproportion between the resources of the two nations had never been greater.[36]

In the second week of February 1385 all the mutual antagonisms and strategic arguments which had divided the English nobility over the past two years came to a head. The occasion was a Great Council which met in the Benedictine abbey of Waltham, a royal foundation some fifteen miles north of London. The assembly had been summoned to consider the French invasion plans, rumours of which had by now reached England. Early reports suggested that a fleet of 600 transports was being prepared to carry an 'enormous' army to England. Even experienced professional soldiers were heard to say that resistance was hopeless. The proceedings opened with a fierce invective by John of Gaunt against the defensive strategy of the government. His anger owed its intensity to a number of factors: irritation with the King and his entourage; loyalty to England's traditional strategy of fighting overseas; fury and embarrassment at the way that the French had cheated him at the conference on the march of Calais. Gaunt was not opposed to peace with France, but since peace was not available on acceptable terms he was determined that the English should take the war to the French. The best way to frustrate the French invasion plans, in his view, was to launch a pre-emptive invasion of France. He was appalled by the prospect of fighting the enemy on English soil, turning it into the kind of wasteland with which he had become familiar on the marches of Scotland and Calais. The Duke was supported in these opinions by his brothers the Earls of Buckingham and Cambridge. They stood for the memory of Edward III and shared the old King's indifference to the constraints of finance and logistics. It was grand but no longer realistic. According to Froissart it was the Earl of Salisbury, a veteran of Edward's reign who had fought at Crécy when John of Gaunt was six years old, who defended the government's strategy of concentrating England's resources on the defence of its coasts. Gaunt and his brothers found to their dismay that the assembly was with Salisbury, with hardly a single exception. It was a turning point. Seeing that their arguments were getting nowhere the three princes walked out in high dudgeon, declaring as they left that they would give no assistance or manpower to the King unless he agreed to fight in France. In their absence the rest of the Council endorsed the strategy of Richard's ministers.[37]

The Waltham conference was followed by a complete breakdown of relations between the King and his uncles. Richard's friends regarded John of Gaunt's outburst as disloyal and hatched a plot to have him arrested and arraigned before the Great Council. When this was frustrated there was another plot to assassinate him at a tournament which was due to be held at Westminster on 13 and 14 February. Well-informed contemporaries, including some members of the royal Council, believed that Richard had lent his support to these schemes. In the event the Duke was forewarned and stayed away. A few days after this incident, on 24 February 1385, Gaunt appeared before the King at the royal manor of Sheen. He arrived with a detachment of soldiers and entered the hall wearing armour under his robes. There he openly accused Richard of having been party to the plot against his life, roundly condemned the King's friends and called for the removal from court of the Earl of Salisbury, who had crossed him at Waltham, and the youthful Earls of Nottingham and Oxford, who were visibly the dominant figures of Richard's circle. The plot against John of Gaunt won him many sympathisers among those who had previously been indifferent or resentful. The Archbishop of Canterbury, Gaunt's old enemy William Courtenay, spoke for these people when he told the King to his face that it was unworthy of his office to scheme against his own uncle. The King responded with a volley of abuse and a threat to confiscate the Archbishop's temporalities. Later that day Richard drew his sword on the Archbishop as their barges passed on the Thames and had to be restrained by those around him. It was the Queen Mother who intervened to restore harmony and avert what looked like an incipient civil war. The Black Prince's formidable widow, once reputed the most beautiful woman in Europe, now at fifty-six so obese that she could hardly move, was probably the only person in England who could have performed this office. It was the last time that she would do so.[38]

The French royal Council met to make its detailed plans for the invasion of England in March 1385, about three weeks after the tempestuous gathering of the English magnates at Waltham. The sixteen-year-old King presided but it was the Duke of Burgundy who assumed the direction of affairs. The two French armies which were to carry out the invasion were both ordered to muster at Arras and then to proceed to Sluys for embarkation. The French had by now resolved to land both armies in Scotland about three months apart. Jean de Vienne was confirmed as commander of the advance guard and was assigned a force of 1,000 men-at-arms and 600 crossbowmen. He was ordered to be ready by late April. The main force commanded by Clisson (referred to in the French administrative records as the 'second army') was to muster in mid-July. There is no reliable evidence of its projected strength but the preparations made during the summer suggest a force of some five or six thousand mounted men including bowmen. The plan was to join forces with the Scots and mount a major invasion of England from the north at the end of the summer. Meanwhile it would be necessary to suppress the operations of the English and their allies in France. About 1,400 men were assigned to the Duke of Bourbon for a *chevauchée* on the northern march of Gascony. Another 2,500 were to be recruited by Philip in Burgundy and Flanders to guard the march of Calais and the coast of Flanders and maintain the blockade of Ghent. The rest of France's military manpower was to be retained in France to defend the country against a pre-emptive attack from England.[39]

An elaborate supply operation was already in progress. A purchasing and shipping organisation was set up at Harfleur and Sluys. Victuals, mainly wine, dried vegetables, meat and the inevitable 'biscuit' distributed to men at sea, were brought down the Seine and the Somme to be accumulated in great depots at the river mouths. Local commissioners toured the markets requisitioning supplies from traders and growers. Throughout western France the government's buying agents were busy acquiring equipment: carts, mobile grain mills, barrels, tools, palisading for field-works, cloth for uniforms, gangways and hoists for loading horses, large quantities of armour, swords, crossbow bolts, cannon and gunpowder. Convoys of barges and coasters carried all this material along the coast and through the Flemish canals to Sluys for trans-shipment onto the invasion fleets. The roads of western Flanders had to be resurfaced to take the wear of so many heavily laden carts. Nothing on this scale had been seen before in France.[40]

The plans for requisitioning ocean-going transports are less well recorded, but since both armies were taking horses with them a very large number of ships was required. More than 180 were needed to carry Jean de Vienne's army alone. The second army would require many more. Where were they to come from? The French royal fleet had not been employed in major operations for several years and its ships were by now in a dilapidated state. Only two royal galleys were found fit to serve in the invasion fleet. There were some Scottish ships, perhaps as many as twenty-five. A number of German vessels were hired or requisitioned in French ports. One large sailing ship was bought by the Duke of Burgundy in Middelburg, because his agents there told him that otherwise it would be sold to a syndicate of Englishmen. The King of Castile had refused to supply the services of his galley fleet, which was committed to the war in Portugal, but at least thirty Castilian merchantmen in Flemish ports joined the fleet. More than 120 ships were requisitioned in Normandy, Picardy and La Rochelle. But most of the transport fleet must have been found from the merchant marine of Flanders with its impressive numbers of large sailing cogs and ocean-going barges. Olivier de Clisson no doubt recalled the last French invasion project in 1369, which he had opposed on the ground that France had insufficient experience of amphibious warfare. It had failed partly because the Flemings declined to help. Fifteen years later the appearance of several hundred Flemish ships in a new French invasion fleet marked a major shift in the balance of naval power in northern Europe.[41]

The cost of all this effort strained even the tax-rich government of France, which was forced to resort to a variety of fresh financial expedients in order to make ends meet. In April 1385 the King ordered the issue of a new devalued coinage. There were sound economic reasons for this decision but its timing suggests that the government's main concern was to boost the languishing profits of the mints. It was reported to have been 'wonderfully profitable' to the Crown. Very shortly afterwards Charles VI's ministers substantially increased the rate of the *taille*. To tide the war treasurers over until these new sources of revenue came in, commissioners were appointed to raise a forced loan from prominent officials, courtiers and churchmen. The loan was an impressive demonstration of the new-found solidarity of the French governing elites. Only the first of a number of rolls of creditors survives but that records loans to the Crown exceeding 300,000 francs (or £60,000). The Constable, Olivier de Clisson lent the enormous sum of 80,000 francs (about £13,300) out of his own pocket. The chronicler of Charles VI records that these loans were subsequently repaid from revenue, 'a circumstance almost unheard of'.[42]

On 12 April 1385 the French court marked another milestone in the process by which the principalities of the Low Countries were reduced to satellites of France. A double marriage was celebrated in the cathedral church of Cambrai. Philip of Burgundy's heir John married the daughter of the regent of Hainault and Holland, and his eldest daughter Margaret married the regent's son, William of Bavaria. The matches, which had been negotiated over several months, created a close alliance between the houses of Burgundy and the Bavarian Wittelsbachs. It also removed the last vestiges of English influence at the court of Hainault, a humiliating snub for John of Gaunt, who had been negotiating to marry William to one of his own daughters. Ultimately, in the next century, it would bring the francophone principality of Hainault and the Dutch-speaking territories of Holland and Zeeland into a consolidated Burgundian principality embracing substantially all of modern Belgium and Holland. The ceremonies were followed by a magnificent banquet in the bishop's palace and a tournament in the market square, in which Charles VI joined in with knights from France, the Low Countries, Castile and Scotland. Canon Robesart, a Hainaulter by upbringing, an Englishman by adoption, mingled with the courtiers, defending as best he could the interests of Richard II and informally canvassing proposals for a diplomatic solution to fifty years of war. The current truce had less than three weeks to run.[43]

On 19 April 1385, as the revellers dispersed, the diplomatic conference briefly resumed on the march of Picardy. It is difficult to believe that either side took the proceedings seriously. Neither John of Gaunt nor the Earl of Buckingham would have anything to do with them. The Englishmen present made it clear that their main priority was to get back to England in time for the Garter festivities at Windsor on St. George's Day. On the French side the Duke of Burgundy did not appear but directed the proceedings from the distance of Arras. The business was entrusted to those workhorses of past negotiations, the Bishops of Hereford and Bayeux, neither of whom had authority to discuss more than an extension of the truce. Although wrapped up in diplomatic obscurities the essence of the deal proposed by the Bishop of Bayeux was that there should be a long truce of at least four years between the three principal belligerents, England, France and Castile. Territorial claims would be left in abeyance. The other belligerents would be abandoned to their fates. The Duke of Burgundy would have a free hand to deal with Ghent, while the English would have a free hand to deal with the Scots. Portugal would be left at the mercy of Castile. A Great Council was assembled in London to consider this cynical scheme but it proved to be of no interest and was formally rejected in the middle of May. The series of diplomatic conferences which had begun three years before in the aftermath of the Peasants' Revolt and the rising of the Parisian *maillotins* finally came to an end. The first acts of war had already occurred.[44]

The first target of the French was Ghent. The town, having lost control of the Scheldt, was now dependent mainly on supplies brought in by sea. These had to be landed on the south shore of the Hondt and brought in by a network of tracks and waterways across the Vier Ambachten. The Duke of Burgundy maintained large garrisons at Biervliet and Aardenburg. They attacked the convoys of carts and barges carrying supplies to Ghent and horribly mutilated their drivers. Their operations were assisted by the general breakdown of order in northern Flanders. Armed bands of robbers and cut-throats, drawn from the thousands made destitute by six years of civil war, roamed across the region indiscriminately robbing and killing all whom they came upon. The men of Ghent planted forts across the region, whose garrisons challenged and occasionally defeated both raiders and brigands. Sir John Bourchier's English company mounted their own patrols and scored several notable successes. But the French gradually tightened their blockade. Although the town had laid in large quantities of foodstuffs during the winter truce, these were rapidly running out. In desperation Francis Ackerman tried to lay siege to the harbour town of Biervliet without success. He led a large force of townsmen on a reckless night-time expedition against Aardenburg at the end of May. They surreptitiously crossed the ditch and planted their scaling ladders against the walls, and had just begun to climb them when the alarm was raised and the attackers driven off. After this incident Ackerman decided to renew his appeal to England. He needed more professional troops to help him break through the ring of hostile forces around the town. In early June 1385 two agents left Ghent to make the increasingly hazardous voyage to London. The senior of them was an anglophile clergyman called William Van Coudenberghe, who had represented the revolutionary government on previous missions to the English court and was known to be held in high regard there. It was his task to persuade the English government that the fate of Ghent depended on them.[45]

Richard II's councillors were at their wits' end to find the means of defending their own country. England's naval resources were now at their lowest point in living memory. The defence of the Channel was in the hands of commercial syndicates of privateers. Their operations consisted mainly of aimless cruises directed at defenceless coastal settlements and

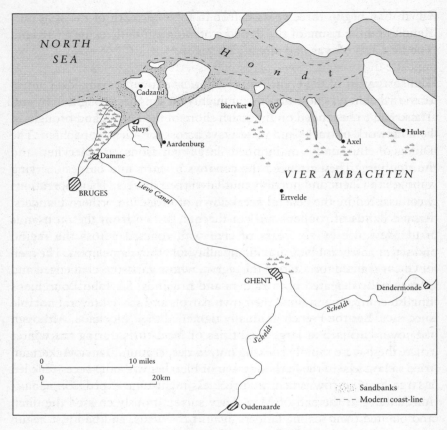

NORTH
SEA

H o n d t

Cadzand

Biervliet

Hulst

Sluys

Aardenburg

Axel

Damme

VIER AMBACHTEN

BRUGES

Lieve Canal

Ertvelde

GHENT

Dendermonde

Scheldt

Scheldt

0   10 miles

0   20km

Sandbanks
- - - Modern coast-line

Oudenaarde

19 Sluys, Damme and the Vier Ambachten, 1385

isolated merchantmen at sea. In the face of the threatened invasion, the
Council resolved in February 1385 to break with the policy of the past
few years and to return to organised naval campaigns, supported by
requisitioning. What was envisaged was nothing less than a direct attack
on the French invasion fleet's base at Sluys. At the end of April, just
before the truce expired, nearly eighty ships and barges sailed from
Orwell and Harwich with 3,500 seamen and nearly 2,000 soldiers on
board. Thirty of the ships were requisitioned merchantmen. The rest
appear to have been furnished by Robert Parys's syndicate. The
command was taken by Sir Thomas Percy, veteran of many French
campaigns, who was now serving as Admiral of the North.[46]

   In the fourteenth century, before the silt closed the rivers of Flanders
to navigation and the engineers drained the ground, the estuary of the

542

Zwyn was a long, shallow inlet from the North Sea, bounded by the island of Cadzand on the north and by desolate mud-flats on the south. A channel, about a mile wide, broadened out into a large inland lagoon opposite the town of Sluys, providing a perfect natural anchorage. The English Admirals sailed directly for the mouth of the estuary. On 12 May 1385 they penetrated through the channel to the harbour and attacked the mass of shipping gathered in the anchorage. Several ships were captured or burned. Most seem to have been trading vessels. Some belonged to neutrals. Not long after, the English launched fire-ships on the tide towards the massed transports of the French invasion fleet waiting in the lagoon but the French succeeded in fending them off. The chronicler Thomas Walsingham sourly put these disappointing results down to idleness, timidity and bickering. This was unfair but it was probably a widely held view. A second English fleet, consisting of privateers from the west country ports of Plymouth, Dartmouth and Fowey, had better success. They set out in late May to harass the long French line of supply from the Seine to the Zwyn. They sank at least four French supply vessels in the Seine estuary and captured another four, including one magnificently fitted-out vessel which the English persuaded themselves was the flagship of the Constable of France.[47]

The English fleets failed to prevent Jean de Vienne's army of Scotland from sailing. The French Admiral arrived at Sluys in the first week of May 1385. His army, which mustered in the town on the following day, finally comprised 1,315 men-at-arms with 300 French and Genoese crossbowmen and some 200 'gros varlets'. With the usual hangers-on they must have numbered some 2,500 men altogether. They brought with them their horses, 600 suits of light armour with helmets and lance tips to help equip the Scots, and 50,000 *livres* in gold florins, the first part of the subsidy to be paid to Robert II and the lords of the Scottish march. They also brought mining equipment and field artillery: seven 'portable' cannon together with stocks of gunpowder, cannonballs and lead shot, and a hundred 'fire-throwing irons', which appear to have been a primitive form of arquebus. Having arrived punctually at Sluys they were compelled to sit on the quayside for a fortnight while storms and the enemy fleet standing off the coast combined to pen them into the harbour. But, on about 22 May 1385, the flotilla sailed out of the estuary on a light wind past the foundations of Philip of Burgundy's Groot Kasteel, evading the English Admirals lying in wait for them, and broke out into the open sea. About three days later they landed at Leith and Dunbar and made for Edinburgh.[48]

The English Great Council met on 4 June 1385 in the presence of the King. The scene was the Benedictine abbey of Reading. The discussions were dominated by the news from Scotland. The English had originally intended to ignore the Scots, leaving them to be contained by the Duke of Lancaster and the wardens of the north, but these plans were swept aside when the English discovered that both of the French armies of the summer were destined for Scotland. The current situation in the north was that a separate truce covering the Scottish march had been agreed between the Earl of Northumberland and Sir Archibald Douglas, which was due to expire on 15 July. It looked as if the Franco-Scottish invasion of England would begin some time after that date. The magnates gathered at Reading decided to raise the largest army on the Scottish march that could be recruited. The muster was fixed for 14 July at Newcastle. The seventeen-year-old King proposed to take command in person, his first experience of military operations. The idea seems to have been to invade Scotland as soon as the truce expired and before Olivier de Clisson could reach the northern kingdom with the main body of the French army.[49]

The emissaries of Ghent must have reached England with Ackerman's appeal for help shortly after the Great Council had closed. Their arrival evidently caused some embarrassment among the King's ministers. They did not doubt the urgency of the situation around the town or the importance of maintaining the threat from Ghent in the French army's rear but their hands were tied by the decision which had just been made at Reading. They replied that no reinforcements could be sent to the Low Countries until the Scottish campaign was over. But they committed themselves to helping later in the season. The King's half-brother, Sir Thomas Holand, was the kind of man that Ackerman and his allies had asked for the year before. He had been retained for the Scottish campaign, but he was ordered to be ready to lead a force of men to Ghent as soon as the army of Scotland had returned. Thirty sailing ships and fourteen barges were requisitioned in readiness for his departure.[50]

These decisions raised a number of problems which seem to have been barely considered at Reading. The foremost of them was finance. The threat of a Franco-Scottish invasion finally put paid to the possibility of the King leading an expedition to the continent. This meant that he had to abandon the second of the two subsidies granted by Parliament, which was conditional upon his undertaking a continental campaign. The decision to raise an army to invade Scotland therefore provoked an immediate financial crisis. A six-week campaign could be expected to cost about £20,000. Within days the captains would be appearing at the Exchequer to claim their advances. The Council decided to address the problem by issuing its demands for military service in Scotland in the form of a summons of the feudal levy. This enabled them to demand payment of scutage, an archaic fine in lieu of service which was traditionally paid by those who held land by knight service but did not fight. It had not been demanded for more than half a century. The demand may have been made as the prelude to a round of financial horse-trading. In the event the demand for scutage was dropped. In return the captains agreed to forfeit the *regards* (or recruitment bonuses) to which they were traditionally entitled. Some of the leading magnates also helped by furnishing part of their retinues on credit. These compromises did something to relieve the government's penury but at the expense of every other front. Creditors and war contractors with assignments from the customs revenues found their claims rejected throughout the summer as the Exchequer scrambled for cash to meet the demands of the new army. The garrisons of Calais and Berwick went short. So did Sir John Bourchier's company at Ghent.[51]

On 10 July 1385 Charles VI of France received the Oriflamme from the Abbot of Saint-Denis before setting out to join his army at Arras. Richard II had already reached Nottingham on his way north. The English King left behind him a caretaker administration at Westminster, comprising the handful of councillors whose age or profession prevented them from taking part in the Scottish campaign: Archbishop Courtenay, the Bishops of London and Winchester, John Lord Cobham, Sir Robert Knolles and the Mayor of London, Nicholas Brembre. They were charged with making contingency plans for keeping the sea and defending the English coasts. The defence of the Thames estuary and north Kent was left to the Londoners to organise and pay for. Southampton, the favoured target of French raiders, was told to see to its own defence. The county levies were arrayed in Suffolk after a squadron of French ships had been reported off Orfordness. There was no attempt to organise coast-guards, to array troops inland or to set up warning beacons on hill-tops, precautions that had routinely been taken in the years when England was threatened by coastal raiders. If Olivier de Clisson had had the information and the flexibility to switch his destination at the last moment Richard II's kingdom would have been caught defenceless.[52]

In Edinburgh Jean de Vienne was encountering unexpected difficulties. He had arrived keen to take the initiative and anxious to start raiding across the border. He found the Scots unco-operative. They were determined to wait until the expiry of the local truce on the march and they needed time to make their own preparations. There were also wearing disputes about strategy, which reflected the allies' contrasting experiences of war. The French wanted a sustained campaign which would tie down significant English forces. They wanted to attack the major walled towns and castles of the English borderlands. They believed in careful advance planning and disciplined movement. The Scots wanted to fight the kind of campaign which they had always fought, involving fast movement by formless hordes of men, maximum physical destruction and the capture of valuable cattle. They were not inclined to suffer the risks and casualties of assaulting fixed defences or the delays associated with siege warfare. Many of these differences are reflected in an elaborate treaty governing the conduct of the coming campaign, which was sealed in Edinburgh on 1 July by the leading captains of both allies. Walled places were to be assaulted only by agreement between the captains of each army and after a careful reconnaissance to assess the risks. Ordinances of war were promulgated providing for the resolution of disputes between French and Scottish soldiers. Rules were formulated for keeping discipline in the ranks and resolving arguments about plunder. The document, which was drawn up in French, had all the hallmarks of French practice and French administrative order. It appointed 23 July 1385 as the date for the opening of the campaign.[53]

The delay made the French soldiers restless and provoked a certain amount of friction with the Scots. The French knights who provided Froissart with his information were taken aback by the primitiveness of the country in which they found themselves. 'What Prussian march is this to which our Admiral has taken us?' they asked. They were amazed to find that Edinburgh, which had been described to them as the Paris of the north, had no more than 400 houses. They were unimpressed by the 'red-faced and bleary-eyed' King Robert. They found his subjects a 'savage race' without courtesy or chivalry and his country bare of everything that made life sweet. The beds were hard and the buildings mean. There was no wine. They hated the beer and rye bread. Those who had lost their horses during the sea passage from Sluys found it impossible to buy adequate replacements in Scotland without paying six or ten times the price in France. Writing to the French royal Council Jean de Vienne observed that Scotland seemed to have 'nothing in it but wild beasts, forests and mountains'. The resentment was mutual. For although the leaders of the French expeditionary force were warmly welcomed by the Douglases and the Morays, men who inhabited the same mental world as they did, ordinary Scots viewed their presence with undisguised hostility. They wondered what a foreign corps of just 1,600 men could do for them that they could not do for themselves. They complained that the French could not speak their language. They objected to their habit of riding several men abreast through fields of growing corn instead of keeping to beaten paths. The Scots treated the newcomers like enemies who would pillage and burn their property like the English. They refused to sell them food and set upon their foragers in isolated places.[54]

On 8 July 1385 Jean de Vienne persuaded Robert II to bring forward the opening of hostilities. He was allowed to lead a mounted raid across the east march into Northumberland, anticipating by a few days the expiry of the truce. The French troops rode south from Edinburgh with white St. Andrew's crosses on large black patches crudely sown onto their tunics. About 3,000 Scots joined them. Crossing the Tweed east of Melrose abbey the French caught their first glimpse of the savagery of the northern war. For several miles on either side of the border they saw nothing but uncultivated wasteland, inhabited only by a few wretches who had been unable to escape in time. The Scots fell on these stragglers and cut their throats. The combined force conducted a cautious reconnaissance around Roxburgh before renouncing the task of assaulting it as impossible. They then rode east down the Tweed into Northumberland and came before Wark. The castle of Wark stood on a steep ridge on the south bank of the river, overlooking one of the principal fords. It was an old fortress, dating from the twelfth century, which had been neglected for years and had already suffered serious damage in earlier Scottish raids. There was an acrimonious argument between the French and Scots about whether to attack the place. This ended with the French assaulting the walls on their own as the Scots stood by and watched. After suffering heavy casualties they succeeded on the second day of the attack in forcing the defenders from the parapets with crossbow fire and carrying the walls from scaling ladders. The raiders took the captain prisoner, massacred the garrison and did as much damage as they could to the buildings before abandoning the castle. A few years later it was reported to be 'worthless on account of war damage'. The capture of Wark proved to be the only notable achievement of this raid. The whole affair generated much ill feeling between the French and the Scottish corps. Shortly they went their

547

separate ways. The Scots withdrew across the border while the French, accompanied only by the Earl of Douglas and his men, pressed on eastward towards Berwick and then south along the coast road, destroying towers and fortified houses and wasting the lands of the Earl of Northumberland. They penetrated into England as far as Morpeth. There, in the last few days of July, they learned that Richard II had reached Newcastle. They turned back and made for Edinburgh.[55]

The presence of the English King had proved to be a powerful recruiting agent. When, on 30 July 1385, Richard marched north out of Newcastle he was accompanied by the largest army to be raised in England since the Crécy campaign of 1346. There were nearly 14,000 men, two-thirds of them archers. The roll call included the retinues of every English earl and almost all the more prominent English captains who were still capable of fighting. With pages and supporters, there must have been between 20,000 and 25,000 men. They marched in battle order in the traditional three battalions. The Duke of Lancaster, who led by far the largest retinue, took his position in the vanguard, accompanied by his brother the Earl of Buckingham and the Marshal of England, Thomas Mowbray, Earl of Nottingham. The King marched in the centre of the next battalion with his uncle the Earl of Cambridge and the Earl of Warwick on the wings. The rear was taken up by the men of the north, led by the contingents of Percy, Neville and Clifford, and by the Bishop of Durham, a prominent figure with his crozier in his hand and the banner of St. Cuthbert, patron of the north, at his side. On 6 August the English army entered Scotland and the King unfurled his banner. In the small town of Hoselaw in Teviotdale Richard marked his entry on to Scottish soil by bestowing new honours on his favourites and relatives. Edmund Langley, Earl of Cambridge, became Duke of York. Thomas of Woodstock, Earl of Buckingham, became Duke of Gloucester. Robert de Vere, Earl of Oxford, became Marquis of Dublin, the first time that this title had been used in England. Michael Pole was made Earl of Suffolk and Simon Burley became Earl of Huntingdon. John, Lord Neville of Raby, became Earl of Cumberland. John of Gaunt's eldest son Henry Bolingbroke was named Earl of Derby. No fewer than 300 men received knighthood at the King's hands. Richard probably hoped to win goodwill among the nobility by these creations in much the same way as his grandfather Edward III had done by his lavish peerage creations at the outset of the war in 1337.[56]

The following days made a mockery of this ambition. The English advanced through Lothian across a six-mile front towards Edinburgh.

The inhabitants of Lothian fled in the path of the approaching mass of men, taking all their foodstuffs with them and destroying what they could not carry. The Scottish and French soldiers retreated before them, refusing to offer battle but harassing their flanks, picking off stragglers and foragers. Unable to come to grips with their enemy, the English turned to destruction. They burned everything in their way. They trampled down the growing corn. Prisoners who fell into their hands were put to death. The usual immunity accorded to monastic buildings was refused on the ground that they were occupied by Clementists. Melrose, the greatest Cistercian foundation in Scotland, was spared for the moment but Dryburgh and Newbattle were almost entirely destroyed. On 11 August, after five days' march, the English reached Edinburgh. They found it completely deserted apart from the garrison of the castle. The Scots looked down impotently from the castle walls as the invaders torched the houses and churches of the town. Only Holyrood Abbey was spared at the special request of John of Gaunt, who had been sheltered there during his exile in Scotland in 1381.

By now, however, Richard's army was beginning to suffer from hunger. There had been no time to organise a proper supply train. The foragers found nothing to take. Disease began to spread among weakened men, aided by the hot weather. It was a repetition of the misfortunes of John of Gaunt's invasion of the previous year. Gaunt urged the King to press on across the Firth of Forth. Since the bulk of the Scottish forces with their French auxiliaries were retreating south through the forest of Ettrick, Gaunt's plan suggests, like so much else about this campaign, that his main object was to pre-empt a French descent between the Firth of Tay and the Moray Firth, where the most suitable landing places were to be found.

Richard, however, had had enough. He turned on his uncle, abusing him to his face and accusing him of treason. It was all very well, he is reported to have said, for great lords like him who had brought wagons of food for themselves. The rest of the army would starve. Was Gaunt deliberately trying to destroy him? 'I shall return home with my men,' Richard declared. 'But I am one of your men,' the Duke replied. 'I see no evidence of that,' the King said. The army turned back by the way that it had come. At Melrose they found that the soldiers who had been left to protect the abbey from pillagers had all been murdered. Richard responded by having the church and conventual buildings reduced to a mass of charred stumps. The English army returned to Newcastle on 20 August 1385, where it disbanded. They had passed less than two weeks in Scotland without either taming the Scots or contributing anything to the destruction of Jean de Vienne's army. The task of defending the north against the inevitable Scottish retaliation was passed to the Percy Earl of Northumberland, with just 1,200 men based at Berwick plus the garrisons of Roxburgh and Carlisle.[57]

The Scots' retaliation had already begun. While the English had been arguing strategy in Edinburgh the Scots had crossed the defenceless western march into Cumberland. On about 15 August 1385 King Robert's second son Robert, Earl of Fife, led his men at low tide across the treacherous sands at the head of the Solway Firth accompanied by Jean de Vienne and his French corps, the borderers of the Earls of Douglas and March and Sir Archibald Douglas and 'the whole youth and flower of Scotland's chivalry'. A screen of men was left to invest the city of Carlisle and burn its suburbs and outlying villages while the rest of the horde rode on south through Cumberland and Westmoreland, penetrating well beyond Penrith into territory which had not been raided from Scotland for several decades. Terrible damage was done to the region. The tax records for years to come told the same tale of depopulation and destruction of crops, buildings and animals. The Scots staggered back towards the border, bowed beneath the weight of their loot. Froissart's French informants told him with calculated ambiguity that the spoil from just four English towns was worth more than all the wealth of Scotland. On their way back they came before Carlisle, the principal walled city of the west march. Jean de Vienne had probably always had this place in mind as the main objective of the campaign. On 7 September his men brought up their artillery against the gates and assaulted the walls from scaling ladders. The walls of Carlisle were weak and in disrepair but the town had a strong garrison and had recut its ditches before the enemy arrived. The assault was beaten back. Several French prisoners were taken. The invaders had run out of time. The Earl of Northumberland's son, Sir Henry Percy, appeared across the Pennines with an army of borderers from the eastern march. The French and Scots made off. According to Froissart, the French were close to starvation. They began to seize food belonging to the inhabitants of the Scottish Lowlands. This provoked angry argument and fighting between French and Scottish troops. The campaign, which had once seemed so promising, ended with a whimper as a half-hearted attempt was made to capture Roxburgh. It was the last opportunity that Jean de Vienne would have to achieve a notable success in Scotland. The facts are obscure but it seems that, as at Wark, the Scots would not join in an assault. The

Admiral responded that if the fortress was taken by French efforts it must be held in the name of Charles VI. The Scots indignantly rejected this idea. Both corps shortly left the field in disgust.[58]

The sailing of the second French army had been fixed for 1 August 1385. In the course of July more ships joined the invasion fleet gathered in the anchorage at Sluys. Banners fluttered in the wind from several hundred masts. The larger hulls, which had been reserved for the leading captains of the army, were brightly painted in their colours. The immense quantity of food and equipment commandeered during the summer had reached the port and was in the process of being loaded. The preparations were almost complete when the project received a mortal blow from an unexpected quarter. On 15 July Francis Ackerman and Peter Van den Bossche left Ghent by night with a small force of 1,300 men including Sir John Bourchier and his company to disrupt the invasion preparations. They reconnoitred the defences of Bruges and Sluys but found them too well guarded. At Damme, however, they had better fortune. The river port of Damme, half-way between Sluys and Bruges, marked the limit of the navigable section of the River Zwyn. Silt had progressively closed its harbour to ocean-going vessels and the town was a shadow of what it had once been. But it remained an important distribution centre for the grain and victualling trades. It was also the nodal point of the canal system in western Flanders. The place was protected by a modern circuit of walls and ditches but the captain was away in Bruges and no proper watch was being kept in his absence. Ackerman's men crossed the water-filled ditches, scaled the walls and took possession of the town before the garrison knew they were there. The inhabitants were massacred. French troops from Bruges, Sluys and Aardenburg soon appeared outside. They tried to recover the place before the invaders could organise its defence. They rushed the barriers beyond the gates. But they were driven back. In the following days they launched a succession of assaults, all of which failed. Shortly a relief force arrived from Ghent to drive off the assailants. By the end of July 1385 Damme was defended by a garrison from Ghent several thousand strong. The artillery already in the town was deployed on the walls and more was brought in from Ghent. A cornucopia of supplies was found in the warehouses of the port to sustain the defenders through a long siege.[59]

On the day that Damme fell the French court was at Amiens celebrating the marriage of their seventeen-year-old King. The bride, Isabelle of Bavaria, who was two years younger than he was, had been brought from Germany by her uncle to be submitted to Charles's inspection. The meeting, sudden betrothal and hastily arranged marriage, all carefully stage-managed by the Duke of Burgundy and accomplished in the space of three days, was perhaps as near to a love-match as a king of France could be allowed to come. Charles did not have long to enjoy his bride's company. The first reports of the capture of Damme reached Amiens on the following day, 18 July. The implications did not take long to sink in. The presence of a large army from Ghent four miles from Bruges and seven from Sluys in a region readily accessible from England was a grave threat to the embarkations as well as to the wider interests of the Duke of Burgundy. And, as a contemporary tartly noted, 'whatever touches the Duke of Burgundy, the King makes it his business to do.' The army of invasion was redirected to Damme and the passage to England was deferred until it had been recovered. On 21 July the Queen was led off to the castle of Creil in the valley of the Oise, while Charles VI and his uncle marched away with the Constable and the household officers to Arras to join the rest of the army. On 31 July the whole French army was encamped in the flat landscape around Damme.[60]

Richard II's councillors at Westminster learned of the capture of Damme a few days after the French did. They appreciated its significance at once. The longer Damme held out the harder it would be for the French invasion fleet to sail this season. At the end of July, therefore, the caretaker administration desperately tried to fit out an expeditionary force to disrupt and prolong the French siege. The Admirals' fleet in the North Sea had reached the end of its indentured service and was on its way home. So Knolles and Brembre, together with the rich London financier William Walworth, set about requisitioning a new fleet in the west country. They proposed to embark troops for Flanders on this fleet as soon as they could be found. Providentially six Portuguese galleys armed with guns, the first fruits of Richard II's alliance with John of Avis, had just arrived in the west country to support the defence of England. It was a generous gesture in view of the limited scale of English assistance to Portugal to date and the fact that no treaty between them had yet been ratified. The galleys were brought round the coast to London and their masters plied with gifts. Plans were devised to send them into the Zwyn to burn part of the French fleet. A Dutch pilot who knew the waters of the estuary was hired to guide them in. A barge was chartered in Southampton and despatched to scout about the mouth of the Zwyn and report on the progress of French operations. There was no money in the government's coffers to pay for any of this. The cost appears to have been advanced by Brembre himself.[61]

The French commanders at Damme knew that the town had to be recaptured quickly if the invasion project was to be saved. They threw assault parties against the walls almost every day, sustaining terrible casualties in the process. They built great stone-throwers which battered the walls, gradually reducing whole sections to rubble. The defenders under Ackerman's command fought back furiously. They waited until the ladder parties had almost reached the summit before throwing them off into the ditches. They fought them off with axes and swords from the parapets. Their cannon let loose a murderous fire from the flanks. The English archers on the ramparts shot dense volleys of arrows into the approaching French cohorts. Conditions in the French lines were appalling. Damme was sited on marshy, low-lying ground. It was hot. The stink of death and excrement and the buzzing of flies was everywhere. The town ditch was filled with sewage. The French men-at-arms sickened and died or withdrew to recover in Bruges. Charles VI left for the cleaner air of the Château de Mâle, leaving his tents behind to conceal his departure. The valiant resistance of the defenders of Damme gradually roused the ancient friends and fellow-travellers of Ghent in western Flanders. In Bruges tensions rose on the streets. The gates were watched for strangers and men of low degree who were 'not knights, squires or clergy or other persons of substance or repute'. At Sluys there were riots against the French. Some of the inhabitants were detected trying to organise a general rising to kill the garrison in their beds at night and then break the dykes and set fire to the French fleet.[62]

Inside Damme supplies, too prodigally distributed at the outset, were beginning to run out. Ackerman sent frantic appeals to the English and to his fellow citizens in Ghent. The English were already doing their best but their relief force was unlikely to be ready for some time. From Ghent, which was only some twenty miles away, Ackerman might have expected more. But the townsmen had fallen to quarrelling among themselves. Many believed that their rebellion was doomed and the enterprise at Damme hopeless. They included the richest citizens: men of property whose estates beyond the town had been wasted by the war; leading grain shippers and victuallers, whose ruin had been completed by the French raids in the Vier Ambachten. These men wanted to throw themselves on the mercy of Charles VI and the Duke of Burgundy. They kept their voices low for fear of Peter Van den Bossche's informers but without Ackerman's demagogic skills to whip up the fear and anger of the crowd the revolutionaries steadily lost ground. In Damme Ackerman sensed his party's power slipping away. He determined to abandon his men in the town and escape. On the night of 16 August 1385 he had one of the gates opened and rode out with his principal lieutenants and a large part of the garrison including Bourchier's English company. He told the watch that they going to reconnoitre the French siege lines. Instead his men picked their way past the encampments of the besiegers without being noticed. When they reached open ground they rode off as fast as possible for Ghent.

Those who were left behind fought on for a time, sustained by the knowledge that they could expect no mercy from the French. On 26 August they too tried to escape. They sent a *parlementaire* into the French lines to propose talks. A brief cease-fire was ordered while this was considered. That night the defenders stole out of the town across the marshes to the east. They were accompanied by many of the inhabitants. But they were seen by the watchmen in the French lines, who sounded the alarm. A large number of French knights in the lines rushed for their weapons, mounted their horses and gave chase through the night. Several hundred people are said to have been cut down and killed in this murderous man-hunt. The rest of the French army waited until daybreak. On 27 August they assaulted the walls, pouring over the parapets and through the gates, killing everyone they found in the streets with a weapon in his hands and setting fire to much of the town. When order was restored about 200 men of Ghent were found still in Damme. They were led off to Bruges and beheaded outside the town jail.[63]

At the end of August 1385 it might still have been possible to mount the invasion of England. But the Duke of Burgundy's first priority was to follow up his victory while the men of Ghent were in disarray. On 1 September he marched east with the army, bringing the King in his baggage train. That evening they established their headquarters in the castle of Ertvelde about seven miles north of Ghent. The fires of the army encamped around the village could be plainly seen from the walls of the town. Olivier de Clisson rode up to the gates to reconnoitre the defences. He devised a plan to attack the citadel and force a way into the town but the defenders opened the sluices of the canals and flooded the low-lying ground around the walls. The French discovered what Louis de Mâle had painfully learned in the last five years of his life. Ghent could not be taken by assault and starving it out would be a very long process. For more than a week they systematically wasted the Vier

Ambachten. Villages, forts, mills were all destroyed. The dykes along the coast were broken, submerging much of the cultivable land. The soldiers killed all who did not flee in time except for those who seemed worth a ransom. But the Duke of Burgundy would not allow even these to live. He had every one of them beheaded in front of the King and his principal officers. Their dignity as they went to their deaths impressed even their executioners. 'The King of France could put every Fleming to death,' one of them told Charles to his face, 'and their desiccated bones would still rise up to fight him.'[64]

The capture of Damme and the Duke of Burgundy's attempt on Ghent saved England from a French invasion. The sailing of the army had now been held up for nearly six weeks. The army paymasters were running out of cash. The supplies which had been stored for the fleet in Sluys had been diverted to feed the army during the siege of Damme and those on the ships were rotting. To replace them would take time. It would also cost money which the French royal Treasury did not expect to have until the final instalment of the *taille* was received in October. By then the autumn gales would have begun. On 10 September 1385 the French royal Council met in the King's presence at Ertvelde and decided that the invasion would have to be put off to the following year. The stores were unloaded from the ships at Sluys. Those that were still usable were deposited for the winter in the newly built cellars of Philip of Burgundy's Groot Kasteel. The army was paid off two days later.[65]

It was a grave reverse but worse was to follow. The requisitioned ships of Normandy and Picardy sailed for their home ports in the course of September. Many of these ships took the opportunity to load cargoes in Sluys. The first convoy sailed into a storm in the Channel on 13 September 1385. Nine sailing ships and both serviceable galleys were driven onto the shore near Calais and fell into the hands of the English together with some 500 of their crews. This was probably the first news that the English received that the invasion plan had been abandoned. The following convoys had to run the gauntlet of English attacks from both sides of the Channel. On 16 September a fleet of English sailing ships and oared barges waiting at Calais intercepted a convoy of about eighty sail and captured about a quarter of them. Two days later the same fleet, reinforced this time by the captures of the past few days and supported by the ships of the Cinque Ports, attacked another convoy of forty-five sail. Most of these vessels escaped but three of them were captured after a sea-fight lasting five hours: two large and magnificent sailing ships with fortified hulls and topmasts, which had been assigned to serve as flagships for Charles VI and Clisson, and a great Baltic cog which was found to be carrying 5,000 francs in cash. Sir William Beauchamp, the captain of Calais, who was mainly responsible for these operations, was credited with forty-eight prizes in the space of two weeks.[66]

The cancellation of the invasion left Jean de Vienne and his men stranded in Scotland. The end of their adventure was as acrimonious as the beginning. The French Admiral wrote to Charles VI and Philip of Burgundy to say that he was willing to winter in Scotland until the new army of invasion arrived in the following year, provided that reinforcements, supplies and money for their wages were sent out from France. But his men had grown to loathe Scotland and its inhabitants. They said that by next summer they would have starved to death if they were not murdered in their beds by the natives. They insisted on going home. They then found that the Scots would not let them leave until they had satisfied those who claimed to have suffered damage at their hands. These included not just those whose timber or foodstuffs had been taken by the French or whose grain had been trodden beneath the hooves of their horses, but the bulk of the Scottish men-at-arms, who claimed to have been fighting for the French King's account and demanded war wages and compensation for horses lost on the campaign. The men-at-arms were eventually satisfied with their share of the 50,000 francs subsidy which Jean de Vienne had brought with him to Scotland. Ten thousand francs of this was paid to Robert II. Six thousand francs was retained to compensate the French soldiers for the horses lost during their passage to Scotland. The rest was distributed according to their deserts among Robert's ministers and the leading Scottish captains by a joint commission of French and Scottish knights. The other claimants had to wait until the French government paid the value of their claims to Robert II's agents in Bruges. The French eventually left in groups towards the end of the year as shipping became available. They returned without money or horses but full of tales of the rudeness, ingratitude and greed of the Scots.[67]

The French government learned some painful lessons from the events of the summer of 1385. One of them was forcefully pointed out by Jean de Vienne when in due course he reported on his mission to the French royal Council. Successive kings of France had greatly overrated the power of the Scots, the Admiral thought. In his view the country's resources were no greater than those of a single French province like Artois or a minor principality like Savoy. He had seen their whole military array, he said, and it included no more than about 500 properly equipped men-at-arms. There were up to 30,000 more who would come when summoned but they were poorly armed and trained and would flee at the first sight of an English army. By comparison, having stood on a hillside and watched the host of Richard II march through Lothian, he reckoned England's strength in men-at-arms at about 6,000. The main problem, however, was that the devastated wastes of the Scottish lowlands were incapable of supporting a French army of any size. If Clisson had ever reached Scotland in the summer, said Jean de Vienne, his troops would have ended up fighting against the Scots or starving them out of their homes. The Admiral strongly advised against another attempt to land a large army in Scotland and in fact the French never again tried to attack England through Scotland until the beginning of the eighteenth century. For their part the Scots gave up hope of fighting a major campaign in England with their French allies. When they learned that the French army of invasion had been disbanded they entered into negotiations with the English King's representatives on the march and agreed a local truce until 1 July 1386. With successive extensions this truce lasted until the summer of 1388. For practical purposes Scotland was out of the war for the next two years.[68]

The other lesson which the French learned was that it was unsafe to attempt the invasion of England without first securing complete control over Flanders. The Duke of Burgundy realised now that he could not capture Ghent by force. He would therefore have to make concessions of a kind which did not come easily to a man of his authoritarian instincts. Even before his withdrawal from Ertvelde Philip had arranged for the King to write an emollient letter to those in Ghent who were thought to be opposed to the die-hards in the town's government. Charles offered to confirm the town's charters and privileges if its citizens would surrender to him and undertook to grant an amnesty for all acts done during the six-year civil war. One of Philip's Flemish-speaking staff covertly installed himself in the Franciscan nunnery at Gentbrugge, beneath the eastern rampart of the town, to work on sympathisers among the citizens. By the end of September 1385 a group of guildsmen, led by a grain shipper and a butcher, was already engaged in secret discussions in Paris with the Duke and other members of the French royal Council.[69]

CHAPTER XII

The Path of Portugal
1385–1388

In the spring of 1385 John of Trastámara had stretched the resources of
Castile to their limits to overcome the resistance of his opponents in
Portugal. In the previous year he had collected no fewer than eight
monedas from his Castilian subjects in spite of their bitter complaints.
In 1385 he exacted twelve. His officials were preparing one of the
largest fleets ever assembled by a Castilian king. Ten galleys and twenty
large converted merchantmen were already lying in the Tagus off
Lisbon. Another five galleys had been hired from the King of Aragon.
Five more galleys and some two dozen armed merchantmen were being
fitted out to join them. On land the Castilian King's army was expected
to be nearly twice as large as the one which had besieged Lisbon in
1384. In addition to the resources of his own kingdom John of
Trastámara's lieutenants could call on the military support of most of
the inland towns in northern and central Portugal and by far the greater
part of the nobility. The invasion plan was the classic two-pronged
attack which had so often been deployed in Castile's wars against
Portugal. The main army of invasion was directed to assemble near the
border city of Badajoz in April. These men would cross the River
Guadiana near Elvas under the King's personal command and make
directly for Lisbon. A second, smaller army was to be formed by the
Archbishop of Toledo at Ciudad Rodrigo in the north and reach the
Portuguese capital by the longer route through Viseu and Coimbra.[1]

It was in these difficult circumstances that the Master of Avis decided
to abandon the claim to rule Portugal as regent of the imprisoned
Infante João and take the crown for himself. Popular support for the
Infante had been an important factor in the rejection of Beatrice. But an
absent sovereign who was in the power of the enemy was no longer a
plausible source of authority or even a useful figurehead. The Cortes of
Portugal gathered at the beginning of March 1385 at Coimbra.
Ostensibly a national assembly, the participants were in fact drawn
exclusively from the supporters of the nationalist cause. Its deliberations

558

were dominated by the delegates of the thirty-one towns represented, which had always been the bedrock of the Master's support. A month was taken up with legal wrangling. Legally John's claim had little to be said for it. He was a bastard whereas the Infante's João's father was generally believed to have been secretly married to Inez de Castro. Even if the marriage had never happened, as John's advocate contended, there was no legal basis for brushing aside the claims of Beatrice and her issue. She had her own advocates even in such a gathering. Law, however, could not resolve what was in reality a Portuguese civil war. It could only anoint the partisans. The decisive factors were political. The crowd outside had already shown where their sympathies lay. They acclaimed John of Avis as King as he arrived at the beginning of the proceedings. They spoke for the streets of Lisbon and Oporto where his real power lay. On 6 April 1385 the Cortes declared him King of Portugal. Five days later, on the 11th, he was crowned in the cathedral. He was twenty-seven years old. Among his first acts were the appointment of the twenty-four-year-old Nun' Alvarez Pereira as Constable of Portugal and the issue of a new coinage in his own name. The coinage was not just a public demonstration of sovereignty. In conditions where effective tax collection was impossible, devaluation and minting profits were expected to raise much of the money needed to fight the Castilians. The new King declared his international allegiance at once. Fresh instructions were sent to Lourenço Fogaça and Alonso de Albuquerque, who were still struggling with their creditors in England, to complete the negotiations for an Anglo-Portuguese treaty. Another embassy left for Rome to declare Portugal's allegiance to Urban II.[2]

Weighed down by problems of recruitment and finance John of Trastámara was unable to assemble his army of invasion for more than two months after the date originally planned. The delay proved fatal to his ambitions, for the Castilians lost the initiative never to regain it. Moving quickly to exploit the moment of euphoria following his coronation, John of Avis and his Constable overran almost all the territory north of the Duero in the space of six weeks. The thirteenth-century fortress of Guimarães, one of the strongest of the region, surrendered after the Castilian King had proved unable to organise a relief force in time. Its captain, who was one of John of Trastámara's most prominent allies among the Portuguese nobility, went over to John of Avis. Men of his kind had assumed that the Castilian King would prevail by sheer force of numbers and resources. Once these certainties were dented, support for the house of Trastámara began to drain away. There were wholesale desertions among the Portuguese troops serving in Castilian garrisons, whose wages had not been paid for nearly a year.[3]

Towards the end of May 1385 the Castilian King tried to shore up his support in Portugal with a military demonstration. He ordered the Archbishop of Toledo, who was in command at Ciudad Rodrigo, to send the forces at his disposal across the border to waste the territory around Guarda and Viseu. Some 300 men-at-arms, supported by light horse and infantry, perhaps 1,000 men in all, took part in this raid. Returning laden with booty on 29 May they were confronted by the combined garrisons of a number of nearby castles, arrayed on foot in front of the gates of the small walled town of Trancoso. The Portuguese were greatly outnumbered but they had the advantage of the defensive. The Castilian men-at-arms dismounted and charged them on foot across the rough ploughed fields. At the same time they sent their light horsemen round the Portuguese position to attack their infantry from the rear. The soft terrain broke up the formation of the Castilian men-at-arms while the infantry rushed the Portuguese lines in no order at all. Both groups were repelled and in the pursuit which followed almost all of them were killed.[4]

The news from Guimarães and Trancoso unnerved John of Trastámara. He had entered Portugal in the last days of May with a small advance guard and stopped a few miles beyond the Guadiana at Elvas, where he proposed to wait for the bulk of his army to arrive. He was unwell, as he had so often been at critical moments of his reign. Illness made him hesitant and vacillating. A few days after arriving at Elvas he abruptly abandoned his existing plans and decided instead to draw the whole of his army together for a single thrust into Portugal by the north, where most of John of Avis's own forces were now concentrated. This decision entailed fresh disruption and delay. The muster had to be moved from Badajoz to Ciudad Rodrigo, more than a hundred miles away, and postponed to July. The Castilian King reached Ciudad Rodrigo, probably towards the end of June, only to receive the news of yet another military reverse, this time at Mertola in the Algarve. Mertola was a small walled town just inside Portugal which was occupied by a Castilian garrison. It had been under siege for some weeks by a horde of locally recruited Portuguese infantry supported by a small contingent of men-at-arms. A relief force of about 300 Castilian men-at-arms and 800 infantry had been sent from Seville to raise the siege. Over-confidence seems once more to have been their undoing. They

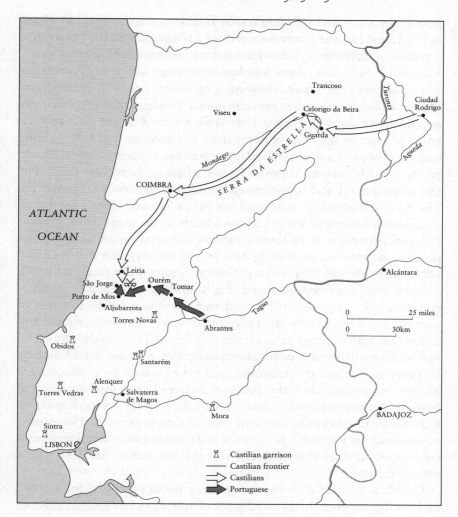

20 The Castilian invasion of Portugal, July–August 1385

were decisively defeated in a pitched battle outside the town and withdrew with heavy losses.[5]

In the massive fortress which his father had built at Ciudad Rodrigo, above the banks of the River Agueda, John of Trastámara called his Council together to consider yet another change of plan. Ostensibly the argument was about strategy. The alternatives were to invade Portugal and march on Lisbon, which would probably provoke a pitched battle with John of Avis; or to adopt a more cautious approach, disbanding part of the army and standing on the frontier until the naval blockade in the Tagus and the garrisons north of Lisbon starved the Portuguese capital into submission. Behind this debate lay more fundamental issues. Many of John's councillors had had misgivings about his Portuguese ambitions from the outset. These men, who were probably the majority of the Council, included the chronicler Ayala, who describes the arguments in vivid language. They were alarmed by the cost and the political risks of the coming campaign. Tax receipts had fallen a long way short of expectations. Recruitment had been exceptionally difficult, partly for that reason. Many of Castile's best soldiers were dead. The rest were unpaid and unenthusiastic and their leaders inexperienced. The King's health was poor and his heir a minor. They were by no means as confident of victory as the leaders of the army were. John of Avis was believed to have about 2,000 men-at-arms under his command plus an uncertain number of light horse and infantry. But they included some battle-hardened English and Gascon cavalry and a force of English archers, whose presence caused much anxiety among the Castilian commanders. A major battle would risk everything on the fortunes of a single day without any assurance of success. There were substantial arguments on the other side. Grave as John of Trastámara's financial and military difficulties were, abandoning the invasion would destroy his party in Portugal at a stroke and make the annexation of the country all but impossible. But the pacifists believed that annexation had become impossible anyway. Better, they said, to wage a war of attrition with small numbers of men and then compromise with the enemy, acknowledging John of Avis's Crown and exacting substantial territorial concessions in exchange. Especially as the alternative could be defeat and bankruptcy.[6]

Unable to decide finally between either school of thought, John ended up by adopting both. In the third week of July 1385 he crossed the River Turones into Portugal, declaring that his intention was to conduct a short punitive raid into Portugal with his whole army. He planned, he said, to penetrate as far as the mountain passes north of Coimbra in order to save his honour and then to retreat to Castile, leaving the further prosecution of the war to raiding parties from the border fortresses and to the ships and garrisons around Lisbon. In spite of the ambitious target given to the recruiting officers the Castilian army was quite small, probably between 4,000 and 5,000 men-at-arms. Of these about 1,200 were French. In due course they were reinforced by John's Portuguese allies and by men-at-arms drawn from the Castilian garrisons in

Portugal. However, the total number of men-at-arms never exceeded 6,000. In addition there were about 2,000 *jinetes*, lightly armed cavalry from Andalusia, and a large host of pikemen, crossbowmen and other infantry whose number can only be guessed. The whole force, including camp-followers, may well have approached the 30,000 men attributed to it by the principal Portuguese chronicler, but that included many troops of poor quality. The King himself made a sorry sight, racked with illness and carried after his men in a litter. On about 21 July the Castilians captured the important border fortress of Celorigo da Beira. Then they marched down the rich valley of the Mondego, destroying everything before them. The slaughter of his troops at Lisbon and Trancoso had provoked fury among the King's followers. They avenged their companions by brutally killing or mutilating all the Portuguese who had not had the time or wit to flee before they arrived. As the Castilian army approached, John of Avis retreated south from Coimbra. When this move was reported to him, John of Trastámara changed his plans once more. Concluding that the Portuguese King did not, after all, intend to fight a pitched battle, John resolved to pursue him into the interior.[7]

At the end of July 1385 John of Avis joined forces with his Constable, Nun' Alvarez Pereira, at the bridge of Abrantes on the Tagus. There a council of war was held which in some ways mirrored the proceedings of John of Trastámara's Council at Ciudad Rodrigo. Most of the Portuguese King's advisers, like those of his rival, were against hazarding everything on a battle. They preferred to wait for the arrival of further reinforcements from England which were reported to be on their way. The main advocate of the offensive was the Constable, Nun' Alvarez. He pointed out that most of John of Avis's garrison in Lisbon had been withdrawn to swell the numbers of his army. Unless the Castilian King was stopped, he would join forces with the garrisons of the Castilian fortresses around Lisbon. There would then be nothing to prevent him from taking the capital by assault. Having made his points before a sceptical Council the Constable walked out. He would lead his own men against the enemy, he announced, whatever the rest of them decided. John of Avis overruled his councillors and accepted Nun' Alvarez's advice. The truth was that he had little choice. He could not afford to avoid a battle, any more than his Castilian rival could, if he was to maintain his support in Portugal. So, in the second week of August 1385, the Portuguese army moved east to Porto de Mos, a castle standing on high ground overlooking the River Lena, just east of the main highway from Coimbra to Lisbon. The Castilian army was reported to be encamped to the north around the fortress-town of Leiria, which had once served as the southern bastion of the Christian kingdom against the Moors.[8]

In the early morning of 14 August 1385 the Portuguese moved forward to block the road at a point eight miles south of Leiria and about the same distance north of the insignificant village of Aljubarrota. Their army was much the smaller of the two. Ayala, an experienced soldier in the Castilian King's entourage, reckoned its total strength at about 2,200 men-at-arms and about 10,000 pikemen, bowmen and other infantry. Not all of the English in Portugal were present. Some are known to have been doing garrison duty beyond the Duero. But an English chronicler, who appears to have been reading a news-letter from Portugal, records that the English contingent numbered 700 men including archers and this is broadly consistent with other evidence. In addition there was a small Gascon company recruited in England, which was led by a prominent Périgourdin nobleman, Guillaume de Montferrand. The Portuguese Constable had carefully reconnoitred the ground on the previous day. He drew up the vanguard of the army across the highway at the northern extremity of a narrow ridge. The road sloped steeply away in front of them towards Leiria. On either side of the vanguard the Constable placed his wings, with their outer flanks protected at each extremity by a creek. The English and Gascon cavalry were placed under the command of Guillaume de Montferrand on the left wing and Portuguese men-at-arms on the right. Behind each wing the Portuguese and English bowmen stood on slightly higher ground where they could see the action and fire their weapons over the heads of the cavalrymen in front. John of Avis himself took up position with the rearguard immediately behind the Constable's battalion. The Portuguese chronicler who tells us these things remarks that the terms used for these units, van, rear, right and left wings, had been borrowed from the military jargon used by the officers of the Earl of Cambridge three years before. Both the Portuguese forces and their Castilian adversaries were now organised on the model of their English and French allies, with a constable in command of operations and marshals to serve as their deputies and maintain discipline. It was part of the long process by which the armies of the Iberian peninsula adopted the organisation, equipment and battle tactics of the leading protagonists in the western European war.[9]

Towards the end of the morning of 14 August 1385 the forward units of the Castilian army approached along the road from Leiria. When

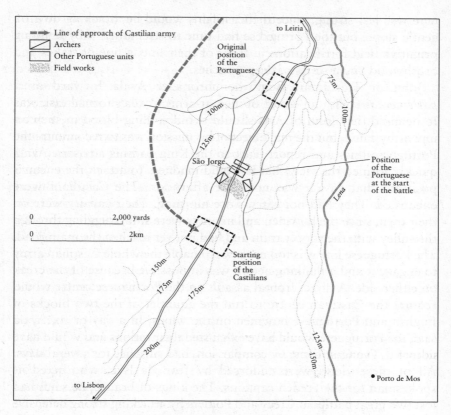

21 The battle of Aljubarrota, 14 August 1385

they saw the Portuguese ahead of them they halted while John of
Trastámara came up from behind to take stock. Before them the road
crossed a stream and rose steeply towards Nun' Alvarez's lines. A frontal
assault was out of the question. It was decided to manoeuvre the
Castilian army round the Portuguese positions and approach the enemy
along the high road from the south. This was probably the only course
open to them but it involved a difficult and time-consuming march of
about five miles through thickly wooded terrain by some twenty to
thirty thousand men encumbered with several hundred carts full of
supplies and equipment. It also had to be carried out in the midday sun
by troops who had been on the road since daybreak. While the
Castilians carried out this manoeuvre the Portuguese Constable turned
his whole army around to face the new threat and repositioned them
about a mile further south, near the village of São Jorge. Their position

here was less strong, since the Castilians would be attacking down a gentle slope, but the Portuguese had time to strengthen it by building primitive field fortifications in front of their line: a line of stakes and brushwood and a series of deep trenches.

John of Trastámara sent the chronicler Ayala forward as a *parlementaire* with an escort of men-at-arms. Ayala's formal task was to demand that John of Avis should avoid spilling blood in such an unworthy cause, but the real object of his mission was to reconnoitre the Portuguese lines and report back to the King and his advisers. Ayala quickly formed the view that it would madness to attack the enemy's positions that day. It was now late afternoon. The Castilians were exhausted. They had not eaten since morning. Their cavalry were on their own, since the bowmen and infantry were still struggling through the valley with the supply train and had not yet reached the main road. The Portuguese line was too narrow to enable the whole Castilian army to engage it and a flanking action was impossible because of the creek on either side. A direct frontal assault on the Portuguese centre would require the Castilian centre to run the gauntlet of the two blocks of English and Portuguese bowmen on the wings. In a day or so, Ayala said, the Portuguese would have exhausted their rations and would have to move. The Castilians, by comparison, had supplies for several days. All of these views were endorsed by Jean de Rye, who acted as spokesman for the French captains. The kings of France, he said, had lost two great battles at Crécy and Poitiers by attacking strong defensive positions without taking the time to organise their own order of battle and impose discipline on their men. Others in the Castilian King's tents scoffed at their caution. The Portuguese army, they said, was far inferior to their own. It was sheer cowardice not to seize the moment to inflict a decisive defeat on them. The chance would not necessarily come again.

All of Jean de Rye's fears were borne out by the event. John of Trastámara was persuaded to defer the battle until the following day but his tents were well behind the front line, out of earshot of his principal commanders, and his orders took some time to reach them. By the time that the couriers reached the forward units of the Castilian army the fighting had already begun. The Master of the Castilian military order of Alcántara took the initiative. Accompanied by a large force of light cavalry and supported by the heavy cavalry of the French, he tried to force his way through the wings of the Portuguese army to attack their position from the rear. He did not realise how strong the Portuguese position was until it was too late. The horsemen were forced back by concentrated arrow fire from the flanks. John of Trastámara had no choice now but to try to save the day by ordering in the rest of his available troops. The Castilian vanguard charged the centre of the Portuguese line. As the attackers tried to cross the Portuguese field fortifications the two Portuguese wings closed in on them, decimating them with murderous flanking fire before they had even reached the enemy. Those that penetrated as far as the Portuguese lines succeeded in driving them back with their first impact but the rearguard under John of Avis advanced to confront them. The Castilian formation broke up into small splinter groups which flailed about right and left without support from their comrades. Within about an hour the Castilian King's standard was seen to fall.

John of Trastámara's bodyguard quickly transferred him from his litter onto a horse and sped away. The King's departure was the signal for what was left of the Castilian army to flee. They had suffered terrible casualties. John of Trastámara's Aragonese constable was among the dead, along with both marshals of the army, the newly appointed Admiral of Castile and several of the principal officers of his household. Jean de Rye, who had done his best to avert the tragedy, was found among the dead. Geoffrey de Parthenay, the captain of the Bretons, died in the mêlée. Almost all the Castilian King's Portuguese allies were killed. Several famous and colourful figures from past campaigns were among the casualties: Arnaud du Solier, the notorious Limousin brigand of the 1360s, who had passed the last fifteen years of his life as a Castilian prince; Juan Ramírez de Arellano, the Navarrese captain who had served Charles the Bad, Edward III and both Trastámaran kings of Castile in his time. Writing to the city of Lisbon, John of Avis announced that 2,500 men-at-arms of the enemy, nearly half of their cavalry, were dead. Reports reaching England suggested that, when light horse and infantry were included, the total Castilian casualties were three times that number. John of Trastámara arrived with his attendants at the castle of Santarém, nearly fifty miles from the battlefield, in the early hours of the following morning. There he embarked on an armed barge in the Tagus and made for Seville by sea. The Castilian fleet blockading Lisbon withdrew shortly afterwards. Over the following weeks all the Castilian garrisons around the capital and most of those in the north and centre of the kingdom were either evacuated or captured by the victorious Portuguese.

The battle of Aljubarrota was the foundation of Portuguese independence and the beginning of the greatest period of the country's history. The house of Avis was destined to rule Portugal for two centuries and the threat of absorption by Castile did not reappear until after it had become extinct in 1579. On a virgin site close to the battlefield, which became known as Batalha, John of Avis founded the Dominican monastery of Santa Maria da Vitoria which his successors travailed to complete until well into the sixteenth century. Constructed by Portuguese, English and Flemish architects to plans derived in large measure from contemporary English buildings, this magnificent monument served to commemorate his victory and in due course to serve as his tomb. The battle sealed the Anglo-Portuguese alliance even before wax and ribbon could do so. It also transformed the balance of power among the southern allies of England and France and consolidated Portugal's position as a naval power capable of challenging Castile on Europe's Atlantic seaboard. For Castile Aljubarrota was a national catastrophe. John of Trastámara withdrew to the fortress of Carmona east of Seville rather than show his face in the city. His self-confidence, which had never been very great, was shattered by the defeat. The prestige of his dynasty and of the Castilian military nobility which had been its principal pillar took many years to recover. The cavalry arm of his army took years to rebuild and the Crown's finances were left in embarrassing disorder for a long time to come. For the rest of the decade France, which had so far been the main beneficiary of the alliance with Castile, was obliged to devote considerable resources to shoring up its southern ally while receiving very little in return.[10]

Shortly after the battle of Aljubarrota John of Avis wrote to the Duke of Lancaster with an account of the campaign and an appeal for help. The Portuguese King knew that for the moment he had disabled the Castilians but he was far from confident for the future. Castile was a richer and more populous country than Portugal. The Castilian nobility were burning to avenge their defeat. John urged the Duke of Lancaster to press his claim to the Castilian throne while its current occupant was in disarray and he had the assurance of Portuguese support. 'There will never be a better chance than now to realise your ambitions,' he told John of Gaunt. Yet when this letter reached England in the first few days of September 1385 the Duke was no longer certain what his ambitions were. The Portuguese ambassador in England, the indispensable Lourenço Fogaça, was present when John's letter was read out and reported that the Duke's first reaction was to make his excuses. Gaunt had given little thought to his Castilian ambitions for the past two years, he said. He had been heavily committed to the affairs of the Scottish border. The current problems of the English royal house required all his attention. He may also have reflected that his declining political influence in England made it hard to see how an English expeditionary army to Castile would be financed. According to the Portuguese sources from which this information comes it was only the pleading of his wife and daughter which caused Gaunt to change his mind. This may be true. But the evidence suggests that by this time Gaunt no longer expected to dethrone the Trastámaran dynasty. The battle of Aljubarrota had changed many things, but Gaunt's main purpose now was to sell his claims to his Castilian rival for the highest possible price, in cash and in diplomatic advantage. He resolved to bring his daughters Philippa and Catherine with him to Castile. They would prove to be valuable diplomatic bargaining counters. Over the following weeks Gaunt began to make detailed plans for a seaborne expedition to Castile in the spring of 1386.[11]

Parliament had been summoned to meet at Westminster on 20 October 1385. The meeting was one of the longest for many years and among the most ill-tempered. The proceedings were overshadowed from the outset by the continuing financial crisis of the Crown and the quarrels of the English political class, intensified by the humiliating outcome of the campaign in Scotland which many of those present had witnessed at first hand. Michael Pole, now Earl of Suffolk, expounded England's dilemmas in his opening speech, as he had done with eloquence and force on every such occasion for the past two years. Attacking France at home was the most effective way of defending England, he repeated, but it was too expensive. Pole was right but being right won him no friends. His address was followed by a concerted attack on the government by a coalition of those who wanted to reduce the burden of taxation and others whose main ambition was to prosecute the war on a more ambitious scale and return to the glorious days of Edward III. The ultimate objectives of these two groups were entirely incompatible but they found a common target in the King's financial administration and in the closed group of courtiers around him, who were believed to be diverting public funds into their own pockets. It was the programme of 1376, informed by all the old delusions. Attention was focussed on the peerage promotions and associated grants which the King had made on his entry into Scotland. Some of them were thought to be undeserved. All of them were thought to be extravagant. There was strong opposition to the promotions of

Neville, Burley, Pole and Robert de Vere. The first two were obliged to abandon their new dignities before Parliament even met. Pole's promotion was confirmed even if some people, according to the snobbish Thomas Walsingham, remembered that his father was a wool merchant and moneylender and thought him 'better suited to commerce than knighthood'. No one would have said that of Robert de Vere, Earl of Oxford. But his promotion to be Marquis of Dublin, coupled with a proposal to send him in state to Ireland at a cost of some £45,000, was confirmed only after weeks of wrangling.[12]

The attack broadened out in the course of November 1385 into a general assault on the government's management of its finances and on the propensity of the eighteen-year-old King to listen to his friends rather than his Council. A commission of three bishops and six lay peers was appointed to examine the government's accounts. The commission, presided over by that old enemy of royal government William of Wykeham, reported so fast that it is hard to believe that there was any serious investigation of the problem. The commissioners were very critical. They concluded that with honest and efficient administration the revenues of the customs, alien priories and royal demesne might be significantly increased. They thought that some heads of government expenditure were too high and ought to be reduced, notably the staff of the King's household, royal grants, naval operations and garrisons. The Commons embraced these proposals with open arms. They insisted on the appointment of four additional councillors, including Wykeham himself and the aged former Treasurer Thomas Brantingham, with a special commission to investigate the disappearance of the enormous sum of £120,000 which was believed to be unaccounted for in the Exchequer's records. They forced the King to agree to a complete stop on all royal grants from revenue for a year. If they had had their way they would have made him revoke existing grants. The Commons finally agreed to grant one and a half subsidies, worth about £55,000. By the standard of recent Parliamentary grants this was generous, but it came with stringent conditions. The financial reforms proposed by Wykeham's commission were to be put into effect. There were also elaborate provisions designed to ensure that the funds did not fall into the wrong hands. Three receivers of the subsidy were appointed and two supervisors to watch over them, all of whom were made answerable to Parliament. These men were charged to pay out nothing in satisfaction of past debts or services of any kind, nothing for any other purpose than the war.[13]

In the midst of these debates the realities of the war beyond England's shores forced itself on the men at Westminster. About a week after the opening of Parliament news arrived of a fresh crisis in Ghent. On 26 October 1385 there had been a major demonstration organised by the growing party within the town which was weary of the war and of the English alliance. The guilds who were behind the peace movement summoned their members to parade through the streets with banners of the Lion of Flanders, shouting their slogans and making for the Friday Market. Their leaders had by now obtained letters from the King of France and the Duke and Duchess of Burgundy reciting the very favourable terms which had been offered to them in Paris. They planned to read these out in public. The only obstacles to peace were the presence of Sir John Bourchier's English garrison, and the personal position of Francis Ackerman and Peter Van den Bossche. Their power-base in the town had been undermined by the discreditable retreat from Damme, but they still commanded a powerful and violent following. There is some evidence that Ackerman was willing to compromise. But Van den Bossche was not. He planned to occupy the market-place with his own supporters in advance of the public meeting. Bourchier and his English soldiers would be on hand to help. The peace party, however, outmanoeuvred him. They brought forward the time of their demonstration and occupied the ground first. There was an ugly moment when both sides stood at opposite ends of the market-place, each defended by phalanxes of armed men. But there was no mistaking the sentiment of the majority. More than four-fifths of those present moved into the lines of the peace party. Van den Bossche withdrew in fury with his men, leaving the English men-at-arms and archers to escape as best they could. The peace party swiftly took control of the government of the town. Three days later, on 29 October, they wrote to the French King proposing talks. A conference was arranged for December between the new leaders of the town and the councillors of the King of France and the Duke of Burgundy.[14]

For the moment the die-hards refused to give up. They appealed to the English government. Sir John Bourchier, fearing for his life in an increasingly hostile city, sent urgently to England for reinforcements. Their letters reached Westminster in the first week of November. The Council obtained Parliamentary authority to send 1,000 men to shore up their only remaining northern European ally. It was proposed to finance this force by borrowing. Sir Hugh Drayton and Sir Hugh Despenser, experienced soldiers who had both commanded companies in Flanders during the Bishop of Norwich's crusade, were ordered to sail from Sandwich as soon as their men could be assembled. They appear to have been planning to fight their way through to Ghent from Calais.[15]

It was in this difficult atmosphere that John of Gaunt rose to press the case for invading Castile. Gaunt had no doubt that he was entitled to his countrymen's support. He recited his many services to the English Crown. He expounded the claims of his wife to the succession of King Pedro. He pointed to the opportunity which the Portuguese victory at Aljubarrota offered for knocking Castile out of the war. He suggested, perhaps rather disingenuously, that he could draw the flower of Scottish chivalry and the lords of Albret and Armagnac to his banner, thereby contributing indirectly to the security of the Scottish and Gascon marches as well. It is perhaps surprising that he met with so little opposition given the degree of scepticism which previous projects of the kind had aroused among the Commons. The reasons must be a matter for speculation. In some quarters there was undoubtedly a strong desire to be rid of John of Gaunt, whose presence in England was an obstacle to the disparate political ambitions of a younger generation. But the decisive factors were probably less personal. There was a better strategic case to be made for the 'path of Portugal' in the aftermath of Aljubarrota than there had been when the idea had last been mooted in the winter of 1382–3. John of Trastámara's distractions in Portugal had in fact kept the Castilian galley fleet in southern waters since 1380, just as Gaunt had predicted that they would. The King of Portugal, moreover, was offering the English King the services of a comparable galley fleet of his own and had already given an earnest of performance by despatching six galleys to the Channel in the summer. There was no other method of striking at the enemy at affordable cost now that the English position in Flanders had all but collapsed.

John of Gaunt was the richest man in England after the King and could be expected to bear much of the financial burden himself. Hard bargaining drove the subsidy from public funds well below the £40,000 that John of Gaunt had asked for. The deal ultimately agreed between Richard and his uncle allowed the Duke 20,000 marks (£13,333) unconditionally out of the proceeds of the Parliamentary subsidy. Another 20,000 marks was lent to him on somewhat complex terms. If he made peace with his rival the treaty was to provide for the payment of 200,000 *doblas* (about £40,000) in compensation for the Castilian naval attacks on England. In that event the loan would be cancelled. But if the Duke became King of Castile or surrendered his claim on any other terms, the sum would be repayable within three years. The upshot was that the Commons received some assurance that wider English interests would be served by the campaign. Privately Richard II assured his uncle that none of these stipulations would be enforced. So, subject to some rather distant contingencies, Gaunt received a subsidy of £26,666. This must have been a modest proportion of the total cost of the expedition. The Duke's financial affairs in this period are particularly opaque but it is likely that most of the cost of the expedition was raised by borrowing against the revenues of his English estates.[16]

The last echoes of the 'path of Flanders' were heard in December 1385. On 7 December, as Parliament closed at Westminster and Drayton and Despenser set out with their men for the coast, more than 200 prominent citizens of Ghent arrived at Tournai to negotiate with the Duke of Burgundy and the councillors of the King of France. They made a grand entrance, mounted on expensive horses with a great suite of attendants, and declined to dismount when they came into the presence of the Duke. Evidently, as French observers noted with irritation, they had not come to grovel. Nor did they need to. On 18 December, after ten days of negotiation in the buildings of St. Martin's abbey, the representatives of Ghent agreed to submit. The terms, when they were announced, were generous. Ghent retained the charters and privileges granted to it by former Counts of Flanders. There were to be no proscriptions and no executions. Philip issued a general pardon to the inhabitants, however prominent their part in the events of the past six years. The blockade was lifted. Confiscated assets were restored. Exiles were to be allowed to return home. Prisoners would be released. In a gesture of great symbolic power the Duke declared that he would not even force the men of Ghent to do anything against their conscience, which was a veiled promise not to interfere with their allegiance to the Roman Pope. But in a larger sense the defeat of Ghent was plain for all to see. The war had been a disaster for the town. The peace, for all its formal concessions to their interests, did little to mitigate the disaster. The town lost the power which it had once held over the towns of eastern Flanders and the waterways of the Scheldt. The cloth-workers' guilds lost ground to the grain-shippers and victuallers, as the town's famous textiles industry moved into terminal decline. Ghent would never again be the political and economic force that had dominated Flanders for the past hundred years.[17]

Politically the immediate result of the peace was a complete severance of Ghent's political and commercial relations with England. The expedition of Drayton and Despenser was cancelled just as it was about to sail and their men diverted to reinforce the garrison of Berwick. In the Château de Gavre, Sir John Bourchier and his English company resigned themselves to the new reality. They had no intention of fighting a last-ditch battle against overwhelming odds. So they negotiated a safe-conduct with the representatives of the Duke of Burgundy and, gathering up the English King's standards, they left for Calais.[18] After three years of absolute power Peter Van den Bossche had made too many enemies in Ghent to sleep soundly in his bed once he had lost it. He fled with Bourchier and settled in England, where he lived on a pension from Richard II and continued to support the English cause against his fellow countrymen. He served with the English garrison of Guines in the summer of 1386 and with the English fleet in the following year. Occasional letters trying to stir up trouble in Ghent were intercepted by the Duke of Burgundy's agents. Peter's old ally Francis Ackerman, for years the main pillar of the English alliance in Ghent, stayed in Ghent but he would have done well to follow his colleague's example. In July 1386 he was assassinated by a relative of one of his old rivals.[19]

In the Castilian city of Valladolid another monarch was confronting the problems of high taxation, military failure and public resentment. The Cortes met in about the middle of November 1385 in the church of Santa María la Mayor, which was then the cathedral. John of Trastámara appeared before his subjects dressed in black mourning robes. He delivered a remarkable oration in which he lamented the sins of the Castilians and his own failure to govern them as he should have done. He had lost many of his finest soldiers. He had brought dishonour and ruin to his realm, 'the pain and shame of which we feel in our heart'. He ordained penitential processions in Castilian cities and declared that for his part he would wear his mourning robes until God had signalled his forgiveness by granting him victory over his enemies. The Cortes approved some radical reforms. They forced the King to delegate many of his prerogatives to a council of twelve, drawn from the three estates of Castile, ostensibly so that he could concentrate his failing energy on the conduct of the war. They introduced a tough scheme of conscription which made every man liable to be called up for military service from his twentieth birthday to his sixtieth and provided for regular inspections to ensure that they were properly trained, mounted and equipped.

Taxation proved to be the most contentious issue. John of Trastámara already knew that his Portuguese rival had sent ambassadors to England to press for a joint invasion of Castile. He acknowledged that the heavy taxes which he had levied to date were profoundly unpopular and that they were economically damaging. But he could see no prospect of relief while the war continued. Indeed in the present crisis it would be necessary to increase them. The Cortes agreed to increase the rate of the *alcabala* (or sales tax) to twenty per cent, double the current level, and to authorise a forced loan of up to ten million *maravedis* (about £44,000). But as in France sales taxes were profoundly unpopular in the streets. This one provoked such uproar in Castile's towns that the representatives went back on their decision almost as soon as they had made it. Instead of higher indirect taxes on commodities, they offered a tax on moveable property, which was less burdensome to the poor but proved to be administratively unworkable. Within two months the King had been forced to return to a variant of the original plan but even at the slightly reduced rate of 16.6 per cent the new sales tax proved impossible to collect. Merchants closed their shops. Fairs were deserted. Out of sight of the collectors the black market flourished. John had reached the limits of his subjects' taxable capacity as Charles VI and Richard II had before him. In December 1385, shortly after the Cortes of Valladolid closed, a Castilian embassy left Valladolid for France to plead for the urgent despatch of a French expeditionary army to the peninsula. John could not afford to pay these men as the existing treaties with France required. For the first time, he was obliged to plead with his French allies for financial as well as military support.[20]

At about the time that John of Trastámara's ambassadors were receiving their instructions Philip of Burgundy made contact with the English court through an unusual intermediary. Leo VI of Lusignan was one of the figureheads of the revived crusading movement of the late fourteenth century. He was the titular King of Armenia, a prince of French ancestry who had lost his kingdom to the Mamluk Sultans of Egypt in 1375 and passed several years in a Cairo prison before being released and settling in Paris. His life's ambition was to recover his realm at the head of a western army. In the short time that he had been in France he had won a good deal of support for this project, especially from the young King and from the Duke of Burgundy. One of the many impediments in the way was the continuing war with England. So Leo made it his mission to reconcile the two countries. In spite of his poor French and non-existent Latin, Leo had some advantages as a mediator.

He was a 'wise and crafty man', according to a contemporary English source. He was also charming, exotic and genuinely neutral. Leo appeared at Richard II's court at Eltham in the midst of the Christmas festivities to announce his mission to the King. He made a strong impression on Richard, whose own aversion to the war was growing year by year. Leo also worked assiduously on the chief advocates of the war in England. He passed the feast of the Epiphany with the Duke of Gloucester at his fine new manor at Pleshey in Essex. He was with the court at Westminster when the King's Council was persuaded to authorise talks with the representatives of the King of France after eighteen months in which there had been virtually no diplomatic contact between the two countries. Leo's proposals have not survived but they were attractive enough for Richard to start making arrangements to cross the Channel and meet the King of France as soon as agreement had been reached.[21]

The conference opened on 1 March 1386 in the familiar surroundings of Leulinghem church. The English side was led by Michael Pole. He was supported by Walter Skirlaw, the Keeper of the Privy Seal and veteran of many previous conferences. The French were represented by another experienced diplomat, Nicholas de Bosc, Bishop of Bayeux, assisted by a formidable team of officials which included the Chancellor of France and the First President of the Parlement. Their main objective was made very clear by their instructions. They were to avoid agreeing a permanent peace. Instead they were to press for a long-term truce of at least six years and preferably more, which would bring an end to the war while avoiding the need to buy out English claims with expensive territorial concessions. The English ministers, in spite of their misgivings about the truce, were sufficiently disillusioned with the war to go along with this. The rock on which it all foundered was Castile. The French would not commit themselves to any proposals for a long-term truce unless John of Gaunt's expedition was cancelled. They thought that the English could be persuaded to agree to this. They could not believe that Richard's ministers would allow the conference to fail on such an issue. Indeed Charles VI and his court were already making their way north in preparation for the arrival of the King of England to seal the agreement.[22]

They under-estimated John of Gaunt's determination. He was intent on pressing on with his invasion of Castile and Richard II was not prepared to force on him the loss of face involved in backing down. Urban VI's crusade against the Spanish adherents of Avignon had been proclaimed in St. Paul's churchyard in London on 18 February 1386. Gaunt himself had been recruiting men-at-arms for at least two months. The Admirals' officers were passing from port to port through southern England requisitioning ships for his passage from Plymouth. An English agent, Sir John Parr, was with John of Avis at the prolonged siege of Chaves in northern Portugal, negotiating the loan of transports and warships from Portugal. On 5 and 6 March 1386 there were two days of jousting at Smithfield to honour the leaders of the expedition. Shortly after the celebrations closed Richard II in full Council formally declared his uncle to be King of Castile 'so far as it lay with him to do so', and gave him precedence as a fellow monarch at the banquet which followed. In London, a Great Council gathered on 15 March to consider the English response to the French negotiating position at Leulinghem. Forced to choose between an admittedly unsatisfactory truce and the Castilian campaign the magnates opted for the latter, with what misgivings we cannot know. On 19 March, as Charles VI's cortege approached Boulogne, the peace conference broke up. The English were given until Easter (22 April) to say whether they were prepared to return for another session in the summer, when the Scots and the Castilians could be present. But the die was already cast. By the time that Pole and Skirlaw returned to Westminster at the end of March the Duke of Lancaster was already on the road to Plymouth. The embarkation of his army for Castile was due to begin on 15 April 1386.[23]

At Westminster Richard's councillors sat down with the ambassadors of John of Avis to conclude the long-delayed alliance of England and Portugal. The terms were agreed by the beginning of May. They were read out before the King in the Chapter House of St. George's Chapel, Windsor, and again a week later before a great concourse of noblemen and officials in the Star Chamber of the palace of Westminster. The treaty was couched in very general terms, with mutual promises of military assistance against enemies within and without. It said very little about the parties' immediate plans. The real point of the deal was apparent from the separate declaration which the Portuguese ambassadors executed a few days later, in which they undertook that in return for English participation in the invasion of Castile the King of Portugal would send ten war galleys of 180 oars, each with a full complement of officers and crew and thirty crossbowmen, to serve at his expense under the English Admirals' command. The galleys were already being made ready in Portugal. Their first task would be to escort John of Gaunt's fleet of transports across the Bay of Biscay to Castile.[24]

The French King held his own Great Council in Paris on about 24 April 1386. The Dukes of Berry, Burgundy and Bourbon were all present, together with the principal officers of the Crown and a crowd of captains and officials. They confirmed the decision made in the previous autumn to make another attempt to invade England with a view, according to the King's proclamation, to putting an end to the war once and for all. The King proposed to sail with them, accompanied by all three of his uncles. The enterprise was conceived on an even more magnificent scale than the abortive expedition of 1385, which had itself provoked the wonder of contemporaries. This time there would be no question of passing through Scotland. The plan was to embark the army at Sluys and sail for eastern England, probably between the Thames estuary and the Wash. An army of between 6,000 and 8,000 men-at-arms and about 3,000 bowmen seems to have been envisaged. This marked a substantial increase on the invasion force planned for the previous year. It was made possible by keeping much smaller forces in Flanders and western France and stripping men from the march of Gascony. A good deal of thought had been devoted to the problems of landing on a hostile coast, an exceptionally dangerous operation which no French army had attempted since Louis IX's landings in Egypt more than a century before. The landings were likely to take several days, during which the first contingents to reach the shore would be vulnerable to the inevitable counter-attack. To meet this difficulty it was proposed to construct an immense wooden fort which could be carried across the North Sea in prefabricated sections and erected within three hours of a landing. These field-works, which were manufactured in Normandy over the summer months, were designed to be large enough to protect the landing site, with twenty-foot-high walls and thirty-foot towers. The whole project called for heavy and sustained expenditure over the remainder of the year. The announcement of the government's plans was accompanied by orders to impose a fresh *taille* in every province of France at a rate twenty-five per cent higher than that of the previous year. Taking account of the ordinary receipts from the *aides* and a smaller supplemental *taille* imposed in July, the French Treasury must have raised approximately three million *livres* (about £600,000) from taxation in 1386.[25]

Having committed themselves to all of this the French King's Council turned to the problems of John of Trastámara. His ambassadors had been in the French capital since about February. They were waiting for a response to their appeals. Charles VI's councillors found it hard to believe that John of Gaunt would persist with his expedition to Castile once it became clear that England itself was threatened with invasion but they could not risk leaving Castile exposed. Olivier du Guesclin, the late Constable's brother, and Pierre de Villaines, the French Count of Ribadeo, were authorised to raise 1,000 men-at-arms and to leave urgently for the peninsula. Both men were experienced captains who had already served for long periods in Castile. The first contingents sailed to Santander from La Rochelle early in May. The French government promised that if necessary another 2,000 men-at-arms would follow under the Duke of Bourbon as soon as they could be spared. They undertook to pay the first 100,000 francs of their wages by way of loan to the King of Castile. But they made it perfectly clear that the invasion of England had first claim on France's resources. Indeed Bourbon himself was among its designated leaders. This meant that the extra troops were unlikely to reach Castile until well into the following year. In the meantime John of Trastámara's ambassadors were pressed with the advice which French strategists had so often given to Castilian commanders: if the English landed they must learn from the French disasters of the previous generation and at all costs avoid giving battle.[26]

Decision-making was hampered on both sides of the Channel by lack of accurate and up-to-date intelligence. The most valuable sources of information available to the English Council were ships sent to cruise off the French coast and report on the movements of transports. They, however, could not detect the early stages of the enemy's preparations or their detailed plans. The English were beginning to make more extensive use of spies, of whom better things were expected. Their efforts were organised from Calais and Middelburg and concentrated in the Low Countries, where a large population of seamen and merchants with fluid loyalties and good international contacts were willing to serve any master who would pay them. Hennequin du Bos was in some ways a characteristic member of this fickle underworld. He was the bastard son of Jean de Jauche, lord of Gommegnies, the Hainaulter who had commanded the English fortress at Ardres on the march of Calais for many years. He had been brought up in France, joined the expedition of Jean de Vienne to Scotland in 1385 and then changed sides after being captured at Carlisle. Hennequin was sent into France via Middelburg in about March 1386 and seems to have successfully infiltrated the households of the Count of Saint-Pol and Jean de Sempy, the French governor of western Flanders, both of whom were closely involved in the preparations for the invasion. But he was caught reconnoitring around Montreuil not long after the start of his mission and after three successful escapes was finally executed in Paris in 1390. The confession extracted from him in the cells of the Châtelet is a mine of information about other English spies. At the height of their activity, in 1386 and 1387, they were operating across much of northern and western France. They picked up their information by taking menial jobs in the households of prominent French noblemen and by wandering about the recruiting and mustering areas disguised as horse-dealers, cloth-merchants, monks, hermits, soldiers of fortune or itinerant tradesmen. Their reports were passed by word of mouth to the English captain of Calais, who sifted the information and passed it on to Richard II's ministers at Westminster.[27]

For all the high hopes invested in them their reports were not worth much judging by the confused changes of plan on both sides of the Channel. Richard II's councillors began to receive casual reports of French naval activity in March. They concluded that an invasion of England was imminent more than a month before any firm decision had even been made in France. Commissions of array were issued for all the counties of England as early as 15 March. When eventually the French royal Council did resolve upon an invasion they planned to embark their army at Sluys. But the belief at Westminster was that the French intended to concentrate their strength in Picardy. Their concern was therefore focussed on the Channel, Calais and the Kent coast while the real target area in East Anglia was left exposed. Large sums of money were expended on revictualling Calais, carrying out emergency work on its defences and sending reinforcements across the Channel to defend the town against an attack that was never part of French plans. The famous jewelled shrine of St. Thomas Becket was moved from Canterbury cathedral to Dover castle. During the first half of May and again in late June the inhabitants of the coastal districts of Kent were ordered to abandon their homes and take refuge in Dover, Rye and Sandwich, taking with them all the foodstuffs they could carry.[28]

English maritime strategy was a picture of confusion. The major naval enterprise of the summer was to be the carriage of John of Gaunt's army to Castile. His fleet of transports, escorted by both Admirals, was expected to sail from Plymouth in late April and to return in June. This operation was likely to denude England of all its larger ships. Major naval operations in home waters were not expected to begin until July, when the Admirals planned to have thirty sailing ships and twenty-four oared barges fitted out for cruising off the French coast, supported by a supply train of victualling ships. In the event the sailing of Gaunt's fleet was delayed and the rest of the Council's plans had to be remade when firm intelligence began to come in about the French government's invasion plans. The Admirals were diverted to commerce raiding. They put to sea at the end of May with some two dozen fortified sailing cogs and ranged along the coast of Flanders from Calais to Sluys until early August. They attacked merchant ships which were thought to belong to French or Castilian owners. They boarded neutral vessels to see whether they were carrying French or Castilian cargoes 'as the law of the sea ordains and as the King's Admirals and lieges have been accustomed to do from time immemorial'. The cruise produced a considerable amount of plunder but almost as much neutral and allied property was taken, for which the English government was later obliged to pay compensation. While they were engaged in these operations the ports of England were cleared out to create a new and larger fleet to defend the country against the threatened invasion. The new fleet was to be assembled in the Thames, where it would be in a position to defend the capital and move either north to East Anglia or south to the Downs when the direction of the French attack became clearer.[29]

The French and Castilian governments were no better informed than the English. Philip of Burgundy had at least one Flemish agent operating in England in the summer of 1386. An elaborate ring of spies was operated from Mechelen in Brabant by a person who is known only by his code-name: the 'beardless man' ('*l'homme sans barbe*'). This shadowy figure, whose activities can be traced from 1384 to 1394, appears to have derived most of his information from the tavern drinkers of Calais, Flemish exiles in England and the talkative English community in the port of Middelburg. The results were not impressive. Writing to the *bailli* of Bruges in April, Philip of Burgundy confessed that he knew little or nothing about the scale or timing of John of Gaunt's expedition and pressed him to find out more. In Castile John of Trastámara sent a squadron of six galleys from Seville to cruise in the Channel, watching for signs of activity.[30]

For some time the prevailing view among Charles VI's councillors was that the signs of continuing activity around Plymouth were an elaborate feint, designed to mask a projected invasion of France. Until they could be sure of Gaunt's destination they were reluctant to denude their home fronts by concentrating all their forces at the northern tip of Flanders. They kept an anxious watch on the three English coastal fortresses in western France. There was a brief panic at the end of May when a new English captain arrived at Cherbourg and the garrison was changed round. French troops were mustered across Normandy to contain an imaginary English descent on the Cotentin. Rather similar fears probably lay behind John de Montfort's decision, at about the same time, to blockade the harbour and fortress of Brest. Large-scale siege operations were begun against the fortress on about 20 June 1386. A ring of ships with fortified superstructures was chained together and anchored across the entrance to the harbour. On land a great stone bastion with ten-foot-thick walls and seven turrets was built outside the main gateway of the fortress in the space of three weeks by an immense workforce of masons and labourers, guarded by several thousand soldiers. A fortnight later, at the beginning of July, attention shifted to western Flanders, with troops being mustered to defend the coast around Gravelines against an English descent. The mere presence of the Duke of Lancaster's fleet in Plymouth thus proved to be a more effective protection for England than all the activities of Richard II's Admirals. It not only slowed the pace of French preparations but may have delayed the invasion by as much as two months.[31]

On 9 July 1386 the Duke of Lancaster finally sailed out of Plymouth Sound. His fleet consisted of 104 ships: 75 of the largest English merchantmen afloat; 11 barges chartered for the Duke's service in Germany and the Low Countries, which were probably used to carry the horses; 12 immense Portuguese carracks, including 2 monsters of 600 tons burden; and an escort of 6 Portuguese war galleys. Crammed into these vessels were about 2,000 men-at-arms according to the most reliable contemporary estimate and probably about the same number of archers. With the usual varlets and pages the whole force must have been about 5,000 strong. In addition the Duke had brought with him a mass of attendants who would be needed if he was to cut the figure of a King in Castile: clerks, servants and ministers, minstrels and trumpeters, heralds, painters and tailors, falcons and hunting dogs, as well as the household staffs of his wife and daughters. The Castilian squadron lying off the coast, which had observed the embarkation of the troops, scuttled south to warn John of Trastámara of the coming armada. As for the French, they appear to have known nothing about the Duke's departure until his fleet appeared without warning off Brest on about 12 July. Their worst fears seemed to be confirmed when the army began to disembark, probably in the harbour of Saint-Mathieu, west of the town. Saint-Mathieu was a traditional landfall where English ships crossing the Bay of Biscay would wait for a favourable wind. But Gaunt may well have hoped to confuse both his French and his Castilian adversaries by attacking the French siege works outside the town. Leaving their horses on the ships the army surrounded John de Montfort's new bastion and brought down a section of the walls with mines. They launched a bloody assault against the breach, supported by Portuguese troops from the galleys. Both sides suffered heavy casualties before the French finally sued for terms, agreeing to pay an indemnity of 20,000 francs, demolish John de Montfort's siege works and withdraw. The English remained ashore for just three days. On about 16 July they re-embarked and sailed south.[32]

The arrival of the Anglo-Portuguese fleet at Brest and its subsequent departure for Castile lifted the fog which had concealed each side's preparations from the other. It provided the French King's ministers with their first certain intelligence that John of Gaunt's armada was not directed against France. Within a week the pace of French preparations for the invasion noticeably accelerated. In about the third week of July 1386 the French royal Council directed Jean de Vienne to proceed with all possible speed with the requisitioning of the huge fleet of transports which would be required. The great stocks of victuals and equipment which had been accumulated in the river ports of western France since early June were shipped onto barges to be carried to Sluys. A supplementary *taille* was decreed, the fourth in two years. The *arrière-ban* was proclaimed throughout France. The noise was soon picked up by the English, who now acquired for the first time a clear picture of the French government's intentions. Sluys was quickly identified from ship movements as the embarkation port. The reinforcements sent to defend the march of Calais were urgently recalled to England. On about 28 July men-at-arms across England were ordered to hold themselves ready to concentrate against the French invasion force as soon as the signal was given.[33]

On about 8 August 1386 Richard II presided over another Great Council, this time in the abbey church of Osney at Oxford. The proceedings were overshadowed by the latest news from France and by the alarming deterioration of the government's finances. John of Gaunt's expedition had consumed nearly £34,000 out of the government's coffers, including some £6,300 spent on shipping. This was equivalent to the whole of the receipts from the Parliamentary subsidy. The Scottish march, Calais and coastal defence had all taken their toll on the government's resources. Requisitioning had brought England's export trade to a halt with serious consequences for customs revenues. The government was subsisting on short-term loans at high rates of interest, mainly from Italian bankers in London. To save money the masters of the ships gathered in the Thames against a French invasion had been allowed to lay off most of their crews in the hope that the press gangs would find them again when they were needed. The caretaker crews left on board were no longer being paid. The government's stock was at its lowest point for many years. Malicious reports circulated about Richard's idleness and cowardice and the corruption and peculation of his ministers. They found a ready audience among those who had no idea of the financial straitjacket in which Richard's government was confined. Stung by these accusations, the King put before the magnates at Oxford an aggressive scheme for pre-empting the French invasion force by attacking its transports at Sluys before they sailed. The King proposed to take command of this expedition in person. The assembly reacted coolly. They pointed out that there was no money to pay for it and that only Parliament could authorise further taxation. Undeterred, Richard summoned a new Parliament to meet at the beginning of October. In the meantime he pressed on with his preparations, sending sergeants and clerks along the east coast to requisition more merchantmen and impress crewmen to man the ships lying immobilised in the Thames. Agents were sent to Holland and Germany to hire ships and barges to increase their numbers.[34]

At the beginning of September 1386 the mustering of companies for the army of invasion began at provincial centres throughout France and beyond its borders in Savoy, Lorraine and the francophone provinces of the Empire. Shortly the men began to converge on Arras. Intense expectations had built up around the enterprise, encouraged by an organised campaign of public prayers and processions and official propaganda which portrayed it as the chance to crush the enemy and force a permanent peace on France's terms. The response took even the French King's ministers by surprise. Charles VI left Paris on 7 September 1386. By the time he entered Arras on about the 19th there were already nearly 9,000 men-at-arms encamped around the town. Writing to his financial officials in Paris two days later the King observed that this was more than his councillors had planned for and that fresh companies were still arriving daily. The war treasurers' accounts show that over the following weeks the number of men-at-arms on their payroll rose to nearly 15,000 in addition to those detached for garrison duty in Flanders and Artois. There was also a large force of about 1,100 bowmen on the war treasurers' payroll and about 2,500 bowmen and

500 men-at-arms contributed by the northern towns. It was the biggest external threat to England in its history until the Spanish Armada of 1588. With pages and hangers-on included the total force may well have matched the 28,500 men reported by a well-informed Flemish chronicler. Yet the numbers proved to be the undoing of the enterprise. They imposed an immense strain on the French military organisation and particularly on its shipping and supplies. The tonnage required to carry the great mass of men, animals and material across the North Sea to England exceeded the entire merchant marine of France and Flanders. It had been necessary to send commissioners to charter ships from Castile, Genoa, Venice, Scotland, Germany and the Low Countries. About 1,000 transports had been assembled in the anchorages of Sluys by the end of September 1386. The muster dates and the movements of the King suggest that the original plan was to embark the army at Sluys by the end of September before the autumn gales. The army originally planned might have made it by then. But not the huge host which ultimately gathered round the King in Flanders. The sailing date had to be put back by a month to the end of October, while efforts were made to find more ships and expand the supply train.[35]

The English government was by now receiving regular reports on the build-up. Ships were regularly sent out from London and Middelburg to reconnoitre the Flanders coast. More information was coming in from the captain of Calais. Their reports caused mounting alarm at Westminster. From time to time fragments of firmer intelligence reached them. By early September 1386 the Council had either discovered or worked out for themselves that the French planned to land on the Suffolk coast near Orwell, a region of broad open shingle beaches just sixty miles from London. Shortly after this they learned about the great prefabricated fort which the French planned to erect on the shore, when English ships operating from Calais captured four ships carrying sections of this vast structure and brought them into Sandwich. A stream of orders issued from Westminster in the course of the month. The county levies were arrayed once more, traditionally every able-bodied man aged from sixteen to sixty who was capable of bearing arms. In East Anglia beach defences were constructed along the coast and timber forts at river crossings. Harbour entrances were blocked and fortified. Garrisons were placed in the Solent and on the Yorkshire coast in case the enemy attempted diversions against these places.[36]

The Council met at Westminster in the presence of the King on 10 September 1386 to review their plans. Richard still clung to his scheme for taking the fight to the enemy by landing an army in Flanders but it is clear that his Council had written off the chances of this enterprise. They were already assuming that the French could not be prevented from landing. They proposed to confront them after the landings with an army of about 10,000 men concentrated north of London. The levies of the inland and western counties and the companies of the professional captains were ordered to have their men in the capital by 29 September. Meanwhile the Londoners prepared themselves for a siege. Terrified citizens formed demolition crews to pull down the buildings which had accumulated around the walls and ditches over the decades of domestic peace. Men who were away from home were summoned back. Householders were ordered to lay in three months' food. Abbot Litlington of Westminster and two of his monks put on their armour and joined the defence although Litlington was in his late seventies.[37]

The 'Wonderful' Parliament, as it later became known, opened at Westminster on 1 October 1386. Michael Pole, Earl of Suffolk, rose for the last time in his career to address the assembled Lords and Commons. The government's position could not have been worse. The Treasury was almost empty. Appeals for loans had been made to towns, merchants and prominent ecclesiastics across the country, but even in the current crisis they had fallen on deaf ears. Less than £800 had been raised and all of that came from just four bishops. There were nearly 150 ships waiting for orders in the Thames, most of them fully crewed. Some forty per cent of them were chartered foreign ships. They needed to be paid. Between 7,000 and 10,000 soldiers had arrived over the past few days in response to the King's summons. Most of them had not been paid by their counties before setting out. They arrived in London to find that the King could not pay them either. Fearing that they would riot in the streets the marshals sent them to bide their time in camps at some distance from the capital. Many of them deserted. The rest kept themselves by selling off their equipment, looting villages and terrorising the roads. Pole told Parliament that the King needed no less than four lay subsidies and four tenths from the clergy in order to pay his debts, carry out his pre-emptive landing on the enemy's coast and defend the realm against invasion. This represented about £220,000. It was more than the Commons had ever been asked to grant in a single year and more than twice the value of the ill-famed poll tax of 1381.[38]

Pole's demands may have been a negotiating tactic, the prelude to a gracious compromise. If so his plan went badly wrong. There was uproar in the Commons. They were shocked by the evidence of the government's financial incontinence and confirmed in the prejudice already embedded in their minds that the crisis was due to ministers lining their pockets. Pole had struggled to find economies in the war budget, but border garrisons were the only area where there was any fat to be lost. The truce with Scotland had enabled the garrisons of the northern march to be halved. Expenditure of English revenues on Gascony, which had been running at about £5,000 a year, was stopped completely. The contract for the defence of Cherbourg was let at a much reduced fee and the system of fixed-price contracts was extended to Brest. But economies were impossible at Calais, which now faced a persistent threat from Burgundian Flanders. The cost of its garrison, currently about £25,000 a year, continued to rise inexorably to a peak of over £30,000 in the following years.[39] Nothing had been done to give effect to William of Wykeham's reforms of the royal household and administration, which the Commons had expected to produce the largest savings. Richard had blocked these. Moreover, he had paid no attention to the warnings uttered in the last Parliament about his tendency to take advice from a small group of intimates whom the nobility distrusted. As a result the main targets of the government's enemies were Robert de Vere and Michael Pole himself. Of the two men De Vere was the more profoundly hated for his rudeness and arrogance, his ambition and greed, his tendency to trample on the local interests of the nobility and above all his intimacy with the King. But it was on Pole that the blow fell. Pole was perhaps the outstanding royal servant of the reign but he was vulnerable. He was the government's titular head and spokesman. He was a parvenu. He was personally unpopular. In some quarters he was even thought to be in league with the French. A brief conference between the two houses followed Pole's opening address. They then called 'with one assent' for his dismissal and declared their intention of impeaching him.[40]

At such a moment the King would have benefited by the presence of John of Gaunt, whose loyalty and natural authority had enabled Richard to survive earlier crises. In Gaunt's absence the dominant voice among the nobility was that of his brother Thomas of Woodstock, Duke of Gloucester. He was supported by Richard Fitzalan, Earl of Arundel, and Thomas Beauchamp, Earl of Warwick. Arundel had become a brutal power politician, his character warped by defeat, inaction and frustrated ambition. Warwick, on the other hand, was a surprising man to find at the head of the opposition. His life had been devoted mainly to estate management and to building. He had little interest in the daily grind of government. But, like Gloucester and Arundel, he was an intemperate and embittered man. All three of them loathed the people about the King. They were disgusted by England's declining military fortunes, whose causes they did not begin to understand. Ultimately military defeat would discredit them as well, but for the moment they had the support of most of the Parliamentary peerage. The King made the position worse by withdrawing from Westminster after the opening sessions of Parliament and declining to participate in the debates. From Eltham he issued a defiant declaration that Parliament should mind its own business and get on with the task of granting a subsidy. As for the attack on his ministers, he 'would not dismiss the meanest kitchen boy at their behest'. To emphasise the point he announced his intention to promote De Vere to be Duke of Ireland, the first duke ever to be made from outside the royal family. Rumours began to circulate that Richard was planning to dissolve Parliament or even to have the leaders of the opposition murdered.[41]

The French army had by now been encamped around Lille since the beginning of October. On 18 October Charles VI marched north with his whole host towards Sluys. At about the same time Richard II's ministers at Westminster received accurate intelligence about the embarkation date, currently fixed for the end of the month. This meant that the invasion force could be expected to reach England at the beginning of November. In the encampments north of London the army which had been assembled to defend the realm was disintegrating. The county levies, their ranks already reduced by desertion and mutiny, were sent home for want of money to pay them and told to come back when summoned. The fate of England was in the hands of a thin crust of locally recruited coast-guards along the east coast, the fleet in the Thames and some 5,000 retained troops still waiting outside London.[42]

There were voices of moderation in Parliament urging that this was no time for a confrontation with the King but their protests were lost in the noise of politics. The Lords were determined to press the issue to a conclusion. They carried with them the knights of the shires who traditionally dominated the political debate in the Commons. They appointed as their spokesmen the Duke of Gloucester and the Earl of Arundel's brother, Thomas Arundel, Bishop of Ely, an emotional and volatile clerical politician, then thirty-three years old. The two men had an ill-tempered audience with the teenage King at the royal manor of

Eltham. They told him that, unless he returned to Westminster, Parliament would decline to proceed with any business and its members would disperse to their homes without voting a subsidy. According to a report of the proceedings which circulated shortly afterwards, the King replied that he had always realised that there was rebellion afoot and for his part would rather submit to Charles VI of France than to his own disloyal subjects. This account may well be tinged by propaganda. But Richard was a mercurial personality who was capable of acts of great folly, and the public was in a mood to believe him capable of anything. Gloucester and Arundel responded with an officious lecture about England's past glories. 'Just think', they said, 'how your grand-father, King Edward III, and your father, Prince Edward, sweated and laboured all their lives in heat and cold to conquer France which was theirs by right and is now yours.' They reminded him that generations of Englishmen had braved danger and death in the cause and had spent all their treasure to sustain it. They complained of the impoverishment of the country by heavy and persistent taxation, which destroyed the revenues of the nobility on whom the King depended to fight his wars. 'And all of this has come about through the King's evil ministers, who have mismanaged the affairs of the kingdom and are still mismanaging them.' Richard, they said, should remember the fate of his great-grandfather, Edward II. There was an ancient law which authorised the English nation to depose a king who declined to be guided by the 'wholesome counsel of the lords and nobles of your kingdom' and to set up another in his place.

Richard never forgave them for this speech. But for the moment there was no alternative to submission. The King returned to Westminster. On 24 October 1386 Pole was dismissed and replaced as Chancellor by Thomas Arundel. The Keeper of the Privy Seal, Walter Skirlaw, and the Treasurer, John Fordham, Bishop of Durham, were removed at the same time. The Commons then proceeded to arraign Pole before the Lords on charges of obstructing William of Wykeham's reforms, neglecting the defence of the sea, diverting funds intended for the defence of Ghent and exploiting his office to fill his own coffers at the King's expense. Most of these charges were dismissed. Even Pole's enemies found it hard to blame him for collective decisions of the King's Council. But the charges of abusing his office for his own enrichment were difficult to deny. Pole was sentenced to be imprisoned and to forfeit all his gains. These proceedings occupied the whole of the last week of October.[43]

Charles VI entered Bruges on 21 October 1386 and established his headquarters in the castle of the counts of Flanders. The four-week delay in launching the invasion cost the French dearly. The weather had broken about a week before the King's arrival. The wind blew off the sea into the mouth of the harbour, making it impossible for the ships to get out of the channel to the open sea. Storms caused havoc in the crowded anchorages, driving ships down on each other and causing serious damage. Torrential rain had soaked stores. Food vanished from local markets and prices rose to astronomical levels. The perennial violence, indiscipline and theft associated with any large medieval army had begun to provoke intense hostility in Flanders. The citizens of Bruges guarded their streets with large armed patrols. They tried to shut their gates in the faces of the Dukes of Berry and Burgundy. When the Duke of Berry forced his way in they mobbed him so badly that he was forced to take to his bed for three weeks. Meanwhile the army spread itself out across the rain-sodden plain between Sluys and Damme, waiting for its orders. 'Today the King will come,' they said to each other each morning, 'tomorrow we will sail.'[44]

On 27 October 1386, the day fixed for the sailing of the fleet, the King finally came. The principal captains of the army held a council of war on the following morning. They decided that the final review of the troops would be held on 2 November before embarkation began. The armada would sail for England, weather permitting, on about 9 November. Privately the royal Council was uneasy enough to contemplate a confidential approach to the English government. Leo of Armenia was once again the messenger. He was authorised to cross to England via Calais with fresh diplomatic proposals. In public, however, none of this was allowed to show. All was confident bravado. Froissart, who was with the army at Sluys, reported the elation of the men when the sailing date was announced. The oldest man alive, he wrote, could not have imagined such a scene. Mingling with soldiers of every province and dialect in the crowded camps he reported that morale was high, fed by the accumulated resentments of decades. 'Smash these English swine . . .' they said, 'now is the time to avenge our fathers and mothers and our dead friends.' One of these men was the soldier-poet Eustache Deschamps. He had witnessed the devastation of Champagne in 1380 and the destruction of his family home by the soldiers of Thomas of Woodstock. Deschamps longed for the day when men would say, contemplating the heap of charred ruins which had once been the home of giants: 'long ago this place was called England.' By

8 November 1386, the day before the fleet was due to sail, the army had boarded the ships. The King conducted a review of the fleet from his flagship. The Florentine merchant Buonaccorso Pitti, who had pooled his funds with some compatriots in Paris and hired a ship to join the army as volunteers, counted 1,200 vessels lying in the harbour. There were about 600 cogs of every size for carrying soldiers. There were broad barges with stern ramps for the horses, equipment and stores. The King's flagship bore him past the dense lines of ships, their masts festooned with banners and streamers, their sides brightly painted with the arms and devices of the principal captains: a white hart and a golden crown for the King's ships, interlaced initials of Philip and his wife in three colours on those of the Duke and Duchess of Burgundy, the Duke of Bourbon's motto on his, *Bonne Esperance*. The soldiers and seamen crowded onto the decks, filling the air with the sound of braying horns and trumpets.[45]

The princes and the commanders of the army were not present to witness the scene. They were ashore, attending a tense meeting in the lodgings of the Duke of Berry. The Duke, perennially risk-averse, had for some time had cold feet about the whole enterprise. The fleet would not be able to sail on the next day unless the wind changed. So many men and animals could not be kept cooped up indefinitely in their ships. It was late in the year. The days were short and the nights dark and bitterly cold. The English coast was hazardous. The east coast harbours, most of which were river ports, were hard to reach in foul weather. Confused reports had reached Flanders about the quarrels of the English King with his Parliament but these were only dimly comprehended and no one imagined that the English would not be waiting for them by the coast. Charles VI's reputation, even his life, were at risk. In the evening the meeting broke up without a decision, to allow the shipmasters to be consulted. The most experienced seamen in the fleet deliberated daily over the next four days. On about 13 November they sent a delegation before the King's Council with their advice. Before the fleet could sail, they said, they needed clear skies, a full moon and a following wind. The present weather conditions could last for a long time. It was the season of the south-westerly equinoctial gales, which traditionally lasted until St. Catherine's Day (25 November). In the shipmasters' view the crossing should not be attempted for at least two weeks. Although the seamen did not say so, it was obvious that this meant calling off the expedition for the second time. It would be a humiliating anticlimax. Some of those present were for pressing on. They included the two principal military officers of the Crown, the Constable and the Admiral. Many of the captains of the army supported them. But they were overruled by the politicians.

It is fair to say that bolder men than Jean de Berry recognised that the invasion plan had become too dangerous. Even on the most optimistic assumptions they would not now reach England until December. The truth was that the French had overreached themselves. Their fleet was too large to be handled together at sea. The ships would either collide or lose each other in the long nights and autumn fogs. The army was too large to be properly managed, supplied and paid. It had taken a week to get the huge mass of men and beasts onto the ships. It would take another week to get them off again and a third to re-embark them when the wind changed. Bringing them ashore across the beaches of eastern England would be a time-consuming and dangerous operation. Most of the stores collected for the campaign had been consumed during the long wait. Replacing them would be hard in mid-winter, impossible in England. But the decisive factor was the financial situation, which was now extremely serious. The monthly wage bill greatly exceeded the amounts originally budgeted. Wages were substantially in arrears. The war treasurers had exhausted the proceeds of the *taille* and tapped the credit markets of Flanders for all they were worth. By November no one would lend money for more than a month at the outside. All of these problems were bound to get worse as the campaign continued. Even the vast resources of the French state were not equal to the task which its leaders had set themselves. So, on 16 November 1386, the heralds passed through the encampments with the announcement that the invasion was being deferred until further notice. The fleet was retained at Sluys, guarded by some 1,300 soldiers, until the outcome of the King of Armenia's embassy in England was known.[46]

The news, which reached England about a week later, was greeted there as a miracle. But the English had other things to hold their attention. On 19 November 1386, after nearly three weeks of argument, the English Parliamentary peerage and their allies in the Commons took power out of the hands of nineteen-year-old Richard II. They imposed on him a new 'continual council' which became known as the Commission of Government. It was in effect a council of regency which was to take control over Richard's administration, household and revenues for a period of a year. Ostensibly the object was to force through the reforms of the royal administration which the Commons had been demanding for a decade. In practice its mandate was much wider than that, extending to the whole conduct of government. The Commission's members were the three principal officers of state and eleven Parliamentary peers. But its proceedings were dominated from the outset by the King's enemies: the new Chancellor Thomas Arundel, Bishop of Ely; the King's uncle Thomas of Woodstock, Duke of Gloucester; the Earls of Arundel and Warwick; and old partisans of administrative reform like William of Wykeham. Their appointment was to be announced in every county town. Any resistance to their ordinances and any attempts to help the King escape its tutelage were declared to be punishable as treason. It was for all practical purposes a *coup d'état* by a group which had constituted the unofficial opposition for the past three years. Richard later claimed that Gloucester and Arundel had forced the measure through by intimidating the Commons and threatening him with death. This may have been true. Even at the time the King declared that he would recognise none of its proceedings so far as they trespassed on his prerogatives. His protest was ordered to be recorded on the Parliament Rolls but it was ignored by all but the clerk. Consistently with their belief that the war could be financed by savings on the cost of the royal administration and household, the Commons made a grant which can only be described as derisory: half of a tenth and fifteenth, reserved for the defence of the realm, with another half to be levied in a year's time if that proved inadequate. Taken with the clerical subsidy granted by convocation shortly afterwards, direct taxation would contribute just £26,000 in the financial year 1386/7, less than a twentieth of the tax revenues of the King of France over the past year.[47]

The mood of the new regime was signalled at once. The peace mission of the King of Armenia was announced at Westminster in the middle of the row between the King and the Lords. Leo had arrived at Calais while the French army was still boarding the ships at Sluys and had sent a message to England asking for a safe-conduct. Richard, who liked Leo, would have been glad to receive him and said so but the Parliamentary peers would have none of it. They dismissed him as a charlatan and had him sent away from Calais empty-handed. At the end of November 1386 the French royal Council assembled at Amiens in the presence of the leading captains of the army to receive Leo's report on the failure of his mission. They resolved to hold the fleet at Sluys and to make a third attempt against England when the weather cleared in the spring. The English, who were now receiving regular reports from their spies in Flanders, learned of this decision almost immediately. One of the first acts of the Commission of Government was to organise large-scale naval operations to disrupt the enemy's new invasion plans. On 10 December the Earl of Arundel, one of its most aggressive members, was made Admiral of England with jurisdiction over both admiralties, the first time that a single officer had been appointed to this function in wartime. He was retained to take a fleet to sea for three months in the spring with 2,500 troops on board. Requisitioning of shipping began throughout England before Christmas. The ships were to be in the Thames ready to sail against the enemy by February 1387.[48]

On 25 July 1386 John of Gaunt's armada had arrived off Corunna, a large and sheltered natural harbour on the Galician coast of Castile. Gaunt's exact destination had been a well-guarded secret and it was generally assumed that he would land in Portugal. The arrival of the English in Galicia therefore took everyone by surprise. Orders had been given for all supplies and foodstuffs in coastal areas to be removed into walled places but otherwise the defences were unprepared. The Duke disembarked and set up his standard in which the arms of Castile and León were quartered with those of England and France. The whole army was quickly put ashore with its horses and stores. The only troops in the area were the garrison of Corunna, which looked on impotently from the walls of the citadel at the western extremity of the bay. A short distance away, in the inlet of Betanzos, the six Castilian galleys which had been cruising off Plymouth were lying beached while their officers and soldiers celebrated the feast of St. James, forty miles away in Santiago de Compostela. The crews of the Portuguese warships seized them without difficulty, recovering in the process some English prisoners taken at sea and a large quantity of goods looted from English west country villages. Once the landings were complete John of Gaunt dismissed the English and Dutch ships, which were sent back to England. The Portuguese warships left for Lisbon a few days later.[49]

The selection of Galicia as Gaunt's point of entry into the kingdom had been a careful strategic choice. Separated from the rest of the kingdom by the inhospitable mountain chains of León, Cantabria and the Asturias, the province was remote from the political heartlands of the Castilian monarchy. Its dialect and historical traditions were in many ways closer to those of Portugal than Castile. The Trastámaran dynasty had never been wholly accepted there. Nearly two decades after Pedro's murder the dead King's cause still had partisans in the region.

Yet by 1386 the main source of disaffection was no longer emotional loyalty to the old dynasty, even in a legitimist region like Galicia. More significant was the intensive government and high taxation which had characterised the reigns of the first two Trastámaran kings, and the persistent inflation and devaluations which ate into the revenues of landowners and townsmen alike. John of Trastámara himself believed that the invasion had brought a crisis of loyalty to a head. Addressing the Cortes later in the year he complained that a vicious campaign of slander had been conducted against himself, his councillors and officials, and the leading magnates of the realm; false reports had been deliberately spread about to undermine his government; treasonable letters were passing from hand to hand through the country. These things are unlikely to have been imagined and were certainly not confined to Galicia. What was less clear was how far they would drive the Castilians to embrace the cause of the Duke of Lancaster.[50]

At about the beginning of August 1386 John of Gaunt marched inland to Santiago, leaving a curtain of troops to contain the garrison of Corunna. Santiago was the principal city of Galicia and the site of the shrine of St. James, the patron saint of Castile. It was ungarrisoned and virtually defenceless. The clergy and leading inhabitants received the invader in front of their gates and escorted him processionally to the tomb of the Apostle in the cathedral. Very shortly after this the English occupied the walled town of Orense, a much stronger place on the River Miño, close to the Portuguese border. It was here, towards the end of August, that the Duke established his court and a rudimentary administration. He organised his own chancery under the direction of his Castilian secretary, Juan Gutiérrez, which issued letters and charters laying out his titles in the traditional fashion. He had his own silver coins minted. He forced the cathedral chapter of Santiago to depose their Clementist bishop, who was also John of Trastámara's chancellor. He called on the nobility and towns of Castile to acknowledge him. Many Galicians did so. They came to Santiago and kissed his ringed finger. They offered their reverences and promises and their symbols of submission. Some took service at his court or in his army.[51] Others kept their heads down and tried to ensure that when the crisis had passed they would not be found to have supported the wrong side. Whatever their personal sympathies they were unwilling to acknowledge the Duke of Lancaster only to see him withdraw to England or Portugal and abandon them to the vengeance of his rival. When the men of Santiago opened their gates to the invader they were careful to qualify their submission. They would recognise him as King on condition that he could get himself acknowledged by the rest of Castile. This proved to be the pattern for the rest of Galicia.[52]

For the first few weeks the only serious resistance to the invaders came from the isolated garrison of Corunna. Its commander was a substantial local landowner called Fernán Perez de Andrade. He took a band of French volunteers into the citadel, who had been part of the advance guard sent to Castile with Olivier du Guesclin and happened to be among the mass of pilgrims at Santiago when the English landed. With their assistance, he conducted a spirited fight from the dilapidated walls of the town before eventually making a highly qualified submission to the invader. In early September Perez placed himself nominally under Gaunt's command but kept the gates of Corunna firmly closed against his army. He agreed to recognise Gaunt's claims but only on the equivocal conditions allowed to the men of Santiago, namely that he could establish his authority in the rest of the kingdom.

In September and October 1386 Sir Thomas Morieux, one of the marshals of the English army, conducted a cavalcade through Galicia accepting the surrender of the principal towns and castles. Most of them acknowledged Gaunt's authority on the same terms as Santiago and Corunna. They wanted a quiet life and the Duke did not press for more. He knew the limitations of armed force. He did not have the men to spare for garrison duties and could not afford the heavy casualties associated with assaulting walled towns. Submissions, however guarded, were politically more valuable than conquests. At the same time the ease with which Gaunt overcame much of Galicia was symptomatic of a wider strategic problem. The English army had been retained on six-month contracts. Most of them would expire at about the end of the year. There was no money to pay for further service. The Duke's plans had assumed that a decisive encounter would follow shortly after his landing, making a prolonged campaign unnecessary. The passivity of the Castilian defence disturbed that calculation, forcing him to defer the decisive battle until the following year and leaving him with serious problems of finance, discipline and morale.[53]

The Castilians' failure to challenge Gaunt in Galicia was not initially a deliberate strategy. It arose from their weakness and disarray. The heavy casualties suffered by the Castilian nobility in Portugal over the past two years had made skilled cavalrymen scarce. At the beginning of August 1386 John of Trastámara had some 3,000 men-at-arms at his disposal in addition to bowmen and other supporting troops. This was about half as much again as the army of John of Gaunt but it was substantially less than the combined strength of the English and the Portuguese. Their value was reduced by the fact that they were dispersed across western Castile, owing to the King's unshakeable conviction that the main attack would come through Portugal. Some were far away in the south, in garrisons between Seville and the Portuguese frontier. Others had been sent into Galicia in July but they appear to have been distributed too thinly to make much difference. The King himself was at Zamora on the Duero with a strategic reserve of about 1,000 men-at-arms, most of them belonging to the French companies who had recently arrived with Olivier du Guesclin. In addition to these forces some 1,500 Breton and Gascon mercenaries had been hired by Castilian agents in France and were reported to be making their way through Bas-Languedoc towards the Aragonese passes. It was far from clear how any of these forces would be paid. There had been a generalised tax strike across Castile since the beginning of the year. After the failure of the sales taxes voted by the Cortes the previous autumn the Castilian King tried to collect no fewer than four *monedas* on his own authority in the course of April. But his demands were widely resisted and in the event brought in very little. The King was reduced to begging the principal cities of his realm to send him whatever funds they would be willing to pay unless they wanted to see the English sweep unopposed across the land.[54]

John of Trastámara's situation would have been difficult enough even if his vacillating temperament had not led him to make frequent changes of plan. His first instinct was to negotiate. In August 1386 he sent four of his councillors to the Duke of Lancaster. Ostensibly their mission was to defend their master's cause against the claims of the invader, which they did with much ingenuity and at extreme length, but the real purpose of their visit was to suggest a deal. At a secret session of Gaunt's council at Orense they proposed a marriage between John of Trastámara's heir Henry and Catherine of Lancaster, who was King Pedro's grand-daughter. Their master, they said, would be willing to add in a large cash indemnity for the Duke himself. How seriously John of Gaunt took these offers at this stage is hard to say but he was sufficiently interested to send Sir Thomas Percy, one of the principal captains serving with his army, to discuss them with the Castilian King in person. The talks appear to have been broken off when John of Trastámara decided that he would have to consult the French but by this time they had already been overtaken by more aggressive projects on both sides. In about the middle of August the Castilian King resolved to confront the invaders in Galicia. He marched north from Zamora with his French troops, announcing his intention to go to the relief of Corunna. But, entering the city of León at about the end of the month, he was greeted with the news that Corunna had just surrendered and the English were heading east. John lost his nerve. The planned offensive in Galicia was abandoned. A few hundred men were left in León under the command of his Chancellor, Archbishop Manrique of Santiago. The King himself withdrew to Valladolid with Olivier du Guesclin and the rest of the army.[55]

Here, in the first week of September 1386, John of Trastámara held a nervous council of war with his ministers and principal captains. The main concerns of those present were the small size of the Castilian field army and the danger that, if they entered Galicia, the Portuguese would turn their flank by invading Castile through the valley of the Duero. These fears were heightened by their uncertainty about the Duke of Lancaster's intentions. He might try to penetrate east into the Duero basin; or disappear into Portugal to join forces with John of Avis; or even, as Olivier du Guesclin was inclined to think, re-embark for England to support the defence of the country against the army of invasion now gathering in Flanders. The consensus was that the Castilian King should stand on the defensive through the winter. The English would be held west of the mountains by guarding the passes. Garrisons would be built up opposite the northern sector of the Portuguese frontier. There would be time in the spring to recruit a fresh army to confront the invaders on their own ground. By then the Duke of Bourbon should have arrived with a further 2,000 French men-at-arms. This was probably the only realistic strategy and it would be wholly vindicated in the coming months. It was presumably the French knights present who pointed out that another army of John of Gaunt had been destroyed by very similar methods in France in the winter of 1373–4. But, as in France, the main problem was political. John of Trastámara addressed a long circular to the chief towns of his realm to explain a decision which he knew would offend all their instincts about how a king should respond to the invasion of his territory. John tried to reassure his subjects about Galicia. He told them that his garrisons there were inflicting serious damage on the enemy and that he intended to reinforce them so that they could carry on the fight over the winter. This was a half-truth at best. There is some evidence of Castilian military activity in eastern Galicia during the winter but substantially the whole territory west of the River Miño was being abandoned to the English until the following year.[56]

On 1 November 1386 John of Gaunt met the Portuguese King at Ponte do Mouro, a small village near Moncão on the south side of the River Miño, which marked the boundary between Portugal and Castile. John of Avis had erected in the meadows by the river bank the magnificent campaign tent of John of Trastámara which he had captured with the rest of the booty of the Castilian camp after the battle of Aljubarrota. Here, on 2 November, the two men sat down with their councillors and staffs to plan the joint invasion of Castile. John of Gaunt's objective was to invade the old kingdom of León, the rich grain-growing region lying east of Galicia which extended from the Asturias in the north to the basin of the Duero in the south. It was out of the question to get there by forcing the mountain passes. The two armies would have to turn the mountain barrier by attacking through Portugal. Ideally the campaign would begin early in the new year, before John of Trastámara's reinforcements arrived from France. John of Avis agreed to take the field in person with 5,000 men. He undertook to have them ready by 26 December, the earliest feasible date, and to keep them continuously in the field until the decisive battle with John of Trastámara, up to the end of August 1387 if necessary. If the Duke was prepared to take over the payment of their wages they would be held at his disposal for even longer. In return, once Lancaster had conquered Castile, he was to cede to the Portuguese King a band of Castilian territory about fifty miles wide running almost the whole length of Portugal's eastern march, including Ciudad Rodrigo, Cáceres, Merida, Badajoz and all the major frontier fortresses of Castile. The alliance was to be sealed by the marriage of John of Avis with Philippa of Lancaster, Gaunt's daughter by his first marriage. The wedding would take place as soon as possible, and in any event before the opening of the campaign. The summit meeting concluded with a great banquet at which the two leaders were waited on by the principal dignitaries of their entourage, and their whole following, several hundred strong, was seated according to their rank. The talk, says the chronicler, continued for long after the meal had ended.[57]

The Duke of Lancaster could not have done without Portuguese help but there is no doubt that his treaty with the victor of Aljubarrota gave John of Trastámara a propaganda advantage of which he made skilful use. The Cortes of Castile opened in the city of Segovia a few days after the meeting at Ponte do Mouro. The King delivered an angry oration to the assembled representatives. It was, he said, the duty of all men to defend 'this realm which God has given us and to which I and all of you belong'. The English were arrogant schismatics who had been enemies of the true Church for as long as they had been Christians, murderers ever since the death of Thomas Becket and fomentors of discord among nations from time immemorial. The Duke of Lancaster, who exemplified all the wickedness of his ancestors, was trying to seize the throne without a shadow of a right. If he got his way Castile would be subjected to a foreign government supported by traitors and friends of the tyrant Pedro. Its territory would be partitioned among the kings of Aragon and Navarre, the rebel regime in Portugal and the Muslim rulers of Granada. Its people would be murdered, kidnapped or raped by English soldiers or dishonoured and driven from their homes as the natives of Brittany and Gascony had been. The King ordained ferocious penalties against those caught speaking against the government. People entering or leaving Castilian towns were to be searched at the gates for letters and any which did not bear the royal seal would be opened and read for seditious matter. The main task of the Cortes, however, was to furnish the government with the resources needed to pay his native and foreign troops and to finance the great fleet of galleys, barges and sailing ships which he had planned for the following year. They responded with the largest grant of taxation ever authorised by a Castilian assembly. The *alcabala* was confirmed at the traditional rate of ten per cent. A *servicio* (or extraordinary tax) was granted amounting to eight *monedas* over 1387 and 1388 plus a supplementary *servicio* to be collected in the first year. Moreover, for the first time the Cortes specified the precise value in coin of these taxes instead of reckoning them simply in conventional percentages or *monedas* whose value depended on the efficiency of collection. They were expected to bring in the immense sum of 47 million *maravedis* (about £204,000) and in fact brought in a very substantial proportion of that amount. Total revenues in the year 1387 were about 53 million *maravedis* (about £230,000), the highest level ever attained by the Castilian Crown in the fourteenth century.[58]

The French court had followed events in Spain with growing perplexity. Part of the problem was that they were receiving information from several sources, much of which was inconsistent, inaccurate or out of date. In September 1386 they learned of John of Trastámara's plan to negotiate with his adversary and did not like the sound of it. Three ambassadors, including one of Charles VI's private secretaries, left at once for the Castilian court to protect French interests, quite pointlessly as it turned out since the discussions had been abandoned by the time they arrived. Shortly afterwards exaggerated reports began to arrive of Lancaster's triumphs. Santiago was one of the few Castilian cities whose name was recognised across Europe and its occupation by the English was widely reported. John of Gaunt, it was said, had already made himself 'master of all Castile'. This was followed at the beginning of November by the arrival of a Castilian embassy at Sluys in the last, confused days of the invasion project. They were able to explain that Lancaster had not yet penetrated beyond Galicia, but they were full of anguish about the prospects for the following year if large-scale reinforcements failed to reach the King in time.[59]

Charles VI's ministers were not able to attend to any of this until after the army of England had been disbanded and the King had returned to Paris. All the royal princes, the leaders of the nobility and the officers of the Crown gathered in the capital in December for the traditional Christmas and New Year celebrations. It was a time of balls and banquets, lavish gifts and a duel about scandalous allegations of adultery and rape which had obsessed the court for months. The atmosphere was poisonous. Philip of Burgundy quarrelled with the rest of the King's Council about the three Walloon-speaking castleries of southern Flanders, which he had long ago promised his brother Charles that he would restore to France after Louis de Mâle's death. Pressed on his undertaking by the other princes he refused point-blank to honour it. The dispute was resolved in January, substantially on Philip's terms, but only after a bruising row which had paralysed decision-making for nearly two months. Recriminations about the abortive invasion continued unabated. The Duke of Berry, who had presided over the debates at Sluys, found himself the victim of a campaign of denigration by some of the captains of the army, who blamed him for the whole debacle. A variety of projects and petitioners competed for the attention of the King's councillors. The Constable and the Admiral regarded the defeat of England as the first priority. They were keen to follow up the decision made at Amiens to make a third attempt in the spring. They believed that England, paralysed by its internal disputes, was incapable of defending itself. The Duke of Burgundy supported the idea in principle but was not prepared to enrage his Flemish subjects by making Sluys available again. The dowager Countess of Anjou was pressing for French intervention in the kingdom of Naples on behalf of her young son. The Duke of Berry was, as ever, lukewarm about all of these schemes. The erratic character of the decision-making process and the enmities and tensions beneath the surface are graphically conveyed in the journal of Jean le Fèvre, Bishop of Chartres, who was in Paris fighting the corner of the Countess of Anjou. His was a daily round of visits to princely mansions: appointments refused, decisions deferred, perfunctory audiences, snatched conversations in antechambers and gossip at dinner tables, with no firm news apart from the laconic observations of officials buttonholed as they came out of Council meetings.[60]

The 'matter of Castile' provoked as much dispute as any other issue. The French princes had never expected to have to honour their promises to John of Trastámara. At the time no one in Paris had imagined that John of Gaunt would persist in his expedition. Yet he had not only persisted but had conquered much of Galicia and, according to exaggerated reports circulating in France, was poised to overwhelm the rest of Castile. The Castilian King's leading, perhaps only advocate in the royal Council was the Duke of Bourbon. Others appear to have been indifferent or hostile. The whole issue was 'most intractable', Jean de Berry confided to the good Bishop of Chartres, who had seized the opportunity to lobby him at his prayers in the chapel of the Hôtel de Nesle. On 23 January 1387 Charles VI presided over a Great Council in the Louvre to decide the main lines of French strategy for the coming year. The meeting was evidently difficult, for it continued for the best part of three days. The French ministers knew a good deal by now about the political crisis in England and the takeover of power by Gloucester and Arundel and their friends. How far they understood its implications is difficult to say but they were certainly aware that a powerful fleet was being collected in England. They must also have known, at least in outline, about John of Gaunt's deal with the King of Portugal. The decision was that the undertakings given to John of Trastámara would have to be honoured 'in spite of other important and pressing affairs'. Because of the urgency of John's situation, two protégés of the Duke of Bourbon, Guillaume de Neilhac and Gaucher de Passat, were commissioned to raise 2,000 men-at-arms and to lead them to Castile in March. The Duke of Bourbon promised to follow them shortly afterwards.[61]

The plans for invading England in 1387 were reviewed at the same assembly. They seem to have been just as controversial. The truth was that the French government could not afford them, even without the distraction of Castile. The ultimate decision seems to have represented a compromise between those who would have preferred to abandon the project altogether and the military officers, Olivier de Clisson and Jean de Vienne, who regarded it as the first call on French resources. It was resolved to proceed with the invasion but on a much reduced scale. The King and the great noblemen, whose stately retinues had encumbered past invasion projects, would stay at home this time. Clisson and Vienne themselves were designated as the commanders. Instead of the hordes planned for 1385 and 1386, they were assigned an army of just 3,000 elite troops, including bowmen. They would embark on locally requisitioned ships from a port in western France instead of Flanders. The invasion would be launched in June instead of at the very end of the sailing season. The French royal Council proposed to raise 400,000 *livres* (£80,000) from yet another *taille*. The new tax was generally referred to as the *taille* 'for Castile' but at least three-quarters of it appears to have been earmarked for the invasion of England.[62]

That left the question what to do about the invasion fleet of the previous autumn, now largely redundant and lying under guard in the anchorage at Sluys. Most of the ships were released to trade. A large number of their masters decided to take on cargoes at La Rochelle, the principal wine port of the Bay of Biscay after Bordeaux. They formed themselves into a large convoy to force the English Channel on the outward and again on the return voyage. It would mean running the gauntlet of the waiting ships of the Earl of Arundel and the captain of Calais, a dangerous operation as the fate of the fleet of 1385 had shown. Jan Buuc, the Admiral of Flanders, agreed to organise the venture at his own financial risk in return for a fixed subsidy from the King and a fee from the ships' masters of a franc per ton of cargo. Buuc's orders were to defend his convoy, to reconnoitre the English coast on his way south, to prey on English shipping and perhaps to attack Arundel's ships if he got the chance.[63]

Jan Buuc's fleet, comprising about 200 armed merchantmen from every country of Europe's western seaboard, passed through the Channel unchallenged and must have reached La Rochelle in about the middle of February 1387. Shortly afterwards the Earl of Arundel put to sea with a small squadron of ships to engage in commerce raiding in the Channel while the rest of his fleet assembled in the Downs off Sandwich. They were sighted by Norman seamen and the reports passed urgently to Buuc in La Rochelle. At this stage the convoy was being re-formed for the laden voyage back to Flanders. The Marshal, Louis de Sancerre, who had recently arrived in Poitou to guard the march of Gascony, offered to put an extra 500 men-at-arms onto the ships. But Sancerre wanted half of Buuc's tonnage fee for his pains and Buuc was not prepared to agree to that. So the ships sailed with their original complements. This was a serious misjudgment. By the time Buuc's fleet approached the Channel on its return journey Arundel had forty-seven large ships lying off the Downs with more on the way. There were 2,500 soldiers waiting by the shore to board them, including the retinues of two earls and several famous English captains. As Thomas Walsingham observed, these were not the 'cobblers and tailors' who had traditionally fought from the decks of English warships but experienced men-at-arms.[64]

On 24 March 1387 Arundel's fleet ambushed Buuc off Margate. They fell on his ships in what a contemporary called a 'hate-filled onslaught'. The English ships were outnumbered but they were larger and better armed. They were also supported by about seventy Dutch and German ships in Buuc's convoy, which abandoned the rest as soon as the battle began and changed sides to join forces with their assailants. As many as fifty of Buuc's ships were captured in the first engagement. Having sent these under guard into the port of Orwell, Arundel pursued the rest northward for two days, catching up with them off the island of Cadzand at the entrance to the Sluys channel. There was a second engagement in which several more captures were made and eleven ships were sunk or burned. Others were wrecked as they tried to find refuge on the Flanders coast. On 26 March Arundel arrived off Sluys, penetrated into the outer anchorage and set up a blockade which lasted more than two weeks. The English stopped and seized incoming vessels. They put landing parties ashore to burn and plunder coastal villages and seize rich prisoners for ransom. They even toyed with the idea of trying to occupy Sluys. The Ghent exile Peter Van den Bossche, who was serving with the English fleet, strongly urged this course on Arundel but the English rejected his advice. The Duke of Burgundy's officers were already rushing troops to the scene. If Arundel had succeeded in taking over the port he would not have been strong enough to hold it against the inevitable counter-attack. The fleet was eventually forced to return to England by shortage of water and sickness among the crews. On 12 April 1387 Arundel sailed away with his booty. A total of sixty-eight sailing ships, most of them Flemish, had been captured, plus three huge laden carracks which were probably Castilian, a number of oared barges and at least 8,000 barrels of wine. Among the prisoners taken was Jan Buuc himself. He was imprisoned in the Tower of London and then in Arundel castle while the Earl held out for an impossible ransom and the Council considered whether to release him at all. The Duke of Burgundy was furious about Buuc's refusal to accept Sancerre's offer of reinforcements. He washed his hands of him and the wretched man eventually died, unransomed, in England in 1389.[65]

On 1 May 1387 the Earl of Arundel sailed from Orwell on his second cruise with a larger squadron of nearly sixty ships. This time his objective was Brest, which had now been under siege by John de Montfort for nearly a year. Recently the attack on the town had been intensified. The besiegers had built a large timber fort by the harbour beneath the town and two stone bastions on the landward approaches. Like John of Gaunt the year before Arundel arrived without warning, landed his soldiers close to the town and fell on the French siege works. The timber fort was burned. One of the stone bastions was captured and occupied. Arundel then launched a large-scale foraging raid into western Brittany. The fruits of this brief campaign were said to have been enough to supply the defenders of Brest for several months. Arundel's ships did not, however, have it all their own way. Sir Hugh Despenser, who was in command of part of the fleet, found himself attacked by a squadron from Harfleur on his way home. His vessels were driven aground and forced to surrender. He himself was carried off to Paris as a prisoner. The rest of Arundel's fleet headed north again and passed through the Channel to prey on the shipping lanes of the North Sea. By the time the cruise ended on 12 June 1387, the tally of prizes taken since March had risen to 160.[66]

The sea had been the Commission of Government's chosen theatre of war. Arundel's two cruises did much to establish its reputation for honest competence and Arundel himself as the hero of the hour. The glut of looted wine and other goods lifted morale in London and East Anglia, where most of it was landed. Arundel made as much political capital as he could from the campaign. The strategy of attacking the French bases in Flanders and controlling the narrow seas of the Channel was not of course his. It had been an axiom of English naval policy for two centuries and had been followed by all of Richard II's Admirals since Percy's raid on Sluys in 1385. But Arundel had followed it with verve. The sea battles inflicted the largest marine losses on the Flemings for many years and must have contributed to the unpopularity of the war among Philip of Burgundy's subjects. The blockade of Sluys and the landings nearby had alarmed the Duke and forced him to divert resources to the defence of the coast. The relief of Brest was an object-lesson in the effective use of seapower to achieve a brief, local superiority on land. Yet Richard II's friends, who were inclined to sneer about Arundel's exploits, were not entirely wrong. The results, although highly profitable for those involved, were rather meagre in strategic terms. Although the English had known since March that the French had shifted their invasion plans to the Channel, Arundel's attention remained fixed on the North Sea. Meanwhile a large fleet of French and Castilian merchant vessels, supported by six Castilian war galleys, was beginning to assemble at Harfleur, in the ports of northern Brittany and at La Rochelle. These preparations must have been difficult to hide but, so far as is recorded, Arundel made no attempt to interfere with them. The English ships were paid off on 12 June, only days before Clisson's invasion fleet was due to sail.[67]

John of Gaunt's invasion of León had been planned for January 1387 but did not get under way until the end of March. The reasons are obscure and generated a certain amount of ill-tempered argument at the time. The main problem seems to have arisen from a hitch in the process of getting the Portuguese King released by the Pope from his monastic vows, which in turn delayed his marriage to Philippa of Lancaster. At the end of January John of Gaunt, frustrated by the delay, resolved to bring the issue to a head. He insisted that the marriage should take place before the opening of the campaign, dispensation or no. In the event it was celebrated at Oporto on 14 February. The festivities were muted and hurried. There had been no time to summon the dignitaries who would normally have attended and the occasion was inevitably overshadowed by preparations for the coming campaign. Much of the Portuguese nobility was absent. Even John of Gaunt was too busy to attend.[68]

There are hints in the Portuguese chronicle of Fernão Lopes, which is the main source for these events, that the difficulties about the dispensation may have masked other, more intractable issues, including opposition to the Lancastrian alliance among a section of the Portuguese nobility. The value of the alliance had been much diminished over the winter months by a catastrophe which overcame the English army. Galicia was a subsistence economy at the best of times and winter there was harsh. The men were forbidden to loot but had no money to buy food. Relations between the army and the peasantry, which had begun well, broke down as the men escaped from their quarters and turned to looting in the countryside. Isolated groups of soldiers wandered about looking for food, only to be set upon and murdered by enraged peasants. As supplies dried up the army found itself forced to import bulk supplies of grain by sea from England to avoid starvation. Weakened by hunger and cold, the English, who were always vulnerable to the endemic diseases of the peninsula, succumbed to an unidentified plague. The epidemic claimed its first victims in September and then swept through the ranks of John of Gaunt's army over the following months. By March, according to reports reaching the Castilian court, the English army was reduced to just 1,200 men fit for service. The true number was probably closer to 2,000 but even that was only half the force Gaunt had brought from England. Many of these were ill, badly mounted and inadequately equipped. They made a poor impression on the Portuguese.[69]

After much debate in his Council, John of Avis resolved to increase the size of his army to make up the deficiency of numbers. This involved withdrawing all the garrisons of his kingdom apart from those in the Alemtejo. It was a controversial decision. Several members of the Council had already come to the conclusion that the Lancastrian enterprise was doomed and urged the Portuguese King to do no more than the minimum consistent with the treaty. As it was he entered the campaign with 3,000 men-at-arms, 2,000 crossbowmen, more than 4,000 infantry and an uncertain number of volunteers, perhaps 10,000 men in all or double the force promised at Ponte do Mouro. But the size of the Portuguese army created its own problems. As the contributor of barely a sixth of the combined army John of Gaunt lost status, especially in relation to the prickly and assertive Constable of Portugal, Nun' Alvarez Pereira. This was not just a matter of pride. It diminished his political influence and meant that he was unable to direct the campaign in the way that had been envisaged at Ponte do Mouro. A symbolic issue arose when Nun' Alvarez demanded the right to command the vanguard of the army, a position that John of Gaunt had expected to take for himself. John of Avis tried to dissuade the Constable. He pointed out that the Duke of Lancaster had commanded the vanguard at the battle of Nájera. He outranked the Constable. He was a great lord in his own country and was present in the peninsula as King of Castile, taking precedence before all but John himself. But Pereira was adamant and got his way. The place appointed for the junction of the armies was the broad plain east of the cathedral city of Bragança on the north-east march of Portugal. Towards the end of February 1387 John of Avis set out from Oporto with part of his troops

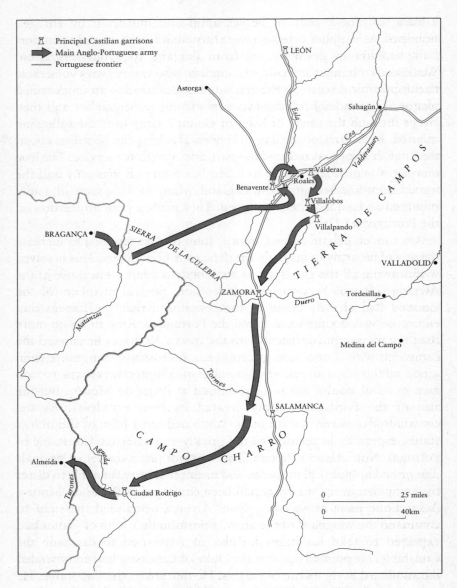

Principal Castilian garrisons
Main Anglo-Portuguese army
Portuguese frontier

LEÓN

Astorga

Sahagún

Esla
Cea
Valderaduey

Válderas
Roales
Benavente
Villalobos
Villalpando

TIERRA DE CAMPOS

BRAGANÇA
SIERRA DE LA CULEBRA

VALLADOLID

ZAMORA
Duero
Tordesillas

Matanzas

Medina del Campo

Tormes

SALAMANCA

CAMPO CHARRO

Almeida
Agueda
Tirones
Ciudad Rodrigo

0   25 miles
0   40km

22 The Anglo-Portuguese invasion of Castile, March–June 1387

while the rest came up from the south with the Constable. John of
Gaunt must have left Orense at about the same time. In the last week
of March the whole army was assembled. On the 25th they began to
move across the River Matanzas into Castile.[70]

John of Trastámara had between 3,000 and 4,000 men-at-arms mobilised, at least half of whom were French or Gascon. This was about the same as the cavalry contingent of the Anglo-Portuguese army. There was also an uncertain number of supporting troops of variable quality. The disposition of these men reflected the defensive strategy which had been agreed with the French captains at Valladolid the previous autumn. They were established in garrisons extending in an arc over some eighty miles from the foothills of the Cantabrian mountains in the north to the River Duero in the south. The northern anchor of the Castilian line was León, where there was a large Castilian garrison under the command of Archbishop Manrique. The southern anchor was the impregnable fortress-city of Zamora on the Duero, for many years one of the principal bastions of Castile against invasion from the west. In the centre the main concentrations of troops were at Benavente and Villalpando. Benavente was a walled town at the hub of the road system of the northern march. It stood across the highways leading north towards the Asturias and the Galician passes, east through Old Castile towards the cities of Palencia and Burgos and south to Zamora and Salamanca. Here John had stationed the largest garrison of the sector under the command of the leading territorial magnate of the region, Alvaro Perez de Osorio. His principal lieutenant was a Norman knight with a taste for foreign adventures, Robert de Bracquemont, who had fought with Louis of Anjou in Italy and had distinguished himself in the defence of Corunna the year before. Between them these two men had about 1,200 men-at-arms: some 600 Castilian cavalry and about 600 Frenchmen. As for Villalpando, that was a considerable town in the fourteenth century with a palace and six churches, commanding an important crossing of the River Valderaduey. It was held in 1387 by Olivier du Guesclin, the leading French captain in the peninsula, with about 1,000 French men-at-arms. The open country in between these fortresses was largely abandoned to the enemy. Castles which were judged indefensible were demolished. Supplies were stripped from the unwalled villages and towns and their populations evacuated into walled places. River bridges were broken, fords blocked with sharpened stakes and guarded by companies of soldiers. The plan was to avoid giving battle unless they could achieve overwhelming local superiority. The Castilians intended to use their garrisons to delay the enemy and protect the local population. They would also serve as reserves from which to form flying columns to harass the flanks of the invading army and pick off their stragglers and foraging parties. It was the strategy which the French had perfected in response to the English *chevauchées* of the previous decade.[71]

The Anglo-Portuguese army was ill-equipped to counter it. Their whole plan depended on forcing the Castilian King to battle. They had brought no siege equipment or artillery. There was a supply train but it was not large enough for an army of this size. The invaders' difficulties were aggravated by the presence of a large number of non-combatants including John of Gaunt's wife, Doña Constanza, and her ladies and domestic staff, all of whom had to be fed. What stocks remained after the first few days quickly rotted, leaving the troops dependent for food on what they could find in the store-rooms of captured towns and castles. This meant that they had to make rapid conquests. Nun' Alvarez Pereira, who directed the army's movements from the outset, understood this well. He decided to make boldly for the strongest point of the Castilian defence. Passing over the Sierra de la Culebra, he marched up the valley of the River Esla and on 2 April 1387 laid siege to Benavente. The siege went badly from the start. Benavente was a strong, walled town, defended by determined troops. The garrison made frequent sorties from the gates, preventing the allies from constructing their siege works. But there was no sign that they would be tempted to fight a pitched battle.[72]

Part of the Anglo-Portuguese army was detached and sent north along the highway towards Astorga to capture smaller walled places and find food. They returned from the north after four days, having taken one small town by assault and ransacked countless abandoned villages but with nothing to show for it except for a few cattle and meagre quantities of stores.[73] The English hated being in Castile for much the same reasons as the French had hated Scotland. Their letters home were full of bile against the land to which they had come. Castile, they said according to Froissart's informants, 'was not a profitable land to fight in like France, with its prosperous villages, serene countryside, beautiful rivers and fine houses.' There was nothing but rocks and crags, harsh desiccating winds, muddy rivers, undrinkable wine and a devious population of half-naked peasants. Opportunities to take prisoners and loot in a country claimed by their commander as his own were necessarily limited. Even the Duke of Lancaster was beginning to write off the prospects of success. According to Froissart he compared his lot to that of Louis of Anjou, who had invaded Italy 'as grandly as ever a prince could' only to encounter stalemate, bankruptcy and death.

After only a week on the march hunger and failure were already straining relations between the English and their Portuguese allies. At a personal level John of Avis remained on good terms with his father-in-law, whom he never failed to treat with deference. Gaunt for his part was generous about the Portuguese. He mourned their heroes when they were killed in skirmishes. He boomed out 'Well done, good Portugal!' when they prevailed. It was a different story among their subordinates. Language must have been a problem. Attitudes were another. The English looked down on the Portuguese, whom they dismissed as verbose, impulsive and lazy. The Portuguese for their part regarded their allies as arrogant, loud-mouthed and rash and were apt to mock their pretensions. There were constant disputes about the division of spoils and the distribution of rations. Relations between the two armies sank so low that it was no longer possible to organise joint foraging expeditions. Easter Sunday fell on 7 April in 1387. A truce was declared around Benavente for the Sunday and Monday to mark the holy season. The English and French knights, some of whom recognised each other from encounters in France, found that they had much more in common with each other than either had with their Iberian allies. They fraternised freely, taking an obvious relish in the ritual jousts organised during the Easter break: stylised fights governed by strict rules, three charges, one blow each in a single encounter. For the Castilians fighting for their homes and the Portuguese for their national independence the issues at stake were closer to home and altogether more serious. The audience traded insults during the sport and real fighting broke out among them.[74]

The French experience of fighting in Castile was very different from the English. They were sustained by the sense that the tide of war was running in their favour. 'The English used to say that we knew more about singing and dancing than fighting,' Froissart has them say, 'but now see how the tables are turned.' For French soldiers Castile was a land of opportunity where riches could be gained in the service of the Trastámaras. Olivier du Guesclin was receiving large sums from the proceeds of the *alcabala* in León. Robert de Bracquemont would later make a rich marriage in Castile and acquire great estates there. Men like these could not understand what the English had to gain from the hopeless endeavour to subdue the whole of Castile. They knew, of course, about John of Trastámara's proposal to settle the succession by marrying the Infante to Catherine of Lancaster. They were sure that the offer was still open. These hints were reported to John of Gaunt and were evidently not rejected out of hand. He put it about that his position was stronger than it seemed. If necessary, he said, he could always summon reinforcements from England and return later in greater force. But Gaunt was whistling in the dark. There was no prospect of raising fresh troops in England as he must have known. The public there was weary of the war with Castile. Contemplating the stout walls of Benavente, Gaunt was quite content to signal his renewed interest in a negotiated settlement. On 10 April, after the Easter truce had expired, the Anglo-Portuguese army abandoned the siege.[75]

John of Trastámara had established his headquarters in the city of Salamanca. From here he would ride out to the fortresses of the Duero, north of the city, to get the latest reports from the front. He was well-informed about the sufferings of the invaders and convinced that they were a certain sign of the restoration of God's favour after the recent disasters. In about the middle of April 1387 the Castilian King held a Great Council to review his campaign strategy. It was attended by the leading magnates of the kingdom and the masters of the military orders. With the support of the assembly the King decided to move onto the offensive as soon as he had received the reinforcements which were expected from France. Guillaume de Neilhac and Gaucher de Passat had left Paris about a fortnight before with an advance guard of just over 1,300 men-at-arms, all that they could raise without courting further delay. They had reached Carcassonne by 22 April. The Duke of Bourbon was due to follow later with the rest of the expeditionary force. Other French captains were reported to have volunteered to bring further companies to Castile. John had been told that he could expect 4,000 French men-at-arms before the campaign was out. These forces would give him for the first time a decisive superiority in cavalry over the combined army of the English and Portuguese. To balance his cavalry arm with adequate numbers of infantry and bowmen the King now issued a general military summons to his subjects. But John, ever cautious and troubled about the immense cost of his French auxiliaries, did not intend to rely on superior strength alone. Towards the end of April, after the exchanges between the English and French knights at Benavente had been reported to him, he appears to have sent an emissary into the English camp to find out whether anything could be built on them.[76]

The Castilian King's emissary must have found the Anglo-Portuguese army in a sorry condition. The campaign had degenerated into a formless mass foraging expedition with no other object than to feed the army. After the abandonment of the siege of Benavente the invaders forded the River Esla and moved east into the Tierra de Campos, the broad plateau of Old Castile watered by the tributaries of the Duero which extended east to the coronation city of the Castilian kings at Burgos. This region, which was still the granary of Spain in spite of the progressive encroachment of cattle farming, had been almost uninhabited before the great internal migrations of the twelfth and thirteenth centuries and it was still sparsely populated when John of Gaunt came to claim the succession of King Pedro. The English and Portuguese troops established themselves in a small country town called Roales. It was an insignificant place defended only by peasants, who abandoned it as soon as the soldiers appeared. But they found enough food there to supply them for a few days while groups of mounted men fanned out across the countryside in search of more. About three weeks had been lost by the time the commanders of the army succeeded in restoring a measure of strategic direction.[77]

At the beginning of May 1387 the campaign was redirected towards the garrisoned towns on the road south towards the Duero, in the hope of finally provoking the defenders to battle. A small siege train was constructed, initially consisting of a mobile timber tower and a stone-thrower. These were hauled into position outside Valderas, a market town on the River Cea some fourteen miles east of Benavente. Valderas was defended by baked clay walls and a stone citadel dating from the twelfth century. There was a garrison of eighty Castilian and Breton men-at-arms and some French bowmen. The captain of the place, apparently frightened by the sight of the siege-tower, decided that it was indefensible and agreed to surrender. He bargained for a safe-conduct out of the castle and undertook that the inhabitants would do homage to the Duke of Lancaster. But the inhabitants would have none of this. They refused to acknowledge the Duke as their king and began to destroy the stores of food and fodder in the town. They then abandoned their homes and marched out of the gates with the garrison. Their departure was followed by a serious incident between the English and Portuguese troops. John of Gaunt had insisted throughout the campaign that captured places should be regarded as his in right of the Castilian Crown, a claim which was accepted by the Portuguese King but not by his army. They laughed at John of Gaunt's claims and refused to accept his right to dispose of the spoils of 'his' kingdom, when they had borne the main burden of the campaign. At Valderas all this came to a head. The two leaders agreed that to avoid riots between the two armies the

English would have a free hand to pillage the town until midday, when the Portuguese would be allowed to take what was left. This agreement was received with indignation in the Portuguese ranks. They burst through the gates before the appointed hour. They began to pillage alongside the English and seized some of the loot which the English had already appropriated. The King was obliged to enter the place in person, sword in hand, to restore order among his men. Valderas was an insignificant capture which the allies shortly abandoned but the incident had a symbolic importance which can hardly have escaped John of Gaunt. It was clear that, for all the resentment against John of Trastámara's government, he would not be welcomed as a liberator, at least in León. His claim to the Castilian Crown was regarded here not with indifference, as it had been in much of Galicia, but with overt hostility.[78]

Enough bread and wine had escaped destruction at the hands of the townsmen of Valderas to relieve the army's hunger for a few days. On about 9 May 1387 they resumed the march south making for Villalobos, another small, walled town about ten miles away. Like Valderas, it was defended by a Castilian garrison, which was reinforced as the invaders approached and supported by cavalry detachments operating outside the town. Like Valderas also, the garrison surrendered after a few days rather than face an assault by superior forces. Some wine and grain were obtained from the inhabitants but foraging had by now become more difficult than ever. To find fodder for the horses foraging parties encumbered by large numbers of pack-animals were having to range fifteen or twenty miles from the army's encampments, escorted by large contingents of cavalry. Flying columns of up to 400 mounted men came out from Benavente and Villalpando to attack them. The Constable of Portugal, seeing his army slowly reduced by attrition, hunger and desertion, made a final attempt to provoke a battle. He took part of the army encamped around Villalobos and marched on the French-held castle of Villalpando. Olivier du Guesclin led his garrison out of the castle as they approached and drew them up in battle order in front of the gates. But there was to be no battle. The French withdrew behind their walls as soon as they saw the size of the Constable's force.[79]

The temperature rose sharply during May. A dull haze hung over the north Castilian plain. The horses began to die for want of fodder and clean water. The men sweltered in the midday sun and were then chilled to the bones during the cold nights. They drank stagnant water and strong red wine brought in from Portugal, which made them ill. Shortly another epidemic disease began to spread through their ranks, aggravated by the dysentery which was inseparable from the life of military encampments. The men sickened and died. According to Castilian estimates at least 300 English men-at-arms died of disease during the march in addition to a large number of archers. These deaths finally broke the morale of the English army. They declared that they had had enough. Their pay was now at least four months in arrears. There were only limited opportunities for taking plunder and ransoms. A substantial number decided to withdraw to Gascony. Their ringleader was Sir John Holand, who as Constable of the army was ultimately responsible for its discipline. Holand was a vain and hot-tempered playboy in his mid-thirties who had recently married John of Gaunt's daughter Elizabeth after getting her pregnant while she was still married to her first husband. It was Holand who came before the Duke to tell him the temper of the men. Everyone knew, he said, that the invasion had failed and that sooner or later there would have to be an accommodation with the Trastámaras. There was no longer a cause to fight for. He himself intended to apply to the Castilian King for a safe-conduct to enable him to take his wife (who was travelling with the army) and anyone else who wanted to leave to the passes of the Pyrenees. As for the rest of the army there was nothing for it, he said, but to abandon the enterprise and return to Portugal. John of Gaunt, who knew as well as Holand did that the campaign was lost, reacted with surprising equanimity. He authorised Holand to send a herald to open discussions with John of Trastámara about the safe-conducts.[80]

Shortly after this interview John of Avis had a remarkably candid discussion with his ally. From his point of view the campaign had become pointless. The only advantage it had ever offered lay in the prospect of annexing territory in western Castile if Gaunt succeeded in toppling the Trastámaras. This now seemed an impossibly remote outcome. The Portuguese King told Gaunt to his face that he had no support in Castile. None of the places that they had attacked had willingly received him. Those that they had conquered were few and insignificant and would be too expensive to hold. To conquer the whole of Castile town by town would require an 'endless' war. Of course, he added, if Gaunt was set on that path he would support him as he had undertaken to do, but the English army was now so small that he risked making himself ridiculous. In his view there were only two choices: Gaunt could call for more troops from England and reinvade later; or he could make a deal with John of Trastámara. The Duke responded with the same weary resignation as he had shown to Holand. He told him about the approaches made by the French knights at Benavente and about Holand's plan to obtain safe-conducts from the Castilians. He said that he had already resolved that if John of Trastámara made an honourable proposal he would accept it. The Portuguese King was taken aback to discover how much had been going on behind his back. But there was no point in recrimination now. The two men agreed that the army would withdraw to Portugal. To avoid the humiliation of returning by the way they had come they proposed to press on towards Zamora and Salamanca and re-enter Portugal further south. By staying on Castilian territory for longer they would not just save their faces but perhaps maintain pressure on John of Trastámara to negotiate with his rival. Few men were deceived. At Villalpando the French commander Olivier du Guesclin went to extremes of courtesy which showed how well he understood the situation. He arranged for Sir Thomas Morieux, one of the marshals of the English army, to be taken under escort with two of his companions to the town of Medina del Campo, where John of Trastámara then was, in order to petition for safe-conducts out of the country.[81]

Five or six days' march, roughly following the old Roman Calzada de la Plata, took the Anglo-Portuguese army eighty miles south across one of the most arid regions of the peninsula. Fording the River Tormes, they arrived on about 19 May 1387 in the plain west of Salamanca. The Castilian commander in the city was the Portuguese Infante Don João, now released from his prison and appointed by the Castilian King as titular regent of Portugal. He had a large body of Castilian troops with him. There was also an important contingent of French men-at-arms under the command of Renaud de Roye, who had recently arrived in Castile. The English and the Portuguese troops remained encamped within a few miles of the city for about a week. French men-at-arms would come into their encampment with cartloads of bread, wine and mutton for their English friends. The English responded by organising tournaments. English, French and Castilians all participated. But the Portuguese seem to have been excluded from both the feasting and the jousting. Their men were still were scavenging along the roads for fallen birds' nests.[82]

John of Trastámara stayed well away from the front at Medina del Campo. Behind the scenes his councillors were talking to Morieux and his companions. The Castilians had nothing to lose by encouraging the drain of manpower to the north and readily granted the safe-conducts.

If Froissart is to be believed they took the opportunity to impose a condition that the holders of Castilian safe-conducts were to undertake not to take up arms against Castile for at least six years. The condition aroused some controversy in the English encampment. But John of Gaunt, distraught by the heavy losses among his friends, did not object. He had criers sent through the camp to announce that all the sick or wounded were at liberty to accept the Castilian King's offer. A large number left at once. Not all of them made it. By the time the convoy of sick reached Villalpando on the road north many could no longer carry on. They were taken into the French fortress by Olivier du Guesclin. In Castile, as the English chronicler Thomas Walsingham observed, both sides were too far from home to take the antagonisms of the real war seriously. Some of these men later recovered and found their way home under French protection. Others succumbed to wounds and disease. The dead included men very close to the Duke. Among them were both marshals of the army, Sir Thomas Morieux and Sir Richard Burley. Morieux, who probably died on the road, was a Norfolk landowner who had married Gaunt's illegitimate daughter Blanche. He had been with the Earl of Cambridge in Portugal and had fought in France, Gascony, Brittany and Scotland. Burley, who died at Villalpando, had served John of Gaunt for twenty years since the days when they had fought together in the army of Nájera. He had wanted to be buried in St. Paul's cathedral in London opposite the tomb which Gaunt had prepared there for himself. The Duke could not have suffered more grievous losses if he had been defeated in battle. The men who withdrew from his army were 'not traitors but men conquered by hardship', he told the King of Portugal, who came up to him on the road to protest against the desertions. Then he bowed his head and wept upon his horse's mane.[83]

In the last week of May 1387 the army began the final part of its march. They headed south-west towards Ciudad Rodrigo and the frontier of Portugal, passing across the undulating plain of the Campo Charro, in modern times a bleak landscape of open scrubland but then a land of vast oak forests where foraging was easier than it had been further north. The Castilians in Salamanca had by now seen with their own eyes the weakness of the retreating army. They became bolder in attacking it. The Infante Don João and his Castilian lieutenants left the city with his cavalry and, travelling at night by obscure paths, succeeded in reaching the walled town of Ciudad Rodrigo the day before the enemy. Some miles from the town they ambushed the Anglo-Portuguese army as they crossed a narrow bridge over a deep stream. It was the most vulnerable moment of any army on the march. The vanguard had already crossed when the French and Castilians came rapidly down a slope and fell on the rearguard stranded on the other bank. The Portuguese bowmen succeeded in holding off the attack for long enough to enable the rest of the army to reach safety across the bridge. The English appear to have taken little part in this engagement.[84] As they approached the River Turones, which marked the frontier of Portugal in this sector, Sir John Holand came up to the rearguard where the King of Portugal and the Duke of Lancaster were stationed in order to take his leave. He had done his duty, as he saw it, by staying with the army up to this point. On the following morning the army crossed into Portugal and made for the Portuguese border fortress of Almeida. Holand rode back along the road to Salamanca and then north to Navarre. With him went his wife, many of the ladies who had been following the army in the entourage of the Duchess of Lancaster and some fifty able-bodied English men-at-arms clutching their Castilian safe-conducts. By the end of June they had crossed the pass of Roncevalles into Gascony.[85]

Meanwhile the French companies of Guillaume de Neilhac and Gaucher de Passat had finally reached Castile. They had been delayed at Carcassonne by the difficulty of obtaining safe-conducts to pass through Aragon. By the time the issue was resolved most of them had decided to take the longer route through Béarn and Navarre. They reached the Castilian town of Logroño on the Navarrese border at the beginning of June 1387. Riding south through León they must have passed Sir John Holand's company on the road. As for the Duke of Bourbon, he was still on his way down the Rhône valley and did not arrive for another month. By the time the French companies finally joined John of Trastámara he had already resolved to make peace with his rival.[86]

On about 10 June 1387, as the Duke of Lancaster was on his way to Coimbra with the remnants of his army, John of Trastámara's ambassadors caught up with him at the castle of Trancoso in eastern Portugal. Given the importance of its mission the composition of the embassy was most unusual. Instead of the traditional prelate or great magnate, it consisted of two low-ranking clerics. One was the Castilian King's Franciscan confessor and spiritual adviser, Fray Fernando de Illescas. The other was the learned doctor of civil and canon laws, Alvaro Martinez, whom Gaunt may have remembered for his prolix arguments at Orense the year before. Their instructions were to conclude a deal as soon as possible before the new French companies arrived on the Portuguese border, even if it meant that revisions would be required later. John of Gaunt appointed two members of his council to deal with them: Sir Thomas Percy, who habitually represented the Duke on such occasions, and Sir John Trailly. The four of them reached agreement so quickly and in such detail that it seems likely that they were working from proposals which had already been exchanged in the course of the campaign.

Within two days a comprehensive treaty had been drawn up. It provided for Catherine of Lancaster to marry John of Trastámara's eldest son, the Infante Don Enrique. A substantial landed endowment was to be provided for the couple in Castile and a declaration made at the next meeting of the Cortes that they would in due course succeed to the throne of Castile. In addition John undertook to pay the Duke of Lancaster no less than 600,000 francs (about £100,000) plus a pension of 40,000 francs (£6,700) a year for the rest of his life or Doña Constanza's if she should outlive him. These enormous sums would double the income of a man who was already by far the richest nobleman in England. The payments were later increased by adding the revenues of three Castilian cities, Medina del Campo, Guadalajara and Olmedo, which were to be made over to Doña Constanza for her lifetime in compensation for the surrender of her own claims. In return for all this the Duke and Duchess agreed to renounce their claims to the sovereignty of Castile and never to reassert them again. The various places that the English had conquered in Galicia were to be restored to the Castilian King's officers against an undertaking that those who had submitted to the invaders would not be penalised.

The parties avoided the thorny question of their allies, which had proved such a formidable obstacle at successive diplomatic conferences in France, by simply ignoring it. This was to be a treaty between John of Trastámara and John of Gaunt, not between England and Castile or indeed between Castile and Portugal. The Castilians agreed to lend their good offices to a broader treaty of peace in due course and to work together for the healing of the schism in the Church. But they remained at war with England and expressly reserved their right to perform all their obligations to France under the Franco-Castilian naval treaty. Their only concession was that they would do no more for France than the terms of those treaties strictly bound them to do. These provisions complied with the letter if not the spirit of John of Trastámara's obligations to his ally. John of Gaunt was more careless of his. He had promised Richard II before leaving England that any treaty that he made with Castile would provide for an indemnity of 200,000 *doblas* to the English government on account of damage done by Castilian coastal raids, but no such provision appeared in the Treaty of Trancoso. As for Portugal, nothing was said about the continuing dispute between John of Avis and his Castilian rival and nothing was done to secure the country against future attacks from Castile. Gaunt even allowed the text of the treaty to include the kingdom of Portugal among John of Trastámara's titles.[87]

After a highly successful campaign, in which the Duke of Lancaster had been visibly discredited and most of his army lost, it is at first sight surprising that the King of Castile should have conceded so much. But there were sound reasons of policy for taking this course. John had already inflicted heavier fiscal burdens on his subjects than they could bear, a fact which not only raised practical difficulties in continuing the war but troubled the soul of this morbidly religious and self-critical man. He was now faced with the prospect of a crippling wage bill for some 3,000 new arrivals from France in addition to the 2,000 or so who were already serving under Olivier du Guesclin. Even with the immense taxes voted by the Cortes at Segovia the Castilian treasury could not have supported this burden for very long. The French garrisons on the march had already made themselves unpopular by their demands for food and supplies. Once their pay stopped they could be expected to start plundering Castile. And after the current campaigning season? As matters stood there was no end in sight to the annual rounds of *servicios* and musters on the frontiers. John of Trastámara was not the only intelligent observer of his times who overrated the offensive capabilities and staying power of the English. He never realised how far they had been hobbled by the financial debility and political squabbles of the past decade. He plainly took seriously the hints dropped by John of Gaunt that he could recruit a fresh army in England. Even after twenty years the Black Prince's astonishing triumph at Nájera cast a long shadow over Castilian war policy. It seemed better to buy off the English in order to deal with the real enemy, Portugal. The King's choice of ambassadors suggests that the policy behind the treaty was very much his own. The decision seems to have been made within the small circle of his closest advisers. So far as the admittedly exiguous surviving documentation shows none of the great lay magnates of Castile or the commanders of the army was involved. On 12 June 1387 the Duke of Lancaster swore to observe the treaty before the Castilian ambassadors at Trancoso. The English negotiators then accompanied the Castilians to Zamora and were present in the bishop's palace on the 23rd when the Castilian King swore his own oath. The die was cast. But the text was not formally published and for some time after the oaths were sworn both parties appear to have been somewhat secretive about its contents. Some amendments were negotiated in the course of the next month and more were agreed in the following year but the basic framework negotiated between Fray Fernando and Sir Thomas Percy remained intact.[88]

John of Trastámara did not initially tell the French about his agreement with the Duke of Lancaster. The Duke of Bourbon arrived at the Castilian court in early July. He announced his intention of advancing into Portugal in pursuit of the Duke of Lancaster and John of Avis. Many prominent Castilians responded to this plan with enthusiasm. The francophile soldier and diplomat Ayala, who tells us this, was one of them. But the King would not contemplate it. He told the French captains that he was grateful for their support but the danger had now passed and he expected them to return as soon as possible to France. Archbishop Manrique would pay them at Burgos for the time they had already passed in Castile but there was no more money available for war wages. Bourbon was furious. He replied that the King of France had sent him to Castile to fight the English and that was what he intended to do. His temper cannot have been improved when rumours began to circulate about the agreement with John of Gaunt. Many years later Jean de Châteaumorand, one of Bourbon's retained knights, dictated a garbled and inaccurate version of these events but his account of Bourbon's parting words has the ring of truth. 'Take care what you do,' he is supposed to have said, 'for your French ally is the most powerful living monarch, as he has more than once demonstrated both in your time and your father's.' The Castilian King retained Olivier du Guesclin in Castile with a reduced company of 300 men. The rest of the French troops were dismissed. Their captains made for home. Angry and frustrated at the way they had been treated they allowed their men to have their head. There were serious incidents of looting and violence as scattered companies of French soldiers crossed the plain of Old Castile towards Burgos. The worst occurred at Sahagún, a small walled town in the north of the Tierra de Campos dominated by a famous Cluniac monastery, which was sacked by the companies of Neilhac and Passat. An estimated 400 people were killed in this incident alone. At

Burgos the French received as much of their due as the Castilian treasury could find to pay them, with deductions in some cases for the damage they had done. Then they rode north across the Pyrenees through Navarre and the county of Foix. The Duke of Bourbon was feted wherever he went. There were bullfights at Tudela, banquets at Pamplona, lavish distributions at Orthez. But nothing could disguise the fact that he had suffered a humiliating political reverse.[89]

In spite of the protestations of loyalty to the French alliance which had been included in the Treaty of Trancoso, everyone could see that John of Trastámara would have no interest in performing his obligations to France once the threat to his throne had been removed. The fact that there was no peace with Portugal meant that his resources would be tied up in the peninsula for some time to come. In the longer term the marriage of the Infante to an English princess seemed likely to bring an end to the dominant role which France had played in the politics of the peninsula for three decades. At the end of the year Charles VI sent Jean de Vienne to Castile to express his displeasure at the turn which events had taken and to reconfirm the naval treaty. The Admiral's instructions were to negotiate the despatch of at least twelve galleys to northern waters in the spring. He found the Castilian King unapologetic. It was only with the utmost reluctance that he was persuaded to confirm the treaty and then he did no more than the minimum. Instead of twelve Castilian galleys the French got a promise of six captured Portuguese galleys commanded by a renegade Portuguese nobleman, and a rather indistinct undertaking to hire more at French expense in the Mediterranean.[90]

Most of the surviving soldiers of the English army were paid off with IOUs at the end of July 1387. They were left to find their own way back by sea to England. The Duke himself remained in Portugal for long enough to oversee the withdrawal of the English garrisons from Galicia. At the end of September he embarked with his personal retinue and household at Oporto on six galleys provided by the King of Portugal and sailed for the Gascon city of Bayonne. There he installed himself in the spacious buildings of the Franciscans. Gaunt intended to remain as close as he could to Castile until the main provisions of the treaty had been duly performed.[91] Raising the large sums of money required to pay off the Duke was always going to require time and delicate negotiations with John of Trastámara's subjects.

The Cortes of Castile met in December 1387 at Briviesca, a modest walled town some twenty-five miles from Burgos where the representatives gathered to escape the plague which had broken out in the Castilian capital. The assembly agreed to continue the *alcabala* and voted a *servicio* of 540,000 gold francs. The tax was widely resisted and had still not been collected in July 1388 when the treaty in its final form was sealed in Bayonne and publicly proclaimed in both Gascony and Castile. The nine-year-old Catherine of Lancaster was married to the Infante in the half-completed shell of Palencia cathedral in September 1388. In another part of the city a new Cortes was being pressed to vote another 20 million *maravedis* to pay off the Duke of Lancaster on top of an estimated 45 million *maravedis* required to prosecute the war with Portugal. They responded very much as their counterparts had done at Westminster, with abrasive demands for more information about what had happened to the last subsidy and overt accusations of dishonesty levelled at the King's officials. Ultimately the Cortes granted the Crown's demands only on condition that their own officers would authorise the collection and disbursement of the new taxes. In October 1388 the first instalment of the indemnity, some 200,000 francs in silver ingots and assorted coins of Castile, Aragon, Morocco and France, was loaded onto pack-animals and sent off to be delivered to John of Gaunt's treasurer at Bayonne. A few days after this the Duke sent to John of Trastámara the gold crown which Richard II had given him more than a year before for his coronation at Burgos.[92]

CHAPTER XIII

War and Peace
1387–1389

On 25 June 1387 Olivier de Clisson was arrested at Vannes on the orders of the Duke of Brittany. He had come to the town to attend an assembly of the baronage of Brittany. The proceedings concluded with a great banquet. At the end of the feast John de Montfort lured Clisson to the Château de l'Hermine, the immense fortress which he was in the process of constructing at the south-eastern entrance to the city, on the pretext of showing off its defences to an acknowledged authority on the art of fortification. There he was seized by armed men, loaded with chains and thrown into prison. The immediate result was the cancellation of the projected invasion of England, in which the Constable was to have taken the leading part. The expedition was almost ready. Some 360 warships and transports had been requisitioned or hired. Most were waiting at Tréguier in Brittany and at Harfleur in the Seine. Others were on their way from La Rochelle. About half the army had already reached their ports of embarkation and more were being mustered across northern and western France. In the course of the following weeks all of them were paid off or transferred to other duties in the confusion which followed the Constable's arrest. In the longer term the incident was to have yet more profound consequences. Years afterwards it came to be seen as the opening of the long-drawn political crisis which engulfed France in the final years of the fourteenth century and the first two decades of fifteenth.[1]

Ever since his appointment as Constable of France in 1380 Olivier de Clisson had been at the centre of the tensions and jealousies which divided the court of Charles VI. Apart from the Duke of Anjou, with whom he had enjoyed cordial relations in his time, Clisson had never been close to the royal dukes who dominated the King's Council. But he was the only major figure at court outside the tight circle of the royal family who had a secure power-base of his own. He was protected by his office, which was conventionally held for life, by his status as the brother-in-arms of the great Du Guesclin and by his reputation, acknowledged even by his enemies, as the most capable French military commander of his generation. He had also achieved a closer personal relationship with the young King than any of his uncles had been able to do. In addition to these solid political advantages Olivier de Clisson possessed one of the greatest fortunes in France. Not only did he own extensive domains in Bas-Poitou and around Josselin in central Brittany but, unusually, he disposed of very large sums in cash. At a time when seigneurial revenues were declining and cash was scarce he had proved to be a capable businessman, making substantial sums from royal grants, spoil and war wages. Clisson shrewdly invested his gains, speculating in land and mortgages and lending out money at interest to the Crown and impecunious noblemen. Few men in France could have advanced 80,000 *livres* to the Crown to pay war wages, as Clisson did in the summer of 1380, or supplied the mints with 600 marks of gold from his own chests (equivalent to 40,000 *livres*) to coin money for the soldiers assigned to the invasion of England in 1385. Wealth of this order was a powerful tool of political influence.[2] Clisson had announced his political ambitions early in the new reign by building the imposing Paris mansion whose gatehouse still towers over the Rue des Archives, following the fashion for grand Parisian residences set by the greatest territorial princes. A man of Clisson's ambitions made enemies easily.

Of all Olivier de Clisson's many hatreds the most persistent and corrosive was his hatred for the Duke of Brittany. With the Duke's submission to Charles VI in 1381 Clisson's unrelenting hostility became a profoundly destabilising factor in French political life. For although both men were now in the same camp, they remained rivals for land, influence and power in Brittany. Clisson was the leader of those in the duchy whose first loyalty had always been to the house of Blois. John de Montfort responded to the challenge by forging a close political alliance with Philip of Burgundy. Philip had never had much time for the upstart and ambitious Constable, who represented the only credible threat to his own hold on power. The Constable had an even more persistent enemy in the Duke of Berry. They had fallen out over Clisson's attempt to enlarge his influence in the north-west corner of Poitou, which was part of Berry's appanage. For all their power and dignities the Dukes of Brittany, Burgundy and Berry felt sufficiently threatened by Clisson to enter into a formal treaty of alliance in 1384 which, without naming the Constable, was plainly directed against him.[3]

It is unlikely that the parties to this pact thought seriously about its wider implications. But, consciously or not, they stood for a political model in which France operated as a coalition of regional principalities. Clisson stood for a very different principle of government. He gathered around him a miscellaneous band of clients and allies whose belief in the undivided authority of the Crown was their main defining characteristic. Many of them had been officials and courtiers of the last King, men who had been marginalised under the regime of the royal princes since 1380. They were viscerally suspicious of John de Montfort. Several of them had been closely associated with the assault on Breton autonomy which had darkened Charles V's final years. Bureau de la Rivière, Charles V's closest friend at the end of his life, owed his survival at court mainly to Clisson's support. Jean le Mercier, one of the outstanding experts on war finance in the previous reign, was only now recovering some of his old influence. The ambitious and authoritarian First President of the Parlement, Arnaud de Corbie, and the diplomat Nicholas du Bosc, Bishop of Bayeux, were administrators and technocrats who had risen, like them, on the favour of Charles V. Their allies included Jean de Vienne and Enguerrand de Coucy, both prominent opponents of the Duke of Brittany's interests at court who had risen to fame in the last years of the old King. The nineteenth-century historian Jules Michelet called these men *'les Marmousets du roi'*, borrowing a throw-away phrase of Froissart's which meant the King's whisperers, the men who spoke softly in his ear. The name has stuck.

There was, however, more to the Marmousets than nostalgia for a time in which they had whispered in the ear of an all-powerful monarch. For at least half a century there had been a significant constituency in French politics for what can loosely be called administrative reform but was in reality a complex mixture of moral puritanism, financial economy and hostility to the endemic corruption of the public service. It was the programme of the Estates-General of 1347, which had been adopted for largely cynical reasons by the King of Navarre and had resurfaced in more violent form during the civil wars of the 1350s and the urban risings of 1381 and 1382. It had much in common with the programme of the political opposition in England. Within the French political class it drew its support mainly from elements in the civil service, the Parlement and the Church, the background from which most of the Marmousets came. Men of their frame of mind were never likely to approve of the administration of the royal dukes. The Duke of Anjou in his lifetime had pillaged the royal treasury to finance his personal expenditure and his ambitions in Italy. The Duke of Burgundy had conducted French policy largely in his own interest, procuring immense grants in his own favour from the French royal treasury. The Duke of Berry did not have his brothers' diligence or political ambitions but he had the same persistent appetite for money. The grant of 300,000 francs made to him in 1385 was the largest gift of its kind in the first decade of the reign. The King was now eighteen years old and nominally of full age but convention required him to wait until his twentieth year before he could be left to conduct his affairs in person. Charles found these constraints increasingly irksome as he grew older. His impatience was assiduously nourished by the Constable. Every year, according to his nephew Jean Harpeden, Clisson would would remind the King that he was a year closer to the day when he would be able to shake off the tutelage of his uncles.[4]

The origin of the crisis of June 1387 lay in some complex and manipulative dealings about the succession to the duchy of Brittany. Charles of Blois's widow, the old Countess of Penthièvre, had died in September 1384 at her castle overlooking the Loire at Guérande. She was followed to the grave by John de Montfort's wife, Joan Holand, who had died about a fortnight later after a marriage of eighteen years in which she had borne him no children. These deaths meant that Charles of Blois's elder son John, a prisoner of the English for more than thirty years, was now not just the heir presumptive of Brittany but as Count of Penthièvre entitled to possession of all his mother's vast domains including some of the principal fortresses in the north of the peninsula. John de Montfort was determined to prevent the Penthièvre lands falling into the hands of his enemies. So, at the beginning of October 1384, he confiscated the Countess's domains on the pretext that as a prisoner the heir was not in a position to perform his feudal obligations. He sent his officers to take possession of the fortresses. Shortly after this Montfort attacked Champtoceaux, one of the principal fortresses of the lower Loire guarding the march of Anjou east of Nantes. Champtoceaux was held by Marie, dowager Countess of Anjou, who was John of Blois's sister. The attack failed but within a few weeks the Duke was reported to be collecting troops and equipment for another attempt.[5]

Olivier de Clisson's interests were closely bound up with the fortunes of the house of Blois. He responded to John de Montfort's move by a series of bold strokes. He sent his agents into England to do a deal with the new Count of Penthièvre. In January 1385 these men met John of Blois behind the walls of his prison at Gloucester castle. John executed a general authority empowering Clisson to act as his lieutenant in

France. Armed with this instrument the Constable occupied John of Blois's lands in Brittany, expelled the officers of the Duke and installed his own garrisons in their place. The wider terms of Clisson's arrangements with John of Blois are not recorded but the sequel makes it clear what they were. Clisson proposed to raise the money required to pay John's ransom. Once he was released John would marry Clisson's daughter and sole heiress, Marguerite. This meant that Clisson's descendants would in due course inherit Penthièvre and, unless the Duke remarried and fathered an heir, Brittany as well. Shortly after his agents had returned from England Clisson entered into a parallel arrangement with the dowager Countess of Anjou. The Countess, who was in constant financial difficulty, appointed Clisson as her lieutenant in Anjou, probably in return for another large cash advance. The Constable thus acquired practical control of a large block of territory in the lower Loire in addition to his extensive ancestral holdings on the left bank of the river, his domains in central Brittany and the territories of the house of Penthièvre in the north. The effect of these transactions was to present John de Montfort with the most dangerous threat to the security of his duchy since he recovered possession of it in 1379.[6]

One of the Duke's first acts after learning of his enemy's alliance with John of Blois was to make his own approaches to the English. He sent his ambassadors to England in the spring of 1385 to try to negotiate some arrangement which would keep the prisoner of Gloucester incarcerated indefinitely. They received short shrift at the hands of Richard II's Council. Some of the English King's councillors had never forgiven John de Montfort for the betrayal of 1381. Some simply saw no advantage to England in keeping him in power. Brest was still valued, arguably beyond its real worth, but the rest of Brittany was of declining strategic importance now that the great continental *chevauchées* of the past had been abandoned. The King himself looked at the issue in purely financial terms. John of Blois was a valuable asset which he was keen to realise. In March 1386 Richard granted the prisoner to his favourite, Robert de Vere, ostensibly to enable him to defray the costs of his forthcoming expedition to Ireland. De Vere opened negotiations with Clisson. Matters were far enough advanced by August 1386 for Pope Clement VI to issue a dispensation for the prisoner's marriage to Marguerite. John de Montfort became increasingly desperate. He sent one emissary after another across the Channel to patch up relations with the English and obstruct the progress of his rival's negotiations, but he had very little to offer the English now that he was reconciled to the French Crown. His agents at Westminster made no progress at all.[7]

During the winter of 1386-7 Olivier de Clisson's plans to bring John of Blois back to Brittany suffered some reverses. The parties could not agree upon the ransom. Clisson's efforts to raise extra money in France were skilfully obstructed by the Duke of Berry. Then the Commission of Government came to power in England and the whole political mood changed. The commissioners, most of whom loathed Robert de Vere, had no interest in helping him to make money out of the Count of Blois. It suited their more aggressive ideas about the conduct of the war to revive the alliance with John de Montfort. In February and March 1387 the Duke of Brittany's ambassadors were back at Westminster, locked in discussion with English diplomats. The discussions may even have got as far as a draft treaty. As an earnest of future co-operation the Commission promised that John of Blois would not be released without the Duke's consent. There was a large element of hypocrisy on both sides. The English distrusted the Duke and he for his part had no intention of allying himself with the English if he could attain his objects without such dangerous friends. On 8 May 1387 he entered into a written treaty with the Duke of Berry, the second of its kind within three years. This time there was no doubt about their target. The two men bound themselves to defend each other against their enemies and in John's case against Olivier de Clisson and John of Blois in particular, together with 'all other persons who may covet his rights and possessions or challenge or obstruct his enjoyment of them'. The Duke of Burgundy was not party to this instrument but he was in close touch with John de Montfort during this period and there can be little doubt that he approved of it.[8]

When the news broke that the Constable had been arrested at Vannes it was widely assumed that John de Montfort had been put up to it by the English. In fact the Duke's desperate stroke had all the marks of an impulsive act with little thought for the consequences and not much in the way of advance planning. Guillaume d'Ancenis, one of the Breton lords who was present at Vannes, told Froissart that the Duke had originally intended to kill Clisson. He was only dissuaded from this course by Clisson's brother-in-law, the lord of Laval, who spent all night talking the Duke out of it with appeals to both sentiment and political calculation. All that is known for certain is that two days after the event, on 27 June 1387, the Constable put his seal to a document which could only have been extorted from him by the direst threats. It recorded that at the request of his friends and kinsmen the Duke of Brittany had pardoned him all his 'acts of extortion, rebellion and insubordination' against his natural lord. The conditions were that Clisson was to renounce his alliance with John of Blois and abandon his plan to marry him to his daughter. He was to order his allies among the Breton nobility to submit to the Duke. All Clisson's castles in the duchy were to be delivered up to the Duke's officers. Two of them, including Josselin, would be transferred permanently to the Duke, and a third for his lifetime. All of John of Blois's castles in the county of Penthièvre were to be garrisoned by the Duke or demolished. On top of all this Clisson was to pay a cash indemnity of 100,000 gold francs. The delivery of the fortresses and the cash were accomplished by the Constable's agents within four days. At the beginning of July Clisson was released from captivity after sealing a post-dated confirmation purporting to have been made of his own free will. Two castles forming part of his inheritance, including his family seat at Clisson, were then restored to him.[9]

The news of Clisson's arrest provoked a grave crisis at the French court. Charles VI left the capital at the end of June for Normandy, where he would be closer to events. The Duke of Burgundy hastened south from Flanders to join him there. Messengers were sent ahead to Vannes to demand the Constable's immediate release. By the time Charles reached Rouen Clisson had been released and was on his way to meet him, full of bile and thoughts of vengeance. The first thought of the King's uncles was to exploit the Constable's humiliation in their own interest. According to Froissart, the Duke of Burgundy smugly informed him that it was his own fault for going to Vannes in the first place when he should have been overseeing the final preparations for the invasion. The story is probably apocryphal but Philip's attitude was certainly not helpful. As for the Duke of Berry, he took the opportunity, with his brother's support, to force on the Constable a settlement of their long-standing disputes in Poitou. But the two royal dukes had miscalculated almost as badly as John de Montfort himself. They under-estimated the outrage which John de Montfort's act would provoke. Older men, who had lived through the civil wars of the 1350s, compared the event to the murder of Charles of Spain by the King of Navarre in 1354. The smell of treason intensified passions, especially among those who had been due to participate in the invasion. The King, now a wilful nineteen-year-old, had always venerated the Constable and regarded his arrest as a personal slight. Over the following months the royal dukes found themselves swept along in the tide of indignation.[10]

The first sign of the new mood at court was that the obstacles which had hitherto impeded Olivier de Clisson's attempts to raise the money for John of Blois's ransom were suddenly lifted. On 1 October 1387 Clisson's representatives met the agents of Robert de Vere at Calais and sealed an agreement to pay 120,000 gold francs in instalments. Clisson proposed to advance half of this sum from his own chests. The rest was guaranteed by an impressive list of French royal councillors headed by the Dukes of Burgundy and Berry themselves. John was finally released in November and married Marguerite de Clisson two months later. In Brittany Clisson's partisans, sensing that events were moving their way, had already begun to attack the castles in the north of the peninsula which John de Montfort had seized from the house of Penthièvre. The Constable was at the French fortress of Pontorson on the north-west march of the duchy, gathering his forces and preparing to recover his own property by force. John de Montfort shut himself in the citadel of Nantes and put his castles in a state of defence.[11]

Faced with the imminent prospect of a civil war in the west, the royal Council met in the King's presence at the end of November 1387 in the walled city of Noyon, north of Paris. The Duke of Burgundy was present but if he tried to save his protégé he failed. The Council resolved to deliver an ultimatum to the Duke of Brittany. The chosen emissary was no friend of John's. Bernard de la Tour, Bishop of Langres, was an old councillor of Charles V who had been associated with the late King's aggressive policies in Brittany. The King, he was to say, intended to take the case against the Duke into his own hands. In the meantime all the property seized from Clisson was to be surrendered to his officers. The Bishop confronted the Duke in the castle of Nantes at the end of December. Bereft of allies and faced with the forfeiture of his duchy, John railed against the Constable. He protested that Clisson had been guilty of many offences against him and that he had imprisoned him as a recalcitrant vassal, not as Constable of France. But the envoy was implacable and with ill grace the Duke submitted. He agreed to appear before the King in April 1388 at Orléans to answer for his conduct. Pending Charles's judgment he delivered up the disputed castles and pledged his county of Montfort as security for the repayment of the 100,000 francs. Then he turned in desperation to the English.[12]

In England the conduct of foreign policy had been reduced to chaos by the conflict between Richard II and the commissioners who conducted the government in his name. From the outset the King had declined to co-operate with the Commission. In February 1387 he had abandoned Westminster altogether, embarking upon a long progress through the Midlands which lasted with brief intervals until the autumn. Here, in the company of Pole, De Vere and other friends, he plotted to reclaim power. Around them gathered a small group of advisers who began to look increasingly like an alternative government: the quarrelsome and headstrong Alexander Neville, Archbishop of York, scion of one of the leading landed families of the north, who was himself a member of the Commission but had repudiated its authority almost as soon as it had been appointed; Sir Robert Tresilian, the corrupt and authoritarian Chief Justice of the King's Bench; and the rich wool merchant and ex-mayor of London, Nicholas Brembre, who was probably helping to finance the King's wanderings. None of them had any following in the country and none were men to look to for balanced advice. Neville and Tresilian, to whom the King listened most, were unbending ultras with little political experience. Pole and De Vere were widely hated and had too much at stake personally. Brembre was an astute city boss with some support among the London guilds but very little in the streets.

The main issues at stake between the King and the Commission were the King's management of his finances and the control which his friends exercised over royal patronage. But attitudes to the war with France continued to divide the political community and assumed growing significance. The King's misgivings about the Commission's foreign policy were well known but his views acquired a new hardness of purpose once Gloucester and Arundel had made the effective prosecution of the war a major element in their pitch for political support. The events of the past year, culminating in the *coup* of November 1386, had taught Richard that he would never be able to exercise effective control over his realm while the war drained his funds and made him dependent on a fractious Parliament which was periodically dominated by his enemies.

The Commission had found the combination of efficient government and uncompromising hostility to France no easier to manage than Michael Pole had done when he was in power. They had instituted some reforms in the government's financial administration and made a start on reducing the mountain of accumulated debt. The royal household had been starved of funds in favour of other departments. But it was already apparent that there was no concealed source of money from which the war could be financed without recourse to taxation. The small Parliamentary subsidy voted by the Wonderful Parliament had been exhausted by the cost of continental garrisons and the three-month cruise of the Earl of Arundel. By June 1387 the Commission had run out of money. In spite of the renewed threat of invasion from France no more major operations were planned for the rest of the year apart from another flotilla to resupply Brest under the command of Henry Percy, which was not expected to leave England until September. Even that was clouded by uncertainty. Percy's indenture contained an unusual provision which envisaged that the Commission might be unable to supply the necessary shipping and permitted the commander in that event to abandon the whole enterprise.[13]

Meanwhile Richard II was actively dealing with the enemy. He had made contact with the French court through the regent of Hainault at the beginning of the year. By May he was dealing with Charles VI directly through a succession of low-grade members of his household staff, who had been chosen so as not to attract attention. Their object was to set up a summit meeting between the two kings on the march of Calais. This much appears to have been agreed. But what proposals were to be discussed there? The French government was well aware of the weakness of Richard's personal position. Their terms reflected the fact. They wanted the surrender of all of England's barbicans on the coast of France: Cherbourg, Brest, Calais and its outlying fortresses. The growing insistence on the problem of Calais bore the mark of Philip of Burgundy, whose possessions in Flanders and Artois were directly threatened by the English enclave. In any case, the French royal dukes observed, the place was worthless given what it cost the English King to maintain. Why should the English want to keep it unless they were contemplating a future cross-Channel invasion? In exchange the French were willing to renew their previous offers to restore most of the territory conquered from the English south of the Charente and the Dordogne, but they maintained their position that the whole duchy would have to be held as a fief of France. What Richard had in mind is much less clear. His domestic enemies accused him of planning to concede all the French demands but his immediate priority appears to have been to obtain a long truce of, say, five years during which concessions of this kind could be more carefully considered. Most of these ideas had featured in past conferences between the two sides. They were of course anathema to the leading members of the Commission. But the indications are that Richard intended the meeting to take place at the end of the year after the Commission's mandate expired.[14]

If Richard had been willing to allow the Commission's authority to lapse without recriminations he could probably have recovered power peacefully and might even have carried through his diplomatic programme. But the King and his advisers were bent on a showdown with the leaders of the aristocratic opposition. In particular Richard was determined to settle scores with Gloucester and Arundel, against whom he had nursed an unrelenting hatred ever since they had lectured him at Eltham the year before. In August 1387 Richard and his Council held two meetings, at Shrewsbury and Nottingham, with the seven judges of the superior courts. Behind closed doors and with the participants sworn to secrecy, ten carefully drafted questions were submitted to them for their opinion. All of them reflected the King's outrage at the way he had been treated by the Wonderful Parliament. They related to the validity of the Parliament's acts and to the legal status of the Commission of Government which it had appointed. The judges' advice, recorded in a document to which each of them put their seals, was one of the most uncompromising statements of the royal prerogative to be uttered before the reign of Charles I. The statute appointing the Commission of Government was declared to have been 'contrary to the royal dignity and prerogative of our Lord the King' because his assent to it had been given under duress. Those responsible for forcing the enactment upon him and taking the government out of his hands were declared to be guilty of common law crimes equivalent to treason and punishable by death. The judges went on to declare that Parliament had had no right to propose business of its own and insist on discussing it before addressing the business of the King; that the King was entitled to dissolve Parliament and dismiss its members whenever he pleased; and that the judgment pronounced against Michael Pole was erroneous 'in its entirety'. Later, when they were taxed with this document by an angry Parliament, the judges claimed to have been coerced. There is some evidence that they were, even if the coercion amounted to no more than angry words and browbeating.[15]

Armed with the judges' views the King prepared to confront his enemies. The sheriffs, who were also present at Nottingham, were not optimistic about the chances of raising an army. They reported that the Commission of Government had the support of 'all the commons' of the counties. Undeterred, Richard sent his household staff through the Welsh march, the Midlands and East Anglia, regions traditionally close to the Crown, to retain men. He put Robert de Vere in control of the militantly royalist palatinate of Chester, where he prepared to recruit a large company of mounted archers. Rumour had it that by October as many as 20,000 men had bound themselves to come armed for his service when summoned. In London Nicholas Brembre worked covertly on his friends and allies among the guilds and extracted oaths to raise the city against the King's enemies when the time came.

Unfortunately for Richard, before the time came his plans became public knowledge. The activities of his recruiting agents inevitably created a fair amount of noise. The Commission responded by ordering the arrest of the King's messengers and the seizure of their letters. In October some of Richard's own entourage lost their nerves. They became alarmed at the bloody course on which he was set, which they believed could only lead to civil war. One of them was Robert Wickford, Archbishop of Dublin, who had been present at the secret sessions with the judges. In October Wickford went to the Duke of Gloucester and told him everything. Shortly afterwards Richard's dealings with the French court came to light when a chamber knight, Sir John Golafre, was stopped and searched as he passed through Calais on his way back from France. Golafre himself escaped but his luggage was found to contain copies of Richard's letters to Charles VI and safe-conducts issued by the French King for the summit meeting. Within days reports were circulating that Richard was preparing to sell out of the English positions in northern France in exchange for armed support against his domestic enemies. It was the second time in a year that rumours of this kind had circulated in England. The allegation was untrue. But it was generally believed.[16]

Richard had no time to summon the retainers whom he had recruited during the summer. He resolved to strike quickly with the support of the Londoners. A clerk was sent to the capital with a warrant for the arrest of the Duke of Gloucester and his allies and an order addressed to the Mayor to execute it. The Mayor, Nicholas Exton, quailed before such a task. He consulted the aldermen and councillors. They resolved that the city had no business executing a writ of this kind. At Westminster Gloucester must have learned very quickly what was going on. His first instinct was to placate his nephew with protestations of loyalty. His second, when these were brushed aside, was to confer with his fellow commissioners Arundel and Warwick. The judges' advice left them with no other way of saving their skins than defiance and armed resistance. Towards the end of October Arundel, the most powerful of the three, withdrew to his estates in Surrey and Sussex. He eventually shut himself with a large armed force in the ancient twelfth-century castle of Reigate, twenty miles south of London. Gloucester and Warwick left to recruit troops in Middlesex and Essex. The rest of the Commission of Government remained, frozen, at Westminster.[17]

Early in November 1387 the King arrived at the royal palace at Sheen by the Thames, west of London. Here he resolved to make for the capital before the situation got out of control. Archbishop Neville and Michael Pole, who had been sent ahead to prepare the ground, reported that in spite of the business of the warrant the King's support there was solid. On 10 November the King made his formal entry into the city, escorted by the aldermen and councillors and the guildsmen in their colours with all the panoply of deference. Later that day Richard, accompanied by Neville, De Vere and Pole and escorted by his household troops, arrived at Westminster. On the following morning Gloucester and Arundel were summoned to appear before him. At once Richard's position fell apart. Neville and Pole had badly misjudged the mood of the Londoners. Mayor Exton was an astute trimmer whose main object was to stay out of trouble. Behind the sycophantic facade the aldermen were reported to be 'as wobbly as reeds'. Support for the opposition was building up in the streets, where Arundel was still the hero of Margate and Cadzand. The freemen of the wards would not stir in Richard's interest. Richard had no forces of his own with which to confront the rebels apart from his household troops and the retainers of those who were with him at Westminster, a few hundred men at the most. Attempts to recruit more failed miserably. Ralph, Lord Basset, an old retainer of the Black Prince who had fought at Poitiers, spoke for many when he told the King that he was always ready to fight for truth and justice but would 'not have his head broken for the Duke of Ireland'. On 12 November the Earl of Northumberland was sent with an armed escort to arrest the Earl of Arundel at Reigate. But his heart was not in it. Finding the place bristling with soldiers and the gates shut against him he withdrew without completing his mission. As soon as he had gone Arundel left Reigate and, marching through the night, joined forces with Gloucester and Warwick in the Bishop of London's park at Haringey, north of London. A large number of armed volunteers from the gentry of the surrounding counties joined them there in the course of the day.[18]

At Westminster panic set in among the King's friends. There was a disorderly meeting of the King's Council on 14 November. It was attended not just by the King's inner circle but by at least eight members of the Commission of Government who were still at Westminster and some respected outsiders such as the Earl of Northumberland. Pole railed against the Earl of Warwick, whom he blamed for the disaster, and tried to interest the others in a scheme to assassinate him. Neville, supported by Sir Thomas Trivet, was for marching against the rebels with the King's household troops and the levies of London. The rest knew that the game was up. The great majority of those present advised Richard to capitulate. Their spokesman was the Earl of Northumberland. He believed that it had been a mistake for Richard to treat Gloucester and Arundel as his enemies and said so.[19]

The King resolved to play for time. The commissioners present were deputed to go before the rebel lords to find out their demands and propose a meeting with the King. Later that day they rode in a body to Waltham Cross in Essex, where Gloucester, Warwick and Arundel had now set up their headquarters. The three lords drove a hard bargain. They declared Neville, Pole, De Vere, Tresilian and Brembre to be the 'wickedest of traitors' and presented an 'appeal of treason' against all five of them. They demanded that the five should be held in custody and tried before Parliament. Otherwise they were ready to march on Westminster with their army. The meeting with the King took place on 17 November 1387. Gloucester, Arundel and Warwick rode into the palace enclosure at Westminster at the head of 300 mounted men. The King was seated on his throne at the far end of Westminster Hall, surrounded by the officers of state and the other members of the hated Commission of Government. The hall was packed with onlookers. The three lords entered by the east end and advanced towards the throne. The King, always a consummate actor, rose and took each of their hands in turn 'as is the custom among friends'. Richard accepted their appeal and gave them a date in February when they would be permitted to prove their case before Parliament. Meanwhile he undertook to detain the five accused and to give his protection to both sides. After the public audience was concluded Richard received the three Appellants in his private chamber and drank wine with them.[20]

When the Appellants had gone the King withdrew to the royal manor of Sheen to organise the raising of an army. Simon Burley proposed to raise 1,000 men in the Cinque Ports, of which he was Warden. There is some, highly circumstantial, evidence that Pole tried to recruit men among the garrison of Calais where his brother commanded the citadel. Robert de Vere left for Chester armed with letters authorising him to raise up to 6,000 men and to pledge the King's credit for their wages. In the last few days of November 1387 he and his lieutenant, Sir

Thomas Molyneux, were busy recruiting troops in Cheshire, Lancashire and north Wales. Within a fortnight of the audience in Westminster Hall the mask was cast aside. Richard wrote to De Vere and Molyneux asking them to come south urgently with as many troops as they had been able to collect. He would meet them with his own forces on the road. It is far from clear where Richard expected his own forces to come from. Nothing had come of the attempt to raise troops in the Cinque Ports and Pole was sent away empty-handed from Calais by the King's officers in the town. All the indications are that in spite of their fickleness to date Richard was counting on the Londoners. On 1 December the Mayor and aldermen of London appeared before the King at Windsor. Richard asked them directly how many troops they would raise for his cause. Exton, unable to evade the issue any longer, made his excuses. The Londoners, he said, were mere craftsmen and merchants. They would defend their walls. But they could not be expected to supply a field army. Then he asked to be relieved of his office.[21]

The traditional fiction that the King's misdeeds were due to his advisers was becoming difficult to maintain. Gloucester and Arundel, if they had had their own way, would have deposed Richard there and then. They were thinking of their own future security and perhaps, in Gloucester's case, of the succession. In the first few days of December 1387 the three original Appellants marched north from London at the head of their troops. They were joined at Huntingdon by John of Gaunt's eldest son Henry Bolingbroke, Earl of Derby, and by Thomas Mowbray, Earl of Nottingham. Both men were relatively inexperienced politicians then twenty-one years old. Bolingbroke had the closest possible links with the Crown. He was the King's first cousin and had been brought up with him. He was in many ways closer to the stereotype of fourteenth-century kingship than Richard was: earnest, flamboyant and generous, a famous knight, enthusiastic jouster and persistent crusader with none of Richard's disabling nervous introspection. In 1387 he seems to have been moved mainly by resentment of Robert de Vere, whose influence, already very great, would have been overwhelming if he had defeated the Appellants in the field. This was a major issue for Bolingbroke. His father was the dominant landowner in both Lancashire and Cheshire, where De Vere and Molyneux were recruiting their army and threatening to create a rival source of patronage. Mowbray's motives were probably more straightforward. Like Bolingbroke he had been brought up at court.

Unlike him he had been close to Richard and would be again. He had no particular affection for the Appellants personally and no ideological commitment to their cause. But he was ambitious, probably living beyond his means, and no more willing than Bolingbroke to become dependent on De Vere's favour for his advancement. The support of these two men for the rebellion brought it a great accession of strength but was destined to undermine its cohesion. The fault lines in the alliance became clear at Huntingdon when Gloucester and Arundel put forward their plan to depose the King. For Bolingbroke and Mowbray, De Vere was the enemy, not Richard. The Earl of Warwick agreed and for the moment the idea was put aside.[22]

De Vere's army, about 4,000 men from north-western England and the northern march of Wales, mustered at Flint and Pulford in the first week of December 1387. A few days later they began their march south through Shrewsbury, Worcester and Evesham. The Appellants' army appears to have outnumbered De Vere's by a considerable margin, particularly in men-at-arms. Its core comprised the military retinues of the five leaders, men united mainly by bonds of personal loyalty to their leaders. But the wide geographical distribution of the men who fought with them suggests a broad-based support for their cause extending well beyond the territorial interests of its leaders, 'stout hearts from every part of the land' as a friendly chronicler put it with only slight exaggeration. In the middle of December the Appellants' host moved west from Huntingdon. Their object was to stop De Vere in the Midlands and prevent a junction with the King. De Vere's was to avoid battle and conserve his forces for the decisive conflict around London. On 19 December 1387, however, he found his route blocked beyond Evesham. The Appellants had divided their forces and occupied all the main road and river crossings in the western Cotswolds. De Vere decided to turn south and make a dash for the Thames crossings. Under cover of a thick autumnal mist he arrived at the stone bridge over the Thames at Radcot only to find it held against him by Bolingbroke. Trapped between Bolingbroke's army in front of him and Gloucester and Arundel coming up behind, De Vere tried to fight his way out. His army was routed in the space of a few minutes. Many of his men were drowned in the marshes of the Thames trying to get away. The rest surrendered. They were stripped of their arms and released. De Vere himself swam his horse across the river and disappeared into the night.[23]

Richard had remained at Windsor through the campaign, immobilised for lack of troops. The battle of Radcot Bridge was a

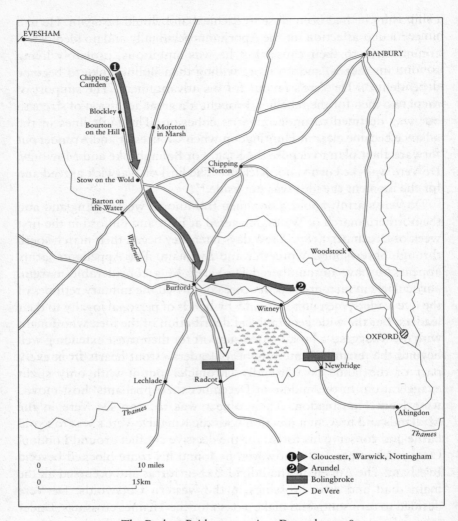

EVESHAM

BANBURY

Chipping
Camden

Blockley

Bourton
on the Hill

Moreton
in Marsh

Chipping
Norton

Stow on the Wold

Barton on
the Water

Windrush

Woodstock

Burford

Witney

OXFORD

Newbridge

Lechlade

Radcot

Thames

Abingdon

Thames

| 0 | | 10 miles |
| 0 | | 15km |

❶▶ Gloucester, Warwick, Nottingham
❷▶ Arundel
▬ Bolingbroke
⇨ De Vere

23 The Radcot Bridge campaign, December 1387

disaster for him. His friends, who knew that they could expect no mercy
from the Appellants, fled as soon as the news reached them. Neville
made off to the north dressed as a simple priest and after many
vicissitudes found his way to Brabant. Pole escaped to Hull and thence
to France where he took refuge at the court of Charles VI. Robert de
Vere, according to one report, succeeded in making his way into
Richard's presence disguised as a groom. He was bundled off to the
royal castle at Queensborough on the Isle of Sheppey, where he found

640

a ship for the continent. Tresilian remained in England. He disguised himself as a beggar, put on a false beard and hid in the house of a friend by the walls of Westminster. As for Richard himself, he made for London and took refuge in the Tower. Nicholas Brembre went with him, hoping to rouse the citizens to his cause. But Brembre's pleas were swept aside by the Mayor and aldermen. They had no confidence in the support of the mob and no desire to see their gates stormed and their homes pillaged by the army of the Appellants. On 27 December 1387 the Appellants arrived with their army in full war array in the open fields by the suburban village of Clerkenwell. The gates of the city were opened before them. On 30 December they took possession of the Tower with a force of 500 heavily armed men and confronted the King.[24]

Richard received them seated on an improvised throne in an upper room of the White Tower. It was a humiliation which he never forgot. The five rebellious magnates appeared surrounded by armed men and supporters, who made so much noise that the King had to withdraw with his enemies into the nearby Chapel of St. John. There, with the crowd baying outside the door, they confronted him with his correspondence with Robert de Vere, which had been found in De Vere's baggage at Radcot Bridge, and with intercepted letters from the King of France taken from the satchels of a diplomatic messenger who had recently arrived from France. They accused him of dishonouring his promises of November, plotting their deaths and betraying his kingdom with the support of 'traitors'. They added, according to a well-informed chronicler, 'many other things which did not become public knowledge'. The evidence is not consistent but there are good reasons for believing that among the 'other things' they told him was that they intended to depose him. For two or three days Richard's fate hung in the balance. Ultimately the Appellants changed their minds, mainly it seems because they could not agree on his successor. There is reason to believe that Gloucester hoped to take the throne for himself. But that was unacceptable to his colleagues and particularly to Bolingbroke. His own claims were stronger than anyone's apart from his father who was abroad and possibly the young Roger Mortimer, Earl of March (descended from Edward III's second son, Lionel Duke of Clarence), who was still a minor. It must also have occurred to them that they were in a position to impose their will without deposing the King. According to the monastic chronicler Henry Knighton, whose house had close links to the house of Lancaster, Bolingbroke took Richard to the walls of the

Tower to show him the strength of their army. 'And this host', he said, 'is not even a tenth of the number who wanted to come here to destroy the men who have betrayed you and all your kingdom.'[25]

On New Year's Day 1388 Richard II rode to Westminster to preside over a meeting of the Council at which the new regime was inaugurated. Nicholas Brembre, the only one of the five accused ministers who had not fled, was arrested. So were ten knights of the King's household including Simon Burley, Thomas Trivet, Nicholas Dagworth and William Elmham, along with several of Richard's chaplains. A month later it was the turn of the judges, who were arrested in their courtrooms, dismissed from their posts and put in the Tower. The whole of the King's household was dismissed and its more prominent members obliged to swear not to set foot in the court again. A new Council was appointed to conduct the day-to-day business of government, consisting mainly of former members of the Commission of Government. The only notable friend of the King among them was Walter Skirlaw, who was presumably included because of his diplomatic experience.[26]

On 3 February 1388 Parliament opened in the palace of Westminster. In the opening speech, delivered by Chancellor Arundel, the business of the assembly was declared to be to decide 'how, by the Grace of God, the great disputes, troubles and dissensions which had divided the realm for want of good government might be peacefully resolved, the King better advised, the country better governed and peace and order restored and maintained.' The White Chamber was packed as the door opposite the throne was opened and the five Appellants entered arm-in-arm, dressed in uniform golden robes, to present their appeal against the former ministers of the King. The appeal was read out, followed by thirty-nine detailed articles of accusation which took the clerk some two hours to read. These are said to have produced a powerful impression on the assembly. The tenor of the charges was that the five ministers had appropriated the King's powers into their own hands and excluded from his counsels the great men of the realm who ought by rights to have been his principal advisers.

As the document got down to detail three broad categories of accusation emerged. First there was the familiar, and largely justified accusation that the ministers, especially De Vere and Pole, had used their influence over the King to divert his patronage in their own direction. Secondly they were accused of trying to help the King shake off the power of the Commission of Government. But the most significant group of accusations was the third, which bore the stamp of

Gloucester and Arundel and concerned the conduct of war and diplomacy. The ministers were accused of appointing incompetent captains to important fortresses in south-western France, as a result of which many of them had been lost. They were said to have failed to organise any proper defence against the French invasion fleet of 1386. They had allowed John of Blois to be ransomed by the French when the national interest dictated that he should continue to be held as a prisoner in England. Finally they stood accused of trying to reach an accommodation with France. The Appellants alleged, and apparently believed, that Richard's negotiations with Charles VI had been intended as the prelude to an assault on the King's domestic enemies with French armed support. These articles suggest a coherent strategy for carrying on the war. The eyes of their authors were fixed on Calais, Brest and Cherbourg, the great English 'barbicans' of the Atlantic coast of France. The Appellants regarded these places as gateways for future cross-Channel invasions, the seeds of an eventual English military revival. Richard and his friends, as they saw it, had been preparing to surrender them, thus making recent defeats irreversible. These convictions do much to explain Gloucester's and Arundel's behaviour during these months. All the evidence suggests that of the five Appellants it was they and Warwick, the 'undivided trinity' as a supportive pamphleteer called them, who dominated the trial of the King's ministers. And it was they who later pressed for the net to be spread wider to encompass the minnows of the King's administration, men who had done no more than execute the decisions of others. They knew enough history to appreciate that if the King remained on his throne they might one day be exposed to his vengeance. They were determined to deter his servants with a lesson so terrifying that none would dare to do his bidding in the same way again.[27]

It was a contemporary, the chronicler Henry Knighton, who first called it the 'Merciless Parliament'. The trials of the accused opened before the Lords on 5 February 1388. Even the new judges, whom the Appellants had themselves appointed, had misgivings about the procedure employed, for which they could find no authority in either civil or common law. The Lords brushed aside this objection, resolving that so 'high a crime' should be tried according to the law of Parliament, which they proceeded to devise for the occasion. On 13 February Neville, Pole, De Vere and Tresilian were all convicted of treason in their absence. Neville, as a cleric, was condemned to lose all his assets. The other three were sentenced to be drawn and hanged. The first to suffer this fate was the unfortunate Tresilian, who was seen watching the comings and goings from the roof of the house in Westminster in which he had taken refuge. The crowd invaded the building, found him hiding under a table and dragged him from his screaming wife and daughter crying 'We havet hym! We havet hym.' Tresilian was drawn from the Tower to Tyburn that afternoon. On the scaffold his robes were found to be lined with magic charms to protect his life. They hanged him naked. The trial of Nicholas Brembre, which had been interrupted by Tresilian's discovery, was a travesty. The accused was not allowed counsel or even a copy of the charges. His attempts to defend himself were shouted down by the Commons and ruled out of order by the Lords. When the King tried to speak up on behalf of his friend members of both houses threw down their gauntlets on the paving to support their allegations. Even so, a commission of twelve peers charged to consider the articles of accusation reported that Brembre had done nothing deserving of death. The Appellants finally got their way by sending for the Mayor of London and selected aldermen, who were asked for their views about the guilt of the accused and rather hesitantly opined that if the treasons charged had occurred, they 'supposed that he must have been aware of them'. At this, Brembre was condemned unheard and followed Tresilian to the scaffold.[28]

At the beginning of March 1388 the Lords proceeded to the lesser figures. John Blake, Tresilian's law clerk, who had drafted the articles sealed by the judges, was drawn and hanged. The under-sheriff of Middlesex was convicted of trying to raise the Londoners in support of the King but his real offence was that he had been designated by the King the previous October to indict Gloucester and Arundel for treason. He was beheaded with thirty strokes of the axe. Next came the judges, who were arraigned on 6 March. They at least were allowed to defend themselves but their protestations that they acted under duress were ignored. They were condemned to death and then reprieved on the petition of the bishops and sentenced instead to exile in Ireland. By the time that the judges were dealt with the momentum of the trials was already failing. Divisions had begun to appear among the Parliamentary peers and even among the Appellants themselves. Richard's confessor, Thomas Rushook, Bishop of Chichester, was alleged by the Commons to have been one of the men behind the questioning of the judges at Nottingham and had certainly been present when they had given their advice. But the Lords refused to proceed with his trial and finally evaded the issue by adjourning it until after Easter. On 12 March four of

Richard's household knights were brought before the Lords together with his private secretary and three of his chaplains. The proceedings against them aroused so much controversy that the case against the knights was deferred along with Rushook's. The charges against the chaplains were dropped altogether.[29]

The final act in the Appellants' campaign of revenge was played out in April and May 1388, when Burley and the other three chamber knights were brought back to face the charges laid against them by the Commons. The main case against them was that they had helped the King to resist the Commission of Government and the rebellion of the Appellant lords. There was also a charge, which was close to the hearts of Gloucester and Arundel, that they had treasonably caused the King to negotiate with France and arranged safe-conducts to allow his messengers to travel to the French court. Burley, who had been closer to the King than anyone, was attacked with special venom. He was said to have taken advantage of Richard's youth to usurp the royal power and enrich himself. In the Lords, which had to judge them, these charges aroused intense controversy. Burley had many supporters there. For although he had unquestionably acquired great power and riches through his influence over the King he had had a distinguished career as a soldier in France in the service of the Black Prince and as an administrator in England. The King and Queen and two of the Appellant Lords, Bolingbroke and Mowbray, laboured mightily on his behalf and won over most of the Lords. After a fortnight of fruitless deliberation Edmund Langley, Duke of York, rose to his feet and declared that he would vouch for Burley's loyalty by fighting a duel with anyone who denied it. Gloucester replied that Burley had been false to his allegiance and offered to prove it with his own sword-arm. York, white with anger, called Gloucester a liar and Gloucester replied in kind. The two brothers would have come to blows if the King had not separated them and adjourned the proceedings for the rest of the week. When they resumed, on 5 May, the Commons were baying for blood while the Lords, weary after the longest Parliamentary session in recent memory, were anxious to get the business done. Gloucester, Arundel and Warwick browbeat them into submission. Burley was convicted and sentenced to death. The King, declaring that Burley was innocent on all charges, thought of refusing to confirm the sentence. But Gloucester told him to his face that if he wanted to keep his crown on his head he had better stop trying to save his old friend. The sentence was carried out on the same day. The three other chamber knights met the same fate a week later. The only concession made to the condemned men was that they were spared being drawn to the place of execution on a hurdle and were beheaded, not hanged. Even that mercy was denied to one of them, John Salisbury. He had been one of the emissaries sent to negotiate with the French court the year before and had earned the special hatred of the Appellants. Rushook was declared guilty of treason but on account of his status as a clerk was spared execution. He was sent to join the judges in Ireland. Six other members of Richard's household remained to be tried. But neither House had the stomach to prolong the hearing into the summer. So the accused were bailed to appear before the next Parliament.[30]

As soon as they had wrested power from the King the Appellants repudiated his foreign policy and put an end to his attempt to make peace with France. The ports were closed and orders given to stop Richard's messengers at the Channel. The captain of Calais castle, Pole's brother Edmund, was replaced along with several other royal captains in the Calais pale who were thought to have connived in the King's plans. The summit meeting of the two sovereigns was silently abandoned. The men who had helped to set it up were pursued with particular savagery and those who had found safe havens abroad were excluded from the general pardon which closed the proceedings, even down to the minor messengers and clerks who had acted as go-betweens. Philip of Burgundy had written to the Duke of Gloucester from Compiègne three days before the battle of Radcot Bridge to remind him of recent diplomatic proposals and to ask what was going on. His letter was not even answered.[31]

As the proceedings of the Merciless Parliament ground on, however, it became clear that the Commons were not prepared to pay for the warlike ambitions of Gloucester and Arundel from public taxation. They continued to believe that the war could be financed from the King's own resources if they were honestly managed, whereas by now Arundel and Gloucester had enough experience of government to realise that it could not. On 21 February 1388 Parliament interrupted their reprisals against the servants of the King to authorise a naval campaign under the command of the Earl of Arundel. But three weeks passed before the Commons could be persuaded to make an interim grant of taxation and then it was small and grudgingly given. They allowed the government just half a standard subsidy. The terms suggest that they had in mind a series of cruises in the Channel against French shipping and coastal settlements with no serious land operations.[32]

The Appellants may have planned to come back for more later. But any prospect of that vanished in April, when a number of peasant risings broke out in Kent and other parts of southern England. They were provoked by a mixture of local and national grievances, but the burden of war taxation and the government's inability to defend the coasts were much the most bitterly felt. For a brief moment it seemed possible that there would be another general rising on the model of 1381. The Lords and Commons were alarmed. When they returned to Westminster after the Easter recess one of the few points on which they were agreed was the impossibility of imposing further burdens on taxpayers. They drew up a remarkable joint protest against the continual demands for war taxation:

By the coast in different parts of your kingdom the houses of your poor commons have been burned, people and whole villages ransomed, ships entirely destroyed and the land abandoned and impoverished, so that you no longer have the means to defend your realm or maintain your royal estate to the great grief of all the wiser men about you. The men who have rebelled against you know of no other remedy than to seize the leading men who control your Council and to charge them with treason against you and your realm . . .

Among the more specific proposals of the petitioners was that a commission of peers should be appointed to 'strictly examine' the way the war was being conducted before it brought further ruin on the community. The targets of this petition were plainly Gloucester and Arundel. No one else could have been described as 'the leading men who control your Council'. When, in the closing days of the session, Parliament turned to the future government of the realm they approved the appointment of a new 'continual council' of five on which neither man was included. On 4 June 1388 the most fractious Parliament in recent memory was dissolved.[33]

In spite of their exclusion from the continual council Arundel and Gloucester remained the dominant figures in the government. They continued to devise grand strategies for prosecuting the war which were far in excess of anything contemplated by the Commons. The catalyst was a fresh crisis in Brittany, which had been developing throughout the sessions of the Merciless Parliament. Faced with a serious threat of invasion from France John de Montfort returned to the double-dealing which he had always used in these straits. He showed just enough interest in the English advances to encourage them and to put pressure on Charles VI to make concessions; but not quite enough to compromise himself irretrievably in French eyes or alienate the Dukes of Burgundy and Berry. In about November 1387 John wrote to Richard II reminding him of the proposals which his agents had discussed with the Commission of Government earlier in the year and declaring his readiness to support an English invasion of France. The Duke of Gloucester knew from experience how difficult it was to trust to John's good faith but he needed allies too much to question it now. In January 1388 Richard Fotheringhay, the captain of John de Montfort's castle at Rising in Norfolk, was sent by the Council on a secret mission to Brittany with proposals for a military alliance. Fotheringhay found John at Vannes in March. A draft treaty was drawn up. The document has not survived but its contents can be reconstructed from other sources. The Duke signalled his willingness to receive an English army in Brittany and to deliver up a number of fortresses to its commanders. He agreed to bring his own army to join forces with them. To ease the perennial problems of shipping he promised to provide mounts for the invaders once they had landed. For the moment at least, John behaved as if he meant it. On 11 April 1388 the King of France arrived at Orléans with a large entourage of noblemen, bishops and jurists to hear the Duke of Brittany answer for his imprisonment of the Constable. John failed to appear and sent neither spokesmen nor explanations in his place. Clisson delivered a bitter tirade against his rival before the assembled court, concluding with a challenge to a duel. He threw down his gauntlet on the ground, followed by all the principal members of his household. It was a dramatic gesture but an empty one. A defendant was traditionally entitled to more than one summons before he could be condemned in default. There was nothing to be done. On 27 April the court left for Paris.[34]

In the hands of Gloucester and Arundel the modest naval operations contemplated by the Commons developed into a major continental campaign, involving co-ordinated attacks on France from Brittany and Gascony. Preparations were already well under way by the time Richard Fotheringhay returned to England in April 1388. The Earl of Arundel was to sail from the Solent in May and land in Brittany with an army of 1,500 men-at-arms and 2,000 archers. In addition he was granted the custody of Brest with its substantial garrison, bringing his total strength to nearly 4,000 men. At the same time plans were in hand to mount a large-scale diversionary campaign in Gascony with the aid of John of Gaunt. This ambitious project seems to have been devised at a very late stage in conjunction with Sir Thomas Percy, who had recently arrived in England as John of Gaunt's personal representative. Percy undertook that Gaunt would take the field with 1,000 men-at-arms and 1,000 archers. He was expected to find 800 of the men-at-arms among the Gascon nobility. The remaining 200 men-at arms and all the archers were to be recruited in England and sent out by sea. The shipping position, although tight, was healthier than it had been for many years. The requisitioning of ships was completed in six weeks by the end of April 1388, the first time that such a thing had ever been achieved. It produced more than a hundred large ships and barges, half as many again as the Admiral's original target, in addition to ten war galleys sent by the King of Portugal which joined Arundel's strength a little later.[35]

At this critical juncture the dominant factor in the strategic plans of the French government was not England or even Brittany but the personal ambitions of the Duke of Burgundy in the Low Countries. These ambitions revolved around the security of the duchy of Brabant, the largest and richest principality of the German Low Countries, which had for many years been a protectorate of Flanders. Its ruler, the Duchess Jeanne, was old and ill, childless and politically incapable. Real power was exercised by the Duke of Burgundy. He and his wife were the designated heirs to the duchy. Their officers dominated the Duchess's council. Their troops were the backbone of its defence against her enemies.

The chief of these enemies was William, Duke of Guelders and heir to Jülich, the most persistent and aggressive opponent of French influence in the region. William's territories lay beyond the eastern march of Brabant between the Meuse and the Rhine. There was a history of sporadic border warfare between Guelders and Brabant going back many years but it had recently acquired a fresh intensity. The Duke skilfully exploited the eddies and currents of the Anglo-French war. He timed his main offensives to coincide with the French invasion projects of 1386 and 1387, when he knew that they would be unable to send troops to Jeanne's aid. He began a noisy exchange of embassies with the English and in June 1387 made a formal military alliance with them, doing homage to Richard II and promising to contribute 500 men-at-arms to his continental ventures. A month after the alliance was made Duke William announced it in letters addressed to Charles VI ('so-called King of France') and to Philip of Burgundy and the Duchess Jeanne. He declared war on all three of them.[36]

This event offered Philip of Burgundy the chance to employ French manpower and French money in a major campaign against his only serious challenger in the Low Countries. In the midst of the crisis provoked by the arrest of Olivier de Clisson, Jeanne's ambassadors came before the French court and received what amounted to a French guarantee of Brabant's territory. In the autumn of 1387 the French began to commit troops to Brabant's north-eastern march. An active war of skirmish and ambush was fought out in the Meuse valley during the winter. But Philip was not content with consolidating the border of Brabant. He wanted a full-scale invasion of Guelders by a French army, which would establish his power as completely in Brabant as the Roosebeke campaign had done in Flanders. His grip on the French government had been much weakened by the events of the past year but he worked assiduously on the young King, remaining almost continually by his side through the winter and spring and staking all his influence at court on the outcome.[37]

The Duke of Burgundy's project aroused strong opposition in Paris. An invasion of Guelders responded to no obvious strategic interest of France. It distracted resources and attention from the far more dangerous activities of the Duke of Brittany. And it denuded France of troops at a time when it was facing a serious threat from England in the west. Charles's ministers had also been concerned for some time about the threat from John of Gaunt in Bayonne. They had no idea of the scale of his losses in Castile. They assumed that he still had at his disposal the substantial army which had landed at Corunna in 1386. Considerable forces had already been deployed along the march of Gascony in order to contain him. The Channel provinces, by comparison, were wide open. There was only a thin curtain of troops defending the march of Brittany. The only warships in commission were the six galleys sent by the King of Castile, which were currently on their way north across the Bay of Biscay with a mixed complement of Portuguese exiles, Castilian seamen and French men-at-arms. A larger fleet of French ships and oared barges was being prepared for service at the Clos des Galées in Rouen but would not be ready until July. The French were well informed about Arundel's preparations in England and had some knowledge of the English government's dealings with John de Montfort. They guessed that English operations mounted from Gascony might be co-ordinated with landings in Brittany. The prospect filled them with alarm.[38]

In the face of these multiple threats the Duke of Burgundy's sole concern was to save his project for invading Guelders. He bent all his efforts to avoiding a major confrontation with England or Brittany. He

opened negotiations with the English government at Calais, initially
without the consent of Charles VI, with a view to arranging a separate
truce covering his own territories in Flanders. He was probably behind
the approaches which the Duke of Berry made at about the same time
to John of Gaunt with proposals for another local truce in the south-
west. He actively promoted a compromise with John de Montfort in
the face of determined opposition from the Constable and other
influential men at court. All of these issues came to a head in May 1388.
The Earl of Arundel's preparations at Southampton were approaching
completion. On the march of Brabant the current truce with the Duke
of Guelders was about to expire and bells were ringing across Jeanne's
principality to summon men to arms. The French royal Council met in
Paris in the middle of the month. All three of the King's uncles were
present as well as most of the leading prelates and noblemen of the
realm and the more important permanent officials. The Duke of
Burgundy pressed for the German campaign to proceed. He was
supported by the King, who was excited by the prospect of military
glory; and by much of the military nobility, who deplored the dishonour
involved in cancelling a widely trumpeted expedition to Guelders and
looked forward to the profits that would be had fighting beyond the
borders of France. Ranged on the other side were the King's permanent
officials, the risk-averse Duke of Berry and presumably Olivier de
Clisson, whose personal interests were as much engaged as Philip's. The
result was a compromise but one which was broadly satisfactory to
Philip. The Guelders campaign was deferred until the Breton problem
could be resolved. But the Council agreed to offer an olive branch to
John de Montfort. Enguerrand de Coucy, who was thought to be the
most gracious emissary available, was sent with a small delegation of
royal councillors on an urgent mission to Brittany. In the meantime
another *taille*, the second in a year, was imposed on the long-suffering
French taxpayers.[39]

In the few days that remained before the sailing of Arundel's fleet
Philip of Burgundy and his allies travailed mightily to patch up an
agreement which might keep John de Montfort loyal, the English out of
Brittany and the Duke's German ambitions alive. Enguerrand de Coucy
worked his charm upon the Duke of Brittany. By the end of May he
had persuaded him to meet the Dukes of Burgundy and Berry in the
Loire town of Blois. At the beginning of June John de Montfort was
rowed up the Loire in a fleet of armed barges, accompanied by no fewer
than 1,200 barons, prelates, liveried retainers and bodyguards. John

was determined not to appear as a petitioner. He was met on the quayside at Blois by the two royal dukes with their own equally magnificent escorts. In the castle, terms were hammered out for John's submission to the Crown. Their tenor can be inferred from subsequent events. If John would agree to appear before the King and excuse himself for his conduct over the past year Charles would pardon his crimes and convert the current criminal proceedings against him into a civil dispute with the Constable. The King would decide it himself. This would save the King's dignity while lifting the threat of forfeiture hanging over John's duchy. John would still be exposed to the risk of having to restore what he had taken from Olivier de Clisson but there is reason to think that the royal dukes dropped a hint that the King might decide in his favour.

John wrote a humble letter to the King apologising for his failure to appear at Orléans, which he claimed was due to illness. He was then conducted in state to Paris. There, on about 8 June, the King received him in the great hall of the Louvre under the resentful eyes of courtiers who had never ceased to regard him as a traitor and a creature of the English. For the Duke of Burgundy it was a moment of extreme satisfaction. Shortly afterwards the French royal Council sent out summonses for the army of Guelders. The muster was fixed for the middle of August at the bridge-town of Montereau, south-east of Paris. The proceeds of the *taille* were diverted to the new venture. As for John de Montfort, when the King at length issued his award in July it was found to be almost entirely in favour of Olivier de Clisson. The two rivals were publicly reconciled, drinking from a loving cup at a splendid banquet given by the King. John had been duped. But by this time Philip of Burgundy's object had been achieved. The strategic foundation of the Earl of Arundel's expedition had crumbled away.[40]

Arundel knew nothing of these events. His fleet sailed out of the Solent on 10 June 1388, a month late, escorted by the galleys of Portugal. His army consisted of nearly 3,600 men, slightly more than the strength for which he had contracted. About a third of the transports had been designated as victuallers for what was evidently expected to be a long campaign. It was the best-prepared English seaborne expedition for many years. Arundel was accompanied by Sir Thomas Percy with 150 men destined to serve as an advance guard for the army of Gascony and by Richard Fotheringhay, armed with a clutch of powers to conclude the treaty which had been negotiated with the Duke of Brittany in March. The armada made first for the coast of

Normandy. From there the ships worked their way south from headland to headland, picking up prizes where they could, but they were unable to land. Everywhere the ports were defended and the coast-guards out. In about the third week of June Arundel finally succeeded in landing on the undefended island of Bréhat, off the north coast of Brittany. There he learned to his dismay about John de Montfort's meeting with the King in Paris. Since the army had come without mounts, counting on the Duke's officers to provide them, there was nothing to be done in Brittany. Arundel and his principal officers were forced to remake their plans. After some debate they decided to attempt a landing on the Biscay coast of France. On 23 June the English fleet reached Brest. From there, towards the end of the month, it made a south-easterly course heading for the Bay of Bourgneuf, a traditional hunting ground for English commerce raiders. The spoil here was spectacular. They stormed the castle of Noirmoutier and burned much of the island before accepting *patis* to withdraw. The islands of Batz and Bouin and four inland towns suffered the same fate. After ten days in the bay they had taken great quantities of gold, wine and cattle and burned no fewer than 140 merchant ships. In the middle of July Arundel's fleet turned south again. Sir Thomas Percy sailed on to Bayonne to confer with John of Gaunt. The rest of the fleet anchored in the Anse de l'Aiguillon, the vast enclosed bay north of La Rochelle, bounded by the windswept sand and marsh of the Aunis.[41]

The whole army disembarked, followed by the ships' crews. Taking some 400 men with him, Arundel penetrated inland in shallow barges through the lacework of creeks and canals and fell upon the town of Marans, some five miles inland on the left bank of the Sèvre Niortaise. The French were taken by surprise. The Seneschal of Saintonge was away at Bayonne trying to negotiate a local truce with the Duke of Lancaster. The local population abandoned the open country and fled to the security of the castles and walled towns. Arundel advanced with his army towards La Rochelle, which lay twelve miles south across the flats. At least part of the fleet followed him off the coast. A few miles from the port the English were repulsed by the garrison, supported by a crowd of armed citizens, and retreated back to Marans. There Arundel waited for about three weeks while his followers burned or looted all that they could find. The English commander's precise intentions are obscure. The Aunis was a poor and sparsely populated region, a treeless wasteland with no adequate roads and very little food or plunder. Without proper equipment there was no question of trying to besiege

La Rochelle. Without horses his men were unable to roam far from their base. The most plausible explanation of his movements was that he hoped to co-ordinate his operations with John of Gaunt and possibly also with the Anglo-Gascon companies of the centre. According to Froissart, he had landed a messenger in Brittany with letters for Perrot de Béarn, the principal *routier* captain of the Limousin.[42]

While Arundel in Saintonge dreamed of these great possibilities, in England the war policy for which he had stood collapsed. In April 1388 the Scots refused to renew the current truce, which was due to expire on 19 June. Unlike previous crises in Anglo-Scottish relations this one was not provoked by the French, who had had very little contact with their Scottish allies since Jean de Vienne's ill-tempered departure in 1385. With John of Gaunt far away on the marches of Castile, Richard II's Council concentrating all its resources and energies on Arundel's expedition and Parliament still unwilling to support the cost of an active war policy, the opportunity was too obvious to need pointing out. England's weakness was particularly evident in the north, where the Parliamentary assault on Richard II's friends had left a dangerous vacuum of power at the top. The Nevilles, who had been the dominant figures in the defence of both marches for much of the decade, were tainted by the fall of Archbishop Neville and displaced by their long-standing rivals the Percys. For Scotland the potential gains from reopening the war were considerable: a chance to secure its possession of the lowland enclaves reconquered in the past ten years; a place at the conference table if negotiations between the principal belligerents were resumed; and the prospect of loot and status, which had become the cement of border society. The only brake on the aggressive instincts of the borderers was the King, Robert II, now a sick old man, averse to the risks of war and resentful of the tutelage of his son Carrick, but only fitfully capable of resisting him. In February 1388 Carrick suppressed the last vestiges of his father's independence by ordering his arrest. From then until his death two years later Robert became a cipher in the hands of successive cliques of noblemen which formed around his sons. The change was marked by an immediate move to the offensive on the border. At the end of April 1388 the puppet-King presided over a council of the leading noblemen of his realm at Edinburgh. Agreement seems to have been reached on a large-scale invasion of northern England in the summer.[43]

The gravity of England's situation does not seem to have occurred to the Duke of Gloucester or the Council until early June. On 8 June 1388 commissions of array were issued in every county north of the Trent to meet the threat from Scotland. In the next few days news came in of the build-up of enemy galleys, ships and barges in the Seine. England had been denuded of her biggest ships and most of her seamen to furnish Arundel's fleet. Heavy calls on the Treasury for funds were answered by the classic devices of every bankrupt government: borrowing, assignments on the customs revenues, a temporary stop on payments to the Calais garrison. There had been a recent reminder of the dangers posed by this kind of financial stringency when one of the outlying forts of Calais had been lost after locally recruited garrison troops deserted to the enemy for want of pay. On 12 June, just two days after Arundel sailed from Southampton, the Council's courage failed. They could not fight on three fronts at once. Meeting in London, they decided that there was no alternative but to approach the French government and ask for a general truce. The Duke of Gloucester, who was present at the meeting, was required to write an awkward letter to the Duke of Burgundy, reminding him of the unanswered letter which Philip had addressed to him in December and purporting to take up the proposals which had been so abruptly dumped when the Appellants came to power. It must have cost him much pain to write it.[44]

On 29 June 1388 two Scottish armies simultaneously invaded England. One came through the east march towards Newcastle. The other entered the west march and made for Carlisle. A third, seaborne expedition left the Clyde to plunder Ulster and the Isle of Man. The wardens of the north were unready. There was no serious resistance anywhere. The damage in the east march was the worst for a hundred years according to a sober contemporary reporter. More than 400 men were taken for ransom and carried back to Scotland. Many more were burned in their houses or cut down as they fled. Reports of the scale of the destruction in the north reached Westminster at about the same time as intelligence suggesting that the threatened French descent on the south coast was now imminent. In the middle of July there was another crisis meeting of the Council. They took a number of drastic decisions. The fleet and army of the Earl of Arundel were recalled to England to be deployed against the Scots. The northern magnates were told to wait by the coast for his arrival. A fresh army would be raised in England to reinforce them. As in 1385 the King would take command in person. Meanwhile all the other military enterprises in hand were abandoned. A plan to send 200 archers to reinforce the Duke of Guelders was dropped. Preparations for the army of Gascony ceased. A Great Council was summoned to meet at short notice at Oxford on 27 July to find ways of funding the sudden increase in the burden of war expenditure in the north of England. These hurried and ill-considered decisions proved impossible to carry out. Ships were sent out from Dover and Dartmouth to scour the seas for the Earl of Arundel and inform him of his recall. Either they failed to find him or else he received the message and ignored it. The Great Council duly met but could do nothing. The magnates reminded the King's ministers of what they already knew, that they had no power to authorise taxation. They suggested that Parliament should be summoned but the earliest that it could meet was September. By then it would be too late.[45]

At the beginning of August 1388 the French fleet entered the Solent with its Castilian auxiliaries and did considerable damage to Portsmouth and the Isle of Wight.[46] At almost the same moment there was another, even more formidable invasion from Scotland. The main thrust of the new Scottish attack was in the west march. The Earl of Fife, Robert II's second son, accompanied by Sir Archibald Douglas, entered Westmoreland on 3 August with the usual elite corps of knights, followed by an immense horde of lightly armed horsemen, infantry and camp-followers, 'the whole power of Scotland' according to a report sent to Richard II. The defence consisted of local levies, greatly out-numbered and poorly led by the warden of the west march, John Lord Beaumont. He was a well-connected nonentity with few local supporters and little military experience, who had only just taken up his appointment. The invaders reached Carlisle within hours. They brushed aside the Cumberland levies who tried to stop them, killing 100 of the defenders and carrying off 300 prisoners including the sheriff. At the opposite end of the border James, Earl of Douglas, entered Northumberland with a much smaller but more select force, probably about 3,000 strong. They were drawn mainly from the retinues of the great Lowland families and the Lothian knights who had followed the banner of Douglas and his father since the 1350s. Douglas was later said by his enemies to have separated himself from the main army and conducted this operation without authority from the King. But it is more likely that he was concerting his movements with those of the Earl of Fife. His object seems to have been to pin down English forces, most of which were concentrated east of the Pennines, and prevent them from going to Beaumont's aid in Cumberland.

In the event Douglas achieved much more than that. In the first few days of August he marched rapidly south through Northumberland, burning farms and villages as he went and penetrating beyond the Tyne almost as far as Durham. Returning northward he conducted a brief demonstration before the walls of Newcastle. The city was defended by the warden of the east march, Sir Henry Percy. Percy, the eldest son of the Earl of Northumberland, was a famous paladin who had been knighted by Edward III at the age of thirteen and had passed his whole career fighting on the Scottish border, in France and at sea. Still only twenty-four years old, he had already earned the nickname 'Hotspur' for his impulsive tactics and speed of movement. In the course of a skirmish outside the gates of Newcastle Douglas captured Percy's pennon. As the Scots withdrew he sent an abusive message to his adversary, boasting that he would plant it on the walls of Dalkeith castle. Percy replied that it would never leave Northumberland. Behind the walls of Newcastle he had gathered the retainers of his house and the levies of Yorkshire and Northumberland. They must have numbered between 5,000 and 8,000 men. Another host had gathered at Durham under the command of its Bishop, Walter Skirlaw, and was on its way. On 5 August Percy received reports that Douglas's army was encamped by the River Rede, close to the tower of Otterburn some thirty miles away. In the early afternoon he led his men out of the town and set off in pursuit, leaving behind him orders that the Durham host should follow after him.

Shortly before dusk on 5 August 1388 the English army passed the village of Elsdon, some three miles east of the Scottish encampment. They were hungry and exhausted after the long march. The light was failing. The English archers would be useless in such conditions. But Hotspur was unwilling to allow the Scots to escape under cover of darkness. He believed that the advantage of surprise would carry the day. True to his name he ordered an immediate attack. He split up his men into two divisions. One, under his own command, would deliver a frontal attack on the Scottish positions. The other was placed under the command of Sir Mathew Redmayne. He was ordered to take a circuitous route by the north to attack the Scots in the rear. The Scots were finishing their dinner, their weapons by their sides, and were about to settle down for the night when a mounted scout rode into the camp with the news that the English were almost upon them. 'Hawys armys spedyly,' he cried. In the rush the Earl of Moray forgot his helmet. Douglas had no time to put on any armour at all. The Scottish camp stood at the foot of a ridge. The Scots scrambled up the slope and formed themselves up in battle order at the summit. Percy's division mounted the ridge on foot in no particular order and fell on the Scottish lines shouting 'Percy!' and 'St. George!' Douglas's men recoiled before the first impact but held firm and then counter-attacked in the declining light, forcing the English into retreat. Douglas, the 'true lantern of the Scots' according to the poet of the battle, was felled in the mêlée with three lances in his body. According to a celebrated but probably apocryphal tale, which was told to Froissart by two knights who had fought in the battle, as Douglas's companions dragged his naked and half-conscious body from the field he ordered them to pick up his banner from the ground and hold it aloft, crying 'Douglas!' above the din so that the Scots should not be demoralised by his death. In savage hand-to-hand fighting, aggravated by the difficulty of distinguishing friend from foe in the dark, the Scots pressed their advantage. At the foot of the hill the English disengaged and tried to reform. But the Earl of Dunbar, who was in command of the Scottish reserve, mounted his horse and led a cavalry charge down the slope, scattering them across the fields.

Most contemporaries blamed Percy for the defeat. Their criticisms had much force. In his haste to engage the enemy he had attacked them before Redmayne's division had closed in from the north and while the Bishop of Durham and the rest of the English army were still some way off. Redmayne reached the Scottish camp shortly after the fighting had begun. His men wasted time slaughtering the grooms and servants whom the Scots had left to guard their possessions and then lost their way in the darkness. Early next morning they found the corpses of their compatriots scattered across the fields by the Rede while the Scots stood triumphant on the ridge above. Redmayne's force attacked the exhausted Scots and drove them off, pursuing them north as far as the border. As for Bishop Skirlaw, he was met on the road in the middle of the night by a messenger carrying the news of the rout and turned back at once for Newcastle. Both sides had suffered heavy casualties. The English lost an estimated 550 dead and many captured. Henry Percy and his brother Ralph and twenty-one other knights were among the haul of prisoners. On the Scottish side casualties were almost as high. They lost about 500 men-at-arms. The prisoners included Sir James Lindsay and several other prominent leaders of the border wars.[47]

In its day Otterburn was a famous battle. Few events so forcibly brought home to English opinion how far things had changed since Edward III's heyday. It was the first major Scottish victory in the field since Bannockburn. It inspired patriotic epic poems in Scotland from the stilted Latin verses of Thomas Barry, written shortly after it was fought, to the *Ballad of the Battle of Otterburn*, which was still being sung in various recensions long after the borders wars had finished. 'I never heard the olde song of Percy and Duglas that I found not my heart moved more than with a trumpet,' Sir Philip Sidney would write two centuries later in the reign of Elizabeth. Jean Froissart, who had known James Douglas as a young boy when staying as his father's guest at Dalkeith, went to much trouble to interview those who had fought in the battle and devoted some of his most inventive prose to spreading its fame among a continental audience. Fought hand-to-hand between evenly matched forces of noblemen with famous captains on both sides and no archers to distort the outcome, the battle stood for everything that he most admired in chivalric warfare.

Of all the campaigns, battles and skirmishes, great and small, that I have recounted in this history, this encounter of which I now speak was the most strenuous and best fought for there was not a man there, knight or squire, but did his duty to the uttermost.

Strategically, it is true that there had been little at stake. Douglas had been heading home anyway. The victory was not followed up. The losses of the two sides roughly balanced out both in numbers and importance. Hotspur was eventually released after nearly a year in captivity in exchange for Sir James Lindsay plus 7,000 marks in cash. But politically the battle would have enormous ramifications. The death of the head of the house of Douglas without an heir left a void in the political and military leadership of the Scottish border and a legacy of political instability which persisted for many years. The elaborate network of service and loyalty built up in the Lowlands over four decades by the Knight of Liddesdale and the Earls of Douglas suddenly disintegrated. Vast domains extending along the border from Berwick to Lauderdale and north as far as Aberdeenshire were contested between the different branches of the Douglas family and the leading members of the Scottish nobility. At Carlisle the Earl of Fife abandoned the siege of the city and withdrew to Scotland with his army as soon as the news of Douglas's death was brought to him.[48]

Beyond the sea the last continental campaign mounted by England in the fourteenth century ended with a whimper. The Marshal, Louis of Sancerre, who was in command of French forces on the Gascon march, entered La Rochelle towards the end of July, accompanied by some of the leading noblemen of Poitou and a force of about 1,100 mounted men. Arundel challenged him to fight an arranged battle but the experienced Sancerre had no intention of squandering his tactical advantages and returned an evasive reply. There was no sign of help from John of Gaunt. The Duke of Lancaster had no plans to mount major military operations against France and without the promised reinforcements from England he was hardly in a position to do so. In any case Arundel's aggressive designs conflicted with all of his political instincts and cut across his negotiations with Castile.

The last page of John of Gaunt's prolonged and complex diplomatic dealings with John of Trastámara was not turned until 8 July 1388, when the final text of the treaty was sealed in the Franciscan convent of Bayonne. The treaty of Bayonne, like all previous versions of Gaunt's agreement with John of Trastámara, bound them both to work for peace between England and France. There is every reason to believe that Gaunt took this seriously. On 17 July 1388 the Castilian King ratified the instrument in the fortress town of Castrojeriz, west of Burgos. As soon as the instrument of ratification was in his hands Gaunt opened negotiations with the representatives of the Duke of Berry. The two sides met in August near the English-held fortress of Mortagne on the north shore of the Gironde. There, on 18 August 1388, they agreed a truce until March of the following year covering the whole of France south of the Loire. The truce put an end to Arundel's operations. His army re-embarked on its ships and sailed away. On 3 September 1388 the fleet arrived at Winchelsea. Apart from the plunder of the Bay of Bourgneuf it had achieved nothing.[49]

When, on 10 September 1388, Parliament met to consider the crisis, it became clear that whatever confidence the political community had once had in the regime of the Appellants had vanished. The assembly was held at Cambridge, in the Augustinian priory of Barnwell, presumably because it was far away from the political tensions of Westminster and the city of London. Comparatively few of those who had been elected in February were re-elected in September. The proceedings are ill-recorded as a result of the loss of the official roll but it is clear that the prosecution of Richard's chamber knights, which had been adjourned at the conclusion of the Merciless Parliament, was dropped. The decision reflected the widespread disillusionment of the Commons with the conduct of the leading Appellants. They were particularly dissatisfied with the results of Arundel's expedition. It had cost a great deal of money, about £34,000 or nearly twice the value of the half-subsidy voted by the Merciless Parliament. The Commons blamed Arundel for leaving a month after the appointed date, which had arguably cost him the support of the Duke of Brittany. They demanded to know why he was asking for four months' pay when he had served only three. The proposed economies and reforms, which had been expected to transform the government's finances, had not materialised and the government of the Appellants was suspected of hiding or embezzling the resources of the Crown just as earlier governments had been. There was some justice in this view. The Appellants had persuaded the Merciless Parliament to allow them to take £20,000 from the wool duties for their labours 'in the salvation of the King and all the realm', a sum which exceeded the entire proceeds of the half-subsidy granted in March. The lion's share of this probably went to the impecunious Duke of Gloucester but Arundel's appetite was not much less. He helped himself to a bonus of 1,000 marks and doubled his own fee as captain of Brest. These minor scandals served only to confirm the Commons in the conventional myth that honest government would find a way to finance the war from its own sources.[50]

As for the Council, their heart had not been in the prosecution of the war since June. But they were obliged to face both ways. They were already in touch with the court of France about the possibility of a long-term truce but needed a credible threat of military action if they were to have any counters to bargain with. They struggled to persuade the assembly to fund another campaign against France. Their pleas fell on deaf ears. A plan to send another war fleet to sea that very month appears to have been announced at the opening of the assembly but almost immediately abandoned. Another, rather vaguer plan took its place, involving an unspecified continental expedition in the spring of 1389. The Commons were only interested in action against the Scots. When eventually they voted a subsidy it was only a single tenth and fifteenth, much less than the Chancellor had demanded, and it was reserved for a campaign of retaliation in the north in the following year. Parliament was dissolved on 17 October 1388. Gloucester, Arundel and Warwick managed to retain control of the government for a few months longer but they had already abandoned most of their original programme. Shortly afterwards the English government agreed to attend a conference with the representatives of Charles VI on the march of Picardy. At about the same time John of Gaunt was empowered to open negotiations for a separate peace between England and Castile.[51]

*

At the beginning of September 1388 the French army marched on Guelders. The Duke of Burgundy led the advance guard north from Châlons-sur-Marne. The King, accompanied by the Constable, the Dukes of Berry and Bourbon, and most of the leading noblemen of France marched out of Montereau a few days later. With a combined strength of 16,000 men-at-arms, it was the largest cavalry force to be formed in France since the Bourbourg campaign of 1383. The scale of the campaign, which was vastly in excess of what was really required, was due mainly to the participation of the King, who had insisted on taking part against the better judgment of his uncles. They would have preferred a smaller army with a much reduced baggage train which would have been easier to supply. The difficulties were aggravated by the choice of route. The logical course would have been to concentrate the army at Lille and pass through eastern Flanders and Brabant. But the damage and cost of the passage of a great French army through their territory horrified the towns of Brabant, in spite of the fact that its ostensible purpose was to defend them against their enemies to the east. They threatened to empty the country and close the gates of the towns in the face of the French advance. So Philip, whose influence there depended partly on their goodwill, was obliged to reroute the army, entering Germany further east through the Ardennes and passing through the duchy of Luxembourg. This meant marching through steep, heavily wooded valleys with poor roads and very little in the way of supplies to feed such a large host.[52]

The Guelders campaign did nothing to satisfy the King's thirst for military glory. The army marched through pouring rain for a fortnight before climbing through the arid and unpopulated passes of the Schnee-Eifel, where they found the air bitterly cold and the ground hard and already covered in snow. On 25 September 1388 the French penetrated across the fertile lowlands of Juliers making for the southern march of Guelders. There they encamped along the road south of the town of Erkelenz while their leaders debated what to do and supplies were brought up after them. They remained there for three weeks. The rain fell incessantly, reducing tents to damp rags and turning the ground into a marsh. The horses had to pick their way through the mud. The wagon trains bringing supplies across the hills from the Meuse and the Rhine were immobilised by floods and mudslides. Duke William had hired bands of irregulars, most of them companies of German brigands from beyond the Rhine, to challenge the French advance. They followed the movements of the French from the hilltops, descending without warning

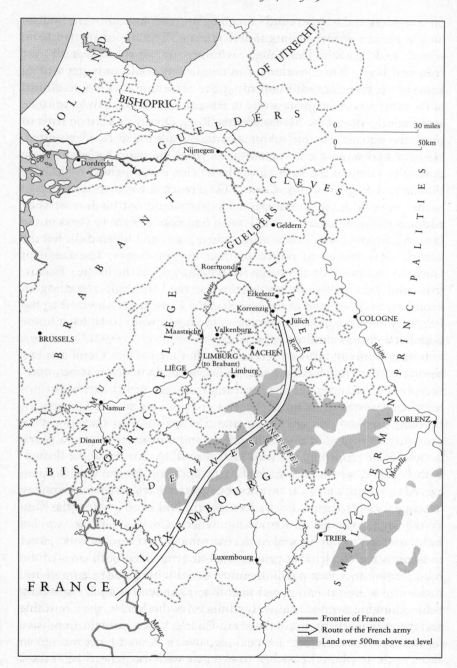

24 The French invasion of Guelders, September–November 1388

on stragglers and foragers and launching murderous night-time attacks
on the French encampments. Food ran out. The life of the soldiers,
complained Eustache Deschamps, who was one of them, was all 'rot,
cold and bog'. When winter set in conditions could only get worse.
Some of the French captains openly spoke of turning back home. Ahead
of the army stood the fortress-city of Roermond, blocking their advance
at the confluence of the Meuse and the Roer. Olivier de Clisson tried to
break the stalemate by provoking a battle outside the walls of this place.
He detached some 4,000 men-at-arms from the main force and rode
down the valley of the Roer towards the city, accompanied by Jean de
Vienne and Enguerrand de Coucy. The French drew themselves up in
battle order in the plain but the defenders would not be drawn. They
adopted the same tactics as the French had done for thirty years in the
face of English armies. They held to their walls and when dusk fell the
French were forced to return to their encampments. The Duke of
Guelders followed the campaign from Nijmegen on the Rhine. 'Floods,
frost and rain will fight my battles for me,' he said, according to
Froissart, to those who urged him that the French were invincible; 'by
February even the most aggressive of them will want to be back home
with his wife and children.'

In fact William did not need to wait that long. On 7 October 1388
he offered the French King a face-saving formula which was promptly
accepted: an apology for the insulting language of his letters but not
for their substance; some territorial concessions to the Duchess of
Brabant, but only on condition that the lordships in question were
promptly regranted to one of his allies; and a promise to give a year's
notice before reopening the war. That was all. As for the wider dispute
with Brabant, which was ostensibly the occasion for the war, William
agreed to submit that to arbitration but on terms which gave him plenty
of scope for obstruction. On 12 October the Duke came before the King
at the small village of Korrenzig, where Charles had set up his
headquarters, to put his seal to the instrument. No trouble was spared
to impress the recalcitrant prince. Men-at arms lined both sides of the
road leading to a vast pavilion embroidered with golden *fleurs de lys*.
Inside the King sat enthroned in full armour with a squire standing
behind him holding his helmet, surrounded by his uncles, the Constable
and the principal captains of the army. Charles's face wore the impassive
mask, expressionless and unspeaking, which he had been trained to
show to those whom he wished to overawe with the majesty of France,
coldly raising his cap and at once replacing it on his head. '*Et ne jocqua*

riens', added the chronicler. Yet, although William of Guelders received his pardon on bended knee, everyone knew that it was a charade designed to mask the failure of the French army.

If anyone doubted it their eyes were opened on the march back to France. The French were prevented from taking the Roman road which followed the west bank of the Meuse because the men of Maastricht and Liège guarded the bridges and refused to let them cross. In Luxembourg they found themselves surrounded by hatred. The countryside had been emptied of all foodstuffs. The towns closed their gates. The Duke of Guelders's companies, seeing the disorder in the ranks and scenting the chance of ransoms, harassed the retreating troops at every point. Bridges were guarded against the invader by large troops of infantry. The rivers were in full flood after six weeks of continuous rainfall. Fords were impassable. Men and horses lost their footing and drowned as they tried to wade through the torrents. Carts lost their wheels and axles in potholes. Lame horses had to be abandoned. Towards the end of October the bedraggled and starving host reached the French frontier, to all outward appearance a defeated army.[53]

The immediate consequence of the debacle in Germany was a palace revolution at the French court. The professional administrators had always chafed at the personal power of the Duke of Burgundy. The Guelders campaign brought them new and powerful allies. It had been Philip of Burgundy's venture, conceived in his personal interest and pressed on the French King's Council against the judgment of many of its more experienced members. The choice of route had been Philip's too. So had the decision to negotiate with the Dukes of Juliers and Guelders instead of wasting their dominions with fire and sword, which undoubtedly served the Duke's political interests in the Low Countries but deprived the captains of the army of the loot on which they had counted. Above all the inglorious outcome of the campaign had proved an intense disappointment to the King, who soon came to resent the pressure that his uncle had brought to bear upon him earlier in the year.

On 3 November 1388, a week after his return from Guelders, Charles VI presided over a Great Council in the hall of the archbishop's palace at Reims. It was attended by all of the great nobles who had participated in the campaign and by a cohort of permanent officials and lawyers who had been summoned for the occasion from Paris. The moment and the place were symbolic. It was the anniversary of the King's coronation, which had occurred in the same city eight years before. In a month's time he would be twenty years old, the age at which he could govern in person. Yet it evidently came as a shock when, at the outset of the proceedings, the aged Cardinal-Bishop of Laon, Pierre Aycelin, rose to propose that the time had come for the King to dispense with his guardians. Aycelin was a widely respected figure who had been close to three successive kings of France. The King's uncles sat dumbfounded as the murmur of approval spread through the hall. The Archbishop of Reims spoke in support of the Cardinal's proposal. So did the captains of the army. Charles, who had known what was afoot, was ready with his response. Turning to the Dukes of Berry and Burgundy he thanked them for their diligence and loyalty over the past eight years, declared that he would always welcome their advice and assistance in time of war and then dismissed them. The Duke of Berry rose to his feet. He and his brother were ready to abide by the wishes of the King, he said; but they would like to discuss the matter properly with him after his return to Paris. However, the decision had been made. For the next four years the Dukes of Burgundy and Berry were excluded from the government of the realm. Their advice was sought on major issues and sometimes accepted but they lost the power to initiate policy and became no more than occasional voices in the proposals of other men. They believed that the whole thing had been plotted in advance between the King and Clisson, supported by their enemies at court.[54]

This was more or less true. A year later, when John of Gaunt's chamberlain, Sir Richard Abberbury the Younger, was at the French court on his master's business, he was taken aside by Olivier de Clisson. 'Do you see the King?', the Constable asked him; 'What do you think of him?' Before the astonished Englishman had a chance to answer, he went on:

I'll have you know that it was I who made him a real King. It was I who took the government out of the hands of his uncles. Let me tell you that when he took over the conduct of affairs there was no more than two francs in his treasury. And now you see him rich, fortunate and generous. He must have handed out a million francs in gifts since then and all this has been my doing. Without me, he would still be in the state he was in before.[55]

Clisson of course had important personal interests at stake. His own position in Brittany was seriously threatened by the hostility of the Dukes of Berry and Burgundy and by their persistent support for John de Montfort. But the dismissal of the royal dukes was a good deal more than a jealous intrigue. The audible approval which greeted the Cardinal of Laon's address at Reims suggests that Clisson and his friends had broad-based support in the French political community. In particular there was strong support for a programme of administrative and financial reform, which was unlikely to make progress while the Dukes of Burgundy and Berry were in power. The essential problem was the state of the royal finances. The Constable put his finger on it in his boastful exchange with Richard Abberbury. The current burden of taxation was politically unsustainable. There had been no fewer than six *tailles* in the past four years in addition to the regular burden of *aides* and the *gabelle du sel*. Yet money was short. There would have to be large cuts in government expenditure.

With the departure of the royal dukes and their protégés the personality of the King became a more significant factor in French politics. It was already clear that Charles VI would be a very different kind of ruler than his father. At twenty, he was a broad-shouldered, athletic young man with a patchy beard and a head of blond hair which was already beginning to recede. Charles was a keen soldier with a strong taste for warfare. He was an excellent horseman who could handle a lance or pull a bow as well as any of his companions. He also had a strong awareness of his status. Over the centuries the French monarchy had acquired a crust of religious symbolism and ritual. Like most of his predecessors, Charles VI had to act out in public the part of an icon of state. The cold dignity with which he had received the Duke of Guelders at Korrenzig was no different from the face he showed to his own subjects or to the joyful crowds who would one day press into the streets of Avignon to see him borne like a graven image to the gates. 'I never saw a prince look so frigid or attended by men whose aspect was so much like his own,' the Datini factor in the city reported to his master in Prato. Shielded behind the walls of his palaces from the gaze of the crowds, Charles impressed petitioners and ambassadors with his willingness to listen and his memory for names and faces. Yet even that was a mask. For as Charles grew older his private life was increasingly at odds with the carefully cultivated image. He ignored the convention that the King did not fight in tournaments. He threw raucous drunken parties continuing late into the night. He wore fancy dress among friends, to the visible dismay of his more conservative ministers. He rose late. He was recklessly extravagant and a notorious womaniser. The King was never a cipher. But well before his world was clouded by illness and insanity his capacity for public business was limited. He was idle, slow-witted and easily bored. This made him malleable in the hands of those whom he trusted.[56]

The dominant figures in the King's counsels were now Olivier de Clisson, who remained the politician closest to the King, the Duke of Bourbon, who was the only one of the King's uncles to retain his old influence, and Pierre ('Le Bègue') de Villaines, the former captain of the French mercenaries in Castile. Day-to-day administration was in the hands of a group of former servants of Charles V who acquired a firm hold on the King's affections and controlled all access to him. Bureau de la Rivière, who was constantly at the King's side, became his most influential chamberlain. Jean le Mercier was appointed 'Grand Master of the Royal Household' and took over responsibility for the royal finances. Arnaud de Corbie resigned from the presidency of the Parlement to become Chancellor of France. Two rising men became notable figures for the first time. Jean de Montaigu, the scion of a large bureaucratic dynasty, became the King's private secretary. The title of Provost of the Merchants of Paris was revived after an abeyance of five years for the principal royal officer of the capital and conferred on a young lawyer in the King's service, Jean Juvénal des Ursins. These men formed a tight corps who acquired a firmer control over the cumbrous machinery of government than any previous ministry. A well-informed if unfriendly observer remarked on their unusual solidarity. They acted collectively, consulting each other in private and supporting each other's decisions in council. No one was allowed to rise in the King's government unless he was willing to join them on their own terms.[57]

'And then feasts, jousts and dances began to be held in France, more than for many years,' wrote the contemporary biographer of Jean de Boucicaut; 'for the young, the vigorous and the noble were all urging the youthful King to enjoy himself, as is natural for a fresh spirit in its prime.' Charles celebrated his emancipation in a succession of grand festivities in and around Paris over the following year. None of them, however, had the symbolic resonance of the spectacular, week-long celebrations at Saint-Denis by which the regime celebrated its own accession to power and courted popularity among the military nobility, the leading figures in the royal administration and the Parisian elite. The occasion was the knighting at the King's hands of the sons of the Duke of Anjou, the eleven-year-old Louis, titular King of Naples, and his brother Charles. The celebrations were carefully stage-managed propaganda for the royal house, deliberately contrived to show its fortunes in the hands of a younger generation. The leading place in the public ceremonies was taken by the King himself and by his contemporaries among the royal princes: his younger brother Louis,

Duke of Touraine; and his cousins Pierre de Navarre, younger son of Charles the Bad, Henry, son of the Duke of Bar, and John, Count of Nevers, the eighteen-year-old heir of the Duke of Burgundy. The participants jousted for three days in the lists set up in front of the abbey gate and banqueted in a huge timber hall, nearly 600 feet long, which had been specially erected in the great courtyard. All was conducted in accordance with carefully ordained rituals reconstructed from the tales of Lancelot and the legends of the Holy Grail. Invitations had been sent to England, but the only English guests present were exiles: Robert de Vere, Earl of Oxford, who was living in Paris on a pension from Charles VI; and Matilda Holand, Countess of Saint-Pol, Richard II's half-sister, now naturalised in France, who was given the honour as the most beautiful woman present of leading the King's horse into the lists. Both of them must have remembered an earlier occasion, on St. George's Day 1377, when, beneath the eye of the senile Edward III, England had celebrated the coming of a new generation on the eve of one of the most sombre periods of her history. Like the young men of 1377, many of the gilded figures at Saint-Denis were destined to meet untimely deaths during the next three decades at the hands of assassins, executioners or lynch-mobs, or on the battlefields of Nicopolis or Agincourt. The festivities ended on 6 May 1389 with a remarkable ceremony dedicated to the memory of Bertrand du Guesclin, who had died nine years before. The sword and armour of the dead captain were presented to the abbey church in the glow of hundreds of burning torches by the military officers of the Crown, accompanied by a crowd of Bertrand's kinsmen and retainers. Louis of Touraine and the young princes of the royal house came forward to offer their own swords as if to mark the direct succession from the great days of Charles V to those of his son.[58]

The new administration immediately set about reforming the machinery of government and hacking away at the luxuriant undergrowth of jobbery which had led to an exponential growth in the royal payroll over the past decade. The Dukes of Berry and Burgundy demanded a formal share of the Crown's revenues now that they could no longer help themselves. They also wanted an undertaking that the jobs of their protégés would be safe. They were courteously heard out but their wishes were ignored on both points. Over the next four years the flow of new grants to Philip the Bold fell to less than a fifth of its previous level. Grants to Jean de Berry were reduced to a trickle. A large number of superfluous functionaries, perceived opponents of the new regime and advocates of the high-tax policies of the past five years, many of whom had owed their places to Berry and Burgundy, were removed from office. Over the following months a stream of regulations and ordinances issued from the King's Council. There was a wholesale change in the personnel of the Parlement and a radical reform of its processes. An attempt was made to limit the staff of provincial *baillis* and seneschals and to abolish the innumerable perquisites by which they supplemented their fees and salaries. The bloated and endemically corrupt financial administration, which was believed to consume up to half of the revenues which it handled, received particular attention. The revenues of the royal demesne were dramatically increased. There was an assault on the endemic corruption and lax accounting of the purchasing offices of the royal household, where so many royal officials had made their fortunes in the past. The Chambre des Comptes recovered the rigorous audit role for which it had once been famous.

It is not easy to change an administrative culture developed over generations but there is a good deal of evidence to support Olivier de Clisson's claim that the King's finances were transformed, at least in the short term. For the first time since the death of Charles V it was possible not only to meet the daily expenses of government but to make large, regular payments to the treasurer of the royal household to support the King's largesse and his increasingly ostentatious court. It was even possible to establish a substantial monthly reserve against unforeseen future expenditure. At the same time the level of taxation was reduced by about a third, a move which contributed largely to the popularity of the new regime. Collection of the latest *taille* was abandoned in January 1389. No further special taxes of this kind would be imposed for the next seven years. When the Duke of Berry issued an order that the collection of the *taille* should proceed in any event in his own domains the King's Council countermanded it.[59]

One of the first acts of the new government upon assuming power was to take up the English offer of a fresh diplomatic conference.[60] The views of the Marmousets on foreign policy were not very different from those of the Duke of Burgundy. But the Marmousets' need for peace was more urgent than his. The fate of their financial reforms and ultimately their own survival in government depended on bringing an end to the annual armies and fleets of the past two decades and achieving large cuts in the cost of maintaining fixed garrisons on the frontiers. At the same time less tangible factors were altering the climate of opinion. The closing years of the fourteenth century were a time of intense moral pessimism, characterised by a growing preoccupation with sin and personal redemption, the insecurity of life and the ubiquity of death, not only among educated clerics but also in influential sections of the nobility. Their outlook owed much to the pervasive sense of decline which weighed heavily on the French political community. The mood was darkened by other developments in the world beyond France: the papal schism; the advances of the Ottoman Turks in the Balkans; the periodic epidemics of bubonic plague. Corruption, decay, the vanity of political and national ambitions: these are abiding themes of the outpourings of the poet Eustache Deschamps and of the writings of political moralists like the anonymous author of the *Songe du Vergier* and the prolific Philippe de Mézières. The same themes constantly reappear in the works of the young lyric poet Christine de Pisan, the lawyer Honoré Bonet and the orator and scholar Jean Gerson. These writers were not simply preaching to their own kind. All of them belonged to the political world. They had careers to make and patrons to please, most of whom belonged to the higher reaches of the government and the Church. The *Songe* was almost certainly the work of one of Charles V's *maîtres des requêtes*. Deschamps lived all his life on the margins of the court and in the armies and civil service of the Valois monarchy. Philippe de Mézières had been one of Charles V's councillors. Bonet was present at diplomatic conferences as a legal adviser. Gerson, a prominent figure in the most intensely political university of Europe, preached regularly before the King.

Hatred of the English was probably as strong as ever in France at the end of the fourteenth century. Yet support for the war declined steeply in these years. It was associated with the wider divisions of Christendom, with a murderous and increasingly pointless military stalemate, an intolerable burden of taxation and the corruption of manners and politics that commonly accompanied high levels of public expenditure. In the last years of his life even Froissart, the authentic voice of aristocratic sentiment and chivalry's greatest contemporary advocate, turned against what he saw as the mindless greed and indiscriminate violence of the warrior class. In the autumn of 1389 Philippe de Mézières presented Charles VI with his immense allegorical work, the *Songe du Vieil Pélerin*. Written in the aftermath of the King's dismissal of his uncles, Philippe's book was a long plea for peace between England and France, the repair of the papal schism and the promotion of a fresh crusade against the renascent power of Islam. He regarded the youth and inexperience of Charles VI and Richard II as their greatest asset. Let them put aside the hatreds of their forbears and their elders, men stained with blood, nourished and enriched by war, before they grew to share them. Let them meet and settle the issues directly with each other without the intervention of lawyers and diplomats who served only to keep old quarrels evergreen. Philippe de Mézières was now a Celestine lay brother and referred to himself throughout his work as the 'Ancient Recluse'. Yet his was not a voice in the wilderness. His ceaseless lobbying and his ability to appeal to the most powerful emotions of his contemporaries won him influential converts including the King.[61]

On 3 May 1389 there was a scene at Westminster reminiscent of the events at Reims in the previous November and quite possibly inspired by them. A Great Council had gathered in the Marcolf Chamber, the small painted hall at the edge of the river in the palace enclosure. Richard II entered the hall to open the proceedings with a prepared statement. He observed that he was now past the age of twenty at which a man was entitled to enter into his inheritance (he was in fact twenty-two) and he called on the magnates present to declare whether he was not entitled to govern in person. They all answered that he was. They could hardly have said anything else. The former Appellants were sitting among the councillors, but without warning and without their allies among the Parliamentary Commons and the city trades there was little that they could do. Richard declared that throughout the twelve years of his reign he had been controlled by others. These years, he said, had been characterised by an unending succession of taxes 'and I have not noticed that my realm is any stronger for it.' He therefore proposed to take over the conduct of affairs himself. Turning to Chancellor Arundel he demanded the surrender of his seals. The astonished prelate handed them to the King. The Treasurer and the Keeper of the Privy Seal were summarily dismissed along with the Chancellor. Gloucester, Arundel and Warwick were removed from the Council. Arundel was also deprived of the Admiralty and the captaincy of Brest. The new judges imposed on the King by the Appellants were told that they would be removed as soon as others could be found to take their places. A purge of the civil service was ordered, which resulted in the dismissal of all those whom the Appellant lords had installed in the administration. No fewer than 400 people whom Richard regarded as creatures of his enemies were dismissed from his household.[62]

Richard played his hand with considerable political skill. Apart from the purges of his opponents in the administration, he did not embark upon a campaign of revenge against the men who had put them there.

The accumulated resentments of the past three years were concealed behind a mask of graciousness. The sentences of the Merciless Parliament were allowed to stand. The judges who had advised the King at the notorious Nottingham council of 1387 were allowed to rot away in their Irish exile. Robert de Vere, Michael Pole and Alexander Neville were left to end their days on the continent. In place of these headstrong, opinionated men, Richard appointed an uncontroversial administration headed by William of Wykeham and Bishop Brantingham of Exeter, elderly professional administrators who took up with overt misgivings the offices that they had last held eighteen years before under Edward III. So far as these men stood for anything they stood for honest, economical government and an ideal of public service not unlike that of the Marmousets in France.

Meanwhile the King discreetly built up his own party. John of Gaunt was recalled from Gascony and plied with deference and favours. The Duke of Lancaster's political skills and his standing among the English nobility would be badly needed in the following years. At the same time Richard made new allies among a younger generation of English noblemen and helped them to build up their power-bases in the country. His raffish and violent half-brother Sir John Holand became Earl of Huntingdon in 1389 and was helped to build up large holdings of land in the west of England. His cousin Edward, the able and ruthless son of Edmund Langley, Duke of York, became Earl of Rutland in the following year and a trusted military and diplomatic adviser. Richard, according to a jaundiced contemporary, 'loved him better than any man living'. Bolingbroke and Mowbray, the more moderate of the ex-Appellants, were retained on the Council and Mowbray became as close to the King as he had been when they were boys. Even Gloucester and Arundel were readmitted to the Council after a few months, although they never recovered their old influence.[63]

In another, perhaps conscious echo of events in France Richard announced on 16 May that if a truce with France was agreed he would dispense with the second instalment of the Parliamentary subsidy which was due to be collected in June. It was, he said, 'his own decision, made without advice from anyone'.[64] This was probably true. Richard was well aware of the corrosive political consequences of high taxation and the destabilising effect of a war that made his government dependent on repeated grants in Parliament. As time went on the King's opposition to the war became not just a political calculation but a matter of conviction with a significant moral dimension. The King threw himself whole-heartedly into the peacemaking process which Gloucester and Arundel had only tolerated for want of any immediate alternative. Richard's resumption of power at Westminster, following upon the Marmousets' takeover in Paris, proved to be the decisive moment in the long, frustrating history of Anglo-French diplomatic exchanges.

The latest peace conference had opened at Leulinghem on the march of Calais shortly after Christmas 1388. Both delegations were led by diplomatic veterans. Walter Skirlaw, Bishop of Durham, had been involved as a Chancery clerk and then Keeper of the Privy Seal in every Anglo-French negotiation for a decade. He had first met his opposite numbers, Nicholas du Bosc and Arnaud de Corbie, at the final session of the Bruges conference in 1378. These men had been over the ground many times. By now there was very little between the two principal belligerents. The old intractable issues, homage and sovereignty and territorial claims in the south-west, had been put to one side while the parties endeavoured to agree the terms of the long-term truce which they both desperately needed. Calais ceased to be a sticking point once the Duke of Burgundy fell from power. Castile, for years the main obstacle to a long-term truce, faded from view after John of Gaunt's settlement with the House of Trastámara. The only significant obstacle in the way of the ambassadors at Leulinghem was the renascent power of Scotland. The English had always refused to treat Scotland as an issue to be debated with the French. It was their affair, an internal issue with a subordinate kingdom whose quarrel with England was older than the French war. 'They are such close neighbours of ours that we can visit them without getting our feet wet, as they can us,' said the English ambassadors. The problem was that the Scots were not represented at Leulinghem and the French were bound by treaty not to make any long-term arrangements without them. How far the French were prepared to go to protect the interests of these difficult allies remained to be seen. In mid-January 1389 the conference was adjourned while Nicholas du Bosc and his colleagues returned to Paris for consultations.[65]

In the meantime relations between England and Scotland sharply deteriorated. On 20 January 1389 a Great Council met at Westminster. Plans for the great punitive expedition to the north, which had been in contemplation since the middle of the previous year, were approved and the opening of the campaign fixed for 1 August. Thomas Mowbray, Earl of Nottingham, was nominated as warden of the west march. A commission of four prominent northern lords was charged with the defence of Northumberland. Unfortunately, in order to save money, they were retained from June only. As a result the only organised military forces on the scene were the garrisons of Berwick, Roxburgh and Carlisle. Seizing their opportunity, the Scots resumed their attacks. There was a series of exceptionally destructive raids in the course of March and April. Once again the brunt of these operations was borne by Cumberland and the city of Carlisle. Two hundred people were reported to have been burned alive in their houses on the west march. 'Everything that the marchers had has been burned and smashed in the continual raids of the Scots,' they complained; 'most of them have nothing left to live on and are on the point of abandoning this desolate wasteland.' Lord Beaumont, who was in command at Carlisle, mounted a brief counter-raid into Teviotdale but otherwise no one stirred in defence of the north. The northern lords, Percy, Neville, Clifford and Roos, had been promised funds to pay their men but received nothing. So far as can be discovered they stayed at home. Too late Mowbray was ordered urgently to the north to take command of the defence of the Scottish border. Scotland was becoming an expensive headache. Operations on the northern marches would soon start to eat up cash at a rate of more than £20,000 a year. The advances of war wages for the King's great punitive expedition would come to more than double that. This was the situation when Richard II took power into his own hands at the beginning of May 1389.[66]

At Calais the diplomatic breakthrough came within a few days of Richard's palace revolution. The English ambassadors reached an informal agreement with their French opposite numbers on the status of Scotland. The French dropped their insistence on Scottish participation in the conference. This cleared the way for the formal sessions to reopen at the beginning of June. The Earl of Salisbury, a vocal advocate of peace with France and at sixty-one the last survivor of the great captains of the reign of Edward III, was added to the strength of the English embassy and sent out to Calais with fresh instructions on the major issues. When the diplomats gathered in the church of Leulinghem on 5 June 1389 they reached agreement almost at once. On 18 June they put their seals to a truce which was to take effect in August and to last for three years, during which a permanent peace would be negotiated. The Scots were left to their fate. The King of Scotland was named as an ally of France. So were the Scottish lords of the border, who were treated as the independent power which they had by now in practice become. But the French government's agreement was not conditional on their assent. To persuade them to co-operate the English, abetted by the French, hit upon a combination of diplomacy and force. Mowbray, who had by now taken up his command on the Scottish march, was at Roxburgh. He was about to lead a large mounted raid into Scotland with the combined forces of the east and west marches. A French embassy would follow on behind with an ultimatum: unless the Scots agreed to be bound by the truce the King of France would abandon them.[67]

Events did not work out entirely according to plan. The military side was a fiasco. Mowbray fell out with the northern lords, who regarded him as a brash outsider and resented the fact that he was being paid at rates far higher than their own. Most of them refused to serve under him. As a result, when Mowbray marched north from Roxburgh on 25 June, he was accompanied by only 1,500 mounted men. He found himself heavily outnumbered by the Scots and faced with a determined and effective rearguard action directed by the Earl of Fife. Unable to pursue his advance into Lothian, Mowbray was forced to retreat eastward and shut himself ingloriously behind the walls of Berwick. In the meantime Fife outflanked him and entered Northumberland at the head of a large Scottish army, penetrating south as far as the Tyne. The region had been left almost entirely defenceless and suffered considerable damage. In about the middle of July the Scots withdrew to dump their spoil and prisoners and to regroup for another attack on an even larger scale.[68]

The French ambassadors reached the Scottish border towards the end of July 1389. They found the Scottish King at Dunfermline. Pierre Fresnel, the young civil lawyer who led the embassy, had a good deal of experience of Scottish affairs and was well aware of the tensions which the French alliance generated. He had been present in 1384 on the last occasion when a French embassy had come to Scotland to force an unwelcome truce on its allies, and again in 1387 when it had suited French interests to push the Scots into reopening the war. Two years later Robert Stewart was a shadow of the man Fresnel had known. The Earl of Carrick, his elder son, who had been the dominant figure at the Scottish court on his last visit, had fallen out with the leading lords of the border over the Douglas inheritance and had then been disabled in a riding accident. As a result he had been replaced by his younger brother the Earl of Fife. Fife, who took the title of 'Governor', was an abler politician and a far better soldier than Carrick. He was also the most persistent protagonist in Scotland of the border war. His ally, Sir Archibald Douglas, who had appropriated the earldom of Douglas with most of its lands and followers, was now by far the richest and most powerful of the border lords. Between them these men effectively controlled the Scottish kingdom. They were not easily persuaded to sign up to the truce. They had fought a successful war against the English for more than a year without any significant assistance from France. The raids were profitable and extremely popular among the lowlanders. They had enabled the border lords to invest in fine horses and armour, to maintain their followings in the region and to sustain their dominant position in Scottish politics. While Fresnel was at the Scottish court he was taken with his staff to see the army which was preparing to invade England. The men were drawn up in disciplined units, well mounted and armed. Many of them had pledged their farms and chattels to buy their equipment. Seeing the French party among them the troops jeered and bellowed their anger over the heads of their fellows. It took great patience and an aggressive combination of threats and blandishments to move the Scots from their chosen course. Ultimately, however, the Scottish leaders were not prepared to risk losing the French alliance and facing the undivided strength of the English alone. Douglas himself, newly installed in possession of other men's lands and sullenly resented by his rivals, had too much to lose if the fortunes of war should turn against him. So the projected invasion force was disbanded. On about 2 August 1389 Robert II put his seal to the truce of Leulinghem.[69]

At the opposite extremity of the vast swathe of Europe which had been drawn into the Anglo-French war, the kings of Castile and Portugal received notice of the truce at the end of July 1389. John of Avis, like Robert II of Scotland, was covered by the terms of the truce provided that he agreed to accede to it. He at least had been consulted in advance, for his agents had been at Westminster in November 1388 when Walter Skirlaw's instructions were being prepared. The ambiguity of his position probably suited him. Ever since John of Gaunt's departure for Bayonne nearly two years before, he and his Constable, Nun' Alvarez Pereira, had conducted an intermittent war against John of Trastámara's border fortresses and the few surviving Castilian garrisons in Portugal, choosing their moment to attack, profiting from the enemy's penury and distraction with other affairs. Campo Maior, the last significant Castilian stronghold in the Alemtejo, surrendered in December 1388 during the first session of the Leulinghem conference. On 23 August

1389, about a month after the text of the truce had reached the peninsula, John of Avis crossed the northern frontier and laid siege to the Galician town of Tui, an important bridgehead into a region which was still the most disaffected part of John of Trastámara's kingdom. In vain the Castilian King sent messengers to invite him to honour the truce. Battered by artillery and repeatedly assaulted, Tui finally surrendered on about 14 November while John of Trastámara was still struggling to collect an army for its relief.[70]

A fortnight later the ambassadors of the two kingdoms agreed upon a truce of three years on substantially the terms agreed at Leulinghem. The truce marked the final triumph of John of Avis. Its terms provided that in exchange for the surrender of his conquests in Galicia the Castilians were to withdraw all of their remaining garrisons in Portugal. The humiliation of Castile and the exhaustion of the country after forty years of continual war were there for all to see. John of Trastámara felt it personally. Addressing the Cortes at Guadalajara the following February he described the terms which he had agreed with the Portuguese as dishonourable to himself and to his crown. But they had been unavoidable. The country had been drained of treasure to pay the wages of the King's French mercenaries and the immense indemnities due to the Duke of Lancaster. The experienced captains and cavalrymen required to put another army into the field no longer existed. His conscience, he said, would not allow him to prolong the struggle any longer. In the wider scheme of things the siege of Tui was a minor affair. But it proved to be the last regular campaign of the Hundred Years War in the fourteenth century and the last of all to be fought in the Iberian peninsula.[71]

CHAPTER XIV

The Gascon March
1381–1393

When, in May 1389, Charles VI announced his intention of visiting the three southern seneschalsies of his kingdom, the event focussed attention on a region which had been a political backwater for a decade.[1] The Duke of Anjou had left Languedoc in the spring of 1379 to attend to the affairs of Brittany. After that he had had very little to do with the government of the province until he was finally relieved of it in April 1380. Anjou had been a formidable figure there for sixteen years. His equally formidable successor Bertrand du Guesclin had died on his way south to take up his duties. The disappearance of these two men left a void which was never filled. In Languedoc and the neighbouring provinces of the march, power fell into the hands of a succession of ambitious local potentates operating in alliance with the Anglo-Gascon companies. The conquest of what remained of the English duchy came to a halt.

The foremost of these potentates were the Counts of Armagnac and Foix. For many years the prolonged vendetta between these two powerful southern families had been one of the major sources of political instability in the region. Gaston III Count of Foix (known as Gaston Phoebus) was a subtle politician who had inherited his territories at the age of twelve in 1343 and had governed them since his fifteenth year. He was a man of many contradictions: the cerebral ruler, dictating staccato letters to four secretaries; the urbane host presiding over one of the most famous small courts of Europe; the obsessive miser hoarding coin in the keep at Orthez; the heavily built man of action who collected fine books and wrote in exquisite French a prayer book and a treatise on hawking; the cautious politician, given to sudden outbursts of uncontrollable rage. These were all different aspects of the same enigmatic figure. Here was a man who passed a lifetime in building up a great autonomous principality only to murder with his own hands the son who was destined to inherit it. Gaston Phoebus's domains comprised three distinct blocks of territory in the Pyrenees: the viscounty of Béarn

and adjoining areas of southern Gascony in the west; the small territory
of Nebouzan around Saint-Gaudens further east; and the county of Foix
at the headwaters of the Ariège south of Toulouse. In addition to these
he had inherited from his mother a substantial block of territory between
the valleys of the Tarn and the Agout, north-east of Toulouse, including
much of the southern Albigeois. Most of Gaston Phoebus's territories
were mountainous and poor. But they produced large numbers of hardy
mountain troops for his armies. His demesne revenues were small, but
he waxed rich on the profits of his wars and the patronage of the free
companies. He learned quicker than most French noblemen of his time
that cash had become a sounder investment than land. His accumulating
chests of coin enabled him to engage in a lucrative traffic in prisoners of
war and to lend money at interest to needy princes and captains as well
as to seize his own political opportunities when they arose.[2]

Much of Gaston Phoebus's long reign was animated by the ambition
to create a consolidated Pyrenean state along the southern flank of
Gascony and Languedoc. The chief obstacles in his way were the counts
of Armagnac and their long-standing protégés the counts of
Comminges. Between them these two noble houses possessed most of
the territory which separated the scattered fractions of Gaston's
Pyrenean empire. The counts of Comminges were also Gaston's chief
adversaries in the Albigeois. In 1375 the last of the male line of the
house of Comminges died, leaving a ten-year-old girl as his sole heiress.
Open war broke out between the Counts of Armagnac and Foix for the
hand of the heiress. Gaston Phoebus invaded Comminges with a mixed
army of his own subjects and Gascon *routiers* from the garrisons of the
Pyrenees. Sir Thomas Felton, the English Seneschal of Gascony, weighed
in on his side. The Count of Armagnac counter-attacked with his own
army, also largely recruited from professional *routiers*. In 1378, after
three years of fighting, Armagnac seized the young heiress and forcibly
married her to his eldest son. Her guardian, the dowager Countess, who
had tried to stop him, was taken away under guard and locked up in
what Armagnac described as a 'delectable place' in his domains.[3]

When eventually peace was restored in March 1379 Armagnac
appeared to have won. The real victor, however, was Gaston Phoebus.
He was, it is true, obliged to acquiesce in his rival's possession of the
Comminges inheritance. But he was allowed to retain a number of
strategic positions which he had occupied in Comminges itself and also
obtained effective possession for the first time of his mother's dower
lands in southern Albigeois. Shortly after the peace had been sealed he

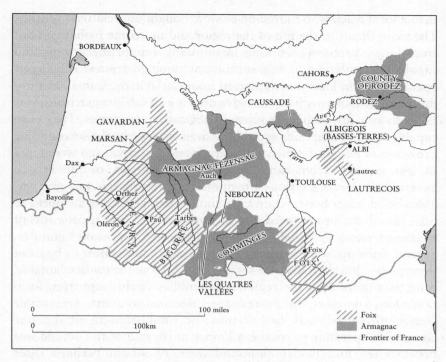

25 Principal territories of the Counts of Armagnac and Foix, 1375–1382

consolidated his position by annexing the whole of the territory of Bigorre lying immediately east of Béarn. His dream of controlling a single consolidated block of territory across the northern face of the Pyrenees was all but achieved, but the cost of his triumph was a decade of tension and instability in southern France. Gaston's garrisons now looked out on three fronts at those of the Count of Armagnac: in the Gave de Pau on the northern march of Béarn, in the upper valley of the Garonne where Foix merged into Comminges, and on the Tarn. 'Ah, Sire Jean,' said the knight who accompanied Froissart on the road to Orthez some years later, 'what fine skirmishes and tough fights I have seen around here between the men of Armagnac and Foix, for in those days there was not a town or castle that they had not stuffed with men-at-arms to harass and despoil each other.'[4]

The Comminges war had been fought against a background of mounting *routier* activity across the whole of southern and central France. In the late 1370s there were several hundred *routier* garrisons operating in the region. Most of them were small gangs with no more than a local reach who moved on or were bought out relatively quickly. The main threat to the life of the region did not come from them but from larger garrisons working in mutually supporting groups and capable of combining to field substantial mounted armies. The largest operation of this kind was conducted from Carlat in the Cantal. In 1379 this place, together with its extensive network of satellite garrisons, was home to as many as thirteen substantial Gascon companies. They were capable of mounting raids several hundred strong into the surrounding provinces of Périgord, Quercy, Rouergue and Auvergne and were more or less immune from interference by the officers of the French government. The one serious attempt to recapture Carlat, in 1377, was abandoned when Bertrand du Guesclin, summoned from the north to offer his advice, pronounced it to be impregnable. Similar networks of *routier* garrisons operated on a smaller scale in Quercy and Limousin. Several attempts were made by the provincial authorities to buy out these places. But they all failed for the same reason: the *routier* captains' price was more than the regional assemblies could raise from local taxpayers, and more distant taxpayers declined to assist. A plausible contemporary estimate had it that the total strength of the free companies operating in southern France at the end of the decade was between ten and twelve thousand men, of whom perhaps three thousand were trained men-at-arms.

The effect on the region was catastrophic. Its internal trade dried up. Fields out of sight of walled places were abandoned to weeds and brambles. Refugees and beggars crowded into the towns. Delegations sent to participate in provincial assemblies travelled by night with armed escorts and were sent on their way with public prayers for their safety. By the end of the 1370s the first symptoms reappeared of the vicious circle which had destroyed so much of provincial France in the 1350s. War damage destroyed the tax base, thereby preventing provincial communities from defending themselves and exposing them to fresh attacks. Auvergne, its Estates declared in 1379:

has been reduced to such a state of poverty and destitution that its walled towns and castles can no longer be defended. These places are ill-manned and so feeble that any substantial force could conquer them. Two-thirds of the open country is abandoned and uninhabited and the rest will soon be in the same state.

The mountains of Auvergne and their western foothills were the worst affected regions. But conditions were not much better in Périgord, Quercy or Rouergue.[5]

The *routier* war acquired a new and more formidable aspect once the Duke of Anjou had left for the north. The government of Languedoc was left to drift. Tax exhaustion drastically reduced its revenues. The settlement of the Comminges war and the treaty between Castile and Navarre, which occurred almost simultaneously in March 1379, released large numbers of footloose bands of soldiers back onto the market. They shortly acquired an impressive leader in the person of Bertucat d'Albret. Bertucat returned from Navarre with his followers in the spring of 1379 and quickly regained his old ascendency over the Gascon companies of the march. These included most of the *routier* garrisons in Quercy, which were commanded by his long-standing lieutenants, as well as Carlat and its satellites, which had been founded back in 1373 by his old brother-in-arms Bernard de la Salle. Under Bertucat's direction they achieved a level of co-ordination which had not been seen since the days of Séguin de Badefol in the 1360s.

Bertucat's first act was to cash in all his existing positions in order to move the companies into new and less exhausted territory. In this endeavour he found a ready collaborator in John II, Count of Armagnac. Armagnac had close links with the companies. One of the captains at Carlat was his bastard half-brother Bernard. Several other captains had been employed by him in the Comminges war. He made a series of agreements with the provincial assemblies of the region by which he undertook to arrange the evacuation of all *routier* garrisons of Auvergne and the Gascon march and to guarantee the region against further incursions. At the end of August 1379 the Count struck a deal with Bertucat to buy out all the garrisons associated with him in Quercy and the Cantal for a lump sum, payable in instalments, taking a commission, a financing profit and a charge for his military services. Armagnac probably hoped to make a profit out of this deal. But his real purpose was to create a new *routier* army to deploy against the Count of Foix.[6]

The Count of Armagnac raised the first instalments due to the companies without too much difficulty. He successfully induced them to leave their strongholds and directed them to concentrate in the valley of the Tarn near Montauban. The ultimate objective was probably Gaston Phoebus's garrisons in the Albigeois, two days' march upstream from Montauban. However, Armagnac quickly found, as others had before him, that such dangerous auxiliaries were hard to control. There is some evidence that he was unable to raise the remaining instalments of the money he had promised them. But for whatever reason, towards the end of 1379 Bertucat took matters into his own hands. He withdrew from Armagnac's service and led the combined companies off on a pillaging campaign across southern France which lasted some six months. Passing swiftly through the valleys of the Tarn and the Agout Bertucat fell on the coastal plain of Languedoc in the middle of December. Within a few weeks his men had occupied at least six walled places around Béziers and Narbonne and plundered much of the rich region by the Mediterranean until they were finally bought out by the cities of Bas-Languedoc. Then, retreating north through the granite hills of the Cevennes, they invaded the Gevaudan at the end of March 1380 and seized the castle of Montferrand and the great square keep of Châteauneuf-de-Randon, lying east and west of the cathedral city of Mende. The old castle of Chaliers, dominating the valley of the Truyère south of Saint-Flour, followed about six weeks later. From there they flowed back into Auvergne.[7]

Re-established in their old hunting grounds in central France Bertucat's companies found allies among a new generation of captains, some of whom would be famous figures in the following years. Six miles south of Limoges the impressive ruins of the thirteenth-century fortress of Chalusset can still be seen standing on a spur of rock above a bend in the River Briance. In April 1380 Chalusset was occupied by Perrot de Fontans, known as 'Le Béarnais' (or Perrot de Béarn). This place shortly became one of the largest *routier* garrisons in France with 500 men-at-arms on its strength. They were capable of deploying up to 300 cavalry on a single raid. Perrot himself waxed rich on the profits. His grandiose fortified mansion and exquisite gardens at Brassempouy in the southern Landes of Gascony were visible symbols of his prosperity. Perrot's long-standing companion-in-arms Mérigot Marchès acquired even greater notoriety. In 1380 he was established at Le Roc de la Borde in Auvergne. From here he extended his operations into Bas-Limousin and the great corridor of the Dordogne by which the traffic of soldiers and booty passed constantly between Gascony and Auvergne. He took over the existing *routier* garrison of Charlus-Champagnac above the gorges of the upper Dordogne. Later in the year he joined forces with Perrot de Béarn to capture the castle of Mercoeur, the treasury and principal residence of the Dauphin of Auvergne, who was then serving with the French army in Brittany. By Mérigot's own account this coup yielded 30,000 *livres* of spoil.[8]

A few of the new strongholds which the companies occupied at the end of the 1370s were recaptured by Bertrand du Guesclin on his march

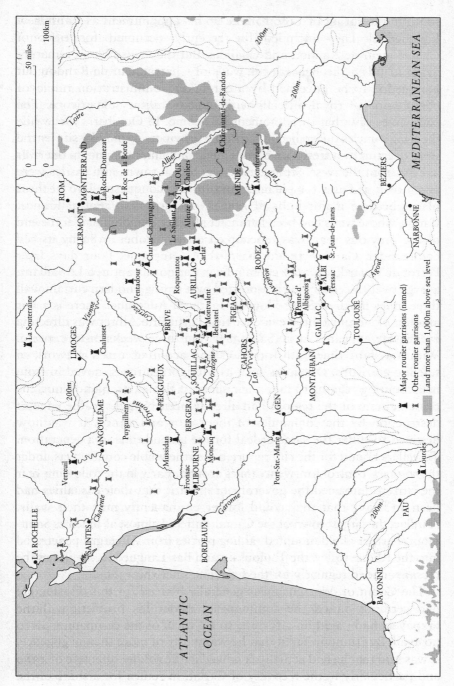

26 Principal *routier* garrisons, 1379-1392

south in the spring of 1380 to take up his appointment as Captain of Languedoc. They included the recently occupied fortresses of Châteauneuf-de-Randon and Chaliers. But the Constable's premature death in July 1380 beneath the walls of Châteauneuf-de-Randon left Languedoc to be governed by a caretaker administration run by a commission of royal officials with limited military experience. The companies saw that their moment had come. In October 1380, while the King's uncles quarrelled in Paris, the provinces of the Massif Central were overrun by a fresh tide of mounted companies coming up the river valleys from the west. Strategically placed hill-towns and castles were taken over as bases for pillaging and further conquests. Two of these places became major hubs of *routier* operations in central France. Carlat, whose walls had been left intact after its abandonment at the end of the previous year, was reoccupied on 6 October 1380 by its old commander, Garcie-Arnaud, bastard of Caupenne. Four days later Perrot de Galard, a *routier* captain from Périgord, captured Le Saillant, a large twelfth-century keep protected by a strong, modern curtain wall three miles north of Saint-Flour in southern Auvergne. There is a fair amount of circumstantial evidence that Bertucat d'Albret was directing events. He appeared at Le Saillant within three weeks of its capture. Within a short time both fortresses had acquired a new network of satellite garrisons. Outsiders such as Mérigot Marchès moved in from neighbouring regions to take their share of the spoils. Saint-Flour, the principal city of the region, had already been brought to the edge of destruction by the companies of the 1350s and 1360s. It was now destined to suffer the same ordeal for the second time in a generation. Travellers bound for the city reported that the whole country was under the *routiers*' control for twenty miles around. Early in the following year the citizens informed the government in Paris that their casualties had been so heavy that they could longer permanently man their walls. Aurillac, the largest town of the Cantal, suffered almost as much as Saint-Flour. Further afield mounted raiding parties from Auvergne penetrated into the Rhône valley, the Toulousain and Bas-Languedoc. At Nîmes the *tocsin* sounded regularly for the first time since the 1360s.[9]

The Count of Armagnac was generally blamed for this disaster. He had certainly failed the communities under his protection. Their taxpayers had paid him a fortune to rid them of the companies, all to no avail. But rumour had it that he was guilty of more than negligence. It was said that he had actually connived in the *routier* offensive of 1380 and particularly in the recovery of Carlat, in return for a share of the loot. There is no way of verifying these reports. But it was certainly true that the companies who had pillaged Bas-Languedoc included several whose captains had been retained by Armagnac in the past, a fact which must have confirmed the growing sentiment that the Count was the enemy. As early as the autumn of 1379 Albi, and probably other cities of Languedoc, were appealing for protection to the Count of Foix.[10]

Gaston Phoebus seized the opportunity to advance his own strategic interest. In October 1380 the Bascot de Mauléon, a *routier* captain who had been associated on and off with Gaston Phoebus for a quarter of a century, surprised Thuriès, a powerful castle dominating the gorges of the River Viaur north of Albi in territory traditionally controlled by the Count of Armagnac. The Bascot later told Froissart that he and his companions had got into the gatehouse dressed as women, one of many tall stories which the chronicler had from this boastful Gascon. The place was immediately besieged by the royal seneschal, but after some weeks he was obliged to withdraw empty-handed. Armagnac responded by putting Perrot de Galard's company into the fortress of Terssac on the Tarn west of Albi. The bastard of Savoy, another prominent *routier* captain who had once been one of the captains of Carlat, was sent to occupy other strongholds of the region in Armagnac's name. Other companies piled in after them, proclaiming their nominal allegiance to one or other count. Between them they transformed the Albigeois into a battleground. The Bascot de Mauléon claimed to have made 100,000 francs from pillage and *patis* over the three years that he held Thuriès.[11]

It was in these circumstances that in November 1380 the Duke of Berry was nominated as royal Lieutenant in Languedoc. The news caused consternation in the south. The cities of Languedoc had only recently got rid of the Duke of Anjou on the understanding that his successor would be a man without Anjou's expensive status and ambitions. Berry represented the worst of all worlds. The people of Languedoc, said Froissart, had heard that he was 'an extravagant spender who took money and gold wherever he could find it'.[12] He was quite as magnificent as Anjou but without Anjou's energy and judgment or his charismatic personality. Berry's appointment was unfortunate for another reason. His wife was the Count of Armagnac's sister and he himself was a close ally of the house of Armagnac. It had been an axiom of royal policy during the reign of Charles V that one of the main functions of the King's Lieutenant in Languedoc was to maintain a balance between the two great feudatories of the region. This had never been more important than it was in 1380. With this legacy the Duke of Berry would have faced formidable problems in Languedoc whatever he did. But he made his position much worse by remaining in Paris until well into the following year. In his absence the Count of Foix made his own bid for power.

January 1381 was a time of intense political activity in Languedoc. The caretaker administration had summoned assemblies in each of the three seneschalsies to consider the government's demands for a reinstatement of royal taxes. The towns were still suffering from the fiscal legacy of the Duke of Anjou. Their representatives resented Berry's appointment, distrusted the provisional government of the province and doubted its ability, perhaps even its willingness to confront the companies. As a result the commissioners met with a complete refusal everywhere, except in the seneschalsy of Nîmes, which granted a hearth tax at the derisory rate of four *gros*. The commissioners claimed, technically correctly, that Charles V's dying decree did not apply to the *aides*. But when they tried to collect them they met with furious protests. The Duke of Berry's representative in the province was beaten up by a mob in the streets of Narbonne. Behind the scenes, at the provincial assemblies and in the consulates of the towns, the agents of the Count of Foix were actively drumming up support for an alternative government under his own control.

The crisis came during the deliberations of the Estates of the seneschalsy of Toulouse. The Count of Foix was represented there by one of his councillors, Aimery de Roquefort. Aimery openly denounced the administration in front of the assembly. Holding up his instructions he declared that Gaston Phoebus was willing to take charge of the defence of Languedoc personally in return for a grant equal to the wages of 400 men-at-arms and a loan of 200,000 francs. With this, he declared, Gaston Phoebus would lead 1,000 men-at-arms against the companies 'whether French or English, from God or Satan' and would give them such a drubbing that they would not dare to steal so much as a capon. After much debate the assembly resolved to call on the King to appoint Gaston Phoebus as his Lieutenant. They would have no one else, they said. If the Duke of Berry insisted on exercising his office they would resist him by force. A delegation was sent to Paris to deliver this unpalatable message.[13]

Gaston Phoebus did not wait for the answer. The thousand men were already on their way. On about 15 January 1381 he appeared outside the walls of Toulouse at the head of a mixed army of Béarnais and

Gascon mercenaries. He was welcomed into the city and nominated by the citizens as their captain. Within a short time he had established effective control over the whole of the Toulousain and much of the neighbouring seneschalsy of Carcassonne and had installed his own garrisons at strategic points across the region. From Mazères on the border of Foix, where he established his headquarters, Gaston Phoebus wrote to the King declaring that he would obey any Lieutenant that he chose to send except for the Duke of Berry. 'Whoever advised you to appoint your uncle as Lieutenant in Languedoc advised you very poorly,' he wrote. At the end of April delegates drawn from all three seneschalsies of Languedoc gathered in Gaston Phoebus's presence at Mazères. There they agreed to pay him the subsidy which they had denied to the commissioners of the King of France.[14]

In Paris the King's Council followed these events with dismay. Paralysed by the tax strike in both north and south they were unable to intervene. They could not even supply an escort to enable the Duke of Berry to appear with suitable dignity in his new lieutenancy. Berry eventually left the capital for Auvergne in the middle of February 1381 to raise what troops he could find in his own domains. The Council announced that another army would march south to join him in the summer under the nominal command of the King. The thirteen-year-old Charles was already sufficiently conscious of his royal dignity to express outrage at the conduct of the Count of Foix and rebellious towns of Languedoc. He received the Oriflamme from the abbot of Saint-Denis at the beginning of April, surrounded by the pomp of the royal court. It was all bluff. Tax revenues did not resume their halting flow until the following year. For the moment there was no money with which to fight a civil war in Languedoc. Privately the Council had already decided to offer Gaston Phoebus whatever he wanted provided that he would recognise the authority of the Duke of Berry.[15]

The Duke of Berry arrived at Le Puy in June 1381. There he gathered around him about 2,500 men with whom to invade his own lieutenancy. Apart a small personal retinue the army was composed entirely of *routiers* in the employment of the Count of Armagnac. In about the last week of June the Duke entered Albi. From here he sent his ambassadors forward to open negotiations with the man who had declared just five months before that he would never tolerate his presence as Lieutenant in Languedoc. Gaston Phoebus now showed all the cunning for which he was famous. He had at least 2,000 and probably nearer 3,000 men under arms, but challenging the government by force of arms was an irrevocable step which he had no intention of taking if he could secure his political position by other means. So he did a deal with the Duke of Berry which gave him most of what he wanted. He recognised Berry as Lieutenant. In return he received an ample pension, a promise that the Duke's service would include as many of his own men as Armagnac's and an undertaking that Armagnac's interests would never be favoured over his own. The Duke ratified these terms on 15 July 1381 at Revel, a small walled town east of Toulouse. On the following day, desperately short of money, he discharged all of Armagnac's companies. They withdrew northward, burning and looting as they went, apparently intending to join Armagnac's garrisons in the Albigeois. But five days later, on 21 July, they were ambushed on the banks of the Tarn at Rabastens by the army of Gaston Phoebus under the command of Aimery de Roquefort. Most of Armagnac's captains were taken prisoner. Their followers were massacred. Some 300 survivors were caught and hanged or drowned in the river. The rest deserted and dispersed into the hills.[16]

In theory Gaston Phoebus had done nothing against the King's Lieutenant. The army which he had defeated had been paid off and was in the service of his enemy. But the Duke was furious. The battle left the Count of Foix the arbiter of Languedoc's fortunes. He commanded the only large organised military force in the province. His political position in the south was much stronger than Berry's. Most of the cities of Languedoc were still refusing to receive the Duke within their walls. The Viscount of Narbonne, who had declared for the Duke, found his authority repudiated by the citizens and his garrison in the city attacked with artillery. When the authorities of Béziers proposed to receive the Duke in September 1381 a furious mob attacked the town hall, killed most of the consuls and left the building in flames. Even in Rouergue, at the heart of Armagnac's territory, the consuls of Saint-Antonin were swept aside by a mob which took over the citadel, proclaimed their support for the Count of Foix and admitted a garrison sent to their assistance by the rebellious city of Toulouse. The Duke of Berry's nakedness was there for all to see when the two men met at the beginning of August. He appeared with his modest household retinue while the Count of Foix was accompanied by a clattering escort of 2,000 mounted men.[17]

On 22 September 1381 Gaston Phoebus presided over another meeting of the Estates of the three seneschalsies of Languedoc. It was held like the last one in his own town of Mazères. Here he set about mediating between the province and the man assigned to govern it. The compromise which emerged from their deliberations can hardly have been welcome to the Duke, but he had little choice but to accept it. There was to be no more piecemeal intimidation of small local assemblies or individual towns. In future taxes would be collected only with the consent of the Estates of all three seneschalsies. The proceeds were to be spent on what amounted to a standing army to be recruited from 'known residents', not *routiers*, and controlled by the consulates of the towns. These men were to be deployed against the companies only. An elaborate scheme of mutual military support was devised for reporting and dealing with incidents as they occurred. The whole system was to be supported by taxpayers at a rate of up to one man-at-arms, one crossbowman and one mounted infantryman for every thirty households. This, according to the current census of taxable households, should have produced up to 3,000 men from across the whole province. There was no disguising the effect of these conditions. They limited the new Lieutenant's tax revenues to the cost of local defence. There would be no more question of supporting a princely household or mounting aggressive campaigns against the surviving English territories in Gascony. After prolonged negotiations the Duke of Berry submitted shortly after Christmas 1381. In the new year the Duke himself was able to preside over the Estates at Béziers. It was not a triumphal occasion. The representatives of Toulouse declined to appear. The rest, after prolonged debate and with obvious ill grace, conceded a modest hearth tax of one and a half francs per hearth (equivalent to about 45,000 francs) to support operations against the companies. Even this proved almost impossible to collect.[18]

The main loser by these events was the Count of Armagnac. He lost much of his territorial power and almost all his political influence. Militarily he never recovered from the disaster at Rabastens. For a year after the battle a destructive guerilla war was fought out between the partisans of the two counts in the Albigeois and the Toulousain. Not until June 1382 was an uneasy peace forced on the rivals by the Estates-General. The Estates promised to find 40,000 francs to buy out some twenty companies of *routiers* operating in Languedoc and the Rhône valley, most of them associated with either Armagnac or Foix. Over the next few months the companies gradually dispersed or withdrew into the Massif Central. By this time Armagnac had been brought to the edge of ruin. He even contemplated throwing in his lot with the King of England. Some deaths are for the best, the lord of Albret wrote when the Count died in 1384. If he had lived any longer he would finally have destroyed the fortunes of his house.[19]

The English King's officers in Bordeaux were idle spectators of most of these events. The financial travails of the English government during the 1380s were felt very hard in Gascony. The English Exchequer continued to pay the wages of the Seneschal's personal retinue, which was never more than 200 strong. But otherwise English revenues made little contribution to the defence of Gascony after 1379. Times were difficult in Bordeaux. Much of the hinterland on which the city had depended was now under French occupation. Wine production was reviving but prices were weak. Hemmed in against the sea the English Seneschals had little manpower and no money. Their local revenues had declined to less than £1,400 sterling a year of which barely £400 was available for war expenditure. John Lord Neville, who held office from 1378 to 1381, was the last Seneschal of the fourteenth century who was able to deploy a field army, however small, or even to maintain significant garrisons. Even he was no longer able to do this by the end of his term of office. Writing to the King in April 1380 Neville pleaded for cash. He had captured the artillery depot left by the Duke of Anjou in 1377. He had won over the lords of twenty-three castles, he said, and was negotiating with the captains of thirty more. Like every commander in his position he claimed to be on the verge of great conquests if only funds could be found to pay for them. His pleas fell on deaf ears. After his recall to England the defence of the Gascon march was left to the citizens of the towns, who manned their own walls; and to the owners and captains of nearby castles, who supported themselves by preying on the inhabitants whom they were supposed to protect. The survival of the English duchy was due less to its own efforts than to the immobility of the Duke of Berry's government in Languedoc. At his trial in Paris in 1391 the Limousin captain Mérigot Marchès gave it as his opinion that the French could have conquered the entire territory if they had been prepared to keep 1,200 men-at-arms and 300 crossbowmen in the field for a year. There were at least a hundred castles which would have surrendered without even putting up a fight.[20]

Having no army to speak of the English King's officers in Bordeaux were entirely dependent for offensive operations on irregulars. The Seneschals maintained a large *routier* company of their own which was based at Fronsac, a powerful fortress on the north bank of the Dordogne, just west of Libourne. The captain of Fronsac was always either the Seneschal himself or one of the principal English officers of his council. The garrison, which appears to have been at least partly composed of Englishmen, drew no wages from the Constable of Bordeaux, instead taking their reward from the loot of Périgord, Angoumois and Saintonge. A handful of English adventurers who had settled in the duchy made a career out of the border war. Henry Green, the English captain of Puyguilhem in northern Périgord, controlled six garrisons in addition to his own, whose reach extended to the Dordogne and beyond. Fronsac and Puyguilhem, however, were exceptions. Generally the English worked through the Gascon companies operating beyond the march. The nobility of the Bordelais recruited their own companies in the hope of recovering lands which they had lost to the French or supplementing their diminished incomes by the profits of war. Raymond de Montaut and his nephew Amanieu, who were substantial territorial magnates on the north-east march, maintained a large garrison at Mussidan on the River Isle from which they raided across much of southern Périgord. Another company, whose leader cannot be identified, recovered the walled town of Saint-Macaire, one of the sentinels of Bordeaux on the Garonne in 1382. Further upstream in the Agenais the Caumonts, the Graillys and the lords of Lesparre had a joint company which progressively infiltrated the province. By 1384 they had established a permanent base for themselves in the important river port of Port-Sainte-Marie and were collecting the tolls of the Garonne and the Lot.[21]

Further afield Gascon companies created networks of mutually supporting garrisons in all the provinces which the Black Prince had ruled at the height of his fame, except Poitou. They represented an important military presence in regions which the English no longer administered but still claimed as their own. Most of them had close connections with the English government in Bordeaux. Perrot de Béarn was well enough known there for the Seneschal of Gascony to call him one of 'your men' when reporting his doings to Richard II. Mérigot Marchès had served as the squire of an English knight at the siege of Limoges in 1370. He had knelt in homage before John of Gaunt 'hands within hands'. A *routier* band which did not have at least a nominal allegiance to the King of England was unusual enough to call for comment. Geoffrey Tête-Noir, one of the few Breton captains still operating in southern France, established himself in about 1378 in the old Plantagenet castle of Ventadour in Bas-Limousin and survived there for more than a decade building his own network of satellite garrisons.

In a world filled with black deeds, Tête-Noir's band acquired a uniquely villainous reputation. The moralist Philippe de Mézières singled him out as the archetypal low-born brute who assumed the status of a knight without ever being one, a man whose skill, cruelty, cunning and sheer boldness brought him to 'great power and vile tyranny'. Tête-Noir may well have been worse than his peers but it is clear that the main reason why he was regarded as beyond the pale was precisely that he disclaimed any political allegiance at all. He never professed to be anything other than a bandit, fighting, says Froissart, 'against English and French interests alike'.[22]

As their resources dried up the English King's ministers at Westminster and Bordeaux made increasing use of the companies. In the spring of 1381 Bertucat d'Albret visited England to negotiate with John of Gaunt and Richard II's ministers. In broad terms Bertucat's proposal was that he should be granted the enormous inheritance of his cousin Bérard d'Albret, lord of Langoiran, who had recently been killed in an ambush leaving no heirs. Most of this property lay in French-occupied territory in the Bordelais. In addition Bertucat wanted to take over the even more extensive territories which had once been held by the lords of Caumont, comprising scattered domains lying between the Garonne and the Dordogne. They were currently occupied by the Beauforts of Limeuil, who had received them from the Duke of Anjou after their reconquest in the early 1370s. In return Bertucat proposed to use his companies to conquer these places and to make trouble for the French elsewhere. He also claimed to be in a position to procure the surrender of Bergerac and La Rochelle. How serious these claims were is hard to say, but Bertucat was certainly in league with the captain of Bergerac and appears to have had allies in La Rochelle. The English government was extremely interested. They granted him a string of strategic towns and castles along the lower course of the Dordogne in addition to the coveted lordships on the condition that he recaptured them. Like everything that Bertucat did, this was a commercial venture. To finance the reconquest he borrowed heavily from the London branches of the Italian banks and a syndicate of city financiers with interests in the wine trade. These debts were eventually secured on the proceeds of a royal licence to export wine by sea from French-occupied territories in the Dordogne valley.[23]

Bertucat returned to Gascony early in 1382 and set to work. An army of mercenaries was recruited in Bordeaux. The plan was to overrun Entre-Deux-Mers, the district immediately east of the city where Bérard d'Albret's former domains were concentrated. He would then move into the Dordogne valley. There was evidently some resistance in the Entre-Deux-Mers but it was muted.

Whether by accident or design Bertucat d'Albret's return from England marked the beginning of a fresh surge of *routier* activity across the whole of southern France. The largest concentration of *routier* companies remained the ten to fifteen garrisons associated with Carlat, which had always looked to Bertucat d'Albret for direction. They worked together as a single federated company and exercised almost total control over a large swathe of territory in Auvergne and the Cantal extending south into Rouergue and the Gevaudan and east into the Velay. Closely associated with them were the garrisons of at least eight castles in the neighbouring province of Quercy which had been occupied by Bertucat's own companies and were commanded by two of his lieutenants: Noli Barbe or Barbet, captain of Pinsac on the Dordogne, and Bernard Douat, whose main base was at Montvalent a short distance upriver. North of the vast territory ransomed by the confederation of Carlat there were two distinct groups of garrisons operating from Bas-Limousin who co-operated with the captain of Carlat when it suited them. One group was controlled by Perrot de Béarn and Mérigot Marchès, who generally worked closely together; the other by the Bretons of Geoffrey Tête-Noir at Ventadour. Between them these captains controlled some forty major garrisons on the western slopes of the Massif Central in addition to a large number of minor keeps, church towers and fortified farmhouses which served as local depots and collection centres. Operating on a much smaller scale and over a shorter range there were approximately fifty or sixty garrisons active in the provinces bordering on the Gascon march, in the Agenais, Périgord, Angoumois and Saintonge.[24]

The only organised attempt at defence on the French side was in Auvergne, where the French Marshal Louis de Sancerre struggled to contain the rising tide of brigandage. His difficulties perfectly illustrated the unequal task faced by organised armies in forcing well-prepared guerillas out of remote mountain fortresses spread across a vast and inhospitable terrain. The Marshal arrived in Auvergne in July 1382 but he was obliged to spend much of his time haggling with the communities of the province about money and military service before he could do anything. The campaign, when eventually it got under way, was a disaster. Arriving at Saint-Flour in August, Sancerre announced his intention of dealing with the four garrisons closest to the town. But he was unable to raise more than 400 men. Two castles were captured but the *routiers* ambushed the army as it approached the third and destroyed its siege train, forcing Sancerre to withdraw. Le Saillant, the fourth and largest of the occupied fortresses, was not even attacked.

Sancerre's departure from the region was the signal for a fresh explosion of *routier* activity. On 18 October 1382 Gascon companies captured the castle of the bishops of Clermont at Alleuze, an incident which for years afterwards was regarded as symptomatic of the problems of defending the French countryside against the free companies. Before the landscape was softened by the construction of the Grandval reservoir, Alleuze stood on a high cliff overlooking the gorges of the River Truyère south of Saint-Flour. Its four tall circular towers still dominate the country for miles around. It would have been impregnable if the bishops had not persistently declined to spend money on repairs or garrison troops. In 1382 Alleuze was defended by a man who had passed most of his career in the accounts department of the bishop's household, assisted by two peasant servants with no experience of war, one of whom was reputed to be a hundred years old. As the *bailli*'s lieutenant observed, it was 'a good fortress but useless'. The place was taken in broad daylight by just twelve men from the garrison of Carlat. They emerged from the forest, felled a servant working by the gate with a crossbow bolt and walked in. Shortly afterwards a horde of masons and carpenters appeared to carry out repairs, make the place habitable and build a new curtain wall. Bernard, bastard of Garlans, the man responsible for this coup, was put in command of all the companies operating around Saint-Flour. On 23 October, five days after his arrival, this man entered Saint-Flour under the protection of a safe-conduct and a crowd of bodyguards and explained to the consuls over a good dinner what his presence in their region would cost them.[25]

Saint-Flour paid *patis* under a succession of agreements with the confederation of Carlat. These deals came at a crushing price and rarely offered much protection. They did not protect outsiders coming to the town, who had to buy safe-conducts. The *routier* captains could not always control their men. Treaties would expire or one or other party would be accused of breaking them. *Patis* would fall into arrears. The captains would then issue letters of marque, a procedure borrowed from international law and gradually sanctioned by practice, which authorised them to enforce the debt against anyone from the same locality. Mounted men would once more descend on the town to carry off animals and people and destroy crops and buildings while desperate

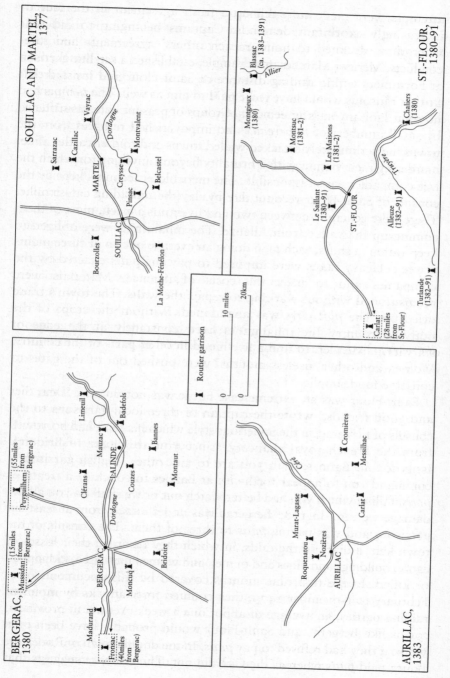

SOUILLAC AND MARTEL, 1377

Sarrazac
Cazillac
Vayrac
Dordogne
Creysse
Montvalent
MARTEL
Belcastel
Pinsac
Bourzolles
SOUILLAC
La Mothe-Fénélon

ST.-FLOUR, 1380-91

Blassac (ca. 1383-1391)
Allier
Montgieux (1380)
Montsuc (1381-2)
Les Maisons (1381-2)
Chaliers (1380)
Truyère
Le Saillant (1380-91)
ST.-FLOUR
Alleuze (1382-91)
Turlande (1382-91)
Carlat (28 miles from St-Flour)

Routier garrison

0   10 miles
0   20km

BERGERAC, 1380

Limeuil
Badefols
Mauzac
LALINDE
Clérans
Dordogne
Couzes
Bannes
Montaut
[55 miles from Bergerac] Puygauilhem
[15 miles from Bergerac] Mussidan
BERGERAC
Madurand
Moncuq
Bridoire
Fronsac (40 miles from Bergerac)

AURILLAC, 1383

Cromières
Messilhac
Cère
Murat-Lagasse
Carlat
Roquenatou
Nozières
AURILLAC

27 Cities under siege, 1379-1389

697

attempts were made to patch up a fresh agreement in the face of increasingly exorbitant demands. Captains belonging to different federations declined to honour each others' agreements and safe-conducts. Mérigot Marchès, for example, established a satellite garrison at Fortuniers within raiding distance of Saint-Flour and insisted that further ransoms would have to be paid to him as well. The *tuchins* had no regard for anyone's agreements. Groups of peasant outcasts stiffened by small numbers of *hobereaux* and impoverished refugees from the towns indiscriminately attacked walled towns and *routier* castles alike, murdering their victims with a brutality beyond anything for which the free companies were responsible. The meticulous accounts kept by the consuls of Saint-Flour recount day by day the unfolding catastrophe. There were generally between two and five raids a week, most of them coming up the valley from Alleuze. The inhabitants were obliged to keep watch in shifts, each man doing an average of two or three nights a week. Heavy taxes were imposed to pay the *patis* exacted by the companies and to meet the costs of defence. Materials were requisitioned without warning to repair the walls. The town's trade dried up. The *plat pays* was abandoned. Without the crops of the outlying country the inhabitants lived constantly at the edge of starvation. Men left to find a livelihood in other parts of the country. Women and other 'useless mouths' were pushed out of the gates to conserve food supplies.[26]

Saint-Flour was an extreme case but it was not unique. 'Dear Sirs and good friends,' wrote the captain of three local garrisons to the consuls of Bergerac, in the imperious style which his clerk had borrowed from the French royal chancery, 'since you are closer to Bridoire, Issigeac and Bannes, than you are to any other English garrison, I command you to appear forthwith at Bannes to conclude a treaty of *patis*, failing which you had better watch out or we shall do you all the damage we can.' In 1382 Bergerac was under attack from at least six garrisons and was paying *patis* to three of them. The consuls of the town kept a diary of the raids, in which they recorded their losses of cattle, buildings and vines and of men and women mutilated, kidnapped or killed. In the first nine months covered by this document, from February to November 1379, they counted forty attacks by mounted raiding parties, an average of about one a week. Yet life in provincial towns like Bergerac and Saint-Flour would probably have been even worse if they had refused to pay *patis*. In the double town of Rodez the Bourg paid *patis* whereas the Cité did not. The evidence suggests that the Bourg survived more or less unscathed. But the Cité listed more than twenty garrisons in 1383 whose continuing depredations were reducing its inhabitants to penury. 'Make for the forts, take with you your food, drive your cattle out of the region . . .' the town crier would proclaim from the cathedral steps on market days when a raid was expected. It was the same in Albi, hemmed in by ten Anglo-Gascon garrisons in the service of the Counts of Armagnac and Foix, where the citizens were forbidden to go out of the gates unarmed. Rather later Saint-Antonin in the Rouergue was said to be under attack by seven Anglo-Gascon garrisons, Figeac by fourteen.[27]

The kidnapping of townsmen and travellers found outside the walls without safe-conducts was a terrifying experience. Men would find themselves seized by brigands who emerged suddenly from the forest and led them off to some nearby castle with their hands tied behind their backs and their legs fastened together beneath the belly of a horse. Most of them were not worth the cost of their keep. They had to be deliberately ill-treated to make their relatives pay up. Geoffrey Tête-Noir and Perrot de Béarn were notorious for the stinking pits in which they would confine their prisoners. A pastrycook who was tried for brigandage at the Châtelet in 1391 told his judges that his job was to beat them up or starve them until they agreed to pay. He reckoned that some sixty of his victims had died in the process. Yet the great majority of prisoners were peasants and labourers whose ransoms were pitifully small. In 1382 an inquiry into *routier* operations in the castlery of Casteljaloux in Languedoc found that the average ransom was twenty francs for a live prisoner and twelve for a corpse. Many could not even afford that. They were put to work or murdered.[28]

Bertucat d'Albret never completed his grand scheme of conquest. He was taken prisoner in a skirmish in the summer of 1382 and, although he appears to have been ransomed quite quickly, his health was broken. He died in September of the following year. His death deprived the English of an ally of great cunning and organisational skill and brought an end to any prospect of their recovering Bergerac. Bertucat's successor was a hitherto obscure *routier* captain from the Landes called Ramonet de Sort. Ramonet called himself Bertucat's 'nephew'. He appears in fact to have been the son of one of the old warrior's companions-in-arms from the early years of his career. Bertucat had appointed him as his lieutenant in Quercy when he departed for England in 1381 and at some stage adopted him as the heir to all his assets outside the Bordelais. It is a tribute to Bertucat's force of personality and the strength of the

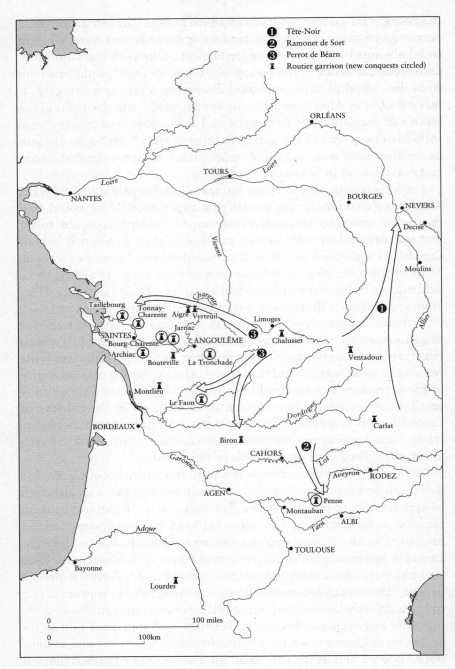

❶ Tête-Noir
❷ Ramonet de Sort
❸ Perrot de Béarn
♟ Routier garrison (new conquests circled)

ORLÉANS

Loire

Loire

TOURS

NANTES

BOURGES

NEVERS

Decise

Vienne

Moulins

Charente

Taillebourg
Tonnay-
Charente   Aigre Verteuil   Limoges
SAINTES Jarnac   ❸
Bourg-Charente ANGOULÊME Chalusset
Archiac
         Bouteville La Tronchade   ❸
                                          Ventadour
Montlieu

Le Faon   *Dordogne*
                                          Carlat
BORDEAUX
                   Biron
Garonne   CAHORS   ❷
                        Lot
                   Aveyron RODEZ
AGEN   Penne
         Montauban   ALBI
Adour   *Tarn*
              TOULOUSE

Bayonne

Lourdes

0   100 miles
0   100km

28 *Routier* operations, autumn 1383

leagues which he created that after his death his choice was by and large respected by his companies. Ramonet became the captain-in-chief of sixteen garrisoned castles in Quercy and at least two in Périgord. Ultimately he seems to have stepped into Bertucat's shoes even in Auvergne, although he personally commanded only one fortress there. What is clear is that Ramonet de Sort, although fighting for profit like all of his kind, saw himself as an English partisan just as Bertucat had. He signed himself 'Captain for the King of England'. His ransom treaties reserved his obligations to Richard II and declared that he would be at liberty to make war again if the King's representative ordered him to do so. His men cried 'St. George!' as they went into battle.[29]

Whether or not it was Ramonet's doing his appearance on the scene coincided with another increase in the range and boldness of the *routiers*' operations. In September 1383 the combined companies of Carlat and Ventadour launched a long-distance raid up the valley of the Allier which penetrated as far as the Nivernais, more than 150 miles north of their base. At one point they were reported to be heading across the Morvan hills into Burgundy. The companies' attempts to extend their reach northward were usually frustrated by the diligence of the Duke of Bourbon's officers in the Bourbonnais, the strong local cohesion of the nobility of Poitou and the impassable barrier of the Loire. There would be other attempts in the coming years to penetrate north of the river but none of them succeeded. To the south and west, however, the companies fared better. In about October 1383 Ramonet de Sort himself led a large raiding force from Quercy south across the *causses* and laid siege to Penne d'Albigeois, an important royal castle dominating the gorges of the Aveyron. A formal siege involving forces on this scale was something new in the history of the companies, who had traditionally avoided difficult or time-consuming operations. After several weeks Ramonet captured Penne and made it a base for fresh raids deep into the Toulousain. From the Limousin the Anglo-Gascon companies advanced south into the Bergeracois and west into Saintonge. Perrot de Béarn established himself for a time in the great fortress of the Gontauts at Biron, well south of the Dordogne. In Saintonge his subordinates and allies acquired a string of at least six fortresses along the River Charente, paralysing the main navigable waterway of the region in what was clearly a concerted campaign of expansion.[30]

Because the companies' activities were confined to the southern and central provinces they had little impact on politicians in Paris where the main strategic decisions on the conduct of the war were made. The only influential figures there with a real interest in the problem were the Duke of Bourbon, whose domains were in the front line of their operations, and Marshal Sancerre, who passed much of his career in the region. South of the Dordogne the control of the Gascon march and the suppression of the companies remained the responsibility of the Duke of Berry as royal Lieutenant in Languedoc. His attention was generally engaged elsewhere and his government was disabled by penury. The *aides* and the *fouage* were reimposed in Languedoc in 1383 but anarchy and brigandage continued to depress receipts. The number of taxable households in the three seneschalsies had been 31,000 when the Duke of Anjou departed, a figure which itself represented a reduction of more than 60 per cent since 1370. In 1387 it was only 23,000 and still falling. Much of what was collected was appropriated by the war treasurers in Paris to finance successive attempts to invade England or taken by the household treasurers of the Duke of Berry to fund his opulent style of life. In the 1370s the taxpayers of Languedoc had supported almost all the cost of the campaigns against the English possessions in Gascony. In the 1380s they could not even find the cost of their own defence and internal administration. These problems would have challenged a far abler and more diligent man than John, Duke of Berry. Berry, however, was neither able nor diligent. He was a poor administrator with no grasp of finance and no interest in warfare, who passed just twenty-three months in Languedoc during the nine years when he was Charles VI's Lieutenant there. He very much preferred Paris.[31]

The root of the problem was the fragmentation of the defence at a time when the companies had learned to co-ordinate their operations and concentrate their forces. None of the Duke of Berry's council in Toulouse had the stature to direct the defence of an area extending from the Rhône to the Atlantic and from the Dordogne to the Pyrenees. The job therefore had to be done piecemeal by local officials. They had to find men and money for the task within their own districts from the communities that they were protecting. Since these were the very communities which had suffered most from the operations of the companies they were rarely in a position to pay much. The history of these years is an unending round of arguments with towns and local assemblies, leading to the recruitment of tiny armies for strictly local operations, generally for no more than a few weeks at a time. When the captain of Penne d'Albigeois appealed for help to the Seneschal of Toulouse during the siege of 1383 no one stirred. Even within the same province Clermont would not willingly come to the aid of Saint-Flour or Cahors to that of Figeac or Martel. A number of attempts were made to combine the resources of the provinces of the Massif Central. None of them was successful. In June 1381 the Duke of Berry bullied the provincial Estates of Auvergne into forming a league with four neighbouring provinces to raise a combined army of 500 men for four months. The venture foundered on the particularism of the various provincial assemblies. The Estates of Rouergue, which had been invited to participate, declined to do so. The Estates of Gevaudan, Velay, Vivarais and Valentinois agreed but contributed less than ten per cent of the cost between them. Another attempt was made at the end of 1382. This time Rouergue participated but the enterprise succeeded no better. In October 1384 a fresh league was formed with the same membership but only against the vocal opposition of the Estates of Auvergne, whose representatives regarded it as a device for making them fund the defence of other provinces. They had to be thrown into prison to make them change their minds. There was no suggestion on any of these occasions that contributions should be made by the taxpayers of the three seneschalsies of Languedoc or the King's treasury in Paris.[32]

The French King's ministers in Paris did not wake up to the gravity of the situation until the federated companies of Auvergne and Quercy began to break out into the lowland provinces. The loss of Penne d'Albigeois and the fortresses of the Charente came as a shock in Paris. But there was no change of policy until the mid-1380s. In 1385 the Duke of Bourbon was appointed as royal Lieutenant in the whole march region north of the Dordogne with powers matching those of the Duke of Berry south of the river. Bourbon's political stature and his reputation as a soldier made possible the first effective collective effort against the companies for many years. About two-thirds of his expenses were met by the King. Further financial contributions were imposed across the territory of his lieutenancy. Much of the baronage of the Bourbonnais, Limousin, Poitou and Saintonge brought their retainers to his army. Including 'varlets', a corps of Genoese crossbowmen, and Jack Wyn's Welsh legion, Bourbon's strength must have come to more than 3,000 men, the largest force which had fought on the Gascon march since the days of the Duke of Anjou. The Duke passed five months, from June to November 1385, in the valley of the Charente and achieved an almost complete sweep of *routier* garrisons in Saintonge. Le Faon, west of Angoulême, was taken by storm. The small forts of Archiac and

La Tronchade were demolished and their garrisons put to death. Bourg-Charente surrendered after the besiegers suborned some of the garrison and poisoned the garrison's water supply. The lower town of Montlieu was battered into submission with stone-throwers and the defenders of the citadel induced to surrender by threats to 'string them up by their throats'. The great stone bridge over the Charente at Taillebourg was stormed in a combined attack by land and water and every one of its defenders killed. The garrison of the nearby citadel surrendered three days later. Verteuil, one the strongest fortresses of the region, defended by a garrison of nearly a hundred men, was abandoned after Bourbon's men had bombarded it for more than two months and undermined the walls. At the end of the campaign only one Anglo-Gascon company had successfully resisted the French army and that was the garrison of the immense thirteenth-century fortress of Bouteville. This place, and the small town of Jarnac on the Charente just north of it, were now the only surviving strongholds of the companies north of the Gironde. The Duke of Bourbon left what amounted to a permanent field force of some 600 mounted men to guard the marches of Poitou, Périgord and Limousin under the command of a group of knights of his personal household. The march of Gascony was entrusted after his departure to Marshal Sancerre. He was destined to serve as permanent military governor in Saintonge and Angoumois until 1389, with a standing army which varied from 1,400 men to over 2,000. These steps effectively blocked the northward expansion of the Anglo-Gascon companies.[33]

The defence of Languedoc proved to be a more difficult problem. In the spring of 1384 the Seneschals of Toulouse and Carcassonne appealed to the King's Council over the head of the Duke of Berry for help against the companies, which were by now penetrating into the region from the Albigeois in the north and Bigorre in the south. The royal Council appointed Gaucher de Passat, a protégé of the Duke of Bourbon then serving as one of the captains of the King's bodyguard, as temporary Captain-General of Languedoc. Gaucher de Passat arrived in the south in June 1384 and set up his headquarters at Gaillac in the Albigeois. There he joined forces with the Seneschals of Toulouse, Carcassonne and Rouergue and set about clearing the companies around Albi. His efforts in the Albigeois met with mixed results. Most of the companies of the region had already agreed to evacuate their strongholds for money. The most that can be said is that the presence of his army ensured that the agreements were observed. But Gaucher failed in his main objective, which was to recapture Penne d'Albigeois, the one fortress in the region which had declined to do a deal with the local communities. In the hands of Ramonet de Sort's lieutenants the place proved to be impregnable and Gaucher was obliged to abandon the siege after a few days. It was ultimately bought back from the garrison of Ramonet de Sort at very great cost in the following year. Gaucher de Passat left for Toulouse towards the end of 1384 and for the next year spread himself thinly across the whole vast area of Jean de Berry's lieutenancy, firefighting from the Agenais to the Pyrenees. He was a competent soldier but he did not have the stature of a Duke of Bourbon and received little or nothing from the royal treasury. As a result he depended entirely on local contributions and local recruits. None of them would fight outside their home provinces. So Gaucher had to raise and finance a fresh army in each region in which he operated. He never disposed of more than 400 men-at-arms. By the time he was recalled the situation in Languedoc was worse than ever.[34]

After much pressure from the King's Council the Duke of Berry was induced to revisit his province in August 1385. Apart from one brief visit he had been absent for three years. Characteristically, his response to the growing crisis that he found in Languedoc was to pass the problem to someone else. In October 1385 the Duke appointed his nephew John III, the new Count of Armagnac, as Captain-General in Languedoc and all the march regions south of the Dordogne. Berry delegated to him his entire civil and military powers and charged him to recruit a permanent force of 700 men-at-arms for the defence of the province, more if the English were to invade from Gascony. For these services Armagnac was promised a large monthly fee together with an even larger life pension than he already enjoyed. Early in 1386 the Duke of Berry withdrew once more to the north leaving John to get on with it. Unfortunately the Count of Armagnac was very close in outlook to the *routier* captains he was pitted against. He was a natural adventurer: ambitious, aggressive, insubordinate and devious. His appointment was a serious misjudgment. Armagnac appears to have raised most of the 700 men-at-arms and deployed them in garrisons on the northern marches of Languedoc and in the Pyrenean county of Bigorre. But having done this he complained that the treasurers in Paris were not paying his pension and treated this as an excuse to do nothing more. The money raised for the soldiers' wages was diverted into his own pocket. As a result most of the men deserted. Those in Rouergue and the Velay stayed at their posts but under-strength and without proper equipment. Some of them had to sell or pledge their horses to feed themselves.

The Anglo-Gascon companies seized their chance. There was a dramatic increase in the range and frequency of their raids. The Duke of Berry's councillors in Toulouse reported that the offensive was being actively pushed by the new Seneschal of Gascony, Sir John Harpeden, and there is some evidence that it was. In the Agenais the Durforts of Duras, who were the main allies of the English, prowled about the country with a company of 500 men-at-arms while Harpeden negotiated with the lords of the *plat pays* and distributed circulars inviting the whole province to submit. By the autumn of 1386 the Anglo-Gascon companies had established control over most of the Agenais and the neighbouring province of Quercy. The French royal administration virtually ceased to exist in both provinces. Cahors and Montauban were reported to be on the verge of submitting to the English. These conditions quickly spread into the seneschalsies of Toulouse and Carcassonne. One of the captains of the Carlat confederation, the Bourc de Montsac, was active there in the spring of 1386. By September he had established ransom districts right up to the gates of Toulouse. All of this had a catastrophic effect on the receipts of the French provincial treasurers. Tax collectors were unable to venture out on the roads without a large armed escort. Collection entirely ceased in Quercy and almost entirely in Rouergue. The *taille* imposed to finance the invasion of England was effectively abandoned in Languedoc in April 1386. Over the whole province the yield of the *aides* fell by a quarter.[35]

Behind the walls of the towns the familiar structures of authority disintegrated. Families migrated elsewhere. Watches were no longer kept. Garrison commanders were caught trying to sell out to the enemy. Something of the atmosphere of suspicion, fear and insecurity in the small towns of the region emerges from the confession of Jean Fossanas, a Gascon who was captured in a skirmish and accused of treason. Fossanas was probably a peasant by origin. He had found work as a 'varlet' at Espiens in the Agenais, one of the castles held by the companies of Nompar de Caumont and the Captal de Buch, who employed him in a variety of low-level missions. His graphic tales of treachery and espionage are in their own way more revealing than the recollections of the more flamboyant figures whose boasts fill the pages of Froissart. A town is identified as a target. A man is sent to explore the walls, looking for dark corners and unblocked openings. A promising site is found beneath the shadow of the church tower and then judged too high. Three men enter the place disguised as casual labourers to see how a gate might be captured. Three more head for another town which may prove easier. Fossanas himself goes to check the gateways of Tournon, a substantial walled town. This is regarded as highly promising. Three inhabitants are found who are prepared to betray the place for 1,500 francs and the right to take the 'best' mansions there for themselves. A date is fixed for the assault. A letter is received from a man in Lectoure, who offers to help the company to enter his town when it is his turn on the night watch. He is not even asking for money. He just wants to be allowed to take a fine house of his choice and to 'have his way' with two fellow citizens who have crossed him. So the companies of Nompar de Caumont and the lord of Duras turn their attention to Lectoure. Two suitable points of entry are found. Two hundred men from the combined companies are detailed to take part. Help is summoned from other *routier* federations of the south. Reinforcements are expected from as far away as Lourdes, the principal Anglo-Gascon garrison in the Pyrenees. A specialist in difficult escalades arrives from one of the Count of Foix's garrisons in the Albigeois. The attempt fails at the last minute because all the dogs of the town start barking as the scaling party approaches. At this point the brief autobiography of Jean Fossanas ends. We know nothing of his fate. He was probably one of the many insignificant figures of the irregular war who were not worth a ransom and were obscurely hanged at midday at the gate of some southern town.[36]

The situation of Languedoc and the march was conveyed to the Duke of Berry in his Parisian mansion in a succession of panic-stricken reports from his councillors in Toulouse. The Gascon march, they reported, which had been in the western Agenais only months before, was now just five miles from Toulouse. The president of the Duke of Berry's council travelled to Paris personally to deliver an account of events and to hand in his resignation. The Duke protested that he was too busy to deal with the matter on the spot. He blamed the Count of Armagnac. Armagnac for his part was unrepentant. In September 1386 he too left Languedoc to participate in the invasion force gathering at Sluys, taking much of the chivalry of the south with him. He made no arrangements for the defence of the province in his absence and left no one behind to represent him apart from two members of his own council in Rodez, who closed their ears and declined to answer letters. The Duke of Berry's councillors could have been forgiven for exaggerating their tale of distress but the sombre picture painted in their reports is borne out by other evidence. Cahors is known to have paid *patis* to Ramonet de Sort, whose companies were able to dispose of their spoil in the city's markets and pass freely to and fro across the famous fortified bridge over the Lot. The conditions in the region left them with no alternative, the citizens replied, when the King's ministers expressed outrage. The citizens of Montauban, surrounded by fourteen *routier* garrisons, had no more choice than the Cahorsins. They not only paid *patis* to Ramonet's garrisons but declared that they would not admit the Duke of Berry or Gaucher de Passat into their citadel.[37]

In 1387 the Count of Armagnac embarked on an attempt to recruit a *routier* army which was in some ways like his father's disastrous scheme of 1379. The target this time was not the Count of Foix but the King of Aragon. Some years earlier Armagnac had bought from that impecunious adventurer Isabella of Mallorca the rather tenuous claim of her family to the crown of Aragon. It was a speculation characteristic of both sides. Isabella had no claim to sell, for she had already sold what rights she had to the late Duke of Anjou. And Armagnac for his part had nothing but promises to give her in exchange: a pension, a title, and a share of the spoils, all on condition that the venture succeeded. But the transaction had given the Count what he wanted, a legal and political cover for what was in reality a crude plundering expedition. On 5 January 1387 Peter IV of Aragon died. Armagnac, who had just returned from the mud and frustrations of Sluys, devised a plan to serve his own interests and those of Languedoc at one and the same time. He proposed to rid southern France of the Anglo-Gascon companies by buying them out of their fortresses in the Massif Central at the expense of local taxpayers and leading them into Aragon. Preliminary approaches were made to the captains of the confederation of Carlat in the spring of 1387. Support was obtained from the Avignon Pope, who had his own interest in suppressing the brigandage of the south. Shortly afterwards Armagnac unveiled his plans at a series of provincial assemblies. Characteristically, the whole project was conceived and implemented without disclosing the ultimate object of the venture and without reference to the Duke of Berry, who was in Paris occupied by other affairs. Berry would certainly not have approved if he had known what Armagnac planned to do with his *routier* army. The new King of Aragon, John I, was a strong francophile married to a French princess. At the very moment that the Count of Armagnac was devising his scheme to unleash an army of bandits over John's kingdom, the King's Council was planning to send an embassy to John I in Barcelona with proposals for a closer alliance.[38]

At the beginning of July 1387 there was a great assembly in the cloister of the Franciscans, beneath the ramparts of the city of Rodez. The Count of Armagnac presided. The papal legates were present. There were delegates from all three seneschalsies of Languedoc and the five outlying provinces of Auvergne, Velay, Gevaudan, Quercy and Rouergue, an unprecedented collaboration covering the whole of Jean de Berry's lieutenancy. Shortly an agreement was reached. The Count undertook to guarantee the evacuation of thirty major fortresses controlled by sixteen *routier* captains in Auvergne, Quercy and Bas-Limousin. This represented about three-quarters of the companies operating in central France including almost all of those associated with Carlat. He agreed to obtain the *routiers'* undertakings, supported by written oaths if possible, not to make war again in France or in the Dauphiné, Provence or the states of the Avignon papacy. He would then unite them in a great army and lead them out of France by 1 November 1387. In return the communities of the Midi agreed to pay him a lump sum of 250,000 francs, by far the largest single payment ever made for an evacuation. In addition the papal legates offered a clerical subsidy from the dioceses of the south. The conventions agreed at Rodez said nothing about the destination of Armagnac's army. Even the *routiers* who were to take part were not told. They had to be content with the information that they would be required to serve on a 'campaign which His Lordship intends to undertake, which will be worthy and honourable for him and profitable for his companions, but which he cannot disclose yet for fear that the news will undermine the venture.' In Paris the King's ministers were already suspicious. The Duke of Berry asked for assurances that the *routiers* would be led out of France by the Rhône and not over the Pyrenees. He was presumably put off with lies. The Council sent an emissary to examine the terms of Armagnac's agreements with the companies. He would have found only circumlocution and silence. The Pope appears to have guessed what was afoot. He withdrew his support and cancelled the clerical subsidy.[39]

The Count of Armagnac's evacuation plan was combined with proposals for dealing with the garrisons closer to the Gascon march by force. Either they had refused to participate in the scheme or they were assumed to be hostile to it. Towards the end of the summer, after the delegates at Rodez had dispersed, there was a co-ordinated French offensive against the Gascon march north and south of the Dordogne. In Saintonge Marshal Sancerre siezed Jarnac, then the only remaining English-held town on the Charente, and marched on Blaye and Saint-

Emilion, the major English strongholds on the north shore of the Gironde. He failed to take either town. But, while Sir John Harpeden rushed reinforcements to the Gironde, Armagnac invaded the Agenais by the valley of the Lot at the head of a large army of cavalry and mounted crossbowmen. He had overrun most of the garrisoned places in the Lot valley before the English succeeded in organising a coherent defence. He then penetrated down the Dordogne into southern Périgord. A total of twenty-eight castles and walled towns and villages were taken from Anglo-Gascon partisans in the space of a few weeks. It was a substantial achievement but the only one in the four years during which Armagnac was effectively governor of Languedoc.[40]

There were several difficulties about the agreements which Armagnac had made at Rodez. In the first place they depended entirely on the Count's diplomatic skills and business acumen. He had to buy out the companies from their fortresses and pay their war wages, all out of his fixed fee. The financial side of the venture was never properly thought through. The three seneschalsies of Languedoc were the richest of the Midi and in spite of the events of the past three years the least war-damaged. However, in order to get their agreement, Armagnac had limited their contribution to the proceeds of a two and a half francs hearth tax. This was later raised to three francs per hearth with a theoretical yield of 69,000 francs, which was about a quarter of Armagnac's lump sum fee. The main burden fell on the two provinces of Auvergne and the Rouergue, who had to raise 50,000 francs each from a much smaller and poorer population. The Estates of Rouergue refused to contribute more than 9,000 francs. The communities of the Velay had to be forced to grant anything at all. The contribution of Auvergne, which had fewer than 3,000 taxable households, was found to require a hearth tax of twenty-two francs, an unheard-of rate which was received with uproar when it was announced to the provincial Estates at Clermont. The tax ultimately imposed was fifteen francs per hearth and even that proved to be impossible to collect.[41]

Armagnac's laborious negotiations with the captains were supposed to be completed by September 1387. In fact they dragged on for more than a year. The captains constantly changed their minds. They quarrelled among themselves. Many of them were subjects or retainers of Gaston Phoebus, Count of Foix, who lobbied actively against the venture and persuaded some significant *routier* leaders not to participate. In the end Armagnac succeeded in agreeing terms with seven of the principal captains, accounting for twenty-two of the thirty castles named in the conventions of Rodez. They included Ramonet de Sort, Mérigot Marchès and the captains of Carlat and Alleuze. These were admittedly the most important *routier* leaders in Quercy and Auvergne. But they did not include six important companies which for some reason had been left out of the conventions of Rodez, among them the large garrison of Le Saillant north of Saint-Flour. Nor did they include the important groups of garrisons in Bas-Limousin controlled by Perrot de Béarn and Geoffrey Tête-Noir, both of whom enjoyed close relations with Gaston Phoebus and had declined to take part. As if to demonstrate his independence, in February 1388 Perrot achieved the greatest stroke of his career by capturing Montferrand, one of the three principal towns of Auvergne. According to Froissart, the deed was done by the company of Chalusset, reinforced by detachments from a large number of the other Gascon companies in Auvergne. A handful of men entered the town on market day disguised as merchants and opened the gates for sixty of their companions at dead of night. It was wet, windy and bitterly cold. The captain of the town had sent his son out to do the rounds. But the street patrol bribed him to let them go to bed. When the companies left three days later, 400 horses were needed to carry the plate, carpets, silk and cloth looted from the inhabitants. No town of comparable importance had fallen to the companies for more than twenty years.[42]

Most of the *routier* captains had promised the Count of Armagnac to observe a truce while the money was raised to pay them. But the collection of the money took much longer than they had expected. As time went on, the truces expired or were simply abandoned by captains who could no longer restrain their men.[43] Shortly the distress in the unwalled villages of the *plat pays* was as great as anything seen before the Count of Armagnac's gathering at Rodez. Limoges was the city of St. Martial, the third century apostle of the Limousin, whose relics, preserved in the great Benedictine abbey of the upper town, were exhibited on the high days of the Church. On 30 June 1388, the feast day of the saint, hysterical crowds of pilgrims crammed into the abbey church praying for relief from the physical and mental scars of war in an emotional atmosphere heightened by plague, harvest failure and incoherent reports of distant negotiations for a truce. As the saint's head encased in enamelled plate was lifted above the heads of the crowd the companies' victims came forward, some of them completely naked, to proclaim some fresh miracle due to his intercession and to present wax models of themselves as votive offerings at the shrine: prisoners of

Perrot de Béarn cast into deep pits at Chalusset; men chained hand and foot by Tête-Noir's men at Ventadour; travellers carried off by horsemen when they were found on the road without a safe-conduct; a priest kidnapped in the Rhône valley by armed men returning from Castile; countless victims held in dungeons for weeks, months or even years to force their kinsmen to ransom them; all liberated by the power of St. Martial, their leg-irons shattered, their prison doors opened, their guards paralysed. Occasionally there was a victim from the other side of the divide, an Englishman saved from drowning in his heavy armour or a Gascon saved at the last moment from the hangman. The impotence and despair of a whole generation are reflected in these naive tales of miracles commemorated in one place on a single day. They could have been matched over a longer period at many other popular shrines, where a growing proportion of pilgrims and votaries were now victims of the war.[44]

By the end of 1388 the Count of Armagnac was becoming as frustrated at the slow progress of his plans as everyone else. Unfortunately his receipts from the provincial treasurers were still well short of what he had promised to the companies. In order to get men released for his army of Aragon he had to agree to some untidy compromises. Large payments on account were made to the captains of Carlat and Alleuze in order to persuade them to keep the peace and detach part of their strength for service across the Pyrenees. Mérigot Marchès was paid a lump of 4,000 francs plus 1,000 francs worth of horses and was granted a town in Rouergue. According to his own account he was also given a private assurance that if his garrisons resorted to their old ways in order to keep themselves the matter would be overlooked provided they stayed away from Armagnac's domains in Rouergue. Ramonet de Sort drove an even harder bargain. In addition to a share of war profits he received a grant in perpetuity (subject to royal confirmation) of all sixteen castles in Quercy which were occupied by his companies plus the town of Gourdon. This meant that only Roquenatou, Ramonet's one fortress in Auvergne, would be evacuated and then only when he was paid for it. In December 1388 the first contingents of Armagnac's *routier* army were ready. Over the following months they were escorted south by Armagnac's lieutenants in small bands and by different routes towards the marches of Roussillon. The Count sent his brother Bernard, a close collaborator in all his ventures, to take command of the horde of brigands gathering by the Mediterranean.[45]

*

By this time the political landscape of France had radically altered in ways that boded ill for the Count of Armagnac. When Charles VI shook off the tutelage of his uncles in November 1388 everyone knew that the Duke of Berry's days as Lieutenant in Languedoc were numbered. The Count of Armagnac, whose fortunes were closely bound up with his uncle's, was removed as Captain-General within weeks of the *coup* at Reims and replaced by Marshal Sancerre. For Berry himself the blow fell at a meeting of the royal Council in the Louvre on 18 May 1389. The King declared that he was moved by the 'clamour' of complaints reaching him from Languedoc. A commission of senior councillors would leave at once for the south to report on conditions there and take over the civil and military government of the region until more durable arrangements could be made. The Duke of Berry was not formally dismissed. The matter was too delicate for that. But messengers were despatched to proclaim the change in market squares across Languedoc. The Duke took it badly. He blamed Olivier de Clisson and never forgave him for the insult. 'One day', he declared, 'their fortunes will wane.' Four months later, on 1 September, he formally resigned his lieutenancy into the King's hands.[46]

Charles VI left two days later for the Midi. His servants spared no effort to project his image as a just and mighty prince with all the sacerdotal ritual and symbolism at which the Valois monarchy was so skilled. He was carried through city gates beneath a canopy of gold cloth and walked on carpets of flowers. He was welcomed everywhere by kneeling dignitaries, processions, choirs and crowds of curious onlookers who had never previously beheld a king. He was received in state by the Pope in the cavernous gloom of the audience hall of the palace at Avignon. At the end of November 1389 he entered Toulouse. During the six weeks which the King passed in the city the administration left by the Duke was purged of his friends, just as it had been in the north. All three provincial seneschals of Languedoc were replaced and a new government was put over them in which the leading figure was Marshal Sancerre. Two days before Christmas the Duke of Berry's private secretary and factotum, Jean de Bétizac, whose main crime was that he was a homosexual who had grown rich out of his master's incompetent and unpopular administration, was burned alive in a public square in Toulouse in spite of the Duke's frantic efforts to save him.[47]

The immediate consequence of the change of government in Languedoc was to inject new energy into its dealings with the companies. The Council resolved upon a two-track policy involving negotiation with those companies who were prepared to negotiate and the use of overwhelming force against the rest. In May 1389 Enguerrand de Coucy was sent to the Massif Central with 400 men-at-arms and 200 crossbowmen to serve as the kernel of a permanent army for use against the companies. Their first objective was Geoffrey Tête-Noir's castle at Ventadour. Tête-Noir's long history of savage and unpredictable behaviour made him an obvious target. But by the time Coucy reached Ventadour he was dead. He had been caught in a skirmish outside the castle gates and struck by a crossbow bolt which penetrated his helmet and entered his skull. When the French army arrived outside the walls in July the fortress was defended by his two nephews, Alain and Pierre Le Roux. Their only concern was to save their skins. Their uncle had always eschewed any national allegiance but without one they knew that they would be treated as bandits, not as prisoners of war. One of their first acts on taking over was to execute a written declaration that they held Ventadour for Richard II. They had this document carried to England, where it still sits in the Public Record Office, but by the time this disingenuous declaration reached Westminster it was too late. The English had just entered into the truce of Leulinghem and had no further interest in such captious friends. The French for their part were determined to establish the principle that those who fought on after the truce were common criminals who could expect no mercy. The siege of Ventadour lasted nearly nine months. The exact circumstances in which it came to an end are obscure but the evidence suggests that the garrison mutinied and sold their two captains together with the castle and its stores to the government for about 12,500 *livres*. The garrison received safe-conducts and an armed escort back to Brittany. The Le Roux brothers were taken to Paris and beheaded as traitors at Les Halles. Their fate was intended to impress the other *routier* captains and no doubt did. Even Perrot de Béarn, who had refused to deal with the Count of Armagnac, thought it wise to observe the truce. Mérigot Marchès actually surrendered his fortresses early.[48]

Frustrated by the slow progress of the buy-outs the government appointed a commission of three men to take the process out of the hands of the Count of Armagnac. The leading commissioner was one of the King's chamberlains, Jean de Blaisy. He was a Burgundian knight, 'famous among soldiers, beloved of princes' according to Philippe de Mézières. Blaisy set about his task with energy. He travelled south at the beginning of September 1389 and began to look into the Count of

Armagnac's murky dealings with the companies. In November the two men confronted each other at Le Puy. It must have been an uncomfortable occasion. Armagnac had no desire to see his project taken over by the Crown, but he had run out of money and was unable to pay the garrisons their due. He agreed to appoint Jean de Blaisy as his agent to enforce the agreements with the *routier* captains. He also agreed to add to the list the six major garrisons of Auvergne which had been left out of the conventions at Rodez. In return he received a promise of financial support to make good the deficit. Armagnac had probably received no more than about half of the 250,000 francs promised at Rodez. When his accounts were examined it was found that he was 50,000 francs short of the amount required to buy out the companies with nothing left over for other expenses. The issue was discussed with the King's advisers. They ordered a further levy on the provinces of the south. The Pope was persuaded to authorise a concurrent tax on the clergy. It was apparently proposed to find the rest of the money from the confiscated assets of Jean de Bétizac. During the winter Jean de Blaisy rode through Auvergne, Rouergue and Quercy with a small cavalry escort, negotiating with one garrison after another. Hostages were taken from those which had received part-payments. Money to pay the balances due to them was collected with painful slowness from the long-suffering taxpayers of the south.[49]

The most awkward problem was finding alternative employment for the displaced garrisons. Armagnac's plan to lead them into Aragon was by now public knowledge. In October 1389 Bernard of Armagnac finally gathered the cohorts waiting in Roussillon and set out for the Col du Perthus and the coastal road into Catalonia. Charles VI could not overtly approve of the invasion of Aragon. But neither could he repudiate it without undermining the strategy for disposing of the companies. There was no honourable way out. So the King resorted to a cynical evasion. In February 1390, as the companies of Bernard of Armagnac began to waste northern Catalonia, John of Aragon sent his ambassadors across the Pyrenees to protest. They confronted the French King at Béziers as he was making for the Rhône valley on his way back to Paris. They demanded that he recall his subjects from Aragon and called on him for armed support against the invaders in accordance with their treaties. Charles professed to be ignorant of these treaties. They had, he said, been concluded by the Dukes of Berry and Burgundy during his minority. He would make enquiries of them after his return to the north. In fact he did nothing. In March 1390 4,000 more *routiers*

were reported to be on their way south to join their companions in
Catalonia. The Count of Armagnac himself was said to be planning to
join them after Easter. In desperation the Aragonese King turned to
another ally, Gaston Phoebus, Count of Foix. Gaston Phoebus had
plenty of reasons for wanting to see the Count of Armagnac humiliated.
He promised to commit 3,000 men from his own companies to the
fight. In the event, however, Bernard of Armagnac's campaign fell apart
before either Armagnac or Foix arrived on the scene. In mid-winter,
with no standing crops in the fields and the barns and stores emptied
out in the invader's wake, the companies in Aragon soon ran out of
food. They began to suffer badly from hunger. In the spring of 1390
the Aragonese gradually drove the main body of the *routier* army back
across the Pyrenean passes. The brothers abandoned the campaign. The
whole venture had been a disaster for them both. Bernard of Armagnac
was obliged to sell his most valuable asset, the county of Charolais in
Burgundy, to defray his losses.⁵⁰

Armagnac's deal with the companies in Auvergne was already on the
verge of collapse when the Gascon companies began to flow back across
the Pyrenees into France. The first serious challenge came from
Ramonet de Sort. He had given hostages for the surrender of
Roquenatou, but when the time came he declined to deliver the place.
In Quercy he refused to surrender any of his castles, on the ground that
the Count of Armagnac had granted them to him. Jean de Blaisy for his
part declined to recognise the grant, which had in any event been subject
to royal confirmation. Ramonet responded by refusing to join Bernard
of Armagnac in Aragon and threatening to make war on Jean de Blaisy
and his fellow commissioners in France. Some of Ramonet's companies
refused to become involved in this spat. His two principal lieutenants,
Noli Barbe and Bernard Douat, both agreed to deliver up their fortresses
anyway. But Ramonet himself was intransigent. In December Blaisy
challenged him to a trial of the issue by single combat. Both men were
in earnest. A place was appointed for them to fight, at Le Puy. A date
was fixed, at the end of December 1389. Lists were built. The Duke of
Bourbon's 'great horse' was brought to the city for Blaisy to use. The
French knight's jousting armour was repaired and his arms embroidered
on his horse's tunic. At the last moment the rivals were persuaded to
settle on the terms that the dispute would be submitted to the
arbitration of the Pope. Ramonet can hardly have hoped for much from
that quarter but he gained valuable time while Clement VII conducted
the formal hearings which his lawyerly instincts demanded. Meanwhile

Ramonet resumed his plundering. In March 1390 two castles in Quercy were captured by associates of his: Cazillac, near Martel in the north of the province; and Montbrun, an impressive fortress dominating the valley of the Lot south of Figeac which belonged to the Crown's principal supporter in the region, the Marquis of Cardaillac. Ramonet de Sort's example was quickly taken up by others. The captain of Turlande in Auvergne who, like Ramonet, had accepted a part payment and delivered hostages, began to raid the territory of those who had defaulted in paying their *patis*. The lord of Mussidan resumed his attacks on the city of Périgueux and its dependencies in the valley of the Vézère.[51]

As for the companies which had followed Bernard of Armagnac to Aragon, once the campaign had failed they were simply abandoned on the march of Roussillon, a defeated rabble, their hopes of booty disappointed and their wages unpaid. Bent on revenge against the house of Armagnac, the men marched north under the leadership of Mérigot Marchès. In about May 1390 Mérigot occupied La Roche-Vendeix, a castle belonging to the Dauphin of Auvergne at one of the highest points of the Monts Dore. Another group sacked the small town of Peyrusse on the marches of Quercy and Rouergue and occupied its castle. Bands of men from both centres spread terror and destruction across much of Rouergue during the summer, doing great damage to the domains of the Count of Armagnac. Froissart imagined Mérigot rejoicing in the rediscovery of his old ways:

What joy it was to ride off across the fields after a rich abbot or prior here or a wealthy merchant there or to come upon a mule train . . . loaded with silk cloth of Brussels or pelts from the Lendit fairs, spices from Bruges and luxuries from Damascus or Alexandria. The peasants of Auvergne and Limousin would come to our gates laden with wheat, bread, straw for our horses, good wine, beef, mutton and fat lambs, chicken and every kind of poultry. Truly we stuffed ourselves like kings . . . And when we rode out the whole countryside trembled at the sight of us.

It was a literary conceit but a realistic one. The historian had met plenty of captains who spoke like this.[52]

It did not help that the breakdown of Armagnac's agreements with the companies coincided with a hiatus in the English administration in Bordeaux, on which the French had been counting for support. The English Seneschal, Sir John Harpeden, died in office in the spring of 1389. John of Gaunt left the duchy for England the following

November. This meant that the enforcement of the truce was left to the bipartite commissions of 'conservators' established in each region to enforce the truce. As Charles VI's ministers tartly remarked, Richard's conservators were the very men who were responsible for much of the violence. Ramonet de Sort, Perrot de Béarn, the lord of Mussidan and the captains of Carlat and Alleuze had all been nominated as conservators for the regions controlled by their fortresses. The principle of turning poachers into gamekeepers could hardly have been carried further. On the rare occasions when they were able to agree with their French colleagues their rulings were ignored by their fellow brigands. Yet at Westminster no one wanted to see the truce fail. In October 1389 two knights of the King's household, Sir William Elmham and Sir Richard Craddock, were sent out from England to serve as additional conservators. They brought with them instructions to ensure that the truce was observed but, it seems, insufficient powers. They returned to England at about the end of February 1390 to report on the situation, accompanied by one of the principal *routier* captains in Quercy, Bernard Douat. Parliament was then in session at Westminster. In its closing days Gascony was the main item of business.[53]

On 2 March 1390 Richard II, with the approval of the Lords and Commons, transferred Aquitaine to his uncle for life, solemnly investing him in full Parliament with the cap and wand of office. John of Gaunt's investiture as Duke of Aquitaine was intended to give the King's uncle an independent principality worthy of his status and wealth, and to confer on the duchy itself something of the prestige which it had enjoyed in the time of his brother the Black Prince. But although Gaunt had wanted the title and bore it for the rest of his life his administration in Gascony was a disappointing failure. The grant was resented by the towns, especially Bordeaux, which had privileges uniting them in perpetuity to the English Crown. They claimed that Richard was not entitled to grant the duchy to anyone other than the heir to the throne and sent a delegation to complain to him in England. At the same time deep offence was caused by Richard's decision to revoke prior grants made by his officers in order to reconstitute the ducal demesne for Gaunt's benefit. The victims of this measure included some influential Gascon noblemen whom neither Richard nor Gaunt could afford to offend. They refused to recognise the authority of Gaunt or his officers. The dispute was in some ways the mirror image of the quarrel of the cities of Languedoc with the Duke of Berry a decade earlier. It was temporarily resolved by a climb-down at Westminster. Richard issued a declaration undertaking that the duchy would revert to direct rule by the Crown on Gaunt's death. Gaunt for his part swore to respect the liberties of the duchy. The revoked grants were reinstated. Unfortunately these events left a legacy of mutual suspicion which was aggravated by Gaunt's inability to visit his duchy in person. Instead he was represented there by a succession of overbearing viceroys. Sir William Scrope, who was sent out as Gaunt's Seneschal in the summer of 1390, was a capable professional soldier who had already served a term as Seneschal some years earlier. But his abrasive manner quickly reopened old wounds. The city of Bordeaux accused him of trampling on their liberties. In August 1392 they declared that they would no longer obey him. Scrope was eventually recalled but his replacement, Harry Hotspur, was another high-handed soldier whom the Gascons liked no better.[54]

Far away in England and preoccupied with other affairs, John of Gaunt found it exceptionally difficult to enforce the truce in the south-west. A show of force against the Gascon captains of the march was out of the question. His representatives in the duchy had no force to show. Instead it was necessary to engage in a long and slow process of persuasion. Sir Richard Craddock was sent back to Gascony on the day after John of Gaunt's investiture, accompanied by the new Mayor of Bordeaux, Sir John Trailly. They were armed with instructions to make the local conservators perform their duties. They brought letters under the King's privy seal addressed to each of the principal *routier* captains of the march ordering them to surrender their fortresses or be disowned as traitors and rebels. The language of these documents was deliberately designed to prevent their recipients from claiming to be fighting a lawful war if they ever fell into French hands. In July 1390 the French government sent two ambassadors to Westminster to protest about the activities of the *routier* captains on the Gascon march. Their arrival provoked an anxious debate at a specially convened meeting of Richard II's Council at Windsor. In fact, however, the worst was already over. Craddock and Trailly appear to have put an end to the depredations of the lord of Mussidan in Périgord. The dispute with Ramonet de Sort in Quercy was resolved, although at high cost to the French. Montbrun had to be bought out for 12,000 francs. A number of garrisons in Rouergue surrendered in June 1390 and some of the major companies of Quercy followed suit six weeks later. In the autumn of 1390 Sir William Elmham returned to Gascony bearing letters addressed to the Seneschal which conferred draconian powers to punish recalcitrant captains. Craddock and Elmham were destined to spend the next two years serving as the English government's special envoys to the free companies, travelling continually between England and Gascony, negotiating with the French conservators and plying the captains with threats and promises.[55]

Mérigot Marchès succumbed to neither one nor the other. At the beginning of August 1390, not long after Craddock had left him, an army of some 600 soldiers and 300 labourers descended on La Roche-Vendeix under the command of Enguerrand de Coucy's lieutenant, Robert de Béthune, Viscount of Meaux. The siege of the place lasted little more than two months. At the beginning of October 1390 Mérigot surrendered it in return for a promise that the garrison would be allowed to leave with their lives. Then he slipped away, carrying with him some seven or eight thousand francs' worth of gold, silver plate and jewellery, all that remained of the gains of the past few years. He pawned a valuable jewelled helmet to raise money and hid the rest in various secret places in the Cantal. Then he vanished into the hills, plotting with old friends the capture of one fortress after another. All his plans were abandoned or failed. On New Year's Day 1391 Mérigot was captured by Jean de Tournemire, a retainer of the Count of Armagnac, while attempting to retake Tête-Noir's old castle at Ventadour by night. Tournemire lodged him in the keep of the Count's castle at Rodez and called on the Estates of Auvergne to buy him for the considerable sum of 7,000 francs. Otherwise, he said, Mérigot would be released like a plague bacillus into the hills of Auvergne. Jean de Blaisy eventually succeeded in borrowing the price from moneylenders in Clermont. Mérigot was handed over and taken to the Châtelet prison in Paris.

In spite of the loss of several leaves of the manuscript, the record of his interrogation there is among the most interesting judicial documents of the fourteenth century. Mérigot did not dispute the main facts alleged against him. It was undeniable that he had waged war in France for at least twenty years before his capture. Mérigot's acts were treason if he was a subject of the King of France. They were treason even for a subject of the King of England if Richard II had disowned him. The legal issue was far from straightforward. Although born in Limousin at a time when it was under French sovereignty Mérigot had entered the service of the English after the province had been passed to Edward III by the treaty of Brétigny. This awkward problem was resolved by declaring that Mérigot had voluntarily chosen the allegiance of the English when the rest of his family had acknowledged the sovereignty of France. He could, and no doubt should, have followed their example even if it meant sharing their exile in neighbouring provinces. But Mérigot was doomed anyway by his activities since the truce, which had on the face of it been disowned by the sovereign whom he claimed to have served. He told his judges that when Richard Craddock had visited him at La Roche-Vendeix he had handed him a letter from John of Gaunt containing secret instructions to hold on to his fortresses until the truce had expired. The court did not believe him. Mérigot was condemned to death as a 'traitor to King and kingdom, persistent robber and arsonist'. His judges were determined to make a spectacle of his death. On 12 July 1391 he was dragged along the ground on a hurdle to the market of Les Halles and beheaded. His head was displayed at the scene on a pike, his limbs exhibited above the four main gates of Paris and his torso suspended from the public gibbet at Montfaucon.[56]

The capture of La Roche-Vendeix and the arrival of Sir William Scrope at Bordeaux were the signals for the general dissolution of the major Gascon companies. The castle of Peyrusse surrendered shortly afterwards to the Count of Armagnac. Carlat, Alleuze, Turlande and Le Saillant were all peacefully exchanged for money in the course of January and February 1391. Mérigot Marchès' family, outraged by his treatment, continued to resist for a time. His wife defended the castle of Saint-Exupéry in Auvergne, which was part of her own inheritance, until late in 1391. His brother Danti reoccupied La Roche Donnezat (the modern La Roche Blanche), a powerful fortress south of Clermont, and withstood a siege of several months before selling out in November 1392. The newly created Marshal Jean de Boucicaut directed mopping-up operations against the remaining garrisons.

Where did the unemployed soldiers go? There is some evidence of a general migration of displaced Gascon *routiers* back to Gascony. Others moved to Italy, the only place in western Europe which still offered a flourishing market for mercenaries. A few tried to return to their old ways in central France. They were treated without mercy. The fate of the garrison of La Rolphie in Périgord, which fell in November 1391, was probably typical: the lord of Mussidan's captain was beheaded and the entire garrison hanged. Richard II had disowned them all. John of Gaunt's representatives in Bordeaux folded their arms and declined to intervene. The last of the great Gascon captains to hold out in the central highlands was Perrot de Béarn. He remained in possession at Chalusset until January 1393, when he finally sold the castle to the Estates of Limousin. He is last heard of some eighteen months later, when he briefly occupied two castles in Saintonge from which he was promptly expelled by the officers of John of Gaunt.[57]

Low-level brigandage was never entirely brought to an end. Some of the evacuated castles proved impossible to demolish owing to engineering difficulties or the claims of former owners. Some lesser places were later reoccupied, generally it seems by local gangs. A group of Gascon soldiers briefly occupied the cliff-top town of Domme in 1393 but fled when not one but two substantial armies were at once directed against it. With the withdrawal of English support concerted *routier* operations on the scale seen in the mid-1380s came to an end. In the northern provinces the much resented obligation of countrymen to serve watches on the walls of local towns had been abolished in all inland regions from the Somme to the Loire in April 1390 within a year of the truce of Leulinghem. In about 1396, watch duty was finally suspended in the towns near the Gascon march as well. In Paris Eustache Deschamps celebrated in mediocre verse the end of an age of constant tensions: watches by night, gate duty by day, continual ditch-digging; the perennial presence of armed soldiers and the barked orders of their captains; learning to distinguish the sounds of the night from those of animals and men, and forever listening out for the scrape of ladders against stone walls.[58]

CHAPTER XV

Men-at-Arms

In November 1389 Jean de Boucicaut and two other French paladins, Renaud de Roye and Jean de Sempy, sent heralds across western Europe with a challenge to the knights and squires of all nations to fight them in the lists 'without pride, hatred or ill will' over a period of thirty days on the march of Calais. The truce of Leulinghem was followed by a sudden upsurge of interest in jousting, of which Jean de Boucicaut's great tournament was only the first and most famous symptom. The habit of fighting died hard. Elaborate and conventionally choreographed pageants provided opportunities for men to exhibit their status and test their courage, strength and horsemanship in one-to-one combat. These occasions had less than ever to do with the actual practice of war. But they became potent symbols of national rivalry, somewhat like modern sporting internationals. Indeed this one was initially viewed with misgiving on both sides of the Channel, precisely because it was seen as a continuation of the war by other means at a time when both governments were committed to peace. The King of England would not issue safe-conducts until the last minute. The councillors of Charles VI raised no objection but muttered in private. They were afraid that it would stimulate national rivalries and, worse, deal a damaging blow to French prestige if their champions were defeated. Anxious remarks were made about the short stature of Boucicaut and his friends.

The tournament opened in spite of the misgivings on 21 March 1390 outside the abbey enclosure of Saint-Ingelvert near Ardres, surrounded by the flat wastes of the coastal plain of Picardy. A hundred and twenty English knights and squires responded to the challenge in addition to more than forty Castilians, Germans and Scots. They included most of the great names of English chivalry: Holand, Bolingbroke, Beaufort, Mowbray, Percy, Fitzalan, Clifford, Courtenay. Yet it was war, not sport, and old animosities were never far below the surface. On a tree outside their brightly painted pavilions the three French champions hung two shields decorated with their 'arms of peace' and 'arms of war'. The challengers were required to strike one or other to signify whether they would fight with tipped lances, blunted swords and wooden bucklers, or with real weapons of war. They all chose the arms of war. The participants heard mass at the beginning of each day and then fought each other according to stylised rules in measured-out lists, watched by the heralds and a crowd of supporters and ladies pressed against the barriers. Yet lances and swords were broken, helmets shattered and horses killed. None of the contestants died but many were wounded, some, like John Holand, Earl of Huntingdon, so badly that their companions feared for their lives. Jean de Boucicaut and Renaud de Roye were both forced to withdraw to their tents for several days to nurse their injuries.[1]

The men who organised the jousts of Saint-Ingelvert had many emulators. A rather similar although less grand tournament was fought in May 1390 between English and Scottish knights. Like the participants at Saint-Ingelvert they fought with sharpened lances. According to the official chronicler of Saint-Denis groups of itinerant English men-at-arms travelled through France challenging all comers to fights at which both sides regarded their national honour as engaged and considerable ill feeling was generated. In the autumn of 1390 Richard II sent invitations across western Europe to a three-day tournament at Smithfield beneath the walls of London, which was destined to be an even more extravagant affair. The English King took part himself. Large contingents attended from both France and the Low Countries. Blunted weapons appear to have been used but there were plenty of other outlets for the repressed violence and patriotism of the participants. At the closing banquet at Windsor castle some of the French knights refused Richard II's gifts and jeered audibly as Philip of Burgundy's son-in-law, the young Count of Ostrevant, was admitted to the Order of the Garter, discarding the jewelled badge of Charles VI's livery as he did so.[2]

The Count of Foix once observed that there were 'more great feats of arms done these fifty years than in the three centuries before'. What above all united those who fought at Saint-Ingelvert was the sense of having participated in great events, a view almost universally shared by the generation of soldiers who had lived through the war. Even the English and the Gascons, who had had the worst of the fighting since 1369, behaved as if the deeds of their greatest contemporaries redeemed them from the stigma of failure. At the lowest point of England's fortunes in the 1380s there were still Englishmen drawn to the fighting by the impulse to earn fame in a struggle which their descendants would speak of with awe. In July 1383 Peter Courtenay, a younger son of the Earl of Devon who had already won a reputation for recklessness among his contemporaries, appeared before the French King in Paris and demanded the right to fight a duel against Gui de la Tremoille. Courtenay had no quarrel with La Tremoille. His object, he said, was to demonstrate the superiority of English chivalry and vindicate the reputation of the English nation by fighting a prominent counsellor of the Duke of Burgundy whose status was roughly comparable to his own. Gui de la Tremoille was willing. When taxed with the fact that there was no issue between the two men he replied that it was enough that Courtenay was an Englishman and he a Frenchman. The French royal Council disapproved and after a certain amount of hesitation the King was prevailed upon to forbid the duel. Courtenay was loaded with gifts and went on his way, boasting that there was no one in France willing to take him on. Ultimately he had to settle for a less prominent opponent who fought him on the march of Calais later in the year and won. What is interesting about this story is the way in which it personalised the war with France. Courtenay, a comparatively obscure English nobleman, wanted to take his country's quarrel for a brief moment upon his own shoulders in order to stand out among those who were fighting a famous war.[3]

The cult of war and personal prowess was never more powerful than in the 1380s when both countries were on the verge of exhaustion and astute politicians on both sides had begun to realise that force of arms would never decide the issue. In France the extravagant public celebration of the life and deeds of Bertrand du Guesclin in the abbey of Saint-Denis in May 1389 was an extraordinary moment. Nine years after the great Constable's death and a month before the truce which would bring the war to an end, the French court marked the passing of a heroic period in their country's history. 'With him died all chivalry; with him perished all courage; with him was all honour buried,' sang Eustache Deschamps, one of the earliest authors of the Constable's remarkable posthumous fame. A mediocre professional versifier called Cuvelier ('that poor fellow', a contemporary called him) wrote an enormous biographical poem full of picturesque fictions which would be copied, abridged and plagiarised for more than a century to come. Thus did a minor Breton squire and sometime mercenary captain take his place with Hector, Joshua and Charlemagne as the Tenth Worthy, the man whose deeds Joan of Arc herself would honour half a century after his death by sending a ring to his widow, then a very old woman still living in Brittany.[4]

Cuvelier's life of Du Guesclin was addressed to an age obsessed with the recording of its own history and convinced of its political and moral significance. The Chandos Herald, a better poet and a more accurate historian than Cuvelier, wrote his verse life of the Black Prince in about 1385, placing his hero among the great warriors of history, alongside Julius Caesar, King Arthur and the mythical Clarus King of India. The bloody deeds of Sylvester Budes's Breton company in Italy were celebrated in rhyming couplets by his chaplain 'for love and honour of gallantry in arms and our Holy Mother the Church'. The anonymous 'Book of Deeds' of the French Marshal Jean de Boucicaut was commissioned by his companions in arms in his lifetime. Nor was it only soldiers who were commemorated in this way. The prolix and inaccurate verse life of John de Montfort written by his secretary is one of the earliest literary monuments of Breton patriotism. Philip Duke of Burgundy commissioned the life of his father Charles V by Christine de Pisan 'so that the noble life and great deeds of the wise King should be recorded in a book and the memory of his example preserved for ever.'[5]

By far the most remarkable monument to this mood of historical narcissism was the chronicle of Jean Froissart, one of the great literary masterpieces of the late middle ages. Froissart was a clerk of bourgeois stock who came from Hainault, a francophone principality of the German Empire. In 1361, when he was about twenty-four years old, he arrived at the English court as a chaplain in the household of Queen Philippa. Living at what was then the most glittering court of Europe he conceived the ambition of writing a great history which would serve as a 'perpetual memorial of the gallant and noble adventures which have happened in the wars of England and France and the lands around'. After the Queen's death in 1369 Froissart left England and began to write, following the course of the war more or less as it was fought. By the time of his death in about 1404 he had completed four books, carrying the story from the last years of Edward II until the death of Richard II in 1399 and filling fifteen stout volumes in the only complete modern edition. Froissart travelled widely in search of material, spending by his own reckoning a quarter of his income on hotel bills. He was welcomed at the courts of England, France and Scotland, of Aquitaine and Béarn. He was a determined collector of letters of introduction. He buttonholed the famous and the powerful wherever he went. He never passed by the chance to interview an eye-witness, however humble. As a historian Froissart had many faults. He was often taken in by braggards with fishermen's tales. He was hampered by his ignorance of geography and uncertain grasp of chronology. And, like Thucydides, he could not resist dramatising his tale with theatrical incidents, spurious detail and long, invented speeches. But at his best he is remarkably well-informed.

What is, however, most striking about Froissart's work is the fame which he achieved among his contemporaries while he was writing it. Arriving at the court of the Count of Foix in November 1388, the chronicler was greeted by Gaston Phoebus as an old friend. Although they had never met, the Count said, he felt that he already knew him well having heard so many men speak of him. Gaston went to some trouble to get his own version of the facts into Froissart's pages. He was not the only one. 'You write that down,' snapped one of the Black Prince's courtiers after regaling the chronicler at dinner with his thoughts. 'Master Jean, tell me,' enquired the Bascot de Mauléon as they sat together in the great hall at Orthez castle, 'do you have enough information about me?' 'Have you got the story of Mauvoisin castle in your history?' asked the Béarnais knight Espan de Lion as they passed beneath it on the road to Lourdes. 'No,' said Froissart, 'tell me.'

The chronicler had no doubt that his work would outlive him. 'In future years when my body has rotted in its grave,' he wrote, 'this noble and exalted history will be widely read and taken up with pleasure by gallant and noble men everywhere.' He was right. More than a hundred contemporary or near contemporary manuscripts of the *Chronicles* survive and many more once existed. Copies found their way into royal and noble libraries across Europe. The Duke of Anjou appropriated a copy of Book I, which was being decorated in a Parisian illuminator's workshop for presentation to Richard II of England. The Duke of Berry had a superbly bound copy in red leather with brass clasps. More than a century after the chronicler's death Henry VIII, the last King of England to entertain the old continental ambitions of Edward III and Henry V, commissioned a translation from the courtier-poet Lord Berners. 'What condign graces and thanks ought men to give to the writers of histories who with their great labours have done so much profit to human life,' Berners wrote in his preface; '. . . what pleasure shall it be to the noble gentlemen of England to see, behold and read the high enterprises, famous acts and glorious deeds of their valiant ancestors?'[6]

*

The three-part division of medieval society into those who fought, those who prayed and those who laboured retained a strong hold on the imagination of contemporaries long after it had ceased to represent reality. In the fourteenth century it was still taken for granted that the King's wars were the business of the nobility. The springs of valour, wrote Christine de Pisan, were courage, honour and fear of disgrace, all qualities which could be expected only among men of gentle birth. Peasants and townsmen marching with the army were good for nothing but brute labour. Philippe de Mézières agreed. The common people came only 'for presumption or loot'. Indeed it was part of the 'horrible tyranny' of the companies that they were largely recruited from such people. But for all its constant repetition this was a literary conceit. The differences between the King's armies and the free companies were a good deal less striking than the similarities and they continually learned from each other. Most prominent *routiers* were the sons of noblemen, even if many were younger sons or bastards. And the military service of the Crown was far from being the exclusively noble vocation of literary convention.[7]

Men-at-arms, the trained cavalrymen who provided the attacking force of every royal army, were in principle recruited from the ranks of the nobility, an elastic term embracing the large class of untitled but substantial provincial landowners whom in England one would call 'gentry'. As a rule of practice the principle was sound, if only because this class was the main source of men with the experience of handling horses and weapons and the resources to buy them. But it was never formally or consistently applied. In England, nobility was too loosely defined to be an absolute qualification for cavalry service. Knights, it is true, were readily distinguishable. They had been formally dubbed. They were expected to have a minimum income from land and a higher standard of mount and equipment. They received a better rate of pay. But most men-at-arms were not knights. They were squires, a protean term widely used by poets and novelists, tax assessors and by the draftsmen of successive sumptuary laws designed to keep men of inferior degree in their place. The status of a squire defied definition. All that could be said with confidence was that it necessarily excluded those who were too poor to arm or mount themselves. A certain gentility was no doubt expected but it was not easy to insist on it. Many of those who served as squires in Sir Robert Knolles's campaign of 1370–1 were recruited from pardoned outcasts, criminals and jailbirds. Until the last years of the fourteenth century English squires did not even have coats of arms. In 1389 Richard

II granted the status of gentleman and the title of squire to one John de Kingston together with the right to bear the arms *argent ove une chapeure d'azure, ovesque une plume d'ostrich, de geules.* It is the first surviving royal grant of arms, but what is striking about the grant is the occasion for it. John de Kingston had received a challenge to a duel from a French knight and needed his enhanced status in order to accept it. This man had obviously been fighting as a man-at-arms in France. He had won nobility by military service, not the other way round. Many others did the same without troubling themselves with points of form. As the herald Nicholas Upton observed a generation later,

... many poor men have become noble through their service in the wars of France by their own wisdom, strength or valour or by the divers other virtues which ennoble a man. Such men have taken coats of arms for themselves and their heirs by no other authority than their own.[8]

Even in France, where nobility was better defined, it proved impractical to limit the recruitment of men-at-arms to gentlemen. Royal ordinances had permitted the mustering of townsmen as men-at-arms since the 1350s and the practice was certainly older than that. When, in January 1374, Charles V issued his famous ordinance governing the recruitment and conduct of his armies he advised his captains to be cautious about hiring 'men of low estate' because they tended to be ill-equipped and undisciplined. But the only rule that he imposed was that a cavalrymen should be fit for the job, known personally to his captain and 'of a standing fit for service at our wages'. In France, as in England, captains raised their own companies of men-at-arms and presented them to the marshals at the outset of each campaign. The captains themselves were usually noblemen and no doubt preferred to recruit men of their own kind, but growing difficulties of recruitment made this a counsel of perfection. The heralds who assisted the marshals' officers at the muster could probably recognise the knights but they were outnumbered ten to one by squires whose status was impossible to verify. Froissart said of his contemporaries in France very much what Nicholas Upton would say about the English. A man without land or money who had an able body and agile limbs would find plenty of noblemen to employ him in the wars. 'You cannot imagine what fine adventures and great fortunes can be had by the pursuit of arms,' the chronicler wrote in his preface, 'but you will find in this book if you but read it, how men became knights and squires and advanced themselves in their profession more by their prowess than by their lineage.'[9]

These developments were assisted by the tactical revolution of the fourteenth century which progressively diminished the role of the heavily armed cavalryman in battle. In about 1340 Sir Geoffrey Luttrell had had himself painted on a page of his famous Psalter in the British Library seated on a caparisoned charger as his wife and daughter handed him his pennon and buckler. It is the classic image of the fourteenth-century man-at-arms. Yet at the time that the Luttrell Psalter was commissioned English men-at-arms had been fighting their battles on foot for many years. They remounted only to finish off a defeated enemy or pursue him from the field. The last notable mass cavalry charge to be carried out by an English army in this period came in the closing moments of the battle of Poitiers in 1356, when Sir James Audley and the Captal de Buch remounted their horses to complete the rout of the French army. As for the French they increasingly copied the English tactical system. Their only major pitched battle in this period, against the Flemings at Roosebeke, was fought on foot. Men-at-arms fought in infantry formations, in the English case in tactical co-operation with archers. They carried their lances on foot, using them as pikes. Their war-horses were left at the back with the grooms and pages. Swordsmanship and brute force were more important than horsemanship. Ancient skills, slowly mastered from an early age and nurtured by men of wealth and leisure, retained all their old prestige but became progressively less valuable on campaign.

When Froissart spoke of the opportunities which war opened up to young men of talent he was thinking of men-at-arms. But the dream was shared on a humbler scale by others with no pretensions to nobility and few expectations of fame. They were bowmen, pages and 'varlets' and specialised tradesmen such as artillerymen, carpenters and miners.

Longbowmen were a significant part of every English army and had a critical place in English battle tactics. Traditionally recruited at the rate of one archer for every two men-at-arms, the proportion tended to increase and by the end of the 1380s was nearer one for one. These men were drawn from the peasantry of the Welsh marches and rural England and occasionally from the streets of the towns, especially London. They were rarely gentlemen. But they had to practise their art constantly and to possess a horse, simple armour and a sword and buckler, all of which meant that they were generally men of some standing in their own communities. A few rose from humble beginnings to great eminence. That conservative spirit Sir Thomas Gray had noticed in the 1350s that the fighting in Normandy was being done mainly by 'mere commoners' many of whom had enlisted as archers and ended up as knights and even captains. Sir Robert Knolles, who accumulated one of the largest military fortunes of his time, was a man of exceedingly obscure origins who almost certainly began his career as an archer. The same was probably true of his fellow Cheshire men Sir David Craddock and Sir Nicholas Colfox, both of whom were the sons of Nantwich townsmen, and Sir Hugh Browe, whose father was a yeoman of Tushingham. The Italian *condottiere* Sir John Hawkwood almost certainly first enlisted as an archer. He was the son of a rich Essex tanner and began his career as the apprentice of a London tailor.[10]

Bowmen were a less significant component of French armies. The conventional proportion appears to have been one for every four men-at-arms. Moreover, they were usually outsiders, generally Italian crossbowmen. Charles V maintained a permanent corps of Genoese cross-bowmen. To maintain their quality their numbers were limited in 1373 to 800 men, who were recruited by the Doria, the Grimaldi and other specialised war contractors. For the major campaigns and local operations numbers were made up by recruiting in the larger towns. Most towns maintained companies of crossbowmen drawn from their own citizens, whose main purpose was to defend their walls but who were available for field service when required. For the great army recruited for the invasion of England in 1386 about 2,500 French crossbowmen were conscripted to supplement the 1,100 Genoese crossbowmen, the largest force of archers deployed by the French since the 1340s.[11]

Like their English counterparts and for much the same reasons, crossbowmen were generally men of some substance. Pages and varlets by comparison represented the lowest form of military existence. They were not paid by the war treasurers. They were not included in the muster strengths before the campaign or the body counts after an engagement. They were unmourned by their companions when they died, as they did in great numbers since they were vulnerable to disease, wore only rudimentary armour and were not worth taking for ransom. Yet there was on average one of them for every man-at-arms, which meant that they must have constituted at least a third of every major field army. Pages were simple body servants employed by men-at-arms to follow them to war. Most of them were boys with no military function, whose main task was to carry their master's helmet and lance on the move, to attend to his food and comforts and care for the horses and equipment. Varlets (sometimes called *gros varlets* or, more revealingly, *pillards* – 'looters') were usually slightly older men who performed many of the same functions but also carried weapons and counted as combatants. They fought beside their masters. They acted as foragers and camp guards. Some of them were even mustered as men-at-arms. The varlets were men of little training who stood out even in the ugly world of fourteenth-century warfare for their casual violence, brutality and incendiarism. Uprooted from their communities to fight in distant campaigns they were generally paid off when the campaign was over and released into the murky underworld at the margins of military life until another campaign brought them the chance of another job. A few served indiscriminately on both sides.

The lives of many of these men are told in the vast record of pardons preserved in the registers of the French royal chancery. But they were the lucky ones with the influence and money to buy forgiveness. The judicial register of the Châtelet prison in Paris, which survives for a period of just over two years between 1389 and 1392, contains the biographies of a large number of soldiers' servants and varlets, patiently recorded by the clerk of the court in the brief interval between their arrest for house-breaking or cutting purses and their death on the public gibbet at Montfaucon. Most of these wretches had been thrown onto the uncertain job market of *fin-de-siècle* Paris in the aftermath of the truce of Leulinghem. Jacquet de Lyembois had served for two decades as the varlet of various men-at-arms when he was brought in for stealing four *écus* from his last master, a Genoese captain of crossbowmen. His confession revealed a rootless petty criminal living by theft and frauds in the intervals between military employments. He had not returned to his home at Douai since his teens. Girard de Sancerre, a soldier's servant for twenty years, had led a very similar existence in the intervals of serving with the armies in Flanders, Guelders and Languedoc. Jean Petit, brought in for picking pockets in the street, had served with men-at-arms in his native Normandy and joined the Guelders campaign of 1388, supplementing his wages with thefts from his fellow soldiers. Oudinot Guigne was arrested for breaking into a house in Montmartre with a gang of thieves. He turned out to have served continually in the wars for sixteen years, carrying the helmet of a squire in the retinue of the Viscount of Rochechouart. The picture of the unemployed, violent and thieving soldier's varlet became so familiar to the judges of the Châtelet that it came to serve as a badge of infamy, justifying torture and death when mere misfortune might have deserved more sympathy. Jean de Noyon, an unskilled labourer brought in for stealing a silver salt-cellar, had served just twice in the armies, both times in order to raise cash to support his family. But that was enough to persuade his judges that he was an incorrigible recidivist. They sent him to the gallows. At the end of most of these accounts, after a brief record of the date, time and manner of their execution, appeared the usual notation for the accountant: 'no worldly possessions'.[12]

Increasingly the distinction which mattered on both sides was not between noble and non-noble but between professional and occasional soldiers. Philippe de Mézières distinguished three classes of men-at-arms: the first comprised noblemen who served only when the King was at the head of his host; the second were men who were in continuous service against the enemy; and the third were non-nobles, 'even labourers', who had made a profession of arms and served for loot and pay.[13] Allowing for a certain overlap between the categories this is a broadly accurate picture of military life in both England and France. In the later fourteenth century the first class tended to dwindle in favour of the second and third. The older tradition which treated military service as a duty owed to their rank by men who were mainly occupied in land management and local politics survived, but was no longer capable of supplying the numbers of trained men required for a long and debilitating war. By the end of the following century it would be almost extinct. The jumped-up archers of whom Sir Thomas Gray complained and the soldiers' varlets arrested by the sergeants of the Châtelet were all professionals of their kind, men who lived by war and little else. At the opposite extreme the same was true of the three French knights responsible for organising the jousts of Saint-Ingelvert as well as a fair number of their English adversaries.

The change was due partly to demographic and economic factors, but mainly to a significant shift in the character of the war. French writers of the period distinguished between war 'with the host' and war 'on the frontiers'.[14] War with the host was fought by large field armies commanded by the King or a prince of his blood in which most of the participants were occasional soldiers serving to justify their status. The war on the frontiers was fought mainly by professionals in permanent service. The last three decades of the fourteenth century were pre-eminently the age of the frontier war. Gone were the impressive hordes serving for a few weeks each year which had stood in line at Buirenfosse and fought at Crécy and Poitiers. Gone were the great pitched battles in which princes gambled the fate of nations. Charles V reconquered most of Aquitaine in the 1370s with small, elite armies of mounted men which remained in service for months at a time, winter and summer. It was a war of sieges, border raids and skirmishes, aimed primarily at controlling territory and fought by troops drawn from permanent garrisons and fixed bases. Endurance, mobility, surprise, rapid concentration and dispersal were their tools. Beginning with the occupation of Brittany and Lower Normandy before 1360 English strategy had haltingly moved in the same direction. For a time, after the war reopened in 1369, the English tried to combine a strategy of border operations conducted from fixed bases with a reversion to the great continental field armies which had been so successful in the heyday of Edward III and the Black Prince. But the commanders of these armies had no answer to the French strategy of avoiding battle and emptying the countryside of supplies. They were unable to withstand the relentless harassment of their flanks and foraging parties as they moved through the forests and the *plat pays* of France. For a mixture of tactical and financial reasons the English abandoned large-scale field operations in France altogether after 1381.

The kings whose presence had been the main draw for noblemen now rarely took the field in person. Charles V never commanded his own armies. Edward III made a number of abortive plans to do so, but his last campaign was fought in 1360. Richard II commanded an army in Scotland in 1385 and two in Ireland in the following decade but never fought in France. It is no coincidence that the only occasions when the war briefly reverted to the older pattern of immense, largely non-professional armies serving for short periods were the campaigns led by the youthful Charles VI between 1382 and 1388. Many of those who enlisted in these royal armies had never fought a major campaign before. The Datini factor in Avignon, whose main business was selling arms to French soldiers, reported in the summer of 1386 that he was doing a roaring trade selling chain mail and helmets to southerners heading for Sluys to take part in the French invasion of England. These were gentlemen, but they evidently lacked even the most basic military equipment. Yet, although such men made up a large proportion of Charles VI's armies in the 1380s, the kernel of these great hordes remained the corps of professional soldiers formed in the continual dog-fights on the marches of Calais, Brittany and Aquitaine and in the French expeditionary armies in Italy and Castile. When the host was paid off these were the men who returned to garrison duties, 'not like others who mark the end of their great exertions by returning to a life of ease and idleness' as the contemporary biographer of Jean de Boucicaut smugly remarked.[15]

The new pattern of the war called for much longer periods of service by people with different skills. In England even major field armies commonly contracted to serve for a full year. The men who joined Knolles's army of 1370 indented for two years and some of those who followed John of Gaunt to Castile in 1386 were away for three. Service in the garrisons of the march could keep a man abroad for a decade or more. These were difficult conditions for men with sheep to shear, grain to harvest and influence to cultivate at home. There was a progressive divergence between the outlook and way of life of the professional soldier and the rest, which was accentuated by the growing luxury and refinement of civilian life. As early as the 1350s a note of contempt for soldiers who were too fond of the creature comforts of their homes crept into the works of hardened professionals like Geoffrey de Charny. The wars of the late fourteenth century, respecting neither the season of the year nor the hour of day, made far greater demands on those who fought in them. It required constant training, great physical endurance and weapons-handling skills of a high order. The poet Eustache Deschamps thought that in time of truce or peace a soldier's life should be passed in jousting, military exercises, mock assaults and hunting. It was, perhaps, a counsel of perfection, but there is no doubt that many soldiers took it seriously. Jean de Boucicaut, who became Marshal of France in 1391, kept fit by constant exercise. He vaulted onto his horse in full armour without using the stirrup. His did muscle exercises in heavy chain mail. He went on long cross-country runs. He watched his weight, taking small helpings and little wine at meals. He may have been more dedicated than most and indeed we know that he was sometimes mocked for it. It was, however, professionalism like Boucicaut's that persuaded the Provençal jurist Honoré Bonet that bearing arms should be the sole occupation of a soldier. In his widely read treatise on the law and practice of war Bonet gave it as his opinion that a soldier should not even own land lest it distract him from his trade. In the last three decades of the fourteenth century the main burden of the war was borne by men for whom fighting was their main and often their sole occupation.[16]

Between 1385 and 1387 the commissioners of the Constable of England toured England taking evidence in the famous litigation between Sir Richard Scrope and Sir Robert Grosvenor about the right to display the arms *azure a bend or*. A fair number of the witnesses who gave evidence before them were professional soldiers, some of whom had enjoyed long and full careers. The squire Nicholas de Sabraham, who gave his age as 'over sixty', had served with Balliol and Bohun in Scotland in the 1330s, with Edward III at Crécy and Calais, then in Normandy, Brittany and Gascony in the 1350s and before Paris in 1359. In times of peace and truce he found other wars to fight. He turned to crusading, fighting at Alexandria under the King of Cyprus. He invaded Castile with the Black Prince. Later he served in the defence of Constantinople and fought with Sir John Hawkwood's company in Italy and with the Teutonic Knights in Prussia. Interestingly, Sabraham never had himself dubbed as a knight. Yet he was clearly a professional soldier deriving most if not all his income from war wages and the profits of war. Cheshire, the county from which many of these witnesses came, was a highly militarised society. But much the same pattern emerges from the evidence in other cases before the Court of Chivalry. Sir Nicholas Goushill, a witness in the hotly contested dispute between John Lord Lovell and Thomas Lord Morley, declared that he had borne arms for thirty-five years in Scotland, Ireland and all over France, serving in the retinues of at least seven different captains. The thumbnail autobiographies at the beginning of such depositions suggest that many other veterans enjoyed active careers extending over thirty years or more. Most had taken up arms in their teens, sometimes as young as thirteen or fourteen, and carried on year after year for as long as their health allowed. Generally they retired from active service by the age of fifty but some served for much longer. Sir John Richford, who had first seen action at the battle of Sluys in 1340 when he was fifteen, had recently served in Richard II's army of Scotland at the age of sixty.[17]

The great majority of these men fought in the 'war with the host'. But the ultimate professionals, in England as in France, were those who fought the 'war on the frontiers'. The Cheshire knight Sir Hugh Browe put his finger on the difference when he told the Constable's commissioners that he could not say whether the Scropes had worn the disputed coat of arms in war, for they performed their military service in the great expeditionary armies whereas he, Browe, had served for twenty years entirely 'in the garrisons and companies of France'. Browe had served most of his time in Brittany, where he had been Knolles's captain at Derval. A generation of retainers of the Prince of Wales served as provincial seneschals and garrison commanders in Rouergue, Quercy and Poitou. They left home as untried youths for the marches of France and were rarely seen by their friends and kinsmen. The Cheshire squire

John Stratton, who probably went to Gascony with the Prince in 1355, married there and apart from a short sojourn in England in the late 1370s remained until his death in 1397, serving in the armies of successive seneschals. Another Cheshire man, Sir William Mainwaring, left for Gascony in 1371 and served there until he died in 1399, making only rare and brief visits to England. Henry Bolingbroke's friend Sir John Norbury had begun his career with the English companies in Brittany in the 1360s and over the next three decades served for long periods as a professional garrison commander at Libourne, Fronsac and Brest as well as fighting with the English mercenary corps in Portugal in 1385 and in Bolingbroke's retinue in Prussia in the 1390s. He must have spent the greater part of his adult life overseas. These are just a few of the professional soldiers whose careers have left regular traces in the records but they are representative of thousands more who were too lowly or unremarkable for their lives to be retraced or who embarked hopefully on a career brought suddenly and inconspicuously short by an arrow in the throat or an axe in the skull. 'We are men of all sorts,' said Norbury to the Portuguese King, 'but all looking for the life of arms and adventure.'[18]

A broadly similar pattern emerged in France, where the conduct of war was increasingly entrusted to men who did very little else. In 1372 Charles V was directly paying fifty garrisons, most of them on the marches of Normandy, in addition to the standing armies maintained on the marches of Calais and Aquitaine and the permanent companies of Bretons, Genoese and Welshmen. These men were more or less permanently under arms. The border campaigns were led by captains whose names appear in French muster rolls year after year. Some of them, like their English counterparts, served the King for decades. Yon de Garencières was already an experienced soldier when he commanded a French military mission in Scotland in 1336. Yet he attended the jousts of Saint-Ingelvert more than half a century later and was still bringing his men to the King's armies in 1392. The Breton captain Maurice de Tréséguidy had been among 'the Thirty' who fought in the famous arranged battle of 1351. He was still active at the end of the century, when he fought with the French army against the Turks at Nicopolis. Marshal Boucicaut's military career spanned thirty-seven years from his first campaign in Castile in 1378 at the age of twelve to his capture on the battlefield of Agincourt in 1415. Similar histories can be found among the military retainers of the great princely houses. Guy de Pontailler, who rose to be Marshal of Burgundy, first appears in the muster rolls in Saintonge in 1351 and did not retire from active service until after the abortive invasion of England in 1386. These were the wonderful old men whom the Knight of La Tour Landry described for his daughters, travelling from one noble household to the next, holding the company spellbound with tales of a lifetime's adventures. The Duke of Bourbon's standard-bearer Jean de Châteaumorand fought in his master's retinue almost every year from 1370 to 1390. After the forty-year truce with England in 1396 he took service with the Byzantine Emperor, acting as captain of Constantinople for three years between 1399 and 1402. Châteaumorand survived into a forgetful dotage, regaling the Duke's biographer with colourful and inaccurate anecdotes about his master and dying well into his eighties in 1429. The careers of humbler men are more difficult to discover. But the same continuity of personnel penetrated down to a level well below the commanders. A great captain like Bertrand du Guesclin was able to call on the same men-at-arms year after year to serve in his retinue. It is clear from the mass of pardons for miscellaneous acts of violence which survive in the French chancery registers that regular service in the armies was a career chosen by many minor landowners on the margins of gentility. References to their 'long service in the wars' were a commonplace of such documents. This man had 'fought armed and mounted in our wars in Flanders, on the march of Picardy and in Scotland with our Admiral'. That one had 'always served us and our forbears and ridden with Du Guesclin in his time'.[19]

The motives of men who chose the life of a career soldier were too varied for generalisation. The pursuit of fame, honour and adventure is a persistent theme of the literature of the period. The bonds of patronage and dependence propelled men into war service behind the banner of some great man. Flight from debt, crime or domestic catastrophe were all important recruiting agents. In both countries landless younger sons were often drawn to the soldier's life. There was always a large number of noble bastards on the French King's payroll.[20] The prolonged decline in incomes from land and the scale of war damage and social disruption in regions such as Picardy, Flanders and Brittany must have added to the attractions of a military career.

Money was an almost universal factor in men's calculations. The daily wage of French men-at-arms and bowmen rose steadily during the latter half of the fourteenth century in response to the difficulties of recruitment and the broader economic pressures which pushed up earnings everywhere after the Black Death. The standard wages paid by the French war treasurers for field service were fixed in the 1360s at twenty *sous* a day for an ordinary knight, the equivalent of four shillings sterling. A banneret received twice as much, a squire half. These rates, which were about a third higher than those paid before 1360, remained in force until the 1390s when they were increased again by some fifty per cent. By comparison with other paid employment, they were generous, equating to the income of a small manor. But they had to be set against the substantial costs of army life. A man-at-arms or a crossbowmen was required to bring his own horse, clothing, armour and weapons. French troops, who were generally fighting on their own territory or that of their allies, were expected to pay their way on campaign. That meant buying food and lodging for themselves and fodder, straw and shoeing for their horses, and paying the wages and keep of their servants. These expenses must have varied considerably from one occasion to the next but the fragmentary evidence which survives suggests that they consumed a large proportion of a man's earnings.

The more prominent professional soldiers did better. Captains of companies received, on top of their wages, a fixed monthly fee known as an *état* which served as a recruitment bonus and a mark of status. The rate varied according to the dignity and importance of the captain but was in principle one franc per man per month. Garrison commanders, who were almost always professionals, also received more. On the march of Normandy, for example, the captain of Bayeux, who served for seven years from 1371 to 1378, was paid 300 *livres* a year and 400 *livres* in the difficult year 1372. In addition he received his *état* and about 1,000 *livres* in gifts from the King over the period of his captaincy plus irregular receipts such as fines for minor breaches of discipline and fees for inspecting other garrisons of the region. The captain of Caen, which was the seat of the Lieutenant and the most important French fortress in Lower Normandy, received 1,000 *livres* a year in the same period.[21]

Although it is impossible to prove, it seems likely that regular pay at adequate rates contributed much to the reputation and success of French arms in the latter part of the fourteenth century. Certainly that is what is suggested by the contrasting experience of England. The customary rates of pay in England had been fixed in the early part of the reign of Edward III at two shillings a day for a knight bachelor, twice that for a banneret and half for a squire. A mounted archer got six pence a day, half the rate paid to a squire. These rates had served well enough before 1360. But by 1369 they were low, about half what was being paid to soldiers fighting in the armies of the King of France. With the resumption of the war it was found necessary to offer significant increases in order to attract recruits. The army which served under John of Gaunt in Picardy in 1369 was paid at one and a half times the 'customary' rates. In the following year the army of Sir Robert Knolles was paid double rates for the opening period of the campaign. However, the English government's resources proved to be incapable of sustaining war wages at this level. Troops serving in garrisons or at sea continued to be paid at single rates. And from 1372 onward increasing financial stringency forced Edward III's ministers to revert to single rates even for their continental field armies. The last expeditionary army which is known to have received more than the customary wage rates was the small army of the Earl of Pembroke which sailed for Gascony in May 1372. At the same time, the government put an end to the century-old system by which the King paid compensation for horses lost on campaign. This measure, which was adopted in France at about the same time, achieved significant financial savings but the change greatly increased the financial risks associated with military service, especially for the higher ranks who had more and dearer mounts.[22]

The result of the sharp deterioration in English terms of service was that men-at-arms were more difficult to recruit and constituted a declining proportion of England's continental armies. Belted knights were particularly rare as gentry families with the means to support the status increasingly declined to do so. The rewards were simply not good enough to justify the heavy investment in training, equipment and horseflesh. The figures are remarkable. In the early campaigns of Edward III in the Low Countries and Brittany, between 1338 and 1343, about a quarter of the men-at-arms were knights. This was still the rule of thumb, at least in theory, when the war was resumed in 1369. Eleven years later when the Earl of Buckingham invaded France the proportion had fallen to six per cent. By comparison the proportion of knights in French field armies remained roughly constant at about eleven or twelve per cent from the 1350s to the end of the century.[23]

The English King's ministers were well aware that low pay was one reason for their recruitment problems. But instead of increasing the basic rate they responded by spending more on recruitment bonuses. 'Regards', as these bonuses were called in England, were paid to captains who contracted to furnish companies of men-at-arms for the King's service. The traditional rate was 100 marks per quarter for every thirty men-at-arms. This was a very substantial sum, nearly four times the standard *état* paid to French captains. It represented at least a third of the wage bill of a company of men-at-arms. From 1370 the traditional rate was doubled and generally remained at that level even when war wages were reduced. The combination of high recruitment bonuses and low wages had a baleful effect on English armies. The main beneficiaries were the professional captains and war contractors who could make substantial fortunes by finding recruits. They either indented directly with the Crown or entered into subcontracts with great magnates to furnish troops for their immense retinues. In either case they pocketed the regard. Quite frequently they also paid war wages to their men at rates even lower than the Crown rates which they were themselves receiving. The predictable result was to depress the quality of recruits. The Northumberland knight Sir John Strother, who contracted to find thirty men-at-arms for the retinue of the Earl of March in 1374, may have found some of them in the traditional way among his friends and tenants but a substantial part of his retinue was hired in the great pool of unemployed soldiery in and around London. Half of his known recruits could not even call themselves squires. Sir Hugh Hastings, who raised a company for the Earl of Buckingham's invasion of France in 1380, made up his numbers in much the same way, also in London. Very few military subcontracts survive, and these ones represent a very small sample, but there is a good deal of anecdotal evidence that across England captains were recruiting men by scraping the barrel of military manpower. John Lord Neville of Raby was accused in the Good Parliament of taking a retinue to Brittany which was well below its nominal strength and composed of 'inadequate fellows such as boys and other worthless people for which he drew full payment of his wages'. How far Neville was personally responsible for this state of affairs, as opposed to the captains whom he retained, is impossible to say. But he was certainly not the only man to lead a ragged band of roughs to war alongside the traditional elite of trained cavalrymen. The Duke of Gloucester personally supervised the muster of the men-at-arms recruited for the naval campaign of 1387 in order to ensure that it did not include 'cobblers and tailors from London and the cities, such as had previously been recruited on low pay in order to put money into the purses of their captains'.[24]

Profits of war contributed a growing proportion of military earnings even in France, where war wages were relatively high. Writing about the soldiers who returned from Castile in 1387 Froissart observed that the men who had thrown themselves into the daily round of pillage and robbery could be recognised at once by their grand horses, satchels of gold and silver and bulging chests full of valuables; whereas those who had simply subsisted on their wages returned impoverished, ill-mounted and bedraggled. The successes of French arms in this period brought a rich crop of ransoms to successful military entrepreneurs. A much larger number helped themselves to plunder and *patis* not only when operating in Flanders, Italy and Spain but in their own country as well. For English soldiers, fighting on conquered land and paid irregularly at wretched rates, the prospect of loot and ransoms was the critical element in every financial calculation. Indeed pay rates were commonly fixed on that assumption. Sir Robert Knolles's army of 1370, which contracted to serve for two years, was offered generous pay for the first three months but thereafter was expected to live entirely on the profits of war. Unlike French soldiers, who kept whatever they could take, English soldiers had traditionally been required to surrender a proportion of their takings to the captain whom they served. He in turn was required to surrender the same proportion of what he received to his own captain and so on up to the King. A serious attempt was made to compensate soldiers for their reduced opportunities and poor rates of pay by increasing the proportion of their takings which they were allowed to keep. Traditionally a half, it rose in the last three decades of the fourteenth century to two-thirds. In practice widespread evasion and fraud increased it still further.[25]

The main consequence of this growing emphasis on profits of war was to broaden still further the gulf between professional and occasional soldiers. Professionals were not only more skilful and persistent in the pursuit of loot and prisoners but tended to fight the kind of war in which these were easier to come by. The French policy of emptying the countryside in the path of the enemy and avoiding major engagements ensured that there was little money to be made out of field service in the late fourteenth century. The lion's share of war profits was made by garrison troops and by the permanent forces of the march who were almost invariably professionals. They were derived from the *patis* exacted within riding distance of occupied fortresses; from safe-conducts sold to merchants and refugees; and from plunder and prisoners taken in the constant raids into the surrounding country. Sir Hugh Browe, the man who told the commissioners in *Scrope* v. *Grosvenor* that he had served throughout his career in garrisons and companies of France, made a modest fortune for his efforts which he laid out in buying land and influence in his native Cheshire. The Craddock family, which had served over two generations as administrators and garrison commanders on the march of Aquitaine, came back rich enough to build the splendid new chancel of Nantwich church. Sir Thomas Trivet was one of the many garrison commanders who showed how money could be made even in defeat by a captain who chose the right moment to sell out. By comparison very few of those who joined the great continental *chevauchées* made any money at all beyond their wages and regards. The Kent knight Sir Thomas Fogg was a career soldier who had known both the best and the worst of England's fortunes. He had made considerable sums as a professional garrison commander in Lower Normandy and Brittany before 1370. But his service was consistently unprofitable during the following decade when he fought in the main English expeditionary armies on the continent and briefly at Calais. He was captured on John of Gaunt's march through France in 1373–4 and spent several years on parole trying to raise his ransom. Fogg was a lifetime retainer of Gaunt, just as he had previously served his father-in-law Henry of Grosmont. But years later in his old age he would tell anyone who cared to listen that half a lifetime of service to the Duke of Lancaster had cost him 10,000 marks of his fortune.

As the chronicler Froissart once observed, losses were part of the chances of war: '*une fois perte, autrefois gaing*'. In the reign of Richard II, however, Fogg's was a far commoner story than the dazzling tales of the Knolleses and Calveleys of an earlier generation. Few new fortunes were being made in the 1380s even by professionals. Cherbourg and Brest probably remained profitable for their non-resident captains and perhaps for the soldiers stationed there right up to their final surrender in the 1390s. But they were the exceptions. Ransom districts were exhausted and depopulated. Calais and its satellites were hemmed in by French garrisons which prevented the establishment of ransom districts in Picardy and Artois. The English had lost all of their other fortresses north of the Loire and nine-tenths of the territory that they had once held in the south-west. On the shrunken borders of Aquitaine there was still money to be made from *patis*, but except perhaps at Fronsac it was being made by Gascons, not Englishmen and by *routiers* rather than regular troops.[26]

Armies were communities on the move whose structures of authority tended to replicate those which were familiar in ordinary life. They depended on traditional notions of hierarchy and status which did not readily accommodate professional soldiers. Bertrand du Guesclin, the most famous professional soldier of his day, was a former freebooter who came from the lowest level of Breton society consistent with gentility. He was famously awkward in the presence of men who outranked him socially. According to Froissart Du Guesclin had serious misgivings about accepting appointment as Constable in 1370. 'The office of Constable,' he told Charles V,

carries great power and status. Whoever would do the job properly must perforce exercise command over great and small alike. Look at your brothers here, at your nephews and cousins, all of them men used to commanding men-at-arms in raiding forces and field armies alike. How am I supposed to exercise command over them?

In fact, he never did. His own campaigns were fought mainly with his own military retinue and other companies of professionals, largely without the participation of the higher nobility. When he fought with the princes of the royal blood or the heads of the great noble houses, they took command and he served as their adviser. Many of the campaigns of the last three decades of the fourteenth century were led by men whose social standing was no higher than Du Guesclin's and who did not have the authority of his office. Yet the great Constable's concerns were widely shared. In 1387 the French royal Council appointed Guillaume de Neilhac and Gaucher de Passat, two minor noblemen who had served the Crown as professional captains for many years, to command an army of 2,000 men-at-arms in Castile. These two made much the same point as Du Guesclin had done seventeen years before: 'this is too great an enterprise for mere knights like us.'[27]

Their concern about their authority was not fanciful as English experience showed. The English produced a number of talented commanders in the late fourteenth century who had risen from relatively humble beginnings. Many of them had served their apprenticeship like Du Guesclin with the free companies in France and Castile. They had no difficulty in taking command of the minor campaigns fought by small task forces composed of men like themselves. But the great *chevauchées* which represented the high points of the war were a different matter. One campaign after another threw up serious problems of organisation, discipline and command, often originating in the tensions generated by the presence of professional captains. Sir John Chandos was a man of gentle but obscure birth who had risen entirely by royal patronage. He was a famous soldier, widely admired on both sides, who rose to become Constable of Aquitaine and the Prince of Wales's principal military lieutenant in the duchy. Yet in 1364, when Chandos was in command of the Anglo-Breton army at the battle of Auray, Sir Hugh Calveley refused to comply with his order to take command of the rearguard, a task which he regarded as demeaning. Calveley eventually backed down. Five years later in 1369, when Chandos was serving as the Prince's lieutenant on the march of Poitou, the young Earl of Pembroke refused to serve under him. His advisers persuaded him that it was not fitting for an earl, even one almost entirely lacking in military experience, to serve under the command of a banneret. Unlike Calveley, Pembroke did not back down. As a result the two men had to divide their forces and operate in different sectors of the march.

The appointment of Sir Robert Knolles to command the expedition sent to France in 1370 was a notable break with tradition which proved to be a turning point in more ways than one. Knolles, like Du Guesclin, was a freebooter by origin and inclination. His whole career marked a reversal of traditional hierarchies, symbolised by the manner in which, years before, he had been dubbed as a knight at the hands of two of his own subordinates after the capture of the city of Auxerre. For some men this was the world turned upside down. The captains serving under Knolles in 1370 included a knight of the Garter, a baron and the heir of another and several other distinguished noblemen. Anticipating trouble Knolles took the unprecedented precaution of requiring them to swear an oath to co-operate with him before the expedition left England. The experiment was not a success for reasons which went some way to vindicate traditional notions of rank. For all his military skills and formidable personality and in spite of the King's letters patent and the captains' oaths Knolles was unable to impose his authority on his companions. As a result his army fell apart in the course of the campaign.[28]

Fourteenth-century practice smoothed the impact of rank and personality by making the command of armies to some extent a collective exercise. Every military commander surrounded himself with a council of advisers to guide him and transmit his decisions to the rest of the army. Philippe de Mézières thought that an army commander's council should comprise ten or twelve experienced knights of whom at least four or five should be with him at all times in addition to a lawyer or two to resolve disputes among the men. Some such practice was invariably followed in both English and French armies. Even the experienced and self-confident Bertrand du Guesclin had a small group of trusted companions 'by whose views he was guided in all things'. After 1371 men of Knolles's kind would be obliged to exercise their military skills in English armies at one remove as members of a council of war, where their influence was often very great but less conspicuous. The Earl of Buckingham commanded the great continental *chevauchée* of 1380 with hardly any military experience behind him. The real direction of the campaign was supplied by Sir Robert Knolles, his brother-in-arms Sir Hugh Calveley and two other professional captains, William Lord Latimer and Sir Thomas Percy. The crusade of the Bishop of Norwich was another campaign conducted under the nominal leadership of an august novice, guided by a council of war packed with professional soldiers.[29]

A large part of the organisational difficulties encountered by army commanders arose from the absence of any effective chain of command. On the march and in battle the larger field armies were formed into 'battalions', each under a single commander who was generally a great nobleman, or in France one of the military officers of the Crown. A battalion had no fixed size. It was, as Honoré Bonet said, as large or as small as the marshals chose to make it. The larger ones could be several thousand strong. But battalions were essentially formless. The company remained the basic building block of the armies of both sides and there were no intermediate officers between its captain and the battalion commander. Companies were generally highly cohesive social units united by powerful bonds of mutual loyalty and dependence. Varying in size from half a dozen men to several hundred, most of them were recruited in a limited geographical area where their captain was a prominent figure. They generally included large numbers of his kinsmen, neighbours, friends and tenants. They fought under his banner or pennon. They took his name as their war-cry: 'Guesclin! Clisson! Sancerre! Sempy! Laval!' They followed his orders even if it meant abandoning the rest of the army on the field or engaging in independent operations of their own. 'By the laws of war,' said Froissart, 'no man can be blamed for following his own lord and captain.'[30]

In both countries attempts were made to create more cohesive armies by replacing the old solidarities of the military aristocracy with more formal lines of authority. In France there had already been several experiments in this direction, beginning with the elaborate ordinance of John II in 1351. The most ambitious scheme of reform was devised by

Charles V of France. His ordinance of 1374 on the organisation of the armies required every captain to hold a commission from the King or his lieutenants. It insisted that a company should comprise a hundred men-at-arms, no more or less, divided into *chambres* of ten men each. Larger companies were to be split up and smaller ones amalgamated and placed under a captain nominated by the King. Every captain would be held personally responsible for the indiscipline of his men. No one was to withdraw from the army without leave. The scheme produced mixed results. But a hierarchy of units began to take shape; and the notion slowly took root that the company was part of a larger unity whose loyalty was owed to the Crown not just to its own captain. Writing in the early 1350s the famous French paladin Geoffrey de Charny still saw the army not as an organic body united by common bonds of discipline but as a group of men engaged in the pursuit of honour and reward subject to a common code of values which exalted individual courage and achievement. He thought it a nice question whether a man who disobeyed orders in pursuit of personal glory was entitled to demand his contractual remuneration. Few people would have had any difficulty with that question a generation later. In the 1380s the jurist Honoré Bonet considered that a man-at-arms was bound to obey the commander of the army in which he served on pain of death. A man who attacked prematurely or withdrew from the army without leave to pursue his own adventures was liable to be summarily beheaded by the constable's order even if his insubordination resulted in a triumph of arms. Froissart's view about the primacy of the captain's authority was becoming old-fashioned even as he wrote it. The disciplinary functions of the constable and the marshals underwent a notable expansion in this period. A growing range of offences was brought within their purview: cowardice, desertion, feigned illness and self-inflicted wounds and fighting within the ranks.[31]

Very similar developments were occurring in England. In 1385, at the outset of Richard II's campaign against the Scots, a comprehensive set of ordinances of war was issued in his name as the army passed Durham. Its very first clause provided that 'all manner of men of whatever nation, rank or condition they be, shall obey the orders of the King and his Constable and Marshals on pain of his life and goods.' Much of the rest of the document was concerned to limit the autonomy of individual companies and to restrain the countless acts of indiscipline to which men were provoked by the pursuit of private profit and glory. Companies were assigned to battalions whose commanders they were required to obey. No man was to shout out his own name or his captain's as his war-cry. None was to cry 'havoc' in the host without authority, the traditional signal to break ranks and begin the competitive scramble for prisoners and booty. None was to march ahead of his battalion or to go off on mounted raids without specific orders. Quarrels about the distribution of spoil were to be referred to the Constable and the Marshals rather than settled by violence. A range of penalties was decreed for infractions, from death at one extreme to the confiscation of a horse and armour or the loss of an ear at the other. It is possible that less elaborate codes of discipline had been issued in earlier campaigns but these are the earliest English ordinances of war to survive and they were used as a model for all subsequent documents of the same kind.[32]

The new solidarity received visible expression in the growing use of uniforms. Companies still followed the heraldic banner of their captain and embossed his arms on their carts and tents as they had always done. Philip of Burgundy had 2,000 miniature pennons of his arms made in 1383 to be distributed among the men of his battalion in the campaign in Flanders. Another 4,000 were made in 1386 for the battalion which he intended to lead to England. His fellow commanders probably did the same for their battalions. But national emblems increasingly superseded the disparate war-cries and confused mass of heraldic emblems and livery colours which had enabled an earlier generation to distinguish friend from foe. In French royal armies the use of the upright white cross against a black or red background, which had begun tentatively in the 1350s, had become compulsory for urban contingents by 1369. It was the general practice in all French royal armies by the end of the century. Richard II's Durham ordinances required every man in the army regardless of rank or nationality to wear a large red cross of St. George over his armour, back and front, and prescribed the death penalty for any enemy who was caught wearing one. Gascons wore the St. George's cross just as Englishmen did to show that they were on the same side. In Scotland somewhat similar ordinances had been issued by the commanders of the Franco-Scottish host a few weeks earlier calling for the St. Andrew's saltire to be worn on their tunics by both national contingents.[33]

For most men-at-arms in both countries the story of a campaign opened with an indenture. This was a written agreement with a captain by which the man-at-arms agreed to serve in his company. In England the system of indentures had by now attained a high degree of elaboration and was all but universal. The man-at-arms undertook to present himself at the muster when summoned, 'sufficiently' armed, mounted and equipped. If he contracted to bring other soldiers with him the exact number and type were stated. If the company was to serve overseas, provision was made for shipping. The period of service was specified. Terms were agreed for the distribution of spoil, generally matching the terms of the captain's own indenture with the King. Rates were agreed for war wages and regards together with the intervals at which they were to be paid. Some of these documents bear the marks of hard bargaining with several hands and untidy erasures and insertions on stained paper.

The fourteenth century was a law-minded age and the indenture was only the first of a number legal instruments to be executed before a soldier set out to war. In an age in which perjury was common and the proceedings of the courts were frequently turned by favour, bribery or violence, the judicial records are filled with stories of property seized from men who were away at the wars. It was the responsibility of the captain to obtain letters of protection for anyone of his company who was leaving landed wealth behind him. These letters, which were issued in hundreds in the weeks preceding every great continental campaign, stayed all legal proceedings against men who were absent on the King's service. The richer soldiers with more complicated affairs would also petition for letters of attorney, which allowed them to appoint representatives to conduct their affairs while they were away. Finally there was a will to be made, often hurriedly on the night before leaving home or at the port while the ships were being brought to the beaches and quaysides for loading. Richard Lord Poynings was surely not the only member of John of Gaunt's army of Castile to write his will 'de ma main en haste' by Plymouth Sound as he waited for the order to embark.[34]

A soldier's paid service began at the muster. The word comes from the French *montre* ('show'). Its purpose was to record the strength and status of the men presented by company captains and to inspect their horses, armour and weapons. The result was recorded by a clerk in a muster roll which served as the basis on which the captain would be paid for his company. Immediately after the muster the captain was entitled to receive an advance for his men. In France, the practice was to pay a month's wages at the muster with fresh advances following at regular intervals during the campaign. English armies received more generous advances, a quarter's wages and regards being normal and six months' not uncommon. But in England the perpetual penury of the government meant that the advance was sometimes all that a man saw of his wages for many months or years. The procedure for taking the muster was much the same in both countries. In England it was generally taken at the port of embarkation by chamber knights who were not part of the army and were thought for that reason to be more independent. In France the muster was generally held in an open space beneath the walls of a town such as Arras, Angers or Tours, located some way back from the theatre of war at the hub of a regional road network. The work was done by officers appointed by the Constable, the Marshals and the Master of the Archers, men who were sworn to do their duty and like their English counterparts were chosen from those who would not themselves be serving in the army. Froissart has a graphic description of a muster of the English garrison of La Rochelle in 1372 which must have been very familiar to the soldiers who read him. Some sixty men paraded before the mustering officer on horseback in full armour, which they had spent hours polishing the night before. The mustering officer passed down the line finding fault here and there. 'You there, where's the rest of your gear? Find it if you don't want your pay docked.' 'Yes sir.' Elaborate precautions were taken against fraud. Musters were required to be held in the open air in daylight. The roll was drawn up in several counterparts. Men-at-arms were listed by name and status. Horses were branded on the thigh to ensure that the same beasts were not re-presented by another company.[35]

Yet, in spite of the growing administrative elaboration, mustering officers and pay clerks were frequently incompetent or corrupt and fraud was endemic. Timeless tricks feature regularly in the literature and ordinances of the period. The same equipment was passed from company to company as each presented itself in turn to the mustering officers. Captains borrowed men from each other to make up the contract strength and lied about their status. The mustering officer could not be everywhere at once. Substantial companies were sometimes mustered before clerks whose knowledge of equipment and horseflesh must have been very limited and who seem to have been easily gulled. John Lord Neville of Raby presented his company at Southampton in 1375 to a clerk who failed to notice serious deficiencies of both numbers and quality. The possibilities of fraud did not end there. Captains were supposed to have their pay reduced *pro rata* for men who deserted or died after the muster and were expected to repay their advances. But the ample records of the English financial administration reveal few cases in which this actually happened. French practice appears to have been more rigorous. Their musters were more strictly supervised. There were regular 'reviews' in the course of the campaign, generally on the first day of each month, at which the exercise was repeated in order to take account of casualties, desertions and losses of equipment, a practice which was not systematically adopted in English armies until the fifteenth century. But even in France there were constant complaints about the negligence and corruption of mustering officers. The war treasurers were widely believed to take bribes for overlooking irregularities. Charles V complained in 1373 that his companies of Genoese crossbowmen were serving at well below their payroll strength and that many of them were not Genoese or even crossbowmen but 'worthless, low-grade fellows hired for a pittance'. It was notorious, his councillor Philippe de Mézières later recalled, that captains drew pay for 500 men-at-arms, who never had more than 250 in their companies and some absconded with their advances as soon as they had received them.[36]

A man-at-arms' most expensive possessions were his horses and his armour. When the Black Prince directed in his will that his body should be escorted to the grave by two of his great war-horses and two men wearing his armour, he was exhibiting even in death the soldier's two principal marks of status as well as following a practice which was becoming conventional among men of his caste. A squire was expected to have a 'covered' war-horse and a knight two of them. These were great beasts with the strength, agility and speed to carry a heavily armoured man-at-arms into battle. In addition to his war-horse a man-at-arms needed a palfrey to ride on the march and, if he could get shipping space for them, a sumpter for his baggage and a rouncy for his servant. This represented a considerable investment in horseflesh. Surviving horse valuations suggest that the average knight rode on a horse worth between £20 and £30 while his squire had an animal worth nearly £10. The largest and finest war-horses (known as destriers) could cost as much as £100. A man's horse was a visible sign of his standing. But it might also make the difference between life and death. When Sir John Falconer was killed in a skirmish outside Benavente in the Castilian campaign of 1387 his companions knew that it was his low-grade horse which had done for him.[37]

Armour was becoming increasingly elaborate, especially in France where much attention was devoted to protecting soldiers from the destructive power of the English longbow. Most armour was still made of chain mail which was cheaper and lighter than plate and allowed freer movement and better ventilation. Mail remained 'the good, the better and the best of the trade' as an experienced arms dealer observed in

1385, but its defects were well known. The excavations carried out in the grave-pits at Wisby in Sweden, where a Danish army wiped out a ramshackle force of Swedish peasants and townsmen in July 1361, have provided powerful evidence of the lethal effect of archery on old-style armour. A large number of the victims had been killed by missiles shot into the air which fell vertically from above, splitting the links of their mail hoods and penetrating the skulls beneath. Mail hoods had already disappeared in France and England largely for this reason. Light steel or iron helmets (known as 'bacinets') with long neck-pieces at the back and moveable vizors over the eyes had become the universal item of equipment of the fighting man. As time went on the coat of mail was in turn superseded by plate body armour. Carefully contoured to present oblique surfaces to an enemy, well-made plate was practically impervious to arrows and bolts and gave a high degree of protection against lances, swords and axes. In the following century it would develop into elaborate articulated suits of armour, made of light, carburised steel hardened in the blast-furnaces of Italy and Germany. But in the late fourteenth century complete suits of plate armour were still too heavy and rigid for comfort. They appeared on funerary monuments and in tournaments but rarely in battle. Charles VI wore mail on campaign. John of Gaunt and his companions appeared in mail for their conference with the King of Portugal at Ponte de Mouro. Like most of their men-at-arms they wore it in combination with plate pieces: breast-plates, thigh and arm pieces and gauntlets covering the forearm and wrists.[38]

There is some evidence that the sums expended on horseflesh declined in the later fourteenth century, at least in England, possibly as a belated response to changes of battle tactics.[39] Armour protection, on the other hand, became ever more costly. The Datini branch in Avignon offered bacinets at 6 *livres* with vizor, 4 without, with an extra 4½ *livres* for the *camail* of chain mail which was suspended from the bacinet to protect the throat and shoulders. A complete mail coat cost more than 14 *livres*. Scattered fragments of evidence suggest that in France it cost about 25 *livres* (say £6) to buy basic armour for a man-at-arms with no pretensions to status. This represented about two months' war wages for a French squire. In England even the humble archer, protected by nothing more than his helmet and a boiled leather jacket, cost more than £2 to equip. At the opposite extreme the Duke of Burgundy could pay 100 francs (about £17) for a single suit of chain mail made in Milan. Thomas Duke of Gloucester's armour was valued after his death at £103. All this was on top of the cost of buying at least one long sword, a long dagger (in effect a short sword) and several ten-foot wooden lances with metal-tipped points. In 1339, at the time of Edward III's first continental campaign, the Hainault chronicler Jean le Bel had been astonished by the cavalcades of English men-at-arms wearing the latest plate pieces on their armour. He associated their swagger with a generation of English victories over France. But there is some anecdotal evidence that English men-at-arms of the late fourteenth century were no longer willing or able to lay out the great sums required. Half a century later other foreign observers, this time Portuguese, remarked on the shoddy equipment with which the army of John of Gaunt set out on their disastrous invasion of northern Castile.[40]

The growing demand for armour generated by half a century of war was met by an increasingly elaborate network of dealers supported by substantial industries. In both England and France armourers had traditionally worked from small workshops in a few centres, predominantly Paris and London. Their resources were quickly overwhelmed and their prices rose steeply, especially after the announcement of major campaigns. Supply expanded rapidly to fill the gap. In France the royal arsenal at Rouen turned out mass-produced armour and weapons in great quantity. Major industrial armouries grew up in Italy, Germany and the Low Countries, which acquired a virtual monopoly over certain lines such as plate pieces. The Datini firm sold large quantities of Italian plate armour into France. Bohemian dealers set up depots in London, one of which was found in 1387 to be holding a stock of nearly 700 pieces. By the end of the fourteenth century the trade had developed on highly organised and specialised lines: steel plate from Milan or Prague, helmets from Montauban, padded jackets from Toulouse, crossbows and bacinets from Genoa, gunpowder artillery from Châlons and Troyes, sword-blades from Germany and daggers from Castile. The Duke of Burgundy acquired his best swords from the famous cutlers of Bordeaux, just like his English and Gascon adversaries. The poet Eustache Deschamps cursed them all, these 'swine' who waxed fat on the tools of death.[41]

For most English armies the campaign opened with the departure of the mounted columns from Calais, their banners unfurled as they passed Ardres or Marquise into French territory. For the French, whose strategy was inevitably reactive, it opened less flamboyantly with the march to the front from a more or less distant mustering point. Their commanders must have started out with a rough mental image of the geography of the region in which they were operating and a broad strategic plan. Yet the lack of even rudimentary maps must have made detailed campaign planning exceptionally difficult. When the Earl of Buckingham entered France in July 1380 he had barely set foot in the country before and most of his companions were as ignorant of it as he was. Froissart reports that a halt had to be called on the first day for a council of war about 'which roads they should take to accomplish their objectives'. It is clear that the Earl was heavily dependent on the recollections of his more experienced military advisers and on information obtained from scouts, prisoners and local guides. In this he was not at all unusual. The valiant captain, advised the ancient knight in *Les Cent Ballades*, rides often over the country where he is to fight and imprints the roads and fords on his memory. These, together with bridges and major cities, were the main points of reference. But there was much ignorance about them. Even Olivier de Clisson, marching north in the first days of the campaign of 1382, had to ask his companions about the course of the River Lys which marked the frontier of Flanders. 'I do not know this land of Flanders,' he explained; 'I have never been here in my life.' It is clear that Clisson had no maps. These difficulties were aggravated by the roughness of the roads and the changeable character of landscapes in an age when rivers could flood a valley overnight or change their course in a season and abandoned land was quickly covered by impenetrable forest and scrub. Bridges were routinely broken by the enemy and had to be repaired by throwing improvised timber carriage-ways across the stumps. In front of every army went a great corps of pioneers armed with picks, spades, axes and scythes to smooth the way for the wagons and hack away at the dense vegetation. Edward III's pioneer corps in 1359 was 500 strong. The French army had 1,800 pioneers in Flanders in 1382 and no fewer than 3,000 when crossing the Ardennes in 1388.[42]

The problems of supply tended to dominate the strategy of English commanders, determining the route of the army and often the fate of a whole campaign. The English had an elaborate victualling system for supplying their permanent garrisons in France by sea. Calais was supplied from a permanent depot on the Isle of Thanet. Brest and Cherbourg were dependent on supplies shipped out from southern England and the Channel Islands. Even inland fortresses such as Derval, Saint-Sauveur and Fronsac were occasionally victualled from England. Supplying field armies on the move in hostile territory was a more difficult problem which the English never mastered. In his prime Edward III had tried several times to organise a supply train for his armies operating inland in France. Great wagon trains, loaded with biscuit, dried vegetables and salted meat and fish, accompanied the expeditions of 1339, 1340 and 1346. The Reims campaign of 1359–60 was the most ambitious exercise of its kind involving, according to the chronicler Jean le Bel, more than 10,000 horse-drawn carts. In 1346 and 1359 plans were laid to seize harbours to serve as coastal depots from which the carts could be refilled. These ambitious plans invariably failed. Experience showed that the food was either consumed or wasted within a very short time. The coastal depots proved difficult for the English to capture, or else the supplies reached them too late. With the arrival of all-mounted armies in the 1350s the wagon trains found it hard to keep up. John of Gaunt tried again when he invaded France in 1373, but his wagons were unable to cross the flooded rivers of northern France and the army ran out of food within a month of leaving Calais. During the difficult winter of 1386–7, when Gaunt was in northern Castile, an attempt was made to bring in cargoes of grain from England to supply his starving army. This was an ambitious undertaking in mid-winter, which may have refilled the stores of the Duke's household but made little impression on the rest of the army.[43]

English armies in France encountered growing difficulties in living off the land. A large army on the move ate as much as the population of a substantial town. It was likely to exhaust the available supplies in any locality in a very short time. Whenever they could, English armies in France marched in columns following separate routes several miles apart in order to ease the burden on foragers. Even so they had to move on quickly to fresh territory or starve. Fodder for horses was even harder to find than food for men. Sieges posed special difficulties of supply. A siege army was rooted to the spot, its foragers forced to look for supplies over ever greater distances the longer the siege lasted. This was one reason why the English rarely attempted them. The French knew how to exploit these weaknesses. They became adept at emptying the countryside around the armies of the English. Their persistent cavalry attacks on foraging parties were highly effective. John of Gaunt's army of 1373–4 was destroyed by hunger without ever engaging significant numbers of the enemy. The army with which he invaded Castile in 1387 suffered the same fate. In 1381 Gaunt's brother Thomas of Woodstock was forced by supply problems to abandon the siege of Nantes and ultimately to return to England.

French armies operating on their own territory were in a different position. In theory they were forbidden to live off the land and in practice unable to do so for very long, for the same iron laws of supply applied to them. Few regions of France were capable of sustaining dense concentrations of soldiers from local resources whether they were friends or foes. Unlike the English, however, the French could bring supplies overland through friendly country from considerable distances, especially where there were navigable rivers. Philippe de Mézières thought that field armies should be supplied by a central commissariat, buying in bulk and issuing rations. He even gave some thought to the appropriate military diet. But in practice this was only ever done for the armies recruited for the abortive invasions of England in 1385 and 1386. Both of these enterprises involved immense supply operations supervised by royal officials across much of northern and western France. They marked a departure from the general rule, which was that French troops did not receive rations but were expected to buy their own supplies out of their advances.

It was left to private enterprise to ensure that there were goods for the soldiers to buy. Every French army was followed by a great tail of commercial victuallers who themselves depended on an extensive network of suppliers and carriers. They set up markets every evening at the edge of the encampments. The formula proved capable of almost infinite expansion. Operations in the Low Countries, a region 'without wheat, grain, vines or fruit to despoil', presented a particular challenge. The huge French host, more than 30,000 strong, which was recruited to confront the Bishop of Norwich's crusade in 1383 was kept supplied throughout the campaign by an extensive system of seaborne and riverborne convoys organised by a Parisian wholesale grocer called Nicholas Boulard. When Charles VI invaded Guelders in 1388 the indispensable Boulard was once more in charge. He is said to have laid out more than 100,000 écus on the victualling operation. Huge bulk purchases were made in Germany, Burgundy and Champagne and carried on barges down the Rhine and the Meuse. Wholesalers from Utrecht and the towns of Brabant brought in more from across the Low Countries. The campaign was a logistical disaster but not for want of organisation.[44]

The fact that every company, indeed every individual, had to fend for himself meant that the hardships of the march were very unevenly distributed. The richest soldiers and those who were associated with the household of a great nobleman were often able to maintain a level of personal comfort which defied the elements and the problems of transport. We cannot know how long the French supply train would have lasted if it had ever landed in England in 1386, but the Duke of

Burgundy's household would have fared better than most. The list of stores laid in for them included 812 casks of wine, 105 beef and 447 mutton carcasses, 450 salted geese and 100 fresh ones, 4,550 fish, 294 hams, 22,000 eggs, 840 whole French cheeses and 136 English ones. The Duke was one of the more munificent commanders but his practices probably differed only in degree from those of other princely captains. Philippe de Mézières railed against army commanders who maintained sumptuous tables for their guests, offering banquets that were eaten off silver plate and lasted several hours amid the squalor of a military encampment. We are told that in the midst of the disaster that overcame the Anglo-Portuguese army in Castile in 1387 King John of Portugal 'never failed to have his three dishes of beef a day, minced, roasted or boiled'. For the mass of the army, however, marching through hostile territory in the latter part of the fourteenth century was a physically draining experience involving serious hardship even if there were no engagements. Those old soldiers who recorded their experiences remembered the aching ribs and backs, the discomforts of sleeping on the ground and rising in the clothes that they had worn for weeks, the intense cold in winter, the bright summer days in which the hot sun beat down on men encased in thick leather and metal, the long periods of famine, the foul billets and crowded camps.[45]

Many of them must also have remembered the boredom of long days in the saddle or uneventful watches from the walls of garrisoned towns and castles. The dullness of much military life was at the root of most disciplinary problems. Soldiers occupied themselves with chatter and reminiscences. They sang songs, a handful of which are recorded out of many more that were once known by heart. Kings and princes and their intimates had their own amusements. Edward III hunted for boar with his leading captains during the Breton campaign of 1342–3. For the campaign of 1359–60 he brought a pack of hounds and a team of falconers with him from England. Several of John of Gaunt's captains are reported to have brought their hunting dogs and falcons with them to Castile in 1386. Others brought dogs for company, like the French knight killed in the Poitou campaign of 1372 whose aged hound refused to abandon his grave. The Duke of Berry paid ten francs to a nearby householder to feed the animal for the rest of its days.[46]

Very occasionally one hears of wives accompanying their husbands on campaign. John of Gaunt's wife Doña Constanza accompanied him to Castile in 1386 in her capacity as joint pretender to the throne and the wives of his captains served to decorate her court. But they also took part, presumably by choice, in the exceptionally arduous campaign across the plain of northern Castile when they might have stayed in comfort in Portugal. It was commoner for women to accompany their husbands in garrisons or on the marches. Sir Richard Totesham had his wife with him in the citadel of La Roche-Derrien during the siege of 1347. She was nearly killed as the French artillery demolished the chamber in which she was feeding their baby. Some of these women were plainly formidable personalities in their own right. Sir Robert Knolles's wife Constance helped him to run his garrisons in Brittany, visiting England on his behalf to find supplies and recruits. James Mascy's wife took command of the citadel of Millau during her husband's absences. Sir Digory Say's French wife actively participated in the defence of Gençay against her fellow countrymen, supported by his French step-daughter. Renaud lord of Pons left his wife in command of the town. She held it against him when he defected to the French in 1371. This lady certainly earned the golden goblet with the Lancastrian symbol of the white hart, which John of Gaunt presented to her in gratitude. Others preferred to acquire mistresses *in situ*, like Sir John Cresswell at Lusignan if the author of *Mélusine* is to be believed, or Sir John Devereux, who appropriated the wife of a local worthy when he was captain of La Souterraine. Most soldiers no doubt found relief as soldiers always have, in rape or prostitution, but some formed powerful and long-lasting attachments to their concubines. The English mercenary William Gold, one of Hawkwood's lieutenants in Italy, was distraught when his French girlfriend of two decades left him. The archives of the Gonzaga lords of Mantua contain a cache of letters in which he tried to enlist their help to find her. 'Sweet love conquers the proudest hearts . . .', Gold wrote. 'It vanquishes the strong. It casts down the tallest towers. It drives men to violence. And all of this has befallen me for Janet's sake, so much does my heart long for her.'[47]

There was probably only one pastime apart from sex which almost all soldiers had in common regardless of rank, and that was gambling, which reached epidemic proportions in the field armies and garrisons of both sides. The Black Prince had a special purse for gambling money on his campaign in Languedoc in 1355. Philip of Burgundy, Bertrand du Guesclin and Olivier de Clisson were all inveterate dice-players. The Count of Savoy gambled away at least 2,000 francs in 1386 while waiting to embark with the French army of England. These were gorgeous personages and their losses probably did no harm except to themselves, but among ordinary soldiers gambling became a serious disciplinary problem. Soldiers gambled at everything: generally at dice but also at archery, *paume* and any other sports and games where they could find someone to wager money against them. As Geoffrey de Charny observed, games were no longer games when played for money. Quarrels over stakes and winnings were the source of countless fights and acts of treachery or negligence. A remarkable number of fortresses were reported to have been lost and encampments attacked while the sentries were busy gaming.[48]

'Lance, mine and assault ladder' were the chief tools of war according to the contemporary authors of *Les Cent Ballades*, all of them experienced professional soldiers.[49] The experience of men in battle is hard to reconstruct. The rare eye-witness accounts, if they descend to detail at all, rarely rise above a jumble of discrete incidents. Froissart, the great descriptive artist of these years, was good at absorbing the experience of others and injecting his own imaginative insights. But so far as can be discovered from his work he never saw a town assaulted or witnessed a pitched battle. The only army which he may have followed on the march was the French army which fought in Flanders and Artois in 1383. It is not easy for one who has never taken part to imagine the collective courage and indifference to death which enabled the French garrison of Limoges to fight on in the open spaces of the city against overwhelming odds or the English to fight their way up the scaling ladders placed against the walls of Ypres as artillery fire raked them from the sides and the men ahead of them were hurled to their deaths in the ditch below.

It is above all the physical intimacy of these encounters which differentiates them from most modern warfare. The chronicler Geoffrey Baker, who derived his account from at least one eye-witness, tells us that at the battle of Poitiers the Earl of Salisbury 'glowed in the warm blood which covered his sword' while men around him 'trod in their own guts and spat out their teeth'. Thomas Walsingham's narrative of an encounter near Montebourg in 1379 between some 500 or 600 French troops and an English raiding force from Cherbourg was probably derived from a news-letter and embellished with what the chronicler had heard from others about the reality of fighting:

The French, who were much stronger than we were, forced us back with the impact of their first assault. Our archers protected us, covering the French with a dense cloud of arrows which wounded many of them and killed more. But they never flagged. They kept on coming at us, fighting with courage and spirit and forcing their way forward with their weapons, determined that if death was their fate they would die gloriously. There was a tremendous noise as the two armies met and swords crashed down on helmets and trumpets blared, while confusion reigned everywhere. Sir John Harleston, the English commander, was the first to fall. He threw himself into the French line and was cut down as the enemy swarmed about him like bees. Overwhelmed, he was left half-dead on the ground, trampled underfoot by men and horses . . . As the battle raged and the French began to get the better of it Sir Geoffrey Worsley, an experienced and determined knight, appeared at our sides with the reserve. He charged the French positions with his men, breaking up their line. Brave men every one of them, they laid about the French with their axes, slaughtering them like cattle. Not a blow was wasted. Not a man brought his weapon down in vain. Not once was it necessary to finish off an enemy with a second blow. The strongest helmets were smashed open. Some were so shattered that the two sides were as if fused together . . . and the man's head inside crushed to nothing. Meanwhile another company of men who had been detailed to guard our horses and baggage in the rear . . . grabbed their weapons and seized more from the bodies of French soldiers lying on the field in order to fall upon the enemy from behind. Sir Geoffrey's men, rampaging through the French positions, scattered them, breaking up their order and forcing them to surrender.

About 120 French troops were killed in this engagement and about the same number captured, nearly half of their whole force.[50]

In spite of the closeness and violence of fourteenth-century fights the numbers killed were surprisingly low. Most of the deaths occurred after the battle in the pursuit, when the vanquished were finished off as they lay helpless on the ground or tried to flee from the field. At the battle of Roosebeke the French army suffered modest losses but is said to have killed 3,000 Flemings as they lay wounded on the ground and many more as they fled for their lives along the roads. But if death was disproportionately the fate of the vanquished, injury was indiscriminate. The weapons used in medieval fights inflicted appalling injuries which left those who survived permanently disfigured or disabled. Sir Hugh Hastings, who died aged less than forty of disease contracted at the siege of Calais in 1347, appears on his famous brass in Elsing parish church in the prime of health and strength. But the recent exhumation of his remains showed that he was a human wreck. He suffered from advanced inflammation of the joints and most of his front teeth had been knocked out by blows to his mouth. Sir William Scrope the elder was completely disabled at the age of about twenty-two by wounds received at the battle of Morlaix (1342) and died two years later without recovering. Olivier de Clisson famously lost an eye at the battle of Auray (1364). Recovery from a serious wound was rarely complete and professional soldiers were easily recognised by scars. A muster roll drawn up in Provence in 1374 which, unusually, records the appearance as well as the names of the men, suggests that at least a quarter of them were scarred by the wounds of past campaigns, generally on their hands or faces. Breton soldiers returning from the wars were described by a contemporary as disfigured, mutilated, often part-blind and lame, with faces like the bark of a tree and stuffing still coming out of their jackets where swords had entered.[51]

Few aspects of fourteenth-century military life are as obscure as the treatment of disease and wounds. Medieval physicians worked in the tradition established by the second century Greek theorist Galen as their successors continued to do until the eighteenth century. Although they must often have supplemented their science with folk remedies of one kind or another we know very little about them except that they seem to have been largely ineffective. Dysentery and other infectious diseases endemic in crowded, ill-drained encampments were among the main sources of loss in medieval armies. The recovery rate was low. The prognosis was better for wounds. They were the province of the surgeons, men who lacked the formal learning and professional prestige of the physicians but were probably more useful. Their training had a significant empirical element which included some dissection and a good deal of observation, much of it derived from treating war wounds. Henri de Mondeville, the famous French surgeon of the early fourteenth century, had derived at least part of his knowledge from serving with the armies of Philip the Fair. His treatise on surgery, written in about 1312, was among the first to put forward a recognisably modern approach to the treatment of wounds based on the control of haemorrhage, the cleaning of the wound and closure with sutures, combined with nourishing diet and rest. Some of Mondeville's ideas remained controversial in his own day and for a long time afterwards. The ancient notion (derived ultimately from Galen) that wounds should be kept open and encouraged to suppurate with caustic materials, thick ointments or poultices, so as to produce the 'laudable pus' by which evil humours were supposedly expelled, continued to command support among most academic teachers and writers until well after the end of the middle ages.[52]

As with so much medieval science, theory is better recorded than practice, which may have been more impressive. The evidence, fragmentary as it is, suggests that contemporaries were capable of distinguishing between some wounds and others and of applying the treatments appropriate to the conditions. It was well understood that the main priority was to wash out the wound with pure water or a natural disinfectant and to keep it clean. The great Duke of Lancaster, John of Gaunt's father-in-law, knew that dirt and flies were the main enemies of the injured man, that wounds should be cleaned out with running water and dressed with compresses of ointment and clean white bandages. The contemporary French surgeon-physician Guy de Chauliac, whose famous and influential *Grande Chirurgie* is said to have set back the academic study of wound treatment by two centuries, observed with a sneer that this kind of unlearned stuff was common wisdom among professional men-at-arms. According to Guy their practice was to clean out wounds with wine or spirits or oils from crushed herbs applied with wads of woollen cloth or cabbage leaves. This is borne out by other evidence. The regulations for supplying the town of Montauban against a siege in 1348 called for, among other things, a stock of cotton fabric, wads of wool, olive oil and 'swint' (ointment) for dressing wounds but also pepper, ginger and spices, dried grapes, figs and almonds to make poultices. Ointments, mainly herbal, were a staple of the medicine chests taken on campaign and were kept in readiness in garrisoned towns and castles. Other disinfectants employed included exotic resins, natural turpentine, honey and even, for inaccessible wounds beyond the reach of the scalpel, diluted compounds of arsenic. Guy de Chauliac dismissed the men who followed such practices as mere 'mechanicals' or 'empiricals' but they were doubtless doing what seemed to work. They were also surprisingly alert to the advantages of a good diet and plenty of rest. These must have been hard to provide in the field. But we have it on the authority of Philippe de Mézières that a reinforced diet was available for sick and wounded men at least in French armies. During his march around Paris in 1360 Edward III even arranged for sick English and allied soldiers to be allowed to withdraw to Burgundy to recuperate away from the war zone, a rare example of solicitude for wounded men who were more commonly abandoned to weaken and die by the roadside.[53]

Guy de Chauliac implies that men-at-arms treated each other's wounds. In most cases they probably did. The Breton knight Geoffrey Budes was severely wounded in the unsuccessful assault on the walls of Ussel in February 1371. As he climbed the scaling ladder he was struck by heavy boulders thrown down from above and fell into the castle ditch with a broken arm, a fractured and dislocated hip and lacerations all over his body. He was rescued and taken to Clermont where his bones were reset with bitumen without medical intervention, apparently by his companions. The surgeons who later examined him in Paris found that some of the lacerations were still unhealed but that the fractures had mended perfectly. There were clearly occasions when professional attention was essential. Princes took their personal surgeons with them. Philip of Burgundy's surgeon was summoned urgently to his side as he set out for the campaign in Poitou in 1372. John of Gaunt's surgeon was retained to serve him wherever he might be needed 'well and properly arrayed for war'. But these men were there to treat their master and his household and personal retainers. Only occasionally do we hear of surgeons being provided for humbler men. Some garrisons took local practitioners permanently into their service. But there is no evidence of organised medical services before 1415, when a corps of nearly two dozen surgeons served with the English army at Agincourt. Most soldiers who suffered battlefield fractures from swords or axes probably died of gangrene or other rapidly spreading infections long before help could reach them.[54]

Among those who survived their injuries arrow and bolt wounds were probably the commonest traumas calling for surgical attention. Crossbow bolts were made of iron. Arrows were tipped with metal which was frequently barbed. Extracting them was a delicate operation with a high risk of failure. A soldier's head was vulnerable because vizors were commonly left open to allow the wearer to see better and to hear or shout orders. Guy de Chauliac had an array of instruments for extracting arrow-heads but warned that deep wounds to the head were usually incurable. This was probably too pessimistic, but the record of surgery was certainly uneven. Two barber-surgeons from York laboured in vain to remove the barbs from the head of King David of Scotland after his capture at the battle of Neville's Cross in 1346. The barbs remained there for twenty years, when they are said to have been removed by the miraculous intervention of St. Monan. On the other hand when an arrow penetrated six inches into the head of Prince Henry (the future Henry V) at the battle of Shrewsbury in 1403 it was successfully removed with a specially made instrument in a complicated and time-consuming operation of which a remarkable account survives written by the surgeon himself. But this was hardly a typical case. Prince Henry was an important patient and the surgeon was one of the most celebrated practitioners in England. Victims of arrow wounds were more commonly advised that it was safer to leave the metal in the wound and put up with the discomfort. 'In surgery is perilous the cure but men might touch the arrow or come thereby', wrote Chaucer in *The Franklin's Tale*.[55]

Horses were if anything even more vulnerable than men, but we hear even less about their treatment. Horses suffered lance and arrow wounds and frequent fractures. They succumbed to camp diseases. They could not bear prolonged periods without food and water as men often had to. They sickened when floods brought down thick, muddy water from the hills. Major expeditions such as those of John of Gaunt in 1373–4 and the Earl of Buckingham in 1380–1 often resulted in catastrophic horse losses. Veterinary surgeons, so far as we can tell, were invariably 'mechanicals', not learned men, and consequently they have left few traces of their work. Some may have been little better than the author of the short manual on the care of horses preserved at Corpus Christi College, Cambridge, who advised prayer for all the more serious maladies. But a certain amount of practical veterinary lore must have been common among men-at-arms and their grooms who lived and worked all the time with horses. The *Menagier de Paris*, whose didactic instructions to his wife tell us so much about the life of prosperous urban households, also had advice to give to his grooms about the illnesses and treatment of horses, which he had presumably derived from observation over the years. Jean de Béarn, the Anglo-Gascon *routier* who commanded the Pyrenean fortress of Lourdes for much of the 1370s and 1380s, commissioned a treatise on veterinary science from a learned Catalan and dedicated it to Richard II. It is an academic compilation, largely derived from old Byzantine sources, which cannot have been of much practical use, but it at least suggests that there was serious interest in the subject. The sole surviving manuscript contains some striking illustrations of procedures for treating fractures, wounds and other ailments of horses which are more instructive than anything in the text.[56]

Of all the hazards encountered by medieval soldiers none was as fundamental to the balance of risk and reward as the danger of capture. In the course of a long professional career a prominent soldier was quite likely to be captured at least once and quite possibly more than once. Bertrand du Guesclin was captured four times in the space of eight years. He took considerable risks with his safety, especially in his early career, but his experience was by no means unusual. The French knight Tristan de Maignelay was captured by the English at the battle of Mauron in 1352 and again four years later when carrying the Dauphin's standard at the battle of Poitiers. The Gascon hero Jean de Grailly, Captal de Buch, was captured by the French at the battle of Cocherel in 1364 and again at Soubise in 1372. Bertucat d'Albret was captured at least twice. The Gascon knight Bernard de Montet, who petitioned Richard II for help in 1382, claimed to have been captured six times in twelve years.[57]

The treatment of prisoners of war was governed by an elaborate mixture of legal rules and customary practice, which was progressively refined as the war continued. Human prisoners were legitimate spoil of war in the same way as armour, baggage or horses. They were at the mercy of their captors. This was more than an abstract idea derived from law-books. In the concluding stages of any decisive battle the survivors of the defeated army, exhausted, wounded or fleeing from the scene, were routinely massacred in cold blood unless their equipment showed them to be rich enough to be worth taking. If a man surrendered, it was an act of grace to spare him. The transaction was treated as a contract by which he put himself at the victor's disposal in return for his life. The deal was commonly completed with explicit formulae which were universally understood and sealed by the delivery of a pledge, such as the prisoner's helmet or right gauntlet, mementoes which would serve as visible evidence in case of dispute. 'Be my prisoner, rescued or not, my lord of Langoiran, or you will die', cried Bérard d'Albret's captor, who had ambushed him on the Gascon march in 1379 and torn his helmet from his head as he lay on the ground. Bérard, who knew that his companions were close at hand, expected to be rescued. So he said nothing, whereupon his enemy drove the point of his dagger into his skull and killed him.[58]

Not all prisoners were ransomed. Some were appropriated by the King, generally on paying compensation to the captor, and detained indefinitely for political reasons. The leading Scottish prisoners taken at the battle of Neville's Cross in 1346 were held in captivity for long periods because Edward III believed that by holding them he would reduce the Scots' ability to resist him. The sons of Charles of Blois were incarcerated in England for more than thirty years for very similar reasons. Henry of Trastámara famously refused to treat with his English and Gascon captives after the battle of La Rochelle and instead kept them in prison in Castile for years. By custom the King of France was entitled to take over any prisoner worth more than 10,000 francs. He exercised this right more sparingly than his rival, but he was perfectly capable of it when it suited him. When the Captal de Buch was captured for the first time, in 1364, Charles V discharged him without payment in the hope of making an ally. On the second occasion, in 1372, the King refused to release him at all, even against a proper ransom, until he agreed to abandon his English allegiance. The Captal protested that his treatment was contrary to the law of arms. So did several of his courtiers, among them the French knight who had taken him. He received only 1,200 francs for his pains, which was much less than the prisoner's value on the open market. But in point of law the King was right. So the Captal remained in the grim keep of Corbeil until his death in 1377.[59]

The moral of this story was that the practice of ransoming prisoners raised many issues other than money. Outside the ranks of the chivalrous class it was never free of controversy. A minority of churchmen felt that it put a price on mercy and treated human beings as chattels. A more significant criticism, because it was more widespread, was that the ransoming of captured soldiers served to strengthen the enemy and prolong the war. The prospect of ransoms also encouraged indiscipline in the army, as soldiers broke ranks and disregarded orders in the pursuit of prisoners. When French opinion turned against the whole knightly class after the disastrous defeat at Poitiers in 1356, one of the main accusations against them was that the ransom system was a conspiracy between men-at-arms on either side. It was said that they had more in common with each other than with the populations which supported them and preferred to make money out of the enemy than to destroy them. Similar complaints were heard in England when people began to turn against the war later in the century. By and large, however, the conventions of chivalry prevailed. Even such significant figures as Charles of Blois and Bertrand du Guesclin were ransomed if a suitable price could be fixed. 'Among Christians, great and small,' wrote Honoré Bonet, 'the general custom is to take ransoms from one another.'[60]

Just as a prisoner had no right to be released against a ransom, so the mere fact of surrender implied no promise to pay one. That required a further agreement. Because the maintenance and custody of his prisoner could be expensive the lesser prisoners were in practice released quite quickly, often within a day or two of their capture, after a rough and ready estimate of their worth and a truncated discussion over a camp fire. These occasions were games of bluff on both sides. Captors threatened to keep the prisoner in captivity when they were in no position to do it. For their part, prisoners gave low estimates of their own worth, like the French knight captured by John Lord Neville at

Carlisle during Jean de Vienne's campaign of 1385, who hid his status behind lies and a false name. This man was exposed by a fellow prisoner, a turncoat who told his captors who the man was and what to charge. But, in general, captors had perforce to take their prisoners at their own estimation, a process which commonly resulted in quite modest ransoms. The chronicler Jean le Bel reports that most of the great horde of French prisoners taken at the battle of Poitiers got away lightly for this reason. The more notable captives fared worse. Their horses and equipment were too grand. Their arms were emblazoned on their tunics and readily identifiable by the heralds. They were almost invariably detained while enquiries were made, a full ransom negotiated and security obtained for its payment. This could be a difficult and long-drawn-out process, as prisoners kept in isolation in a foreign country, without friends or advisers to support them, struggled to weigh up the prospect of indefinite detention against the dangers of a ruinous freedom.[61]

Conventionally there were limits to what a captor could demand. When Jean de Grailly's captor appealed to Charles V to release him against '*finance courtoise*' he was invoking a widely held belief that among noblemen ransoms should be reasonable. Pope Gregory XI made the same point when he demanded that the ransom of his nephew Roger Beaufort (who had been captured at the fall of Limoges) should be reduced to a level consistent with the 'laws of arms and the practices of noblemen'. Although the existence of such a principle was generally acknowledged, there was never any firm consensus as to what '*finance courtoise*' was. According to Honoré Bonet a ransom should be:

... reasonable and knightly and such as the prisoner is capable of paying according to the usage of arms and of his country and pitched at such a level as will not disinherit his wife, children, relations and friends, for justice demands that they should have the wherewithal to live after the ransom has been paid.

This formula begged many questions and, as Bonet himself observed, the ideal was widely ignored in practice. Most captors made a rough assessment of what the prisoner could raise by selling assets and added something for the contribution which might be expected from his relatives and friends and, in the case of politically important prisoners, from his sovereign.[62]

At a time when cash was scarce and revenues from land were declining, even modest ransoms could be hard to raise. Many prisoners were ruined by the excessive demands made on them and the stiff terms on which credit was available from the few people who were in a position to provide it. Cash-rich entrepreneurs, often successful soldiers of fortune, provided loans and guarantees. The Earls of Arundel, Warwick and Suffolk and Edward III's mistress Alice Perrers were among the English investors who put money into loans to prisoners of war, taking mortgages on their estates. A syndicate of English noblemen led by John of Gaunt undertook to advance the ransom of the Earl of Pembroke in 1375. Some of these transactions involved buying the captor's rights over the prisoner, an arrangement which treated him as a marketable security. Shares in Olivier du Guesclin, the Constable's younger brother who was captured near Cherbourg in 1378, were divided between at least seven parties, some of whom were certainly financiers. There was an active secondary market in prisoners' obligations, which were often executed in bearer form and traded at discounts according to the due dates of payment and the practical likelihood of recovery. Edward III himself was a persistent but not particularly successful speculator in this market. In France rich Parisian merchants and officials bought up land and chattels from distressed prisoners at bargain prices, like the syndicate that bailed out Tristan de Maignelay. Bertrand du Guesclin, Olivier de Clisson and Gaston Phoebus of Foix all carried on a regular brokerage business, advancing cash for ransom payments and buying up prisoners at a discount to release or sell them at a profit.

Without financial accommodation of this kind the ransoming of prisoners would hardly have been possible, but it came at a heavy price. There was interest to pay. Hostages were required as security. Pledges were taken and charges executed. Foreclosures were frequent. The Norman knight Robert de Brucourt, who was captured at the battle of Auray in 1364, was held at Saint-Sauveur-le-Vicomte for eleven years until he agreed to pay a ransom which was ten times the annual revenues of his domains in Lower Normandy. The money was raised by selling the property to Bertrand du Guesclin on terms which left him and his wife with two-thirds of the income for life to live on. Their heirs were left with nothing. Sir John Bourchier, who was captured on the Breton march in 1371, passed more than two years immured in the fortress of his captor before agreeing to a ransom of 12,000 francs, about three times the revenues of his English estates. Writing to his wife from his prison, he excused himself for having brought ruin on both of them by promising a sum so far beyond their means. He was afraid for his health, he said, if he remained incarcerated for much longer. 'My true, beloved wife, I charge you by the love we bear each other to sell or mortgage all that we have, sparing nothing, for he whose health is broken has truly nothing left at all.' Once the terms were agreed, Bourchier's captor sold him at a discount for ready cash to Olivier de Clisson, while in England Lady Bourchier struggled for four years to raise the first instalment of the debt which would allow her husband to be released on parole. The records of both England and France are full of petitions by men who claimed to have lost everything as a result of being captured in the King's service. Some of them may have been exaggerated but there is enough anecdotal evidence to suggest that stories like Brucourt's and Bourchier's were commonplace in both countries.[63]

The conditions in which prisoners of war were kept varied widely according to the means and generosity of the captor. The duty to protect his prisoner, which the captor assumed on the battlefield, entailed allowing him a minimum of comfort according to his status. Indeed, under the law of arms ill-treatment dissolved a prisoner's obligations and entitled him to escape. But what counted as ill-treatment? Honoré Bonet thought that the captor's obligation extended to supplying food, drink and a bed to lie on and to taking reasonable care for the prisoner's health, but no more. He was entitled to confine his prisoner in a locked cell if he chose and was under no obligation to let him out for exercise or recreation. Strictly speaking a prisoner of war could be kept in leg-irons. This practice was regularly employed by *routier* garrisons to put pressure on prisoners and their relatives and is said to have been normal in Castile and Germany. But it was regarded with abhorrence by most noblemen in France and England and appears to have been used only against prisoners who had defaulted or against their hapless hostages. Sir Matthew Gournay, who captured Louis de Chalon at the battle of Auray in 1364, eventually lost patience with his prisoner's inability to raise his ransom and had him put in leg-irons and kept on short rations. As a result his relatives found the money. His fate could easily have been worse. The Count of Denia, an Aragonese nobleman captured at the battle of Nájera, was obliged to deliver up his son to Gaston Phoebus of Foix as security for a loan. Fifteen years later, the loan still unpaid, Denia's son was reported to be confined to a foul dungeon, loaded with chains and fetters.[64]

Outside the notorious prisons of the free companies, however, the treatment of prisoners was generally well above the minimum standard which the law of arms required. Gaston Phoebus did not treat other prisoners like Alfonso de Denia. The Albret brothers whom he captured at the battle of Launac in 1362 received a promise that he would not 'martyr their bodies'. They were allowed out on parole to hunt in his forests and go where they wished in his domains provided that they were back by sunset. The Count of Saint-Pol met his future wife while living comfortably on parole at the English court at Windsor. Sir Thomas Percy, a prisoner of the battle of Soubise, was held in the forbidding fortress of the Marché de Meaux but he was at least allowed the run of the courts and corridors. In 1375, when rumours began to circulate that the Captal de Buch was being maltreated at Corbeil, it was said that the English had retaliated by inflicting the same treatment on Roger Beaufort. Both governments reacted with indignation to these reports. The papal legates at Bruges received formal assurances that Beaufort was being 'held in a good chamber without chains or leg-irons and supplied with proper and decent provisions according to his needs'. From Paris the French King's Chamberlain Bureau de la Rivière sent a report on the conditions of the Captal's imprisonment, countersigned by the Captal himself. These were of course famous prisoners in the custody of the King whose maltreatment would have had serious repercussions. But lesser men appear to have received broadly comparable treatment in the castles of their captors. The fact that 4,000 francs of Sir John Bourchier's ransom was attributed to the cost of his upkeep over some two and a half years suggests that he lived in reasonable comfort. He certainly had several servants with him, including his English squire, who were free to come and go with messages and errands.

Even in these relatively benign conditions illness, boredom and depression were formidable enemies. Medieval castles were cold in winter and insanitary in summer. Confined within the walls of the castle of Machecoul, Bourchier complained that he was losing the use of his limbs, which was probably due to a combination of unfitness and premature arthritis. After his release he was able to rebuild his fortunes in royal service, ultimately becoming Richard II's governor in Ghent, but many prisoners died in captivity or returned home with their health and spirits broken. Fourteenth-century men-at-arms were usually educated men but their habits did not fit them for a life without activity or companionship. Few of them could have matched the mental discipline of Sir Thomas Gray, who occupied himself in writing his chronicle while confined as a prisoner of war in Edinburgh castle, or Charles of Orléans in the following century, who wrote much of his finest poetry in captivity in the Tower of London.[65]

Given the disastrous consequences of capture for so many prisoners it is surprising that there were not more defaults. Escape from captivity was rare, especially in England. The most famous example was that of Hugh de Châtillon, Charles V's Master of the Archers, who was captured on the Somme during John of Gaunt's *chevauchée* of 1369. In about 1371 Hugh escaped from Nottingham castle, one of the strongest fortresses in the kingdom, with the assistance of a Flemish sea captain hired by his wife, and managed to get back to France via Scotland. Most prisoners who escaped took the easier course of absconding while on parole. A captor was practically bound to release his prisoner on parole once he had entered into a ransom agreement because there was usually no other way in which he could raise the money. Captors took hostages or guarantees where they could or insisted on part-payment first, but these precautions were not always possible. In many cases the captor's only security was the prisoner's undertaking to remain a 'good and loyal prisoner', to return to captivity if his ransom had not been paid within the time agreed and not to bear arms against his captor's sovereign while his ransom was outstanding. Every effort was made to pile on the moral pressure to comply with these promises. A prisoner would be made to swear to keep faith on pain of being 'reviled as a false knight, traitor and perjurer in every place where he may go'. The promises of prisoners were recorded in writing, drawn up under their seal and witnessed by notaries. Their oaths were sworn in the presence of the most impressive witnesses that could be found. When Sir Thomas Percy was paroled in July 1373 to find his ransom in England he was brought to the Louvre to swear his oath before Charles V, Bertrand du Guesclin and a great congress of princes and noblemen. Percy failed to raise the money and was back in captivity by December.[66]

Particular importance was attached to the prisoner's promise not to fight against his captor's sovereign while on parole. When Arnoul d'Audrehem was captured at Nájera he was arraigned before a jury of knights on the ground that part of the ransom due after his capture at Poitiers eleven years earlier was still outstanding. He defended himself on the ground that in Castile he should be regarded as fighting against King Pedro of Castile, not the Prince. Sir Thomas Felton was technically a prisoner on parole at the beginning of 1381 when Richard II's Council appointed him to command the expedition to reinforce the Earl of Buckingham in Brittany. The outstanding balance of his ransom had to be hurriedly paid to Marshal Sancerre before the expedition sailed. A complex arrangement was devised with the assent of both governments, which illustrates how far contemporaries would go to adapt the conduct of war to the private interests of prominent captains. To enable Felton to invade France part of his debt was discharged in exchange for the release of Guillaume des Bordes, the former French captain in the Cotentin, who was bought by Richard II from his captor and transferred to Felton for the purpose. The rest was paid with Charles VI's leave by a syndicate of French merchants in return for licences to sell 10,000 barrels of wine onto the English market, which would otherwise have been closed to them. Among men of the standing of Percy and Felton default was unthinkable. Ironically the same was true of Hugh de Châtillon. The evidence suggests that after his escape from Nottingham castle he actually paid his ransom in order to be able to accept appointment as Captain-General of the French forces on the march of Calais.[67]

Defaults were more common among younger men and occasional soldiers as well as at the rougher end of the profession. They returned home and went to ground or devised colourable grounds for defying convention. Bertrand du Guesclin himself was more than once accused of breaking his parole before he became Constable. Always conscious of his controversial past, Bertrand was inordinately sensitive to the charge and once famously had a man hanged in his armour from his own battlements for repeating it. He was not alone. Yon de Garencières, one of the grand old men of the court of Charles V and VI, had once fought a duel over a very similar accusation. Sir James Pipe, the English captain of the 1350s who occupied the margins of military respectability, had twice defaulted on his parole. There was no doubt much to be said on both sides of these particular disputes but manifest defaulters were unwelcome even to their own side. They dishonoured their kinsmen and companions, provoked reprisals from the enemy and exposed hostages and guarantors to imprisonment and even death. For this reason defaulters received no protection from their own government. In both England and France the Constable and the Marshals maintained courts, with juries of knights and specialised advocates, to hear cases under the law of arms, many of which were about prisoners and ransoms. A similar court was held by the Black Prince's Constable in Aquitaine and after his departure by the Seneschal. When the much-captured Tristan de Maignelay absconded while on parole in France, leaving two hostages behind in England, he was arrested on the orders of Marshal Audrehem and kept in prison until he had paid his ransom. In Anjou in the mid-1350s defaulting French prisoners of war were being pursued by hue and cry and smoked out of caves on the orders of the French royal Seneschal. The courts and jails of England were equally available to French captors and evidently much used. Even so, outraged captors increasingly resorted to self-help. Many of them fought duels to vindicate claims against prisoners of war. A defaulting nobleman's arms could be 'reversed', which involved displaying them in public places, upside down or broken, an insult so serious that in the following century it came to be accepted that only a King or his lieutenant could authorise it. The evidence is entirely anecdotal, but recorded defaults become rarer in the later years of the century and it seems likely that peer pressure and the threat of enforcement at home had much to do with this.[68]

Contemporary attitudes to the conduct of war were informed by an approach to the boundaries of the public and the private sphere which is alien to modern thinking. War was an occasion for private profit and private loss. Military service, the treatment of prisoners and hostages and the surrender of fortresses all depended on contract. In this respect they resembled other aspects of this brutal conflict, which were based on complicated relationships of personal dependence at a relatively low level. Lawyers had long ago declared that only a sovereign could lawfully authorise war and by the end of the fourteenth century the principle was increasingly acknowledged in practice. Mérigot Marchès paid with his life for ignoring it. Yet the role of the state in the conduct of its own wars was constricted by the essentially private interests of those who actually fought in them. The power of sovereigns was limited by the narrow financial margins on which they operated even in rich and intensively governed countries like France and England, constraints which left a large role for private enterprise. It was a world of hierarchy tempered by opinion, of violence fettered by bureaucracy, of law which reflected force without limiting it, of officers and tribunals existing side by side with authorised anarchy. Yet it is perhaps right to remember that although these are major themes of fourteenth-century warfare they are by no means peculiar to the fourteenth century. In Europe they persisted until nation-states acquired the financial resources to assert a monopoly of organised violence. Public war and private business remained inextricably mixed in most European countries until the seventeenth century. Some aspects of the same mentality, such as naval privateering and the purchase of military commissions, survived until well into the nineteenth. In England private companies were still being recruited for the army in the Napoleonic Wars. The modern treatment of prisoners of war as the exclusive responsibility of the state dates from the same period. The first, very limited, Geneva Convention was not drawn up until 1863.

CHAPTER XVI

The Truce of Leulinghem
1389–1396

The three-year truce had been agreed in June 1389 on the understanding that the time would be used to agree the terms of a final peace. However, for more than a year almost nothing happened, chiefly because of the slow pace of decision-making in England. At Westminster the whole issue was exceptionally sensitive. The fate of the ministers and household staff who had conducted Richard II's negotiations with France in 1387 was in everyone's mind. No one dared to agree anything without express Parliamentary approval. There was a long delay while Richard II waited for the return of John of Gaunt from Gascony and another while the issues were considered by a Great Council and then by Parliament. As a result the English negotiating position was not settled until March 1390. It was in substance a development of the line which they had taken at successive conferences in the 1380s. Richard and his ministers wanted the return of as much as possible of the territory in the south-west which had been ceded to them by the treaty of Brétigny. French claims to ultimate sovereignty in Aquitaine were by now resisted only for the sake of form. The English expected to have to concede the point and concentrated on limiting the political, judicial and military obligations associated with French sovereignty. The actual performance of homage was a sensitive issue for Richard, as it had been for previous English kings. He was not prepared to do homage to a king of France in person. Nor was he willing to do military service or to have his decisions challenged before the French King's judges in the Parlement in Paris.

These were difficult questions, both legally and politically. The diplomats returned to the church of Leulinghem in April 1390 but more than two months of negotiations failed to produce agreement on any of them. The solution envisaged by the English was that Richard should hold Aquitaine as a fief of France but that the homage and the services due to Charles VI should be performed on carefully circumscribed conditions by whoever was in actual occupation of it. By this Richard meant John of Gaunt, to whom the duchy had recently been granted. This was not enough for the French. Their ambassadors' instructions were very clear. They were to insist that any territories held by the English King in France would have to be held in return for liege homage. Liege homage, the closest bond of feudal dependence known to the law, implied the full range of obligations owed by a vassal to his lord including military service. The French ambassadors were empowered to make generous territorial concessions in return, but they would not discuss them until the question of homage had been settled. The English ambassadors protested rather disingenuously that this was a new demand and insisted that the issue should be deferred. The French stood their ground. On this unsatisfactory note the proceedings were adjourned at the beginning of July until October and then again until the new year while the English Parliament was summoned to consider the matter.[1]

In England the attempt to replace a temporary truce with a formal peace raised many ghosts and proved to be extremely controversial. Froissart visited England a few years after these events and spoke to many of those involved. He believed that the Duke of Gloucester was the main source of opposition and everything that is known about the Duke's activities in these years bears out this judgment. Gloucester's political defeat in 1389 had diminished his power but it had not altered his views. He loathed the French with an intense loathing. In his dealings with the princes of France he felt overshadowed by their magnificent bearing and disadvantaged by his imperfect command of French. He regarded the whole history of Anglo-French relations since 1368 as a tale of French deceit: tricky diplomacy, dishonest truces, unmanly avoidance of battle. Because the English had not been outfought in the field he could not accept that they had been defeated in the war. So he saw no reason for England to abandon its insistence on all the terms agreed at Brétigny in 1360.[2]

It is difficult to know how much support Gloucester's views enjoyed among his fellow-countrymen. Froissart thought that they were shared by the whole political community outside the King's circle. Like many of his contemporaries in France he put this down to the endemic greed, vanity and sheer love of fighting of the English military class. In the long allegory which Philippe de Mézières addressed to Charles VI in 1389 he pictured Queen Truth preaching the virtues of peace to a gathering of Englishmen. The merchants, townsmen and common people listened appreciatively. But the 'old men-at-arms and archers' whom Philippe called the 'Black Boars' muttered angrily among themselves, neither willing to agree nor daring to dissent. It was a gross over-simplification, like most arresting images. But it is fair to say that a generation of English moralists expressed very similar views about their own countrymen. In his great Latin poem *Vox Clamantis*, the London poet John Gower blamed the persistence of war on the pursuit of fame and booty and savagely satirised a generation of professional soldiers who were indifferent to the suffering of their victims. 'Your tears are laughter in my ears,' they cry from his pages. Richard II's chamber knight Sir John Clanvowe, one of the negotiators of the truce of Leulinghem, with twenty-five years experience of war and diplomacy behind him, would have agreed. He thought that his contemporaries 'held them worshipful that been grete werreyours and fighteres and that distroyen and wynnen manye landis'.[3]

Yet Clanvowe's own career suggests a more ambiguous picture. A deeply spiritual man who wrote poetry and moral tracts, Clanvowe eventually turned against the war and died in Greece in 1391 on his way to expiate his sins in the Holy Land. He was an unusual figure but not by any means unique. Englishmen of his class were touched, although perhaps less profoundly, by the same mood of guilt, pessimism and insecurity, the same fears for the unity of Christendom and for their own salvation which had produced such a strong shift of opinion against the war in France. Lollardy, the spiritual movement inspired by John Wycliffe, had overtly pacifist overtones and made a number of converts among the military nobility including in all probability Clanvowe himself. Even Sir Robert Knolles, perhaps the most feared freebooter of the fourteenth century, performed a pilgrimage to Rome in 1389 'for the quieting of his conscience' and dispersed much of his great fortune in endowing a bridge, a college and an almshouse.

The great majority of the English military nobility no doubt thought about the war in more conventional terms than this. But the truth is that even conventional opinion was divided. Much of the corps of career soldiers among the English nobility were probably instinctive opponents of peace with France. In Cheshire, admittedly an extreme case, military service was a long-standing tradition not only among gentry families but among the rich peasants and small landowners who had supplied archers for service in Wales, Scotland, Ireland and France for more than a century. Peace was a serious threat in this populous county with a mainly pastoral economy offering few other possibilities of employment. The same must have been true of other areas where strong local connections with a particular captain had generated a tradition of war service. Beyond these belligerent enclaves, however, the continental view of England as a pervasively military society was much exaggerated. The financial rewards of fighting were in steep decline. The general experience was that military service was not popular among the gentry of the counties. It is unlikely that more than a quarter of English knights and squires had ever served in France and most of those had fought in just one campaign. In 1387 the Earl of Arundel had had great difficulty recruiting an army of 'good, reputable men' to fight under his command at sea without the usual admixture of London roughs. The gentlemen whom he approached served with overt reluctance. They turned up late for the muster, pleading that they needed to say goodbye to their friends or settle their affairs. Some of them appeared with borrowed equipment. Even among those who served regularly in the armies the balance of profit and loss was highly uncertain and there was little direct correlation between experience of war and opposition to the peace. The Duke of Gloucester was the foremost proponent of the war but he had much less experience of fighting in France than Michael Pole, Simon Burley or indeed John of Gaunt, all of whom had been supporters of the King's peace policy. As the poet Chaucer, who had himself fought in France in the heyday of Edward III, reflected in old age: 'there is full many a man that crieth "War! War!" that woot full little what war amounteth.'[4]

The evidence suggests that by the 1390s most of the English political community wanted peace with France. For more than a decade the Parliamentary Commons had objected to large-scale continental campaigns and refused to fund them from tax revenues. There is no reason to doubt that this reflected the collective sentiment of most of the knightly class who tended to dominate the proceedings of the Commons on issues of this kind. A significant fraction of the Parliamentary peerage had believed for some time that the war was unwinnable and after the debacle of 1388 theirs was probably the majority view. The main obstacle was not the vested interests of the soldiery in continuing the war, still less an endemic love of violence. It arose from political concerns about the terms on which peace was available. Great Councils and Parliaments, although they had experienced lawyers and diplomats among them, rarely understood the exigencies of diplomatic horse-trading or appreciated how limited were the areas in which compromise was possible. There was much distrust of France, even among those English politicians who were in principle for peace. There was a real fear of the wider implications of allowing Richard II to do liege homage for Aquitaine to the King of France. Everyone knew that this had proved an inherently unstable relationship in the past, which had led to the confiscation of the duchy in the reigns of all three Edwards. There was also a pervasive feeling that homage would compromise Richard's autonomy as sovereign in England. Although Richard was not proposing to do homage for England these fears were not irrational. The neat distinction which the lawyers drew between the King's two capacities was in practice hard to draw. The King embodied the state in his person. He could not, for example, make war on France in his capacity as King of England while in his capacity as Duke of Aquitaine he performed his duty to sustain the King of France. Issues such as a vassal's obligation of military or court service were particularly sensitive.

The Duke of Gloucester's skill lay in marrying his own enthusiasm for continuing the war, which was shared by only by a minority of his contemporaries, with other sentiments which were widespread and emotionally powerful: suspicion of the government and of John of Gaunt, concerns about England's autonomy in a post-war world, ignorance of the alternatives. Gloucester had some significant allies among the Parliamentary peerage including his old colleague the Earl of Arundel, the chief of the 'Black Boars' according to Philippe de Mézières; perhaps the Earl of Warwick as well; and some magnates and professional captains of like mind who could not bring themselves to acknowledge the finality of defeat. Their mixture of aggressive patriotism, nostalgia for past glories and appeals to English independence of a foreign power struck a chord among the population at large, especially in London where visceral hatred of France was still strong. Gloucester did not challenge the peace programme directly. He could see that that was hopeless while it was so strongly supported by the King and the Duke of Lancaster. But he sniped at it from a distance. He looked with suspicion at every embassy's instructions. When the ambassadors returned he raised countless detailed objections to the proposals they brought back with them. And he rallied the opposition at the successive assemblies at which Richard II and his ministers sought to build up support for their foreign policy.

In the meantime relations between the two countries were complicated by a sudden revival of France's old imperial ambitions in Italy. Traditionally French policy in the peninsula had been driven by their support for the Angevin claims to the kingdom of Naples and their championship of the Avignon papacy, two axioms of French foreign policy which were closely linked. At the time of the truce of Leulinghem both depended on a twelve-year-old boy, Louis II of Anjou. Louis was destined to pass his entire life as the symbol of France's broken dream of becoming the dominant power in Italy. He was the elder son of the great Duke of Anjou who had died in 1384 trying to expel the Hungarian usurper Charles of Durazzo from the kingdom of Naples. In 1389 the situation in the southern kingdom was complicated and delicate. Louis was formally recognised by the French King and the Avignon Pope Clement VII as King of Naples but was living in exile at Avignon with a diminutive court dominated by his formidable mother Marie of Blois. In southern Italy his partisans maintained a tenuous and insecure hold on most of the city of Naples with the aid of a small army of German and Gascon mercenaries financed from the coffers of the papal chamber. Charles of Durazzo was dead. His cause was sustained by his widow Margaret, who ruled from the city of Gaeta as regent for another boy-king, the young Ladislas of Durazzo. Their supporters still clung on to the two principal fortresses of the capital, the Castel Nuovo and the Castel Sant'Elmo, and their officials controlled most of the rest of the kingdom. In Avignon Clement VII and Marie of Blois desperately looked about for a way of sending Louis II back to his kingdom with an army that would enable him to consolidate his hold on Naples and push his power outwards into the hinterland. For Marie it represented the last chance of vindicating the claims of her family. For Clement the position was even more critical. As long as his Roman rival held Italy there was no prospect of dislodging him from the papal throne. The House of Anjou was his only significant ally in the peninsula. For years the pleas of Clement and Marie had fallen on deaf ears in Paris. Charles VI's uncles were content to pay lip-service to Louis II's cause. They had very little interest in installing him on the Neapolitan throne. Between them they had persistently vetoed Marie of Blois's appeals for funds.

The dismissal of the Dukes of Berry and Burgundy in November 1388 led to a radical reorientation of French foreign policy away from northern Europe, which had been Philip's preoccupation, towards Italy. No longer inhibited by the enormous presence of his uncles, Charles was able to indulge his affection for his cousin Louis of Anjou and his instinct for the grand gesture. Early in 1389 he presided over a meeting of his Council which resolved to support Louis II's return to Naples with a subsidy of 300,000 florins. Another 300,000 florins was promised by Clement VII from the revenues of the French Church and more than 200,000 from the Angevin domains in France and Provence. The letter in which Charles announced the change of policy to the Neapolitans blamed his former coolness towards them on his uncles. Read out in the cathedral immediately after the annual miracle of the liquefaction of the blood of St. Januarius, it provoked tremendous enthusiasm among the fickle crowd.[5] But this was not the limit of the French King's ambitions. Over the following months his plans for the reconquest of the Angevin kingdom of Naples were subsumed in a vaster design involving nothing less than the establishment of the French royal house as the dominant power throughout the Italian peninsula.

The prime mover in this enterprise was the King's younger brother Louis, Duke of Touraine, a man destined to become one of the pivotal figures in French politics over the next two decades. In 1389 Louis was a slightly built, precocious young man of seventeen. Orphaned as small children, the two brothers had been brought up together by the officers of their common household under the distant tutelage of their uncles. Louis, by convention the first man in the kingdom after the King and the senior member of his Council, had suffered for eight years the same frustrating combination of high status and practical impotence as Charles himself. The experience created a lifelong bond between them. Yet they emerged from it as very different personalities. Both men shared the conventional social and religious pieties of their age and the skills and graces deemed fitting for a prince. Both were extrovert and self-indulgent, persistent gamers and womanisers. But Louis was already emerging as a politician of exceptional ability and ambition, politically astute, calculating, highly intelligent and articulate in company, with an outstanding memory and great powers of concentration. He was perennially short of money. He had been granted the small duchy of Touraine in the Loire valley on terms that it was all that he would ever receive from the royal demesne. It yielded little more than the cost of its administration. Like the Duke of Gloucester in England, Louis was constantly reminded of the contrast between his high birth and his poor endowment in a society in which land and riches were the main source of status and political power. His position was particularly painful by comparison with the splendid state of his uncles with their rich appanages and their tendency to patronise the younger princes about them.[6]

In January 1387 Louis had been betrothed to his fourteen-year-old cousin Valentine, the daughter of Gian Galeazzo Visconti, despot of Milan. Her father had recently seized power in Milan by overthrowing and then murdering his uncle, Bernabò, a coup which resounded across

Europe and won for its author the richest principality of Italy, embracing most of the basin of the River Po and the Lombard plain. Louis's betrothal brought him fine prospects: a large cash dowry, the county of Vertus in Champagne, which had belonged to the Milanese dynasty, the Italian principality of Asti on the marches of Lombardy and Piedmont, and the alliance of the most powerful prince in the peninsula. These advantages became progressively more valuable as Gian Galeazzo embarked on a series of wars of conquest in northern Italy which brought his power to the marches of Florence and Venice and threatened the northern cities of the papal state. But the alliance between Louis of Touraine and the despot of Milan also set up considerable tensions at the French court. The murdered Bernabò had influential kinsmen in France, including the Queen, Isabelle of Bavaria, who was his grand-daughter; and John III, Count of Armagnac, whose sister was married to one of his sons. These considerations, and perhaps also a budding jealousy, may explain why the Dukes of Berry and Burgundy delayed the ratification of Louis's marriage contract for nearly two years. One of Louis's first acts after his brother assumed power was to execute the document and send it urgently to Milan. Valentine arrived in France, laden with jewels and cash, in August 1389. The marriage was celebrated at Melun in the same month.[7]

Two weeks after his marriage Louis of Touraine accompanied his brother on his state visit to Avignon and Languedoc. On 1 November the brothers were present in the chapel of the papal palace when Louis of Anjou was crowned King of Naples. In the secret sessions with the Pope and the cardinals which followed the French King unveiled his plan to conquer central and southern Italy. A great French army would cross the Alps to enter the peninsula by the north, led by the King in person and accompanied by the Pope. There they would join forces with Gian Galeazzo and march on Rome, forcibly installing Clement VII on the throne of St. Peter. The French King was not of course proposing to undertake such an enormous enterprise without tangible rewards for the French royal house and its allies. According to information which reached Rome much later, after the secret was out, the plan was that Charles VI should be crowned by Clement as Holy Roman Emperor in the basilica of St. Peter. Gian Galeazzo Visconti, who had given private undertakings to switch his allegiance to the Avignon Pope, would be rewarded with a new north Italian kingdom extending from the Alps to the Apennines. Louis of Touraine's own reward can be inferred with reasonable certainty. Clement VII had already dangled before Louis's agents the prospect of a principality built around the Adriatic towns of Rimini and Pesaro and a group of cities in eastern Emilia, provided that he could conquer them from his rival. The French, however, aimed higher than that. They saw these places as the germ of the 'Kingdom of Adria', which Clement had once promised to create for the Duke of Anjou and might surely be induced to confer on Louis of Touraine. Precisely what territory would be comprised in the new kingdom was a delicate question but there is a good deal of evidence that Charles hoped to carve a rich principality for his brother out of the eastern and northern marches of the papal state, including the cities of Bologna, Ferrara, Perugia, Ravenna and Todi.[8]

Over the following months the French government made a serious attempt to put these plans into effect. Louis II of Anjou sailed from Marseille in July 1390, urged on his way by processions in the streets of Avignon and blessings pronounced by a cardinal-legate from the deck of his flagship. On 6 August his fleet of some forty galleys and sailing ships entered the Bay of Naples. The first results were highly satisfactory. A large number of troops was recruited from Angevin loyalists in the capital. In October the Castel Sant'Elmo was recaptured from the garrison of Margaret of Durazzo followed, some weeks afterwards, by the Castel Nuovo. In Paris, shortly after Christmas, an enlarged meeting of the King's Council agreed upon the final arrangements for the march on Rome. The King and his brother and the Dukes of Burgundy and Berry would all participate. The French army would assemble at Lyon by 15 March 1391 at least 12,000 strong. Pope Clement was expected to contribute another 1,500 mercenaries and Gian Galeazzo a further 1,000. Since every man-at-arms was required to bring two fighting attendants this implied a total strength of nearly 20,000 mounted men. After the Council Louis of Touraine left at once for Italy, accompanied by the Duke of Burgundy and the Admiral, Jean de Vienne, to confer with his father-in-law in Milan.[9]

The whole Italian adventure depended critically on English acquiescence, which proved to be its undoing. There could be no question of leaving France exposed to invasion from across the Channel while its government and most of its chivalry were far away in Italy. Charles VI and his ministers had made their plans on the assumption that there would be a peace treaty with England by the time that the army of Italy was ready. By the autumn of 1390 the slow progress of negotiations made this assumption highly questionable. So the King of

France and his brother made their own attempt to break the deadlock. Richard II's tournament at Smithfield was due to open in October. Waleran de Luxembourg, Count of Saint-Pol, one of the small group of French councillors concerned with negotiations with England, was a famous jouster, close to the Marmouset ministers in France and well-liked in England. He had obtained a safe-conduct to come to London accompanied by no fewer than 200 horsemen. Charles VI and Louis transformed Saint-Pol's visit into an official mission. They sent him on his way with a company that included the King's private secretary, Yves Derrien, and one of his heralds as well as a fine jousting horse and two teams of minstrels to ensure that he made a suitably impressive show. It was symptomatic of the growing preference of both courts for a more intimate, less formal style of diplomacy than had been customary before the recent truce. Charles empowered Saint-Pol and Derrien to put a new proposal before the English King and his Council. South of the Dordogne the French government was willing to restore all the provinces ceded at Brétigny except for southern Quercy. North of the river they offered Périgord, southern Saintonge and the county of Angoulême. In addition there would be a cash indemnity of 1,200,000 francs for the regions which they proposed to retain. In terms of territory this was the most generous French offer to date. Even the francophobe chronicler of St. Albans was impressed. Charles also gave Saint-Pol a letter for Richard proposing a summit meeting between the two kings on the march of Calais. This idea had been proposed before, in 1387. It was much in favour among those who believed, like Philippe de Mézières, that only the two young kings could slough off the accumulated legacy of old resentments and suspicions which was obstructing the negotiations between their councillors. Saint-Pol stayed in England for several weeks after the tournament had closed. By the time he left it seems to have been agreed that the conference between the two kings would be held on the march of Calais at Candlemas, 2 February 1391.[10]

When Saint-Pol returned to France in early December he was accompanied by an English embassy led by Sir Thomas Percy. Percy was well known at the court of France and had many friends there. His instructions were to obtain further details of the French offer and to finalise the arrangements for the summit meeting. The discussions were extremely affable. The French, as their negotiators candidly observed, were not strong enough to defeat England, while England was manifestly unable to defeat France. To prolong the stalemate could serve no purpose other than to impoverish both countries. Reports reaching Avignon suggested that there were high hopes of a final peace in February, in time for the French King to depart for Italy in the following month.[11]

This was a serious miscalculation. Richard II's ministers appear to have known nothing about Charles VI's Italian adventure until a very late stage. When they discovered they were dismayed. French domination of Italy would be a serious blow to English interests. It would bring about a radical shift in the European balance of power in France's favour. At a time when the Popes remained a major diplomatic force in European affairs it would oblige future English governments to deal with a papal court which was beholden to France. Besides, although this was a minor factor in the broader scheme of things, the English were no friends of Gian Galeazzo Visconti. They regarded him as an ally of France. Indeed, they had given asylum and pensions to two of the sons of Bernabò who were then living in exile in London. So, when the French plans became known at Westminster early in 1391, the Candlemas conference was abruptly put off. Fresh instructions were urgently sent to Percy in Paris. He was told to protest against the planned invasion of Italy, which Richard's ministers professed to regard as a breach of the truce, and to propose that the summit meeting should be put off to midsummer. The postponement of the meeting necessarily involved suspending the Italian campaign, as the English knew. There was no alternative unless the meeting of the two kings was indefinitely postponed or the command of the army of Italy delegated to some less exalted personage. Postponing the summit would have undermined the policy of peace and low taxation on which ultimately the government of the Marmousets depended. The possibility of appointing another commander seems never to have been seriously entertained. It would probably have been impossible to recruit allies in Italy or an army of the necessary strength without the draw of the King's presence.

Forced to choose, Charles VI's Council quickly came to the conclusion that peace with England was a higher priority. They heard Percy out and then deputed the Duke of Bourbon to negotiate with him. On 24 February 1391 an agreement was drawn up. Charles VI and Richard II would meet on the Calais march on midsummer day, 24 June 1391. Nothing was said in the document about Italy. But the implications did not need to be spelled out. At the end of February 1391 a messenger was despatched urgently to Avignon with the news that owing to the overriding importance of making peace with England the Italian campaign would not after all take place. Ostensibly it was no more than a postponement. In fact within three months Charles abandoned the projected campaign altogether. France's Italian dreams were henceforth to be left to Louis of Touraine to pursue for himself.[12]

Judging by the gifts heaped on him before he left Paris Sir Thomas Percy had accomplished his difficult mission with great skill. Yet the ease with which it was accomplished suggests that other factors were at work in addition to pressure from England. The situation in Italy was much less favourable to France's ambitions than it had been when the projected invasion was first conceived. Urban VI had died in Rome in October 1389. Two weeks later the cardinals of the Roman obedience had elected as his successor Pietro Tomacelli, who took the name Boniface IX. The new Pope was very different from his predecessor. He was an aristocratic Neapolitan prelate in his mid-thirties, tall and imposing with a gracious manner, who proved to be an adept politician. Within a short time he had undone most of the mistakes of the rebarbative Urban. He repaired relations with the cardinals, conciliated the populace of Rome, re-established control over the disaffected cities of the papal state and made his peace with the house of Durazzo. As a result the Roman papacy was a far more formidable opponent of French interests in the peninsula in 1391 than it had been two years earlier. At the same time the city of Florence was building up a powerful coalition against Gian Galeazzo along the despot's southern borders. It is not clear how much of this was known in France but, given their regular diplomatic contacts with Milan, Florence and Naples, Charles VI's ministers must have known a fair amount. Some of them must already have had their misgivings about the planned invasion. The absence in Lombardy of its chief advocate and beneficiary, Louis of Touraine, no doubt made these men bolder. The whole project had been lightly undertaken and pursued with very little by way of advance planning or political forethought. Only an excuse was required to bring about the immediate cancellation of the whole enterprise.

The excuse was supplied by the mounting domestic difficulties which the Italian project provoked within France. There were too many people with an interest in making trouble in the King's absence. The Duke of Brittany, John de Montfort, was ostensibly committed to joining the expedition. Charles VI had insisted on this. But Montfort's relations with a government dominated by Olivier de Clisson were inevitably strained and he was openly contemptuous of the whole venture. When it came to the point he showed no sign of participating, and in the autumn of 1390 he took advantage of the government's preoccupations to strike out against his enemies in Brittany. The most serious incident was the seizure of the major fortress of Champtoceaux on the Loire from Olivier de Clisson, which provoked howls of anger in Paris. Difficult and ultimately inconclusive negotiations with John de Montfort were in progress throughout the first three months of 1391. He was ultimately pressured into surrendering the place to the Duke of Bourbon as stakeholder. But the growing signs of a revival of the old vendettas in Brittany raised all the old concerns about John's links with England, and must have undermined the Constable's enthusiasm for a campaign that would take him a thousand miles from home.[13]

Another recalcitrant, John III, Count of Armagnac, was causing even greater concern, not least because he and his brother Bernard were close to the Duke of Brittany. They were in the last stages of negotiating a political alliance providing for mutual military assistance against 'all their enemies and any others who may seek to injure or dishonour them'. Charles VI's ministers almost certainly knew about this. They may also have known that Armagnac was being actively courted by Richard II's representatives in Bordeaux with a view to a possible change of allegiance. These acts were symptomatic of the Count of Armagnac's progressive estrangement from the government of the Marmousets after the fall of his patron, the Duke of Berry. Armagnac's kinship with the heirs of Bernabò Visconti had inspired in his breast a deep loathing of Gian Galeazzo and a visceral hostility to his allies in France. But he was not content with simply withholding his support. In October 1390, after prolonged negotiations, he agreed to enter the service of the city of Florence, which was then at war with the despot of Milan. He undertook to furnish the city with 2,000 men-at-arms and 3,000 mounted infantry, most of whom would be recruited from the *routier* companies of southern France and Provence. As matters stood these men would have found themselves fighting in Italy on the opposite side to the King of France. In February 1391 the Count of Armagnac was at Avignon with a large and unruly army of mercenaries arguing with the Duke of Berry, who had been sent from the court of France to dissuade him. Some of Armagnac's Breton companies were bought off by the French government. Another Gascon captain, the ageing Bernard de la Salle, was put up to ambush Armagnac in the Alpine passes, an adventure that cost him his company and his life. In the event Armagnac's was the only French army to fight in Italy in 1391. The Count descended on the Lombard plain from the Susa pass in June. Within six weeks most of his men were dead, slaughtered by the

Milanese army at the disastrous battle before the Lombard fortress of Alexandria. Armagnac himself died of heat-stroke as he tried to escape by swimming across a stream.[14]

The midsummer meeting of the kings of England and France never happened. The reasons are obscure but it is clear that the problems, whatever they were, lay mainly on the English side. In April 1391 a Great Council met at Westminster. According to the chronicle of Westminster Abbey there was 'much consideration and debate about alternative solutions'. It soon became apparent that the goodwill between the two courts was not shared by the wider political community in England. The magnates at Westminster expressed misgivings about the size of the French King's military escort. They were suspicious of French trickery. Might they not surprise Calais or the outlying forts if negotiations failed? The main concern of the magnates, however, was about the loss of control involved in allowing Richard to agree a final peace with only a handful of intimate advisers at his side. They feared that the King would commit them to an unwelcome peace and then present it to them as a *fait accompli*. This had of course been the object of the exercise, but the magnates were not having it. They wanted as much as possible of the treaty worked out between the diplomats with limited authority before the meeting so that they could consider it for themselves before anything was irrevocably agreed.[15]

Preparations had already been put in hand for the summit meeting. Immense sums, equivalent to the cost of a minor military campaign, were paid out to the King's uncles and courtiers to enable them to appear splendidly accoutred and escorted in the wastes of the Calais marshes. But a preliminary conference on the march of Picardy failed to resolve the magnates' concerns about direct negotiations between the two kings. Several months were consumed in fruitless shuttlecock diplomacy between Westminster and Paris. In September 1391, with less than a year to go before the truce expired, Richard gave in to his domestic critics. A new French embassy came before him at the royal manor of Eltham, led by the elderly veteran Pierre le Bègue de Villaines. They agreed to put off the summit meeting until after the terms of peace had been substantially agreed by others. The Duke of Lancaster would lead a particularly grand embassy to France the following March to negotiate with Charles VI in person. The English King's personal role would be confined to resolving minor outstanding points at the end of the process.[16]

John of Gaunt was by now a confirmed advocate of peace. A treaty would secure his gains in the Iberian peninsula. It would represent his only chance of becoming the independent ruler of an enlarged principality of Aquitaine after the manner of his famous brother the Black Prince. The continuation of the war would undermine his treaty with John of Trastámara and threaten the position of his daughter, who had recently become Queen of Castile. But self-interest is unlikely to have been Gaunt's only motive or even his main one. All that we know about his views suggests that he thought that the war was no longer in England's interest and no longer within its means. When the plan for a fresh diplomatic conference was reported to Parliament in November the Lords were enthusiastic. Gaunt, they said, was 'the most sufficient man in the realm' for such a task. But however 'sufficient' and however committed personally, the very fact of Gaunt's appointment meant that his powers could be limited in a way that Richard's would not have been if he had negotiated personally. The ultimate power of decision was reserved to a larger body, a Great Council or the Lords in Parliament, who had very mixed feelings about the negotiations. It was necessary to contemplate the disagreeable possibility that the truce might expire before agreement on terms of peace had been reached. The Commons granted Richard half of a tenth and fifteenth to cover the cost of the summit meeting if Gaunt's efforts succeeded. But they also granted a further tenth and fifteenth for war purposes if it did not.[17]

The English negotiating line was settled in the course of a long and argumentative Great Council at Westminster. It extended over five days from 12 to 16 February 1392. The King presided. All three of his uncles attended. The English demands as they emerged were probably more aggressive than Richard would have wished. They included the return of the whole of the territory ceded to England at Brétigny, except for the county of Ponthieu, and the payment of all the arrears of John II's ransom. The English ambassadors were authorised to concede that Poitou, which was part of the Duke of Berry's appanage, should remain his for life. But they were to insist that the province, the richest part of the Black Prince's empire, should revert to Richard or his heirs after the Duke's death. The major issue as always was the legal status of these territories. The Council was ready to make large concessions. They empowered the ambassadors to agree to French sovereignty over all the English territories in France. The Duke of Gloucester fought a solitary battle to exclude Calais from this concession but ultimately agreed that even this might be conceded. The new subsidies meant, when the clerical subsidy and a contribution from the wool duties was added, that Gaunt could confront the French King with a potential war chest of between £80,000 and £100,000 if the peace talks failed. Plans were put in hand for a major military campaign on the continent. Surveys were ordered of shipping and manpower. Preliminary arrangements were made to array men-at-arms and archers for service in France. Richard declared his intention of taking command in person.[18]

The long-awaited conference opened at Amiens on 25 March 1392 with a carefully choreographed ceremony. Charles VI entered the city by the Paris gate, south of the cathedral, riding side by side with Leo of Armenia. They were preceded through the gate by a corps of mounted archers, a long column of squires, some 2,000 knights, then heralds and musicians, the liveried bodyguard of the King riding two abreast and the military officers of the Crown. Behind them came the King's uncles, his brother and cousins, a great crowd of noblemen and twenty-two prelates, all with their own large and clattering escorts. Philip de Mézières, a long-standing critic of diplomatic conferences, had been particularly harsh about these 'Gallic pomps', and the English had affected an ostentatious contempt for them ever since the first conference at Bruges seventeen years before. John of Gaunt arrived in the city shortly after the French court, accompanied by his brother Edmund Langley, Duke of York, the veteran diplomat Walter Skirlaw, Bishop of Durham, and John Holand, Richard's half-brother and now Earl of Huntingdon. They had an impressive suite of their own, more than a thousand strong, but they made no attempt to match the magnificence of their hosts. They presented themselves before Charles VI and his court in the hall of the bishop's palace still in their travelling gear.[19]

The ambassadors got down to business on the following day in the more intimate surroundings of the Malmaison, the building used for meetings of the town council. It was, by an irony of which the participants were probably unaware, the house in which Edward III had stayed when he came to Amiens to do homage to Philip VI in 1329. After four days of negotiation the two sides agreed to exchange documents recording their current negotiating position. The English document was broadly in line with what had been agreed at the Great Council at Westminster. The French document was substantially based on the offer made by the Count of Saint-Pol in the autumn of 1390. The differences between the two related to Calais, Poitou and the vexed question of tenure. The French wanted Calais surrendered or demolished and insisted on retaining Poitou. Tenure was to be by liege homage. Nothing less would do. They proposed, according to an English chronicler, that any difficulties associated with this should be resolved by separating the duchy from the English Crown and ceding it to John of Gaunt and his heirs in perpetuity. All of this suggested there had been no movement by either side in the course of the conference and indeed virtually no movement for the past eighteen months. John of Gaunt's problem was that he was constrained by his instructions. The French King, who was there in person with his Council, had a freer hand but saw no reason to make concessions when none were forthcoming from John of Gaunt. Privately the Dukes of Berry and Burgundy assured Gaunt that the French document was not their last word on the subject. Further concessions might be made if Gaunt's own powers were enlarged. The Duke of Lancaster rather reluctantly agreed on that basis to put the latest French offer before the English King. The rest of the conference was given over to discussion about the next stage. It was agreed that the ambassadors of each side would meet again at Leulinghem on 1 July 1392 to consider the English response. In the meantime the truce was extended by a little over a year until 29 September 1393.[20]

In spite of the lack of agreement the conference at Amiens was an important milestone. At a personal level it established a large measure of trust between the closest kinsmen and advisers of the two kings. They were grand enough to dispense with the stilted formality which had divided less exalted diplomats at previous conferences. In France the goodwill generated by the conference continued for long after it had closed. An influential element in Charles's Council favoured substantial further concessions to the English. Jean Gerson spoke for these men when, in one of his earliest sermons before the royal court (delivered about two months after the conference), he urged the King to accept some of the English demands, however exorbitant. Peace had no price, he declared. 'Glory in these losses for they will bring you lasting peace.'[21]

This attitude reflected a shared sense of insecurity provoked by the wider problems of Christendom, an intangible but increasingly significant factor in the relations of England and France. The truce of Leulinghem had been followed by a remarkable upsurge of popular enthusiasm for the crusade after a century in which the crusading spirit had been moribund in most of western Europe. In 1390 the Duke of Bourbon had organised an expedition with Genoese naval support against the port of Mahdia, a notorious lair of pirates in the Hafsid kingdom of Tunis, 'which port is known as Africa' said Froissart with his customary indifference to geography. This extraordinary venture attracted some 1,500 noble volunteers. The expedition was overwhelmingly French but included a small number of Englishmen, among them Sir William Neville, Sir John Clanvowe and the illegitimate sons of John of Gaunt and Sir Thomas Percy, all of them men close to Richard II's court. The expedition ended in heavy casualties and a humiliating retreat but the outcome did nothing to deter others. English and French noblemen left to join the twice-yearly campaigns of the Teutonic Knights in Poland and Lithuania in the last period when these murderous *Reisen* could be called crusades. Henry Bolingbroke, Earl of Derby, left for Prussia in July 1390 with more than a hundred companions. The Duke of Gloucester would have fought in Prussia in the winter of 1391–2 if his fleet had not been partially destroyed by a gale and driven back to the coast of Northumberland. Jean de Boucicaut went at the end of the year. While the princes debated peace at Amiens Thomas, Lord Despenser, was fighting on the Prussian march, accompanied by prominent English captains whose combined retinues must have numbered several hundred men. To some extent these men were seeking an escape from boredom and an outlet for aggressive energy which was no longer satisfied by war on the marches. But there was an important and genuine spiritual element which transcended nationality and inspired a new solidarity between the chivalry of England and France.[22]

The Barbary crusade and the Prussian campaigns were comparatively minor enterprises by comparison with the ancient dream of driving back the Turks and liberating the Holy Land. The advance of Islam in the Balkans provoked much anguish in France and to some extent in England also. A succession of offensives in the 1380s had brought the Ottoman Turks to the marches of Hungary and the shores of the Adriatic. In 1389 Sultan Murad had destroyed the Christian empire of Serbia on the battlefield of Kossovo. These were not the remote regions which they later became. Hungary was ruled by a French dynasty. The coastal settlements of Albania and Croatia were for practical purposes colonies of Venice. In the course of the 1390s the crusading dream briefly recovered something of its lost status as a universal western ideal. At the close of the conference at Amiens Charles VI had raised with John of Gaunt the possibility of an international crusade into the Balkans. There is no doubt that both men took the project seriously. Philippe de Mézières's Order of the Passion, conceived many years before as a crusading order which would unite England and France against the Infidel, was at last drawing real recruits. All the royal princes at Amiens on both sides would become members or patrons of the order, together with many of the lay delegates, ministers and captains who had been present at the conference. More than eighty noblemen joined the order or were persuaded to support it. A majority were French but twenty-eight were English.[23]

The generosity of spirit reflected in Gerson's sermon struck a strong chord at the court of Richard II but it generated intense scepticism in the English provinces. On 25 May 1392 John of Gaunt presented the French terms to a Great Council in the Lincolnshire town of Stamford. Unusually, the bishops had not been summoned to this gathering. In addition to the lay peerage, there were knights from the shires and a large number of experienced captains. The result was a rather military assembly in which professional soldiers or those who hoped to become professional soldiers were probably over-represented. The Duke of Lancaster described the territorial concessions that the French were willing to make. He raised the issue of homage and suggested it could be dealt with by a perpetual grant of the duchy of Aquitaine to himself. He had hardly finished his account of the proposals before the opposition made itself heard. The tone was set by the Duke of Guelders, who had recently arrived in England and was present with the King. The Duke had lost none of his visceral resentment of the French. He took the opportunity to deliver a fierce harangue against the proposals. The assembly, he said, ought to reject any treaty whatever with 'those bombastic deceivers'. He would be the first to join the fight if Richard should take it up again. His words, according to the Westminster chronicler, were applauded by 'men of mettle and courage' and disparaged by 'the indolent and chicken-hearted'. It is clear, however, that both groups were extremely critical of the terms. Opposition was particularly strong among the knights. They objected to the idea of separating Aquitaine from the English Crown by granting it to John of Gaunt and his descendants. The loss of the whole hereditary domain of the kings of England in France seemed to them to be too high a price to pay to resolve the argument about homage. There was also a more general suspicion of France and of John of Gaunt, who appeared to have used his position as England's chief negotiator to serve his own interests as Duke of Aquitaine. At the conclusion of the proceedings the Duke of Gloucester declared, to a general murmur of approval, that there could be no question of agreeing to such proposals until they had been put before Parliament. The whole occasion had been badly mismanaged. For Richard and John of Gaunt it was the worst possible outcome. Politically they needed a consensus in support of any treaty. Since it was clear that the French would not be shifted on the question of liege homage some way had to be found of making that acceptable to English political opinion. That would take time and the next diplomatic conference was due to open in less than six weeks.[24]

The conference opened at Leulinghem in July 1392. The whole session was taken up with a tactical dispute about which side should disclose its hand first. The French delegation were strictly instructed to make no new offer of its own until it had received a considered response to the offer made at Amiens. The English replied that although they were empowered to modify some of the positions taken up by John of Gaunt at Amiens, the current French offer did not deserve serious attention. They were equally strictly instructed to say nothing until they had received a better one. In order to break logjams like this each government had agreed to confide more informal and flexible instructions to one of their ambassadors who could be counted on to know his sovereign's real wishes. Unfortunately Guillaume de Melun, who was the ambassador charged with this function on the French side, was delayed on the road. As a result Sir Thomas Percy, who had been charged with the same function by Richard II, left in high dudgeon before his arrival. Both delegations recognised the absurdity of the situation. The English offered to tell their opponents what concessions they would be in a position to make if they got a better offer. The French were unmoved. The obvious solution, they suggested, was for the two kings to negotiate personally when none of these problems would arise. The English agreed but pointed to the political difficulties in their own country. They would work on it, they said, but nothing should be said in the formal record for fear of infuriating 'certain members' of Richard's Council.[25]

Guillaume de Melun's presence would probably have made no difference. The main reason for the French ambassadors' reticence at Leulinghem was that their government was in the throes of an unforeseen political crisis which had paralysed decision-making in the French capital. On the night of 13 June 1392 an attempt was made to assassinate Olivier de Clisson. It happened in the Rue Saint-Pol in Paris, a narrow road which ran beneath the west wall of the royal palace. The Constable had been attending the festivities in the palace to mark the feast of Corpus Christi. Shortly after midnight he was making his way home on horseback, accompanied by a small group of friends and two servants with burning torches. A band of armed men sprang from a side-street shouting 'Kill them! Death to Clisson!' They seized the torches from the servants' hands, threw them to the ground and fell on the Constable. Clisson's companions fled while he tried to fend off his assailants with a dagger, the only weapon he had. He suffered three sword gashes to his legs before a heavy blow to his head propelled him from his horse into the open doorway of a baker's shop. The attackers, who believed that they had killed him, made off. In fact Clisson had suffered only superficial wounds and within a short time he had completely recovered. Moreover he had recognised the leader of the gang as Pierre de Craon, a violent and quarrelsome nobleman from Anjou who had recently been banished from court as a result of an obscure scandal.[26]

The attack on the Constable provoked a hysterical response. Charles VI arrived at the scene of the attack within a few minutes accompanied by a crowd of servants, courtiers and soldiers. The King, who had always been close to Olivier de Clisson, regarded the incident as a slight to his Crown. The victim was the highest officer of his court. The attack had occurred within a few yards of his palace only minutes after Clisson had left his presence. As soon as dawn broke the Provost of the Châtelet was sent in pursuit of the attackers with a troop of armed men. Pierre de Craon had ridden through the night to Chartres, where his servants were waiting with fresh horses, and then found his way to his fortress of Sablé in Maine. It was here that he learned that the Constable had survived the attack. Realising that the King's officers would soon be after him he fled to Brittany and threw himself on the protection of the Duke. John de Montfort had better sense than to offer asylum to such a dangerous guest. So Craon made for the English fortress of Brest and boarded a ship. There were rumours that he had taken refuge in England. Letters were addressed to the Duke of Brittany and the King of England demanding the surrender of the fugitive. In Paris Craon was summarily condemned in his absence and his property confiscated. His Paris house and a suburban mansion belonging to him were razed to the ground. The Admiral of France was sent to Maine to seize his estates and drive his wife and daughter from their home. Three of his accomplices had their hands cut off at the scene of the crime before being beheaded at Les Halles. They were followed a few days later by the aged porter of his house who appeared to have committed no crime at all other than failing to detect and denounce his master in time. Then, in early July, Pierre de Craon appeared in Barcelona and took passage for the Levant. By now, however, the news of his crime had reached the court of Aragon. A few hours out from the port he was taken off his ship by four galleys sent in pursuit by the French Queen of Aragon and brought back to the city, where he was thrown in prison to await the pleasure of the King of France.[27]

In Paris the fate of Craon himself had by now receded into the background. Charles VI's ministers had seen the chance to turn the King's rage against a more significant target, John de Montfort. So far as is known the Duke of Brittany had had nothing to do with the plot, but it proved difficult to persuade the Constable of that. The long-standing vendetta between the two rivals for control of Brittany had by now reached a fresh peak of intensity. After two childless marriages John de Montfort had married Charles of Navarre's daughter Joan. She had recently given birth to a son, the first of eight children born to the couple. The birth of the future John V of Brittany lifted the threat that the duchy would pass to Clisson's son-in-law John of Penthièvre and assured the permanence of the dynasty so far as any fragile infant life could do so in the unhealthy conditions of the fourteenth century. It also meant that Clisson's ambitions could be achieved only by deploying the power of the Crown against the Duke of Brittany. The Constable's public reconciliation with his rival, engineered by the Dukes of Burgundy and Berry in 1388, had never been more than skin-deep on either side. Relations between them progressively deteriorated until by the summer of 1391 open war had broken out in Brittany between their Breton partisans.[28]

For the French King's Council there were wider issues than the dispute between two jealous and obstinate men. John de Montfort's relations with the French royal government had become increasingly tense as the struggle between England and France seemed to be coming to an end. In the new world of international peace John would need a constitutional settlement with France. Old bones of contention were being dug up: the form of the Duke's homage to the King and of his vassals' homage to him, the control of crucial border fortresses, the Duke's exercise of regalian rights to coin money and nominate bishops, the perennial irritants of Breton appeals to the Parlement of Paris and the incursions of French officials in the duchy's affairs. With the Dukes of Burgundy and Berry, his traditional patrons, out of power, the King's government dominated by his chief enemy and Richard II showing no interest in England's traditional role as guarantor of Brittany's territorial integrity, John de Montfort had very little to bargain with. In January 1392 there had been a difficult meeting between Charles VI and the Duke in the Loire city of Tours, followed by an agreement which satisfied neither of them. The Duke promised yet again to make peace with his domestic enemies. Agreement was reached, largely on John's terms, on some of the more difficult constitutional questions. A marriage was negotiated between John's infant son and the King's one-year-old daughter Jeanne. But the discussions were disagreeable and the atmosphere tense. When all was done, John de Montfort executed a private deed before a notary declaring that his own concessions had been forced on him by threats. None of Charles's ministers regarded the issues as closed. When John de Montfort wrote to the King protesting that Pierre de Craon had not received his protection and was no longer in Brittany, Charles VI and his brother were at first inclined to believe him but the Council were adamant that Craon would never have attempted such a bold stroke against the King without the support of the Duke of Brittany. Charles, angry and easily led, was persuaded. It became an obsession in the inner counsels of the King that John de Montfort should be punished for Craon's crime.[29]

The King's Council met in Paris at about the beginning of July 1392 to decide what to do. The proceedings were dominated by the Constable and by the two leading figures of the administration, Bureau de la Rivière and Jean le Mercier. All three of them were determined that the King should lead an army into Brittany to avenge the injury done to his honour by John de Montfort. To fund the substantial cost of war wages Clisson undertook to lend the government at least 80,000 francs in cash from his own resources. The King and his brother were already won over to the plan. So were the Constable's allies and the Marmousets' many protégés in the royal administration. The only voice urging caution was that of the Duke of Bourbon. He thought that the decision was a mistake. The case against John de Montfort seemed contrived. The attack was out of all proportion to the offence. The whole affair owed too much to the private rancours of Olivier de Clisson. 'The Duke of Brittany is a great lord,' Bourbon urged, 'he might yet do you good service.' But Charles would brook no dissent.

Contemporaries were shocked. There was no precedent for embarking on a major campaign by the fiat of the King and his ministers alone. It looked like a partisan decision, a conscious rejection of the show of deliberation and consensus which had always lent legitimacy to such decisions in the past. The Duke of Berry kept his own counsels, but among his intimates he made no secret of his disapproval. The Duke of Burgundy, who had not been consulted, was furious. He wrote to Bureau de la Rivière and other prominent ministers to protest. To some extent Philip was moved by an older conception of the public order which declined to treat private war between noblemen as a matter of state. After all, the Constable had not been attacked in the execution of his duties but on his way home after a ball and good dinner. Philip regarded the quarrel between Clisson and Craon as a matter for them, which need not concern either Brittany or France or indeed the King's other subjects. He was concerned about the wider political implications to which the King's councillors appeared to have given no thought at all. The decision to pick a fight with John de Montfort at this moment could serve only to drive him into the arms of the English and wreck the prospect of peace. There was substance in these fears. John's first act on hearing of Charles VI's decision was to send his agents urgently to England with proposals for a fresh military alliance. They came with offers to surrender the principal fortresses of the duchy into English hands and instructions to hire up to 5,000 mercenaries. The English government's response is not recorded but there is some evidence that the Duke's proposals were seriously considered by Richard II's ministers.[30]

The French King's army, about seven or eight thousand strong, gathered on the banks of the River Sarthe at the end of July 1392 beneath the walls of the cathedral city of Le Mans. It was overwhelmingly composed of 'official' contingents. In spite of their misgivings, all the royal princes were present except for the Duke of Berry, a friend and ally of John de Montfort who had contrived to have himself sent on a diplomatic mission to Avignon. The King's brother Louis, who had been made Duke of Orléans on the eve of the campaign, appeared with a substantial battalion of his own. The officers of state and the court nobility were there with their retinues. The march provinces of Normandy, Anjou and Maine contributed important contingents. But most of the rest of the French nobility stayed away. The French-speaking nobility of eastern Brittany, traditionally loyal to the Crown, had been summoned but few of them came. Among the troops at the muster there was a detectable sense of unease. It was reported that the great noblemen about the King were pressing him 'night and day' to reconsider. Charles's only response was to separate himself from the crowd of petitioners and surround himself with his Marmouset ministers. Even the news, which reached the camp at about the beginning of August, that Pierre de Craon was in Barcelona and not in Brittany failed to shake his resolve. 'Whoever advises me to stop,' he declared, 'advises me against my wishes and is no friend of mine.'[31]

On 5 August 1392, as the army began to march south through the forest of Le Mans, Charles VI had a maniacal fit. A man ran out from the forest, seized the bridle of his horse and began to shout of treason and betrayal, commanding him to stop. The man, who may have been mad, was driven off by Charles's bodyguards but the incident unsettled the King. He had been suffering for some weeks from exhaustion, lack of sleep and periodic bouts of fever. As the sun rose in the sky it became hot and close. The King sweltered in his thick velvet tunic. Clouds of fine sand and dust thrown up by the hoofs of thousands of horses got into men's nostrils and lungs. Riding ahead to escape the dust Charles entered a clearing close to the village of Pontvallain, accompanied only by his brother Louis and a few attendants. Behind him the page bearing the King's lance had fallen asleep in the saddle and allowed the lance to fall from his hands, the tip striking another man's helmet with a clang of metal on metal. The King started. Thinking he was being attacked, he drew his sword and felled the page. Then he began to strike out at anyone within range. It dawned on his companions that he no longer recognised them. None dared fight back. Three more men were killed. Several others were wounded. The rest fled or played dead. His brother Louis tried to approach him, only to be struck on the head with the sword and chased through the forest. For an hour Charles charged to and fro until his sword broke and his mount was too exhausted to continue. One of his household knights finally came up behind him, jumped behind his saddle and seized him by the arms while others took away his fractured sword and dragged him from his horse, his eyes still rolling in their sockets. The King, subsiding into a coma, was carried back to Le Mans tied down to a litter. Messengers rode along the Angers road turning back each company in turn. The Brittany campaign was over.[32]

Charles's fit was the first serious manifestation of a life-long illness which, so far as we can judge across an interval of more than six centuries, appears to have been a form of paranoid schizophrenia. The King's contemporaries were mystified. The doctors crowded round the bed of the comatose King in the monastery of St. Julian at Le Mans. They pronounced that his hopes of recovery were poor. A variety of explanations was canvassed. The King's entourage initially suspected poison and interrogated his servants. The Duke of Burgundy blamed Charles's household officers for allowing him to lead a dissolute life at court, with its unending sequence of late nights and mornings, banquets and balls. Among the population at large the origins of the King's illness were almost universally thought to be supernatural: a thunderbolt of God or sorcery worked by obscure and malevolent enemies.

Much of this speculation was put aside when Charles recovered consciousness after three days. He was lucid but remained weak and lethargic for several weeks. For the next thirty years of his life the French King was destined to live a life of intermittent sanity, interrupted by ever longer and more frequent 'absences', the delicate euphemism used by his contemporaries to describe the prolonged periods when the King would wander through the corridors of his palaces howling and screaming, not knowing who or what he was. Yet the truth was that even in his periods of lucidity Charles VI was no longer capable of governing his realm. He was gracious and could be articulate. He acted his role. But politically he was generally content to allow the factions around him to fight their battles over his head as if he were no more than a distant spectator of a performance that no longer concerned him. For France the political consequences were catastrophic, far worse than they would have been if Charles had died. So long as the King lived everything had to be done in his name. The situation was too uncertain to warrant a formal regency, which might have provided a measure of continuity and conserved the strength of the Valois monarchy. Instead power was uneasily contested between his closest relatives and was exercised intermittently by cliques with no real legitimacy in law or security in fact. The great institutions of the Valois state were riven with jealousies and divisions which mirrored those of the princes to whom their members were bound by ties of patronage and self-preservation. The ultimate consequence was a civil war of which the main beneficiary would be Henry V of England.[33]

In August 1392 the Duke of Burgundy moved swiftly to seize control of the government. His first acts were to announce the cancellation of the attack on Brittany and disband the army. An embassy was sent to Brittany bearing a letter from the Dukes of Burgundy and Bourbon full of gracious apologies for a campaign which had been 'instigated by the Devil and by evil counsellors'. These measures provoked an immediate row with the Constable, who had been the leader of the 'evil counsellors' in question and was the financier and chief beneficiary of the campaign. Clisson at once reneged on his promise to fund the payment of war wages. The result was that the captains had to be sent away unpaid, a highly unpopular course which did nothing for Clisson's political credit. Towards the end of August, when the King was well enough to travel, he was carried to the royal castle of Creil, isolated on its island in the Oise north of Paris. In the capital a Great Council was hastily assembled from those notables who were at hand to approve the new arrangements for the government of the kingdom. The King's closest blood relation was Louis of Orléans, now in his twenty-first year. He made a determined bid for power. If Charles had been dead or permanently incapacitated his claim would have been unanswerable. But with the King nominally in command of his affairs the Duke of Burgundy prevailed by the sheer force of his personality and the strength of his following. Orléans was young, inexperienced and cocky. He was also widely regarded as dissolute and unstable, addicted to gambling, surrounding himself with wild friends and throwing debauched parties. His obsessive interest in sorcery and the black arts was an open secret. In some minds the connection may already have been made between the King's illness and the evil spells of his brother's circle. These things tended to overshadow Louis's undoubted abilities. His claims were brushed aside.[34]

At the end of September 1392 the King was brought back to Paris and installed in the Hôtel Saint-Pol while the Dukes of Burgundy and Berry set about consolidating their power and purging their enemies from the royal household and administration. The leading Marmouset ministers were suspended from their functions. Bureau de la Rivière and Jean le Mercier were shut in the Bastille. Le Bègue de Villaines was taken to the fortress of Crèvecoeur. Jean de Montaigu fled to the papal court at Avignon. Clisson, who was at the royal castle of Montlhéry, was tipped off as the soldiers came down the Orléans road to arrest him, and fled to his domains in Brittany. Philip of Burgundy loathed these men. They were parvenus with ambitions above their station who had excluded him and his brother from power since 1388, indulged the King's vices, undermined his health, monopolised his patronage and finally engineered the disastrous decision to invade Brittany. For the Duke of Berry they were also the men responsible for the judicial murder of his friend and minister Jean de Bétizac. The Marmousets had done good service to the King. But they had the vulnerability of all self-made men who rose to high office in the middle ages. 'There is no greater menace in this world,' intoned that faithful mirror of conventional sentiment Eustache Deschamps, 'than a poor man raised to high estate.' The leading Marmousets had grown rich, with ostentatious ways and fine houses, 'lording it over the highest in the land' in the words of the prim chronicler of Saint-Denis. Exaggerated stories were put about by their enemies. Olivier de Clisson was reported to have made a will after the recent attempt on his life in which he disposed of no less than 1.7 million francs in cash and moveables alone, a sum not far short of the entire revenues of the realm for a year. A commission of inquiry was appointed to find evidence of corruption. They were instructed to examine every case where more than 1,000 francs had been granted to a single person since the famous council at Reims which had brought the Marmousets to power. The results of their labours are not known but the allegations against the Marmousets are not borne out by the financial records which survive. Charles VI was certainly over-generous to his friends and his ministers were never shy of accepting tips or grants for their services. But the services were genuine enough and the scale of the rewards not out of line with what a successful official could expect to earn in the fourteenth century.[35]

Clisson's fate was ultimately settled by a deal between Philip of Burgundy and John de Montfort. In return for the removal of his enemy from the French government John undertook to cut off all contact with the English. In December 1392 an obliging Parlement condemned Clisson in default for embezzlement and stripped him of his office of Constable. He was eventually replaced by Philip, Count of Eu, an inexperienced young man whose main qualification for the job was that he was betrothed to Jean de Berry's daughter. There was at least a serious political case against Clisson, whose obsessive vendetta against John de Montfort was a threat to the internal peace of France and the prospect of peace with England. But the rest of the Marmousets were simply victims of the royal dukes' thirst for revenge after four years in the political wilderness. Bureau de la Rivière and Jean le Mercier were accused of stealing more than 120,000 francs from the royal treasury, of carrying on a treasonable correspondence with the English and of taking bribes from Richard II's ministers. If Burgundy and Berry had had their way both men would have been executed. Indeed, for several days in October, crowds gathered expectantly in the Place de Grève to enjoy the spectacle. But the disgraced ministers were saved, probably by the intervention of the Duke of Bourbon and Louis of Orléans. Nothing was ever proved against them and after more than a year in prison they were released and exonerated. It was a discreditable episode.[36]

The Dukes of Berry and Burgundy maintained effective control of the royal administration until Philip's death in 1404. The royal Council was never wholly under their control but they ensured that it always included a strong caucus of their creatures. Beneath the Council Philip of Burgundy's officials and clients secured direct control of the main organs of government, especially the financial institutions and the royal secretariat. Philip's only real political rival was Louis of Orléans. Louis had been wrong-footed in the power struggle which followed the return of the court from Le Mans but he was still a force to be reckoned with and likely to become stronger with the passage of time. Over the following months he forged an alliance with a group of councillors who had been close to the Marmousets in their better days and were beyond the reach of Burgundy's anger: the Duke of Bourbon, Enguerrand de Coucy, the Admiral Jean de Vienne and the Provost of the Merchants of Paris, Jean Juvénal des Ursins. The strong personal bond between Louis and his brother, which survived through all the King's vicissitudes, gave him a measure of influence during the King's periods of lucidity. The grant of the duchy of Orléans, one of the King's last acts of largesse before his illness, had brought him a bigger and more prestigious appanage which he rounded out by judicious purchases in the Beauce and the Loire valley over the following years. Louis could never match the immense wealth of the Duke of Burgundy but he was now getting a substantial income from his domains, augmented by a generous pension from the royal treasury. He maintained a large household at the Hôtel de Bohême near the market of Les Halles. He took the field with an impressive military retinue. He cultivated a political following, distributing largesse with an open but discriminating hand. He even moderated the wilder aspects of his behaviour, at least in public.[37]

The price of Louis's acquiescence in the new regime was its support for his Italian ambitions. It is unlikely that Philip of Burgundy had any personal enthusiasm for this project but it was worth indulging a potentially disruptive political rival if only to get rid of him. In November 1392 the ambassador of Gian Galeazzo Visconti was in Paris trying to interest the French government in reviving the plans of conquest which had been so abruptly dropped the year before. Since that setback the French viceroy in Naples, Louis of Montjoie, and the child-King Louis II of Anjou had built on their early successes. With the aid of regular shipments of bullion from the papal treasury and the Angevin territories in France and Provence they had maintained their position against the companies of Ladislas of Durazzo and his mother. By the autumn of 1392 the whole of Calabria had submitted to them. In Paris the Christmas season was the traditional time for great plans. Louis of Orléans and his supporters devised a fresh scheme for a dual invasion of Italy in the joint interest of himself and the Avignon Pope.

He planned to cross the Alps into the Lombard plain in the following summer at the head of an army of 6,000 men, there to join forces with the despot of Milan. Their combined forces would enter the states of the Church from the north by the march of Bologna. Simultaneously the Duke of Bourbon would sail from Marseille with a small company of troops and money to hire more in Italy. According to reports reaching Florence Bourbon planned to march up the coast with some 4,500 men and invade the papal state from the south, making for the march of Viterbo. There he would be able to concert operations with the surviving companies of Breton and Gascon *routiers* around Viterbo and Urbino, the only significant forces in central Italy which still acknowledged the Avignon Pope.[38]

In the new year an intense diplomatic offensive was launched in support of Louis's Italian adventure. A French embassy headed by Philip of Burgundy's friend and confidant Gui de la Tremoille left for Milan to propose a fresh military alliance to Gian Galeazzo. Jean de Vienne went to canvass support in Florence and Genoa and probably in Bologna. Enguerrand de Coucy was sent to Avignon with another embassy charged with agreeing terms with Clement VII. Yet another mission travelled to Aragon to hire war galleys and transports. Louis's initial objective in 1393 was the same as it had been in 1389: to carve a 'kingdom of Adria' out of the papal state for his own benefit. But as his plans matured they became even more ambitious. He began to intrigue with a faction of Guelph noblemen to deliver up the Republic of Genoa to him as well, thus giving him a major port and an additional point of entry into the peninsula. In the event all these pipe dreams encountered an unexpected obstacle in Clement VII himself. Clement was delighted at the prospect of his rival's expulsion from Italy by French arms but sceptical about whether Louis could do it. Where was he going to find the troops? How would he pay them without open-ended financial support from the French Crown? Did he have enough allies among the Italian cities? These were good questions. Orléans's ambassadors, questioned by the Pope in the council chamber of the papal palace, had no answers to them. Clement was reluctant to agree to the dismemberment of the papal state for the benefit of a prince of the *fleur de lys*, least of all for such an uncertain return. It was true that he had made a secret grant in very similar terms to Louis of Anjou in 1379, as Louis's ambassadors reminded him. He had also given tacit encouragement to a very similar project two years earlier. But the Pope had come to regard these things as embarrassing mistakes which would serve only to rally the communities of central Italy to Boniface IX. It is difficult to fault his judgment on any of these points but the consequences were embarrassing. The Duke of Bourbon, who attended some of these exchanges on his way to Marseille, walked out. He returned in disgust to Paris, to the fury of the Pope and the Duchess of Anjou, both of whom had laid out large sums on shipping and supplies for his army. Much of the next two years was to be consumed in ultimately fruitless attempts to resolve the impasse.[39]

To Philip of Burgundy, all of this was an unwelcome distraction from the business of concluding a lasting peace with England. He had begun to apply himself to the question as soon as Charles VI had recovered consciousness in the monastery of St. Julian at Le Mans. The King's illness raised some delicate issues. There was no concealing the gravity of what had happened. Richard II's representatives had been present at Le Mans when Charles suffered his crisis and were even admitted to the bedchamber of the comatose King until they were hurriedly shooed out by the Duke of Burgundy. English spies were busy picking up gossip about the court. The English government was unlikely to agree to a permanent treaty if there were doubts about who had authority to speak for the King of France. To soothe these anxieties Philip made use of a highly unconventional intermediary. Robert de Mennot, known as 'Robert the Hermit', was a Norman seer who had passed most of his adult life in the east. He had recently arrived in France claiming to have been commanded by God to reconcile England and France and direct their combined energies against the Turk. Robert was a man of great eloquence and charm whose preaching had already had some impact in France. Philippe de Mézières, who was probably responsible for introducing him to the French King's councillors, called him the 'special messenger of God to both monarchs'. The Duke of Burgundy shrewdly judged that he would appeal to the impressionable and high-minded King of England and perhaps circumvent the cumbrous conventions of diplomatic exchange. He was not disappointed. Robert clearly did impress Richard, much as that other crusade propagandist Leo of Armenia had done before him. The upshot of his mission and of a more formal embassy which reached England at the end of September was an agreement that a fresh conference would open at Leulinghem on 9 February 1393. Both sides would be represented there at the highest levels below the kings themselves.[40]

The conference finally opened at Leulinghem, two months late, in April 1393. On the English side it occurred against a difficult political background. The departure of Richard's ambassadors had been preceded by an acrimonious debate in Parliament about their instructions, in some ways reminiscent of the Stamford debate the year before. The English sources are reticent about this. There is some evidence that the Duke of Guelders may once again have served as the unofficial leader of the war party. He was certainly invited to send his ambassadors to lay his views before Parliament and may have done so. If so they had some effect, judging by reports reaching the French King's ministers in Paris. The English government apparently had much difficulty in containing the hostility of the knights in the Commons. In some parts of England, where the tradition of military service was strong, the peace conference was viewed with grave foreboding and threats of violence. In the north-east and the Midlands resistance was being organised by professional captains who had made their careers in France. The ringleader, Sir Thomas Talbot, who had lands in Yorkshire, Cheshire and Lancashire, had been captain of Berwick and then Guines and had fought in the jousts of Saint-Ingelvert. The other participants who can be identified came from a very similar background. The Lancashire knight Sir William Clifton, another jouster at Saint-Ingelvert, had been captain of Ham in Picardy. Sir John Mascy belonged to a famous military family from Cheshire, several of whom had served for long periods in Gascony. Richard's ministers were well aware of the problem that was brewing. They sent the Earl of Huntingdon and a local magnate, Sir John Stanley, to the north-east to reason with the leading contrariants, but they trod warily, unwilling to proceed to tougher measures for fear of precipitating a crisis which might require the conference to be postponed.[41]

Richard II's chief representative at Leulinghem was John of Gaunt. He was supported by the Duke of Gloucester, who had been added to the team in order to disarm critics of the peace process at home. They were given wide discretion to make concessions. The King himself remained in Kent, in close touch with events. On the French side were the Dukes of Burgundy and Berry. They did not quite have *carte blanche*, in spite of their dominant position on the French King's Council. But Charles VI established his court at Abbeville, a day's ride south of Calais, so that the Council could meet whenever decisions were required. The two royal uncles set up their headquarters at Boulogne and travelled several times a week to Leulinghem to meet Lancaster and Gloucester. The bleak flats around the village were transformed into a scene of unparalleled splendour. The Duke of Burgundy had an immense tented pavilion, looking like a miniature walled town with avenues and streets, which was said to have a capacity of 3,000. The Duke of Lancaster's pavilion was reported to be even grander, with chapels, arcades, law courts and markets and bell-towers sounding out the hours. At nearly £5,000, the English embassy was the most expensive mission to France for many years.

On the opening day of the conference the whole mass of noblemen, officials and clerks crammed into the church for the reading of the ambassadors' procurations. The humble thatched church had been decked out with unbecoming tapestries depicting the great battles of the ancient world. John of Gaunt had them taken down and replaced with symbols of the Passion of Christ, an unmistakable reference to Philippe de Mézières's crusading order. Leo of Armenia, who was present in the entourage of the French royal dukes, had recently returned from eastern Europe with reports on the situation there. Robert the Hermit preached his message of peace and unity at the fringes of the conference. The advances of the Turks were in everyone's mind. Eustache Deschamps faithfully reflected the mood in a long lament on the divisions of Christendom, written in the opening days of the conference. It was full of conventional sentiments but infused with real optimism. Men felt that they were about to witness great events. Michel Pintoin, the monk of Saint-Denis who had recently been appointed official historiographer, was summoned to Leulinghem by the Duke of Berry to record the occasion in his chronicle. Jean Froissart took lodgings at Abbeville to be close to the gossip of the court.[42]

As soon as the opening ceremonies were over the four royal dukes dispensed with the usual elaborate forensic procedures and began a series of closed sessions with only a limited number of participants. The exchanges, according to the Duke of Burgundy, were 'friendly and straightforward'. The English made it clear at once that they would not in any circumstances agree to surrender Calais. The French royal dukes, who had already decided that this point might have to be conceded, accepted this with good grace. Most of the rest of the time was given over to debate about the legal status of the English possessions in France and to haggling about the new borders of the duchy of Aquitaine. The driving force on the English side was the Duke of Lancaster. Gloucester played the part assigned to him, but his heart was not in it and he made no attempt to hide the fact. Years later he told Froissart that the French were constantly producing documents full of tricky ambiguities. 'You French have ways of colouring your words . . .', he claimed to have told

Robert the Hermit to his face; the same terms 'mean war when you want war and peace when you want peace'. He was content to do his sovereign's bidding, he added, but if Richard II had listened to his advice he would long ago have taken back his territory in France by force and imposed a peace on his own terms.[43]

By the end of April 1393 the four royal dukes had made enough progress to enable detailed proposals to be submitted to both governments. The conference adjourned for three weeks for consultations. When the proceedings resumed at the end of May 1393 agreement in principle was reached almost immediately. On 16 June 1393 a protocol was drawn up and sealed, which recorded the terms to be included in a treaty of peace together with a small number of matters which it had not been possible to agree and which were reserved for direct negotiation between the two kings. The terms were remarkably generous to the English. They were to have the whole of the vast territory ceded to them at Brétigny in 1360 with the exception of Poitou, northern Saintonge and the county of Ponthieu in the north. This included Périgord, the Angoumois, Limousin, Rouergue and Quercy, and the Pyrenean enclaves of Bigorre, Gaure and Tarbes. It was more generous than any of the territorial settlements which the French had previously proposed. They also abandoned their insistence on the surrender or destruction of Calais and agreed to pay an indemnity of between 1,200,000 and 1,500,000 francs as compensation for the territories ceded at Brétigny which they were retaining. The English for their part finally gave way on the question of homage. The duchy of Aquitaine was to become once again one of the twelve peerages of France and would be held in return for liege homage. The one point on which they insisted was that it would be necessary to define the incidents of this homage more carefully. Did it include military service? Would the King of England be expected to attend Charles VI's courts and councils as a peer of France? And what of the French King's right to have judicial appeals from English-held territories heard in his courts? These were important and difficult questions. It was agreed that a commission of experts from each side would meet during the summer to consider them. This left four main matters to be agreed between Richard II and Charles VI personally when they met: the legal status of Calais; the fate of La Rochelle, France's only Atlantic port south of the Seine; the thorny question whether Richard II would have to perform his homage in person now that Aquitaine had been granted to John of Gaunt; and the precise amount of the cash indemnity. The four dukes swore that the terms would in due course be

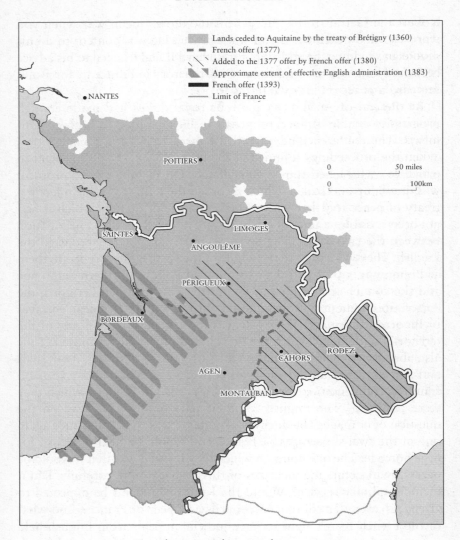

29 French territorial proposals, 1377–1393

embodied in a formal treaty of peace. The Duke of Gloucester, for all his misgivings, swore with the rest. Before they separated they agreed a timetable for the completion of the remaining stages. The commission of legal experts would meet in August. The four royal dukes were to reconvene at Leulinghem on 29 September to resolve any outstanding issues. The meeting of the two kings was fixed for February 1394.[44]

*

It was a measure of the latent threat which English hostility still represented for France that the Leulinghem protocol of June 1393 should have conceded so much to a defeated enemy. The herald who brought the news of the agreement to Richard II from Calais graphically described for Froissart's benefit the joy on his face when he opened the Duke of Lancaster's letter. Yet the English were unable to follow up their diplomatic triumph. In the last days of the conference Charles VI suffered another attack of insanity. He had violent fits. He no longer recognised his wife or any of those around him. He could not even remember who he was. The King's second 'absence' was a far more serious affair than the first. It lasted for nearly six months, during which Charles disappeared from sight. Among the public at large the suspicion of sorcery hardened into certainty, and the first voices were raised identifying Louis of Orléans and his wife as the people responsible. Had the King not tried to kill Louis in that forest clearing ten months before? Did Louis not have most to gain by his brother's incapacity? Was he not notorious for his interest in the black arts? Did Valentine not come from Italy, in popular imagination the European homeland of magicians, sorcerers and necromancers? There were reports that the Duchess of Orléans was the only person whom the King continued to recognise in his delirium. The gossip, almost certainly originating in the King's own circle, was magnified by repetition. Sorcery, charms, curses were a delusion of the 'common people' according to the chronicler of Saint-Denis. But they were a potent delusion throughout the middle ages, shared by many who were 'common' only in the sense that they were laymen without the weight of theological learning which had long ago persuaded the Church that such things could not happen to a king. Over the following years several magicians would be employed to heal him of an illness which was itself ascribed to magic. In the autumn of 1393 Charles's attendants summoned from Guyenne a self-proclaimed sorcerer by the name of Arnaud Guillaume, the first of a succession of such people who would be invited to cure the sick monarch, only to be condemned as heretics and brutally put to death at Montfaucon or Les Halles when their books, charms and incantations failed.[45]

Richard II's ministers must have had a fair idea from their own sources about what was going on. But it was not until September 1393 that one of the French King's councillors was sent to England to explain the situation. By then it was clear that the main obstacle to the completion of the peace was not the health of the French King but political opposition in England. The decision of Richard's Council to ignore the unrest in the north proved in hindsight to have been unwise. Sir Thomas Talbot and his friends nailed their manifesto to the doors of parish churches in Cheshire, Lancashire and the neighbouring counties. They accused the two royal dukes of plotting to abandon the King's claim to the throne of France without his authority. They threatened to murder them together with any other supporters of the peace whom they could lay hands on. Opposition to the peace merged with a variety of local grievances: the wider economic ills of agricultural communities; in Cheshire, hostility to a heavy local tax imposed in return for the renewal of the county's charters and unspecific fears for its liberties; in Lancashire, the innumerable slights, jealousies and resentments provoked by John of Gaunt's position as the dominant local landowner. By June 1393 the rebellion had reached formidable proportions. About 20,000 men according to contemporary estimates had gathered at rallying-points across the region. The Duke of Lancaster hurriedly returned to England at the end of June and passed the next three months in the north. The rebellion was put down with an adept mixture of firmness and tact. Many of the poorer rebels were bought off by offers of service with the Duke in Gascony. There was very little fighting. But the incident revealed the fault lines in English politics. The Duke of Gloucester was committed to the peace terms by his oath. Indeed, as justiciar of Chester he was bound to support his brother in putting down an armed uprising. But he was thought to have been lukewarm in his efforts. The Earl of Arundel, who had important interests of his own in the region and held views very similar to Gloucester's, was even more equivocal. He put a large force into his castle of Holt, about ten miles south of Chester, and waited on events. John of Gaunt was convinced that Arundel was preparing to support the rebels and would have done so if a favourable opportunity had arisen. He would later openly accuse the Earl of treason.[46]

Seven months passed after the protocol of Leulinghem, during which the momentum achieved at the conference was lost. The commission of experts met in August 1393, a bench of lawyers presided over by a bishop on each side. After two months of deliberation they failed to reach agreement. The law is a conservative profession. After much learned research into the manner in which appeals from Gascony had been conducted when they had last been heard in the 1330s, the French jurists declared that there was no reason why the same practices should not be followed now. Since the practices of the 1330s had led to the confiscation of the duchy and precipitated the war this was not acceptable to their English counterparts. It was perhaps unrealistic to expect technical experts to resolve what was really an issue of principle. The meeting of the four royal uncles, which might have revisited this question, had had to be postponed on account of the continuing illness of the King of France. Charles did not recover his senses until shortly after Christmas 1393.

Richard II remained personally committed to a permanent peace. The first of England's Atlantic barbicans was already in the course of evacuation. The fortress-town of Cherbourg was sold back to the heir of Charles the Bad of Navarre. The troops in the castle delivered the place up to a Navarrese garrison and sailed back to England at the beginning of 1394. Desultory negotiations were in train for the abandonment of Brest to John de Montfort. There was even talk of abandoning Calais in spite of the adamant line which English representatives had taken on the subject at successive diplomatic conferences. John of Gaunt was reported to have declared that the place 'grieved more England and did more hurt thereto than profit for the great expenses about the keeping thereof'.[47]

The real test of English opinion came with the meeting of Parliament at Westminster on 27 January 1394. In his opening address the Chancellor, Archbishop Arundel, reported on the progress of negotiations with France. He had the terms of the Leulinghem protocol read out before the assembly. He told his hearers that they would be expected to offer their advice, but there would be a price to pay if the government's proposals were rejected. If they were not willing to approve the peace they would be duty-bound to furnish the King with the means of continuing the war. The gathering which listened to these words was not a particularly martial one. Very few of them had a vested interest in the continuance of the war. Almost all of the fifty-three lay peers summoned had fought at one time or another under the command of the King or the royal princes as it was their duty to do, but only a handful of them could have been described as professional soldiers. Of the seventy-three knights of the shires who sat in the Commons thirty-four were not proper, belted knights at all. Less than half had had any significant military experience. Of those only fourteen are known to have fought in France and two in Castile, and only four had been professional captains. The opponents of the peace had lost their natural spokesman when the Duke of Gloucester put his name to the protocol at Leulinghem. It therefore fell to the Earl of Arundel to speak for the opposition. He was supported from the wings by the Duke of Guelders, who had come specially to England for the occasion.[48]

The debate began as soon as the Chancellor had finished speaking. His brother, the Earl of Arundel, launched into a stinging attack on the terms brought back by the ambassadors from Leulinghem and on their principal author, John of Gaunt. There were, he said, 'certain matters close to his heart which he could not honourably conceal'. The Duke of Lancaster was too close to the King. Richard was always in his company. The King even wore Gaunt's livery collar and ordered his retainers to do the same. Fortified by the King's support, Gaunt was overbearing in Council and in Parliament, intimidating colleagues and preventing them from speaking their minds. Arundel criticised the use of tax revenues to support Gaunt's expedition to Castile and the release of his debts to the Crown. He complained about the grant to Gaunt of the duchy of Aquitaine, which he believed disinherited the King. Finally he turned on the peace terms. His criticisms are not recorded in the official roll. But according to the usually well-informed chronicler of Westminster Abbey the Earl seized on the question of homage. If Richard performed liege homage to the King of France, he declared, even if it was only for his domains in France, England would become a subordinate kingdom. 'Every Englishman having the King of England as his lord would pass under the heel of the King of France and be held for ever more under the yoke of slavery.' John of Gaunt himself was not present in the Chamber to hear the Earl of Arundel's words. It was the King himself who took up his defence. If he was close to John of Gaunt, Richard said, that was only natural for an uncle and his nephew. It had been his own decision to wear Gaunt's livery collar as a 'symbol of the love and confidence between them' after the Duke's return from Spain. He pointed out that the subsidy for Gaunt's expedition to Castile and the grant of Aquitaine had both been approved in full Parliament. The Duke of Lancaster, he declared, had spent more of his own money on the King's affairs than he owed to the Treasury. As for the agreement with the French, everything that Gaunt had done at Leulinghem had been done in accordance with his instructions and approved by the Council, of which Arundel himself was a member. In any event nothing was irrevocable yet. The lords, who had witnessed this extraordinary exchange, declared that Gaunt's honour was safe. They forced the Earl to withdraw his allegations and apologise. Shortly after this there was another row between the two men. This time it was the Duke of Lancaster's turn to accuse his rival. Gaunt was angry about the covert support given to the Cheshire rebels in the previous summer. He alleged that Arundel had deliberately withheld his support during the crisis. He hinted that powerful individuals were sheltering the leader of the rebellion, Sir Thomas Talbot. Arundel responded with what the St. Albans chronicler called a 'forceful and plausible speech' defending his own conduct. But the Lords appear to have supported Gaunt on this issue also, for at the end of the debate Arundel walked out. Shortly afterwards he obtained the King's licence never to attend the Council or Parliament again.[49]

Arundel's mistake was to turn his attack on the treaty into a general assault on the King and his principal adviser. If his language had been more measured the Lords might not have humiliated him in the way they did. For it is clear that many of them had strong misgivings of their own about the terms agreed at Leulinghem. They too were concerned about the Duke of Lancaster's role at the conference and about the political implications of recognising French sovereignty over Aquitaine. The Lords discussed the terms jointly with the 'more mature and substantial' knights sitting in the Commons. They issued a joint declaration approving the idea of making peace with France in principle but rejecting the essential features of the deal which Lancaster had negotiated. They were against Richard doing liege homage for his domains in France as opposed to simple homage. They said that if he was to do homage of whatever kind to the King of France it would be necessary to have guarantees against manipulative appeals of the kind which had led to the confiscation of the duchy in the past. They also foresaw that sooner or later the treaty would break down. A conflict would then arise between Richard's rights as King of England and his duties as a vassal of France. They wanted to deal with this by inserting a provision reviving the English claim to the throne of France if it happened. These provisos would have destroyed the whole basis of the deal.

The agreement fared no better in the Commons. The Speaker was the Lincolnshire knight Sir John Bussy, an experienced Parliamentarian and a retainer of the Duke of Lancaster, who may already have acquired his later reputation as a government fixer. But even Bussy was unable to save the protocol. The Commons followed the lead of the knights and issued a declaration in very similar terms to the Lords. England, they said, 'should not be burdened by the said homage and ressort'. The Duke of Lancaster came in for a good deal of abuse in both Houses. The fact that as Duke of Aquitaine he was personally the main beneficiary of the agreement escaped no one's attention. Someone suggested that if a lesser figure had put forward such terms he would have been convicted of treason on the spot, 'but the Duke of Lancaster does as he pleases'. As for the Duke of Gloucester, he had lost much of his popularity by his participation in the conference. It was even put about that Gaunt had bribed him with the promise of an increased endowment. The Commons spurned the Chancellor's suggestion that heavy taxation would be required if the terms were rejected. The most that they were willing to do was to allow the government to collect half a lay subsidy, which had been already granted the year before in case war broke out with France. They obviously regarded the renewal of the war as unlikely. Like the Lords they seem to have thought that there were better terms to be had. They were mistaken about this, as John of Gaunt could have told them and no doubt did.

In April 1394 the ambassadors returned to Leulinghem. Lancaster, accompanied this time by the youngest of his brothers, Edmund Langley Duke of York, represented Richard II. They reported the response of Parliament to Charles VI's uncles. The royal dukes remained locked in conference until the end of May and then separated without agreement. All that could be salvaged from two years of intensive negotiation was another truce, this time for four years, and a promise that John of Gaunt would participate with the Dukes of Burgundy and Orléans in a joint crusade against the pagans of the eastern Baltic or the Ottoman Turks in the Balkans. An opportunity had been lost.[50]

The English rejection of the peace process to which the King had devoted the last five years of his life proved to be a turning point in Richard II's public life. He was now twenty-seven years old. A handsome but rather frail and boyish-looking man, he flushed readily according to a contemporary account, and spoke with a slight stammer. Cultivated, sensitive, speaking excellent French, fastidious in his personal habits and addicted to luxury, temperamentally averse to war, he had very little in common with the majority of the English baronage. In public his manner was distant and kingly. But, like Charles VI of France, he combined this with undignified carousing with his intimates in private. The moody impulsiveness and irritability of his youth had grown worse with the years. On 7 June 1394, a few days after the return of the ambassadors from Leulinghem, his wife Anne of Bohemia died at the royal manor of Sheen. Richard had been close to Anne and after her death became increasingly introspective and emotional. He refused to enter any room where she had been. He ordered Sheen to be razed to the ground. Politically he became more unpredictable in his reactions and less inclined to take any counsel but his own. There was a revealing incident at the Queen's funeral in Westminster Abbey when the Earl of Arundel, who had arrived late, asked for permission to leave early. The

King, who had till now kept his hatred of Arundel under control, seized a cane from an attendant and laid about the Earl, cutting his head and knocking him to the ground before ordering him to be imprisoned in the Tower of London. He was only released after providing a bond for his good behaviour in the enormous sum of £40,000. Richard's anger against others who crossed him began to provoke a noticeable edginess at court. Even John of Gaunt, who had dominated Richard's government since his return from Gascony, found that his relations with his nephew became cooler and more distant after the failure of the negotiations with France. The Duke felt it necessary to write to his nephew shortly after the incident involving Arundel, urging him not to believe slanders that he was told were being uttered against his loyalty at court. Behind these personal animosities there lay an inordinate sensitivity to criticism which became progressively more pronounced as the years passed. The King's public appearances became more theatrical, the forms of address employed in his presence more extravagant, his official portraiture more icon-like, an image of divinely ordained kingship reinforced by elaborate court rituals borrowed from the ceremonial of the Church and the splendour of the court of France.[51]

For nearly a year after the collapse of the Leulinghem agreement of 1394 all the main protagonists turned away to attend to other problems. Richard II turned to the affairs of Ireland, which was now in serious danger of being lost to the Irish chiefs. On 16 June 1394, a few days after his ambassadors' return from Leulinghem, he announced his intention of crossing to Ireland with an army, the first time that an English King had visited the Irish lordship since the reign of King John nearly two centuries before. The army which ultimately embarked at Milford Haven in October was at least 5,000 strong and included most of those about the King who had been involved in the negotiations with France. John of Gaunt immersed himself in the problems of Gascony, where the most serious revolt yet against his authority had broken out in April 1394. Resentful of the authoritarian ways of Gaunt's lieutenants and frightened by inaccurate reports from England that Richard was about to cede the duchy to his uncle in perpetuity as part of a deal with France, the Estates of Gascony had repudiated his authority. In future, they declared, they would obey only officials who were directly answerable to the King. Towards the end of October, with the French negotiations for the time being in abeyance, Gaunt sailed with some 1,500 men men from Plymouth. He would be away from

England for more than a year. At the court of France the Duke of Burgundy threw himself into the business of broking a permanent resolution of the Breton civil war.[52]

The only visible symptom of the earlier goodwill between the two courts was the crusade. The Duke of Burgundy was the driving force behind this project. He conceived ambitious plans for an elite army of knights to confront the Turks in Hungary and drive them from the Balkans. This venture was intended as the prelude to an even more grandiose plan for the liberation of the Holy Land. A budget of 520,000 francs (£87,500) was drawn up to pay for Philip's retinue alone. Heavy taxes were demanded from his domains in Burgundy, Flanders and Artois. A Hungarian embassy was in France for much of the summer of 1394. There was intense diplomatic activity across Europe over the following winter as plans were concerted between the rulers of France, Hungary, Germany, Venice and Byzantium. John of Gaunt showed every sign of taking this project seriously. His son-in-law John Holand, Earl of Huntingdon, accompanied a French embassy to Hungary to make preliminary arrangements. His illegitimate son, Sir John Beaufort, left on a similar mission to Prussia. His agents haggled about logistics and naval support with the Venetians.[53]

On 16 September 1394 Clement VII died suddenly of a heart attack in the papal palace at Avignon at the age of only fifty-two. He was little mourned. 'If God has thought fit to receive him into Paradise', intoned the Datini factor in the city, 'he has doubtless done so.' Clement's death proved to be a turning point in the relations of the principal western European states.

For sixteen years the declared policy of the French government had been to impose Clement's authority in Italy by force in the belief that once he was securely installed in Rome the rest of Europe would acknowledge him. This policy, which was known in France as the *voie de fait* (or 'path of force'), had its supporters even in 1394 when it had manifestly failed. Louis of Orléans, whose Italian ambitions depended on it, was still calling for the grant of the 'kingdom of Adria' right up to the Pope's death. His allies on the royal Council pressed for ways to be found of financing it. Enguerrand de Coucy, who was one of those councillors, had been nominated as Louis's captain-general in Italy.[54] However, behind Louis's back, support for the *voie de fait* was draining away. Men distressed by the spectacle of Christendom divided against the Turk were in no mood to support either claimant to the papal throne, least of all by force. The schism provoked intense moral misgivings in France, where the government's role in sustaining the Avignon obedience was increasingly controversial. Even the Duke of Berry, a friend of Clement VII and long-standing supporter of Avignon, thought the schism had 'lasted too long' and declared that the French monarchy was shamed by it. The *voie de fait* created special difficulties for the Duke of Burgundy. Most of his Flemish subjects were partisans of Rome. It was therefore a destabilising factor in his northern dominions. In Paris it was associated with a rival centre of influence around his nephew Louis of Orléans. It also threatened to poison his dealings with England and obstruct his attempts to organise a crusade in eastern Europe.

Ever since the Dukes of Berry and Burgundy had returned to power in August 1392 there had been growing support within the French government for an alternative policy. The dukes gave some consideration to the possibility of submitting the issue to arbitration or to a general council of the Church. But the difficulty about this course was that it would almost inevitably require an adjudication that one or other Pope was unlawfully elected, and no one was likely to contemplate that with equanimity. 'Who would want to be judged to have been a schismatic for the last twenty years?' asked a Castilian prelate. Instead the dukes lighted on the policy which became known as the *voie de cession* (or 'path of abdication'). The object of the *voie de cession* was to induce both pretenders to the papal throne to withdraw so that a single, incontestable candidate could be elected in their place. Early in 1394 the French royal Council encouraged the University of Paris to devise proposals for healing the schism. The University, which had never whole-heartedly accepted Clement VII, considered a number of proposals but finally came down firmly in favour of the *voie de cession*. In June they presented their conclusions to the King in a document laced with abuse of Clement and his court.[55]

Reverence for Charles V's memory protected the Pope's position in his lifetime. Charles VI's response to the University's intemperate advice was to declare that he would take no action and desired never to receive such a document again. But Clement's death produced an immediate change of mood. The messenger from Avignon bought the news to the King at the Hôtel Saint-Pol in the middle of the mass. A Council meeting was hastily arranged. A rider was despatched with an urgent message for the cardinals, begging them to defer the election of a successor so that thought could be given to ways of healing the schism. It would be easier, they reasoned, to force one Pope to abdicate than two. The letter reached the cardinals on 26 September 1394, just as the doors of the conclave were about to be sealed. Guessing what its contents would be, they declined to receive it. Two days later they elected the Aragonese cardinal Pedro de Luna, who took the name Benedict XIII. The cardinals were as anxious as the French royal Council to bring an end to the schism. Their choice was almost certainly determined by their belief that Pedro would share their views. Before proceeding to the election each of them had sworn an oath that whichever of them was chosen would work for the unity of the Church, even to the point of abdicating the throne if a majority of the cardinals called on him to do so. Pedro had sworn the oath before his election and swore it again afterwards.[56]

The new Pope's historical reputation has been overshadowed by his miserable end, but in his time he was an impressive figure. Elected at the relatively advanced age of sixty-six, he was a distinguished canon lawyer, a cultivated man of great personal holiness and a politician endowed with formidable energy and intellect and indomitable will. He had a profound knowledge of the politics of Europe, having been a cardinal for nineteen years, much of it spent in the diplomatic service of the papacy in France and Spain. But Benedict was never likely to be an easy man to work with. He was prickly and conceited. He was strongly attached to the dignity of his office and determined not to be pushed around. His election was initially welcomed in France, where he was hailed as a potential collaborator in the government's ideas for healing the schism. However, within a very short time doubts began to emerge. An embassy sent by the new Pope to Paris arrived laden with good intentions and professions of support. Another followed in its tracks in the new year. But although they were instructed to canvass various possibilities with Charles VI's councillors, Benedict's emissaries were conspicuously silent about the *voie de cession*. The Pope, they were to say, had his own ideas about how to heal the schism, 'sound and speedy' ideas which, however, he proposed to keep to himself until a sufficiently eminent embassy was sent to Avignon to receive them.[57] The truth was that if Benedict had ever been sincere about abdicating for the sake of Christian unity he changed his mind as soon as he was elected to the papal throne. At various times over the following years he professed interest in a negotiated settlement, an arbitration on carefully contrived terms or a revival of the *voie de fait*. But he never again contemplated a resolution which involved his own abdication, even as part of a deal which disposed of his rival as well.

The French King's uncles and ministers declined to wait to hear Benedict's 'good and speedy' ideas. Fortified by the support of the cardinals, they resolved to force his hand. On 2 February 1395 an assembly of the French Church met in Paris to advise the King how to bring an end to the schism. More than a hundred representatives of the higher clergy and the leading universities of France were present. It is clear that sentiment was divided. Even among the universities' representatives there was an important minority who were concerned about the implications of secular governments determining what was ultimately a question of canon law. But the King's uncles were determined to get the advice they wanted. The sessions were held in the Sainte Chapelle of the royal palace on the Île de la Cité and attended by the Chancellor of France and a host of royal councillors. They procured the election as president of the assembly of Simon de Cramaud, the intelligent and worldly Bishop of Poitiers. Simon was a famous orator and fixer who was fast becoming one of the most influential figures on Charles VI's Council. He knew what was expected of him. He manipulated the procedure of the assembly, carefully selecting the speakers, cutting short debate whenever it moved into awkward territory and marginalising dissenters. After two weeks of this the assembled churchmen declared the *voie de fait* militarily and politically impracticable and pronounced by a large majority in favour of the *voie de cession*. It was decided to send the most impressive possible embassy to Avignon with an intimidating retinue of soldiers and attendants. The Dukes of Berry, Burgundy and Orléans would all take part. A separate delegation from the University of Paris was to accompany them. Their instructions were to present Benedict XIII with the decision of the assembly and to call for his abdication as soon as a similar commitment could be extracted from his rival. The French King's ministers did not under-estimate the difficulty of bringing this about. An agreement would be required among the states of Europe, including those which belonged to the Roman obedience. The logic of their position was not spelled out but must have been clear enough to contemporaries. In the (highly probable) event that neither Pope would co-operate the principal nations of Europe would have to be persuaded to withdraw their obedience from both claimants. Ultimately, as Simon de Cramaud had recognised in his own speech to the assembly, it would probably be necessary to force both of them from their seats.[58]

France's adoption of the *voie de cession* was an extremely unwelcome development from Louis of Orléans's point of view. It brought about a revolution in French policy towards Italy which had important consequences for the play of factions in the Hôtel Saint-Pol. Louis's Italian schemes all ultimately depended on a close alliance with his father-in-law, Gian Galeazzo Visconti of Milan. Everything changed with the abandonment of the *voie de fait*, for it meant that Gian Galeazzo was no longer an indispensable collaborator. At the same time Louis's enemies were gathering strength at court. Foremost among them was the 25-year-old Queen, Isabelle of Bavaria. Forced by her husband's illness to fend for herself among the cabals of the Hôtel Saint-Pol, Isabelle was becoming a force to be reckoned with. She shared the hostility of her Wittelsbach relations to Gian Galeazzo. She resented the ambitions of her brother-in-law and his Visconti wife and the ostentatious preference of the King for Valentine during his bouts of insanity. She may also have shared the widespread prejudice which blamed the pair for his ill-health.

At the time of the Paris assembly Enguerrand de Coucy was in Italy. He was actively engaged in the conquest of Liguria in the interests of Louis of Orléans and his father-in-law. Coucy and his Italian allies had occupied the port of Savona with nearly 3,000 troops, the first stage of a carefully planned offensive against Genoa itself. In December 1394 Enguerrand negotiated a fresh alliance between Louis of Orléans and Gian Galeazzo which, like earlier agreements of its kind, envisaged the invasion of the papal state in Italy. Louis, who was well aware of what was being done in his name, must have been counting on his personal influence over his brother to get support for this venture in Paris. But the French King was a broken reed by now, even when he was lucid. The republic of Genoa had astutely countered Enguerrand de Coucy's moves against the city by sending its ambassadors to the court of France to offer the lordship of the republic to Charles VI himself. Better the distant lordship of the King of France than the closer embrace of the all-powerful despot of Milan and his aggressive son-in-law. At the end of February 1395 the Genoese ambassadors were in Paris waiting on the French King's answer. While they waited the Queen joined forces with Philip of Burgundy to put an end to Louis's Italian dreams. Charles VI was prevailed upon to accept the Genoese offer in principle, subject to negotiating the details. The conduct of French policy in Italy was abruptly taken out of Louis's hands. He was forced to give up Savona and his Genoese ambitions in return for a cash payment. Enguerrand de Coucy was ordered to desist from his operations in Liguria and then recalled to France. In Paris Louis and his friends, marginalised in

Council, nursed their resentments and grew progressively more hostile to the government of the King's uncles.[59]

On 22 May 1395 the three French Dukes entered Avignon across the Pont-Saint-Bénézet, followed by a suite of more than 5,000 soldiers and attendants. Five days later, on 27 May, the Pope, in the presence of the assembled cardinals and officers of his court, unveiled his own plan for healing the schism. This proved to be the so-called *voie de convention*. It involved a meeting between the two popes and their colleges of cardinals at some neutral place on the borders of France at which their claims could be debated and resolved. Benedict professed himself confident that if the conference were once held his rivals could not fail to perceive the legitimacy of his own claims. The royal dukes begged to differ. They thought that the Pope's proposal was naive. It could lead only to delay, sterile argument and failure. Over the following days there was a series of futile meetings. Benedict played for time, asking for written memoranda and proposing special commissions to study the issue. The Duke of Berry, who served as the French spokesman, dismissed all this as a waste of time. Charles VI had resolved upon the *voie de cession* and would accept nothing less. Berry declined to enter into lengthy debates on the issue. He called for the Pope's immediate assent.

Having got nothing out of Benedict the Duke of Berry assembled the cardinals at Villeneuve-lès-Avignon on the French side of the Rhône and browbeat them into declaring, each in turn, his own opinion. A large majority pronounced in favour of the *voie de cession*. Most of them, including the solid core of French cardinals, were probably voicing their true preference. Some of them dared not say anything else. One protested against the whole proceeding and another agreed but with qualifications which rendered his support valueless. Armed with the cardinals' declarations, the French royal princes returned to the audience hall of the papal palace to insist on their position. The Pope demurred. He asked to speak to each of the three Dukes privately and then to their principal councillors. He protested with dignity that lay governments could not ordain the fortunes of the papacy, least of all a single lay government. He objected to the high-handed way that he had been treated. He declared that the cardinals were saying one thing to the French princes and another to him. On 24 June 1395 the cardinals came before him in a body to declare their conviction that the *voie de cession* was the only solution. A week later, at another audience, they threatened to give the Pope formal advice to abdicate, thereby obliging him to comply if he was to honour the oath that he had sworn at the time of the conclave. There was an embarrassing scene. Benedict declared that the cardinals had no power to act in that or any other respect without his consent. He forbade them to have any further dealings with the French royal dukes or to sign the declarations, and confiscated the drafts which they had brought with them. The Pope was isolated but immoveable. On 8 July 1395 he put an end to all further discussion. At a final audience in the presence of the French delegations and the whole body of cardinals he announced that he would have nothing to do with the *voie de cession*. He would 'rather be burned alive'. 'Holy Father', the Duke of Berry responded, 'do you want to have any authority in France?' After nearly two months in the papal city the three royal dukes returned empty-handed to Paris.[60]

Even in their greatest moments of hubris the Dukes of Berry and Burgundy knew that France could not achieve the concerted withdrawal of both popes alone. If the *voie de cession* was to be pursued it would be necessary to reach an accommodation with England, which was the principal patron of the Roman obedience. The King's uncles were counting on the support of Richard II. There were good reasons for their confidence. The English government, although firmly committed to the Roman obedience, was certainly not committed to the current incumbent. At the time of his election in 1389 they had seriously considered declining to recognise either pontiff and in effect pursuing their own version of the *voie de cession* five years before it was adopted in France. Since then, there had been a succession of disputes with Boniface IX about taxation, patronage and jurisdiction. John of Gaunt expressed his own views with characteristic bluntness. Buttonholed during the sessions of the Amiens conference by the Provençal jurist Honoré Bonet, who was there as part of the French delegation, Gaunt observed that it was unreasonable to expect the English to abandon the Roman obedience while the two countries were at war and Avignon remained a dependency of France. But, he added, he personally thought little of either claim and believed that the ultimate solution would be the abdication or deposition of both Popes once the war was over. 'I am telling you that when peace is made between our Kings there will be one Pope, not before.' Richard II held very similar views and made no secret of them when French diplomats visited his court.[61]

Towards the end of February 1395, shortly after the Paris assembly closed, a French embassy was sent urgently to England with instructions to find their way to Richard II in Ireland. The moment was somewhat delicate. It was well known that ever since the death of Anne of Bohemia Richard's councillors had been looking about for a diplomatically advantageous marriage for him. Several possibilities had been rather noisily explored. Currently the favoured choices were a daughter or sister of the King of Navarre or else Yolande, the sole surviving child of the King of Aragon. England's negotiations with the Spanish kingdoms were extremely unwelcome to the French court for a number of reasons. In the first place a marriage alliance with either Navarre or Aragon would further undermine French influence in the Iberian peninsula, a sore point at a time when English princesses were already married to the kings of Castile and Portugal. An alliance with Yolande of Aragon would be particularly objectionable, for the lady was already betrothed to Louis II of Anjou. Louis was counting on Aragonese naval support for his continuing struggle to reconquer the Kingdom of Naples from the House of Durazzo. Worst of all, Richard's current marriage plans would remove the opportunity to negotiate a marriage between Richard and a French bride as part of a wider agreement between the two kings to restore the peace of western Europe and heal the papal schism. French agents were hastily despatched to Pamplona and Barcelona to obstruct the English proposals there, which they did with some success. Meanwhile the French ambassadors in Ireland were instructed to suggest any of three eligible cousins of Charles VI. They reached Richard towards the end of April 1395, probably at Waterford, where he was in the process of receiving the submissions of the Irish chiefs and winding up a highly successful campaign. The English King's initial reaction is not recorded. None of the ladies on offer was as desirable, diplomatically speaking, as the Iberian princesses. But before Richard had a chance to consider their offer with his councillors the French significantly increased the stakes.[62]

Richard II returned to England in May 1395. Shortly after his arrival another French embassy appeared before him with instructions to offer him the hand of Charles VI's eldest daughter Isabelle, who was then just five years old. The bearer of this proposal was none other than the visionary moral reformer and crusade propagandist Robert the Hermit. He brought with him a personal letter from the King of France, dated 15 May 1395, which was couched in ecstatic and emotional terms. Charles begged the English King to help him 'rebuild the walls long ago sundered by mortal war of the united temple of God that is France and England'. He wrote of his 'tearful recollection of our forbears' war, which had now lasted sixty years, years in which so many evils have occurred, so many Christian souls have perished, so many churches been destroyed and women raped.' God in his special goodness had reserved to him and to Richard, men hitherto innocent of bloodshed, the task of reconciling their two nations in spite of the opposition of those around them. 'Let us make ourselves God's auxiliaries and hold fast to the vocation to which he has called us as young men to bring about the sweet peace for which all Christendom longs.' This remarkable diplomatic document, with its extravagant rhetoric and high-blown phrases, was certainly not drafted by Charles himself or any of his ministers or officials. The sentiments are authentic, but the author was probably the Ancient Recluse of the Celestine convent in Paris, Philippe de Mézières. It was accompanied by a document which was unquestionably his. Philippe's *Letter to Richard II* was a prolix treatise, written in the same discursive and allegorical style, which had been commissioned by the French King and composed at lightning speed over the past two months. Its main purpose was to encourage Richard to override the domestic opponents of peace with France. Specifically, Philippe tried to persuade the English King to abandon his existing marriage plans in favour of a union with Isabelle which would serve the wider interests of peace between England and France. He foresaw a time when, the peace made, the two kings would join forces to heal the papal schism and expel the Turks from eastern Europe.[63]

This direct appeal to Richard's emotions was shrewdly judged and very much in line with what was known about the English King's views. Richard had never shown much interest in participating personally in a crusade but he had been attracted by the crusading ideal ever since he had first received Leo of Armenia at his court. His long-standing belief that the war was a disaster for England and Christendom was based at least in part on moral conviction. But it was increasingly reinforced by other, more prosaic considerations. The King's financial situation had progressively deteriorated throughout the 1390s, a problem which was masked by windfall receipts in the early part of the decade but was causing serious concern by 1395. Parliament had been reluctant to authorise public taxation since the truce of Leulinghem. Yet the garrisons at Calais and Brest and on the Scottish march remained a heavy financial commitment in spite of the suspension of hostilities. At the same time Richard was expensively reinforcing his political position at home by increasing the size and splendour of his household and the number of his retainers in the shires. So when Richard replied that he was 'well pleased' with the French King's letter of 15 May his words were more than the conventional diplomatic courtesies.[64]

From an early stage Richard resolved upon the marriage to Isabelle and took charge personally of the task of driving the project forward. In July 1395 Jean Froissart arrived in England after an absence of nearly three decades, armed with a sheaf of introductions, to collect evidence for his history. He found the country alive with gossip about current negotiations with France. A few days after landing at Dover the chronicler joined the court at Leeds Castle and was presented to Richard II, whom he had last seen at his baptism in Bordeaux cathedral. His account of his reception graphically reveals the tensions at the English court. The Gascon knight Jean de Grailly, who rode with him up the London road from Leeds, filled him in on the current state of English politics. The King, he said, was enthusiastic about the French marriage. Like Charles VI and his ministers he was looking at the proposal in the wider context of a European peace. The language which Jean de Grailly attributed to him might have been lifted from the French King's letter. The war with France had lasted too long, Richard had told his advisers. 'Too many gallant men have died, too many evil deeds perpetrated, too much destruction and bloodshed inflicted. All Christendom is weakened by this war.' But the project had also reignited old quarrels. Beyond the royal court dissenting voices were already making themselves heard. Some declared themselves to be astonished that the King should think of marrying the daughter of his enemy. Some opined that the princess was too young, others that she would be too French. Much of what Grailly told Froissart was confirmed by Sir Richard Stury, a councillor with whom the chronicler had a long discussion some days later. Both of the chronicler's informants regarded the Duke of Gloucester as the main threat to the King's position. 'Malicious and devious' according to one, 'proud, arrogant and dangerous' according to the other, Gloucester was still bitterly resented for his role in the judicial murders of 1388 and feared for his ability to appeal to the country at large. The Duke of Lancaster, potentially Richard's strongest ally, was far away in Bordeaux. Gloucester, cowed by his brother's power in England and frightened of his influence over the King, plotted to keep him there indefinitely.[65]

For a few months a semblance of unity was maintained by pitching the English terms for the marriage alliance too high. A 'solemn' embassy was instructed to proceed to Paris, the first English embassy of its kind to appear in the French capital for many years. It was led by Robert Waldby, the absentee Archbishop of Dublin, who was one of England's foremost experts on Gascon affairs. He was accompanied by that veteran of past diplomatic conferences John Gilbert, Bishop of St. David's. But the real principals were Richard's close friends and collaborators, Edward Earl of Rutland (Edmund Langley's son) and Thomas Mowbray, Earl of Nottingham. The ambassadors were instructed to demand a dowry of two million gold francs (£333,334) but were given discretion to come down to a million. At the same time, if the atmosphere seemed right they were to propose a second royal marriage between Rutland himself and Isabelle's younger sister Joan. It was their territorial demands which were the main obstacle to progress. The English ambassadors were instructed to call for the surrender of the whole of the territory ceded to England at the treaty of Brétigny including Poitou, northern Saintonge and Ponthieu, which had been withheld from the French offer of 1393, all of it to be held free of homage. Normandy was to be settled on the eldest son of the marriage and Anjou and Maine on the second, to be held 'as fully and completely as any King of England had ever held them', which presumably meant as fiefs of France. Scotland was to be conquered with French assistance and settled on the third son if there was one. On top of all this Richard wanted to be allowed to maintain his existing coat of arms with the arms of France crossed with those of England. These extravagant demands, if they had been met, would have recreated an English state in France comparable with the twelfth-century empire of the Angevins at its grandest. It is unlikely that anyone in England seriously expected them to be met. They were designed to exploit the obvious desire of the French government for a settlement and were no doubt expected to provoke a round of horse-trading. Richard's ministers must have hoped that in the course of the bargaining the French might be induced to abandon their insistence on liege homage which had created so much political difficulty for him in England.[66]

If so they were destined to be disappointed. The English ambassadors made their formal entry into Paris at the end of July 1395, shortly before the return of the Dukes of Berry and Burgundy from Avignon. They remained there for a month. We are told that they were magnificently entertained, that their accommodation cost the French treasury the enormous sum of 500 *livres* a day and that their stay was punctuated by splendid banquets in the presence of the King. There is no record of their discussions with the French ministers. But it is clear that the Dukes of Berry and Burgundy were in no mood to entertain the English demands even in the aftermath of their humiliation at the hands of Benedict XIII. Instead of engaging in the bargaining that the English Council had anticipated they rejected the ambassadors' demands out of hand and declined to discuss them further. Short of liege homage, the only deal which they were willing to contemplate was a long truce.[67]

Richard now had to confront the dilemma which his extravagant proposals had merely deferred. A long truce would mark a grave diplomatic defeat. It would bring France almost all the advantages of peace for a generation but without requiring it to make any of the territorial concessions which had been so painfully negotiated over the past twenty years. The parties would simply stand on the territory which they held. Charles VI would retain all the provinces of the south-west which had been conquered since 1369, including those which his ministers had offered to restore in 1393. The English King would be left with nothing but the narrow strip of territory along the Atlantic coast and the shores of the Gironde, which was all that remained of the duchy of Aquitaine. The only advantage for England in such a deal was that it would enable the domestically contentious issue of liege homage to be parked. Richard would undoubtedly have preferred to concede the issue of liege homage but he had tried to persuade Parliament to endorse this course in January 1394 and failed. So, determined to have peace in one way or the other, he resolved upon a long truce with no *quid pro quo* at all other than the hand of Isabelle of France. Initially he tried to limit the truce to five years but when the ambassadors returned to Paris in October 1395 the French royal Council insisted on longer. Over the next six months Richard conceded twenty years and then twenty-eight. He does not appear to have consulted anyone about this radical break with England's traditional negotiating line, beyond his Council and his closest relatives and friends.[68]

In Paris progress was slow. Diplomatic business was repeatedly interrupted during the winter as Charles VI moved erratically between lucidity and depressive violence. His attendance at audiences and Council meetings became increasingly irregular. Court factions fought for influence as the King's servants kept him immured in his rooms at the Hôtel Saint-Pol, while outside the palace walls speculation ran riot. Reports that he had been bewitched by the Duchess of Orléans, which had first surfaced in 1393, became so persistent that Valentine was obliged to withdraw from Paris to her husband's estates. It was not until February 1396 that the French King appeared to have recovered well enough for the business to resume. On 9 March terms were finally agreed with the English representatives. Isabelle was to marry Richard II with a dowry of 800,000 gold francs (£133,333). Neither Isabelle herself nor any children of the marriage were to have any claim to appanages in France. So much for Richard's proposal that they should be endowed with Normandy, Anjou and Maine. The current truce was to be extended for twenty-eight years until 29 September 1426 and was to apply to the allies of both sides. Elaborate arrangements, born of the bitter experience in the past two decades, were made for its enforcement. In the south-west, where *patis* and ransoms were still legally due to the *routier* captains, a bipartite commission was set up to 'moderate' the more onerous agreements.

Thus it was that sixty years of war were brought to an end with a whimper. There was no agreement about territory or homage or even the English claim to the crown of France. None of the great issues which had divided England and France since the days of Philip the Fair and Edward I were addressed. At the French court the outcome was viewed with much satisfaction. The Duke of Burgundy marked the occasion with a magnificent banquet in the Hôtel d'Artois. Three days later, on 12 March 1396, Richard was betrothed by proxy to Isabelle at a ceremony in the Sainte-Chapelle performed by that great apostle of the *voie de cession*, Simon de Cramaud. The princess, who was not yet seven years old, at once became known in accordance with French court etiquette as Queen of England. In Paris the mood was full of joy and optimism. Men said that the war which had been provoked by the marriage of Isabelle of France to Richard's great-grandfather Edward II would now be closed by his marriage to another Isabelle. Especially, they added, as the English would not be getting an inch of territory out of the deal.[69]

The great question was whether Richard would be able to carry the English political community with him once this fact was appreciated. The King did not expect the truce to be popular. He recalled John of Gaunt from Gascony at the end of 1395 at least in part in order to bolster his political position. He even toyed with the idea of seeking French military assistance to put down a rebellion in England. Charles VI's ministers, who were well informed about English politics in this period, were concerned. They sent their ambassadors, accompanied by the formidable figure of Robert the Hermit, to reason with the Duke of Gloucester, whom they correctly identified as the most dangerous of the dissentients. Gloucester received his visitor with frigid courtesy at his manor of Pleshey in Essex and listened to his emotional oratory over two full days. But he remained as belligerent as ever. Robert, he observed, might have the ear of kings and princes in both countries but he, Gloucester, knew better than to take his advice on a matter of this importance. He blamed his brothers Lancaster and York for the way things had turned out. He had tried to reason with

York, he said, but without success. Lancaster was not even worth arguing with. The King had not asked for his own views but if it had been up to him he would never have allowed the French to get away with their treacherous repudiation of the treaty of Brétigny. After the difficulties of the last few years no one under-estimated Gloucester's power to make trouble. Richard told the Count of Saint-Pol that his uncle still had powerful allies among the nobility and was actively engaged in trying to stir up the Londoners. Yet, once the deed was done, it proved difficult to rally opposition to an agreement that resolved nothing and conceded nothing but merely brought an end to the fighting. Richard was careful to avoid giving Gloucester a platform. The truce was not formally proclaimed until 1398, when the previous four-year truce was about to expire. Judging by contemporary reports very little information about it was available. Unusually for a major diplomatic initiative, the King did not consult Parliament or even, so far as is known, a Great Council. For the moment opposition remained muted, to the obvious relief of politicians in both countries.[70]

On 28 March 1396, some three weeks after the English ambassadors had put their seals to the agreements in Paris, the Duke of Burgundy presided over a meeting in the Hôtel Saint-Pol in Paris at which the final arrangements were made for the departure of the Balkan crusade. The long delay had deprived the venture of most of its leaders. John of Gaunt, in failing health and preoccupied by political problems in Gascony and England, had pulled out in the autumn. Philip of Burgundy and Louis of Orléans had withdrawn not long afterwards, almost certainly because their presence was required in France for the final stages of the negotiations with England. Philip of Burgundy's 25-year-old heir John, Count of Nevers, was appointed as the nominal leader of the expedition. In reality the command was exercised by his immediate subordinates: Enguerrand de Coucy; the Constable, Philip Count of Eu; the Admiral, Jean de Vienne; and the Marshal, Jean de Boucicaut. In spite of the presence of some German knights and a few hundred English and Gascon soldiers under Gaunt's illegitimate son John Beaufort, the crusade remained a largely French affair. The names of the captains who served in it read like a roll-call of the French campaigns of the past three decades in France and Flanders, Spain, Italy and Scotland. In the course of May at least three armies comprising some 10,000 men in all gathered on the Rhône and the Saône before passing through Germany and northern Italy to converge on Hungary.[71]

At the beginning of August 1396, as the crusaders reached the Danube, Richard II travelled to Calais with his Chancellor and principal advisers to meet the Duke of Burgundy. His main purpose was to agree the final arrangements for taking delivery of his child-bride. He also wanted, he said, to visit the town, which he had never seen; to seal his personal friendship with the dominant personality in the French government; and to talk about the healing of the papal schism, a subject on which he had so far offered congenial words but no firm commitment. Richard was dazzled by the grandeur of the Valois court and by the wealth and apparent solidity of the French state. Never one to do things by halves, he went to great lengths to impress Philip with his own substance. He had the streets of Calais lined with citizens in livery to receive him. He built a vast audience chamber of timber for their first meeting. He presided at mass in St. Nicholas's church wearing his crown and carrying his sceptre. And he agreed, to Philip's great satisfaction, to declare his conversion to the *voie de cession*, a decision made without any formal consultation with the English Church for no other reason than to curry favour with the Duke of Burgundy. The two men agreed that Richard would meet Charles VI on the march of Calais at the end of September, when outstanding issues would be discussed and appropriate announcements made to the world at large. Isabelle of France would be delivered to him on the same occasion.

In spite of the splendour of the display at Calais there was a noticeable edginess in Richard's dealings with the French King's uncle. He knew that there were strong misgivings in England about the truce, the wisdom of the French marriage and the *voie de cession*. The Duke of Gloucester and his friends looked on sullenly as Richard extended the hand of friendship to the enemies of his father and grandfather. The University of Oxford, which like most of the English Church regarded the Avignon papacy as a political creature of the French government, had only recently rejected the *voie de cession* outright after a debate which had unleashed a fierce tide of anti-French sentiment among clerical pamphleteers in England. At Calais Richard seemed to be glancing over his shoulder all the while at the state of opinion in England and looking for security in a closer relationship with France. In a moment of candour, he told the Duke of Burgundy that although he and the men who were with him were content with what they had agreed, none of them could be sure that the English people would endorse it.[72]

The meeting of the kings, which had been talked about on and off since 1387, finally happened at the end of October 1396. The site chosen was the bleak borderland at the edge of the pale of Calais between Guines and Ardres, which became famous more than a century later as the site of Henry VIII's Field of Cloth of Gold. An immense operation had been required on both sides of the Channel, costing the equivalent of a short military campaign. The French budget for the occasion was 100,000 francs (£16,666) in addition to the substantial sums which would be spent on food and accommodation by the towns through which the royal cortege would pass on its way across northern France. The English were reported to have spent even more: 40,000 marks (£26,666) according to one estimate, a quarter of which went on gifts for Charles VI and the French royal princes. A vast palisaded encampment was prepared, filled with some 240 gaily coloured pavilions and two great tented reception halls. The ceremonies were carefully choreographed. On the morning of 26 October 1396 Richard II rode out of Calais towards the camp accompanied by the Dukes of Berry and Orléans, while Charles VI approached with the Dukes of Lancaster and Gloucester from Saint-Omer. Each of them was escorted by 400 knights and squires armed only with swords and daggers and by unarmed pages. Artillery, longbows and crossbows were, by agreement, kept out of sight and far away. On the following afternoon the two monarchs met at a post driven into the ground in the middle of the encampment. Their entourages dismounted and knelt on the ground as they shook hands and kissed. The royal dukes offered them sweetmeats and spiced wine. Precious gifts were exchanged. Both kings then walked hand in hand to the French pavilion nearby, followed by their advisers. There they conferred in private for four hours. The ceremony was repeated on the following day in spite of a torrential rainstorm and was followed by another long conference. The kings swore a great oath to observe the truce, never to arm or allow others to arm against each other and to bend all their energies to achieving a formal peace 'with no cavilling, trickery or special pleading'. The following day was a Sunday. It was on the Monday that a tearful Princess Isabelle, dressed in a blue velvet dress sewn with golden *fleurs de lys* and wearing a diadem of gold and pearls, was carried by the Dukes of Berry and Burgundy to Richard's pavilion. She was taken away by a delegation of English ladies led by the Duchesses of Lancaster and Gloucester. Four days later, on 4 November 1396, she was brought to the church of St. Nicholas in Calais where Richard married her. She was five days short of her seventh birthday. Her dolls were included in her trousseau. The first instalment of the dowry, 300,000 gold francs, was weighed out on the day of the ceremony and a receipt delivered.[73]

The final meeting occurred on the evening of the following day in a council chamber of the citadel of Calais. Richard II presided. The Dukes of Berry and Burgundy and the Count of Melun were present on the French side and the Dukes of Lancaster and Gloucester and the Earl of Rutland on the English. The assembled princes issued what amounted to a joint communiqué covering points which had presumably been agreed during the conferences of the past few days. In the first place they declared that there would be an immediate reduction of a quarter in all *patis* currently being levied on the Gascon march. The concession, although undoubtedly humane, was made at the direct expense of the Gascon professional soldiers to whom most of these *patis* were owed. Secondly they declared that in spite of the long truce to which Richard had committed himself, negotiations for a permanent peace were not dead. No firm commitment was made, however, on any of the major issues which had divided England and France. The matter was left to the mutual goodwill of the two kings and their representatives. The four royal dukes would meet again on 1 April 1397 to resume the previous discussions. Finally it was agreed to send a joint embassy to Rome and Avignon. The King of Castile had already agreed to participate in this delegation and it was proposed to invite the German King to do so as well. The ambassadors were to be led by the egregious Robert the Hermit. Their instructions were to declare to the two claimants to the papal throne that the kings were determined to impose the *voie de cession*. By the end of September 1397 they would expect them to have abdicated so that a third could be elected in their place.[74]

These major concessions to France's current foreign policy objectives were accompanied by another, even more remarkable, which was not disclosed in the joint communiqué. A month before the summit meeting, on 29 September 1396, Charles VI's government had sealed a five-year military alliance with the Florentine Republic. The French committed themselves to intervene in Italy to defend the city-state, whose territory was then hard-pressed by Gian Galeazzo Visconti's captains and allies. In return they were to be allowed to appropriate, with limited exceptions, whatever they could conquer in the domains of Gian Galeazzo in Lombardy. A few days later, on 4 October, Charles VI committed himself to accepting the sovereignty of Genoa. Under the terms of the formal treaty, which was sealed by the King's agents in the ducal palace in Genoa on the day before his meeting with Richard II, the Genoese transferred the sovereignty of the city and its territory to the King of France, who undertook to defend them against the Visconti state of Milan. A French nominee was to be appointed as their governor. The King had already made plans for putting his undertakings into effect. He proposed to lead an army across the Alps in the spring. These acts marked the final repudiation of France's alliance with the despot of Milan and the Italian policy of Louis of Orléans. Gian Galeazzo's herald, who was seen standing among the group of heralds at the side of the marquee where the Kings were banqueting, was abruptly stripped of his master's arms, dismissed from the King's presence and told never to appear at court again. Meanwhile Charles VI pressed the English King to supply an English contingent to support his invasion of Lombardy. It was an extraordinary suggestion. The project served no discernible English interest. It was contrary to England's traditional policy of trying to contain France's ambitions beyond its frontiers. But Richard agreed to participate, apparently at his own cost. A substantial English force was promised, 15,000 men according to reports reaching Italy, commanded by two of Richard's closest collaborators, the Earls of Rutland and Nottingham.[75]

It is this brief moment of concord which seems to be represented in the Wilton Diptych in the National Gallery in London, one of the most beautiful objects to survive from the late middle ages and an image rich in enigmatic political symbolism. The Diptych, which Richard II must have commissioned shortly after his marriage to Isabelle, is a small portable altar-piece. The King is shown at the age of his coronation, an idealised young man wearing a jewelled crown. He is being presented to the Virgin and Child by St. John the Baptist and the two English royal saints, St. Edmund and St. Edward the Confessor, while angels crowd around, their eyes fixed upon him. It is a strikingly narcissistic image of sacral kingship, very characteristic of the official portraiture which Richard deliberately promoted in the final years of his reign. The King and the angels are all wearing his emblem of the white hart together with the livery collars of broom pods which Charles VI had adopted as his own emblem. Behind the Virgin one of the angels holds a banner with a pennant of St. George, at the top of which there is an orb, enamelled with an image of England, a green, wooded island dominated by a white, turreted castle and surrounded by a sea of silver leaf. Here, two centuries before Shakespeare gave the words to John of Gaunt, was the sceptred isle, 'this fortress built by nature for herself against infection and the hand of war . . . this precious stone set in the silver sea . . . this England.'[76]

CHAPTER XVII

Epilogue
1396–1399

On 25 September 1396 the last great crusading army to leave western Europe for the east was wiped out by the Ottoman Sultan Bayezid at Nicopolis on the Danube together with its Hungarian and Wallachian allies. The French contingent represented only part of the forces of the Christian coalition and the overall command belonged to the Hungarian King, Sigismund. But the French heavy cavalry had insisted on leading the attack before the rest were ready and without properly reconnoitring the enemy's positions. They bore the brunt of the fighting and acquitted themselves with extraordinary courage and endurance. But they were defeated by superior tactics, discipline and force of numbers. Jean de Vienne was killed defending the standard of Notre-Dame in the heat of the battle. Many died with him. Thousands more who survived the battle were killed by the pursuing Turkish *spahis*. Others were drowned in the Danube as they tried to escape or were massacred in the prisoners' pens when it was all over. All the leaders of the French host were captured and held for ransom: John, Count of Nevers, Gui de la Tremoille, the Constable Philip, Count of Eu, Marshal Boucicaut, Enguerrand de Coucy, Henry of Bar and Jacques de Bourbon, Count of La Marche. Sigismund was more fortunate. He abandoned his treasury and his army on the field and escaped by boat with the Grand Master of the Hospitallers, eventually finding his way home via the Black Sea with the aid of the Venetians. When the kings of France and England met with their uncles and ministers on the march of Calais they were still completely ignorant of the catastrophe that had overcome the army more than a month before. It was not until the beginning of December that the first refugees from the battlefield found their way back to France with the news.[1]

In England the Duke of Gloucester could scarcely contain his delight. The heavy casualties were bound to weaken France militarily. The outcome, he told his intimates, confirmed what he had always said about 'those French shits'. They were no good at fighting when they allowed themselves to be tested in battle. Philippe de Mézières, whose life's work was undone by the defeat, came to a curiously similar conclusion. The '*desconfiture lacrimable*' of Nicopolis, he thought, was God's punishment of the chivalry of France for its moral failings. They had been destroyed by the same sin of pride which had brought French armies to destruction at Crécy and Poitiers. The shock transformed the political mood in western Europe. It put an end to the brief moment of moral anguish which had turned so much of the knightly class against the Anglo-French war in the 1390s. And it removed a fruitful area of co-operation between the two nations. There would be fresh calls for crusading armies from the west over the following years and some small-scale expeditions to reinforce the defence of the beleaguered city of Constantinople. But there was no more talk of the great Anglo-French army which would liberate Jerusalem after the Turks had been swept from eastern Europe. What remained were the crude political and strategic realities which had always existed.[2]

The first test of English public opinion came with the opening of Parliament at Westminster on 22 January 1397. Unfortunately the Parliament roll appears to have been heavily edited to exclude overt evidence of opposition to the King's policies. But the record, even in its truncated form, shows that there were serious misgivings about Richard's diplomacy. The traditional opening address was delivered by the new Chancellor, Edmund Stafford, Bishop of Exeter. It was more than usually anodyne. The real business of the session was not explained until two days later, when both houses were summoned to what seems to have been a closed meeting in the refectory of Westminster Abbey. There they learned from the Chancellor about Richard's plans to send an army to support the ambitions of Charles VI in Italy. The King wanted a fresh Parliamentary subsidy to pay for it. The Commons were visibly dismayed. When they withdrew to consider the Chancellor's demands there was evidently a good deal of hostility. Word of this reached Richard's ears and provoked an outburst of rage of a kind which was now becoming familiar. On 25 January the Commons came before the King in full Parliament to deliver a barbed apology. They declared that they had not presumed to criticise Richard's Italian plans, which were entirely a matter for him. But for their part they would have nothing to do with them. If he wanted to invade Italy with the King of France he could pay the cost himself. Richard, instead of replying through his Chancellor, responded in person. He told them why he had undertaken to join in the Italian campaign. After years of misery and destruction arising from the war, he said, England needed a long and secure peace. This was most likely to be achieved by the closest possible alliance with France. The Italian expedition would increase Charles VI's affection for him and for his realm. It would encourage him to come to Richard's assistance if one day he should need it. Besides, he said, in an apparent reference to the war between Milan and Florence, as two of the 'most worthy and valiant Christian princes' the rulers of England and France had a moral duty to protect the weak against tyrants. He acknowledged that he could not make them contribute to the cost but he was entitled to direct his own retainers and employ his own money for whatever purposes he pleased.[3]

In February 1397 Charles VI of France relapsed once more into madness and the Italian project was put off indefinitely. The news, which must have reached Richard during the sittings of Parliament, may well have come as a relief. But Richard was busy cementing his relations with the French court on other fronts. As soon as he returned from Calais he opened negotiations with the Duke of Brittany for the restoration of Brest. Agreement was reached on 16 March 1397 to abandon the place in return for an indemnity of 120,000 francs (£20,000) on the sole condition that it was not to be used as a base for offensive operations against England or English shipping. Brest was finally delivered up to the Duke's representatives in June, after more than half a century of military occupation. Reports circulated in England that Calais would be next. These were almost certainly untrue but they found ready audiences among the growing number of people who were dismayed by Richard's craven policy towards France. Meanwhile, in April, the joint Anglo-French embassy in which Richard had promised to participate set out on its hopeless mission to Avignon and Rome with an ultimatum calling on the two claimants to the papal throne to abdicate.[4]

For all his lauding of the benefits of closer relations with France Richard II got very little in return for his concessions. Once the French King's ministers had achieved their own objectives they naturally lost interest in the negotiations for a permanent peace, on which the English had been counting to achieve theirs. The conference between the royal dukes on either side, which was to have occurred on 1 April 1397, was postponed at the request of the French for 'various reasons'. Richard sent the Earls of Rutland and Nottingham and Sir William Scrope to Paris to press for a fresh date by June at the latest. They were brushed off with excuses: the Duke of Berry had not been consulted; ministers were preoccupied with other urgent business. The conference never met.[5]

The Duke of Gloucester, already disgusted by the King's marriage and convinced that Richard had been duped by the French, was shocked by the surrender of the Atlantic barbicans on the coast of France. They represented in his eyes the best guarantee of England's ability to return to the strategy of destructive *chevauchées* in France when the English recovered their self-confidence, as they surely would. At the beginning of July 1397 the garrison of Brest returned to England full of bile against the government. The last captain of the town had been the royal favourite John Holand, Earl of Huntingdon, an absentee like his predecessors who had allowed their pay to fall into arrears. Under the terms of Richard's deal with the Duke of Brittany they had also lost their lucrative *patis* in western Brittany. The men conducted embarrassing demonstrations in the palace of Westminster and rioted in the streets of London until they were cleared away to billets in the suburbs. The Duke of Gloucester publicly took their part. Froissart quotes a long rant of the Duke, addressed to his retainer Sir John Lakenheath, which is so lifelike that it is tempting to believe that the chronicler had heard him speak like this.

By God, if I live for two more years in good health this war will be fought out again. If I have anything to do with it we shall be done with all these truces and suspensions of arms, these covert understandings . . . If we only had a real king in England, someone who would fight the French for the heritage which they have tricked out of him, that man would find 100,000 archers and 6,000 men-at-arms behind him ready to put their lives and substance at his service across the Channel. But No, we have don't have a king like that here in England. If only we did he would not hesitate to show himself in France. There has never been a better time to invade France than now. If we attacked them now they would fight back. The people of this realm love a good battle. They would throw themselves boldly into the fray for the fat lucre to be had from it, just as they used to do in the time of my father and my brother the Prince of Wales. I am the last-born of the royal princes of the house of England. But if only I were able to make my voice heard I would be the first: the first to go back to war, the first to right all the wrongs which in our silliness and softness we have let them do to us. Our lord the King has actually allied himself by marriage with his enemy. That's no way for a true warrior to behave. No, not on your life it isn't. The man's arse is too heavy to be shifted. All he ever wants to do is to eat, drink and sleep, dance and caper about and laugh the hours away with women. What sort of life is that for a man of action? For a man who is serious about honour and arms, or has any vigour left in him . . . What we want is battle. Battle and victory are the only things that are going to make us rich and allow us to recover what is ours. But instead we will just have to languish on as we do now and have done ever since my nephew became King of England. Things cannot go on like this. Surely the country will sooner or later wake up to what is happening. This King is levying heavy taxes on merchants. They are very angry about it. Yet no one knows what he does with the money. He dishes it out to men who do him rotten service while his people suffer. I tell you that before long we will see a great uprising in this country. People are already starting to complain. They are not going to put up with all this business much longer . . . You'll see if I am not right about that, Lakenheath, you mark my words.[6]

The Duke of Gloucester spoke like a man standing alone, deserted by his former allies. Richard's calculation that he could circumvent English hostility to a formal treaty by agreeing a long truce seemed to be working. Gloucester tried to stir up opposition to Richard's foreign policy among the Londoners. But London was cowed by recent disputes with the King and weakened by a severe depression in the wool trade. Gloucester tried to frighten them with reports of the imminent loss of Calais. Richard was able to persuade the city's representatives that nothing of the sort was intended. According to Froissart the Duke tried to interest the Earl of March, arguably the heir presumptive to the throne, in the idea of serving as the figurehead for a *coup* to be organised in conjunction with the Earls of Arundel and Warwick. But the young man took fright before Gloucester had a chance to develop these proposals. How much substance there was in these rumours is impossible to say. Froissart probably got his information from French diplomats at Richard's court such as the Count of Saint-Pol, who had often supplied him with material for his chronicle. Like other councillors of Charles VI Saint-Pol was becoming concerned about the stability of Richard's government. Gloucester, Arundel and Warwick were bitter men. But no hard evidence was ever discovered of a plot against Richard's government. The probability is that the reports reflected nothing more than Gloucester's tendency to talk big.[7]

Richard II, ever paranoid about hidden treasons, took them at face value. Conferring with a small caucus of his closest advisers he resolved upon a pre-emptive strike. On 10 July 1397 the King held a banquet in the Earl of Huntingdon's mansion at Coldharbour in the city. Gloucester, Arundel and Warwick were all invited. Only Warwick appeared. On the surface all was friendship and reconciliation but at the end of the meal he was arrested. Arundel had smelled a rat and stayed away. He shut himself in his castle at Reigate but Richard, using the Earl's brother the Archbishop of Canterbury as a go-between, persuaded him to give himself up. As for Gloucester, his protestations of illness were quite genuine. He was lying bedridden at Pleshey. Richard, remembering the events of 1387, believed that his uncle must have assembled a large force of men-at-arms around the castle. He hastily gathered an army of his own, consisting of his household knights, retainers of the peers who had been present at the banquet and a large number of Londoners recruited at short notice by the Mayor. They marched through the night and arrived before dawn at Pleshey. The old Bohun castle stood on a motte overlooking the river. All was quiet. Most of Gloucester's household were away on leave. There was no sign of the great armed camp that the King had expected to find. The Duke, roused from his sleep, came out to meet him, accompanied by his distraught wife and surrounded by the canons of the nearby college. Richard went up to his uncle, took him by the arm and arrested him in person. According to the Canterbury annalist, Gloucester begged for an assurance that his life would be spared. 'You shall have the same mercy as you showed to Simon Burley,' Richard replied. All three noblemen were initially taken to the Tower of London. Shortly afterwards Warwick was sent to the Earl of Rutland's castle at Carisbrooke on the Isle of Wight. Gloucester was taken to the citadel of Calais, probably the most secure place in Richard's dominions and far away from curious eyes and wagging tongues.[8]

Richard had arrested the three former Appellants because he believed that they were plotting to reverse the settlement with France. Even when it became apparent that Pleshey was not an armed camp and that neither Warwick nor Arundel had the strength or following to contemplate rebellion, the King persisted in the belief that evidence of a plot would be found. He issued a proclamation reassuring his subjects that he was not trying to settle old scores. Yet once it became clear that there was no plot Richard had to find other grounds for keeping them in custody. Inevitably this meant raking over the embers of the crisis of the previous decade. It was a dangerous course politically. Hundreds of prominent men in London and the counties had supported the Appellants at the time. Men feared for their lives and property if the events of the previous decade were now to be reopened. There was a serious risk that they would be propelled into armed rebellion. Processions and public prayers for the prisoners were organised throughout the realm. Yet the King had no choice unless he was to take the even greater risk of releasing his enemies to lead a new opposition to his rule. So on 13 July, two days after the arrests, he summoned 2,000 archers from Cheshire. Some ten days later he withdrew to the security of Nottingham castle. There, in the great hall, he met his closest political allies on 5 August 1397 to decide what to do with the prisoners. The outcome was a decision to prosecute them before Parliament in September for various acts of treason committed between 1385 and 1389. Charges were drawn up. In another echo of the earlier crisis, the procedure selected was an 'Appeal', the same as the one which the three lords had devised for use against the King's ministers a decade before. Its main advantage had been demonstrated then: it allowed the accused to be summarily condemned to death with almost no opportunity to be heard in their defence.[9]

This was a convenient solution in the case of Arundel and Warwick. But the public trial of the King's uncle, even by this cursory procedure, posed grave problems for Richard as he shortly began to realise. John of Gaunt would be expected to preside, as Lord High Steward of England. It was far from clear that he would be prepared to condemn his own brother. Even if Gloucester could be arraigned he would no doubt defend himself with his usual eloquence. He had many supporters, especially in London. He might make a considerable impression on his hearers. The whole affair could easily turn into an inquest into the conduct of the King's foreign policy. So, in about the middle of August, Richard and his cousin Rutland determined to murder him. They told Mowbray, who as captain of Calais had Gloucester in his custody, to see to it. What happened next came to light as a result of a judicial inquiry at the beginning of the following reign. Mowbray departed for Calais. At about the end of August the King, assuming that his orders had been carried out, had it announced throughout England that Gloucester had died on the 25th of the month of natural causes. In fact Mowbray had had cold feet. He returned shortly afterwards from Calais and shame-facedly admitted that he had not been able to bring himself to do the deed. The King was furious. Mowbray was terrified of his revenge. He went back to Calais, resolved to put Gloucester to death 'for dread of the King and eschewing his own death'.

At about the beginning of September 1397 the Duke of Gloucester was persuaded to make a confession, presumably by promises of royal mercy. Sir William Rickhill, one of the Judges of the Common Bench, was woken from his sleep in the middle of the night at his home in Kent by a royal messenger and told to go at once to Calais, where Mowbray would give him his instructions. Rickhill arrived at Calais castle early in the morning of the 8th and was admitted to Mowbray's presence. Mowbray gave him a writ, sealed in London some three weeks before, ordering him to record what the Duke had to say. Gloucester dictated a document in English to his chaplain in the course of the day and delivered it to the judge that evening. It was a remarkable statement. He admitted all that was alleged against him. He had taken the leading role in the events of 1386-8. He had 'acted wickedly and against the King's estate and regality'. He had come armed into the King's presence and abused him in the hearing of his subjects. He had briefly, in December 1387, deposed him from his throne. For all of which crimes he threw himself upon the King's mercy and begged to be spared. Shortly after Rickhill had left with the document Gloucester was taken from the castle to an inn in the town where one of Richard's household staff was waiting for him in a back room. He had with him some servants of Rutland and Mowbray. They told him that the King had ordered him to be killed. They gave him time to confess his sins to a priest. Then they held him down and smothered him with a feather mattress.[10]

Parliament met at Westminster on 17 September 1397. Richard was later accused of having used the sheriffs to fix the elections and there is some circumstantial evidence that he had. A great many royal retainers, pensioners and office-holders sat among the Commons together with many clients of the King's friends and ministers. The rest were overawed by the King's attendants and business managers. A great gathering of armed men was held in Richard's presence at Kingston on Thames just before the opening of Parliament. The kernel of the army was the King's corps of Cheshire archers, rough countrymen, says Thomas Walsingham, who clattered arrogantly along the roads knocking down those who got in their way and swaggering through the streets of London. Since Westminster Hall was being rebuilt the assembly was held in a large marquee in Palace Yard with open sides through which the ranks of soldiers could be seen flanking the building. When the Chancellor, Bishop Stafford of Exeter, rose to deliver the opening address, he took as his theme the words of the prophet Ezekiel. 'There shall be one King over all of them,' he intoned, 'and they shall not be two nations any longer.' There followed a remarkable oration on the plenitude of the King's power and the subject's duty of obedience, which said almost nothing about the business for which Parliament had been summoned. The Commons signalled their complaisance on the following day. They elected as their speaker one of Richard's most trusted ministers, the eloquent, manipulative and sycophantic Sir John

Bussy. He managed most of the proceedings that followed. On Bussy's proposal the enactment establishing the Commission of Government in 1386 was repealed. The pardons which the King had been induced to grant to the Appellants at the conclusion of the Merciless Parliament of 1388 were revoked. The additional pardon which had been granted to the Earl of Arundel in 1394 was also revoked. The assembly then declared to be treason any case in which a man plotted the death or deposition of the King or 'rode against the King to wage war within his realm'.[11]

These preliminaries set the scene for the trial of the three prisoners and of Archbishop Arundel, who had served as their principal adviser during the crisis of 1386–8. The proceedings were brutal even by the standards of the Merciless Parliament on which they were modelled. The Earl of Arundel's case was dealt with first, on 21 September 1397. His old enemy the Duke of Lancaster presided. Gaunt had the accused stripped of every mark of status and hectored him as he tried to defend himself. The Earl responded with vigour and dignity. But he had no defence except for his pardon and that had been revoked, by 'King, Lords and us, the faithful Commons' as Bussy interjected. 'And where are the faithful Commons?' Arundel famously retorted. It did him little good. He was sentenced to death after a hearing which cannot have lasted more than a few minutes once the charges had been read. He was beheaded on Tower Hill on the same day. Three days later his brother the Archbishop was condemned unheard and banished from the realm for life. The Pope was later prevailed upon to remove him from his see and appoint the King's treasurer in his place. On 24 September the Lords embarked on the posthumous trial of the Duke of Gloucester. The forms were nicely observed. Mowbray, summoned to produce the prisoner, declared that he could not because he was dead. On the following day an edited version of Gloucester's confession was read out in Parliament. He was then declared to have been a traitor and his whole estate forfeited to the King. The Earl of Warwick came last. Brought before the Lords on 28 September, he made a wretched spectacle. Now aged about sixty, he had lost all interest in politics. 'Sobbing and whining', he admitted all that was charged against him and begged for his life. He was sentenced to death but reprieved and banished to the Isle of Man.[12]

After Warwick's condemnation Parliament was adjourned until the new year. When the proceedings reopened, on 27 January 1398, it was in the small provincial town of Shrewsbury, far away from the tensions of London and close to the palatinate of Cheshire, where the King's armed strength was concentrated. The whole proceedings of the Merciless Parliament were now declared null and void and the proscriptions renewed against the lesser supporters of Gloucester and his friends. The selection appears to have been fairly arbitrary. The main victims were Sir Thomas Mortimer, Sir John Cheyne and John, Lord Cobham, all of whom were victims of obscure grudges. Mortimer's offence was to have killed one of De Vere's lieutenants at the battle of Radcot Bridge. He had taken refuge in Scotland and was beyond the King's vengeance. Cheyne was an old soldier who had fought in France and was probably arraigned because he had been a retainer and councillor of the Duke of Gloucester. Cobham, a long-standing servant of the Crown now more than eighty years old, was arraigned for having been a member of the Commission of Government of 1386–7. He defended his conduct in a series of sharp exchanges with the King and the Duke of Lancaster. Condemned like the others, he refused to thank the King for commuting his death sentence to lifelong banishment to Jersey. 'I had hoped to enjoy eternal life rather sooner,' he said. As for the former Appellants' followers, who were many, Richard had announced that with the exception of fifty men they would all have pardons, provided that they came forward to admit their offences. But the King refused to identify the fifty men in what was clearly a deliberate attempt to sow insecurity and fear among those who had crossed him in the past or might think of doing so in future. Over the following year more than five hundred men sued out for their pardons, paying substantial fees for the privilege. For Richard these events marked the release of the suppressed hatreds of a decade but they also polarised English opinion and destroyed the unspoken compromise on which English politics had been based since 1389. As Richard later wrote to the Byzantine Emperor, he had 'collected the might of his prowess, stretched forth his arm against his enemies and by God's grace and his own valour had trodden on the necks of the proud and arrogant and ground them down like plants underfoot, not just to the bark but even unto the root.'[13]

The verdicts against the former Appellants and their friends were the prelude to a deliberate reinforcement of the King's powers and an assertion of central control over the counties which even at the time men called Richard's 'tyranny'. Richard rewarded his friends and supporters in a lavish distribution of honours which was designed to make them (in the words of their letters patent) 'the strength of the King's sceptre'. No fewer than five new dukes were created by promotions from the existing peerage. Mowbray became Duke of Norfolk and Rutland Duke of Albemarle. The King's half-brother John Holand, Earl of Huntingdon, became Duke of Exeter while Holand's brother Thomas, Earl of Kent, became Duke of Surrey. John of Gaunt's son Bolingbroke was raised from Earl of Derby to Duke of Hereford. Gaunt's son by Catherine Swynford, who had only recently been legitimised and raised to the peerage as Earl of Somerset, became Marquess of Dorset. Three of the King's closest friends entered the peerage for the first time: Sir William Scrope, one of the chief authors of the trial of the former Appellants, became Earl of Wiltshire; the King's long-standing adjutant, Sir Thomas Percy, became Earl of Worcester; and Thomas, Lord Despenser, became Earl of Gloucester. Ralph Neville, the chief rival to the Percys on the northern march, was made Earl of Westmoreland. The wealth of the condemned men, including the vast domains of Warwick and Arundel, was distributed among the promoted dukes to support their new dignities. Richard undoubtedly believed that his destruction of his enemies would bring internal peace to England after the divisions of the past two decades. Outsiders were more sceptical. There is a good deal of evidence that the new regime was disliked and resented and that far from closing a violent chapter in England's history the King's revenge had reopened all the old wounds. According to Thomas Walsingham Arundel's execution was watched by a sympathetic crowd on Tower Hill. Miracles were reported at his tomb in the Austin Friars' church in the city. The new promotions were widely derided as 'duketti'.[14]

Gloucester's views about the relative strength of France and England were absurd but he was plainly right about the King's marriage and the long truce with France. No experienced diplomat can have been surprised by the French government's refusal to resume negotiations for a permanent peace once they had got a binding cessation of hostilities. Indeed, Richard himself seems to have resigned himself to the fact by the summer of 1397. The issue was quietly dropped. But, although the French change of front produced an inevitable cooling in relations with France, both sides remained committed to the truce. Measures were taken to enforce it on the Gascon march, where the perennial anarchy of the region continued to generate violent incidents. A joint diplomatic campaign was undertaken to extend it to Castile and Portugal, where a desultory border war had continued ever since John of Gaunt had made his peace with John of Trastámara; and to Scotland, where an ineffective government struggled to maintain control and the border lords would only sign up to the truce from year to year. Relations between the French and English courts remained correct, even cordial. The forms of friendship were observed. A regular flow of visitors passed across the Channel in both directions. But after the French broke off negotiations for a permanent peace Richard II was no longer willing to identify himself with their wider European ambitions. There was no more talk of sending an English army to join Charles VI in Lombardy. In July 1397, when Charles VI briefly recovered his reason, the French tried to revive the project and sent Renaud de Trie to England to ask for English support. But Richard would have nothing to do with it. In the following year he even made overtures to Gian Galeazzo Visconti.[15]

Richard proved equally changeable on the subject of the schism. Having undertaken to the Duke of Burgundy to press forward with the *voie de cession*, he did nothing more to promote it after the summer of 1397. According to Charles VI's ministers, when the joint Anglo-French embassy reached Rome to present their ultimatum to Boniface IX, the English clergymen on the mission, far from joining in French attempts to push Boniface off his throne, spent much of their time canvassing for ecclesiastical promotion. In May 1397 an English embassy attended the meeting of the German Diet in Frankfurt, ostensibly to drum up support for the French government's plans to deal with the schism. But their main objective seems to have been to recruit allies for England among the German states and to promote a fantastic scheme, devised by two of the electors, to present Richard II as a candidate for the German throne. In July 1398, after a council of the French church had deliberated for more than a month in Paris under the eyes of Charles VI's ministers, it was announced that France would withdraw unilaterally from the obedience of the Avignon Pope and would recognise no claimant until there was one whose rights were incontestable. Shortly afterwards a French army arrived in Avignon to lay siege to Benedict XIII in his palace with the support of the college of cardinals and the population of the city. The French pressed Richard for similar action against Boniface IX. But Richard did nothing and ultimately he made his own terms with the Roman Pope.[16]

The scarcity of documents for these years makes it hard to reconstruct the French ministers' attitude to Richard's wayward and changeable diplomacy. But it is clear that even if they could not have Richard II as an ally they were determined that he should not be an enemy. France's growing ambitions in other directions depended on the maintenance of the truce with England. Genoa received a French governor in 1397. The Queen and the Duke of Burgundy pressed on with their attempts to challenge Gian Galeazzo Visconti's dominance of the north Italian plain even after it had become clear that the King would be incapable of leading an army across the Alps with or without English assistance. Further south Louis of Anjou struggled to hold on to the kingdom of Naples with intermittent French support, as the revived power of the house of Durazzo gradually overran his territory and penned him into his capital. Some 1,200 French troops were sent in 1398 under Marshal Boucicaut to support the defence of Constantinople. All of these ventures depended on France remaining at peace with England. But the main priority of the French government in these years was to enable the Duke of Burgundy to close his grip on the vast jigsaw of principalities of the German Low Countries lying east and north of Flanders, territories which he was in the process of acquiring for his family by treaty, inheritance or political pressure: Brabant, Hainault, Holland, Zeeland, Limbourg, Luxembourg and the semi-autonomous episcopal cities of Tournai and Cambrai. The whole of this region would fall under Burgundian control in the early fifteenth century. Philip was counting on the long-term acquiescence or at least the passivity of Richard's government in the face of what on the face of it was a rapid and threatening expansion of France's reach in northern Europe. In March 1398 Philip's spokesman, laying out his master's claims to the government of the duchy before the Estates of Brabant in Brussels, made no secret of this. The sheer scale of Philip's territorial interests, he said, was the best guarantee of their security against their enemies beyond the Rhine. 'If needs be my Lord and his heirs will have all the strength of France and England behind him.'[17]

The Dukes of Berry and Burgundy had another reason to be tender towards Richard II. The truce with England made it possible for them to divert large sums of money from the King's revenues into their own coffers. The occasion for war taxation had gone in the 1390s but the taxes had not. The *aides* and the *gabelle* continued to be collected after the truce of Leulinghem albeit at a somewhat reduced rate. The *taille*, which was probably the most resented of French taxes, was revived. A *taille* was levied in 1396 and another in the following year. The revenues of the French state remained exceptionally high for a country at peace, while war expenditure fell to the lowest levels since the 1330s. The Duke of Burgundy, who was the main beneficiary of this policy, doubled his pension from the King within a few weeks of resuming power in

1392 and more than doubled it again by 1397. By the end of the decade he was taking an annual income from the royal Treasury of nearly 80,000 gold francs (about £13,000) in addition to gifts and loans worth at least as much again. These funds enabled Philip to maintain his magnificent state and to pursue his political ambitions beyond France's eastern and northern frontiers while sheltering his Flemish and Burgundian subjects from the high levels of taxation which prevailed in France. The receipts of the other princes were smaller but still impressive. They enabled the Queen to acquire an ample landed endowment in the Île de France; the Duke of Berry to fill his mansions in Paris, Berry and Auvergne with treasures; and the Duke of Orléans to acquire great landed domains in the Loire valley and Champagne. A river of pensions, gifts and subsidies flowed into the purses of their clients among the court nobility and the higher officials. The magnificence of these years is reflected in the banquets, the buildings, the painted manuscripts, the fabrics and jewellery which dazzled the impressionable Richard II, drew craftsmen, adventurers and professional gamblers from across Europe and made Paris at the end of the fourteenth century the centre of European fashion and luxury.[18]

What disturbed the comfortable calculations of the Duke of Burgundy was a dramatic breakdown of Richard's relations with a significant fraction of the English baronage and a fresh crisis in the relations between Louis of Orléans and his uncles.

After the Westminster Parliament of September 1397 Richard II stayed away from Westminster, leading his court in an itinerant existence in the Midlands and the west of England. The enormous dowry of his wife, the confiscated assets of the former Appellants, the proceeds of the sale of pardons and a variety of financial expedients filled his coffers and made him for the time being independent of Parliamentary taxation. Over the following months the King set about consolidating his power. He installed friends and clients in the sheriffs' offices. He built up a body of retainers of his own in the counties. Meanwhile the day-to-day government of the realm was carried on through a small council consisting almost entirely of permanent officials: the three officers of state, all of them ecclesiastics cast in the compliant mould of the English Church; the King's old friend and collaborator William Scrope, now Earl of Wiltshire; the lawyers Lawrence Drew and Ralph Selby; and the notorious trio of Sir John Bussy, Sir Henry Green and Sir William Bagot. Walsingham famously described Bussy as 'brutal beyond measure, overweeningly ambitious and covetous of other men's property' and thought that Bagot and Green were no better. Richard's cousin the Earl of Rutland became the pre-eminent royal favourite. According to Sir William Bagot the King even mused about abdicating in his favour.[19]

The peerage both old and new was largely excluded from the King's counsels. Most of them were viewed from Richard's small circle of friends with suspicion and distrust which at times verged on paranoia. In a private conversation with the King shortly after he had been ordered into exile on the continent Archbishop Arundel told him that he expected that 'other lords' would follow him before long. To the Archbishop's astonishment Richard replied that this was quite possible and that he himself could well be expelled from the realm by his subjects. It is plain that the King believed himself to be in constant danger of an aristocratic *coup*. He maintained a personal bodyguard of three hundred unruly Cheshire archers, a small standing army which followed him everywhere, with several hundred more in reserve. Walsingham called them 'rustic brutes . . . who in their home country would have been thought unworthy to pull their masters' boots off'. The King's Cheshire guard was only the most visible symptom of his intense insecurity. 'Sleep securely while we wake, Dick, and dread nought while we live,' the captain of his guard was heard to say one day to the nervous King. In March 1398 Richard even instituted a system of censorship by which in theory all letters leaving the country (apart from those dealing with purely commercial business) were to be laid before the Council together with all incoming letters addressed to 'lords and great men'.[20]

How far were Richard's fears justified? In 1397 there was probably very little risk of a *coup* but sooner or later Richard's ambitions and methods were bound to generate tensions which would be difficult to contain. Since the twelfth century no English king had succeeded in ruling for very long without the support of the higher nobility. In a society in which wealth and influence were founded on the possession of land, the distribution of the holdings among the major aristocratic families was a matter of great sensitivity. The current pattern of landholding in England, which dated from the tumults of the reign of Edward II and the early years of Edward III, had subsisted for two or three generations. But Richard appeared to be intent on a major redistribution in favour of the Crown and a new nobility which shared his own exalted idea of the Crown. The Earl of Warwick had been dispossessed of the great lordship of Gower in south Wales by a judgment of the King's Bench in 1396 which bears all the marks of political manipulation. The forfeiture of the entire Beauchamp and Fitzalan estates followed with the fall of Warwick and Arundel the next year. There was more to come. The young Thomas Despenser, the King's friend and ward whom he had raised to be Earl of Gloucester, was encouraged to claim the vast inheritance confiscated from his ancestors on the fall of Edward II seventy years before. When the young Earl of March was killed in a skirmish in Ireland in 1398 Richard was able to lay hands on the whole Mortimer inheritance in England, Wales and Ireland, including the great Welsh lordship of Denbigh. It is no accident that much of the land that changed hands in these upheavals was in the Welsh march, a region of large, consolidated lordships, yielding valuable revenues and large numbers of soldiers, whose proprietors exercised a degree of personal control that was unusual elsewhere. Richard, who already controlled Chester and Flint, seems to have been consciously trying to enlarge his 'citadel' by building up the domains of the Crown and its allies on the march of Wales and the adjacent parts of north-western England. But even in other regions, where the patterns of landholding were more fragmented, Richard's indifference to long established titles, his ruthlessness in revoking earlier pardons and settled judgments and his determination to revenge himself on those who had been responsible for the humiliations of the 1380s, left few men in England who could feel that their lives were entirely safe or their property secure.[21]

Richard II's peerage promotions of September 1397 concealed profound divisions even among those whom he counted as his friends. Some of them completely associated themselves with Richard's revolution from conviction or ambition or a mixture of the two. Others had more equivocal loyalties. Two of the new dukes, Mowbray and Bolingbroke, had themselves been among the Appellants of 1387. They had received a fresh pardon for their offences, but Mowbray for one doubted whether such instruments were worth much. He had agreed to take part in the prosecution of his former colleagues but had become increasingly uncomfortable about it as the time approached. He had resisted the King's orders to murder the Duke of Gloucester for as long as he could. He had failed to appear on the first day of the proceedings against Arundel and Warwick. He had publicly objected to the proposal to annul the acts of the Merciless Parliament. Henry Bolingbroke was in some ways in a different position. Richard had never liked him and had never drawn him into his inner circle of advisers or employed him on diplomatic business or other great matters of state. According to Sir William Bagot at his trial in 1399, Richard once told him that Henry 'was a worthless man at heart and always will be'. But he was the heir to the richest and most powerful noble house in England and second in the line of succession to the throne after his father. He also had a considerable personal following, not only among the many retainers and clients of the house of Lancaster but among a wider public attracted by his charm and his reputation as a jouster and crusader. The truth was that Richard was afraid of him. One day Bolingbroke would come into his father's inheritance and would be entitled to play a prominent role in public affairs whether as friend or enemy. The King entertained real fears that his cousin would become a focus of opposition to his rule. For his part Bolingbroke is most unlikely to have approved of the Duke of Gloucester's murder or to have been under any illusions about who was responsible for it. Nor can he have felt confident that Richard's growing appetite for forfeitures and his sustained assault on the great aristocratic estates would not one day be turned against the house of Lancaster. The atmosphere at court was poisoned by the King's capricious hatreds, his insecurity and suspicions and terrible outbursts of rage, and by the craven obeisance of those around him. 'Which of you if Richard had wanted something would have refused to comply or dared to cross him?' his councillor Sir William Bagot asked his accusers at his trial in 1399.[22]

It was almost certainly Bagot who proposed a scheme to destroy the house of Lancaster not long after the adjournment of the Westminster Parliament. The plan was to arrest Lancaster and Bolingbroke while the court was at Windsor and put them to death. A compliant Parliament would then be prevailed upon to annul the seventy-year-old statutes which reversed the attainder of Thomas of Lancaster in 1322. Since these statutes were the legal foundation of the Lancastrian estate the result would be to revest the whole of John of Gaunt's vast landed domain in the Crown. Few things revealed more about the shattering of ancient loyalties than this volte-face by a man who had been a retainer of John of Gaunt, had served in Bolingbroke's household and years later would be buried beneath a brass showing him wearing the liveried collar of Lancaster. According to Mowbray, who had been privy to the discussions, Bagot's plan was actively supported by the King, egged on by Scrope and some of the more ambitious new peers who hoped to share in the spoils. The scheme was dropped partly because of opposition from some of Richard's courtiers, including Mowbray himself, and partly because Mowbray told Bolingbroke about it. The two men met by chance on the road from London to Brentford in December 1397. 'We are both about to be undone,' Mowbray said. 'Why?', asked Boling-broke. 'Because of Radcot Bridge,' the other replied. Then he disclosed the whole affair. Bolingbroke said that he could not believe that the King was capable of such treachery. Had he not sworn by St. Edward to be a good lord to him? 'The King has said many things to me on God's body and I do not trust him any better for that,' Mowbray replied.[23]

Mowbray's words on the Brentford road set off a chain of events which has become famous through the pages of Shakespeare's *Richard II*. Bolingbroke reported the encounter to his father, who confronted the King in the new year and demanded an explanation. Richard, caught out while his designs on the house of Lancaster were still half-formed, was forced to abandon them. He denied everything and cast the blame on Bagot, a convenient and loyal scapegoat who was in due course pardoned for his offence and required to enter into bonds undertaking never to propose such a thing again. Richard blamed Mowbray for the debacle and set out to destroy both men. He summoned Bolingbroke before him and demanded to know what Mowbray had said. Bolingbroke produced a 'bill' or memorandum recording the encounter. Mowbray's language, if Bolingbroke had correctly reported it, was certainly slanderous and arguably treasonable. Richard professed to be outraged that anyone should think him capable of compassing the death of the Duke of Lancaster and his son. He directed that the matter should be referred to the adjourned session of Parliament, which was about to meet at Shrewsbury.

Mowbray had evidently not expected this. He had disclosed Bagot's scheme to Bolingbroke because he regarded him and his father as potential allies against the King. He now concluded that they were determined to ruin him. He laid an ambush for John of Gaunt as he travelled to Shrewsbury and by his own admission would have killed him if Gaunt had not been forewarned and altered his route. He then fled, leaving Bolingbroke to lay his allegations before the Shrewsbury Parliament unanswered. Richard dismissed Mowbray from his service. He stripped him of the offices of Earl Marshal and Admiral of England and ordered his arrest. A special commission, presided over by the Duke of Lancaster and filled with Mowbray's enemies, was created by statute to deal with the matter after the assembly had been dissolved and was vested with all the powers of Parliament for that purpose. Shortly after

Parliament dispersed Mowbray gave himself up and was imprisoned at Windsor castle. The Commission heard out both men. Bolingbroke expanded his allegations against Mowbray, accusing him of having treacherously neglected the defence of Calais and embezzled the King's funds. Moving into territory which he must have known was exceptionally sensitive for the King, he added the charge that Mowbray had been responsible for the murder of the Duke of Gloucester. Mowbray denied everything. The Commission, unable or perhaps unwilling to take evidence on these matters, ordered the issues to be tried 'by the laws of chivalry'. A judicial duel was to be held at Coventry on 16 September 1398. Since the charge was treason the occasion was likely to end with the death or execution of one or other combatant.[24]

On the appointed day the two champions appeared before the Constable and the Marshal of England at Gosford Green beneath the walls of Coventry. They entered the lists encased from head to toe in armour manufactured by Europe's foremost armourers. The two men announced their names and stated their quarrel. Each swore to the truth of his own version of events. The King watched from a stand, surrounded by the members of the Parliamentary commission and by a crowd of courtiers, officials and dignitaries. Their numbers were swollen by men who had travelled from Scotland, France, the Low Countries and all over England to witness the spectacle of the age. The duel was to be fought on foot in accordance with the usual practice. When the heralds gave the signal Bolingbroke advanced towards his enemy, making a sign of the cross and holding his lance against his thigh. Mowbray stood motionless waiting for the attack. But, unknown to most of those present, Richard had already decided that he could not risk a fight to the finish. A victory for Mowbray would have revived controversy over the responsibility for the murder of the Duke of Gloucester, while a victory for Bolingbroke would have boosted the political standing of a dangerous rival. Before the two combatants came to blows the King rose from his seat and cried 'Ho'. Everything stopped. The contestants' weapons were taken away. They were conducted back to their seats.

For two hours nothing happened. Then the Brittany herald appeared and called for silence. Sir John Bussy, reading from a long roll, announced that the King had resolved to take the resolution of the dispute upon himself. By the authority of the Parliamentary Commission he condemned both men. Bolingbroke was declared guilty of no offence, but Richard banished him from the realm for ten years 'for the peace and tranquillity of himself, his kingdom and his subjects'. There was an immediate uproar from the crowd, most of whom were Bolingbroke's supporters. The herald had to call for silence again before Bussy could be heard announcing that Mowbray had been found guilty of repeated acts of disloyalty towards the King. For these he was banished for life to fight on the marches of Christendom in Prussia, Hungary or the middle east for the rest of his days. 'We might as well have gone to the Parliament at Shrewsbury after all,' Mowbray was heard to say to his followers as they left the field, 'if we had, we should both have been put to death like the Earl of Arundel.'[25]

The dispute between Mowbray and Bolingbroke had been followed in France with fascination and dismay. Charles VI's Council was fed with regular news and gossip by French diplomats visiting England and by members of the young Queen's French household. Isolated in a foreign country, surrounded by a people who regarded them as schismatics and enemies, these people took a profoundly gloomy view of the future of their adoptive country. Pierre Salmon, a clerk in Isabelle's household, was afraid to travel in the English countryside without an escort because of the collapse of law and order and the unpopularity of the French. In Paris there was mounting concern about the situation. At the time of the Shrewsbury Parliament a delegation of French knights had been present in England charged with the delivery of gifts and messages of goodwill to Richard and his Queen. They returned in the spring of 1398 with reports that the whole country was 'shaken by discord and rebellion and threatened by black storms'. The Duke of Berry wondered out loud about the implications for the truce. The declining yield of the *aides* troubled him, he said, 'in view of the way that the English are carrying on their affairs'. In August, shortly before Bolingbroke and Mowbray were due to fight their duel, the French royal Council sent one of their number, Nicholas Paynel, to England to discuss current issues between the two governments. He was instructed to raise the question of the duel with Richard as a matter of urgency. Charles VI, he was to say, was distressed by the prospect of a fight to the death between two men so closely related to the King, especially as the occasion for it seemed so trivial. 'Hurtful words are sometimes lightly uttered by decent men whose loyalty can at bottom be relied upon. In such matters a King may be wise to show a little flexibility and worldly indulgence.' The Count of Saint-Pol, who had so often acted as an informal go-between, was sent to England, presumably with a similar message. He was with the

King at Coventry. The Duke of Burgundy was surely responsible for their instructions. How little he understood Richard's complex, brooding personality. The English King's response is not recorded.[26]

In October 1398 Bolingbroke sailed from Dover for France, followed by a large household and a considerable baggage train. He settled in Paris, where he could remain close to English affairs. Bolingbroke was a well-known figure in France. He had jousted with the paragons of French chivalry at Saint-Ingelvert and fought beside them in Prussia. He was warmly received at court, feasted by the King's uncles and installed with his household in the deserted grandeur of Olivier de Clisson's mansion. From here he set about finding allies among the French princes. He made a confidant of the Duke of Berry. Within a short time of his arrival he was negotiating with the Duke for the hand of his daughter Marie, the widow of the Count of Eu who had died at Nicopolis. Reports of Bolingbroke's reception in France and his possible engagement caused much irritation at the court of Richard II. The Earl of Salisbury, who was in the French capital to discuss the instalments of Queen Isabelle's dowry, was instructed to protest. The Duke of Burgundy intervened to avert a diplomatic row with England. The offer of Marie's hand was withdrawn.[27]

On 3 February 1399 John of Gaunt died at the age of fifty-nine at his castle at Leicester. The chroniclers barely paused to reflect on the disappearance of a man who had dominated English politics for most of the past twenty-five years. His death was quickly overtaken by more dramatic events. On 18 March 1399, just two days after Gaunt's funeral in St. Paul's, Richard declared before a Great Council at Westminster that Bolingbroke's banishment was extended to the rest of his life and that all the possessions of the house of Lancaster were forfeited to the Crown. The men gathered to hear this announcement swore to uphold the decision. Even the Earl of Rutland, who was one of the main beneficiaries of the deed, observed that it would 'astonish the world'. The victim of the King's decree was the first man in the realm. It was a direct affront to universal notions about the security of property rights. It was promulgated without any form of legal process. No justification was ever asserted for it. Richard claimed the authority of the Parliamentary Commission. But he was obliged to tamper with the record of the Shrewsbury Parliament in order to confer powers on the Commission which had never been envisaged when it was created. Richard's motive was no doubt the same as the one which had impelled him to banish Bolingbroke in the first place: fear of an opponent and potential rival. But there was also a large element of territorial empire-building. The duchy of Lancaster and the three Lancastrian lordships in Wales were major building blocks in the King's expanding 'citadel' in the Welsh march and north-western England. At the same time Richard took steps to exclude Bolingbroke from the succession to the throne. Even as a disinherited exile Bolingbroke would always find ambitious men to support him if he was likely to be the next King of England. The only other person with a colourable claim was the infant heir of the Mortimer Earls of March, whose right was derived from the daughter of Edward III's second son Lionel of Antwerp, Duke of Clarence. Richard had once toyed with the idea of promoting the claims of the Mortimers but in 1399 his preferred successor was his cousin and favourite Rutland. Richard never formally designated an heir but in his will he made it clear that he expected to be succeeded by Rutland's ageing and ineffective father Edmund Langley, Duke of York, whom Rutland would sooner or later succeed.[28]

Sir William Bagot was one of many in England who was frightened by the turn that events were taking. Determined to hunt with the hounds and run with the hare, Bagot wrote a private letter to Bolingbroke in Paris with an oblique warning of what was about to happen. The King, he said, was his sworn enemy. There was no other course open to him now but force. The news of Bolingbroke's dispossession reached the French capital a few days after this missive, probably at about the end of March. Bolingbroke resolved to assert his right to his father's inheritance by force. He had some able professional soldiers with him in Paris. They included Sir Thomas Erpingham, who had fought with John of Gaunt in Scotland, at Brest and in Portugal and Castile, and had accompanied Bolingbroke's crusade in Prussia in 1390; and Sir John Norbury, another veteran of the Prussian crusade with nearly three decades of soldiering behind him who had been one of the captains of the English troops at Aljubarotta. Bolingbroke made contact with his friends and retainers in England. He approached Archbishop Arundel, then in exile in the Dutch town of Utrecht, who came to join him in Paris. The Archbishop brought with him his nephew Thomas Fitzalan, the heir of the executed Earl of Arundel, who had recently escaped from custody in England. What he needed was a port of embarkation on the French coast and allies in the French government, who would allow him to pursue his preparations undisturbed. The business of Marie de Berry had shown that he could not expect any help from the Duke of Burgundy. The Duke of Berry, never a man to challenge his brother's views, merely urged caution and resignation on his English protégé. So Bolingbroke turned to the Duke of Orléans.[29]

After years of finding his ambitions thwarted and his voice unheard, Louis of Orléans had recently embarked on an overt campaign of opposition to the government of his uncles. Louis forged personal alliances with the Emperor and the German princes which cut across Burgundian policy in the Low Countries. He resisted the attempts of Burgundy and Berry to force Benedict XIII from his throne and secretly reached an accommodation with the beleaguered Avignon Pope. He became a persistent contrariant, opposing whatever the Duke of Burgundy favoured. Tempers frayed in the royal Council. 'Hatreds, jealousies and quarrels' were reported between Louis and the Duke of Burgundy. The pacific Duke of Berry was harangued by his nephew with a violence of language which shocked the older man's attendants. For much of this time Charles VI was 'absent' behind the closed doors of his apartments in the Hôtel Saint-Pol. But in February 1399 the King recovered his senses after nearly a year of illness and remained intermittently sane for several months. Shortly afterwards a virulent epidemic of bubonic plague hit the capital, causing most of the princes to flee to their suburban mansions or distant domains. It was a critical moment. Louis stayed in Paris and made his bid for power. He worked on his enfeebled brother in his intervals of coherence. Charles's official correspondence described the two men as 'inseparable'. Shortly Louis acquired a degree of ascendency over the King which enabled him briefly to take control of the machinery of government. For a few months Louis took over the conduct of French diplomacy. He also set about entrenching his position for the future, partially refashioning the administration and putting his own clients into critical departments, especially the financial departments hitherto dominated by protégés of the Duke of Burgundy.[30]

Louis of Orléans's attitude to England was as complex as anything else in his impulsive life. To some extent his hostility to Richard II was the mirror image of Philip of Burgundy's support for him, but there was more to it than that. Richard himself had deeply imbibed the anti-Orléanist propaganda of Philip of Burgundy's circle. He took it as fact that Louis was bent on usurping the French throne and that Charles's illness had been caused by his experiments with sorcerers. He had openly spoken about it at the summit meeting with the French King on the march of Calais. For his part, Louis had no reason to think well of Richard II or the deal which France had done with him in 1396. It had been Philip's deal, designed to protect Philip's interests. In Louis's mind it was associated mainly with the scheme for a joint Anglo-French attack on his father-in-law, a venture which was aimed indirectly against himself. In 1398 the land-hungry Duke of Orléans found another quarrel with Richard II when he began to interest himself in the provinces of the Gascon march. Louis became the King's lieutenant on the march and took over control of the French garrisons there. He was probably behind the French invasion of Périgord in that year, which resulted in the expulsion of Archambaut VI, the last of its independent counts. He was certainly responsible for Archambaut's dispossession by order of the Parlement, which occurred while he was in power in Paris, and for procuring the grant of the county to himself shortly afterwards. The Counts of Périgord had had a guarded understanding with Richard's officers in Bordeaux for some years. Archambaut at once made his way to England to find help.[31]

Louis of Orléans had assiduously courted Henry Bolingbroke ever since his arrival in Paris. He gave a great banquet in his honour. He supported his attempts to marry Marie de Berry even after the project had been vetoed by her father and uncle. The two men exchanged gifts of horses and jewellery. Bolingbroke was popular at the French court and widely regarded as the victim of a gross injustice. In May 1399 Richard clumsily added to the number of Bolingbroke's supporters. He dismissed his Queen's governess, Margaret Dame de Courcy, together with most of her French attendants, whom he accused of extravagance and indiscretion. At the same time he transferred Isabelle's household from Windsor to the dismal fortress of Wallingford in Oxfordshire. The news of this action caused outrage in France. It may well have cost Richard the support of the Duke of Berry and the King himself. On 17 June 1399 Louis of Orléans entered into a secret alliance with Henry Bolingbroke by which each of them bound himself to support the other against his enemies. In point of form the English King was excluded from the enemies against whom the treaty was directed but this was a sham, as both parties knew. Later, when the two men had fallen out, Bolingbroke declared that he had told Louis at the time about his plans to invade England and had received the French prince's promise of support. The evidence, such as it is, suggests that this was true. But Bolingbroke seems to have told Orléans that he planned a rebellion, not a *coup d'état*. When other councillors of Charles VI expressed their misgivings he swore that he had no intention of trying to topple Richard from his throne.[32]

In an act of uncharacteristic self-confidence or perhaps of hubristic folly, Richard II chose this moment to fulfil a long-standing commitment to return to Ireland and complete the subjugation of the Irish chiefs which he had begun four years before. On 29 May 1399 the King sailed from Milford in Wales, accompanied by a small army which incorporated the whole of his Cheshire guard; and by most of his closest friends among the nobility including Rutland, Salisbury and the new Earls of Worcester and Gloucester. He also took with him Bolingbroke's eldest son Henry of Monmouth (the future Henry V) as a hostage for his father's good behaviour. As soon as the news of Richard's departure had reached Paris Bolingbroke and Archbishop Arundel left the city with their companions. They paused at the royal abbey of Saint-Denis to receive the blessing of the Abbot and the community upon his enterprise, a courtesy arranged for him by the Duke of Berry. The Abbot clearly knew what Bolingbroke was about for he asked him to arrange for the restitution of one of the abbey's confiscated priories in England. The English party then made for Boulogne. About 300 men-at-arms had gathered there by the water's edge. Some ten or twelve English merchant ships were commandeered in the port to embark them. Bolingbroke gave out he was bound for Castile. But it is unlikely that anyone was deceived. No one lifted a finger to stop him. The garrison of Boulogne looked on impassively.[33]

In England the government had been left in the incapable hands of Edmund Langley, Duke of York. With him was a small group of Richard's councillors: the new Earl of Wiltshire, William Scrope, assisted by Bussy, Bagot and Green. They had no inkling of what was happening until 28 June, when the first reports reached Westminster of hostile forces gathering in Picardy. The sheriffs were ordered to raise troops urgently in their counties and send them to gather under the Duke of York's command at Ware in Hertfordshire. By that time Bolingbroke's fleet had already sailed. The ships hovered for a time off the south coast. A detachment was landed at Pevensey on the Sussex coast to seize the Lancastrian castle there. The Duke of York ordered the recapture of Pevensey. Then, believing that the rest of Henry's fleet had headed west, he set off after them. In fact Bolingbroke had sailed east from Pevensey, passed through the Channel and landed on about 30 June at the mouth of the Humber in Yorkshire. Most of the confiscated castles and estates of the house of Lancaster were concentrated in the north. Within days their stewards and keepers had rallied to their former master. Bolingbroke made first for the

Lancastrian castle of Pickering and then for his father's castle of Knaresborough. By the middle of July he had occupied the immense Lancastrian fortress of Pontefract. Lancastrian retainers came to join him from across the northern counties.

On 16 July 1399 Henry met the Earl of Northumberland and his son Hotspur in the Augustinian house at Doncaster. Henry went to great lengths to draw the Percys to his cause. He disclaimed any intention to depose Richard or seek the crown for himself. He declared that he sought no more than the inheritance of his father. He laid out a moderate programme for restraining the government of the King, reforming his household and dismissing his Cheshire guard. Weakened and impoverished by the relative calm on the Scottish border and stripped of their traditional authority in the north, the Percys were natural allies of Bolingbroke. Like other noblemen, they could see that they might be the next victims of Richard's destruction of solid titles to land. They threw in their lot with the invader. Their example was followed by much of the baronage of the north. By the end of July Bolingbroke's army had swollen from the original 300 men to about 3,000, almost all from the Midlands and north of England. The rest of the country held its breath and waited to see which side would gain the upper hand.[34]

The Duke of York's messenger reached Richard II at Dublin on about 10 July 1399 with news of the landings. There was a scramble to return to England, which was frustrated by shortage of shipping. Most of the fleet which had brought the King to Ireland in June had withdrawn and there were no ships of any size available in Ireland. So an advance party was formed and put under the command of the Earl of Salisbury. Salisbury was appointed governor of Cheshire and north Wales. His orders were to take what few ships were available and make for the royal fortress of Conway on the north Wales coast. There he was to recruit fresh forces in the principality and use them to secure Cheshire for the King. Salisbury left on his mission on about 17 July, leaving the King to find his own way across the Irish Sea. The delay proved to be disastrous to Richard's cause. Rumours spread that he had fled or died. As a result many of his natural supporters gave up or acknowledged Bolingbroke. The Welsh companies who had been summoned to meet Salisbury at Conway had been led to believe that they would find the King there. When they discovered their error they melted away. 'We will not fight for you,' they told the Earl.[35]

The only other forces available to confront Bolingbroke's swelling army were those recruited by the Duke of York. About 3,000 men had answered York's summons at Ware. By the middle of July they had reached Oxford. The Duke of York, who had no idea where or when Richard would return, held a council of war. It was decided to split the army into two in order to cover the most likely eventualities. One force was sent with Scrope, Bussy and Green to occupy Bristol. York himself marched west with the rest, apparently making for south Wales. When these movements were reported to Bolingbroke he set out in pursuit. York seems to have learned of Bolingbroke's approach somewhere near Gloucester. At this point his nerve failed him. Bolingbroke's army was considerably larger than his own. So he turned south to join Scrope at Bristol. On 27 July Bolingbroke caught up with him at Berkeley castle. The two men met in the nearby parish church under a flag of truce. York's heart was not in the campaign. He had never been close to Richard. He is unlikely to have approved of Richard's methods of government, still less of his forfeiture of the Lancastrian domains. He was no soldier. His forces were divided and his troops were beginning to desert in large numbers. So he agreed to throw in his lot with his nephew. The two of them marched on Bristol with their combined forces. The constable of the castle opened his gates to them. Sir William Bagot managed to escape and find a ship bound for Ireland. But Scrope, Bussy and Green were found in the castle and arrested. They were summarily tried on the following morning, 29 July, and beheaded outside the castle gates before an enthusiastic crowd.[36]

Richard II sailed into Milford Haven on about 26 July 1399. He was accompanied by Rutland, Despenser, the Holand brothers and most of the army which had been with him in Ireland. By the time that Richard finally landed his cause was lost. He headed east towards Carmarthen and installed himself in Whitland Abbey, not far from the town. As the successive tidings arrived of Bolingbroke's triumphant advance, his men began to desert in large numbers. Despenser was sent to find more troops among his tenants in Glamorgan. None of them would fight for him. Shortly, the news arrived of the Duke of York's desertion and the surrender of Bristol. Richard no longer trusted anyone. Doubting the loyalty of his troops and believing that he was about to be betrayed to his enemies, he lost his nerve. He thought of fleeing to Gascony and then dropped the idea. Finally, in the first few days of August, he fled in the middle of the night disguised as a priest and accompanied by only fifteen companions to join the Earl of Salisbury at Conway. When Sir Thomas Percy, the steward of his household, found him gone the next morning he wept uncontrollably, broke his rod of office and told the King's followers that they were free to go.[37]

Richard arrived at Conway to find that the army which Salisbury was supposed to have recruited in north Wales did not exist. Salisbury controlled nothing beyond the walls of the castle and its twin fortress of Beaumaris across the bay. Neither place was properly victualled or garrisoned for a siege. Meanwhile Bolingbroke had effortlessly occupied Chester. Richard sent the Holand brothers there to protest at his acts and, perhaps, to explore the scope for a compromise. But they were at once arrested and confined in Chester castle. The Frenchman Jean Creton, a *valet de chambre* of the Duke of Burgundy who was serving in Salisbury's household, remembered their ashen, tearful faces and their inability even now to accept that all was lost ('I will summon men from all of Wales'). In the second week of August 1399 Henry Percy, Earl of Northumberland, who had now emerged as Bolingbroke's principal lieutenant, advanced on Conway castle with a substantial force of men-at-arms and archers. Holt, Flint and Rhuddlan, the only substantial fortresses between Conway and Chester, surrendered to him with little or no resistance. Leaving his army encamped a few miles from Conway, Northumberland approached the castle by boat with a handful of attendants. He was admitted and brought into Richard's presence.

What happened next is obscured by the conflicting propaganda of the two sides. It is, however, very likely that, whatever his original intentions may have been, Bolingbroke had by now decided to depose Richard and seize the crown for himself. It would have been too dangerous to leave Richard on his throne to choose his moment for revenge. Although Northumberland would later deny it, it is inconceivable that he was not privy to Bolingbroke's plan. According to the most plausible account Northumberland tricked Richard into leaving the protection of the castle. He offered him a deal under which he would retain his throne on three conditions: that Bolingbroke would be allowed to receive his inheritance; that a Parliament would be summoned to Westminster at which five of Richard's leading councillors, including the Holands and the Earl of Salisbury, would be tried for treason; and that Bolingbroke himself would preside at their trial as hereditary Lord High Steward of England. Richard reflected on these proposals for several days and finally accepted them. Before leaving the castle he made Northumberland swear on the consecrated host that no deceit would be practised on him. The truth was that each of them was intent on double-crossing the other. Northumberland knew that the days of Richard's reign would be numbered once he fell into Bolingbroke's hands. Richard for his part assured his attendants that he had no intention of abiding by the agreement he had made with the Earl. 'Rest assured that whatever assurances I may give him he will suffer death for this outrage . . . believe me, there will be no Parliament at Westminster on this matter.' Northumberland escorted the King with every outward mark of deference to the castle of Flint, where Richard had a brief and frigid interview with Bolingbroke. He was then taken to Chester. Any pretence that he was a free agent was now abandoned. He was locked in a turret of Chester castle and then brought south to London, where he was lodged under guard in the Tower.[38]

Richard II finally sealed the instrument of abdication in the Tower in Bolingbroke's presence on 29 September 1399. According to a sympathetic chronicler he insisted to the end that he would not resign his crown to his rival but only to God, from whom he had received it. At the conclusion of the interview he took it from his head and placed it on the ground. The instrument was presented to Parliament on the following day. Unusually for a medieval ruler, Richard was fascinated and obsessed by the past. He was well aware of the tradition of aristocratic rebellion of which he was the latest victim and knew a good deal about the history of King John, Henry III and Edward II. 'What a strange and fickle land this is,' he told the chronicler Adam of Usk who visited him in his prison, 'which has banished, killed or ruined so many of its kings, rulers and great men and has ever been tarnished with strife and envy.'[39]

Bolingbroke was crowned at Westminster as King Henry IV on 13 October 1399. On this occasion there was very little retribution against the defeated party. Several of Richard's closest counsellors were already dead. Mowbray, who had left England for the Holy Land a year before, had died of disease on his way back through Venice a week before the abdication, apparently ignorant of all that had happened in his absence. The acts of Richard's last Parliament were formally reversed and the confiscated estates of Gloucester, Arundel and Warwick were restored to their heirs. John Hall, a lowly servant of Mowbray's who had stood at the door as the Duke of Gloucester was suffocated, was tried in Parliament and condemned to be drawn, hanged and quartered 'since the Duke of Gloucester was so great a man'. Sir William Bagot, who had escaped to Ireland when Bristol fell to Bolingbroke, was brought back in irons but was saved from the same fate by his eloquence and his past connections with the house of Lancaster.[40]

The six surviving peers who had presented the Appeals against Gloucester, Arundel and Warwick in 1397 and connived in the forfeiture of the Lancastrian estate were tried in Parliament in an atmosphere of anger and emotion which revealed more than anything else how far the last two years of Richard's reign had aroused antagonisms within the political community. They were stripped of their new lands and titles but their lives were spared and they were allowed to retain what they had had before 1397. Four of them, Salisbury, Despenser and the two Holands, were lynched by mobs the following January when they tried to start a rebellion against the new regime and restore Richard II to his throne. Their folly cost them not only their own lives but Richard's. Few deposed kings of the middle ages survived long into the reigns of their successors. Their continued existence offered a rallying point for rebellion which was too potent to be ignored. The deposed King was taken to the Lancastrian castle of Pontefract at the beginning of January and was dead within days of his arrival. There was no judicial inquiry into Richard's death as there had been into Gloucester's. But the weight of the evidence is that he was starved to death by his jailers on the instructions of Henry IV. The new King had his body carried processionally to London with his face exposed in an open bier so that all would know that he was truly dead.[41]

The first news of events in England reached the French court through Flemish and Italian merchants. Then, during October and November 1399, the Dame de Courcy arrived in Paris with her entourage from Wallingford, followed by a trickle of other French refugees who had served in English royal and noble households. They brought with them fuller accounts, spiced with the embellishments of Richard II's friends and supporters. Many came back with tales of the hatred of the English population for France and its people. 'I would not want all the wealth of England if I had to spend my life there, so much do they resent the French,' said one of them, who had worked as a clerk in Bolingbroke's household. Some of the returning exiles wrote up their experiences into rhetorical histories of the revolution, overtly designed to stir up sympathy for Richard II. The Earl of Salisbury's French valet Jean Creton, who had witnessed the dramatic events at Conway castle, venerated Richard as the man who 'loved the French people with all his heart'. He returned to France to write a prolix narrative in verse of Richard's martyrdom. Another Frenchman, serving in the household of Richard's friend John Holand, Duke of Exeter, penned a tendentious account of the last two years of Richard's reign under the title of *The Betrayal and Death of*

Richard II. These accounts were widely read outside England and almost universally believed. They fed a generalised hostility to England and its people which found its way into the final pages of Froissart's chronicle and the verses of Eustache Deschamps.[42]

The sense of shock which is palpable in French accounts was due in part to outrage at the idea of deposing an anointed king, something which the English had now done twice in the past century but which the French never contemplated even at the lowest point of their mad King's fortunes. 'O *detestabile monstrum*', cried the official chronicler of Saint-Denis. But an even more important factor in French minds was the widespread misconception that Richard had been deposed because of his support for peace with France. The charges levelled against Richard in Parliament in fact made no allegations about his conduct of foreign policy but in France men were convinced that he was accused of abandoning Brest and Cherbourg to their former owners and of entering into the twenty-eight-year truce without the consent of his subjects. Charles VI's ministers had for years regarded Richard II as the solitary barrier against the tide of English francophobia. They were obsessed by the English King's dispute with the Duke of Gloucester, which had received extensive publicity in their country. They assumed that Bolingbroke's supporters must have hated Richard for the same reasons as Gloucester had. For many years the received opinion on the continent was that the deposition of Richard II was a declaration of war. So, when the news of Henry IV's coronation was confirmed, the French King's ministers at once reinforced the garrisons on the marches of Calais and Aquitaine. The Duke of Burgundy sent his brother Berry a summary of the latest reports from across the Channel. He found them so troubling that he insisted that Berry should burn it as soon as it had been read. 'Truth to tell, my dear brother,' Berry replied, 'it is a great tragedy and a signal misfortune for our country. For as you well know, Lancaster governs by the will of the English people and the English people like nothing better than war.'[43]

Royal House of England

(not complete)

EDWARD III
(d. 1377)
m.
Philippa of Hainault
(d. 1369)

Edward, Prince of Wales ('the Black Prince')
(1330–76)
m.
Joan of Kent
(d. 1385)

Isabella
(1332–79)
m.
Enguerrand de Coucy

Lionel of Antwerp, Duke of Clarence
(1338–68)
m.
(1) Elizabeth de Burgh
(d. 1363)
(2) Violante Visconti

John of Gaunt, Duke of Lancaster
(1340–99)
m.
(1) Blanche of Lancaster
(d. 1368)
(2) Constance of Castile
(d. 1394)
(3) Catherine Swynford
(d. 1403)

Edmund of Langley, Earl of Cambridge,
later Duke of York
(1342–1402)
m.
(1) Isabella of Castile
(d. 1392)
(2) Joan Holand
(d. 1434)

Mary
(1344–62)
m.
John de Montfort, Duke of Brittany

Margaret
(1346–61)
m.
John, Earl of Pembroke
(d. 1375)

Thomas of Woodstock, Earl of Buckingham,
later Duke of Gloucester
(1355–97)
m.
Eleanor Bohun
(d. 1399)

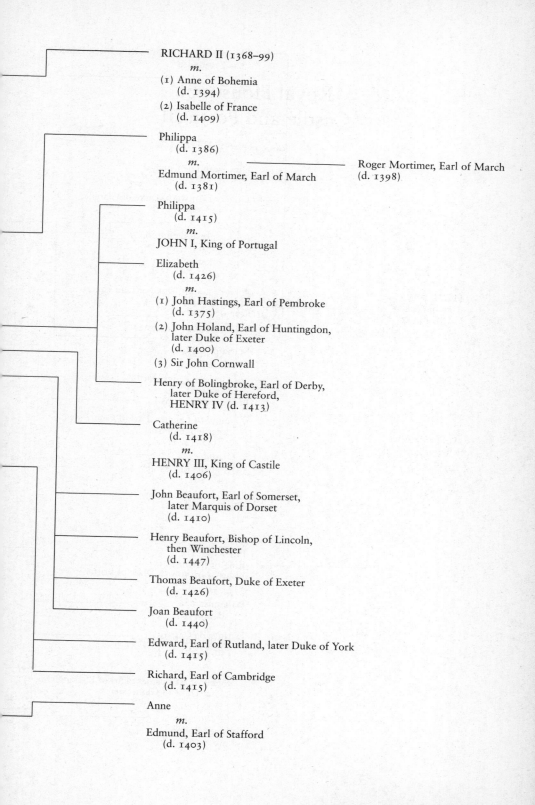

RICHARD II (1368–99)
    m.
(1) Anne of Bohemia
    (d. 1394)
(2) Isabelle of France
    (d. 1409)

Philippa
    (d. 1386)
    m. ——————————— Roger Mortimer, Earl of March
Edmund Mortimer, Earl of March   (d. 1398)
    (d. 1381)

Philippa
    (d. 1415)
    m.
JOHN I, King of Portugal

Elizabeth
    (d. 1426)
    m.
(1) John Hastings, Earl of Pembroke
    (d. 1375)
(2) John Holand, Earl of Huntingdon,
    later Duke of Exeter
    (d. 1400)
(3) Sir John Cornwall

Henry of Bolingbroke, Earl of Derby,
    later Duke of Hereford,
    HENRY IV (d. 1413)

Catherine
    (d. 1418)
    m.
HENRY III, King of Castile
    (d. 1406)

John Beaufort, Earl of Somerset,
    later Marquis of Dorset
    (d. 1410)

Henry Beaufort, Bishop of Lincoln,
    then Winchester
    (d. 1447)

Thomas Beaufort, Duke of Exeter
    (d. 1426)

Joan Beaufort
    (d. 1440)

Edward, Earl of Rutland, later Duke of York
    (d. 1415)

Richard, Earl of Cambridge
    (d. 1415)

Anne
    m.
Edmund, Earl of Stafford
    (d. 1403)

Royal Houses of
Castile and Portugal

(not complete)

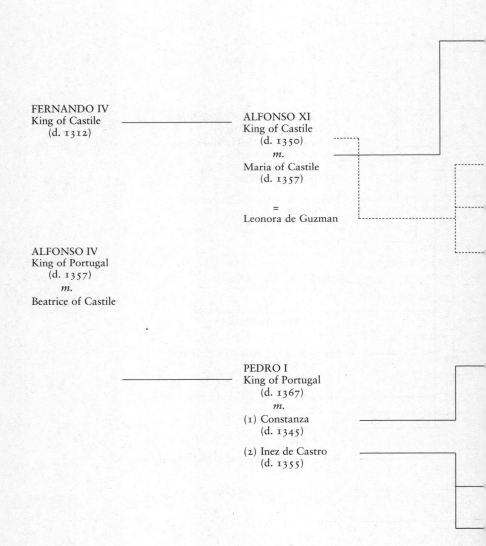

FERNANDO IV
King of Castile
(d. 1312) ——————————— ALFONSO XI
King of Castile
(d. 1350)
m.
Maria of Castile
(d. 1357)

=
Leonora de Guzman

ALFONSO IV
King of Portugal
(d. 1357)
m.
Beatrice of Castile

——————————— PEDRO I
King of Portugal
(d. 1367)
m.
(1) Constanza
(d. 1345)

(2) Inez de Castro
(d. 1355)

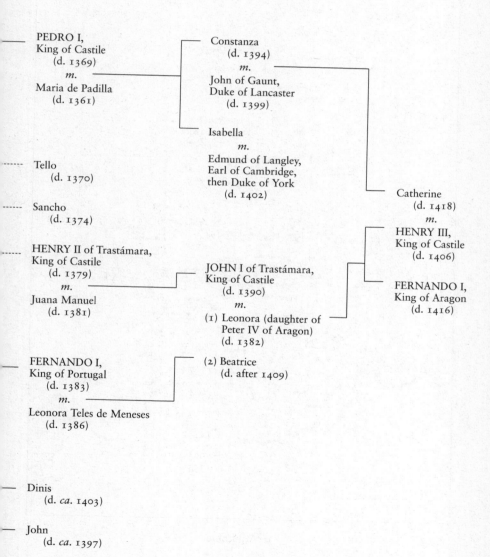

PEDRO I,
King of Castile
(d. 1369)
m.
Maria de Padilla
(d. 1361)

Constanza
(d. 1394)
m.
John of Gaunt,
Duke of Lancaster
(d. 1399)

Isabella
m.
Edmund of Langley,
Earl of Cambridge,
then Duke of York
(d. 1402)

Catherine
(d. 1418)
m.
HENRY III,
King of Castile
(d. 1406)

Tello
(d. 1370)

Sancho
(d. 1374)

HENRY II of Trastámara,
King of Castile
(d. 1379)
m.
Juana Manuel
(d. 1381)

JOHN I of Trastámara,
King of Castile
(d. 1390)
m.
(1) Leonora (daughter of
Peter IV of Aragon)
(d. 1382)

FERNANDO I,
King of Aragon
(d. 1416)

FERNANDO I,
King of Portugal
(d. 1383)
m.
Leonora Teles de Meneses
(d. 1386)

(2) Beatrice
(d. after 1409)

Dinis
(d. ca. 1403)

John
(d. ca. 1397)

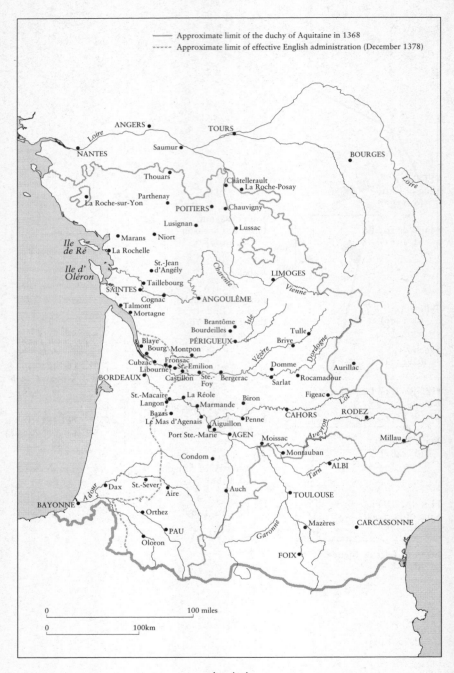

— Approximate limit of the duchy of Aquitaine in 1368
---- Approximate limit of effective English administration (December 1378)

ANGERS

TOURS

NANTES

Saumur

BOURGES

Thouars

Châtellerault

La Roche-Posay

La Roche-sur-Yon

Parthenay

POITIERS

Chauvigny

Lusignan

Lussac

Marans

Niort

Ile de Ré

La Rochelle

St.-Jean d'Angély

LIMOGES

Ile d'Oléron

Taillebourg

Vienne

SAINTES

Charente

Cognac

ANGOULÊME

Talmont

Mortagne

Brantôme

Isle

Tulle

Bourdeilles

PÉRIGUEUX

Brive

Blaye

Bourg

Montpon

Vézère

Dordogne

Cubzac

Fronsac

Domme

Aurillac

Libourne

St.-Emilion

Rocamadour

BORDEAUX

Castillon

Ste.-Foy

Bergerac

Sarlat

St.-Macaire

La Réole

Biron

Figeac

Lot

Langon

Marmande

CAHORS

RODEZ

Bazas

Penne

Le Mas d'Agenais

Aiguillon

Millau

Port Ste.-Marie

AGEN

Moissac

Aveyron

Condom

Montauban

Tarn

ALBI

St.-Sever

Dax

Auch

TOULOUSE

BAYONNE

Adour

Aire

Orthez

Mazères

CARCASSONNE

PAU

Garonne

Oloron

FOIX

0   100 miles

0   100km

II Aquitaine

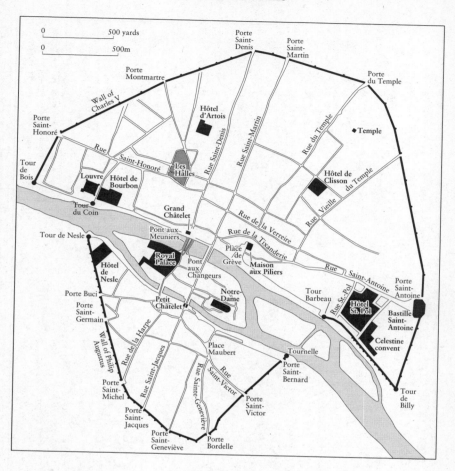

0   500 yards

0   500m

Porte Saint-Denis

Porte Saint-Martin

Porte du Temple

Porte Montmartre

Wall of Charles V

Porte Saint-Honoré

Hôtel d'Artois

Rue Saint-Denis

Rue Saint-Martin

Rue du Temple

Temple

Tour de Bois

Rue Saint-Honoré

Les Halles

Louvre

Hôtel de Bourbon

Hôtel de Clisson

Rue Vieille du Temple

Tour du Coin

Grand Châtelet

Rue de la Verreire

Pont aux Meuniers

Rue de la Tixanderie

Tour de Nesle

Royal Palace

Place de Grève

Maison aux Piliers

Hôtel de Nesle

Pont aux Changeurs

Rue Saint-Antoine

Porte Saint-Antoine

Porte Buci

Petit Châtelet

Notre-Dame

Tour Barbeau

Rue St.-Pol

Hôtel St. Pol

Porte Saint-Germain

Wall of Philip Augustus

Rue de la Harpe

Rue Saint-Jacques

Place Maubert

Bastille Saint-Antoine

Celestine convent

Tournelle

Porte Saint-Michel

Rue Sainte-Geneviève

Rue Saint-Victor

Porte Saint-Bernard

Tour de Billy

Porte Saint-Jacques

Porte Saint-Victor

Porte Saint-Geneviève

Porte Bordelle

III Paris

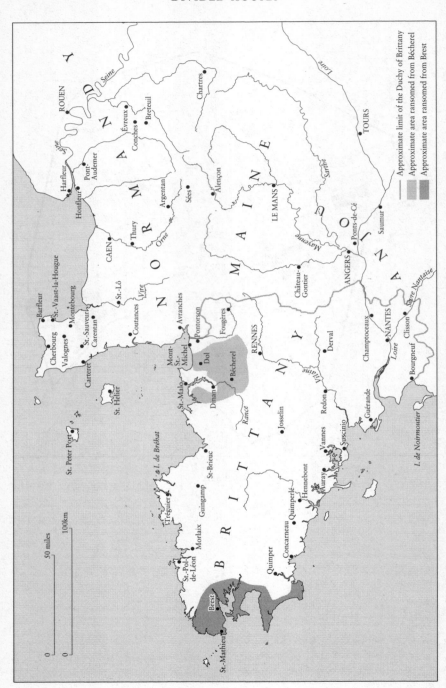

IV Brittany and the Cotentin

Approximate limit of the Duchy of Brittany
Approximate area ransomed from Bécherel
Approximate area ransomed from Brest

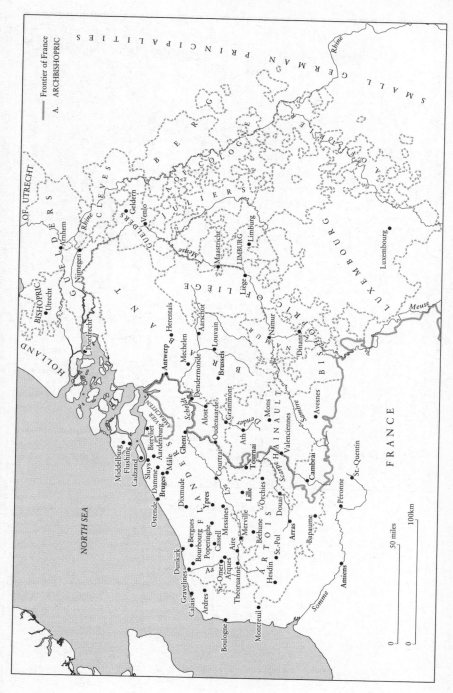

Frontier of France
A. ARCHBISHOPRIC

SMALL GERMAN PRINCIPALITIES

BERG

J. OF COLOGNE

JULIERS

BISHOPRIC
OF UTRECHT

CLEVES

GUELDERS
G

Arnhem
Rhine
Nijmegen
Utrecht
Dordrecht

HOLLAND

Geldern
Venlo

Rhine

LIMBURG

Maastricht

Limburg

LIÈGE

Liège

Meuse

LUXEMBOURG

Luxembourg

Meuse

NAMUR

BRABANT

Herentals
Aarschot
Louvain
Brussels
Mechelen
Antwerp

NORTH SEA

Middelburg
Flushing
Cadzand

Sluys
Damme
Bruges
Male
Aardenburg
Biervliet

WATCHTERN

Scheldt
Ghent
Dixmude
Ostende

Dendermonde
Alost
Oudenaarde
Grammont

Mons
HAINAULT
Valenciennes

Dinant

BISHOPRIC

Avesnes

Sambre

Courtrai
Ypres
Messines
Poperinghe
Cassell
Bergues
Bourbourg
Dunkirk
Gravelines
Calais
Ardres
St Omer
Arques
Théorouanne

Lys
Merville
Lille
Aire

ARTOIS
Hesdin
St-Pol
Bethune

Orchies
Douai
Arras
Bapaume

Cambrai

Tournai
Ath

Scarpe
Scheldt

St-Quentin

Péronne

FRANCE

Boulogne
Montreuil

Somme

Amiens

50 miles
100km
0

v Flanders and the Low Countries

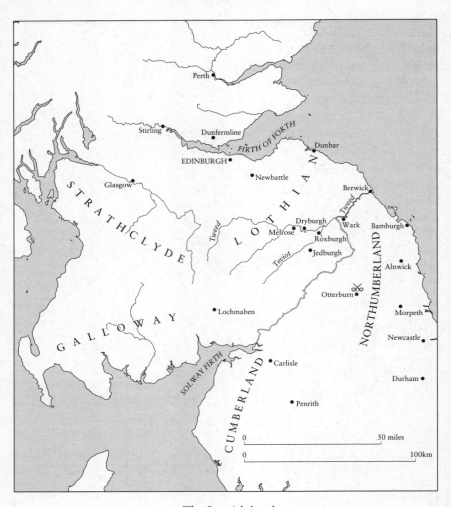

VI The Scottish border

Land over 1,000m above sea level

Corunna
Betanzos
Santiago
GALICIA
LEÓN
Miño
Tui
Orense
Ponte do Mouro
Bragança
Braga
OPORTO
Douro
Trancoso
Viseu
Almeida
Guarda
COIMBRA
Benavente
Esla
Valladolid
Zamora
Tordesillas
Medina del Campo
Salamanca
Segovia
Ciudad Rodrigo
Avila
Duero

Santander
Bilbao
Vitoria
Sto. Domingo
de la Calzada
BURGOS
Logroño
Soria
Saragossa
Ebro

Bayonne
St.-Jean-
Pied-
de-Port
PAMPLONA
Estella
Olite
Tudela

NAVARRE
ARAGON

Aljubarrota
Santarém
Salvaterra
de Magos
LISBON
Setubal
Vimieiro
Estremoz
Evora
Vila Viçosa
Elvas
Badajoz
Alcántara
Cáceres
Tagus
Guadiana
TOLEDO

Murcia

Mertola
Huelva
Faro
I. of
Saltes
Cape
St. Vincent
SEVILLE
Tinto
Guadalquivir
Sanlúcar de
Barrameda
GRANADA
GRANADA

PORTUGAL
ALEMTEJO
CASTILE

Tamega

0   100 miles
0   200km

VII Castile, Navarre and Portugal

875

Note on Money

In most western European countries it is necessary to distinguish between money of account, which was simply a conventional measure of value, and money of payment, that is to say the coins in which payments were actually made.

England used a silver standard. The unit of account was the pound sterling (£), equal to one and a half marks of silver. The pound was divided into twenty shillings (s), each of 12 pennies (d). There was a variety of silver coins in circulation, of which the most significant was the silver groat, worth four pennies sterling. There was also a gold coinage based on the noble, which was conventionally worth 6s 8d, but was rarely used. English coin maintained a stable metal content throughout this period.

France also used a silver standard. The French units of account were the *livre tournois* (*l.t.*), or pound of Tours, and the *livre parisis* (l.p.), or pound of Paris. Like the pound sterling, they corresponded to a conventional weight of silver. The pound sterling was worth five *l.t.* and four *l.p.* Both of these units of account were divided, like the English units, into twenty shillings (*s*, or *sols*) each of twelve pennies (*d*, or *deniers*). For most of this period, the main French coins in circulation were the silver *gros* and, for larger transactions, the gold franc. Between 1365 and 1385, these coins maintained a stable value in money of account. The *gros* was worth one *s.p.* The franc was nominally worth one *l.t.*, in fact slightly less. English government accounts convert francs into sterling at six to the pound. In 1385 a new coinage was issued. The gold franc was replaced by the *écu* (or *couronne*, after the image on its obverse side), and the *gros* by the silver *blanc*, which remained the standard silver coin of France until the sixteenth century. These were worth less than their predecessors, and the gentle course of devaluation continued through the 1380s and 1390s.

In the duchy of Aquitaine the accounts of the English administration were reckoned in *livre bordelais* (*l.b.*) or pounds of Bordeaux, but this unit was rarely used for any other purpose. Traditionally, the pound of Bordeaux was worth the same as the pound of Tours, i.e. 4s sterling, but in about 1370 it was devalued to 2s 8d.

In Castile, the unit of account was the *maravedi*, which represented a value in silver equal to the silver dinar of the old Almoravid rulers of Andalusia and Morocco, last struck in 1170. A *maravedi* was divided into ten pennies (or *dineros*). £1 sterling was worth about 230 *maravedis*. The standard silver coin of Castile was the *real*, but larger transactions were generally reckoned in gold *doblas*. The metal content of the *dobla* was relatively stable in this period, and the coin was generally worth about 4s sterling, i.e. five to the pound.

The gold florin of Florence circulated widely throughout western Europe. This famous coin, first minted in 1252, was the nearest thing to an international standard of value in fourteenth-century Europe, but it had become discredited by imitations and forgeries. The genuine article was worth 2s 10d sterling.

In the text, sterling equivalents are generally given for sums reckoned in French, Castilian or Italian currency. Purchasing power is notoriously elusive, and modern equivalents even more so. Silver had become scarce throughout Europe, with the result that in countries operating a silver standard the value of the unit of account tended to rise. In England, a gallon of red Gascon wine cost 8d. A building craftsman, who had earned 3d or 4d a day in the 1350s, could expect 5d or 6d by the end of the century, roughly equivalent to the earnings of an archer. An ordinary warhorse generally cost about £10 in the 1370s, while a carthorse could be had for £1, about the same as half an acre of good agricultural land.

Abbreviations

AC	Archives Communales
ACA	Archivo de la Corona de Aragon (Barcelona)
AD	Archives Départmentales
AHG	*Archives historiques . . . de la Gironde*
AHP	*Archives historiques du Poitou*
AHSA	*Archives historiques de la Saintonge*
AHVF	*Atlas historique des villes de France*
AN	Archives Nationales (Paris)
ASFDB	European State Finance Database
BEC	*Bibliothèque de l'École des Chartes*
BL	British Library (London)
BN	Bibliothèque Nationale (Paris)
CCR	*Calendar of Close Rolls*
CFR	*Calendar of Fine Rolls*
CPR	*Calendar of Patent Rolls*
EHR	*English Historical Review*
GEC	*Complete Peerage*
ODNB	*Oxford Dictionary of National Biography*
PPC	*Proceedings and Ordinances of the Privy Council*
PRO	Public Record Office (London) [The National Archives]
RISS¹	*Rerum Italicarum scriptores*
RISS²	*Rerum Italicarum Scriptores* (new edition)
VCH	*Victoria History of the Counties of England*

References

Printed sources (Bibliography, Sections B and C) are cited by title or by author/editor and title. Secondary works are cited without title by author alone.

References marked with an asterisk* are to the documentary notes or appendices of the work cited.

CHAPTER I

1 Mézières, *Songe*, i, 395–8.
2 Wykeham: *Anonimalle*, 97. Latimer: *GEC*, vii, 470–2; Jones (1970), 17–18, 50–2; *CPR 1367–70*, 187.
3 McFarlane (1972), 14; McFarlane (1973), 134–5; Goodman (1992), 341–9.
4 Chaplais (1957), 85–9; Chaplais (1989), 147–50; Bériac; cf. list of officers in Chandos Herald, *Prince Noir*, ll. 4189–4252.
5 Garrison strength: 1,132 in 1371–2 (*Compte Gunthorp*, 20–5); 1,162 in 1373 (PRO E101/179/12, mm. 4–5vo); 1,220 in 1375–6 (E101/180/4, mm. 4vo–8vo). Townsmen: *Parl. Rolls*, v, 381 (209). Economy: Holmes (1975), 81; Lloyd (1973), 240–1. French forces: Rey (1965), ii, 375–7. Deschamps, *Oeuvres*, iii, 93–5.
6 Storey-Challenger, 169–87, 196–9, *275–83, *288–307; PRO C36/79, pp. 547–52.
7 *Foed.*, iii, 491; *CPR 1358–61*, 329. Defences: Mesqui (1997), 336. Supply: e.g., PRO E101/31/6 (Feb. 1370), C76/56, m. 14 (July 1373); *Delisle, ii, 263–4. Great company: Sumption, ii, 566–7; *Gr. chron.*, ii, 134.
8 *GEC*, x, 823–4; Froissart, *Chron.* (SHF), viii, 125. Morice, *Preuves*, ii, 34; *Lobineau, ii, 580.
9 Garrisons: *CPR 1367–70*, 123; *Parl. Rolls*, v, 302–3, 304–6 (21, 27); Morice, *Preuves*, ii, 34; Morice, *Preuves*, ii, 36–7; Jean IV, *Actes*, no. 152. Court: Jones (1970), 17–18, 39–51. Richmond: Jones (1970), 174–6.
10 *Rot. Scot.*, i, 811–14, 894–5; *Acts Parl. Scot.*, i, 518–21, xii, 12–13. Diplomacy: *Exch. R. Scotland*, ii, 328, 348; *Foed.*, iii, 862–3, 873, 878; *Cal. Doc. Scot.*, iv, no. 154; David II, *Acts*, no. 441.
11 *Rot. Scot.*, i, 955, 965; *Foed.*, iii, 3–4, 20; *Parl. Rolls*, v, 369 (177).
12 Neville, Ch. 3 (a valuable work).
13 *Parls. & Councils*, i, 19–22. 1369: PRO E101/30/1, 2, E101/31/25.
14 *Vernier, 130–1 ('Flamens'); Froissart, *Chron.* (KL), xv, 185, *xviii, 491.
15 Christine de Pisan, *Livre des fais*, i, 44, 80, 118, 132–3, 185, ii, 50–2. Crécy: Mézières, *Songe*, ii, 382. Portrait: *Inv. mobilier Charles V*, no. 2217.
16 Cazelles (1982), 308–9, 366, 402–10, 424, 461–2, 473–5, 482, 545–7; *Notices et extraits BN*, i, 344.

CHAPTER II

1 *Mandements*, nos. 495, 507; Anselme, vi, 205; *Chron. premiers Valois*, 201; *Arch. St.-Quentin*, ii, no. 713; Froissart, *Chron.* (SHF), vii, 157–8; *Chron. Bourbon*, 72–3; AN JJ102/240.

2 *Anglo-Norman Letters*, 198–9; *Ord.*, v, 699–702; *Hist. gen. Lang.*, x, 1453–4; *Doc. Millau* [2], nos. 318, 325–6, 328–9 332, 336, 359–60.

3 PRO E403/436, mm. 24, 25, 26 (26, 31 Jan.; 3 Feb.); E403/438, m. 25 (14 June); Delpit, *Coll. doc.*, 132–68, 175 (no. 28); *Parl. Rolls*, v, 258 (7, 8).

4 *Anglo-Norman Letters*, 200. Felton: *Reg. Black Prince*, iv, 99, 161, 207, 246; *Cal. Pap. R. Petitions*, i, 452; Chandos Herald, *Prince Noir*, ll. 1910–14, 1936–8, 4201–2. Calveley: ACA reg. 916, fol. 36. Chandos: Sumption, ii, 569, 571; *Compte r. Navarre*, 219; Froissart, *Chron.* (SHF), vii, 104.

5 Calveley: Froissart, *Chron.* (SHF), vii, 117–18; *Gr. Chron.*, iii, 146. Reinforcements: *Foed.*, iii, 861–2.

6 Froissart, *Chron.* (SHF), vii, 120, 122, 339; *Anglo-Norman Letters*, 198; Chandos Herald, *Prince Noir*, ll. 3933–4; *Douze comptes d'Albi*, i, 94 (no. 1666); cf. BN Doat 131, fols. 21–22. Bertucat: Rouquette, 178; *Comptes Rodez*, ii, 69, 70; AC Martel EE1/23; Lacoste, iii, 206n[1]; *Boudet (1893)*, 345 (Auvergne).

7 Froissart, *Chron.* (SHF), vii, 143–5; BN Doat 131, fols. 21–22 (St.-Nicolas). Citadel: J.-U. Devals, *Monuments historiques de Montauban* (1841), 49–50.

8 AN JJ 102/91; *Anglo-Norman Letters*, 199–200. For French garrisons see, e.g., Cahors (*BEC*, xv, 199) and Figeac (BN Fr. 20586/32). Armies: *Anglo-Norman Letters*. 201; Froissart, *Chron.* (SHF), vii, 114, 123–4, 335, 341; *Moranvillé (1888)*, 221–4. Cf. *Mandements*, nos. 510, 525; *Douze comptes d'Albi*, i, 94 (nos. 1657, 1662, 1664); copy musters and receipts at AD Lot F45–8.

9 Chandos: *Douze comptes d'Albi*, i, 96 (no. 1688); Froissart, *Chron.* (SHF), vii, 143, 339–40; *Hist. gén. Lang.*, ix, 808. Réalville: AN JJ 100/242–3, 102/305; Froissart, *Chron.* (SHF), vii, 123–4, 135, 341. Walkefare: *Reg. Black Prince*, iv, 308, 334, 388; Froissart, *Chron.* (SHF), vii, 123, 340–1; AN JJ 108/183, J642/2 (his name). The French were besieging Réalville and Caussade on 13 April: BN Doat 241, fol. 661.

10 Froissart, *Chron.* (SHF), vii, 139–46, 356–7; Artières, 'Nouveaux docs', 280–1; *Chron. Bourbon*, 74. Cf. *Doc. Millau* [2], no. 313; *Petit Thalamus*, 383–4; BN Coll. Languedoc 159, fol. 127vo. Date: *Comptes Rodez*, ii, 70. Topography: Lartigaut, 176.

11 Froissart, *Chron.* (SHF), vii, 142–9, 357–61; Lacoste, iii, 208–9; AC Cajarc CC6, fol. 147; *Anglo-Norman Letters*, 200 (Domme is 'H'); *Ord.*, xv, 443; BN PO 1009 De Dome/8; *Rupin*, 368–9; *Hist. gén. Lang.*, x, 1489–90.

12 'Inv. Arch. Cahors', nos. 507–9; AC Cajarc CC6, fols. 147vo, 148, 148vo; Froissart, *Chron.* (SHF), vii, 146–7, 358–9.

13 PRO E101/29/24, E101/315/35; Froissart, *Chron.* (SHF), vii, 116; Knighton, *Chron.* 196. Last protections issued 28 Feb.: *Foed.*, iii, 857, 859, 862.

14 Froissart, *Chron.* (SHF), vii, 116–17, 118, confirmed by acct. of Robert Beverley (PRO E101/315/35) and John's excuses in Jan. 1372 (Morice, *Preuves*, ii, 34). Solidor: Gregory XI, *Lettres (France)*, no. 775.

15 The defectors before April 1369 were the lords of Castelnaud, Biron, Badefols and Montferrand: AN J655/18 (lost: see summary in the 17th cent. MS inventory of Dupuy and Godefroy). On these families: Maubourguet, 310–11, 324–6. Count: AN JJ 100/778, 102/305; BN Doat 241, fol. 661; BN Doat 244, fols. 29–38; BN Fr. 22382, fol. 5; *Mandements*, no. 686; *Rec. titres Périgueux*, 374–8. Raid, Brantôme: AC Périgueux BB13, fol. 47; Chandos Herald, *Prince Noir*, ll. 3927–30; Froissart, *Chron.* (SHF), vii, 118–19, 150–3, 362–4.

16 *Rec. doc. Poitou*, iv, pp. x–xii. Service with Chandos: Froissart, *Chron.* (SHF), vii, 122, 137 (lords of Châtellerault, Angle, Parthenay).

17 *Mandements*, no. 535; *Rec. doc. Poitou*, iii, 389–91; Froissart, *Chron.* (SHF), vii, 114,

120, 136. On De Bueil: *Mandements*, no. 510; *Moranvillé (1888), 219; Froissart, *Chron.* (SHF), vii, 120. On Kerlouet: *Mon. proc. canonisation Ch. de Blois*, 108, 109. Ambush: *Chron. norm.*, 192; Froissart, *Chron.* (SHF), vii, 120–2; *Rec. doc. Poitou*, iv, 406.

18 Froissart, *Chron.* (SHF), vii, 137–8, 160; *Delisle, ii, 169. Audley: BN Doat 197, fol. 51.

19 *Controversy Scrope Grosvenor*, i, 261, 262, 271, 275, 286, 286–7, 319, 322; AN JJ100/292, JJ105/374; *Rec. doc. Poitou*, iii, 376–7, 413–14, iv, 113; Froissart, *Chron.* (SHF), vii, 137, 138–9, 349–51.

20 Froissart, *Chron.* (SHF), vii, 160–2; *Controversy Scrope Grosvenor*, i, 261, 262, 269, 271, 275, 286, 299, 302, 316, 319, 322; *Mandements*, no. 544, 559, 568–70, 661; *Moranvillé (1888), 215, 232–3, 242n; BN Clair. 73, p. 5735; Froissart, *Chron.* (SHF), vii, 162; *Rec. doc. Poitou*, iii, 387–8, iv, 53–4; AN KK242, fols. 4vo, 19. On legal status of La Roche-sur-Yon: AN JJ102/4.

21 Ch.-Gontier garrison: *Mandements*, no. 570; *Frag. chron. norm.*, 9; Morice, *Preuves*, i, 1632–3. Attack on St.-Sauveur: *Mandements*, no. 661; Morice, *Preuves*, i, 1633–4; *Frag. chron. norm.*, 9; *Gr. chron.*, ii, 134; *Chron. premiers Valois*, 203–4.

22 Froissart, *Chron.* (SHF), vii, 190, 386–7.

23 Froissart, *Chron.* (SHF), vii, 155–6, 366–8; Froissart, *Chron.* (KL), xvii, 480; *Chron. Bourbon*, 23, 74–5. Date: *Titres Bourbon*, i, nos. 3120, 3123; *Petit, 263n[1]. On B. de La Salle: Sumption, ii, 563; 'Ciquot de la Saigue' is another name for him, see Froissart, *Chron.* (SHF), vii, 398. On his companions: Durrieu (1885), 110–11. On Devereux: Chandos Herald, *Prince Noir*, ll. 1983–93; AN JJ112/345, 11/177; *Rec. doc. Poitou*, iv, 113–14; *Chron. Bourbon*, 23, 26. La Souterraine had been occupied since at least 1361: AN JJ112/345.

24 Devals, 28–30, *70; *Hist. gén. Lang.*, x, 1411–12, 1427; BN PO 268 Belfort/12; BN Doat 87, fols. 239–253; *Ord.*, xii, 113–15; PRO C47/25/5 (16), C61/91, m. 1 (pensions to exiles). Ratier's past: *Livre Tannée* fol. 92 in AC Cahors (I owe this information to Mr Guilhem Pépin). Moissac: BN PO 2615 de la Salle à Toulouse/3. Walkefare: Froissart, *Chron.* (SHF), vii, 104; BN Clair. 137/40; BN Coll. Languedoc 159, fol. 137vo.

25 Rouquette, 198; BN Doat 197, fols. 42–44; *Doc. Millau* [2], no. 332–4, 339, 359; *Hist. gén. Lang.*, x, 1426–7; *Douze comptes d'Albi*, i, 121, 136, 140, 143–4 (nos. 259, 276, 572, 728, 813); *Moranvillé (1888), 223. On Compeyre: *Ord.*, v, 236–7; *Doc. Millau (2)*, no. 240; Miquel, i, 149, ii, 169.

26 AN JJ100/460; *Storey-Challenger, 195–9, 310–12; PRO E36/79, pp. 485, 543, 547–51, 552, 563; E403/438, m. 14 (2 May). *Chronographia*, ii, 337–9; Froissart, *Chron.* (SHF), vii, 111–12. Gascony: *Foed.*, iii, 864–5.

27 Calais: *Anonimalle*, 59, 60; Froissart, *Chron.* (SHF), vii, 133–4, 347–8; *Foed.*, iii, 866; PRO C61/82, m. 12; E403/438, mm. 14, 17–18, 21 (2, 5, 7, 8, 18 May); E101/396/13; E101/396/13 (71); *Cal. Letter Books G*, 242–3. Gascony: PRO E403/438, m. 19 (16 May). Expeditionary force: PRO E403/438, mm. 21, 25 (18 May, 16 June); E101/68/4 (87); *Foed.*, iii, 871 (first orders issued on 5 May: PRO E101/29/35, 36). King's role: Cambridge, UL Ms. Dd. III.53, fols. 76vo–77; *Reg. Appleby*, no. 179.

28 *Parl. Rolls*, v, 221 (2), 223 (8).

29 *Doc. Clos des Galées*, i, 662–6, 668–72; PRO E403/438, mm. 24, 29 (13 June, 7 July); E364/3, m. 4d (atte Wood); E101/29/36; E101/36/14; E101/396/13; *Foed.*, iii, 874–5, 876; *Chron. premiers Valois*, 202; AN JJ100/240; *Doc. Clos des Galées*, i, no. 685.

30 *Doc. Clos des Galées*, i, nos. 659–70, 673–4, 677, 683–4, 687, 690–1, 697–8, 708, 710–12, 865; *Mandements*, no. 507; Anselme, vii, 758. Clisson: Froissart, *Chron.* (SHF), vii, 158.

31 Monaco: Anselme, iv, 490; compare *Doc. Clos des Galées*, ii, no XXXII (84). Grimaldi galleys served from 1370: *ibid.*, i, nos. 780, 791, 810, 816, 819. Castile: *Foed.*, iii, 850–2, 869–70; Ayala, *Crón.*, ii, 14–17; Lopes, *Crón. D. Fernando*, 137–9, 143. Visits: *Mandements*, nos. 562 (p. 278).

32 *Mandements*, no. 549–50, 553–4, 557–8; *Itin. Ph. le Hardi*, 57; 'Séjours', 222;

Gr. Chron., ii, 132–3; *Itin. Ph. le Hardi*, 57; *Moranvillé (1888), 224–32; *Chron. premiers Valois*, 202; *Chron. Bourbon*, 72–3; *Anonimalle*, 59–60; Froissart, *Chron.* (SHF), vii, 348.

33 *Chron. premiers Valois*, 202–3; BN Clair. 12, p. 747, 56, p. 4303, 74, p. 5819, 100, p. 7757, 109, p. 8521, etc.; *Mandements*, nos. 566–7; *Chron. Bourbon*, 73; Froissart, *Chron.* (SHF), vii, 164–5; 'Chron. Pays-Bas', 247–8; *Itin. Ph. le Hardi*, 58.

34 *Anonimalle*, 60–1; *Itin. Ph. le Hardi*, 58; *Gr. Chron.*, ii, 133; *Chron. Bourbon*, 73; Froissart, *Chron.* (SHF), vii, 166–7, 183–5, 374–5, 385–6; *Chron. norm.*, 190; *Chron. premiers Valois*, 205; Walsingham, *Hist. Angl.*, i, 308. Philip's squire: AD Côte-d'Or B1430, fol. 168.

35 PRO E101/29/40; E403/438, mm. 35, 36 (14 Aug., 1 Sept.); *Foed.*, iii, 878. Spies: *Issue R. Brantingham*, 493.

36 PRO E403/438, mm. 37–8 (12, 15 Sept.), and cf. Sherborne (1964), 720–3; *Anonimalle*, 61; *Eulogium*, iii, 336; Walsingham, *Hist. Angl.*, i, 308; *Gr. Chron.*, ii, 135; *Itin. Ph. le Hardi*, 59.

37 The principal captains were employed elsewhere after about 12 Sept.: *Moranvillé (1888), 234, 235. The Duke of Burgundy left Hesdin for Paris on the 13th: *Itin. Ph. le Hardi*, 59. Fleet: *Chron. Bourbon*, 73; 'Séjours', 222.

38 PRO E403/438, mm. 37–8 (15 Sept.); E403/460, m. 26 (23 Sept.); E101/36/14; Cochon, *Chron.*, 123. Germans: Froissart, *Chron.* (SHF), vii, 126–9.

39 Froissart, *Chron.* (SHF), vii, 192–3, 388; *Chron. premiers Valois*, 205–6; *Gr. Chron.*, ii, 136; Cochon, *Chron.*, 123; *Mandements*, no. 642 (note), 747.

40 Froissart, *Chron.* (SHF), vii, 192–3; *Chron. premiers Valois*, 205–6; *Gr. Chron.*, ii, 136; *Mandements*, nos. 598, 642 (note); *Doc. Clos des Galées*, i, nos. 715; Walsingham, *Hist. Angl.*, i, 308.

41 *Anonimalle*, 62; Froissart, *Chron.* (SHF), vii, 193–5, viii, 182; *Issue R. Brantingham*, 5, 368, 376, 445, 450, 466. Cf. *Gr. Chron.*, ii, 136; *Chron. norm.*, 191; *Cal. Inq. P.M.*, xii, 307.

42 Christine de Pisan, *Livre des fais*, i, 204; *Gr. chron.*, ii, 137. Prisoners of war: see, e.g., *CPR 1381–5*, 381. On Owen: Froissart, *Chron.* (SHF), ix, 76–7; *Record of Caernarvon*, ed. H. Ellis (1838), 133; *CFR*, vii, 319; *Cal. Inq. Misc.*, iii, no. 712. On Wyn: Oxford, Corpus Christi Coll., Ms 495, fol. 16 (in Gaunt's service); Froissart, *Chron.* (SHF), vii, 115; *Gr. chron.*, ii, 137.

43 BN Fr. 26008/793; PO 1186 (de Fontaines en Normandie, 18, 19); 656 de Chambly/3; BN Clair. 13, p. 819, 17/6879; BN Clair. 13, p. 819; 17, p. 6879; *Cron. Tournay*, 166–7; 'Chron. Pays-Bas', 249–50; *Doc. Clos des Galées*, i, nos. 721–2, 727–30; *Gr. chron.*, ii, 139–40; *Foed.*, iii, 883.

44 *Doc. Millau* [2], nos. 336–7, 341, 343–4, 346, 348, 351–6, 361; Rouquette, 223, 230, *467–9, *477–9; Chaplais, 'Some documents', 58–78; *Comptes Rodez*, ii, 115–17.

45 *Chron. norm.*, 191; *Hay du Chastelet, 434–6; *Rec. doc. Poitou*, v, 113; Froissart, *Chron.*, vii, 136, 181, 190–1.

46 Froissart, *Chron.* (SHF), vii, 167–8, 170–81; *Chron. norm.*, 191–2.

47 *Chron. norm.*, 194–5; Froissart, *Chron.* (SHF), vii, 196–207, 389–95; Walsingham, *Hist. Angl.*, i, 312.

48 Froissart, *Chron.* (SHF), vii, 213–14; *Chron. Bourbon*, 75–8. Cf. Moranvillé (1888), 235–7; BN Clair. 7, p. 335; 13, p. 873; 16, p. 1087; 45, p. 3375; 71, p. 5525; 99/15, 100/9, 102/121, 103/164, 115/33, etc.

49 Froissart, *Chron.* (SHF), 372; *Chron. Bourbon*, 77–8.

50 Froissart, *Chron.* (SHF), vii, 215–20, 401–3; *Chron. Bourbon*, 78–86 (confuses Cambridge with Thomas of Woodstock, later Earl of Buckingham); *Petit, 262; *Chron. norm.*, 192–3; AC Martel EE1/23. Cambridge was at Limoges on 2 Feb.: PRO C61/84, m. 3. For arbalest of Chantelle, see Rabelais's *Pantagruel*, Lib. II, cap. 5. Release of duchess: *Titres Bourbon*, nos. 3222, 3227, 4780.

51 BN PO 1258 Fumel/19, 21, 22, 23; 1050 Emerat/2; 1936 du Merle/34; BN Doat 197,

fols. 78–79vo; *Ord.*, v, 310–14, xv, 637–8; *AHG*, xxxiv, 197–207; AN JJ102/104; *Petit Thalamus*, 388. Aiguillon had an English garrison by spring 1370: *Hist. gén. Lang.*, x, 1431–3. Port Ste-Marie held out until 1372: *Petit Thalamus*, 388.

52 BN PO 1065 Espagne/33, 35; 2507 de la Roche/24, 25; *Rec. titres Périgueux*, 369–71, 379–84; *Inv. AC Périgueux*, 231–2; *Inv. Trés. Périgueux*, nos. 34–5; *Denifle, 545n^6.

53 *AHG*, i, 158–9; *Petite chron. Guyenne*, para. 61; BN PO 24 Albret (doss. 603)/18, 23; 3057 Ysalguier/15; AN JJ100/889.

54 Delpit, *Coll. doc.*, 136 (nos. 49–57), 148–9 (no. 355), 164–8; James, 33 (App. I).

55 BN Doat 125, fols. 97–99vo; *Comptes Rodez*, ii, 99–100, 101–2; Lacoste, iii, 214–16; *Denifle, 545n^6.

56 Contamine (1972), 138; Cuvelier, *Chanson*, i, 360 (l. 18296).

57 *Ord.*, iii, 433–9, v, 17 (Art. 9); Rey (1973), 502–3.

58 Broome, 'Ransom', 37; Henneman (1976), 180, 188, 209–10, 216, 239–40. Towns' sixth: e.g. *Mandements*, nos. 181, 183, 196, 208, 222, 223, 225, 234, 243, 258, 271, 370, 388, 415, 417, 424, 437, 459, 482, 487, 492, 543, 548, etc.; *Inv. AC Montferrand*, i, 395; *Arch. St.-Quentin*, ii, 695; *Arch. admin. Reims*, iii, 317. Other grants: *ibid.*, nos. 163, 166, 169, 173, 174, 192, 212.

59 *Mandements*, no. 562 (p. 277); *Arch. admin. Reims*, iii, 273–6; *Ord.*, iii, 436–7. Henneman (1976), 119–20, 209, 228–9, 236, 278–80, 291–2; Rey (1965), i, 70–3, 178–80; Rey (1973); Autrand (1981), 213–14, 220–1; C. Hirschauer, *Les états d'Artois* (1923), i, 16–23. Appanages: *Mandements*, no. 537, *Rey (1965), i, 371–2; for Burgundy, see *Plancher, iii, PJ nos. 14, 16; for Berry, *Mandements*, no. 376, 486. Reserve: Rey (1965), ii, 446–7; Cazelles (1882), 531–4.

60 Rey (1965), ii, 447–8. Sources of war treasurers' receipts: *Moranvillé (1888), 211–13.

61 *Mandements*, nos. 562–3, 609 (p. 312); *Chron. premiers Valois*, 202; 'Chron. Pays-Bas', 248.

62 AN X^{1a} 1469, fol. 388; *Gr. Chron.*, ii, 138–9; *Mandements*, nos. 609, 625, 637, 679 (p. 342); BN PO 674 de la Chapelle/19.

63 *Aides*: AN J655/40; *AHG*, i, 159. *Gabelle*: Dognon, 606–14. *Fouage*: *ibid.*, 621, 624–9. Grants: *Hist. gén. Lang.*, x, 1380–2, 1396–7, 1403–4, 1408, 1413; *Douze comptes d'Albi*, i, 67, 69–70 (nos. 917, 938–9, 944, 950) (the reference to 2½ francs is to the forced loan granted against the subsidy at the same time); *E. Molinier, 328–9.

64 *Douze comptes d'Albi*, i, 132, 133, 139 (nos. 494, 518, 702, 704); BN Lat. 9175, fols. 130–149, esp. fols. 135vo–136; *Arch. Montpellier*, ii, no. 923; *Hist. gén. Lang.*, x, 1415–17; *Arch. Montpellier*, i, no. 3920; Henneman (1976), 261–4.

65 *Rey (1965), i, 371–7 and *Ord.*, v, 541 (Arts. 18–22), analysed in Rey, *op. cit.*, i, 36–9.

66 Of estimated tax revenues of Languedoil in 1372, in round figures 631,000 *l.t.* (38%) was earmarked for garrisons, military officers, and operations, 83,000 *l.t.* (5%) was granted to walled towns, generally for defence, and 350,000 (21%) for the repayment of debt most of which must have represented past war expenditure: Rey (1965), i, 37–7, *370–7. Household: *Gr. chron.*, ii, 138; cf. *Mandements*, no. 669. English expenditure: Sherborne (1977)[1], 140.

CHAPTER III

1 Froissart, *Chron.* (SHF), vii, 320–1.

2 *Parl. Rolls*, v, 151–2 (35), 181 (9), 209 (9), 223 (10).

3 Customs: Ormrod (1990), 207 (Table 4). Staple fees: *Parl. Rolls*, v, 300–2, 304–5 (17–18, 27); Holmes (1975), 79–81, 83, 110–11. Demesne and prerogative: Ormrod (1995), 147 (fig. 23) (full figures at ESFDB/orm/engdo30); Harriss (1975), 489. In the Exchequer year 1371–2 (when figures are undistorted by advances) alien priories yielded £3,061/13/8d: PRO E401/506, 508. Overheads: Harriss (1975), 487.

4 Ormrod (1990), 204 (Table 1), 205 (Table 2); Ramsay, ii, 294 (Table V).

5 Wykeham, *Register*, ii, 82–8; Walsingham, *Hist. Angl.*, i, 309.

6 PRO E401/495 (14 Nov., 16 Dec., 31 Jan., 3, 24 Feb., 5, 6 Mar.); E401/499 (5, 7, 12, 17, 29 May; 14 June, 4 Aug.). Windfalls: Harriss (1975), 489–94, 499; for Violante Visconti's portion, see PRO E401/495 (24 Feb., 5, 6 Mar.). Expenditure from reserve: PRO E403/436, mm. 24, 25, 26 (26, 31 Jan., 3 Feb.); E403/438, m. 25 (14 June); E361/4, mm. 21–22 (Wakefield) (not including advances to troops who had not yet accounted for them); E364/5, m. 6d. (Calais, payments for 22 months, 1369–71, annualised); PRO E101/30/1 (Ireland). Chaucer, *Works*, iv, 231.

7 *Cat. Arch. Navarra (Comptos)*, vii, nos. 744–56; *Compte r. Navarre*, 63, 136, 361.

8 Secousse, *Preuves*, 380–1 (confession of Jacques de Rue), 412, 428–9 (confession of Pierre du Tertre); *Compte r. Navarre*, 374.

9 Secousse, *Preuves*, 301–4; *Gr. chron.*, ii, 133–4, 140–1, 379, 433–4 (confession of Pierre du Tertre); *Chron. premiers Valois*, 204; John IV, *Actes*, no. 145; Morice, *Preuves*, i, 1637–8. Charles V was at Jumièges on 16 and 24 Aug.: 'Séjours', 222.

10 *Compte r. Navarre*, 39–40, 302–3, 361; PRO E101/29/28; E101/315/34; E403/438, m. 35 (28 Aug.); *Foed.*, iii, 879. St.-Sauveur: *Cal. Inq. P.M.*, xiv, no. 116; *Foed.*, iii, 993; *Compte r. Navarre*, 39; Secousse, *Preuves*, 428 (confession of Pierre du Tertre); BN Fr. 26008/771; *Delisle, ii, 200–1. Works: *Frag. chron. norm.*, 9; *Compte r. Navarre*, 224; *Foed.*, iii, 903; *Mandements*, no. 699. Hilton's presence at Château-Gontier: *Borderie, iv, 113. Emissaries: *Issue R. Brantingham*, 371, 374, 382, 406, 421, 422.

11 *Anonimalle*, 62 (the text says 6,000 archers, but this must be a copyist's error for 2,000; see proportion of men-at-arms to archers in Knolles's indenture: PRO E101/68/4 (90)); *Issue R. Brantingham*, 382, 406, 421, 430; Secousse, *Preuves*, 427 (confession of Pierre du Tertre). English preparations: PRO C76/53, m. 28; E101/30/6; E101/31/6. Knolles: Froissart, *Chron.* (SHF), vii, 220; E101/68/4 (90); *Foed.*, iii, 894–5.

12 PRO E101/68/4 (90); E101/30/25; *Foed.*, iii, 894–5, 896, 897–8; CPR 1367–70, 397–8, 411–17, 430–55 passim; CFR 1369–77, 167; *Anonimalle*, 63; PRO E101/30/25; cf. Knolles's ordinances for the campaign, BL Cotton Caligula D.III, fols. 115–115vo. Buxhill: CFR 1369–77, 321; *Foed.*, iii, 963. Bourchier: PRO C61/67, m. 2; C61/77, m.4; Chandos Herald, *Prince Noir*, l. 2335. Grandison: Froissart, *Chron.* (SHF), v, 261, 401, vii, 40; Beltz, 177. Minsterworth: *Cal. Inq. Misc.*, iii, no. 885. Caun: *Chron. norm.*, 121–2; *Chron. premiers Valois*, 81, 107. Redmayne: *Hist. Parl.*, iv, 183–4. Clanvowe, Atte Lee: *Controversy Scrope Grosvenor*, i, 172, 184–5.

13 *Foed.*, iii, 886, 888, 894; *Issue R. Brantingham*, 99, 445, 446; 452, 459, 482, 119–20, 130, 141, 142. Hewitt's force cost £5,856, *ibid.*, 452, 459, 482, 119–20, 130, 141, 142; for his loans (£2,680): PRO E401/500 (18, 20 Feb.), E401/501 (21 May); £1,000 was repaid before his departure, *Issue R. Brantingham*, 139; Date of decision: Oxford, Corpus Christi Coll., Ms. 495, fol. 15 (warrants for expedition from 18 April 1370).

14 Knolles: PRO E403/441, m. 5 (4 Nov.); *Issue R. Brantingham*, 267–8. Gascony: *ibid.*, 212, 231, 271, 445, 446, 452, 459, 482, 119–20, 130, 141, 142; PRO E364/5, m. 5d (Lancaster). Naval patrols: PRO E101/30/13, m. 2; E101/396/13 (6); E364/4, m. 4d (Wodeburgh); E364/3, m. 6d (Brian); E101/30/21, 29, 36. Customs: Ormrod (1990), 207 (Table 4). Clerical subsidies: *Rec. Convoc.*, iii, 300–3; *Concilia*, iii, 85.

15 PRO E401/500 (22 Jan. *et seq.*); E401/501, passim; *Issue R. Brantingham*, 146, 169–70, 173–9, 184–91, 194, 214, 216, 221, 228, 251; *Cal. Letter Books G*, 263; *Antient Kalendars*, i, 221 (no. 11), 226–7 (no. 16); CPR 1367–70, 451; CCR 1369–74, 149–50; E403/444, m. 9 (14 Nov.); *Concilia*, iii, 87–8; *Reg. Appleby*, nos. 249, 251–3; *Anonimalle*, 63; Walsingham, *Hist. Angl.*, i, 309; *Parl. Rolls*, vi, 129 (42). Arundel loans: McFarlane (1973), 88–91; Given-Wilson (1991), 1–2, 5–17, 18–22.

16 *Gr. chron.*, ii, 140–2; *Issue R. Brantingham*, 442; Secousse, 307–11.

17 PRO E101/29/36; E101/30/6, 20, 25; E101/30/34; C76/53, m. 28; E364/3, m. 6 (Châteauneuf); E364/4, m. 2 (Stokes); *Issue R. Brantingham*, 115–16, 151–6; 149, 154, 183, 267–8; Secousse, *Preuves*, 427 (confession of Pierre du Tertre). Transports: *Foed.*, iii, 890; PRO E101/30/6.

18 *Compte r. Navarre*, 39, 152, 281–3, 299, 302–3; *Frag. chron. norm.*, 9; Secousse, *Preuves*,

427 (confession of Pierre du Tertre); *Issue R. Brantingham*, 166–7, 167.

19 Secousse, *Preuves*, 427–8 (confession of Pierre du Tertre); *Issue R. Brantingham*, 167, 186, 191–2, 202–3, 225, 263; *Anonimalle*, 66; Walsingham, *Hist. Angl.*, i, 309; PRO E101/29/36, 39; E101/30/13, m. 4.

20 PRO E101/29/39; E101/30/22; E101/30/29, mm. 3–6; E364/3, m. 6 (Châteauneuf); E403/441, m. 4 (26 Oct.); Higden, *Polychron.*, viii, 375; *Foed.*, iii, 899–900; *Anonimalle*, 66; Walsingham, *Hist. Angl.*, i, 312; Walsingham, *Chron. Maj.*, i, 22–4; *Anglo-Norman Letters*, 267; *Issue R. Brantingham*, 244, 248, 268–70, 273–4, 275–6, 277; Secousse, *Preuves*, 428 (confession of Pierre du Tertre). Charles had returned to Cherbourg by 24 Aug., when the Earl of Suffolk, one of the hostages, left: E101/315/39.

21 Froissart, *Chron.* (SHF), vii, 220–1, 403–4; Chandos Herald, *Prince Noir*, ll. 4001–18; *Chron. premiers Valois*, 206; Anselme, vi, 757. Cf. Delachenal, iv, 254; Lehoux, i, 226–7.

22 Christine de Pisan, *Livre des fais*, i, 185, ii, 208–9 (App. 17); Froissart, *Chron.* (SHF), vii, 221, 255; *Chronographia*, ii, 390.

23 AN KK251, fols. 26, 28, 38vo; Froissart, *Chron.*, vii, 212; Cuvelier, *Chanson*, i, 412–14; *Hay du Chastelet, 330–1; *Moranvillé (1888), 247; *Rec. doc. Poitou*, iv, 121–3; Gregory XI, *Lettres (France)*, no. 277.

24 *Col. doc. Murcia*, viii, no. 55; Ayala, *Chron.*, ii, 12–13; *Letters B. du Guesclin*, nos. 335–6, 344; *Petit Thalamus*, 384; Froissart, *Chron.* (SHF), vii, 227; BN Coll. Languedoc 86, fol. 131; BN PO 2615, de la Salle à Toulouse/3. Anjou's movements: AD Hérault A5/64; AN JJ102/243, 156/260. Bertrand was at Moissac on 26 July and Toulouse on the 27th: *Letters B. du Guesclin*, nos. 346–7. On 8 Aug. both were at Agen: BN PO 1015, Doria/6; AN JJ102/116. Strength: *Hist. gén. Lang.*, ix, 818; *L. Menard, iii, 3; *Delachenal, iv, 264n[2,3], 265n[1,2]; BN PO 1015, Doria/5, 6, 7. Castilian retainers: Morice, *Preuves*, i, 1650–1, 1654–5. Beynac: BN Doat 197, fols. 55–58vo. Sarlat: *Ord.*, v, 339–42; J.-J. Escande, *Histoire de Sarlat* (1912), 73–4. Limeuil: AN JJ102/319.

25 AN JJ101/139 (Sarlat); AC Périgueux CC13/1; BN Doat 241, fol. 488vo; BN PO 1407, Gresignac/4; *Chronographia*, ii, 390; Cuvelier, *Chanson*, ii, 361; Froissart, *Chron.* (SHF), vii, 227–8, 230–1.

26 Delpit, *Coll. doc.*, 152–3 (nos. 402–6); Jeanne de Penthièvre, *Actes*, no. 308–9, 320; *Plaine, 44–6; Clément-Simon, 18–21. Rochechouart: Froissart, *Chron.* (SHF), vii, 164; *Moranvillé (1888), 219; *Mandements*, nos. 613, 615, 659. Distribution of Viscount's lands: AN JJ81/773; Anselme, ii, 858E; Froissart, *Chron.* (SHF), vii, 169, 170–1. Chalusset: AN J400/63; *Mandements*, nos. 619, 692; *Moranvillé (1888), 239.

27 Froissart, *Chron.* (SHF), vii, 228, 339, 358, 397, 411; AN J242/16 (8); AN KK251, fols. 5vo, 26vo, 39, 45vo. Nobles in army: e.g. lord of Pierre-Buffière and Raymond de Mareuil's uncle the lord of Malval: Froissart, *Chron.* (SHF), vii, 209, 228, 339, 358, 397, 411; AN J242/16 (13). Berry's agents: AN KK251, fol. 26vo, 27.

28 AN KK251, fols. 23vo, 24, 39vo; *Moranvillé (1888), 246, 247; *La Roque, iv, 1568; *Doc. Limoges*, i, 68.

29 AN KK251, fol. 27; Froissart, *Chron.* (SHF), vii, 228–9, 241–2; Higden, *Polychron*, Cont. (iv), 374; 'Privilèges de Limoges', 116–22.

30 Froissart, *Chron.* (SHF), vii, 241. Anjou's movements: BN PO 1407, Gresignac/4; *L. Menard, iii, 3. Berry's finances: *Moranvillé (1888), 245–7; AN KK251, fols. 3vo; Lehoux, i, 248–50. Anjou's finances: *AHG*, i, 157–9; BN PO 2130, Noyers/16; *E. Molinier, 339–42. Du Guesclin's movements: *Letters B. du Guesclin*, no. 351–2; BN PO 2202, Partenay/5; AN KK251, fols. 31vo. Berry's movements: AN KK251, fol. 24, 27, 40–40vo; BN Clair. 85/89.

31 *Chron. premiers Valois*, 208; Froissart, *Chron.* (SHF), vii, 239–40, 243–4; Walsingham, *Hist. Angl.*, i, 311.

32 *Petit Thalamus*, 385; *Chron. norm.*, 195; *Cron. Tournay*, 173; *Chron. premiers Valois*, 209–10; *Ann. Limoges de 1638*, 271–2; Froissart, *Chron.* (SHF), vii, 244–5, 249–50; Walsingham, *Hist. Angl.*, i, 311–12; *Vitae paparum*, i, 376. Garrison: *Chron. norm.*, 195; *Moranvillé (1888), 245; * Hay du Chastelet, 330–1.

33 Froissart, *Chron.* (SHF), vii, 250, 252; *Chroniques de Saint-Martial de Limoges*, ed. H. Duplès-Agier (1874), 154. Laws of war: Keen (1965), 120–4.

34 Froissart, *Chron.* (SHF), vii, 250–1, 251–2; *Chron. premiers Valois*, 210; Chandos Herald, *Prince Noir*, ll. 4043–52; *Ann. Limoges de 1638*, 273–4;*Vitae paparum*, i, 376; *Doc. Limoges*, i, 71–4. Fate of prisoners: *Gall. Christ.*, ii, 534; BN Coll. Languedoc 159, fol. 138; *Ausgaben apost. Kammer*, 381; *Rec. doc. Poitou*, iv, 41n; *Foed..*, iii, 923, 1034.

35 *Gr. chron.*, ii, 144–5; *Chron. norm.*, 195; *Anonimalle*, 63–4; *Chron. premiers Valois*, 207; Froissart, *Chron.* (SHF), vii, 232–9, 245.

36 Cazelles (1972), 346–7; Berty, 124–5; Christine de Pisan, *Livre des fais*, ii, 37, 40, 114; Bournon (1880), 93–4; Sauval, i, 448; *Gr. chron.*, ii, 143; F. de Fossa, *Le Château Historique de Vincennes*, ii (1908), 5–17.

37 *Gr. chron.*, ii, 145–6; *Chronographia*, ii, 342; Froissart, *Chron.* (SHF), vii, 245–8; BN Fr. 26009/1054 (Sées); *Comptes Tours*, ii, no. 332–3.

38 *Gr. chron.*, ii, 147–8; *Mandements*, nos. 1967; cf. nos. 728–34, 737, 1968; AN X1a 1469, fol. 445vo.

39 *Gr. chron.*, ii, 141–2; PRO E30/260; *Anglo-Norman Letters*, 266–7. French safe-conduct: *Cat. Arch. Navarra (Comptos)*, viii, nos. 297; *Letters B. du Guesclin*, no. 359.

40 *Comptes Tours*, ii, nos. 332–5, 348, 514; AN JJ109/15; *Moranvillé (1888), 249; *Gr. chron.*, ii, 147–8; Froissart, *Chron.* (SHF), viii, 1–2; *Gr. chron.*, ii, 147–8; AN 103/214 (Vaas, Rillé); *Chron. norm.*, 196–7 (Vaas, Rillé, Louroux); Walsingham, *Hist. Angl.*, i, 310.

41 *Mandements*, nos. 704, 714, 743; *Coville (1894), 387–8; *Letters B. du Guesclin*, no. 393; Morice, *Preuves*, i, 1643–5; *Chronographia*, ii, 343, 390. Sancerre's army: AN JJ109/15; *Comptes Tours*, ii, no. 514; *Chron. Bourbon*, 25. His strength: *Mandements*, no. 718; *Moranvillé (1888), 247–9. Musters from 21 Sept. to 2 Oct. in BN PO and BN Clair.: BN PO 1936, du Merle/36; 1947, Mesnil-en-Normandie/44; 2014, Montenay/9; 2182, Painel/32; 2272, La Pierre/2; 2339, de Porcon/15; 2753, St.-Germain/75; 1004, Dinan-en-Bretagne/3, 4; BN Clair. 176, p. 6027; etc.

42 Froissart, *Chron.* (SHF), viii, 2–3; PRO E101/30/38, 39; *Doc. hist. Maine*, no. 238; *Foed.*, iii, 903.

43 Walsingham, *Hist. Angl.*, i, 310; 'Trésor des Chartes, Anjou et Craon', 224–5 and *Chron. norm.*, 196–7 (Vaas, Rillé, Louroux); Froissart, *Chron.* (SHF), xiv, 5 (Beaufort).

44 Walsingham, *Hist. Angl.*, i, 310; *Anonimalle*, 64; Cuvelier, *Chanson*, i, 377 (ll. 19193–19207); *Chron. norm.*, 196–7; *Chron. premiers Valois*, 208; *Chronographia*, ii, 343, 390. Dates: Morice, *Preuves*, i, 1644–5; *Letters B. du Guesclin*, no. 364. Fitzwalter's position: *Chron. norm.*, 198; *Chron. Bourbon*, 25.

45 *Letters B. du Guesclin*, no. 370; *Chron. Bourbon*, 25–6; *Chron. norm.*, 198–9; *Gr. chron.*, ii, 148.

46 *Anonimalle*, 64–5; Walsingham, *Chron. Maj.*, i, 106; PRO E101/30/38, 39 (St.-Sauveur); Froissart, *Chron.* (SHF), viii, 7–8, xiv, 5–7; *John of G. Reg. (1372–6)*, no. 981; *Chron. Bourbon*, 26–7; *Gr. chron.*, ii, 148–9; *Chron. norm.*, 198–9, 199n[1]; *Letters B. du Guesclin*, no. 364; *Hay du Chastelet*, 336;*Moranvillé (1888), 247.

47 Walsingham, *Hist. Angl.*, i, 310; *Chron. norm.*, 198; *Gr. chron.*, ii, 150; *Anonimalle*, 64–5 (confused); *Chron. premiers Valois*, 208; *Chronographia*, ii, 344; *Parl. Rolls*, v, 344 (129). Grandison: *GEC*, vi, 66–7. Fitzwalter: PRO C76/54, m. 10, C76/56, m. 13. Debts: *CPR 1374–7*, 191; *CCR 1374–77*, 71, 267, 274–6, 276–7, 457. Workesley: Walker (1990)[1], 75.

48 *Chron. Bourbon*, 28–9; *Comptes Tours*, ii, no. 498; *Chron. norm.*, 199, 199n[1]; *Letters B. du Guesclin*, no. 371; Froissart, *Chron.* (SHF), xiv, 8.

49 Walsingham, *Hist. Angl.*, i, 310–11; Walsingham, *Chron. Maj.*, i, 16, 106–8, 984–6; Froissart, *Chron.* (SHF), viii, 24; *CCR 1369–74*, 394; *CPR 1370–74*, 394, 420–1; *CPR 1374–77*, 20–1; *Foed.*, iii, 963–4; *Cal. Inq. Misc.*, iii, no. 885; *CFR 1369–77*, 232.

50 Secousse, *Preuves*, 375 (confession of Jacques de Rue), 390–400, 428; *Anglo-Norman Letters*, 266–7; PRO C76/53, m. 9; *Foed.*, iii, 903, 907–8, 993. Archers: Froissart,

Chron. (SHF), viii, 256.
51 PRO E101/30/38; PRO E101/31/19 (15 Feb.–3 June 1371); *Mandements*, no. 860.
Meeting at Vernon: *Gr. chron.*, ii, 153–5; Secousse, *Preuves*, 316, 324–5.
52 Froissart, *Chron.* (SHF), vii, 252, viii, 9–10, 260–3; *John of G. Reg. (1372–6)*, no. 9
(pp. 6–7); *Anonimalle*, 67; Walsingham, *Hist. Angl.*, i, 312; *Mems. London*, 352.
The Prince was at Cognac on 8 Oct.: *John of G. Reg. (1372–6)*, nos. 773–4. Pembroke
was in England in Feb.: *Parl. Rolls*, v, 236 (4).
53 Appointments: Chandos Herald, *Prince Noir*, ll. 4216–18; Gregory XI, *Lettres (France)*,
no. 146; L.-V.-L. de Rochechouart, *Histoire de la maison de Rochechouart* (1859), i, 143.
On Abberbury: PRO E101/29/24; C61/81, m. 3. Rochechouart: BN Fr. 8604/1;
BN Fr. 31928, fol. 121. Pierre-Buffière: Froissart, *Chron.* (SHF), viii, 6. Hewitt was at
the siege of Moncontour in *ca.* July 1371: Froissart, *Chron.* (SHF), viii, 21. Limoges:
Ann. Limoges de 1638, 276–7.
54 Gregory XI, *Lettres (France)*, nos. 229, 550–2; *Ann. Limoges de 1638*, 276–7;
*Troubat, i, 231; Froissart, *Chron.* (SHF), viii, 22; *Inv. arch. Aurillac*, ii, 12–15;
Mandements, no. 844. On Perrot: Gregory XI, *Lettres (France)*, nos. 687, 689.
55 *Chron. norm.*, 200; *Chron. premiers Valois*, 208–9; *Petit Thalamus*, 385; Froissart,
Chron. (SHF), viii, 12–15, 263–6. On Budes: *Inv. AC Périgueux*, 84, 85; BN PO 548,
Budes/2, 3.
56 *Chron. norm.*, 200; *Chron. premiers Valois*, 209; Morice, *Preuves*, i, 1647; *Hay du
Chastelet, 337–9; *Arch. Montpellier*, i, nos. 3924–5; Gregory XI, *Lettres (France)*, no. 17;
Itin. Ph. le Hardi, 484. Finance: *L. Menard, iii, 3; BN Fr. 26010/1131; *Douze comptes
d'Albi*, i, 182 (1297), cf. 184 (1340, 1361), 185 (1386), 188 (1453), 193 (1549);
Arch. Montpellier, i, nos. 683–4, 3924–5.
57 *Chron. premiers Valois*, 210; *Chron. norm.*, 200; *Petit Thalamus*, 385; Froissart,
Chron. (SHF), viii, 15–17, 267–8, 270–1. Movements: Morice, *Preuves*, i, 1645–7;
*Hay du Chastelet, 337–41, 343–6; AN KK251, fols. 31, 43; *Itin. Ph. le Hardi*, 65;
Inv. AC Montferrand, i, 384–5; BN Fr. 26010/1136; N.a fr. 8604/15–16.
58 *Itin. Ph. le Hardi*, 65; Petit, 274–5; *Mon. proc. canonisation Ch. de Blois*, 281–2;
Chron. norm., 201, *Chron. premiers Valois*, 210; Cuvelier, *Chanson*, i, 415 (ll. 21155–7);
Inv. AC Montferrand, i, 385, 386; *Troubat, i, 231; Froissart, *Chron.* (SHF), viii, 23–4.
Reoccupation: *Reg. St.-Flour*, 113. Anjou left for Lavaur *ca.* 22 or 23 Feb.: *L. Menard,
iii, 4.
59 *Parl. Rolls*, v, 235 (1), 237 (6), 247 (40), 240–1; *Anonimalle*, 67; *Galbraith, 580;
Higden, *Polychronicon*, Cont. (iv), viii, 378; Walsingham, *Hist. Angl.*, i, 312–15;
CCR 1369–74, 287; CPR 1370–74, 61; *Rec. Convoc.*, iii, 309–12, xiii, 167–70;
Songe du vergier, i, 39–40.
60 *Parl. Rolls*, v, 237–8 (6, 10–11); CFR, viii, 110–12, 124–5; Higden, *Polychronicon*, ii, 90;
Ormrod (1988), 67, 80.
61 AN X1a 1469, fol. 448ᵛᵒ (salaries); *Mandements*, nos. 806, 861, 809; BN Clair. 94,
p. 7321; *Chron. Bourbon*, 87.
62 *Doc. norm.*, no. 467, 597, 667; BN PO 2320, Pollehay/3. On the Pollehays: *Compte r.
Navarre*, 170–1; BN PO 245, Beaumanoir/3; *Mon. hist.*, no. 1493; BN Fr. 26011/1282;
Chron. premiers Valois, 212–13.
63 *Chron. premiers Valois*, 212–13; *Chron. norm.*, 201, 203; Christine de Pisan,
Livre des fais, i, 87–8. Conches: BN PO 526, Brun/4; PO 1646, de Lannoy/15; 1699,
de Lestandard/11, etc.; BN Clair. 32, p. 2416; 36, p. 2725; 45, p. 3337; 46, p. 3413; 47,
p. 3491; 55, p. 4197; 63, p. 4899; 69, pp. 4537, 5359, etc.; *Hay du Chastelet, 359–61;
Letters B. du Guesclin, no. 441–2. Breteuil: BN Fr. 26010/1240, 1275; 2342, du Port/3,
4, 5. Artillery: *Mandements*, no. 797; BN PO 1726, de Lions/11, 13, 14, 15.
64 Morice, *Preuves*, ii, 36–7.
65 Urban V, *Lettres (France)*, nos. 2843; *Mon. proc. canonisation*, 2–4; Morice, *Preuves*, i,
1667–8, 1676–8; *Hay du Chastelet, 304; Jean IV, *Actes*, nos. 196, 211 (pp. 221–3);
Jones (1970), 53–4; Froissart, *Chron.* (SHF), viii, 289.

66 *Foed.*, iii, 431, 465–6; *CCR 1354–60*, 481; Froissart, *Chron.* (SHF), vi, 165; Chandos Herald, *Prince Noir*, ll. 2124–30, 2327; Secousse, *Preuves*, 380–1 (confession of Jacques de Rue).

67 Jeanne de Penthièvre, *Actes*, no. 322; *Mandements*, no. 702, 712, 814; Morice, *Preuves*, i, 1640, ii, 70–3; *Letters B. du Guesclin*, no. 357; Jean IV, *Actes*, no. 170–3; *Gr. chron.*, iii, 216–17; *Songe du vergier*, i, 266.

68 Jean IV, *Actes*, nos. 195 (p. 210), 196 (p. 211), 211 (p. 222–4); Jones (1970), 54n[1].

69 Morice, *Preuves*, i, 1356–7, 1654–7, 1662–3; *Istore*, ii, 116; *Anonimalle*, 68; *Chron. premiers Valois*, 214–15; *Istore*, ii, 116; *Rot. Parl.*, ii, 324–5 (22, 23); *Letters B. du Guesclin*, nos. 421; 425; *Hay du Chastelet, 362–7.

70 PRO E364/5, m. 5d (Lancaster); *John of G. Reg. (1372–6)*, nos. 9, 1038; *Lacour, 60–1.

71 Froissart, *Chron.* (SHF), viii, 17–18, 20–1; *Chron. premiers Valois*, 220–1; *Chron. norm.*, 202; *Mandements*, nos. 813–15; *Moranvillé (1888), 255–6; Morice, *Preuves*, i, 1666–7; BN PO 789, Clisson/7, 40. Musters before Marshals at Tours, 5–7 Sept.: BN Clair. 167/155, 156, 177/94, etc.; BN PO 47, Amboise/18; 398, de Blainville/31; 423, du Boschet/6; 1522, Heuse/29; 1699, de Lestandart/6; 1831, Macquerel/8, 10; 1917, Melun/247; etc. Cresswell: BN PO 2881, Cressovalle/2.

72 PRO E364/5, m. 5d (Lancaster); Froissart, *Chron.* (SHF), viii, 21, 32; *John of G. Reg. (1372–6)*, no. 5; BN PO 2881, Cressovalle/2 (Cresswell at Moncontour).

73 *Ann. Limoges de 1638*, 277; *Arch. hist. Limousin*, xii, 23–4; *Moranvillé (1888), 256–7; *Doc. Limoges*, i, 338–45; *Arch. hist. Limousin*, iii, 313–15. Castles round Limoges: *Mandements*, no. 844, 846; BN Fr. n.a. 8604/32; BN PO 2209, Passac/3, 4; BN Fr. n.a. 8604/32; Gregory XI, *Lettres (France)*, nos. 550–2, 602; *Arch. hist. Limousin*, iii, 314.

74 Benoit XII (Benedict XII), *Lettres closes et patentes intéressant les pays autres que la France*, ed. J.-M. Vidal and G. Mollat (1950), no. 2871.

75 *Vitae paparum*, i, 375–6, 413; Salutati, *Ep.*, i (1891), 141–2; Walsingham, *Hist. Angl.*, i, 313; *Mandements*, nos. 741, 763, 935; *Prou (1887), 170–1.

76 Salutati, *Ep.*, i, 143. Turenne: Higounet, 523–6; Gregory XI, *Lettres (France)*, no. 338; PRO C61/84, m. 4; *Justel, 111–12. Limeuil: AN JJ102/319. Relations with France: Gregory XI, *Lettres (France)*, nos. 1, 23, 183; *Gr. Chron.*, ii. 149–50; BN PO 1689, Lesant/3; 1774, Luisant/2; *Hist. gén. Lang.*, ix, 862; *Ausgaben apost. Kammer*, 385

77 *CPR Letters*, iv, 93; Gregory XI, *Lettres (France)*, no. 8. On Langham: *Eulogium*, iii, 334; Birchington, 'Vitae Archiep. Cant.', i, 47–8. On Dormans: *Gr. chron.*, ii, 74.

78 *CPR Letters*, iv, 93–4; Gregory XI, *Lettres (France)*, no. 152.

79 *Ausgaben apost. Kammer*, 363; *Reg. Appleby*, no. 265; *Gr. chron.*, ii, 156–7; 'Dispacci di C. da Piacenza', 37; *Anonimalle*, 69–70; *Foed.*, iii, 929; *Reg. (France)*, no. 454–5; *Chron. premiers Valois*, 214; 'Anglo-French negotiations', 70–1 (7); Gregory XI, *Lettres (France)*, nos. 454–61, 604–5.

CHAPTER IV

1 Russell, 68, 173–4.

2 Provence: *Foed.*, iii, 830; Gregory XI, *Lettres (Autres Pays)*, no. 91. Gutiérrez: Russell, 167–8, 183–4. Marriage: *Anonimalle*, 69; Froissart, *Chron.* (SHF), viii, 30.

3 French in Castile: *Hay du Chastelet, 316–17; Valdeon Baruque, 280–1. *Emperogilados*: *Cortes Castilla*, ii, 213–14 (28); *Col. doc. Murcia*, viii, nos. 97–8; Ayala, *Crón.*, ii, 36; *Col. doc. Murcia*, viii, no. 103; Lopes, *Crón. D. Fernando*, 242.

4 Lopes, *Crón. D. Fernando*, 5, 6; Lopes, *Crón. D. Pedro*, 150, 195; Ayala, *Crón.*, i, 275.

5 Jean IV, *Actes*, 57; PRO E403/444, m. 10 (22 Nov.). Their offices: *Cal. Plea & Mem. R. 1364–81*, 123.

6 *Foed.*, iii, 926, 927–8; PRO E364/5, m. 3d (Neville); E403/441, m. 9 (17 Nov.); E403/446, m. 3 (23 Apr.). On Neville: Given-Wilson (1986), 148; Tout (1920–37), iii, 379, 386n[4]; Morice, *Preuves*, i, 1603, 1606. On Barry: *Issue R. Brantingham*, 154, 182–3, 196, 371, 374, 406, 421; Secousse, *Preuves*, 428; *Compte r. Navarre*, 150, 224,

225; PRO E403/441, m. 11 (28 Nov.).

7 PRO E364/5, m. 5d (Lancaster); Froissart, *Chron.* (SHF), viii, 32: *AHG*, iii, 275–6. On Andeiro, Lopes, *Crón. D. Fernando*, 417–18.

8 *AHG*, iii, 275–6; Froissart, *Chron.* (SHF), viii, 34–5, 288–9. For Anjou's relations with Albret, and his ally Armagnac in this period: **Hist. gén. Lang.*, x, 1476–82; BN Doat 197, fols. 201–2, 266–171.

9 *AHG*, iii, 275–6; PRO E403/444, mm. 17, 21 (12 Dec., 20 Jan.). Army of Brittany: PRO E403/444, mm. 23, 28 (31 Jan., 4 Feb., 6 Mar.); *Foed.*, iii, 933; *Reg. Appleby*, no. 301. Army of Gascony: PRO E101/68/5 (103, 109); C61/85, m. 8; E403/446, mm. 3 (20, 29 Apr.); Cambridge, UL Ms. Dd. III.53, fols. 90, 90–90vo (oath of secrecy). Advances were paid in March and April for 2,355 men-at-arms: PRO E403/444, mm. 28, 29 (6, 8, 13, 17, 23, 30 Mar.), E403/446, m. 3 (22, 24 Apr.). Comparison with surviving indentures suggests that advances were initially paid for two-thirds of the contracted men-at-arms of most retinues: PRO E101/68/4 (92–4), 101/68/5 (95–102). This suggests a total of about 7,000 men, of whom 1,000 were to form part of the separate force (see below) commanded by John of Gaunt: *John of G. Reg. (1372–6)*, no. 51.

10 *Anonimalle*, 69. Army of Castile: *John of G. Reg. (1372–6)*, no. 51, 1000; PRO E159/153 (*brevia directa baronibus*), Mich., m. 5; Easter, m. 13d; E403/446, m. 25 (14 July). Negotiations with Aragon and Navarre: Russell, 190, *557–61 (Gaunt's treaty with Portugal, 10 July 1373, which presumably reflected the instructions of his ambassadors, appointed on 1 March); *Foed.*, iii, 939–40. Portugal: Lopes, *Crón. D. Fernando*, 417–18; PRO E159/154 (*brevia directa baronibus*), Hilary, m. 9; *Russell, 560–1.

11 Russell, 176–85. Procession: *Anonimalle*, 69.

12 *Cortes Castilla*, ii, 202–43; *Col. doc. Murcia*, viii, nos. 84–9; Ladero Quesada, 182; Ormrod (1995), 144–5 and fig. 21 (compare fig. 23).

13 Ayala, *Crón.*, i, 275, ii, 17.

14 Gregory XI, *Lettres (France)*, nos. 260, 383; *Mandements*, no. 791, 803; AN J497/14; *Col. doc. Murcia*, viii, nos. 84 (p. 117), 86 (p. 124); Froissart, *Chron.* (SHF), viii, 30–1.

15 *Doc. Clos des Galées*, i, nos. 716, 723–4, 749, 753, 756, 760, 770, 772, 780, 782, 791, 810, 816, 819, 834–5, 847–8, 854, 881. *Galées huissières*: Anselme, vii, 758; they are probably the ones for which repair bills survive from 1370 and 1371: *Doc. Clos des Galées*, i, nos. 847–8, 881.

16 1369: *Foed.*, iii, 880; *Hist. gén. Lang.*, ix, 813–14; *Doc. Clos des Galées*, i, nos. 765, 767, 868. 1370: *ibid.*, i, nos. 778–80, 783–4, 786–94, 804, 828, 832, 863; PRO E101/29/40 (Gosport); *Foed.*, iii, 909. 1371: CCR 1369–74, 220–1; CPR 1370–74, 107–8.

17 *Chron. Bourbon*, 29–32, 86–7; AN 185A/22, 185B/50.

18 *Inv. AC Toulouse*, 470; **Hist. gén. Lang.*, x, 1462–4 (Art. I). Increase (June 1372): *L. Menard, iii, 4, 5; Dognon, 612.

19 *Acts. Parl. Scot.*, i, 559–60; *Parl. Recs. Scot.*, 122–3; *Foed.*, iii, 925–6.

20 Russell, 186; *Hay du Chastelet, 316–17. Owen was mustering his company in Paris at the end of Jan. 1372: BN Clair. 114/69. On his activities since 1369: Carr (1975), 163–5; Carr (1991), 60, 61–2; *J. François and N. Tabouillot, *Histoire de Metz*, iv (1775), 270–5; *Calmet, iii, 391; *Chron. premiers Valois*, 230.

21 *Mandements*, nos. 854–8, 905; Froissart, *Chron.* (SHF), viii, 36.

22 *Hay du Chastelet, 316–17. On J. de Rye: H.-P.-A. Terrier de Loray, 'Jean de Rye', *Méms. Acad. Sci. de Besançon*, cxxxvii (1889–90), 150–69; G. Daumet, 'Jean de Rye au siège d'Algesiras', *Bull. Hispan. Fac. Lettres Bordeaux*, xii (1910), 265–74; *Foed.*, iii, 851.

23 'Anglo-French negotiations', 69–74; PRO E364/5, mm. 3 (Scrope), 3d (Brian), 5–5d (Savage); *Chron. premiers Valois*, 224–6; *Anonimalle*, 70.

24 Jean IV, *Actes*, nos. 195, 196, 211; Morice, *Preuves*, ii, 34–7; BL Cotton Julius B.VI, fols. 10vo–13vo (probably the draft articles of agreement referred to in John de Montfort's instructions of 25 Feb. to Thomas Melbourne: *Foed.*, iii, 936); PRO E364/5, m. 3d (Neville); E403/446, m. 3 (23 Apr.).

25 Sumption, i, 398–9, 403, 455, ii, 154. Army of 1346: A. Ayton and P. Preston, *The Battle*

of Crécy, 1346 (2005), 167–8, 181–6, 189, 242–51.

26 *Parl. Rolls*, v, 261 (20). Fleet of 1347: *Lettres de rois*, ii, 86–92. 255 English merchantmen were requisitioned in 1369 (PRO E101/36/14); 218 in 1373 (BL Add. Mss. 37494, fols. 17–20ᵛᵒ, 35ᵛᵒ–37ᵛᵒ); and 194 in the winter of 1374–5 (PRO E101/33/27, 31). These figures do not include royal ships or foreign ships. Tonnage (1369): PRO 101/36/14.

27 *Wardrobe Book of William de Norwell*, ed. M. Lyon *et al.* (1983), 386–92 for 1338–40; PRO E101/393/11, fols. 79–116ᵛᵒ for 1359–60. The more generous allowances for knights, bannerets and earls were dropped after 1369, see, e.g., Knolles's army of 2,000 archers and 2,000 men-at-arms in 1370, which had shipping space for 8,000 horses: PRO E101/30/22; *Issue R. Brantingham*, 244, 248, 268–70. In 1378 John Neville of Raby led 280 men-at-arms and 280 archers to Gascony, for whom he was assigned shipping space for 1,114 horses: PRO E403/468, m. 15 (28 May); E364/23, m. 3d (Trivet); E101/38/19.

28 Before 1360: Sumption, i, 178 (twelve men per hull, not including pages and varlets). In April 1375, 194 vessels carried about 2,000 men-at-arms and 2,000 archers with horses to Brittany: see PRO E101/33/27, 31; E403/454, m. 23 (20 Sept.). Assuming that each man-at-arms had one page or varlet, this suggests an average carrying capacity of 30.9 mounted men per hull. Tonnage figures are not recorded for this expedition. Capacity was lower on the longer passage to Gascony. In 1370, 80 ships with a capacity of 6,344 tons carried John of Gaunt to Gascony with 300 men-at-arms and 500 archers, all with horses, i.e. 10 paid troops with their horses and attendants (say 13.75 mounted men altogether) per hull: PRO E364/5, m. 5d (Lancaster) and PRO E101/30/29, mm. 4–6. This equates to 0.17 mounted men per ton of carrying capacity. The corresponding figures for the force led by Walter Hewitt to Gascony in the same year are: 14.3 paid troops (say 20 mounted men) per hull, or 0.25 mounted men per ton: *Issue R. Brantingham*, 119–20, 482, PRO E101/30/29, mm. 3–4. Gaunt's force, being drawn from men of higher rank, travelled in greater comfort and may have had more non-combatant attendants and clerks. In August 1378, 34 ships, including 12 large Dutch barges, carried 280 men-at-arms and 280 archers to Gascony, an average of 16.5 paid troops per hull, say 24.7 mounted men including pages and varlets: see PRO E101/38/19 (ships) and E364/15, m. 4d (J. Neville), E364/23, m. 3d (Trivet) (troops). All of these calculations are complicated by uncertainty about the number of pages and varlets (who do not appear on pay records), the questionable accuracy of medieval tonnage figures, the omission of tonnage figures for barges and the use of some ships as escorts rather than transports. Ships with unrecorded or illegible tonnage have been assumed to correspond to the average. It is impossible to calculate capacities on the short passage to Calais, because of uncertainty about the number of passages performed by each vessel.

29 On John of Gaunt's expedition to St.-Malo (1378), 102 ships and barges carried 4,980 paid troops (say 7,500 men altogether) with few if any horses, an average of 48.8 paid troops (say 73.2 mounted men altogether) per hull: PRO E403/465, m. 20 (5 Apr.), E403/468, m. 15 (28 May); E101/37/25. Tonnage figures cannot be calculated because of the large number of barges employed whose tonnage is not recorded. In July 1381, 41 large vessels of a total of 4,800 tons burden (reckoning the capacity of the two barges at 100 tons each) carried 2,997 paid troops without horses (about 4,500 men altogether) to Portugal, an average of 73.1 paid troops (say 110 men altogether) per hull or 0.94 men per ton including pages and varlets: PRO E101/39/17.

30 Crewing ratios: PRO E101/36/14 (1369); E101/30/29 (1370); E101/32/22 (1372); BL Add. Mss. 37494, fols. 17–20ᵛᵒ (1373); PRO E101/37/25 (1378); E101/38/19 (1378–9); E101/39/2, mm. 1–2 (1380); E101/39/17, m. 2 (1381); E101/40/19 (Portugal, 1386); E101/40/21 (Thames, Oct., Nov. 1386); E101/40/40 (1388). Crew numbers in 1347: *Lettres de rois*, ii, 86–92.

31 *Parl. Rolls*, v, 245 (32), 261 (20), 284–5 (28–9); vi, 133 (50), 179 (47), 200 (33). Pay: PRO E403/444, mm. 23, 24 (31 Jan., 10 Feb.); E403/446, m. 38 (29 Sept.). Requisitions of 1372: PRO E101/32/22; E403/444, m. 24 (10 Feb.); E403/446, m. 38 (30 Sept.); *Foed.*, iii, 938. Requisitioning officers had also been sent to Wales and the north-west: see

PRO E403/444, m. 23 (4 Feb.); but no record of their work survives.

32 *CPR 1370–74*, 68; PRO E403/441, m. 22 (5 Feb.); E30/264; E364/19, m. 4 (Eyrmin). Revolution: Stella, *Ann. Gen.*, 164, 165–6.

33 Coastal defence: PRO C76/55, m. 40; *Foed.*, iii, 940; PRO D364/6, m. 3 (Tiddescombe); E403/446, mm. 9, 11 (15, 29 May); CCR 1369–74, 436. Council: PRO E403/446, m. 10 (15 May). Pembroke: PRO E403/446, mm. 4, 12 (29 Apr., 29 May). Portugal: PRO E403/446, m. 20 (18 June); E364/11, m. 5 (Green). Neville: PRO E101/68/5 (111); cf. E403/446, m. 9 (15 May); PRO E101/32/22. Further ships: PRO C76/55, m. 41; E403/446, mm. 9, 25 (14, 15 May, 15 July). June embarkation: PRO E403/446, mm. 9, 10 (15 May).

34 Froissart, *Chron.* (KL), viii, 435–6; *Moranvillé (1888), 264; *Gr. chron.*, iii, 165; BN Clair. 9, p. 84; 95, p. 7379; *Doc. Clos des Galées*, i, no. 907.

35 *Chron. premiers Valois*, 230–1; 'Chron. Pays-Bas', 259; Froissart, *Chron.* (SHF), viii, 45–6. Date: *Doc. Clos des Galées*, i, 916. Defences of Ch. Islands: PRO E364/14, m. 6 (Appelby); C47/10/9 (20); E364/17, m. 1 (Rose); *Issue R. Brantingham*, 138.

36 *Mandements*, nos. 819, 872, 878, 880; 'Compte inédit de B. du Guesclin', 263; AD Côte d'Or B11749; *Letters B. du Guesclin*, no. 456, 467; *Chron. Bourbon*, 87–8; *Chron. premiers Valois*, 229–30; Froissart, *Chron.* (SHF), viii, 51, 60–1; AN KK 251, fols. 75, 96ᵛᵒ; BN Fr. 7615, fols. 449–451 (Sept. 1371).

37 *Chron. Bourbon*, 87–9; Froissart, *Chron.* (SHF), viii, 51–3; 'Chron. Pays-Bas', 261.

38 PRO E403/446, mm. 3, 4, 12 (20, 29 Apr., 29 May); PRO C61/85, m. 8; Froissart, *Chron.* (SHF), viii, 294.

39 *Chron. premiers Valois*, 232–4; Froissart, *Chron.* (SHF), viii, 37–43, 293–300, 303; 'Chron. Pays-Bas', 259; Ayala, *Crón.*, ii, 31–2; *Gr. chron.*, ii, 164–5; Walsingham, *Hist. Angl.*, i, 314.

40 Froissart, *Chron.* (SHF), viii, 43–4, 300.

41 *Chron. premiers Valois*, 235; Froissart, *Chron.* (SHF), viii, 47–9; Ayala, *Crón.*, ii, 32; *Anonimalle*, 71. Date: BN Clair. 9, p. 511; 95, p. 7379. Florimond: PRO C61/100, m. 6; E101/179/14, m. 13. Pembroke: Ayala, *Crón.*, ii, 32, 66; *Inv. Arch. Bruges*, ii, 240–7; *Letters B. du Guesclin*, nos. 633, 635, 660, 725, 921; *Col. doc. Murcia*, viii, no. 117; *Hay du Chastelet, 454, 456–7; Walsingham, *Hist. Angl.*, i, 319–20; Higden, *Polychron.*, viii, 383; *Royal Wills*, 95. Guichard: Froissart, *Chron.* (SHF), viii, 165–6; Anselme, viii, 9–10. Harpeden: *Anonimalle*, 115–16. Seamen: *Cal. Inq. Misc.*, iv, no. 126.

42 Froissart, *Chron.* (SHF), viii, 50, 53, 54, 56; *Rec. doc. Poitou*, iv, 185–6, 185n[1]; *Letters B. du Guesclin*, no. 474. Anjou: *L. Menard, iii, 4; *Petit Thalamus*, 388.

43 *Foed.*, iii, 942, 944, 947, 947–8, 953; PRO E403/446, m. 20 (17 June), m. 21 (22 June); *John of G. Reg. (1372–6)*, no. 253; *CPR 1370–4*, 238.

44 PRO E101/31/33 (p.s. letter of 22 June); *John of G. Reg. (1372–6)*, no. 63; *Reg. Appleby*, no. 301; Cambridge, UL Ms. Dd. III.53, fols. 47, 54ᵛᵒ; PRO E101/31/33; E101/32/21; E159/153 (*brevia directa baronibus*), Mich., mm. 2, 5, 15d, Easter, m. 13d; E403/446, m. 25 (14 July); C76/55, m. 28; Tout (1934)[2], ii, 265. Cf. advances paid for service at sea to companies previously destined for France: PRO E403/446, mm. 22, 23, 25, 28, 29 (29 June, 3, 14, 15 July, 2, 5 Aug.). The small force waiting at Plymouth for Green's passage to Portugal joined the royal fleet instead: PRO E364/11, m. 5 (Green).

45 *John of G. Reg. (1372–6)*, no. 955; Lopes, *Crón. D. Fernando*, 197–204, 209–21, 227–30, 235. Alliance: *Russell, 557–61.

46 Bécherel: *Anonimalle Chron.*, 68, 70; Froissart, *Chron.* (SHF), viii, 177–8 (wrongly dating the event to 1374). King's army: PRO E101/30/13, m. 7 (issue of equipment to ships for King's expedition to Bécherel); C76/55, m. 27 (recruitment of stone-masons); E403/446, m. 27 (24 July) (recruitment of miners); E403/446, mm. 27,33 (24 July, 16 Aug.); E364/19, m. 4 (Eyrmin, 2nd account); *Lettres de rois*, ii, 180. Treaty: *Foed.*, iii, 9 53–6. Neville's army: Cambridge, UL Ms. Dd. III.53, fol. 47, 47–47ᵛᵒ; PRO E403/446, m. 27 (24 July); C76/55, mm. 30, 24; E403/446, m. 21, 25, 33, 34, 38 (21 June, 15 July, 16, 29 Aug.).

47 *Chron. Bourbon*, 32–5, 87–8; *Istore*, ii, 119; 'Chron. Pays-Bas', 261; Cuvelier, *Chanson*, i, 419–31; Froissart, *Chron.* (SHF), xii, 106 (recollections of the Bascot de Mauléon). Froissart's own account, *ibid.*, viii, 54–60, is unreliable. Date: AN KK 251, fol. 89vo. Verse: Cuvelier, *Chanson*, i, 416 (ll. 21193–5). La Souterraine: *Istore*, ii, 120.

48 Froissart, *Chron.*, (SHF), viii, 56–7; *Chron. Bourbon*, 35–6; AN KK 251, fols. 97, fol. 97vo; *Chronographia*, ii, 391; *Chron. premiers Valois*, 237; *Istore*, ii, 120.

49 *Rec. doc. Poitou*, v, 416–17; Froissart, *Chron.* (SHF), viii, 60–2; *Istore*, ii, 119–20; *Chron. premiers Valois*, 237–8; *Gr. Chron.*, i, 166; *Chron. Bourbon*, 36, 89–90; Cuvelier, *Chanson*, i, 443–7. Regnault: *Rec. doc. Poitiers*, iv, 233–4, 237–8. Date: Cuvelier, *Chanson*, i, 446 (l. 22765); AN KK251, fol. 89vo.

50 Froissart, *Chron.* (SHF), viii, 62–5; *Istore*, ii, 121; *Chron. premiers Valois*, 241.

51 BN Clair. 9, p. 511; 95, p. 7379; Ayala, *Crón.*, ii, 34, 36–8; Lopes, *Crón. D. Fernando*, 231–3; *Mandements*, no. 905; *Chron. premiers Valois*, 235.

52 *Gr. chron.*, iii, 165; *Istore*, ii, 122–3; Froissart, *Chron.* (SHF), viii, 65; *Chron. premiers Valois*, 238–9; *Chron. Bourbon*, 36, 90.

53 *Chron. premiers Valois*, 238–41; *Istore*, ii, 123–5; Froissart, *Chron.* (SHF), viii, 66–71; *Froissart, *Chron.* (KL), xviii, 506; *Col. doc. Murcia.*, viii, no. 103.

54 *Rec. doc. Poitou*, v, 416–17; *Ord.*, v, 565–7; *Chron. premiers Valois*, 241–2; *Itin. Ph. le Hardi*, 85; AD Côte d'Or B11749. Anjou: BN PO 2556, Roucy/7; 2776, de St.-Rion/4; 1910, Geneve/1; 1836, Marcenac/5, 6; 1896, Mauny/8; PO 548, Budes/4; etc.; *Hay du Chastelet, 378; Morice, *Preuves*, ii, 49–50. Anjou was at Le Mas d'Agenais on 7 Sept.: BN PO 2037, Montpezat/11.

55 King's army: PRO E403/446, mm. 28 (2 Aug.), 29 (5, 11 Aug.), 31–3 (16 Aug.); E101/30/13, m. 7; E101/31/33–5, 37, 39–40, 32/12–21, 26, 30 (mm. 2, 6); E364/9, mm. 13 (Warwick), 14 (Hereford); E364/12, m. 9 (Zouche); E101/397/5, fols. 52vo–54; 'Dispacci di C. da Piacenza', 42; Walsingham, *Hist. Angl.*, i, 315; *Eulogium*, iii, 339; *Foed.*, iii, 960, 962; *Parl. Rolls*, v, 258 (9). Neville's army: *Parl. Rolls*, v, 312 (34); PRO C76/55, m. 16; E403/446, m. 38 (29 Sept.).

56 *Itin. Ph. le Hardi*, 86; AN KK 251, fols. 90, 98; Froissart, *Chron.*, viii, *pp. clv–clix, 75–80, 86–8, 97; *Istore*, ii, 126–7; *Chron. Bourbon*, 91–2; *Gr. Chron.*, ii, 166; *Mandements*, no. 918; AN JJ 104/156; *Letters B. du Guesclin*, no. 520.

57 Saintonge: *Itin. Ph. le Hardi*, 86; Froissart, *Chron.* (SHF), viii, 72–5; *Istore*, ii, 125. Angoumois: AN JJ104/2; *Gr. chron.*, ii, 167, 178; Froissart, *Chron.* (SHF), viii, 7, 75; 'Reg. B. de Noces', 543–4. Agenais: BN PO 2037, Montpezat/10–12; BN Fr. 26011/1333; BN Coll. Languedoc 159, fol. 142; *Petit Thalamus*, 388; *L. Menard, iii, 5.

58 *Cal. Letter Books G*, 297; PRO E101/31/35–9, 32/12–19, 21; PRO E101/397/5, fol. 57vo; PRO E403/447 (6 Oct.); *CCR* 1369–74, 463–5. Cost: PRO E403/444, 446 and captains' accounts at E101/31/33–5, 37, 39–40, 32/12–21, 26, 30 (mm. 2, 6) and E364/9, mm. 13 (Warwick), 14 (Hereford); E364/12, m. 9 (Zouche). Prince: *Parl. Rolls*, v, 258 (8). Date: PRO E101/179/7. On Brian: Given-Wilson (1986), 156–7.

59 Neville: PRO E403/446, m. 36 (28 Sept.); E364/19, m. 4 (Eyrmin). Date: PRO E101/179/13; E403/446, m. 38. (29 Sept.); Froissart, *Chron.* (SHF), viii, 106; *Gr. chron.*, iii, 179. Bécherel: *Istore*, ii, 116; *Chron. premiers Valois*, 215. French invasion: Froissart, *Chron.* (SHF), viii, 106–7; *Itin. Ph. le Hardi*, 87; *Chron. Bourbon*, 37–9.

60 *Gr. chron.*, iii, 179–80; Jean IV, *Actes*, no. 208; *Foed.*, iii, 964; *Chron. Bourbon*, 39–40; *Anonimalle*, 71.

61 Ayala, *Crón.*, ii, 37–9, 40–1; Lopes, *Crón. D. Fernando*, 231–3, 243, 245–7, 249, 251–2, 265–6; *Foed.*, iii, 966.

62 *Gr. chron.*, ii, 167–8; Froissart, *Chron.* (SHF), viii, 96–101; *Istore*, ii, 128; *Itin. Ph. le Hardi*, 89; 'Chron. française', 651; AN X^{1a}, fol. 6.

63 'Compte inédit', 264–5; Froissart, *Chron.* (SHF), viii, 101–3, 107–8; *Chronographia*, ii, 391; *John of G. Reg. (1372–6)*, no. 42. Du Guesclin was at Poitiers on 17 Feb. 1373: AN JJ104/87.

64 Mortagne: Froissart, *Chron.* (SHF), viii, 101–3; *AHP*, viii, 417–18, 424–6. Chizé:

Chronographia, ii, 391–2; *Chron. Bourbon*, 40–1; Froissart, *Chron.* (SHF), viii, 107–15; *Istore*, ii, 133–4; *Itin. Ph. le Hardi*, 497; AN KK251, fol. 93vo. La Roche-sur-Yon: AN KK251, fol. 94vo, 127; Froissart, *Chron.* (SHF), viii, 131, 139 (wrongly attributing the siege to the Duke of Anjou). Lusignan: Jean d'Arras, *Mélusine*, 215, 263–5, 813–15; *John of G. Reg.* (1372–6), no. 42; *Rec. doc. Poitiers*, ii, 256–7; AN KK251, fols. 127–9; AN KK252, fol. 21, 31; 'Reg. B. de Noces', 220, 246–8; *Istore*, ii, 130–1; Walsingham, *Hist. Angl.*, i, 317; *Rec. doc. Poitou*, iv, pp. lxvii–lxviii. Gençay: *Rec. doc. Poitiers*, ii, 256, 259; *Rec. doc. Poitou*, iv, 364–7, 402–4.

65 *Rec. doc. Poitou*, iii, 380–4, iv, 67–71, 129–32, iv, 4–7, 41–8, 57–60, 63–5, 77–80, 117–20, 134–43, 157–9, 163–5, 354–8, 364–7, 402–5. On Spridlington: 'Procès-verbal Chandos', 250; he is called a squire in his letters of protection of 1371 (PRO C61/84, m. 2).

66 *Istore*, ii, 133 (Poitevins at Chizé); *Rec. doc. Poitou*, iv, 217–21, 319, 388–90, v, 181–5. Guichard and his family: Deschamps, *Oeuvres*, iii, 320–1, iv, 120; Froissart, *Chron.* (SHF), viii, 115–17; *Rec. doc. Poitou*, iv, 312–16, v, 342; CCR 1377–81, 395; *Testamenta Vetusta*, ed. N.H. Nicolas, i (1826), 109. Harpeden and his family: Anselme, vi, 203; PRO C61/98, m. 3; *Rec. doc. Poitou*, v, 203–7; *Inv. AC Périgueux*, 27. John the Younger at French court: *Chron. r. St.-Denis*, i, 646–8; *Froissart, Chron.* (KL), xiii, 352–4; *Cal. Inq. P.M.*, xvii, no. 289; CFR, xi, 240, 241. Burley: *Rec. doc. Poitou*, iii, 381n^1. Radegonde Béchet and Catherine Senechal: Froissart, *Chron.* (SHF), viii, 88; *Itin. Ph. le Hardi*, 87; *Rec. doc. Poitou*, iv, 366, 402–5, vi, 17–21, 291–2; PRO C61/96, m. 2; C61/97, m. 1; C76/89, m. 12; *Pépin, 114; cf. CPR 1399–1401, 22; CCR 1405–9, 307. Forget: *Rec. doc. Poitou*, iv, 159–62, 282–6.

67 Oxford, Bodley MS Ashmole 865, fol. 423 (statutes of the Order of the Passion), cited by Keen (1976), 43.

68 Bertucat: BN Doat 125, fol. 97–97vo; cf. his own estimate, in 1375, that his company had been 500 strong in 1368, BN Fr. 15515, fol. 294. His garrisons in Quercy and Rouergue: BN Doat 125/97–99vo (Figeac, Cayssor, St.-Espene, St.-Céré-de-Lagarde, Malemort); *Inv. arch. Aurillac*, ii, 13 (Saignes, Anglars); AC Martel CC1^{bis}/3 (Montalzat); AC Martel CC5, fol. 40vo, 6, 11, 11vo, 15vo (Belcastel, Nadaillac, Lamothe-Fénélon); Rouquette, 265 (Espalion). Others: *Inv. arch. Aurillac*, ii, 12–15.

69 BN Doat 125, fols. 42–45vo, 97–101; *Denifle, 839; *Petit Thalamus*, 386; Lacoste, iii, 223–4, 227, 229–33; AC Martel CC1^{bis}; CC5, fols. 1–30 *passim*, esp. fols. 1, 1vo, 2vo, 15vo, 16; *Denifle, 839.

70 AD Aveyron C1886, fols. 3, 26, 30–30vo, 31, 34vo, 35vo, 36, 39, 39vo, 40, 40vo, 41; AC Martel CC1^{bis}/3; CC5, fols. 3vo, 10, 12, 12vo; EE1/40; Rouquette, 266–9; Lacoste, iii, 235; BN Doat 125, fols. 46vo–54, 61–71vo, 101, 113–17; *Petit Thalamus*, 386; *Denifle, 826; Gregory XI, *Lettres (France)*, no. 1294.

71 La Salle: *L. Menard, iii, 317, 318. Bertucat: BN Doat 87, fols. 239–253; BN PO 1577, Jean/12; Rouquette, 270; BN Fr. 15515, fol. 293vo. On Philippe de Jean's wars, see Lacoste, iii, 229, 233, 236–7. He is reported at Comiac (Quercy) in January 1377: *Reg. St.-Flour*, 35–6.

72 Bonet, *Tree*, 153–4 (cf. Keen (1965), Ch. 5); Froissart, *Chron.* (SHF), xiv, 200 (Bonne-Lance); BN Fr. 15515, fol. 291, AN JJ108/104 (Charles of Artois); *Reg. crim. Châtelet*, ii, 177–213 (Mérigot).

73 Subsidies: PRO E101/179/7, fol. 13vo (payments to Bertucat, 1372–3); *John of G. Reg.* (1372–6), no. 42 and *Antient Kalendars*, i, 243 (payments for Lusignan, 1374). Appointments: 'Anglo-French negotiations', 24; *Foed.*, iv, 153. Instructions: *Anglo-Norman Letters*, 266–7; *Foed.*, iii, 903; Secousse, *Preuves*, 428 (confession of Pierre du Tertre); Gregory XI, *Lettres (France)*, nos. 898, 1243.

CHAPTER V

1 *Parl. Rolls*, v, 258 (7–9); CCR 1369–74, 475–7.

2 Runyan, 'Constabulary', 228–9; PRO E101/179/7; E364/15, m. 2 (Rotour); CPR 1374–7, 93. Grain shipments: PRO C61/86, mm. 2, 1; C61/87, mm. 6, 5, 3; C61/88, mm. 7, 6, 5, 4, 3, 1; C61/89, mm. 8, 7; etc.

3 Canterbury Tales, Prologue ll. 276–7 (Works, iv, 9). Convoys: PRO E403/446, m. 35 (27 Sept.); E101/4–11, 28, 32; E364/19, m. 4 (Eyrmin); Parl. Rolls, v, 259–60 (15); James, 25–6. Flemish war: PRO E30/1271, 1275; CCR 1369–74, 169; Foed., iii, 917.

4 1340: Sumption, i, 320–1. Coast-guards: Parl. Rolls, v, 268 (44).

5 BL Add. Mss. 37494, fols. 13, 25ᵛᵒ–27: PRO E101/30/15; Tinniswood, 284; Sherborne (1977)[2], 111. Four royal barges are recorded in 1370: PRO E101/29/39. Only two 'old' barges are recorded in 1373: BL Add. Mss. 37494, fols. 25–25ᵛᵒ, 26ᵛᵒ. New barges: PRO E403/447 (22 Nov.); E364/12, m. 3; C76/56, mm. 33, 30, 29, 8; Cal. Letter Books G, 302; Mems. London, 368–71; BL Add. Mss. 37494, fols. 27–8; CPR 1370–4, 219; Foed., iii, 976. Galley: PRO E403/454, m. 4 (8 May); E101/30/13, m. 9; BL Add. Mss., 37494, fols. 13, 34–34ᵛᵒ.

6 Foed., iii, 931, 965, 966, 971; BL Add. Mss. 37494, fols. 9, 10ᵛᵒ–13, 29; PRO E403/447 (10 Dec.). Doria in France: BN PO 1015, Doria/5–7; Mandements, no. 770. Salisbury: Foed., iii, 971; PRO E101/30/36; E101/32/30, mm. 2, 6.

7 The destination is not explicitly stated but may be inferred. Walter Leicester was charged with requisitioning ships for Gaunt's campaign: BL Add. Mss. 37494, fol. 15. He was the main agent for English dealings with John de Montfort in this period: PRO E403/446, m. 38 (29 Sept.); E101/179/13; PRO E403/447, m. 30 (4 Mar.). On 21 March 1373, a receiver was appointed to accompany Gaunt to take possession of booty and ransoms 'according to the laws of France, Brittany and Aquitaine': PRO C76/56, m. 28. Planned date of embarkation: PRO C76/56, m. 33.

8 Parl. Rolls, v, 258–9 (10–12); Ormrod (1990), 204, 207. French budget: Ord., v, 538–41 (18–19); *Rey (1965), i, 371–7.

9 Walsingham, St. Alban's Chron., i, 30 (Stury).

10 Myers (1969), 301–4; Holmes (1975), 77–8, 87–8; CFR, viii, 197–8, 227, 231, 273; CPR 1370–4, 382, 383, 384–5; Parl. Rolls, v, 300–1 (17), 305–6 (27).

11 Walsingham, St. Alban's Chron., i, 42–6; Parl. Rolls, vi, 26–30 (41–3); Anonimalle, 87; Brinton, Sermons, ii, 321; Gower, Mirrour de l'Homme, ll. 22814–15 (Works, i, 251). Also: C. Given-Wilson and A. Curteis, The Royal Bastards of Medieval England (1984), 136–7, 141–2; J. Bothwell, 'The management of position: Alice Perrers, Edward III, and the creation of a landed estate, 1362–1377', J. Med. Hist., xxiv (1998), 31–51; Holmes (1975), 68–9, 87–9.

12 Lopes, Crón. D. Fernando, 243; John of G. Reg. (1372–6), nos. 52, 1143. Tamworth: PRO E101/32/36. On Tamworth: Walker (1990)[1], 29n; Gr. chron., i, 227; *Plancher, iii (Preuves), no. 300; PRO C76/53, m. 26; Foed., iii, 914.

13 Lopes, Crón. D. Fernando, 251–77; Ayala, Crón., ii, 41–3.

14 Lopes, Crón. D. Fernando, 283–8; Ayala, Crón., ii, 43, 44; 'Dispacci di C. da Piacenza', 49–50 (wrongly reporting the peace as already made); Gregory XI, Lettres (Autres Pays), nos. 1422, 1447–9; *Suarez Fernandez (1956), 64–77.

15 Cat. Arch. Navarra (Comptos), ix, nos. 115, 128, 130, 137; Col. doc. Murcia, viii, no. 118.

16 'Dispacci di C. da Piacenza', 50, 52; AN K1338/51; Ayala, Crón., ii, 58; Lopes, Crón. D. Fernando, 285. Genoa: Stella, Ann. Gen., 165–6.

17 Mandements, nos. 937, 952; Chron. Bourbon, 41; John IV, Actes, no. 218; Froissart, Chron. (SHF), viii, 123–4.

18 Gr. chron., ii, 168–9; Froissart, Chron. (SHF), viii, 122. Fleet: PRO E101/30/13, m. 9; Foed., iii, 71; BL Add. Mss. 37494, fols. 10–13, 23ᵛᵒ–24ᵛᵒ, 24–25ᵛᵒ, 26ᵛᵒ–27, 31. Gaunt: PRO C76/56, m. 33. John de Montfort and St.-Malo: Jones (1981)[2], 173; Gregory XI, Lettres (France), nos. 1073, 1271, 1273–4.

19 Gr. chron., ii, 169, 170; Froissart, Chron. (SHF), viii, pp. lxxii nᶦ, 123–6; Chron. Bourbon, 42. Bourbon left Paris after 23 April: Titres Bourbon, i, no. 3241. Du Guesclin

was in Brittany by April: AN KK251, fol. 94vo. Montfort at Brest: PRO E101/179/14, m. 13 (lieutenant); *Rot. Parl.*, iii, 53 (12); Jones (1970), 147n^4; 'Chron. Brioc.', col. 46; *Istore*, ii, 118–19.

20 *Gr. chron.*, ii, 169; *Istore*, ii, 118–19, 131, 132–3; *Chron. Bourbon*, 42–4; Froissart, *Chron.* (SHF), viii, p. *clxii, 126–7, 129–31, 135–6, 139–40; Morice, *Preuves*, ii, 65; *Hay du Chastelet, 379–81, 382.

21 *Chaucer Life-Records*, 35–6; *John of G. Reg. (1372–6)*, no. 310. Salisbury, Tamworth: PRO C76/56, m. 14; E101/32/36 (before 18 June). Treaty: Chaplais, *English Med. Dipl. Practice*, 517–22.

22 BL Add. Mss. 37494, fols. 13vo, 17–23, 30, 35vo–37vo; PRO E403/449, m. 4 (11 May); *John of G. Reg. (1372–6)*, no. 310; *Istore*, ii, 136; Froissart, *Chron.* (SHF), viii, 137, 148–9, 163.

23 PRO 403/449, m. 15 (13 July); *Antient Kalendars*, i, 238; CCR 1369–74, 502; CPR 1377–81, 74; CPR 1385–9, 205; *Foed.*, iii, 981. Reassigned to Gaunt's army: PRO E403/449, m. 15 (13 July). Salisbury: PRO E101/179/14, m. 13; *AHG*, xii, 328.

24 *Chron. Bourbon*, 49; *Froissart, *Chron.* (SHF), viii, pp. clx–clxiii; *Froissart, *Chron.* (KL), xviii, 509–10; *Rot. Parl.*, ii, 53 (12).

25 *Lemoine, 55–7, 60–1; *Foed.*, iii, 990; *Chron. Bourbon*, 45–6.

26 Froissart, *Chron.* (SHF), viii, p. lxxx n^3, 128, 143–6; *Gr. chron.*, ii, 170; *AHG*, xii, 328; PRO E101/179/14, m. 12, 13; PRO E403/449, m. 20 (26 Aug.) (Courtenay back by 23 Aug.). Relief force: BL Add. Mss. 37494, fols. 10–11, 12–12vo, 23vo–25, 27–28; PRO E403/449, m. 15, 20 (13 July, 26 Aug.). These figures assume that Tamworth served with Salisbury: PRO C76/56, m. 14. Garrison: CCR 1369–74, 517–18. Hostages: John IV, *Actes*, no. 249; *Letters B. du Guesclin*, nos. 724, 727, 736, 740–1; *Rot. Parl.*, iii, 53 (12).

27 *Parl. Rolls*, v, 277 (2). Barges: BL Add. Mss. 37494, fols. 14, 27–8, 29, 34–34vo; PRO C76/56, mm. 34, 30, 8; CPR 1370–74, 343–4; CCR 1369–74, 508, 510; *Cal. Letter Books G*, 310, 311–12.

28 PRO E101/179/14, mm. 12, 13 (threat); *Doc. Clos des Galées*, i, nos. 946–9, 954, 957–8, 960, 964–5, 966, 972–3, 976, ii, no. 57 (5); *Mandements*, no. 1009; CCR 1369–74, 579–80. Castilians: BN PO 638, Châlons/2; PRO E403/449, m. 7 (27 May); *Foed.*, iii, 986, 988; Ayala, *Crón.*, ii, 58. On Sanchez: Valdeon Baruque, 287–8.

29 BL Add. Mss. 37494, fols 2–6, 10–14vo, 23vo–28, 33–37vo; PRO E403/447, 449, 451, *passim*.

30 *John of G. Reg. (1372–6)*, nos. 111, 157, 195, 318–25, 598, 742, 1357–87, 1749, 1784–5; PRO E403/448, m. 15 (13 July); C76/56, mm. 12, 11; BL Add. Mss. 37494, fols. 21–23; *Gr. chron.*, ii, 171; 'Chron. Brioc.', col. 47; Noyal, 'Frag. Chron.', 271; Froissart, *Chron.* (SHF), viii, 148–50, 151–2. Strength: Sherborne (1964), 728 (Table 1.2).

31 *Moranvillé (1888), 266–71, 270–7; *Itin. Ph. le Hardi*, 96–7.

32 *Voyage paléogr.*, 148–50; *Gr. chron.*, ii, 171, *iii, 217; John IV, *Actes*, no. 225; 'Chron. Brioc.', col. 47.

33 *Itin. Ph. le Hardi*, 97; *Arch. admin. Reims*, iii, 385–7; *Moranvillé (1888), 277–8; *Istore*, ii, 137. Jean de Vienne participated in Grimaldi's first cruise (*Doc. Clos des Galées*, i, no. 966), but was with the army in Champagne on 9 Sept. (*Gr. chron.*, ii, 171–2).

34 Froissart, *Chron.* (SHF), viii, 150; *Mandements*, no. 984; *Istore*, ii, 135; *Chron. premiers Valois*, 245; *Moranvillé (1888), 278. Du Guesclin was at Rennes on 20 Aug. (Morice, *Preuves*, ii, 77) and near Ribemont in Champagne at the beginning of Sept. (AN JJ105/298). Clisson was in Champagne on 13 Sept.: *Itin. Ph. le Hardi*, 98. Anjou: BN Doat 198, fols. 55–8; *L. Menard, iii, 6; *Mandements*, no. 984.

35 Noyal, 'Frag. Chron.', 271; *Voyage paléogr.*, 150–1; *Istore*, ii, 136–7; Froissart, *Chron.* (SHF), viii, 157–8, 163; *Gr. chron.*, ii, 171–2; *Anonimalle*, 74; AN JJ104/207, 105/31 (peasants).

36 *Chron. premiers Valois*, 246; *Chronographia*, ii, 347; *Itin. Ph. le Hardi*, 98; AD Côte-d'Or B1441, fols. 19vo, 20, 62vo. Council of war: Froissart, *Chron.* (SHF), viii, 160–3.

37 Froissart, *Chron.* (SHF), viii, 167–8; *Chron. Bourbon*, 53; *Gr. chron.*, ii, 172; *Itin. Ph. le Hardi*, 98. Damage: *Voyage paléogr.*, 151–2; AN JJ106/397.

38 Froissart, *Chron.* (SHF), viii, 142, 158–60; cf. xii, 36–8; *Istore*, ii, 137.

39 *Gr. chron.*, ii, 172, *iii, 217; *Itin. Ph. le Hardi*, 98–9; AD Côte-d'Or B1441, fol. 63vo; *Istore*, ii, 138. Anjou's movements: *Titres Bourbon*, i, no. 3251; *Hist. gén. Lang.*, x, 1498; AN KK251, fols. 107vo, 109; AD Côte-d'Or B1441, fol. 63vo. Topography: M. Litaudon, *Moulins en 1460* (1947), 84–97.

40 *Istore*, ii, 138; *Itin. Ph. le Hardi*, 99; *Chron. premiers Valois*, 247. Cf. *Gr. chron.*, ii, 173–4; Noyal, 'Frag. Chron.', 271.

41 AC Martel CC5, fols. 26, 27, 27vo; EE1/16, 32; Rouquette, 270; *Clément-Simon, 68–70, 73–4, *101–4, *109–13, *117–18. Bordeaux: *Chron. Bourbon*, 55, 56; *Istore*, ii, 138–9; *Gr. chron.*, ii, 172; *Anonimalle*, 74; Walsingham, *Hist. Angl.*, i, 315–16; *Chron. premiers Valois*, 247. Prisoners: *Parl. Rolls*, v, 344 (129). Gaunt was at Bergerac on 15 Dec. (PRO C61/90, m. 2), and at Bordeaux by 3 January 1374 (PRO C61/91, m. 5).

42 *Parl. Rolls*, v, 277 (2–3); BL Cotton, Caligula D.III, fols. 117vo–118.

43 Cascales, 168–9; *Col. doc. Murcia*, viii, nos. 128, 130; Secousse, *Preuves*, 376–7; *Cat. Arch. Navarra (Comptos)*, ix, nos. 334, 859; Ayala, *Crón.*, ii, 59–60, 61; *Chron. premiers Valois*, 247; 'Dispacci di C. da Piacenza', 54–5.

44 Gregory XI, *Lettres (Autres Pays)*, nos. 2096, 2098, 2343–6, 2371, 2501; Zurita, iv, 629–30, 632. One of the ambassadors, Roger-Bernard, Viscount of Castelbon, was in Navarre in March: *Cat. Arch. Navarra (Comptos)*, ix, no. 187. Two others, Garcia Fernández de Villodre and Sancho Ruiz de Quintana Redonda, may have accompanied him, since they were not included in the safe-conduct given to the rest of the embassy to return to Bordeaux: ACA reg. 1240, fol. 148vo.

45 *Anonimalle*, 74; Delpit, *Coll. doc.*, 190; *Gr. chron.*, ii, 173. Wages: PRO E101/68/5 (120), E101/68/6 (121–7, 131, 133, 135); *John of G. Reg.* (1372–6), no. 52 (p. 38); BL Cotton, Caligula D.III, fols. 117vo–118 (promise). Gaunt's claims: PRO E364/10, m. 1 (Lancaster); E364/5, m. 5d (Lancaster).

46 BL Cotton, Caligula D.III, fols. 117vo–118; PRO E403/451, mm. 19, 21, 22 (26 Jan., 7, 16 Feb.); *Foed.*, iii, 997; *Antient Kalendars*, i, 240–1 (no. 10).

47 Cash receipts: PRO E401/514. Cost of Gaunt's expedition: payments to captains who accounted at the Exchequer, at PRO E364/8, m. 6d (Calveley), m. 10d (Despenser); E364/9, m. 1 (Calveley), m. 5 (Percy), m. 12 (Stafford), m. 14 (Willoughby), m. 14 (Warwick); E364/9, m. 15d (Suffolk); E364/10, m. 1 (Lancaster), m. 2 (Basset); E364/13, m. 6 (Bardolf); payments to other captains (advances only), at E403/447 (5, 14, 16, 21 Mar.); E403/449, mm. 4, 11–13, 15, 19 (11 May, 20–30 June, 13, 16 July); shipping costs at BL Add. Mss. 37494, fols. 17–23. Subsidies: *Parl. Rolls*, v, 277 (2–3), 279–80 (12); *Rec. Convoc.*, iii, 328, 329–30; *CFR*, viii, 241–2. Calais: PRO E364/8, m. 7 (Romsey). Ireland: PRO E101/33/3, m. 3. Fleet: BL Cotton Caligula D.III, fols. 117vo–118; *Foed.*, iii, 997, 998, 999, 1001; PRO C76/57, mm. 19, 18; PRO E101/30/13, m. 10, E101/33/9–18, 25; payments at E403/451, mm. 20–9, *passim*.

48 BN Clair. 159/41; *Chron. premiers Valois*, 247. Truce: AN X^{1a}, fol. 110; *Gr. chron.*, ii, 175; Walsingham, *Hist. Angl.*, i, 316; *Foed.*, iii, 1000. French recruitment: *L. Menard, iii, 6; *Doc. Millau* [2], no. 407; Rouquette, 275–6; *Chron. Bourbon*, 56; Higden, *Polychron.*, Cont. (iv), 381; *Inv. mobiliers Bourgogne*, i, no. 2004; AD Côte d'Or B1444, fol. 39. Cf. *Chron. Bourbon*, 56; Troubat, i, 545n^{12}; *Hist. gén. Lang.*, x, 1503–5. Castilians: *Chron. premiers Valois*, 247–8; *Russell, 562.

49 AN X^{1a}, fol. 110.

50 *Foed.*, iii, 1000; BN Coll. Languedoc 159, fol. 147vo; *Chron. premiers Valois*, 248. Gaunt was at Dax with Gaston Phoebus on 19 and 20 March:: *Tucoo-Chala (1959), 403 (nos. 346–7), 353. Charles of Navarre's presence: Secousse, *Preuves*, 376 (confession of Jacques de Rue). Cardaillac's presence is attested by the fact that the sealed original of his powers to discuss the arranged battle, issued in Toulouse on 17 March and presumably given to Gaunt, is in the English public records: PRO E30/1491 (*Foed.*, iii, 1000).

Observance of truce: *Gr. chron.*, ii, 175; *John of G. Reg. (1372–6)*, no. 42.

51 Secousse, *Preuves*, 376–7 (confession of Jacques de Rue); *Tucoo-Chala (1959), 353; AD Pyr.-Atl. E410. Aragon: Russell, 207–8, *562–5.

52 Russell, 216–17, 216n[3]; *Col. doc. Murcia*, viii, nos. 145–6. Gaunt's movements: *John of G. Reg. (1372–6)*, nos. 724, 1766; PRO E364/10, m. 1 (Lancaster). Felton: PRO C61/87, m. 4, C61/88, mm. 8, 7.

53 Secousse, *Preuves*, 377; Ayala, *Crón.*, ii, 48–9 (wrongly dated to 1373), 76; *Cat. Arch. Navarra (Comptos)*, ix, nos. 865–70, 890; Zurita, iv, 635, 639–41; *Col. doc. Murcia*, viii, nos. 165, 169, 126–30; *Documents per l'historia de la cultura catalana mig-eval*, ed. A. Rubio i Lluch, i (1908), 263–5.

54 Ayala, *Crón.*, ii, 62; *Russell, 565; BN PO 266, Bel/2, 3, 13, 14.

55 Ayala, *Crón.*, ii, 63; BN Coll. Moreau 654, fols. 255–264vo; Cambridge, UL Ms. Dd. III.53, fols. 44vo–45; Balasque, iii, 359–61; *Russell, 565; PRO E101/179/14, fols. 10, 13, 25. Rebellion of lord of Castelbon: *Hist. gén. Lang.*, x, 1482–6.

56 Lecoy, ii, 196–8; *L. Menard, iii, 6; Ayala, *Crón.*, ii, 63–4.

57 *Chron. Bourbon*, 56–8, 59; *Istore*, ii, 140; Clément-Simon, 82, *118–21; *L. Menard, iii, 6. Strength: *Hist. gén. Lang.* x, 1503–10 (some of the companies listed in this document had been detached to fight in Aragon).

58 *Chron. Bourbon*, 60; *Gr. chron.*, ii, 175–6; *Ord.*, vi, 105–6. Garrison: PRO E101/179/14, fol. 10; *AHG*, xii, 337.

59 PRO E101/179/14, fols. 9vo, 10, 24; *Foed.*, iii, 1030; *L. Menard, iii, 6, 321; *Arch. Montpellier*, i, 198 (no. 2473); *Inv. AC Toulouse*, i, 540; *Chron. Bourbon*, 61.

60 *Gr. chron.*, ii, 174; Walsingham, *Hist. Angl.*, i, 316; Higden, *Polychron.*, Cont. (iv), 378–9; Froissart, *Chron.*, viii, 179. Future of Gascony: *John of G. Reg. (1372–6)*, no. 42; *Russell, 565–6; PRO C61/88, m. 4; E403/457, m. 8 (4 June); Brinton, *Sermons*, ii, 321.

61 AC Martel EE1/67; *Clément-Simon, 102; Rouquette, 271; *Reg. St.-Flour*, 214.

62 *Doc. Carlat*, i, 287–8, 330–2, ii, pp. xxxiii, cclxxx, cccxlv–cccxlix; *Spic. Briv.*, 447–8; *Reg. St.-Flour*, 113–14; AC Cajarc CC11, fols. 45, 47; BN Doat 199, fols. 113–15. Garcie-Arnaud accompanied Bernard de la Salle to Quercy in 1369: AC Martel EE1/23. He is recorded as captain of Carlat in 1375: BN Doat 199, fols. 113–15, 124–128[vo].

63 Gregory XI, *Lettres (France)*, nos. 1626, 1685, 1725, 1727, 1923–9, 3329, 3502, 3508, 3618; *Ann. Limoges de 1638*, 283; PRO SC1/56/47; AN JJ112/263; *Chron. Bourbon*, 96. Charlus-Champagnac: *Inv. AC Montferrand*, i, 403, 404; *Inv. AC Riom*, 57. La Souterraine: *Chron. r. St.-Denis*, i, 122–4; BN Fr. n.a. 7414, fol. 300 (date).

64 *Chron. Bourbon*, 93–105; Christine de Pisan, *Livre des fais*, i, 155–6; BN N.a.fr. 7414, fol. 221. Cheyne: Froissart, *Chron.* (SHF), vi, 8, 39; Jones (1970), 216; *Doc. Millau [2]*, no. 332. Craddock commanded a company in Gascony in 1379: PRO E101/38/27; C61/93, m. 9. He was captain of Fronsac, 1383–9 (*Foed.*, iv, 153; vii, 642). His father: PRO C61/95, m. 5.

CHAPTER VI

1 Chaucer, *The Tale of Melibeus* (*Works*, iv, 203). Preliminaries: *Clément-Simon, 102; Gregory XI, *Lettres (France)*, no. 1486. Turenne at Avignon: *Ausgaben apost. Kammer*, 450, 452, 548. His local representatives: *ibid.*, 381, 445; *Reg. (France)*, no. 1294; 'Dispacci di C. da Piacenza', 54.

2 *Foed.*, iii, 1004; Chaplais, *English Med. Dipl. Practice*, 787; Gregory XI, *Lettres (France)*, nos. 1613, 1662; 'Anglo-French negotiations', 1–2, 4, 75–6. Gaunt's movements: *John of G. Reg. (1372–6)*, nos. 196–7, 607–8, 611–12, 682–3, 865, 869–70, 1403–4.

3 Pocquet (1967), 152–4; *Gr. chron.*, ii, 173; 'Chron. Brioc.', 48.

4 Rey (1965), i, 233–6; *Chron. r. St.-Denis*, i, 12. Succession: *Ord.*, vi, 26–32, 45–54.

5 *Hist. gén. Lang.*, x, 1509–12; *Songe du vergier*, i, 266; *Itin. Ph. le Hardi*, 106–7.

6 'Anglo-French negotiations', 75–6. Pileo left England *ca.* 10 June: Chaplais, *English Med. Dipl. Practice*, 787.

7 Diplomatic exchanges: 'Anglo-French negotiations', 75–6; PRO E403/454, m. 14
(12 July); Cambridge, UL Ms. Dd. III.53, fols. 43–43vo. Expedition: *Foed.*, iii, 1006;
PRO E403/454, m. 20 (23 Sept.); E364/10, mm. 4 (March), 4d (Despenser), 7d
(Cambridge). On Despenser: *GEC*, iv, 274–5; Froissart, *Chron.* (SHF), i, 257.

8 Fleets: PRO E101/33/9–11, 13–15, 25; E403/454, m. 19 (4 Aug.). Brittany:
PRO E403/454, m. 23 (20 Sept.). Borrowing: *CPR 1374–7*, 5–6; E401/515 (3, 23 Aug.,
18, 20 Sept.); E401/518 (23 Dec.); E403/454, mm. 22 (23 Aug.), 23 (20 Sept.);
Holmes (1975), 77–8; *Parl. Rolls*, v, 300–2, 304, 304–6 (17–18, 24, 27);
Anonimalle, 86–7, 88–90; Walsingham, *Chron. Maj.*, i, 18.

9 *Chron. premiers Valois*, 226, 229, 236; *Delisle, i, 181, ii, 208–12; AN KK350,
fols. 336vo–338; *Terrier de Loray, PJ no. 22; *Coville (1894), 388–9; AN KK350,
fols. 326–55.

10 *Mandements*, nos. 1009, 1057, 1064; Terrier de Loray, 65; *Delisle, ii, 183, 216–17
(one third of a year's *fouage* was worth about Frs. 15,000: *ibid.*, ii, 227). On J. de
Vienne: Contamine (1972), 591–2. On Mercier: *Chron. premiers Valois*, 263.

11 *Anonimalle*, 77; BN Clair. 44/3253, 56/4295, 4297, 83/6509; *Delisle, ii, 183, 217,
218–19, 222, 234–5; *Mandements*, no. 1227; Froissart, *Chron.* (SHF), viii, 190.
Seigneurial castles: *Delisle, ii, 288–9; *Doc. norm.*, nos. 789, 1006; *Delisle, ii, 219;
cf. *Gall. Reg.*, ii, nos. 7593–4 and Rey (1965), i, 372.

12 Buxhill: *Foed.*, iii, 917. Catterton: PRO C76/53, m. 9; *Delisle, ii, 178–80; *Compte r.
Navarre*, 302–3; Walsingham, *St. Alban's Chron.*, i, 356. Trivet: Froissart, *Chron.* (SHF),
vii, 42; PRO E101/30/25; *Controversy Scrope Grosvenor*, 179. Garrison: see *Anonimalle*,
77; Froissart, *Chron.* (SHF), viii, 193, and names cited in the agreements of May 1375
(*Delisle, ii, 242–8). Operations: *Delisle, ii, 219, 232, 340, 341; *Chron. premiers Valois*,
250; AD Côte d'Or B1444, fol. 74; *Anonimalle*, 77–8.

13 PRO E403/454, m. 18 (2 Aug.); E403/456, m. 23 (19 Apr.); E101/33/31, mm. 2–7.

14 'Anglo-French negotiations', 1–2, 6, 7, 76; PRO E403/454, m. 24 (22 Sept.); *Foed.*,
iii, 1015.

15 *Delisle, ii, 185–6, 189, 190, 220–1, 223–31, 227, 237–8, 241; BN Clair. 10/575,
33/2490, 44/3253, 58/4413, 83/6511, etc.; *Terrier de Loray, PJ nos. 24, 25.

16 PRO E101/33/27; E101/33/31, mm. 2–7; E101/33/33; E101/34/3, 5; E403/456, mm. 10
(23 Dec.); *Foed.*, iii, 1021; Cambridge, UL Ms Dd. III.53, fols. 42–42vo (for date of this
letter, PRO E403/456, m. 16 [2 Mar.]); *Cal. Letter Books H*, 4; PRO E101/34/3, 5;
Parl. Rolls, v, 370–1 (180). Ireland: *Parls. & Councils*, i, 82–3.

17 *Delisle, ii, 192, 235–7, 292, 301–2; Froissart, *Chron.* (SHF), viii, 194, 197.

18 Lacabane (1844), 45–6, 49, 52; Tout (1934)[2], ii, 241–4; BN Fr. 9237, p. 781;
*P. Horton-Smith Hartley and H.R. Aldridge, *Johannes de Mirfield* (1936), 90.

19 'Anglo-French negotiations', 9–10, 12, 18; *Foed.*, iii, 1024–5, 1027; PRO E403/456, mm.
15, 20 (24 Feb., 9, 18 Apr.); Petit, 301; *Inv. mobiliers Bourgogne*, i, nos. 2286, 2304;
Walsingham, *Hist. Angl.*, i, 317–18; *Anonimalle*, 79. Latimer: PRO E101/316/38.

20 'Anglo-French negotiations', 10–13, 14, 17–18; 'Dispacci di C. da Piacenza', 73, 75.

21 'Anglo-French negotiations', 15, 18–19; *Gr. chron.*, ii, 176–7. Louis was in Paris
throughout March and April 1375: *Hist. gén. Lang.*, ix, 846n5, *x, 1524.

22 PRO E101/33/27, 31, 33; *Chron. premiers Valois*, 252, 254; Froissart, *Chron.* (SHF),
viii, 196; *Rec. doc. Poitou*, iv, 365–7, xxiv, 291–2; AN KK252, fols. 69, 79, 82vo.
Cognac: *Gr. Chron.*, ii, 178; BN PO 147, Auterives/3; 975, le Dard/2, 1561, d'Isy/3;
1133, Terron en Bretagne/3.

23 *Foed.*, iii, 1018–19; *Chron. premiers Valois*, 254; Froissart, *Chron.* (SHF), viii, 195, 196,
200, 204.

24 'Anglo-French negotiations', 14–20; PRO E403/457, m. 2 (7 May); *Foed.*, iii, 1029.
Jousting: AD Côte d'Or B1444, fols. 79–79vo, 96vo.

25 *Chron. premiers Valois*, 252; *Gr. chron.*, ii, 178. The agreement was made before 17 May:
AN KK252, fol. 71vo. Sancerre: BN PO 2527, Rogerville/3–4; 2063, de la Mote/38; 2919,
de la Vallée/2; *Hist. généal. Harcourt*, iv, 1585–6.

26 The text of the legates' truce does not survive but an amended version of it, with changes made shortly after 17 June, was included in a declaration made by John of Gaunt and Philip of Burgundy on 27 June: *Foed.*, iii, 1033. Subsequent events suggest that the original instrument did not include the provision relating to Montfort's forces in Brittany, but that it did include the provision relating to Saint-Sauveur, which appears to be referred to in a later declaration of the legates: *Foed.*, iii, 1034. The terms are said to have been 'notified and awarded' (*avisé et regardé*) by the legates. The relevant meaning of '*regarder*' in 14th-century French was to make an adjudication: F. Godefroy, *Dictionnaire de la langue française... du ixe au xve siècle*, vi (1889), 734-5.

27 Cognac: 'Reg. B. de Noces', 557; AN KK252, fols. 72, 83vo; *Gr. chron.*, ii, 178. St.-Sauveur: *Delisle, ii, 191-3, 195-6, 284, 341; terms recited at *ibid.*, ii, 242-5, 250, 261-2, 263-4, 272-3; *Chron. premiers Valois*, 253; Froissart, *Chron.* (SHF), viii, 197, 200.

28 *Chron. premiers Valois*, 252-4; *Gr. chron.*, ii, 178; *Delisle, ii, 194, 195-6. Quotation: Christine de Pisan, *Book of Fayttes of Armes*, 128-9.

29 PRO C76/58, m. 18; E403/457, m. 10 (8 June); E101/34/10; *Foed.*, iii, 1029. Gaunt: E101/316/38. Philip: *Itin. Ph. le Hardi*, 117.

30 PRO E403/457, m. 8 (5 June); C76/58, m. 14; 'Reg. B. de Noces, 549-50; *Hist. généal. Harcourt*, iv, 1597.

31 Froissart, *Chron.* (SHF), viii, 200-9; Walsingham, *Hist. Angl.*, i, 318-19. Part of the army was still at St.-Brieuc on 10 June: Jean IV, *Actes*, i, 58n[1].

32 *Foed.*, iii, 1033-4; 'Anglo-French negotiations', 21-2.

33 *Delisle, ii, 216-17, 220-4, 226-9, 239-40, 250-7, 281-2, 285-6, 306-8, 319-20; AN KK350, fols. 228vo-232.

34 *Delisle, ii, 185, 263-6, 272-3, 278; *Foed.*, iii, 1034-5; PRO C76/58, m. 15; Froissart, *Chron.* (SHF), viii, 213-14.

35 Froissart, *Chron.* (SHF), viii, 209-12; Walsingham, *Hist. Angl.*, i, 319; PRO E101/34/6 (text in Holmes (1975), 45n[2]); E403/457, mm. 15, 22 (4, 30 Sept.); E403/461, m. 34 (23 Mar.); C76/58, m. 14; *Foed.*, iii, 1034-5. After English withdrawal: Morice, *Preuves*, ii, 99; *Chron. premiers Valois*, 255, 256; 'Anglo-French negotiations', 34. Montfort in Flanders: *Rek. Gent*, 43; Froissart, *Chron.* (SHF), viii, 217-18.

36 Walsingham, *Hist. Angl.*, i, 317-18; Walsingham, *Chron. Maj.*, i, 356-64; *Anonimalle*, 78-9, 93; *Foed.*, iv, 80-1.

37 *Parl. Rolls*, v, 351-2 (136); *Nicolas, ii, 510-13; *Anonimalle*, 77, 79; *Chron. premiers Valois*, 255; Ayala, *Crón.*, ii, 78; 'Anglo-French negotiations', 36, 79; Cambridge, UL Ms. Dd. III.53, fol. 90vo; *Lecoy, ii, 398-9.

38 Froissart, *Chron.* (SHF), viii, 214-15; 'Anglo-French negotiations', 35-6.

39 *Inv. AC Périgueux*, 58, 85, 86; BN Clair. 3/39, 64/4949, 75/5837, 88/6595 BN PO 323, Beslon/4; 384, du Bois 15; 976, le Dard/2; 1906, Gimuchat/4; 2787, de Talaye/5, 8-10; BN Coll. Languedoc 159, fols. 151, 170.

40 'Anglo-French negotiations', 35-6, 46; *Inv. AC Périgueux*, 57-8, 85-7; *Jurades de Bergerac*, i, 34-7; PRO SC1/56/47.

41 BN Doat 199, fols. 109-176; *Hist. gén. Lang.*, x, 1594-6; Gregory XI, *Lettres (France)*, no. 1981-2, 1985; *Reg. St.-Flour*, 40-1, 44-5.

42 Alauzier (1957)[2], 98-9, 99, 99-100, 100-1; AN KK 252, fol. 28; 'Doc. St.-Antonin', 290; *Inv. AC Rodez (Bourg)*, 2; AD Aveyron, 2E 178 (8), fol. 4-4vo; BN Doat 87, fols. 199, fols. 257-261vo, 263-267vo; *Inv. AC Rodez (Bourg)*, 2. Douat negotiated jointly with Carlat later in the year for the *videment* of Carlat, Castel d'Ozon and Balaguier: *Inv. AC Rodez (Bourg)*, 2; *Doc. Millau* [2], no. 424. Finance: 'Inv. Arch. Cahors', 83n[3]; BN Doat 199, 218-219vo.

43 Deschamps, *Oeuvres*, i, 217-18.

44 Dismissal of Bretons: BN PO 548, Budes/10; 798, Coetlogon/2; 1495, de la Haye/3; 1813, Malestroit/3; 2917, Guesclin, 38. Others: see BN PO 174, de Balastre/2; 573, de Callar/2; 1346, Godelin/2; 1495, de la Haye/3, 4; etc. Aragon: Froissart, *Chron.* (SHF),

viii, 28, 276; Zurita, iv, 633–4, 637–8; Lecoy, ii, 196–200; *Cat. Arch. Navarra (Comptos)*, ix, no. 859, and l, no. 754; *Tucoo-Chala (1959), 355. Berry, etc.: Gregory XI, *Lettres (France)*, no. 1923. Papal state: 'Dispacci di C. da Piacenza', 61, 66; *Ausgaben apost. Kammer*, 518, 568, 570, 571, 572.

45 *Hay du Chastelet, 386; 'Dispacci di C. da Piacenza', 61, 66; *Ausgaben apost. Kammer*, 571; Gregory XI, *Lettres (France)*, no. 1815.

46 *Dumay, 146–7; Königshofen, *Chron.*, 818; *Urkundenbuch Strassburg*, v, no. 1225, 1229, 1234; *Fontes Rerum Bernensium*, ix, no. 972; Froissart, *Chron.* (SHF), viii, 214–16. Coucy's career: Froissart, *Chron.* (SHF), vi, 96, vii, 100, 208–9; *Le joli buisson de jonece*, ed. A. Fourrier (1975), 56; 'Anglo-French negotiations', 83–4 (25); *Duchesne, ii, 415; *CPR 1367–70*, 271; *CPR 1370–4*, 17; *CCR 1369–74*, 87; Gregory XI, *Lettres (France)*, nos. 911, 2750–2.

47 *Ausgaben apost. Kammer*, 572, 576, 606; *Inv. AD Côte-d'Or B*, ii, no. 4421; *Dumay, 146–7; Servais, i, 302–5; *Urkundenbuch Strassburg*, v, no. 1213, 1218.

48 *Urkundenbuch Strassburg*, v, no. 1221–3, 1225–7, 1231–4, 1414; Königshofen, *Chron.*, 815–16, 817–19; 'Chron. S. Thiébaut', p. xxvi; *Calmet, iii, col. ccxcv; *Limburger Chron.*, 71; Justinger, *Berner-Chron.*, 142–5; 'Kleine Basler Annalen', 62; *Chron. Zurich*, 85. Peace of Wattwiller: Froissart, *Chron.* (SHF), viii, p. cxxxvii n[2].

49 BN Fr. n.a. 7414, fols. 241vo–245; BN Clair. 18/1, 36/2733, 46/3419, 55/4165, 101/18, etc.; receipts for war wages at Autun, 14–16 March (BN Clair. 12/739, 17/1181, 92/7145, etc.); Lyon, 2 April (BN Clair. 55/4195, 57/4317, etc.); Vienne, 2 May (BN Clair. 12/757, 106/88, etc.); Pont-St.-Esprit (BN Clair. 17/1181, etc.); *Ausgaben apost. Kammer*, 631; *Hist. gén. Lang.*, x, 1535; Durrieu (1835), 126n[2]; Mirot (1897), 599n[1].

50 Caferro, 145–6, 162–3, 192, 272, 281; Temple-Leader & Marcotti, 84, 87–95, *331–2, *334; *Miscellanea fiorentina di stori e erudizione*, ed. I. del Badia (1902), ii, 172–3.

51 *Ausgaben apost. Kammer*, 579, 596, 641, 645–6; Gregory XI, *Lettres (France)*, no. 3759, 3785–9, 3762–3; *Corpus chron. Bonon.*, iv, 300, 301; 'La guerra dei fiorentini con papa Gregorio XI detta la guerra degli otto santi', ed. A. Gherardi, *Archivio Storico Italiano*, Series III, vii (1), 217–18; 'Dispacci di C. da Piacenza', 86.

52 Mirot (1897), 604–14; (1898), 262–9; Caferro, 189–90; Temple-Leader & Marcotti, 106–8, 118–23; 'Gesta Britonum in Italia', cols. 1468–9.

53 *Foed.*, iii, 1039–40; *Lettere di mercatanti*, 28–33.

54 *Foed.*, iii, 1034, 1040; *Mandements*, no. 1174A; 'Anglo-French negotiations', 24–6; Gregory XI, *Lettres (France)*, no. 2005; *Cotton Manuscrit Galba B.1*, 31–3; *Gr. chron.*, ii, 179; Froissart, *Chron.* (SHF), viii, 191; *Lecoy, ii, 392 (quotation).

55 *Lettere di mercatanti*, 34–5; *Cotton Manuscrit Galba B.1*, 31–2; 'Anglo-French negotiations', 26–37. Date: PRO E364/8, m. 4 (Sheppey).

56 PRO E364/8, m. 4 (Sheppey); 'Anglo-French negotiations', 37–43; *Foed.*, iii, 1048; PRO E101/317/10, 11, 19.

57 *Parl. Rolls*, v, 295 (1, 2); *Anonimalle*, 80–3.

58 Froissart, *Chron.* (KL), xiv, 384.

59 *Anonimalle*, 81–2. On London and the Good Parliament: Nightingale, 243–7; Bird, 17–24; Holmes (1975), 80–4; Lloyd (1977), 218–19, 220, 222–3.

60 Perroy (1933), 28–40; Lunt, ii, 103–7, 351–3, 377–8; Holmes (1975), 11–20, 46–8; *Foed.*, iii, 1049; Brinton, *Sermons*, ii, 315–21.

61 The writs *de expensis* list 39 as knights: *CCR 1374–7*, 428–9. Add: Sir Thomas Hoo (Wrottesley, 171); Sir Thomas Blount (*Foed.*, iii, 857, 888); Sir Thomas Cobham (*Foed.*, iii, 958); Sir John Avenel (*Foed.*, iii, 897); and Sir John Kentwood (*CCR 1374–7*, 471). Individuals: *Controversy Scrope Grosvenor*, i, 112, 126–7, 162 (Saville, Haselrigg, Eynsford); Wrottesley, 133, 165, 171 (Marney, Boteller, Hoo); *Foed.*, Supp., i, 2, 16, 17 (FitzWalter, Wingfield, Blount); *Reg. Black Prince*, iv, 285 (Kentwood); *Foed.*, iii, 323, 326, 731, 765, 812 (Appleby, Fyton, Preston, Gissing); *CPR 1354–8*, 559, 560 (Ludlow, Wood); *Hist. Parl.*, iii, 517 (Kentwood). Waldegrave: *Controversy Scrope Grosvenor*, i, 166; *Anonimalle*, 51–2, 170 (note). Calais, 1369: PRO C76/52, m. 15 (Appleby);

Controversy Scrope Grosvenor, i, 77, 117 (Bonville, Boynton); *ibid.*, i, 166 and *Foed.*, iii, 866 (Ludlow, Waldegrave); *Foed.*, iii, 870 (Burton); *Foed.*, iii, 871 (Hamely); *Foed.*, iii, 873 (Teye, Thorp, Bussy). Pontvallain: *Foed.*, iii, 897. Fleet of 1372: *Foed.*, iii, 958 (Cobham). Gaunt, 1373: PRO C76/56, mm. 20, 27 (Boteller, Saville, Fogg). Brittany, 1375: *Foed.*, iii, 1010 (Giffard); *Foed.*, iii, 1014, 1018 (Aylesbury, Boteller). *Parl. Rolls*, vi, 11 (16) ('longed to participate').

62 Walsingham, *Chron. Maj.*, i, 10–12, 34; Higden, *Polychronicon*, Cont. (iv), 386; *Anonimalle*, 92, 94. March: PRO E403/446, m. 25 (14 July); E403/454, m. 23 (19 Sept.).

63 *Anonimalle*, 83–5. On the members of the Lords' commission: Holmes (1975), 139–55.

64 Walsingham, *Chron. Maj.*, i, 8–12; *Anonimalle*, 79, 85–8, 92, 94–5.

65 *Anonimalle*, 88–90, 93; Walsingham, *Chron. Maj.*, i, 14–18, 356; *Parl. Rolls*, v, 302, 304, 307–11, 313–14, 324, 424, 426 (21–3, 25, 31–4, 46, 90, 92, 96).

66 *Anonimalle*, 90–2, 94; Walsingham, *Chron. Maj.*, i, 14, 40–2; *Parl. Rolls*, v, 298, 307, 314, 326–7 (10, 30, 47); PRO E101/531/28.

67 *Anonimalle*, 93–4; Walsingham, *Chron. Maj.*, i, 22–8, 28, 46–50; Higden, *Polychronicon*, Cont. (iv), 385; *Cal. Letter Books H*, 25, 30; CCR 1374–7, 318, 439–40; *Parl. Rolls*, v, 300–6, 307–12, 313, 424 (17–28, 31–4, esp. 28, 45, 89).

68 *Anonimalle*, 94–5; Walsingham, *Chron. Maj.*, i, 32–6; Brinton, *Sermons*, 354–7; Froissart, *Chron.* (SHF), viii, 225; *Chron. premiers Valois*, 257.

69 *Parl. Rolls*, v, 297–8, 315 (9, 51); CCR 1374–7, 428–9; *Anonimalle*, 94–5; Walsingham, *Chron. Maj.*, i, 56.

70 Prince: *Anonimalle*, 95; *Royal Wills*, 66–9. Attendance: PRO E403/460, mm. 23, 25, 26 (31 July, 22, 23 Sept.). Counter-revolution: Walsingham, *Chron. Maj.*, i, 54; Higden, *Polychronicon*, Cont. (iv), 387; CPR 1374–7, 353–4, 361, 364–5; Holmes (1975), 160n[3]; PRO E101/397/20.

71 Holmes (1975), 160n[1]; Walsingham, *Chron. Maj.*, i, 58–62; *Anonimalle*, 95–100; *Foed.*, iii, 1069; CCR 1374–7, 397.

72 Higden, *Polychronicon*, Cont. (iv), 386–7.

73 Walsingham, *Chron. Maj.*, i, 38; *Parl. Rolls*, v, 315 (50), vi 10 (13); *Chron. premiers Valois*, 259; *Froissart, *Chron.* (KL), viii, 461.

74 *J. Finot, 'Le train de maison d'une grande dame au xive siècle', *Bull. Philol. et Hist. du Com. des Travaux Hist. et Sci.* (1888), at 199–200; 'Anglo-French negotiations', 48–9, 53–4.

75 'Anglo-French negotiations', 53–60, 63–6.

76 Cazelles (1982), 537–41; *Troubat, i, 230–1; *Hist. gén. Lang.*, ix, 855, x, 1512–22, 1534–42; Dognon, 613; Froissart, *Chron.* (SHF), x, 170–1.

77 *Ordonnances*, vi, 219–22; *Doc. Clos des Galées*, i, nos. 1002, 1008, 1013, 1042; *Terrier de Loray, PJ no. 30; Lopes, *Crón. D. Fernando*, 330.

78 Walsingham, *Chron. Maj.*, i, 106–8; *Anglo-Norman Letters*, 164.

79 Froissart, *Chron.* (SHF), viii, 121, ix, 27–8, 127–8; *Mandements*, no. 1414; *Facs. Nat. MSS. Scot.*, ii, no. 46.

80 *Gr. chron.*, ii, 183–4. Attendance: *Itin. Ph. le Hardi*, 135; AD Côte d'Or B1451, fol. 18; Lehoux, iii, 454.

81 *Anonimalle*, 95, 103; 'Anglo-French negotiations', 78; *Parl. Rolls*, vi, 27–30 (42); Walsingham, *Chron. Maj.*, i, 102.

82 Walsingham, *Chron. Maj.*, i, 68–70; *Parl. Rolls*, v, 397 (12), 399–400 (18), 424–6 (89–96); *Rec. Convoc.*, iii, 340 (March); CPR 1374–7, 439–40, 444, 448–9, 453, 455. Mobilisation: PRO C76/59, m. 4; C76/60, m. 7; E403/461, m. 30, 34 (19, 20, 23 Feb.); *Foed.*, iii, 1066, 1071.

83 *Anonimalle*, 100–1; Weske, 259; Walsingham, *Chron. Maj.*, i, 72–4; *Rec. Convoc.*, iii, 342, 343, 344, 345.

84 Walsingham, *Chron. Maj.*, i, 80–98, 104; *Anonimalle*, 103–5, 105–6; *Cal. Letter Books H*, 59–61. Fitzwalter's debts: CPR 1374–7, 191; CPR 1385–9, 204; CCR 1374–7, 71, 267, 274–6, 276–7, 457.

85 Walsingham, *Chron. Maj.*, i, 68, 980; *Parl. Rolls*, v, 400 (19); *Anonimalle*, 101; *CFR*, viii, 391–2. The northern province resisted until June: *Concilia*, iii, 114, 125; *CFR*, ix, 38.
86 Walsingham, *Chron. Maj.*, i, 100; *Select Cas. K.B.*, vi, 178; Oman, xii n[6], xvi–xvii, 164–6; Ormrod (1990), 205 (Table 4); Ormrod (1999), 177 (Fig. 8.7).
87 Minsterworth: *Issues Exch.*, 202, 203; *CPR 1374–7*, 488–9, 491; *Anglo-Norman Letters*, 164–5; Walsingham, *Chron. Maj.*, i, 106–8. Bournaseau: *Froissart, *Chron.* (KL), ix, 511–16; Froissart, *Chron.* (SHF), ix, 127–30.
88 *Cal. Doc. Scot.*, v, nos. 4029–39; *CPR 1374–7*, 495; PRO E101/34/29; E403/461, m. 34 (21 Mar.); E403/462, mm. 3–4 (22 Apr.); *Foed.*, iii, 1071, 1075, 1076, 1078, 1078–9; *Cal. Letter Books H*, 64–6. Councils: PRO E403/461, m. 34 (21 Mar.); E403/462, mm. 1–2, 11 (9 Apr., 16 May).
89 'Anglo-French negotiations', 66–8; PRO E101/317/12, 23; Walsingham, *Chron. Maj.*, i, 114; Froissart, *Chron.* (SHF), viii, 225–6; *Gr. chron.*, ii, 180. Montreuil: *Foed.*, iii, 1076; *Mandements*, no. 1425; Froissart, *Chron.* (SHF), viii, 223–4, 226, 227; *Chaucer Life-Records*, 45–9; *Gr. chron.*, ii, 180; 'Anglo-French negotiations', 80–5; PRO 101/317/30–32, E101/318/1–2. The English delegation maintained direct contact with Coucy during the conference: PRO E403/462, m. 1 (7 Apr.).
90 *Moranvillé (1888), 309–10; *Mandements*, no. 1392; *Delisle, ii, 312. Ship strength: Walsingham, *Chron. Maj.*, i, 132; Walsingham, *Hist. Angl.*, i, 142; Thorne, *Gesta Abbatum S. Augustini*, cols. 2152–3; *Gr. chron.*, ii, 180; Cochon, *Chron.*, 129. Manning: *Mandements*, p. ix; *Chron. premiers Valois*, 262; Froissart, *Chron.* (SHF), viii, 229.
91 PRO E101/34/25; E101/37/15; E403/462, mm. 12, 16–18 (26 May, 20 June); E403/463, m. 1 (2 July). Manning: PRO E403/462, mm. 14, 15, 16, 19 (12, 17, 19, 20 June). Embarkation: PRO DL28/3/1, m. 7.
92 'Voyage de N. de Bosc', 327; BN Coll. Dupuy 306, fol. 77 (recitation of the offer in 1390); 'Anglo-French negotiations', 80–5; *Gr. chron.*, ii, 181.
93 Pageant: Beltz, 11; *Anonimalle*, 106. Death: Walsingham, *Chron. Maj.*, i, 116–22. Cancellation: PRO E101/34/23; E101/37/8, 13, 19, 20. Ambassadors: *Gr. chron.*, ii, 181.

CHAPTER VII

1 *Chron. premiers Valois*, 262–3; Higden, *Polychron.*, Cont. (ii), 229; Walsingham, *Chron. Maj.*, i, 132, 162; *Anonimalle Chron.*, 107; *Rot. Parl.*, iii, 70 (5). On Hamo: *CPR 1377–81*, 40; *Westminster Chron.*, 34; E. Searle, *Lordship and Community. Battle Abbey and its Banlieu, 1066–1538* (1974), 342n[14]. Walls of Rye: *CPR 1367–70*, 203; *CPR 1377–81*, 74–5.
2 Walsingham, *Chron. Maj.*, i, 162–4; *Chron. Bourbon*, 71–2; Froissart, *Chron.* (SHF), viii, 234–6; *CCR 1377–81*, 135; *Cal. Pap. R. Letters 1362–1404*, 396. On Lewes castle: Saul (1986), 29–30, 35–6. On John of Charlieu ('de Cariloco'): *Heads of Religious Houses. England and Wales*, ed. D.M. Smith and V.C.M. London, ii (2001), 222, 235. On Fawsley: Goodman (1971), 111, 17. On Cheyne: *Foed.*, iv, 122–3.
3 PRO E159/154 (Brevia directa baronibus); *Anonimalle Chron.*, 106, 114; Walsingham, *Chron. Maj.*, i, 152. Defence: *Foed.*, iv, 3–4; cf. PRO E403/463, m. 1 (1 July).
4 *Foed.*, iv, 10; Tout (1920–37), iii, 326–32, 342–5; iv, 189–95; v, 397–400; Given-Wilson (1986), 161–2.
5 Walsingham, *Chron. Maj.*, i, 124–30, 156, 164–6; *Foed.*, iv, 13–14; Steel (1954), 37; *CCR 1377–81*, 7; PRO E403/468, m. 10 (5 Aug.).
6 *CPR 1377–81*, 4, 6; *Foed.*, iv, 3, 4, 12; PRO E101/37/5; Froissart, *Chron.* (SHF), viii, 233; PRO E101/36/23; E403/463, m. 1 (29 June).
7 *Moranvillé (1888), 311; *Mandements*, no. 1414; *Doc. Clos des Galées*, i, no. 1028. Southampton: *Chron. premiers Valois*, 263. Jean de Vienne was in Paris on 8 Aug.: *Terrier de Loray, PJ no. 33.
8 *Northern Petitions*, no. 113; *Rot. Scot.*, ii, 2; *Foed.*, iv, 11; BL Cotton Vespasian F.VII, fol. 17; Walsingham, *Chron. Maj.*, i, 158–60; Wyntoun, *Oryg. Cron.*, iii, 9–12; Bower,

Scotichron., vii, 368–73; *Cal. Doc. Scot.*, iv, nos. 242, 252, 851; PRO E403/463, m. 6 (15 Sept.). Herald: PRO E403/463, mm. 2, 4 (11 July, 19 Aug.).

9 PRO E403/463, m. 3 (19 Aug.); Walsingham, *Chron. Maj.*, i, 160–2; Higden, *Polychron.*, Cont. (ii), 229; *Cal. Inq. Misc.*, iv, nos. 128, 136, 384; CCR 1385–9, 365. On Tyrell: *Foed.*, iii, 1019–20.

10 Froissart, *Chron.* (SHF), viii, 233–4; *Chron. premiers Valois*, 263; Walsingham, *Chron. Maj.*, i, 158; PRO E403/463, m. 4 (12 Aug.); Thorne, *Gesta Abbatum S. Augustini*, cols. 2152–3; *Chron. premiers Valois*, 263; Froissart, *Chron.* (SHF), viii, 237–8. Dover garrison: PRO E403/463, mm. 1, 3, 4 (2, 23 July, 7, 19 Aug.).

11 *Rot. Parl.*, iii, 70 (5); *Parl. Rolls*, vi, 98 (64). Gaunt: Walsingham, *Chron. Maj.*, i, 164–6; PRO DL28/3/1, m. 7.

12 *Parl. Rolls*, vi, 98 (64); Turner, 148–52, 162, 164, 177; O'Neill, 8–9; Brown, Colvin & Taylor, 237, 394, 623, 789–90, 843–7; Platt (1973), 127–9; Kenyon, 146–7. Bodiam: *CPR 1385–9*, 42. Scotney: *CPR 1377–81*, 596. Surveys: PRO E403/468, mm. 9, 12 (9 July, 12 Aug.); *Foed.*, iv, 30.

13 Mézières, *Songe*, ii, 404–6; Christine de Pisan, *Livre des fais*, i, 241. Spies: *Parl. Rolls*, vi, 38 (58); PRO E403/463, m. 3 (28 July); E403/471, m. 13 (22 Dec.); *CPR 1381–5*, 190–1; CCR 1385–9, 501.

14 Alien monks: *Parl. Rolls*, v, 48–50 (91), 128–9 (40), 286 (32); PRO C76/61, m. 11; CCR 1369–74, 63; CFR, viii, 13, 346, ix, 16, 161; PRO E403/462, m. 3 (21 Apr.) (Rougecok); Matthew, 110–11, 162–70; *Cal. Pap. R. Letters*, iv, 239–40. Other scares: CCR 1374–77, 139, 416; CCR 1377–81, 201, 514; *Cal. Inq. Misc.*, iv, nos. 54, 152, 346.

15 *Itin. Ph. le Hardi*, 136; *Parl. Rolls*, vi, 22 (39); *Parl. Rolls*, vi, 22 (39); *Garnier, 8–13; *Inv. mobiliers Bourgogne*, i, no. 3229.

16 PRO E403/462, m. 1 (7 Apr.) (message to all major garrisons); *Parl. Rolls*, vi, 22–3 (39); Froissart, *Chron.* (SHF), viii, 237–8. Defences: Brown, Colvin & Taylor, 434–6. The 'normal' garrison strength was *ca.* 1,200 men: PRO E101/179/12, fols. 4–5vo; E101/180/4, fols. 4vo–8vo. The townsmen contributed another 300: *Parl. Rolls*, v, 381 (209). At least 200 reinforcements arrived in June under Sir Thomas Percy: PRO E403/462, mm. 10–11, 13 (16 May, 1 June).

17 Ardres: *Compte Gunthorp*, 46–7; PRO E101/180/5; PRO E101/68/6 (139); E101/180/4, m. 6vo; *Parl. Rolls*, vi, 23–6 (40); Froissart, *Chron.* (SHF), viii, 244–7; *Gr. chron.*, ii, 192; Walsingham, *Chron. Maj.*, i, 166. Gommegnies: *Foed.*, iii, 882, 891, 982, 1016; PRO C76/61, m. 29. Balinghem, La Planque, La Haie: *Gr. chron.*, ii, 192–3; Froissart, *Chron.* (SHF), viii, 247–8. Audruicq: *Parl. Rolls*, vi, 22–3 (39); Froissart, *Chron.* (SHF), viii, 248–9; *Mandements*, no. 1456. Charges: CCR 1377–81, 20; *Parl. Rolls*, vi, 21–6 (38–40).

18 *Gr. chron.*, ii, 193; *Istore*, ii, 143–4; Froissart, *Chron.* (SHF), viii, 238; Cochon, *Chron.*, 129; *Terrier de Loray, PJ., no. 36.

19 AN KK 242, fols. 61, 65vo, 68; KK252, fols. 137–8; BN Fr. n.a. 7414, fols. 265–265vo; *Istore*, ii, 146; *Gr. chron.*, ii, 184–6; *Chronographia*, ii, 392; 'Chron. Pays-Bas', 265; *Inv. AC Périgueux*, 26, 57; BN PO 2012, Moncontour/3; *Rec. titres Périgueux*, 439. On Jean IV de Bueil: *Gall. Reg.*, i, no. 2959; Anselme, viii, 62.

20 Sir Thomas Felton's retinue (based at Bordeaux) was 120 strong: PRO E101/181/1 (24) (assuming an equal number of archers and men-at-arms); Sir William Elmham had 100 men-at-arms at Bayonne: PRO E403/460, m. 23 (31 July). Finance, Bayonne: PRO E403/460, m. 23 (31 July); E403/461, m. 34 (21 Mar.); E403/468, m. 11 (5 Aug.); E403/478, m. 26 (3 Sept.). Finance, Bordeaux: PRO E403/461, m. 4 (21 Mar.); E403/472, m. 18 (16 Aug.). Finance, Bergerac: PRO DL28/3/1, m. 6. Finance, other garrisons: PRO E101/180/9, fols. 33vo, 36–36vo, 50vo, 77–80. Subsidy of 1377: PRO C61/90, mm. 3, 2; E403/461, m. 34 (21 Mar.); E403/462, mm. 3, 5 (21, 28 Apr.); E364/15, m. 2 (Rotour); E364/25, m. 4d (Lumbard); E101/181/1 (23, 24). Council: PRO E403/462, mm. 1–2 (9 Apr.); C61/90, mm. 3.

21 PRO E101/181/1 (23–5, 45); E101/181/5 (2, 6, 8, 12).

22 Bordeaux: PRO E101/180/9, fols. 72vo, 74; Froissart, *Chron.* (SHF), ix, 2–4. Pommiers:

AHG, xxvi, 149–63. Greilly: Froissart, *Chron*., viii, 239–41; *Foed*., iv, 10. Montaut: Anselme, vi, 222; PRO C61/89, mm. 6, 4, 3; E403/460, m. 19 (9 July); *Foed*., iii, 1061–2.

23 *Rec. titres Périgueux*, 439; PRO E101/181/5 (8, 9); E101/181/1 (24); E101/181/4 (18); *Chronographia*, ii, 392. Hélie: *John of G. Reg. (1372–6)*, no. 6; *Jurades de Bergerac*, i, 34; PRO DL28/3/1, m. 4. Bertrand de Buade had been in command since 1375: PRO 101/180/9, fol. 17ᵛᵒ, 36ᵛᵒ; E101/181/5 (6, 8, 9). Topography: *AHVF Bergerac*.

24 *Istore*, ii, 147–8; *Rec. titres Périgueux*, 439–40; *Gr. chron*., ii, 186–8; *Anonimalle Chron*., 116; *Jurades de Bergerac*, i, 54; Froissart, *Chron*. (SHF), ix, 11–12.

25 Froissart, *Chron*. (SHF), ix, 13; AD Hérault A6/118 (troops of Languedoc); BN Fr. n.a. 7414, fols. 267–8. Coucy renounced his homage on 26 Aug. and would not have fought against Richard II before then: *Foed*., iv, 18, 60; *CFR*, ix, 31; PRO C76/61, m. 31; GEC, ii, 69–70. Weather: *Petit Thalamus*, 395.

26 PRO E101/180/9, fols. 48, 51, 52, 52ᵛᵒ; E101/181/1 (65, 66).

27 'Petite chronique', para. 72; Froissart, *Chron*. (SHF), ix, 14–15; *Jurades de Bergerac*, i, 53–4; *Gr. chron*., ii, 189; *Doc. Durfort*, no. 1287; BN PO 2624, Sancerre/29. Duras, Madaillan: *Gr. chron*., ii, 189; PRO 101/180/9, m. 50ᵛᵒ. Bérard: PRO E101/180/10 (41); C61/85, m. 10; *Trés. Chartes Albret*, i, nos. 631–2. Montaut: PRO E101/180/9, fol. 52; E101/181/1 (60); *Gr. chron*., ii, 191. The Montauts and Blaye: PRO C61/70, m. 4; *AHG*, xii, 340. Bertucat: *Gr. chron*., ii, 188; *Chronographia*, ii, 392; 'Chron. Pays-Bas', 266.

28 *Gr. chron*., ii, 188–9; *Istore*, ii, 148–9; Froissart, *Chron*. (SHF), ix, 14, 16–17, 19–20; PRO E101/180/9, fol. 51; E101/181/1 (54, 55, 56). Defence of Castillon: PRO E101/180/9, fol. 79. Siege of St.-Macaire was in progress on 24 Sept. and 8 Oct.: *Trés. Chartes Albret*, i, nos. 631–2. Anjou was at La Réole on 8 October: BN PO 2624, Sancerre/29.

29 *Gr. chron*., ii, 191; Froissart, *Chron*. (SHF), ix, 16, 20–4.

30 Gregory XI, *Lettres (France)*, no 2060; *Gr. chron*., ii, 188–92. Winter garrisons: *AHG*, n.s., i, 3–4 (Duras, Marmande, Montségur, Langon, Landiras, Créon, Ste.-Foy); BN PO 2639, Saulaye/2 and 2690, Ver/9, 14 (St.-Macaire); BN Fr. n.a. 7414, fol. 274 and *Froissart, *Chron*. (KL), xviii, 551–2 (Cadillac); PRO E101/180/10 (41) (Cubsac); *Foed*., iv, 131 and *Anonimalle*, 120 (St.-Mambert near Pauillac, and nearby places); Froissart, *Chron*. (SHF), ix, 24–5. Destruction: *Comptes arch. Bordeaux*, ii, 288, 298, 300–2, 305, 370; Denifle, i, no. 487, ii, 646–7; PRO C61/98, m. 8 (Soudan); Boutruche, 214, 308–9.

31 *Parl. Rolls*, vi, 279–80 (3). Ch. Islands: PRO E101/31/23; E101/89/26B; BL Add. Mss. 37494, fol. 31; C76/56, m. 29; E101/89/27, 28.

32 Richmond: *CPR 1377–81*, 74; *CPR 1377–81*, 74. Auray: *Gr. chron*., ii, 183, 192; *Moranvillé (1888)*, 311. Brest: *Foed*., iv, 34–5 (terms negotiated before 13 Oct.: *Parl. Rolls*, vi, 20 (34)), 36; Morice, *Preuves*, i, 417; PRO E403/463, m. 1 (3 July); E403/465, mm. 2, 10 (7 Oct., 12 Dec.); Froissart, *Chron*. (SHF), viii, 252. English mobilisation: PRO E403/463, m. 5, 6 (28 Aug., 15, 16 Sept.); E403/465, mm. 1, 2, 6 (1, 5 Oct., 4 Nov.); C76/61, mm. 29, 28, 27; E101/37/17; E101/37/16, 23; E101/68/7 (149–153); *Foed*., iv, 18, 19.

33 *Parl. Rolls*, vi, 11 (16). Arundel: Goodman (1971), 3–4. Buckingham: PRO C76/61, m. 21; Froissart, *Chron*. (SHF), x, 34; Goodman (1971), 4–5, 74–104; Walsingham, *Hist. Angl*., ii, 226 (quotation).

34 *Parl. Rolls*, vi, 10–11, 12, 13, 21–30 (13–18, 22, 38–43); Walsingham, *Chron. Maj*., i, 168; *CFR*, ix, 45; *CCR 1377–81*, 20; Froissart, *Chron*. (SHF), viii, 251. Membership: Roskell (1981–3), ii, 10.

35 *Parl. Rolls*, vi, 15 (27); *CPR 1377–81*, 24, 25, 99, 327; *CFR*, ix, 52–3, 61; *Foed*., iv, 22; *Anonimalle*, 116; Prestwich (1984); Given-Wilson (1986), 123–4. Cf. clerical subsidy: *Rec. Convoc*., iv, 7–8, 11, 12–13, xiii, 190–3.

36 PRO C76/61, m. 28; *CCR 1377–81*, 88; *Anonimalle*, 116–17; Walsingham, *Chron. Maj*., i, 170–2; Higden, *Polychron*., Cont. (iv), 395. Date of return: PRO E403/465, mm. 7, 9 (11, 20 Nov., 10 Dec.). Ships: E101/37/23; *Anonimalle*, 117. Troops, London: PRO E403/465, mm. 1, 1–2, 6 (1, 5 Oct, 4 Nov.); E101/36/26 (Ferrers); E101/26/27 (J. Pole);

E101/36/30 (Knolles); E101/36/31, E101/38/1 (Buckingham); E101/42/13 (John de Montfort); E364/12, m. 4 (Cobham); E364/13, m. 2d (Hales); E364/15, m. 4d (M. Pole); E364/17, m. 8 (Talbot). Troops, west: E364/12, m. 3d (J. de Arundel); E364/13, m. 1d (Brian); E364/15, m. 12 (Roches); E364/16, m. 8d (Sandes); E364/22, m. 7 (Devon). New Admirals: PRO C76/61, m. 9.

37 PRO E403/465, m. 9 (10 Dec.). The captains recorded at Brest in January included men from both eastern and western fleets: see note 36 above and PRO E403/465, mm. 18, 22; E101/37/27 (66). Campaign: Walsingham, *Chron. Maj.*, i, 212–16; *Anonimalle*, 117; *Foed.*, iv, 36; PRO E403/468, mm. 16, 20, 21 (28 May, 12 June); E364/12, m. 4d (Knolles); E101/36/30; E364/14, m. 2d (Armesthorpe & Philpot). On Lakenheath: *CPR 1367–70*, 475; *CCR 1369–74*, 359. Return: PRO E101/36/31, E101/38/1.

38 PRO E364/12, m. 4d (Knolles). Townsmen: *Foed.*, vii, 656. Victualling: PRO E101/37/1; E403/465, mm. 21 (5 Apr.), E403/468, 16, 21 (28 May, 12 June); E403/471, m. 13 (23 Dec.); E403/475, m. 24 (23 Mar.). Victualler: PRO C76/62, m. 9; E101/37/27 (67). Defences: PRO E364/18, m. 5 (Norwich); E101/38/8 (7, 18); C76/62, m. 8; *Foed.*, iv. 32. Cost: Jones (1970), 221 (App. E) (to 1381) (figures do not include victualling, munitions and shipping); *Parl. Rolls*, vi, 73–4 (15).

39 Jones (1970), 169 and n³. Abberbury, Golafre: *Foed.*, iv, 37; PRO E101/37/30; E364/13, m. 3 (Abberbury and Golafre); E101/68/7 (171). On them: *Hist. Parl.*, ii, 13, 14–15, iii, 199; *CPR 1385–9*, 156; *VCH Berkshire*, iv, 93–4. Calveley, Percy: PRO E101/38/26. Deputies: PRO E364/18, m. 5 (Norwich); E101/38/26; *CCR 1377–81*, 411; John IV, *Actes*, no. 418; *Parl. Rolls*, vii, 25 (35); Morice, *Preuves*, ii, 450 at 455; cf. 30,000 francs estimated in 1393, *PPC*, i, 49. Later captains of Brest took all the spoil, but the fee was reduced to between 2,000 and 4,250 marks per year: Jones (1970), 219 (App. C); *Foed.*, iv, 133; E101/68/10 (237).

40 Secousse, *Preuves*, 378–9 (confession of Jacques de Rue), 411, 412–13, 429–30 (confession of Pierre du Tertre); Charon, 87–100.

41 *Foed.*, iii, 1057, 1069, 1070, 1074, 1076; PRO E101/317/33; Secousse, *Preuves*, 407, 418, 419–22 (confession of Pierre du Tertre); Charon, 100–4. On Berkeley: *Reg. Black Prince*, iv, 403, 497; PRO C61/81, m. 5.

42 Secousse, *Preuves*, 381–2 (confession of Jacques de Rue), 407, 421, 422, 423 (confession of Pierre du Tertre); *Mandements*, nos. 1468–70, 1819; PRO E364/11, m. 7 (Roches), E364/15, m. 13 (Roches). Roches was still at Bristol on 28 Nov. 1377: PRO E403/465, m. 8 (28 Nov.). J. de Rye: *Mandements*, nos. 1468–70; *Suarez Fernandez (1959), 143. Castilian muster: *Col. doc. Murcia*, viii, no. 225.

43 *Cat. Arch. Navarra (Comptos)*, xi, nos. 138, 156, 162; Secousse, *Preuves*, 379, 382 (confession of Jacques de Rue), 402, 407, 420–1 (confession of Pierre du Tertre); *Doc. norm.*, 381–3.

44 *Mandements*, no. 1819; Secousse, *Preuves*, 381–2 (confession of Jacques de Rue), 407 (confession of Pierre du Tertre); Russell, 259–60.

45 Bayonne: Walsingham, *Chron. Maj.*, i, 218; PRO E403/465, mm. 12, 13, 14 (7 19, 23 Jan., 4, 5 Feb.); and two further vessels added in March: E403/465, m. 22 (5 Apr.); E101/37/27 (36). Arundel's 1st cruise: PRO E403/365, m. 20 (5 Apr.); E101/68/7 (169); C76/62, m. 24. Service of men assigned to 1st cruise expressed in pay records to be for a month before John of Gaunt took command of the whole army: PRO E364/13, mm. 1–1d (W. Neville), 1d (W. Neville, Clanvowe), 3d (Vere, Devereux). 'Great expedition.': PRO C76/62, m. 16; PRO E101/68/7 (162–7); PRO E101/37/25, m. 14.

46 *Anonimalle*, 119 (the reference is to the Great Council which met in London on 26 March: PRO E403/465, m. 17 (19 Mar.)). Douat, Galard: PRO E403/468, m,. 3, 17 (17, 28 May); E101/37/27 (82, 142). Their operations: AC Martel CC5, fol. 32, 33ᵛᵒ; *Denifle, 822; Alauzier (1957/1), 98–100, 101; *Comptes Rodez*, ii, 470, 486; 'Doc. St.-Antonin', 290. Marchès: *Thomas, 383–4. Raymond de Custon, lieutenant of Pierre de Custon, captain of Charlus-Champagnac, was retained by Neville in England on 18 May 1378: PRO E101/180/9, fol. 67; cf. E101/180/10 (56). On Charlus-Champagnac: *Inv. AC*

905

Montferrand, i, 403, 404; *Troubat, i, 230, 231; *Chron. Bourbon*, 104.

47 Mobilisation: PRO E403/465, m. 22 (5 Apr.); E364/13, m. 1–1d (W. Neville), m. 1d
(W. Neville and ors), m. 3d (Vere, Devereux), m. 6 (J. Pole); E364/15, m. 10 (Salisbury);
E364/15, m. 12 (Arundel); E101/37/25, mm. 11–14. Hakenet: PRO E403/463, mm. 5, 6,
8, 10, 13 (28 Aug., 21 Sept., 23 Nov., 12 Dec., 29 Jan.); E403/465, mm. 8, 10, 13 (23
Nov., 12 Dec., 29 Jan.); E403/468, m. 1 (26 Apr.). Operations: Walsingham, *Chron.
Maj.*, i, 218–28; *Foed.*, iv, 40; *Parl. Rolls*, vi, 126–7 (37).

48 PRO E364/11, m. 7; *AHG*, n.s., i, 3–4; *Chronographia*, ii, 348–9; *Gr. chron.*, ii, 284–5,
*iii, 210–11; *Moranvillé (1888), 316–17; Secousse, *Preuves*, 374–87 (confession of
Jacques de Rue).

49 *Gr. chron.*, ii, 305–8, *iii, 211; *Froissart, *Chron.* (KL), xviii, 549–50. Date: 'Séjours',
256–7. Rewards: *Doc. norm.*, no. 1449; AN KK326, fol. 3ᵛᵒ.

50 AD Côte d'Or B1452, fol. 15ᵛᵒ; Secousse, *Preuves*, 403 (confession of Pierre du Tertre);
Gr. chron., ii, 308; Morice, *Preuves*, ii, 380–1; BN PO 232, de Baveux/8; 621,
Caudecotte/3; 765, Cintray/3, 4, 5; 781, de Clere/19; 1064, Esneval/11; 1133, Ferron-en-
Bretagne/8; 1280, de Garencières 15; 2040, Monteuil/4; BN Clair. 152/3807, 203/8649.
Breteuil: Secousse, *Preuves*, 403 (confession of Pierre du Tertre), 440–1; *Gr. chron.*, ii,
309; BN PO 232, de Baveux/8; 765, Cintray/3, 4; 1280, de Garencieres/15; 2040,
Monteuil/4; BN PO 2076, Moustier/24; BN Clair. 176/8. Évreux: BN PO 1064,
Esneval/5; AN JJ113/6–11, 120/155. Beaumont: BN PO 621, Caudecotte/3; 765,
Cintray/5; 781, de Clere/19; Secousse, *Preuves*, 440–1. Bernay: Secousse, *Preuves*, 404–5
(confession of Pierre du Tertre). Pacy: AN JJ114/268, 120/155. Pont-Audemer: *Terrier
de Loray, PJ., nos. 39–40; *Doc. norm.*. no. 1200; BN PO 12, Agneaux/11; 1495, Hay/3;
1377, Gournay/7; 1915, Mellemont/5; 1947, Mesnil-en-Normandie/64; 2647,
Sauvigny/3, 4; 2747, etc.; BN Clair. 165/55, 59, 203/101; BN Fr. 26015/2214. *Chron.
premiers Valois*, 267; *Chron. Bourbon*, 69–70; Secousse, *Preuves*, 447; Cochon, *Chron.*,
149. Bastides: BN PO 348, le Bigot/5; *Mon. hist.*, no. 1568. Fate of du Tertre: Secousse,
Preuves, 389, 404–5 (confession of Pierre du Tertre); *Gr. chron.*, ii,

51 Morice, *Preuves*, ii, 381–4. Carentan: Terrier de Loray, 119. Valognes: BN PO 1496,
Haye-en-Normandie/31. Avranches: *Letters B. du Guesclin*, nos. 780, 853; BN PO 2903,
d'Urssue/7, 9, 11, 20, 23. Gavray: *Letters B. du Guesclin*, nos. 778, 782, 784–5, 828;
Mandements, no. 1743; *Hay du Chastelet, 403, 463; *Chron. premiers Valois*, 266–7;
Chron. Bourbon, 67–8. Mortain: *Mandements*, no. 1705; *Letters B. du Guesclin*, no.
854; Cochon, *Chron.*, 149–50; *Chron. premiers Valois*, 275; *Doc. norm.*, nos. 1234,
1344; BN Fr. 26015/2422. Cherbourg: *Letters B. du Guesclin*, no. 792.

52 *Gr. chron.*, ii, 315–17; Secousse, *Preuves*, 431–3; *Mon. hist.*, nos. 1572, 1575; *Frag.
chron. norm.*, 10. Garrisons: BN PO 1117, du Fayel/5; 1560, d'Isque/8; 1561, d'Ivry-en-
Normandie/10 2703, Siffrevart/7; 3021, Villiers/25. D'Ayens: *Gr. chron.*, ii, 317, *iii,
224–5; *Chron. premiers Valois*, 278; BN PO 598, Blainville/56.

53 *Cat. Arch. Navarra (Comptos)*, xi, nos. 219, 253–4, 267, 276–7, 302, 308, 348, 359,
361, 365, 371, 384, 397, 405, 415, 417, 427, 438, 520; xii, 46, 47, 510; Yanguas, i,
67–8; Russell, 259–61.

54 PRO E101/37/27 (64); E101/37/27 (64). Terms ultimately agreed in July: *Foed.*, iv, 47;
Anglo-Norman Letters, 204–6. On Cherbourg: Masson, 10, 73; 15th-century description
in Blondel, *Oeuvres*, ed. A. Héron, ii (1893), 254.

55 PRO E101/37/27 (68, 118–19, 123–5, 132); E101/68/7 (173); E364/13, m. 8d
(Farringdon).

56 PRO E403/468, m. 6 (4 June). Shipping: PRO E403/468, mm. 3, 6, 15, 16, 17 (20, 28
May, 5 June); E101/37/25, mm. 1–6, 11–14; E101/37/27 (36); E101/318/10; E364/11,
m. 8 (Craling); *Foed.*, iv, 41. Cherbourg: PRO E364/12, mm. 1d (J. de Arundel), 9d
(J. de Arundel) (orders given on 13 June); E101/37/25, m. 7 (advance paid on 12 June).
The troops were ready in mid-June: PRO C76/62, m. 2; E364/13, m. 8d (Farringdon).
Le Crotoy: PRO E403/468, m. 19 (12 June); E101/37/27 (137). Neville: *Foed.*, iv, 45;
Dipl. Corr., 1, 181–2; PRO E101/38/19; E101/37/25, mm. 5–6. His numbers: PRO

E403/468, m. 15 (28 May); E364/23, m. 3d (Trivet).

57 PRO E101/36/39; E101/37/25, mm. 1–5; E101/38/17 (13, 15); E403/468, m. 20 (12 June); *Chron. premiers Valois*, 272–3; Cochon, *Chron.*, 149; Walsingham, *Chron. Maj.*, i, 228; *Cat. Arch. Navarra (Comptos)*, xi, no. 476. English reinforcements: PRO E364/12, m. 9d (J. de Arundel); E364/13, m. 8d (Farringdon).

58 *Doc. Clos des Galées*, i, no. 1060; Morice, *Preuves*, ii, col. 392; Walsingham, *Chron. Maj.*, 220–2; *Hist. Vitae*, 50; PRO C76/63, m. 8; E101/37/27 (143); E101/38/11 *Foed.*, iv, 46, 47–8; Walsingham, *Chron. Maj.*, i, 234–6; *CPR 1377–81*, 306; *Parl. Rolls*, vi, 89–90 (41).

59 *Anonimalle*, 120; Froissart, *Chron.* (SHF), ix, 73–4, 93–5; PRO E403/465, m. 20 (5 Apr.), E403/468, m. 15 (28 May). Dates: PRO 101/37/25, m. 6 (pay clerk of fleet returns to London on 12 Aug.); E364/16, m. 6d (Suffolk) (new knighthoods on 14 Aug.). Topography: Pocquet (1967), 157–8, 159–60.

60 Walsingham, *Chron. Maj.*, i, 234; *Chron. premiers Valois*, 274–5; Higden, *Polychronicon*, Cont. (iv), 397; Froissart, *Chron.* (SHF), ix, 73–4, 81–5, 92–5. Constable's movements: Morice, *Preuves*, ii, 390; AN KK252, fol. 181vo; *Letters B. du Guesclin*, no. 863. Withdrawal: PRO E364/13, m. 6 (Pole); E364/18, m. 7d (Trussell); E101/37/25, mm. 1–5, 11–14.

61 *Masson, 82–3; Morice, *Preuves*, ii, 185–7, 390. Defence: PRO E364/12, m. 9d (J. de Arundel); PRO E101/37/25, mm. 6–9; E101/38/15; E403/468, m. 20 (12 June); E403/475, m. 20 (10 Dec.). Wine fleet: PPC, i, 93 (misdated).

62 *Masson, 82–4; *Letters B. du Guesclin*, nos. 835–6, 840; *Doc. norm.*, nos. 1254, 1257, 1259–1315, 1318–19, 1328, 1330, 1341; *Mandements*, no. 1786. Cost, cash grants: Masson, 23; *Mandements*, nos. 1802–6.

63 *Chron. premiers Valois*, 275–8; Froissart, *Chron.* (SHF), ix, 96–9; *Mandements*, nos. 1802, 1803. N-D du Voeu: *Letters B. du Guesclin*, no. 845. Reinforcements: PRO E101/38/15. Valognes: *Mandements*, no. 1920. Montebourg: *Doc. norm.*, nos. 1335, 1354, 1394, 1412, 1414, 1419–20, 1477; *Moranvillé (1888), 320; *Anonimalle*, 129–30; Walsingham, *Chron. Maj.*, i, 282–8; *Frag. chron. norm.*, 10; *Istore*, ii, 160; *CPR 1377–81*, 495; Masson, 24, 27. Bordes: PRO C76/64, m. 24; E403/487, m. 2 (10 Oct.).

64 Garrison: PRO E101/37/27 (134); *Foed.*, iv, 55–7. Townsmen: AN JJ 148/167; Masson, 25–6, 76, *86, *85–7, *89–90.

65 PRO E101/37/27 (134); E101/38/17 (8, 24); E101/68/8 (178); E364/12, m. 9d (J. de Arundel); E364/13, m. 8d (Harleston); E364/29, m. 6–6d (Windsor); E101/68/9 (222, 225); E101/68/10 (244). Profits of war: the King's claim to a share of ransoms was rejected by a court of chivalry in 1378, apparently on the ground that Cherbourg was held for Charles of Navarre: Given-Wilson (1981), 18–20. Only John Harleston (April–Dec. 1379) agreed to account for spoil, but he was not in practice required to do so: PRO E101/68/8 (178); E364/13, m. 8d (Harleston). Deputies: *Parl. Rolls*, vii, 25 (35); Walsingham, *Chron. Maj.*, i, 732 (John Walsh); *Masson, 89, 90 (John Pritwell, John Austin).

66 *Anonimalle*, 120; PRO E403/468, m. 15 (28 May); E364/23, m. 3d (Trivet); PRO E364/15, m. 2 (Rotour). Gournay at Dax: PRO E101/37/27 (30); E101/180/9, fol. 50vo. Annual expenditure on administrative salaries, previously about 6,000 pounds of Bordeaux (about £800 sterling) fell to about 2,200 pounds of Bordeaux (about £300 sterling) in 1377–8: PRO E101/180/9, fols. 10–11vo, 29–31, 46–47vo. Military expenditure: PRO E101/180/9, fols. 50–53. Operations: *Anonimalle*, 120 (identifiable as Langon from PRO E364/15, m. 5 (Stratton)); Bernis, 'Chron.', 440; PRO E101/180/9, fol. 79vo.

67 *Hist. gén. Lang.*, ix, 868, x, 1588; Lecoy, ii, 253–4, *396–400, *416–39, esp. 426, 428–9, 432–3. Campaign: PRO E101/181/1 (70); *Hist. gén. Lang.*, ix, 868–9; BN Coll. Languedoc 159, fols. 158–158vo; Bernis, 'Chron.', 440; *Anonimalle*, 121.

68 *Anonimalle*, 120–1; Froissart, *Chron.* (SHF), ix, 74–5; *Foed.*, iv, 130–1. Wyn: BN Fr. n.a. 7414, fol. 278. On the Soudan: *Chron. Bourbon*, 222. English positions in Saintonge:

PRO C61/90, m. 3; Favreau (1986), 31. On St.-Mambert: Gardelles, 80n[3].

69 *Jurades de Bergerac*, i, 53–4; PRO E364/15, m. 4d (Neville); Froissart, *Chron.* (SHF), ix, 119–20.

70 *Issues Exch.*, 209; *Foed.*, iv, 131; *Owen, 18–19; Froissart, *Chron.* (SHF), ix, 77–9. For Welsh operations in 1379: *Mandements*, no. 1830 (p. 896); BN Fr. n.a. 7414, fol. 282[vo]; Fr. 9501, fol. 273[vo]. In 1380–1: *Rec. doc. Poitou*, v, 201. In 1382–4: BN PO 3055, Wyn/3–7; *Liv. mirac. Ste.-Catherine*, no. 58. In 1384: *Rec. doc. Poitou*, v, 254. In 1385: *ibid.*, v, 254n[1]. In 1386: BN Fr. 7858, fol. 274. In 1990–2: *ibid.*, pp. 30, 37–9, 84, 92–3, 96–7, 98–9, 104–7, 108–12, 244–7. In 1394–5: BN Fr. 32510, fol. 330. Their fate: e.g. *CPR 1381–5*, 235, 381; AN JJ123/74, 85. Inspiration: *Chron. r. St.-Denis*, iii, 164.

71 Ayala, *Crón.*, ii, 91–2, 93; ACA *reg.* 1261, fol. 120vo. Manrique: Secousse, *Preuves*, 376 (confession of Jacques de Rue); *Cat. Arch. Navarra (Comptos)*, xi, nos. 423, 426, 432–3, 439–40, 525, 529, xii, nos. 99, 113, 160, 208, 248, 325, 530, 578, 586.

72 *Cat. Arch. Navarra (Comptos)*, xi, nos. 420–567 *passim*, 483, 487–528, 539–815 *passim*, 820, 868, 941; xii, nos. 82–7, 315, 356, 388, 429, 1051; l, no. 771; *Cat. Arch. Navarra (Cart.)*, nos. 750–1; Yanguas, i, 377, 586–7; ii, 174, 315, 319; iii, 117–18, 370; Ayala, *Crón.*, ii, 92–3; Froissart, *Chron.* (SHF), ix, 99. *Cat. Arch. Navarra (Comptos)*, xi, nos. 435, 438, 445, 476, 512, 539, and xii, no. 185 record payments to 461 Gascons and Béarnais serving in July 1378, plus the Vic. of Castelbon's company, whose strength is not disclosed. Contracts and advances are recorded for a further 520 men of Gascon, Béarnais and Aragonese companies who were engaged but appear to have defaulted: *ibid.*, xi, nos. 267, 276, 383, 581. The Gascon squire Lope de S. Julian commanded at Pamplona until 1 Oct. 1378: *Cat. Arch. Navarra (Comptos)*, xi, 504, 643, 786. The King's lieutenant Roger-Bernard, Vic. of Castlebon (see *ibid.*, xi, no. 911, xii, no. 984), and the Bastard of Armagnac were both in Pamplona for the siege: *ibid.*, xi, nos. 806, 808, 879. Bowmen: *Cat. Arch. Navarra (Comptos)*, xi, no. 886, cf. 302.

73 Ayala, *Crón.*, ii, 93; M. Berthe, *Famines et épidémies dans les campagnes navarraises à la fin du moyen age* (1984), 384–91.

74 PRO E101/180/10 (34, 48); PRO E101/37/29; *Foed.*, iv, 131–2; *Dipl. Corr.*, 181–2. Charles in Bordeaux: *Cat. Arch. Navarra (Comptos)*, xi, nos. 782, 806, 808, 879, xii, no. 742. Aragon: Russell, 269–70.

75 PRO E101/37/29; *Foed.*, iv, 132; Froissart, *Chron.* (SHF), ix, 108–10.

76 *Cat. Arch. Navarra (Comptos)*, xi, nos. 824, 832, 868–78, 911, 915, 917ff, 920, 940–1, xii, no. 274; Froissart, *Chron.* (SHF), ix, 110.

77 *Cat. Arch. Navarra (Comptos)*, xi, 911, 915, 920, 940–1, xii, no. 628; Froissart, *Chron.* (SHF), ix, 110. On Tudela: B. Leroy, 'Tudela en 1381–3 à travers le régistre du notaire Martin Don Costal', *Principe de Viana*, xlvii (1986), 723–37.

78 Froissart, *Chron.* (SHF), ix, 110–15; *Cat. Arch. Navarra (Comptos)*, xi, no. 909, xii, no. 63.

79 *Dipl. Corr.*, 181–2; *Cat. Arch. Navarra (Comptos)*, xii, nos. 197, 391, 401.

80 *Col. doc. Murcia*, viii, no. 247; Ayala, *Crón.*, ii, 101–3; *Cat. Arch. Navarra (Comptos)*, xii, no. 421, 509, 562, 602, 617, 652, 661, 665, 691, 782. On Ramírez: *Cat. Arch. Navarra (Comptos)*, ii, no. 1074, iii, nos. 1121, 1123; PRO E403/380, mm. 6, 7 (24, 27 May); Valdeon Baruque, 284; Yanguas, iii, 8–9.

81 Russell, 277–8. Trivet: *Cat. Arch. Navarra (Comptos)*, xii, nos. 767, 902.

82 Ayala, *Crón.*, ii, 103–5; Froissart, *Chron.* (SHF), xiv, 187–8; *Chron. r. St.-Denis*, i, 470–2; Secousse, *Preuves*, 499.

83 Unless otherwise stated, the following account of the contested papal elections is based on Valois (1896–1902), i, Ch. 1 and W. Ullmann, *The Origins of the Great Schism* (1948).

84 Niem, *De Scismate*, 9, 85.

85 Gayet, *Schisme*, ii, 164.

86 *Gr. chron.*, i, 318–22; Valois (1896–1902), i, 90–3, 96–7, 100–1, 101n[1].

87 Valois (1896–1902), i, 106–8.

88 *Anonimalle Chron.*, 118–19; Walsingham, *Chron. Maj.*, i, 248–50; *CCR 1377–81*, 163,

164, 173; *Parl. Rolls*, vi, 104 (78); Perroy (1933), 103–28.

89 *Gr. chron.*, ii, 320–1; *Chart. Univ. Paris.*, iii, 561; *Chron. premiers Valois*, 280; Cochon, *Chron.*, 132; Valois (1896–1902), i, 94–6, 114–28, 132–7. 'Misguided...': F. Bliemetzrieder, 'Ein Aktenstück zu Beginn des abendländischen Schismas', *Studien und Mitteilungen aus dem Benediktinerorden*, xxviii (1907), 30–7, at 34.

90 Valois (1896–1902), i, 133 and n[4], 262–303; *Gr. chron.*, ii, 344–6.

91 Valois (1896–1902), i, 18 and n[3], 71–2, 97–8, 98n[4], 149n[3], 157–8, 162–3, 166–9; Niem, *De Scismate*, 30, 38–9. Durrieu (1880)[2], 11–14, 29–31.

92 Valois (1896–1902), i, 169–73;*L. Fumi, 'Un nuovo avviso della battaglia di Marino', *Studi e documenti di storia e diritto*, vii (1886), 57–8; *Urkundenbuch Strassburg*, v, no. 1354; *Cron. siculum*, 35–6; *Diurnali Monteleone*, 22–3; *Chronographia*, ii, 374–5; *Vitae paparum*, i, 476–7. Budes: Mirot (1898), 300; *Chron. premiers Valois*, 282.

93 *Chron. premiers Valois*, 282–3; Froissart, *Chron.* (SHF), ix, 157–8; Donato di Neri, *Cron. Senese*, ed. A. Lisini *et al.*, *RISS*[2], xv.6 (1937), 679; Labande, 90, 94–5, 104–5, 110–11, 118–21; Mirot (1898), 300; Durrieu (1885), 137–71.

94 *Pap. L. Scotland, Clement VII*, 27; Valois (1896–1902), i, 196–7, 269–71, 273–93; *Chron. premiers Valois*, 278–80; Perroy (1933), 133.

95 *Gr. chron.*, ii, 365; N. de Pauw, 'L'adhésion du clergé de Flandre au pape Urbain VI et les évêques urbanistes de Gand (1375–1395)', *Bull. Comm. Royale d'Histoire*, lxxiii (1904), 692–702.

96 Portugal: J.C. Baptista, 'Portugal e o cisma de occidente', *Lusitania Sacra*, i (1956), 65–203, at 109, 114; Lopes, *Crón. D. Fernando*, 409–10; 'Dispacci di C. da Piacenza', 302–3. For the diplomatic background: Valois (1891); Perroy (1933), 215–17; Russell, 296–300; *Valois (1891), 513–15. Castile: Ayala, *Crón.*, ii, 140–50; the treaty of Bicêtre between Castile and France had been made (by Ayala) a month before, *Choix de pièces*, i, 14–20. Aragon: *Vitae paparum*, iv, 302–4. Navarre: J. Zunzunegui, *El reino de Navarra y su obispado de Pamplona durante la primera epoca del cisma de occidente* (1942), 139–42.

97 *Gr. chron.*, ii, 283; *Froissart, *Chron.* (KL), xviii, 545–7, 553–4; PRO E101/318/1, 2; *Mandements*, nos. 1631–3, 1635, 1638; *Lecoy, ii, 450; PRO E364/13, mm. 2d, 3 (Cobham), 4d (Skirlaw), 5, 5d (Segrave); 'Voyage de N. de Bosc', 307–27.

CHAPTER VIII

1 Saint-André, *Libvre*, 505–6; 'Extr. J. Trésor', 384n[2]; 'Chron. Brioc.', 49; *Gr. chron.*, ii, 349–53, *iii, 213–19.

2 Pocquet (1967), 152–3; Morice, *Preuves*, ii, 408.

3 See *Gr. chron.*, iii, 216–18 and Henneman (1996), 90–2.

4 *Chron. premiers Valois*, 283–4. John of Blois: PRO E403/447 (4 Mar.); E403/449, m. 16 (13 July); E403/461, m. 29 (13 Feb.); E403/471, m. 21 (17 Mar.).

5 Cazelles (1972), 539–40; Cazelles (1982), 560–8; Vuitry, ii, 653–64.

6 *Gr. chron.*, ii, 355, *iii, 215, 218–19; 'Chron. Brioc.', 49–50; *Chron. premiers Valois*, 283 (quotation); 'Chron. Brioc.', 52. Jeanne's arguments are reflected in B. d'Argentré, *Histoire de Bretagne*, 3rd ed. (1618), 588–90; *Songe du vergier*, i, 261–3.

7 *Parl. Rolls*, vi, 71, 73–9, 80–1 (9, 15–26, 29), 110–11 (5), 147–9 (10); Walsingham, *Chron. Maj.*, i, 246; *Hist. Vitae*, 52; *Eulogium*, iii, 345; *Foed.*, iv, 51. Date of dissolution: Tout (1920–37), iii, 342n[2].

8 Council: *Parl. Rolls*, vi, 110–11 (5). Berwick: *Letters N. Reg.*, 419–20; *Anonimalle*, 125–6; Walsingham, *Chron. Maj.*, i, 264–6; Fordun, *Chron.*, 382. Calais: *Parl. Rolls*, vi, 73–4 (15). Cherbourg: PRO C76/63, m. 10; E101/318/10; *Foed.*, iv, 57–8. Brest: PRO E101/38/28. Gascony: *Froissart, *Chron.*, xviii, 550–2 (April 1380).

9 *Doc. Clos des Galées*, ii, nos. 1069–96; *Foed.*, iv, 49, 51–2, 56; *CPR 1377–81*, 168; PRO E101/38/26; E403/472, m. 15 (1 Apr.). Finance: *Parl. Rolls*, vi, 110–11 (5), 124 (30), 148–9 (10); *Foed.*, iv, 57–9; *Cal. Letter Books H*, 119–21, 122–3; *CPR 1377–81*, 635–8,

390; *Antient Kalendars*, ii, 4 (no. 2); Steel (1954), 18, 39, 40; PRO C76/63, mm. 6, 4, 3; Walsingham, *Chron. Maj.*, i, 270.

10 PRO C76/63, m. 3; E403/471, m. 21 (17 Mar.); PRO E403/472, m. 16 (1 Apr.).

11 'Chron. Brioc.', 49, 52–3; Morice, *Preuves*, ii, 402–3, 406, 408–9.

12 *Gr. chron.*, ii, 355–61, 363; 'Chron. Brioc.', 52–3, 214–18; Walsingham, *Chron. Maj.*, i, 270; *Hay du Chastelet, 468, 469–70.

13 *Moranvillé (1888), 319–20; 'Chron. Brioc.', 52–3; Morice, *Preuves*, ii, 402–3, 406, 407, 408, 409.

14 *Parl. Rolls*, vi, 110–12 (3–7), 113–14 (11–12); 148 (10); Froissart, *Chron.* (SHF), ix, 138; Morice, *Preuves*, ii, 220–3.

15 *Parl. Rolls*, vi, 114–17 (13–18), 148 (10); CFR, ix, 139–40, 145, 158–9.

16 Morice, *Preuves*, ii, 223–5, 226–7, 392–4, 396–410; *Doc. Clos des Galées*, i, nos. 1078, 1082, 1084, 1089, 1094–1117; *Gr. chron.*, ii, 363–4.

17 Steel (1954), 40; Fenwick, *Poll Taxes*, i, p. xx, xxv–xxvi; CFR, ix, 162–4; Oman, p. xii n[6].

18 Walsingham, *Chron. Maj.*, i, 294; Morice, *Preuves*, ii, 221, 224, 226, 230; PRO E101/39/1; E101/318/21; E364/13, m. 2 (Stanley), 4d (Skirlaw). 'Guidance': *Foed.*, iv, 67; and draft treaty in John IV, *Actes*, i, no. 307. The fleet made first for the Seine: *Hay du Chastelet, 480 (letter dated 28 July off the mouth of the Orne).

19 Walsingham, *Chron. Maj.*, i, 294–304; Morice, *Preuves*, ii, 225; *Hay du Chastelet, 480; *Letters B. du Guesclin*, no. 866.

20 Morice, *Preuves*, ii, 224–5, 396–410; *Gr. chron.*, ii, 362–3; 'Séjours', 262. Anjou was at Montargis on 7 Aug.: *Hist. gén. Lang.*, ix, 870.

21 Correspondence of Louis of Anjou in *Hay du Chastelet, 467–80, Morice, *Preuves*, ii, 223–31, and *Letters B. du Guesclin*, nos. 866, 868–9, 875; Walsingham, *Chron. Maj.*, i, 294–304 (apparently based on a news-letter from an Englishman with the Admirals); 'Chron. Brioc.', 53–5; itinerary in John IV, *Actes*, i, 64. The fleet returned to Southampton on 14 Aug.: PRO E101/39/1.

22 *Letters B. du Guesclin*, nos. 866, 868; *Hay du Chastelet, 474–5, 480; BN Fr. 10238/126; John IV, *Actes*, i, no. 325; Morice, *Preuves*, ii, 233–6, 394. Desertions: Contamine (1972), 169–70. Anjou's movements: *Hay du Chastelet, 478; BN Clair. 90/3731. Du Guesclin's attempted resignation: *Chron. Bourbon*, 112–15; cf. Deschamps, *Oeuvres*, ii, 331 (ll. 196–212).

23 PRO E101/318/10, 21; E364/25, m. 4 (Hambrugg); E403/472, mm. 17, 18 (6 June, 16 July, 1, 6 Aug.); *Foed.*, iv, 65–6.

24 *Foed.*, iv, 67–8, 69; PRO E364/13, mm. 6–6d (Rous, Brocas, Codford); Cambridge, UL Ms. Dd. III.53, fol. 89 (Robesart's letters of credence to the rulers of Flanders, Brabant, Hainault and Juliers). St.-Pol in England: *Foed.*, iii, 1024, 1025; *Anonimalle*, 76–7; Walsingham, *Chron. Maj.*, i, 348–50; Froissart, *Chron.* (SHF), ix, 135–6.

25 PRO E364/13, mm. 6–6d (Rous, Brocas, Codford); *Chronographia*, ii, 369; *Gr. chron.*, ii, 370–1; *Chron. Tournai*, 215; Froissart, *Chron.* (SHF), ix, 137; *Chron. premiers Valois*, 281. Coucy's service began on 1 Oct.: Morice, *Preuves*, ii, 408. St.-Pol's fate: Walsingham, *Chron. Maj.*, i, 348–50; *Gr. chron.*, ii, 370–1; *Chron. r. St.-Denis*, i, 36.

26 CPR 1377–81, 420–1; *Parl. Rolls*, vi, 165 (27); PRO E101/38/30, mm. 1–3; *Anonimalle*, 131–2; Walsingham, *Chron. Maj.*, i, 324–40; Froissart, *Chron.* (SHF), ix, 209–11. Arundel died on 15 or 16 Dec.: *Cal. Inq. P.M.*, xv, 179–89. Cornwall: PRO E101/38/30, m. 4.

27 Tax base: *Hist. gén. Lang.*, *x, 1440–3; BN Lat. 9176, fols. 121–125vo. Anjou's demands: Dognon, 611–14; Mascaro, 'Libre', 71; *Hist. gén. Lang.*, ix, 866–9, *x, 1588–90 (misdated), 1602, 1609–12, 1630–2; BN Lat. 9175, fols. 241–53; *Arch. Montpellier*, i, no. 3928, ii, nos. 82, 85, 90, 841–2; *L. Menard, iii, 14–16, 19; *Douze comptes d'Albi*, i, 270 (482); Bardon, 107–9. Messenger: BN Coll. Languedoc 159, fol. 157.

28 BN Fr. 10238/126; *Hist. gén. Lang.*, x, 1443, 1444; A. Germain (1847), 7; *A. Germain (1851), 388–401; *Petit Thalamus*, 398; Mascaro, 'Libre', 71, 72; *Gr. chron.*, ii, 368–9.

29 L. Menard, iii, 19–26 (esp. 23), 36–45, *64; *Hist. gén. Lang., x, 1432–9, 1605, 1609–12; Arch. Montpellier, i, nos. 683–4 (income tax).

30 Arch. Montpellier, i, no. 2746; Petit Thalamus, 399; Gr. chron., ii, 371–6; Chron. premiers Valois, 281–2; AN JJ119/147, 121/185.

31 Mascaro, 'Libre', 73; *Blanc, 206–8; Gr. chron., ii, 376–7; Chron. r. St.-Denis, i, 92–4, 572; Thes. nov. anecd., i, 1601 (will).

32 Mandements, nos. 1899–1900; Troubat, i, 714–16, 725–31, *229–33; Inv. AC Montferrand, i, 406, 408. Tuchins: Chron. r. St.-Denis, i, 306–8; Reg. St.-Flour, 80–1, 98, 106; Boudet (1895), 20–45.

33 *Troubat, i, 233; Cazelles (1982), 566–7; Ord., vi, 442–9.

34 Parl. Rolls, vi, 147–52 (10–15). Scrope: Foed., iv, 75; Higden, Polychron., Cont. (iv), 402.

35 *Froissart, Chron., ix, 510–11, xviii, 550–2; PRO E403/472, mm. 19, 20 (9, 23 Sept.); PRO E364/15, m. 4d (Neville), m. 5 (Stratton), m. 6d (Trailly), m. 12 (Roches), m. 12 (Sandys and Craddock); E364/16, m. 5d (Lamb); E364/17, m. 5 (Etton); E364/23, m. 3d (Trivet); Dipl. Corr., 12, 183–4, 194.

36 John IV, Actes, i, no. 326, 333–4; Hanserecesse, ii, 217; *Hay du Chastelet, 479; Foed., iv, 77–8; Morice, Preuves, ii, 241–2; PRO E403/478, mm. 21, 22 (21, 23, 28 May). Buckingham's expedition: Anonimalle, 132; PRO 364/15, mm. 13 (Calveley), 13 (Bassét), 13d (Buckingham), 13d (Holgrave); E364/16, mm. 1d (Percy), 2 (Stassa & Merkeryn), 3d (Drayton & Frank); E364/19, m. 6 (Hastings), m. 6 (Wenk), m. 8 (Verteyne); and the companies of Latimer, Knolles and Harleston (no audited accounts) to whom advances were paid: PRO E403/478, mm. 21, 22, 29 (21, 23, 28, 29 May).

37 Parl. Rolls, vi, 153–4 (16,17); Foed., iv, 92 ('travailler pur final esploit de notre guerre'). On Gildesburgh, Controversy Scrope Grosvenor, i, 217–18; Hist. Parl. 1386–1421, iii, 186–7.

38 King's fleet: PRO E101/36/14; E101/37/25, m. 1; E101/37/27 (52, 149); E101/38/13, 24; CPR 1377–81, 543–4; PRO E364/20, m. 3 (Lincoln). Barges: Foed., iv, 24, 106; PRO E101/37/25, mm. 1–5. 1379; E101/38/30. There is no sign of the barges in the (unfortunately damaged) fleet account for 1380: PRO E101/39/2, mm. 1–2, 7–8. Facilities: PRO E101/38/24.

39 255 ships had been requisitioned in 1369: PRO E101/36/14. 158 ships were requisitioned at different times in 1377: PRO E403/463, mm. 12, 16–18 (26 May, 20 June), E101/37/14–20, 24; 188 in the summer of 1378, the largest number requisitioned in the early years of Richard II: PRO E101/37/24, 25; 155 in the winter of 1378–9: PRO E101/38/18; ca. 90 in the autumn of 1379: PRO E101/38/30, mm. 1–3; 123 in the summer of 1380: PRO E101/39/2, mm. 7–8. Tonnages calculated from the fleet lists of 1369: PRO E101/36/14; and 1380: PRO E101/39/2.

40 Barges: e.g. fleets of 1378 (PRO E101/37/25, mm. 1–5) and 1380 (PRO E101/37/25); Canterbury Tales, Prologue, ll. 408–9 (in Works, iv, 13). Privateers: CPR 1377–81, 405; PRO E364/18, m. 3d (Hauley); Parl. Rolls, vi, 274 (15); Foed., iv, 170; PRO C76/68, m. 25; CCR 1381–5, 367–8, 380; Westminster Chron., 40. On Hauley: see Hist. Parl., iii, 328–31; New Maritime History of Devon, ed. M. Duffy et al., i (1992), 91.

41 Parl. Rolls, vi, 179–80 (47), vii, 23–4 (28), 51 (30). Foreign charters: e.g., in 1373, BL Add. Mss. 37494, fols. 21–23; in 1378, PRO E364/11, m. 8 (Craling); E101/318/10. Fleet of 1380: PRO E101/39/2, mm. 2–5, 7–8.

42 Foed., iv, 82; Walsingham, Chron. Maj., i, 364; Hist. Vitae, 59; PRO C76/64, m. 11; E364/15, m. 13d (Buckingham). Treaty: *Terrier de Loray, PJ. no. 67. Measures were taken to defend the Isle of Wight (one of the targets specified in the treaty) against a Franco-Castilian galley fleet on 22 April 1380: CPR 1377–81, 510.

43 Lopes, Crón. D. Fernando, 303–10, 317–24; Ayala, Crón., ii, 125.

44 Dias Arnaut, 19–26; Lopes, Crón. D. Fernando, 347–84.

45 Lopes, Crón. D. Fernando, 417–18; *Russell, 566.

46 John of G. Reg. (1379–83), no. 327 (pp. 109–10); Cambridge, UL Ms. Dd. III.53, fol. 33vo; Ayala, Crón., ii, 131; *Dias Arnaut, 296–324.

47 Walsingham, *Chron. Maj.*, i, 408; *Foed.*, iv, 86–7; Cambridge, UL Ms. Dd. III.35, fols. 33vo, 35vo. Portugal had at least 21 galleys and a galiot in 1381: Lopes, *Crón. D. Fernando*, 439.

48 Lopes, *Crón. D. Fernando*, 418–19, 487; *Foed.*, iv, 93–5.

49 Lopes, *Crón. D. Fernando*, 419–20; *Col. doc. Murcia*, xi, no. 37; Ayala, *Crón.*, ii, 131–2.

50 *Petit Thalamus*, 400; *Gr. chron.*, ii, 377–8; *Inv. AC Montferrand*, i, 411; *Chronographia*, ii, 393; *Chron. Bourbon*, 118–19; Froissart, *Chron.* (SHF), ix, 232–3;

51 *Terrier de Loray, PJ nos. 67 (p. liv), 71 (pp. lxi, lxii); Walsingham, *Chron. Maj.*, i, 368–70 (exaggerated); *Mandements*, no. 1940; *Doc. Clos des Galées*, i, no. 1145; PRO E403/481, m. 11 (11 Dec.) (reporting 25 galleys). Buckingham: *ibid.*

52 *Terrier de Loray, PJ. no. 71 (p. lxii); Walsingham, *Chron. Maj.*, i, 372–4; *Hist. Vitae*, 60.

53 *Terrier de Loray, PJ. no. 71 (pp. lxii–lxiii); *Foed.*, iv, 97; Higden, *Polychron.*, Cont. (ii), 241; Ayala, *Crón.*, ii, 130; *Cal. Letter Books H*, 153; *Mems. London*, 444–5. On Philpot: Walsingham, *Chron. Maj.*, i, 224–8, 364–6; Steel (1954), 21, 38, 43.

54 *Parl. Rolls*, vi, 200 (34).

55 *Terrier de Loray, PJ. no. 71; *Doc. Clos des Galées*, i, nos. 1078, 1082, 1084, 1089, 1094–1117, 1162, 1134, 1136, 1143.

56 Froissart, *Chron.* (SHF), ix, 238, 239, 240, 243, 247, 251, 253–4; PRO E364/16, m. 1d (Percy). Froissart's dates are corroborated by record evidence. Discharge from the ships was completed on 22 July: PRO E403/481, m. 11 (11 Dec.). The army was at Aire (38 miles from Calais) on '27 or 28 July': *Inv. AD Pas-de-Calais*, ii, 121.

57 *Mandements*, no. 1935, 1937; *Plancher, iii, PJ., no. 69; Petit, 359–60; *Gr. chron.*, ii, 379; Froissart, *Chron.* (SHF), ix, 242–4, 246–7, 248, 250, 251. Ports: *Foed.*, iv, 86. Coucy: BN Clair. 30/2221; cf. 13/847, 14/923, 31/2344, 35/2640, 59/4565, 99/34, etc.

58 Desobry; Froissart, *Chron.* (SHF), ix, 252–5; Deschamps, *Oeuvres*, v, 5–7, 17, 42–3.

59 Froissart, *Chron.* (SHF), ix, 255, 256, 258–68; *Chronographia*, ii, 393–4; *Inv. AC Montferrand*, i, 411; *Chron. premiers Valois*, 286; Walsingham, *Chron. Maj.*, i, 382–4. Date: *Itin. Ph. le Hardi*, 148. Knighthoods: PRO E101/39/7.

60 BN PO 549, Bueil/14, 18, 22; 845/Conti 3; 1775, de Varie/7; 1798, Maille/43; BN PO 1868, Martel 32; 2861, Tour d'Aubergne/18; BN Clair. 8/479, 9/543, 12/131, 747, 22/1547, 1605, 30/2191, 32/2385, 35/2609, 36/2677, 70/5461, 71/5557, etc.; Petit, 360–1, 449; *Inv. mobiliers Bourgogne*, ii, no. 459; Froissart, *Chron.* (SHF), ix, 277, 284, 286; *Comptes Tours*, ii, no. 943. Death of King: BN Coll. Bourgogne 24, fol. 45vo; *Gr. chron.*, ii, 382.

61 Christine de Pisan, *Advision Cristine*, 98; *Gr. chron.*, ii, 382; *Comptes hôtel*, 35, 37, 208, 210; *Chron. r. St.-Denis*, i, 22–4.

62 *Ord.*, vi, 26–30, 45–54; Charles's will at *Gr. chron.*, iii, 183–99, 219–24 (esp. 196–7, 199). Cf. P. Dupuy, *Traité de la majorité de nos rois et des régences dy royaume* (1655), 190–2; O. Martin, *Histoire de la coutume de la prévôté et vicomté de Paris*, i (1922), 172–3.

63 AN X^ia 1471, fol. 382–382vo; *Gr. chron.*, ii, 382–3; *Chron. r. St.-Denis*, i, 8, 24–6, 30–2, 36–8, 40; *Hist. gén. Lang.*, x, 1646. Clisson was appointed on 1 Oct. 1380: AN K57^A/17.

64 Berry: *Chron. r. St.-Denis*, i, 90. Naples: Gatari, *Cronaca Carrarese*; *RISS²*, xvii. 1, 181–3, 185–6; Niem, *De Scismate*, 39–42; Jarry (1906).

65 *Chron. r. St.-Denis*, i, 6–16, 26–8, 40–2, 90–2; AN X^ia 1471, fol. 382vo; *Ord.*, vi, 529–32; Froissart, *Chron.* (SHF), ix, 287–8; Luce (1875). Vincennes cash: *Mandements*, no. 1956.

66 *Notices et extraits BN*, i, 342; *Ord.*, vii, 710–11; Finot (1889); Mirot (1905)[1], 5n¹.

67 *Arch. Montpellier*, i, no. 1823; *L. Menard, iii, 32; *Inv. AC Montferrand*, i, 415; *Chron. r. St.-Denis*, i, 20–2; *Arch. St.-Quentin*, ii, no. 754 (p. 349); *Choix de pièces*, i, 20; *Chronographia*, ii, 397; Mirot (1905)[1], 21n¹; *Gr. chron.*, iii, 1.

68 *Chron. premiers Valois*, 289; Froissart, *Chron.* (SHF), x, 1; *Chron. r. St.-Denis*, i, 14, 16–18, 40; BN Clair. 23/120; Morice, *Preuves*, ii, 257–62, 291–2; *Chron. Bourbon*, 120.

69 Froissart, *Chron.* (SHF), ix, 268–70, 279–80, 287–8, x, 1–3, 18–19; Walsingham, *Chron. Maj.*, i, 388; *Chron. r. St.-Denis*, i, 56–8; Froissart, *Chron.* (SHF), x, 18–19.

70 Froissart, *Chron.* (SHF), x, 4–9; Higden, *Polychron.*, Cont. (iv), 403–4; Morice, *Preuves*, ii, 294–6.

71 *Gr. chron.*, iii, 1; *Chron. r. St.-Denis*, i, 28–30; *Chron. Bourbon*, 119–20; 'Chron. Brioc.', 56; Froissart, *Chron.* (SHF), x, 9.

72 *Chron. Bourbon*, 121; Froissart, *Chron.* (SHF), x, 13, 17–18. Reinforcements: *Parl. Rolls*, vi, 188 (4); PRO E403/481, mm. 20–1 (28 Feb., 2 Mar.). *CCR 1377–81*, 485 suggests that Buckingham's call for reinforcements had reached England in early Nov. Nantes topography: Leguay, 171–2 and plan of the 15th-century city at 262. Paris: *Gr. chron.*, iii, 1; *Chron. r. St.-Denis*, i, 34; 'Chron. Brioc.', 57; John IV, *Actes*, no. 354.

73 *Gr. chron.*, iii, 1–2; *Chron. premiers Valois*, 291.

74 Déprez, 9–29; Geremek, 23–29; *Chron. r. St.-Denis*, i, 100; Le Roux de Lincy, 180; *Gr. chron.*, ii, 143.

75 *Chron. r. St.-Denis*, i, 44–56; *Gr. chron.*, iii, 2–3; *Chronographia*, iii, 2–3; *Chron. premiers Valois*, 291–2; *Ord.*, vi, 527–8. Date: AN X^{Ia} 1471, fol. 443; Mirot (1905)[1], 36 and n[4].

76 *Coville (1894), 390; *Froissart, *Chron.* (KL), xviii, 558; *Chron. premiers Valois*, 292–3; Mirot (1905)[1], 41–5. Reports: see *Chron. r. St.-Denis*, i, 40; *Choix de pièces*, i, 58–9.

77 *Ord.*, vi, 552–4, 564–6. Grant: *Arch. admin. Reims*, iii, 512–16; *Hist. gén. Lang.*, x, 1646; *Gr. chron.*, iii, 11; *Chron. premiers Valois*, 293–4; *Istore*, ii, 172; *Choix de pièces*, i, 9–13; *Coville (1894), 391–5; Mirot (1905)[1], 51–6.

78 Ireland: *Doc. Affairs Ireland*, no. 265; PRO E403/475, mm. 18, 22 (12 Oct., 23 Feb.); Higden, *Polychron.*, Cont. (ii), 241, Cont. (iv), 402–3. Scotland: *Northern Petitions*, nos. 115–17; Bower, *Scotichron.*, vii, 380, 396; *Hist. Vitae*, 59, 60–1; *Foed.*, iv, 96–7, 100; PRO E364/14, m. 7 (Waltham), m. 8d (Segrave and Beauchamp), 9d (Skirlaw); PRO E403/478, mm. 25, 26, 26–7 (25 July, 17 Aug., 8 Sept.).

79 Cost of Buckingham's army. War wages for six months (£60,807): PRO E403/475, m. 23 (22 Mar.); E403/478, mm. 21, 22, 23, 27, 29 (21, 23, 28, 29 May, 26 June, 10, 12 Sept.). Shipping costs (£15,639): PRO E403/475, m. 23 (17 Mar.); E403/478, mm. 18, 19, 22, 23, 24, 28 (30 Apr., 1 May, 2, 18 June, 6 July, 12 Sept.); E403/481, mm. 1, 11 (1 Oct., 11 Dec.). Back wages: PRO E403/475, mm. 23, 24 (12, 23 Mar.); E403/478, mm. 18, 22, 28, 29, 30, 31 (30 Apr., 30 May, 12, 13 Sept.). Other commitments: the estimate assumes £10,000 on reinforcing Buckingham (PRO E403/481, mm. 20–21, 22, 24 (28 Feb., 2, 13 Mar., 1 Apr.)) plus an estimated £2,000 on associated shipping; £24,000 p.a. on Calais (*Parl. Rolls*, vi, 73 (15)); £5,500 p.a. on Brest and £8,000 p.a. on Cherbourg, for which see above; £10,000 due under the Earl of March's indenture for Ireland, to Feb. 1381 (PRO 101/246/13); £6,000 on Scotland (PRO E403/478, mm. 25, 26–7 (25 July, 8 Sept.)); and about £20,000 on Portugal (PRO E403/481, mm. 20, 24 (23, 26 Feb., 5, 6 Apr.), E403/484, m. 1, 2, 12, 13 (23, 30 Apr., 2 Aug.)). Total: £278,000. Revenue: Ormrod (1995), 147 (fig. 23) (full figures at ESFDB/orm/engd030); Ormrod (1999), 164 (full figures, net of collection costs, at ESFDB/orm/engd007). Parliament: *CCR 1377–81*, 477–8.

80 Walsingham, *Chron. Maj.*, i, 400; *Parl. Rolls*, vi, 187–8, 190 (1, 3, 4, 10, 11); *Foed.*, iv, 99.

81 *Parl. Rolls*, vi, 190–2 (12–16). Quotation: *Eulogium*, iii, 345. For the earlier assessments, see Oman, p. xii n[6].

82 *Parl. Rolls*, vi, 199 (30); *Rec. Convoc.*, iv, 40–3. The northern province granted a similar tax in January: *CFR*, ix, 252; *Rec. Convoc.* xiii, 202.

83 PRO E403/481, mm. 19, 20–1 (14, 23, 26, 28 Feb., 2 Mar.); E403/484, m. 13 (2 Aug.); E101/68/8 (200), E101/68/9 (201–12); E364/23, m. 8 (Hannay), E364/30, m. 1d (Welle); *Foed.*, iv, 103–4.

84 *Chron. Bourbon*, 122–7; Froissart, *Chron.* (SHF), x, 19–24; Higden, *Polychron.*, Cont. (ii), 240–1; Walsingham, *Chron. Maj.*, i, 390; 'Chron. Britannicum', 114. French reinforcements: Morice, *Preuves*, ii, 297–8. Desertion: *CCR 1377–81*, 485.

85 Morice, *Preuves*, ii, 280–1, 298–301; Froissart, *Chron.* (SHF), x, 42.
86 PRO E101/68/8 (187, 200); E101/68/9 (201–12); E364/21, m. 3 (Veel & Passelew); E364/22, mm. 5d (Roches), 7d (West); E403/481, mm. 20–1 (28 Feb., 2 Mar.); C76/65, m. 16; cf. *Foed.*, iv, 106, and *CPR 1377–81*, 607 (impressment of smiths). Barges were being prepared for the siege until at least 17 March: PRO E364/16, m. 10 (Orwell).
87 PRO E364/15, m. 13d (Buckingham); E364/16, m. 1d (Percy); E364/15, m. 13 (Calveley); John IV, *Actes*, no. 362; Froissart, *Chron.* (SHF), x, 25–8, 34–9, 42–3; *Chron. Bourbon*, 130–5. Buckingham arrived at Vannes before 27 Feb. 1381: *CPR 1377–81*, 235; John de Montfort left Vannes before 5 March: *Actes*, no. 356.
88 PRO E364/15, m. 13 (Basset); E364/15, m. 13d (Buckingham). Cf. E364/16, m. 1d (Percy), m. 6 (Wenk), m. 8 (Verteyne); E364/19, m. 6 (Hastings); PRO E101/318/32; E364/16, m. 10 (Orwell), m. 10d (Orwell). College: R. Gough, *The History and Antiquities of Pleshy* (1803), 180.
89 Felton: PRO E364/21, m. 3 (Veel & Passelew), E364/22, mm. 5d (Roches), 7d (West); *John of G. Reg. (1379–83)*, nos. 522–3, 1095. Cambridge: PRO E403/481, m. 25 (6 Apr.); *Foed.*, iv, 118. Gaunt: *Foed.*, iv, 110–11; *John of G. Reg. (1379–83)*, nos. 500–1, 1223; PRO E403/484, m. 3 (10 May); E364/14, m. 11d (Bp. Hereford). Montfort: *CFR*, ix, 274–5; *Cal. Inq. Misc.*, vi, no. 23; PRO E364/21, m. 3 (Veel & Passelew). Clisson: Froissart, *Chron.* (SHF), x, 169; Jones (1972), 13–19. Joan: PRO C76/66, m. 30; Morice, *Preuves*, ii, 380; *Foed.*, vii, 360, 414; PRO C81/481/2881.

CHAPTER IX

1 Deschamps, *Oeuvres*, i, 113, 203; cf. iii, 131–2.
2 *Inv. Arch. Bruges*, ii, 367–70; 'Chron. Com. Fland.', 235; Nicholas (1987), 240–1; 'Chron. Com. Fland.', 235–6 (dates unreliable); Froissart, *Chron.* (SHF), ix, 165–78, 182–6; *Rek. Gent*, 115; *Cron. Tournay*, 218–19; *Istore*, ii, 164, 183, 221–6; *Chron. rimée*, 12; *Memorieboek Ghent*, i, 105–8; 'Chron. Pays-Bas', 266. Background: Nicholas (1971), 138–41; Nicholas (1987), Ch. 9. On Van den Bossche: see Nicholas (1988), 144–6.
3 *Istore*, ii, 164, 183–5; Froissart, *Chron.* (SHF), ix, 192–4, 199; *Itin. Ph. le Hardi*, 146; *Chron. r. St.-Denis*, i, 108; Dixmude, *Merkw. Geb.*, 2–3; *Cron. Tournay*, 219; *Chron. rimée*, 13–16.
4 *Chron. Rimée*, 16–23; Froissart, *Chron.* (SHF), ix, 187–92; *Cron. Tournay*, 220; *Istore*, ii, 228; AD Côte-d'Or B11737; BN Coll. Bourgogne 21, fol. 11vo; *Rek. Gent*, 441–5.
5 Froissart, *Chron.* (SHF), ix, 231–2; *Istore*, ii, 233; 'Chron. Pays-Bas', 268; *Itin. Ph. le Hardi*, 147.
6 *Cron. Tournay*, 234–5; *Istore*, ii, 189, 234; Froissart, *Chron.* (SHF), ix, 227–8, 230; *Chron. rimée*, 42–4.
7 *Chron. rimée*, 42–5, 52–5, 101; *Hanserecesse*, ii, 234; 'Chron. Com. Fland.', 236–8; *Istore*, ii, 173–4, 192–3, 236–40; Froissart, *Chron.* (SHF), x, 52–9; *Gr. chron.*, ii, 380, iii, 3; *Cron. Tournay*, 237; *Rek. Gent*, 449–50.
8 Gower, 'Confessio Amantis', Prol. ll. 499–528 (*Works*, ii, 18–19); *Parl. Rolls*, vi, 36–7 (54), 47–8 (88). Background: R. Faith, 'The "Great Rumour" and peasant ideology', *The English Rising of 1381*, ed. R.H. Hilton and T.H. Aston (1984), 43–73.
9 Brinton, *Sermons*, i, 194–200; Walsingham, *Chron. Maj.*, i, 152–4; *Parl. Rolls*, vi, 275 (17); C. Petit-Dutaillis, 'Les prédications populaires. Les Lollards et le soulèvement des travailleurs anglais en 1381', *Études d'histoire du moyen age dédiées à Gabriel Monod* (1896), 373–88; G.R. Owst, *Literature and Pulpit in Medieval England*, 2nd ed. (1961), Ch. VI; Langland, *Piers Plowman*, i, 13–18 (B Text, Prol.).
10 Oman, 27–9, 164–6 (App. II); *CFR*, ix, 248–50; *Parl. Rolls*, vi, 324–5 (6); *Anonimalle*, 134–5; Brooks, 252, 254–5.
11 *Anonimalle*, 136–7; Walsingham, *Chron. Maj.*, i, 412; Froissart, *Chron.* (SHF), x, 98, 100–2, 108.

12 Walsingham, *Chron. Maj.*, i, 412–14; *Anonimalle*, 136–7; R.H. Hilton, *Bond men made free* (1973), 180–4; Brooks, 256, 260–7. Haselden: *Parl. Rolls*, vi, 233–58 (54); *CPR 1381–5*, 76. Trivet: Réville, 185, 187.

13 *Anonimalle*, 137–9; Walsingham, *Chron. Maj.*, i, 544–8; Knighton, *Chron.*, 222–4; Froissart, *Chron.* (SHF), x, 95–7. On Ball's past career: *CPR 1361–4*, 470; *Concilia*, iii, 64–5, 152–3.

14 Saul (1997), 469; *Anonimalle*, 139; Froissart, *Chron.* (SHF), x, 108–10; Knighton, *Chron.*, 210–12.

15 *Cal. Letter Books H*, 163; Oman, 165 (App. II); Tout (1920–37), iii, 364; B. Putnam, *The Enforcement of the Statute of Labourers* (1908), 155–6.

16 *Anonimalle*, 138–9; Walsingham, *Chron. Maj.*, i, 414–16.

17 *Anonimalle*, 140–3, 144; Walsingham, *Chron. Maj.*, i, 418; *Westminster Chron.*, 4; Knighton, *Chron.*, 214–16; *Mems. London*, 449–50. Horne: *Réville, 190–8; Bird, 52–61.

18 Oman, 99–128.

19 *John of G. Reg. (1379–83)*, nos. 530–6, 541, 548–51, 559–61, 563–4, 1096–7, 1186–8; Knighton, *Chron.*, 230, 232–6; PRO C49/F12/11; *Walker (1991), 68–9; *Anonimalle*, 152–3, 155–6.

20 *Anonimalle*, 143–50; Froissart, *Chron.* (SHF), x, 109–10, 116–24; Walsingham, *Chron. Maj.*, i, 422–40; Knighton, *Chron.*, 212, 218–20; *Westminster Chron.*, 4–12; *Mems. London*, 450–1; *Eulogium*, iii, 353–4.

21 *Anonimalle*, 149; Walsingham, *Chron. Maj.*, i, 514–16, 544–6; *Westminster Chron.*, 14–18; PRO E101/531/40; E364/21, m. 3 (Veel & Passelew), E364/22, mm. 5d (Roches), 7d (West); E403/484, m. 8 (25 June); *CPR 1381–5*, 18, 23, 69–71. Wraw: *Réville, 175–82.

22 *Parl. Rolls*, vi, 217–18, 221–2, 225–6 (17, 25–8, 36–7, 40).

23 1380: *Foed.*, iv, 83–4; PRO E101/318/20, 28; 'Voyage de N. de Bosc', 327–8. 1381: *Foed.*, iv, 122; PRO E101/318/36–38, E101/319/3; 'Voyage de N. de Bosc', 309–14, 317–27. 1382: *Foed.*, iv, 141; Le Fèvre, *Journal*, 26; 'Voyage de N. de Bosc', 326; Russell, 329–30.

24 PRO E101/39/17, mm. 1–2; E101/39/18, 22; Lopes, *Crón. D. Fernando*, 452–3. On Gournay: Leland, *Itin.*, i, 159; Cuvelier, *Chanson*, i, 217–23. On Beauchamp: Chandos Herald, *Prince Noir*, ll. 2250–2; Walker (1990)[1], 264.

25 'Dispacci di C. da Piacenza', 302–3; *Col. doc. Murcia*, xi, no. 67; Ayala, *Crón.*, ii, 151–2; Lopes, *Crón. D. Fernando*, 421; Russell, 315, 318; Froissart, *Chron.* (SHF), x, 164–5; *Choix de pièces*, i, 14–20; Ayala, *Crón.*, ii, 140–2; Valois (1896–1902), ii, 206 (but his argument does not convince). Olivier du Guesclin: AN JJ142/189, JJ143/299; Froissart, *Chron.* (SHF), x, 165. Charles, Infante of Navarre: ACA *reg.* 1271, fol. 149; *ibid.*, *reg.* 1276, fol. 96.

26 *Col. doc. Murcia*, xi, nos. 69–70, 72–3; Lopes, *Crón. D. Fernando*, 422–4, 475.

27 Lopes, *Crón. D. Fernando*, 425–50, 453; *Col. doc. Murcia*, xi, no. 78; Ayala, *Crón.*, ii, 152–3, 204; ACA *reg.* 1276, fols. 44vo–46.

28 Lopes, *Crón. D. Fernando*, 455–6, 459–61; Valois (1896–1902), ii, 207–8; Froissart, *Chron.* (SHF), x, 157–8; Perroy (1933), 122.

29 Ayala, *Crón.*, ii, 154–5; Lopes, *Crón. D. Fernando*, 455, 465–7.

30 ACA *reg.* 1276, fols. 44vo–46; Ayala, *Crón.*, ii, 152, 153–5; Lopes, *Crón. D. Fernando*, 449, 463–4; *Col. doc. Murcia*, xi, nos. 79–81, 83, 86, 112.

31 *Col. doc. Murcia*, xi, nos. 79, 81, 83; Lopes, *Crón. D. Fernando*, 467, 471–3.

32 *Parl. Rolls*, vi, 247–8 (66). Squire: PRO E404/12/82 (10 Dec.); E403/487, m. 14 (18 Dec.). Portuguese financial commitment: *Foed.*, iv, 94.

33 *Westminster Chron.*, 24; *Parl. Rolls*, vi, 247–9 (65–70).

34 'Dispacci di C. da Piacenza', 293, 303–4; Niem, *De Scismate*, 42–3; 'Diario d'anonimo fiorentino', 425; *Cron. siculum*, 37–8; *Diurnali Monteleone*, 25; Bouard, 47; Valois (1896–1902), ii, 8–12; Labande, 122–5; Léonard, 462–5. On events in Naples, see also

Diurnali Monteleone, 28–9; *Cron. siculum*, 38–9; and Gobelinus, *Cosm.*, 89–92.

35 Le Fèvre, *Journal*, 8–14, 21, 23. Clement VII's financial contribution: *ibid.*, 24; Valois (1896–1902), II, 24–9; Favier (1966), 614–15.

36 Le Fèvre, *Journal*, 3, 44; Gobelinus, *Cosm.*, 93; *Valois (1896–1902), ii, 39 and n² ('60,000 horses'), 444, 445. Companies: Labande, 141–2, 145–7.

37 E.-G. Léonard, 'La captivité et la mort de Jeanne Iʳᵉ de Naples', *Mélanges d'archéologie et d'histoire*, xli (1924), 43–77, at *68–9, 75–7; *Cron. siculum*, 46; *Vitae paparum*, i, 486–7; 'Diario d'anonimo fiorentino', 446; *Diurnali D. de Monteleone*, 32–3; 'Dispacci di C. da Piacenza', 317–20. And see Valois (1896–1902), ii, 41–60; Labande, 148–50. Hawkwood: Caferro, 220–1, 232–6, 237–40; Temple-Leader & Marcotti, 176–82.

38 Mirot (1905)[1], 64–5, 66n¹.

39 *Chronographia*, iii, 7–8; *Gr. chron.*, iii, 11–12; *Chron. r. St.-Denis*, i, 134; *Choix de pièces*, i, 24–6; *Coville (1894), 396–8; Mirot (1905)[1], 90–1.

40 Cochon, *Chron.*, 162–6; *Chron. premiers Valois*, 298–9; *Chéruel, 544–9; Mirot (1905)[1], 98–103. Pintoin: *Chron. r. St.-Denis*, i, 134.

41 *Chronographia*, iii, 22–6; *Gr. chron.*, iii, 12–13; *Chron. r. St.-Denis*, i, 136–40; Pitti, *Cron.*, 63–4; Mirot (1905), 115–26, 129–34. Hôtel d'Anjou: *ibid.*, 129n¹.

42 *Chronographia*, iii, 26–30, 28–9; *Chron. r. St.-Denis*, i, 140, 146–8; *Gr. chron.*, iii, 13–14; Pitti, *Cron.*, 64–5; Mirot (1905)[1], 95–7, 109–10, 127–9. Musters: *Itin. Ph. le Hardi*, 513; *Auctarium Chart. Univ. Paris.*, i, 618. Amiens: *Doc. Amiens*, i, 225–6.

43 Cochon, *Chron.*, 166–8; *Chron. premiers Valois*, 299–301; *Gr. chron.*, iii, 14–15; *Chron. r. St.-Denis*, i, 144; *Chronographia*, iii, 30–1.

44 *Chronographia*, iii, 30–1; *Chron. r. St.-Denis*, i, 148–50; *Chron. premiers Valois*, 301; *Doc. Amiens*, i, 225–6.

45 *Chronographia*, iii, 32–3, 36–7; *Chron. r. St.-Denis*, i, 152–6; *Chron. premiers Valois*, 302; Froissart, *Chron.* (SHF), x, 212; *Gr. chron.*, iii, 17–18; *Choix de pièces*, i, no. 18.

46 *Chron. premiers Valois*, 303–4; Cochon, *Chron.*, 168; Mirot (1905)[1], 157n⁵; *Coville (1894), 398–401.

47 Grammont: Froissart, *Chron.* (SHF), x, 142; *Istore*, ii, 244. For the third siege (June–July 1381): *Cron. Tournay*, 237–8, 239–40; Froissart, *Chron.* (SHF), x, 141, 145; 'Chron. Com. Fland.', 239; *Istore*, ii, 175, 199–200, 244–5; 'Chron. Pays-Bas', 273. Contagion: Pitti, *Cron.*, 63; *Doc. Amiens*, i, 225–6.

48 Froissart, *Chron.* (SHF), x, 145–7, 201–8; *Chron. Liégeoise de 1402*, 390–1; Quicke, 312–21. Provisioning raids: *Rek. Gent*, 257, 283, 284–301; Dixmude, *Merkw. Geb.*, 10–11; *Rek. Baljuws*, 387. Letters of support: F. Vercauteren, *Luttes sociales à Liège* (1943), 98.

49 Froissart, *Chron.* (SHF), x, 80–1, 139–40, 147, 150–1; *Rek. Gent*, 272–3, *451–2; *Rek. Baljuws*, 405–6; *Vlaamsche kron.*, 28–33; and see Nicholas (1988), 123–44, 153–9.

50 *Vlaamsche kron.*, 31, 33; Froissart, *Chron.* (SHF), x, 140, 202–7; *Rek. Baljuws*, 137–45, 486.

51 Froissart, *Chron.* (SHF), x, 84, 260; *CPR 1345–8*, 9; *CPR 1348–50*, 568; PRO E403/462, m. 8 (6 May); E403/493, m. 9 (30 Dec.); Palmer (1972), 245–6.

52 *Foed.*, iv, 141; *Parl. Rolls*, vi, 269–70, 271 (3, 9); *Westminster Chron.*, 24; PRO E364/15, m. 4 (Hereford); E403/487, m. 18 (10 Feb.).

53 *Palmer (1972), 245–6; *Parl. Rolls*, vi, 269–70, 271 (3, 9); *CCR 1381–5*, 121–2; *Foed.*, iv, 143; PRO E364/15, m. 7d (Cobham); *Westminster Chron.*, 24.

54 *Palmer (1972), 246; Froissart, *Chron.* (SHF), x, 207–11, 215–16; *Cron. Tournay*, 242; 'Chron. Pays-Bas', 275; *Istore*, ii, 177; Quicke, 318–19, 321. Spies: *Palmer (1972), 245–7.

CHAPTER X

1 *Istore*, ii, 204–5, 246–7, 257–8; 'Chron. Com. Fland.', 239–41; *Cron. Tournay*, 242–3; 'Chron. Pays-Bas', 275; *Vlaamsche kron.*, 34–6; *Gr. chron.*, iii, 15–17; *Chron. r. St.-*

Denis, i, 118, 168–70; *Chron. premiers Valois*, 302–3; Walsingham, *Chron. Maj.*, i, 604–8 (based on reports of English merchants); Froissart, *Chron.* (SHF), x, 220–34 (much embellished). Louis's English troop: **Chron. rimée*, 103.

2 *Istore*, ii, 177–8, 205–6, 247–8; *Cron. Tournay*, 244–5; 'Chron. Com. Fland.', 240, 241; *Vlaamsche kron.*, 36–8; **Chron. rimée*, 104. Outports: Froissart, *Chron.* (SHF), x, 236. Ypres: Dixmude, *Merkw. Geb.*, 12.

3 Froissart, *Chron.* (SHF), x, 244–9, , 259–61, 272–3; *Istore*, ii, 178, 206, 258; *Cron. Tournay*, 243–4; *Chron. r. St.-Denis*, i, 170–2.

4 *CCR 1381–5*, 53; Lopes, *Crón. D. Fernando*, 559.

5 Parliament: *Parl. Rolls*, vi, 269–70, 271–2 (1–4, 9–11); *CCR 1381–5*, 133–4. Finance: Steel (1954), 46, 436, 455; *Foed.*, iv, 147. Flanders: PRO E101/319/2. Fogaça: *Dipl. Corr.*, 19, 192; *Foed.*, iv, 149.

6 *Chronographia*, iii, 34–5; Froissart, *Chron.* (SHF), x, 238–9, 250–1, 261; *Istore*, ii, 207, 248–9.

7 *Jurades de Bergerac*, i, 75 (news-letter from seneschal of Périgord); **Froissart, *Chron.* (KL), xviii, 543–5 (misdated 1376); *Foed.*, iv, 147–8; Le Fèvre, *Journal*, 37.

8 Conference: PRO E101/319/4; Walsingham, *Chron. Maj.*, i, 806; *Chron. r. St.-Denis*, i, 124–6. Charles VI's ambassador Jean de Rye was in Castile at the end of 1381: ACA reg. 1271, fol. 174. Gilbert was in London from 29 June to 6 July: PRO E101/319/4. The decision must have been made during that week. Gaunt left London for the Midlands before 11 July and did not return until Oct.: Goodman (1992), 93. Richard II's letter of 26 Aug. to Peter IV of Aragon shows that the government had decided to support Gaunt's plans by that date: *Dipl. Corr.*, 19. Oudenaarde: PRO E101/318/9; E403/490, m. 9 (11 July); cf. *Rek. Gent*, 306. Fogaça: *Foed.*, iv, 149. Cease-fire: *Chron. r. St.-Denis*, i, 124–6.

9 ACA reg. 1274, fol. 27vo; Lopes, *Crón. D. Fernando*, 475–6.

10 Froissart, *Chron.* (SHF), x, 159–64; Lopes, *Crón. D. Fernando*, 466–7, 519–21; Walsingham, *Chron. Maj.*, i, 656.

11 Lopes, *Crón. D. Fernando*, 471–2, 487–520, 523. On John of Avis: Lopes, *Crón. D. Pedro*, 93, 275, 277–8.

12 Lopes, *Crón. D. Fernando*, 470; cf. Ayala, *Crón.*, ii, 157 (giving an estimate of 2,000 in July); Froissart, *Chron.* (SHF), x, 184–91. Treasuries: *Provas casa r. portuguesa*, i, 388.

13 Lopes, *Crón. D. Fernando*, 559; Ayala, *Crón.*, ii, 156, 204–5.

14 Lopes, *Crón. D. Fernando*, 523–4; Ayala, *Crón.*, ii, 157. Strengths: *ibid.*, and Lopes, *Crón. D. Fernando*, 470, 531–2. John's itinerary: Suarez Fernandez (1977), i, 398.

15 Froissart, *Chron.* (SHF), x, 192–3; Lopes, *Crón. D. Fernando*, 531–2.

16 Lopes, *Crón. D. Fernando*, 523–4, 534–6, 561; Ayala, *Crón.*, ii, 158–60; Suarez Fernandez (1977), i, 97–101.

17 *Quadro elementar*, i, 248–9; Lopes, *Crón. D. Fernando*, 541–4. Exiles: Russell, 343n[1]. Sotherey: PRO E403/505, m. 12 (24 Nov.).

18 PRO E101/319/4; *Chron. r. St.-Denis*, i, 174–8; *Chronographia*, iii, 38–9; *Chron. premiers Valois*, 304–5; *Chron. r. St.-Denis*, i, 178. Date of Council of Compiègne: 'Séjours', 416; *Itin. Ph. le Hardi*, 152. Muster: BN PO 2987, Vienne/52.

19 *Foed.*, iv, 153; *Dipl. Corr.*, 19–20; *CCR 1381–5*, 210–11.

20 Gaunt: Goodman (1992), 93; PRO E403/490, mm. 13, 14, 15 (13 Sept.). Fogaça: PRO E403/493, m. 3 (30 Oct.); *CPR 1381–5*, 191, 216. Flanders: PRO E101/319/2, 6; *Rek. Gent*, 344; *Rek. Gent*, 329; *Parl. Rolls*, vi, 280 (3); Walsinghman, *Chron. Maj.*, i, 624; *Foed.*, iv, 153.

21 Walsingham, *Chron. Maj.*, i, 490–4, 626; Froissart, *Chron.* (SHF), xi, 91; *Dipl. corr.*, 10–11, 187; Wykeham, *Reg.*, ii, 198–211.

22 Walsingham, *Chron. Maj.*, i, 572, 620–4.

23 Burley: Saul (1997), 113–14. Pole: *ODNB*, xliv, 709–10; *Parl. Rolls*, vi, 226 (38).

24 *Westminster Chron.*, 112.

25 'Séjours', 417; *Istore*, ii, 207; *Gr. chron.*, iii, 18. Helchin: 'Chron. Pays-Bas', 276; Froissart, *Chron.* (SHF), x, 249–50. Postponement: BN PO 2987, Vienne/52.

26 *Parl. Rolls*, vi, 281–4, 289, 296–7 (9–13, 15, 23, 46).

27 *Gr. chron.*, iii, 20–3; *Cron. Tournay*, 357–8; Froissart, *Chron.* (SHF), x, 274–5; *Cartul. Artevelde*, 364–5, 368–70; *Rek. Gent*, 330, *462.

28 *Gr. chron.*, iii, 23; *Chronographia*, iii, 39; *Rek. Gent*, 461–3. Troops: BN Clair. 15/996, 19/1303, 36/2740, 58/4427, 60/4623, etc. Dates: 'Séjours', 417; AD Côte d'Or B1460, fols. 143-3vo.

29 PRO E403/493, mm. 3, 4 (25, 31 Oct., 4 Nov.); C76/67, m. 22; Froissart, *Chron.* (SHF), x, 264, 267–9, xi, 27–8, 68–9; *Westminster Chron.*, 30.

30 'Séjours', 417; *Istore*, ii, 209–10; *Chronographia*, iii, 39. On Charles: *Chron. r. St.-Denis*, i, 22–4; *Comptes Écurie*, i, 38; *Gr. chron.*, iii, 23; *Istore*, ii, 210–11; Froissart, *Chron.* (SHF), x, 254 (quotation).

31 *Gr. chron.*, iii, 24–5; Pitti, *Cron.*, 60–1; Ayala, *Crón.*, ii, 164; *Chronographia*, iii, 40–1; *Istore*, ii, 211. Burgundy contingent: AD Côte d'Or B1460, fols. 144–58. His finances: BN Coll. Bourgogne 53, fols. 3vo, 4, 222; *Inv. mobiliers Bourgogne*, ii, nos. 594–721.

32 *Froissart, *Chron.* (KL), x, 467–8; *Mirot (1905)[1], 162–4, 166n^2, 170–5; *Dumay, 169–70, 170–1; Froissart, *Chron.* (SHF), xi, 32–3. For Nicholas's past: *Gr. chron.*, i, 221, iii, 43; *Chron. r. St.-Denis*, i, 240.

33 Froissart, *Chron.* (SHF), x, 286–8, 291–3. Ypres struggles: *Rek. Gent*, 454–7; *Rek. Baljuws*, 275–7.

34 *Gr. chron.*, iii, 25–30; *Istore*, ii, 211–13, 249–50; *Chron. r. St.-Denis*, i, 192–202; Froissart, *Chron.* (SHF), xi, 1–5, 8–26, 28–32, 33–5; *Chronographia*, iii, 41–2; *Chron. Bourbon*, 168–9; Dixmude, *Merkw. Geb.*, 14; *Cron. Tournay*, 248; 'Séjours', 417; Vandenpeerenboom, vii, 395–9.

35 *Gr. chron.*, iii, 27–8; *Istore*, ii, 213; *Chron. Bourbon*, 169–70; *Liv. mirac. Ste.-Catherine*, no. 58.

36 Froissart, *Chron.* (SHF), xi, 27–8, 38–9, 41–59; *Rek. Gent*, 331, 335; *Istore*, ii, 180–1, 214–16, 250–3; *Cron. Tournay*, 249–52; *Chron. Bourbon*, 170–4; *Chron. premiers Valois*, 306–7; Pitti, *Cron.*, 60–2; Ayala, *Crón.*, ii, 164–5; *Gr. chron.*, iii, 30–1; *Chron. r. St.-Denis*, i, 208–28; *Chronographia*, iii, 43–6. Bodyguard: BN Fr. n.a. 20528, fols. 129, 135. Broken on wheel: *Rek. Baljuws*, 286.

37 *Cron. Tournay*, 254; Froissart, *Chron.* (SHF), xi, 59, 61–4; *Chron. premiers Valois*, 307; *Chron. r. St.-Denis*, i, 224; *Gr. chron.*, iii, 31–2, 34–5; Pitti, *Cron.*, 62; *Chron. rimée*, 106–9; *Hanserecesse*, ii, 309–10; *Cron. Tournay*, 252–3; *Rek. Baljuws*, 104–6, 114, 240, 245, 250, 287–9, 433–4, 489–90, 492, 497–8, 533–4, 536–7, 544.

38 *Gr. chron.*, iii, 33–8; Froissart, *Chron.* (SHF), xi, 61–2, 66–8, 69–70, 72–3; *Froissart, *Chron.* (KL), x, 494–6; *Chron. r. St.-Denis*, i, 228–30; *Istore*, ii, 181, 217–18, 253; *Cron. Tournay*, 253, 254; Deschamps: *Oeuvres*, i, 201–2, cf. 92–7. The Duke of Burgundy paid off his troops on 20 December: AD Côte d'Or B1460, fol. 143vo.

39 *Chron. rimée*, 106–9. Cf. *Froissart, *Chron.* (KL), x, 495; Froissart, *Chron.* (SHF), xi, 73–4, 112–13; *Cron. Tournay*, 257; Walsingham, *Chron. Maj.*, i, 672 (Gravelines).

40 *Hanserecesse*, ii, 309; Walsingham, *Chron. Maj.*, i, 652; Froissart, Chron. (SHF), xi, 83–5; *Lefranc, 440; *Rek. Baljuws*, 104, 105 (executions). On the English community: Nicholas (1979). Staple: CCR 1381–5, 185, 188, 265; *Groot Charterboek der Graven van Holland en Zeeland*, ed. F. van Mieris, iii (1755), 383–4 (misdated); *Bronnen tot de Geschiedenis van den Handel met Engeland*, ed. H.J. Smit, i (1928), 345–7. Total exports of wool to all destinations fell in 1382–3 by about a quarter: Carus-Wilson & Coleman, 51. Prices: Lloyd (1973), 46.

41 'Ann. Arch. Datini', xii, 32; *Chron. rimée*, 107; *Gr. chron.*, iii, 29, 37; Froissart, *Chron.* (SHF), xi, 73.

42 *Gr. chron.*, iii, 39–53; *Chron. r. St.-Denis*, i, 230–48; *Chronographia*, iii, 47–52; Pitti, *Cron.*, 66–7; *Chron. premiers Valois*, 308–11; Froissart, *Chron.* (SHF), xi, 74–81; *Chron. Bourbon*, 175–9; *Ord.*, vi, 685–8; Mirot (1905)[1], 179–95.

43 *Chron. r. St.-Denis*, i, 242, 246–8; *Gr. chron.*, iii, 44, 48–52; *Ord.*, vii, 746–51.

44 *Chron. r. St.-Denis*, i, 248–54; Mirot (1905)[1], 196–7, 201; Froissart, *Chron.* (SHF), xi,

81–2; *Hist. gén. Lang.*, ix, 914, x, 124–5; *Rouquette, 497–8; *Inv. AC Toulouse*, 474; Dognon, 616–18; Lehoux, ii, 154–6; Rey (1965), i, 166–7, 324–5.

45 *CPR 1381–5*, 256; *Foed.*, iv, 156; *Perroy (1933), 408; *Dias Arnaut, 336–48; PRO E403/493, m. 14 (13 Feb.); *Parl. Rolls*, vi, 318 (22). In his will of 1398, Gaunt ordered that debts arising from the campaign should not be paid: *Armitage-Smith, 422.

46 Walsingham, *Chron. Maj.*, i, 662–4; Knighton, *Chron.*, 324, 330–2; *Westminster Chron.*, 32–6; *Eulogium*, iii, 356–7; Froissart, *Chron.* (SHF), xi, 87. Imposters: *Foed.*, iv, 163. Recruits: see the letters of protection at PRO C76/67, mm. 16–18.

47 *Foed.*, iv, 157–8; *Parl. Rolls*, vi, 309–10 (3); *Istore*, ii, 218, 221, 254, 281. Ackerman: *Foed.*, iv, 158–8; PRO E403/493, m. 18 (18 Mar.), E403/496, mm. 4, 8 (1 May, 8 July); *Rek. Gent*, 345; *Chron. rimée*, 110–11. Aardenburg: 'Chron. Com. Fland.', 242; Froissart, *Chron.* (SHF), xi, 82–3.

48 *Parl. Rolls*, vi, 309–10, 311–13 (3, 9–11), 316–18 (20–22), 332 (18); *Westminster Chron.*, 32–4, 34–6; Walsingham, *Chron. Maj.*, i, 662; *Eulogium*, iii, 356.

49 *Parl. Rolls*, vi, 317–18 (20–1); Walsingham, *Chron. Maj.*, i, 664–6; *Russell, 567. Money: PRO E403/493, m. 17 (17 Mar.), E403/496, m. 6 (9 May); Lunt, ii, 543.

50 Lopes, *Crón. D. Fernando*, 547, 559, 561–80; *Dias Arnaut, 357–95. Cost: *Col. doc. Murcia*, xi, nos. 124, 133.

51 PRO E403/499, m. 21 (31 Mar.); Walsingham, *Chron. Maj.*, i, 670–2; *Foed.*, iv, 164, 165; 'Medieval Treatise', 359–60; Walsingham, *Chron. Maj.*, i, 670–2. The estimates in *Gr. chron.*, iii, 53 (8,000 at the start of the campaign, based on French reconnaissance) and Froissart, *Chron.* (SHF), xi, 114 (3,000 waiting in England in early June), are broadly in line with the 8,000 archers and 3,500 men-at-arms reported by Richard II's ambassador to the King of Aragon: *Russell, 567.

52 'Medieval Treatise', 360–1; Walsingham, *Chron. Maj.*, i, 672–84; *Westminster Chron.*, 38–40; *Hist. Vitae*, 77–8; *Istore*, ii, 282–3, 285–6, 293–4; 'Chron. Com. Fland.', 242; Dixmude, *Merkw. Geb.*, 17–18; Froissart, *Chron.* (SHF), xi, 95–7, 102–11; *Cron. Tournay*, 258–9; BN Fr. 25705/44, 45. Flemish mission: PRO E403/496, mm. 5, 6, 12, 14 (7, 9 May, 14, 29 July); E403/499, mm. 12, 13 (13 Dec., 9 Jan.). All thirteen receive payments from the Exchequer for their expenses up to 10 April, but only seven thereafter. I infer that the other six are those referred to as advising Despenser on campaign: see Froissart, *Chron.* (SHF), xi, 94 and *Parl. Rolls*, vi, 333 (19).

53 *Istore*, ii, 287–8, 294–6, 309, 310–11; Dixmude, *Merkw. Geb.*, 18. Decision: *Parl. Rolls*, vi, 333 (19); Walsingham, *Chron. Maj.*, i, 686.

54 *Istore*, ii, 286–7, 288–9, 290, 293–4, 305, 308–9, 309–10; Froissart, *Chron.* (SHF), xi, 112; Dixmude, *Merkw. Geb.*, 18; Vandenpeereboom, v, 4–8.

55 *Istore*, ii, 288–9, 296–9, 311–15; Walsingham, *Chron. Maj.*, i, 690–2.

56 *Parl. Rolls*, vi, 333–4 (19); Walsingham, *Chron. Maj.*, i, 686, 688, 692; *Westminster Chron.*, 44; *Mems. London*, 479–80.

57 BL Add. Chart. 3345, 6749; BN Fr. 25705/47, 49, 50; BN Fr. 32510, fols. 250–251vo; BN Clair. 67/72; *Parl. Rolls*, vi, 334 (19, 20); *Westminster Chron.*, 40.

58 *Istore*, ii, 289–91, 299–301, 316. Provisional agreement: *Perroy (1933), 407.

59 *Gr. chron.*, iii, 55; *Itin. Ph. le Hardi*, 159; *Istore*, ii, 284, 301–5, 316–20, 332; *Chronographia*, ii, 57; Walsingham, *Chron. Maj.*, i, 692–4; Knighton, *Chron.*, 326.

60 *Parl. Rolls*, vi, 334 (19), 336–7 (22); *Istore*, ii, 291, 305–6, 320; Walsingham, *Chron. Maj.*, i, 694–6; *Westminster Chron.*, 44; Froissart, *Chron.* (SHF), xi, 122–3.

61 John of G. Reg. (1379–83), no. 909; PRO E403/496, m. 15, 16 (15, 25 Sept.); *Westminster Chron.*, 48.

62 *Chron. r. St.-Denis*, i, 262; *Chronographia*, ii, 57; *Gr. chron.*, iii, 55–6; *Istore.*, ii, 324–7. Numbers partially confirmed by the war treasurers' accounts: BN Fr. 7858, fols. 221–253vo; Fr. 32510, fols. 250–70.

63 *Itin. Ph. le Hardi*, 159–60; 'Séjours', 420–1; *Chronographia*, ii, 57–8; *Gr. chron.*, iii, 56–9; *Istore*, ii, 323–4, 327–8; Pitti, *Cron.*, 69–70; *Parl. Rolls*, vi, 331 (17).

64 Walsingham, *Chron. Maj.*, i, 702–4; *Foed.*, vii, 408–11; *Westminster Chron.*, 48; *Parl.*

Rolls, vi, 337 (23); PRO C76/68, mm. 21, 20, 19, 18; E403/496, m. 15 (15 Sept.); E403/499, m. 17 (3 Mar.); E101/39/29. Bourbourg: *Itin. Ph. le Hardi*, 160.

65 Pitti, *Cron.*, 70–1; Walsingham, *Chron. Maj.*, i, 696–700; Knighton, *Chron.*, 326–8; *Gr. chron.*, iii, 59–60; *Istore*, ii, 335; Froissart, *Chron.* (SHF), xi, 136–8, 145–50; *Chron. Bourbon*, 186–7; *Itin. Ph. le Hardi*, 160. Agreement: John IV, *Actes*, no. 462. Prisoners: *Rec. ord. Pays-Bas*, ii, no. 372. Payments: *Westminster Chron.*, 45–6; *Parl. Rolls*, vi, 338–41 (24–5); Bibl. Arsenal MS 4522, fols. 4–4vo.

66 *Parl. Rolls*, vi, 328–30 (15), 336–41 (22–5); John IV, *Actes*, no. 463; Walsingham, *Chron. Maj.*, i, 700–2; *Westminster Chron.*, 46; *Gr. chron.*, iii, 60–1; *Istore*, ii, 330. Chronology: Morice, *Preuves*, ii, 471–2 (retainer for the defence of the frontier at the end of the campaign); *Itin. Ph. le Hardi*, 160.

67 Pitti, *Cron.*, 70; *Chron. r. St.-Denis*, i, 284–94; Froissart, *Chron.* (SHF), xi, 149–50; *Chron. Bourbon*, 187. The total paid out by Guillaume d'Enfernet, the principal paymaster of the army, was 1,550,848 *livres*: Bibl. Arsenal MS 4522 (Preuves), fol. 10vo. The expenditure of the other war treasurer, Jean le Flament, is not known but was certainly smaller: see BN Fr. 32510, fols. 260–270. Borrowing: see BN PO 322, de Besames/2; 495, Bray/17; 1090, Eury/4; 1243, Frere/3; 1725, de Linières/15; 2289, Picquet/3; 2957, Venderesse/2.

68 *Istore*, ii, 329–30; *Cron. Tournay*, 261–2; 'Chron. Pays-Bas', 280–1; Walsingham, *Chron. Maj.*, i, 710–12; *Foed.*, vii, 412, 417; *Parl. Rolls*, vi, 337 (23); *Westminster Chron.*, 48–50.

69 *Westminster Chron.*, 522; PRO E403/499, m. 9 (9 Oct.); *Russell, 567; *Dipl. Corr.*, 194–5; *Perroy (1933), 407–8; *Parl. Rolls*, vi, 327 (13), 328–41 (15–25); CCR 1381–5, 350, 351, 351–2, 368–9; CPR 1381–5, 368–9; CFR, x, 33–4.

CHAPTER XI

1 *Parl. Rolls*, vi, 323–4 (4), 371 (18).

2 *John of G. Reg.*, nos. 564, 643.

3 Carrick: Wyntoun, *Oryg. Cron.*, iii, 9; *Exch. R. Scotland*, ii, 554, 587, 621–2; *Foed.*, vii, 403–4; *John of G. Reg.* (1379–83), no. 1186; *Rot. Scot.*, ii, 38; M. Brown, 69–70. Raids: *Westminster Chron.*, 40–2, 50; Walsingham, *Chron. Maj.*, i, 706, 714; *Foed.*, vii, 403–4. Orléans agreement: *Foed.*, iv, 167–8, vii, 406–7; 'Voyage de N. de Bosc', 332–3; *Parl. Rec. Scot.*, 131–2; 'Séjours', 419 (date).

4 Froissart, *Chron.* (SHF), xii, 6–7; *Westminster Chron.*, 54, 62; Nightingale, 279–81; Ormrod (1999), 161–2.

5 *Foed.*, vii, 412–15, 417–18; *Westminster Chron.*, 48–50, 54–6, 524; *Parl. Rolls*, vi, 337 (23); Walsingham, *Chron. Maj.*, i, 712–14; PRO E364/18, m. 3 (Montagu).

6 'Voyage de N. de Bosc', 328–30; BN Fr. 7619, fols. 191–192vo; *Westminster Chron.*, 48–50, 524; *Gr. chron.*, iii, 61; *Parl. Rolls*, vi, 371 (17); *Cron. Tournay*, 263; *Hist. gén. Lang.*, x, 1691–2 (proposal to make Gaunt Duke of Aquitaine; cf. Deschamps, *Oeuvres*, iii, 63); *Istore*, ii, 331, 336; Froissart, *Chron.* (SHF), xi, 154–6 (conflates the sessions of Jan. and Aug.–Sept. 1384); *Foed.*, vii, 418–22. Dates: PRO E364/17, m. 2 (Beauchamp), m. 5 (Bp. Hereford, Skirlaw, Sheppey), m. 5d (Holand); BN PO 549/Bueil, 97. Leulinghem: *Chron. r. St.-Denis*, i, 343, ii, 74–6.

7 *Gr. chron.*, iii, 62; Plancher, iii, 73–4. Brabant: Laurent & Quicke, 81–6.

8 AD Côte-d'Or B11751; Vandepeereboom, ii, 324–37; *Inv. Arch. Bruges*, iii, no. 658; *Rec. Ord. Pays-Bas*, i, no. 27. Groot Kasteel: *Inv. mobiliers Bourgogne*, ii, nos. 1069, 1071, 1084; *Inv. AD Nord*, i (2), 352–3; Nieuwenhuysen, ii, 436–41; Paviot (1995)[1], 281–3. Topography: R. Laurent, 135–42. Oudenaarde: *Cron. Tournay*, 264; 'Chron. Com. Fland.', 244; *Istore*, ii, 350, 363; Froissart, *Chron.* (SHF), xi, 179–81.

9 PRO E364/18, m. 3 (Montagu, Northumberland); E101/40/5; Fordun, *Chron.*, 383; *Westminster Chron.*, 58; Bower, *Scotichron.*, vii, 394–6; Wyntoun, *Oryg. Cron.*, iii, 18–19; Knighton, *Chron.*, 332–4. On Lochmaben: *Cal. Doc. Scot.*, iv, nos. 223, 231;

Northern Petitions, no. 113. French embassy: *Foed.*, vii, 423; BN PO 1246/Fresnel 5, 7; *Doc. Clos des Galées*, i, nos. 1191, 1193; 'Voyage de N. de Bosc', 333; Froissart, *Chron.* (SHF), xi, 165, 166–8, 173. Gaunt raid: Walsingham, *Chron. Maj.*, i, 718–22; *Westminster Chron.*, 66; Knighton, *Chron.*, 334; Bower, *Scotichron.*, vii, 396, 402; *Parl. Rec. Scot.*, 133, 134. Cambridge's participation: *Parl. Rolls*, vi, 365 (9). The English had withdrawn to Northumberland by 23 Apr.: *Foed.*, vii, 425.

10 Lopes, *Crón. D. Fernando*, 591–3, 601–3, 611–12; Ayala, *Crón.*, ii, 175–8, 181–2.
11 Ayala, *Crón.*, ii, 182–3; Lopes, *Crón. D. Fernando*, 593–7, 602–3, 605–10; *Crón. D. João*, i, 5, 10–13.
12 Lopes, *Crón. D. João*, i, 3–40, 46–50, 54–5, 69–72, 104–5; Ayala, *Crón.*, ii, 175, 179–81, 183–4, 187. John of Trastámara at Guarda: Suarez Fernandez (1977), i, 169.
13 Lopes, *Crón. D. João*, i, 50–1, 110–13, 141–2; Ayala, *Crón.*, ii, 176, 187–8, 189, 192–3; Santarém, *Quadro elementar*, i, 262.
14 Le Fèvre, *Journal*, 51, 53, 54; *Foed.*, vii, 439–41; Ayala, *Crón.*, ii, 189–90; *Lopes de Meneses, 248; BN PO 2087/Nade 3; BN PO 2030/Montmaur 11. On Montmor: *Gr. chron.*, iii, 163–76; *Doc. Clos des Galées*, i, nos. 868, 1344, 1459, 1460, 1483–4, 1501, 1547.
15 Lopes, *Crón. D. João*, i, 83–4, ii, 181; CCR 1381–5, 358.
16 Ayala, *Crón.*, ii, 189–90, 193–8; Lopes, *Crón. D. João*, i, 86–91, 116–23, 184–95; *Col. doc. Murcia*, xi, nos. 143, 146–7.
17 *Parl. Rolls*, vi, 362–3 (3–4).
18 *Parl. Rolls*, vi, 365 (9); *Westminster Chron.*, 66–80; Walsingham, *Chron. Maj.*, i, 722–6. Arundel's wool interests: Goodman (1971), 109, 114.
19 *Parl. Rolls*, vi, 365–6, 370–1 (10, 16–18); *Westminster Chron.*, 82–4.
20 Froissart, *Chron.* (SHF), xi, 166–74, 170–1; *Cron. Tournay*, 262 ('par licensse du Roi'); Walsingham, *Chron. Maj.*, i, 728; *Westminster Chron.*, 86, 100; *Rot. Scot.*, ii, 63; *Excerpta Historica*, 142–4; PRO SC1/56/96 (Sept.). Charny: *Gall. Reg.*, ii, no. 5871. Blaisy: *Froissart, *Chron.* (KL), xx, 329; *Hist. gén. Lang.*, x, 1812, 1814. James, Earl of Douglas: Bower, *Scotichron.*, vii, 402. Truce: PRO E403/502, m. 10 (2 July); *Foed.*, vii, 434–5; Froissart, *Chron.* (SHF), xi, 169–70, 171–5.
21 *Rot. Scot.*, ii, 66–8; *Parl. Rolls*, vii, 25 (33). Cost (Edward III): PRO E101/68/6 (140, 142); E101/73/1 (21); E364/9, m. 14 (Stapleton); E364/10, m. 5 (Percy); E364/13, m. 5 (Musgrave); E364/25, m. 3 (Curwen); Kirby, 138. Cost (1384): BL Cotton Chart. 16/64. The cost fell slightly in 1385–6: PRO E101/68/239, 242; E101/73/2 (29–35); E364/22, m. 5d (Despenser & Drayton); E364/23, m. 7 (Tempest & Talbot); E364/32, m. 5d (Swinburne); E364/33, m. 3 (Swinburne). Castles: Brown, Colvin & Taylor, 568–9, 599, 819–20.
22 Froissart, *Chron.* (SHF), xi, 176.
23 'Voyage de N. de Bosc', 331–41; *Hist. gén. Lang.*, x, 1691–2.
24 Deschamps, *Oeuvres*, iv, 55, v, 48–9, 79–80. Cf. *Instructions for British Servicemen in France* (issued by the Foreign Office, 1944): 'The French are more polite than most of us. Remember to call them "Monsieur, Madame, Mademoiselle", not just "Oy!".'
25 *Parl. Rolls*, vi, 384–5 (4); *Foed.*, vii, 441–3, 444–5; *Westminster Chron.*, 88, 98; Deschamps, *Oeuvres*, iii, 62–4; Froissart, *Chron.* (SHF), xi, 154 (conflates the sessions of Jan. and Aug.–Sept. 1384); 'Voyage de N. de Bosc', 342. The treatment of Calais in the draft treaty can be inferred from *Parl. Rolls*, vi, 371 (17).
26 *Foed.*, vii, 444; *Westminster Chron.*, 98, 104. Great Council: PRO E403/502, m. 12 (15 July); E403/505, m. 1 (4 Oct.). Parliament: CCR 1381–5, 586–7, 599–600; *Parl. Rolls*, vi, 384 (2), 386–7 (10). Clerical subsidy: *Rec. Convoc.*, iv, 82. *Ibid.*, iv, 81 records that Parliament was still in session on 17 Dec., after the Commons had received their expenses.
27 Carrick: *Acts Parl. Scot.*, i, 186. Berwick: *Westminster Chron.*, 104; Walsingham, *Chron. Maj.*, i, 734.
28 Wool exports in 1384–5 were 57% of those in the preceding year, and 68% of the five-

year average: Carus-Wilson & Coleman, 51–2. For the effect on revenue, see Ormrod (1999), 177 (Fig. 8.7).

29 Ayala, *Crón.*, ii, 195–6, 199–200; Lopes, *Crón. D. João*, i, 220–31, 271–6, 268–71, 288, 290–3; *Sandoval, 58–60; *Col. doc. Murcia*, xi, nos. 143–4, 148–9, 153; ACA *reg.* 1289, fol. 28vo–29.

30 *Foed.*, vii, 436; Lopes, *Crón. D. João*, i, 84; CCR *1381–5*, 549–50, 552; CCR *1385–9*, 22, 31; CPR *1385–9*, 9. Recruits: Froissart, *Chron.* (SHF), xii, 138; Lopes, *Crón. D. João*, i, 84, ii, 11–12; *Foed.*, vii, 453, 455, 472–3. Russell, 369–73, 375–6, 385 underestimates their number. PRO C81/1018–1033 and PRO C76/69 record 182 letters of protection issued between Aug. 1384 and Mar. 1385 to men-at-arms recruited for Portugal. A few defaulted. Letters of protection were not usually sought by landless men, or even by all landed ones. No letters were issued to archers, who were certainly recruited in considerable numbers.

31 *Col. doc. Murcia*, xi, nos. 148 (p. 297), 189 ('los omes de armas quel rey de Francia, nuestro hermano, nos enbia en ayuda nuestra'); Froissart, *Chron.* (SHF), xii, 124–7; Ayala, *Crón.*, ii, 201, 203–4, 232, 237; *Chron. r. St.-Denis*, i, 438–40; ACA *reg.* 1749, fols. 100, 142; 'Ann. Arch. Datini', xii, 81.

32 Brandon, 'Chron.', 2–3; 'Chron. Com. Fland.', 244–5; Froissart, *Chron.* (SHF), xi, 182, 311. Pension: PRO E403/499, m. 13 (8 Jan.), E403/505, mm. 12, 16 (24 Nov., 20 Dec.). On Van Herzele: Haegeman, 78.

33 *Foed.*, vii, 448–9; Froissart, *Chron.* (SHF), xi, 182–3; PRO E403/505, m. 12 (1 Dec.), E403/508, m. 18 (15 July); C76/69, m. 14; Haegeman, 145n^120, 146n^123; Brandon, 'Chron.', 5.

34 Valois (1896–1902), ii, 81–6, 91–112; Le Fèvre, *Journal*, 56, 60–7, 73–4, 77, 78–80, 87; *Choix de pièces*, i, 58–9; Durrieu (1880)[1].

35 *Chron. Bourbon*, 181–2; *Terrier de Loray, PJ nos. 89–90; *Plancher, ii, PJ no. 112 (relating to the subsidy granted by the Estates of Burgundy in Nov. 1384: see *ibid.*, iii, PJ nos. 81, 84 and BN Coll. Bourgogne 53, fol. 34); Froissart, *Chron.* (SHF), xi, 281 (Clisson quote); Walsingham, *Chron. Maj.*, i, 764.

36 Rey (1965), i, 261–2, 325–6, 390–404. *Taille*: *Bréard, PJ. no. 58 (pp. 100–3); *Doc. Clos des Galées*, i, no. 1198.

37 PRO E403/505, m. 19 (11, 16 Feb.); *Westminster Chron.*, 110–12; Froissart, *Chron.* (SHF), xiii, 16. '600 transports': Walsingham, *Chron. Maj.*, i, 752.

38 *Hist. Vitae*, 85–6; Walsingham, *Chron. Maj.*, i, 750, 754–6; *Westminster Chron.*, 110, 114–16.

39 *Chron. r. St.-Denis*, i, 348–50. Date: see the itineraries of the main participants, *Itin. Ph. le Hardi*, 175–6; Lehoux, iii, 467; Troubat, ii, 796; Jean de Vienne's appointment was formally made on 16 March: *Terrier de Loray, PJ no. 92; and Louis de Bourbon's on the 17th: see below. Vienne's army: Terrier de Loray, PJ nos. 90, 92. His payroll strength of 1,615 mounted men was carried on 183 ships, a ratio of 8.3 men per ship: see Terrier de Loray, PJ., nos. 101, 104, 111, 115, 116. The same ratio for the 600 ships assigned, according to English reports, to the second army (Walsingham, *Chron. Maj.*, i, 752) indicates a payroll strength of about 5,300 mounted men. For their destination, see Froissart, *Chron.* (SHF), xi, 240, 281 and *Cron. Tournay*, 276. Their information is borne out by the absence of any special equipment, such as was constructed in 1386, for landing on a hostile coast; and by the almost complete absence of preparations to defend the English coast: see below. Bourbon: *Titres Bourbon*, no. 3602; *Chron. Bourbon*, 136–7. Flanders and Ghent: Froissart, *Chron.* (SHF), xi, 199–200; *Cron. Tournay*, 274–5; *Inv. mobiliers Bourgogne*, ii, nos. 840–1040.

40 *Doc. Clos des Galées*, i, nos. 1203–5, 1207, 1209, 1213–29, 1231–51, 1253–5, 1257–85, 1288–93, 1296–1309, 1312–40, 1350–4, 1355–61; *Bréard, PJ. nos. 64, 74, 77; *Terrier de Loray, PJ. no. 98, Mirot (1915), 275–85.

41 Terrier de Loray, PJ no. 115; Walsingham, *Chron. Maj.*, i, 752, 770; Roncière, ii, 71–2; *Doc. Clos des Galées*, i, nos. 1237, 1285, 1294, 1306–8, 1310, 1313, 1342–3, 1354, ii,

no. 72; *Inv. AD Nord*, vii, 209; Ayala, *Crón.*, ii, 203–4; Mirot (1915), 272–3.

42 *Ord.*, vii, 123–4, 759; *Chron. r. St.-Denis*, i, 346–8; Juvénal, *Hist.*, 45; BN Fr. 7619, fols. 229–231vo; *Palmer (1968)[3], 422–5; *Chron. r. St.-Denis*, i, 350.

43 Laurent & Quicke, 118–36; Vaughan, 86–8. Festivities: Froissart, *Chron.* (SHF), xi, 193–5; *Istore*, ii, 384–6; 'Voyage de N. de Bosc', 345.

44 'Voyage de N. de Bosc', 343–7; *Itin. Ph. le Hardi*, 176–7; *Foed.*, iv, 466, 470. Great Council: PRO E403/508, mm. 6, 9 (9, 18 May).

45 Froissart, *Chron.* (SHF), xi, 199–202, 218–21; Brandon, 'Chron.', 5–6; Walsingham, *Chron. Maj.*, i, 738. Biervliet: BN Clair. 48/3561, 79/6221. London mission: Brandon, 'Chron.', 6; PRO E403/508, m. 17 (8 July). On Coudenberghe: Perroy (1930).

46 PRO E101/40/9; E101/68/10 (240, 241); E364/20, m. 5 (Raddington), m. 7 (Percy); C76/69, mm. 12, 10; E403/510, m. 10 (17 Nov.); *CPR 1385–9*, 73.

47 *Hanserecesse*, iii, nos. 198, (esp. para. 7), 200, 203–5, 403, 407–8; *Chron. r. St.-Denis*, i, 360–2; PRO E403/508, m. 7 (12 May); E364/35, m. 2d (Hannay & Warblington); Walsingham, *Chron. Maj.*, i, 752–4. Topography: R. Laurent, 2–5, 90–6, 136–43.

48 *Terrier de Loray, PJ.*, nos. 101, 104, 110–11, 115, 116; *Doc. Clos des Galées*, i, nos. 1207, 1252, 1264, 1275; *Inv. mobiliers Bourgogne*, ii, nos. 1178–83; Fordun, *Chron.*, 383; *Chron. r. St.-Denis*, i, 360–2; Walsingham, *Chron. Maj.*, i, 752–4; Bower, *Scotichron.*, vii, 402–3; Froissart, *Chron.* (SHF), xi, 213; *Cron. Tournay*, 273.

49 *Westminster Chron.*, 120; PRO E403/508, m. 2 (19 Apr.); *Rot. Scot.*, ii, 70–1, 73; *Foed.*, vii, 473, 474–5. Cf. Richard's itinerary in Saul (1997), 470.

50 *Cron. Tournay*, 275, 280; Brandon, 'Chron.', 6; PRO C76/70, m. 39; E364/30, m. 4 (Hereford); E403/508, m. 18 (15 July).

51 *Foed.*, vii, 471–2, 473, 474–5. Scutage: PRO E403/508, mm. 12, 18 (15 June, 11 July); *Parl. Rolls*, vii, 26 (40); Lewis (1958); Palmer (1968)[2]; Steel (1954), 51–2.

52 Richard's itinerary in Saul (1997), 470; PRO E403/508, m. 22 (18 Sept.); E403/510, mm. 6, 22 (31 Oct., 18 Sept.); *Cal. Letter Books H*, 269–71; *CCR 1381–5*, 551; *CCR 1385–9*, 6; *Foed.*, vii, 474.

53 *Chron. r. St.-Denis*, i, 364–6; *Acts Parl. Scot.*, i, 554–5.

54 Froissart, *Chron.* (SHF), xi, 214–18, 253–4, 275–6; *Chron. r. St.-Denis*, i, 364. Lost horses: *Foed.*, vii, 485.

55 *Chron. r. St.-Denis*, i, 366–8; Froissart, *Chron.* (SHF), xi, 255–8; Bower, *Scotichron.*, vii, 404. Crosses: *Acts. Parl. Scot.*, i, 555. On Wark: *Cal. Inq. P.M.*, xvi, no. 871; *Cal. Doc. Scot.*, iv, no. 318. The French were in Edinburgh on 3 Aug.: *Terrier de Loray, PJ.* no. 104.

56 *Westminster Chron.*, 124–6; *Armitage-Smith, 437–8; *Foed.*, vii, 481–4; Knighton, *Chron.*, 336–8; *Hist. Vitae*, 89; Palmer (1971)[3], 489–90. Itinerary: Saul (1997), 470.

57 *Westminster Chron.*, 126–30; Walsingham, *Chron. Maj.*, i, 760–4; Knighton, *Chron.*, 336–8; *Hist. Vitae*, 88–9; Fordun, *Chron.*, 383; Wyntoun, *Oryg. Cron.*, iii, 28–9; Bower, *Scotichron.*, vii, 406, 408. Itinerary: Saul (1997), 470. The Scots were at Carlisle on 15 August: *Northern Petitions*, no. 84. Defence of north: PRO E403/510, m. 20 (7 Jan.).

58 *Northern Petitions*, no. 84; Bower, *Scotichron.*, vii, 404, 408–10; Knighton, *Chron.*, 336; Wyntoun, *Oryg. Cron.*, iii, 29–30; *Reg. crim. Châtelet*, 382–3, 386–7; Froissart, *Chron.* (SHF), xi, 267–9, 270–1, 274–5. Carlisle: Brown, Colvin & Taylor, 599; *Northern Petitions*, no. 84; *Rot. Parl.*, iii, 30 (1); *CCR 1381–5*, 542; *CPR 1385–9*, 42–3, 110; PRO E159/162 (*brev. dir. bar.*), Mich., m. 16d. Destruction: PRO E159/164 (*brev. dir. bar.*), Mich., m. 11d.; E159/166 (*recorda*), Mich., m. 20; *CPR 1385–9*, 25–6; *CPR 1385–9*, 230.

59 Preparations: *Puiseux, 22–3; *Doc. Clos des Galées*, i, nos. 1228, 1256, 1285, 1348, 1385, ii, no. 72. Damme: *Cron. Tournay*, 272; Brandon, 'Chron.', 6; 'Chron. Com. Fland.', 244–5; Froissart, *Chron.* (SHF), xi, 232–5, 240. Topography: R. Laurent, 111–15.

60 *Chronographia*, iii, 75–6; Froissart, *Chron.* (SHF), xi, 237–9, 248; *Cron. Tournay*, 272, 273–4; *Puiseux, 22–3; 'Séjours', 428; *Itin. Ph. le Hardi*, 180. Quotation: *Chron.*

Bourbon, 147. Marriage: Froissart, *Chron.* (SHF), xi, 223–32, 235–7; *Chron. r. St.-Denis*, i, 356–60.

61 PRO E101/40/11; E403/510, m. 6 (31 Oct.); C76/70, m. 39; *Westminster Chron.*, 128; Walsingham, *Chron. Maj.*, i, 768.

62 *Istore*, ii, 386; *Chron. r. St.-Denis*, i, 372–4; *Cron. Tournay*, 274–6; Froissart, *Chron.* (SHF), xi, 239–41, 243; *Inv. Arch. Bruges*, iii, 18; *Doc. Clos des Galées*, i, no. 1461; 'Chron. Pays-Bas', 282.

63 *Cron. Tournay*, 276–8; 'Chron. Com. Fland.', 245–6; *Istore*, ii, 386; *Chron. r. St.-Denis*, i, 374–8; Froissart, *Chron.* (SHF), xi, 243–6, 282–5; *Chronographia*, iii, 76; *Chron. premiers Valois*, 312.

64 *Chron. premiers Valois*, 312; *Chron. r. St.-Denis*, i, 380–4; Froissart, *Chron.* (SHF), xi, 246–7; *Cron. Tournay*, 278; Brandon, 'Chron.', 7, Cochon, *Chron.*, 177–8; *Inv. AD Nord*, ii, 135 (dykes).

65 *Puiseux, 22–3; *Doc. Clos des Galées*, i, no. 1356, ii, nos. 70–1; Froissart, *Chron.* (SHF), xi, 247–8.

66 *Westminster Chron.*, 134–6; Walsingham, *Chron. Maj.*, i, 768–70 (my translation differs from the editor's); Knighton, *Chron.*, 338–40. Loss of galleys confirmed by *Doc. Clos des Galées*, i, no. 1461.

67 *Cron. Tournay*, 273; Froissart, *Chron.* (SHF), xi, 276–80. Subsidy: *Foed.*, vii, 484–6; *Inv. doc. Écosse*, 30.

68 Froissart, *Chron.* (SHF), xi, 280–1. Truces: *Rot. Scot.*, ii, 75, 84, 93; *Foed.*, vii, 526–7; PRO E101/675/56.

69 *Froissart, *Chron.* (KL), x, 562–3, 571–2; Froissart, *Chron.* (SHF), xi, 286–9; *Istore*, ii, 372–5; Brandon, 'Chron.', 7–8.

CHAPTER XII

1 Ayala, *Crón.*, ii, 202, 218, 221; Lopes, *Crón. D. João*, ii, 11. Tax: *Col. doc. Murcia*, xi, nos. 154, 167, 175. Army: *ibid.*, xi, nos. 158, 170, 172; Suarez Fernandez (1977), i, 203. Ships: ACA *reg.* 1289, fols. 166, 168; *Suarez Fernandez (1959), 144–9;

2 Ayala, *Crón.*, ii, 213; Lopes, *Crón. D. João*, i, 341–73, ii, 10–11; 181–3; *Foed.*, vii, 518–19.

3 Ayala, *Crón.*, ii, 214–17, 223; Lopes, *Crón. D. João*, ii, 12–37. Finance: *Col. doc. Murcia*, xi, no. 175.

4 Ayala, *Crón.*, ii, 218–19; Lopes, *Crón. D. João*, ii, 38–45. Date: Batlle.

5 Ayala, *Crón.*, ii, 219–22; *Col. doc. Murcia*, xi, nos. 175–6.

6 Ayala, *Crón.*, ii, 222–5.

7 Lopes, *Crón. D. João*, ii, 58–60 (nos. 82, 84); Ayala, *Crón.*, ii, 225–6, 436 (date). Illness: *ibid.*, 228; *Col. doc. Murcia*, xi, no. 178.

8 Ayala, *Crón.*, ii, 227–8; *Coron. Condestabre*, 112–16; Lopes, *Crón. D. João*, ii, 60–66, 70–1.

9 Ayala, *Crón.*, ii, 227; Lopes, *Crón. D. João*, ii, 71, 83–6; *Col. doc. Murcia*, xi, no. 178. English: *Westminster Chron.*, 132; *Documentos das chancelarias reais anteriores a 1531 relativos a Marrocos*, ed. P. de Azevedo, i (1915), 6–7 (garrisons). Organisation: Lopes, *Crón. D. Fernando*, 523–4; Ayala, *Crón.*, ii, 157.

10 *Col. doc. Murcia*, xi, no. 178; Ayala, *Crón.*, ii, 228–36, 237, 238, 240, 241; *Coron. Condestabre*, 122–3; Lopes, *Crón. D. João*, ii, 96–9, 103, 108–9, 122–8; *Westminster Chron.*, 132. Fieldworks: Paço.

11 Lopes, *Crón. D. João*, ii, 183–4; PRO E403/508, m. 22 (18 Sept.).

12 *Parl. Rolls*, vii, 4–5, 11–19 (5, 16–17); Walsingham, *Chron. Maj.*, i, 780–2; CPR 1385–9, 123. Burley, Neville: see Palmer (1971)[3], 489–90.

13 *Parl. Rolls*, vii, 6–7, 26–7 (10, 41–3); *Westminster Chron.*, 146; *PPC*, i, 84–6 (date: Palmer (1971)[3], 480–1); *Palmer (1969), 100–1.

14 Froissart, *Chron.* (SHF), xi, 290–3. Ackerman: *Cron. Tournay*, 280. Negotiations:

*Froissart, *Chron.* (KL), x, 562–3; *Rek. Gent*, 487–95.

15 PRO E403/510, mm. 7 (7 Nov.); C76/70, m. 32, E403/519, m. 23 (14 Sept.); *Westminster Chron.*, 146. Loan: *Parl. Rolls*, vii, 38 (6); *CPR 1385–9*, 60, 74.

16 *Westminster Chron.*, 142; *Crón. D. João*, ii, 184–5. Finance: *Foed.*, vii, 495, 679–80; *Cal. Reg. Wakefield*, no. 807; PRO E403/512, m. 26 (26 July).

17 *Rek. Gent*, 493–5; *Cron. Tournay*, 281; *Chron. r. St.-Denis*, i, 410; *Rec. Ord. Pays-Bas*, i, nos. 71, 81. Pope: *Froissart, *Chron.* (KL), x, 572, 573–4; *Thes. nov. anecd.*, i, 1625. Economic consequences: Nicholas (1971), 334–40; Nicholas (1987), 14–16.

18 Drayton, Despenser: PRO C76/70, m. 32; E101/40/18; E403/510, mm. 7, 8 (7 Nov.), E403/519, m. 23 (14 Sept.); *Foed.*, vii, 488–9; *Westminster Chron.*, 146–8; Walsingham, *Chron. Maj.*, i, 786–8. Bourchier: *Prevenier (1961), 305; Froissart, *Chron.* (SHF), xi, 294–5, 311–13.

19 Nicholas Barbot, see: PRO E403/517, m. 16 (27 July); E403/521, m. 18 (8 Feb.); E403/527, m. 4 (6 Nov.); E403/532, m. 9 (10 Dec.). Coudenberghe: Perroy (1930), 273–5. Others: PRO E403/527, m. 2 (22 Oct.); E403/530, m. 17 (23 July). Van den Bossche: *CCR 1385–9*, 204; PRO E101/40/29; *Cartellieri, 130; Froissart, *Chron.* (KL), xx, 364 and *Chron.* (SHF), xi, 312–13, xiii, 7, 9, 140, 141. Ackerman: Froissart, *Chron.* (SHF), xiii, 7–11; *Istore*, ii, 383.

20 *Cortes Castilla*, ii, 315–19, 329–35; *Col. doc. Murcia*, xi, nos. 183, 185, 187–8. Date: *ibid.*, nos. 180–1. Embassy: Ayala, *Crón.*, ii, 241, 242.

21 *Westminster Chron.*, 154; *Chron. r. St.-Denis*, i, 418–26; *Foed.*, vii, 491–4, 497; *CPR 1385–9*, 503. On Leo: Jorga, 462–3; Paviot (2003), 18–19.

22 'Voyage de N. de Bosc', 349–55, 359. Charles's movements: 'Séjours de Charles VI', 430–1; *Chron. r. St.-Denis*, i, 428–9.

23 *Westminster Chron.*, 164–5; *Foed.*, vii, 490–1, 499–504; PRO C76/20, mm. 29, 22, 20; E101/40/13, E101/42/18; E101/319/23–4; E403/510, m. 23 (25 Mar.); C76/20, mm. 29, 22; *Foed.*, vii, 501–2. Parr: PRO C81/1031/13; Lopes, *Crón. D. João*, ii, 156–7. Great Council: PRO E403/510, m. 23 (31 Jan.). Conference: 'Voyage de N. de Bosc', 352–5, 359. Charles's movements: 'Séjours', 430–1; *Chron. r. St.-Denis*, i, 428–9.

24 *Foed.*, vii, 515–18, 521–3; Lopes, *Crón. D. João*, ii, 185–6, 187.

25 *Chron. r. St.-Denis*, i, 428–30; Terrier de Loray, PJ. no 119; *Palmer (1972), 249; Froissart, *Chron.* (SHF), xiii, 4–5; Walsingham, *Chron. Maj.*, i, 794–6; Knighton, *Chron.*, 348; *Puiseux, 18–19, 25; *Doc. Clos des Galées*, i, no. 1372. Charles VI wrote on 21 Sept. that the numbers of men-at-arms mustered to date (9,000) exceeded those planned: see AN K53B/57. Between 3,000 and 4,000 bowmen actually served (see below), which probably represented roughly the number called for. Finance: Terrier de Loray, PJ. no 119 ('le parisis pour le tournois'); Rey (1965), i, 392, 404.

26 Froissart, *Chron.* (SHF), xii, 299–302, xiii, 44–5; *Chron. r. St.-Denis*, i, 440–2; Ayala, *Crón.*, ii, 243–5; *Daumet, 176–7; *Col. doc. Murcia*, xi, no. 195 (pp. 380, 381). In the event, Pierre de Villaines remained in France: BN Fr. 7858, fol. 256vo.

27 Spy ships: PRO E101/40/21, m. 12; E403/512, m. 23 (17 Sept.); E403/515, m. 8, 10, 11 (5, 23, 28 Nov.). Hennequin: *Reg. crim. Châtelet*, i, 379–93, esp. at 382–5, 386–9.

28 *CCR 1385–9*, 60, 77; *CPR 1385–9*, 175, 180; PRO C76/70, m. 18; E403/510, mm. 29–30 (9, 12, 14 Apr.); E403/512, mm. 1–2 (4, 5, 7, 9 May); E101/40/24–9; Walsingham, *Chron. Maj.*, i, 790–2. *Eulogium*, iii, 358–9; Thorne, *Gesta Abbatum S. Augustini*, cols. 2182–3.

29 PRO C76/70, m. 25; E101/40/19, 21, 22; E364/24, m. 1 (Darcy); E403/524, m. 21 (28 Aug.); BL Harley Charters, 49 D.3; Knighton, *Chron.*, 346; Walsingham, *Chron. Maj.*, i, 792–4; PRO E403/512, m. 14 (7 July); E403/524, m. 21 (28 Aug.); *Dipl. Corr.*, 41, 199–200; *Baldwin, 507–10 (quotation). Thames: *Foed.*, vii, 507.

30 AD Côte d'Or B1465, fol. 108; *Inv. AD Nord*, iv, 1; Haegeman, 175–9; Mirot (1915), 442. Galleys: Lopes, *Crón. D. João*, ii, 188, 199.

31 *Chron. r. St.-Denis*, i, 430. Cherbourg: PRO E101/40/13; C76/70, m. 18; BN Clair. 9/487, 16/1077, 22/1585, 25/1805, 26/5971, 44/3257, 46/3423, etc. Brest: Knighton,

Chron., 342; *Chron. r. St.-Denis*, i, 430–4; Morice, *Preuves*, ii, col. 526. Flanders: BN Fr. 32510, fols. 278ᵛᵒ–279; BN Clair. 6/239, 19/1283, 41/3045, 65/5047, 91/3865, 92/3907, 102/152, etc. Palmer (1972), 73, attributes the delay, less plausibly, to the illness of the Duke of Burgundy in early May.

32 PRO E101/40/19; *Westminster Chron.*, 164; Knighton, *Chron.*, 340–4; Walsingham, *Chron. Maj.*, i, 788; Lopes, *Crón. D. João*, ii, 187–8; 'Chron. Brioc.', 58; *Chron. r. St.-Denis*, i, 434–6. Lopes's figure for archers, at 3,000, is probably too high. Ayala's figures for both categories are lower: *Crón.*, ii, 249. Russell's calculation (at p. 418), based on a comparison with the tonnage per man in the Earl of Cambridge's fleet of 1381, makes insufficient allowance for the presence of horses in 1386.

33 Terrier de Loray, PJ., no. 120; *Doc. Clos des Galées*, i, nos. 1375–7, 1379, 1385–6, 1395, 1405, 1415, 1390–3, 1396–1402, 1437–40. *Taille*: Rey (1965), i, 392 and n⁴. *Arrière-ban*: AD Côte d'Or B1465, fol. 109ᵛᵒ; BN Fr. 20590/78. English measures: PRO E101/40, 24, 26; E403/512, m. 17 (28 July); Walsingham, *Chron. Maj.*, i, 792.

34 Great Council: PRO E403/512, m. 12 (2 July); *Reports Dignity Peer*, iv, 721–4; cf. Richard's itinerary in Saul (1997), 471. Finance: PRO E403/512, m. 3 (10, 12 May), m. 23 (18 Sept.), mm. 25, 26 (19 May, 19 June, 26 July); Ormrod (1999), 162 (Table 8.3); ESFDB/orm/engd030; Steel (1954), 54–6. Fleet: PRO E101/40/21, mm. 3–4, 6–7; E403/512, mm. 19, 20, 21 (2, 25 Aug., 6 Sept.). Richard's plans: *Reports Dignity Peer*, iv, 721–4; *Parl. Rolls*, vii, 35 (1).

35 BN Fr. 7858, fols. 255–295; AN K53B/57; *Cron. Tournay*, 286 (urban contingents); BN Fr. 32510, fols. 276–80 (garrisons). Shipping: *Cron. Tournay*, 285, 290; 'Cronaca prima d'anonimo', *RISS*², xviii.3, 102 (correspondents' reports reaching Florence on 25 Oct.); *Chron. r. St.-Denis*, i, 450 (900 ships). Postponement: 'Ann. Arch. Datini', xii, 93; CCR 1385–9, 214; Mézières, *Songe*, ii, 437; *Doc. Clos des Galées*, i, nos. 1395, 1423, 1429, 1430, 1434, 1435, 1437.

36 Spy ships: PRO E403/512, mm. 21, 23 (6, 17 Sept.); E403/515, mm. 1, 3, 8, 10, 11 (2, 17 Oct., 5, 23, 28 Nov.); E101/40/21, m. 12. Defence: PRO E403/512, m. 21, 22 (6, 15 Sept.); CPR 1385–9, 190, 214, 259; CCR 1385–9, 169, 190; *Cron. Tournay*, 360. Fort: Knighton, *Chron.*, 348; Walsingham, *Chron. Maj.*, i, 796. Levies: PRO E403/512, m. 21 (6 Sept.).

37 PRO E403/512, m. 21 (6 Sept.); C76/71, m. 19; CCR 1385–9, 264–5; CPR 1385–9, 216, 217, 242; *Foed.*, vii, 545–6. London: *Cal. Letter Books H*, 285–6; Walsingham, *Chron. Maj.*, i, 792; Westminster Abbey Muniments, cited by Saul (1997), 155n²⁶.

38 Knighton, *Chron.*, 354. Loans: *Foed.*, vii, 543–5; PRO E403/512, m. 21 (6 Sept.); PRO E401/564 (15 Sept.). Ships: PRO E101/40/21, mm. 5–6. Troops: CCR 1385–9, 187; PRO E403/515, m. 1 (2 Oct.); Knighton, *Chron.*, 348–50; Walsingham, *Chron. Maj.*, i, 796–8. PRO E403/515, mm. 1–9, 11, 12, 14, 16, 26 (2 Oct.–1 Apr.) records payments to 4,637 retained men, more than 70% of them archers; plus ten companies whose strength is not stated. The commissioners of array were asked to produce about 6,120 archers, but the number actually produced was smaller: CCR 1395–9, 217, 242, 315, 322.

39 North: PRO E364/23, m. 7 (Tempest & Talbot); E364/32, m. 5d (Swinburne). William Scrope's expenditure as Seneschal of Aquitaine from 1382 to 1385 had been financed from the English Exchequer: PRO E364/18, m. 7 (Scrope). His successor, Sir John Harpeden, had to rely entirely on local revenues: PRO E364/21, m. 3 (Stratton); E364/27, m. 7d (Gedney). Cherbourg: PRO E364/20, m. 1d (Holand); E364/23, m. 6 (Scrope). Brest: Jones (1970), 219 (App. C); PRO E101/68/10 (237, 238); *Parl. Rolls*, vii, 39 (7). Calais: PRO E364/22, m. 6 (de Burgh); E364/25, m. 5 (Walden).

40 Walsingham, *Chron. Maj.*, i, 794, 798–800, 878; Thorne, *Gesta Abbatum S. Augustini*, 2181–3; *Parl. Rolls*, vii, 37–46 (6–17); Knighton, *Chron.*, 352–4; *Eulogium*, iii, 359–60. Cf. *Somers Tracts*, ed. W. Scott (1809), i, 15, a 17th-century narrative probably based on a lost contemporary account: see Taylor, 272–3.

41 Knighton, *Chron.*, 352–4; *Eulogium*, iii, 359–60; Walsingham, *Chron. Maj.*, i, 798–800.

42 *Cron. Tournay*, 283–4; CCR 1385–9, 190, 322; CCR 1385–9, 193–4; Knighton, *Chron.*,

348–50; Walsingham, *Chron. Maj.*, i, 796–8.

43 Walsingham, *Chron. Maj.*, i, 798; Knighton, *Chron.*, 354–68; *Eulogium*, iii, 359–60; *Foed.*, vii, 548; *Parl. Rolls*, vii, 37–46 (6–17). Skirlaw, Fordham: *CPR 1385–9*, 232; Tout (1920–37), vi, 24, 53.

44 *Cron. Tournay*, 284–5, 286–7, *359; *Chron. r. St.-Denis*, i, 458; Knighton, *Chron.*, 348; *Inv. Arch. Bruges*, iii, 102–3; *Memorieboek Ghent*, i, 119; Froissart, *Chron.* (SHF), xiii, 75, 83, 94–7.

45 *Cron. Tournay*, 285–8, 290, 296, *359, *360; *Dipl. Corr.*, 42–3; Froissart, *Chron.* (SHF), xiii, 75; Deschamps, *Oeuvres*, i, no. 26, ii, no. 211, v, nos. 835, 836, 845; Pitti, *Cron.*, 71–2; *Chron. r. St.-Denis*, i, 450.

46 *Cron. Tournay*, 288–92, 296; *Chron. r. St.-Denis*, i, 452–4, 460, 480; Pitti, *Cron.*, 72; 'Ann. Arch. Datini', 94; Cochon, *Chron.*, 180–1.

47 Invasion: PRO E403/515, m. 11 (28 Nov.); Walsingham, *Chron. Maj.*, i, 804. The ships in the Thames were dismissed on 24 Nov.: PRO E101/40/21, mm. 5–6. Coup: *Parl. Rolls*, vii, 345–7 (11). Finance: *Parl. Rolls*, vii, 46–7, 48, 53 (18, 20, 35); *Statutes*, ii, 44–6; *Rec. Convoc.*, iv, 107–8.

48 Leo: Walsingham, *Chron. Maj.*, i, 804; *Foed.*, vii, 549; *Dipl. Corr.*, 42–3. New invasion: *Cron. Tournay*, 285, 294, 295–6; PRO C76/71, m. 16. Arundel: PRO C76/71, m. 18; E364/21, m. 6d (Arundel); E403/515, mm. 11, 18, 20, 25 (26, 28 Nov., 4 Feb., 19 Mar.).

49 Ayala, *Crón.*, ii, 249, 252; Lopes, *Crón. D. João*, ii, 188–9, 199; *Russell, 570; *Col. doc. Murcia*, xi, no. 196; Knighton, *Chron.*, 344–6; PRO E403/512, m. 19 (2 Aug.); E101/40/19. Removal of supplies: *El libro becerro de la catedral de Oviedo*, ed. P. Floriano Llorente (1963), 101–7, 174–5.

50 *Cortes Castilla*, ii, 349–50.

51 Lopes, *Crón. D. João*, ii, 198–9, 200, 202; Ayala, *Crón.*, ii, 250, 303.

52 Lopes, *Crón. D. João*, ii, 198–9, 200, 202; Ayala, *Crón.*, ii, 250, 253, 303; Froissart, *Chron.* (SHF), xii, 314–19, xiii, 18, 56, 57, 58, 59, 65, 66, 67; *Cron. Tournay*, 283; Knighton, *Chron.*, 344. Date: *CPR 1396–9*, 489.

53 Ayala, *Crón.*, ii, 249–50; Froissart, *Chron.* (SHF), xii, 309–10, 319–20, xiii, 18, 53–72; Lopes, *Crón. D. João*, ii, 198. Surrender of Corunna reported to John of Trastámara between 4 and 7 September: *Col. doc. Murcia*, xi, no. 193–5. Six-month contracts: PRO E101/169/10 (250B).

54 Lopes, *Crón. D. João*, ii, 180–1; *Russell, 569–71; *Col. doc. Murcia*, xi, nos. 193, 195; ACA *reg.* 1674, fols. 108vo, 111; 'Ann. Arch. Datini', xii, 92; BN Coll. Doat, 203, fols. 50–61. Shortage of cavalry: Ayala, *Crón.*, ii, 252; cf. survey of military obligations in 1390, *ibid.*, ii, 306–14. Finance: *Col. doc. Murcia*, xi, nos. 189–90, 193–4.

55 Ayala, *Crón.*, ii, 253–61, esp. at 255, 261; *Choix de pièces*, i, 74–6; *Russell, 570; *Col. doc. Murcia*, xi, nos. 193–5; Froissart, *Chron.* (SHF), xiii, 44–5.

56 *Col. doc. Murcia*, xi, no. 195; Ayala, *Crón.*, ii, 252–3; Froissart, *Chron.* (SHF), xiii, 44–5, 72–4. Military activity: *Catalina Garcia, ii, 330n[1].

57 Lopes, *Crón. D. João*, ii, 202–6.

58 *Cortes Castilla*, ii, 336, 349–59. Finance: *Col. doc. Murcia*, xi, nos. 199, 200; Ormrod (1995), 145 (fig. 21), based on calculations of Ladero Quesada at ESFDB/orm/casdoo1.

59 *Choix de pièces*, i, 74–6; *Cron. Tournay*, 283.

60 Le Fèvre, *Journal*, 326–33; *Rec. ord. Pays-Bas*, i, no. 136; *Chron. r. St.-Denis*, i, 452, 458, 480; Froissart, *Chron.* (SHF), xiii, 84–5, 92–3, 96–101; Juvénal des Ursins, *Hist.*, 58, 61; AD Côte d'Or B1465, fol. 95 (Burgundy's support).

61 Le Fèvre, *Journal*, 331–3; BN Fr. 25705/149; Juvénal des Ursins, *Hist.*, 61; BN Fr. 25705/149; BL Add. Chart. 3358; *Choix de pièces*, i, 76–8 (quotation). Cf. *Chron. Bourbon*, 188–91 (inaccurate in detail). On Neilhac and Passat: Troubat, 732–3, 735; Contamine (1972), 583–4.

62 *Chron. r. St.-Denis*, i, 480; Juvénal des Ursins, *Hist.*, 61. Clisson left Paris for Brittany at the end of January to start recruiting troops for the invasion of England: Juvénal, *loc. cit.*; Le Fèvre, *Journal*, 333. Finance: BN Fr. 25705/149; *Chronographia*, iii, 85;

Le Fèvre, *Journal*, 337; Rey (1965), i, 404. The commitment to Castile was limited to 100,000 *livres*.

63 AD Nord B584/16591*bis* (cited in Paviot (1995)[1], 36n[9]); BN Fr. 32510, fol. 309vo; *Cron. Tournay*, 311.

64 PRO E403/515, m. 25 (11 Mar.) (prisoners landed at Sandwich); BN Fr. 26022/996 (sighting); *Cron. Tournay*, 310–11. Arundel's fleet: PRO E364/21, m. 6d (Arundel); E101/40/33, 34, 35; Walsingham, *Chron. Maj.*, i, 808.

65 *Westminster Chron.*, 180–4; *Cron. Tournay*, 311–15; Froissart, *Chron.* (SHF), xiii, 136–46; Walsingham, *Chron. Maj.*, i, 808–12; Knighton, *Chron.*, 388–90. Cf. on Sluys blockade: *Rek. Gent*, 377; *Hanserecesse*, iii, 207; *Inv. Arch. Bruges*, iii, 100–1; *Haegeman, 157n[17]. Buuc's fate: *CCR 1385–9*, 329; *CPR 1388–92*, 146.

66 *Westminster Chron.*, 184; Walsingham, *Chron. Maj.*, i, 812; Knighton, *Chron.*, 390; *Chron. r. St.-Denis*, i, 476–8; PRO E101/40/35, 36; Terrier de Loray, PJ., no. 124.

67 Walsingham, *Chron. Maj.*, i, 808–10, 812. Fee: PRO E364/21, m. 6d (Arundel). Sluys: *Handelingen*, no. 34; BN PO 326/Bethune 54; BN Clair. 56/182, 59/4479, 60/4269, 86/6773, 87/6869, etc. La Rochelle: *Doc. Clos des Galées*, i, nos. 1459–60, 1462–4, 1467; ii, nos. 73, 75. Galleys: Duro. 12 June: PRO E101/40/35, 36.

68 Lopes, *Crón. D. João*, ii, 205, 207–8, 212–13, 251–63; *Russell, 571–3.

69 Lopes, *Crón. D. João*, ii, 214, 223; Froissart, *Chron.* (SHF), xiv, 84–6; Ayala, *Crón.*, ii, 251, 263; *Col. doc. Murcia*, xi, no. 210; Walsingham, *Chron. Maj.*, i, 892. Imports: PRO C76/71, mm. 11, 13. The first recorded victim of plague was Lord Fitzwalter, who died on 26 September 1386: *Cal. Inq. P.M.*, xvi, nos. 377–93.

70 Lopes, *Crón. D. João*, ii, 213–15; *Itin. D. João*, 31.

71 Ayala, *Crón.*, ii, 252–3, 263–4; Lopes, *Crón. D. João*, ii, 215–17, 228, 229. On Bracquemont: Anselme, vii, 816–17; Froissart, *Chron.* (SHF), xii, 312, xiv, 85–6, 89. On Villalpando: Russell, 477n[1].

72 Lopes, *Crón. D. João*, ii, 215; Ayala, *Crón.*, ii, 263–4.

73 Lopes, *Crón. D. João*, ii, 216–20; Ayala, *Crón.*, ii, 263–4

74 Lopes, *Crón. D. João*, ii, 223, 230, 231, 233; Froissart, *Chron.* (SHF), xiii, 196, xiv, 88, xv, 7, 22.

75 Froissart, *Chron.* (SHF), xiv, 133. Guesclin: *Cat. doc. Burgos*, nos. 267, 269, 271–3, 276–8, 280–2. Bracquemont: Anselme, vii, 816–17. 10 April: *Itin. D. João*, 31.

76 Ayala, *Crón.*, ii, 264; *Col. doc. Murcia*, xi, no. 210. Neilhac, Passat: BN Fr. n.a. 8604/76, 84; BN Fr. 26022/1008–9; 'Ann. Arch. Datini', xii, 97, 98; AN J916/3. John's movements: Suarez Fernandez (1977), i, 408–9. Gaunt's emissary: see *John of G. Reg. (1379–83)*, no. 1234.

77 Lopes, *Crón. D. João*, ii, 220; Ayala, *Crón.*, ii, 264.

78 Lopes, *Crón. D. João*, ii, 221–4; *Col. cédulas*, v, 395–413; Ayala, *Crón.*, ii, 264. Date: *Itin. D. João*, 32.

79 Lopes, *Crón. D. João*, ii, 224–8. Date: *Itin. D. João*, 32.

80 Ayala, *Crón.*, ii, 264–5; Lopes, *Crón. D. João*, ii, 224, 230; *Westminster Chron.*, 190; Walsingham, *Chron. Maj.*, i, 892; Froissart, *Chron.* (SHF), xiv, 98–102, 114–16. Pay: Goodman (1992), 122–3. On Holand: Knighton, *Chron.*, 338, 340, 342; *Westminster Chron.*, 122, 144, 192.

81 Lopes, *Crón. D. João*, ii, 229–30; Froissart, *Chron.* (SHF), xiv, 103–4.

82 Lopes, *Crón. D. João*, ii, 232, 233–4. Roye: ACA reg. 1675, fol. 100vo; *John of G. Reg. (1379–83)*, no. 1233. Dates: *Itin. D. João*, 32.

83 Walsingham, *Chron. Maj.*, i, 892; Froissart, *Chron.* (SHF), xiv, 105–12. Deaths: *ibid.*, xiv, 111–12; Ayala, *Crón.*, ii, 265; *Westminster Chron.*, 190; *Cal. Inq. P.M.*, xvi, nos. 514–15, 610–23. On Morieux: *John of G. Reg. (1379–83)*, nos. 543, 558; *Controversy Scrope Grosvenor*, i, 56. On Burley: see *Political Poems*, i, 109; Walker (1990)[1], 266; *Reg. Gilbert*, 109.

84 Lopes, *Crón. D. João*, ii, 233–6;

85 Lopes, *Crón. D. João*, ii, 233–6; Ayala, *Crón.*, ii, 265–6; *Cat. Arch. Navarra (Comptos)*,

xvi, nos. 1057, 1106, 1108. Dates: *Itin. D. João*, 32.

86 Neilhac, Passat: ACA *reg.* 1751, fols. 17, 42vo, 51vo; *Cat. Arch. Navarra (Comptos)*, xvi, nos. 902, 905, 914, 939, 959, 967, 974; Ayala, *Crón.*, ii, 266. Bourbon: 'Ann. Arch. Datini', 99; *Petit Thalamus*, 411; ACA *reg.* 1751, fol. 74.

87 Ayala, *Crón.*, ii, 268–9; Lopes, *Crón. D. João*, ii, 237–8; *Treaty of Bayonne*, 3–15. Amendments: *ibid.*, 25–47 (see clause xxiiii at page 46 for the grant to D. Constanza).

88 *Col. doc. Murcia*, xi, no. 213; Ayala, *Crón.*, ii, 266–7; Froissart, *Chron.* (SHF), xiv, 123–4; Lopes, *Crón. D. João*, ii, 238; *Eulogium*, iii, 367; *Treaty of Bayonne*, 15–18, 19, 19–47 (note clauses xxv and xxvi).

89 'Ann. Arch. Datini', 101; *Chron. Bourbon*, 195–9; Ayala, *Crón.*, ii, 266–8. Sahagún: Froissart, *Chron.* (SHF), xiv, 126–32. Guesclin: *ibid.*, xiv, 125; *Cat. doc. Burgos*, nos. 282. Deductions: *ibid.*, no. 273. Bourbon in Navarre: *Cat. Arch. Navarra (Comptos)*, xvi, nos. 1147, 1149–50, 1234, 1264–5, 1301, 1308, 1319, 1326.

90 *Terrier de Loray, PJ nos. 126–7; Froissart, *Chron.* (SHF), xv, 200–2, 216–19. Portuguese: BN Fr. 32510, fol. 305; BN PO 2030 Montmaur/24–26. On the commander (Gonzales de Tenreiro): *Crón. D. João*, i, 62, 317, 337–8, ii, 150.

91 *John of G. Reg. (1379–83)*, nos. 1235–9; Ayala, *Crón.*, ii, 269, 270; Lopes, *Crón. D. João*, ii, 244–5.

92 Ayala, *Crón.*, ii, 271–2, 278–81; *Cortes Castilla*, ii, 395–6, 399–412; *Col. doc. Murcia*, xi, no. 254; *Colección de documentos ineditos para la historia de España*, li (1867), 39–46; Suarez Fernandez (1977), 286–8, 296. Final treaty: *Treaty of Bayonne*, 49–66. On the Crown: Knighton, *Chron.*, 340.

CHAPTER XIII

1 Froissart, *Chron.* (SHF), xiii, 229–32, xiv, 4; 'Chron. Brioc.', 59; *Chronographia*, iii, 86; Morice, *Preuves*, ii, col. 552; Le Fèvre, *Journal*, 365, 368; *Chron. r. St.-Denis*, i, 480–2. Expedition: *Chron. Tournai*, 317–18; Froissart, *Chron.* (SHF), xiii, 220–1, 228; *Doc. Clos des Galées*, i, nos. 1459–60, 1462–4, 1467, 1518; ii, nos. 73, 75; BN PO 789/Clisson 10, 11; 1499/Hazay 6, 17; 2291/Pise 3, 4, 5; BN Fr. 26022/1045, 1047, 1047, 1048; BN Fr. 32510, fols. 299–299vo.

2 Lefranc, 267–8, 270n[1], 273–9, *438–9; *Ord.*, vii, 123. For pledges, bonds, cash and plate in his possession at his death in 1407: 'Inv. meubles Clisson'; Palmer (1968)[3], 422.

3 *Lefranc, 445–50; *Choix de pièces*, i, 51–2.

4 Grants: Nieuwenhuysen, i, 157–8, 194, ii, 373–4; Vaughan, 34, 57–8, 95, 229–31; Lehoux, ii, 26–7, 162. Harpeden: *Froissart, *Chron.* (KL), xiii, 352–4.

5 John IV, *Actes*, no. 521; Le Fèvre, *Journal*, 56, 58, 72.

6 *Foed.*, vii, 454; Morice, *Preuves*, ii, 482–3; John IV, *Actes*, no. 551 (p. 401); Le Fèvre, *Journal*, 96.

7 *Cal. Inq. Misc.*, iv, no. 296; PRO C76/69, mm. 3, 1; C76/70, mm. 32, 26, 24, 7; C76/71, m. 24; *Foed.*, vii, 503; *CPR 1385–9*, 132; Le Fèvre, *Journal*, 312.

8 Le Fèvre, *Journal*, 331, 332, 333; *Foed.*, vii, 553; PRO C76/71, m. 6; John IV, *Actes*, no. 613, 620–1; *PPC*, i, 48; AD Côte d'Or B1467, fol. 30vo; B1469, fol. 33.

9 Froissart, *Chron.* (SHF), xiii, 228, 233–40, 246, 247–8, 282; *Chron. r. St.-Denis*, i, 480; Morice, *Preuves*, ii, 540–2, 552–5; John IV, *Actes*, no. 646 (p. 439).

10 'Séjours', 436; *Itin. Ph. le Hardi*, 189; *Chron. r. St.-Denis*, i, 484; Juvénal des Ursins, *Hist.*, 62; Froissart, *Chron.*, xiii, 250–1, xiv, 1–2; *Lefranc, 445–50; *Choix de pièces*, i, 80; AD Côte d'Or B1467, fol. 240vo.

11 Jones (1972), 18, 19; Morice, *Preuves*, ii, 528–9; *Chron. r. St.-Denis*, i, 498; John IV, *Actes*, p. 68 and nos. 639–43, 646–51.

12 *Itin. Ph. le Hardi*, 190; *John IV, *Actes*, p. 439n[1] and nos. 646–7; 'Chron. Brioc.', 60–1; *Chron. r. St.-Denis*, i, 489–91. On Bernard, *Gall. Christ.*, iv, 625.

13 PRO E101/68/11 (253).

14 *Dipl. Corr.*, no. 78 and p. 206; Edinburgh Univ. Lib., Ms. 183, fols. 66[vo], 66A[vo], 84[vo]–85

(arrangements for summit); BN Coll. Dupuy 306, fol. 77vo (French memorandum, 1390); *Parl. Rolls*, vii, 95–6 (Art. XXXI); 'Inv. lettres rois d'Aragon', no. 10; *CPR 1385–9*, 503; *Westminster Chron.*, 204; Walsingham, *Chron. Maj.*, i, 846.

15 *Parl. Rolls*, vii, 89–90, 91–3 (Arts. XVII, XXV), 105–9. Secrecy: *Westminster Chron.*, 202; Favent, 'Hist.', 7.

16 Walsingham, *Chron. Maj.*, i, 826–8; *Westminster Chron.*, 186, 206; Favent, 'Hist.', 4–6, 8; *Parl. Rolls*, vii, 90, 91, 95, 96 (Arts. XIX, XXII, XXIV, XXIX, XXXII, XXXIII), 115, 116 (Arts. XIV, XVI); *Cal. Letter Books H*, 314–15, 317; Knighton, *Chron.*, 404–6, 426–8.

17 *Parl. Rolls*, vii, 94 (Art. XXXVI); Favent, 'Hist.', 6, 8; Walsingham, *Chron. Maj.*, i, 828–30; *Westminster Chron.*, 210.

18 *Westminster Chron.*, 206–10; Favent, 'Hist.', 9; Knighton, *Chron.*, 400–4, 406, 408–12; Walsingham, *Chron. Maj.*, i, 824, 828–30. Array: *Cal. Letter Books H*, 321.

19 *Westminster Chron.*, 208–10, 212; Walsingham, *Chron. Maj.*, i, 830–2.

20 *Westminster Chron.*, 210–14; Favent, 'Hist.', 10; Walsingham, *Chron. Maj.*, i, 832–6; Knighton, *Chron.*, 412–14.

21 *Parl. Rolls*, vii, 97–8 (Art. XXXVIII), 114 (Art. XI); *Westminster Chron.*, 214–16; Walsingham, *Chron. Maj.*, i, 836, 840–2; Knighton, *Chron.*, 416–18; Favent, 'Hist.', 11; *Cal. Letter Books H*, 321. Richard was at Sheen on 22 Nov.: Saul (1997), 471. On the story put out by the Appellants that Pole was trying to escape via Calais: Palmer (1972), 109–12. Cheshire: Morgan (1987), 188; Walker (1990)[1], 167–71.

22 *Westminster Chron.*, 218–20; *Parl. Rolls*, vii, 408 (Art. VII). On Bolingbroke: McFarlane (1972), ch. 1–2; Morgan (1987), 191–2; Walker (1990)[1], 167–71. On Mowbray: Goodman (1971), 158–63.

23 Morgan (1987), 188, 190–1; Goodman (1971), 34–41; *Cal. Reg. Wakefield*, no. 824; *Westminster Chron.*, 220–4; Walsingham, *Chron. Maj.*, i, 838–40, 842; Knighton, *Chron.*, 418–24; Favent, 'Hist.', 11.

24 *Westminster Chron.*, 214, 220–6, 320, 342–4, 492; Walsingham, *Chron. Maj.*, i, 842–6; Knighton, *Chron.*, 416, 424–6; *Issues Exch.*, 234; Favent, 'Hist.', 12–13, 17.

25 *Westminster Chron.*, 226–8; Walsingham, *Chron. Maj.*, i, 842, 846–8; Knighton, *Chron.*, 426; *Clarke, 157 (Chronicle of Whalley Abbey); *Parl. Rolls*, vii, 414 (Gloucester's confession, 1397).

26 *Westminster Chron.*, 228–32, 306–8; Walsingham, *Chron. Maj.*, 848–50; Favent, 'Hist.', 13–14; *CCR 1385–9*, 583, 593–5; Knighton, *Chron.*, 426–8, 430.

27 *Parl. Rolls*, vii, 63 (1), 84–98 (esp. Arts. VIII, XV, XXIII, XXVIII–XXXII); Favent, 'Hist.', 14–15, 21.

28 Knighton, *Chron.*, 414, 432; *Parl. Rolls*, vii, 99–104; Favent, 'Hist.', 17–18; *Westminster Chron.*, 280–4, 308–14.

29 *Parl. Rolls*, vii, 106–12, 117–18; Favent, 'Hist.', 19–20, 23; *Westminster Chron.*, 286–8, 314–18.

30 *Parl. Rolls*, vii, 112–17, 408 (6), 414, 416 (8); *Westminster Chron.*, 328, 330, 330–32, 338, 340; Favent, 'Hist.', 21–2, 23, 24; Walsingham, *St. Albans Chron.*, i, 852.

31 *CCR 1385–9*, 388; *CPR 1385–9*, 427, 503, 522; PRO C76/72, m. 5, C76/74, m. 13; *Parl. Rolls*, vii, 95–6.

32 *Parl. Rolls*, vii, 66 (11); *Westminster Chron.*, 286, 314, 316–18.

33 Knighton, *Chron.*, 442–50. Date: Palmer (1972), 237–8. Council, dissolution: *Parl. Rolls*, vii, 68–9 (23), 82 (52); *Westminster Chron.*, 332.

34 John IV, *Actes*, nos. 613, 673; PRO E101/319/33; E403/518, m. 18 (26 Jan.); *Foed.*, vii, 586–7; 'Séjours', 439; *Itin. Ph. le Hardi*, 192; *Chron. r. St.-Denis*, i, 507–9. John's itinerary: *Actes*, 68. On Fotheringhay: *ibid.*, nos. 277, 279, 727; *CPR 1381–5*, 402; *CPR 1385–9*, 259.

35 Brittany: PRO E101/68/11 (257, 258); C76/72, m. 13; E403/518, m. 26 (11 Mar.). Gascony: PRO E159/166 (Trinity, *brev. dir. bar.*), m. 16; C61/100, m. 5; *Westminster Chron.*, 322 (Holand should read Percy), 345. Shipping: PRO C76/72, m. 13, 3, 2;

E403/518, m. 26 (11 Mar.); E403/521, mm. 6–7, 15, 16, 17 (30 Nov., 14 Dec., 30 Jan., 3 Feb.); E101/40/40. Arundel originally planned a fleet of 62 vessels: PRO E101/68/11 (257).

36 Laurent & Quicke, 138–64; *Gedenk. Gesch. Gelderland*, iii, no. 122; *Choix de pièces*, i, 78–9; *Cartellieri, 128–9; Laurent & Quicke, 200n².

37 Froissart, *Chron.* (SHF), xiv, 180–3, 192–6; Dynter, *Chron.*, iii, 120–3, 126–7; *Itin. Ph. le Hardi*, 190–3. Troops committed: BN Fr. 32510, fols. 299ᵛᵒ–300; BN PO 2878, La Trémoille/4, 6, 8, 10, 13; Clair. 32/79, 103/120, 112/150; Plancher, iii, 570.

38 Gascony: *Choix de pièces*, i, 83–6; *Mon. hist.*, no. 1687; *Arch. Montpellier*, ii, 104–5; BN Fr. 20416/6, 26022/1138, 1140–3, 1152–4; BN Fr. 32510, fols. 303–303ᵛᵒ. Channel: BN Fr. 32510, fol. 305; BN PO 2030 Montmaur/24–26; *Daumet, 176–7; *Doc. Clos des Galées*, i, no. 1526. Fleet: *Doc. Clos des Galées*, i, nos. 1491, 1505, 1511–17, 1526; BN Fr. 26023/1224, 1229; BN Fr. 32510, fol. 305ᵛᵒ (musters on 9 July). Intelligence: *Ord.*, vii, 188; BN Fr. 25706/176.

39 Negotiations at Calais: *Foed.*, vii, 581–2; PRO E364/22, m. 2d (Beaupyne), E364/22, m. 8 (Rouhale); *Handelingen*, no. 56; *Rec. Ord. Pays-Bas*, i, no. 184. Gascon truce: PRO E101/184/1, fol. 36ᵛᵒ, 37; *Foed.*, vii, 595–6. Brabant: Laurent & Quicke, 211–12. Council: Froissart, Chron. (SHF), xv, 10–16, 28–31; *Chron. r. St.-Denis*, i, 524–8; 'Chron. Pays-Bas', 283; *Ord.*, vii, 186–9. Attendance, date: Le Fèvre, *Journal*, 523–4; *Itin. Ph. le Hardi*, 192; Lehoux, iii, 472; Troubat, 800. Taille: *Ord.*, vii, 186–9.

40 *Chron. r. St.-Denis*, i, 508–12; 'Chron. Brioc.', 61; *Itin. Ph. le Hardi*, 193–4; Froissart, *Chron.* (SHF), xv, 52–9. Musters (13–20 Aug. 1388): BN PO 1089, Estouteville/12; 1783, Lyons/2; 1814, Malet/28; 1925, Menon/4; Clair. 138/61; etc. Award: Morice, *Preuves*, ii, 552–5; 'Chron. Brioc.', 62.

41 *Westminster Chron.*, 340; *Westminster Chron.*, 350–2; Froissart, *Chron.* (SHF), xv, 16–18, 20–1, 62–3. Forces: PRO E101/41/5; E403/519, mm. 8, 11 (14 May, 2 June); E403/521, mm. 6–7 (30 Nov.); PRO E101/319/33. Powers: *Foed.*, vii, 586–7. Brest: PRO E101/41/8. Noirmoutier: *Rec. doc. Poitou*, xxiv, 88–90. The knightings at Batz recorded by the Westminster chronicler occurred on 28 June: PRO E101/40/33, mm. 1d, 3, 4, 10, 11d. The landing in Aunis was probably the occasion for a knighting on 16 July: PRO E101/41/5, m. 14. Bayonne: *Frag. chron. norm.*, 11 (corroborated by Percy's presence with John of Gaunt in August: PRO E101/184/1, fol. 37). Topography: Tranchant, 17–31.

42 *Westminster Chron.*, 352; Froissart, *Chron.* (SHF), xv, 63–76.

43 *Foed.*, vii, 572–3, 583; *Cal. Doc. Scot.*, iv, no. 387; PRO E101/319/30, 35. Percies: *Cal. Doc. Scot.*, iv, no. 377; Storey, 596–600, 611–12. Carrick: Boardman (2004), 107–8; Boardman (1996), 142, 157n⁶⁴; Froissart, *Chron.* (SHF), xv, 120–1 (wrongly giving the venue as Aberdeen).

44 *CPR 1385–9*, 456, 475, 502–3. Finance: Steel (1954), 59–60. Calais fort (Poil): *Westminster Chron.*, 320–2; *CPR 1385–9*, 495, 522.

45 Scotland: *Westminster Chron.*, 344; Bower, *Scotichron.*, vii, 412–14; Wyntoun, *Oryg. Cron.*, iii, 32–4; *CCR 1385–9*, 603–4. Guelders: PRO E403/519, mm. 19 (17 July). Recall of Arundel: PRO E403/519, mm. 19, 20 (17, 18 July).

46 *Westminster Chron.*, 344; *Frag. chron. norm.*, 11; *CPR 1385–9*, 547.

47 Edinburgh UL, Ms. 183, fol. 94–94ᵛᵒ; Knighton, *Chron.*, 504, 504–6; *Westminster Chron.*, 346–52; *Hist. Vitae*, 119; Bower, *Scotichron.*, vii, 414–18 and the confused Latin poem by Thomas Barry, at *ibid.*, 420–62; Wyntoun, *Oryg. Cron.*, iii, 35–9; Froissart, *Chron.* (SHF), xv, 120–74 (much embroidered); Walsingham, *Chron. Maj.*, i, 854–6. Topography: A.H. Burne, *More English Battlefields* (1952), ch. 12.

48 *Westminster Chron.*, 400; Bower, *Scotichron.*, vii, 418. Sir Philip Sydney: *The Defence of Poesie* in *Prose Works*, ed. A Feuillerat, iii (1912), 24.

49 *Westminster Chron.*, 352; Froissart, *Chron.* (SHF), xv, 193–6; PRO E101/41/4. The knightings referred to by the Westminster chronicler in connection with this challenge may be those recorded in the muster roll for 27 July: see PRO E101/40/33, mm. 10, 15.

Castile: *Treaty of Bayonne*, 49, 62–4. Truce of Mortagne: *Foed.*, vii, 595–8; PRO E101/184/1, fols. 36vo, 37. Later extended to 31 July: *Chavanon, 109.

50 *Westminster Chron.*, 354; *Westminster Chron.*, 368–70. Arundel: PRO E403/519, mm. 2, 7, 8, 11–12, 23 (13 Apr., 11, 14 May, 2 June, 14 Sept.), E403/521, mm. 6–7, 15, 16, 17 (30 Nov., 14 Dec., 30 Jan., 3 Feb.); E159/167 (Mich., *brev. dir. bar.*), m. 51. Appellants' rewards: PRO E403/519, m. 21 (11 Sept.); *Parl. Rolls*, vii, 67 (16); PRO E364/24, m. 5 (Arundel); E364/27, m. 4d (Arundel). Members: Tuck (1969), 226–7.

51 Plans: *Concilia*, iii, 205; *Rec. Convoc.*, iv, 125. Subsidy: Knighton, *Chron.*, 508. Conference: *Foed.*, vii, 608. Castile: Ayala, *Crón.*, ii, 286. The power referred to was probably delivered to Sir Richard Abberbury *fils*, one of Gaunt's officers, who was in England for consultations in October and returned to Bayonne in November: PRO E101/184/1, fol. 37; E403/521, mm. 1, 6 (19 Oct., 28 Nov.).

52 *Chronographia*, iii, 94–5; *Cron. Tournai*, 324–5; Froissart, *Chron.* (SHF), xv, 99–100, 105–6; Laurent & Quicke, 221–5. Dates: 'Séjours', 441; *Itin. Ph. le Hardi*, 198.

53 *Itin. Ph. le Hardi*, 198–201; 'Séjours', 441; *Cron. Tournai*, 325–31 ('ne jocqua pas' at 329); *Hist. Gelriae*, 87–99; Froissart, *Chron.* (SHF), xv, 174–92, 197–8 (quotation at 187); *Chron. r. St.-Denis*, i, 528–54; Juvénal, *Hist.*, 67; Stavelot, 'Chron.', 92–3; Outremeuse, *Myreur*, vi, 709; Deschamps, *Oeuvres*, i, 123–4, iii, 25, v, 121. Treaties: *Rec. Ord. Pays-Bas*, i, nos. 192, 196; *Oorkonden*, no. 24; *Gedenkwaardigheden*, iii, no. 132. Supply train: AD Côte d'Or B1469, 1475.

54 *Chron. r. St.-Denis*, i, 555–62; Juvénal, *Hist.*, 68–9; Froissart, *Chron.* (SHF), xv, 179; *Moranvillé (1888), 358–9. On Aycelin: Cazelles (1982), 478; Valois (1888), 75, 88.

55 *Froissart, *Chron.* (KL), xiii, 352–4.

56 *Chron. r. St.-Denis*, i, 562–6, 568; Mézières, *Songe*, ii, 212–14, 318–19; 'Ann. Arch. Datini', xii, 118.

57 *Chron. r. St.-Denis*, i, 568, 570, ii, 10; Juvénal, *Hist.*, 69–70; Valois (1888), 94–6. Bourbon's role: Troubat, ii, 277–92. Montaigu's early career: Borrelli de Serres, iii, 325–6. On Juvénal: R. Delachenal, *Histoire des avocats au Parlement de Paris* (1885), 358–9; Favier (1974), 141–2.

58 *Livre fais Bouciquaut*, 34; *Chron. r. St.-Denis*, i, 584–604; Deschamps, *Oeuvres*, iii, 255–6 (quotation); De Vere: *Barroux, 45 (no. 99); BN PO 1633, Lancastre/2.

59 *Chron. r. St.-Denis*, i, 566–72. Grants: Pocquet (1940–1), 115; Nieuwenhuysen, ii, 374, 378; AN J187B/35 (10,000 gold francs granted to Berry, Sept. 1389). Admin. reform: *Ord.*, vii, 224–5, xii, 162–6; Autrand (1981), 23, 24, 127–8, 279n²⁴. Financial admin.: Rey (1965), ii, 95–104, 175–6, 438–40, 449–54, 472–6, 573–4; *Ord.*, vii, 256–64, 228–30, 236–43, 245–9, 768–70, xii, 167–8, 170–6; Juvénal, *Hist.*, 74–5. *Taille*: *Ord.*, vii, 284, 768; Rey (1965), ii, 392, 404.

60 *Foed.*, vii, 608.

61 Mézières, *Songe*, i, 394–403; ii, 373–7. Date: Jorga, 467–8.

62 *Westminster Chron.*, 390–2; Knighton, *Chron.*, 528–30; Walsingham, *Chron. Maj.*, i, 864–6; *Foed.*, vii, 618–19; Tout (1920–37), iii, 454–9.

63 *Westminster Chron.*, 392, 404, 492, 510; *Foed.*, vii, 641. Holand: Saul (1997), 243–4. Rutland: *Parl. Rolls*, vii, 145–7 (23); Creton, *Met. Hist.*, 309. Council: *PPC*, i, 11, 12, 17.

64 *Foed.*, vii, 620–1.

65 PRO E364/22, m. 6d (Rouhale), m. 8 (Clanvowe); E364/23, m. 1 (Bp. Durham), m. 8 (Dagworth); *Westminster Chron.*, 374–6; Walsingham, *Chron. Maj.*, i, 862; *Foed.*, vii, 608, 610–12. Bruges: PRO E364/13, m. 4d (Skirlaw); *Mandements*, nos. 1631, 1633, 1635.

66 *Westminster Chron.*, 376–8, 382–4, 394–6; Knighton, *Chron.*, 526–8; Walsingham, *Chron. Maj.*, i, 862; *CPR 1388–92*, 60, 203; *Northern Petitions*, nos. 118–19. Retainers: *Rot. Scot.*, ii, 96. Beaumont was being paid £8,600 a year for the custody of the West March: PRO E403/521, mm. 18, 20, 24 (11, 22 Feb., 31 Mar.). Ralph, Lord Neville, and John, Lord Roos, received £6,000 a year for the same service from July 1389: PRO E403/524, m. 14 (17 July). Mowbray received £12,000 a year in time

of war for the custody of the East March: PRO E364/30, m. 4 (Nottingham). PRO E403/524, m. 14 (17 July).

67 PRO C76/73, m. 3; E101/319/39; *Dipl. Corr.*, no. 99; *Foed.*, vii, 622–30. Mowbray: *Cal. Doc. Scot.*, v, no. 4426.

68 *Westminster Chron.*, 396; Walsingham, *Chron. Maj.*, i, 862, 868; Wyntoun, *Oryg. Cron.*, iii, 40–1; Bower, *Scotichron.*, vii, 442–4.

69 Walsingham, *Chron. Maj.*, i, 868–70; Wyntoun, *Oryg. Cron.*, iii, 41–3; Bower, *Scotichron.*, vii, 444; *Westminster Chron.*, 398. Dates: PRO E364/30, m. 4 (Nottingham); E101/319/38. On Fresnel: *Chart. Univ. Paris.*, iii, 264; 'Voyage de N. de Bosc', 332–3 (treaty, 1383); BN PO 1246, Fresnel/5, 7, *Foed.*, vii, 423 (embassy, 1384); BN PO 1913, Meilhac/2 (embassy, 1387); *Foed.*, vii, 631 (embassy, 1389).

70 PRO E403/521, m. 11 (8 Dec.) (consultation); Ayala, *Crón.*, ii, 288–9. The truce was published in Castile on 27 July: Suarez Fernandez, i, 306. Campo Maior: Lopes, *Crón. D. João*, ii, 280–2. Tui: *ibid.*, ii, 287–9; *Itin. D. João*, 41; Ayala, *Crón.*, ii, 289–90, 303.

71 Ayala, *Crón.*, ii, 290–1, 303–4, 307; PRO E30/1589.

CHAPTER XIV

1 *Hist. gén. Lang.*, x, 1770–74.

2 Murder: Froissart, *Chron.* (SHF), xii, 81–9; Tucoo-Chala (1959), 316–21. Territory: see Tucoo-Chala (1959), 41, maps I, VII (end). Financial dealings: Tucoo-Chala (1959), 88–92, 136–48, 270, 283–300, 306.

3 Bernis, 'Chron.', paras. 97–105; Higounet, 548–53, *650–8; Tucoo-Chala (1959), 307–11.

4 *Hist. gén. Lang.*, x, 1619–24; Tucoo-Chala (1959), 311–15 and map VII (end); Bernis, 'Chron.', para. 108; Froissart, *Chron.* (SHF), xii, 31.

5 Carlat: *Reg. St.-Flour*, 71–3; *Gr. chron.*, ii, 183; BN Coll. Doat 194, fols. 167–8; AN X[ia] 1471, fol. 53. Attempted buy-outs (1377–8): *Inv. AC Montferrand*, i, 391, 406; *Comptes Rodez*, ii, 159, 160, 167–8; *Doc. Millau*, no. 424. Numbers: Mézières, *Songe*, ii, 407. Damage: *Reg. St.-Flour*, 65; *Troubat, i, 233.

6 Armagnac's captains (Bastard of Landorre, Perrot de Béarn): 'Délibérations Albi', xlvii, 360, 364–5. Cantal: *Reg. St.-Flour*, 71–3; *Hist. gén. Lang.*, ix, 871. Quercy: BN Coll. Doat 200, fols. 253–258vo. Armagnac's role: *Preuves Polignac*, ii, 70–4; BN Coll. Doat 87, fols. 239–53; BN Coll. Doat 200, fols. 253–258vo.

7 BN Coll. Doat 87, fols. 239–53; *Comptes Rodez*, ii, 184–5; 'Délibérations Albi', xlvii, 544. Bas-Languedoc: *Hist. gén. Lang.*, ix, 871; Mascaro, 'Libre', 73; BN Coll. Languedoc 159, fol. 165; *Petit Thalamus*, 400; *Inv. AC Montferrand*, i, 409–10; *Reg. St.-Flour*, 77, 79, 80, 80–1, 82. The recorded participants in this venture (Bertucat, Benoit Chapparral, the Bastards of Armagnac, Landorre, Savoy and Perulle) had all been party to the agreement for the surrender of Carlat: *Doc. Carlat*, i, 283–4; *Hist. gén. Lang.*, ix, 871. Perrot de Galard, the principal captain in Quercy, also participated: see *Petit Thalamus*, 400; *Comptes Rodez*, ii, 183–4.

8 Perrot: *Froissart, Chron.* (KL), xviii, 552; *Flandin-Bléty, 311–13. Date: AN JJ141/28; *Ann. Limoges de 1638*, 284, 286–7. Strength: *Reg. crim. Châtelet*, i, 123. On Perrot: *ibid.*, ii, 187; *Jurades de Bergerac*, i, 76; *Foed.*, vii, 725 (name); *Chron. Bourbon*, 200. Mérigot: *Thomas, 384–5; *Reg. crim. Châtelet*, ii, 187, 194; *Troubat, i, 230; *Livre de vie*, 406, 411; Froissart, *Chron.* (SHF), ix, 141; *Reg. St.-Flour*, 261, 271. Mérigot also held Châteauneuf-de-St.-Nectaire: *Reg. crim. Châtelet*, ii, 177–8; BN Coll. Doat 203, fols. 106–108vo. St.-Exupéry belonged to his wife: Froissart, *Chron.* (KL), xiv, 175, 181. Mercoeur: AN JJ141/272; *Hist. gén. Lang.*, x, 1823–5; *Reg. crim. Châtelet*, ii, 204–5; Froissart, *Chron.* (KL), xiv, 264.

9 Du Guesclin: *Inv. AC Montferrand*, i, 408, 411; *Reg. St.-Flour*, 74*, 82–3, 84, 89, 91–2; *Petit Thalamus*, 400; *Chron. Bourbon*, 116–18; *Gr. chron.*, ii, 377–8; *Hist. gén. Lang.*, ix, 882. Carlat: *Reg. St.-Flour*, 99. For Garcie-Arnaud's involvement: *Reg. St.-Flour*, 192,

261, 275; *Doc. Carlat*, i, 290–5. Le Saillant: *Reg. St.-Flour*, 78, 99, 104–5, 218; Boudet (1893), 17–18; *Savaron, 466. Mérigot: *Reg. St.-Flour*, 158, 163, 168, 190–1. St.-Flour: *Reg. St.-Flour*, 101; Boudet (1893), 17–18. Aurillac: *Inv. arch. Aurillac*, ii, 8–9, 16. Nîmes: * L. Menard, iii (*Preuves*), 33–6; *Petit Thalamus*, 403. Cf. the complaints of the Estates at Mazères (Sept. 1381): *Inv. AC Narbonne*, 361, 362; and Béziers (Jan. 1382): *Lehoux, ii, 53n³.

10 BN Coll. Doat 199, fols. 92–3; 'Délibérations Albi', xlvii, 544.

11 Thuriès: *Douze comptes d'Albi*, i, 310, 314–15, 337, 343–9; Froissart, *Chron.* (SHF), xii, 107–8; *Hist. gén. Lang.*, x, 1676–8; 'Délibérations Albi', xlvii, 550. Perrot: *ibid.*, xlvii, 364–5; *Douze comptes d'Albi*, ii, 26, 28. Bastard of Savoy: *ibid.*, i, 313.

12 Froissart, *Chron.* (SHF), xii, 66.

13 Dognon, 615; *Hist. gén. Lang.*, x, 1646; BN Coll. Doat 49, fol. 547vo; *Douze comptes d'Albi*, i, 313–14; *Baudouin, 374–5; *Chron. r. St.-Denis*, i, 92–4.

14 Bernis, 'Chron.', para. 109; *Baudouin, 375; *Hist. gén. Lang.*, x, 1644–6, 1724–5, 1817–18; AN JJ 142/84; 'Délibérations Albi', xlvii, 550, 551–2, xlviii, 265; Tucoo-Chala (1959), 324; *Compayré, 262–3; *Douze comptes d'Albi*, i, 317;*L. Menard, iii, 35.

15 *Hist. gén. Lang.*, x, 1645–8; Lehoux, iii, 461; *Chron. r. St.-Denis*, i, 94; *Gr. chron.*, iii, 8; *Choix de pièces*, i, 6–9; *Mon. hist.*, no. 1616.

16 *Hist. gén. Lang.*, x, 1655–6; *Comptes Rodez*, ii, 515; *Cabié (1879), 18; ACA reg. 1746, fol. 140vo; Bernis, 'Chron.', para. 110–12; AN J 186A/52; Froissart, *Chron.* (SHF), xii, 67–8. Cf. *Baudouin, 375–6; *Comptes Rodez*, ii, 509; *Hist. gén. Lang.*, x, 1653–4 (misdated), 1782; *Rouquette, 493–4; Cabié (1901)[1], no. 4 (para. 4), no. 5 (para. 4). Gaston had 2,000 men with him at Limoux on 4 Aug.: Bernis, 'Chron.', para. 115.

17 *Hist. gén. Lang.*, ix, 906–8, x, 1653–4, 1749–50; Froissart, *Chron.* (SHF), xii, 68; Mascaro, 'Libre', 74–6; *Petit Thalamus*, 403, 403–4; AN JJ 135/91; Bernis, 'Chron.', para. 115.

18 *Inv. AC Narbonne*, 359–62; *Hist. gén. Lang.*, x, 1655–7, 1663, 1665; *Arch. Montpellier*, ii, no. 93; Lehoux, ii, 54–6. Census: *Hist. gén. Lang.*, x, 1442–5.

19 BN Coll. Doat 201, fols. 109–12; *Hist. gén. Lang.*, x, 1664–8, 1670–1, 1691–2; 'Délibérations Albi', xlviii, 267–8; *Foed.*, iv, 167.

20 PRO E364/17, m. 3 (Loryng), E364/21, m.3 (Stratton), E364/27, m. 7d (Gedney). Wine: James, 33, 37. Neville: *Froissart, *Chron.* (KL), xviii, 550–2 (April 1380). Mérigot: *Reg. crim. Châtelet*, ii, 196–7.

21 Fronsac: *Foed.*, iv, 42, 152, 153; PRO C61/96, m. 17; C61/99, m. 6; *Jurades de Bergerac*, i, 48–9; *Livre de vie*, 405, 409, 414, 417. Green: *Jurades de Bergerac*, i, 70; *Livre de vie*, 416. Mussidan: *Inv. AC Périgueux*, 26, 88; *Dessalles (1847), 2; *Titres Périgueux*, 441–6; *Jurades de Bergerac*, i, 56, 57–8, 58–9, 62–3, 69–70, 78–9; *Livre de vie*, 407, 408. St.-Macaire: PRO C61/95, m. 1; C61/96, m. 15. Agenais: BN Coll. Doat 201, fols. 197–203vo; 203, fols. 39–47; PRO E101/184/1, fols. 10, 11vo–12; *Foed.*, vii, 446–7. Tolls: PRO C61/97, m. 11.

22 Perrot: *Froissart, *Chron.* (KL), xviii, 552. Mérigot: *Reg. crim. Châtelet*, ii, 186–7. Tête-Noir: *Troubat, 232, 233; Froissart, *Chron.* (SHF), ix, 140–1, xi, 144–5, xv, 209; 'Mirac. S. Martialis', 414; Mézières, *Songe*, i, 530.

23 Bertucat: PRO E403/487, m. 5 (25 Oct.); *John of G. Reg. (1379–83)*, nos. 522–3, 1095; *Jurades de Bergerac*, i, 60–1; *Trés. Chartes Albret*, i, nos. 618, 633–5; *Lettres de rois*, ii, 221–4; Boutruche, 392. Bérard's death: Froissart, *Chron.* (SHF), ix, 120–22. Caumont lands: Gregory XI, *Lettres (France)*, nos. 1036–8, 1066–80. Bergerac: *John of G. Reg. (1379–83)*, nos. 522–3, 1095. La Rochelle: *Foed.*, iv, 133; PRO C61/96, m. 14. Grants: PRO C61/95, mm. 19, 18, C61/96, m.1; E61.96, mm. 13, 12. Finance: the loans were refinanced and secured in 1383: PRO E30/301–6, 1346, 1364; PRO C61/96, m. 2; *Cat. Arch. Navarra (Comptos)*, xv, no. 910.

24 Bordelais: *Reg. St.-Flour*, 164; PRO C61/96, mm. 3; C61/97, m. 11; BN Coll. Doat 201/167–170vo, 172–176vo. Noli Barbe: AC Martel BB7, fol. 3vo; CC1bis/46; CC5, fols. 2vo, 30vo; EE1/59, 60; Lacoste, iii, 282. Douat: *Chron. Bourbon*, 153, 156–7; AC Martel

BB6, fols. 1, 3vo; CC5, fols. 35vo 37; EE1/48. Numbers: list of 30 castles prepared for the purposes of *rachat* in 1387 at *Preuves Polignac*, ii, 131–2. It excludes (i) Le Saillant and five other castles, which were dealt with separately (*Hist. gén. Lang.*, x, 1811–14); and (ii) Chalusset and Ventadour, and associated castles of Perrot de Béarn and Tête-Noir. Périgord, Agenais: *Jurades de Bergerac*, i, 55–120; *Livre de vie*.

25 *Reg. St.-Flour*, 173–82, 183, 185, 186–7, 190–1, 261, 292–303; *Savaron, 466–71; *Inv. AC Montferrand*, i, 417–18; Froissart, *Chron.* (SHF), ix, 141–2 (wrongly attributing the capture to Mérigot Marchès).

26 *Reg. St.-Flour*, 160–1, 163, 190–1, 276, 282; Boudet (1893), 21–6; 'Délibérations Albi', xlviii, 248–50, 252–3, 269, 434–5. *Tuchins* in Auvergne: Boudet (1895); *Chron. r. St.-Denis*, i, 306–8; *Reg. St.-Flour*, 185–6, 187, 190. And in Languedoc: *Hist. gén. Lang.*, ix, 910–13; *L. Menard, iii, 59–77, esp. at 65–8, 72–4, 76; *Vitae paparum*, i, 487–8.

27 Bergerac: *Jurades de Bergerac*, i, 42, 43, 44, 47, 48–9, 51–2, 69–70, 72–3, 77–8; *Livre de vie*, 405–11, 421–4. Rodez: *Rouquette, 498–500; BN Coll. Doat 202, fols. 148–151vo. Albi: 'Délibérations Albi', xlviii, 248–79, 420–9. St.-Antonin: BN Coll. Doat 146, fols. 289–294. Figeac: BN Coll. Doat 125, 126vo–129vo.

28 *Mirac. S. Martialis*, nos. 4, 13, 22, 29, 35–6, 42, 47–8, 54–5, 61–2, 71; *Liv. mirac. Ste.-Catherine*, nos. 28–9, 32, 57, 71, 78; *Reg. crim. Châtelet*, ii, 95; AD Pyr.-Atl. E49 (Casteljaloux).

29 Bertucat: PRO E403/490, m. 15; C61/97, m. 4. Ramonet's father was probably the man of the same name who served as Bertucat's second in a duel in 1361: see BN Coll. Doat 196, fol. 121–126vo. Ramonet's origins: Lacoste, iii, 270–2; *Cat. Arch. Navarra (Comptos)*, xv, nos. 905, 907, 910; BN Coll. Doat 198, fols. 331–332; *Jurades de Bergerac*, i, 85–7, 102–3 (Bannes, Issigeac); *Livre de vie*, 415. In Oct. 1384, the English chancery treated Ramonet de Sort as captain of the garrisons on the marches of Quercy and Rouergue, but not those of Auvergne: *Foed.*, vii, 447. By 1389, he was recognised as one of the principal captains in Auvergne, together with the captains of Carlat and Alleuze: *Foed.*, vii, 640. He personally commanded at Roquenatou: BN Coll. Doat 203, fols. 281–282vo. English allegiance: *Inv. arch. Aurillac*, ii, 11; BN Coll. Doat 203, fols. 281–282vo; BN Coll. Doat 194, fols. 54–55; Froissart, *Chron.* (SHF), xiv, 222.

30 Northward raids: *Flandin-Bléty, 312; *Inv. AD Côte d'Or*, i, 425; ii, 260; AD Côte d'Or B1461, fols. 134vo, 138, 138vo, B5504; B5505, B5508. Penne: AN JJ141/33; *Hist. gén. Lang.*, x, 1708–10; Lacoste, iii, 276. Ramonet's involvement is confirmed by the treaty of surrender in 1385: BN Fr. 7619, fols. 361–366vo. Bergeracois: *Inv. AC Périgueux*, 88; *Jurades de Bergerac*, i, 76, 107–8; BN Coll. Doat 201, fols. 212–212vo (Biron). Saintonge (Tonnay-Charente, Taillebourg, Bourg-Charente, Jarnac, Aigre, Verteuil, Montlieu, Archiac, Bouteville, Le Faon, La Tronchade): AN JJ124/111; *Liv. mirac. Ste.-Catherine*, nos. 57, 71; *Foed.*, vii, 446–7; *Reg. St.-Jean d'Angély*, i, 308, 316, 319, 322, 324; Froissart, *Chron.* (SHF), xi, 208–10, 252; *Chron. Bourbon*, 136. Bouteville had been occupied since 1379 at least: Barbot, i, 223–5. Verteuil was occupied in 1383: AN JJ126/200. Tonnay-Charente in early 1383: 'Compte Clos des Galées', 68–9; *Doc. Clos des Galées*, i, nos. 1195, 1208; Cochon, *Chron.*

31 *Hist. gén. Lang.*, x, 1440–3; *Preuves Polignac*, ii, 133; *Arch. Montpellier*, ii, no. 242; 'Délibérations Albi', xlviii, 453–4. Berry's itinerary: Lehoux, iii, 460–74.

32 *Hist. gén. Lang.*, x, 1708–10 (Penne); *Preuves Polignac*, ii, 75–7; *Comptes Rodez*, ii, 514–20; *Inv. AC Montferrand*, i, 426.

33 *Titres Bourbon*, ii, no. 3602; Froissart, *Chron.* (SHF), xi, 207–12, 237, 251–3; *Livre fais Bouciquaut*, 44–5, 47–9; *Chron. Bourbon*, 136–54; Christine de Pisan, *Livre des fais*, i, 156–7. Contributions: *Inv. AC Montferrand*, i, 424, 427 (Auvergne); BN PO Châteaumorand/2. Participants: Troubat, 134–5. Welsh, Bouteville: *Rec. doc. Poitou*, v, 254n[1]. The siege of Verteuil began before 28 Aug. (BN Fr. 20389/52) and ended at the beginning of Nov. (BN Clair. 163/86). Jarnac: AN JJ135/89. Permanent field force: BN Fr. 20389/43, 50. Sancerre: BN Fr. 7858, fols. 297–306vo; Fr. 32510, fols. 288vo–290, 301–303vo.

935

34 Froissart, *Chron.* (SHF), xii, 183–203; *Gall. Reg.*, iii, no. 13779; 'Délibérations Albi', xlviii, 430–1, 437, 438–9, 441–2; BN Coll. Doat 202, fols. 148–151vo; Mascaro, 'Libre', 84. Penne: *Hist. gén. Lang.*, ix, 922–3; Cabié (1901)[2]; BN Fr. 7619, fols. 361–366vo. On Passat: Contamine (1972), 583–4; Troubat, 735.

35 *Hist. gén. Lang.*, x, 1705–8, 1711–16, 1721–3; *Doc. Agenais*, no. 24; *Froissart, Chron.* (KL), xviii, 551–2; *Doc. Durfort*, ii, no. 1296. Berry's movements: Lehoux, ii, 150n², iii, 463–8. For the Bourc de Monsat: see *Preuves Polignac*, ii, 131. Escorts: *Mon. hist.*, no. 1661. *Taille*: *L. Menard, iii, 88–9.

36 *Hist. gén. Lang.*, x, 1713–14; BN Coll. Doat 201, fols. 197–203vo (Fossanas).

37 *Hist. gén. Lang.*, x, 1711–16, 1722–3. President: BN Fr. 26021/911. Southern lords in invasion army: BN Coll. Doat 203, fols. 32–36. Cahors: Lacoste, iii, 284–6. Montauban: *Hist. gén. Lang.*, ix, 926, *x, 1740.

38 BN Coll. Doat 202, fols. 292–293; *Preuves Polignac*, ii, 131–2, 133–4, 140–4; *Hist. gén. Lang.*, x, 1728–9; *Inv. AC Montferrand*, i, 431. Papal emissaries: *Comptes Rodez*, ii, 328. Aragon claim: Durrieu (1885), 31–2; Lecoy, ii, 271–2. Alliance: Le Fèvre, *Journal*, 332.

39 *Preuves Polignac*, ii, 130–45; *Cal. Pap. R. Letters*, iv, 256; BN Coll. Doat 193, fols. 148–150vo, 194, fols. 288–289, 180–180vo.

40 PRO E101/183/13 (3); E101/184/1, fols. 10vo–11, 11vo, 12, 12vo, 23; BN Coll. Doat 201, fols. 212–212vo lists Armagnac's conquests.

41 *Preuves Polignac*, ii, 132–3, 145–8; BN Coll. Doat 203, fols. 295–309vo; *Monicat, 229–30; *Inv. AC Montferrand*, i, 431–2, 432, 433.

42 Froissart, *Chron.* (SHF), xiv, 138–41, 210, 205–24. Treaties with captains: Mérigot Marchès answered for Charlus-Champagnac and Châteauneuf-de-St.-Nectaire (BN Coll. Doat 203, fols. 106–108vo), but not for St.-Exupéry in Auvergne, which was his wife's (Froissart, *Chron.* (KL), xiv, 175); Raymond-Guillaume de Caupenne answered for Carlat, Murat-Lagasse and Valcaylès (*Doc. Carlat*, i, 290–5); the Bastard of Garlans for Alleuze (*ibid.*, i, 295–8); Chopin de Badefol for Turlande (*ibid.*, i, 298–301); Guillaume de Clarens and Robert de la Lats for Orgueil and Penne (BN Coll. Doat 193, fols. 65–67vo). The castles for which Ramonet answered are not listed in the agreement with him (BN Coll. Doat 193, fols. 148–150vo) but included Roquenatou in Auvergne (BN Coll. Doat 203, fols. 281–282vo); and sixteen castles in Quercy (BN Coll. Doat 198, fols. 331–332). They appear to have included twelve listed in the conventions of Rodez: Le Roc de Verdale, Vayrac, Pinsac, Costeraste, La Garenie, Sabadel, Montvalent, Creysse, Palaret, Loubressac, Gréalou, Frayssinet.

43 See, e.g., BN Coll. Doat 193, fols. 221–3; Coll. Doat 203, fols. 216–233vo.

44 *Mirac. S. Martialis, passim; Liv. mirac. Ste.-Catherine*, nos. 28–9, 32, 57–8, 71, 73, 78.

45 The shortfall was 50,000 francs in Dec. 1389: *Monicat, 237. Payments on account: *Doc. Carlat*, i, 342–4; *Reg. crim. Châtelet*, ii, 199–200, 212. For the purpose of these payments, see the case of Chopin de Badefol, captain of Turlande, who refused a part payment because he did not want to be bound by the truce: BN Coll. Doat 193, fols. 221–223. Ramonet: BN Coll. Doat 198, fols. 331–332; 203, fols. 286–189vo; 204, fols. 1–3, 7–8vo; *Inv. AC Rodez (Cité)*, 40. Armagnac's army: BN Coll. Doat 193, fols. 209–210; 194, fols. 265–6; *Inv. AC Rodez (Cité)*, 40; 'Inv. lettres rois d'Aragon', nos. 39, 41, 53, 62, 65; 'Ann. arch. Datini', xii, 117, 118.

46 BN Fr. 32510, fol. 309vo; *Hist. gén. Lang.*, x, 1770–4; *Chron. r. St.-Denis*, i, 646–8; AN P2296, fol. 201vo; J188B/14.

47 'Séjours', 445; Mascaro, 'Libre', 93–4; *Petit Thalamus*, 415; *Chron. r. St.-Denis*, i, 626–30. Purge: *Gall. Reg.*, i, nos. 2965–6, 4877–8; v, 21407–8; *Hist. gén. Lang.*, ix, 951–2, 957–8.

48 BN Fr. 4482, pp. 28–29; BN PO 13, Aggriffin/2, 3; 293, du Berat/2, 3; 384, du Bois/28;477, le Bouteiller/17, 18; 1277, Garait/2; 2953, Viel/2; 3041, Voyer/36; BN Fr. 32510, fol. 314vo. Death of Tête-Noir: Froissart, *Chron.* (SHF), xv, 208. Le Roux brothers: *Ann. Limoges de 1638*, 286; PRO E101/41/12; Froissart, *Chron.* (KL), xiv, 104–5 (execution, but the rest of this account is fictitious). Perrot: *ibid.*, xiv, 168–9.

Mérigot: *Reg. crim. Châtelet*, ii, 178, 198–9; *Inv. AC Rodez (Cité)*, 39.
49 *Doc. Carlat*, i, 319–22, 334–42, 345–59, 363, 364, 366, 375–6, 377, 379. On Blaisy: Mézières, 'Épistre lamentable', 515. Six garrisons: *Hist. gén. Lang.*, x, 1811–14. Bétizac assets: Mascaro, 'Libre', 94–5.
50 'Inv. lettres rois d'Aragon', nos. 41, 44, 62, 65, 67, 70–1, 75; ACA *reg.* 1957, fols. 143, 148; 1958, fols. 51vo–52vo; 1760, fol. 23; 1970, fol. 67; 2053, fols. 136–7; Zurita, iv, 737–41, 744–6. Gaston Phoebus: *Tucoo-Chala (1959)*, 367–9. The brothers were both in Paris in mid-June 1390: AN J247/28, 29, 30. Charolais: *Dumay, 200–4; *Doc. Carlat*, i, 325; BN Coll. Doat 194, fols. 139–139vo.
51 Ramonet: *Doc. Carlat*, i, 360, 376–7, 381, 385; BN Coll. Doat 198, fols. 331–2. Barbe, Douat (Pinsac, Montvalent, Creysse): *Doc. Carlat*, i, 348–9. Cazillac, Montbrun: BN Coll. Doat, 194, fols. 313–15vo; AN X^{Ia} 44, fol. 110; *Doc. Carlat*, i, 325–7. Date: Alauzier (1957)[1], 103. Cf. raids from Belcastel: AC Martel CC1, fol. 41. Turlande: BN Coll. Doat 193, fols. 221–3. Mussidan: *Inv. AC Périgueux*, 185, 247–8.
52 *Reg. crim. Châtelet*, ii, 199, 200; Zurita, iv, 746; *Doc. Millau* [2], no. 473; *Inv. AC Rodez (Bourg)*, 3; *ibid. (Cité)*, 40; Rouquette, 371–5, *508–9; Froissart, *Chron.* (KL), xiv, 164 (quotation).
53 Harpeden, Gaunt: PRO E364/31, m. 5 (Traylly); *Westminster Chron.*, 402, 406. Conservators: *Chavanon, 116–17; *Foed.*, vii, 640. Elmham, Craddock: PRO E101/41/20. Douat: PRO E403/527, mm. 22, 23 (7, 22 Feb.).
54 *Foed.*, vii, 659–63; *Parl. Rolls*, vii, 143–5 (21, 22). Gaunt and the Gascons: PRO E30/1232, 1234; C61/101, mm. 4, 3; C61/104, mm. 14, 13; *Arch. mun. Bordeaux*, i, 233–4; *Foed.*, iv, 171, vii, 687–8, 727–8; *Anglo-Norman Letters*, no. 150.
55 Craddock, Trailly, Elmham: *Foed.*, vii, 656; PRO E101/319/40; E364/24, m. 3d (Craddock, Elmham); E403/532, mm. 21, 26 (23 Feb., 10 Nov.); E403/536, m. 20 (4 Mar.); E403/538, m. 8 (6 July); E403/546, m. 16, 23,24–5 (4 Dec., 2, 11 Mar.); E101/320/4; *Reg. crim. Châtelet*, ii, 192, 196; *Inv. AC Périgueux*, 185 (EE11: the date should be June 1390); *Chavanon, 116–17. Surrenders: *Doc. Carlat*, i. 332, 346–9. French protest: BN PO 2030, Montmaur/40, 41; PO 2431, de Rancé/4, 5; PRO E403/530, mm. 16, 17 (23 Aug., 26 Sept.); PRO E403/530, m. 16 (23 July); CCR 1385–9, 469.
56 La Roche-Vendeix: BN Fr. 4482, pp. 30, 33, 34, 37, 40–2, 43, 44–5, 84, 92–3, 96–7, 98–9, 104–7, 108–12, 115–16, 119–23, 126–8, 270; BN Coll. Doat 204, fol. 77; *Inv. AC Riom*, 57–8; *Doc. Carlat*, i, 322–3; *Reg. crim. Châtelet*, ii, 193. Mérigot's fate: BN Coll. Doat 194, fols. 248–248vo; *Inv. AC Rodez (Bourg)*, 3; *Moranvillé (1892), 84–7; *Inv. AC Montferrand*, i, 434, 435, 436, 439; *Doc. Carlat*, i, 378; *Reg. crim. Châtelet*, ii, 177–213, esp. 189–90, 193–4, 196, 205–11, 212–13.
57 Surrenders: Rouquette, 374; *Doc. Carlat*, i, 328–9, 343, 344, 345–6; *Hist. gén. Lang.*, x, 1820. Mérigot's family: *Inv. AC Montferrand*, i, 434, 435–6, 439; *Reg. St.-Flour*, 228–9; *Livre fais Bouciquaut*, 84–5; *Savaron, 472. Tax: *Inv. AC Rodez (Cité)*, 40, 41; BN Coll. Doat 87, fols. 292–296; *Rouquette, 510–12. Mopping-up: *Rec. Titres Périgueux*, 451; *Inv. trés. Périgueux*, no. 451; *Inv. AC Périgueux*, 187. Perrot: *Ann. Limoges de 1638*, 286–7; BN PO 1394, La Grange/20; *Livre fais Bouciquaut*, 86–7.
58 Domme: Lacoste, iii, 308–9; *Livre fais Bouciquaut*, 85–6; BN Fr. 32510, fols. 325vo–326vo. Watches: *Ord.*, vii, 334–5, viii, 356; Deschamps, *Oeuvres*, i, 307–8.

CHAPTER XV

1 *Chron. r. St.-Denis*, i, 672–82; Froissart, *Chron.* (KL), xiv, 55–8, 105–51; *Livre fais Bouciquaut*, 65–74; *Chronographia*, iii, 97–100; 'Joutes de St.-Inglebert'; *Foed.*, vii, 663, 665–6. On arms of peace and war: Keen (1984), 205–6.
2 *Foed.*, vii, 666; PRO E403/530, m. 6 (25 May); *Cal. Doc. Scot.*, iv, no. 411; *Westminster Chron.*, 436; *Chron. r. St.-Denis*, i, 672. Smithfield: *Lettres de rois*, ii, 261–2; *Westminster Chron.*, 450, 450–2; *Chron. r. St.-Denis*, i, 686–8; Froissart, *Chron.* (KL),

xiv, 253–69; *Chron. premiers Valois*, 315–16.

3 Froissart, *Chron.* (SHF), xii, 3; *Gr. chron.*, iii, 53–5; *Chronographia*, iii, 54–6; *Chron. r. St.-Denis*, i, 392–6; Juvénal, *Hist.*, 53.

4 Deschamps, *Oeuvres*, ii, 324–35 (quotation at ll. 254–6); cf, *ibid.*, ii, 27–8, iii, 100–2, iv, 111, vi, 42–3; Mézières, *Songe*, ii, 243 ('poor fellow'); Luce (1890), i, 231–43; *Procès de condamnation et de réhabilitation de Jeanne d'Arc*, ed. J. Quicherat, v (1849), 109.

5 Chandos Herald, *Prince Noir*, 50; Guillaume de la Penne, 'Gesta Britonum'; *Livre fais Bouciquaut*, 10–11; Christine de Pisan, *Advision Cristine*, 114; St.-André, *Libvre*.

6 Froissart, *Chron.* (SHF), i, 1, xii, 2–3, 35, 109, xvi, 234; 'Dit du Florin', in *Oeuvres. Poésies*, ed. A. Scheler, ii (1871), 226–7 (hotel bills); Le Fèvre, *Journal*, 7 (D. of Anjou); *Inventaires de Jean Duc de Berry (1401–1416)*, ed. J. Guiffrey, i (1894), no. 967; *The Chronicle of Froissart, translated out of French by Sir John Bourchier Lord Berners*, ed. W.P. Ker, i (1901), 1, 6.

7 Contamine (1997), 3–6; Christine de Pisan, *Livre des fais*, i, 200–1; Mézières, *Songe*, i, 530–1.

8 Coats of arms: Saul (1981), 16–25; *CPR 1388–92*, 72. Upton, *De Studio Militari*, ed. E. Bisshe (1654), 257–8.

9 *Ord.*, iii, 232 (28), v, 658, 659 (4). Froissart, *Chron.* (SHF), i, 3.

10 Bell, 10 (Table 1) (proportions); Gray, *Scalacron.*, 152, 156; Bennett (1983), 182 (Cheshire). Hawkwood: Temple-Leader, 6–7; Caferro, 38–9; *Westminster Chron.*, 520.

11 Mézières, *Songe*, ii, 403. Genoese: *Ord.*, v, 651 (26); Contamine (1972), 154–5. 1386: BN Fr. 7858, fols. 255–95; *Cron. Tournai*, 286.

12 Contamine (1972), 20–2, 178; Wright, 72–4. Proportions: *Cat. Arch. Navarra (Comptos)*, xii, nos. 621, 623–4 (service in Navarre, 1378); PRO E101/68/11 (253) (service under Hotspur, 1387); E101/41/4 (service under Arundel, 1388); Contamine (1972), 20–1, 21n[65] (France). Serving both sides: e.g. AN JJ111/115, JJ124/120. Crimes: Wright, 72–3; Gauvard, i, 413, ii, 528–40; *Reg. crim. Châtelet*, i, 130–7, 225–39, 456–62, 505–15.

13 Mézières, *Songe*, i, 530.

14 Mézières, *Songe*, ii, 403 ('guerre en l'ost ou en frontières'); *Cent Ballades*, 165 ('d'ost de guerre ou de frontière').

15 'Ann. Arch. Datini', xii, 92; *Livre fais Bouciquaut*, 39–40.

16 Charny, *Book*, 122–8; Deschamps, *Oeuvres*, i, 223–4; *Livre fais Bouciquaut*, 19–20, 24–6, 47–8, 57; Bonet, *Tree*, 131.

17 *Controversy Scrope Grosvenor*, i, 124–5, 241–2; Caferro, 200 (Sabraham in Italy); Ayton (1995), 91–3.

18 Browe: *Controversy Scrope Grosvenor*, i, 82; although in fact Browe had also served in the St.-Malo campaign of 1378 (PRO E101/36/32, m. 3) and in Buckingham's *chevauchée* of 1380 (PRO C76/65, m. 28). Stratton: M.W. Labarge, *Gascony. England's First Colony, 1204–1453* (1980), 178; *AHG*, xvi, 156–8, 165–9; PRO E101/68/8 (183); E101/180/9, fol. 52; E101/181/1 (60); E101/181/4 (37); E403/472, m. 16 (1 Apr.). Mainwaring: Morgan (1987), 155–6, 158, 165. Norbury: *ibid.*, 160; PRO E101/180/9, fol. 78vo; E101/181/1 (18, 24); C61/90, m. 1; John IV, *Actes*, nos. 418, 461, 1099–1100; Froissart, *Chron.* (SHF), xii, 138–9.

19 Permanent forces: *Rey (1965), i, 371–7. Garencières: *Exch. R. Scot.*, i, 451, 453, 454; Froissart, *Chron.* (KL), xiv, 127, 150, xv, 30. Others: Contamine (1972), 590–1; Lalande; Dumay; Troubat, ii, 700. *Livre Chev. de La Tour*, 226. Du Guesclin: *Letters B. du Guesclin*, App. I; Gauvard, ii, 855–9.

20 Contamine (1972), 178–9.

21 Contamine (1972), 619–30, 641–3; Rey (1965), ii, 402–4. *États*: *Ord.*, v, 660 (15, 16); Mézières, *Songe*, ii, 403; and examples at *Mandements*, no. 1830 (1378); *Terrier de Loray, PJ no. 93 (1385); BN Doat 203, fols. 135–136vo (1386). Garrison commanders: *Gall. Reg.*, i, no. 4722; AN JJ112/14; *Mandements*, no. 513.

22 Ayton (1994), 109–10, 120–5; Contamine (1972), 146. 1369: PRO E101/68/4 (87) (Gaunt, 1369); E101/68/4 (90) (Knolles, 1370); E101/68/5 (103) (Gascony, 1372);

E101/68/5 (95) (Edward III, 1372); E101/68/5 (111) (Brittany, 1372); E101/68/6 (120–1, 126) (Gaunt, 1373); E101/37/27 (43) (St.-Malo, 1378); E364/13, m. 13d (Buckingham) (Buckingham, 1381); E101/68/8 (197) (Portugal, 1381); E101/68/10 (250B) (Castile, 1386). Garrisons: for Calais see *Compte Gunthorp*, 20–6 (1371–2); PRO E101/68/6 (143) (1376); E101/68/8 (175). Sea: PRO E101/68/7 (149, 150, 162–167).

23 Sherborne (1964), Tables 1.1–1.4, 745–6; Bell, Tables 1, 3, 5; Powicke, 170–8; Saul (1981), 39–47, 50–9; S.M. Wright, *The Derbyshire Gentry in the Fifteenth Century* (1983), 8; Prince (1931), 361 (1338–9); PRO E36/204, fols. 105vo–110vo (1342). France: Contamine (1972), 180 (the author's figures do not bear out his conclusions).

24 Regards: Prince (1933), 293–4; Ayton (1994), 111–20; PRO E101/68/4 (90) (Knolles, 1370); E101/68/5 (103) (Pembroke, 1372); PRO E101/68/5 (95) (projected campaign of Edward III, 1372); E101/68/6 (120–1, 126) (Gaunt's campaign, 1373); E364/13, m. 13d (Buckingham) (France, 1380); E101/39/17, m. 1 (Portugal, 1381). Subcontracts: Sherborne (1964), 742–3; Goodman (1980), 116–20; Walker (1985), 103–5; Walker (1990)[1], 70–1. John of Gaunt was probably typical of great magnates in paying over his regard to his retainers and subcontractors: Walker (1990)[1], 67–9; PRO E159/153 (*brev. dir. bar.*), Mich. m. 5. Neville: *Parl. Rolls*, v, 311–12 (34). Buckingham: Walsingham, *Chron. Maj.*, i, 808.

25 Froissart, *Chron.* (SHF), xiv, 132. Proportion retained: Ayton (1994), 127–37; Keen (1965), 146–7; 'Private indentures', 27–8; Contamine (1972), 197–8.

26 Browe: *Hist. Parl.*, ii, 384, 385; Bennett (1983), 187, 189. Craddock: Morgan (1987), 175–6. Fogg: Sumption, ii, 274, 286; John IV, *Actes*, no. 19; PRO C76/56, m. 27; *Parl. Rolls*, v, 344 (129); *Anglo-Norman Letters*, no. 309. Froissart, *Chron.* (KL), xv, 186.

27 Froissart, *Chron.* (SHF), vii, 255; *Chron. Bourbon*, 189–91.

28 Chandos: Froissart, *Chron.* (SHF), vi, 156–7; vii, 168. Knolles: *Foed.*, iii, 897–8; *GEC*, v, 977–9, xii, 942 (peers: Fitzwalter, Zouche); *GEC*, vi, 67 (K.G., Sir Thomas Grandison). Knolles's knighthood: *Gr. chron.*, i, 227.

29 Mézières, *Songe*, i, 514–15; *Chron. Bourbon*, 91 (Du Guesclin).

30 Bonet, *Tree*, 130; Contamine (1972), 78–81, 224; Froissart, *Chron.* (SHF), viii, 187–8.

31 *Ord.*, iv, 67–70, v, 658–61; Contamine (1972), 81–3, 143–4, 188, 201, 224–5; Bonet, *Tree*, 122–3, 132–3; Orgeval, 42–50.

32 *Black Book*, i, 453–8; Keen (1995).

33 *Inv. mobiliers Bourgogne*, ii, nos. 803, 1401, 1614. French cross: *Cron. Tournai*, 167; Contamine (1972), 668–70. St. George's cross: *Black Book*, i, 456 (xviii); *Chronographia*, ii, 391. St. Andrew's cross: *Acts Parl. Scot.*, i, 554–5.

34 Prince (1933), 296–7 (for French practice, see Contamine (1972), 58–60); Walker (1990)[1], 55n[66] (will).

35 France: *Ord.*, iv, 68, v, 658–9; BN Lat. 9175, fols. 130–49, esp. at 141–142, 149–149vo (closing ordinance of the Estates of Languedoc, Dec. 1369); Contamine (1972), 86–7, 89–91, 110–11, 146–7. England: Prince (1933), 292–3; Ayton (1994), 55–6; Froissart, *Chron.* (SHF), viii, 78–9.

36 England: *Parl. Rolls*, v, 311–12 (34); vi, 256–7 (93). France: *Ord.*, v, 650–1 (23–4, 26); Mézières, *Songe*, i, 458–60, ii, 401–2, 403–4; Contamine (1972), 92–3, 144–6.

37 *Royal Wills*, 67, 68 (Black Prince); Ayton (1994), 57–8, 194–8, 202–6, 219–20, 224–7, 229–31; Lopes, *Crón. D. João*, ii, 216 (Falconer). Cf., for France, Contamine (1972), 17–19, 655–7.

38 'Ann. Arch. Datini', xii, 78 (arms dealer); B. Thordeman, *Armour from the Battle of Wisby, 1361* (1939), i, 185–92; Strickland & Hardy, 277–8. Charles: *Comptes Écurie*, i, nos. 66, 143, 152, 170, 223–30, 252, 507, 715–20, 939, 1029–35; *Comptes hôtel*, 219; and see his coat of mail (1383) in the cathedral museum at Chartres. Gaunt: *Crón. D. João*, ii, 202. Cf. equipment supplied for service at sea in 1385: *Doc. Clos des Galées*, i, no. 1207.

39 Ayton (1994), 197.

40 Brun, 215–16, 218–20; Contamine (1972), 656–7; Morgan (1987), 154–5 (archer); *Inv.*

mobiliers Bourgogne, i, no. 356; H.A. Dillon and W.H. St. John Hope, 'Inventory of the goods and chattels belonging to Thomas, Duke of Gloucester', *Archaeological Journal*, liv (1897), 275, 305–7; Le Bel, *Chron.*, i, 155–6 (1339); Lopes, *Crón. D. João*, ii, 223 (Castile, 1386).

41 London: *Cal. Letter Books G*, 44,191, *H*, 44, 59; *Foed.*, iii, 1050; *The London Assize of Nuisance*, ed. H.M. Chew and W. Kellaway (1973), 160. English provinces: H. Swanson, *Medieval Artisans* (1989), 70–2. Paris: G. Fagniez, *Études sur l'industrie à Paris aux xiiie et au xive siècle* (1877), 8, 9, 15, 16; *Inv. mobiliers Bourgogne*, i, nos. 590, 680, 691, 695, 893, 914, 916, 921, 926, 963, 1082, 1084–91, 1441, 1462, 1585–6, 1819–24, 2224, 2263, 2265, 2786, 3078, ii, nos. 140, 467, 545, 3010. Arsenal: *Doc. Clos des Galées*, i, 95–7. Bordeaux: *Inv. mobiliers Bourgogne*, i, no. 1371, ii, no. 824. Italy: I. Origo, *The Merchant of Prato* (1960), 35–7. Bohemia: *Cal. Plea & Mem. R., 1381–1412*, 128. Specialisation: Gaier, 164–5, 166–7. Price rises: *Parl. Rolls*, v, 224 (13) (1369); *Cal. Letter Books H*, 69, 160 (1377, 1381); *Foed.*, vii, 546 (1386). Deschamps, *Oeuvres*, vii, 36–8.

42 Froissart, *Chron.* (SHF), v, 200, viii, 163, ix, 239–40, xi, 2, 5, xv, 107, 115–16; *Cent Ballades*, 19.

43 Calais: PRO C76/56, m. 22, C76/58, m. 4, C76/59, m. 5, C76/64, m. 16, C76/68, m. 21. Brest: see, e.g., PRO E101/37/1. Cherbourg: see, e.g., PRO E101/603/4; C76/63, m. 10, C76/67, m. 22, C76/69, m. 11, C76/70, m. 18, C76/71, m. 18, C61/99, m. 18. Derval: PRO C76/53, mm. 26, 23, 22. St.-Sauveur: PRO E101/31/6 (Feb. 1370), C76/56, m. 14 (July 1373). Fronsac: PRO C76/99, m. 7. Field armies: Hewitt, 50–62; Sumption, i, 285, 510–11, 525, ii, 425, 426–7, 432, 442–4; Le Bel, *Chron.*, ii, 312 (1359). Gaunt, 1373: *Istore*, ii, 136; Froissart, *Chron.* (SHF), viii, 148–9. Castile, 1386–7: PRO C76/71, m. 13, C61/100, m. 8.

44 *Ord.*, v, 659 (7), 660 (10); Mézières, *Songe*, i, 512–13; Contamine (1972), 124–5. Low Countries: Deschamps, *Oeuvres*, v, 29; *Chron. r. St.-Denis*, i, 264, 532; Juvénal, *Hist.*, 67; AD Côte d'Or B1469, 1475.

45 *Inv. mobiliers Bourgogne*, ii, nos. 1545–56; Mézières, *Songe*, ii, 402; Lopes, *Crón. D. João*, ii, 234. Hardship: see, e.g., Charny, *Book*, 122–8; *Livre Chev. de La Tour*, 225; Deschamps, *Oeuvres*, i, 75–6.

46 Songs: Taylor, 264–6. Dogs: Knighton, *Chron.*, 44; Le Bel, *Chron.*, ii, 313; Froissart, *Chron.* (SHF), xii, 311–12; *Menagier*, 69.

47 Lopes, *Crón. D. João*, ii, 236 (D. Constanza); Lescot, *Chronique*, ed. J. Lemoine (1896), 77–8 and *Grandes chroniques de France*, ed. J. Viard, ix (1937), 298–9 (Totesham); *Foed.*, iii, 480 (Constance Knolles); *Doc. Millau* [2], no. 337, 341 (Mascy); *Rec. doc. Poitou*, iv, 364–7, 402–4 (Say). Dame de Pons: Froissart, *Chron.* (SHF), viii, 18–19; *John of G. Reg. (1372–6)*, no. 1090. Mistresses: *Rec. doc. Poitou*, iv, 114–15 (Devereux); Jean d'Arras, *Mélusine*, 811 (Cresswell); *Cal. S.P. Venice*, i, nos. 67, 69–71, 74 (Gold).

48 London, Duchy of Cornwall Office, Journal of John Henxteworth, fol. 1; *Letters B. du Guesclin*, nos. 496, 515, 522, 720, 763; *Itin. Ph. le Hardi*, 489; Pitti, *Cron.*, 72–3; Charny, *Book*, 112. Sentries: e.g., Walsingham, *Chron. Maj.*, 172; *Chron. Bourbon*, 91, 125.

49 *Cent Ballades*, 14.

50 *Chronicon Galfridi le Baker*, ed. E.M. Thompson (1889), 148, 152; Walsingham, *Chron. Maj.*, i, 284–8.

51 Roosebeke: *Chronographia*, iii, 307; *Chron. r. St.-Denis*, i, 220. Hastings: S. Hooper et al., 'The grave of Sir Hugh de Hastyngs, Elsing', *Norfolk Archaeology*, xxxix (1984), 88–99. Scrope: *Controversy Scrope Grosvenor*, i, 51, 127, 145; *Cal. Inq. P.M.*, viii, no. 546. Clisson: Froissart, *Chron.* (SHF), vi, 165. Provence: Hébert, 21, 22, 23. Bretons: St.-André, *Libvre*, 396.

52 Henri de Mondeville, *Die Chirurgie*, ed. J.L. Pagel (1892), 140, 206, 332; M.C. Pouchelle, *The Body and Surgery in the Middle Ages*, tr. R. Morris (1990), 58–9; Rawlcliffe, 75–6.

53 Lancaster, *Livre*, 202, 207–8; Chauliac, *Gr. Chirurgie*, 15–16; *E. Forestié, 'Hughes de

Cardaillac et la poudre à canon', *Bull. Soc. Archéol. Tarn-et-Garonne*, xxix (1901), 193, 217–18 (Montauban). Ointments, disinfectants: e.g., *Doc. Clos des Galées*, ii, no. XXVII (542); *Inv. mobiliers Bourgogne*, ii, no. 1343; Lang, 121–30; Secousse, *Preuves*, 503 (arsenic). Diet: Mézières, *Songe*, i, 513. Rest: *Foed.*, iii, 473.

54 Budes: *Mon. proc. canonisation Ch. de Blois*, 281–2. Personal surgeons: PRO C81/333/19764 (Edward III); *Foed.*, iii, 403 (Black Prince); *Inv. mobiliers Bourgogne*, i, nos. 1411n[3]; *Itin. Ph. le Hardi*, 494, 495, 558; *John of G. Reg. (1379–83)*, nos. 48, 691. Humbler men: BN PO 2490 Riquelme/2 (sieges in Garonne campaign, 1346); *Doc. Clos des Galées*, i, no. 591 (wounds received in 'various assaults', 1363). Surgeons who served in *routier* garrisons often claimed to have been constrained: AN JJ90/385 (Creil, *ca.* 1358); *S. Luce, 'Négociations des anglais avec le roi de Navarre', *Mems. Soc. Hist. Paris*, i (1875), 113, 122–5 (St.-Cloud, 1358). Agincourt: Rawcliffe, 141.

55 Chauliac, *Gr. Chirurgie*, 201, 206–8, 255; *Works*, iv, 493 (ll. 1114–15). David: PRO E101/25/10; Bower, *Scotichron.*, vii, 260. Henry: Lang, 121–30.

56 Cambridge, Corpus Christi Coll. MS 297, cited in *Menagier*, 306n[141]; BN Esp. 214, fols. 1–73; Poulle-Drieux, 35; Davis, 104–5. On Jean de Béarn: PRO C61/97, m. 5.

57 S. Luce, *Histoire de Bertrand du Guesclin. La Jeunesse de Bertrand* (1876), 312–14, 149–52; *Letters B. du Guesclin*, nos. 97–8; Sumption, ii, 555–6. Maignelay: Robert of Avesbury, *de gestis mirabilibus regis Edwardi*, ed. E.M. Thompson (1889), 416; *CPR 1354–8*, 235; AN JJ91/499; *Foed.*, iii, 359. Captal: Sumption, ii, 511, 522, 574, and above. Montet: PRO C61/96, m. 15.

58 Bonet, *Tree*, 152; Keen (1965), 156–7; *Black Book*, i, 457 (xxii); Froissart, *Chron.* (SHF), ix, 122; xv, 146, 154.

59 Sumption, i, 553–4, 574; Contamine (1972), 198; Timbal, *Régistres*, 306. Captal: Froissart, *Chron.* (SHF), viii, 239–40; *Istore*, ii, 124.

60 Bonet, *Tree*, 152; 'Complainte sur la bataille de Poitiers', ed. C. de Beaurepaire, *BEC*, xii (1851), 257, 261.

61 Carlisle: *Reg. crim. Châtelet*, i, 383; PRO C61/70, m. 32. Poitiers: Bel, *Chron.*, ii , 237–8.

62 Froissart, *Chron.* (SHF), viii, 239–40 (Greilly); *Foed.*, iii, 923 (Beaufort); Bonet, *Tree*, 153.

63 Jones (1996), 198 (Arundel, etc.); *CPR 1385–9*, 204 (Perrers); *Inv. Arch. Bruges*, ii, 243–4 (para. VII) (Pembroke); Given-Wilson (1981) (Guesclin). Secondary market: Timbal, *Régistres*, 332; Given-Wilson (2001), 814–24, 830–3; Perroy (1951)[2], 575–6. Ransom brokerage: Timbal, *Régistres*, 346–51 (Maignelay); Tucoo-Chala (1959), 284–9; *Hunger, 152–70 (Brucourt); Jones (1996), 194–9, *206–7 (Bourchier).

64 Keen (1965), 178–81; Bonet, *Tree*, 153, 159–60; Froissart, *Chron.* (SHF), viii, 47–8, 5, xv, 152–3; *Chron. premiers Valois*, 235. L de Châlons: AN 105/273. Denia: Gutiérrez de Velasco, 288–9; *Tucoo-Chala (1959), 398 (no. 279). Cf. Timbal, *Régistres*, 362.

65 BN Doat 195, fols. 34–34vo (Albrets); Froissart, *Chron.* (SHF), ix, 135–6 (St.-Pol); *Froissart, *Chron.* (KL), xviii, 508–9 (Percy); 'Anglo-French negotiations', 13 (Captal); *Jones (1996), 205, 207 (Bourchier); Gray, *Scalacron.*, 5.

66 Châtillon: Anselme, viii, 46; *Parl. Rolls*, v, 364 (165); *CPR 1377–81*, 276; Froissart, *Chron.* (SHF), viii, 182; *Anonimalle Chron.*, 62; Noyal, 'Frag. Chron.', 272. Percy: *Froissart, *Chron.* (KL), xviii, 506–9. Cf. the oath of the Scottish knights Sir Walter Halliburton and Sir David Anand in 1350: *CCR 1349–54*, 223.

67 Audrehem: *Chron. premiers Valois*, 180–1. Felton: *Foed.*, iv, 107. For the sale of Bordes: *CCR 1377–81*, 311, 409, 495, 549. Châtillon: Anselme, viii, 46; his letters of appointment are dated 9 March 1372: *Mandements*, no. 870.

68 Du Guesclin: *Letters B. du Guesclin*, nos. 38–9, 43; *Chron. Bourbon*, 89. Garencières: *Foed.*, iii, 228. Pipe: Gray, *Scalachron.*, 178–80. Maignelay: *CPR 1354–8*, 235; Timbal, *Régistres*, 349. Smoking out: *Rec. doc. Poitou*, iii, 295–8. Constable's court: Keen (1965), 25–30; *CPR 1345–8*, 468; *Foed.*, iii, 251, 343; *Issues Exch.*, 159; *Gr. chron.*, iii, 130–1. Duels: e.g., *Foed.*, iii, 228 (Richard Totesham and Yon de Garencières, 1351);

Chron. Bourbon, 98–100 (lord of Montravel and Perrot de Lignaige, 1375); BN Doat 203, fols. 267–272vo (Jacques Breton and Louis de Cera, 1386). Reversed arms: Keen (1965), 55–6; *Songe du vergier*, i, 293.

CHAPTER XVI

1 *PPC*, i, 19–21 (formal instructions), 22–4 (permitted concessions); BN Coll. Dupuy 306, fols. 77vo–78vo; *Moranvillé (1889), 367–9. Dates and participants: PRO E364/24, m. 1 (Durham); BN PO 1053, d'Erians/17, 20–22; BN Clair. 177/137–9. Parliament was summoned on 12 Sept. 1390 to consider (among other things) the terms of peace: *CCR 1389–92*, 99; *Parl. Rolls*, vii, 174 (1).
2 Froissart, *Chron.* (KL), xiv, 314–15, 384–5, xv, 80–1, 110, 120–1, 154, xvi, 1–5.
3 Mézières, *Songe*, i, 402; Gower, *Vox Clamantis*, Lib. V, caps. 5, 7, Lib. VII, caps. 1, 4, in *Works*, iv, 208–9, 214–18, 273, 279; *The Two Ways*, ed. V.J. Scattergood, *The Works of Sir John Clanvowe* (1965), 69.
4 Clanvowe: *Westminster Chron.*, 480. Lollardy: see A. Hudson, *The Premature Reformation* (1988), 368–70; *Select English Works of John Wyclif*, ed. T. Arnold, iii (1871), 137–8; *Registrum Johnanis Trefnant Episcopi Herefordensis*, ed. W.W. Capes (1916), 369–70, 377–9; McFarlane (1972), Part II. Knolles: *Foed.*, vii, 641; *ODNB*, xxxi, 956. Cheshire: Bennett (1983), 165–8, 173–4, 180–3, 190–1; Morgan (1978); Morgan (1987), 121–78. It has been estimated that there were about 10,000 families in England from which men-at-arms were drawn: C. Given-Wilson, *The English Nobility in the Late Middle Ages* (1987), 72. The largest number that ever served in a continental army in this period was 3,000 in John of Gaunt's expedition of 1373–4. Of forty Gloucestershire knights and squires known to have been active in the reign of Richard II, nine had served in France, seven of whom had served for a single campaign: Saul (1981), 288–92 (the only systematic regional survey); cf. Walker (1990)[1], 42–50. Arundel: Walsingham, *Chron. Maj.*, i, 810–12. 'War!': *The Tale of Melibeus*, in *Works*, iv, 203.
5 *Cron. siculum*, 84–6.
6 Christine de Pisan, *Livre des fais*, i, 172–4; *ibid.*, *Livre corps policie*, 46; Juvénal, *Hist.*, 88; *Chron. r. St.-Denis*, iii, 738; Nicolas de Baye, *Journal*, ed. A. Tuetey, ii (1888), 294. Touraine: BN Fr. n.a. 3653, nos. 406–7; *Jarry (1889), 418.
7 Jarry (1889), 47–8, *392–406; Bouard, 83, 85–99; *Chron. r. St.-Denis*, i, 608–10.
8 *Chron. r. St.-Denis*, i, 622–4. Charles's plans: *Westminster Chron.*, 464–6; Walsingham, *Chron. Maj.*, i, 908–10; *Choix de pièces*, i, 112–17 (esp. 114–15); *Jarry (1889), 406–7, 419–30; *Romano, 611–23; *Durrieu (1880)[2], 41–52 (esp. 42–3), 61–8 (esp. 63–4); *Champollion-Figeac (1844), 28–39. Cf. 'Ann. arch. Datini', 119; *Valois (1896–1902), ii, 177n²; *Dok. Gesch. Schismas*, 50, 61–2; *Mirot (1933), 537–41.
9 'Ann. arch. Datini', xii, 122, 123, 123–4, 127; *Cron. siculum*, 94, 97,88–100; *Diurnali Monteleone*, 55; Valois (1896–1902), ii, 168; *Dok. Gesch. Schismas*, 61. Army: Froissart, *Chron.* (KL), xiv, 282; AD Côte-d'Or B1479, fol. 14vo, B1480, fol. 38; *Mirot (1933), 537, 538;*Terrier de Loray, PJ. nos. 133–4; *Pièces rel. Louis d'Orléans*, nos. 20–1.
10 *Lettres de rois*, ii, 261–2; *Westminster Chron.*, 450; BN PO 1053 d'Erians/19; *CCR 1389–92*, 216; *Pièces rel. Louis d'Orléans*, no. 17 (pp. 53, 56); BN Fr. 25706/259. Offer: Walsingham, *Chron. Maj.*, i, 904. The territorial proposals were later said to be substantially the same as those made at Amiens in March 1392: *Moranvillé (1889), 372–3. Summit: *Dipl. Corr.*, 224 (correctly dated to 1390); *Parl. Rolls*, vii, 174 (1); *Dok. Gesch. Schismas*, 50–1. On St.-Pol's past diplomatic activities, 1389–90: *Foed.*, vii, 634, 667.
11 PRO E403/532, m. 9 (10 Dec.); Walsingham, *Chron. Maj.*, i, 904; *Dok. Gesch. Schismas*, 50–1.
12 PRO E364/24, m. 2 (Percy & Clifford); E403/532, mm. 16, 20 (9, 23 Feb.); *Chron. premiers Valois*, 316–17; *Moranvillé (1889), 369–70; 'Ann. arch. Datini', 127; *Dok.

Gesch. Schismas, 67; *Valois (1896–1902), ii, 179n[6]. Bernabò: PRO E403/524, mm. 14, 20 (16 July, 23 Aug.); E403/527, mm. 20, 22 (25 Jan., 7 Feb.); E403/530, mm. 14, 16 (13, 23 July).

13 Froissart, *Chron.* (KL), xiv, 282–3; Morice, *Preuves*, ii, 555–6, 573–4; BN Fr. 20405/9, 20885/77–82; John IV, *Actes*, nos 786 (p. 494), 983A (p. 573).

14 John IV, *Actes*, nos. 779A-B, 780; *Foed.*, vii, 693; 'Ann. arch. Datini', 127–30; *Durrieu (1880)[2], 62–3, 75–7, 80–102, 234–47; Bouard, 128–9.

15 *Westminster Chron.*, 456–8; cf. Walsingham, *Chron. Maj.*, i, 904.

16 PRO E403/533, mm. 6, 7, 8, 9, 11, 14 (6, 10, 13, 27 May, 6, 16 June, 11 July, 12 Aug.); PRO E364/24, m. 6d (Stury, Stanley); BN PO 671, Chantemelle/26–29; 2633, Saqueville/33, 37–9; *Westminster Chron.*, 478; *Dipl. corr.*, no. 135; *Moranville (1889), 370–1; *Parl. Rolls*, vii, 196 (10).

17 *Parl. Rolls*, vii, 196, 197–8 (10, 15). Clerical subsidy: *CFR*, xi, 33, 71–4.

18 *Baldwin, 493–6; *Moranville (1889), 371–2.

19 *Chron. r. St.-Denis*, i, 736–40. Mézières: *Songe*, ii, 293.

20 *Moranville (1889), 371–4, 377; *Chronographia*, iii, 102–4; Froissart, *Chron.* (KL), xiv, 376–88; Walsingham, *Chron. Maj.*, i, 918–20; *Westminster Chron.*, 486, 490 (muddled). Truce: *Foed.*, vii, 719–20.

21 Gerson, *Oeuvres*, vii (2), 446, 447–9.

22 Barbary: *Chron. r. St.-Denis*, i, 648–71; *Chron. Bourbon*, 218–57; Froissart, *Chron.* (KL), xiv, 151–9, 211–53, 269–80; *Chronographia*, iii, 100; *Westminster Chron.*, 432, 448–50; Stella, *Ann. Gen.*, 194. Poland: *Rechnungen*, 3, 4, 5, 6, 10, 28, 35, 109–29; *Expeditions*, xliii, xlv; *Westminster Chron.*, 444–8, 478, 480–4; BN PO 1913, Meingre/7; [A. Molinier], 'Campagne de Boucicault en Prusse', *BEC*, xxxviii (1878), 491–2.

23 Froissart, *Chron.* (KL), xiv, 389; *Moranville (1881), 30–2.

24 *Westminster Chron.*, 488–90; Walsingham, *Chron. Maj.*, i, 920–2; Knighton, *Chron.*, 544; Froissart, *Chron.* (KL), xiv, 388–9. For those summoned, see PRO E403/538, m. 9 (12 July).

25 *Foed.*, vii, 721–3; Moranville (1889), 376–8; *Dipl. Corr.*, no. 151; Le Bis, 'Pratique', no. 1.

26 *Lefranc, 450–2; Froissart, *Chron.* (KL), xv, 4–14; *Chron. r. St.-Denis*, i, 2–4; *Chronographia*, iii, 104. On Craon: *Broussillon, ii, nos. 1235–8, 1249, 1252, 1255, 1264, 1269, 1300; *Jarry (1889), 417; *Chron. premiers Valois*, 330–1; Froissart, *Chron.* (KL), xv, 1–4; Juvénal, *Hist.*, 44; 'Mémoire de P. de Craon', 105, 106–7. His financial difficulties: *Broussillon, ii, p. 227 and nos. 1242, 1256, 1258–9, 1261, 1265, 1268, 1271, 1292; Henneman (1996), 290[78].

27 Froissart, *Chron.* (KL), xv, 11–13, 15, 13–21; 'Chron. Brioc.', col. 6; 'Ann. arch. Datini', xii, 137; *Chron. premiers Valois*, 322–3; *Broussillon, ii, nos.1273–6, 1278–80; *Chron. r. St.-Denis*, ii, 6–8; *Courteault, 441–2.

28 'Chron. Brioc.', col. 62; *Chron. r. St.-Denis*, i, 720–2; John IV, *Actes*, no. 983 (p. 576).

29 'Chron. Brioc.', cols. 63–8; Morice, *Preuves*, ii, cols. 577–8, 581–8, 594; Froissart, *Chron.* (KL), xv, 362–8; 'Séjours', 453–4; John IV, *Actes*, nos. 795–9, 803–5. *Chron. r. St.-Denis*, ii, 8–10; Bouchart, *Gr. chron. Bretagne*, ii, 185 (late). Cf. for preliminary embassies: *Terrier de Loray, PJ nos. 135–6; BN PO 584 Canard/15, 1320 Giac/28, 1878 Martreuil/9, 2828 Thigonville/3; BN Clair. 140/59, 204/104.

30 *Chron. r. St.-Denis*, ii, 10–12; 'Chron. Brioc.', cols. 67–8; *Chron. premiers Valois*, 330–1; Juvénal, *Hist.*, 89–90; *Chron. Bourbon*, 261–3; Froissart, *Chron.* (KL), xv, 22–3, 25–6. Loan: BN Fr. 4482, p. 242. The army must have been summoned not later than the beginning of July, for companies began to muster at Le Mans from the 18th: BN Clair. 42, p. 3142; 51, p. 3857vo; Morice, *Preuves*, ii, 597–616. Alliance proposed: *PPC*, i, 41–7, 89–93.

31 Rey (1965), ii, 387n[2]; Morice, *Preuves*, ii, 597–616; *Pièces rel. Louis d'Orléans*, no. 39; *Chronographia*, iii, 104–5; BN Fr. 4482, pp. 167–235; BN Clair. 841, pp. 167–235; Froissart, *Chron.* (KL), xv, 28–9, 34, 32–4.

32 Chron. r. St.-Denis, ii, 18–20; Froissart, Chron. (KL), xv, 29–30, 35–43; 'Ann. arch. Datini', xii, 138; Chron. premiers Valois, 323–4; Chronographia, iii, 105; Chron. Bourbon, 264–5.

33 Chron. r. St.-Denis, ii, 22–4; Froissart, Chron. (KL), xv, 43–5, 48–51; Chron. premiers Valois, 324–5. Cf. Jarry (1889), 430 (processions).

34 Froissart, Chron. (KL), xv, 47, 49; BN Fr. 4482, pp. 242, 269; 'Chron. Brioc.', col. 68; Chron. r. St.-Denis, ii, 24–6; 'Séjours', 457; Itin. Ph. le Hardi, 229; Chronographia, iii, 106. Louis's ways: Mézières, Songe, ii, 466–9; Juvénal, Hist., 88, 96; *Carbonnières, 816–17; Deschamps, Oeuvres, vii, 120–1.

35 Chron. premiers Valois, 324–5, 335; Valois (1888), 97–103; Chron. r. St.-Denis, ii, 10, 26–8; Froissart, Chron. (KL), xv, 53–4, 56–71; Chronographia, iii, 106–7; Deschamps, Oeuvres, iv, 122; Moranvillé (1888), 158–9; Rey (1965), ii, 573–7.

36 John IV, Actes, no. 930 (p. 543); 'Chron. Brioc.', 69; Froissart, Chron. (KL), xv, 71–4, 96–7, 98–9, 202–4; Chron. r. St.-Denis, ii, 28–30; Istore, ii, 411; 'Chron. Pays-Bas', 287; Juvénal, Hist., 92, *774; Chronographia, iii, 106–7; Moranvillé (1888), 159–62, *373–4; Choix de pièces, i, 117–19, 128; AN X^{1a} 1477, fol. 409vo (involvement of Bourbon and Orléans); BN Clair. 191/27.

37 Valois (1888), 98–100; Vaughan, 44–5; Jarry (1889), 82–93, 98–100, 103–6; Nordberg, 13, 15–16, 41–60; Juvénal, Hist., 96.

38 *Jarry (1889), 419–24, 434–5; Chron. Siculum, 99–110, 111; 'Ann. arch. Datini', xii, 142, xiii, 58–9. Clementist companies in march of Viterbo: *Durrieu (1880)[2], 59–60.

39 'Ann. arch. Datini', xiii, 58–9, 61, 63–5, 65–9; *Jarry (1889), 426–30; Jarry (1892), 248; Jarry (1896), 40–5, *368 [1, 2], *396–7; Choix de pièces, i, 112–17; 'Inv. lettres rois d'Aragon', nos. 93–6; *Durrieu (1880)[2], 61–8; Favier (1966), 627, 628; Titres Bourbon, ii, no. 3923.

40 Chron. r. St.-Denis, ii, 22; PRO E403/538, m. 12 (10 Sept.) (spies); Mézières, Letter, 86, 103, 105, 106, 108; Anglo-Norman Letters, no. 10; Dipl. Corr., nos. 150–1; Le Bis, 'Pratique', nos. 1–2. On Robert: Jorga, 479–80; Froissart, Chron. (KL), xv, 188–90.

41 Edinburgh U.L., Ms. 183, fol. 144vo; Chron. r. St.-Denis, ii, 74; Froissart, Chron. (KL), xv, 108–9; Foed., vii, 746; PRO C47/14/6 (44); Walsingham, Chron. Maj., i, 944. Participants: Bellamy (1964–5), 261–3. On the Mascys: Morgan (1987), 76, 108, 110–11, 135, 137, 138, 164.

42 Foed., vii, 738–9; Froissart, Chron. (KL), xv, 110–12, 116–17, 120; Chron. r. St.-Denis, ii, 74–8; Inv. AD Nord, iv, 19; Walsingham, Chron. Maj., i, 940; Deschamps, Oeuvres, vii, 293–311, esp. 308. Gaunt was the only English ambassador identified by name when the conference was first proposed in Aug. 1392: Dipl. corr., no. 150. Gloucester appears to have been added by early Jan. 1393: PRO E403/541, m. 12 (9 Jan.). English expenditure: PRO E403/541, mm. 17, 22 (25 Feb., 1 Apr.); E403/543, mm. 5, 12, 16, 17, 18 (10 May, 4, 12 June, 15, 22 July); E403/546, m. 7 (12 Nov.). Dates: 'Séjours', 459–60; Itin. Ph. le Hardi, 232; Froissart, Chron. (KL), xv, 110–12.

43 Chron. r. St.-Denis, ii, 78; Froissart, Chron. (KL), xv, 109–23.

44 Chron. r. St.-Denis, ii, 82; John IV, Actes, no. 930; Foed., vii, 748; Chron. premiers Valois, 331; Anglo-Norman Letters, no. 133; *Palmer (1966)[2]; PRO E36/188, pp. 85–6; Dipl. Corr., no. 197. For earlier French proposals: 'Voyage de N. de Bosc', 309–15, 324–5, 326–7; Moranvillé (1889), 372–3.

45 Froissart, Chron. (KL), xv, 122–3, 127–8, 260; Chron. r. St.-Denis, ii, 86–94; Juvénal, Hist., 98, 100–1; Chronographia, iii, 110.

46 'Ann. arch. Datini', xiii, 75; Chron. r. St.-Denis, ii, 94; Walsingham, Chron. Maj., i, 944–8, 956; Parl. Rolls, vii, 264–6 (20, 21); Foed., vii, 746. Date of G. de Melun's mission: PRO E403/546, m. 3 (12 Oct.). Local grievances: Morgan (1987), 193–4; Walker (1990)[1], 171–3. Lancaster and Gloucester returned from France on 20 June: Westminster Chron., 514.

47 Lettres de rois, ii, 268–9; PRO E364/26, m. 2d (Durham); E364/27, m. 2d (Sergeaux, Newton, Rouhale, Puy); E30/1583, 1629; Foed., vii, 753; Dipl. Corr., no. 197;

Chronographia, iii, 110. Cherbourg: PRO E30/316; *Foed.*, vii, 756–7, 759–60, 764–5; *Cat. Arch. Navarra (Comptos)*, xx, 367, 645; PRO E101/41/24. Brest: Morice, *Preuves*, ii, 576; PPC, i, 47–50. Calais: *Eulogium*, iii, 369; *English Chron.*, 7.

48 PRO E403/546, m. 20 (17 Feb.). Statistics extracted from *Hist. Parl.*.

49 *Parl. Rolls*, vii, 249, 258–9, 264–5 (1, 11, 20, 21); Walsingham, *Chron. Maj.*, i, 956. Arundel licence: CPR 1391–6, 405.

50 *Parl. Rolls*, vii, 259–60, 262–3 (12, 16, 17); *Westminster Chron.*, 516–18; PRO C76/78, m. 18; E101/320/9; E364/27, m. 5d (Hereford); *Itin. Ph. le Hardi*, 236; *Foed.*, vii, 766, 769–76. Crusade: *Cartellieri, 145–6, 148–9. I do not accept the argument of Palmer (1971), ch. 9, that the Leulinghem agreement was destroyed by Gascon opposition to the transfer of Aquitaine to John of Gaunt. The idea that John of Gaunt might do homage for Aquitaine instead of Richard II had been raised by the French on several occasions as a method of dealing with Richard's reluctance to do homage. It was seriously contemplated by the English between 1390 and 1392, but killed by the hostility of the Council of Stamford. Only for a brief period in 1392 did Richard consider separating Aquitaine from his Crown.

51 See *Hist. Vitae*, 134, 166–7, and the portrait panel and funeral effigy in Westminster Abbey, both dating from *ca*. 1395; Usk, *Chron.*, 18; Brown, Colvin & Taylor, 998 (Sheen); Walsingham, *Chron. Maj.*, i, 960–2; *Foed.*, vii, 784, 785; CCR 1392–6, 368; *Anglo-Norman Letters*, no. 29.

52 *Cal. Letter Books H*, 412; CPR 1391–6, 451–2; PRO E101/402/20, fols. 31–40vo (mutilated at end). York: *Foed.*, vii, 789–90. Gaunt: PRO E30/1232 (notarised narrative of the city of Bordeaux); Froissart, *Chron.* (KL), xv, 135; *Anglo-Norman Letters*, no. 19. Palmer (1972), 158–60 accepts the statement in Froissart, *Chron.* (KL), xv, 157–9, that the revolt was provoked by the grant of the duchy to Gaunt and his heirs in perpetuity. But the original grant (*Foed.*, vii, 659–60) was for life only, and no grant in wider terms was ever enrolled on the Gascon roll. Froissart's story is also inconsistent with the notarised narrative and with Richard II's declaration on 10 September 1394 that he had never granted Aquitaine to Gaunt for any longer term than his life: see *Arch. mun. Bordeaux*, i, no. 66. D. of Burgundy: AN J243/79; BN Coll. Bourgogne 53, fols. 227, 230, 100, p. 55; *Itin. Ph. le Hardi*, 236–7; John IV, *Actes*, nos. 982–983B, 985; Morice, *Preuves*, ii, 633–43, 655–6; 'Chron. Brioc.', cols. 73–6.

53 Delaville le Roulx, i, 229–32, *ii, 18–20 ; Palmer (1972), 200–4, 240–2; Paviot (2003), 24–31; Vaughan, 61–4. Venetians: *Cal. S.P. Venice*, i, nos. 115, 117.

54 'Ann. arch. Datini', xiii, 95, 96; *Durrieu (1880)[2], 69–74; Bouard, 172; Jarry (1896), ch. 3, 4.

55 *Chron. r. St.-Denis*, ii, 94–100, 130–82; *Chart. Univ. Paris*, iii, nos. 1680, 1680, 1683–4; Valois (1896–1902), ii, 224–71; Vaughan, 184–6; *Goñi Gaztambide, 170; Kaminsky, 53–6.

56 *Chron. r. St.-Denis*, ii, 184; *Vet. script. ampl. coll.*, vii, 479–80, 483; Ehrle, 'Afterconcils von Perpignan', v, 403; Valois (1896–1902), iii, 16.

57 *Vet. script. ampl. coll.*, vii, 437–8, 483–7; *Chron. r. St.-Denis*, ii, 204–6; Ehrle, 'Neue Materialen', vi, 160–2.

58 *Chron. r. St.-Denis*, ii, 218–44; *Vet. script. ampl. coll.*, vii, 438–58, esp. 449; Kaminsky, 124–34; Cramaud, *De substraccione*, 231–2.

59 Jarry (1896), 78–9, 83–94, 120–1, 127–8, 154–5, *370[4], *403–20; *Jarry (1892), 558–70; Bouard, 183, 188–9; *Chron. r. St.-Denis*, ii, 400–2; *Choix de pièces*, i, 134–6; *Perroy (1933), 412–14. Queen's role: Bouard, 190–1; Pitti, *Chron.*, 94.

60 *Vet. script. ampl. coll.*, vii, 487–530; 'Ann. arch. Datini', xiv, 14–22. Session of 8 July: Valois (1896–1902), iii, 62–3; S. Baluze, *Miscellanea*, ed. J.D. Mansi, ii (1762), 594.

61 PPC, i, 14b; Palmer (1968), 518–19; Bonet, *Somnium*, 92; *Valois (1896–1902), iii, 76n^3, 620–3.

62 Froissart, *Chron.* (KL), xv, 155; PRO E364/28, m. 6d (bp. St. David's); E159/172 (Brev. bar., Hilary), m. 1, and *ibid.* (Brev. bar., Mich.), m. 3; E403/549, m. 15, 17 (22 Mar.,

3 Apr.); *Foed.*, vii, 794–5; *Palmer (1971)[2], 16–17; *Anglo-Norman Letters*, no. 109. For Navarre, see Froissart, *Chron.* (KL), xv, 155. For Aragon, see 'Inv. lettres rois d'Aragon', no. 105; Alpartil, *Chron.*, 16–17. Cf. Palmer (1971)[2], 2–8, 13–16 (overstates the significance of negotiations with Aragon).

63 *Anglo-Norman Letters*, no. 172; *Froissart, *Chron.* (KL), xviii, 573–5; *Foed.*, vii, 802–5; Mezières, *Letter*, esp. 77, 140–2, 145; Palmer (1971)[2], 8–10.

64 Given-Wilson (1986), 214–15, 270–1, 282–6; Tout (1920–37), vi, 108; *Froissart, *Chron.* (KL), xviii, 574.

65 Froissart, *Chron.* (KL), xv, 140–2, 146, 154–6, 164, 165–6.

66 *Foed.*, vii, 802–5; *Palmer (1972), 256–7. Retinues: BN Fr. 7621, fol. 187; *Chron. r. St.-Denis*, ii, 328.

67 PRO E364/29, m. 1 (bp. St. David's, Nottingham, Rutland, abp. Dublin), m. 7 (Scrope); *Chron. r. St.-Denis*, ii, 328; Froissart, *Chron.* (KL), xv, 183.

68 PRO C76/80, m. 18; *Chron. r. St.-Denis* , ii, 358–62; *Foed.*, vii, 811–12.

69 *Foed.*, vii, 813–30; Chaplais, *English Med. Dipl. Practice*, nos. 262, 270, 276; *Chron. r. St.-Denis*, ii, 412–14. Bewitched: *ibid.*, ii, 402–8; Lehoux, ii, 351n[1].

70 Walsingham, *Ann.*, 187–8; *Foed.*, vii, 811, viii, 43; PRO E101/402/15, m. 5; Froissart, *Chron.* (KL), xv, 238, 195–202, 272–3; *Le Bis, 'Pratique', no. 4[7].

71 *Atiya, 144–8; *Itin. Ph. le Hardi* , 250; *Cron. volgare*, 208; Froissart, *Chron.* (KL), xv, 218–21, 230, 318–20; *Chron. r. St.-Denis*, ii, 428–30; *Livre fais Bouciquaut*, 90; *Chronographia*, iii, 129–30; Palmer (1972), 239–40; Paviot (2003), 31–2, 36–7. Numbers: see Atiya, 67.

72 *Foed.*, vii, 834; Chaplais, *English Med. Dipl. Practice*, no. 57 (b); *Chron. r. St.-Denis*, ii, 444–50; Froissart, *Chron.* (KL), xv, 273–6; *Anglo-Norman Letters*, no. 174. Dates: PRO E101/320/16; E101/403/10; *Itin. Ph. le Hardi*, 255. Oxford, pamphleteers: Perroy (1933), 366–78; Valois (1896–1902), iii, 76–9, esp. *78n[2].

73 *Choix de pièces*, i, 133–4; Le Bis, 'Pratique', no. 3; Walsingham, *Ann.*, 188–94; *Chron. r. St.-Denis*, ii, 450–72; Froissart, *Chron.* (KL), xv, 297–307; Meyer, 'Entrevue'; Chaplais, *English Med. Dipl. Practice*, no. 197. Oath: *Froissart, *Chron.* (KL), xviii, 582–3. Dolls: *Mirot (1902), 155. Dowry: *Foed.*, vii, 846–7.

74 *Perroy (1933), 414–15. Castile: *Goñi Gaztambide, 171–2; Kaminsky, 158. Robert: Valois (1896–1902), iii, 115n[3].

75 J.C. Lunig, *Codex Italiae Diplomaticus*, i (1725), 1101–4; Pitti, *Cron.*, 104–6; 'Ann. arch. Datini', xiv, 35; *Chron. r. St.-Denis*, ii, 464–6; Jarry (1896), 170–4, 191–3, 215n[5], 517–32; Bouard, 214–18, 221; *Parl. Rolls*, vii, 312–13 (9–10); *Arch. Stat. Lucca Reg.*, ii.2, no. 1615. Gian Galeazzo's attacks on Florence: *Cron. volgare*, 212–13.

76 *Richard II*, Act II, Scene 1, ll. 40–50.

CHAPTER XVII

1 Atiya, 82–99; Froissart, *Chron.* (KL), xv, 330–2; Paviot (2003), 40–2.

2 Froissart, *Chron.* (KL), xvi, 2; Mézières, 'Épistre lamentable', 444, 446–7, 451–2, 454, 458.

3 *Parl. Rolls*, vii, 312–13 (7–11).

4 *Chron. r. St.-Denis*, ii, 532. Brittany: Jones (1970), 137–9; *Lettres de rois*, ii, 282–3; PPC, i, 66–7; *Foed.*, vii, 852–3; John IV, *Actes*, nos. 1097–1100. Calais: Froissart, *Chron.* (KL), xvi, 15. Embassy: PRO C76/81, m. 4; E364/32, m. 4d (Holme); E364/34, m. 4d (Retford); E364/36, m. 1 (Sturmy).

5 *Foed.*, vii, 850–1; Chaplais, *Eng. Med. Dipl. Practice*, no. 58.

6 *Chron. r. St.-Denis*, ii, 476; *Chron. traïson*, 1–2; Froissart, *Chron.* (KL), xvi, 2–5.

7 Froissart, *Chron.* (KL), xvi, 7–8, 15–20.

8 Walsingham, *Ann.*, 201–6; *Eulogium*, iii, 371–2; *Hist. Vitae*, 137; *Chron. traïson*, 7 (Coldharbour); CCR 1396–9, 197; CPR 1396–9, 241.

9 Walsingham, *Ann.*, 207; *Foed.*, viii, 6–7; PRO CHES 2/70, m. 7d; *Parl. Rolls*, vii, 403 (2),

viii, 82 (4), 83 (6), 84 (8).

10 *Parl. Rolls*, vii, 411-14 (7), viii, 43-7 (92), 87 (11-15), and Bagot's 'bill' of 1399 in *Great Chron. London*, 76. The full version of Gloucester's confession is at *Rot. Parl.*, iii, 378-9. For the announced date of death, see Lincolnshire inquisition (the only one to be returned during the session of Parliament): *Cal. Inq. P.M.*, xvii, no. 1036.

11 *Parl. Rolls*, vii, 341, 344-9 (1, 8-13), viii, 19 (36); Walsingham, *Ann.*, 208, 420; *CCR 1396-9*, 210; *Foed.*, viii, 14; *Hist. Vitae*, 140; Usk, *Chron.*, 22-4. Membership: *Hist. Parl.*, i, 197-208.

12 *Parl. Rolls*, vii, 403-16 (1-8); *Eulogium*, iii, 374-7; *Hist. Vitae*, 141-5 and Usk, *Chron.*, 26-32, 34 (drawing on a common source); Walsingham, *Ann.*, 214-16, 219-20; *CPR 1396-9*, 211. On Bussy: *ibid.*, 209, 210.

13 *Parl. Rolls*, vii, 363-4 (47), 417-20 (9-10); Usk, *Chron.*, 20, 38, 40; *Hist. Vitae*, 138-9, 142, 144, 147; Walsingham, *Ann.*, 224-5; *Eulogium*, iii, 376; PRO C67/30; *Official Correspondence of Thomas Beckington*, ed. G. Williams, i (1872), 285-7. On Cheyne: Roskell (1981-3), ii, 79-81.

14 *Parl. Rolls*, vii, 358-9 (35); Walsingham, *Ann.*, 216-19, 222-3; *Eulogium*, iii, 377; Saul (1997), 388-90.

15 Gascony: *Foed.*, viii, 43; Le Bis, 'Pratique', no. 4 [7-14]; PRO DL28/3/5, fol. 11; Castile, Portugal: *Daumet, 207-9. Scotland: Chaplais, *Eng. Med. Dipl. Practice*, no. 58 (p. 85); *Foed.*, vii, 850, viii, 17-18, 35-6, 50-1, 54-7, 65-6, 69-70, 72. Italy: *Arch. Stat. Lucca Reg.*, ii.2, nos. 1810, 1855, 1872, 1895; Bueno de Mesquita, 634-6, *637; *Cal. S.P. Milan*, i, no. 2; Bouard, 231 (confused chronology).

16 *Perroy (1933), 416-18, 384-7; Valois (1896-1902), iii, 150-84, 190-200. German throne: Walsingham, *Ann.*, 199-200; *Foed.*, vii, 854-6; Perroy (1933), 342-3, 382-3; Bueno de Mesquita, 631-4.

17 Italy: *Chronographia*, iii, 149-50; *Moranvillé (1888), 357; Bouard, 213-14, 219-20, 224-6, 227-30, 233-8. Constantinople: *Livre fais Bouciquaut*, 132-5; *Chron. r. St.-Denis*, ii, 690-2; Delaville le Roulx, i, 359-64. Low Countries: Laurent & Quicke, ch. III, V, VII-X; Vaughan, 100-11; *Froissart, *Chron.* (KL), xiii, 342-5, esp. 343 (date: *Itin. Ph. le Hardi*, 272; Cartellieri, 84-5).

18 Rey (1965), i, 392, ii, 437-42, 454-7, 467-8, 472-86, 579-604, 608-12; Nieuwenhuysen, i, 194-5, ii, 372-83 (his figures do not include gifts in kind or direct payments on ducal projects such as the new castle at Sluys); Pocquet (1939)[2]; Pocquet (1940-1); Vaughan, 230-2; Nordberg, 20-22; Avout, 62-3; David, 55-71, 148-55.

19 *Foed.*, viii, 281; *Parl. Rolls*, viii, 18 (30), 19 (35); Walsingham, *Ann.*, 209, 222-3; Given-Wilson (1986), 135, 214-26; Saul (1997), 383-4; Tuck (1973), 198-9.

20 *Parl. Rolls*, viii, 23 (50); Davies, 268-9; Gillespie (1979), 19; Walsingham, *Ann.*, 208, 237; *Clarke, 163-4; *CCR 1396-9*, 288.

21 *Glamorgan County History*, iii, 253-5; *Parl. Rolls*, vii, 381-7 (62-6), 388-9 (71-2); Dunn (2002), 166-9; Davies, 257-64.

22 *Parl. Rolls*, vii, 354-5 (27), viii, 424; Walsingham, *Ann.*, 304-5.

23 *Parl. Rolls*, vii, 369-70 (53), 420-2 (11) (Mowbray's account to Bolingbroke), confirmed in its essential respects by *CPR 1396-9*, 285, 317; *CCR 1396-9*, 291, 292; Walsingham, *Ann.*, 308 (Bagot's admissions at his trial in Oct. 1399).

24 *Eulogium*, iii, 379; *CPR 1396-9*, 285, 317; *CCR 1396-9*, 249, 281-2, 291, 292; *Parl. Rolls*, vii, 369 (53), 389 (73), 392 (79); Usk, *Chron.*, 48; *Chron. traïson*, 12-17.

25 *Parl. Rolls*, vii, 421-5 (11); *Chron. traïson*, 12-23. Armour: Froissart, *Chron.* (KL), xvi, 95-6; cf. PRO DL28/1/6, fol. 43.

26 Salmon, 'Lamentacions', 65; *Chron. r. St.-Denis*, ii, 668-72; *Vote de soustraction*, i, 53; *Le Bis, 'Pratique', no. 4[2-5]; *Chron. traïson*, 19.

27 *Chron. r. St.-Denis*, ii, 674-6; *CCR 1396-9*, 339; *Foed.*, viii, 48-50; Froissart, *Chron.* (KL), xvi, 115, 132, 141-51; AN KK253, fol. 80; Creton, 'Metr. Hist.', 374-5. For Salisbury's mission: *Foed.*, viii, 52; PRO E364/32, m. 5 (Bp. Carlisle).

28 *Parl. Rolls*, vii, 398-400 (87, 89), 428; viii, 81-3 (3-6); *Great Chron. London*, 76; *Foed.*,

viii, 77.

29 *Great Chron. London*, 77; *Chron. r. St.-Denis*, ii, 676, 704–6; Walsingham, *Ann.*, 241–2. Companions: Given-Wilson (1986), 190. Erpingham: Curry, 60–2. Norbury: *Hist. Parl.*, iii, 844–6; M. Barber, 66–8.

30 D. of Burgundy: Juvénal, *Hist.*, 135; *Chron. r. St.-Denis*, ii, 564–70; *Choix de pièces*, i, 140–2; Nordberg, 152, 157–8, 163–4, 166–7. Papacy: *Vote de soustraction*, 51–2; Alpartil, *Chron.*, 88–91; Lehoux, ii, 413; Ehrle, 'Neue Materialen', vii, 93–4. Louis's takeover: *Chron. r. St.-Denis*, ii, 678, 684, 692; AN J517/2^{A} (memorandum of *ca.* Sept. 1399); Lehoux, ii, 416–17, 418–19; Salmon, 'Lamentacions', 47–8; Nordberg, 44, 53–4, 55–6. Itineraries at *Itin. Ph. le Hardi*, 286–93; Lehoux, ii, 416n^{1}, iii, 487–9; Troubat, ii, 813.

31 Richard's views: Salmon, 'Lamentacions', 55–6; Coville (1932), 337–8. Périgord: *Gall. Reg.*, iii, no. 13375; BN Fr. n.a. 20027/194; Lalande, 77–81, esp. 78; *Chron. r. St.-Denis*, ii, 648–50; Dessalles (1847), 301–7, *77–93. The formal grant was not made until Jan. 1400: *ibid.*, *93–6.

32 Jarry (1889), 227–8; *Choix de pièces*, i, 157–60; Monstrelet, *Chron.*, i, 46–66, esp. 49–52, 54–5, 59; Juvénal, *Hist.*, 141. Queen's household: *Chron. r. St.-Denis*, ii, 704; *Chron. traïson*, 24–6; Froissart, *Chron.* (KL), xvi, 89–90; *Foed.*, viii, 83.

33 *Chron. traïson*, 28–9; Walsingham, *Ann.*, 238–9, 242, 247–8; Dunn (2003), 73; *Chron. r. St.-Denis*, ii, 706; Usk, *Chron.*, 52.

34 CCR 1396–9, 518, 596; *Foed.*, 89–90; *Chron. traïson*, 38; *Kirkstall Chron.*, 121–2; Hardyng, *Chron.*, 349–50; Walsingham, *Ann.*, 242–3; *Walker (1991), 75–6; Given-Wilson (1993), 252–3. Dates: PRO E101/42/12 (summons to Ware); PRO DL28/4/1, fol. 15 (landing).

35 Walsingham, *Ann.*, 245; PRO CHES 2/73, m. 1; Creton, 'Metr. Hist.', 312–18.

36 Walsingham, *Ann.*, 243–7; *Hist. Vitae*, 153–4; *Chron. traïson*, 38–40. York's strength: Given-Wilson (1993), 247–51.

37 Creton, 'Metr. Hist.', 318–27; Usk, *Chron.*, 58–60; Walsingham, *Ann.*, 248–9; *Hist. Vitae*, 155; *Chron. traïson*, 42–5.

38 Creton, 'Metr. Hist.', 328–78.

39 Sayles, 'Lancastrian narratives', 264–8; *Parl. Rolls*, viii, 11–15 (10–17); Usk, *Chron.*, 62–4, 66–8.

40 Walsingham, *Ann.*, 303–6, 308–9, 321; Usk, *Chron.*, 48–50, 60, 74–6; *Kirkstall Chron.*, 122. Mowbray: *Cal. S.P. Venice*, i, no. 128; *Cal. Inq. P.M.*, xviii, no. 264.

41 *Parl. Rolls*, viii, 80–9 (1–16); *Great Chron. London*, 77–83; Walsingham, *Ann.*, 306–8, 309–11, 313–20, 323–9, 330–1; Usk, *Chron.*, 86–90; *Hist. Vitae*, 160–1; *Eulogium*, iii, 385–7.

42 Froissart, *Chron.* (KL), xvi, 211–12; Creton, 'Metr. Hist.', 382, 410; Deschamps, *Oeuvres*, vi, 133–4, 184–5.

43 *Chron. r. St.-Denis*, ii, 716–20, 738; Creton, 'Metr. Hist.', 410; Juvénal, *Hist.*, 141–2; *Cartellieri, 152. Received opinion: see Jean Juvénal des Ursins, *Ecrits politiques*, ed. P.S. Lewis, ii (1985), 152–3; *El Victorial*, ed. J. de M. Carriazo (1940), 182; Robert Blondel, *Oeuvres*, ed. A. Héron, i (1891), 258–9, 272, 439–40, 456–7; *Débat des Hérauts d'Armes de France et d'Angleterre*, ed. L. Pannier (1877), 49. Garrisons: BN Fr. 32510, fols. 338–338vo. Cf. 'Ann. Arch. Datini', xv, 33; Froissart, *Chron.* (KL), xvi, 212; Juvénal, *Hist.*, 142.

Bibliography

A MANUSCRIPTS

Barcelona: Archivo de la Corona de Aragon

Real Cancillería
Registros: 916, 1261–92, 1674–5, 1746–57

Cahors: Archives Départementales du Lot

Archives communales de Cajarc
CC6, fols. 77–156vo: Accounts [1369–70]
CC10–16: Accounts [1368–9, 1373–4, 1376–8, 1379–81]

Archives communales de Martel
BB 6–7: Consuls and councillors, proceedings [1379–83, 1389]
CC1, 1bis: Finance (correspondence)
CC 5–6: Accounts [1371–4, 1377–8, 1382–3]
EE 1: War (correspondence)

Cambridge: University Library

Dd. III.53, fols. 1–94: Privy Seal office formulary (early 15th century)

Dijon: Archives Départementales de la Côte-d'Or

Série B: Chambre des Comptes de Bourgogne
  1430–1554: Treasurers, Receivers-General and household [1367–1408]
  4418–21: Bailliage of Dijon [1370–5]
  11736–8, 11748–68, 11875–6: War (indentures, musters, miscellaneous)

Edinburgh: University Library

MS 183: Privy Seal and Signet Office formulary, compiled for John Prophet, *ca.* 1410

London: British Library

Additional Charters
  1–208: Collection Courcelles
  232–505, 1397–1516, 2028–4578: Collection Joursanvault
Additional Manuscript 37494: Account of Adam Hartingdon (controller's roll)
Cotton Charters
Cotton MSS:
  Julius B.VI Diplomatic documents, Brittany
  Caligula D.III War; diplomatic documents, Gascony
  Vespasian F.VII Diplomatic documents, Scotland
Harley Charters
Harley MSS 3988, fols. 28–67: Treatise on letter-writing, *ca.* 1400.

949

London: Public Record Office [The National Archives]

Chancery
C47 Chancery miscellanea
C49 Council and parliamentary proceedings
C61/82–106 Gascon rolls [1369–99]
C76/52–83 Treaty (formerly French) rolls [1369–99]
C81 Chancery warrants
  C81/414–582: Writs of Privy Seal [1369–99]
  C81/923–1084: Bills of Privy Seal [1369–99]
  C81/1339–55: Signet warrants [1377–99]
Exchequer
E30 Diplomatic documents
E36 Treasury Books
  E36/79–80: English possessions in France [1361–72]
  E36/188: Transcripts of treaties [1419]
E101 Accounts various
  E101/29/25–101/42/26, 101/531/25, 28–31, 40: Army, navy and ordnance [1369–99]
  E101/68/4–101/69/1: Indentures of war [1351–99]
  E101/89/26B–101/90/14: Channel Islands [1372–77]
  E101/178/14–101/184/7: English possessions in France [1369–99]
  E101/315/33–101/320/19: *Nuncii* [messengers and diplomatic agents] [1369–99]
  E101/396/9–101/403/31: Wardrobe and household [1368–99]
E159/145–175 Memoranda rolls [1368–99]
E361/4–5 Enrolled accounts, wardrobe and household [1350–99]
E364/3–36 Enrolled accounts, foreign [1369–1402]
E401/495–615 Receipt rolls [1369–99]
E403/436–562 Issue rolls [1368–99]
E404/9–14 Warrants for issue [1368–99]

Palatinate of Chester
CHES 2/57–73 Exchequer of Chester, Enrolments [1386–99]
CHES 25/24 Indictment roll [1353–99]
CHES 30/11–16 Plea Rolls [1368–1399]

Duchy of Lancaster
DL28/1/9–10 Henry of Lancaster, Duke of Hereford, Household accounts [1396–8]
DL28/3/1–3 John, Duke of Lancaster, Receiver general's accounts [1376–7, 1392–3, 1397–9]
DL34 Letters and diplomatic documents

Special Collections
SC1 Ancient correspondence

Montpellier: Archives Départmentales de l'Hérault

A5–7 Registers of the Seneschalsies of Toulouse and Beaucaire [1352–1407]

Oxford: Corpus Christi College

Ms. 495: Warrants of John, Duke of Lancaster [1365–70]

Paris: Archives Nationales

Série J Trésor des Chartes, Layettes
  186: Berry   603: Castille
  382: Jean, duc de Berry   642–4: Angleterre
  400: Forteresses   677: Écosse
  592: Aragon

Série JJ Trésor des Chartes, Régistres
  JJ99–154 [1369–1400]
Série K Monuments historiques, Cartons
Série KK Monuments historiques, Régistres (comptes)
  30: Charles VI, Chambre aux deniers (Hôtel)
  242: Louis, duc d'Anjou (Trésorerie)
  251–54: Jean, duc de Berry (Chambre aux deniers, Hôtel)
  322: Haute Auvergne (évacuation de Carlat, Murat, et autres lieux)
  326: Charles de Navarre (Hôtel)
  327: Taille (vicomté de Pont-Authou)
 . 350: Aides (diocèse de Bayeux)
Série P Chambre des Comptes
  1334: House of Anjou
  2295–7: Mémoriaux D, E, F [1359–1412]
Série X Parlement de Paris
  X¹ᵃ: Parlement civil
    22–32: Jugés, lettres et arrêts
    1469–77: Plaidoiries et Conseil [1364–95]
    9182–6: Grands Jours [1367–98]
  X²ᵃ: Parlement criminel
    8–13: Registers [1367–1400]

Paris: Bibliothèque de l'Arsenal

Ms. 4522: War Treasurers' accounts, various, extracts (transcriptions)

Paris: Bibliothèque Nationale

Collection de Bourgogne:
  21, 23–5: Chambre des Comptes de Dijon, analyses of documents
  52–3: Chambre des Comptes de Dijon (accounts, transcribed extracts)
Collection Clairambault:
  1–227: Titres scellés
  841: Armées du roi Charles VI (états de paiements, etc.)
Collection Doat (Languedoc):
  1–6: Inventaire   131: Moissac
  49: Narbonne   146: Najac, St.-Antonin
  87: Montauban   193–207: Foix, Armagnac and Albret
  110: Albi   241–4: Périgord
  125: Figeac
Collection Dupuy
  306: Recueil de pièces concernant les relations politiques de la France et de l'Angleterre
    aux XIVᵉ et XVᵉ siècles
Collection de Languedoc (Bénédictins):
  86: Miscellaneous transcriptions   159: Accounts
Collection Moreau, 625–733: Collection de Bréquigny
Collection du Périgord:
  9–10: Counts of Périgord   46–7: Towns
Collection de Touraine, 8
Manuscrits français
  4482: War Treasurers' accounts, Arnoul Boucher [1390–2]
  4493: War Treasurers' accounts, Guillaume d'Orgemont [1395–6]
  7858: War Treasurers' accounts, various (transcriptions) [1340–1495]
  9501: War Treasurers' accounts, various, extracts (transcriptions) [XIII–XVI cent.]
  10237–8: Miscellaneous correspondence [XIV–XVI cent.]
  15515, fols. 281–351: proceedings against Charles of Artois, count of Pézenas [1375]

20366–426: Collection de Gaignières (pièces originales, maisons royales de France)
20586–7: Collection de Gaignières (pièces historiques)
20692, fols. 140–147: War Treasurers' accounts, various, extracts [1380–4]
25705–7: Chartes royales [royal warrants and orders,1380–1402]
25764–6: Musters and reviews [1347–1422]
26008–30: Quittances et pièces diverses
26485–9545: Pièces originales [cited as PO, 1–3061]
31884–976: Trésor généalogique de Dom Villevieille
32510: Chambre des Comptes, war accounts and musters, extracts (transcriptions)
n.a. 3653–5: Chambre des Comptes, Inventaire Aubron
n.a. 7414: War Treasurers' accounts, various, extracts (transcriptions) [1360–1515]
n.a. 7615–21: Portefeuilles de Fontanieu (transcriptions) [1368–99]
n.a. 8603–4: Cabinet des Titres, musters and reviews [1295–1399]
n.a. 20026–8: Chambre des Comptes [1346–1464]
n.a. 20528, pp. 25–118: War Treasurers' accounts, Jean le Flament [1377–83]
Manuscrits latins 9175–6: Languedoc, taxation (transcriptions) [1360–99]
Pièces originales: see MS Fr. 26485–29545

Pau: Archives Départementales des Pyrennées-Atlantiques

Série E (Titres de famille)
13–236: Albret   800–81: Périgord, Limousin
288–367: Béarn   882: Rouergue

Périgueux: Archives Départmentales de la Dordogne

Archives Communales de la ville de Périgueux
BB13: Régistres mémoriaux, Livre Noir [1360–1449]

Rodez: Archives Départmentales de l'Aveyron

C1886–7: Estates of Rouergue, war subsidy accounts [1371–80]
2E 178 (8): Najac, Accounts [1350–83]

B PRINTED RECORD SOURCES

Actes royaux des Archives de l'Hérault, i, 1151–1422, ed. A. Caramel (1980)
Acts of the Parliaments of Scotland, ed. T. Thomson and C. Innes, 12 vols (1814–75)
'Anglo-French negotiations at Bruges, 1374–1377', ed. E. Perroy, Camden Miscellany, xix
    (Camden Third Series, lxxx) (1952)
Ancient Petitions relating to Northumberland, ed. C.M. Fraser (1966)
Anglo-Norman Letters and Petitions, ed. M.D. Legge (1941)
'Annales Avignonaises de 1382 à 1410, extraites des archives de Datini', ed. R. Brun, Méms.
    Inst. Historique Provence, xii (1935), 17–142, xiii (1936), 58–105, xiv (1937), 5–57, xv
    (1938), 21–52, xvi (1939), 154–92
Antient Kalendars and Inventories of the Treasury of His Majesty's Exchequer, ed. F.
    Palgrave, 3 vols (1836)
Archives administratives de la ville de Reims, ed. P. Varin, 3 vols in 5 (1839–48)
Archives anciennes de la ville de Saint-Quentin, ed. E. Lemaire, 2 vols (1888–1910)
Archives historiques du Département de la Gironde, 59 vols (1859–1936)
Archives historiques du Poitou, 64 vols (1872–2005)
Archives historiques de la Saintonge et de l'Aunis, 50 vols (1874–1967)
Archives municipales de Bordeaux, i, Livre des Bouillons (1867); v, Livre des Coutumes, ed.
    H. Barckhausen (1890)
Archives de la ville de Montpellier, ed. J. Berthelé and M. Oudot de Dainville, 13 vols
    (1895–1984)

Archivio di Stato in Lucca. Regesti, ed. L. Fumi and G. degli Azzi Vitelleschi, 4 vols (1903–33)

Artières, J. (ed.), 'Nouveaux documents relatifs à l'occupation anglaise (1369)', *Mémoires de la Société des Lettres, Sciences et Arts de l'Aveyron*, xvi (1900)

Auctarium chartularii Universitatis Parisiensis, ed. H. Denifle, E. Chatelain, *et al.*, 6 vols (1894–1964)

Ausgaben der apostolischen Kammer unter den Päpsten Urban V und Gregor XI, ed. K.H. Schäfer (1914)

Beaurepaire, F. de (ed.), 'Les sources de l'histoire du moyen age à la Bibliothèque de la Ville de Rouen', *Cahiers Léopold Delisle*, xiii (1964), fasc. 2

Black Book of the Admiralty, ed. T. Twiss, 4 vols (1871–6)

Broome, D.M. (ed.), 'The Ransom of John II, King of France', *Camden Miscellany*, xiv (Royal Historical Society, Camden Third Series, xxxvii) (1926)

Calendar of Close Rolls, 45 vols (1892–1954)

'Calendar of Diplomatic Documents, formerly in the Treasury of the Receipt of the Exchequer, Chapter House, Westminster', *Forty-fifth Report of the Deputy Keeper of the Public Records* (1885), Appendix I, 283–380; *Forty-eighth Report of the Deputy Keeper of the Public Records* (1887), Appendix I, 561–619

Calendar of Documents relating to Scotland, ed. J. Bain, 5 vols (1881–1988)

Calendar of Entries in the Papal Registers relating to Great Britain and Ireland. Papal Letters, ed. W.H. Bliss, C. Johnson *et al.*, 19 vols (1894–1998)

Calendar of Entries in the Papal Registers relating to Great Britain and Ireland. Petitions to the Pope, i (1342–1419), ed. W.H. Bliss (1896) [all published]

Calendar of Fine Rolls, 22 vols (1911–63)

Calendar of Inquisitions Miscellaneous, 8 vols (1916–2003)

Calendar of Inquisitions Post Mortem, 23 vols (1904–2004)

Calendar of Letter Books of the City of London, ed. R.R. Sharpe, 11 vols (1899–1912)

Calendar of Patent Rolls, 70 vols (1891–1982)

Calendar of Plea and Memoranda Rolls preserved among the archives of the Corporation of the City of London at the Guildhall, ed. A.H. Thomas and P.E. Jones, 7 vols (1924–61)

Calendar of the Register of Henry Wakefield, Bishop of Worcester, ed. W.P. Marett (1972)

Calendar of State Papers and Manuscripts existing in the Archives and Collections of Milan, ed. A.B. Hinds, i (1912) [all published]

Calendar of State Papers and Manuscripts relating to English affairs existing in the Archives and Collections of Venice and in other Libraries of Northern Italy, ed. R. Brown *et al.*, 38 vols (1864–1947)

Cartulaire historique et généalogique des Artevelde, ed. N. de Pauw (1920)

Carus-Wilson, E.M., and Coleman, O. (ed.), *England's Export Trade* (1963)

Catálogo del Archivo General de Navarra, Catalogo de la Sección de Comptos, ed. J. Ramón Castro and F. Idoate, 52 vols (1952–74)

Catálogo de los cartularios reales del Archivo General de Navarra, Años 1007–1384, ed. F. Idoate (1974)

Catálogo documental del Archivo Municipal de Burgos: Sección histórica, ed. J.A. Bonachia Hernando and J.A. Pardos Martines (1983)

Catalogue analytique des archives de M. le baron de Joursanvault, 2 vols (1838)

Catalogue des rolles Gascons, Normans et François conservés dans les archives de la Tour de Londres, ed. T. Carte, 2 vols (1743)

Chaplais, P. (ed.), 'Some documents regarding the fulfilment and interpretation of the treaty of Brétigny (1361–1369)', *Camden Miscellany*, xix (Royal Historical Society, Camden Third Series, lxxx) (1952)

Chaplais, P. (ed.), *English Medieval Diplomatic Practice*, i: *Documents and Interpretation* (1982)

Chartrier de Pons, ed. G. Musset, 2 vols, *AHSA*, ix, xxi (1881–92)

Chartularium Universitatis Parisiensis, ed. H. Denifle and E. Chatelain, 4 vols (1889–97)

Chaucer Life-Records, ed. M.M. Crow and C.C. Olson (1966)

Choix de pièces inédites relatives au règne de Charles VI, ed. L. Douët d'Arcq, 2 vols (1853–4)

Colección de cédulas, cartas-patentes, provisiones, reales órdenes y otros documentos concernientes a las provincias vascongadas, ed. T. González, 6 vols (1829–33)

Colección de documentos para la historia del reino de Murcia, viii, *Documentos de Enrique II*, ed. L. Pascual Martínez (1983); xi, *Documentos de Juan I*, ed. J.M. Diez Martinez (2001)

'Compte du Clos des Galées de Rouen au xive siècle (1382–1384)', ed. C. Bréard, Société de l'Histoire de Normandie, *Mélanges. Documents*, 2ᵉ série (1893), 51–154

'Compte inédit de Bertrand du Guesclin', ed. J. Marchand, *BEC*, lxxxviii (1927), 260–5

Compte des recettes et dépenses du roi de Navarre en France et en Normandie de 1367 à 1370, ed. E. Izarn (1885)

Compte de William Gunthorp, Trésorier de Calais, 1371–1372, ed. E. Perroy (1959)

Comptes de l'archevêché de Bordeaux, ed. L. Drouyn, 2 vols, *AHG*, xxi, xxii (1871–2)

Comptes de l'argenterie des rois de France au xivᵉ siècle, ed. L. Douët d'Arcq (1851)

Comptes consulaires de la Cité et du Bourg de Rodez, 1ᵉʳᵉ partie: *Cité*, ed. H. Bousquet, 2 vols (1926–43)

Comptes de l'Écurie du Roi Charles VI, ed. G-M. Leproux, 2 vols (1995–6)

Comptes de l'hôtel des rois de France, ed. L. Douët d'Arcq (1865)

Comptes du Trésor, ed. R. Fawtier (1930)

Concilia Magnae Britanniae et Hiberniae, ed. D. Wilkins, 4 vols (1737)

Controversy between Sir Richard Scrope and Sir Robert Grosvenor in the Court of Chivalry, 2 vols, ed. N.H. Nicolas (1832)

Cortes de los antiguos reinos de León y de Castilla, 5 vols (1861–84)

Cotton manuscrit Galba B.1, ed. L. Gilliodts-van Severen (1896)

David II, *The Acts of David II, King of Scots*, ed. B. Webster (1982)

'Délibérations du conseil communal d'Albi de 1372 à 1388', ed. A. Vidal, *Revue des langues romanes*, xlvi (1903), 33–73; xlvii (1904), 75–90, 348–73, 535–64; xlviii (1905), 240–79, 420–70

Delpit, J., *Collection générale des documents français qui se trouvent en Angleterre* (1847)

Diplomatic correspondence of Richard II, ed. E. Perroy (Royal Historical Society, Camden Third Series, xlviii) (1933)

'Dispacci di Cristoforo da Piacenza, procuratore mantovano alla corte pontificia (1371–83)', ed. A. Segre, *Archivio Storico Italiano*, 5th series, xliii (1909), 27–95, xliv (1909), 253–326

Documents on the Affairs of Ireland before the King's Council, ed. G.O. Sayles (1979)

Documents historiques rélatifs à la vicomté de Carlat, ed. G. Saige and Cte. de Dienne, 2 vols (1900)

Documents inédits concernant la ville et le siège du baillage d'Amiens extraits des régistres du Parlement de Paris et du Trésor des Chartes, i, *xivᵉ siècle (1296–1412)*, ed. E. Maugis (1908)

'Documents inédits sur Saint-Antonin pendant la guerre de cent ans', ed. C. Dumas de Rauly, *Bull. Archéol. et Hist. de la Soc. Archéol. de Tarn-et-Garonne*, viii (1880), 273–301

Documents inédits pour servir à l'histoire de l'Agenais, ed. P. Tamizey de Larroque (1874)

Documents inédits pour servir à l'histoire du Maine au xivᵉ siècle, ed. B. de Broussillon (1905)

'Documents inédits sur la ville de Millau'[1], ed. J. Artières, *Mémoires de la Société des Lettres, Sciences et Arts de l'Aveyron*, xv (1894–9), 317–65, xxi (1921), 552–91.

Documents inédits sur la ville de Millau [2], ed. J. Artières (1930)

Documents sur la maison de Durfort, ed. N. de la Peña (1977)

Documents normands du règne de Charles V… conservés au département des Manuscrits de la Bibliothèque Nationale de France, ed. M. Nortier (2000)

Documents relatifs au clos des galées de Rouen et aux armées de la mer des rois de France de 1293 à 1418, ed. A. Chazelas, 2 vols (1977–8)

Documents relatifs à l'histoire municipale des deux villes de Limoges, ed. L. Guibert, 2 vols (1897–1902)

Dokumente zur Geschichte des grossen abendländischen Schismas (1385–1395), ed. S. Steinherz (1932)

Douze comptes consulaires d'Albi du xive siècle, ed. A. Vidal, 2 vols (1906–11)

Ehrle, F. (ed.), 'Aus den Acten des Afterconcils von Perpignan 1408', *Archiv für Literatur- und Kirchengeschichte des Mittelalters*, v (1889), 387–492

Ehrle, F. (ed.), 'Neue Materialen zur Geschichte Peters von Luna (Benedicts XIII)', *Archiv für Literatur- und Kirchengeschichte des Mittelalters*, vi (1892), 139–308, vii (1900), 1–310

Excerpta Historica or Illustrations of English History, ed. S. Bentley (1833)

Exchequer Rolls of Scotland, ed. J. Stuart *et al.*, 23 vols (1878–1908)

Expeditions to Prussia and the Holy Land made by Henry, Earl of Derby, ed. L. Toulmin Smith (1894)

'Extraits des archives historiques de la ville de Fontenay-le-Comte', ed. B. Fillon, *AHP*, i, 117–42

'Extraits de journaux du Trésor (1345–1419)', ed. H. Moranvillé, *BEC*, xlix (1888), 149–214, 368–452

Facsimiles of the National Manuscripts of Scotland, ed. W.G. Craig, 3 vols (1867–73)

Fenwick, C.N. (ed.), *The Poll Taxes of 1377, 1379 and 1381*, 2 vols (1998–2001)

Foedera, conventiones, literae et acta publica, ed. T. Rymer, 7 vols (1816–69) [references to vols 3 and 4 are to this edition]; 20 vols (1727–9) [references to vols 7 and 8 are to this edition]; and Supplement in *Appendices to the Report on Rymer's Foedera*, Section E, *Chronological Catalogue of Materials Transcribed for the New Edition of the Foedera*, 2 vols (1869).

Gallia Christiana, 16 vols, ed. D. de Sainte-Marthe, F. Hodin, *et al.* (1716–1865)

Gallia Regia, ou état des officiers royaux des baillages et des sénéchaussés de 1328 à 1515, ed. G. Dupont-Ferrier, 7 vols (1942–65)

Gascogne dans les régistres du Trésor des Chartes, ed. C. Samaran (1966)

Gayet, L. (ed.), *Le Grand Schisme d'Occident, d'après les documents contemporains déposés aux archives secrètes du Vatican*, 2 vols (1889)

Gedenkwaardigheden uit de Geschiedenis van Gelderland, ed. I.A. Nijhoff, 7 vols (1830–75)

Gregory XI, *Lettres secrètes et curiales du Pape Grégoire XI (1370–1378) intéressant les pays autres que la France*, ed. G. Mollat, 3 fascs. (1962–5)

Gregory XI, *Lettres secrètes et curiales du Pape Grégoire XI (1370–1378) relatives à la France*, ed. L. Mirot, H. Jassemin *et al.* (1935–57)

Handelingen van de Leden en van de Staten van Vlaanderen (1384–1405), ed. W. Prevenier (1959)

Hanserecesse. Die Recesse und andere Akten der Hansetage von 1256–1430, ed. K. Koppmann, 8 vols (1870–97)

Histoire généalogique de la maison de Harcourt, ed. G.-A. de La Roque, 4 vols (1662)

Historical Papers and Letters from the Northern Registers, ed. J. Raine (1873)

'Indentures of retinue with John of Gaunt, Duke of Lancaster, enrolled in Chancery', ed. N.B. Lewis, *Camden Miscellany* (Royal Historical Society, Camden Fourth Series, i) (1964), 77–112

Inventaire analytique des chartes et documents appartenant aux Archives de la Ville de Gand, ed. P. van Duyse and E. de Busscher (1847)

Inventaire analytique et chronologique des chartes et documents appartenant aux archives de la ville d'Ypres, 7 vols, ed. I.L.A. Diegerick (1853–68)

Inventaire des archives communales de la ville d'Aurillac antérieures à 1790, ed. G. Esquier, 2 vols (1906–11)

Inventaire des archives de la ville de Bruges. Inventaire des Chartes, ed. L. Gilliodts-van Severen, 9 vols (1871–82)

Inventaire chronologique des documents relatifs a l'histoire d'Ecosse conservés aux Archives du Royaume à Paris, ed. A. Teulet (1839)

'Inventaire des lettres des rois d'Aragon à Charles VI et à la cour de France, conservées aux Archives de la Couronne d'Aragon à Barcelone', ed. J. Vielliard and L. Mirot, *BEC*, ciii (1942), 99–150

'Inventaire de meubles et de titres trouvés au Château de Josselin à la mort du Connétable de Clisson', *BEC*, lxvi (1905), 193–245

Inventaire du mobilier de Charles V, Roi de France, ed. J. Labarte (1879)

'Inventaire raisonné et analytique des archives municipales de Cahors. 2ᵉ partie, XIVᵉ siècle', ed. E. Albe, *Bull. Soc. Études du Lot*, xli.2 (1920), 1–48; xliii.2 (1922), 1–28; xlv.2 (1924), 29–99.

Inventaire des sceaux de la Collection Clairambault à la Bibliothèque Nationale, ed. G. Demay, 2 vols (1885–6)

Inventaire des sceaux de la Collection des Pièces Originales du Cabinet des Titres à la Bibliothèque Nationale, ed. J. Roman, i (1909)

Inventaire du trésor de la maison du consulat de Périgueux (1598 et additions), ed. J. Roux (1934)

Inventaires mobiliers et extraits des comptes des ducs de Bourgogne de la Maison de Valois (1363–1477), ed. B. and H. Prost, 2 vols (1902–13).

Inventaire-sommaire des Archives Communales antérieures à 1790.
Ville de Clermont-Ferrand. Fonds de Montferrand, ed. E. Teilhard de Chardin, 2 vols (1922)
Ville de Narbonne. Série AA, ed. G. Mouynès (1877), and *Annexes* (1871)
Ville de Périgueux, ed. M. Hardy (1897)
Ville de Riom, ed. F. Boyer (1892)
Ville de Rodez. ed. H. Affre (1877)
Ville de Toulouse, i, ed. E. Roschach (1891)

Inventaire-sommaire des Archives Départementales antérieures à 1790.
Basses-Pyrennées, ed. P. Raymond, 6 vols (1863–76)
Côte d'Or. Archives civiles. Série B: Chambre des Comptes de Bourgogne, ed. C. Rossignol and J. Garnier, 5 vols (1863–78)
Nord. Archives civiles, Série B: Chambre des Comptes de Lille, ed. Dehaisnes, J. Finot, A. Desplanque, *et al.*, 9 vols (1899–1913)
Pas-de-Calais. Archives civiles, Série A, 2 vols, ed. J.-M. Richard (1878–87)

Issue Roll of Thomas de Brantingham, bishop of Exeter, Lord High Treasurer of England…, A.D. 1370, ed. F. Devon (1835)

Issues of the Exchequer, ed. F. Devon (1837)

Itinéraires de Philippe le Hardi et de Jean sans Peur, ed. E. Petit (1888)

Itinerários de el-rei dom João, ed. H. Baquero Moreno (1988)

Jeanne de Penthièvre, *Recueil des Actes de Charles de Blois et Jeanne de Penthièvre, duc et duchesse de Bretagne (1341–1364), suivi des Actes de Jeanne de Penthièvre (1364–1384)*, ed. M. Jones (1996)

John IV, Duke of Brittany, *Recueil des actes de Jean IV, duc de Bretagne*, ed. M. Jones (1980–3)

John of Gaunt's Register, i, *1372–1376*, ed. S. Armitage-Smith (1911); ii, *1379–1383*, ed. E.C. Lodge and R. Somerville (1937)

Jurades de la ville de Bergerac, 14 vols, ed. G. Charrier (1892–1941)

Languedoc et le Rouergue dans le Trésor des Chartes, ed. Y. Dossat, A.-M. Lemasson and P. Wolff (1983)

Larson, A., 'English Embassies during the Hundred Years War', *EHR*, lv (1940), 423–3

Le Bis, I. (ed.), 'Pratique de la diplomatie. Un dossier d'ambassadeurs français sous Charles VI (1400–1403)', *Ann-Bull. Soc. Hist. France* (1985–6), 97–214

Le Fèvre, Jean, bishop of Chartres, *Journal de Jean le Fèvre*, ed. H. Moranvillé (1887)

Lettere di mercatanti toscani scritte nel secolo xivº non mai fin qui stampate, ed. P. Ferrato (1869)

Letters, Orders and Musters of Bertrand du Guesclin, 1357–1380, ed. M. Jones (2004)

'Lettres originales de Charles VI, conservées aux Archives de la Couronne d'Aragon à Barcelone', ed. J. Vielliard and Robert Avezou, *BEC*, xcvii (1936), 317–73

Lettres de rois, reines et autres personnages des cours de France et d'Angleterre, ed. L-A. Champollion-Figeac, 2 vols (1839–43)

Literae Cantuarienses, ed. J.B. Sheppard, 3 vols (1887–9)

Livre de vie, ed. E. Labroue, *op. cit.*, 405–25

Livre Noir et les établissements de Dax, ed. F. Abadie, *AHG*, xxxvii (1902)

Mandements et actes divers de Charles V (1364–1380), ed. L. Delisle (1874)

'Medieval Treatise on Letter-writing, with Examples, from the Rylands Latin MS. 394', ed. W.A. Pantin, *Bull. J. Rylands Lib.*, xiii (1929), 326–82

'Mémoire de Pierre de Craon', ed. J. Pichon, *Mélanges de littérature et d'histoire recueillis et publiés par la Société des Bibliophiles français*, i (1856), 92–119

Memorials of London and London Life in the XIIIth, XIVth and XVth centuries, ed. H.T. Riley (1868)

Memorieboek der Stad Ghent, ed. P.C. van der Meersch, 4 vols (1852–61)

Mirot, L. and Deprez, E., 'Les ambassades anglaises pendant la guerre de cent ans. Catalogue chronologique (1327–1450)', *BEC*, lix (1898), 530–77, lx (1899), 177–214, lxi (1900), 20–58 [for corrections, see Larson, A.]

Monuments historiques. Cartons des rois, ed. J. Tardif (1866)

Monuments du procès de canonisation du bienheureux Charles de Blois duc de Bretagne, 1320–64, ed. F. Plaine (1921)

Morice, P.-H., *Mémoires pour servir de preuves à l'histoire ecclésiastique et civile de Bretagne*, 3 vols (1742–6)

'Morley vs. Montagu (1399): A case in the Court of Chivalry', ed. M.H. Keen and M. Warner, *Camden Miscellany*, xxxiv (Royal Historical Society, Camden Fifth Series, x) (1997)

Northern Petitions illustrative of Life in Berwick, Cumbria and Durham in the Fourteenth Century, ed. C.M. Fraser (1981)

Notices et extraits de quelques manuscrits de la Bibliothèque Nationale, ed. J.B. Hauréau, 6 vols (1890–3)

Oorkonden in de Archives Nationales te Parijs aangaande de betrekkingen der Geldersche vorsten tot Frankeich, ed. A. Hulshof (1912)

Ordonnances des rois de France de la troisième race, ed. D. Secousse et al., 21 vols (1729–1849)

Papal Letters to Scotland of Clement VII of Avignon, 1378–1394, ed. C. Burns (1976)

Parliamentary Records of Scotland in the General Register House, Edinburgh, i, ed. W. Robertson (1804)

Parliament Rolls of Medieval England, ed. C. Given-Wilson et al., 16 vols (2005)

Parliaments and Councils of Mediaeval Ireland, ed. H.G. Richardson and G.O Sayles, i (1947)

Pays de la Loire moyenne dans le Trésor des chartes. Berry, Blésois, Chartrain, Orléanais, Touraine, 1350–1502 (Archives nationales, JJ 80–235), ed. B. Chevalier (1993)

Pièces rélatives à la vie de Louis I, Duc d'Orléans et de Valentine Visconti, sa femme, ed. F.M. Graves (1913)

Preuves de la maison de Polignac. Recueil de documents pour servir à l'histoire des anciennes provinces de Velay, Auvergne, Gévaudan, Vivarais, Forez, etc., ixe-xviiie siècle, ed. A. Jacotin, 5 vols (1898–1906)

'Private indentures for life service in peace and war, 1278–1476', ed. M. Jones and S. Walker, *Camden Miscellany*, xxxii (Royal Historical Society, Camden Fifth Series, iii) (1994)

'Privilèges de la Cité de Limoges', ed. E. Ruben, *Bull. Soc. Archéol. Limousin*, xvii (1867), 116–22.

Proceedings and Ordinances of the Privy Council of England, ed. N.H. Nicolas, 7 vols (1834–7)

'Procès-verbal de délivrance à Jean Chandos commissaire du roi d'Angleterre des places françaises abandonnées par le traité de Brétigny', ed. A. Bardonnet, *Mems. Soc. stat. sci. et arts dep. Deux-Sèvres*, 2e série, vi (1866), 2e partie, 119–282

BIBLIOGRAPHY

Provas da história da casa real portuguesa, ed. A. Caetano de Sousa, 6 vols (1739–48)

Quadro elementar dar relações politicas e diplomaticas de Portugal, ed. Barros e Sousa de Mesquita, visconde de Santarém, 18 vols (1842–60)

Rechnungen über Heinrich von Derby's Preussenfahrten, 1390–91 und 1392, ed. H. Prutz (1893)

Records of Convocation, ed. G. Bray, 20 vols (2005–6)

Recueil de documents concernant la commune et la ville de Poitiers, 2 vols, ed. E. Audouin, AHP, xliv, xlvi (1926–8)

Recueil des documents concernant le Poitou contenus dans les registres de la Chancellerie de France, ed. P. Guerin and L. Célier, 14 vols, AHP, xi, xiii, xvii, xix, xxi, xxiv, xxvi, xxix, xxxii, xxxv, xxxviii, xli, l, lvi (1881–1958)

Recueil des Ordonnances des Pays-Bas. Ordonnances de Philippe le Hardi, de Marguerite de Mâle et de Jean sans Peur, 1381–1419, ed. J. Bartier and A. van Nieuwenhuysen, 2 vols (in progress) (1965–74)

Recueil de pièces servant de preuves au Mémoires sur les troubles excités par Charles II, dit le Mauvais, roi de Navarre et comte d'Evreux, ed. D. Secousse (1755)

Recueil de titres et autres pièces justificatives employées dans le Mémoire sur la constitution politique de la ville de Périgueux (1775)

Register of Edward the Black Prince, 4 vols (1930–33)

Register of John Gilbert, Bishop of Hereford (AD 1375–1389), ed. J.H. Parry (1913)

Register of Thomas Appleby, Bishop of Carlisle, 1363–1395, ed. R.L. Storey (2006)

'Registre de Barthélemi de Noces, officier du duc de Berri (1374–77)', ed. E. Teilhard de Chardin, BEC, lii (1891), 220–58, 517–72

Régistre criminel du Châtelet de Paris, 2 vols (1861–4)

Régistres des comptes municipaux de la ville de Tours, ed. J. Delaville le Roulx, 2 vols (1878–81)

Régistres consulaires de Saint-Flour, ed. M. Boudet (1898)

Régistres de l'échevinage de Saint-Jean d'Angély, 3 vols, ed. D. d'Aussy, AHSA, xxiv, xxvi, xxxii (1895–1902)

Rekeningen der Baljuws van Vlaenderen, ed. N. de Pauw, *Jehan Froissart's Cronyke van Vlaenderen*, ii (1900–6)

Rekeningen der stad Gent. Tijdvak van Philips van Artevelde (1376–1389), ed. J. Vuylsteke (1893)

Reports from the Lords Committees... touching the Dignity of a Peer, 5 vols (1820–9)

Rotuli Parliamentorum, ed. J. Strachey et al., 7 vols (1767–1832)

Rotuli Scotiae, ed. D. Macpherson et al., 2 vols (1814)

Royal and Noble Wills. A Collection of all the Wills... of the Kings and Queens of England, Princes and Princesses of Wales and every Branch of the Blood Royal, ed. J. Nichols (1780)

Runyan, T. (ed.), 'The Constabulary of Bordeaux: the accounts of John Ludham (1372–73) and Robert de Wykford (1373–75)', Pontifical Institute of Mediaeval Studies, *Mediaeval Studies*, xxxvi (1974), 215–58, xxxvii (1975), 42–84

Salutati, Coluccio, *Epistolario*, ed. F. Novati, 4 vols (1891–1911)

Secousse, D.: see *Recueil de pièces*

'Séjours de Charles V (1364–1380)', ed. E. Petit, *Bull. Philol. et Hist. du Com. des Travaux Hist. et Sci.* (1887), 197–226

'Séjours de Charles VI (1380–1400)', ed. E. Petit, *Bull. Philol. et Hist. du Com. des Travaux Hist. et Sci.* (1893), 405–92

Select Cases in the Court of King's Bench, ed. G.O. Sayles, 7 vols (1936–71)

Spicilegium Brivatense. Recueil de documents historiques relatifs au Brivadois et à l'Auvergne, ed. A. Chassaing (1886)

Statutes of the Realm, ed. A. Luders, T.E. Tomlins, et al., 11 vols (1810–28)

Thesaurus novus anecdotorum, ed. E. Martène and U. Durand, 5 vols (1717)

Timbal, P.-C. (ed.), *La guerre de cent ans vue à travers les régistres du Parlement de Paris* (1961)

Titres de la maison ducale de Bourbon, ed. A. Huillard-Bréholles, 2 vols (1867–74)

Treaty of Bayonne (1388) with Preliminary Treaties of Trancoso (1387), ed. J. Palmer and B. Powell (1988)

Trésor des Chartes d'Albret, i, *Les archives de Vayres*, ed. J. Marquette (1973)

'Trésor des Chartes. Titres originaux, Anjou et Craon. Table analytique', ed. P. Marchegay, *Archives de l'Anjou*, ii (1853), 153–243

Urban V, *Lettres secrètes et curiales du pape Urbain V (1362–1370) se rapportant à la France*, ed. P. Lecacheux and G. Mollat (1902–55)

Urkundenbuch der Stadt Strassburg, ed. W. Wiegand, H. Witte, G. Wolfram, 7 vols (1869–1900)

Veterum scriptorum et monumentorum historicorum, dogmaticorum moralium amplissima collectio, ed. E. Martène and U. Durand, 9 vols (1724–33)

Vote de soustraction d'obédience en 1398, ed. H. Millet and E. Poulle, i (1988) [all published]

'Voyage de Nicolas de Bosc, Éveque de Bayeux, pour négocier la paix entre les couronnes de France et d'Angleterre', ed. E. Martène and D. Durand, *Voyage littéraire de deux réligieux Bénédictins*, ii (1724), 307–60

Voyage paléographique dans le département de l'Aube, ed. H. Arbois de Jubainville (1855)

Wrottesley, G., *Crécy and Calais from the Original Records in the Public Record Office* (1898)

Wykeham's Register, ed. T.F. Kirby, 2 vols (1896–9)

C NARRATIVE AND LITERARY SOURCES

Asterisks * mark editions having important documentary notes or appendices.

Alpartil, Martin de, *Chronica Actitatorum temporibus Benedicti XIII*, ed. F. Ehrle (1906)

Annales manuscrites de Limoges dites Manuscrit de 1638, ed. E. Ruben, F. Achard and P. Ducourtieux (1872)

Anonimalle chronicle, 1333–1381, ed. V.H. Galbraith (1927)

Arras, Jean d', *Mélusine, ou La noble histoire de Lusignan*, ed. J.-J. Vincensini (2003)

*Ayala, Pedro Lopez de, *Crónicas de los reyes de Castilla. Don Pedro, Don Enrique II, Don Juan I, Don Enrique III*, ed. E. de Llaguno Amirola, 2 vols (1779–80)

Bel, Jean le, *Chroniques*, ed. J. Viard and E. Déprez, 2 vols (1904–5)

Bernis, Michel de, 'Chronique des comtes de Foix', ed. H. Biu, 'Du panegyrique à l'histoire: l'archiviste Michel de Bernis, chroniqueur des comtes de Foix (1445)', *BEC*, clx (2002), 385–473

Birchington, Stephen, 'Historia de Vitis Archiepiscoporum Cantuariensium', ed. H. Wharton, *Anglia Sacra* (1691), i, 1–48

Bonet, Honoré, *L'apparicion Maistre Jehan de Meun et le Somnium super Materia Scismatis*, ed. I. Arnold (1926)

Bonet, Honoré, *The Tree of Battles of Honoré Bonet*, ed. G.W. Coopland (1949)

Bouchart, Alain, *Grandes chroniques de Bretagne*, ed. M.-L. Auger and G. Jeanneau, 3 vols (1986–8)

Bower, Walter, *Scotichronicon*, ed. D.E.R. Watt, 9 vols (1989–98)

Brandon, Jean, 'Chronique', ed. Kervyn de Lettonhove, *Chroniques relatives à l'histoire de la Belgique sous la domination des ducs de Bourgogne*, i (1870), 1–166

'Breve chronicon Flandriae', *Corpus Chronicorum Flandriae*, iii, 1–30

Brinton, Thomas, *The Sermons of Thomas Brinton, Bishop of Rochester*, ed. M.A. Devlin, 2 vols (1954)

Brut, or the Chronicles of England, ed. F.W.D. Brie (1906–8)

Cent Ballades (Les). Poème du XIVᵉ siècle composé par Jean le Séneschal avec la collaboration de Philippe d'Artois, Comte d'Eu, de Boucicaut le Jeune et de Jean de Crésecque, ed. G. Raynaud (1905)

Chandos Herald, *La vie du Prince Noir*, ed. D.B. Tyson (1975)

Charny, Geoffroy de, *The Book of Chivalry*, ed. R.W. Kaeuper (1995)

Chaucer, Geoffrey, *The Complete Works*, ed. R.W. Skeat, 7 vols (1894)

Chauliac, Guy de, *La Grande Chirurgie*, ed. E. Nicaise (1890)

Chronicles of London, ed. C.L. Kingsford (1905)

'Chronicon Briocense', ed. P.-H. Morice, *Preuves*, i, 7–102

'Chronicon Britannicum', ed. P.-H. Morice, *Preuves*, i, 1–7, 102–17

'Chronicon Comitum Flandrensium', *Corpus Chronicorum Flandriae*, i, 34–257

Chronik der Stadt Zurich, ed. J. Dirauer (1900)

Chronique Liégeoise de 1402, ed. E. Bacha (1900)

Chronique du bon duc Loys de Bourbon, ed. A.-M. Chazaud (1876)

'Chronique du doyen de S. Thiébaut de Metz', in Calmet, *Hist. de Lorraine*, v, pp.vi–cxvii

'Chronique française', ed. D. Secousse, *Preuves*, 636–55

Chronique du Mont-Saint-Michel (1443–1468), ed. S. Luce, 2 vols (1879–1883)

**Chronique normande du xive siècle*, ed. A. and E. Molinier (1882)

'Chronique des Pays-Bas, de France, d'Angleterre et de Tournai', *Corpus Chronicorum Flandriae*, iii, 110–569

Chronique des quatre premiers Valois (1327–1393), ed. S. Luce (1862)

Chronique du réligieux de Saint-Denis, ed. L. Bellaguet, 6 vols (1839–52)

**Chronique rimée des troubles de Flandre à la fin du xive siècle*, ed. E. Le Glay (1842) [references to the documentary appendix are to this edition]

Chronique rimée des troubles de Flandre en 1379–1380, ed. H. Pirenne (1902) [references to the text are to this edition]

Chronique de la traïson et mort de Richard Deux Roy Dengleterre, ed. B. Williams (1846)

'Chronique d'Uzerche (1320–1373)', ed. G. de Manteyer, *Mélanges Paul Fabre* (1902), 403–15

Chronographia regum Francorum, ed. H. Moranvillé, 3 vols (1891–7)

Cochon, Pierre, *Chronique Normande*, ed. C. Robillard de Beaurepaire (1870)

Coronica do Condestabre. Estoria de Dom Alvarez Pereyra, ed. A. de Almeida Calado (1991)

Corpus chronicorum Bononiensium, ed. A. Sorbelli, 4 vols *RISS²*, xviii.1 (1905)

Corpus chronicorum Flandriae, ed. J.J. de Smet, 4 vols (1837–65)

Cramaud, Simon de, *De substraccione obedience*, ed. H. Kaminsky (1984)

Creton, Jean, 'A metrical history of the deposition of Richard the Second', ed. J. Webb, *Archaeologia*, xx (1824), 1–441

Cronica volgare di Anonomo Fiorentino, ed. E. Bellondi, *RISS²*, xxvii.2 (1915)

Cronicon siculum incerti authoris ab anno 340 ad annum 1396, ed. J. de Blasiis (1887)

Croniques de Franche, d'Engleterre, de Flandres, de Lile et espécialment de Tournay, ed. A. Hocquet (1938)

**Cuvelier, Chronique de Bertrand du Guesclin*, ed. E. Charrière, 2 vols (1839) [all references to the documentary appendix are to this edition]

Cuvelier, *La chanson de Bertrand du Guesclin*, ed. J.-C. Faucon, 3 vols (1990–1) [all references to the text are to this edition]

Deschamps, Eustache, *Oeuvres complètes*, ed. Queux de Saint-Hilaire, 11 vols (1878–1903)

'Diario d'anonimo fiorentino', ed. A. Gherardi, *Cronache dei secoli XIII e XIV* (1876), 207–588

Diurnali del Duca di Monteleone, ed. M. Manfredi, *RISS²*, xxi.5 (1958)

Dixmude, Olivier van, *Merkwaerdige gebeurtenissen vooral in Vlaenderen en Brabant van 1377 tot 1443*, ed. J.-J. Lambin (1835)

Dynter, Edmond de, *Chronique des ducs de Brabant*, ed. P.F.X. de Ram, 3 vols (1854–60)

English Chronicle of the Reigns of Richard II, Henry IV, Henry V and Henry VI, ed. J.S. Davies (Camden Soc., lxiv) (1856)

Esquerrier et Miègeville, Arnaud, *Chroniques romanes des comtes de Foix composées au xve siècle*, ed. H. Courteault and F. Pasquier (1893)

Eulogium historiarum, ed. F.S. Haydon, 3 vols (1858–63)

Favent, Thomas, 'Historia Mirabilis Parliamenti (1386)', ed. M. McKisack, *Camden Miscellany*, xiv (Royal Historical Society, Camden Third Series, xxxvii) (1926)

Fontes Rerum Bernensium, 11 vols (1877–1956)

Fordun, John, *Chronica gentis Scotorum*, ed. W.F. Skene (1871)

Fragments d'une chronique inédite relatifs aux événements militaires arrivés en Basse-Normandie, de 1353 à 1389, ed. L. Delisle (1895)

*Froissart, Jean, *Oeuvres de Froissart. Chroniques*, ed. Kervyn de Lettenhove, 25 vols (1867–77) [cited as Froissart, *Chron.* (KL)]

*Froissart, Jean, *Chroniques de J. Froissart*, ed. S. Luce, G. Raynaud, L. and A. Mirot, 15 vols (1869–in progress) [cited as Froissart, *Chron.* (SHF)]

Gerson, Jean, *Oeuvres complètes*, ed. P. Glorieux, 10 vols (1960–73)

Gobelinus Persona, *Cosmidromius*, ed. M. Jansen (1900)

Gower, John, *Complete Works*, ed. G.C. Macaulay, 4 vols (1899–1902)

* *Grandes chroniques de France. Chronique des règnes de Jean II et de Charles V*, ed. R. Delachenal, 4 vols (1910–20)

Gray, Sir Thomas of Heton, *Scalacronica, 1272–1363*, ed. A. King (2005)

Great Chronicle of London, ed. A.H. Thomas and I.D. Thornley (1938)

Hardyng, John, *Chronicle*, ed. H. Ellis (1812)

Higden, Ranulph, *Polychronicon*, Continuations (i) 1340–77, ed. T. Hearne, in Hemingford, *De rebus gestis Edwardi I, II, & III*, ii (1731), 421–52; (ii) 1337–81, ed. T. Hog, in Murimuth, Adam, *Chronica* (1846), 171–243; (iii) 1352–1376, ed. J.R. Lumby, Higden, Ranulph, *Polychronicon* (Appendix), viii (1882), 407–28; (iv) 1348–1381, by John of Malvern, ed. J.R. Lumby, *ibid.*, 355–406; (v) 1355–77, ed. J. Taylor, 'A Wigmore Chronicle, 1355–1377', *English Historical Literature in the Fourteenth Century* (1987), 284–300

Historia Gelriae auctore anonymo, ed. J.G.C. Joosting (1902)

Historia Vitae et Regni Ricardi Secundi, ed. G.B. Stow (1977)

Istore et croniques de Flandres, ed. Kervyn de Lettenhove, 2 vols (1879–80)

'Joutes de Saint-Inglebert, 1389–1390. Poème contemporain', ed. J. Pichon, *Partie inédite des chroniques de Saint-Denis* (1863), 59–78

Justinger, Conrad, *Die Berner-Chronik*, ed. G. Studer (1871)

Juvénal des Ursins, Jean, *Histoire de Charles VI, roi de France*, ed. D. Godefroy (1653)

Kirkstall Abbey Chronicles, ed. J. Taylor (1952)

'Kleine Basler Annalen, 1308–1415', ed. A. Bernoulli, *Basler Chroniken*, v (1895), 49–71

Knighton, Henry, *Chronicle, 1337–1376*, ed. G.H. Martin (1995)

Königshofen, Jacob Twinger von, *Chronik*, ed. K. Hegel, *Chroniken der deutsche Stadte*, viii–ix, *Die Chroniken der oberrheinischen Stadte* (1870–1)

Lancaster, Henry of, *Le Livre de Seyntz Medicines*, ed. A.J. Arnould (1940)

Langland, William, *The Vision of William concerning Piers the Plowman*, 2 vols (1886)

Leland, John, *The Itinerary of John Leland in or about the years 1535–1543*, ed. L. Toulmin Smith, 5 vols (1906–10)

Limburger Chronik, ed. A. Wyss, *Monumenta Germaniae Historica, Deutsche Chroniken*, iv.1 (1883)

Livre du chevalier de La Tour Landry, ed. A. de Montaiglon (1854)

Livre des fais du bon messire Jehan le Maingre, dit Bouciquaut, ed. D. Lalande (1985)

Livre des miracles de Sainte-Catherine-de-Fierbois (1375–1470), ed. Y. Chauvin, *AHP*, lx (1976)

Lopes, Fernão, *Crónica de D. Fernando*, ed. G. Macchi (1975)

Lopes, Fernão, *Crónica de D. Pedro*, ed. G. Macchi (1966)

Lopes, Fernão, *Crónica del Rei dom João I da boa memória*, ed. A.B. Freire and W.J. Entwhistle, 2 vols (1915–77)

Malvern, John of: see Higden, Continuation (iv)

Mascaro, Jacme, 'Libre de Memorias', ed. C. Barbier, *Revue des Langues Romanes*, 4ᵉ série, iv (1890), 36–100

Menagier de Paris, ed. G.E. Brereton and J.M. Ferrier (1981)

Meyer, P. (ed.), 'L'entrevue d'Ardres', *Ann.-Bull. Soc. Hist Fr.*, xviii (1881), 209–24

Mézières, Philippe de, 'Épistre lamentable et consolatoire sue le fait de la desconfiture lacrimable... devant la ville de Nicopoli', ed. Kervyn de Lettenhove in Froissart, *Chroniques*, xvi, 444–523

Mézières, Philippe de, *Le songe du vieil pélerin*, ed. G.W. Coopland, 2 vols (1969)

Mézières, Philippe de, *Letter to King Richard II. A Plea made in 1395 for Peace between England and France*, ed. G.W. Coopland (1975)

Miracula S. Martialis anno 1388 patrata, ed. V.V.F. Arbellot, *Analecta Bollandiana*, i (1882), 411–45

Monstrelet, Enguerrand de, *Chronique*, ed. L. Douet d'Arcq, 6 vols (1857–62)

Niem, Dietrich von, *De Scismate*, ed. G. Erler (1890)

Noyal, Jean de, 'Fragments inédits de la chronique de Jean de Noyal', *Bull. Soc. Hist. Fr.* (1883), 246–75

Outremeuse, Jean d', 'Geste de Liège', ed. A. Borgnet, *Corps des Chroniques liégeoises. Ly myreur des histors* (1864–87), v, 583–694, vi, 639–710

Penne, Guillaume de la, 'Gesta Britonum in Italia', Martène and Durand, *Thesaurus*, iii, 1457–1502

Peter IV, King of Aragon, *Chronique Catalane*, 406.

Petit Thalamus de Montpellier, La chronique romane, ed. F. Pegat, E. Thomas, and E. Alicot (1840)

'Petite chronique de Guyenne jusqu'à l'an 1442', ed. G. Lefèvre-Pontalis, *BEC*, xlvii (1886), 53–79

Pisan, Christine de, *The Book of Fayttes of Armes and of Chivalrye*, tr. William Caxton, ed. A.T.P. Byles (1932)

Pisan, Christine de, *Le livre de l'advision Cristine*, ed. C. Reno and L. Dulac (2001)

Pisan, Christine de, *Le livre du corps de policie*, ed. A.J. Kennedy (1998)

Pisan, Christine de, *Le livre des fais et bonnes meurs du sage roy Charles V*, ed. S. Solente, 2 vols (1936–40)

Pisan, Christine, *The 'Livre de la paix' of Christine de Pisan*, ed. C.C. Willard (1958)

Pitti, Buonaccorso, *Cronica*, ed. A. Bacchi de la Lega (1905)

Political Poems and Songs, ed. T. Wright, 2 vols (1859–61)

Rerum Italicarum Scriptores, ed. L.A. Muratori, 25 vols (1723–51)

Rerum Italicarum Scriptores, ed. L.A. Muratori, n.e., 34 vols (1900–79)

Saint-André, Guillaume de, *Le Libvre du bon Jehan*, ed. J.-M. Cauneau and D. Philippe (2005)

Salmon, Pierre, 'Les lamentacions et épistres de Pierre Salmon', ed. G.-A. Crapelet, *Les demandes faites par le Roi Charles VI... avec les réponses de Pierre Salmon* (1833), 41–167

*Sayles, G.O. (ed.), 'The deposition of Richard II: three Lancastrian narratives', *Bull. Inst. Hist. Research*, liv (1981), 257–70

Songe du vergier, ed. M. Schnerb-Lièvre, 2 vols (1982)

Stavelot, Jean de, 'Chronique latine', ed. S. Balau, *Chronique Liégeoises* (1913–31), i, 69–143

Stella, Giorgio, *Annales Genuenses*, ed. G.P. Balbi (1975)

Thorne, William, *De Rebus Gestis Abbatum Sancti Augustini Cantuariae*, ed. R. Twysden (1652), cols. 1753–2202

Usk, Adam, *The Chronicle of Adam Usk, 1377–1421*, ed. C. Given-Wilson (1997)

Villani, Matteo and Filippo, *Historia universalis*, ed. L.A. Muratori, *RISS¹*, xiv (1729), 1–770

Vitae paparum Avenionensium, ed. E. Baluze, n.e., G. Mollat, 4 vols (1916–22)

Vlaamsche kroniek van Vlaanderen, ed. N. de Pauw, *Jehan Froissart's Cronyke van Vlaenderen*, iii (1909)

[Walsingham, Thomas], *Annales Ricardi Secundi et Henrici Quarti Regum Angliae*, ed. H.T. Riley, in Trokelow (J. de), *Chronica et Annales* (1866), 155–420

Walsingham, Thomas, *Historia Anglicana*, ed. H.T. Riley, 2 vols (1863–4)

Walsingham, Thomas, *The St. Albans Chronicle. The Chronica Maiora of Thomas Walsingham*, i, 1376–1394, ed. J. Taylor, W.R. Childs and L. Watkiss (2003)

Westminster Chronicle, 1381–1394, ed. L.C. Hector and B.F. Harvey (1982)
Wigmore Chronicle: see Higden, Continuation (v)
Wyntoun, Andrew of, *Orygynale Cronykil of Scotland*, ed. D. Laing, 3 vols (1872–9)

D SELECTED SECONDARY WORKS

Asterisks * mark works having important documentary notes and appendices.

Ainsworth, P.F., *Jean Froissart and the Fabric of History. Truth, Myth and Fiction in the Chroniques* (1990)
Alauzier, L. d', 'Comptes consulaires de Cajarc (Lot) au XIV⁰ siècle', *Bull. Philol. et Hist. du Com. des Trav. Hist.* (1957)[1], 89–103
Alauzier, L. d', 'Trois prises de Fons par les Anglais au xiv⁰ siècle', *Bull. Soc. Études du Lot*, lxxviii (1957)[2], 168–74
Alban, J.R., and Allmand, C.T., 'Spies and Spying in the Fourteenth Century', *War, Literature and Politics in the Late Middle Ages*, ed. C.T. Allmand (1976), 73–101
Allmand, C., *The Hundred Years War. England and France at War, c.1300–c.1450* (1988)
Anselme, Le P., *Histoire généalogique et chronologique de la maison royale de France*, 3rd edn., 9 vols (1726–33)
Armitage-Smith, S., *John of Gaunt* (1904)
Artonne, A., 'Froissart historien. Le siège et la prise de la Roche-Vendeix', *BEC*, cx (1953), 89–107
Arvanigian, M., 'A Lancastrian polity? John of Gaunt, John Neville and the war with France', *Fourteenth Century England*, ed. W.M. Ormrod (2004), 121–42
Aston, M., 'The impeachment of Bishop Despenser', *Bull. Inst. Hist. Research*, xxxviii (1965), 127–48
*Atiya, A.S., *The Crusade of Nicopolis* (1934)
Atlas historique des villes de France (1982–in progress)
Autrand, F., *Naissance d'un grand corps de l'état. Les gens du Parlement de Paris* (1981)
Autrand, F., *Charles VI. La folie du Roi* (1986)
Avout, J. d', *La querelle des Armagnacs et des Bourguignons* (1943)
Ayton, A., *Knights and warhorses. Military service and the English aristocracy under Edward III* (1994)
Ayton, A., 'Knights, esquires and military service. The evidence of the armorial cases before the Court of Chivalry', *The Medieval Military Revolution*, ed. A. Ayton and J.L. Price (1995), 81–104
*Balasque, J. and Dulaurens, E., *Études historiques sur la ville de Bayonne*, 3 vols (1862–75)
*Baldwin, J.F., *The King's Council in England during the Middle Ages* (1913)
Barber, M., 'John Norbury (c. 1350–1414): an Esquire of Henry IV', *EHR*, lxviii (1953), 66–76
Barber, R., *Edward Prince of Wales and Aquitaine* (1978)
Barbot, A., *Histoire de la Rochelle*, ed. D. d'Aussy, 3 vols, *AHSA* xiv, xvii, xviii (1886–90)
Bardon, A., *Histoire de la ville d'Alais de 1341 à 1461* (1896)
Barker, J.R.V., *The tournament in England, 1100–1400* (1986)
Barnie, J., *War in Medieval English Society. Social Values in the Hundred Years War, 1377–99* (1974)
*Barroux, M., *Les fêtes royales de Saint-Denis en mai 1389* (1930)
Batlle, C., 'La fecha de la batalla de Trancoso', *Anuario de Estudios Medievales*, iii (1966), 525–32
*Baudouin, A., 'Commencements de la querelle du comte de Foix et du duc de Berry en 1380 et 1381', *Mems. Acad. Sci. Inscr. et B-L de Toulouse*, 7⁰ série, iii (1871), 360–78
Bayley, C.C., 'The Campaign of 1375 and the Good Parliament', *EHR*, liii (1940), 370–83
Beauchet-Filleau, H., P. and J., *Dictionnaire historique et généalogique des familles du Poitou*, 2nd ed., 7 vols (1891– in progress)

Beardwood, A., *Alien Merchants in England, 1350–1377* (1931)

Bell, A.R., *War and the Soldier in the Fourteenth Century* (2004)

Bellamy, J.G., 'The Northern Rebellions in the Later Years of Richard II', *Bull. J. Rylands Lib.*, xlvii (1964–5), 254–74

Bellamy, J.G., 'Sir John de Annesley and the Chandos inheritance', *Nottingham Mediaeval Studies*, x (1966), 94–105

Beltz, G.F., *Memorials of the Order of the Garter* (1841)

Bennett, M.J., *Community, Class and Careerism. Cheshire and Lancashire Society in the age of Sir Gawain and the Green Knight* (1983)

*Bennett, M.J., 'Edward III's entail and the succession to the Crown, 1376–1471', *EHR*, cxiii (1998), 580–609

Bériac, F., 'Une principauté sans chambre des comptes ni Échiquier: l'Aquitaine (1362–1370)', *La France des principautés. Les Chambres des Comptes, XIVe et XVe siècles* (1996), 105–22

Berty, A., *Topographie historique du vieux Paris. Région du Louvre et des Tuileries* (1866)

Billot, C., *Chartres à la fin du moyen age* (1987)

Bird, R.R., *The Turbulent London of Richard II* (1949)

Blair, C., *European Armour* (1958)

*Blanc, A., 'Le rappel du duc d'Anjou et l'ordonnance du 25 avril 1380', *Bull. Philol. et Hist. du Com. des Trav. Hist.* (1899), 191–212

Boffa, S., *Warfare in Medieval Brabant, 1356–1406* (2004)

Bois, G., *Crise du feodalisme* (1976)

Boardman, S., *The Early Stewart Kings. Robert II and Robert III, 1371–1406* (1996)

Boardman, S., 'Coronations, Kings and Guardians: Politics, Parliaments and General Councils, 1371–1406', *The History of the Scottish Parliament*, i, *Parliament and Politics in Scotland, 1235–1560*, ed. K.M. Brown and R.J. Tanner (2004)

Booth, P.H.W., *The Financial Administration of the Lordship and County of Chester, 1272–1377* (1981)

Borderie, A. le Moyne de la, *Histoire de Bretagne*, 6 vols (1905–14)

Borrelli de Serres, L.-L. de, *Recherches sur divers services publics du xiii*e *au xvii*e *siècle*, 3 vols (1895–1909)

*Bouard, M. de, *Les origines des guerres d'Italie. La France et l'Italie au temps du grand schisme d'occident* (1936)

Boudet, M., 'Assauts, sièges et blocus de Saint-Flour par les Anglais pendant la guerre de cent Ans (1356–1391)', *Revue d'Auvergne*, x (1893), 337–67

Boudet, M., *La Jacquerie des Tuchins (1363–1384)* (1895)

Boulay, F.R.H. du, 'Henry of Derby's expeditions to Prussia, 1390–1 and 1392', *The Reign of Richard II. Essays in Honour of May McKisack*, ed. F.R.H. du Boulay and C. Barron (1971), 153–72

Bournon, F., 'L'hôtel royale de Saint-Pol', *Mems. Soc. Hist. Paris*, vi (1880), 55–179

Bournon, F., *La Bastille* (1893)

Bouton, A., *Le Maine. Histoire économique et sociale, XIV*e, *XV*e *et XVI*e *siècles* (1970)

Boutruche, R., *La crise d'une société. Seigneurs et paysans du Bordelais pendant la guerre de cent ans* (1963)

Brachet, A., *Pathologie mentale des rois de France* (1903)

*Bréard, C., *Le Crotoy et les armements maritimes des xiv*e *et xv*e *siècles* (1902)

Breuils, A., 'Jean I, Comte d'Armagnac et le mouvement national dans le midi au temps du Prince Noir', *Revue des Questions Historiques*, lix (1896), 44–102

British Atlas of Historic Towns, iii, *The City of London from Prehistoric Times to c. 1520*, ed. M.C. Lobel (1989)

Brooks, N., 'The organisation and achievements of the peasants of Kent and Essex in 1381', *Studies in Medieval History presented to R.H.C. Davis*, ed. H. Mayr-Harting and R.I. Moore (1985), 247–70

*Broussillon, B. de, *La Maison de Craon, 1050–1480. Étude historique accompagné du cartulaire de Craon*, 2 vols (1893)

Brown, M., *The Black Douglases. War and Lordship in Late Medieval Scotland, 1300–1455* (1998)

Brown, R.A., Colvin, H.M., and Taylor, A.J., *The History of the King's Works*, i–ii, *The Middle Ages* (1963)

*Brun, R., 'Notes sur le commerce des armes à Avignon au xiv⁰ siècle', *BEC*, cix (1951), 209–31

*Bueno de Mesquita, D.M., 'The foreign policy of Richard II in 1397: some Italian letters', *EHR*, lvi (1941), 628–37

*Cabié, E., *Événements relatifs à l'Albigeois pendant la querelle du comte de Foix et du duc de Berry de 1380 à 1382* (1879) [extr. *Revue du Tarn* (1879)]

*Cabié, E., 'Notes et documents sur les différends des comtes de Foix et d'Armagnac en 1381', *Annales du Midi*, Année 13 (1901)[1], 500–29

Cabié, E., 'Campagne de Gaucher de Passac contre les routiers du sud-ouest de la France, 1384–1385' *Rev. Hist. du Tarn*, xviii (1901)[2], 61–71, 168–79

Caferro, W., *John Hawkwood. An Englush Mercenary in Fourteenth-century Italy* (2006)

*Calmet, A., *Histoire ecclésiastique et civile de Lorraine*, 7 vols (1745–57)

Campbell, J., 'Scotland and the Hundred Years War in the 14th century', *Europe in the Late Middle Ages*, ed. J. Hale, R. Highfield and B. Smalley (1965), 184–216

*Carbonnières, L. de, *La procédure devant la chambre criminelle du Parlement de Paris au xiv⁰ siècle* (2004)

Carr, A.D., 'Welshmen and the Hundred Years War', *Welsh History Review*, iv (1968), 21–46

Carr, A.D., 'Rhys ap Robert', *Denbighshire Historical Society, Transactions*, xxiv (1975), 155–70

Carr, A.D., *Owen of Wales. The End of the House of Gwynedd* (1991)

*Cartellieri, O., *Philipp der Kühne, Herzog von Burgund* (1910)

*Cascales, F., *Discursos historicos de la muy noble y muy leal ciudad de Murcia* (1775)

Catalina Garcia, J., *Castilla y León durante los reinados de Pedro I, Enrique II, Juan I y Enrique III*, 2 vols (1891–3)

Cazelles, R., *Nouvelle histoire de Paris de la fin du règne de Philippe Auguste à la mort de Charles V, 1223–1380* (1972)

Cazelles, R., *Société politique, noblesse et couronne sous Jean le Bon et Charles V* (1982)

*Champollion-Figeac, L.-A., *Louis et Charles, ducs d'Orléans. Leur influence sur les arts, la littérature et l'esprit de leur siècle* (1844)

Chaplais, P., 'The Chancery of Guyenne, 1289–1453', *Studies presented to Sir Hilary Jenkinson*, ed. J. Conway Davies (1957), 61–95

Chaplais, P., 'The Court of Sovereignty of Guyenne (Edward III–Henry VI) and its antecedents', *Documenting the Past. Essays in Medieval History Presented to George Peddy Cuttino*, ed. J.S. Hamilton and P.J. Bradley (1989), 137–53

Charon, P., 'Relations entre les cours de France et de Navarre en 1376–1377', *BEC*, cl (1992), 85–108

*Chavanon, J., 'Renaud VI de Pons, Vicomte de Turenne et de Carlat', *AHSA*, xxxi (1902), 1–202

Chénon, E., 'Date exacte de l'occupation de Saint-Sévère par les anglais sous Charles V', *Mems. Soc. Antiq. Centre*, xxxvii (1914–16), 48–51

Chéruel, A., *Histoire de Rouen pendant l'époque communale, 1150–1382*, 2 vols (1844)

Chotzen, T.M., *Recherches sur la poésie de Dafydd ab Gwilym, barde gallois du xiv⁰ siècle* (1927)

Chotzen, T.M., 'Yvain de Galles in Alsace-Lorraine and in Switzerland', *Bull. Board of Celtic Studies*, iv (1927–9), 231–40

*Clarke, M.V., 'The deposition of Richard II', *Bull. J. Rylands Lib.* xiv (1930),125–81

Clément-Simon, G., *La rupture du traité de Brétigny et ses conséquences en Limousin* (1898)

Cokayne, G.E., *The Complete Peerage*, ed. V. Gibbs *et al.*, 12 vols (1910–59)

*Compayré, C., Études historiques et documents inédits sur l'Albigeois, le Castrais et l'ancien diocèse de Lavaur (1841)

Contamine, P., 'The French nobility and the war', The Hundred Years War, ed. K. Fowler (1971), 135–62

Contamine, P., Guerre, état et société à la fin du moyen age. Étude sur les armées des rois de France, 1337–1494 (1972)

Contamine, P., L'Oriflamme de St.-Denis aux xive et xve siècles (1975)

Contamine, P., La vie quotidienne pendant la guerre de cent ans (1976)

Contamine, P., 'Les fortifications urbaines en France à la fin du moyen age: aspects financiers et économiques', Revue historique, cclx (1978), 23–47

Contamine, P., La guerre au moyen age (1980)

Contamine, P., La noblesse au royaume de France de Philippe le Bel à Louis XII. Essai de synthèse (1997)

Contamine, P., 'Froissart: art militaire, pratique et conception de la guerre', in Pages d'histoire militaire (xive–xve siècles) (2005), 249–65

*Cordey, J., Les comtes de Savoie et les rois de France pendant la guerre de cent ans (1911)

Costa Gomes, R., A corte dos reis de Portugal do final da idade média (1995)

Coulborn, A.P.R., 'The Economic and Political Preliminaries of the Crusade of 1383', Bull. Inst. Hist. Res., x (1932–3), 40–4

*Courteault, H., 'La fuite et les aventures de Pierre de Craon en Espagne, d'après des documents inédits des archives d'Aragon', BEC, lii (1891), 430–48

*Coussemaker, E. de, 'Analectes historiques sur la Flandre maritime', Bull. Com. flamande de France, vi (1872–5), 36–48, 66–89

*Coville, A., Les états de Normandie. Leurs origines et leur developpement au xive siècle (1894)

Coville, A., Jean Petit. La question du tyrannicide au commencement du xve siècle (1932)

Coville, A., Gontier et Pierre Col et l'humanisme en France au temps de Charles VI (1934)

Curry, A., 'Sir Thomas Erpingham. A life in arms', Agincourt, 1415. Henry V, Sir Thomas Erpingham and the triumph of the English archers ed. A. Curry (2000), 53–77

Cuttler, S.H., The Law of Treason and Treason Trials in Later Medieval France (1981)

*Daumet, G., Étude sur l'alliance de la France et la Castille au xive et au xve siècles (1898)

David, H., Philippe le Hardi, duc de Bourgogne et co-régent de France de 1392 à 1404. Le train somptuaire d'un grand Valois (1947)

Davies, R.R., 'Richard II and the Principality of Chester, 1397–9', The Reign of Richard II. Essays in Honour of May McKisack, ed. F.R.H. du Boulay and C. Barron (1971), 256–79

Davis, R.H.C., The Medieval Warhorse (1989)

*Delachenal, R., Histoire de Charles V, 5 vols (1909–31)

Delaruelle, E., Labande, E.-R., and Ourliac, P., L'église au temps du Grand Schisme et de la crise conciliaire (1378–1449) (1962)

Delaville le Roulx, J., La France en Orient au xive siècle. Les expéditions du Maréchal Boucicaut, 2 vols (1886)

*Delisle, L., Histoire du château et des sires de Saint-Sauveur-le-Vicomte (1867)

*Denifle, H., La guerre de cent ans et les désolations des églises, monastères et hôpitaux en France, 2 vols (1897–9)

Déprez, E., Hugo Aubriot, Praepositus parisiensis et urbanis praetor (1367–1381) (1902)

Desobry, J., 'Pour des queues d'hermine. L'abbaye du Mont-Saint-Quentin et la chevauchée de Buckingham (1380)', La guerre, la violence et les gens au moyen age, ed. P. Contamine and O. Guyotjeannin (1996), ii, 119–26

Dessalles, L., Périgueux et les deux derniers comtes de Périgord (1847)

Dessalles, L., Histoire du Périgord, 3 vols (1883–5)

Devals, J.-U., Histoire de Montauban sous la domination anglaise (1843)

*Dias Arnaut, S., A crise nacional dos fins do século XIV. A sucessão de D. Fernando (1960)

Dieudonné, A., 'La monnaie royale depuis le réforme de Charles V jusqu'à la restauration monétaire par Charles VII, spécialement dans ses rapports avec l'histoire politique', *BEC*, lxxii (1911), 473–99, lxxiii (1912), 263–82

Dognon, P., *Les institutions politiques et administratives du pays de Languedoc du XIIIᵉ siècle aux guerres de religion* (1895)

Drouyn, L., *La Guyenne militaire*, 3 vols (1865)

Duchesne, A., *Histoire généalogique des maisons de Guines, d'Ardres, de Gand et de Coucy*, 2 vols (1631)

*Dumay, G., 'Guy de Pontailler, sire de Talmay, gouverneur et maréchal de Bourgogne (1364–1392)', *Mems. Soc. Bourguignonne de Géographie et d'Histoire*, xxiii (1907), 1–222

Dunn, A., 'Richard II and the Mortimer Inheritance', *Fourteenth Century England*, ii, ed. C. Given-Wilson (2002), 159–70

Dunn, A., *The Politics of Magnate Power in England and Wales* (2003)

Duro, C.F., 'Una escuadra de galeras de Castilla del siglo XIV', *Bol. R. Acad. Hist.*, xii (1888), 243

Durrieu, P., 'La prise d'Arezzo par Enguerrand VII, sire de Coucy en 1384', *BEC*, xli (1880)[1], 161–94

Durrieu, P., *Le royaume d'Adria* (1880)[2]

Durrieu, P., *Les Gascons en Italie* (1885)

Eiden, H., 'Norfolk, 1382: A sequel to the Peasants' Revolt', *EHR*, cxiv (1999), 370–7

Emden, A.B., *A Biographical Register of the University of Oxford to A.D. 1500*, 3 vols (1957)

Entwistle, W.J., 'The English archers at Aljubarrota, 1385', *Revista de Historia*, xvi (1928), 197–205

Favier, J., *Les finances pontificales à l'époque du grand schisme d'occident, 1378–1409* (1966)

Favier, J., *Paris au XVᵉ siècle* (1974)

Favreau, R., *La ville de Poitiers à la fin du moyen age* (1978)

Favreau, R., *La commanderie du Breuil-du-Pas et la guerre de cent ans dans la Saintonge méridionale* (1986)

Fino, J.-F., *Forteresses de la France médiévale*, 3ᵉ edn. (1977)

Finot, J., *Recherches sur les incursions des anglais et des grandes compagnies dans le duché et le comté de Bourgogne à la fin du XIVᵉ siècle* (1874)

Finot, J., 'La dernière ordonnance de Charles V', *BEC*, l (1889), 164–7

Finot, J., *Étude historique sur les relations commerciales entre la Flandre et l'Espagne au moyen age* (1899)

Flandin-Bléty, P., 'Trahison ou pacification? À propos d'une rémission de 1389', *La "France Anglaise" au moyen age. Actes du IIIᵉ congrès nationale des sociétés savantes (Poitiers, 1986), Section d'histoire médiévale et de philologie*, i (1988), 285–313

Fournier, G., *Le château dans la France médiévale* (1978)

Fowler, K., 'Les finances et la discipline dans les armées anglaises en France au xive siècle', *Actes du Colloque internationale de Cocherel, 16, 17 et 18 mai 1964, Les Cahiers Vernonnais*, no. 4 (1964), 55–84

Fowler, K., 'Truces', *The Hundred Years War*, ed. K. Fowler (1971), 184–215

Fowler, K., 'L'emploi des mercenaires par les pouvoirs ibériques et l'intervention militaire anglaise en Espagne (vers 1361–vers 1379)', *Realidad e imagenes del poder. España a fines de la edad media*, ed. A. Rucquoi (1988), 23–55

Fowler, K., *Medieval Mercenaries*, i, *The Great Companies* (2001)

Fréville, E. de, 'Des Grandes Compagnies au quatorzième siècle', *BEC*, iii (1841–2), 258–81, v (1843–4), 232–53

Friel, I., 'Winds of Change? Ships and the Hundred Years War', *Arms, Armies and Fortifications in the Hundred Years War*, ed. A. Curry and M. Hughes (1994), 183–93

Gaier, C., *L'industrie et le commerce des armes dans les anciens principautés belges du XIIIᵐᵉ à la fin du XVᵐᵉ siècle* (1973)

*Galbraith, V.H., 'Articles laid before the Parliament of 1371', *EHR*, xxxiv (1919), 579–82

Gardelles, J., *Les châteaux du moyen age dans la France du sud-ouest* (1972)

*Garnier, J., *L'artillerie des ducs de Bourgogne d'après les documents conservés aux archives de la Côte d'Or* (1895)

Gauvard, *'De grace especial'. Crime, état et société en France à la fin du moyen age* (1991)

Geremek, B., *Les marginaux parisiens aux xive et xve siècles* (1976)

Germain, A., *Une émeute à Montpellier au XIVe siècle* (1847)

*Germain, A. *Histoire de la commune de Montpellier*, 3 vols (1851)

Germain, R., *Les campagnes bourbonnaises à la fin du moyen age* (1984)

Gillespie, J.L., 'Richard II's Cheshire Archers', *Trans. Hist. Soc. Lancashire & Cheshire*, cxxv (1974), 1–39

Gillespie, J.L., 'Richard II's Archers of the Crown', *Journal of British Studies*, xviii (1979), 14–29

Given-Wilson, C., 'The ransom of Olivier du Guesclin', *Bull. Inst. Hist. Research*, liv (1981), 17–28

Given-Wilson, C., *The Royal Household and the King's Affinity. Service, Politics and Finance in England, 1360–1413* (1986)

Given-Wilson, C., 'Wealth and credit, public and private: the Earls of Arundel, 1306–1397', *EHR*, cvi (1991), 1–26

Given-Wilson, C., *Chronicles of the Revolution, 1397–1400* (1993)

Given-Wilson, C., 'Richard II, Edward II and the Lancastrian Inheritance', *EHR*, cix (1994), 553–71

Given-Wilson, C., 'Edward III's prisoners of war: the battle of Poitiers and its context', *EHR*, cxvi (2001), 802–33

Glamorgan County History, iii, *The Middle Ages*, ed. T.B. Pugh (1971)

*Goñi Gaztambide, J., 'La embajada de Simon de Cramaud a Castilla en 1396', *Hispania Sacra*, xv (1962), 165–76

Goodman, A., *The Loyal Conspiracy. The Lords Appellant under Richard II* (1971)

Goodman, A., 'The military subcontracts of Sir Hugh Hastings', *EHR*, xcv (1980), 114–20

Goodman, A., 'John of Gaunt', *England in the Fourteenth Century. Proceedings of the 1985 Harlaxton Symposium*, ed. W.M. Ormrod (1986)

Goodman, A., *John of Gaunt* (1992)

Goodman, A. and Tuck, A. (ed.), *War and Border Societies in the Middle Ages* (1992)

Gordon, D., *Making & Meaning. The Wilton Diptych* (1993)

Green, D., 'The later retinue of Edward the Black Prince', *Nottingham Mediaeval Studies*, xliv (2000), 141–51

Green, D., 'Edward the Black Prince and East Anglia: an unlikely association', *Fourteenth Century England*, ed. W.M. Ormrod (2004), 83–98

Gresser, P., *La Franche-Comté au temps de la guerre de cent ans* (1989)

*Guichenon, S., *Histoire généalogique de la maison de Savoie*, n.e., 4 vols (1778–80)

Guenée, B., *Un roi et son historien. Vingt études sur le règne de Charles VI et la Chronique du Réligieux de Saint-Denis* (1999)

Guenée, B., *L'opinion publique à la fin du moyen age* (2002)

Guenée, B., *La folie de Charles VI, Roi Bien-Aimé* (2004)

Guillemain, B., *La cour pontificale d'Avignon, 1309–1376* (1966)

Gutiérrez de Velasco, A., 'Los ingleses en España', *Estudios de Edad Media de la Corona de Aragon*, iv (1950), 215–319

Haegeman, M., *De Anglofilie in het Graafschap Vlaanderen tussen 1379 en 1435. Politieke en economische aspecten* (1988)

Harriss, G.L., *King, Parliament and Public Finance in Medieval England, to 1369* (1975)

Harriss, G.L., *Shaping the Nation. England 1360–1461* (2005)

*Hay du Chastelet, P., *Histoire de Bertrand du Guesclin, Connestable de France* (1666)

Hébert, M., 'L'armée provençale en 1374', *Annales du Midi*, xci (1979), 5–27

Henneman, J.B., *Royal Taxation in Fourteenth Century France. The Captivity and Ransom of John II, 1356–1370* (1976)

Henneman, J.B., *Olivier de Clisson and Political Society in France under Charles V and Charles VI* (1996)

Hewitt, J., *The Organisation of War under Edward III* (1966)

*Higounet, *Le comté de Comminges de ses origines à son annexion à la couronne* (1949)

Higounet-Nadal, A., *Périgueux aux xive et xve siècles. Étude de démographie historique* (1978)

Histoire générale de Languedoc: see Vic, C. de and Vaissète, J.

History of Northumberland, issued under the direction of the Northumberland County History Committee, 15 vols (1893–1940)

History of Parliament. The House of Commons, 1386–1421, ed. J.S Roskell, L. Clark and C. Rawcliffe, 4 vols (1992)

Holmes, G.A., *The Estates of the Higher Nobility in Fourteenth Century England* (1957)

Holmes, G.A., *The Good Parliament* (1975)

*Hunger, V., 'Les seigneurs de Maisy du XIe au XVIIIe siècle', *Bull. Soc. Antiq. Normandie*, xxxi (1916), 65–181.

James, M.K., *Studies in the Medieval Wine Trade* (1971)

*Jarry, E., *La vie politique de Louis de France, Duc d'Orléans* (1889)

Jarry, E., 'La "voie de fait" et l'alliance franco-milanaise (1386–1395)', *BEC*, liii (1892), 213–53, 504–70

*Jarry, E., *Les origines de la domination française à Génes (1392–1402)* (1896)

*Jarry, E., 'Instructions secrètes pour l'adoption de Louis I d'Anjou par Jeanne de Naples (janvier 1380)', *BEC*, lxvii (1906), 234–54

Jones, M., *Ducal Brittany, 1364–1399* (1970)

Jones, M., 'The ransom of Jean de Bretagne, Count of Penthièvre: an aspect of English foreign policy, 1386–1388', *Bull. Inst. Hist. Res.*, xlv (1972), 7–26

Jones, M., '"Mon Pais et ma Nation": Breton Identity in the Fourteenth Century', *War, Literature and Politics in the Late Middle Ages*, ed. C.T. Allmand (1976), 144–68

*Jones, M., 'The Diplomatic Evidence for Franco-Breton Relations, c. 1370–1372', *EHR*, xciii (1978), 300–19

Jones, M., 'The finances of John IV, Duke of Brittany', *The Crown and Local Communities in England and France in the Fifteenth Century*, ed. J.R.L. Highfield and R. Jeffs (1981)[1], 51–71

Jones, M., 'The defence of medieval Brittany', *Archaeological Journal*, cxxxviii (1981)[2], 149–204

Jones, M., 'La mort de Walter Huet (1373)', *Bull. Soc. d'études et de recherches historiques du pays de Retz*, iv (1984), 28–34

Jones, M., 'Les capitaines anglo-bretons et les marches entre la Bretagne et le Poitou de 1342 à 1373', *La "France Anglaise" au moyen age. Actes du IIIe congrès nationale des sociétés savantes (Poitiers, 1986), Section d'histoire médiévale et de philologie*, i (1988), 357–75

Jones, M., 'The Breton nobility and their masters from the civil war of 1341–64 to the late fifteenth century', in M. Jones, *The Creation of Brittany. A late Medieval State* (1988), 219–37

Jones, M., 'Fortunes et malheurs de guerre. Autour de la rançon du chevalier anglais Jean Bourchier', *La guerre, la violence et les gens au moyen age*, ed. P. Contamine and O. Guyotjeannin (1996), i, 189–208

Jorga, N., *Philippe de Mézières, 1327–1405, et la croisade au xive siècle* (1896)

Jurkowski, M., Smith, C.L., and Crook, D., *Lay taxes in England and Wales, 1188–1688* (1998)

*Justel, C., *Histoire généalogique de la maison de Turenne* (1645)

Kaminsky, H., *Simon de Cramaud and the Great Schism* (1983)

Kerhervé, J., *L'État Breton aux 14e et 15e siècles. Les ducs, l'argent et les hommes*, 2 vols (1987)

Keen, M.H., *The Laws of War in the Late Middle Ages* (1965)

Keen, M.H., 'Chivalry, nobility and the man-at-arms', *War, Literature and Politics in the Late Middle Ages*, ed. C.T. Allmand (1976), 32–45

Keen, M.H., *Chivalry* (1984)

Keen, M.H., 'The jurisdiction and origins of the Constable's Court', *War and Government in the Middle Ages. Essays in Honour of J.O. Prestwich*, ed. J. Gillingham and J.C. Holt (1984), 159–69

Keen, M.H., 'English Military Experience and the Court of Chivalry: the Case of Grey v. Hastings', *Guerre et société en France, en Angleterre et en Bourgogne, xive–xve siècle*, ed. P. Contamine, C. Giry-Deloison and M. Keen (1991), 123–42

Keen, M.H., 'Richard II's ordinances of war of 1385', *Rulers and Ruled in Late Medieval England. Essays Presented to Gerald Harriss*, ed. R.E. Archer and S. Walker (1995), 33–48

Kenyon, J.R., 'Coastal Artillery Fortification in England in the Late Fourteenth and Early Fifteenth Centuries', *Arms, Armies and Fortifications in the Hundred Years War*, ed. A. Curry and M. Hughes (1994), 145–9

King, D.J.C., *Castellarium Anglicanum*, 2 vols (1983)

Kirby, J.L., 'The keeping of Carlisle Castle before 1381', *Trans. Cumberland and Westmoreland Arch. and Ant. Soc.*, liv (1955), 131–9

Labande, E.-R., *Rinaldo Orsini, Comte de Tagliacozzo* (1939)

*Labroue, E., *Livre de vie. Les seigneurs et les capitaines du Périgord Blanc au XIVe siècle* (1891)

Labroue, E., *Bergerac sous les anglais. Essai sur le consulat et la communauté de Bergerac au moyen age* (1893)

*Lacabane, L., 'De la poudre à canon et de son introduction en France', *BEC*, vi (1844), 28–57

*Lacabane, L., 'Mémoire sur les deux prétendues délivrances de Condom en 1369 et 1374', *BEC*, 3e série, ii (1851), 97–130

Lacaille, H., 'Enguerrand de Coucy au service de Grégoire XI, 1372–1374', *Ann.-Bull. Hist. France*, xxxii (1895), 185–206

Lacoste, G., *Histoire générale de la province de Quercy*, ed. L. Combarieu and F. Cangardel, 4 vols (1883–6)

Lacour, R., *Le gouvernement de l'apanage de Jean, duc de Berry, 1360–1416* (1934)

Ladero Quesada, M.A., 'Castile in the Middle Ages', *The Rise of the Fiscal State in Europe*, ed. R. Bonney (1999), 177–99

Lalande, D., *Jean II le Meingre dit Boucicaut (1366–1421). Étude d'une biographie héroïque* (1988)

Lang, S.J., 'John Bradmore and his book *Philomena*', *Social History of Medicine*, v (1992), 121–30.

Lapierre, A., *La guerre de cent ans dans l'Argonne et le Rethélois* (1900)

Lartigaut, J., *Puy-l'Évêque au moyen age* (1991)

Laurent, H. and Quicke, F., *Les origines de l'état bourguignon. L'accession de la Maison de Bourgogne aux duchés de Brabant et de Limbourg, i, jusqu'à l'acquisition du duché de Limbourg et des terres d'Outre-Meuse (1383–1396)* (1939)

Laurent, R., *Les ports de la Côte et du Zwin* (1986)

Lebeuf, J., *Histoire de la ville et de tout le diocèse de Paris*, ed. F. Bournon, 7 vols (1883–93)

Le Breton, C., *L'Avranchin pendant la guerre de cent ans* (1879)

*Lecoy de la Marche, *Les relations politiques de la France avec le royaume de majorque*, 2 vols (1892)

*Lefranc, A., *Olivier de Clisson, Connétable de France* (1898)

Leguai, A., *De la seigneurie à l'état. Le Bourbonnais pendant la guerre de cent ans* (1969)

Leguay, J.-P., *Un réseau urbain au moyen age: les villes du duché de Bretagne aux xive et xve siècles* (1981)

*Lehoux, F., *Jean de France, duc de Berri. Sa vie, son action politique*, 4 vols (1966–8)

*Lemoine, J., 'Du Guesclin à Jersey', *Rev. Hist.*, lxi (1896), 45–61

Lennel, F., *Histoire de Calais*, 3 vols (1908–1913)

Léonard, E.-G., *Les Angevins de Naples* (1947)

Leroux, A., 'Le sac de la cité de Limoges et son relèvement, 1379–1464', *Bul. Soc. Archéol. Hist. Limousin*, lvi (1906), 155–233

Le Roux de Lincy, A., 'Hughes Aubriot, Prévot de Paris, sous Charles V', *BEC*, xxiii (1862), 173–213

Lewis, N.B., 'Article VII of the Impeachment of Michael de la Pole in 1386', *EHR*, xlii (1927), 402–7

Lewis, N.B., 'The Organisation of Indentured Retinues in Fourteenth Century England', *Trans. Roy. Hist. Soc.*, 4th series, xxvii (1945), 29–39

Lewis, N.B., 'The Last Medieval Summons of the English Feudal Levy, 13 June 1385', *EHR*, lxxiii (1958), 1–26

Lloyd, T.H., *The Movement of Wool Prices in Medieval England* (1973)

Lloyd, T.H., *The English Wool Trade in the Middle Ages* (1977)

*Lobineau, G.A., *Histoire de Bretagne*, 2 vols (1707)

Loirette, G., 'Arnaud Amanieu, sire d'Albret et ses rapports avec la monarchie française pendant le règne de Charles V (1364–1380)', *Annales du Midi*, Année xliii (1931), 5–39

*López de Meneses, A., 'El canciller Pero López de Ayala y los reyes de Aragón,' *Estudios de Edad Media de la Corona de Aragón*, viii (1967), 189–264

Luce, S., *La France pendant la guerre de cent ans*, 2 vols (1890)

*Luce, S., 'Louis, duc d'Anjou, s'est-il approprié, après la mort de Charles V, du trésor laissé par le roi son frère?', *BEC*, xxxvi (1875), 299–303

Lunt, W.E., *Financial Relations of the Papacy with England*, 2 vols (1939–62)

Martin, H., 'Engerrand d'Eudin, Capitaine Royale de Loches, Sénéchal de Beaucaire, Gouverneur de Dauphiné (13..–1391), *Bull. Soc. Archéol. Touraine*, xxxii (1957), 131–59

Mancest-Batiffol, L., 'La prévoté des marchands de Paris à la fin du XIVe siècle', *BEC*, lii (1891), 269–84

Masson d'Autume, M. de, *Cherbourg pendant la guerre de cent ans* (1948)

Matthew, D., *The Norman Monasteries and their English Possessions* (1962)

Maubourguet, J.-M., *Le Périgord méridional des origines à l'an 1370. Étude d'histoire politique et religieuse* (1926)

McFarlane, K.B., *Lancastrian Kings and Lollard Knights* (1972)

McFarlane, K.B., *The Nobility of Later Medieval England* (1973)

McHardy, A.K., 'Some reflections on Edward III's use of propaganda', *The Age of Edward III*, ed. J.S. Bothwell (2001), 171–92

*Menard, L., *Histoire civile, ecclésiastique et littéraire de la ville de Nismes*, 7 vols (1744–58)

*Menard, V., *Histoire réligieuse, civile et militaire de Saint-James de Beuvron* (1897)

Merlet, L., 'Biographie de Jean de Montagu, Grand Maître de France (1350–1409)', *BEC*, xiii (1852), 248–84

Mesqui, J., *Châteaux et enceintes de la France médiévale*, 2 vols (1991–3)

Mesqui, J., *Châteaux forts et fortifications en France* (1997)

Miller, E., *War in the North. The Anglo-Scottish Wars of the Middle Ages* (1960)

Miquel, J., *L'architecture militaire dans le Rouerge au moyen âge et l'organisation de la défense*, 2 vols (1981)

Mirot, L., 'Sylvester Budes (13??–1380) et les Bretons en Italie', *BEC*, lviii (1897), 579–614; lix (1898), 262–303

Mirot, L., *La politique pontificale et le retour du saint-siège à Rome* (1899)

*Mirot, L., 'Un trousseau royal à la fin du xive siècle', *Mems. Soc. H. Paris*, xxix (1902), 125–58

Mirot, L., *Les insurrections urbaines au début du règne de Charles VI (1380–1383)* (1905)[1]

Mirot, L., 'Isabelle de France, reine d'Angleterre, comtesse d'Angoulême, duchesse d'Orléans, 1389–1409', *Revue d'histoire diplomatique*, xviii (1904), 544–73, xix (1905)[2], 60–95, 161–91, 481–522

Mirot, L., 'Une tentative d'invasion en Angleterre pendant la guerre de cent ans (1385–1386)', *Revue des Études Historiques*, lxxxi (1915), 249–87, 417–66

Mirot, L., 'Dom Bévy et les comptes des trésoriers des guerres. Essai de restitution d'un fonds disparu de la Chambre des Comptes', *BEC*, lxxxvi (1925), 245–379

*Mirot, L., 'La politique française en Italie sous le règne de Charles VI (1380–1422)', *Rev. des Études Hist.*, c (1933), 493–542

*Molinier, A., 'Description de deux manuscrits contenant le règle de la Militia Passionis Jhesu Christi de Philippe de Mézières', *Archives de l'Orient Latin*, i (1881), 335–64

*Molinier, E., *Étude sur la vie d'Arnoul d'Audrehem, maréchal de France, 130.-1370*, *Mems. Acad. Inscr. et Belles-Lettres*, 2ᵉ sér., vi, 1ᵉʳᵉ partie (1883)

*Monicat, J., *Les Grandes Compagnies en Velay, 1358–1392*, 2ᵉ ed. (1928)

*Moranvillé, H., 'Description de deux manuscrits contenant la règle de la *Militia Passionis Jhesu Christi* de Philippe de Mézières', *Archives de l'Orient Latin*, i (1881), 335–64

*Moranvillé, H., *Étude sur la vie de Jean le Mercier* (1888)

*Moranvillé, H., 'Conférences entre la France et l'Angleterre (1388–1393)', *BEC*, l (1889), 355–80

*Moranvillé, H., 'La fin de Mérigot Marchès', *BEC*, liii (1892), 76–87

Moranvillé, H., 'L'inventaire de l'orfèvrerie et des joyaux de Louis Iᵉʳ duc d'Anjou', *BEC*, lxii (1901), 181–222

*Moranvillé, H., 'Charles d'Artois', *BEC*, lxviii (1907), 433–80

Morel-Fatio, A., 'La donation du duché de Molina à Bertrand du Guesclin', *BEC*, lx (1899), 145–77

Morgan, P., 'Cheshire and the Defence of the Principality of Aquitaine', *Trans. Hist. Soc. Lancs and Cheshire*, cxxviii (1978), 139–60

Morgan, P., *War and Society in Medieval Cheshire, 1277–1403* (1987)

Mortimer, I., *The Fears of Henry IV* (2007)

Murray, J.M., *Bruges, Cradle of Capitalism, 1280–1390* (2005)

Myers, A.R., 'The wealth of Richard Lyons', *Essays in Medieval History presented to Bertie Wilkinson*, ed. T.A. Sandquist and M.R. Powicke (1969), 301–29

Myers, A.R., *London in the Age of Chaucer* (1972)

Myres, J.N.L., 'The Campaign of Radcot Bridge in December 1387', *EHR*, xlii (1927), 20–33

Neville, C.J., *Violence, Custom and Law. The Anglo-Scottish Border Lands in the Later Middle Ages* (1998)

Nicholas, D., *Town and Countryside. Social, Economic and Political Tensions in Fourteenth Century Flanders* (1971)

Nicholas, D., 'The English trade at Bruges in the last years of Edward III', *J. Med. Hist.*, v (1979), 23–61

Nicholas, D., *The Metamorphosis of a Medieval City. Ghent in the age of the van Arteveldes, 1302–1390* (1987)

Nicholas, D., *The van Arteveldes of Ghent. The Varieties of Vendetta and the Hero in History* (1988)

Nicholson, R., *Scotland. The Later Middle Ages* (1974)

*Nicolas, N.H., *A History of the Royal Navy*, 2 vols (1847)

Nieuwenhuysen, A. van, *Les finances du duc de Bourgogne Philippe le Hardi (1384–1404)*, i, *Le montant des ressources* (1983); ii, *Économie et politique* (1984)

Nightingale, P., *A Medieval Mercantile Community. The Grocers' Company and the Politics and Trade of London, 1000–1485* (1995)

Nordberg, M., *Les ducs et la royauté. Études sur la rivalité des ducs d'Orléans et de Bourgogne, 1392–1407* (1964)

Oman, C., *The Great Revolt of 1381*, n.e. (1969)

O'Neill, B.H. St. J., *Castles and Cannon. A study of Early Artillery Fortifications in England* (1960)

Orgeval, Le Barrois d', *La justice militaire sous l'ancien régime. Le tribunal de la Connétablie de France du xive siècle à 1790* (1918)

Ormrod, W.M., 'An Experiment in Taxation: The English Parish Subsidy of 1371', *Speculum*, lxiii (1988), 58–82

Ormrod, W.M., *The Reign of Edward III. Crown and Political Society in England, 1327–1377* (1990)

Ormrod, W.M., 'The Domestic Response to the Hundred Years War', *Arms, Armies and Fortifications in the Hundred Years War*, ed. A. Curry and M. Hughes (1994), 83–101

Ormrod, W.M., 'The Western European Monarchies in the Later Middle Ages', *Economic Systems and State Finance*, ed. R. Bonney (1995), 123–60

Ormrod, W.M., 'Finance and Trade under Richard II', *Richard II. The Art of Kingship*, ed. A. Goodman and J. Gillespie (1999), 155–86

Owen, E., 'Owen Lawgoch–Yeuain de Galles: some facts and suggestions', *Trans. Hon. Soc. Cymmrodorion* (1899–1900), 6–105

Oxford Dictionary of National Biography, 60 vols (2004)

Paço, A. do, 'Système de fortifications de campagne découvert sur le champ de bataille d'Aljubarrota (14 août 1385)', *Bull. Études Portuguaises*, n.s., xxiv (1963), 11–24

Palmer, J.J.N., 'The Anglo-French Peace Negotiations, 1390–1396', *Trans. Roy. Hist. Soc.*, 5th ser., v (1966)[1], 81–94

*Palmer, J.J.N., 'Articles for a Final Peace between England and France, 16 June 1393', *Bull. J. Rylands Lib.*, xxxix (1966)[2], 180–5

Palmer, J.J.N., 'England and the Great Western Schism, 1388–1399', *EHR*, lxxxiii (1968)[1], 516–22

Palmer, J.J.N., 'The Last Summons of the Feudal Army in England (1385)', *EHR*, lxxxiii (1968)[2], 771–5

Palmer, J.J.N., 'Prêts à la couronne', *BEC*, cxxvi (1968)[3], 419–25

Palmer, J.J.N., 'The impeachment of Michael de la Pole in 1386', *Bull. Inst. Hist. Res.*, xlii (1969), 96–101

Palmer, J.J.N., 'English foreign policy, 1388–99', *The Reign of Richard II. Essays in Honour of May McKisack*, ed. F.R.H. du Boulay and C. Barron (1971)[1], 75–107

Palmer, J.J.N., 'The Background to Richard II's Marriage to Isabel of France (1396)', *Bull. Inst. Hist. Res.*, xliv (1971)[2], 1–17

Palmer, J.J.N., 'The Parliament of 1385 and the Constitutional Crisis of 1386', *Speculum*, xlvi (1971)[3], 477–90

Palmer, J.J.N., *England, France and Christendom, 1377–99* (1972)

Palmer, J.J.N., 'The Authorship, Date and Historical Value of the French Chronicles on the Lancastrian Revolution', *Bull. J. Rylands Lib.*, lxi (1978–9), 145–81, 398–421

Palmer, J.J.N., 'Book I (1325–1378) and its sources', *Froissart, Historian*, ed. J.J.N. Palmer (1981), 7–24.

Patourel, J. Le, 'L'occupation anglaise de Calais', *Revue du Nord*, xxxiii (1951), 228–41

Patourel, J. Le, 'The King and the Princes in Fourteenth Century France', *Europe in the Late Middle Ages*, ed. J. Hale, R. Highfield and B. Smalley (1965), 155–83

Paviot, J., *La politique navale des ducs de Bourgogne, 1384–1482* (1995)[1]

Paviot, J., *Portugal et Bourgogne au XVe siècle* (1995)[2]

Paviot, J., *Les ducs de Bourgogne, la croisade et l'orient (fin xive–xve siècle)* (2003)

*Pépin, G., 'Towards a new assessment of the Black Prince's principality of Aquitaine: a study of the last years (1369–1372)', *Nottingham Medieval Studies*, l (2006), 59–114

Perroy, E., 'Un évêque urbaniste protégé par l'Angleterre: Guillaume de Coudenberghe, évêque de Tournai et de Bâle', *Revue d'Histoire Ecclésiastique*, xxvi (1930), 103–9

*Perroy, E., *L'Angleterre et le grand schisme d'occident. Étude sur la politique religieuse de l'Angleterre sous Richard II (1378–1399)* (1933)

Perroy, E., *The Hundred Years War*, tr. W.B. Wells (1945)

Perroy, E., 'Louis de Male et les négociations de paix franco-anglaises, 1371–1377', *Revue Belge de Philiologie et d'Histoire* (1949), 138–50

Perroy, E., 'L'administration de Calais en 1371–1372', *Rev. du Nord*, xxxiii (1951)[1], 218–27

Perroy, E., 'Gras profits et rançons pendant la guerre de cent ans: l'affaire du comte de Denia', *Mélanges d'histoire du moyen age dédiés à la mémoire de Louis Halphen* (1951)[2], 573–80

*Petit, E., *Ducs de Bourgogne de la Maison de Valois*, i, *Philippe le Hardi*, 1ère partie (1909)

Phillpotts, C., 'The fate of the truce of Paris, 1396–1415', *J. Med. Hist.*, xxiv (1998), 61–80

Pirenne, H., *Histoire de Belgique*, 4th edn, 6 vols (1947)

*Plaine, F., *Jeanne de Penthièvre* (1883)

*Plancher, U., *Histoire générale et particulière de Bourgogne*, 4 vols (1739–81)

Platt, C., *Medieval Southampton* (1973)

Platt, C., *The Castle in Medieval England and Wales* (1982)

Pocquet du Haut-Jussé, B.A., 'Les faux États de Bretagne de 1315 et les premiers États de Bretagne', *BEC*, lxxxvi (1925), 388–406

Pocquet du Haut-Jussé, B.A., *Les papes et les ducs de Bretagne*, 2 vols (1928)

Pocquet du Haut-Jussé, B.A., 'Les dons du roi aux ducs de Bourgogne Philippe le Hardi et Jean sans Peur, 1363–1419. Le dons des aides', *Annales de Bourgogne*, x (1938), 261–89.

Pocquet du Haut-Jussé, B.A., 'Les aides en Bourgogne sous Philippe le Hardi et Jean sans Peur, 1363–1419', *Revue historique de droit français et étranger* (1939)[1], 388–422

Pocquet du Haut-Jussé, B.A., 'Les dons du roi aux ducs de Bourgogne Philippe le Hardi et Jean sans Peur, 1363–1419. Les dons ordinaires', *Méms Soc. pour l'Hist. du Droit et des Institutions des Anciens Pays Bourguignons*, vi (1939)[2], 113–44

Pocquet du Haut-Jussé, B.A., 'Les dons du roi aux ducs de Bourgogne Philippe le Hardi et Jean sans Peur, 1363–1419. Les dons extraordinaires', *Méms. Soc. pour l'Hist. du Droit et des Institutions des Anciens Pays Bourguignons*, vii (1940–1), 95–129

Pocquet du Haut-Jussé, B.A., 'La dernière phase de la vie de Du Guesclin. L'affaire de Bretagne', *BEC*, cxxv (1967), 142–89

Port, C., *Dictionnaire historique, géographique et biographique de Maine et Loire et de l'ancienne province d'Anjou*, n.e., 4 vols (1965–96)

Poulle-Drieux, Y., 'L'Hippiatrie dans l'Occident Latin, du xiiie au xve siècle', *Médecine humaine et vétérinaire à la fin du moyen age*, ed. G. Baeujouan *et al.* (1966), 11–168.

Powell, E., *The Rising of 1381 in East Anglia* (1896)

Powicke, M., *Military Obligation in Medieval England. A Study in Liberty and Duty* (1962)

Prestwich, M., 'An estimate by the Commons of royal revenue in England under Richard II', *Parliamentary History*, iii (1984), 147–55

Prestwich, M., *Armies and Warfare in the Middle Ages. The English Experience* (1996)

*Prevenier, W., *De Leden en de Staten van Vlaanderen (1384–1405)* (1961)

Prevenier, W., 'Les perturbations dans les relations commerciales anglo-flamandes entre 1379 et 1407. Causes de désaccord et raisons d'une réconciliation', *Économies et sociétés au moyen age. Mélanges offerts à Edouard Perroy* (1973), 477–97

Prince, A.E., 'The Strength of English Armies in the Reign of Edward III', *EHR*, xlvi (1931), 353–71

Prince, A.E., 'The Indenture System under Edward III', *Historical Essays in Honour of James Tait* (1933), 283–97

Prince, A.E., 'The payment of army wages in Edward III's reign', *Speculum*, xix (1944), 137–60.

*Prou, M., 'Compte de Raoul de Louppy, gouverneur du Dauphiné de 1361 à 1369', *BEC*, xlvii (1886), 567–73

*Prou, M., *Étude sur les relations politiques du pape Urbain V avec les rois de France Jean II et Charles V* (1887)

*Puiseux, L., *Étude sur une grande ville de bois construite en Normandie pour une expédition en Angleterre en 1386* (1864)

Quicke, F., *Les Pays-Bas à la veille de la période bourguignonne, 1356–1384* (1947)

Ramsay, J.H., *A History of the Revenues of the Kings of England, 1066–1399*, 2 vols (1925)

Rawcliffe, C., *Medicine and Society in Later Medieval England* (1999)

Reid, R.R., 'The office of Warden of the Marches; its origin and early history', *EHR*, xxxii (1917), 479–96

Renouard, Y., *Bordeaux sous les rois d'Angleterre* (1965)

Réville, A., *Le soulèvement des travailleurs d'Angleterre en 1381* (1898)

Rey, M., 'Les émissions d'écus à la couronne à l'Hôtel des Monnaies de Paris vers la fin du xive siècle et dans les premières années du xve (1385–1413)', *Mélanges d'histoire du moyen age dédiés à la mémoire de Louis Halphen* (1951), 595–603

Rey, M., i, *Le domaine du roi et les finances extraordinaires sous Charles VI, 1388–1413*; ii, *Les finances royales sous Charles VI. Les causes du déficit, 1388–1413* (1965)

Rey, M., 'Aux origines de l'impôt: les premiers comptes des aides dans l'élection de Langres', *Économies et sociétés au moyen age. Mélanges offerts à Édouard Perroy* (1973), 498–517

Rigaudière, A., 'Le financement des fortifications urbaines en France du milieu du xive siècle à la fin du xve siècle', *Revue historique*, cclxxiii (1985), 19–95

Rigaudière, A., *Saint-Flour. Ville d'Auvergne au bas moyen age* (1982)

*Romano, G., *Niccolo Spinelli di Giovinezza, diplomatico del secolo XIV* (1902)

Roncière, C. de la, *Histoire de la marine française*, 6 vols (1899–1932)

Roosbroeck, R. van, Weerd, H. van de, Maeyer, R. de, Essen, L. van der *et al.* (eds.), *Geschiedenis van Vlaanderen*, 6 vols (1936–49)

Roskell, J.S., *The Impeachment of Michael de la Pole, Earl of Suffolk, in 1386, in the context of the reign of Richard II* (1954)

Roskell, J.S., *The Commons and their Speakers in English Parliaments, 1376–1523* (1965)

Roskell, J.S., *Parliament and Politics in Late Medieval England*, 3 vols (1981–3)

*Rouquette, J., *Le Rouergue sous les Anglais* (1887)

Rupin, E., *Roc-Amador. Étude historique et archéologique* (1904)

Russell, P.E., *The English Intervention in Spain and Portugal in the Time of Edward III and Richard II* (1955)

*Sandoval, X. de, *Batalla de Aljubarrota. Monografía histórica y estudio crítico-militar* (1872)

Saul, N., *Knights and Esquires. The Gloucester Gentry in the Fourteenth Century* (1981)

Saul, N., *Scenes from provincial Life. Knightly Families in Sussex, 1280–1400* (1986)

Saul, N., *Richard II* (1997)

Saul, N., 'A farewell to arms? Criticism of warfare in late fourteenth-century England', *Fourteenth Century England*, ii, ed. C. Given-Wilson (2002), 131–45

Sauval, H., *Histoire et recherche des antiquités de la ville de Paris*, 3 vols (1724)

*Savaron, J., *Les origines de la ville de Clairmont*, ed. P. Durands (1662)

Scattergood, V.J., 'Chaucer and the French war: *Sir Thopas* and *Melibee*', *Court and Poet. Selected Proceedings of the Third Congress of the International Courtly Literature Society (Liverpool, 1980)*, ed. G.S. Burgess (1981), 287–96

Schoos, J., *Der Machtkampf zwischen Burguns und Orléans unter den Herzögen Philipp dem Kühnen, Johann ohne Furcht und Ludwig von Orléans* (1956)

Scots Peerage (The), ed. J. Balfour Paul, 9 vols (1904–14)

Servais, V., *Annales historiques du Barrois de 1352 à 1411*, 2 vols (1865–7)

Shears, F.S., *Froissart, Chronicler and Poet* (1930)

Sherborne, J., 'Indentured retinues and English expeditions to France, 1369–80', *EHR*, lxxix (1964), 718–46

Sherborne, J., 'The English navy: shipping and manpower, 1369–89', *Past and Present*, xxxvii (1967), 163–75

Sherborne, J., 'The battle of La Rochelle and the war at sea, 1372–75', *Bull. Inst. Hist. Res.*, xlii (1969), 17–29

Sherborne, J., 'The cost of warfare with France in the later fourteenth century', *Bull. Inst. Hist. Res.*, l (1977)[1], 135–50

Sherborne, J., 'English barges and balingers of the late fourteenth century', *Mariner's Mirror*, lxiii (1977)[2], 109–14

Sherborne, J., 'Charles VI and Richard II', *Froissart: Historian*, ed. J.J.N. Palmer (1981), 50–63

Sherborne, J., 'John of Gaunt, Edward III's retinue and the French campaign of 1369', *Kings and Nobles in the Later Middle Ages*, ed. R.A. Griffiths and J. Sherborne (1986), 41–61

Sherborne, J., 'The defence of the realm and the impeachment of Michael de la Pole in 1386', *Politics and Crisis in Fourteenth Century England*, ed. J. Taylor and W. Childs (1990), 97–116

*Söchting, W., 'Die Beziehungen zwischen Flandern und England am Ende des Vierzehnten Jahrhunderts', *Historische Vierteljahrschrift*, xxiv (1927–9), 182–98

Steel, A., *The Receipt of the Exchequer, 1377–1485* (1954)

Steel, A., *Richard II* (1962)

Storey, R.L., 'The Wardens of the Marches of England towards Scotland, 1377–1489', *EHR*, lxxii (1957), 593–615

*Storey-Challenger, S., *L'administration anglaise du Ponthieu après le traité de Brétigny, 1361–1369* (1975)

Stow, G.B., 'Chronicles versus records: the character of Richard II', *Documenting the Past. Essays in Medieval History presented to George Peddy Cuttino*, ed. J.S. Hamilton and P.J. Bradley (1989), 155–76

Strickland, M., and Hardy, R., *From Hastings to the Mary Rose. The Great Warbow* (2005)

Sturler, J. de, *Les relations politiques et les échanges commerciaux entre le duché de Brabant et l'Angleterre au moyen age* (1936)

*Suarez Fernandez, L., 'Política internacional de Enrique II', *Hispania*, xvi (1956), 16–129.

*Suarez Fernandez, L., *Navegación y comercio en el Golfo de Vizcaya. Un estudio sobre la política marinera de la casa de Trastámara* (1959)

Suarez Fernandez, L., *Historia del Reinado de Juan I de Castilla*, 2 vols (1977–82)

Sumption, J., *The Hundred Years War*, i, *Trial by Battle* (1990), ii, *Trial by Fire* (1999)

Tait, J., 'Did Richard II murder the Duke of Gloucester?', *Historical Essays first published in 1902 in commemoration of the Jubilee of the Owens College, Manchester*, ed. T.F. Tout and J. Tait (1907)

Taylor, J., *English Historical Literature in the Fourteenth Century* (1987)

*Temple-Leader, J., and Marcotti, G.O., *Sir John Hawkwood (l'Acuto). Story of a Condottiere*, tr. L. Scott (1889)

*Terrier de Loray, H.-P.-A., *Jean de Vienne, Admiral de France* (1877)

Thibault, M., *Isabeau de Bavière, reine de France. La jeunesse, 1370–1405* (1903)

*Thomas, A., 'Un exploit inconnu de Mérigot Marchès', *Annales du Midi*, v (1893), 381–5

Tinniswood, J.T., 'English galleys, 1272–1377', *Mariner's Mirror*, xxxv (1949), 276–315

Touchard, H., *Le commerce maritime Breton à la fin du moyen age* (1967)

Tout, T.F., *Chapters in the Administrative History of Medieval England*, 6 vols (1920–37)

Tout, T.F., 'The English Parliament and public opinion', *Collected Papers*, ii (1934)[1], 173–90

Tout, T.F., 'Firearms in England in the Fourteenth Century', *Collected Papers*, ii (1934)[2], 233–75

Towson, K., '"Hearts warped by passion": the Percy-Gaunt dispute of 1381', *Fourteenth Century England*, ed. W.M. Ormrod (2004), 143–53

Tranchant, M., *Le commerce maritime de La Rochelle à la fin du moyen age* (2003)

*Trautz, F., *Die Könige von England und das Reich, 1272–1377* (1961)

Troubat, O., *La Guerre de Cent Ans et le Prince Chevalier. Le "Bon Duc" Louis II de Bourbon, 1337–41*, 2 vols (2001)

*Tucoo-Chala, P., *Gaston Fébus et la vicomté de Béarn* (1959)

*Tucoo-Chala, P., *La vicomté de Béarn et le problème de la souveraineté* (1961)

Tuck, A., 'Richard II and the border magnates', *Northern History*, iii (1968), 27–52

Tuck, A., 'The Cambridge Parliament, 1388', *EHR*, lxxxiv (1969), 225–43

Tuck, A., *Richard II and the English Nobility* (1973)

Tuck, A., 'War and the Medieval North', *Northern History*, xxi (1985), 33–52

Tuck, A., 'Richard II and the Hundred Years War', *Politics and Crisis in Fourteenth Century England*, ed. J. Taylor and W. Childs (1990), 117–49

Tuck, A., 'Richard II and the House of Luxemburg', *Richard II. The Art of Kingship*, ed. A. Goodman and J. Gillespie (1999), 205–29

Turner, H.L., *Town Defences in England and Wales* (1971)

Valdeon Baruque, J., *Enrique II de Castilla: La guerra civil y la consolidación del regimen (1366–1371)* (1966)

Valois, N., *Le conseil du Roi aux xive, xve et xvie siècles* (1888)

*Valois, N., 'Discours prononcé le 14 juillet 1380 en présence de Charles V par Martin, évêque de Lisbonne, ambassadeur du roi de Portugal', *BEC*, lii (1891), 485–516

Valois, N., *La France et le grand schisme d'occident*, 4 vols (1896–1902)

*Vandenpeereboom, A., *Ypriana. Notices, études, notes et documents sur Ypres*, 7 vols (1876–83)

*Varenbergh, E., *Histoire des relations diplomatiques entre le comté de Flandre et l'Angleterre au moyen age* (1874)

Vaughan, R., *Philip the Bold* (1962)

Vaultier, R., *Le folklore pendant la guerre de cent ans d'après les lettres de rémission du Trésor des Chartes* (1965)

*Vernier, J.-J., 'Philippe le Hardi, duc de Bourgogne. Son marriage avec Marguerite de Flandre en 1369', *Bull. Com. Hist. Département du Nord*, xxi (1900), 89–133

*Vic, C. de and Vaissète, J., *Histoire générale de Languedoc*, n.e., 16 vols (1874–1905)

Victoria History of the Counties of England (1899–in progress)

Vries, K. de, 'The reasons for the Bishop of Norwich's attack on Flanders in 1383', *Fourteenth Century England*, ed. W.M. Ormrod (2004), 155–65

Vuitry, A., *Études sur le régime financier de la France avant la Révolution de 1789*, n.s., 2 vols (1878–83)

Walker, S., 'Profit and Loss in the Hundred Years War: the Subcontracts of Sir John Strother', *Bull. Inst. Hist. Res.*, lviii (1985), 100–106

Walker, S., *The Lancastrian Affinity, 1361–1399* (1990)[1]

Walker, S., 'Sir Richard Abberbury (c. 1330–1399) and his kinsmen: the rise and fall of a gentry family', *Nottingham Medieval Studies*, xxxiv (1990)[2], 113–40

*Walker, S., 'Letters to the Dukes of Lancaster in 1381 and 1399', *EHR*, cvi (1991), 68–79

Walker, S., 'Richard II's views on kingship', *Rulers and Ruled in Late Medieval England. Essays Presented to Gerald Harriss*, ed. R.E. Archer and S. Walker (1995), 49–63

Walker, S., 'Janico Dartasso: Chivalry, Nationality and the Man-at-Arms', *History*, n.s. lxxxiv (1999), 31–51

Wathey, A., 'John of Gaunt, John Pycard and the Amiens Negotiations of 1392', *England and the Low Countries in the Late Middle Ages*, ed. C. Barron and N. Saul (1995), 29–42

Watt, D.E.R., *A Biographical Dictionary of Scottish Graduates to A.D. 1410* (1977)

Weske, D.B., *Convocation of the Clergy* (1937)

Wilkinson, B., 'The Peasants' Revolt of 1381', *Speculum*, xv (1940), 12–35

Wolff, P., *Commerces et marchands de Toulouse (vers 1350–vers 1450)* (1954)

Wright, N., *Knights and Peasants. The Hundred Years War in the French Countryside* (1998)

Yanguas y Miranda, J., *Diccionario de antiguedades del reino de Navarra*, 4 vols (1840–3)

Zink, M., *Froissart et le temps* (1998)

Zurita, J., *Anales de Aragón*, ed. A. Canellas Lopez, 9 vols (1967–78)

E DATABASES

European State Finance Database [http://www.le.ac.uk/hi/bon/ESFDB]: 'English revenues' (by W.M. Ormrod)

Index

Aalst, 486

Aardenburg, 488, 551; captured (1383), 494; attacked (1385), 541

Abberbury, Sir Richard (the elder), 95, 96, 311, 362, 366

Abberbury, Sir Richard (the younger), 666–7

Abbeville, captured (1369), 35; 36, 39, 41, 43, 805, 806

Aberdeen, 9

Abrantes, 563

Ackerman, Francis, 416, 452, 456, 494, 509, 533–4, 541, 544, 551, 553–4, 571, 574

'Adria, kingdom of', 547, 781–2, 803, 816

Agen, 50, 51, 143, 152

Agenais, province, 20, 33, 299, 301, 331, 707, 710; campaigns (1370), 50, 77; (1372), 155; (1377), 709–10; *routier* operations (1381–7), 693, 695, 705, 706

Agincourt, battle (1415), 669, 737, 763

Aiguillon, 51, 143

Airaines, 35

Aire, 39

Albi, 22, 687, 689, 699, 704

Albigeois, province, 680; *routier* operations (1379–84), 683, 687, 690, 691, 699, 707; campaign (1384), 704–5

Albret, lords of, 50, 769

Albret, Arnaud-Amanieu, lord of, 17, 19, 20, 21, 27, 51–2, 58, 121, 284, 296, 444, 572, 691–2

Albret, Bérard III d', lord of Langoiran, Cubzac and Vayres, 299, 301, 304, 494–5, 765

Albret, Bertucat d', in Auvergne (1369–70), 21, 52; in Quercy (1369–73), 21, 34, 164–8, 170; in Limousin (1371), 96; evacuation treaty (1373), 168, 209, 242; and Anjou's campaign (1377), 297–8, 299–300, 301–2, 315; in Navarre (1378–9), 321; mission to Navarre (1382), 321;

evacuation treaty (1379), 483–4; in Auvergne (1380), 686; in England (1381–2), 423, 694; in Bordelais (1382), 694–5; death (1382), 699; mentioned, 169, 765

Albuquerque, Fernando Afonso de, Master of the Order of Santiago (Portugal), 522, 532, 533, 559

Alcántara, 158

Alcántara, Order of, Master: see Nuñez de Guzman

Alcobaça, abbey, 381

Alcoutim, treaty (1371), 119, 124

Alemtejo, region, 383, 432–3, 463–4, 466, 522, 607, 677

Alençon, Charles, Count of, 87, 106, 400

Alès, 369

Alexandria (Egypt), 256, 717, 736

Alexandria (Lombardy), 787

Aljubarrota, battle (1385), 564–8

Alleuze, castle, 696, 698, 711, 712, 718, 721

Almada, 469

Almeida, 158, 618; captured (1381), 436, 468

Alnwick, castle, 426

Anagni, 303, 343–4

Alsace, province, 245–7

Amiens, 789–90, 791, 792, 793, 822; conference (1392), 6, 55, 142, 188, 446–7, 449, 491, 551, 552, 593, 601

Anagni, 343–4

Ancenis, Guillaume d', 629

Andeiro, Juan Fernández, 120; embassies to Portugal (1372), 122, 144–5, 150, 158, 179; (1380), 381, 382, 383–4, 409; treaty of London (1373), 177, 183; English in Portugal (1381–2), 431, 463–4, 466, 467; treaty of Salvaterra de Magos (1383), 492–3, 496; murder (1383), 520

Andrade, Fernán Perez de, 596

Angers, 28, 31, 181, 359, 750

Angle, Guichard d', Earl of Huntingdon, 81, 82, 98, 120, 121, 142, 148, 162, 279, 349

Angle, Jean, bastard of, 148

Anglesey, 45

Angoulême, 20, 21, 24, 26, 27, 29, 46, 48, 74, 77, 80, 703; captured (1372), 155

Angoumois, province, 4, 21, 78, 127, 279, 693, 695, 704, 783, 807; campaign (1372), 154–5

Anjou, province, 7, 17, 18, 26, 28, 56, 88, 110, 627, 772, 794, 797, 826, 828

Anjou, Charles, Duke of (d. 1285)

Anjou, Fulk Nerra, Count of (d. 1040), 109

Anjou, Louis I, Duke of (d. 1384), character, 16–17; and finances of Languedoc, 58, 59–60, 80, 368–9, 370, 687, 688; campaigns in Aquitaine (1369–70), 18–19, 21, 22, 25, 27, 31, 32–3, 34, 45–6, 50–2; (1371), 97–8; (1372), 127, 143, 152, 155; (1374), 203, 204–7, 215, 249–50, 253; (1377), 270, 294–303; (1378), 315, 331–2, 351, 374, 692; and evacuation of Figeac (1373), 167, 168; and Bertucat d'Albret (1373–7), 168; and John of Gaunt's raid (1373–4), 189, 192, 194, 196, 199–202, 212; and Congress of Bruges (1374–7), 214, 228; and companies (1375–7), 239, 243–4, 269; and papal schism (1378–9), 343, 346–7, 782, 802; and Brittany (1379), 360–1, 363–5, 679; and revolt of Montpellier (1379–80), 368–71, 396; recall from Languedoc (1380), 371–2; regency (1380–2), 390, 391–2, 394–5, 396, 402, 403, 441–2; and Italy (1380–2), 392–4, 396, 432, 438–41, 442, 534, 609, 610, 626; mentioned, 30, 75, 104, 112, 113, 116, 121, 130, 150, 174, 243, 313, 351, 400, 445, 446, 490, 624, 668, 679, 683, 694, 702, 703, 708, 727

Anjou, Louis II, Duke of (d. 1417), 668, 779, 781, 782, 802, 823, 846

Anjou, Marie of Blois, Countess of, 535, 601–2, 628, 779, 804

Annandale, district, 10, 518

Anne of Bohemia, Queen of England, 472, 814, 823

Annesley, Sir John, 259

Anonimalle Chronicle, 425

Anse, 168

Anse de l'Aiguillon, 653

Antwerp, 13, 454, 488

Appleton, William, 427

Aquitaine, principality, duchy, feudal status, proposals for partition, xv, xvi, 212–13, 226–8, 266–7, 515, 525, 774–5, 777–8, 788, 806–8, 810–12, 813; government, 3, 4, 94–6, 108, 119, 120–1, 156, 207, 692, 717–18, 718–19; finances, xvii, 63, 94, 108, 109–10, 171–2, 197–9, 587, 692; English settlers, 161–3, 736–7; strategic problems of English, 64, 207, 305, 374–5; campaigns (1345–6), xvi; (1355–7), xvi; (1369), 18–35, 45–52; (1370), 69–70, 74, 76–84; (1371), 97–9, 108–9; (1372), 127–8, 137–43, 145–50, 153–5, 158–61; (1373–4), 183, 194–6; (1374), 205–7; (1375), 228–9; (1377), 294–304; (1378), 315–16, 322, 330–3; (1385), 538; (1387), 708–10; French invasion plan (1382), 469, 477; routier operations, 163–4, 169–70, 692–4, 694–5, 718, 719–21, 743; John of Gaunt in (1374), 199–202; (1387–9), 622–3, 648–9, 650, 652, 655; (1394–5), 815–16; mentioned, 16, 36, 44, 67, 70, 113–14, 175, 262, 284, 351, 356, 412, 462, 509–10, 615, 618, 680

Aragon, diplomatic relations with England and Castile, 122, 196–7, 202–3, 333–4, 336, 338, 339, 374–5, 382, 469–70, 558, 600, 823; invaded by routiers (1374), 204, 243–4; (1389–90), 708, 712, 715–16, 717; mentioned, 17, 20, 117, 119, 321, 331, 349, 431, 469, 567, 618, 795, 803

Aragon, King of: see Peter IV

Aragon, Queen of: see Yolande of Bar

Aragon, Cardinal of: see Benedict XIII

Arc, Joan of, 104, 726

Archiac, captured (1385), 703–4

Arcueil, 85

Ardres, siege (1369), 35, 39; captured (1377), 292, 307; mentioned, 579, 723, 831

Armagnac, Counts of, 50, 400, 679, 680

Armagnac, Bernard VII, Count of (d. 1418), 712, 715–16, 717

Armagnac, Bernard, bastard of, 683

Armagnac, John I, Count of (d. 1373), xvii, 19, 27, 34, 51, 58, 166, 168, 208, 284

Armagnac, John II, Count of (d. 1384), 572, 680–1, 683–4, 686–7, 689–90, 691–2, 699

Armagnac, John III, Count of (d. 1391), 705, 707, 708–11, 712, 713, 714–16, 717, 720, 721, 781, 786–7

armour, 93, 263, 273, 318, 391, 478, 484, 487, 543, 677, 730, 731, 739, 749, 751–3, 852

arms (heraldic), 713–14, 728–9, 735–6

Arras, 84, 188, 375, 478–9, 482, 503, 505,

538, 545, 548, 552, 584, 750
arrière-ban, 502
Artevelde, Jacob Van, Captain of Ghent
  (d. 1345), 451, 452
Artevelde, Philip Van, Captain of Ghent
  (d. 1382), 451-4, 457, 458, 460, 462, 470,
  476-8, 480, 482, 483-6, 487, 533
artillery, 43, 49, 73, 103, 109, 204, 205,
  218, 222, 223-4, 231, 232, 233, 285, 292,
  294, 299, 303, 310, 318, 321, 325, 346,
  374, 434, 456, 458, 482, 485, 501, 504,
  507, 543, 550, 551, 678, 690, 692, 753,
  758, 759
Artois, province, 5, 15, 55, 387, 484, 516,
  556, 584, 633, 743, 759, 816
Artois, Charles of, 169
Artois, Margaret, Countess of, 417
Arundel, John of, 285, 286, 327, 329, 366,
  367-8, 375, 379
Arundel, Richard Fitzalan, Earl of (d. 1376)
  ('Copped Hat'), 70-1
Arundel, Richard Fitzalan, Earl of (d. 1397),
  282, 287, 306, 315, 316, 323-5, 385, 423,
  502, 525, 587-8, 593-4, 602, 603-6, 632,
  633-7, 639, 642-3, 644-5, 659-61, 672,
  673, 674, 768, 777, 778, 810, 811-13,
  814-15, 838-40, 842, 844, 862, 863
Arundel, Thomas Fitzalan, Bishop of Ely,
  then Archbishop of Canterbury, 588, 589,
  593, 642, 811, 842, 848, 849, 853, 855,
  858
Arundel, Thomas Fitzalan, Earl of (d. 1415),
  862
Ashburnham, Sir Roger, 288
Asti, 781
Astorga, 610
Ath, treaty (1356), 13
Attichy, 479
attorney, letters of, 749
Aubricourt, Eustache d', 95-6
Aubriot, Hughes, 401, 445
Audley, Sir James, 29, 30
Audrehem, Arnoul d', 87, 90, 771, 772
Audruicq, captured (1369), 35; recaptured
  (1369), 39; (1377), 293-4, 307
Aunis, 653
Auray, 182, 213, 215, 229, 234, 238, 251,
  270; battle (1364), 67, 105, 745, 760, 768,
  769; siege (1377), 306
Aurillac, 208, 686
Austria, Leopold, Duke of, 245-6
Auvergne, province, *routier* operations, 21,
  163, 210-11, 239, 242, 244, 682, 683,
  684, 686, 695-8, 701, 721; taxation,

Estates, 59, 208, 242, 372, 395, 703, 720;
  mentioned, 22, 26, 34, 67, 78, 91, 98, 166,
  270, 689, 709-11, 712, 715-17
Auxerre, captured (1359), 67, 745
Avignon, 80, 102, 111, 112, 114, 153, 179,
  212, 227, 244, 265, 340, 341, 347, 393,
  431, 439, 440, 503, 667, 713, 734, 752,
  779, 781-2, 784, 786, 797, 800, 803, 816,
  817, 818, 819, 821-2, 832, 836, 845
Avila, Cortes (1381), 436
Avis, John, Master of: see John I of Avis,
  King of Portugal
Avranches, 318, 320, 360
Ayala, Pedro Lopez de, 349, 379, 386, 432,
  521, 562, 564, 566, 621
Aycelin, Pierre, Bishop of Laon, Cardinal,
  666
Ayens, Ferrando d', 318, 321
Ayton, 527

Badajoz, 432, 436, 463, 466-7, 558, 560,
  599; treaty (1382), 468, 469, 470, 492,
  496-7
Badefol, Séguin de, 164, 683
Bagot, Sir William, 847-8, 850-1, 855, 858,
  860, 862
Baker, Geoffrey, 759
Baker, Thomas, 420
Balaguier, castle, 242, 316
Balinghem, fort, 40, 41
Ball, John, 420, 422-3, 429
Balliol, Edward, 736
Bamburgh, castle, 426
Bañares, 180
Bannes, castle, 698
Bannockburn, battle (1314), 658
Bar, Henry of, Lord of Marle, 669, 834
Bar, Robert, Duke of, 389, 669
Barbe, Noli, 695, 716
Barcelona, 122, 202, 336, 338, 374, 381-2,
  469, 708, 795, 797-8, 823
Barfleur, 312
Bari, 534
Barry, Ralph, 120, 131
Barry, Thomas, 659
Bas-Berry, 145, 372
Bas-Languedoc, 597, 684, 686-7
Bas-Limousin, district, 112, 170, 195, 316,
  684, 693, 695, 709, 711
Bas-Poitou, district, 65, 105, 106, 107, 110,
  175, 625
Basel, 246
Basset, Ralph Lord, 636
Batalha, Abbey of S. Maria da Vitoria, 568

Batz, island, 653
Bauffès, Jean, Bishop of Dax, 317–18
Bavaria, William of: see Hainault, Count of
Bayeux, 220, 222, 236, 349, 739
Bayeux, Bishop of: see Bosc, Nicholas de
Bayezid, Sultan, 834
Bayonne, xi, 4, 115, 116, 126, 135, 156,
    203, 204–5, 206, 226, 295, 296, 300, 310,
    313, 314, 316, 322, 324, 355, 367, 378,
    622, 650, 653, 677; naval forces, 135, 156,
    203, 313, 314–15, 316, 324, 367, 378;
    siege (1374), 203–4; treaty (1388), 623,
    660
Bazadais, district, 20, 51, 303, 304
Bazas, captured (1370), 51–2; (1378), 331
Béarn, 317, 533, 618, 679–81, 726
Béarn, Bernard de, 117
Béarn, Perrot de: see Fontans, Perrot de
Béarn, Jean de, 764
Beatrice of Portugal, Queen of Castile,
    380–1, 382, 383–4, 435, 466, 467, 468,
    493, 496–7, 519, 520, 532, 558–9
Beaucaire, Seneschal of (1377): see Beuil,
    Jean de
Beauchamp, Sir William, 431, 556
Beauffès, Jean, bishop of Dax, 317–18
Beaufort (Champagne), 44
Beaufort-la-Vallée (Anjou), castle, 88, 91
Beaufort, Sir John, Earl of Somerset (Feb.
    1397), Marquis of Dorset (Sept. 1397),
    723, 816, 829
Beaufort, Nicholas [Roger] de, lord of
    Limeuil, 77, 112
Beaufort, Roger [Roger] de, 80, 81, 83, 112,
    694, 767, 770
Beaumanoir, family, 105, 228
Beaumanoir, Jean de, 375
Beaumaris, castle, 861
Beaumont-le-Roger, siege (1378), 319, 320
Beaumont, Charlot de, 321, 324, 329
Beaumont, John lord, 280, 656, 675
Beauregard, castle, 136
Beauvais, Cardinal of: see Dormans, Jean de
Bécherel, castle, 7, 8, 26, 103, 259; siege
    (1371–2), 107–8, 109, 119–20, 131, 145,
    153, 156, 219, 261
Béchet, Radegonde, wife of Sir Digory Say,
    161, 163, 758
Belcastel, castle, 242
Belfort, Ratier de, 33
Belleperche, captured (1369), 32; siege
    (1370), 48–50, 52
Bellknap, Sir Robert, Chief Justice of
    Common Pleas, 425

Belon, Jean, 30–1
Benavente, 614; siege (1387), 610–11, 612,
    613, 751
Benedict XII, Pope, 110
Benedict XIII, Pope (Avignon), 343, 818,
    819, 821–2, 826, 845, 856
Bénodet, Bay, 311
Benon, castle, 154
Bergerac, siege (1377), 295, 296–300, 301
Bergues, 486, 498, 506
Berkeley, castle, 860
Berkeley, Sir Edward, 312–13
Berkhamsted, 95
Bermeo, 124
Bernay, siege (1378), 319–20, 322
Berne, 246
Berry, province, 32, 46, 78, 82, 87, 210,
    244, 372
Berry, John, Duke of, campaigns (1369), 18,
    22, 25–6, 34; (1370), 74, 78–81; (1371),
    97–9; (1372), 126–7, 137, 145–6, 149,
    152, 154, 155, 156, 159; (1375), 231;
    (1380), 389; finances, 80, 268, 442, 627,
    669; and regency (1380–8), 390, 392, 441;
    Lieutenant in Languedoc (1380–9), 394,
    687–92, 702–9; and the war (1380–8),
    590, 591–2, 601–2, 651, 662; and Anglo-
    French diplomacy (1380–8), 515, 517,
    528–9, 660; and O. de Clisson, 625, 629,
    630, 631, 666, 795; and the Marmousets
    (1388–92), 666–7, 669–70, 786, 796–7;
    and government of France (1392–9), 801;
    and papal schism (1392–9), 817, 819,
    821–2; and Anglo-French diplomacy
    (1392–9), 790, 805, 806, 826, 831–2; and
    Bolingbroke (1398–9), 854, 855–6, 858,
    864; mentioned, 16, 56, 60, 161, 162, 270,
    400, 402, 535, 578, 648, 713, 715, 727,
    757, 836, 846, 853
Berry, Jeanne d'Armagnac, duchess of, 161
Berry, Marie de, see Eu, Countess of
Berwick, 10, 72, 277, 285, 329, 426, 519,
    545, 548, 550, 574, 659, 675, 676, 805;
    treaty (1357), 9; captured (1378), 356;
    (1384), 531
Betanzos, 594
Béthune, Robert de, Viscount of Meaux, 720
Bétizac, Jean de, 713, 715, 800
Bette, Simon, 450, 452
Beuzeville, 219
Beverhoutsveld, battle (1382), 456–7, 484
Beverley, 426
Beynac, 77
Béziers, 168, 684, 690, 691, 715

Bicêtre, 85, 432
Bigorre, district, 680–1, 704, 705, 807
Bihorel, 444
Bilbao, 124
Billericay, 429
Biron, castle, 701
Blackheath, 423, 424
Blainville, Jean ('Mouton') de Mauquenchy, lord of, Marshal of France, 72, 74, 87, 324
Blaisy, Jean de, 526, 527, 714–15, 720
Blake, John, 644
Blanchetaque, ford, 6, 43
Blaye, 297, 301, 332, 709
Blois, 652
Blois, county, 56
Blois, house of, 104–5, 352–3, 375, 625, 627–8
Blois, Charles of, Duke of Brittany, xv, 7, 28, 104, 352, 766
Blois, John of: see Penthièvre
Boccanegra, Ambrogio, Admiral of Castile, 139–41, 178, 187
Boccanegra, Gil, Admiral of Castile, 124
Boccanegra, Simon, Doge of Genoa, 124
Bocking, 420–1
Bodiam, castle, 288
Bohemia, 245, 753
Bohun, family, 10, 518, 839
Bohun, William de, Earl of Northampton, 2, 736
Bolingbroke, Henry, Earl of Derby (1385), Duke of Hereford (1397), Appellant (1387–8), 638–9, 641–2, 645, 673; dispute with Mowbray (1398–9), 849–53; exile, invasion of England (1398–9), 853–6, 857–62, 864; mentioned, 548, 723, 737, 791, 844
Bologna, 45–6, 248–9, 289, 782, 803
Bonet, Honoré, 168–9, 671, 735, 746, 747, 766, 767, 769
Boniface IX, Pope, 785, 804, 822, 845
Bonne-Lance, 169
booty, 164, 166, 168–9, 210, 236–7, 241–2, 310–11, 378, 386, 502, 508, 550, 599, 611, 613–14, 625, 653, 684, 707–8, 748, 749, 776
Boquet, Jean, 290
Bordeaux, xvi, 4, 52, 81, 91, 95, 108, 159, 195–6, 197, 202, 206, 207, 213, 277, 295–7, 300–1, 303, 330–2, 332, 334, 335–6, 355, 692, 718–19, 753, 825
Bordelais, district, 21, 141, 158–9, 169, 171, 296, 301–2, 303–4, 331, 332, 693, 694–5
Bordes, Guillaume des, 328–9, 772

Bos, Hennequin du, 579
Bosc, Nicholas de, Bishop of Bayeux, 349, 528, 540, 576, 626, 674
Bossche, Peter Van den, 416, 451–2, 456–7,480, 482, 487, 494, 499, 504, 518, 533–4, 551, 553, 571, 574, 604
Boucicaut, Jean de, Marshal of France, 668, 721, 723–4, 726, 735, 737, 791, 829, 834, 846
Bouin, island, 653
Boulard, Nicholas, 756
Boulogne, 5, 37, 39, 173, 179, 528, 577, 805, 858
Boulogne, Guy of, Cardinal of Porto, 179–80
Bourbon, Louis, Duke of, campaigns (1369), 38; (1370), 48–50, 79; (1372), 126–7, 136–7, 138, 145–6, 148, 151, 152, 156–7; (1373), 181, 194; (1374), 205–6, 210–11; (1379), 357, 358–9, 360, 365; (1380), 389; (1382), 483, 485; (1385), 703–4, 705; (1386), 591; (Castile, 1387), 579, 598, 602, 612, 618, 621–2; (1388), 662; (Tunisia, 1390), 790; and regency (1380–8), 390–2, 394, 441, 469; and Marmousets (1388–92), 668, 801, 802; and John de Montfort (1391–2), 786, 796; and Italy (1392), 784–5, 803–4; mentioned, 16, 74, 270, 372, 400, 578, 716, 738, 799
Bourbon, Isabelle de Valois, Duchess of, 32, 49, 50
Bourbonnais, province, 32, 48, 49, 50, 79, 194, 201, 372, 701
Bourbourg, 497, 504, 506–9, 662
Bourchier, Sir John, 68, 532, 541, 545, 551, 554, 571, 574, 768–9, 770
Bourchier, Lady, 769
Bourdeilles, 295; siege (1369), 27, 28–9
Bourg-Charente, siege (1385), 704
Bourges, 60, 78, 81, 98, 145, 146
Bourgneuf, Bay of, 30, 105, 107, 238, 276, 653, 660
Bournaseau, Pierre, 277
Bouteville, 704
Bowet, Henry, later Archbishop of York, 471, 510
Brabant, 13, 154, 414, 449, 450, 452, 454, 516, 529, 581, 640, 649–51, 662, 664, 806; Estates, 846
Brabant, Jeanne, Duchess of, 664
Bracquemont, Robert de, 609, 611
Braga, 144, 150; treaty (1372), 157
Brantingham, Thomas, Bishop of Exeter, 101, 570, 673

Brantôme, 77, 239; siege (1369), 27; (1376), 240–1

Brassempouy, 684

Bray-sur-Somme, 188

Braybrooke, Robert, Bishop of London, 475

Bréhat, 653

Brembre, Nicholas, 459, 514, 532, 545, 552, 553, 632, 635, 637, 641, 642, 644

Brentford, 851

Brentwood, 420–1

Bressuire, 91–2

Brest, Neville at (1372–4), 156, 157, 182, 215; sieges (1373), 182, 184–6, 188, 189; (1377–8), 306, 308–10; (1386–7), 382–3, 582–3, 605–6; English occupation (1378–97), 304, 305–6, 309–11, 315, 316, 323, 352, 355, 356, 405, 412, 587, 628, 633, 643, 648, 743, 754, 824; surrender (1397), 811, 836, 837, 864; mentioned, xv, 120, 229, 234, 238, 251, 270, 362, 365, 366, 411, 533, 628, 653, 661, 672, 737, 794, 855

Breteuil, castle, siege (1378), 103, 107, 318, 320, 322

Brétigny, treaty (1360), xi, xvi, xvii, 2, 4, 15, 27, 30, 36, 113, 130, 142, 163, 214, 225–7, 244, 267, 720, 774, 775, 783, 788, 807, 826, 829

Breton companies, 29, 34, 76, 97, 98, 104–5, 151, 160, 200, 243–7, 248–9, 299, 306, 343, 346–8, 440, 445, 497, 533, 597, 613, 693–4, 726, 737, 761, 786, 795, 803

Brian, Sir Guy, 156, 171, 173, 223, 274

Bridoire, 698

Brighton, 282

Brinton, Thomas, Bishop of Rochester, 255, 262, 420

Briones, treaty (1379), 339–40

Brioude, 168

Bristol, 522, 860, 862

Brittany, duchy, 6–7; civil war (1341–64), xv, xvi; Earl of Cambridge in (1369), 26–7; projected English invasion (1372), 119–20, 121, 129, 131, 135, 144, 145, 149, 153; campaigns (1372), 156–7; (1373), 175, 180–2, 183, 184, 185–6, 192; (1374–5), 215–16, 222–3, 228–9, 230, 232, 234–5, 237–8, 257; (1377), 270; (1378), 305–6, 315, 325–7; (1380), 379, 396–7, 398–9, 406, 409–12; (1387), 605–6; and projected invasion of England (1387), 624; forfeiture and double invasion (1378), 351–4, 356–9, 360–6; projected French invasion (1392), 794–8, 799; mentioned, 2, 5, 13, 31, 37,
56, 64, 87, 88, 91, 114, 207, 243, 304, 714, 726, 736, 740, 741, 743, 771

Brittany, John IV de Montfort, Duke of, and England, 7–8; and Charles of Navarre (1369), 65; and Charles V, 103–5; and O. de Clisson, 105–8, 624–5, 627–31, 785–6, 801; with Gaunt in France (1373–4), 187–9; in Brittany (1374), 197, 213–14; forfeiture (1378), 351–2; recovery of Brittany (1379), 358–9, 360, 361–6, 375; and Buckingham's expedition (1380–1), 375, 396–7, 411; submission to Charles VI (1380), 399, 409–10, 412; and Bourbourg campaign (1383), 505, 507–9; siege of Brest (1386–7), 582–3, 605; and England (1388–92), 647–8, 651–2, 653; and the Marmousets (1392), 785–6, 794, 795–7; mentioned, 400, 451–2

Brittany, Joan Holand, Duchess of (d. 1384), 7, 412, 627

Brittany, Mary Plantagenet, Duchess of (d. 1361), 7

Brittany, Joan of Navarre, Duchess of (d. 1437), 795

Brive, captured (1373), 195, 208, 212; (1375), 205

Briviesca, Cortes (1387), 622–3

Browe, Sir Hugh, 731, 736, 742

Brucourt, Robert de, 768–9

Bruges, 14, 142, 174, 305, 416, 551, 553, 556, 717; conference (1373), 212; Congress (1374–7), 213, 215–16, 221, 224–8, 229–31, 233–4, 235–6, 249–52, 253, 255, 265–7, 278, 279–80, 344–5, 349–50, 453, 515, 674, 770, 789; truce (1375), 235–6, 238, 244; and civil war in Flanders (1379–85), 413–18, 456–8, 474, 477, 480, 482, 486–9, 517, 551, 554; and projected invasions of England (1385–6), 551, 553, 590

Bruges, franc of, 498

Brussels, 450, 717, 846

Buckingham, Earl of: see Woodstock, Thomas of

Budes, Geoffrey, 762

Budes, Sylvester, 97, 244, 248–9, 347

Bueil, Jean de, Seneschal of Beaucaire (1374–7), 28–9, 46, 47, 191, 299

Burgos, 141, 150, 196, 202, 338, 609, 613, 621–2; Cortes (1387), 622–3

Burgundy, Philip Duke of, campaigns (1369), 18, 38–42, 53; (1370), 97–9; (1372), 152, 154, 156, 163; (1373), 188–9, 191–2, 194; (1374), 200; (1377), 270, 285,

287, 291–4; (1378), 318, 319–20; (1380), 287–90; (1382), 479, 485; (1383), 503, 748; (1385), 535, 537–8, 539; (1386), 581, 590, 591, 748, 756–7; and Congress of Bruges (1374–7), 214–15, 224–5, 226, 228, 230, 235, 250, 253; and regency (1380–8), 390–2, 394–5, 396, 402, 441–2, 444–8, 490–1, 552, 556, 578, 601, 666–7; and civil war in Flanders (1379–85), 392, 417, 418, 460, 469, 474, 479, 485, 516–17, 531, 533–4, 540, 541, 553–5, 557, 571, 573–4; Anglo-French diplomacy (1382–8), 460–1, 469, 509, 514–15, 528, 529, 575, 633, 646, 655; and John de Montfort (1380–99), 396–7, 625–6, 629, 630–1, 647–8, 795, 801, 816; Guelders campaign (1388), 649–52, 662, 665; and *Marmousets* (1388–92), 669–70, 797, 798–9, 801; and Louis of Orléans, Italy, 781, 782, 802, 803, 846, 856; in government (1392–9), 799, 801–2; and Anglo-French diplomacy (1392–99), 790, 799–800, 804, 805–6, 830–2, 846, 853–4, 864; and Nicopolis crusade (1396), 816, 829; and papal schism (1392–9), 817, 819, 820, 822, 826, 828, 856; mentioned, 16, 74, 351, 400, 512, 540, 581, 605, 715, 726, 752, 753, 758, 763
Burley, Sir Richard, 617
Burley, Sir Simon, 29, 50, 161, 162, 177, 284, 472–3, 478, 514, 548, 570, 637, 642, 645, 777, 839
Bury St. Edmund's, 426
Bury, Adam, 260
Bussy, Sir John, 813, 841–2, 847–8, 852–3, 858, 860
Buuc, Jan, Admiral of Flanders, 603–5
Buxhill, Sir Alan, 68, 88, 92–3, 173, 219, 253
Byzantium, 738, 764, 816, 843

Cáceres, 599
Cadillac, 302, 303
Cadzand, island, 543, 604, 636
Caen, 87–8, 89, 218, 222, 233, 234, 321, 446, 739
Cahors, 24, 25, 166, 168, 243, 703, 706, 707–8
Caia, 467
Cairo, 575
Calais; siege (1347–8), xv, 132, 760; English occupation, 4–6, 63, 163, 199, 252–3, 273, 355, 356, 405, 516, 527, 528, 579–80, 587, 643, 754, 824; staple, 5, 217, 253,

254, 258, 260, 261, 308, 453, 477, 488; operations (1369), 35–6, 37–42, 43; (1377), 270, 285, 287, 291–4; negotiations about, 525, 529, 788, 789, 806, 807, 811; Richard II at (1396), 830, 831, 832; mentioned, xvi, 15, 55, 64, 73–4, 75, 84, 85, 102, 114, 132, 142, 155, 163, 176, 177, 183, 184, 186, 188, 199, 215, 217, 249, 250, 252–3, 253–4, 256, 258, 260, 261, 273, 278, 279, 294, 305, 308, 323, 367, 379, 385, 387, 406, 430, 453, 458, 461, 471, 478, 482, 483–4, 488, 497, 500, 504, 507, 508, 509, 515, 527–9, 533, 538, 545, 572, 574, 583, 585, 590, 593, 603, 631, 633, 635, 637, 638, 646, 651, 655, 674, 675, 723, 725, 734, 736, 737, 743, 753, 754, 755, 762, 772, 783, 784, 787, 809, 834, 836, 838, 839, 840, 852, 856, 864
Calais, treaty (1361), xvii, 4, 36, 163, 267
Calatrava, Order of, 158
Calveley, Sir Hugh, 20–1, 27, 28, 33, 88, 91, 92, 120, 122, 144, 187, 206, 211, 291, 292, 294, 311, 323, 330, 356, 358, 632, 364, 365, 368, 375, 399, 496, 498, 504, 507, 510, 743, 745,746
Cambrai, 540, 846
Cambridge, 377
Cambridge, Earl of: see Langley, Edmund
Campo Fregoso, Domenico, Doge of Genoa, 174
Campo Fregoso, Pietro, Admiral of Genoa, 174
Campo Maior, 677
Canterbury, 174, 263, 286, 288, 421–2, 580, 839
Canterbury, cardinal of: see Langham, Simon
Canterbury, ecclesiastical province, Convocation of, 62, 70, 408, 525
Captals de Buch: see Grailly
Carcassonne, 51, 59, 492, 612, 618, 689, 704, 706
Cardaillac, Marquis of, 201, 242, 717
Carentan, 320, 328, 329
Carlat, castle, occupied by companies (1369–71), 208; (1373–9), 208–10, 241, 242, 270, 682, 683; (1380–91), 686–7, 695, 696, 697, 701, 706, 708, 709, 711, 712, 718, 721
Carlisle, 10, 518, 527, 550, 579, 655, 656, 659, 675, 766–7
Carmona, 115, 569
Carpentras, 244, 440

Carrick, John Stewart, Earl of, 513, 531, 654, 676

Carteret, 237

Cascante, 337–8

Cassell, Mont Cassell, 498, 505–6

Castelbon, Roger-Bernard, Viscount of, 204, 334, 337, 338

Casteljaloux, 699

Castelmary, castle, 19, 46

Castile, xii, 114–16, 118–19, 122–4, 126, 129–30, 132, 196, 197, 202–3, 568, 610, 611, 613

Castillon-sur-Dordogne, siege (1377), 302–3

Castle Cornet, castle, 136, 185, 304

Castle Donnington, castle, 311

Castro, Alvaro Perez de: see Perez de Castro

Castro, Inez de, 381, 382, 493, 519, 559

Castro Urdiales, 124

Castrojeriz, 660

Cataneo, Martin, 174

Catherine of France, daughter of Charles V, 279

Catherine of Lancaster, Queen of Castile, 569, 597, 611, 619, 623

Catterton, Thomas, 219, 231–3, 235, 236, 238, 259, 260, 261

Caudrot, 240

Caumont, family, 693, 694

Caumont, Nompar de, 706, 707

Caun, Thomas, 69

Caupenne, Garcie-Arnaud, bastard of, 208–9, 210, 241, 242, 686

Caussade, 27

Cavendish, Sir John, Chief Justice of King's Bench, 426

Cazillac, 717

Celorigo da Beira, 563

Cent Ballades (Les), 754, 759

Cervole, Arnaud de, 164, 246

Cesena, sack (1377), 249, 344

Chaliers, 684, 686

Chalon, Louis de, 769

Châlons-sur-Marne (Châlons-en-Champagne), 491, 622, 753

Chalusset, castle, 78, 684, 711–12, 721

Chambre des Comptes, 373, 670

Champagne, province, campaigns (1373), 191–2; (1380), 387, 388–90, 590; mentioned, 405, 442, 447, 756, 847

Champtoceaux, castle, 105, 106, 358, 410, 627, 786

Chandler, William, 300–1, 302

Chandos, Sir John, Constable of Aquitaine, 6, 20–2, 24–6, 28, 29, 46, 47–8, 51, 66, 69, 75, 78, 105, 109, 170, 744–5

Chandos Herald, 49, 483, 726

Chantelle, 49

Charenton, 446, 448

Charles IV of Luxembourg, Holy Roman Emperor, 84–5, 346

Charles V, King of France, character and health, 14–16, 214, 391; buildings, 60, 84–5, 400, 474; advisers, 16–17, 113, 352–3, 626, 668; and military operations (1369), 18, 27, 31, 38, 39, 42, 44–5, 56–7, 61; (1370–1), 74, 86, 110; (1372), 127–8, 129, 149; (1373–4), 189, 200; (1377), 285, 300; and Bertrand du Guesclin, 53, 385, 744; and Charles of Navarre, 65, 94, 312, 314, 317–18, 320–1; and Brittany, 104–5, 106, 353–4, 357; and negotiations with England, 114, 214, 266, 267–8; and papal schism, 343–4, 345–6; and Languedoc, 371, 413; death (1380), 390, 391–2, 395; biographer, 726; mentioned, xvii, 13, 53

Charles VI, King of France, character, 390–1, 478–9, 627, 667, 689, 752; accession (1380), 390, 397–8, 448; and tax rebellions (1380–3), 489, 491; marriage (1385), 551–2; campaigns (1382), 478, 482; (1383), 503, 506; (1385–6), 545, 553, 555, 578, 584, 588, 590, 591, 578; (1388) 664–5; and negotiations with England, 469, 576, 577, 671–2, 787, 789, 790, 791, 805, 823–4, 827, 830–1, 833, 856; majority (1388), 665–6, 668–9; and O. de Clisson, 441, 630, 668, 694; and Marmousets, 801; in Languedoc (1389), 679, 713, 715; and Louis of Orléans, 780, 856; and Italy, 779–81, 784, 820; and Brittany, 796; insanity, xii, 798–800, 804, 809, 811, 827, 836, 856

Charles of Durazzo, King of Naples, 393, 438–9, 440–1, 779

Charles II of Evreux, King of Navarre ('the Bad'), personality and ambitions, 64, 311–12; negotiations with England (1369–71), 64–7, 71–4, 86–7, 93–4, 102–3, 261; and Gaunt's claim to Castile, 122, 179–80, 196–7, 200–1, 202–3; alliance with England (1377–9), 312–14, 321–3, 324, 333, 334–40; loss of Norman domains (1378), 317–21; mentioned, xvi, 626, 630, 795

Charles III of Evreux, King of Navarre, 202, 314, 317, 340, 533, 811, 823

Charlieu, John of, Prior of Lewes, 282

Charlus-Champagnac, castle, 316, 684

Charny, Geoffrey de (d. 1356), 747, 759
Charny, Geoffrey de (d. 1398), 526, 527, 735
Charolais, county, 192, 716
Charroux, abbey, 148
Chartres, 54, 390, 704
Château-du-Loir, 91
Château-Gontier, 6, 8, 26, 31, 66
Château-Larcher, 162
Cháteaumorand, Jean de, 146, 156, 365, 621, 738
Châteauneuf-de-Randon, 385, 684, 686
Châtellerault, 28, 87, 137; captured (1370), 76
Châtillon, Hugh de, Master of the Royal Archers, 35, 43, 771, 772
Chaucer, Geoffrey, xii, 63, 142, 172, 174, 182–3, 212, 256, 279, 377–8, 763–4, 777
Chauliac, Guy de, 762, 763
Chauvigny, 137; captured (1372), 148, 149
Chauvigny, Guy de, 29
Chaves, siege (1386), 577
Cherbourg, 65, 66, 67, 71, 72, 73, 126, 304, 312, 318, 320, 322; siege (1378), English occupation (1378–94), 322–4, 329–30, 340, 355, 356, 405, 533, 581–2, 587, 633, 643, 743, 754, 759, 811, 864; siege (1378), 327–9
Cheshire, Chester, county, 638, 636–7, 642–3, 776, 805, 810, 812–13, 843
Cheshire archers, 839–40, 841, 848, 858, 859
Cheyne, Sir John, 843
Cheyne, Sir Robert, 210–11
Cheyne, Sir Thomas, 282
Chinon, 136–7
Chiriton, Walter, 459
Chizé, battle (1373), 160, 161, 162
Cinque Ports, 135, 173, 216, 282, 316, 555, 637, 638
Cintruénigo, 337
Ciudad Rodrigo, 158, 466, 496, 558, 560, 561, 563, 599, 617–18
Clanvowe, Sir John, 69, 776, 791
Clarence, Lionel, Duke of (d. 1368), 641, 855
Clarence, Thomas of Lancaster, Duke of (d. 1421), 207
Clarendon, 74
Clark, John, 306
Clement VI, Pope, 111, 112
Clement VII, Pope (Avignon), 344, 345–50, 393–4, 434–5, 439–40, 489, 503, 628, 708, 716, 779–80, 781–2, 802–3, 816, 817

Clerkenwell, St. John's Priory, 425, 429
Clermont (Auvergne), 34, 98, 211, 703, 710, 720, 762–3
Clermont de l'Hérault, 370
Cléry-sur-Somme, 387
Clifford family, 10, 406, 548, 675, 723
Clifton, Sir William, 805
Clisson, 65
Clisson, Marguerite de, dame de Penthièvre, 628, 631
Clisson, Olivier de, Constable of France, character, 105–6, 758; early career (to 1380), 37, 65, 85, 87, 90, 91, 162, 760; business activities, 625, 768–9, 801; and John de Montfort, 105–7, 108, 109, 119, 157, 352–3, 624–5, 627–31, 648, 651–2, 785–6; campaigns (to 1380), 109, 138, 142–3, 160, 189, 191, 192, 213, 228, 234–5, 237–8, 243, 270, 306, 325–6; and forfeiture of Brittany (1378–9), 352–3, 357, 358, 363; Constable (1380), 392; siege of Nantes (1380–1), 396–8, 409; Roosebeke campaign (1382), 480–2, 484–5, 754; and regency (1380–8), 412, 439, 441, 469, 624–5, 625–6, 627; and projects to invade England (1385–7), 535, 538–9, 544, 556, 557, 603; attack on Ghent (1385), 554; and Guelders campaign (1388), 664; and the Marmousets (1388–92), 626, 666–8, 670, 713; and invasion of Brittany (1392), 793–5, 796–7, 799, 800; disgrace (1392), 801; mentioned, 854
coastal defence, 63, 131, 135, 143, 173, 199, 221, 278, 283, 287, 289, 353, 545, 605
Cobham, John lord, 288, 545, 843
Coca, 436
Cocherel, battle (1364), 103, 765
Cocking, John, 66, 72
Cognac, 81, 94–5, 155, 215; siege (1375), 229, 230, 231, 233
Coimbra, 158, 178, 558, 562–3, 618; Cortes at (1385), 558
Colfox, Sir Nicholas, 731
Comines, 480, 482–3, 487
Comminges, Counts of, 112, 680–1, 683
companies, xi, xvi, 21, 22, 28, 31, 32, 34, 44, 48, 50, 52, 55, 66, 84, 88, 96–7, 102–3, 104, 110, 117, 136, 137, 145–6, 160, 163–70, 200, 204, 207–11, 219, 239–49, 250–1, 268, 298, 315–16, 321, 337, 339, 343, 346, 347–8, 368, 384–5, 440, 533, 654, 662–3, 665, 679, 680, 681–7, 688,

689, 691, 693–712, 713–17, 719–22, 728, 743, 744, 769, 786, 803

Compeyre, 19; battle (1369), 33–5

Compiègne, 54, 396, 447–8, 469, 477, 479, 646

Comtat Venaissin, 247, 248

Concarneau, 182

Conches, castle, siege (1371), 103,107

Constanza of Castile, Duchess of Lancaster, 115–16, 117, 122, 610, 619, 757–8

Conway, 859–61, 863

Cooling, castle, 288

Corbeil, 84, 317, 766, 770

Corbie, 487

Corbie, Arnaud de, First President of the Parlement, then Chancellor of France, 447, 476, 626, 668, 674

Corella, 337

Cornwall, 278, 288, 325, 368, 411

Cortes (Castile), 115, 117, 123, 124, 384, 433, 436, 574–5, 595, 597, 599–600, 619, 620, 622–3, 678

Cortes (Navarre), 336

Cortes (Portugal), 435, 558–9

Corunna, siege (1386), 594–6, 598, 609

Cotentin, 6, 64, 66–7, 73–4, 94, 132, 136, 154, 215, 218–21, 222, 279, 313, 320, 325, 328–30, 360, 404, 582

Coucy, Enguerrand de, Earl of Bedford, Count of Soissons, 244–6, 279, 300, 367, 387, 389, 409, 439, 441, 444, 445, 448, 484, 485, 534–5, 626, 651, 664, 714, 720, 802, 803, 816, 820, 829, 834

Coudenberghe, William van, 541

Coulombier, Jean de, 125

Courcy, Margaret, Dame de, 857, 863

Courtenay, Matilda: see St.-Pol, Countess of

Courtenay, Sir Peter, 495, 723, 725

Courtenay, Sir Philip, 237, 495

Courtenay, William, Bishop of London, 257, 272–3, 274, 275, 425, 429, 537, 545

Courtrai, 414, 416, 449, 457, 480, 484, 486–7, 488; battle (1302), 477, 487

Coventry, 429, 852, 853–4

Craddock, Sir David, 731, 743

Craddock, Sir Richard, 211, 718, 719–20, 721, 743

Cramaud, Simon de, Bishop of Poitiers, 819, 828

Craon, Amaury de, 30–1

Craon, Pierre de, 794–8

Crécy, battle (1346), xv, 1, 13, 16, 41, 53, 174, 191, 224, 256, 375, 431, 536, 548, 566, 733, 736

Creil, castle, 15, 60, 146, 552, 800

Cresswell, Edmund, 300, 301, 302

Cresswell, Sir John, 6, 92, 138, 142, 152, 159, 161, 211, 237, 758

Creton, Jean, 861, 863

Cros, Jean de, Bishop of Limoges, 79–80, 83

crossbow, crossbowmen, 43, 151, 434, 538, 547, 696, 714, 763

Cubzac, castle, 301

Cumberland, county, 10, 285, 405, 518, 550, 656, 675

Curiel, castle, 141

Custon, Raymond de, 316

Cuvelier, 725, 726

Dacre family, 10

Dagworth, Sir Nicholas, 198, 642

Dalyngrigg, Sir Edward, 288

Damascus, 717

Damme, 277, 417, 488; occupied by Ghent (1385), 551, 552–4, 555

Dartford, 421

Dartmouth, 74, 145, 184, 202, 310, 378, 379, 409, 411, 412, 429, 431, 543, 656

Datini, Francesco di Marco, 667, 734, 752, 753, 816

Dauphiné, province, 56, 709

Daventry, 506

David II, King of Scotland, xvi, 9, 128, 763

Dauphiné, 56, 709

Dax, 201, 204, 295, 331

Dax, Bishop of: see Beauffès, Jean; Gutierrez, Juan

Denbigh, lordship, 849

Dendermonde, 449, 458, 476, 486

Denia, Alfonso de Villena, Count of, 769

Derby, Earl of: see Bolingbroke, Grosmont, Gaunt

Derrien, Yves, 783

Derval, 78, 91, 238, 736, 754; siege (1373), 182, 188, 189, 192

Deschamps, Eustache, xii, 6, 162, 243, 388, 413, 487, 528, 590, 664, 671, 722, 725, 735, 753, 800, 806, 864

Despenser, Edward lord, 216, 223

Despenser, Henry, Bishop of Norwich, 470–2, 493, 494–6, 497–504, 507–10

Despenser, Sir Hugh, 571–2, 573–4, 605

Despenser, Thomas lord, Earl of Gloucester (1397), 791, 844, 849, 860, 863

Devereux, Sir John, 32, 96, 99, 120, 138, 140, 142, 145–6, 152, 159–60, 169, 211, 234–5, 758

Devizes, 353

Devon, 278, 323, 412
Devon, Hugh Courtenay, Earl of, 272, 725
Dieppe, 37, 446
Dijon, 318
Dinan, 325, 360, 363–4
Dinis, Infante of Portugal, 381
discipline, military, 746–8
Dixmude, Thierry, lord of, 497–8
Dominguez, Vasco, 177
Domme, siege (1369), 25, 27, 78; captured (1393), 722
Doncaster, 859
Doria family, 176, 731
Doria, Antonio, 174
Dormans, Jean de, Bishop of Beauvais, Cardinal, 17, 113–14, 130
Dormans, Mile de, 399, 476
Douai, town; castlery, 13, 732
Douat, Bernard, 242, 315, 316, 695, 716, 718
Douglas, house of, 10, 513, 531, 547, 676
Douglas, Sir Archibald, Earl of ('the Grim') (d. 1400), 128, 269, 518, 526, 527, 544, 550, 656, 677
Douglas, James, Earl of (d. 1388), 548, 550, 656–9
Douglas, Sir James, lord of Dalkeith, 527
Douglas, William, Earl of (d. 1384), 269, 405
Douglas, Sir William ('the Knight of Liddesdale'), 659
Dover, 183, 284, 286–7, 288, 290, 478, 580, 656, 677
Drayton, Sir Hugh, 571, 573–4
Drew, Lawrence, 847
Dryburgh, 549
Dublin, 13, 889
Dublin, Marquis of: see Vere, Robert de
Dunbar, 543
Dunfermline, 676
Dunkirk, 497, 506; battle (1383), 498
Duras, 303
Duras, lords of: see Durfort
Duravel, siege (1369), 24
Durfort, Gaillard de, lord of Duras, 299, 301, 303, 331, 706, 707
Durham, 68, 657; ordinances (1385), 747–8
Durham, bishops of: see Fordham, John; Hatfield, Thomas; Skirlaw, Walter

Edinburgh, 270, 277, 518, 526, 543, 545, 546, 547, 548, 549, 550, 654, 770
Edward I, King of England, 11, 12, 61, 828
Edward II, King of England, 273, 589, 726,

828, 848, 849, 862
Edward III, King of England, personality and dotage, 1–2, 175–7; early wars, xv, xvii; claim to French Crown, xv, 36, 130, 225; campaigns (1369), 36, 36, 41; (1372), 121, 135, 144, 153, 155–6; and Enguerrand de Coucy, 244–5, 300; and Good Parliament, 257, 262–3; last illness and death, xi, 270–1, 280, 283; mentioned, 7, 16, 26, 113, 120–1, 213, 223, 237, 536, 757, 768, 789
Edward, Prince of Wales and Aquitaine ('the Black Prince'), character and health, 3, 20; campaigns (1356), xvi; (1367), xvii, 620 (1370), 81–3, 94; resigns principality of Aquitaine (1372), 156; in English politics (1371–6), 101, 115, 256, 257–8, 261–2; death and obsequies (1376), 262, 263, 751; biographer, 726; mentioned, xi, 22, 36, 46, 48, 49, 50, 51, 69, 79, 159, 589, 758
Edward of Cambridge, Earl of Rutland (1390), Duke of Albemarle (1397), in Gascony (1369–70), 26–7, 28, 29–30, 35, 48–50, 51, 69, 81, 82, 95, 97, 181; campaign (1372), 121, 144; at Congress of Bruges (1375), 249; defence of Kent (1376), 284; in Portugal (1381–2), 381, 383–4, 412, 431–2, 343, 435–7, 459, 461, 463–9, 470, 475, 492, 564; and Scotland (1384–5), 518, 548; and English politics (1385–9), 536, 645; Anglo-French diplomacy (1392–6), 789, 814; heir of Richard II, 855; and Bolingbroke's invasion (1399), 858–60; mentioned, 673, 832, 833, 836, 839, 840, 844, 848, 854, 855, 858, 860
Egypt, 575, 578
Elmham, Sir William, 204, 206, 300, 301–3, 376, 496, 504, 507, 510, 514, 642, 718, 719–20
Eltham, palace, 1, 41, 262, 576 588–9, 634, 787
Elvas, 558, 560; siege (1381), 436; Anglo-Portuguese army at (1382), 466–7
Entre-Deux-Mers, 301, 303, 654–5
Erkelenz, 662
Erpingham, Sir Thomas, 855
Ertvelde, 554–5, 557
Espagne, Arnaud d', 51
Esparza, Ramón de, 322, 324
Essex, 386, 420–1
Estates-General (Languedoil), 53, 55, 56–8, 60, 368–9, 396, 399, 402, 404–5, 442, 447, 492, 626, 691

Estella, 312, 334, 339
Estrange, Guillaume de l', 350
Estremoz, 383, 435
Eu, Philip, Count of, Constable of France, 801, 829, 834, 854
Eu, Marie de Berry, Countess of, 854, 855, 857
Evesham, 639
Evora, 464, 522
Evreux, siege (1378), 64, 312, 319, 322
Exton, Nicholas, 635, 636, 638
Eymet, battle (1377), 299, 301, 332
Eynesford, Sir John, 256

Fadrique, bastard of Henry of Trastámara, 381, 382
Falaise, 446
Falconer, Sir John, 751
Farringdon, Sir William, 155, 323, 496, 504, 507, 510
Fawsley, Sir John, 282
Faye, Guy de, Bishop of Maillezais, 154
Fécamp, 57, 316
Felton, Sir Thomas, Seneschal of Gascony, (1371–7), 20, 77, 113, 137, 140, 141, 152, 158–9, 171–2, 197, 200–1, 202, 207, 240, 277, 295–9, 329, 680; and Buckingham's expedition (1381), 409–12, 771–2
Fiennes, Moreau de, Constable of France, 39, 74–5
Fernando, King of Portugal, 118–19, 122, 14, 157–8, 177–80, 183, 349, 379–84, 431–2, 434–7, 462–8, 470, 492–3, 496–7, 519, 521, 522
Ferrers, Sir Ralph, 223, 292
Fieschi, Antonio, 134
Fife, Robert Stewart, Earl of, 550, 656, 659, 676–7
Figeac, attacked (1369), 26, 52, 699, 703; occupied by *routiers* (1371–3), 165–8
FitzNicol, John, Admiral of Brittany, 119
Fitzwalter, Walter lord, 68, 89–90, 92, 274
Flamenc, Nicholas, 480
Flanders, county, neutrality (1369–79), xv, 13–14, 37, 56, 100, 277; naval war with England (1371), 172–3; naval resources, 183, 511–12, 523, 535; John de Montfort in (1375–7), 238; and papal schism, 348, 350; civil war, French occupation (1379–85), 373, 392, 413–14, 442, 449–58, 460, 470–1, 474–89, 490, 493–6, 497–510, 513, 514, 516–17, 524, 529, 531, 538–9, 541, 542–3, 551–5, 557, 571–2, 573–4, 759; and the war

(1385–96), 578, 581–2, 584–7, 590–4, 598, 601, 603–4, 633, 649, 651, 662, 748, 754; mentioned, 260, 316, 405, 732, 738, 742, 816
Flanders, Louis de Mâle, Count of, 13–14; and Philip of Burgundy, 40, 215, 460, 474; and papal schism, 348, 417, 471; and John de Montfort, 238, 365; and France, 5, 14, 417, 277, 417, 460–1, 474–5, 478, 515; and civil war in Flanders (1379–85), 413–18, 449–53, 455, 456–7, 479, 482–3, 486; death (1384), 516
Flanders, Louis of Nevers, Count of, xv
Flanders, Margaret, Countess of, Duchess of Burgundy, 13, 215, 516
Flint, lordship; castle, 639, 849, 861, 862
Florence, 134, 247–8, 340, 413, 445, 519, 785–6, 803, 836
Fobbing (Essex), 420
Fogaça, Lourenço, Chancellor of Portugal, 459–60, 462, 465, 470, 522, 432–3, 559, 568
Fogg, Sir Thomas, 743
Foix, county, 622
Foix, Gaston II, Count of, 117
Foix, Gaston Phoebus III, Count of, 121, 201, 202, 317, 321–2, 333, 533, 679–81, 683, 687–91, 699, 707, 710, 716, 724, 727, 768, 769
Fondi, 344–5
Fontans, Perrot de ('Le Béarmais'), 654, 684, 686, 687, 693, 695, 699, 701, 711–12, 714, 718, 721
Fontenay-le-Comte, 163
Fontenay, Thomas de, 364
foraging, 25, 42, 84, 89, 137, 160, 181, 191, 195, 219, 302, 327, 329, 388, 407, 409, 532, 547, 549, 605, 609, 611–14, 617, 664, 732, 734, 755
Fordham, John, Bishop of Durham, 548, 589, 658
Forget, Agnes, 163
Fossanas, Jean, 706–7
Fotheringhay, John, 146
Fotheringhay, Richard,
fouage, generally, 395, 403–4; Gascony, xvii, 20, 27, 78, 94; Languedoc, 97, 127, 243, 247, 368–9, 371, 491, 688, 691, 710, 702; Languedoil, 55–9, 214, 222, 236, 240, 402; Brittany, 358, 364; Auvergne, 372
Fowey, 120, 310, 325, 543
Frankfurt, Diet (1379), 348; (1397), 845
Fraubrunnen, abbey, 246
Fresnel, Pierre, Bishop of Meaux, 676, 677

Friuli, 393

Froissart, Jean, 216, 671, 681, 626–7, 775, 806, 825; quoted, 14, 22, 25, 28, 39, 40, 44, 48, 49, 61, 75, 79, 82–3, 98, 138, 141, 146, 153–4, 162, 169, 191, 236, 239, 244, 254, 270, 301, 307, 333, 366, 387, 388, 394, 421, 450, 452, 490, 493, 513–14, 526, 527, 533, 534, 535, 536, 546, 550, 590, 610, 611, 617, 626, 629, 630, 654, 658, 659, 664, 671, 687, 694, 706, 711, 717, 729, 730, 741–2, 743, 744, 746, 747, 750, 754, 759, 790–1, 806–7, 809,. 837–8, 864

Fronsac, 296, 297, 692–3, 737, 743, 754

Furnes, 498

Gaillac, 704

Galard, Perrot de, 96, 315–16, 686, 687

Galard, Marguerite de, dame de Limeuil, 77

Galen, 761

Galicia, province, 117, 432, 594–9, 601, 602, 606–7, 609, 614, 619, 622, 678

Galloway, 10, 518

gambling, 758–9, 800, 847

Garlans, Bernard, Bastard of, 696

Garencières, Yon de, 757, 772

Garnetot, 66, 93

Garro, Arnaud-Garcia, lord of, 314, 322, 324

Garter, Order of the, 68, 244–5, 280, 300, 540, 724, 745

Gascony, province, 21, 51–2, 680

Gaunt, John of, Duke of Lancaster and Aquitaine, character, 3–4; campaigns (1369), 35, 36, 38–44, 56, 63, 69, 132, 740, 771; (1370–1), 69–70, 74, 81–3, 94–5, 97–8, 108–10, 113, 115, 758; (1372), 144; (1373–4), 170, 175, 180, 181–4, 186, 187–96, 197–203, 204, 207–8, 374; (1378), 315, 316, 323, 324, 325–7, 354, 355; claim to Castile, 115–16, 119, 120–1, 122–3, 157, 177–80, 196–7, 200–2, 239, 349, 381, 408, 437, 459; and Congress of Bruges (1374–7), 212–13, 214, 221, 224–6, 230, 233–4, 235, 238, 249–50, 253, 267; and Good Parliament (1376), 256–8, 260, 265; government of England (1376–7), 263–5, 271–6; and minority of Richard II (1377–86), 283–4, 287, 307, 359, 472–4, 514, 524, 531, 537–8, 587, 694; and Peasants' Revolt (1381), 422, 425–8; and expedition to Portugal (1381–2), 381–4, 431, 437–8, 459, 462, 466, 467, 469–70, 475, 492,

497; and Flanders (1382–3), 478, 495; and Norwich Crusade (1383), 472, 475, 478, 504–5, 507, 508–10; and Scotland (1380–6), 406, 412, 426, 504, 512–13, 518–19, 544, 548–9; and Anglo-French negotiations (1382–6), 431, 460–1, 478, 515, 527–30, 536–7, 540; expedition to Castile (1385–8), 568–9, 572–3, 576–7, 578–9, 580–3, 594–601, 606–21, 622–3, 660, 735, 749, 752, 753, 755; in Gascony (1388–9), 648–9, 650–1, 653, 654, 660–2, 673, 717–18, 774; Duke of Aquitaine (1390–8), 718–19, 721–2; and Anglo-French negotiations (1390–6), 774–5, 777, 778, 787, 788–9, 790–3, 805–7, 809, 822, 828–9, 831–2; and English politics (1390–8), 673, 810, 811–16, 825, 828–9, 840, 842–3, 850–1; death, 854; mentioned, 1, 7, 15, 44, 93, 162, 169, 288, 295, 351, 360, 454, 540, 693, 763, 768, 833

Gaure, 807

Gaveston, Piers, 177

Gavray, siege (1378), 320

Gençay, captured (1375), 159, 161, 163, 215, 228, 758

Genoa, Genoese, 18, 38, 45, 49, 118, 124–5, 132, 134–5, 137, 174, 180, 181, 186, 187, 245, 285, 291, 386, 387, 459, 503, 543, 585, 703, 731, 732, 737, 751, 753, 790, 803, 820, 832, 846

Gentbrugge, 557

Gentilly, 85

Gerard, Hughlin, 289

Germany, Germans, xi, xvi, 42, 141, 244, 245–7, 348, 350, 375, 440, 449, 456, 532, 539, 582, 584, 585, 604, 649, 662, 723, 752, 753, 756, 769, 779, 816, 829, 845, 846, 856

Gerson, Jean, 671, 790, 792

Gevaudan, province, 166, 242, 385, 684, 695, 709; Estates, 703

Ghent, xiv, 3, 14, 274, 348; revolt (1379–85), 413–18, 449–58, 460, 469, 470, 474, 476–80, 482, 483, 486–9, 494–5, 497–9, 500, 504, 509–10, 514, 516–17, 528, 529, 533–4, 538, 540, 541, 544–5, 551–5, 557, 571–4, 589, 770; Friday Market, 451, 571; Château de Gavre, 574

Gilbert, John, Bishop of Hereford, then St. David's, 461–2, 475, 540, 826

Gildesburgh, Sir John, 375, 407

Glendower, Owen, 11

Gloucester, 345, 354, 355, 359, 407, 438,

627, 628

Gloucester, Duke of: see Woodstock, Thomas of

Gloucester, Earl of: see Despenser, Thomas

Golafre, Sir John, 311, 635

Gold, William, 758

Gonzaga family, lords of Mantua, 758

Gorey, castle, 136, 184–5, 304

Gosport, 126

Gournay, Sir Matthew, 141, 204, 331, 431, 465, 769

Goushill, Sir Nicholas, 736

Gower, lordship, 849

Gower, John, xii, 177, 419, 776

Grailly, Archambaud de, Captal de Buch (d. 1412), 297, 706

Grailly, Jean de, Captal de Buch (d. 1377), 25, 81, 103, 137, 140, 141, 142, 146, 148, 149–50, 151–2, 155, 301, 730, 765–6, 770

Grailly, Jean de (fl. late 14th cent.), 825

Grammont, 449

Granada, 150, 436

Grandison, Sir Thomas, 68, 88, 89–90, 91–2

Granton, Robert, 161

Gravelines, 488, 582; captured (1383), 497, 506, 507–8, 509

Gravesend, 283, 386

Gray, Sir Thomas, 730, 733, 770

Great Councils (England), (Feb. 1370), 67, 69, 71; (Jan. 1372), 121–2, 129, 131, 155; (Oct. 1374), 221; (May 1375), 230; (Oct. 1376), 264, 266; (Apr. 1377), 295; (June 1378), 323; (June 1379), 355; (Sept. 1379), 366; (Mar. 1382), 453; (Jan. 1383), 494; (Oct. 1384), 530; (Feb. 1385), 536–7; (May 1385), 540; (June 1385), 544; (July 1385), 655–6; (Mar. 1386), 577; (Aug. 1386), 583; (May 1389), 672; (June 1389), 674; (Dec. 1389), 774; (Apr. 1391), 787; (Feb. 1392), 788, 789; (May 1392), 792; (Mar. 1399), 854

Great Councils (France), (Mar. 1369), 18, 37; (May 1369), 113; (Aug. 1369), 39, 56–7, 59; (Dec. 1371), 126–7; (May 1375), 227; (Nov. 1378), 345; (Apr. 1386), 578; (Jan. 1387), 602; (May 1388), 651; (Nov. 1388), 665–6; (Dec. 1390), 782; (Sept. 1392), 800

Green, Sir Henry, 847–8, 858, 860

Green, Henry, captain of Puyguilhem, 693

Greenwich, 283, 424

Gregory XI, Pope, 111–14, 179, 212–13, 229, 247–8, 265, 303, 340, 347, 349, 767

Greystoke, Ralph, lord, 405

Grimaldi family, 37, 125, 731

Grimaldi, Marco, 134

Grimaldi, Rainier, 38, 136, 141, 186

Grosmont, Henry of, Earl of Derby (1337), Earl (1345) then Duke (1351) of Lancaster, xvi, 2, 3, 75, 121, 206, 535, 762

Grosvenor, Sir Robert, 735–6

Grutere, Gilbert de, 450, 452

Guadalajara, 619; Cortes (1389), 678

Guarda, 520–1, 560

Guelders, 649–52, 662–5, 756

Guelders, William, Duke of, 649, 651, 655, 664, 667, 792, 805, 811

Guérande, 157, 627; treaty (1365), 352

Guernsey, 136, 143, 185, 304

Guesclin, Bertrand du, Constable of France, in Castile (1368–70), 28, 75, 117, 282; Constable (1370), 74–5, 86, 744; campaigns (1370), 76–7, 81, 86–7, 89–90, 91, 92, 97; (1371), 97–8, 103, 104–5, 106–8, 109; (1372), 126–7, 136–8, 142–3, 145, 148–9, 151, 152, 156, 159, 160, 162; (1373), 181, 182, 184–5; (1373–4), 189, 191, 194–5, 199–200; (1374), 205, 213; (1375), 228–9, 230, 233, 236, 237–8; (1376–7), 240–1, 251, 270, 299, 682; (1378), 319, 325–6, 327–8; (1379), 357, 363–5; Captain-General in Languedoc, death (1379–80), 371, 384–5, 679, 684–6; posthumous reputation, 669, 725–6; mentioned, 53, 80, 130, 254, 319, 624, 738, 744, 746, 758, 764, 766, 772

Guesclin, Olivier du, 244, 579, 596, 597, 598, 609, 611, 614, 616, 617, 620, 621, 768

Guigne, Oudinot, 732

Guillaume, Arnaud, 809

Guimarães, captured (1385), 559, 560

Guines, 130, 212, 574, 805

Guingamp, 104

Guise, 367

Guy, Bishop of Luçon, 154

Gutiérrez, Juan, dean of Segovia, later bishop of Dax, 116, 120, 123, 431, 435, 595

Gyé-sur-Seine, 192

Hainault, Hainaulters, 367, 431, 435, 449, 450, 455, 540, 579, 726, 753, 846

Hainault, Albert of Bavaria (Wittelsbach), Regent, then Count of (d. 1404), 367, 454, 633

Hainault, Margaret of Burgundy, Countess of, 540

Hainault, William of Bavaria (Wittelsbach), Count of Ostrevant, then Hainault (d. 1417), 540
Hakenet, Nicholas, 316
Hale, Sir Frank, 36
Hales, Sir Robert, 423, 424, 425, 427
Halewyn, Daniel de, 458, 480
Halidon Hill, battle (1333), 256
Hall, John, 862
Ham, 805
Hamo of Offington, 281–2
Harcourt, Godfrey, lord of, 6
Harcourt, Louis, lord of, 76
Harelbeke, 450
Harelle (1382), 444
Harewell, John, Bishop of Bath and Wells, Chancellor of Aquitaine, 284
Harfleur, naval base, 18, 39, 41, 45, 129, 136, 150, 173, 186, 189, 279, 285, 385, 387, 538, 605, 606, 624; attacked (1369), 42–3; (1378), 324
Haringey, 636
Harleston, Sir John, 329, 375, 760
Harpeden, Sir John (the elder), 109–10, 139–40, 142, 162, 706, 710, 717
Harpeden, John (the younger), 162, 627
Harwich, 534, 542
Hase, Louis de, Bastard of Flanders, 497
Haselrigg, William, 256
Hastings, attacked (1377), 282
Hastings, Sir Hugh (d. 1347), 760
Hastings, Sir Hugh (d. 1396), 741
Hatfield, Thomas, Bishop of Durham, 73
Hauterive, Roger de, bailli of Ghent, 416
Havering, royal manor, 1, 263, 271
Hawkwood, Sir John, 247–9, 348, 440–1, 731, 736, 758
Hawley, John, 378
Haye, Henry, Seneschal of Angoumois, 151
Hédé, castle, 397
Hennebont, 120, 396; siege (1373), 182
Henry II of Trastámara, King of Castile, 17, 38, 75, 115, 116–17, 119, 121, 123–5, 129–30, 141, 142, 150, 158, 177–80, 196–7, 200, 201–5, 212, 238, 313, 321, 323, 333, 338–9, 379–80, 384, 765
Henry III of Trastámara, King of Castile, 384
Henry III, King of England, 74, 862
Henry IV, King of England: see Bolingbroke
Henry V, King of England: see Monmouth, Henry of
Henry IV, King of France, 208
heralds, 26, 49, 98, 159, 225, 232, 234,

235, 238, 263, 278, 285, 411, 435, 462, 483, 485, 498, 507, 508, 526, 582, 592, 615, 723, 724, 726, 729, 748, 767, 783, 789, 809, 833, 852–3
Hereford, Henry Bolingbroke, Duke of: see Bolingbroke
Hereford, Humphrey de Bohun Earl of (d. 1373), 35, 36, 38, 40, 41
Hertford, 426
Herzele, Rees Van, 534
Hesdin, castle, 39, 42, 458
Hewitt, Sir Walter, 69, 74, 80, 81, 95, 96, 108, 110, 149–50, 151–2, 187, 191, 211
Hexham, 10
Higden, Ranulph, 101
Hilton, Roger, 66, 72
Holand, Sir John, Earl of Huntingdon (1389), Duke of Exeter (1397), 615, 616, 618, 673, 723, 724, 789, 816, 837, 844, 860, 861, 863
Holand, Thomas, Earl of Kent (1360), Duke of Surrey (1397), 366, 431, 544, 844, 860, 861, 863
Holland, 72, 135, 145, 153, 183, 449, 450, 512, 540, 584, 846
Holt, castle, 810, 861
Holy Land, 435, 471, 776, 791, 826, 862
Holyrood Abbey: see Edinburgh
Hoo, William, 507
horses, 132–3, 728, 731, 739, 740, 742, 749, 750, 751, 755, 764, 890–1
Hoselaw, 548
Hospitallers, Grand Master: see Naillac, Philibert de, 834
Houghton, Adam, Bishop of St. David's, 271, 534, 355
Hungary, xii, 393, 791, 816, 829, 834, 853
Huntingdon, 638, 639
Huntingdon, Earl of: see Holand, Sir John

Illescas, Fernando de, friar, 618
Imworth, Richard, 428
indentures of war, 69, 633, 748–9
Ingham, Sir Oliver, 296
Ireland, 12–13, 63, 199, 223, 355, 368, 405, 407, 570, 628, 644, 646, 734, 736, 776, 815, 822–3, 849, 858, 859, 860, 862
Ireland, Duke of: see Vere, de
Isabel Plantagenet, Countess of Bedford and Soissons, 244
Isabella, Infanta of Castile, Countess of Cambridge, then Duchess of York, 115, 431
Isabella of Mallorca, 708

Isabelle of Bavaria, Queen of France, 551–2, 781, 820, 846, 847

Isabelle of France, Queen of England, 823–5, 827–8, 830, 831, 833, 853, 854, 857

Issigeac, 698

Jacquerie (1358), 419

Jarnac, 704, 709

Jauche, Jean de, lord of Gommegnies, 292, 294, 579

Jean, Philippe de, 168

Jeanne of Anjou, Queen of Naples, 344, 347–8, 393, 438–40

Jedburgh, abbey, 10, 519

Jersey, 136, 185, 304, 843

Joan of France, 826

João, Infante of Portugal, 381, 432, 434, 496, 519, 520, 521, 558, 559, 616, 617

John I, King of Aragon, 708

John, King of Castile, 336, 339, 349, 380, 382–3, 432–4, 436, 461, 466–8, 492–3, 496, 515, 519–21, 522, 523, 531, 533, 535, 558, 559–68, 574–5, 578–9, 581, 582, 595–600, 602, 609–23, 660, 678, 788, 844

John II, King of France, xvi, 9, 16, 17, 54, 267, 270, 386, 404, 746

John I of Avis, King of Portugal, 464–5, 520–2, 532, 552, 559–64, 566–8, 577, 598, 599, 607, 611, 615, 620–1, 677–8

Josselin, castle, 106, 625, 630

jousts, jousting: see tournaments

Jülich, 649

Juliers, county, 662

Jumièges, 65

Juvénal des Ursins, Jean, 668, 802

Kenilworth, castle, 4

Kennington, 257, 262, 275, 437

Kent, county, 37, 135, 153, 183, 286, 287, 288, 386, 421–5, 429, 497, 507, 545, 580, 647, 805, 840

Kent, Joan, Countess of, Princess of Wales and Aquitaine, 275, 283, 423

Kent, Earl of: see Holand, Thomas

Kentwood, Sir John, 411

Kerlouet, Jean de, 28–9, 46, 47, 76

Kilkenny, Council (1360), 12, 13

Kingston, John de, 729

Kingston-on-Thames, 841

Knaresborough, castle, 4, 426, 859

knighthood, 467, 548, 859

Knighton, John, 641, 643

Knolles, Constance, 758

Knolles, Sir Robert, 7, 24, 26, 67–70, 72–5, 80, 84, 85–93, 107, 111, 169, 182, 184, 189, 192, 211, 238, 286, 309, 310–11, 356, 375, 399, 423, 426, 428–9, 496, 506, 510, 523, 545, 552, 731, 735, 740, 742, 745–6, 776

Knyvet, Sir John, 175–6, 252

Korrenzig, 664, 667

Kossovo, battle (1389), 791

La Brosse, 29

La Faigne, 90

La Grange, Jean de, Abbot of Fécamp, then Bishop of Amiens and Cardinal, 224–6, 228, 250, 342, 344

La Heuse, Baudrain de la, 43

La Hogue, 67, 72

La Marche, Jean de Bourbon, Count of (d. 1393), 79

La Marche, Jacques de Bourbon, Count of (d. 1438), 834

La Pallice, 139

La Réole, 74, 299, 331; siege (1374), 205–6

La Rochelle, 4, 37, 109, 110, 119, 121, 137, 138, 146, 149–50, 152, 261, 385, 539, 603, 606, 624, 653–4, 659–60, 694, 750, 807; battle (1372), 139–41, 142; captured (1372), 150, 153–4, 157, 163, 284, 290, 765

La Roche, Hugh de, 81, 83

La Roche-Blanche: see La Roche-Donnezat

La Roche-Derrien, siege (1347), 758

La Roche-Donnezat, 721

La Roche-Posay, 46, 76, 137; captured (1369), 28

La Roche-Senadoire, 210–11

La Roche-Vendeix, siege (1390), 717, 720–1

La Roche-sur-Yon, 110; siege (1369), 30–1, (1372), 159–60

La Rolphie, siege (1391), 721

La Salle, Bernard de, 32, 50, 52, 96, 165–6, 168, 169–70, 208, 210, 245, 248, 347–8, 440, 683, 786

La Salle, Hortingo de, 32

La Souterraine, 32, 96, 145, 148, 210, 758

La Tour, Bernard of, Bishop of Langres, 631

La Tour Landry, Geoffroy de, 738

La Trémoille, Gui de, 725, 803, 834

La Tronchade, fort, captured (1385), 704

Ladislas of Durazzo, King of Naples, 779, 802

Lakenheath, Sir John, 309, 837–8

Lalinde, 77, 239

Lamb, John, 333
Lancaster, Blanche, Duchess of, 3, 116
Lancaster, dukes of: see Grosmont, Gaunt
Langham, Simon, Archbishop of Canterbury, Cardinal, 113–14
Langland, William, 420
Langley, royal manor, 1, 198
Langley, Edmund of, Earl of Cambridge (1362), Duke of York (1385), campaigns (1369–70), 26–7, 28, 29–30, 35, 48–50, 51, 69, 81, 82, 95, 97; (1372), 121, 144; (1374–5), 216, 221, 223–4, 229, 232–3, 234; (1381–2), 381, 383–4, 412, 431–2, 434, 435–7, 459, 461, 463, 469, 470, 475, 492, 564; coastal defence (1376), 284; heir apparent of Richard II, 855; and Bolingbroke's invasion (1399), 858–60; mentioned, 518, 249, 536, 548, 645, 789, 814
Langon, 206; captured (1377), 302; (1378), 331
Languedoc, province, Estates, taxation, 55, 58–60, 97, 127, 200, 206, 243, 247, 368–9, 371, 491–2, 683, 691; routier operations in, 168, 204, 243–4, 247, 372, 384–5, 683–4, 699, 702, 703–8, 708–12, 714–18; Du Guesclin as Captain-General, 384–5, 679, 686; rebellions (1379–80), 369–71; (1380–2), 392, 394, 461, 687–91; projected royal invasion (1382), 469; wars of Armagnac and Foix (1374–82), 679–81, 686–7; Charles VI visits (1389–90), 713, 781
Laon, 189
Latimer, John, friar, 524
Latimer, William lord, 2, 7–8, 74, 107, 173, 176, 214, 217, 219, 225, 227, 238, 249, 254, 258–61, 263–4, 307, 375, 399, 411, 746
Lauderdale, 659
Launac, battle (1362), 769–70
Laval, family, 105, 228
Laval, Guy, lord of, 182, 354, 357–8, 361, 363, 629
Lawgoch, Owen ('Owen of Wales'), 44–5, 128–9, 135–6, 140–1, 144, 150–1, 245, 246, 269, 284, 299, 333
Le Bel, Jean, 753, 755, 767
Le Blanc, 29
Le Crotoy, 6; captured (1369), 35; English attempt on (1378), 304, 323, 327
Le Faon, castle, siege (1385), 703
Le Fèvre, Jean, Abbot of St.-Vaast, then Bishop of Chartres, 266, 521, 602

Le Mans, 89, 358, 390, 797–8, 802, 804
Le Mas d'Agenais, 155
Le Puy, 242, 369–70, 689, 715, 716
Le Roc de la Borde, castle, 684
Le Roux, Alain and Pierre, 714
Le Saillant, castle, 686, 696, 711, 721
Le Soudun, 29
Lectoure, 707
Lee, Sir Walter atte, 69
Legge, John, 427
Leicester, 4, 854
Leiria, 384, 564
Leith, 543
Leland, John, 289
Leo VI of Lusignan, titular King of Armenia, 575, 590, 593, 789, 804, 806, 824
León, city, 598
Léon, province, 122, 433, 594, 599, 606–18
Leonora Teles de Meneses, Queen of Portugal, 144, 202, 380–1, 383, 463–4, 466, 468, 492, 496, 519–21, 522
Leopold Habsburg, Duke of Austria, 246
Lesparre, Florimond de, 141, 204, 206, 239, 493, 693
Lesterps, 50
Leulinghem, 515; conferences (1384), 515–16, 517, 521, 523, 525, 526, 527–8; (1386), 576–7; (1388–9), 674, 675, 677; (1390), 774–5; (1392), 790, 793; (1393), 804–7, 810; (1394), 814, 815; truce (1389), 677, 678, 714, 722, 723, 732, 774, 776, 824, 846; protocol (1393), 807–9, 811–13
Lewes, 282–3, 285, 287
Libourne, 300, 302, 737
Liège, 450, 452, 454, 665, 775
Lille, 457, 479, 480, 482, 588, 662
Lille, castlery, 13
Limoges, 49, 95, 96, 711–12; submission (1370), 79–80; siege (1370), 81–4, 94, 111, 112, 693, 759, 767; submission (1371), 110
Limousin, province, 4, 20, 32, 50, 74, 77–81, 95–6, 98–9, 110, 120, 163–4, 166, 168, 196, 208, 210, 239, 244, 284, 654, 682, 701, 703, 704, 709, 711, 717, 721, 807
Lindsay, Sir James, 658, 659
Lion, Espan de, 727
Lisbon, x, xi, 118, 144, 379, 380, 519–21, 522; siege (1373), 158, 178–9, 187; English at (1381), 434–6, 463, 469; siege (1384), 523, 531–2, 558, 559; castle of San Jorge, 379–80

Lisbon, Martin, Bishop of: see Martin
Lithuania, 256, 791
Litlington, Nicholas, Abbot of Westminster, 586
Lochmaben, castle, 10, 277–8; captured (1384), 518
Logroño, 179, 196, 201, 313, 336, 338, 339, 618
London, and war finance, 71, 176, 217, 254, 259, 273, 305, 308, 356, 378, 453, 454, 459–60, 523, 532, 583–4, 632, 694; war trades, 323, 377, 460, 753; recruits market, 501–2, 730, 731, 741, 777; and the war, 273–4, 477–8, 605, 778, 829, 838, 840; and national politics, 258, 261, 272, 272–5, 354, 407, 437, 514, 660, 839, 843; internal politics, 260, 284; and Peasants' Revolt (1381), 423–9, 443; defences, 278, 386, 545, 586; spies in, 289, 290–1, 455, 474; and the Appellants (1387–8), 632, 635–6, 637, 638, 641, 644; Aldgate, 424, 425; Cheapside, 122, 275, 428; Coldharbour, 838; London Bridge, 424, 428, 429; Ludgate Hill, 275, 425; Marshalsea Prison, 273, 424; Newgate Prison, 290, 345, 425; Savoy Palace, 4, 95, 101, 122, 275, 425; St. Bartholomew's Priory and Hospital, 428, 429; St. John's, Clerkenwell, 425, 429; St. Paul's Cathedral, 70, 101, 183, 255, 272–3, 274, 275, 283, 425, 617, 854; St. Paul's Cross, 493; Smithfield, 428, 429, 577, 724, 783; Strand, 4, 122, 425; Tower, 68, 144, 260, 273, 277, 279, 294, 423–7, 514, 604, 641–2, 644, 770, 815, 839, 842, 844, 862; mentioned, 1, 9, 43, 67, 70, 95, 120, 122, 174, 197, 213, 222–3, 255, 277, 309, 345, 421, 488, 493, 494, 497, 506, 514, 529, 540, 541, 552, 577, 585, 617, 655, 724, 783, 784, 837, 841, 862, 863
London, treaty (1373), 183
longbow, longbowmen, 96, 329, 730–1, 751
Lopes, Fernão, 118, 383, 606
Lorraine, duchy, 246, 584
Lorraine, John, Duke of, 389
Lothian, district, 285, 548–9, 557, 656, 476
Louis IX, King of France, 15, 391, 393, 578
Louis of France, Duke of Touraine, then of Orléans, 668–9, 780–2, 785, 797, 800–2, 809, 816–17, 819–20, 829, 833, 847, 856–7
Louis the Great, King of Hungary, 393
Lourdes, castle, 707, 764
Louroux, 88

Louvain, 450
Lovell, John lord, 736
Luçon, Bishop of: see Guy
Lucy family, 10
Luna, Pedro de: see Benedict XIII
Lusignan, castle, 29, 159, 758; siege (1374), 160–1, 215
Lussac, battle (1369), 47, 76
Luttrell, Sir Geoffrey, 730
Luxembourg, 662, 665, 846
Lyembois, Jacquet de, 732
Lyon, 245, 491, 782
Lyons, Richard, 176, 217, 254, 258–61, 271, 273, 307, 426, 428

Maastricht, 665
Machecoul, castle, 770
Mâcon, 347
Madaillan, lords of, 301
Mahdia, 790–1
Maidstone, 421, 422, 427
Maignelay, Tristan de, 764, 768, 772
Mainwaring, Sir William, 737
Maillezais, bishop of: see Faye, Guy de
Maillotins, revolt of (1382), 444–9, 541
Mâle, 458
Mâle, Louis de: see Flanders
Malestroit, Jean de, 248, 348
Mallorca, kingdom, 331, 708
Man, Isle of, 655, 842
Manrique, Juan García, Archbishop of Santiago, 598, 609, 621
Mansel, Philip, captain of La Rochelle, 153–4
Mantua, 758
Manuel II Palaeologos, Byzantine Emperor, 738, 843
maps, 754
Marans, 154, 653
march law, 11, 240, 513, 718–20
March, George Dunbar, Earl of (Scotland), 10, 285, 518
March, Edmund Mortimer, Earl of (d. 1381), 216, 253, 256, 260, 264, 271, 405, 741
March, Roger Mortimer, Earl of (d. 1398), 641, 838, 849
Marchès, Mérigot, 169, 316, 684, 686, 692, 693, 695, 698, 711, 712, 714, 717, 720–1, 773
Marcigny, 193–4
Mare, Sir Peter de la, 253, 257–8, 260, 264, 271–2, 275, 284, 307
Marennes, 150–1

Marets, Jean des, 490
Mareuil, Raymond de, 78, 151
Margaret of Durazzo, Queen of Naples, 782, 802
Margate, 604, 636
marshals, 200, 358, 507, 564, 586, 729, 746, 747
Marino, battle (1379), 347
Marlborough, 357
Marmousets, 625–7, 670, 673, 674, 783, 784, 786, 796, 797, 800–2
Marquise, 753
Marseille, 111, 265, 440, 782, 803, 804
Martel, 166, 703, 717
Martin, Bishop of Lisbon, 435, 492
Martinez, Alvaro, 618–19
Mascy, Sir James, 19, 34, 46, 52, 758
Mascy, Sir John, 805
Mauléon, Le Bascot de, 533, 687, 727
Mauny, Olivier de, 142
Mauny, Sir Walter, 36
Mauron, battle (1352), 764–5
Mauvinet, Guillaume, 157
Mayet, 89
Mazères, 689, 690–1
Meaux, Marché fortress, 770
Mechelen, 13, 581
medicine, 761, 762
Medina del Campo, 616–17, 619; Cortes (1381), 433
Melbourne, Thomas, Treasurer of Brittany, 119, 182
Melrose, 549
Melun, 15, 56, 60, 114, 224, 394, 448, 781
Melun, Guillaume de, Archbishop of Sens, 17, 793
Mélusine, 161, 758
men-at-arms, 728–30, 738–9, 740–1, 747, 748–9, 753, 762, 764, 766, 770
Menagier de Paris, 764
Mende, 684
Mennot, Robert de ('Robert the Hermit'), 804, 806–7, 823, 828–9, 832
Menta, Geraud de, 336, 338, 374–5, 381–2, 469
Menton, 37
Mercer, Andrew, 316
Mercer, John, of Perth, 270
Mercier, Jean le, 218, 236, 245, 328, 626, 668, 796, 800, 801
Mercoeur, castle, 684
Merida, 599
Merle, castles, 170
Mertola, siege (1385), 560

Merville, 480
Meschin, Hélie ('Petit Meschin'), 24, 25
Messines, 483
Mézières, Philippe de, 1, 164, 289, 671–2, 694, 714, 728, 733, 745, 751, 756, 757, 762, 775–6, 778, 783, 789, 791–2, 804, 806, 824, 835
Michelet, Jules, 826
Middelburg[h], 172, 488, 534, 539, 579, 581, 585
Middlesex, Under-sheriff of: see Usk, Thomas
Milan, 752, 753, 782, 785, 836
Milan, Dukes of: see Visconti
Mile End, 427, 428, 429, 473
Milford Haven, 269, 815, 858, 860
Millau, 4, 19, 33–5, 45–6, 758
mines, miners, mining, 82, 232, 325, 543, 730, 759
Minsterworth, Sir John, 69, 87, 89, 91–3, 269, 277
Moissac, 22, 33, 51, 76, 143, 199–201, 207
Molyneux, Sir Thomas, 638
Monaco, 37, 125, 320
Moncontour, castle, 40; siege (1371), 109; (1372), 138
Moncuq, castle, 300
Mondeville, Henri de, 761
money, coinage, devaluation, 54, 123, 171, 414, 522, 539, 559, 595
Monmouth, Henry of, 858
Mons, Aimery de, Bishop of Poitiers, 76
Mont-St.-Quentin, abbey, 388
Montague, Sir John: see Salisbury, Earl of
Montaigu, Jean de, 668, 800
Montargis, castle, 15, 60, 363, 364, 365, 474, 477
Montauban, 4, 19, 21–2, 24, 33, 78, 98, 205, 683, 706, 708, 753, 762
Montaut family, 52
Montaut, Amanieu de, 717, 718, 719, 721
Montaut, Raymond de, lord of Mussidan, 239, 240–1, 295, 297, 299, 301, 332, 693
Montbrun, castle, 717, 719
Montebourg, 72, 328–9, 759
Montereau, 652, 662
Montet, Bernard de, 765
Montfaucon, 721, 732, 809
Montferrand, 684, 711
Montferrand, Guillaume de, 564
Montfort, John de: see Brittany
Montiel, castle, 115
Montjoie, Louis de, 347, 802
Montlaur, 34

Montlhéry, 800
Montlieu, siege (1385), 704
Montmartre, 732
Montmor, Jacques de, 521
Montmor, Morelet de, 136, 150, 151, 152
Montpellier, town, 59, 125, 168, 369–71, 395
Montpellier, lordship, 64, 65, 94
Montpon, captured (1370), 77; siege (1371), 97–8
Montreuil, conference (1377), 278–80
Montreuil-Bonnin, 29; captured, 228–9
Montrose, 526
Montsac, Le Bourc de, 706
Montvalent, 315–16, 695
Moray, John Dunbar, Earl of, 657
Morieux, Sir Thomas, 596, 616–17
Morlaix, 120; battle (1342), 760
Morley, Thomas lord, 736
Morpeth, 548
Mortagne-sur-Sèvre, siege (1372), 159, 160
Mortagne-sur-Gironde, siege (1378), 332–3; conference (1388), 660
Mortain, siege (1378), 320, 321
Mortimer, Sir Thomas, 843
Moulins, 194
Mowbray, Sir Thomas, Earl of Nottingham (1385), Duke of Norfolk (1397), 280, 473, 548, 638–9, 645, 673, 674–6, 723, 826, 840–1, 842, 844, 849, 850–3, 862
Murad, Sultan, 791
Muro, 440
Musgrave, Sir Thomas, 285
Mussidan, 693
Mussidan, lords of: see Montaut
musters, 729, 741, 749–51, 761

Naillac, Philibert, Grand Master of the Hospitallers, 834
Nájera, battle (1367), xvii, 20, 68, 105, 138, 180, 256, 282, 296, 331, 431, 607, 617, 620, 769, 771
Nantes, 27, 31, 65, 153, 175, 182, 352, 357, 358, 363, 365, 374, 631; siege (1380–1), 397–9, 404–5, 409, 410, 442, 755
Nantwich, 731, 743
Naples, xii, 347, 393–5, 439–40, 779–80, 782, 802; Castel Nuovo, Castel S. Elmo, 439, 779, 782; Castel dell'Ovo, 347; S. Chiara, 440
Narbonne, 684, 688
Narbonne, Aimery de, Admiral of France, 125
naval warfare, 125–6, 138, 139, 362

Navarre, xi, 118, 122, 197, 200, 201, 277, 321–2, 323, 334, 336–8, 339, 340, 432, 622
naval forces, Bayonne, 203, 316; Castile, 38, 123–4, 129, 139, 141, 150, 158, 180, 186–7, 203–4, 219, 238–9, 268–9, 279, 294, 306, 360, 362, 379, 385–6, 433–4, 436, 462, 523, 532, 558, 581, 594, 600, 606, 622, 650; England, 36–7, 42, 64, 72, 131–4, 135, 138–41, 144, 145, 153, 172, 173–5, 181, 183, 185, 199, 216–17, 221, 222–3, 237, 239, 276, 278, 279, 280, 308–10, 315, 316, 323–7, 362, 367–8, 376–9, 410, 431, 454, 542–3, 544, 580, 582–3, 584, 585, 586, 594, 652–4; Flanders, 14, 183, 494; France, 18, 37, 125–6, 126, 136, 186, 268–9, 279, 281–3, 285, 286–7, 294, 317, 324–5, 362, 385–7, 538–9, 555–6, 582, 585, 590–1, 592, 603, 603–4, 624; Genoa, 124, 134–5, 174; Monaco, 37–8, 125, 136, 320; Portugal, 118, 178, 279, 380, 382, 431, 433–4, 522, 552–3, 577, 582, 594, 622, 649, 652
Navarre, Kings of: see Charles II, Charles III
Navarre, Pierre de, 318, 669
Nebouzan, 680
Neilhac, Guillaume de, 602, 612, 618, 621, 744
Nemours, 317
Nevers, John, Count of, later Duke of Burgundy ('the Fearless'), 669, 829, 834
Neville family, 10, 548, 654
Neville, Alexander, Archbishop of York, 632, 636–7, 640, 643, 654, 673
Neville, John, lord of Raby, Earl of Cumberland (1385), 135, 145, 153, 156–7, 176, 182, 183–6, 260, 261, 305–6, 315, 323, 324, 330, 331–3, 336, 338, 356, 374, 538, 569–70, 675, 692, 741, 750, 766–7
Neville, Ralph, Earl of Westmoreland (1397), 632, 636–7, 640, 643, 673, 844
Neville, Robert, 120, 131
Neville, Sir William, 173, 791
Neville's Cross, battle (1346) xvi, 9, 763, 765
Newbattle, abbey, 549
Newcastle, 10, 518, 544, 548, 549–50, 655, 657, 658
Nicopolis, battle (1396), 669, 737, 834–5, 854
Nieuport, 498
Nîmes, 369, 370, 395, 686
Niort, 32, 137, 138, 149, 154, 159–60
Noirmoutier, 653

Nontron, 294

Norbury, Sir John, 737, 855

Norfolk, Duke of: see Mowbray, Sir Thomas

Normandy, province, xv, 37, 63, 65–7, 71,
85, 87, 231–7, 245, 279, 305, 311–12,
313, 314, 315, 316, 362, 368, 391, 442,
446, 448–9, 539, 578, 582, 630, 652–3,
734, 736, 737, 739, 797, 826, 828;
campaigns (1369), 42–3; (1371), 102–3;
(1374–5), 218–22, 223–4; (1378), 317,
318–30; Estates, 218, 222, 236, 403–4,
405

Northampton, 407–8

Northumberland, county, 10, 68, 285, 513,
526, 547–8, 656–7, 674–5, 676, 791

Northumberland, Henry, lord Percy, Duke of
(1377), 187, 274–5, 283, 286, 356, 426,
531, 544, 548, 636–7, 859, 861–2

Nottingham, 43, 264, 276, 284, 353, 545,
634, 771, 772, 840

Nottingham, Earl of: see Mowbray, Sir
Thomas

Noyon, 84, 631

Noyon, Jean de, 732–3

Nuñez de Guzman, Gonzalo, Master of
Alcántara, 566

Offington, Hamo of, Abbot of Battle, 281

Oléron, island, 139, 150

Olite, castle, 312, 334, 340

Olmedo, 619

Oporto, 118, 383, 522, 531, 532, 559, 606,
607, 622

ordinances of war, 546, 747–8

Orense, 595, 597, 608, 618–19

Orfordness, 545

Orgemont, Pierre d', 279, 491

Oriflamme, 38, 469, 485, 503, 545, 689

Orléans, 85, 447, 469, 474, 477, 491, 513,
517, 534, 631, 648, 652, 770

Orléans, Charles, Duke of, 770

Orléans, Louis, Duke of: see Louis of France

Orléans, Philip Duke of, 189

Orléans, Valentine Visconti, Duchess of,
780, 781, 809, 820, 827

Orthez, 533, 622, 679, 81, 727

Orvieto, 248

Orwell, 542, 604, 605

Osorio, Alvaro Perez de, 609

Ostrevant, Count of: see Hainault, William
of Bavaria, Count of

Otterburn, battle (1388), 657–9

Otto of Brunswick, 439

Oulchy-le-Château, 191

Oudenaarde, 449; siege (1382), 458, 462,
476, 477, 480, 483–4, 486; captured
(1382), 509; (1384), 517

Oxford, 288, 583–4, 656, 860; University,
830; New College, 264

Oxford, Robert de Vere, Earl of: see Vere, de

Oxford, Thomas de Vere, Earl of, 41

Orchies, castlery, 13

Owen of Wales: see Lawgoch

Pacheco, Diego Lopez de, 150, 158

Pacy, 320

Padilla, Maria de, 115

pages, 245, 249, 299, 731

Pailhas, Raymond de, 337

Palencia, 609, 623; Cortes (1388), 623

Pamplona, 312, 313, 314, 336, 337, 339,
469, 622, 823

Paris, and national politics, 400–1;
buildings, 60, 400, 625; institutions, 401,
402, 442, 445, 446, 490, 668, 794, 802;
revolution (1357–8), xvi, 15, 85, 480,
489–90; Estates-General at (1369), 57;
(1380–1), 399–400, 404; Councils at
(1369), 113; (1370), 74, 76, 80; (1371),
126, 129; (1377), 277; (1378), 345–6;
(1382), 469; (1386), 578; (1387), 602–3;
(1388), 651; (1390), 782; (1392), 796;
(1395), 819; (1398), 845; threatened by
Knolles (1370), 85–6, 256; tax revolt
(1380–3), 396, 400, 402–3, 441, 442–3,
444–9, 479–80, 489–91; festivities, 399,
668–9; war industries, 753; attempted
murder of O. de Clisson (1392), 793–5;
Louis of Orléans in (1391), 856–8; Bastille
St.-Antoine, 60, 85, 401, 490; Celestine
convent, 1, 85; Châtelet, 201, 273, 317,
401, 403, 443, 446–7, 489, 580, 699,
720–1, 732–3; Les Halles, 321, 444–5,
714, 721, 794; Hôtel d'Artois, 441, 828;
Hôtel de Clisson, 625, 854; Hôtel de Nesle,
602; Hôtel St.-Pol, 15, 16, 56, 85, 86, 214,
394, 800, 817, 820, 827, 829, 856; Île de
la Cité, 15, 57, 357, 394, 399, 469, 816;
Louvre, 56, 60, 84; Maison aux Piliers,
402, 445; Notre-Dame, 149, 346, 391;
Petit Châtelet, 401; Place de Grève, 402,
403, 445, 801; Porte de la Bordelle, 84, 85;
Porte St.-Antoine, 85, 445, 490; Porte St.-
Denis, 489; Royal Palace (Île de la Cité),
15, 819; Sainte-Chapelle, 262, 819, 828;
Temple Prison, 319, 320; mentioned, 1, 13,
15, 35, 38, 42, 50, 55, 61, 71, 78, 87, 91,
104, 110, 114, 127, 129, 130, 145, 149,

159, 163, 169, 188, 191, 194, 223, 227, 234, 245, 262, 178, 289, 312, 313, 314, 317, 318, 319, 321, 340, 343, 357, 371, 390, 391, 396, 399, 417, 432, 517-18, 535, 557, 575, 580, 591, 601-2, 605, 652, 653, 688, 692, 702, 707, 714, 720-1, 725, 784-5, 800, 802, 818, 820, 826, 827-8, 829, 836, 847, 863
Paris, Treaty (1396), 827-8
Paris, University of, 225, 345, 447, 817, 819
Parlement of Paris, 27, 106, 200, 321, 352, 354, 441, 447, 476, 488, 490, 576, 626, 668, 670, 774, 795, 801, 857
Parliament of England, (1369), 36, 62; (1371), 99-102, 176; (1372), 171, 173, 175; (1373), 186, 196, 198-9; (1376), 177, 252-61, 262-3, 264, 265, 271, 274, 419, 741; (Jan. 1377), 271-2, 274, 275-7; (Oct. 1377), 307-8, 313, 419; (1378), 345, 354-5; (1379), 359-60; (Jan. 1380), 373-4, 375-6, 376-7, 386, 406; (Nov. 1380), 406-8, 419; (1381-2), 429-30, 427-8; (May 1382), 454, 458-60; (Oct. 1382), 469-70, 475-6; (Feb. 1383), 494-5; (Oct. 1383), 510, 511, 512, 514; (May 1384), 523-5, 529; (1385), 569-70, 572-3; (1386), 330, 586-9, 592-3; (Feb. 1388), 637, 642-6, 647; (Sept. 1388), 656, 660-1; (Feb. 1390), 718; (1391), 788; (1393), 805; (1394), 811-14, 827; (Jan. 1397), 835-6; (1397-8), 840, 841-3, 849, 851-2; 853; (1399), 862-3, 864
Parliament of Ireland, 12
Parliament of Scotland, 116
Parr, Sir John, 577
Parthenay, Guillaume Larchevèque, lord of, 159, 161
Parthenay, Geoffrey de, 533, 567
Parys, Robert, 378, 542
Passat, Gaucher de, 602, 612, 618, 621, 704-5, 708, 744
Passion, Order of the, 791-2, 806
patis, 8, 72, 103, 185, 210, 239, 241, 242, 243, 246, 251, 254, 286, 311, 653, 687, 696, 698, 707-8, 717, 742, 743, 828, 832, 837
Paulesholt, 67
Paulhe, 19, 34, 46
pay: see war wages
Paynel, Nicholas, 853
Peasants' Revolt (1381), 413, 419-30, 471, 472, 541
Pedro I, King of Castile, xvii, 38, 115-17, 118, 120, 123, 142, 145, 179, 196, 203,

492, 572, 594, 597, 600, 613, 771
Pedro I, King of Portugal, 118, 381, 464
Pembroke, John Hastings, Earl of, 26-9, 31-2, 46-7, 69, 81, 82, 95, 100-1, 104, 120, 121, 129, 135, 138-43, 740, 745, 768
Penne d'Agenais, siege (1372), 155
Penne d'Albigeois, siege (1383), 701, 702, 703; (1384), 704-5
Penrith, 405, 518
Penthièvre, Jeanne, Countess of, wife of Charles of Blois, 104, 106, 354, 357-8, 361, 627
Penthièvre, John of Blois, Count of, 353, 357, 412, 627-30, 643, 795
Percy family, 10
Percy, Henry, lord: see Northumberland, Earl of
Percy, Sir Henry ('Hotspur'), 280, 550, 633, 657-9, 719, 723, 859
Percy, Richard, Seneschal of Saintonge (1372), 151
Percy, Sir Thomas, Earl of Worcester (1397), 108-9, 142, 146, 149-50, 151, 161, 310, 311, 356, 364, 375, 387, 399, 411, 542, 548, 597, 619, 621, 648-9, 652, 653, 746, 770, 771, 772, 783, 784-5, 791, 793, 884, 860
Pereira, Nun' Alvarez, Constable of Portugal, 465, 522, 559, 563, 564-5, 607-8, 610, 614, 577
Perez de Castro, Alvaro, Count of Arraialos, Constable of Portugal, 492
Périgord, province, 20, 25, 27, 51, 52, 78, 95, 158-9, 162, 163-4, 239, 682, 693, 695, 701, 704, 719, 721, 783, 807, 857; campaigns (1370), 77, 80; (1371), 97-8; (1375-6), 239-41, 251; (1377), 294-5, 297-300, 301, 303; (1387), 710
Périgord, Archambaud V, Count of, 27
Périgord, Archambeau VI, Count of, 857
Périgord, Talleyrand de, 27
Périgueux, 51, 52, 77, 239-40, 717
Péronne, 388, 477
Perrers, Alice, 176-7, 258-61, 263, 270-1, 274, 280, 284, 307, 465, 768
Perrin de Savoie, 24, 25
Perrot de Béarn ('le Béarnais'): see Fontans, Perrot de
Pert, Sir John, 107, 145
Perth, 316; siege (1335), 265
Perthus, Col de, 715
Perugia, 248, 782
Pesaro, 728

Peter IV, King of Aragon, 115, 122, 196–7, 202–3, 233–4, 333, 336, 338, 382, 469–70, 558, 708
Petit, Jean, 732
Pevensey, 287, 288, 858
Peyrusse, 717, 721
Philip IV the Fair, King of France, xv
Philip VI, King of France, xv, 15, 16, 37, 105, 386, 789
Philippa of Hainault, Queen of England, 176, 453, 726
Philippa of Lancaster, Queen of Portugal, 201, 569, 599, 606
Philpot, John, 308, 316, 386, 459, 507, 523
Picardy, province, 5, 37, 42, 84, 221, 305, 323, 366–7, 395–6, 442, 447, 484, 489, 539, 555, 580, 723, 738, 743, 858
Pickering, 859
Picque, Richard, Archbishop of Reims, 666
Pierre-Buffière, castle, 96
Piers Plowman, 420
Pintoin, Michel, 443, 806
pioneers, 754
Pipe, Sir James, 772
Pisan, Christine de, xii, 15, 75, 289, 390, 671, 726, 728
Pitti, Buonaccorso, 445, 446, 449, 485, 508–9, 591
Pleshey, manor, 576, 828, 839
Plymouth, 95, 122, 135, 138, 145, 183, 184, 222–3, 228, 285, 324, 379, 409, 410, 431, 543, 577, 580, 581, 582, 594, 749, 815
Plympton, priory, 95
Poitiers, 29, 30, 47, 76, 138, 142, 151, 152, 161, 294; battle (1356), xvi, 1, 6, 9, 16, 17, 20, 21, 24, 41, 44, 68, 95, 128, 137, 152, 191, 215, 256, 269–70, 296, 375, 431, 566, 636, 730, 733, 759, 764–5, 766, 767, 771, 835; captured (1372), 148–9, 162
Poitiers, bishop of: see Mons, Aimery de
Poitou, province, campaigns (1369), 27–32; (1369–70), 46–8; (1370), 76; (1371), 108–10; (1372), 127, 136–43, 146–52; 153–5, 158–63, 757, 763; mentioned, 4, 15, 20, 21, 49, 79, 81, 87, 91, 109, 164, 171, 181, 215, 228–9, 243, 294, 472, 603–4, 625, 630, 701, 703, 704, 736, 788, 789–90, 826
Pole, Sir Edmund, 646
Pole, Sir Michael, Earl of Suffolk (1385), 420, 472–3, 511–14, 523–5, 529, 530–1, 548, 569–70, 577, 586–7, 589, 632, 634, 636–8, 640, 642, 643, 673, 777
Pole, William, 459
Pollehay, Jean ('Le Moine') and Eustache ('Rifflart') de, 102–3
Pommiers, Guillaume Sans, lord of, 296–7
Pons, Renaud, lord of, 151, 155, 758
Pont, Thibault du, 96, 151
Pont-l'Abbé, 219
Pont-de-Sorgues, 248
Pontailler, Guy de, Marshal of Burgundy, 737
Pont-Audemer, siege (1378), 320
Pont-St.-Esprit, 244, 247
Ponte do Mouro, conference (1386), 599, 607, 752
Pontefract, castle, 4, 426, 505, 859, 863
Pontoise, 448
Pontorson, 107, 361, 365, 368, 631
Ponthieu, county, 4, 6, 35
Ponts-de-Cé, 32
Pontvallain, battle (1370), 89–90, 93, 219, 256, 798
Poperinghe, 483; sacked (1382), 498
Port-Ste.-Marie, 51, 143, 693
Porto de Mos, castle, 563
Portsmouth, 125, 126, 656
Portugal, 117, 118–19, 122, 144–5, 150, 383–4, 492–3, 496–7, 577, 677–8; campaign in (1372), 157–8, 178–9; Earl of Cambridge in (1381–2), 431–8, 462–9; war of succession (1383–5), 519–23, 531–3, 558–68, 737; John of Gaunt in (1386–7), 599, 608, 618–19, 752
Poynings, Richard lord, 749
Prague, 753
Prata, Pileo de, Archbishop of Ravenna, Cardinal, 213–16, 221, 350
Prignano, Bartolomeo: see Urban VI, Pope
prisoners of war, 43, 83, 90, 91–2, 141–2, 159, 169, 186, 192, 232, 244–5, 282–3, 294, 297, 301, 366–7, 601, 610, 680, 699, 711–12, 714, 742, 765–73
professional soldiers, 733–8, 739, 742–6, 759, 760–1, 762, 776, 792, 805, 811
protection, letters of, 749
Provana, Jacopo, 134, 174, 180, 182–3
Provence, province, 244, 533, 709, 780, 786, 802
Prussia, 736, 737, 791, 816, 853, 854, 855
Purnon, 47
Puyguilhem, 693; siege (1338), 224
Pyel, John, 217

Queensborough, castle, 260, 288, 640–1

Quercy, province, campaign (1369–70), 18, 19–20, 21, 22–4, 27, 28, 32–3, 76–7, 170; *routier* operations, 52, 164–8, 205, 242–3, 315–16, 682–3, 695, 699–701, 706, 709, 711, 712, 715, 716–17, 718, 719; Estates, 242–3; mentioned, 783, 807
Quimperlé, 234–5, 237

Rabastens, battle (1381), 690, 691
Rabelais, François, 49
Radcot Bridge, battle (1387), 639–40, 641, 843, 851
Ramírez, Juan, de Arellano, 338, 567
ransoms (personal), 9, 50, 83, 92, 96, 103, 128, 138, 141–2, 160, 161, 168, 232, 235, 242, 274, 282–3, 301, 329, 366–7, 425, 508, 605, 699, 712, 731, 742, 765–9, 769, 770, 771–3
Ratcliffe, 309, 377
Rauzan, lords of, 299
Ré, island, 139
Reading, Great Council (1385), 544
Réalville, siege (1369), 24
recruitment, 68, 184, 532–3, 729, 740–1
Redmayne, Sir Mathew, 69, 237, 657–8
Reigate, 635–6, 838
Reims, 68, 247, 388, 397–8, 447, 479, 491; siege (1359), 755; Council (1388), 665–7
Reims, Archbishop of: see Picque, Richard
Renaud, Jean, Mayor of Poitiers, 137, 148–9
Rennes, 156–7, 181, 357–8, 364, 396–7
Retz, family, 105
Revel, 690
reviews, 153–4, 751
Rhuddlan, castle, 861
Richard I ('Coeur de Lion'), King of England, 22, 205
Richard II, King of England, youth, 265, 275, 279, 280; accession, minority, 281, 283–4; personality, 472, 494, 511, 814–15; and Peasants;' Revolt (1381), 424, 427, 428, 429; marriage (1382), 472; friendships, 473, 524, 537, 606, 826; and John of Gaunt, 537, 572–3, 576–7, 623, 718–19, 812, 828; invasion of Scotland (1385), 545, 548–9; attitude to war, 297, 506, 576, 584, 585–6, 734, 787, 788, 804, 809, 811, 823–5, 827, 837–8, 864; and crisis of 1386–9, 583–4, 587–8, 588–9, 592–3, 631–2, 633–42, 646, 674, 806–7; and papal schism, 822; and treaty of Paris (1396), 828–9, 830–3, 835–6, 844–5; and fall of the Appellants (1397), 838–44;

'tyranny' (1397–9), 847–9; and Bolingbroke (1398–9), 849–55, 861–2; mentioned, 313, 724, 825
Richford, Sir John, 736
Richmond, honour, 7, 131, 184, 305–6, 412
Rickhill, Sir William, 840–1
Rillé, castle, 88, 91
Rillington, Robert, 289
Rimini, 782
Rising, castle, 648
Rivière, Bureau de la, 17, 236, 245, 279, 352–3, 357, 364, 391, 392, 394, 396, 626, 668, 770, 796, 797, 800, 801
Roales, 613
Roanne, 194
Robert II Stewart, King of Scotland, 128, 269–70, 426, 523, 526–7, 530–1, 543, 546, 556, 654, 676–7
Robert of Geneva, Cardinal: see Clement VII, Pope
Robert the Hermit: see Mennot, Robert de
Robert of Namur, 423
Robesart, Thierry ('Canon'), 367, 431, 463, 540
Robynet, John, 276
Rocamadour, 25
Rochechouart, Louis Viscount of, 78, 96, 732
Rochefort, family, 228
Roches, Sir John, 313, 317
Rochester, 255, 421, 427
Rodez, 4, 34, 242, 698–9, 707, 709–11, 720
Roermond, 664
Roger, family; see Clement VI, Pope; Gregory XI, Pope; Beaufort
Roger, Guillaume, Viscount of Turenne, 80, 112, 212, 316
Rohan, family, 105, 228
Rohan, John, Viscount of, 181, 189, 352, 354, 357–8, 361, 363, 364
Rome, 340–1, 346, 438–9, 471, 776, 785, 845; Castel S. Angelo, 346, 347; S. Maria Nuova (Romana), 340; Vatican basilica and palace, 340, 341, 346, 438
Roncevalles, pass, 336, 618
Roos, Sir Robert, 204, 675
Roosebeke, battle (1382), 484–6
Roquefort, 116
Roquefort, Aimery de, 116, 688, 690
Roquemaure, castle, 168, 268
Roquenatou, castle, 712, 716
Rose, Sir Edmund, 136
Rotherhithe, 279
Rottingdean, 282

Rouen, xvi, 32, 38, 39, 40, 42, 56, 59, 65, 321, 403–4, 491, 630; Harelle (1382), 443–4, 447, 449, 479; Arsenal, 37, 43, 125, 173, 186, 268, 279, 316, 317, 324, 360, 377, 386, 387, 650, 753

Rouergue, province, 20, 21, 807; campaigns (1369–70), 18–19, 33–5, 45–6, 52; *routier* operations, 165, 166, 168, 241, 242, 303, 682, 690, 695, 699, 705, 706, 709, 710, 712, 715, 717, 719; Estates, 703

Rougecok, John, 290

Roussillon, province, 374, 712, 715, 717

Roxburgh, 10, 285, 405, 519, 547, 550, 675, 676

Roye, 188

Roye, Mathieu de, 142

Roye, Renaud de, 616, 723–4

Rue, Jacques de, 72, 201, 314, 317, 318, 320, 321, 322

Russell, Hugh, 34

Rushook, Thomas, Bishop of Chichester, 644, 646

Rutland: see Edward of Cambridge

Rye, 42, 77, 281, 282, 287, 288, 316, 580

Rye, Jean de, 129–30, 150, 152, 533, 566, 567

Sablé, 794

Sabraham, Nicholas de, 736

Sahagún, 621

St. Albans, 429, 506

St.-Antonin, 690, 699

St.-Brieuc, siege (1375), 229, 234–5

St.-Cloud, 448

St.-Denis-en-Caux, 36–7

St.-Denis-en-France, abbey, 38, 385, 391, 396, 443, 448, 469, 503, 545, 668, 669, 689, 724, 725, 858

St.-Emilion, 300, 301, 302, 709–10

St.-Exupéry, castle, 721

St.-Flour, 242, 684, 686, 695–6, 698

St.-Gaudens, 680

St.-Germain-en-Laye, 15, 60

St.-Ingelvert, jousts (1389), 723–4, 733, 737, 805, 854

St.-Jean d'Angély, 146, 150, 155

St.-Jean-Pied-de-Port, 322, 334, 336

St.-Lô, 220, 222, 234

St.-Macaire, 693; siege (1374), 206; siege (1377), 295, 302, 304

St-Malo, 26–7, 104, 304, 362, 363, 365, 366; siege (1373), 181–2, 183, 186; (1378), 323, 325–7, 354, 355

St.-Mathieu, 91, 221, 228, 238, 251, 582

St.-Maur, 31, 88, 91, 92

St.-Nicolas-la-Grave, castle, 22

St.-Omer, 5, 39, 84, 188, 250, 480–1, 516, 831

St. Peter Port, 136

St.-Pol, Gui de Luxembourg, Count of (d. 1371), 39, 42–3, 61, 85

St.-Pol, Matilda Courtenay (Holand), Countess of, 366–7, 665, 669

St.-Pol, Waleran de Luxembourg, Count of (d. 1415), 366–7, 579, 770, 783, 789, 829, 838, 853

St.-Pourçain, 194

St.-Quentin, 189, 396

St.-Sauveur-de-Pierrepont, 219

St.-Sauveur-le-Vicomte, castle, 5, 6, 32, 66–7, 72, 87, 88, 91, 93–4, 102, 103, 136, 154, 170, 215, 768; siege (1369), 31–2, 65, 217; (1372), 217–18; (1373), 218; (1374–5), 218–24, 228, 230–3, 236–7, 238, 245, 259, 261, 279, 754

St.-Savin-sur-Gartempe, 46, 76

St.-Vaast-la-Hougue, 328, 329

St.-Valéry, 37

Ste.-Adresse, 37

Ste.-Sévère, 96, 99, 145–6

Saintonge, province, 4, 20, 21, 127, 140, 146, 239, 240, 279, 332, 693, 695, 701, 721–2, 783, 807, 826; campaign (1372), 154–5, 171; (1385), 703–4; (1387), 709–10; (1388), 653–4, 659–60.

Salamanca, 609, 612, 616, 617, 618

Salies, Garcie-Arnaud de, 313, 314, 323

Salisbury, 289, 523–4

Salisbury, John, 646

Salisbury, John Montague, Earl of (d. 1400), 478, 854, 858, 859, 860–1, 863

Salisbury, William Montague, Earl of (d. 1397), 41, 122, 144, 174, 181–7, 278–9, 280, 284–5, 286, 324, 423, 478, 536, 537, 675, 759

Salmon, Pierre, 853

Salomon, John, 488

Saltes, battle (1381), 433–4, 468

Saltwood, castle, 288

Salutati, Coluccio, Chancellor of Florence, 111

Salvaterra de Magos, treaty (1383), 416, 519

Salvatierra, 179

Sancerre, Girard de, 732

Sancerre, Louis de, Marshal of France, 22, 46, 48, 50, 76, 79, 87, 89–91, 110, 127, 145, 146, 156, 162, 194, 230, 240, 246–7,

294, 332, 357, 409, 441, 603–4, 605, 659–60, 695–6, 702, 704, 709, 713, 771

Sánchez de Tovar, Fernán, Admiral of Castile, 187, 204, 433–4, 436, 532

Sandwich, 36, 41, 144–5, 153, 183, 288, 309, 379, 385, 497, 572, 580, 585, 603

Sanlucar de Barrameda, battle (1370), 118

San Sebastian, 204

Santander, 124, 141, 150, 382, 579

Santarém, 178, 384, 437, 520, 521–2, 523, 567; treaty (1373), 179, 180, 379

Santiago de Compostela, 594, 595–6, 601

Santiago, military order (Castile), 158, 432, 436

Santiago, military order (Portugal), 522

Santo Domingo de la Calzada, 179–80, 339

São Jorge, 565

Sarlat, 77

Sarrebruch, John, Count of, 17

Saumur, 28, 31, 46, 91

Sauveterre (Rouergue), 19, 46

Savona, 820

Savoy, county, 556, 584

Savoy, Amadeus VI, Count of (d. 1383), 200, 348

Savoy, Amadeus VII, Count of (d. 1391), 758

Savoy, Bastard of, 687

Say, Sir Digory, 29, 47, 159, 161, 163, 215, 228, 278, 758

Scarborough, 289, 426

Schnee-Eifel, 662

Scotland, Scots, Scottish march, xii, xv–xvi, 1, 2, 12, 36, 60, 63, 68, 116, 156, 187, 271, 316, 333, 348, 373, 407, 412, 426, 495, 504, 512–13, 523, 539, 540, 569, 572, 579, 583, 585, 587, 617, 657, 661, 675–7, 723, 724, 726, 734, 736, 737, 738, 747–8, 763, 765, 776, 824, 826, 843, 844–5, 859; march law, 11, 528, 529, 577, 587, 674, 675, 826; border wars (1377), 285–6, 355; (1378), 356, 405–6; (1383), 513; (1384), 518–19, 530–1, 526–7; (1385), 535, 538, 543, 545–8, 500–1, 556–7; (1358), 544–5, 548–50, 569; (1388), 654–6, 657–9; (1389), 675; Anglo-Scottish diplomacy, 9–11, 412, 514, 526–7; Franco-Scottish diplomacy, 9, 128, 277–8, 513, 517–18, 676–7

Scotney, castle, 288

scouts, 89–90, 91, 159, 657, 754

Scrope, Richard, lord of Bolton, 175–6, 259, 354–5, 359, 373–4, 459, 472, 735–6, 742

Scrope, Sir William (the elder), 760

Scrope, Sir William, Earl of Wiltshire (1397), 719, 721, 836, 844, 847, 850, 860

Segovia, Cortes (1386), 599–60, 620

Selby, Ralph, 847

Sempy, John, lord of, 39, 482, 488, 579, 723

Senechal, Catherine, 2nd wife of Sir John Harpeden, 163

Senlis, 317–18, 504

Sens, 54, 403, 447–8, 491

Seville, 38, 124, 158, 203–4, 268–9, 278, 377, 382, 433–4, 436, 523, 532, 560, 567, 568, 584, 597

Shakespeare, 3, 833, 851

Sheen, royal manor, 1, 280, 537, 636, 637, 814

Sheerness, 283

Sheppey, Isle of, 260, 640–1

ships, *Grace Dieu*, 153, 155, 156; *Dieulagarde*, 174; *Katherine*; *Maudelayne*, 377; *Paul of London*, 174

Shoebury Ness, 283

Shrewsbury, 71, 634, 639, 763, 842–3, 851, 853, 854

Sicily, Kingdom of: see Naples

siege warfare, 49, 218–21, 222–4, 302, 398–9, 409, 500–2, 531–2, 605, 755

Sigismund of Luxembourg, King of Hungary, later King of the Romans and Holy Roman Emperor, 843,

Skipwith, William, 264

Skirlaw, Walter, Bishop of Durham, 362, 366, 576–7, 589, 642, 657, 658, 674, 677, 789

Sluys, 309, 417, 448, 488, 526, 546, 578, 603–4, 736; battle (1340), xv, 126, 331, 431; base for invasion of England (1385–6), 537–8, 551–2, 553, 555, 583, 584–5, 588, 590–2, 593, 601; English naval attacks (1385), 542–3; (1386), 580–1; (1387), 604, 605; Groot Kasteel, 517

Soissons, 188, 189, 191, 245

Solidor, castle, 27, 181, 362

Solier, Arnaud du, lord of Villalpando ('Le Limousin'), 117, 567

Songe du Vergier, 671

Soria, 202–3, 337–8; Cortes (1380), 384

Sort, Ramonet de, 699–701, 705, 707–8, 711, 712, 716–17, 718, 719

Sotherey, Sir John, 280, 465, 469

Soubise, 150; siege (1372), 151–2, 159, 161, 765, 770

Soustons, 204

Southampton, 21, 26, 35, 67, 72, 73, 93, 126, 144, 145, 153, 156, 183, 184, 185, 233, 285, 286, 287, 288–9, 315, 324, 327, 362, 378, 545, 552, 651, 655, 750

Southwark, 95, 273, 424

Souvigny, 194

Spain, Charles of, Constable of France, xvi, 630

spies, spying, 39, 40–1, 129, 141, 166, 173, 259, 278, 289–91, 316, 579–80, 581, 706–7

Spridlington, Walter, 138, 149, 161

Stafford, Edmund, Bishop of Exeter, 835, 841

Stafford, Sir Hugh, Earl of (1372), 47

Stafford, Sir Ralph, 280, 473

Stamford, council (1392), 792–3

Stanley, Sir John, 805

Statute of Labourers, 419, 427

Statute of Winchester, 427

Stepney, 309, 377

Stoke-sub-Hamdon, 431

Stratton, John, 736–7

Strother, Sir John, 741

Stury, Sir Richard, 176, 825

Sudbury (Suffolk), 426

Sudbury, Simon, Bishop of London, then Archbishop of Canterbury, 224, 226, 241, 249, 255, 272, 374, 407, 421, 423, 424, 427, 443

Suffolk, 426, 545, 585

Sully, Louis de, 78

Surgères, siege (1372), 154

surgery, 761–2, 762–4

Suscinio, castle, captured (1373), 182

Sussex, county, 135, 282, 286, 288, 385, 635, 858

Switzerland, 245–6,

Swynford, Catherine, Duchess of Lancaster, 426, 844

Sidney, Sir Philip, 659

Symonds, Sir Thomas, 431, 467

tactics, 564, 730

Taillebourg, siege (1385), 704

Talbot, Sir Thomas, 805, 810, 813

Tamworth, Sir Nicholas, 177–8, 183

Tarbes, 807

Tartas, Guiraud de, lord of Poyanne, 120, 121

taxation, Castile, 123, 432–3, 574–5, 575, 597, 600, 623; England, 61–3, 101–2, 175, 198–9, 255, 276–7, 360, 361, 407–8, 419–20, 423–4, 512, 550; France, xii,

53–60, 97, 102, 127, 175, 214, 236, 242–3, 268, 353–4, 368–9, 371–3, 395–6, 399–400, 404–5, 442–3, 447–9, 490–2, 535–6, 578, 603, 667, 669–70, 682–3, 691, 702, 710, 846–7; Aquitaine, xvii, 108; Scotland, 9

Telo, João Afonso, Admiral of Portugal, 433, 492

Tenorio, Pedro, Archbishop of Toledo, 558, 560

Terssac, castle, 687

Tertre, Pierre du, 66–7, 72, 86, 314, 319–20, 321

Tête-Noir, Geoffrey, 693–4, 695, 699, 711–12, 714, 720

Teutonic Order, 256, 736, 791

Teviotdale, 10, 518, 548, 675

Thanet, Isle of, 507, 754

Thérouanne, 39, 291, 477

Thouars, 137, 149; submitted (1372) 154, 156, 158–9

Thuriès, 687

Thurrock, 283

Thury-Harcourt, castle, siege (1371), 102–3

Toledo, 313, 521

Toledo, Archbishop of: see Tenorio, Pedro

Tordesillas, 521

Toro, Cortes (1371), 117, 123, 124

Totesham, Sir Richard, 758

Toulouse, 22, 25, 33, 34, 59, 76, 80–1, 127, 196, 204, 205, 206, 243, 332, 368–9, 492, 680, 702, 705, 706, 707, 713, 753; revolt (1380–1), 688–9, 690, 691

Touraine, Louis, Duke of: see Louis of France

Tournai, 454–5, 476, 487, 573, 846

tournaments, 230, 411, 478, 540, 577, 611, 616, 667, 668–9, 716, 723–4, 735, 752, 783

Tournehem, 40

Tournemire, Jean de, 720

Tours, 796

Trailly, Sir John, 619

Trancoso, battle (1385), 560, 563; treaty (1388), 618–21, 622

Trascros, 210

Trastámara: see Henry II, King of Castile; John, King of Castile

Trau, Soudan de, 304, 332, 333, 431

Tréguier, 624

Tréséguidy, Maurice de, 445, 737

Tresilian, Sir Robert, Chief Justice of King's Bench, 632, 637, 641, 643–4

Trie, Renaud de, 845

Trivet, Sir Thomas, 219, 232, 336–9, 429, 496, 498, 502, 504, 507, 510, 514, 637, 642, 643
Troyes, 191–2, 389–90, 491, 753
Tudela, 336–9, 622
Tui, siege (1389), 678
Turenne, viscounty, 80, 112, 316
Turks, 671, 737, 791, 806, 814, 824, 834–5
Turlande, castle, 717, 721
Tyler, Wat, 421–2, 428–9
Tyrell, Sir Hugh, 286

Ulster, 655
uniforms, 538, 547, 748
Upton, Nicholas, 729
Urban V, Pope, 111, 113
Urban VI, Pope, 341–50, 393, 435, 438, 441, 467, 471, 559, 576–7, 785
Urbino, 248, 803
Usk, Adam of, 862
Usk, Thomas, Under-sheriff of Middlesex, 644
Ussel, 96, 98–9, 762
Utrecht, 756, 855

Vaas, battle (1370), 88, 90, 93, 274
Vabres, Bishop of: see Vassignac, Etienne de
Vailly, 119
Valderas, 613–14
Valentinois, province, Estates, 703
Valladolid, 141–2; Cortes (1385), 574–5, 598, 609
Vallebreton, Hennequin, 219, 232
Valognes, 320
varlets, 38, 730, 731–2
Vannes, 119, 131, 157, 181, 364, 411, 624, 629, 630, 648
Vasques de Azevedo, Gonçalo, 464, 467, 492
Vassignac, Etienne de, Bishop of Vabres, 19, 46
Velay, province, 67, 369, 695, 705, 709, 710; Estates, 703
Vendée, 4, 29–30, 159
Vendôme, 86, 87–8, 89, 390
Venice, 132, 387, 585, 781, 791, 816, 862
Ventadour, castle, 693, 695, 701, 712, 720; siege (1389), 714
Vere, Robert de, Earl of Oxford (1371), Marquis of Dublin (1385), Duke of Ireland (1386), 473, 548, 570, 587, 588, 628, 629, 631, 632, 634–6, 637–41, 642, 643, 669, 673, 843
Verteuil, castle, siege (1385), 704

Vertus, 388, 781
veterinary services, 764
victuals, victualling, 5, 18, 25, 125, 304, 315, 316, 327, 523, 580–1, 583, 652, 754–7
Vienne, Jean de, Admiral of France, 218, 220, 221–2, 228, 232, 233, 245, 268, 270, 281–2, 285, 286, 304, 313, 320, 357, 386–7, 441, 503, 504, 535, 538, 543, 545–7, 549–50, 556–7, 579, 583, 603, 622, 626, 664, 676–7, 782, 802, 803, 829, 834
Vier Ambachten, district, 449, 452, 494, 541, 542, 553–4
Vila Viçosa, 437, 465, 469
Villaines, Pierre le Bègue de, Count of Ribadeo, 117, 299, 441, 579, 668, 787, 800
Villalobos, 614
Villalpando, 609, 614, 616, 617
Villefranche-de-Rouergue, 19, 242
Villejuif, 85
Villemur, Jean de, 81–2, 83
Villeneuve-lès-Avignon, 112, 340, 821
Villiers, Pierre de, 42
Vimieiro, 464
Vincennes, castle, 60, 85, 128, 345, 346, 394, 439, 442, 444–8, 480, 490
Visconti, family, lords of Milan, 111–12
Visconti, Bernabò, Duke of Milan, 111, 348, 535, 780–1
Visconti, Gian Galeazzo, Duke of Milan, 780, 780–1, 784, 786, 801, 820, 832–3, 845, 846
Viseu, 158, 558, 560
Viterbo, 111, 248, 803
Vitré, 396
Vivarais, province, Estates, 703
Vivonne, Renaud de, 109–10
Vitoria, 179

Waldby, Robert, Archbishop of Dublin, 825
Waldegrave, Sir Richard, 256, 429–30
Wales, Welsh, xvi, 11–12, 135–6, 143, 245–6, 269, 270, 277–8, 284, 290, 299, 368, 776, 848–9, 855, 858, 859–61; companies in French service, 44–45, 128–9, 150–1, 245, 333, 484, 703, 737
Walkefare, Sir Thomas, 19, 23–4
Wallingford, 857, 863
Walsingham, Thomas, 3, 262, 265, 271, 272, 275, 276, 280, 287, 307, 316, 383, 461, 470, 471, 498, 506, 535, 543, 570, 604, 617, 759, 841, 844, 847, 848

Waltham abbey, council (1385), 536–7
Waltham Cross, 637
Walwain, John, 459
Walworth, Sir William, 308, 424, 426, 428–9, 552
war-cries, 25, 80, 149, 151, 465, 658, 701, 746, 748
war wages, 738–41
Wardlaw, William, Bishop of Glasgow, 128, 513
Ware, 858, 860
Wareyn, Walter, 290
Wark, captured (1383), 513; (1385), 547
Warneton, 480
Warwick, Thomas Beauchamp, Earl of, 41–2, 43, 73, 264–5, 309, 423, 548, 587, 593, 635–7, 639, 643, 645, 661, 672, 768, 778, 838–40, 842, 844, 848–9, 862–3
Waterford, 823
Wattwiller, treaty (1376), 246
weapons, 752–3
Wesenham, John, 59
West, Bernard de, 32
Westminster, 1, 36, 73, 99, 121, 129, 135, 145, 156, 171, 221, 252, 257, 264, 271, 274, 275, 282, 283, 304, 323, 359, 366, 373, 428, 437, 458, 475, 494, 506, 510, 518, 530, 531, 537, 569, 577, 585, 586, 589, 636–7, 641, 642, 643–4, 672, 674, 787, 788, 811, 814–15, 835, 837, 841, 854, 862
Westmoreland, county, 10, 68, 550, 656, 844
Weston, William, 292, 294
Wettenhall, Sir Thomas, 19, 33–5, 52
'White Hoods' of Ghent, 415–16
Whitland, abbey, 860
Wickford, Robert, Archbishop of Dublin, 635
Wight, Isle of, 73, 143, 212, 278, 286, 385, 656, 839
Wilton Diptych, 833
Winchelsea, 73, 155, 281–2, 288, 385, 660; battle off (1350), 3
Winchester, 101–2, 512
Windsor,1, 280, 366, 423, 453, 540, 638, 639–40, 719, 724, 770, 850, 852, 857; treaty (1386), 577
Windsor, Sir William, 399
Winter, Peter de, 457, 480
Wisby, battle (1361), 752
women at war, 757–8
Wondelgem, castle, 416
Woodstock, Thomas of, Earl of Buckingham

(1377), Duke of Gloucester (1385), character, 306–7, 473–4; early career, 280, 283; naval campaigns (1377–8), 306, 308–10; campaign in France (1380–1), 305, 375–6, 378–9, 385, 386, 387–90, 396–9, 405, 406, 409–12, 740, 746, 754, 764, 771; and Peasants' Revolt (1381), 429; and Norwich Crusade (1383), 504–5, 507; and Anglo-French diplomacy (1381–94), 431, 514, 527–8, 536, 540, 576; and Scotland (1383–5), 514, 518, 548; and Parliament of 1386, 586–9; Appellant (1387–9), 637–9, 641, 642–3, 644–5, 646–7, 647–8, 654–5, 661; and Richard II's peace policy (1389–96), 672, 673, 741; Anglo-French diplomacy (1389–96), 775–6, 777, 778, 788, 792–3, 805–6, 808, 810, 811, 813–14, 825, 828–9, 830–2, 834–5, 837, 864; abortive expedition to Prussia (1391–2), 791; arrest and murder (1397), 838–41, 842, 843, 849, 852, 862, 863; mentioned, 1, 478
Woolwich, 283
Worcester, 639
Workesley, Sir Geoffrey, 92
Worsley, Sir Geoffrey, 760
Wraw, John, 426, 429
Wycliffe, John, 272–3, 274, 776
Wykeham, William of, Bishop of Winchester, 2, 36, 99, 101, 263–4, 272, 284, 570, 587, 589, 593, 637
Wyn, Jack, 44–5, 128, 333, 484, 703

Yevele, Henry, 288–9
Yoens, Jan, 415–16, 417
Yolande of Bar, Queen of Aragon, 795
Yolande, Infanta of Aragon, 823
York, 426, 763
York, ecclesiastical province, convocation,62, 70, 255
York, Edmund Duke of: see Langley, Edmund
Yorkshire, county, 10, 172, 426, 470, 505, 585, 757, 805, 858
Ypres, 14, 413, 414, 416, 418, 457, 480, 482, 486, 488, 489, 494, 517; siege (1383), 498–504, 759

Zamora, 115, 150, 158, 597–8, 609, 621
Zeeland, 153, 183, 449–50, 488, 512, 540, 846
Zouche, William, lord of Harringworth, 68
Zype, Peter Van der, 500